Third Edition

Intermediate Microeconomics
Theory and Applications

Third Edition

Intermediate Microeconomics
Theory and Applications

Heinz Kohler

Credits are listed at the back of the book on pages C1–2, which constitutes a legal extension of the copyright page.

Library of Congress Cataloging-in-Publication Data

Kohler, Heinz.
    Intermediate microeconomics: theory and applications/Heinz Kohler. —3rd ed.
        p. cm.
    Includes bibliographies and indexes.
    ISBN 0-673-38839-5
    1. Microeconomics. I. Title.
    HB172.K68 1989
    338.5—dc20   89-10382
                                                            CIP

1 2 3 4 5 6 - VHJ - 94 93 92 91 90 89

Preface

Economics is an important subject. Those who master the theoretical knowledge of the discipline are able to wield a powerful set of tools capable of affecting, for better or for worse, the material welfare of vast millions of people. This book, which is aimed at students who have had only an introductory economics course or students in MBA programs, develops all of the theoretical tools traditionally found in microeconomics texts (and more).

Economics is also an exciting subject—as evidenced throughout this book by a continuous link between theory and applications. As the detailed table of contents shows, many of these applications have been integrated into the basic structure of chapters. Such is the case with lump-sum versus selective sales tax (Chapter 2), free trade: who gains, who loses? (Chapter 6), price discrimination (Chapter 7), adverse selection and moral hazard (Chapter 10), teenage unemployment and the minimum wage (Chapter 11), and investing in human capital (Chapter 12), to name just a few of the 30 topics. Some 86 other applications, however, have been set off as self-contained, fairly rigorous "Analytical Examples" or as "Close-Ups" that provide somewhat less rigorous examples of how microeconomics reaches into every nook and cranny of our lives. (The text Applications, Analytical Examples, and Close-Ups are all listed in the Contents.)

TO THE INSTRUCTOR

This book is divided into seven parts. Part 1, "Introduction," reviews crucial lessons of the elementary economics course and lays the groundwork for the remainder of the book. Chap-

ter 1 can easily be assigned without further class discussion of the key concepts of scarcity, choice, optimizing, demand and supply, and the like. Part 2, "The Consumer and the Firm," presents the traditional theory of the household (Chapters 2 and 3) and of the firm (Chapters 4 and 5).

Part 3, "Markets for Goods," presents the traditional theories of price/output determination in markets that are perfectly competitive, dominated by monopoly and cartels, or best described by oligopoly and monopolistic competition (Chapters 6 through 8). In accordance with the wishes of past users of this text, Chapter 8 presents numerous competing theories of oligopoly, ranging from Cournot's quantity adjusters and Sweezy's kinked-demand model to price-leadership models of low-cost firms, dominant firms (Stackelberg), and entry-limiting firms to Hotelling's product-differentiation model, Bertrand's price adjusters, and contestable markets. However, Part 4, "Special Topic: The Economics of Uncertainty," goes further than that. An entirely new chapter (9) is devoted to decision theory and game theory, while another chapter (10) explores the implications of uncertainty with respect to insurance, gambling, search, and futures markets.

Part 5, "Markets for Resources," analyzes the determination of price and employment in markets for labor and capital inputs (Chapters 11 and 12) and thus inevitably presents the economics of intertemporal decision making. An appendix (12A) explores alternative concepts of rent. Part 6, "The Market Economy as a Whole," develops the key concepts of general equilibrium (Chapter 13) and efficiency and equity (Chapter 14). Finally, Part 7, "The Economic Role of

Government,'' notes the importance of government establishing property rights and promoting competition if the market economy is to function well. This leads to the discussion of antitrust policy, regulation (and deregulation), externalities, and public goods (Chapters 15 and 16).

The chapters of this book are self-contained units. It is not necessary to cover them all or even to assign them in the order in which they appear. To the extent that one chapter builds upon material in other chapters, cross-references with page numbers have been provided. Instructors, therefore, can design their own courses using any desired combinations of chapters. Instructors teaching under a quarter system, for example, could assign Chapter 1, but could focus class discussion on Chapters 2–8 and 11–12 (that is, Parts 2, 3, and 5). If time permits, *any* remaining chapters, in any order, can be added to this nine-chapter core.

A number of teaching supports are available to the instructor. Some of these are built into the text: the figures made self-contained by carefully worded captions, chapter summaries, end-of-chapter listings of Key Terms (boldfaced in the text), end-of-chapter Questions and Problems (now averaging 13 per chapter), and Selected Readings. In addition, while the main body of the text itself contains no calculus, whenever appropriate, elaborate calculus treatment has been provided in a Calculus Appendix at the back of this book (along with footnote references in the text). Instructors who are so inclined can thus teach a calculus-based course; others can tell their students to ignore the Calculus Appendix. The end-of-chapter Questions and Problems, similarly, contain some that require calculus, but they are clearly marked by asterisks. The remaining questions are about equally divided among thought questions and technical questions. Finally, note that this third edition introduces a new feature, Hands-On Practice, just prior to the general question section in each chapter. Here students are given practice with numerical or graphic problems; full solutions to these exercises are provided as well. Apart from these built-in features, three other types of supporting

materials are available: an *Instructor's Manual*, a *Student Workbook* (described below), and KOHLER-3, a set of personal-computer diskettes (described below also).

The *Instructor's Manual* contains responses or answers for the even-numbered end-of-chapter Questions and Problems in this text. It also contains, for each chapter of the text, an average of 38 multiple-choice and 18 true-false questions (with answers). These questions do not duplicate those in the *Student Workbook*. Instructors who wish to elaborate upon any of the materials discussed in the text will find some 46 additional, worked-out applications in the *Manual*. More topics yet are covered in the *Workbook* appendices and biographies.

TO THE STUDENT

Students will find a number of aids to the study of the material presented in this book. Some of these aids have been built into the text: the figures made self-contained by carefully worded captions, the chapter summaries, the end-of-chapter listings of Key Terms (boldfaced in the text), the Hands-On Practice exercises (with solutions), the end-of-chapter Questions and Problems, and the Selected Readings. In addition, a Glossary of Key Terms and Answers to Odd-numbered Questions and Problems appear at the end of the book. A separate *Student Workbook* is also available. For each chapter of this book, the *Student Workbook* contains an average of 29 multiple-choice and 12 true-false questions, and numerous problems—as well as answers to all of these.

The *Student Workbook* also contains some 31 biographies featuring the economists who developed the theories and applications contained in the text, and there are 4 major appendices that extend the material presented in the text. (These appendices cover the use of calculus, linear programming, deriving the Leontief inverse matrix, and markets for bonds and stocks.)

Finally, note the availability of KOHLER-3, a set of personal-computer diskettes, described in the following section.

THE KOHLER-3 PERSONAL-COMPUTER DISKETTES

A set of programs for IBM personal computers and compatible machines has been specifically designed to accompany this text. The computer must have graphics capability. Although it is not required, a color display is preferable. The 20 programs are available either on two $5\frac{1}{4}$ inch floppy disks or on a single $3\frac{1}{2}$ inch rigid diskette.

KOHLER-3 covers all aspects of the text. It contains:

1. About 450 multiple-choice questions (along with nearly 200 graphs). For each question, the correct answer is identified and elaborate comments are provided on incorrect responses.

2. Some 200 challenging problems (with solutions when appropriate). These problems involve one of the following:

> **a.** Thought Experiments. You think about the effects of specified events on graphs or tables, then use the computer to check your mental solution. The graphs and tables change in response to your prompts. Examples: the separation of substitution and income effects (Chapter 3), the "random walk" of futures prices (Chapter 10), income redistribution and incentives (Chapter 14), externalities and their remedies (Chapter 16).
>
> **b.** Graphical Exercises. You interpret graphical information. Examples: measuring price elasticities (Chapter 3), isoquant analysis (Chapter 5), monopoly profit maximization or government price fixing (Chapter 7).
>
> **c.** Tabular Exercises. You interpret tabular information. Examples: the production function (Chapter 4), concepts of cost (Chapter 5), marginal revenue (Chapter 7), decision theory and game theory (Chapter 9).
>
> **d.** Solving Equations Algebraically. You learn to solve linear simultaneous

equations algebraically. Examples: supply and demand in markets for goods and resources (Chapters 6 and 11), the Cournot equilibrium or the dominant-firm model. (Chapter 8), general equilibrium (Chapter 13).

> **e.** Other Algebraic Exercises. You learn to use various special programs. Examples: maximization under constraints via linear programming (Chapter 5), determining fair and unfair insurance and gambles (via an expected-monetary-value program, Chapter 10), benefit-cost analysis (via a cash-flow program, Chapter 16).

3. A kit of tools that will enable you to solve all kinds of problems of your own. Most of these tools are found in Appendices A–D; some are built into chapters. They allow you to solve simultaneous equations, do linear programming, work compounding or discounting problems, find expected monetary values, perform matrix operations, and much more.

Initial Start-Up Procedure

The KOHLER-3 diskettes contain detailed operating instructions. For first-time-ever users, however, the following will be helpful:

1. Prior to loading KOHLER-3, in response to the DOS prompt (such as C>), type **BASICA** and press [ENTER]. (Failure to load BASICA and loading BASIC instead will prevent you from seeing graphs on the screen.)

2. At this point, place your diskette into the drive of your choice (for example, A) and, in response to the BASICA prompt (OK), type **RUN "A:KOHLER"** and then press [ENTER]. (Naturally, you replace *A* by another letter if you are not using drive A.)

3. Some program features are automatic. Do not press any key unless told.

4. You can escape the program at any time by pressing [Ctrl] plus [Break]. If you also wish to return to DOS, type **SYSTEM** and press [ENTER].

5. You can always restart the program by the procedure noted in (1) and (2) if you see the DOS symbol. Just press the [F2] key if you see the OK symbol.

Hard Disk Installation Instructions

If you have the two floppy diskettes but your machine has a hard disk, you can install both floppies on it, along with a unified menu, by the procedure below. It is assumed here that the floppy disk is placed in drive A, that drive A is not a high-density drive, and that the hard disk is called C. If this is not the case, you must change the drive names accordingly.

1. Get the DOS prompt C> and place disk #1 in drive A. Then type **COPY A:*.* C:** (with a space before A and before C) and press [ENTER].

2. Repeat step 1 for disk #2.

3. Get the DOS prompt C> and type **ERASE C:KOHLER.BAS** (with a space before C) and press [ENTER].

4. Get the DOS prompt C> and type **RENAME   C:KOHLER-H.BAS   KOHLER. BAS** (with two spaces as shown) and press [ENTER].

Acknowledgments

I would like to express my sincere gratitude to many who have helped me in the creation of this text. Many reviewers took the time to examine at least a part of the project and gave me good advice; many users of the first and second editions have helped me decide where more or less elaborate discussion was in order:

Jack Adams, *University of Arkansas*
Torben Andersen, *Red Deer College, Alberta*
Ernest Ankrim, *Pacific Lutheran University*
Daniel Biederman, *University of Kansas*
G. O. Bierwag, *University of Arizona*
Jacques Blair, *Western New England College*
George S. Bohler, *Embry-Riddle Aeronautical University*
Robert Borengasser, *St. Mary's College, Indiana*
William Brown, *California State University, Northridge*
Earl R. Brubaker, *Naval Postgraduate School*
Louis Cain, *Loyola University, Chicago*
Fikret Ceyhun, *University of North Dakota*
Richard Clarke, *University of Wisconsin, Madison*
James Paul Clay, *Fort Lewis College*
Alvin Cohen, *Lehigh University*
John L. Conant, *Indiana State University*
Eleanor Craig, *University of Delaware*
Jacques Cremer, *Virginia Polytechnic Institute*
Betsy Crowell, *University of Michigan, Dearborn*
Donald J. Cymrot, *Miami University*
James L. Dietz, *California State University, Fullerton*
Gregory M. Duncan, *Washington State University*
Harold W. Elder, *University of Alabama*

Catherine J. Elliott, *College of William and Mary*
Maxim Engers, *University of Virginia*
Richard Ericson, *Columbia University*
James Ferguson, *University of Rochester*
Ronald C. Fisher, *Michigan State University*
Robert J. Flanagan, *Stanford University*
Charles R. Fraley, *Northern Kentucky University*
Terri L. Gollinger, *Loyola University of Chicago*
Tim Gronberg, *Texas A & M University*
Loren Guffey, *University of Central Arkansas*
Karen Hallows, *University of Missouri—Columbia*
James B. Heisler, *Hope College*
James Hess, *University of Southern California*
Elisabeth Hoffman, *University of Arizona*
Oz Honkalehto, *Colgate University*
Lawrence R. Iannaccone, *University of Santa Clara*
Dennis Johnson, *University of South Dakota*
Donn M. Johnson, *University of Northern Iowa*
John Kambhu, *Columbia University*
J. R. Kearl, *Brigham Young University*
Richard Kihlstrom, *University of Pennsylvania*
Y.C. Kim, *Northern Illinois University*
James K. Kindahl, *University of Massachusetts, Amherst*
Terry G. Langan, *University of Minnesota*
R. Ashley Lyman, *University of Idaho*
Rodney Mabry, *Northeast Louisiana University*
Jeff Madura, *University of North Carolina, Charlotte*
Cdr. Lee Mairs, *Navy Postgraduate School*
Scott E. Masten, *University of Virginia*
J. Peter Mattila, *Iowa State University*
Carol McDonough, *University of Lowell*
Brian H. McGavin, *California State University, Northridge*

Acknowledgments

Donna E. Olszewski, *Northeastern University*
Sharon Oster, *Yale University*
Sam Peltzman, *University of Chicago*
Owen Phillips, *Texas A & M University*
Ibrahim Pordy, *San Diego State University*
Larry Pulley, *Brandeis University*
Robert Puth, *University of New Hampshire*
Seyed M. Raji, *Dowling College*
Bee Roberts, *Pennsylvania State University*
Robert S. Rycroft, *Mary Washington College*
F. M. Scherer, *Swarthmore College*
Carl Shapiro, *Princeton University*
Dorothy R. Siden, *Salem State College*
James L. Smith, *University of Illinois, Urbana*
Janet Kiholm Smith, *Arizona State University*
Edward W. Sparling, *Colorado State University*
Helen Tauchen, *University of North Carolina, Chapel Hill*
Thomas S. Ulen, *University of Illinois, Urbana-Champaign*
Johannes Van Lierop, *California State University, Fullerton*
Fred Westfield, *Vanderbilt University*
Hildegard C. Wette, *Northwestern University*
Robert Wolf, *Boston University*

Hassan A. Zavareei, *West Virginia Institute of Technology*

I am equally grateful to Bruce Kaplan, Julie Howell, and Paula Meyers, the acquiring editor, project editor, and designer, respectively, of the book. They have guided this project through the long process of production and have created, as most will agree, a beautiful book.

Permission to use selected materials from earlier books is gratefully acknowledged from the Dryden Press of Hinsdale, Illinois (*Economics: The Science of Scarcity*, 1970); from D. C. Heath and Co. of Lexington, Massachusetts (*Economics and Urban Problems*, 1973; *Scarcity and Freedom: An Introduction to Economics*, 1977); and from the Robert E. Krieger Publishing Company, once of Huntington, New York, and now of Melbourne, Florida (*Welfare and Planning: An Analysis of Capitalism versus Socialism*, 2nd ed., 1979).

Heinz Kohler
Amherst College

Contents

Contents

PART 3 Markets for Goods 175

Contents

PART 4   Special Topic: The Economics of Uncertainty   289

CHAPTER 9   Decision Theory and Game Theory   290

CHAPTER 10   Insurance and Gambling, Search and Futures Markets   326

PART 5   Markets for Resources   355

CHAPTER 11   Labor and Wages   356

CHAPTER 12 Capital and Interest 406

CHAPTER 12A The Concept of Rent 443

Contents

CHAPTER 16   Externalities and Public Goods   558

PART

1

Introduction

1 Scarcity, Choice, and Optimizing

This chapter identifies scarcity as the basic economic problem and reviews its major implication, the need to make choices. The chapter also shows why the best choices are made when applying a universal principle, the principle of optimization, and it notes that all of microeconomic theorizing, ultimately, is built on this simple idea.

1

Scarcity, Choice, and Optimizing

A universal problem exists. Small bands of African Bushmen face it; so do Amazon Indians and Greenland Eskimos. Peasants in China, Egypt, and Peru suffer from it; so do urban dwellers in Moscow, Paris, and New York. All of them, every day, wrestle with the basic economic problem of *scarcity*. This problem, which is central to every elementary economics text, is also central to this intermediate one. This chapter will review the nature of the problem and its implications.

AN IMMENSE DESIRE FOR GOODS

A thought experiment can quickly remind us of what scarcity involves. Suppose a smiling genie popped out of a bottle and offered to be at our service. Suppose he were prepared to bring us, just for the asking, any object we desired and the devoted attention of any person we named. Imagine the abundance of goods that could then be ours! If we were hungry, we could call for food, and it would be there in the wink of an eye. We could conjure up new clothes or that fancy camera we were never quite able to afford.

Presents for family and friends? A flashy sports car for ourselves? Of course. A house on our favorite island in the middle of the sea? A plane to take us there? They could be ours. Lessons to fly that plane? Lessons to gain all kinds of other skills? The best in medical care, concerts at night, visits to beautiful places? All of these we could enjoy. . . .

We need not belabor the point. More than 4 billion people live on this earth, and they do not have genies ready to serve them. But they do spend their individual lives in the pursuit of happiness. To most of them, most of the time, happiness is an elusive goal indeed. Most of them, probably, could not even name the exact ingredients that would produce it. But, surely, the kinds of material things listed in the thought experiment would be mentioned by many. We can guess that most people, if given the chance offered by our genie, would not reject it. Most likely, they would be all too ready to prepare an impressive list of things to have and of things or people to use. And all these people would hope that somewhere hidden in their list would be at least some of the ingredients required for their happiness.

Indeed, economists typically assume that most people on earth harbor desires for a truly staggering variety and quantity of goods. Although no one has ever measured the aggregate size of this desire, one can guess that its extent is immense. All one has to do is imagine people in their various capacities as family members, producers, government officials, and so on, and one can easily picture the lengthy lists of wishes such people would prepare if they did meet an incredible genie who was ready to offer all goods at a zero price.

Two things, in particular, should be noted. First, in this book the term **goods** refers to all the varied means by which people satisfy their material wants. These means may be tangible *commodities* (like food and clothes) that users come to own completely. But goods may also be intangible *services,* either of people (such as teachers and doctors) or of commodities (such as airliners and hotels) that users enjoy temporarily without coming to own the persons or commodities involved.

Second, the term **desire for goods** does not mean *demand* for goods, a concept that refers to desire backed up by purchasing power, which enables people in our society to acquire goods that are for sale at positive prices. Instead, *desire* refers to wishful thinking, to the quantities people would take if no purchasing power were needed because all goods were available at zero prices. It is desire for goods in this sense that economists claim is immense in most places on earth.

RESOURCES—THE INGREDIENTS TO MAKE GOODS

Introductory economics courses teach something else that must be recalled: In the real world, goods are not made by genies with the help of magic; on the contrary, they are made by people with the help of productive ingredients called **resources.** Customarily, resources are classified into three major groups: human, natural, and capital. They are put to work in the **process of production,** a set of activities deliberately designed to make goods available to people where and when they are wanted.

Human resources are people able and willing to participate in the productive process, supplying their mental or physical labor. **Natural resources** are gifts of nature in their natural state; that is, productive ingredients not made by people and as yet untouched by them. Think of sunlight and ocean tides, of virgin land and the plants and animals on it, of schools of fish in the ocean, or of minerals and fuels underground. **Capital resources,** finally, are all the productive ingredients made by people. They include all types of structures used by producers of goods—structures such as factory buildings, schools, or airport control towers. They include equipment of producers, such as computers, milling machines, or fleets of trucks. And they include producer inventories of raw materials, semifinished goods, or even finished goods that have not yet reached their ultimate users.

Three things should be noted concerning the capital concept. First, many items considered by people in general to be natural resources are viewed as capital resources by economists. Consider animals that have been domesticated and specially bred; soil that has been cleared, irrigated, and fertilized; or oil that has been pumped from the ground and shipped far from its original place of deposit. None of these is in its natural state; all of them are in a sense made by people. So they are capital resources, as defined above.

Second, one is almost tempted to carry this reasoning a step further. Economists know that a healthy, educated, and trained labor force (like soil that has been cleared, irrigated, and fertilized) is more productive than it would be without these qualities. Thus one might wish to classify people who are in good physical condition, educated, and trained as produced capital, too! Nevertheless, economists do not classify people as capital resources. In later chapters, however, we will recognize that different people clearly possess different amounts of an invisible kind of

human capital, consisting of the health care, general education, and training embodied in them.

Finally, *capital resources,* as the term is used in this book, do not include **financial capital,** such as money, stocks, deeds, or bonds. For an individual in modern society, such items are important indeed, but they are not directly productive. They are only claims against real resources. People could easily increase such paper claims a millionfold. Yet if no corresponding increase occurred in the form of blast furnaces, locomotives, oil deposits, and so on, people would not be richer at all. They could not produce more on that account. Just as a baker uses butter, eggs, flour, and milk (and not green dollar bills) to bake a cake, so the people in every society must mix *real* capital resources with natural and human ones to produce each and every good they do acquire.

TECHNOLOGY—THE KNOWLEDGE TO MAKE GOODS

Elementary economics textbooks also teach us that the quantities of goods people are able to produce depend not only on the quantities of resources they have and put to use, but also on their **technology,** the set of known methods of production available to them. This knowledge of possible methods of production, like the recipe book available to the baker, sets limits on the quantity of goods that can be produced *per unit* of resources. Such limits are, of course, far from eternally fixed. Consider how, during the past century, people have discovered fertilizers, hormones, and high-yield crops and have used these discoveries, along with wonders of agricultural machinery, to raise incredibly the yield per acre of land. Before we run out of conventional fuel, people may well discover how to use solar power on a large scale. Should that happen, the quantities of goods produced per unit of this particular natural resource would increase dramatically. This would happen, furthermore, not because of

any change in the quantity or quality of this resource (the sun radiates as much energy to us now as it will then). It would happen because of a new entry in our productive recipe book that would enable us to switch to a technique of production previously unavailable. Such an advance in technical knowledge should not be confused with a switch, in response to changing circumstances, from one known technique of production to another. While the former is akin to discovering a new recipe, the latter is about selecting a different one from among those previously known.

LIMITED RESOURCES AND TECHNOLOGY YIELD LIMITED GOODS

Just as a cake is limited in size by the quantities of ingredients and the possible recipes available to the baker, so the "pie" of goods produced by any society is limited by the resources and technology available to it. Obviously, no society has unlimited stocks of resources or of technical knowledge. At any one moment, there are only so many people able and willing to work in the productive process, and limited quantities of human capital are embodied in them. There are only so many acres of virgin timberland and so many known barrels of oil in the ground. There are only so many assembly plants and miles of highway in existence. There are only so many recipes of production from which to choose. Given the best techniques of production available, even the use of all resource stocks at the maximum possible rate (of 24 hours each day) would produce a limited set of newly produced goods in a year. In fact, of course, some resources cannot be used at such a maximum rate. This is most obvious in the case of people.

Yet, as a matter of logic, the inevitably limited size of a society's annual "pie" of goods need not be of concern. Conceivably, this set of goods might be more than sufficient to satisfy all the material desires of all the people. In fact, however, this isn't so, and therein lies the essence of the problem of scarcity.

SCARCITY—THE BASIC ECONOMIC PROBLEM

All nations on earth face the economic problem of **scarcity.** Everywhere, the limited set of goods that can be produced in a year is insufficient to satisfy, simultaneously, the desire for goods by all the people. When an attempt is made to give to all people all the goods they desire at zero prices, there are not enough goods to go around.

The notion of scarcity employed by economists, therefore, is clearly not identical to the concept of shortages that exist at *positive* prices. Nor must it be confused with situations in which quantities supplied seem small compared to other times or places. Economists measure the desire for goods at *zero* prices and do not link scarcity to the production of small quantities of goods. On the contrary, in many nations, many goods are produced in huge quantities indeed. The essence of scarcity lies in the *relationship* between people's desire for goods (at zero prices) and their ability to produce goods. As long as that desire exceeds that ability, no matter how large that ability is, scarcity persists, as Figure 1.1 illustrates.

Because economists are forever telling people that ours is a world of scarcity wherein people can never have all they want, economics is often called "the dismal science." Yet, actually, economists are far from content with being prophets of gloom. While they recognize that scarcity is a built-in fact of life for modern Americans, Chinese, and Russians as well as for isolated Bushmen, Indians, and Eskimos, the main concern of economists is to explore the exact implications of scarcity. This exploration can help people minimize the impact of scarcity.

SCARCITY REQUIRES CHOICE

The most obvious implication of scarcity is the need to choose—which is the second major lesson of an elementary text. Children have to learn painfully that, when confronted with the

FIGURE 1.1

The Scarcity Problem

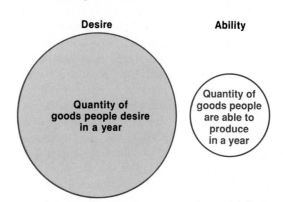

In any nation today, the people's wish to satisfy all their desires for goods is frustrated by the unavailability of sufficient resources and technical knowledge to produce a sufficiently large quantity of goods. While resources and technology allow the production of the "pie" shown by the right-hand circle, people would like to consume the one shown by the left-hand circle. Note: This graph refers to a given year. Over time, the right-hand circle can grow, as more resources and better technology are put to work. Yet the left-hand circle can grow as well, as the number of people or desires multiply, allowing scarcity to persist.

offer of ice cream or cake, "I take both" is not a permissible answer. Adult decision makers in every society, every day, face similar painful choices. Because the present technical knowledge of people falls short of that possessed by genies, there are not enough resources to do everything; hence, people cannot have all the goods they want. But they can choose within the limited realm of the possible. They can decide what will be done with the resources available— and what must be left undone. And there are literally millions of such choices to be made. Consider some of the major types of choices.

First, decision makers in each society must decide on the *rate of resource use;* for example, they must decide how many hours the available number of people or machines should work on the average day. Decision makers must then decide on the *rates of consumption and investment;* that is, they must channel the chosen flow of resource services (such as 800 million labor hours per day) toward making goods available to households in the present or toward the creation of bigger and better stocks of resources and improved methods of production. Decision makers must also determine the *detailed composition of production;* in other words, they must decide on the precise types and quantities of (individual and collective) consumption or investment goods. Some economists refer to the decisions just discussed as the big question of What. People in each society must decide, they say, *what* they will have: leisure or goods, consumption or investment goods, apples or new factories. . . . But people must also consider the question of How; that is, they must decide on how each of these decisions is to be carried out. Such a decision requires that people determine a *scheme of specialization,* or precisely which household provides, and which firm uses, which portion of the total flow of resource services toward what end. Finally, as some economists like to put it, there is the big question of For Whom. People in each society must choose one of many possible ways of *apportioning goods* among themselves.

CHOICE BRINGS BENEFIT AND COST

In a world of scarcity, the kinds of choices previously outlined cannot be escaped. And every choice is a mixture of pleasure and pain, of opportunity gained and opportunity lost. This is so because every use of resources for one purpose means forgoing the opportunity to use them for another purpose that is also desired. Every act of choice gives people something they want and thus brings an advantage, or **benefit,** but with each benefit comes the disappointment of not getting something else that is also wanted—hence, a disadvantage, or **cost.** Because every desire we satisfy ''costs us'' the opportunity of satisfying a different desire, the opportunity lost is also referred to as **opportunity cost.**

Implicitly, we have noted all this in the previous section. Every hour of labor performed means an hour of leisure forgone. Every labor

hour devoted to making a consumption good is an hour taken from making an investment good. Every hour of labor spent raising apples is an hour lost raising corn. Every labor hour spent raising apples in Oregon is an hour lost raising apples in Maine. Every apple given to John Doe is an apple lost to Peggy Brown. In each case, there is an opportunity gained and another one lost.

Figure 1.2, the production-possibilities frontier, is a favorite graph of elementary economics texts because it illustrates the concepts of scarcity and choice as well as the concepts of benefit and cost. Imagine people in a society allocating their annual flow of resources to the production of nothing but military goods, such as submarines

FIGURE 1.2

The Production-Possibilities Frontier

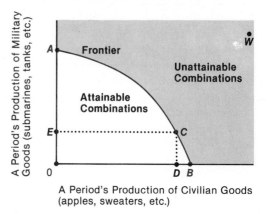

A Period's Production of Civilian Goods (apples, sweaters, etc.)

This production-possibilities frontier shows all the alternative combinations of two groups of goods that people in a society are capable of producing in a given period by using their flow of resources fully and in the best possible way, given their present state of technology. Thus it divides the set of all conceivable combinations of goods into two: attainable ones (unshaded) and unattainable ones (shaded). In a world of scarcity, there is always some impenetrable frontier that restricts people's freedom to get all they want (such as combination *W*). People must choose within the (unshaded) world of the possible, along or underneath the frontier to the world of the impossible. When they do, they derive a benefit, but they also incur an opportunity cost.

and tanks. By using their flow of resources fully and in the best possible way, given their present state of technical knowledge, the people of that society would be able to produce some maximum quantity of such goods, perhaps that shown by the distance $0A$ in Figure 1.2. These same people could, of course, devote all their resources to making goods for civilian uses, such as apples or sweaters. By using all their resources for civilian instead of military purposes, they would, under similar assumptions, produce some other maximum quantity of goods, exemplified by $0B$. These people could also produce any one of the many combinations of military and civilian goods lying on line AB. This line is their **production-possibilities frontier,** which shows all the alternative combinations of the two groups of goods that the people in a society are capable of producing in a given period by using their flow of resources fully and in the best possible way, given their present state of technology. The existence of scarcity is illustrated by the fact that all combinations of goods lying above and to the right of line AB are unattainable, even though they may well be wanted by people. Combinations lying to the left of and below the line are attainable, but they would require less than the total flow of resources or less efficient production methods than the people have available. The production-possibilities frontier inescapably restricts people's freedom to get all they want. They may want combination W, but they cannot penetrate the frontier into the (shaded) world of the impossible. In spite of scarcity, however, it is not impossible for people to choose from within the (unshaded) realm of the possible.

It is now very easy to see how each benefit comes together with an opportunity cost. If the people in this society were to produce quantity $0A$ of military goods, they would have to forgo quantity $0B$ of civilian goods. Thus the opportunity cost of $0A$ military goods would equal $0B$ of civilian goods. Alternatively, if these people were to produce $0B$ of civilian goods, they would have to forgo production of $0A$ of military goods. The opportunity cost of $0B$ of civilian goods would equal $0A$ of military goods. And if they

were to produce (at point C) some of both types of goods, the production of $0D$ of civilian goods would cost AE of military goods, while producing $0E$ of the military goods would cost BD of civilian goods. The benefit of producing a certain quantity of one good always costs people the quantity of another good that might have been made with the resources that were used to make the first.

The citizens of many a society have incurred heavy opportunity costs in order to carry forward certain national goals, whether freely chosen by all of them or imposed upon them by a few. Hitler urged Germany to forgo butter in favor of guns, and he presided over a massive national effort to cut the production of civilian goods in favor of military goods. Stalin, interested in rapid economic growth of the Soviet Union, drastically cut the production of consumption goods and greatly increased that of investment goods. The increased quantities of buildings and machines produced then, he argued, would allow a much greater production of consumption goods later. The people of the United States, in the 1960s, carried on a similar massive redirection of resources. In the midst of much controversy, such tasks as the abolition of poverty and the cleaning up of the environment were slighted in order to carry forward national commitments to land an American on the moon and to fight a war in Vietnam. (Close-Up 1.1 tells part of the story.)

We as individuals, similarly, incur opportunity costs every day, wherever we turn. Just as the nation as a whole has limited resources to spend, each individual has a limited money income. When we spend our money on ice cream, we might have to forgo the opportunity of seeing a movie. Then the movie forgone is the opportunity cost of eating ice cream. When a family spends its money on furniture, it might have to forgo a vacation trip. The vacation trip forgone is the opportunity cost of having the furniture.

Similar costs are incurred by all of us as we allocate the limited *time* available to us. If we watch the evening newscast (or read this book), we might not be able to watch the sunset. Not enjoying the sunset is the opportunity cost of seeing the news (or reading this book). Whatever we do, because there are so many things we like to do and time is limited, we must *pay* for our benefits by incurring opportunity costs. Everything we do has its price! And that is why economics applies to every nook and cranny of human experience, and why price theory, or microeconomics, has been called the heart of economic science.

THE NATURE OF MICROECONOMICS

The preceding sections make it easy to see why the following is such a popular definition of **economics:** *the study of how people allocate scarce resources (that usually have many alternative uses) to produce goods and of how they apportion these scarce goods among themselves.* Other, briefer definitions simply refer to economics as the study of scarcity or of choice, the need for the latter being, of course, implied by the existence of the former.

Practitioners of economics have, in turn, divided the field into **macroeconomics** and **microeconomics.** Macroeconomics, not to be dealt with in this book, studies the "big picture," the aggregate flows of resources and goods and the overall level of prices. Microeconomics, the exclusive subject matter of this book, studies the behavior of decision makers in households, firms, and governments who, individually or in groups, make the kinds of choices that determine not only the detailed composition of the aggregate flows of resources and goods, but also the relative prices among individual resources and goods.

And microeconomists have noted this: Individuals who make decisions in the context of scarcity are typically interested in promoting their welfare as much as possible, given the inescapable constraints that scarcity imposes upon them. To minimize the impact of scarcity on their lives, they sooner or later learn not to waste their resources, to use them ever so frugally, to

economize them. Sooner or later, consciously or unconsciously, the successful decision makers come to employ a special way of thinking.

MARGINALIST THINKING

To see what microeconomists have in mind, ask yourself this: How do we decide on the allocation of our scarce time among the many competing activities we might engage in? How do we decide on the allocation of our scarce money income among the many goods we want? Are we successfully economizing our own "resources"?

Even a moment's reflection reveals one interesting fact: Seldom do we make all-or-nothing decisions. We rarely spend *all* our time studying economics and *none* of it doing other things. We rarely spend all our income buying food and none of it buying other goods. Usually, we engage in a variety of activities in a day, just as we buy many different goods with our income. Groups of people, like the citizens of a nation, do the same thing. They never use all their scarce resources for one purpose only. Hitler did not make the Germans choose *all* guns and *no* butter (combination A in Figure 1.3). Rather, he moved Germany along its production-possibilities frontier from a combination like C (lots of civilian goods, few military goods, but some of *both*) to one nearer to but not at A (lots of military goods, few civilian goods, but some of both). The decisions made did not involve choosing *all* this or *all* that. It was, rather, a matter of *a little more of this* and *a little less of that,* as Figure 1.3 illustrates.

It is easy to see why all-or-nothing decisions are rare and why people often prefer to use scarce resources for a combination of many things. Imagine how you would feel about the allocation of your daily money income if you spent all of it on food only. No matter how much you wished otherwise, you couldn't buy the same amount of food *and* more of other things as well, but by giving up a little of the food you were buying in a day, you could get a little more of other things—like clothing, housing, or medical care. And you would then feel better off.

FIGURE 1.3

Making a New Choice

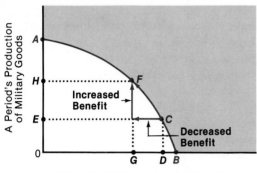

The reallocation of resources in a fully employed economy can be illustrated by a movement along its production-possibilities frontier, as from *C* to *F*. As a result of this movement, one benefit is decreased—in this case, the production of civilian goods from 0*D* to 0*G*. At the same time, another benefit is increased—in this case, the production of military goods from 0*E* to 0*H*.

At that moment you would have utilized, subconsciously no doubt, the very key to the economical use of resources. You would have engaged in **marginalist thinking,** or thinking about the objective possibility and the subjective welfare implication of small changes in variables. In this case you would have determined (a) that a dollar's worth of other goods could, in fact, be gained by forgoing a dollar's worth of food and (b) that the potential gain to your welfare from having a little more of other goods would far outweigh the potential loss to your welfare from doing so. (This loss would be occasioned by the necessity of having to eat less food.) By reallocating your spending accordingly, you would have squeezed from your scarce income a greater total welfare than before. And, without knowing it, you would have employed a principle of smart decision making that, consistently applied, would allow you to achieve not only greater welfare, but the greatest possible welfare.

OPTIMIZING

When there is scarcity, any act of choice brings with it not only a benefit, but also a cost. Therefore, if we replace one choice by another choice, we will *change* both the benefit and the cost that were associated with our original choice. Economists have a special name for such changes in the overall benefit and cost of an activity. They call an increase (or decrease) in an activity's overall benefit, which is attributable to a unit increase (or decrease) in the level of that activity, its **marginal benefit (*MB*).** And they call an increase (or decrease) in an activity's overall cost, which is attributable to a unit increase (or decrease) in the level of that activity, its **marginal cost (*MC*)** (or its marginal opportunity cost). Thus Hitler's decision to expand the production of military goods was occasioned by the judgment that the marginal benefit involved (distance *EH* in Figure 1.3) was worth more than the marginal cost (distance *DG*, the decreased benefit from the enjoyment of civilian goods, the production of which had to be decreased). Similarly, in the earlier example, your hypothetical decision to consume a larger quantity of other goods resulted from your judgment that the subjective value of the marginal benefit of doing so (the increase in your satisfaction caused by consuming more nonfood items than before) exceeded that of the marginal cost (the decrease in your satisfaction caused by having to consume less food in order to consume more nonfood items). The decision involved nothing more difficult than applying the **optimization principle:**

> *People desiring to maximize the welfare they obtain from scarce resources must change the level of any activity as long as they do not value equally its marginal benefit, **MB**, and its marginal cost, **MC**. Whenever they value the marginal benefit more than the marginal cost, an expansion of the activity will raise their total welfare. Whenever they value the marginal benefit less than the marginal cost, a contraction of the activity will raise their total welfare.*

Whenever they consider the marginal benefit and marginal cost of equal value, the best possible (or optimum) level of the activity has been reached.

The advice inherent in the optimization principle can be summarized succinctly, as in Box 1.A.

1.A The Optimization Principle

a. *MB > MC*, **expand activity.**
b. *MB < MC*, **contract activity.**
c. *MB = MC*, **activity level is optimum.**

If one follows this principle, any initial divergence between the values placed on marginal benefit and marginal cost tends to disappear as one changes the level of the activity in question. This surprising result occurs because the values placed on the marginal benefit tend to be smaller, and those placed on the marginal cost tend to be larger, at higher levels of an activity; at lower levels of the activity, the opposite occurs.

DECLINING MARGINAL BENEFIT

All other relevant factors being equal, the greater the overall level of any activity during a given period, the smaller will its marginal benefit usually be.

This **principle of declining marginal benefit** is depicted in Figure 1.4. If you were consuming no food at all during a day, you would, of course, get a zero *total* benefit from food consumption (Point 0, upper graph). But you might place a fairly high value on *changing* your level of food consumption from zero to one unit. The hypothetical increase in satisfaction associated with such a one-unit change in food consumption might be designated as quantity *a*, and this *marginal* benefit is illustrated by block *a* in the lower graph. The height of block *a* would also, of course, show the total benefit associated with a daily food consumption of one unit (point *Q*, upper graph).

But, almost certainly, you would feel quite different under different circumstances. Imagine, instead, that you were consuming four units of food per day and receiving a total benefit of *R*. You would surely place a much lower value on changing your level of food consumption by one unit, from four to five units. This lower hypothetical increase in satisfaction, associated with a unit change in food consumption, might be designated as quantity *e*, and this marginal benefit is illustrated by block *e* in the lower graph. The height of block *e*, of course, also shows by how much the total benefit associated with a daily food consumption of five units (point *P*) would exceed the total benefit associated with a daily food consumption of four units (point *R*).

All this is only common sense. Can you imagine yourself placing the *same* value on getting another unit of food (or attaching the *same* importance to giving up a single unit of food) regardless of your current level of consumption? Of course not. Indeed, one can easily imagine the marginal benefit of food consumption being zero at a sufficiently high level of consumption (to the right of block *e* on the lower graph). At such a point of **satiation,** the total benefit derivable from consumption could not be increased any further. The total benefit would be maximized at some point to the right of *P* in the upper graph. At that point you would feel that nothing could be gained from consuming a unit more and that nothing would be lost by consuming a unit less.

Just as one can increase daily food intake, so can one decrease it. In that case, the operation of the principle of declining marginal benefit reverses: *Because marginal benefit is lower at higher levels of an activity, marginal benefit is higher at lower levels of an activity.* You can see this reversal of the principle by noting how the size of the blocks in Figure 1.4 increases as one goes from the right-hand to the left-hand side of the graphs. This fact also corresponds to our

FIGURE 1.4

Declining Marginal Benefit

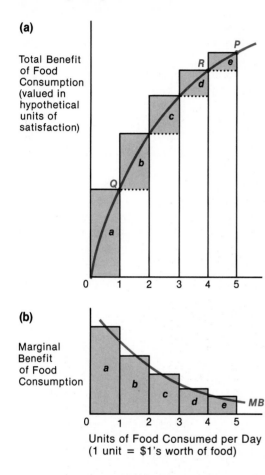

(a)

Total Benefit of Food Consumption (valued in hypothetical units of satisfaction)

(b)

Marginal Benefit of Food Consumption

Units of Food Consumed per Day
(1 unit = $1's worth of food)

This graph illustrates the principle of declining marginal benefit. All other relevant factors being equal, the higher the level of daily food consumption, the lower its marginal benefit (*MB*). The heights of blocks *a* through *e* measure the hypothetical marginal benefit. Note how, in panel (b), the smooth curve drawn through the top of each block declines toward the right, while the total benefit of food consumption in panel (a)—being nothing else but the sum of the marginal benefits—rises by less and less as the amount of food consumed increases by equal units. Note: The principle is not a rigid law. Increased units of any activity may well be associated with at first rising and then constant marginal benefits (not shown here), but the principle asserts that marginal benefits always decline *eventually.*

daily experience. For example, it might make little difference to you whether you got four or five units of food per day. Your evaluation of the marginal benefit might be low (quantity *e*). Yet it might make a big difference to you to get one unit of food instead of two. Under these different circumstances, your view of the marginal benefit might be high (quantity *b*). The marginal benefit of food consumption differs with your circumstances! Place this phenomenon in the context of scarcity, and you make an important discovery: *Declining* marginal benefit is closely related to *rising* marginal cost.

RISING MARGINAL COST

As we noted earlier, we can, in fact, always have more of one good if we are ready to give up some of another. Now we are ready to see fully the implication of making such changes. As we have more and more of one thing, the result is *declining* marginal benefits. But these benefits come to us only because we have less and less of another thing, the *rising* marginal benefits of which we have to forgo. Those forgone and rising marginal benefits of whatever we are giving up are, of course, the *rising marginal costs* of whatever we are getting more of. Given your limited money income, if you buy successively more units of clothing, you must forgo successively more units of food. As you do so, the marginal benefit to you of clothing will decline, but, simultaneously, the marginal cost to you of clothing will rise. This is so because the marginal cost to you of clothing is identical to the forgone marginal benefit to you of food, which will rise as you have less food. Consider Figure 1.5.

Figure 1.5 is based on Figure 1.4 and, to keep things simple, on the assumption that the marginal benefit of food is independent of the quantity of clothing, while the marginal benefit of clothing is unaffected by the quantity of food. Now imagine yourself spending $5 a day on food and clothing. If we defined a unit of each good as *a dollar's worth*, you could buy five units of food and nothing else, deriving a total benefit shown by point P in Figure 1.4. You could, of course, get a first unit of clothing by giving up the fifth unit of food. If you did, you would gain satisfaction from clothing (a quantity we might call f), but your satisfaction derived from food would drop from point P to point R in Figure 1.4; that is, by quantity e. This would be the marginal cost of consuming one unit of clothing per day (note quantity e in the lower graph, Figure 1.5). Similarly, giving up the fourth unit of food (to get a second one of clothing) would involve not only a further (and smaller) gain (quantity g), but also a further (and larger) loss of satisfaction equal to d (Figure 1.4). This loss would be the marginal cost of consuming two units of clothing (note quantity d in the lower graph, Figure 1.5). At this point, the *total* cost of clothing consumption would be $e + d$ (upper graph, Figure 1.5). You can proceed similarly to derive the remainder of Figure 1.5.

THE MAXIMUM NET BENEFIT

It is but a short step now to determine how you could gain the greatest satisfaction from your limited budget; it is just a matter of applying the optimization principle illustrated in Figure 1.6. In the upper two portions of the graph, the smooth curves representing the total and marginal cost of clothing consumption in Figure 1.5 have been redrawn. Added are total and marginal benefit curves for clothing consumption, which are analogous to those for food in Figure 1.4.

Now it can be shown that you would have to consume 2.5 units of clothing per day if you cared to maximize your **net benefit**; that is, the difference between the total benefit and total cost of your activities. If you consumed less, you would find the marginal benefit of clothing consumption, *MB*, exceeding the corresponding marginal cost, *MC*. Note how distance f exceeds e and how g exceeds d. In each case, by consuming more clothing at the expense of food, you would raise your total benefit (by f or g, respectively), but you would raise your total cost

FIGURE 1.5

Rising Marginal Cost

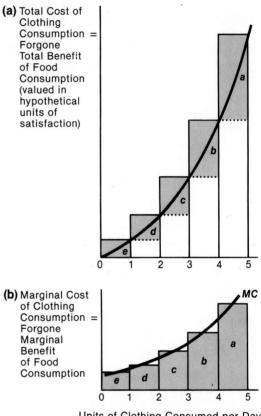

(a) Total Cost of Clothing Consumption = Forgone Total Benefit of Food Consumption (valued in hypothetical units of satisfaction)

(b) Marginal Cost of Clothing Consumption = Forgone Marginal Benefit of Food Consumption

Units of Clothing Consumed per Day (1 unit = $1's worth of clothing)

The declining marginal benefit of increased food consumption implies a rising marginal benefit of decreased food consumption (Figure 1.4); this rising marginal benefit of decreased food consumption constitutes the rising marginal cost of increased clothing consumption if food has to be sacrificed for clothing. Note: It is assumed here that the marginal benefit of consuming any one good is independent of the quantities consumed of any other good.

by less (by e or d, respectively). Because the additional satisfaction from more clothing would exceed the loss of satisfaction from less food, the difference between your total benefit and total cost, or your *net benefit*, would rise (from k toward m). Note how the net benefit is plotted separately in the lowest portion of the graph.

Similarly, you would be foolish to consume more than 2.5 units of clothing per day. If you did, you would find the marginal benefit of clothing consumption falling short of its marginal cost. Note how distance *i* falls short of *b* and how *j* falls short of *a*. In this case, by consuming less clothing but more food, you would lower your total benefit (by *j* or *i*), but you would lower your total cost more (by *a* or *b*). Since the loss of satisfaction from less clothing would be exceeded by the additional satisfaction from more food, your net benefit would again rise (from *o* toward *m*).*

We can now go full circle and return to the issue raised earlier in this chapter. We make so few all-or-nothing decisions precisely because, without knowing it, we are following the optimization principle in much of our daily lives. It is rarely desirable to expand an activity in order to maximize the total benefit from it. Note how, in the top graph of Figure 1.6, the total benefit of clothing consumption would indeed continue to rise beyond the optimum if you purchased a fourth or fifth unit. But it is the *greater* rise in total cost (the greater loss in some other benefit) that would make such action inadvisable.

Whoever follows the principle of optimization can thus reach the best possible (or *optimum*) position—not where the *total* benefit is maximized, but where the total benefit of an activity

This graph illustrates the principle of optimization: Anyone desiring to maximize the net benefit of an activity must expand or contract that activity up to the point at which its marginal benefit just equals its marginal cost. This optimum is reached at 2.5 units of clothing consumption in this example. Note how the *equality* of marginal benefit and marginal cost in panel (b) is associated with the widest divergence of total benefit and total cost in panel (a) and, thus, with the greatest net benefit in panel (c). Note also that we abstract from the possibility that low levels of an activity may be associated with at first rising or constant marginal benefits and with at first falling or constant marginal costs in order to focus on the essentials.

*For a calculus-based treatment of this material, see Section 1A of the Calculus Appendix at the back of this book.

FIGURE 1.6

Optimization

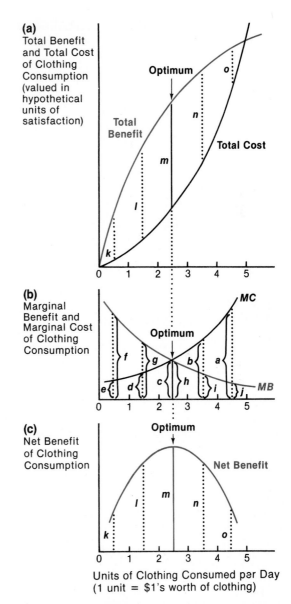

Units of Clothing Consumed per Day
(1 unit = $1's worth of clothing)

exceeds the total cost by the greatest amount, yielding the maximum *net* benefit (distance *m*). This principle is widely applicable beyond the seemingly trivial example utilized here.

A UNIVERSAL PRINCIPLE

The optimization principle is the universal principle of rational behavior for all who want to maximize welfare under conditions of scarcity. The people of all societies, be they members of households, managers of firms, or government officials, must apply it when deciding how to allocate their scarce resources in the best way. You must apply it if you care to allocate most effectively your scarce money income between food and clothing or your scarce time between tennis and study. Managers must apply it if they care to allocate their scarce resources most effectively between the production of cars and trucks or potatoes and wheat. Government officials must apply it if they care to allocate their scarce resources most effectively between health care and education or subways and cleaning up the environment. All these activities have marginal costs, all of which eventually rise as the activity level is increased. All these activities have declining marginal benefits also. And that is why all decision makers must be careful not to do too much of any one thing at the expense of other things that are also wanted. No matter how good or sacred any activity may seem, in a world of scarcity there is some logical stopping point beyond which an activity should be expanded no further. This is not the point of satiation, but the point at which, in people's judgment, the marginal cost and marginal benefit have come together. Those who heed this rule will be most effective in achieving their objectives, whatever they may be. But there are complications.

COMPLICATIONS

Making the best of all possible choices looks simple enough in Figure 1.6. The position of the optimum is obvious no matter which one of the three graphs is considered because the example is a simple one. All the necessary data have been plotted and the necessary curves have been drawn for us, placing us in the position of an omniscient observer. A single decision maker is involved. Unfortunately, the real world is much more inconveniently arranged. Decision makers may not know what the relevant benefits and costs are, they may disagree about the precise magnitudes of marginal benefit and marginal cost, or they may clash over who will reap the benefit and who will bear the cost. (See Close-Ups 1.2 and 1.3.)

All this, however, does not invalidate the usefulness of the optimization principle. It is helpful even in less than ideal circumstances. It helps decision makers avoid the grossest of errors in allocating their scarce resources—not a mean accomplishment in a world of scarcity—and it helps economists predict at least the direction of any changes that decision makers are likely to make. Thus economists expect that people will often be unable to equate benefits and costs precisely at the margin. Yet they also expect that people will change their behavior whenever the possibility of a more satisfactory state of affairs (of reaping a larger net benefit under different circumstances) has become too obvious to be ignored. And if people who are eager to promote their own welfare at least follow the optimization principle to the best of their ability (and that seems in fact to be the case), economists who are aware of this fact have in their hands a powerful tool of understanding and prediction. Consider, for instance, one of the most important models of the elementary economics course, that of perfectly competitive supply and demand.

SUPPLY AND DEMAND REVISITED

The supply and demand model is illustrated in Figure 1.7 and predicts, in this example, an equilibrium price of $3 per bushel of potatoes and an equilibrium quantity of 900 million bushels per year. The similarity of this graph with panel (b) of Figure 1.6 is more than accidental. Behind the demand line lies the declining marginal ben-

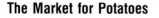

FIGURE 1.7

The Market for Potatoes

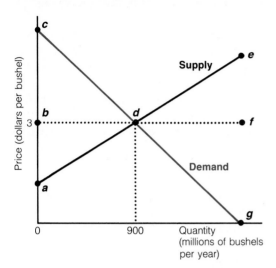

In a perfectly competitive potato market, large numbers of well-informed and independently acting buyers as well as sellers are trading a homogeneous product, being free to enter into or exit from the market at will. The equilibrium price equals $3 per bushel, and the equilibrium quantity equals 900 million bushels per year, in this example.

efit of potato consumers and the assumption that these consumers are trying to maximize their utility. To these consumers, the market price (represented by the dotted horizontal line from b to f) equals the marginal cost of acquiring potatoes; as long as they consider the marginal benefit (along segment cd) to be worth more than this marginal cost (along segment bd), potatoes are bought; once the marginal benefit (along segment dg) is considered worth less than this marginal cost (along segment df), potatoes are not bought. Similarly, behind the supply line lies the rising marginal cost of potato producers and the assumption that these producers are trying to maximize their profit. To these producers, the market price (again represented by the dotted horizontal line) equals the marginal benefit of selling potatoes; as long as this marginal benefit (along segment bd) exceeds the associated marginal cost

of production (along segment ad), potatoes are produced and offered for sale; once the marginal benefit (along segment df) falls short of marginal cost (along segment de), potatoes are not produced.

Or consider the claim that perfectly competitive markets produce **economic efficiency,** a state of affairs in which it is impossible to make someone better off without harming anyone else (or, put differently, in which all conceivable mutually beneficial deals among parties have been carried out). The truth of this claim can be seen in Figure 1.7 and can also be stated in terms of the optimization principle. Until the equilibrium quantity of 900 million bushels is reached, the marginal benefit to consumers (along segment cd) exceeds the marginal cost to producers (along segment ad); thus mutually beneficial deals can be struck (such as selling at $3 per bushel). Beyond the equilibrium quantity, no such deals can be struck because marginal benefit (along dg) is less than marginal cost (along de).

Finally, consider any external event, such as the imposition of an excise tax on potato producers that raises their marginal costs (and, thus, the supply line) vertically by $1. The model predicts a rise in price and a fall in the quantity produced; once again, this could be easily explained by the optimizing behavior of consumers and producers alike.

Throughout the remainder of this book, similar models or theories of human behavior will be introduced and, again and again, the optimization principle will play a key role in them. Before we proceed, however, we should understand clearly the nature of the journey we are about to take, because it is often misunderstood.

THEORIZING: MAKING MAPS OF REALITY

Some professors tell the story of a mythical student who demanded ''just the facts, all the facts.'' Anyone who wants to understand a modern market economy (such as that of the United

States) and who wants to judge the degree of its success in allocating scarce resources in the best possible way does well not to ask for *all* the facts. It is too easy to drown in an infinite morass of incoherent detail. Contrary to the often heard cliché, facts do *not* speak for themselves.

Paradoxically, true understanding is always gained through the orderly *loss* of information. To gain such understanding of our economy, we must simplify, even ruthlessly so. We must first take something like a satellite picture of the market economy, a picture that brings into sharp relief the broad outlines of reality but fails to convey important details. Once we have come to understand the *essence* of the market economy as described in Parts Two and Three, we can move our vantage point and consider additional features of the bewildering complexity around us in the remaining chapters.

The process of abstracting from reality, of focusing on only its most important features, is called *theorizing*. Theorizing is akin to producing a geographic map. Because all of us have used maps, we are already familiar with the benefits of theorizing. Notice how geographers never provide us with a detailed picture of the world. Nowadays they draw their maps from satellite and aircraft photographs, and, before we know it, they show us the whole United States on a piece of paper 12 inches square. What could be more unrealistic? Yet realism would force the map makers to include every town, every brook, every house and tree, even every blade of grass in the landscape. This would be manifestly absurd. If we insisted on realism in maps, none of us would have the slightest idea even of the broad outlines of our physical environment. Literally, we would be lost. It is just when we create the unrealistic, when we forget about the many towns and brooks and houses, when we refuse to consider trees and blades of grass, that we create the useful. Up to a point, the more unrealistic it is, the more useful our map becomes! As we delete most of the detail and concentrate on the essentials, we extract ourselves from the chaos of fact and see things to which we were blind before. Economic theorizing does the same sort

of thing. It produces a set of propositions intended to serve as an explanation of the major phenomena observed in the economy. Like a map, such **theory** is a simplified representation of reality.

Yet we should note one thing at the outset: While it is true that theory is indispensable for those who seek to understand a complex world, it is also true that not every theory is automatically a good one. Just as early map makers produced bad maps that falsified even the broad outlines of reality (and contributed to confusion rather than understanding), so theorists are quite capable of producing simplified representations of the economic world that mislead rather than enlighten. This is, of course, no argument against drawing maps or constructing theory; it is an argument for making the best possible ones. And this brings us to an important question: How can we tell whether a theory is good or bad?

GOOD THEORY VERSUS BAD THEORY

There are two schools of thought on the best way to test a theory. Some judge a theory by testing the validity of its *assumptions;* others by testing the validity of a theory's *predictions*.

Testing a Theory by Its Assumptions

One way to evaluate a theory is to inquire into the truth of the assumptions on which a theory is based. If the assumptions are patently false or distort reality greatly, one can rate the theory as bad and refuse to use it as a guide to reality.

In the preceding discussion, for example, we made the assumption that owners of firms maximize profits. Some economists have argued that this is simply not so. When asked about their motivation, owners of firms, these critics say, reveal a great variety of goals besides maximum profit: a large share of their market, maximum *sales,* prestige (gained, perhaps, by improving environmental quality or giving to charity), personal power, a good life, growth of their firms, technical leadership, *average* profit (to discourage competitors, labor unions, and government regulators), stability (or the avoidance of unpleasant surprises)—the list goes on. Indeed, critics continue, firms that are corporations are run by managers and not owners; and managers couldn't care less about profit. They care a great deal about high salaries, large staffs, luxury offices, business trips to Las Vegas, and the like. These things raise costs and *reduce* profit.

In the same fashion, those focusing on assumptions to validate theory might investigate any other assumption made (such as the maximization of utility by households or the particular role played by government). They might note many exceptions, and they might, therefore, reject out of hand and right now *whatever* theory might be built upon these assumptions in the chapters to come. But one can test the validity of a theory in an altogether different way.

Testing a Theory by Its Predictions

There are those who argue that the nature of theoretical assumptions is quite irrelevant to judging the usefulness of theories. All geographic maps are totally at odds with what people know about reality, yet these maps work—they help people find their way. In the same way, economic theories may well be based on the weirdest of assumptions; what matters is whether they allow us to make accurate predictions about past or future phenomena of which observations have not yet been made.

Milton Friedman (1912–   ), who won the 1976 Nobel Prize in economics (and whose Biography appears in Chapter 1 of the *Student Workbook* that accompanies this text), has been the undisputed leader of those who would validate a theory solely on the basis of its ability to generate successful predictions. Consider, for example, his view of the profit maximization assumption. Friedman knows that many of the nonprofit goals noted above are in fact not as important as alleged. Yet proving the validity of the profit-maximizing assumption does not matter to him at all. Friedman would retain any

theory based on the profit-maximizing assumption, even if the behavior of firms were apparently determined by the nonprofit goals listed above or even if owners made decisions at random—*as long as accurate predictions were derivable from this theory.* And why should such accurate predictions be generated? Because, among all the owners of firms, some may in fact (and quite unintentionally) make the kinds of decisions that maximize profits. Their firms may well prosper and grow in the long run. And all other firms may grow less, shrink, and disappear. If this were so, Friedman argues, one would be justified in assuming a nonexistent world in which owners of firms *consciously* maximized profits. A theory based on this false assumption would nevertheless produce accurate predictions about the survival of profit-maximizing firms in the real world.

Thus Friedman considers the widely held view that realistic assumptions are the criteria for a valid theory as fundamentally wrong and the cause of much mischief. Truly significant theories, he argues, necessarily have assumptions that are wildly inaccurate as descriptive representations of reality. The more significant the theory, the more unrealistic its assumptions must be. A theory is important, he says, if it explains much by little, if it abstracts crucial elements from the mass of complex and detailed circumstances surrounding the phenomena to be explained, and permits valid predictions on the basis of them alone. This is also the position adopted in this book.

Positive Theory Versus Normative Statements

The stress on prediction as a test for the value of a theory has an added advantage. It calls attention to a crucial distinction. We will restrict ourselves here to **positive theory,** theory that makes purely descriptive statements and predictions. Positive theory is the essence of science. It explains what is and what causes what; it predicts what will be the consequences of any change in circumstances. Such positive theory must not be confused with

normative statements, or prescriptive statements akin to preaching. Such value judgments tell us what ought to be, what is good, and what is bad.

Every theorist has, of course, personal preferences. Often these norms act as a filter for the analytic perceptions of the theorist. All of us, being human, tend to filter out aspects of reality that challenge our norms and to overemphasize those that support them. Often we are blind to what we dislike, overperceptive to what we like. We may end up presenting as theory (as a map of reality) what is in fact our own wishful thinking.

The only known remedy for this deplorable habit of confusing our wishful thinking with reality is the criticism of others. However blind they are to the impact of their norms on their thought (as we are to that of our norms on our thought), we all seem to have an acute perception of the impact of the norms of others on their thought. We must always do our best not to shape positive conclusions to fit strongly held normative preconceptions and not to reject positive conclusions when their normative implications are unpalatable to us. Normative statements that masquerade as positive theory are the worst possible kind of ''theory.''

SUMMARY

1. Most people on earth harbor desires for a truly staggering variety and quantity of goods. One can appreciate the extent of this desire by imagining the quantities of goods people would take if all goods were available at zero prices.

2. Goods are produced with resources—human, natural, and capital.

3. Technology sets limits on the quantity of goods producible per unit of resources.

4. Limited resources and limited technology combine to yield limited quantities of goods in any given period.

5. In all nations today, the quantity of goods that can be produced in a given period with available resources and technology falls short of the quantity required to fulfill, simultaneously, the desire for goods by all the people. This condition constitutes the economic problem of scarcity.

6. The most obvious implication of scarcity is the need to choose. People in each society must decide on one of many possible rates at which to use their resources. They must direct their flow of resources toward consuming or investing. They must choose the detailed composition of their production and a scheme of specialization among themselves. They must choose one of many ways of apportioning their output.

7. Choice brings a mixture of pleasure and pain because every use of resources for one purpose means forgoing the opportunity to use them for another desired purpose. Where there is scarcity, opportunity cost thus accompanies any benefit derived from a particular use of resources. This fact can be illustrated by the production-possibilities frontier.

8. Microeconomics, the exclusive subject matter of this book, studies the behavior of decision makers in households, firms, and governments who make the kinds of choices that determine not only the detailed composition of the aggregate flows of resources and goods, but also the relative prices of individual resources and goods.

9. Modern economists stress that successful economizing requires a special (marginalist) way of thinking about the objective possibility and subjective welfare implication of small changes in variables. People can always allocate another unit of their fully used resources toward one activity if they take a unit away from another activity. They can always have a marginal benefit if they are ready to pay a marginal cost.

10. The optimization principle tells people who wish to maximize their welfare under what circumstances it is wise or foolish to expand one activity at the expense of another. The optimization principle tells people whenever a subjective evaluation of one activity shows:

a. $MB > MC$, one should expand the activity.

b. $MB < MC$, one should contract the activity.

c. $MB = MC$, the activity level is optimum.

11. As a consequence of the principle of declining marginal benefit, any initial divergence between marginal benefit and marginal cost tends to disappear as one changes the level of an activity.

12. Declining marginal benefits associated with increased levels of an activity imply rising marginal benefits associated with decreased levels of that activity. If such decreased levels are the opportunity cost of increasing some other activity, the rising marginal benefits forgone from the sacrificed activity become the rising marginal costs of the increasing activity.

13. The net benefit of any activity can be maximized by following the optimization principle.

14. The optimization principle is a universal principle of rational behavior that sets, for all activities, a logical stopping point beyond which that activity should be expanded no further.

15. Optimizing can, however, be an elusive goal, especially when crucial information needed by individual decision makers is absent or when they clash over who is to reap the benefits or bear the costs.

16. Nevertheless, the optimization principle is the basis for many microeconomic models or theories that help us understand or predict the behavior of people. This is illustrated with the familiar model of supply and demand. Many similar illustrations will be found in the remainder of the book, which explores every nook and cranny of the modern market economy.

17. Anyone who wants to understand the modern market economy and wants to judge the degree of its success will find it impossible to gather and digest *all* the relevant facts. Yet the desired understanding can be gained by a process called *theorizing*. This process is much akin to the making of a geographic map because a map, like a theory, becomes a useful guide to reality precisely because it is unrealistic.

18. A comprehensive theory that explains the major phenomena observed in the market economy can be built from simple assumptions, such as the attempt by firms to maximize their profits. Two schools of thought disagree on the issue of what makes a theory good or bad. Some would test the goodness of a theory by the validity of its *assumptions* (an approach rejected here); others would focus on the validity of its *predictions*. In either case, one must be careful to distinguish between *positive theory* (description and prediction) and *normative statements* (prescription or preaching).

KEY TERMS

benefit

capital resources

cost

desire for goods

economic efficiency

economics

financial capital

goods

human capital

human resources

macroeconomics

marginal benefit (*MB*)

marginal cost (*MC*)

marginalist thinking

microeconomics

natural resources

net benefit

normative statements

opportunity cost

optimization principle

positive theory

principle of declining marginal benefit

process of production

production-possibilities frontier

resources

satiation

scarcity

technology

theory

HANDS-ON PRACTICE

Exercise #1

The public health director of a large city has an annual budget of $400,000 and wants to spend it to save as many lives as possible. Two approaches, in particular, seem most promising: cancer screening of the population or purchasing and deploying mobile cardiac arrest units throughout the city. The projected facts are given in Tables 1.1 and 1.2.

TABLE 1.1

Cancer Screening Program

Population Screened	Total Annual Cost	Total Lives Saved
60–70 year olds	$ 80,000	35
50–70	$160,000	65
40–70	$240,000	85
30–70	$320,000	95
20–70	$400,000	100

TABLE 1.2

Mobile Cardiac Arrest Units

Number of Units	Total Annual Cost	Total Lives Saved
1	$ 80,000	100
2	$160,000	150
3	$240,000	175
4	$320,000	190
5	$400,000	200

The public health director hires you to resolve a dispute between him and his staff. He argues that the entire budget should be spent on mobile cardiac arrest units (saving 200 lives) rather than on cancer screening (saving only 100 lives). His staff proposes to apply a "principle of optimization" instead and spend some money on each program.

Solution:

Measuring marginal benefit, MB, and marginal cost, MC, in terms of lives saved or not saved, you could fill in Table 1.3 as follows. Note that the first cardiac arrest unit saves 100 lives but costs $80,000 and, thus, requires giving up screening the lowest-risk population group for cancer (and *not* saving $100 - 95 = 5$ lives of 20–29-year-olds). Similarly, the second cardiac arrest unit saves an additional $150 - 100 = 50$ lives, but costs $95 - 85 = 10$ lives (of 30–39-year-olds).

TABLE 1.3

Mobile Cardiac Arrest Units

Number of Units	MB	MC
1st	100	5
2nd	50	10
3rd	25	20
4th	15	30
5th	10	35

Proceeding with the purchase of cardiac arrest units as long as $MB > MC$, you should recommend purchasing three units, spending $240,000 and saving 175 heart attack victims. By implication, you would spend $160,000 on screening 50–70-year-olds for cancer, saving an additional 65 lives, or a total of 240 lives.

Alternative Solution:

You could have filled in Table 1.4 instead. Note that screening the 60–70-year-olds saves 35 lives but costs $80,000 and, thus, requires giving up the 5th cardiac arrest unit (and 10 lives). Similarly, screening the 50–59-year-olds in addition saves an extra $65 - 35 = 30$ lives, but costs $190 - 175 = 15$ lives of heart attack victims who do not find the 4th unit in place.

Proceeding with cancer screening as long as $MB > MC$, you should recommend screening the two highest-risk groups, spending $160,000 and saving 65 lives. By implication, you would

TABLE 1.4

Cancer Screening

Age of Group Screened	*MB*	*MC*
60–70 years	35	10
50–59	30	15
40–49	20	25
30–39	10	50
20–29	5	100

spend $240,000 on cardiac arrest units, saving an additional 175 lives, or a total of 240 lives, as above.

Exercise #2

Figure 1.8 represents a perfectly competitive market for beef. Let supply be represented by $P = 10 + .4Q$.

FIGURE 1.8

The Market for Beef

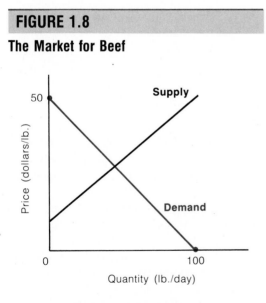

a.   Calculate the equilibrium price and quantity.

b.   Recalculate the equilibrium price and quantity after the government imposes a $10 excise tax per unit of beef sold.

Solution:

a.   The equation of the supply line is given to us directly as $P = 10 + .4Q$. As Figure 1.9 indicates, in this equation, the constant 10 represents the vertical intercept of supply (point *a*), while the coefficient .4 represents the supply line slope (such as the ratio *cb/ab* or 40/100). The equation of the demand line can be derived from the information given in Figure 1.8. Focus on the encircled values reproduced in Figure 1.9 and follow the arrows, writing

$$P = 50 - \frac{50}{100}Q = 50 - .5Q$$

FIGURE 1.9

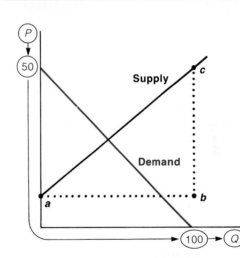

In this equation, the constant 50 represents the vertical intercept of demand, while the coefficient $-.5$ represents the negative demand line slope.

In equilibrium, demand equals supply; hence

$$50 - .5Q = 10 + .4Q \text{ and}$$
$$40 = .9Q \text{ and}$$
$$Q = 44.\overline{44}$$

By implication, $P = 10 + .4(44.\overline{44}) = 27.\overline{77}$.

b.   The solution for part (a) is illustrated in Figure 1.10 by point E. The $10 excise tax shifts the supply line as shown and changes the supply equation to $P = 20 + .4Q$. Hence, in the new equilibrium at point e,

$$50 - .5Q = 20 + .4Q \text{ and}$$
$$30 = .9Q \text{ and}$$
$$Q = 33.\overline{33}$$

By implication, $P = 20 + .4(33.\overline{33}) = 33.\overline{33}$.

FIGURE 1.10

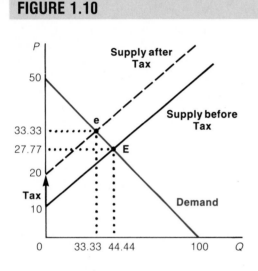

QUESTIONS AND PROBLEMS

1. a.   Which of the following are *natural resources* as defined in this chapter: 100 cubic feet of coal, a highway, a cow, an acre of land, sand at a beach not yet discovered by humans, sunshine, a school of tuna in the ocean, a college building, a can of peas? (*Hint:* Of the nine required answers, three will be *always*, three others *never*, and the remaining three *maybe*). What reasons can you give for your answers?

b.   Which of the following are *capital resources:* an automobile assembly plant, a toy truck, Ford Motor Company stock, a natural waterfall, unsold refrigerators held by an appliance dealer, an inventory of groceries held by a food store, a horse, a truck driver, a wristwatch? (*Hint:* Of the nine required answers, three will be *always*, three others *never*, and the remaining three *maybe*.) What reasons can you give for your answers?

2.   Have another look at Figure 1.1, which illustrates the scarcity problem. Residents of poor countries are almost unanimous in preferring policies that increase the right-hand circle to policies that decrease the left-hand circle; the reverse is found only among some residents of rich countries. Explain, using the principle of declining marginal benefit.

3.   A country faces a production-possibilities frontier (such as Figure 1.2) that relates military goods, M, to civilian goods, C, and that is described by the equation $5C^2 + 2M^2 = 80$.

a.   What are the largest amounts of C and M that can be produced?

b.   How much C must be produced to ensure $C = 4M$?

c.   What is the opportunity cost when the production of C is increased from 2 to 3 units?

4.   Draw a production-possibilities frontier like the one in Figure 1.2. Label the vertical axis "investment goods" and the horizontal one "consumption goods." Choose some point on the curve near the middle to depict a country's present position. What do you think would eventually happen *to the entire curve* if the country's citizens

a.   increased the production of investment goods (and your chosen point moved up and left along the frontier)?

b.   reduced the production of investment goods (and your chosen point moved down and right along the frontier)?

c.   decided to give up the "rat race" and be content with a minimum of both types of goods?

5. Consider the concept of *opportunity cost*.

a. Suppose you had to choose one of *three* items *a*, *b*, and *c*. If you chose *a*, what would be the opportunity cost: *b*, *c*, or both?

b. What do you think is the opportunity cost of each of the following: giving more foreign aid, stepping up the arms race, avoiding air and water pollution?

c. When people say "time is money," what can they possibly mean?

6. Explain the following statements (with the help of Figure 1.6 on optimization):

a. "It may be wise for a household to stop the consumption of any good long before satiation is reached, and it would be stupid to increase consumption beyond satiation."

b. "It may be wise for a nation to stop putting more resources into education long before the extra benefits from such action have fallen to zero."

c. "It is stupid to maximize the total benefit of an activity and equally stupid to minimize its total cost."

d. "It is foolish to maximize the total benefit of an activity and equally foolish to maximize the ratio of total benefit to total cost."

7.   Mr. A: I have been looking at Figure 1.6 on optimization. It's fascinating! Just imagine how one can apply it to other things besides mundane commodities: One could put on the horizontal axis the height of trees or of buildings, the weight of people or of airplanes, the size of people's wealth or of their business organizations, the degree of pollution or the degree of race or sex discrimination in society. Or even people's sinfulness and the length of their lives! In all these cases and a million more, the graph applies. Most things are good when there is little of them and bad when there is much.

Mrs. B: Really, *you* are a little much. Your application of the optimization principle is an outrage. I am with Wordsworth: "High Heaven rejects the lore of nicely calculated less or more." Discuss.

8. Evaluate each illustration of the following statement: "People, clearly, do *not* optimize:

a. Note how speeders end up in the hospital, bank robbers go to jail, and cheating students are thrown out of school."

b. Note how so many people do things I would never do because I know it is bad for me (and them)."

c. Note how so many people act selfishly, impulsively, or out of habit."

9.   Ms. A: Economic analysis can and should be pursued with the same objective detachment that natural scientists are said to bring to their subjects. Economists must never confuse their role with that of advocates, moral teachers, or priests; their goal must be prediction and control of social phenomena; their method must be abstract reasoning, backed up by tangible data and reproducible experiments.

Ms. B: I disagree. Prediction is not the hallmark of all science. (What has the theory of evolution ever predicted?) Economics already is built on normative foundations; note how economists choose the human individual, and not animals or plants, as the relevant unit of study, which is a value judgment. Economists should feel free to state moral beliefs and to engineer social improvements on their basis.

What do you think? Should scientific and humanistic concerns be separated? Is it even possible to separate them?

*10. Consider panel (a) of Figure 1.6. Let the total benefit curve be described by the equation $TB = 4Q - .5Q^2$, while total cost is described by $TC = 2Q + Q^2$. Using calculus, determine:

a. the activity level, Q, that maximizes the total benefit.

b. the activity level, Q, that maximizes the total net benefit.

c. the equations for marginal benefit and marginal cost and then, noting panel (b), confirm answer (b) with their help.

d. the size of the maximum total net benefit, as well as its total-benefit and total-cost components.

CLOSE-UP

SELECTED READINGS

Boland, Lawrence A. "A Critique of Friedman's Critics," *Journal of Economic Literature,* June 1979, pp. 503–22.

> A superb discussion of the methodological issues raised in the last section of this chapter; but note also the continued debate in the December 1980 issue, pp. 1553–57.

Boulding, Kenneth E. *Collected Papers.* Boulder, Col.: Associated University Press, 1971–75, vol. 1, "Is Economics Necessary?"; vol. 2, "Some Contributions of Economics to the General Theory of Value" (Chap. 1), "The Uses of Price Theory" (Chap. 19), "The Economics of the Coming Spaceship Earth" (Chap. 26); vol. 3, "The Economist and the Engineer" (Chap. 14), "Is Scarcity Dead?" (Chap. 20), "The Misallocation of Intellectual Resources in Economics" (Chap. 35), "After Samuelson, Who Needs Adam Smith?" (Chap. 36); vol. 4, "The Menace of Methuselah: Possible Consequences of Increased Life Expectancy" (Chap. 20).

Dennis, Ken. "Boland on Friedman: A Rebuttal," *Journal of Economic Issues,* September 1986, pp. 633–60.

> A severe criticism of both Boland (above) and Friedman (below).

Friedman, Milton. *Essays in Positive Economics.* Chicago: Chicago University Press, 1953.

> A statement, by the 1976 Nobel Prize winner in economics, of the methodological position noted in the text.

Koopmans, Tjalling. *Three Essays on the State of Economic Science.* New York: McGraw-Hill, 1957.

> A methodological discussion at odds with Friedman's view.

McCloskey, Donald N. "The Rhetoric of Economics," *Journal of Economic Literature,* June 1983, pp. 481–517.

> A delightfully written essay on methodology.

Robbins, Lionel. *An Essay on the Nature and Significance of Economic Science.* London: Macmillan, 1935.

> A classic work on methodology.

Samuelson, Paul. "Problems of Methodology: Discussion," *The American Economic Review,* May 1963, pp. 231–36.

> A methodological discussion at odds with Friedman's view, written by the 1970 Nobel Prize winner in economics.

Simon, Herbert A. *Administrative Behavior,* 3rd ed. New York: Macmillan, 1976.

> A study of the decision-making process within economic organizations. The 1978 Nobel Prize winner in economics contrasts optimizing with "satisficing."

Simon, Herbert A. "Rational Decision Making in Business Organizations," *The American Economic Review,* September 1979, pp. 493–513.

> The 1978 Nobel Prize lecture, at odds with Friedman's view.

COMPUTER PROGRAMS

The KOHLER-3 personal computer diskettes that accompany this book contain one program of particular interest to this chapter:

1. Scarcity, Choice, and Optimizing includes a 30-question multiple-choice test with immediate responses to incorrect answers.

CLOSE-UP 1.1

WHEN SPACE WON OVER SEWERS

On July 20, 1969, at 10:56 P.M. Eastern Daylight Time, Neil A. Armstrong, commander of Apollo 11, put the first human footprint on the moon. Since then, 11 others—all Americans—have also walked on the moon. Their success followed the kind of difficult choice depicted in Figure 1.2 by the production-possibilities frontier. By forgoing $24 billion worth of other goods, Americans bought a number of benefits with the Apollo Project: a demonstration of space flight capability, rapid advances in computer technology, and important new knowledge of the solar system. Yet Americans have never been able to agree on whether the benefits were worth the cost. A 1969 poll by CBS News showed that people throughout the nation were just about evenly split on that question. A similar poll taken 10 years later had identical results.

This ambivalence was reflected in Congress. In 1970, a tough fight emerged among those, like Senator Fulbright, who wanted resources used for the construction of sewer and water facilities and others who urged the construction of a space shuttle. This reusable, piloted vehicle would be able to carry large payloads into space, taking off like a rocket. It would orbit like a spacecraft and return to earth, landing like a plane. The program's cost was estimated at $14 to $30 billion; the perceived benefits included the shuttle's use for orbiting, servicing, repairing, and retrieving satellites, as well as ferrying people and materials between the earth and permanent space stations. These space stations might produce vast amounts of solar electric power and become the homes, eventually, of billions of people. Although Senator Mondale described the space shuttle program as one of the most indefensible items in the budget in light of domestic needs, space won over sewers.

Sources: *The New York Times,* July 21, 1969, p. 1, and July 20, 1979, p. 12; National Aeronautics and Space Administration, *Space Settlements: A Design Study* (Washington, D.C.: U.S. Government Printing Office, 1977).

CLOSE-UP 1.2

FISH VERSUS FUEL AT THE GEORGES BANK

Georges Bank, lying from 50–200 miles off Massachusetts, is one of the world's most productive fishing grounds. Some 200 species of fish and shellfish spawn and feed there, including cod, haddock, flounder, lobster, and scallops. In 1978, the U.S. catch was valued at $82 million; that of foreigners at $85 million. Similar catches worth $3.34 billion were likely over the next 20 years.

Yet in 1979 some argued that Americans, if necessary, should forgo this food (incur a marginal cost) in order to get oil and gas from Georges Bank. Over the next 20 years, the drilling leases for 6.3 million acres of offshore tracts were expected to yield 123 million barrels of oil and 870 billion cubic feet of gas, worth $7 billion (a larger marginal benefit).

Quite possibly, the marginal cost of $3.34 billion worth of fish did not need to be incurred at all: oil and gas leases were granted in the "safe" part of the bank, from which currents could carry any oil spill out to sea. Marine life was so diverse that only a few species were spawning at any one time (so few would have their fragile eggs and larvae harmed by any one spill). Even the harm of a spill like those at Santa Barbara and the Bay of Campeche was not expected to be permanent.

Others disagreed with this assessment. The Commonwealth of Massachusetts, along with a coalition of environmentalists and fishermen, sued the U.S. Department of the Interior and successfully delayed the auctioning of drilling rights. By 1989, there were few who were not delighted about this turn of events. The country's largest oil spill that disfigured Alaska's Prince William Sound caused many to reassess the marginal cost of drilling for oil under the sea.

Sources: *The New York Times,* October 12, 1979, p. A30, April 3, 1989, pp. A1 and 12; *The Daily Hampshire Gazette,* September 6, 1984.

CLOSE-UP

CLOSE-UP 1.3

BENZENE AT THE WORKPLACE

Benzene, found in gas and oil, is one of 2,000 suspected *carcinogens* (cancer-producing substances). In concentrations of over 20 parts per million (ppm), it causes leukemia and bone cancer. Yet some 600,000 workers have been affected by benzene in the oil industry and in plants that produce adhesives, paints, pesticides, plastics, rubber, and solvents. Acting under the authority of a 1970 law, the Occupational Safety and Health Administration (OSHA) set a 10-ppm allowable limit of benzene in the air but announced its intention to lower the limit further to 1 ppm. It was estimated that this tightened regulation would prevent one extra cancer death every three years (the marginal benefit). It would cost the industry an extra $500 million in the first year, and $150 million per year thereafter (the marginal cost).

To spend hundreds of millions of dollars in order to prevent a single death, argued the industry, was absurd. With that money, spent elsewhere, one could save *more* lives. (A mobile cardiac unit saves lives at $1,765 each, a motorcycle crash helmet campaign at $3,000 each, and a cervical cancer detection program at $3,520 each). Indeed, a lower court set the OSHA regulation aside on grounds such as these.

Then, in 1979, the U.S. Supreme Court agreed to hear the case of *AFL-CIO Industrial Union Department* vs. *American Petroleum Institute.* Everyone thought this would decide definitively whether government agencies had to justify the benefits of their regulations by reasonable costs, but such was not to be. The court was unable to muster a majority on any of the legal questions before it. By 1988, the controversy continued unabated.

Sources: *The New York Times,* April 29, 1979, and October 14, 1979, p. E20; Antonin Scalia, "A Note on the Benzene Case," *Regulation,* July/August 1980, pp. 25–28; *The Wall Street Journal,* February 27, 1985, p. 14, April 23, 1987, p. 36.

PART

2

The Consumer and the Firm

These chapters analyze some of the behavior of utility-maximizing consumers and profit-maximizing firms. The preferences of consumers are shown to be related to the demand for goods, while technology is related to the costs of firms and, ultimately, influences their supply of goods.

2

The Preferences of the Consumer

In the United States of 1989, over 90 million households spent privately close to $3,500 billion, or almost two-thirds of the gross national income. As a result, they received a vast collection of consumption and human capital goods, ranging from apples, butter, and winter coats to housing and refrigerators, airplane rides, medical care, and vocational training. This chapter will construct a theory that highlights the major factors that explain how households divided their expenditures.

THE MOTIVATION OF HOUSEHOLDS

Throughout this book, we will assume that households follow the optimization principle in order to *maximize the utility* they derive from their economic choices. We will consider each household to be a single decision-making consumer and not concern ourselves with the internal process by which the members of multiperson households come to resolve possible conflicts of interest among themselves.

The utility-maximization assumption is often misunderstood. We are not imagining that all people are totally selfish and driven only by self-love. The utility-maximization assumption is perfectly consistent with people being selfish, selfless, or a mixture of both. Totally selfish people, who have no use for other people unless they can get something out of them, might maximize their utility by working their resources to the utmost and then spending their incomes on an army of gadgets that give pleasure to them alone: cars and snowmobiles; vacuum cleaners and refrigerators; power saws and electric toothbrushes. Yet other people, equally selfish, might prefer a minimum of work and money income and then maximize their utility by sleeping late, swinging in hammocks, lolling at the beach, and spending hours each day in lonesome meditation. Perfect altruists, on the other hand, might spend lives of hard work, only to give away most of their incomes to the church, to the college of their choice, or to the victims of the latest drought, hurricane, or war. They, too, would be maximizing their utility. Their happiness would not be derived from the pleasurable use of gadgets or free time, but from the pleasure of contemplating the help they had given to the sick, crippled, orphaned, or college students who, thanks to their scholarships, need not toil in factory and field. These same altruists could, of course, like our selfish friends, forgo work and income and monetary charity, maximize their leisure time, and give their *personal* attention to those they cared to help. In each of these very different cases, people are maximizing their utility. When citing this goal as the basic motivation of households, we only assume that people will attempt to make as much progress toward their goals in life as they possibly can, whatever these goals might be. Presumably, this is as important to the egotist as to the altruist.

THE CONSUMPTION-POSSIBILITIES FRONTIER

Now envision millions of utility-maximizing consumers confronted with a multitude of markets in which goods are offered at given prices. Naturally, the preferences of consumers play a major role in their consumption decisions. Their tastes do not, however, play the only role, for that which is desired is always constrained by that which is possible.

Imagine a consumer who makes choices about the consumption of two goods only, apples and butter. In light of the existence of millions of goods, this request may seem unbearingly restrictive, but it is made for good reasons. It makes possible the graphical exposition of our theory (graphs become awkward in three dimensions and fail us completely in more than three). More importantly, this approach yields results that can be applied to any number of goods. Consider Figure 2.1. Every point on the graph represents a different combination of two goods, quantities of which are measured along the two axes of the graph. Point *A*, for example, represents 120 pounds of apples and 0 pounds of butter per week; point *B*, 0 pounds of apples and 30 pounds of butter per week; and point *C*, 60 pounds of apples and 60 pounds of butter per week. The graph as a whole, therefore, can be looked upon as the **field of choice,** the set of all the alternative combinations of these two goods over which the consumer might conceivably exercise choice.

Note: The graph is said to be *dense* because every single point in it represents a logically possible combination of our two goods, even though some of these combinations may contain fractions, such as 200.13 pounds of apples and 10.69 pounds of butter per week. Some writers argue that our theory becomes invalid for goods that cannot be subdivided into small units in this way. Surely, this is not so. A household can

FIGURE 2.1

The Field of Choice

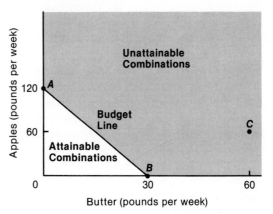

This graph shows all the alternative combinations of two goods over which a consumer might conceivably exercise choice. Given a limited budget ($120 per week) and positive prices of goods ($1 per pound for apples, $4 per pound for butter), many conceivable bundles of goods become unattainable. The budget line is a consumption-possibilities frontier. It divides the field of choice in two: combinations of goods that can be bought (unshaded) and those that cannot be bought (shaded). The budget line, of course, satisfies a simple equation: $(P_a \cdot Q_a) + (P_b \cdot Q_b) =$ Budget, where the P's and Q's refer to the prices and quantities of apples and butter, respectively. This implies that

$$Q_a = \frac{\text{Budget}}{P_a} - \frac{P_b}{P_a} \cdot Q_b$$

where Budget/P_a equals the vertical intercept of the budget line (point *A*) and $-P_b/P_a$ equals its slope.

Note: The units on the two axes are not identical. Compare the position of the 60 on each axis. The purpose of the difference in scale between axes is not to confuse but to keep the graph compact. It is important to be alert to how any graph is constructed.

consume fractions *per week* even of so-called indivisible goods. One can consume .1428571 automobiles or .2 haircuts per week because one can rent goods for limited periods or own them jointly with others (and hence use a car for one day a week only). One can vary the frequency of purchase (and hence buy a haircut once every five weeks). One can also vary the lifetime of so-called indivisible goods by buying different sizes or qualities.

However, not every combination in Figure 2.1—logically conceivable though it may be—is accessible to our consumer because scarce goods do not sell at zero prices, and the consumer has only a limited budget to spend. This budget equals the consumer's income, possibly augmented by borrowing or reduced by saving. Now assume an apple price of $1 per pound, a butter price of $4 per pound, and a budget of $120 per week. Given these facts, our consumer could spend in a week $120 on apples and receive 120 pounds of them, as represented by point A. The consumer could instead spend $120 on butter and receive 30 pounds of it, as indicated by point B. Finally, by fully spending the $120 budget, the consumer could instead buy any other combination of apples and butter lying on the straight line AB. This line is the **budget line** or **consumption-possibilities frontier,** which shows all the alternative combinations of the two goods that the consumer is able to buy in the given period at current market prices by fully using the given budget. Thus the budget line divides the set of all conceivable combinations of goods in two: attainable ones (unshaded) and unattainable ones (shaded). The consumer is constrained by prices and budget to choose within the unshaded world of the possible, along or underneath the consumption-possibilities frontier.

Note that the *slope* of budget line AB reflects the ratio of prices of the two goods: The absolute value of this slope (ignoring its negative sign)[1]* equals distance 0A divided by distance 0B, measured, of course, not in inches but in the units given on our axes. This comes to 120 pounds per week over 30 pounds per week and equals 4/1, or the price of butter, P_b, divided by the price of apples, P_a.

$$|\text{Budget line slope}| = \frac{P_b}{P_a}$$

[1]It is common practice among mathematicians to depict *absolute value* by placing vertical lines before and after a number, as in |4|. This indicates that the number can represent either +4 or −4 but that the sign is irrelevant for the moment.

In our case, because a pound of butter costs four times as much as a pound of apples, 4 pounds of apples exchange in the market for 1 pound of butter.

Similarly, the *position* of budget line AB reflects the size of the consumer's budget. Because we assumed a budget of $120 per week, point A is found by dividing $120 by the apple price of $1 (equals 120 pounds per week). Point B is found by dividing $120 by the butter price of $4 (equals 30 pounds per week).

$$A = \frac{\text{Budget}}{P_a} \text{ and } B = \frac{\text{Budget}}{P_b}$$

The *equation* of budget line AB, finally, can be derived by noting that $(P_a \cdot Q_a) + (P_b \cdot Q_b)$ must always equal the given budget, where the P's and Q's refer to the prices and quantities of apples and butter, respectively. Thus,

$$(P_a \cdot Q_a) + (P_b \cdot Q_b) = \text{Budget}$$
$$P_a \cdot Q_a = \text{Budget} - (P_b \cdot Q_b)$$

This implies the Box 2.A formula.

2.A The Budget-Line Equation
$$Q_a = \frac{\text{Budget}}{P_a} - \frac{P_b}{P_a} \cdot Q_b$$

This budget-line equation tells us that the quantity of apples consumed always equals the maximum possible quantity shown by point A (and equal to Budget/P_a) minus the budget-line slope's absolute value (P_b/P_a) times the quantity of butter consumed.

In our Figure 2.1 example, if $Q_b = 0$,

$$Q_a = \frac{\text{Budget}}{P_a} = \frac{\$120}{\$1} = 120 \text{ (point A)}.$$

On the other hand, if $Q_a = 0$,

$$Q_b = \frac{\text{Budget}}{P_a}\left(\frac{P_a}{P_b}\right) = \frac{\text{Budget}}{P_b}$$

$$= \frac{\$120}{\$4} = 30 \text{ (point } B\text{)}.$$

Similarly, a $Q_b = 20$ implies

$$Q_a = \frac{\text{Budget}}{P_a} - \frac{P_b}{P_a}Q_b = \frac{\$120}{\$1} - \frac{\$4}{\$1} \quad (20)$$

$$= 40.$$

Naturally, any change in prices or budget also changes the slope or position of the budget line. These changing opportunities are shown in Figure 2.2. The graph comes in three panels (a), (b), and (c), and in each of these, the budget line of Figure 2.1 has been reproduced as the dashed line AB. In panel (a), we assume a fall in the butter price from \$4 per pound to \$2 per pound, with the apple price (\$1 per pound) and budget (\$120 per week) remaining the same. As a result, the budget line tilts outward, enlarging the unshaded subset of attainable combinations. Note the arrows and the shrinking of the shaded subset

FIGURE 2.2

Changing Opportunities

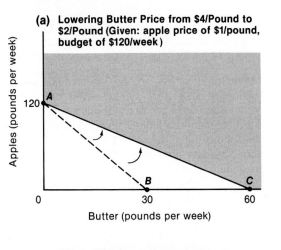

(a) Lowering Butter Price from \$4/Pound to \$2/Pound (Given: apple price of \$1/pound, budget of \$120/week)

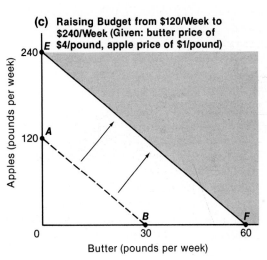

(c) Raising Budget from \$120/Week to \$240/Week (Given: butter price of \$4/pound, apple price of \$1/pound)

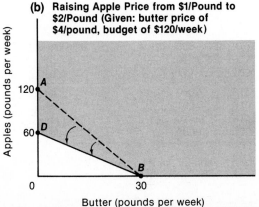

(b) Raising Apple Price from \$1/Pound to \$2/Pound (Given: butter price of \$4/pound, budget of \$120/week)

The consumption-possibilities frontier between the set of consumption goods that can be bought by a consumer (unshaded) and the set that cannot be bought (shaded) is far from fixed. Lower prices, as in panel (a), or a higher budget, as in panel (c), expand consumption possibilities; higher prices, as in panel (b), or a lower budget (not shown) contract them. Obviously, combinations of these events can also occur (not shown).

of unattainable bundles of goods. While $120 per week still buys only 120 pounds of apples per week (at $1 each), it now buys 60 rather than 30 pounds of butter per week (at $2 each). The new budget line, therefore, is *AC*. Its slope is 0*A*/0*C*, equal in absolute value to 120/60 or 2/1, the new ratio of butter price to apple price.

Panel (b) depicts the opposite case of a *rise* in price, but this time the price is of apples rather than butter. Here the price rises from $1 per pound to $2 per pound, with the butter price ($4 per pound) and budget ($120 per week) remaining the same. As a result, the budget line tilts *inward,* reducing the unshaded subset of attainable combinations. Note the arrows and the enlargement of the shaded subset of unattainable bundles of goods. While $120 per week still buys 30 pounds of butter per week (at $4 each), it now buys only 60 rather than 120 pounds of apples per week (at $2 each). The slope of the new budget line, *BD,* is 0*D*/0*B*, equal in absolute value to 60/30 or 2/1, the new ratio of butter price to apple price.

Panel (c) shows the effect of a higher budget only. All prices are assumed unchanged ($1 per pound of apples and $4 per pound of butter). Line *EF* represents a budget that doubles from $120 to $240 per week. As a result, there occurs a parallel outward *shift* of the budget line, enlarging the unshaded subset of attainable combinations of goods. At unchanged prices, $240 rather than $120 per week can buy exactly twice as much of either good. Distance 0*A* doubles to 0*E*, and distance 0*B* to 0*F*.

Naturally, Figure 2.2 does not show all the conceivable combinations of events that can change consumption opportunities. A higher butter price, a lower apple price, a lower budget, or simultaneous changes in prices and budget, for example, are not illustrated. Yet the message is clear: The combinations of goods that are accessible to the consumer are always constrained by prices and budget. The graphs of Figure 2.2 depict this basic fact.

Once we know how a consumer's choices are constrained by prices and budget, can we similarly depict the one bundle of goods, among all the attainable ones, that a utility-maximizing consumer will finally select because it is of the greatest subjective value? The answer is yes, and it leads us directly into a fascinating chapter in the history of economic theorizing.

THE CONCEPT OF UTILITY: A HISTORIC NOTE

As we noted in Chapter 1, most activities have benefits as well as costs. The satisfaction a person derives from the activity of consumption has traditionally been termed **utility.** This term has been closely associated with the philosophy of Jeremy Bentham (1748–1832), whose Biography appears in Chapter 2 of the *Student Workbook* that accompanies this text. Bentham suggested that human conduct be guided by a "felicific calculus," which approves of any action only if the pleasure it brings outweighs the pain it causes. He thought that the pleasure and pain of each action could be measured in units called *utils,* just as weight can be measured in pounds. He even believed it possible to add up these util numbers interpersonally so that 10 utils for John and 5 for Jane make a total of 15 for the pair. He identified the social total of utility produced by all actions as the common good, and he advocated that this total utility be maximized to achieve "the greatest happiness of the greatest number." Yet neither philosopher Bentham nor the economists who embraced or rejected his ideas during his lifetime (and for several decades thereafter) understood the relationship between the value of goods and the utility derived by their consumers. Many economists, in fact, used to think of value as something intrinsic to a good. Karl Marx, for example, thought of value as congealed labor time that was "embodied" in a good. Presumably, if it took 4 units of labor to produce a pound of butter but only 1 unit to produce a pound of apples, a pound of butter was worth four times as much as a pound of apples. The famous beaver/deer example of Adam Smith (according to which the respective times required for hunting these animals determined their market exchange values) let to a similar conclusion. Yet economists were never too happy with this type of explanation. Marx's critics argued that the mere expenditure of labor, even of the minimum necessary amount, was surely not sufficient to establish the value of a good. What if one produced shredded bees' wings that nobody wanted? And Adam Smith found it necessary to distinguish between "value in exchange" and "value in use" when he noted the famous paradox of diamonds and water: While diamonds have a high value in the marketplace (a high value in exchange), they are unnecessary to life (have a low value in use). On the other hand, water is fetching a low market price, while life is impossible without it. Despite its low market value, water has a high utility.

The first major breakthrough in this controversy came a century after Adam Smith, in the move from total utility to marginal utility. To the British economist William Stanley Jevons (1835–1882)—whose Biography also appears in Chapter 2 of the *Student Workbook* that accompanies this text—value was never intrinsic to an object but resulted from a relationship between a valuing person and an object. Even the value so determined was not a fixed number, but varied with the quantity of the object the evaluating person possessed. The great advance made by Jevons was, in fact, the discovery of the **principle of diminishing marginal utility:**

> *Given the quantities of all other goods being consumed, and given a person's tastes, successive additions of equal units of a good to the process of consumption eventually yield ever smaller additions to total utility.*

Thus Jevons distinguished between the total utility associated with a given level of consumption and the **marginal utility,** or the change in total utility produced by a unit change in consumption (or any other activity). Jevons, in short, discovered a special case of the general principle of declining marginal benefit, which we have already met in Chapter 1. Indeed, Jevons did more than that.

The best combination of goods among all those attainable by a consumer, the one that would maximize *total* utility, argued Jevons, was the one that equated the *marginal* utilities of a dollar's worth of every good. Consider a consumer at position A in Figure 2.1. Such a consumer would be consuming 120 pounds of apples per week, receiving a high *total* utility, as represented, perhaps, by a point such as P in the upper graph of Figure 1.4 "Declining Marginal Benefit" (see p. 11). Yet this person's *marginal* utility would be low, represented by the height of block e in that graph. On the other hand, this consumer would be consuming no butter at all. Hence the consumer's total utility from butter consumption would be 0 (as at 0 in the upper graph of Figure 1.4), but the marginal utility would be high (as the height of block a). Surely, Jevons would argue, the consumer's combined total utility from apple and butter consumption could be increased by a $1 reduction in apple consumption (a loss of 1 pound at our assumed price of $1 per pound) and a $1 increase in butter consumption (a gain of 1/4 pound at our assumed price of $4 per pound). While the former would reduce total utility by an amount equal to e (the marginal cost), the latter would raise total utility by a larger amount equal to a (the marginal benefit). Thus a move along the budget line from point A in Figure 2.1 toward point B would raise total utility. Jevons used the optimization principle to show that consumers could reach maximum total utility only by selecting a bundle of consumption goods such that the marginal utility (*MU*) per dollar of any one good was equal to that of any other good (as Box 2.B indicates).

2.B Jevons's Rule
Condition for maximum total utility:
MU *per dollar of apples* = **MU** *per dollar of butter* = **MU** *per dollar of any other good*

Yet, for all its brilliance, the work of Jevons still rested on the belief that utility, whether total or marginal, was a quantity that could somehow be *measured*. The first step away from this belief was taken at the time of Jevons's death.

THE DISCOVERY OF THE CONSUMPTION-INDIFFERENCE CURVE

Another Englishman, Francis Ysidro Edgeworth (1845–1926)—whose biography is also featured in Chapter 2 of the *Student Workbook* that accompanies this text—visualized Figure 2.1 as the unseen base of a mountain. He imagined a third dimension, rising above the plane of paper, in which one might measure the utility total associated with any given combination of our two goods.

Figure 2.3 depicts Edgeworth's vision of the utility mountain (luckily, it is the only three-dimensional graph in this book). Because the consumer has neither apples nor butter to consume at point 0, the mountain has a zero elevation above this point. Now consider segment 0C. As the consumer acquires more and more butter, the quantity of apples remaining at zero, total utility rises, and the mountain begins to take shape. In accordance with the insight of Jevons, Edgeworth imagined total utility rising at a decreasing rate. This was pictured earlier in the upper part of Figure 1.4, "Declining Marginal Benefit," and it is pictured here as the utility mountain rising along curved line 0DEF.

Similarly, as the consumer acquires more and more apples, but the quantity of butter remains at zero (a process that can be pictured by moving along segment 0K), total utility rises by less and less, along 0LMN.

Finally, Edgeworth imagined the elevation of his mountain to increase as quantities of one good were added to any initial *positive* quantity

FIGURE 2.3

The Utility Mountain

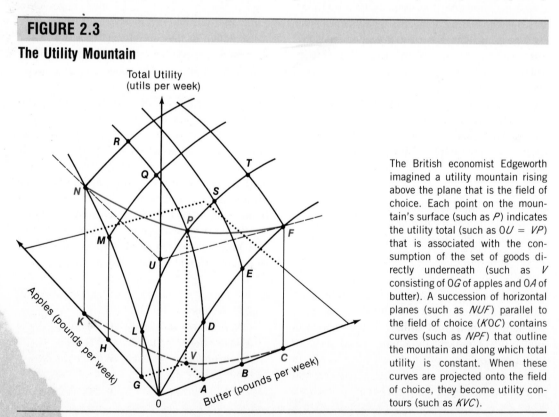

The British economist Edgeworth imagined a utility mountain rising above the plane that is the field of choice. Each point on the mountain's surface (such as *P*) indicates the utility total (such as 0*U* = *VP*) that is associated with the consumption of the set of goods directly underneath (such as *V* consisting of 0*G* of apples and 0*A* of butter). A succession of horizontal planes (such as *NUF*) parallel to the field of choice (*K0C*) contains curves (such as *NPF*) that outline the mountain and along which total utility is constant. When these curves are projected onto the field of choice, they become utility contours (such as *KVC*).

of the other good. Holding apple consumption constant at *G*, *H*, or *K*, respectively, increased butter consumption raises total utility along *LP*, *MQ*, or *NR*. Holding butter consumption constant at *A*, *B*, or *C*, respectively, increased apple consumption raises total utility along *DP*, *ES*, or *FT*. Thus the utility mountain looks like the end of a loaf of French bread!

Fortunately, having once visited the third dimension, we need not stay there. Edgeworth had a wonderful idea: He imagined cutting into the mountain at a given level of utility, such as 0*U*, and doing so along a horizontal plane (such as *NUF*) precisely parallel to the base of the mountain (*K*0*C*). Such a cut touches the mountain along a curved line (such as *NPF*) in the same way as would a horizontal cut into a loaf of French bread. This curved line, noted Edgeworth, can be projected onto the base of the mountain: *Plumb* vertical lines from *N*, *P*, and *F* yield *K*, *V*, and *C*, respectively. Thus the cut along *NPF* is reproduced as dashed line *KVC*. Edgeworth called this projection onto the base a **utility contour** or **consumption-indifference curve.** He argued, correctly, that it shows all the alternative combinations of two consumption goods that yield the same total of utility; all points on the curve correspond to the same height (0*U* in our case) in the third dimension. Because all combinations on the curve have the same total of utility, a utility-maximizing consumer would be indifferent about choosing among them.

Such an indifference curve is very much like the contour line of a real mountain, which a mapmaker might draw to connect all the points of equal elevation. Indeed, just as a mapmaker labels a contour line with a cardinal number (such as 20 feet above sea level), so Edgeworth placed a cardinal utility number (such as 20 *utils*, or units of utility) next to the indifference curve. Note line *KVC* in Figure 2.4. It is a reproduction of line *KVC* of Figure 2.3 and a projection onto the field of choice of all the 20-util total-utility points on the imaginary utility mountain.

Note: Just as mapmakers draw many contours on their maps (for elevations of 10 feet, 20

FIGURE 2.4

Utility Contours

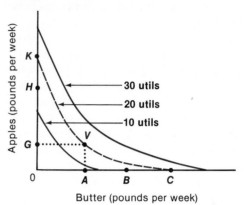

A utility contour, derived from Edgeworth's utility mountain, contains all the points of equal elevation on the imaginary utility mountain. Line *KVC,* for instance, corresponds to the projected curve so labeled in Figure 2.3. It shows all the alternative combinations of apples and butter that yield to the consumer the same total utility (of 20 utils). The curve to the right of *KVC* would be higher in the third dimension than *KVC* and would have a higher total of utility. Similarly, the curve to the left of *KVC* would be lower on the mountain and would have a lower total of utility.

feet, 30 feet, and so on), Edgeworth was aware that one could draw a whole family of utility contours, each one corresponding to a different utility total. If we cut the utility mountain successively at levels below or above *U*, we could derive the utility contours lying to the left or right of line *KVC* in Figure 2.4. They correspond, as their labels show, to lower or higher utility totals.

Caution: Point *V* does *not* indicate that the consumer is indifferent between 0*G* apples and 0*A* butter. Rather, the consumer is indifferent among 0*G* apples plus 0*A* butter, on the one hand, and all other combinations depicted by line *KVC*, on the other hand.

It was but a short step, taken somewhat inconsistently by Vilfredo Pareto and then decisively by Irving Fisher and John Hicks (biographies of all three appear in the *Student Workbook*), to abandon the *cardinal measurement* (1 unit, 2 units, 5 units, 15 units) of utility altogether. A consumer's preferences can be described, these later economists argued, without resort to utility measurement and without knowledge of the utility mountain from which the utility contours are derived. It is not necessary to tell *how much* a consumer values one set of goods compared to another (10 utils versus 20 utils); it is quite sufficient to know whether one set is considered inferior, equal, or superior to another. An *ordinal ranking* (1st, 2nd, 5th, 15th), with the help of any arbitrary scale, will do. One can eliminate the word "utils" after 10, 20, and 30 in Figure 2.4 and still know enough, as long as it is understood that any curve labeled 10 simply refers to sets of goods all of which provide less total utility than sets found on a curve labeled with a higher number, be it 20, 30, or 566.

ANALYSIS OF THE CONSUMPTION-INDIFFERENCE CURVE

Modern economists map the preferences of consumers with the help of consumption-indifference curves, and they construct these curves on the basis of four simple assumptions that do not require any utility measurement. These assumptions are good approximations of people's actual behavior, exceptions being rare.

1. *Consumers are able to rank bundles of goods.* It is assumed, first, that consumers can rank, on a scale of better or worse, all conceivable combinations of goods. When comparing two bundles of goods, they can tell whether they prefer one to the other or find them equally desirable. If preference is indicated, it is not necessary to gauge its intensity.

2. *Consumers prefer more of any good to less.* It is assumed that consumers always prefer a larger to a smaller quantity of any good because they have not yet reached the point of satiation. This implies that larger quantities of a good are associated with rising total utility (or positive marginal utility). Because there are so many goods in the world, this assumption is likely to be satisfied. As our Chapter 1 discussion of the

optimization principle has shown, consuming so much of one good that satiation is reached is unlikely to be optimal. As a result of our second assumption, indifference curves must be *negatively sloped*. Consider panel (a) of Figure 2.5, and focus on the combination of goods represented by point *A*. As long as people are not satiated with any good, any set of goods above and to the right of *A* will be preferred to *A* itself. This is true of point *B* because it contains more pounds of apples and as much butter as *A*. It is true of *C* because it contains more of both goods. It is true of *D* because it contains more butter and as many pounds of apples as *A*. Since an indifference curve is the locus of points that are *equally* desirable, such a curve cannot possibly connect *A* with any of the *preferred* points contained in segment *DAB*.

For analogous reasons, such a curve cannot possibly connect *A* with any of the *inferior* points in segment *EAG*. All points in this segment are inferior because they contain less of one or both goods than does *A*. As a result, an indifference curve conforming to our second assumption cannot be positively sloped, nor can it be vertical or horizontal. An indifference curve containing set *A* must necessarily go through the shaded segments of our graph; that is, be negatively sloped. (Analytical Examples 2.1 and 2.2 have more to say on the subject.)

There is another way of seeing why indifference curves must be negatively sloped: A move from *A* to *D* would raise a consumer's total utility because of an increase in butter consumption, all else being equal. Once at *D*, the consumer could be made to sacrifice an amount of apples just sufficient to offset the utility gained by the move from *A* to *D*. The set of goods so found would be equally desirable as *A* and, as the arrow at *D* indicates, it would lie in the shaded segment below *D*. Similarly, moves from *A* to *B*, *E*, or *G* could be compensated by additional moves in the direction of the arrows; in each case, the same conclusion emerges: An indifference curve through *A* must be negatively sloped. Naturally, the same argument could be made for any other point.

FIGURE 2.5

The Indifference Curve Analyzed

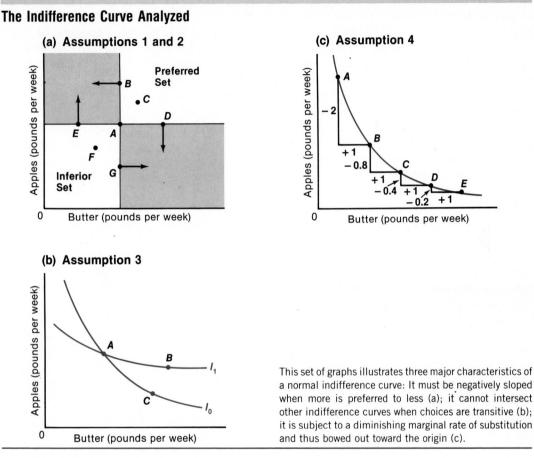

(a) Assumptions 1 and 2

(b) Assumption 3

(c) Assumption 4

This set of graphs illustrates three major characteristics of a normal indifference curve: It must be negatively sloped when more is preferred to less (a); it cannot intersect other indifference curves when choices are transitive (b); it is subject to a diminishing marginal rate of substitution and thus bowed out toward the origin (c).

Note: We are concerned with goods only, not with bads. Our assumption does not deny that people want less of things that they hate and cannot instantly and costlessly discard, such as garbage or pollution. However, our analysis can easily accommodate the existence of bads by considering their opposites to be goods, such as garbage removal or pollution abatement.

3. *Consumers rank bundles of goods in a consistent manner.* It is assumed that consumers are consistent when they rank bundles of goods in order of preference. If set *A* is preferred to *B* and *B* is preferred to *C*, consistency requires that *A* is also preferred to *C*. When choices are made in such a noncontradictory fashion, **transitivity** in choice is said to prevail.

As a result of this assumption, it is impossible for indifference curves to meet or intersect. Consider panel (b) of Figure 2.5. According to indifference curve I_1, set *A* is as desirable as set *B*; according to curve I_0, *A* is as good as *C*. Logic then requires for *B* to be valued as much as *C*. Yet the graph tells us that *B* contains more of both goods than *C*, so it must be preferred to *C* (by assumption 2).

Indifference curves that intersect and meet always lead to such inconsistencies. They are just as impossible as intersecting contour lines on a geographer's map. A given point on a mountain surface cannot be 500 feet and 800 feet above sea level at the same time. In the same way, point *A* in panel (b) of Figure 2.5 cannot correspond simultaneously to the total utility level implied by I_0 and to the different level implied by I_1.

4. *Consumers insist on a diminishing marginal rate of substitution.* Economists define the **marginal rate of substitution (MRS)** as an *indifferent* exchange ratio—the rate at which a consumer is willing to exchange a little bit of one good for a little bit of another good because the exchange involves neither a feeling of gain nor of loss. Economists speculate, assumption 4 tells us, that consumers who acquire successive additional units of one good at the expense of another good will remain indifferent about such substitution only if they have to sacrifice ever smaller quantities of the second good. This is likely to be so because the relative importance people attach to different goods changes with the relative quantities available to them. Typically, the scarcer a good becomes, the greater is its marginal utility relative to that of a good that is becoming more plentiful. Consider panel (c) of Figure 2.5. A person who consumes the set of goods depicted by A might feel equally well off if 2 pounds of apples were sacrificed for an additional 1 pound of butter. Therefore, B is on the same indifference curve as A. Yet this subjective exchange ratio in the consumer's mind is likely to change with circumstances. Once at B, total utility might remain unchanged only if a much smaller sacrifice of apples were made to gain yet another pound of butter. And so on, at C, D, and E. As a result, the indifference curve is bowed out or *convex* with respect to the origin of the graph.

A nonmathematical explanation (admittedly oversimplified) invokes the principle of diminishing marginal utility without relying on the measurability of marginal utility: If the marginal utility of any one good depends only on the quantity of that good, the move from A to B raises the marginal utility of apples (and reduces the willingness to give them up at the old terms) because there is less of them. The same move lowers the marginal utility of butter (and reduces the eagerness to get more of it) because there is more of it. This could explain the decline in the

subjective indifferent exchange ratio, or *MRS*.

In our graph, the marginal rate of substitution of butter for apples, $MRS_{b/a}$, is pictured as the amount of apples the consumer is willing to sacrifice indifferently for an extra unit of butter. This ever changing *MRS* is in fact nothing else but the *slope* of the indifference curve. Between points A and B, its absolute value is 2/1, on the average.[2]

Note: If it takes *one* pound of butter to raise total utility enough to compensate precisely for the total utility decline caused by the loss of *two* pounds of apples (and this is what the consumer's indifference implies), we can therefore write $MU_{1b} = MU_{2a}$. Knowing full well that marginal utility cannot be measured, we can, nevertheless, set each of these equivalences equal to *x utils,* or units of satisfaction, calling $MU_{1b} = x$ and also $MU_{2a} = x$. It follows logically that $MU_{1a} = .5x$ and that $MU_{1b}/MU_{1a} = x/.5x = 2/1$. Thus the absolute value of the slope is seen to equal also the ratio of the unmeasurable marginal utility of a pound of butter to that of a pound of apples.*

$$|\textit{Indifference curve slope}| = MRS_{b/a} = \frac{MU_b}{MU_a}$$

It is but a short step now to find the answer to our original question about the way utility-maximizing consumers divide their expenditure.

---

[2]At any one point, P_0, on a convex indifference curve, the slope is measured by a ratio such as a/b; between two points, P_1 and P_2, the (average) slope is measured by a ratio such as c/d.

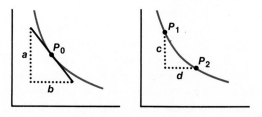

*For a calculus-based treatment of this material, see Section 2A of the Calculus Appendix at the back of this book.

THE OPTIMUM OF THE CONSUMER

Figure 2.6 brings together the various aspects of the consumer's optimum. Panel (a) depicts the field of choice, constrained by prices and budget. Panel (b) depicts a consumer's tastes with the help of a family of indifference curves. Logically, but not practically, one can draw such a curve through every point in the field of choice, thereby relating the consumer's subjective evaluation of any one combination of goods to every

other one in the field. Five curves, labeled I_0 to I_4, have been drawn. Their labels, unlike those of Edgeworth in Figure 2.4, have no cardinal significance. (Bundles of goods on curve I_4 do not necessarily yield *twice* the utility of bundles on curve I_2.) The labels do, however, have an ordinal meaning. (Bundles of goods on curve I_4 do yield *higher* utility, of whatever size, than those on curve I_2.) Thus the labels remind us that all sets of goods above a given curve yield higher utility totals, and all sets below it lower ones, than do the sets on the curve. Combination A,

FIGURE 2.6

The Consumer's Optimum

(a) Opportunities

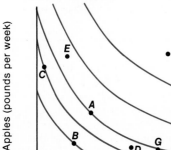

(b) Preferences

(c) The Consumer's Optimum

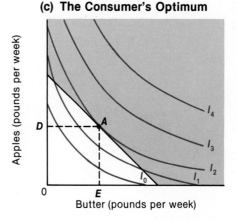

This set of graphs summarizes how utility-maximizing consumers divide their expenditures among different goods. Panel (a) depicts opportunities. It shows how prices and budget define what can be bought. Panel (b) depicts preferences. It shows the subjective value the consumer places on every set of goods relative to every other set. Panel (c) shows the best set of goods (point A) that the consumer can buy within the unshaded realm of the possible. This set lies on the highest indifference curve, I_2, that can be reached along the consumption-possibilities frontier.

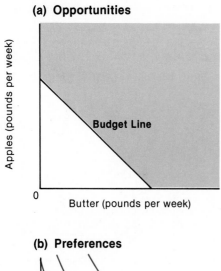

therefore, is preferred to *B, C,* and *D; A* is considered inferior to *E* and *F,* but just as good as *G.*

Panel (c) of Figure 2.6 combines the other two graphs, and the solution becomes obvious. Given the constraints implied by the budget line, the consumer reaches maximum utility by choosing combination *A;* that is, by purchasing *D* pounds of apples and *E* pounds of butter per week.

Note: This combination lies on the highest indifference curve that can be reached along the budget line. *A* is found where the budget line just touches an indifference curve. At optimum point *A,* therefore, the slopes of budget line and indifference curve are the same. This is summarized in Box 2.C below.*

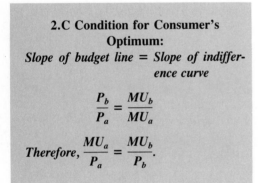

2.C Condition for Consumer's Optimum:
Slope of budget line = Slope of indifference curve

$$\frac{P_b}{P_a} = \frac{MU_b}{MU_a}$$

Therefore, $\dfrac{MU_a}{P_a} = \dfrac{MU_b}{P_b}.$

Indifference-curve analysis thus confirms the conclusion reached by Jevons and discussed above. The condition for consumer's optimum can easily be expanded to any number of goods so that

$$\frac{MU_a}{P_a} = \frac{MU_b}{P_b} = \frac{MU_c}{P_c} = \cdots = \frac{MU_n}{P_n}.$$

This analysis, furthermore, has many important applications. We will consider four of them.

*For a calculus-based treatment of this material, see Section 2B of the Calculus Appendix at the back of this book.

Application 1: Lump-Sum Versus Selective Sales Tax

Governments can raise revenue in many ways. Consider the choice between a **lump-sum tax,** a fixed dollar levy imposed on people regardless of what they do, and a **selective sales tax** levied on the purchase of a particular good only (but in a way that yields the same revenue). Figure 2.7 shows why the lump-sum tax is more efficient. Picture a consumer with budget line *AB* and indifference curves I_0, I_1, and I_2. The optimum position is *C.* Government imposes a selective sales tax on butter consumption only. This raises the price of butter only; the budget line becomes

FIGURE 2.7

Lump-Sum Versus Selective Sales Tax

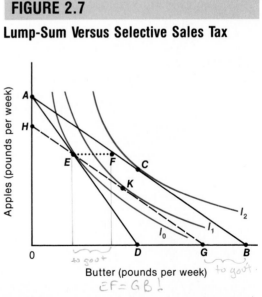

On efficiency grounds, a lump-sum tax on consumers is better than a selective sales tax on a particular good: A move from a selective sales tax to a lump-sum tax that collects the same amount of revenue leaves government equally well off but raises the welfare of consumers (who move from *C* to *K* rather than from *C* to *E*). Note: An analogous argument can be made in favor of lump-sum subsidies rather than subsidies for particular goods.

AD. The consumer finds a new optimum at *E;* utility falls from I_2 to I_0. The government's tax revenue can be depicted by dotted line *EF.* (It is measured in terms of the quantity of additional butter the consumer could buy if the tax were removed and the same quantity of apples were bought as at *E.*)

Now consider the alternative. Let the government impose an equivalent lump-sum tax of *EF* = *GB*. Prices are unaffected; the budget line makes a parallel shift from *AB* to *HG*. The consumer buys combination *K;* utility drops from I_2 to I_1 only. The difference in utility between I_1 and I_0 is the **excess burden** of the selective butter tax, a drop in utility that is unnecessary in order to collect tax revenue *GB* and that could be avoided by the use of a different type of tax.

Application 2: Cash or In-Kind Subsidy

Governments that wish to provide a given amount of subsidy can do so in many ways. Consider the choice between a *subsidy in kind* (for example, vouchers for specific goods), usually preferred by taxpayers, and a *subsidy in cash.* Figure 2.8 shows why a cash subsidy may be better (and certainly will not be worse) *for recipients* than a subsidy in kind. Picture a consumer with budget line *AB* and indifference curves I_0, I_1, and I_2. The optimum position is *C.* Let government provide free vouchers that permit the purchase of *AD* = *BE* of butter only. The budget line becomes *ADE.* The consumer finds a new optimum at *D;* utility rises from I_0 to I_1.

Now consider the alternative. Let the government provide an amount of cash sufficient to purchase *BE* of butter but with no strings attached. The budget line shifts to *FE,* leaving intact all the opportunities along *DE* but providing additional ones along *DF.* (The latter, of course, is what taxpayers often dislike.) In our case, the consumer buys combination *G,* containing less butter than at *C* but bringing utility to an even higher level, I_2 instead of I_1. This shows the possible inefficiency of the voucher approach (as long as we focus only on the recipients' utility).

FIGURE 2.8

Cash or In-Kind Subsidy

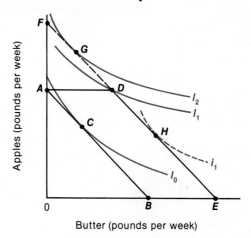

Butter (pounds per week)

On efficiency grounds, a cash subsidy given to consumers may be better for them (and it will not be worse) than an equivalent subsidy in kind: As long as taxpayers do not derive utility from seeing others consume specific quantities of goods, a move from an in-kind subsidy to a cash subsidy of equal value leaves donors equally well off but may raise the welfare of recipients (who may move from *C* to *G* rather than *C* to *D*). Note: An analogous argument can be made with respect to taxes in cash rather than taxes in kind (which collect a number of physical units of a good of equal cash value).

Note: What if the consumer's preferences were depicted by lines I_0 and i_1 (and I_1, I_2 didn't exist)? The consumer would go to position *H* regardless of the form of the subsidy.

Application 3: Rationing and Mandated Purchases

Governments often set maximum purchase limits on particular goods or on all goods. (Consider the wartime rationing of food or gasoline.) Governments also require minimum purchases of particular goods. (Consider requirements to buy automobile safety features, social security, or trash collection services.) All these regulations may or may not affect any particular consumer. Consider Figure 2.9. Picture a consumer with budget line *AB* and indifference curves I_0 and I_1. The optimum position is *C*. Let government impose rationing of butter only. If the maximum allowed were *D* per week, this particular consumer would not be affected at all. (Low-income people often are in this position.) If the ration were *E* per week, it would be *potentially* binding: Purchase opportunities in triangle *BEH* would be eliminated by the ration limit (depicted by dashed line *EH*). In fact, however, this consumer's preferences are such that all of these opportunities are considered inferior compared to *C*, which could still be purchased. A binding limit is depicted by dotted line *FG*. Legally, the consumer could not reach a higher utility than that implied by point *G*, namely, I_0, which is lower than I_1. Preferring point *C*, the consumer may well move from *G* toward *C* by entering the black market for butter.

The case is analogous for mandated purchases. If government *required* the purchase of not less than *F* butter per week, our consumer, already purchasing the larger quantity of butter corresponding to *C*, would not be affected at all.

(High-income people often are in this position.) A required minimum purchase of *E*, however, would be binding. Legally, the consumer could not reach a higher utility than that implied by point *H*, namely I_0. Preferring point *C*, the consumer may well move from *H* toward *C* by cheating on mandated purchases (as by failing to maintain auto safety features or trading them away).

Application 4: Discouraging Gasoline Consumption by Means of a Tax-and-Rebate Program

It has been argued that government can discourage the consumption of any good, such as gasoline, by means of a selective sales tax, even if the

---

FIGURE 2.9

Rationing and Mandated Purchases

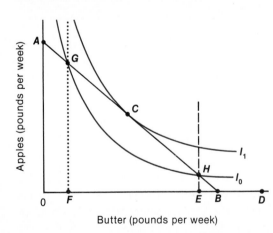

Rationing and mandated purchases alike, if effectively binding for a particular consumer, are bound to lower utility. Note: The argument made here for a single good can be extended to cover more goods than one.

FIGURE 2.10

Selective Sales Tax and Lump-Sum Rebate

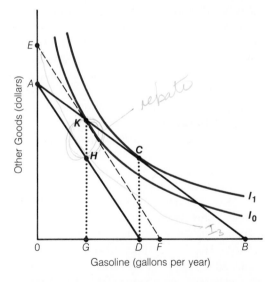

The imposition of a selective sales tax on a good, such as gasoline, reduces consumption of the good, even if the entire tax revenue, here of *HK = AE,* is rebated in a lump sum. Given the original optimum *C* and the new optimum *K,* gasoline consumption falls from *D* to *G* gallons per year in this example.

total tax revenue is immediately rebated to consumers in a lump sum. At first sight, this argument seems nonsensical, yet it is correct. Consider a consumer at original optimum C in Figure 2.10, corresponding to original budget line AB and indifference curve I_1. Let a sales tax double the price of gasoline; the budget line becomes AD. But the consumer will not find a new optimum on this line. Because of the rebate, the consumer will, ultimately, continue to buy a combination of goods lying on line AB and costing the same as the original budget. Because of the changed relative prices, however, the new optimum will lie at a point, such as K, where the marginal rate of substitution of gasoline for other goods will correspond to the new relative prices. In this example, the size of the tax revenue is HK; so is the size of the rebate. Gasoline consumption is down from D gallons per year to G gallons per year; the consumption of other goods is up by the vertical difference between C and K. Consumers are worse off than before because the new optimum K lies on a lower indifference curve, I_0. Government, presumably, considers it worthwhile to pay this cost in order to reap the benefit of a lessened dependence on oil imports or of some similar goal.

SUMMARY

1. Economists theorize that consumers follow the optimization principle in order to maximize the utility they derive from their economic choices. This is *not* to say that economists assume all people to be selfish; utility maximization is nothing else but making as much progress as possible toward one's goals, given limited resources, and this is just as important to the altruist as to the egotist.

2. All conceivable consumption choices can be depicted graphically as a field of choice. However, a consumer's actual choices are always constrained by positive prices and a limited budget. The budget line (or consumption-possibilities frontier) is a graphical device that separates attainable from unattainable combinations of goods. Its slope reflects relative prices of goods; its position reflects the size of the budget.

3. A utility-maximizing consumer must somehow evaluate and compare the utility derivable from the alternative combinations of goods that are attainable. Bentham, who focused on total utility, was not very helpful. Jevons defined the solution in principle: Total utility is maximized when the marginal utilities per dollar of every good consumed are equalized.

4. Edgeworth went a step further and showed that utility totals associated with various combinations of goods can be depicted on the field of choice as utility contours or consumption-indifference curves.

5. Edgeworth-type indifference curves can, however, be constructed without resort to utility measurement, on the basis of four simple assumptions: Consumers are able to rank bundles of goods in order of preference; they prefer more of any good to less; they rank bundles of goods in a consistent manner; and they insist on a diminishing marginal rate of substitution (MRS). The MRS reflects the relative marginal utilities of goods and equals the changing slope of the indifference curve.

6. The optimum division of a utility-maximizing consumer's expenditures can be made evident by combining the budget line (depicting the consumer's opportunities) with a family of consumption-indifference curves (depicting the consumer's preferences). The optimum is found on the highest indifference curve that can be reached along the budget line.

7. The theory of the consumer's optimum has a great number of important applications. Discussed are the choice between a lump-sum and selective sales tax, the choice between a subsidy in cash and one in kind, the effect of rationing and mandated purchases, and the discouragement of gasoline consumption by means of a tax-and-rebate program.

KEY TERMS

budget line
consumption-indifference curve
consumption-possibilities frontier
excess burden
field of choice
lump-sum tax
marginal rate of substitution (*MRS*)
marginal utility (*MU*)
principle of diminishing marginal utility
revealed-preference approach
selective sales tax
transitivity
utility
utility contour

HANDS-ON PRACTICE

Exercise #1

Although utility is not considered measurable, suppose that someone did provide us with the information given in Table 2.1. How would one have to allocate seven available dollars between the two goods if one cared to maximize utility?

TABLE 2.1

Total Spending	Associated Total Utility if Spent on	
	Good A	Good B
$1	60	100
2	110	180
3	150	240
4	180	280
5	200	300
6	210	300

Solution:

One would have to equate the *marginal* utility per dollar spent. Relevant data are given in Table 2.2.

TABLE 2.2

Spending	Associated Marginal Utility if Spent on	
	Good A	Good B
1st dollar	60	100
2nd dollar	50	80
3rd dollar	40	60
4th dollar	30	40
5th dollar	20	20
6th dollar	10	0
7th dollar	?	?

As you can see by checking off the marginal-utility numbers in Table 2.2, one would want to spend the 1st dollar on good B, the 2nd dollar likewise. The 3rd and 4th would be spent on B and A; the 5th on A; the 6th and 7th on A and B. Marginal utility per dollar spent would be 40; total utility would be maximized at 430 when 3 units of A and 4 units of B are bought. (Can you see the similarity to Exercise 1 in Chapter 1?)

Exercise #2

Consider Figure 2.11, which depicts, at point *c*, a consumer's optimum allocation of a weekly

FIGURE 2.11

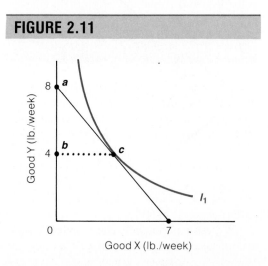

Good Y (lb./week)

Good X (lb./week)

sum of $100 between goods Y and X.

a.   What is the price of good Y? Of good X?

b.   What is the quantity of X consumed?

c.   What is the consumer's marginal rate of substitution between Y and X? What is the ratio of marginal utilities?

d.   Why would the optimization principle be violated at point *a*?

Solution:

a.   The price of Y equals $100/8, or $12.50 (because the maximum quantity of Y the $100 budget can buy is 8 units). Likewise, the price of X equals $100/7, or $14.29 rounded (because the maximum quantity of X the $100 budget can buy is 7 units).

b.   The equation of the budget line is $Y = 8 - (8/7)X$. At point *c*, $Y = 4$; hence, $4 = 8 - (8/7)X$ and $(8/7)X = 4$ and $X = 3.5$. Alternative: Since 4 units of Y are bought at *c* and each Y costs $12.50, $50 are spent on Y, leaving another $50 for X. Given the price of X, 3.5 units of it can be bought.

c.   At point *c*, the *MRS* is given by the slope of indifference curve I_1, but also by the slope of the tangent budget line: 8Y for 7X. This implies that the marginal utility of Y is 7/8 that of X (just as the price of Y is 7/8 that of X).

d.   Point *a* lies on a lower indifference curve I_0 (not shown). The consumer could give up 4Y (distance *ab*) and buy with the funds so saved 3.5X (distance *bc*). Since total utility at *c* exceeds total utility at *a*, the marginal cost (utility of *ab* of Y) is below the marginal benefit (utility of *bc* of X). $MC < MB$ or $MB > MC$ violates the optimization principle.

Exercise #3

Draw a budget line indicating how someone might allocate a $30,000 annual income between other goods and higher education. Let the government now offer $10,000 of higher education to anyone who pays tuition of $3,000 (which implies a $7,000 subsidy). Picture the possibility of someone moving (a) from no education to public education and (b) from private education to public education.

Solution:

Case (a) is pictured in Figure 2.12. The original budget line is *af*.

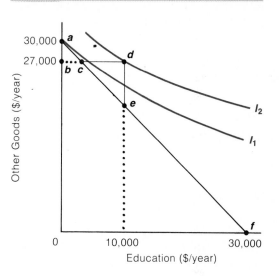

FIGURE 2.12

The original optimum is at *a;* $30,000 are spent on other goods; nothing is spent on higher education. The government's offer changes the budget line to *acdef:* A $3,000 sacrifice of other goods (*ab*) makes possible a $3,000 tuition payment (*bc*) and brings a $7,000 subsidy (*cd*). The consumer reaches a higher indifference curve at *d* on I_2. Case (b) is pictured in Figure 2.13. Now the original optimum is at *f:* $15,000 each are spent on other goods and (private) higher education. The government's offer changes the budget line to *acdeg*. This consumer gains the greatest utility by moving to *d* on I_2, abandoning private for public education. Note how $5,000 less of education is received, along with $12,000 more of other goods. The difference reflects the $7,000 subsidy.

FIGURE 2.13

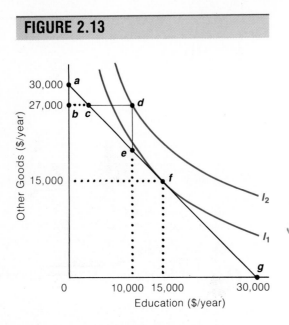

e. Starting with the original budget line, show the effect on the consumer if consumption required 10 hours of time per unit of *a* and 1 hour per unit of *b*, but the consumer had a total of only 150 hours to spend.

2. Consider the effect on your answer to Question 1d if ration points could be traded for money in "white" markets; consider the effect on your answer to Question 1e if time could be traded for money (as by working more or less outside the home in income-earning activities or inside the home in activities that substitute for the spending of income).

3. Again consider the consumer described in the opening paragraph of Question 1. Imagine that the consumer's marginal utility of each good is shown in the table and is dependent only on the amount consumed of that good. Use the rule of Jevons to determine the optimum quantities to be consumed of each good.

QUESTIONS AND PROBLEMS

1. Draw the budget line for a consumer with a monthly budget of $500, which is to be allocated between goods *a* and *b*, priced at $10 and $20 per unit, respectively.

a. Show the effect on this budget line if, simultaneously, the budget and the price of *a* halved, while the price of *b* doubled.

b. If only the price of *a* halved, could the consumer buy more of *b*? Explain.

c. Starting with the original budget line, show the effect on the consumer if government, simultaneously, rationed good *a* at 20 units and good *b* at 10 units per month. What if the rations were 40*a* and 20*b*?

d. Starting with the original budget line, show the effect on the consumer if government handed out 300 ration points per month and required the consumer to pay 5 points per unit of good *a* and 20 points per unit of good *b*, in addition to money.

Units Consumed (in pounds)	Marginal Utility (in utils/pound)	
	Good *a*	Good *b*
5	60	50
10	55	45
15	50	40
20	45	35
25	40	30
30	35	25
35	30	20
40	25	15

4. **Mr. A:** All of the assumptions about indifference curves in this chapter are wrong:

a. Consumers are able to rank bundles of goods? Then why do they say: "These goods are so different, I can't choose," or "I don't care, you choose for me," or "Whichever I choose, I know I'll be sorry"?

b. Consumers prefer more of any good to less? What about *complementary* goods, such as bacon and eggs, cars and roads, cars and gasoline, French fries and ketchup, knives and forks, peanut butter and jelly, rifles and ammunition, right shoes and left shoes, tea and lemon, TV sets and electricity, vermouth and gin? Given an amount of one item of these pairs, an increased amount of the other item will be considered a nuisance at worst and a matter of indifference at best. Or what about goods some people can't stand, such as lipstick, hated foods, pornographic books? I can easily imagine indifference curves that are horizontal, vertical, and even positively sloped. In fact, I think they might be circular.

c. Consumers rank bundles of goods in a consistent manner? I observe people making inconsistent choices all the time, probably because comparing pairs of goods one at a time is not the same thing as making rank orderings of many goods simultaneously. This problem is worse when we turn from individual choices to group choices.

d. Consumers insist on a diminishing marginal rate of substitution? What about *perfect substitutes,* such as two nickels and one dime, red apples and yellow apples, brand A salt and brand B salt, a gallon of Amoco gas and a similar gallon of Mobil gas, and (for some people) a glass of Coors and a glass of Budweiser? What about the phenomenon of *addiction,* whether to alcohol, cigarettes, classical music, gambling, heroin, mountain climbing, rock and roll, or stamp collecting? I can easily imagine indifference curves that are negatively sloped but are straight lines or concave with respect to the origin.

Ms. B: I am speechless.

What about you? What response would you make to each of Mr. A's points?

5. Consider the accompanying diagram of a person's budget line and three indifference curves.
   a. If the price of good *a* were $15, what would be the size of the consumer's budget?
   b. Given your answer to Question 5a, what would be the price of good *b*?

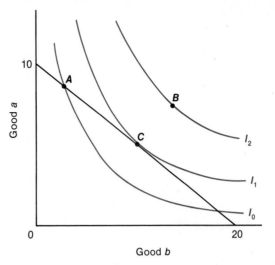

c. What is the consumer's *MRS* at the optimum?
d. Why is point *A* not the optimum? Why not *B*?
e. If utility-maximizing consumers in another city paid half as much for good *a* and twice as much for good *b*, what would their *MRS* be?

6. Consider the graph in Question 5. Let good *a* stand for food and good *b* for all other goods.
   a. Show the effect on the consumer's optimum if the government provided free food stamps for 5 units of food.
   b. What if the government made people buy each $2 worth of those food stamps for $1 worth of money?

7. Still considering the graph in Question 5,
   a. Show that a cash grant smaller than the value of the in-kind subsidy might be able to raise the recipients' welfare just as much.
   b. Make an analogous argument about in-kind fringe benefits often provided by employers (such as life insurance, medical care, or recreational facilities). Why do employers provide fringe benefits rather than cash?

8. A family of indifference curves depicts a person's tastes, but, surely, these tastes are not determined by genes and fixed forever. People

are born with few tastes (a liking for warmth and mother's milk, a dislike of falling, loud noises, and being wet). Thereafter, tastes are learned (from parents and peers, teachers and preachers, business advertising and government propaganda). Tastes, therefore, change with age and also with the cycles of fashion—whether in art, cars, dress, food, or even scientific doctrines.

  a. How might one depict a change in a person's tastes?

  b. How would one account for interdependencies in people's tastes, such as the desire to be like others (bandwagon effect), to be unlike others (snob effect), to see others well off (benevolence), or to see them in misery (malevolence)?

  c. Can a person's tastes ever be wrong? *Hint:* Consider arsonists, dope addicts, the feeble-minded or immature, neurotics, psychotics. If your answer is yes, ask yourself who can be trusted to have the correct tastes and how these tastes could be made effective in people's choices.

  *9. A consumer's utility function is $U = 4Q_a + 15Q_b - Q_a^2 - Q_aQ_b - 3Q_b^2$. The consumer has a budget of 100 and faces prices of $P_a = 10$ and $P_b = 5$. Using calculus, determine

  a. the utility-maximizing quantities of good a and b that the consumer should consume.

  b. the meaning of the Lagrangian multiplier, λ, in this example of constrained maximization.

  10. Consider a family of *community* indifference curves for the residents of New York City, lying in private goods (vertical axis) versus public goods (horizontal axis) space. How would an original optimum be changed if the state or federal government made a *matching grant* that provided a $1 gift for every $1 of their own money that New Yorkers spent on public goods? What would happen to the welfare of New Yorkers if the matching grant actually made at the new optimum were converted into an unconditional grant of equal size that New Yorkers could spend on anything, public or private goods?

  11. Consider the six budget lines in Figure 2.2. Write down the equation for each.

  12. The accompanying table gives points on three different consumption indifference curves. Plot these points in a graph and connect them by smooth curves.

Indifference Curves

I_0		I_1		I_2	
Q_a	Q_b	Q_a	Q_b	Q_a	Q_b
12	.9	12.4	2.0	12.0	5.0
10	1.8	9.3	4.0	9.0	8.0
8	2.8	7.0	6.0	7.8	10.0
6	4.0	5.7	8.0	6.0	14.0
4	5.9	4.7	10.0	5.2	16.0
2	9.2	3.9	12.0		
1	13.0	3.3	14.0		
.9	16.0	2.9	16.0		

  13. Between each of the adjacent points given in the accompanying table, determine the marginal rate of substitution of b for a.

  14. Reconsider the graph drawn in answer to Question 12.

  a. Determine the optimum if the budget line is $Q_a = 8.6 - .78Q_b$.

  b. If $P_a = 10$, what is the budget? What is P_b?

SELECTED READINGS

Becker, Gary S. "Altruism in the Family and Selfishness in the Market Place," *Economica*, February 1981, pp. 1–15.

  Discusses why altruism is so much more important in families than in market transactions.

Cooter, Robert, and Peter Rappoport. "Were the Ordinalists Wrong about Welfare Economics?" *Journal of Economic Literature*, June 1984, pp. 507–30.

  A sharp critique of the common view that rejection of the marginalist revolution of the 1870s (and its interpersonal utility comparisons) in favor of the ordinalist revolution of the 1930s (and its stress on observable *MRS*s instead of unmeasurable *MU*s) was scientific progress, from normative statements to positive theory.

Galbraith, John K. *The Affluent Society.* Boston: Houghton Mifflin, 1958; *The New Industrial State.* Boston: Houghton Mifflin, 1971.

Argues that people's tastes are artificial creations of business advertising and, therefore, not worth respecting. For a contrary view, *see* F. A. von Hayek, "The Non Sequitur of the Dependence Effect," *Southern Economic Journal,* April 1961, pp. 346–48.

Leibenstein, Harvey. *Beyond Economic Man: A New Foundation for Microeconomics,* chaps. 4 and 11. Cambridge, Mass.: Harvard University Press, 1976.

Discusses interdependencies in people's tastes and the process of decision making *within* multiperson households.

Linder, Staffan B. *The Harried Leisure Class.* New York: Columbia University Press, 1970.

Discusses time as an important constraint to people's consumption choices.

Samuelson, Paul A. *Foundations of Economic Analysis.* Cambridge, Mass.: Harvard University Press, 1947.

An early but classic work by the 1970 winner of the Nobel Prize in economics. Chapter 5 contains a detailed, calculus-based treatment of consumer theory; also introduces the revealed preference approach.

Scott, Robert H. "Avarice, Altruism, and Second Party Preferences," *The Quarterly Journal of Economics,* February 1972, pp. 1–18.

A discussion of interdependent utilities.

Stigler, George. "The Development of Utility Theory," *Journal of Political Economy,* August–October 1950, pp. 307–27, 373–96.

An insightful survey of the history of utility theory, written by the 1982 winner of the Nobel Prize in economics.

Weinstein, Arnold A. "Transitivity of Preference: A Comparison among Age Groups," *Journal of Political Economy,* March–April 1968, pp. 307–11.

Reports on an experiment to test the consistency of people's choices; concludes that transitivity is an acquired skill (it increases with age).

COMPUTER PROGRAMS

The KOHLER-3 personal-computer diskettes that accompany this book contain one program of particular interest to this chapter:

2. The Preferences of the Consumer includes a 25-question multiple-choice test with immediate responses to incorrect answers as well as numerous exercises that show how budget, prices, and tastes interact to determine the optimum purchases of goods that maximize a consumer's utility.

ANALYTICAL EXAMPLE 2.1

THE DERIVATION OF INDIFFERENCE CURVES: REVEALED PREFERENCE

Economists have used several approaches to derive actual indifference curves. The **revealed-preference approach,** which was introduced by Paul Samuelson, relies on observing the actual market behavior of people. Consider Figure A. Suppose a person is observed choosing combination *D* when relative prices are given by the slope of line *AB*. By assumption 2, found in the section on the "Analysis of the Consumption-Indifference Curve," this choice reveals as *superior* all bundles of goods in shaded rectangle *CDE*. From what we know about a consumer's optimum, this choice also reveals that all other points on line *AB* and below it are *inferior* to *D*. (All bundles of goods in the shaded triangle were available to the consumer and cost as much as *D* or less but were not chosen.) An indifference curve through *D* must, therefore, go through the remaining unshaded areas.

This area can be narrowed by further observations. Consider Figure B, which elaborates upon Figure A. Suppose the consumer is observed choosing combination *F* (which we know to be inferior to *D*) when relative prices are given by the slope of line *GH.* By reasoning analogous to the above, the unshaded area can be reduced by the dotted area *BFH.* Or suppose combination *K* is chosen when relative prices are given by the slope of line *LM.* Since *D* is available, *K* must be preferred to *D,* and so must be all bundles of goods in the cross-hatched area above and to the right of *K.* In this way, repeated observations narrow the zone of ignorance until the exact indifference curve through *D* is found, looking, perhaps, like line I_0. All this assumes, of course, that the consumer's tastes have not changed during the period of observation.

FIGURE A

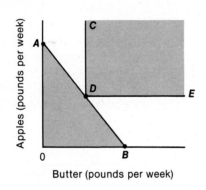

FIGURE B

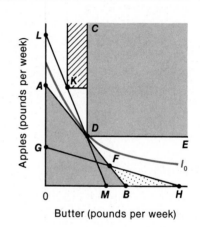

ANALYTICAL EXAMPLE 2.2

THE DERIVATION OF INDIFFERENCE CURVES: EXPERIMENT

Instead of relying on repeated observations of the market behavior of a *single* person *over time* (and assuming stability of this person's tastes), a second approach to the derivation of indifference curves experiments with *many* persons at a *given time* (and assumes that all have identical tastes). In a 1967 experiment at UCLA, students were asked to rank bundles of money ($0–$25) and ball point pens (0–180).

To find the indifference curve going through point *A* in Figure C, all combinations both above and to the right of *A* were ruled out as impossibly equivalent to *A* by the "more-is-preferred-to-less principle" (note the shading). Then subjects were asked to rank *A* versus *B, A* versus *C,* and so on. If *A* was preferred to *B,* combination *B* and all others to the left and below it were eliminated as inferior to *A.* If *C* was preferred to *A,* all points above and to the right of it were likewise eliminated. In this way, the zone of ignorance about the location of the indifference curve through *A* was successively narrowed.

Subjects were motivated to tell the truth by a payoff: After making their choice, a point *X* in the field of choice was selected at random, and subjects received the bundle of goods corresponding to *X* or *A*, whichever was preferred.

Figure D shows one of the indifference maps so derived.

Source: K. R. MacCrimmon and M. Toda, "The Experimental Determination of Indifference Curves," *Review of Economic Studies,* October 1969, pp. 433–51. (Note also the literature about other experiments cited there.)

FIGURE C

FIGURE D

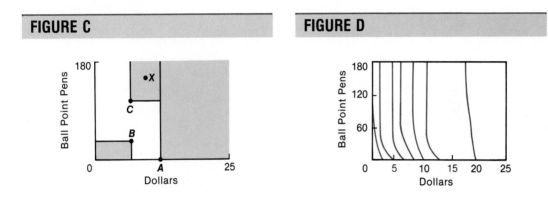

3

The Demand for Goods

In the previous chapter, we isolated the major elements that explain the division of a consumer's expenditures among different consumption goods. The elements consisted of objective factors on the one hand, notably the prices of goods and the size of the consumer's budget, and of subjective factors on the other hand, notably the consumer's preferences. Figure 2.6, "The Consumer's Optimum" (p. 39), brought these elements together and depicted the consumption choices of a consumer who cared to maximize utility. In Chapter 3, we will test the validity of our theory of consumer choice by developing some of its behavioral implications and comparing them with the observed behavior of real-world consumers.

The first of these implications is the famous **"law" of downward-sloping demand,** referring to the tendency of people normally to buy larger quantities of something when its price is lower, all else being equal. Note the careful wording. The term "law" has been placed in quotation marks because it is not in fact a rigid law (although traditionally referred to as such) but a tendency normally observed.

Also note: As every beginning student in economics learns rather quickly, **demand** never refers to a single quantity number but rather to the alternative amounts of an item a person (or group of persons) would buy during a given period at all conceivable prices of this item, all else being equal. We can now appreciate the meaning of this. Let us denote a person's demand for a consumption good x by D_x. As we have shown, D_x depends on (or is a function of) the price of this good, P_x; the prices of any other good, P_y, P_z, and so on; the consumer's budget, B; and the consumer's tastes, T. All of this can be written as

$$D_x = f(P_x, P_y, P_z, \ldots B, T).$$

If we assume that P_y, P_z, $\ldots$, B, and T do not vary, then the demand for x depends on its own price alone.

$$D_x = f(P_x), \text{ given } P_y, P_z, \ldots B, \text{ and } T.$$

Every conceivable price of x will thus be associated with a particular (and probably different) quantity demanded of x; hence *demand* refers to a set of many price-quantity combinations. Our earlier analysis of the consumer's optimum can help us derive such a relationship.

THE DEMAND FOR A GOOD AS A FUNCTION OF ITS OWN PRICE

Picture a consumer whose tastes are summarized by indifference curves I_0 to I_3 in panel (a) of Figure 3.1. Imagine an initial optimum at a, corresponding to a weekly budget of $120 and prices of $2.50 per pound of apples and $6 per pound of butter. (Hence distance $0A$ measures $120 per week divided by $2.50 per pound, or 48 pounds per week. Distance $0B$ measures $120 per week divided by $6 per pound, or 20 pounds per week.) The actual quantity of butter purchased at point a is graphed in panel (b) as point e.

Now let the consumer's tastes and budget remain unchanged, along with the apple price. Let the price of butter fall, successively, to $3, $2, and $1.50 per pound. The budget line will swing around point A from AB to AC, AD, and AE, respectively. (Distance $0C$ measures 40 pounds per week, $0D$ 60 pounds per week, and $0E$ 80 pounds per week, as implied by the lower prices of butter.) The consumer's optimum will move from point a to b, c, and d, respectively, along a path called the **price-consumption line.** This line indicates how the optimum quantities of two consumption goods change in response to a change in the price of one of these goods, all else being equal.

Now consider panel (b). The quantities of butter consumed at the various optima have been plotted separately there, along with the corresponding butter prices. The points so derived, labeled e through h, trace out the familiar downward-sloping demand curve. Naturally, if initially we had assumed different tastes (had

FIGURE 3.1

The Price-Consumption Line

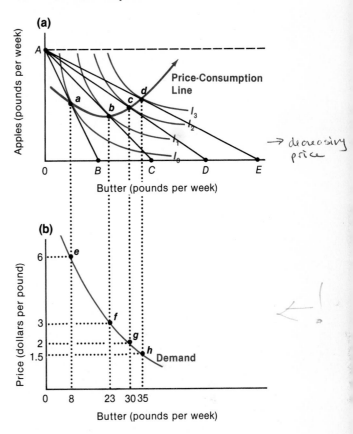

The decreasing price of a consumption good, here butter, is pictured by budget line AB swinging to the right to become AC, AD, and then AE. This decrease in butter price gives rise to an increased quantity of butter demanded, all else being equal. (Tastes throughout are depicted by indifference curves I_0 to I_3; the weekly budget remains $120; the apple price stays at $2.50 per pound.) The price-consumption line in panel (a) traces the alternative optima selected by a utility-maximizing consumer; the implied demand curve for butter, pictured in panel (b), is downward-sloping.

drawn different indifference curves), had assumed a different budget size or apple price (and had thus started from a budget line unlike AB), we would have derived a different demand curve.

That is why a change in tastes, budget, or the price of any other goods *shifts* a given demand curve to the right or left and is referred to as a **change in demand.** In contrast, a change in the good's own price, while tastes, budget, and other prices are unchanged, causes a *movement along* a given demand curve (as between *e* and *f*) and is referred to as a **change in quantity demanded.**

Three things should be noted. First, as long as the price-consumption line, in response to lowered prices of the good measured along the horizontal axis (here butter), follows a path toward the right, the demand curve of this good will be downward-sloping. This will be so regardless of whether the consumption of the other good (here apples) falls (as it does between *a* and *b*) or rises (as it does between *b* and *d*).

Second, the price-consumption line can never cross the dashed horizontal line drawn through point *A*. That line would depict the budget line if the price of butter were to become zero. The consumer could then spend the entire budget on apples, buying the maximum possible quantity of 0*A*, while picking up for nothing any desired quantity of butter. Such a combination would lie on the dashed line. Any combination above that line would remain unavailable because the limited budget, along with the positive apple price, would not allow the acquisition of any apple quantity larger than 0*A*.

Third, a hypothetical case could be made for an upward-sloping demand curve: Imagine indifference curve I_1 touching budget line *AC* above and to the left of point *a*. The lower butter price would then be associated, at a new optimum b′ (not shown), with a *lower* butter quantity purchased. Point *f*, in panel (b), would be below and to the left of point *e*. Such a situation, in which consumers buy less of an item when its price is lower and more when it is higher, all else being equal, is called **Giffen's paradox.** This situation is named after a British statistician, Sir Robert Giffen (1837–1910), and has been observed only on the rarest of occasions. A possible explanation is given later in this chapter.

THE DEMAND FOR A GOOD AS A FUNCTION OF INCOME

A mental experiment analogous to the one in the previous section reveals the likely effect of changes in income on quantity demanded. Consider Figure 3.2. Imagine a consumer, whose tastes are depicted by indifference curves I_0 to I_3 in panel (a), who neither borrows nor saves and whose budget, therefore, equals income. Picture an initial optimum at *a*, corresponding to a weekly income of $40 and prices of $4 per pound of apples and $2 per pound of butter. (Hence distance 0*A* measures $40 per week divided by $4 per pound, or 10 pounds per week. Distance 0*B* measures $40 per week divided by $2 per pound, or 20 pounds per week.) The actual quantity of butter purchased at point *a* is graphed in panel (b) as point *e*.

Now let the consumer's tastes and all prices remain unchanged. Then

$$D_x = f(B), \text{ given } P_x, P_y, P_z \ldots \text{ and } T.$$

Let budget and income rise, successively, to $80, $120, and $160 per week. The budget line will shift out from *AB* to *CD*, *EF*, and *GH*, respectively. The consumer's optimum will move from point *a* to *b*, *c*, and *d*, along a path called the **income-consumption line.** This line indicates how the optimum quantities of two consumption goods change in response to a change in income, all else being equal.

Now consider panel (b). The quantities of butter consumed at the various optima have been plotted separately here, along with the corresponding incomes. The points so derived, labeled *e* through *h*, trace out an upward-sloping **Engel curve.** Such a curve always shows the alternative amounts of an item a person (or group of persons) would buy during a given period at all conceivable incomes, all else being equal. The curve is named after a German statistician, Ernst Engel (1821–1896), who should not be confused with

important distinction

FIGURE 3.2

The Income-Consumption Line

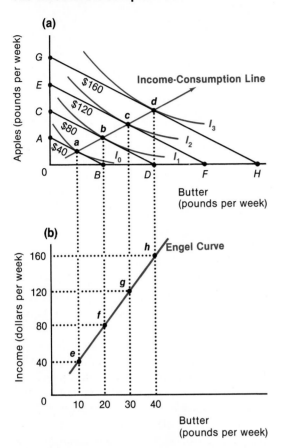

(a)

Apples (pounds per week)

Income-Consumption Line

$160
$120
$80
$40

Butter
(pounds per week)

(b)

Income (dollars per week)

Engel Curve

Butter
(pounds per week)

Increasing income is pictured by parallel shifts of budget line *AB* to *CD, EF,* and then *GH.* This increase in income gives rise to an increased quantity of butter demanded, all else being equal. (Tastes throughout are depicted by indifference curves I_0 to I_3; the prices of apples and butter remain at $4 and $2 per pound, respectively.) The income-consumption line in panel (a) traces the alternative optima selected by a utility-maximizing consumer; the implied Engel curve for butter, pictured in panel (b), is upward-sloping.

Friedrich Engels, the friend of Karl Marx. Ernst Engel studied the budgets and expenditures of large numbers of families. In 1857, he pronounced what is now known as **Engel's Law,** that food expenditures take a smaller percentage of income the larger income is. This tendency has been confirmed ever since throughout the world, not only for families, but also for nations. Engel also noted that clothing and housing tend to take a constant percentage of family incomes, while luxuries (such as education, health care, transportation, recreation, and saving) took increasing percentages of higher incomes.

Two things should be noted about the Engel curve in Figure 3.2. First, while Engel himself related income to various types of money expenditures, our curve relates income to physical quantities bought. As long as prices are given, money expenditures and physical quantities move, of course, together, and one magnitude can always be calculated from the other. (At our assumed price of $2 per pound, the 10 pounds of butter per week at point *e* correspond to $20 of butter *expenditures,* and so on for points *f* to *h.*)

Note, second, that an upward-sloping Engel curve is typical but not inevitable. As long as the income-consumption line, in response to higher income, follows a path toward the right, an upward-sloping Engel curve is implied. At higher incomes, all else being equal, the consumer is then consuming larger physical quantities. Goods of which larger physical quantities are consumed at higher than at lower incomes are called **normal goods.** However, an upward-sloping Engel curve need not be a straight line. To the extent that quantities bought rise *less rapidly* than income, the normal goods involved are called **necessities,** and the Engel curve has an *ever increasing* slope to the right of point *e.* (As income doubled from $40 to $80, for instance, butter consumption would less than double from 10 to, say, only 15 pounds per week.) To the extent that quantities bought rise *more rapidly* than income, the normal goods involved are called **luxuries,** and the Engel curve has an *ever decreasing* slope to the right of point *e.* (As income doubled from $40 to $80, for instance, butter consumption would more than double from 10 to, say, 28 pounds per week.) Not all goods are normal, however. Imagine a set of indifference curves that are vertical displacements of each other (such that their slopes are identical at any given quantity measured on the horizontal axis). In that case, tangency points *b, c,* and *d* would be vertically above *a,* and the Engel curve would be a vertical line, too. No matter what the income, the consumer would consume the identical physical quantity. (Salt might be an example.) Indeed, it is possible for curves I_1 through I_3 to be tangent on higher budget lines above and to the *left* of *a.* The income-consumption line through *a* would then be pointing upward to the left, and the corresponding Engel curve would be likewise sloping upward and left from point *e.* At higher incomes, all else being equal, the consumer would then be consuming smaller physical quantities. Goods of which smaller physical quantities are consumed at higher incomes are called **inferior goods.** Examples might be bulky, but not necessarily nutritious and palatable foods (bread, pasta, potatoes, rice, turnips, pigs' feet), as well as all kinds of low-quality goods that people abandon the moment their income rises (second-hand clothes, reconditioned tires, long-distance bus rides, routine tooth extractions, and, some think, even having children). As it turns out, Giffen's paradox is always associated with inferior goods, although the reverse is not true. Not all inferior goods produce the paradox. To solve the paradox, we must come to understand the distinction between *substitution* and *income effects.*

SUBSTITUTION AND INCOME EFFECTS

Every price change—other prices, money income, and tastes being constant—can be considered to change quantity demanded for two different reasons. This fact was first noted by the Russian mathematician Evgeny Slutsky (1880–1948), but the idea was fully developed by a British economist, Sir John Hicks (1904–1989)

who received the 1972 Nobel Prize in economics. (Chapter 3 of the *Student Workbook* that accompanies this text features biographies of both men.) A change in a good's price, argue Slutsky and Hicks, gives rise to, first of all, to a **substitution effect** because—given any initial level of real income—a utility-maximizing consumer facing a price change is bound to change the composition of the optimal bundle of consumption goods, substituting more of the now relatively cheaper good for less of other, now relatively more expensive goods.

Such a price change also gives rise to an **income effect** because—given *money* income—the price change alters *real* income and, thus, the quantity demanded. If, for example, the price of a good has fallen, other prices and money income being equal—the consumer's real income has in fact risen. Hence the consumer will buy more of the good if it is a normal good but less if it is an inferior good. The income effect, therefore, reinforces the substitution effect (that makes people buy a larger quantity at a lower price) in the case of normal goods but counteracts the substitution effect in the case of inferior goods. If the income effect occurs in the opposite direction of the substitution effect, it can offset it partially, exactly, or more than fully; only the last of these three contingencies produces Giffen's paradox.

While Slutsky and Hicks agree that a good's price change, given other prices, *money* income, and tastes, has a specified total effect on the good's quantity demanded and also that this total effect can be divided into two independent and additive effects, called substitution and income effects, they differ on how this division is to be made. Their disagreement results from differing interpretations of the concept of *real* income. Hicks thinks of real income as some level of utility, specified by some indifference curve. Slutsky thinks of real income as a set of physical quantities of goods, specified by some point in the field of choice. Let us consider the Hicksian approach first; another look at Figure 3.1 on p. 53 proves helpful as a starting point.

Hicks's Approach

Hicks noted that the demand curve in panel (b) was derived on the assumption of a given money income, but that movements along this curve clearly imply changes in the consumer's real income. Thus a fall in the price of butter from $6 per pound to $3 per pound that moves the consumer from point e to point f in panel (b) also moves the consumer from a to b in panel (a) and, thus, from indifference curve I_0 to indifference curve I_1, the latter implying a higher level of utility (and Hicksian real income). Analogous observations can be made for further price decreases, as from $3 to $2 and $1.5 per pound. The consumer moves from f to g to h in panel (b) and, correspondingly, from b to c to d in panel (a). Each point on the panel (b) demand curve that holds money income constant and is, therefore, called an **ordinary demand curve,** is associated with a different level of real income.

Hicks asked himself an obvious question: Is it similarly possible to derive a demand curve for a *constant* level of real income? When he answered his own question, Hicks found a way of separating the substitution effect from the income effect. Consider panel (a) of Figure 3.3. Point a represents a consumer's optimum, corresponding to budget line AB and indifference curve I_0. The implied price of butter is shown by distance $0F$ in panel (b), the quantity of butter demanded is $0H$; point d is a point on the ordinary demand curve for butter. Let the price of butter halve from $0F$ to $0G$ in panel (b); the panel (a) budget line swings around A to become AC. The consumer finds a new optimum at b, is better off in utility terms, and consumes $0L$ units of butter in panel (b). Point f is a second point on the ordinary demand curve that keeps *money* income constant. Yet, Hicks figured, by taking some money income away from the consumer—just enough to compensate for the utility increase occasioned by the price decline—the consumer's real income, in utility terms, could be kept constant. Such a decrease in money income is illustrated by a

hypothetical shift of the new budget line AC to parallel line DE that just touches the original indifference curve. Given this new and lower money income and the new relative prices (embodied in the position and slope of dashed line DE), the consumer would find a new optimum at c and consume quantity $0K$ of butter, shown in panel (b). Thus point e is said to lie on the **Hicksian income-compensated demand curve,** now shown as the color line. This demand curve shows the quantity demanded at alternative prices of a good when the consumer's *real* income is constant because the utility-increasing consequence of a price cut is immediately compensated (and offset) by a cut in money income that leaves overall utility unchanged, while the utility-decreasing consequence of a price increase is similarly compensated by an increase in money income. Note that the Hicksian procedure of sliding the original budget line, such as AB, around the original indifference curve, I_0, until the budget line's slope reflects the new relative prices (as dashed line DE does) permits the division of the total effect of a price change on quantity demanded into the separate substitution and income effects discussed above: In our example, the halving of the butter price from $0F$ to $0G$ (that replaces actual budget line AB by actual budget line AC) raises quantity demanded from $0H$ to $0L$. This is the *total effect;* it is recorded by the ordinary demand curve (as we move along it from d to f).

Yet we now know that a consumer whose real income was held constant would have increased quantity demanded not by HL in panel (b), but only by HK; this horizontal distance between points a and c measures the *substitution effect.* The remaining increase in quantity demanded by KL in panel (b), which represents the horizontal distance between c and b, measures the *income effect.* It recognizes that the consumer in fact gained real income, the difference between the utility levels associated with indifference curve I_0 and I_2 (or the difference between hypothetical budget line DE and actual line AC).

Unlike in this example, the Hicksian substitution and income effects do not always reinforce each other, however. To that matter we must now turn.

In order to facilitate comparisons, panel (a) of Figure 3.4 reviews the case of a normal good (butter). A consumer with tastes depicted by I_0 and I_1 and budget line AB has chosen to consume combination a. The price of butter falls, as shown by the budget line's swing to AC, all other factors relevant to butter demand remaining

equal. The consumer chooses combination b. Conceptually, the horizontal movement from a to b can be divided with the help of artificial budget line DE, the slope of which reflects the new relative prices depicted by line AC. The consumer could have remained equally well off by moving from a to c, substituting more butter for less apples to this extent. (Note how both a and c are found on indifference curve I_0.) This portion of the increased butter demand is the substitution

---

FIGURE 3.3

The Hicksian Income-Compensated Demand Curve for a Normal Good

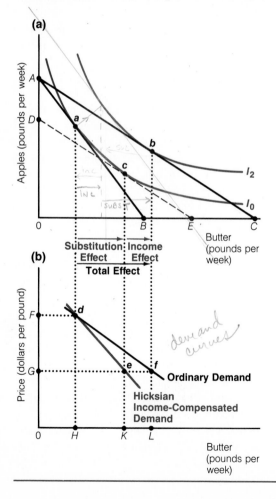

A fall in the butter price, from $0F$ to $0G$ in panel (b), moves an original budget line from AB to AC in panel (a), moves the consumer's optimum from a to $b,$ and raises quantity demanded from $0H$ to $0L$. This *total effect* is divided by Hicks into *substitution and income effects* by noting that the consumer, according to point c, would have demanded only HK more butter at the new relative prices if real income had remained unchanged at utility level I_0 and that the remaining increase in quantity demanded (KL) can be explained by the rise in real income occasioned by the combination of price fall and unchanged money income. The Hicksian income-compensated demand curve takes account of the substitution effect only; it is constructed on the assumption that the welfare effect of price changes has been precisely offset (or *compensated*) by money-income changes in the opposite direction.

effect. It doesn't tell the whole story because the consumer in effect received a real-income increase that can be depicted by a parallel shift of *DE* to *AC*. The consumer chose to buy a butter quantity corresponding to *b*, not *c*. This portion of the increased butter demand is the income effect. In the case of normal goods, it always reinforces the substitution effect. The demand curve for butter is certainly downward-sloping.

Panel (b) illustrates the case of an inferior good (pigs' feet) that does not exhibit Giffen's paradox. A consumer with tastes depicted by I_0 and I_1 and budget line *FG* has chosen to consume combination *d*. The price of pigs' feet falls, as shown by the budget line's swing to *FH*, all other factors relevant to the demand for pigs' feet remaining the same. The consumer chooses combination *e*. Our conceptual subdivision shows a

FIGURE 3.4

Substitution and Income Effects

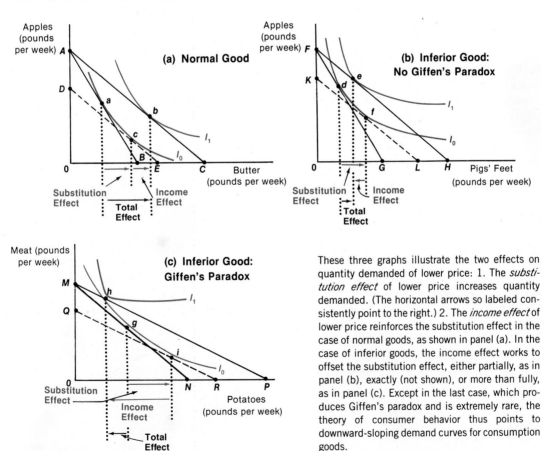

These three graphs illustrate the two effects on quantity demanded of lower price: 1. The *substitution effect* of lower price increases quantity demanded. (The horizontal arrows so labeled consistently point to the right.) 2. The *income effect* of lower price reinforces the substitution effect in the case of normal goods, as shown in panel (a). In the case of inferior goods, the income effect works to offset the substitution effect, either partially, as in panel (b), exactly (not shown), or more than fully, as in panel (c). Except in the last case, which produces Giffen's paradox and is extremely rare, the theory of consumer behavior thus points to downward-sloping demand curves for consumption goods.

substitution effect equal to the horizontal distance between *d* and *f*, partially offset by an income effect equal to the horizontal distance between *f* and *e*. Still, the net effect is an *increased* quantity of pigs' feet demanded (measured by the horizontal distance between *d* and *e*), hence a downward-sloping demand curve for pigs' feet is involved.

Panel (c), finally, illustrates the case of an inferior good (potatoes) that does give rise to Giffen's paradox. A consumer with tastes depicted by I_0 and I_1 and budget line *MN* has chosen to consume combination *g*. The price of potatoes falls, as shown by the budget line's swing to *MP*, all other factors relevant to the demand for potatoes remaining the same. The consumer chooses combination *h*. The substitution effect, equal to the horizontal distance between *g* and *i*, is swamped by the offsetting income effect equal to the horizontal distance between *i* and *h*. The net effect is a *decreased* quantity of potatoes demanded (measured by the horizontal distance between *g* and *h*), hence an upward-sloping demand curve for potatoes is implied.

Indeed, the economic literature abounds with stories (probably incorrect) according to which Giffen himself noted this paradox when studying the Irish famine of 1846–49. In that case, it is often alleged, the price of potatoes went up because of blight, rather than down as in the previous example. The Irish found that buying the same amount of potatoes cost more money and left less for other goods, such as meat. The resultant combination of goods provided insufficient calories for sheer survival. Yet, by spending even less on meat and buying more potatoes, the calorie count could be raised. Thus the higher price of potatoes gave rise to a larger quantity of potatoes demanded.[1] In Asiatic countries, a rela-

tionship similar to that between potatoes and meat has been observed between rice and fish. Apparently, inferior goods that take a small part of the family budget, as our pigs' feet in panel (b), have only a trivial income effect, and in such cases the substitution effect cannot be overpowered by the income effect. In the rare instances in which inferior goods make up a large part of the family budget, however, as when a country's main staple of food is involved, the income effect can overpower the substitution effect. A price fall (or rise) in this good makes people very much richer (or poorer); so they buy a lot less (or more) of the inferior good.

Slutsky's Approach

Slutsky's way of separating substitution effect from income effect differs from the Hicksian approach because of the differing definition of real income noted earlier. Consider Figure 3.5; it is a copy of Figure 3.3 with additional information added. Once again, in panel (a), a consumer's optimum at point *a* (budget line *AB* and indifference curve I_0) changes to point *b* (budget line *AC* and indifference curve I_2) as the price of butter halves from *0F* to *0G* (panel b). Like Hicks, Slutsky also asks how much extra butter the consumer would have demanded if real income had remained unchanged, but unlike Hicks (who answers the question by sliding the original budget line *AB* around the original indifference curve I_0 until the slope at tangency point *c* reflects the new relative prices), Slutsky considers the consumer's real income unchanged if the consumer is able, at the new relative prices, to continue buying the original quantity set (point *a*). Slutsky draws a hypothetical budget line, *MN*, through the original optimum, *a*, and par-

---

[1]We retell the story for its pedagogic value; quite possibly, it was never told by Giffen himself and may not even have happened in Ireland in the way in which it is usually told. See Gerald P. Dwyer, Jr. and Cotton M. Lindsay, ''Robert Giffen and the Irish Potato,'' *The American Economic Review,* March 1984, pp. 188–92, who argue that the Irish *as a group* could not have bought more potatoes because their crop failed and there were no imports, but that the paradox is likely to occur in open economies, such as Singapore's, that import their staple food and may find that they can buy any quantity they want, but at a price determined in the world market.

allel to the actual new budget line, *AC*. Although the consumer *could* continue buying combination *a*, a new optimum at *h* is selected because utility on I_1 exceeds utility on I_0. The butter quantity demanded rises from $0H$ to $0P$; this is Slutsky's substitution effect. Correspondingly, *PL* is the Slutsky income effect. Thus point *g* in panel (b) lies on **Slutsky's income-compensated demand curve,** now shown as the color line. This demand curve shows the quantity demanded at alternative prices of a good when the consumer's *real*

income is constant in the sense that any price changes are always compensated by money-income changes in such a way that the consumer can, if desired, buy precisely the quantities that were bought prior to the price changes.

Conclusion

As panel (b) of Figure 3.5 indicates, the work of Slutsky and Hicks puts before economists an embarrassment of riches so far as demand curves

---

FIGURE 3.5

Slutsky's Income-Compensated Demand Curve for a Normal Good

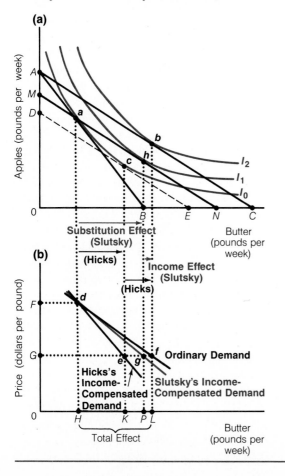

	Total Effect =	Substitution Effect +	Income Effect
Slutsky's Approach:	*HL* =	*HP* +	*PL*
Hicks' Approach	*HL* =	*HK* +	*KL*

A fall in the butter price, from $0F$ to $0G$ in panel (b), moves an original budget line from *AB* to *AC* in panel (a), moves the consumer's optimum from *a* to *b*, and raises quantity demanded from $0H$ to $0L$ (just as in Figure 3.3). This *total effect* is divided by Slutsky into *substitution and income effects* by noting that the consumer, according to point *h*, would have demanded only *HP* more butter at the new relative prices if real income had remained unchanged in the sense of a continued ability (shown by budget line *MN*) to buy the original combination of goods (point *a*). The remaining increase in quantity demanded (*PL*) is explained by a rise in real income occasioned by the combination of price fall and unchanged money income that enables the consumer to buy more of all goods than set *a* contains. Because of the different definition of real income, Slutsky's substitution and income effects differ from those of Hicks, which are shown here for comparison. Slutsky's income-compensated demand curve, therefore, differs from Hicks's as well.

are concerned. There is the ordinary demand curve that holds money income constant (along with other prices and tastes); there are two types of income-compensated demand curves that hold real income constant. The shape of these demand curves, furthermore, will differ depending on whether the good in question is a normal or inferior one and, in the latter case, on whether Giffen's paradox does or does not apply. Unless stated otherwise, we will continue to work with ordinary demand curves, but there are occasions when the alternative types of curves are very important. The Hicksian demand curve, for example, is useful in the analysis of consumer surplus, a subject to which we turn in Chapter 6. Slutsky's approach is often used in empirical work (consider Close-Up 3.1, for example) because it is difficult to know the exact shape of indifference curves (and to calculate money income adjustments to keep Hicksian real income unchanged), while it is easy to observe the quantities contained in an original bundle of consumption goods and to calculate the money income required to buy the same bundle at a new set of prices.

THE DEMAND FOR A GOOD AS A FUNCTION OF ANOTHER GOOD'S PRICE

We can learn even more about the nature of demand from another mental experiment in which we vary neither the price of the good in question nor income or tastes, but in which we vary the price of another good. Thus,

$$D_x = f(P_y), \text{ given } P_x, P_z, \ldots B, T.$$

Consider Figure 3.6, which presents some rather unusual demand curves of this type (in that the quantity demanded of a good is related to the price of another good) and which also illustrates the concepts of independent, complementary, and substitute goods.

First, imagine a consumer of salt and tea whose tastes are depicted by indifference curves I_0 and I_1 in panel (a). With an initial budget line of AB, the optimum is found at a. Consumption of tea equals 0D when the price of salt is $1 per pound (point c). How will the quantity of tea vary, not with the price of tea, but with the price of salt? Let the price of salt fall from $1 per pound to 50¢ per pound, all other relevant factors (tastes, budget, and other prices) remaining unchanged. The budget line swings around B to BC, and a new optimum is found at b. The quantity of tea demanded remains unchanged and is plotted, at the new price, at d in the middle graph. Accordingly, the ordinary demand curve for tea, shown in the lowest graph of panel (a), stays put. When in this way the quantity demanded of one good *does not respond to a changed price of another good,* all else being equal, the goods are said to be **independent goods.** Surely, many pairs of goods—ranging from salt and tea to men's shoes and women's shoes to baby rattles and oil filters—are of this nature.

Now consider panel (b). We imagine a consumer of lemons and tea whose tastes are depicted by I_2 and I_3. With an initial budget line of EF, the optimum is found at e. Consumption of tea equals 0H when the price of lemons is $2 per pound (point g). We let this price fall to $1, all else remaining equal. The budget line swings around F to FG, and a new optimum is found at f. The quantity of tea rises to 0K and is plotted, at the new price, at h in the middle graph. Accordingly, the ordinary demand curve for tea, shown in the lowest graph of panel (b), shifts to the right. When in this way the quantity demanded of one good *varies inversely with the price of another good,* all else being equal, the goods are said to be **complementary goods.** These are goods that "go together," that cooperate with each other in the process of consumption. When the price of one falls and people buy more of it, they buy more of the other good as well. Besides lemons and tea, other examples are autos and gasoline, fishing licenses and fishing poles, ham-

FIGURE 3.6

Independent, Complementary, and Substitute Goods

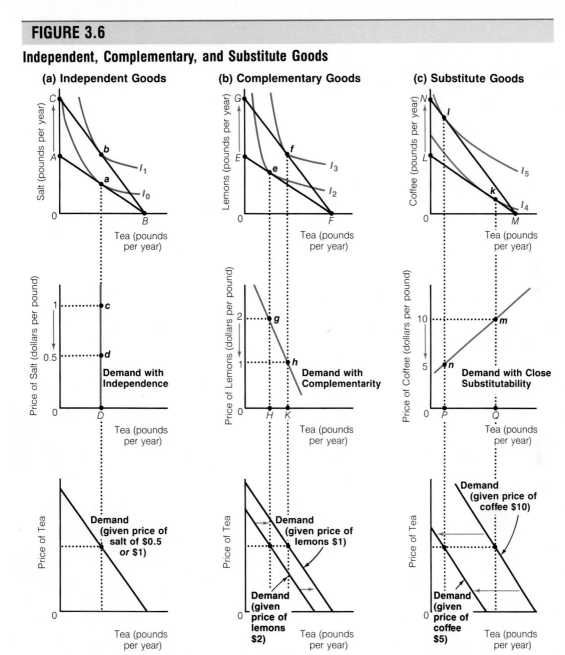

The quantity demanded of a consumption good, such as tea, might be *independent* of the price of another good, such as salt, pictured in panel (a). The quantity might vary *inversely* with the price of another good such as lemons, pictured in panel (b). Finally, the quantity might vary *in the same direction* as the price of another good such as coffee, pictured in panel (c). The unusual demand curves in the second row of three panels (which relate the quantity of tea to the price of *another* good) illustrate relationships of independence, complementarity, or substitutability, respectively, and predict whether the ordinary demand curves in the three bottom panels are unaffected, shift right, or shift left when the price of the other good falls.

burgers and ketchup, hot dogs and buns, knives and forks, shoes and laces, strawberries and shortcake, trousers and belts, turkeys and cranberry sauce.

Finally, consider panel (c). We imagine a consumer of coffee and tea whose tastes are depicted by I_4 and I_5. With an initial budget line of *LM,* the optimum is found at *k.* Consumption of tea equals $0Q$ when the price of coffee is $10 per pound (point *m*). We let this price fall to $5, all else remaining equal. The budget line swings around *M* to *MN,* and a new optimum is found at *l.* The quantity of tea falls to $0P$ and is plotted, at the new price, at *n* in the middle graph. Accordingly, the ordinary demand curve for tea, shown in the lowest graph of panel (c), shifts to the left. When in this way the quantity demanded of one good *varies in the same direction as the price of another good,* all else being equal, the goods are said to be **substitute goods.** These are "either-or" goods that are rivals in consumption. When the price of one falls and people buy more of it, they buy less of the other good because it fulfills the same basic want. Besides coffee and tea, examples are beef and pork, butter and margarine, ice cream and ice milk, motorcycles and bicycles, new houses and old ones, oil and coal, truck and rail freight, tuna and salmon.

Note: The above distinctions among independent, complementary, and substitute goods, although commonly used, are not the only possible ones. Our analysis did not separate the substitution and income effects. One could argue, for instance, that a fall in the price of salt or lemons or coffee, all else being equal, constitutes a rise in real income, and this by itself would lead, in each case, to increased purchases of tea (assuming it is a normal good). One could deduct this income effect on tea purchases from the total effect observed in Figure 3.6 and classify goods as independents, complements, or substitutes only after adjusting for this income effect, on the basis of the pure relative price effect alone.

FROM INDIVIDUAL DEMAND TO MARKET DEMAND

We have seen how the quantity demanded of a good can be related to any one of a number of factors that influence it. Economists are, however, particularly interested in the relationship between the quantity demanded of a good and its own price, as illustrated in panel (b) of Figure 3.1. Moreover, they tend to focus attention not so much on the demand of one individual, but on

TABLE 3.1

Deriving the Market-Demand Schedule

Price (dollars per bushel)	Quantity of Apples Demanded (bushels per year)						
(1)	Household A (2)		Household B (3)		Household C (4)		All Three Households (5) = (2) + (3) + (4)
21	0		5		0		5
18	1		6		0		7
15	2		7		1		10
12	3		8		2		13
9	4	+	9	+	3	=	16
6	5		10		4		19
3	6		11		5		22
0	7		12		6		25

A market-demand schedule can be derived by adding, at each conceivable price, the quantities demanded by all potential market participants, all else, of course, being held equal.

market demand, the sum of the demands of all potential market participants. This sum can be derived quite easily in most instances.

As long as all individuals who demand a given good face identical market prices (and this is more often true than not, even in markets that are not perfectly competitive), individual demands will differ due to differences in budgets and tastes, but they can be added together at each price. Table 3.1 shows the derivation of a market demand schedule. Although thousands, perhaps millions of buyers would appear in the real-world apple market, we need not concern ourselves with such large numbers. For a moment, and only to simplify the arithmetic, we can imagine just three buyers to exist in the market for apples. Their respective demand schedules might be those shown in columns (2) through (4) of Table 3.1.

Their combined market demand is shown in column (5). Naturally, all this information can be graphed, as in Figure 3.7.

Note that the market-demand line will shift to the right (or left) as the number of consumers increases (or decreases). It will also shift with any of the factors that shift an individual consumer's demand, such as changes in income, the prices of complementary or substitute goods, and tastes. Because of the large numbers of buyers in many markets (and certainly in perfectly competitive ones), shifts in a single individual's demand will affect market demand only imperceptibly, but widespread changes in individual demands will shift market demand noticeably. (Imagine what would happen to Figure 3.7 if everyone's income rose, if the price of oranges fell, or if it was reported that apples cure cancer.)

FIGURE 3.7

Deriving Market Demand

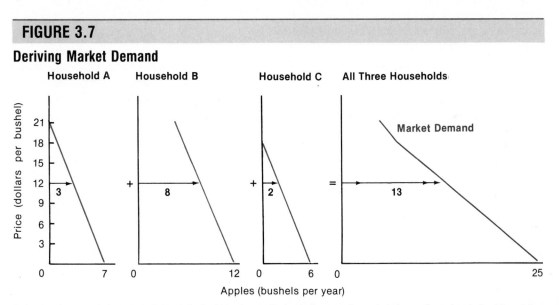

This set of graphs is based on Table 3.1. It shows how, all else being equal, market demand can be derived by adding horizontally, at each conceivable price, the quantities demanded by all potential market participants. All this can, however, be done mathematically as well. Calling quantity demanded Q and price P, the three individual demands can be represented by three equations:

$$Q_A = 7 - (P/3)$$
$$Q_B = 12 - (P/3)$$
$$Q_C = 6 - (P/3)$$

If $P = 12$, $Q_A + Q_B + Q_C = 3 + 8 + 2$; if $P = 0$, $Q_A + Q_B + Q_C = 7 + 12 + 6$, just as the graphs indicate.

While the story told so far is likely to be correct in most instances, we should note a number of exceptions. These exceptions occur when the tastes of people are interdependent in such a way that the quantity demanded by one individual rises or falls with the quantities others are seen to demand (bandwagon or snob effects) or when people try to impress each other by the conspicuous consumption of expensive goods, such as diamonds, mink coats, and Rolls Royces (Veblen effect).

The Bandwagon Effect

Sometimes people like to conform, behave like others, join the crowd, keep up with the Joneses. They want to be fashionable and stylish. When the demand for a good by each individual varies directly with the quantity others are seen to demand, a **bandwagon effect** is said to occur. It is by no means difficult to find examples. Consider how women are swept by the ''need'' for long skirts, then pant suits, then mini-skirts or how men first must have white shirts, then colored shirts, then turtlenecks. Consider how some cannot live without their pet rocks or automobile air conditioners or tape players; how youngsters first crave, and later disdain, hoola hoops, skateboards, crew cuts, and long hair.

In situations such as these, our simple horizontal addition of individual demand curves will not do, for the position of each consumer's demand will vary with market demand. Consider Figure 3.8, which depicts the bandwagon effect. Let D_A represent a market-demand line derived by the horizontal summation of the demands of all individuals, each one of whom believes that the actual quantity of long skirts purchased in the market will be $0A$. Let D_B, D_C, and D_D, similarly, represent hypothetical market-demand lines built on the expectation by all individuals of market sales equal to $0B$, $0C$, and $0D$, respectively. Then only one point on each of these curves (points a through d, respectively) represents a situation in which these quantity expec-

FIGURE 3.8

Market Demand with Bandwagon Effect

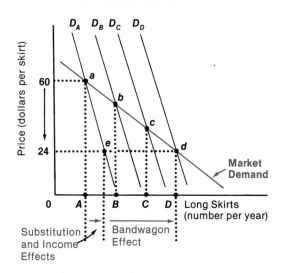

When the demand for a good by each individual varies directly with the quantity others are seen to demand, a *bandwagon effect* is said to occur. The market-demand curve in this case is still downward-sloping but is flatter than it would otherwise be.

tations are realized. The colored line connecting these points is the true market-demand line.

If the price is $60 per skirt, point a on this true market-demand line tells us, people buy quantity $0A$. This is the only price at which the expectations embodied in line D_A are realized. Let price fall to $24 per skirt. Line D_A tells us that substitution and income effects will lead to an increase in quantity demanded from a toward e. Yet the quantity demanded corresponding to point e exceeds $0A$. People would find market sales greater than expected; they would ''get on the bandwagon''; line D_A would begin to shift right. As long as price remained at $24, this shift of demand would cease only at D_D. People would then base their own purchases on expected market sales of $0D$ and, as point d indicates, this is exactly what market sales would be. Thus a downward-sloping market-demand line can still be derived in the presence of the bandwagon effect, but the slope of this line is flatter than it would otherwise be.

The Snob Effect

People do not always conform to behavioral norms. At times, they search for exclusiveness. They seek dignity, prestige, and status through being different. Instead of "being one of the gang," they like to set themselves off from the mass. When the demand for a good by each individual varies inversely with the quantity others are seen to demand, a **snob effect** is said to occur. Consider how people often buy things just because others are *not*—distinctive cars, clothes, food, and houses, for instance.

In such cases, the market-demand curve must be derived in a fashion analogous to that shown in the previous section. Consider Figure 3.9, which graphically depicts the snob effect. Let D_A represent a market-demand line derived by the horizontal summation of the demands of all individuals, each of whom believes that the actual quantity of frogs' legs purchased in the market will be 0A. Let D_B, D_C, and D_D, similarly, represent hypothetical market-demand lines built on the expectation by all individuals of market sales equal to 0B, 0C, and 0D, respectively. Unlike before, at any given price, people now demand less rather than more when market sales are high. As before, only points *a* through *d* represent situations in which these quantity expectations are realized. The colored line connecting them is the true market-demand line.

If the price is $20 per pound, point *a* on this true market line tells us, people buy quantity 0A. This is the only price at which the expectations embodied in line D_A are realized. Let price fall to $9 per pound. Line D_A tells us that substitution and income effects will lead to an increase in quantity demanded from *a* toward *e*. Yet the quantity demanded corresponding to point *e* exceeds 0A. People would find market sales greater

FIGURE 3.9

Market Demand with Snob Effect

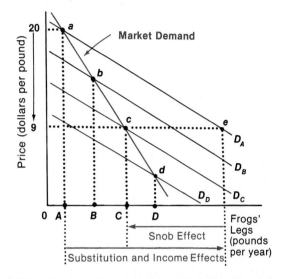

When the demand for a good by each individual varies inversely with the quantity others are seen to demand, a *snob effect* is said to occur. The market-demand curve in this case is still downward-sloping but is steeper than it would otherwise be.

than expected; they would snobbishly withdraw from the market; line D_A would begin to shift left. As long as price remained at $9, this shift of demand would cease only at D_C. People would then base their own purchases on expected market sales of 0C, and, as point *c* indicates, this is exactly what market sales would be. Thus a downward-sloping demand line can still be derived in the presence of the snob effect, but the slope of this line is steeper than it would otherwise be.

Note: The snob effect could never overpower the combined substitution and income effects because this would require quantity demanded at the lower price to be less than at the higher price (point *c* would have to be below and to the left of *a*), and such low market sales would encourage all the snobs to buy more!

The Veblen Effect

Some people allow their decision to buy a consumption good to be influenced not so much by their desire to buy (or not to buy) what others are buying, but by a wish to impress others with the high price they can afford to pay. When the demand for a good by each individual varies directly with the prevailing market price, a **Veblen effect** is said to occur. It is named after the American economist Thorstein Veblen (1857—1929), who wrote about this type of "conspicuous consumption" by people who tried to advertise their wealth. We are not likely to meet many people who drive around in diamond-studded Rolls Royces, but let us consider the argument. To the extent that this effect occurs,

FIGURE 3.10

Market Demand with Veblen Effect

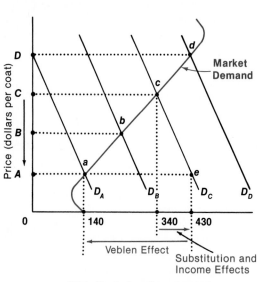

When the demand for a good by each individual varies directly with the prevailing market price, a *Veblen effect* is said to occur. At least a section of the market-demand curve in this case can be upward-sloping.

the market-demand curve could have an upward-sloping section in it. Consider Figure 3.10, which depicts the Veblen effect. Let D_A represent a market-demand line derived by the horizontal summation of the demands of all individuals, each of whom believes that the actual market price of mink coats will be $0A$. Let D_B, D_C, and D_D, similarly, represent hypothetical market-demand lines built on the expectation by all individuals of market prices equal to $0B$, $0C$, and $0D$, respectively. Note how people's demand shifts right with higher expected prices (because of the enhanced possibility of impressing others). Only points a through d represent situations in which these price expectations are realized. The colored line connecting them is the true market-demand line.

If the price is $0C$, point c on this true market line tells us, people buy 340 mink coats per year. This is the only quantity at which the expectations embodied in line D_C are realized. Let price fall to $0A$. Line D_C tells us that substitution and income effects will lead to an increase in quantity demanded from c toward e. Yet the price corresponding to point e falls short of $0C$. People would find market price smaller than expected; they would want to buy less now that mink coats are not expensive enough to impress people; line D_C would begin to shift left. As long as price remained at $0A$, this shift of demand would cease only at D_A. People would then base their purchases on an expected market price of $0A$ and, as point a indicates, this is exactly what market price would be. Thus the Veblen effect can overpower the normal substitution and income effects and produce an upward-sloping market-demand line.

Note, however, that market demand is still likely to be downward-sloping at very high and very low prices, producing the line's backward S shape. At some high price people run into their budget limits and will be unable to buy any mink coats. Thus market demand cannot possibly run upward and to the right forever. At some low price, on the other hand, almost everyone can afford mink coats. Their value for purposes of conspicuous consumption then disappears and so does our entire argument.

EMPIRICAL STUDIES OF MARKET DEMAND

Economists have tested their notions about market demand by engaging in a wide variety of empirical studies. Five types of approaches have been used: consumer interviews, consumer clinics, market experiments, time-series studies, and cross-section studies.

Consumer Interviews

Some investigators have simply collared consumers on the street and in shopping centers and asked them how much they would buy of a good at various conceivable prices of this good. In this way, they have amassed data such as those in columns (2) to (4) of Table 3.1. Such data, however, are nonsensical, unless the consumers interviewed represent a carefully selected sample of the population. Even when this was the case, economists have often been less than happy with the results. Consumers so interviewed tend to make snap judgments that may not reflect their actual behavior in a real rather than a hypothetical market situation. Consumers may also be unwilling to tell the truth, especially if true answers would reveal socially deprecating character traits. To avoid embarrassment, they might give acceptable but untrue answers. Rather than *ask* consumers, other investigators have preferred to *observe* them. This can be done in a variety of direct and indirect ways.

Consumer Clinics

One direct way of observing consumers is to study consumer behavior in consumer clinics or laboratories. Consumers are placed in a simulated market situation, such as an artificial store with goods packaged, displayed, and priced by the experimenter. Consumers are given a fixed amount of money and asked to spend it in this "store." Experimenters vary budgets and prices and note the subsequent behavior of consumers. Once again, however, general confidence in the results is lacking. For one thing, the consumers so tested may be too small a sample of the whole population to allow valid conclusions about all consumers. In addition, consumers so tested know the artificiality of the situation. Would they spend their own hard-earned money in reality in the same way as they spend this manna from heaven? Considering what we know about business people living on expense accounts and about politicians spending the taxpayers' money, one can have doubts. Finally, this type of study is very expensive to undertake.

Market Experiments

A second direct way of observing consumers is to conduct experiments in real markets. A firm may increase the price of a consumption good by 5 percent in one store or city, by 10 percent in another, and reduce it by 5 percent in a third. (The Parker Pen Company once tested the demand for its ink, called Quink, by raising prices in four cities from 15 cents to 25 cents.) Mail-order merchants sometimes print two different prices in a given issue of a national magazine, every even-numbered copy containing, perhaps, a low price; every odd-numbered one a high price. Half the copies distributed in every town will then make one offer, half another. The different mail orders are then tabulated, and the totals are considered to represent two dots on the demand line.

Once more, this approach can yield ambivalent results. It tends to be costly to the experimenter because customers faced with higher temporary prices may be lost permanently. Alternatively, the effects observed in the short run (such as a negligible loss of customers during the test period) may be quite inapplicable to the long run (if the price change were to be made permanent). In addition, the experimenter has no control over all the other factors that also affect demand. Coincidentally with the experiment, people's tastes and incomes may change, as may other prices, and even the weather and local strikes may affect demand.

Time-Series Studies

One indirect way of observing consumers is to study the statistical record of their past behavior. **Time-series studies** investigate economic data pertaining to a given population during different past periods of time. Suppose that a study of the U.S. potato market for the years 1983–86 revealed average annual prices of $3, $1, $5, and $2 per pound, respectively, for each of the four years, while corresponding potato purchases in these four years were found to have been 8 million, 11 million, 2 million, and 7 million tons. One could plot these data as in panel (a) of Figure 3.11. One might be tempted to draw a line that would be as close as possible to the four data plots and call it the market demand for the 1983–86 period. This approach, however, is not necessarily legitimate. Each set of historical price-quantity data reveals only one of the many data combinations that might have occurred during the period in question (and that constitute that period's market demand). It is quite possible that the potato market demand in 1983 looked like line D_1 in panel (b). While it shows the various quantities people would then have demanded at all conceivable prices, only one of these quantities (8 million tons) was realized because only one of these prices ($3 per pound) actually materialized as a result of the position (not shown) of that year's supply. Thus we know with certainty only a single dot on the 1983 market-demand line, the one labeled 1983. Market demands for subsequent years might, similarly, have looked like lines D_2, D_3, and D_4 in panel (b), indicating continual changes in demand during this four-year period. This might have happened in response to changes in the number of

FIGURE 3.11

The Identification Problem

(a) False Market Demand

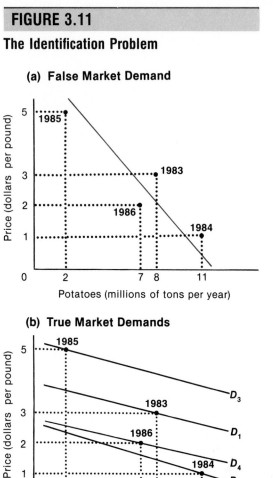

Potatoes (millions of tons per year)

(b) True Market Demands

Potatoes (millions of tons per year)

A time-series study might reveal price and quantity data about the U.S. potato market as plotted in panel (a). It is not necessarily legitimate, however, to identify as the likely market demand for the given period some line like the one drawn in panel (a). True market demands may have looked very different, as shown in panel (b). Each set of actual price-quantity data reveals only one of the many data combinations that might have occurred during the period in question. Presumably, each heavy dot in these graphs corresponds to the given year's intersection of demand and supply (and, thus, reveals only one point on a demand curve).

consumers, in their incomes and tastes, in the prices of other goods, and so on.

One can, however, easily overcome this **identification problem,** the difficulty of identifying a large number of potential data (such as those on a market-demand line) from a few historical data, each of which may belong to a different set of potential data. By also gathering historical data on all the other likely influences on demand and then employing the *least-squares multiple regression technique*, a careful statistician can actually make a fairly good estimate of market demand.[2] This technique yields estimates of some variable, such as market demand, in such a way that the sum of the squared differences between each estimate and the associated magnitude actually observed is minimized. Each estimate conforms to an equation such as

$$D_x = a + bP_x + cY + dP_y + \text{other terms},$$

where a, b, c, and d are positive or negative constants,
D_x is the quantity of x demanded,
P_x is its price,
Y is income,
and P_y is the price of some other good, y.

Once this relationship is estimated, one can hold all terms other than P_x constant and examine the partial relationship between P_x and D_x (which is market demand). We should note that this technique is not foolproof. The statistician will grind out nonsense if an important explanatory variable is forgotten or if several such variables are included that are highly correlated, for example.

Figure 3.12 summarizes an actual time-series study of the potato market in the United States.

---

[2]For a detailed discussion of this technique, see Heinz Kohler, *Statistics for Business and Economics,* 2nd edition (Glenview, Ill.: Scott, Foresman and Co., 1988), chapters 13 and 14.

FIGURE 3.12

The Market Demand for Potatoes: A Time-Series Study

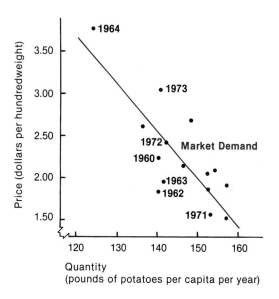

The market-demand line shown in this graph was calculated by the *least-squares multiple regression technique* as $Q = 1.636 - 0.177P + 0.093Y$, where Q measures per capita consumption of potatoes, P their price, and Y is per capita income at 1958 prices.

Source: Daniel B. Suits, "Agriculture" in Walter Adams, ed., *The Structure of American Industry,* 5th edition (New York: Macmillan, 1977), pp. 3–4.

Cross-Section Studies

Instead of looking at the past behavior of a *given* population during *different* periods of time, one can use **cross-section studies** to analyze economic data pertaining to *different* populations during the *same* past period of time. Suppose that a study of the electric power market in four U.S. cities in 1985 revealed four different price-quantity combinations. These, too, might be plotted like the data in panel (a) of Figure 3.11

and a market-demand line might be estimated on the assumption that the people in any one city, if faced with the prices actually prevailing in the other cities, would consume the quantities actually consumed in the other cities. Again, however, possible differences among cities in income and the like could vitiate the result, but, once more, careful multiple regression analysis can help overcome this problem.

Figure 3.13 summarizes actual cross-section studies of urban residential water markets in six regions of the United States. The studies were based on a survey of the 1960 water markets of 218 cities.

FIGURE 3.13

The Market Demand for Water: A Cross-Section Study

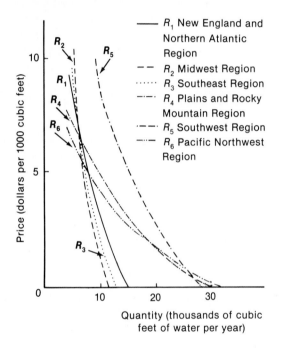

—— R_1 New England and Northern Atlantic Region
– – R_2 Midwest Region
· · · · · · R_3 Southeast Region
—·· – R_4 Plains and Rocky Mountain Region
– – · – R_5 Southwest Region
—·· – R_6 Pacific Northwest Region

The market-demand lines shown in this graph were calculated by the least-squares multiple regression technique. Each demand equation relates the quantity of water demanded per urban household to the average price of water, median household income, precipitation during the growing season (a factor that influences water demand for horticultural purposes), and the average number of residents per water meter.

Source: Henry S. Foster and Bruce R. Beattie, "Urban Residential Demand for Water in the United States," *Land Economics,* February 1979, p. 53. Copyright © 1979 by The Board of Regents of the University of Wisconsin System. Reprinted by permission.

MARKET DEMAND EXAMINED: ELASTICITY

The study of market-demand relationships allows economists to answer a multitude of important questions. All kinds of people in business—ranging from producers of cars, electric power, fountain pens, records, and wheat to providers of educational services, rail transport, spectator sports, and telephone services—want to know what would happen to their sales if their prices changed or people's incomes changed or the prices of other goods changed. All kinds of government officials, concerned with their tax revenues or the ("excessive" or "insufficient") quantities of various goods people buy, want to know what would happen if they took actions that affected prices or incomes. Thus local officials worry about the use of taxis and bridges and · about property taxes; state officials worry about gambling· and liquor; federal officials are concerned about air fares, the consumption of cigarettes and gasoline, and the plight of public transit. Sometimes these decision makers receive bad advice: They are told that nothing can be done to discourage "excessive" numbers of directory assistance calls or "excessive" consumption of gasoline because people *need* the phone numbers and because they *must* drive their cars to work and shop. Such advice, almost always, is incorrect. As the previous sections have shown, the quantities of goods demanded by people are responsive to the prices of these goods, to income, and to the prices of other goods. Changes in these variables will change the quantities demanded. This section will discuss various **elasticities of demand,** exact measures of the responsiveness of quantity demanded to other variables. Because several types of variables can affect quantity demanded, several types of elasticity can be calculated, including own-price elasticity, cross-price elasticity, and income elasticity.

As the following overview indicates, in each case, the elasticity measure equals the percentage change in quantity demanded divided by the percentage change in some other variable that caused the change in quantity demanded, all else being equal.

Overview

Let us call the quantity of good x demanded Q_{D_x}, the absolute change of this quantity ΔQ_{D_x}, and the percentage change $\%\Delta Q_{D_x}$. Let us employ a similar notation for the price of x, P_x, the price of y, P_y, for income, Y, and all other factors that might influence the demand for x. Then we can write the following equation and see the meaning of the various elasticity measures with its help:

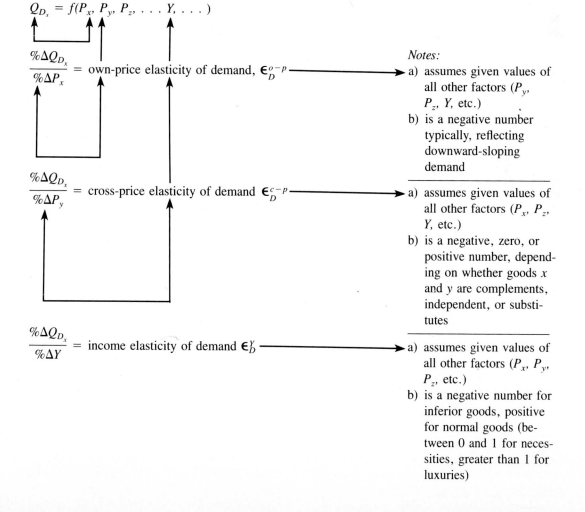

$$Q_{D_x} = f(P_x, P_y, P_z, \ldots Y, \ldots)$$

$\dfrac{\%\Delta Q_{D_x}}{\%\Delta P_x}$ = own-price elasticity of demand, ϵ_D^{o-p} ⟶

Notes:
a) assumes given values of all other factors (P_y, P_z, Y, etc.)
b) is a negative number typically, reflecting downward-sloping demand

$\dfrac{\%\Delta Q_{D_x}}{\%\Delta P_y}$ = cross-price elasticity of demand ϵ_D^{c-p} ⟶

a) assumes given values of all other factors (P_x, P_z, Y, etc.)
b) is a negative, zero, or positive number, depending on whether goods x and y are complements, independent, or substitutes

$\dfrac{\%\Delta Q_{D_x}}{\%\Delta Y}$ = income elasticity of demand ϵ_D^Y ⟶

a) assumes given values of all other factors (P_x, P_y, P_z, etc.)
b) is a negative number for inferior goods, positive for normal goods (between 0 and 1 for necessities, greater than 1 for luxuries)

Arc Elasticity Versus Point Elasticity

The kinds of elasticity numbers defined in the previous section can be calculated in two different ways. If one is interested in finding the responsiveness of quantity demanded to a fairly large change in some variable (such as the good's own price, some other price, or income), one is in effect interested in the elasticity of a given

FIGURE 3.14

**The Market Demand for Apples:
Arc Elasticity**

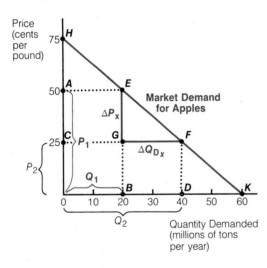

A good's own-price elasticity of demand is measured as the percentage change in quantity demanded divided by the percentage change in the good's own price, all else being equal. The arc elasticity for a range such as *EF* is traditionally calculated as

$$\epsilon_D^{o-p} = \frac{\dfrac{\Delta Q_{D_x}}{\overline{Q}_{D_x}} \cdot 100}{\dfrac{\Delta P_x}{\overline{P}_x} \cdot 100},$$

it being understood that $\overline{Q}_{D_x}$ is the *average* of old and new quantities (such as Q_1 and Q_2) and that $\overline{P}_x$ is the *average* of old and new prices (such as P_1 and P_2).

section of a demand line (such as range *EF* in Figure 3.14). An elasticity measure that refers in this way to a finite section of a demand (or supply) line is called **arc elasticity.** More often than not, however, economists are interested in the effects on quantity demanded of very small changes of the aforementioned variables. Take another look at Figure 3.14 and imagine that ΔP_x shrank and shrank until *G* was just barely below *E*. Naturally, ΔQ_{D_x} would shrink, too, and point *F* would move very close to *E*. In the limit, *F* would merge with *E*. If we made ΔP_x and, therefore, ΔQ_{D_x}, infinitesimal, we would be measuring elasticity at point *E* itself. An elasticity measure that refers in this way to a point on a demand (or supply) line is called **point elasticity.** In the following sections, we will consider both of these concepts.

Arc Elasticity Measures

The Own-Price Elasticity of Demand. Consider Figure 3.14, which shows the market demand for apples. Imagine an original price-quantity combination at *E*, corresponding to an original apple price, P_1, of 50¢ per pound (measured by distance 0*A*) and an original apple quantity, Q_1, of 20 million tons per year (measured by distance 0*B*). Let there be a 25-cent price fall, ΔP_x (measured by distance $EG = AC$), all other factors influencing quantity demanded remaining equal. Quantity demanded will then increase by 20 million tons per year, ΔQ_{D_x} (measured by distance $GF = BD$).

Now it is tempting, indeed, to designate the reciprocal of the *slope* between *E* and *F*, or $\Delta Q_{D_x}/\Delta P_x$, as a measure of the responsiveness of the good's quantity demanded to changes in its own price. In our example, such a measure would equal $+20$ million tons per year/-25 cents per pound. Such a measure, however, suffers from a major problem.

The ratio of quantity change to price change is not a pure number and, therefore, cannot be compared with similar measures of responsiveness for, say, gasoline (measured in gallons) or cloth (measured in yards). Which is bigger: $+20$ million tons of apples/-25 cents per pound or $+100,000$ gallons of gasoline/$-\$0.02$ per gallon? Yet one may wish to know whether consumers are more or less responsive to a change in the price of apples than they are to a change in the price of gasoline. Fortunately, the problem can be overcome by turning the absolute changes in quantity and price into relative (or percentage) changes and, thus, by defining the **own-price elasticity of demand** as the percentage change in quantity demanded of a good divided by the percentage change in the good's own price, all else being equal. (See Box 3.A.)

3.A Own-Price Elasticity of Demand

$$\epsilon_D^{o\text{-}p} = \frac{\%\Delta Q_{D_x}}{\%\Delta P_x} = \frac{\dfrac{\Delta Q_{D_x}}{Q_{D_x}} \cdot 100}{\dfrac{\Delta P_x}{P_x} \cdot 100}$$

Yet, as long as we are measuring arc elasticity, this formula invites a possible confusion. This danger can be illustrated with the help of Figure 3.14 as well.

In our example, it seems, the own-price elasticity of demand in the EF range equals

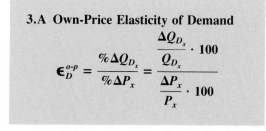

$$\frac{\dfrac{GF}{OB} \cdot 100}{\dfrac{EG}{OA} \cdot 100} = \frac{\dfrac{+20 \text{ million tons}}{20 \text{ million tons}} \cdot 100}{\dfrac{-25\cent \text{ per pound}}{50\cent \text{ per pound}} \cdot 100}$$

$$= \frac{+100}{-50} = -2$$

In the range EF, it seems, a 100-percent quantity change is associated with a 50-percent price change; in percentage terms, the quantity change is twice as large as the price change that causes it, and it is in the opposite direction of the price

change; thus the *negative* 2. But now consider the elasticity number we would have calculated if we had originally started at point F instead of point E on our graph and had *raised* the price by 25 cents, thereby moving to E. In that case, ΔQ_{D_x} would still have been GF and ΔP_x would still have been EG, as above, but with the plus and minus signs interchanged. The value of the original price would have been $P_2 = OC$, while the value of the original quantity would have been $Q_2 = OD$. Thus, by the above procedure, we would have calculated this elasticity value for the FE range:

$$\frac{\dfrac{GF}{OD} \cdot 100}{\dfrac{EG}{OC} \cdot 100} = \frac{\dfrac{-20 \text{ million tons}}{40 \text{ million tons}} \cdot 100}{\dfrac{+25\cent \text{ per pound}}{25\cent \text{ per pound}} \cdot 100}$$

$$= \frac{-50}{+100} = -.5$$

In the range FE, it seems, a 50-percent quantity change is associated with a 100-percent price change; in percentage terms, the quantity change is half as large as the price change that causes it, and it is in the opposite direction of the price change; thus the negative .5. Yet the range EF is the same as the range FE! How can quantity change relative to price change, both measured in percentage terms, be at the same time twice as strong and half as strong?

In order to avoid this confusion, economists interpret the value of Q_{D_x} in the above formula not as the original quantity (as we have so far), but as the *average* of the original and new quantities (and, as the Figure 3.14 caption shows, this fact is indicated by placing a bar above Q_{D_x} so that it looks like $\overline{Q}_{D_x}$. Similarly, economists interpret the value of P_x in the above formula not as the original price, but as the average of the original and new prices ($\overline{P}_x$). When this convention is followed, the same elasticity number is calculated regardless of whether one moves from a point such as E to a point such as F or does the reverse. In our example, this convention yields

$$\mathbf{\epsilon}_D^{o\text{-}p} = \frac{\dfrac{+20 \text{ million tons}}{30 \text{ million tons}} \cdot 100}{\dfrac{-25\cancel{c} \text{ per pound}}{37.5\cancel{c} \text{ per pound}} \cdot 100}$$

$$= \left.\frac{+66.66}{-66.66} = -1 \right\} \text{ for a move from } E \text{ to } F$$

and the identical

$$\mathbf{\epsilon}_D^{o\text{-}p} = \frac{\dfrac{-20 \text{ million tons}}{30 \text{ million tons}} \cdot 100}{\dfrac{+25\cancel{c} \text{ per pound}}{37.5\cancel{c} \text{ per pound}} \cdot 100}$$

$$= \left.\frac{-66.66}{+66.66} = -1 \right\} \text{ for a move from } F \text{ to } E$$

Note: Given the conventional interpretation of the above formula's Q_{D_x} as the average of new quantity, Q_2, and old quantity, Q_1, and of the above formula's P_x as the average of new price, P_2, and old price, P_1 (and realizing that $\Delta Q = Q_2 - Q_1$, while $\Delta P = P_2 - P_1$), one can rewrite the above arc elasticity formula as in Box 3.B.

3.B Own-Price Elasticity of Demand, Alternative Formulation

$$\mathbf{\epsilon}_D^{o\text{-}p} = \frac{\dfrac{\Delta Q_{D_x}}{Q_{D_x}}}{\dfrac{\Delta P_x}{P_x}} = \frac{\dfrac{Q_2 - Q_1}{\left\{\dfrac{Q_2 + Q_1}{2}\right.}}{\dfrac{P_2 - P_1}{\left\{\dfrac{P_2 + P_1}{2}\right.}} = \frac{\dfrac{Q_2 - Q_1}{Q_2 + Q_1}}{\dfrac{P_2 - P_1}{P_2 + P_1}}$$

This expression comes to

$$\frac{\dfrac{40 - 20}{40 + 20}}{\dfrac{25 - 50}{25 + 50}} = \frac{\dfrac{20}{60}}{\dfrac{-25}{75}} = \frac{\dfrac{1}{3}}{-\dfrac{1}{3}} = -1$$

for a move from E to F; and it is

$$\frac{\dfrac{20 - 40}{20 + 40}}{\dfrac{50 - 25}{50 + 25}} = \frac{\dfrac{-20}{60}}{\dfrac{25}{75}} = \frac{-\dfrac{1}{3}}{\dfrac{1}{3}} = -1$$

for a move from F to E. These results are identical with the previous ones.

One final point must be made. As long as the law of downward-sloping demand prevails (and that is mostly the case, excepting instances of Giffen's paradox and Veblen effects), any measure of own-price elasticity will be a negative number. When people's responsiveness to a price change is high, as in one of the above examples, the calculated elasticity number may be -2. When people's responsiveness to a price change is low, the calculated number may be $-.02$, which is a *larger* number than -2. Sometimes economists seek to avoid the likely confusion resulting from smaller numbers (such as -2) designating high responsiveness and larger numbers (such as $-.02$) designating low responsiveness. So they ignore the minus sign and simply look at the *absolute values* involved. The absolute value of $\mathbf{\epsilon} = -2$ is then written as $|\mathbf{\epsilon}| = 2$, which designates high elasticity; the absolute value of $\mathbf{\epsilon} = -.02$ is written as $|\mathbf{\epsilon}| = .02$, which designates low elasticity. (The vertical lines warn us that minus signs are being ignored.)

The Cross-Price Elasticity of Demand. A second important elasticity concept relates the quantities demanded of one good to the price of another good. Such a relationship was illustrated on page 63 by the second row of three panels in Figure 3.6. Economists define the **cross-price elasticity of demand** as the percentage change in quantity demanded of one good, x, divided by the percentage change in the price of another good, y, all else being equal. As with own-price elasticity, the percentage changes are typically calculated by relating the absolute change in quantity, ΔQ_{D_x}, to the average of the old and new quantities, $\overline{Q}_{D_x}$, while relating the absolute change in price, ΔP_y, to the average of the old and new prices, $\overline{P}_y$. (See Box 3.C.)

Estimates of such cross-price elasticity are zero for independent goods, negative for complements, and positive for substitutes. (See Close-Up 3.2.)

The Income Elasticity of Demand. Decision makers are also interested in measuring how changes in income affect the quantities demanded of a good. Such a relationship was illustrated on p. 55 by the Engel curve in panel (b) of Figure 3.2. Economists define the **income elasticity of demand** as the percentage change in quantity demanded of a good, x, divided by the percentage change in consumer income, Y, all else being equal. Once again, the percentage changes are typically calculated by relating the absolute change in quantity, ΔQ_{D_x}, to the average of the old and new quantities, $\overline{Q}_{D_x}$, while relating the absolute change in income, ΔY, to the average of the old and new incomes, $\overline{Y}$. (See Box 3.D.)

Estimates of income elasticity are positive for normal goods (less than unity for "necessities" and greater than unity for "luxuries"); they are negative for inferior goods.

Point Elasticity Measures

Each one of the elasticities just discussed can also be measured at a point of a demand line, rather than along a section of it.

A Simple Rule to Remember. The size of point elasticity can be determined almost instantly at any point on any demand (or supply) line, whether it is straight or curved or sloping to the right or to the left, by using three simple steps:

1. Place a tangent—a straight line that *just touches* (but does not intersect) the demand (or supply) line—on the point at which elasticity is to be measured.

2. Along this tangent, measure the distance (in any convenient units of length) from this point to the horizontal axis (or abscissa) and also the distance from this point to the vertical axis (or ordinate).

3. The elasticity at the point in question equals the distance from the point to the abscissa ($P{\rightarrow}A$), divided by the distance from the point to the ordinate ($P{\rightarrow}O$). *PAPO* is a key word to remember!

We will prove the *PAPO* rule by measuring the own-price elasticity at point E in Figure 3.14. Because the demand line in question is a straight line, step 1 above has already been performed. A tangent placed at point E coincides with demand line HK. The distance along the tangent from our point to the abscissa equals $EK;$ the distance along the tangent from our point to the ordinate is EH (step 2). Hence elasticity at E equals EK/EH (step 3).

Rewriting the elasticity definition, we get

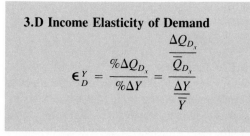

$$\epsilon_D^{o\text{-}p} = \frac{\Delta Q_{D_x}}{Q_{D_x}} \cdot \frac{P_x}{\Delta P_x} = \frac{\Delta Q_{D_x}}{\Delta P_x} \cdot \frac{P_x}{Q_{D_x}}$$

Inserting the appropriate values from Figure 3.14 (we imagine that EG and EF are so tiny that $P_1 = P_2$ and $Q_1 = Q_2$), this point elasticity becomes

$$\epsilon_D^{o\text{-}p} = \frac{GF}{EG} \cdot \frac{EB}{BO} \, .$$

Because EGF and EBK are similar triangles,

$$\frac{GF}{EG} = \frac{BK}{EB} \text{ and}$$

$$\epsilon_D^{o\text{-}p} = \frac{BK}{EB} \cdot \frac{EB}{BO} = \frac{BK}{BO} = \frac{EK}{EH} \, .$$

Elasticity Is Not Slope.   It is important to keep the concepts of elasticity and slope separate. Consider Figure 3.15. At every point on demand-line AB, the slope is the same and equals the ratio $0A/0B$. Yet the *PAPO* rule tells us that elasticity at A equals AB divided by zero, or (what economists usually call) infinity. Elasticity at C equals CB/CA (which is 1.86); elasticity at M equals MB/MA (which is 1); elasticity at D equals DB/DA (which is .2); elasticity at B equals zero divided by BA, or zero. Elasticity, unlike the slope, changes from point to point along this straight demand line!

The variability of elasticity explains why it is usually nonsensical to talk about "*the* elasticity of a demand line." Every point on most market-demand lines has a different elasticity. Exceptions are extremely rare. Among these would be:

1.   a vertical demand line (elasticity of zero at every point),

2.   a horizontal one (elasticity of infinity at every point),

3.   one shaped like a rectangular hyperbola, or

4.   a straight, upward-sloping line (exhibiting Giffen's paradox or the Veblen effect) that also passes through the origin.

The latter two exceptions have an elasticity of unity at every point. Can you confirm the four statements about elasticity just made with the help of the *PAPO* rule?

FIGURE 3.15

How Elasticity Can Vary

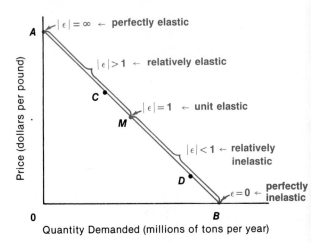

Along a straight, downward-sloping demand line, the own-price elasticity of demand takes on a different value at every point. With the help of the *PAPO* rule, derived from the definition of this type of elasticity, the absolute values of the elasticity can be shown always to produce the same pattern. Elasticity equals infinity (and demand is said to be "perfectly elastic") where demand intercepts the ordinate (point A). Elasticity equals zero (and demand is said to be "perfectly inelastic") where demand intercepts the abscissa (point B). Elasticity equals unity at midpoint M. (By definition, at the midpoint, $MB = MA$, hence MB/MA equals one.) Between M and A, the absolute value of elasticity always exceeds unity. (This must be so because the *PAPO* rule makes us divide one distance, such as CB, by a smaller distance, such as CA.) Demand in this region is said to be "relatively elastic," and elasticity rises increasingly above unity as one moves from M toward A. Between M and B, the absolute value of elasticity always falls short of unity. (This must be so because the *PAPO* rule makes us divide one distance, such as DB, by a larger distance, such as DA.) Demand in this region is said to be "relatively inelastic," and elasticity falls increasingly below unity as one moves from M toward B. All of the above holds true regardless of the slope of the demand line.

Practice Problems.   Panels (a) through (i) of Figure 3.16 provide an opportunity to practice measuring point elasticity. In each case, the point elasticity is to be determined at point P, and in all cases the *PAPO* rule can be applied to get a quick answer. Panels (a) and (b), for instance, feature

FIGURE 3.16

Determining Point Elasticity

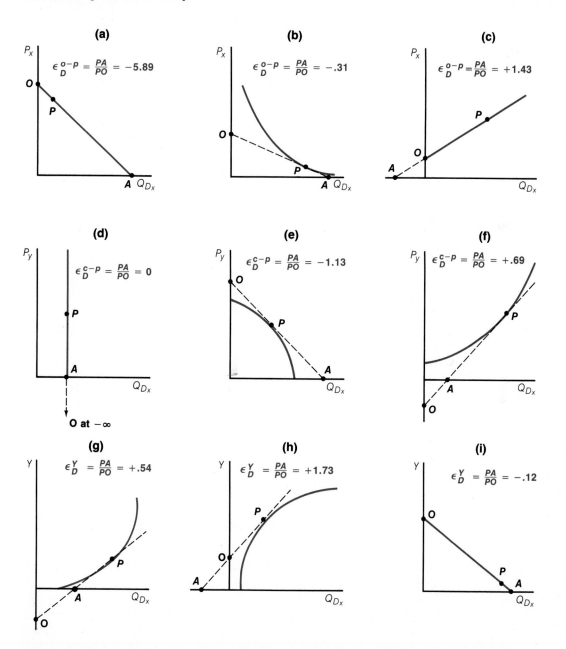

Regardless of whether demand lines relate the quantity of a good demanded to the good's own price (panels a–c), to the price of another good (panels d–f), or to income (panels g–i) and regardless of whether these relationships are linear or not, point elasticity can be determined instantly with the help of the *PAPO* rule (as the ratio *PA/PO*).

FIGURE 3.17

Elasticity, Expenditure, and Revenue

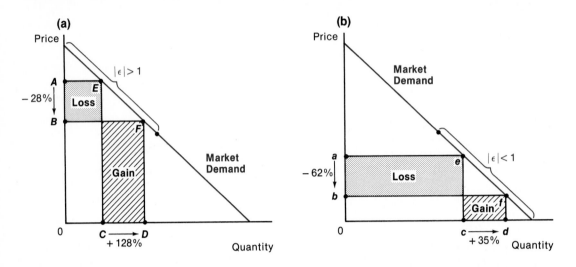

When market demand is relatively (own-price) elastic, as shown in panel (a), a price cut of any size produces increased consumer expenditures and a net gain in the revenues of firms. When market demand is relatively (own-price) inelastic, as shown in panel (b), a price cut of any size produces decreased consumer expenditures and a net loss in the revenues of firms. Increases in price have the opposite effects.

ordinary downward-sloping demand curves, one linear, the other one curved. In panel (a), the elasticity is measured directly along the straight demand line and comes to −5.89. Thus, in the immediate vicinity of *P*, a 1-percent change in price causes a 5.89-percent change in quantity demanded (in the opposite direction from the price change). In panel (b), the desired elasticity must be measured along tangent *OA* that touches the demand curve at *P*; and the elasticity turns out to be −.31. Here a 1-percent change in price causes only a .31-percent change in quantity demanded, all else being equal. The remaining calculations have been performed similarly. Note that panel (c) pictures an unusual upward-sloping demand line (reminding us of Giffen's paradox or Veblen effects), while panels (d) through (f) feature, respectively, relationships of independence, complementarity, and substitutability between two different goods (first noted in Figure 3.6). Panels (g) through (i), finally, picture Engel curves. Panel (g) pictures such a curve

for a necessity; at *P*, a 1-percent change in income causes a .54-percent change in quantity demanded in the same direction. Panel (h) pictures a luxury instead; a 1-percent change in income at *P* goes with a 1.73-percent change in quantity demanded in the same direction. Panel (i) features an inferior good; at *P*, a 1-percent change in income causes quantity demanded to change by .12 percent, but in the *opposite* direction.*

Elasticity, Expenditure, Revenue

What we have just learned about elasticity has important implications: Whenever the absolute value of the own-price elasticity of demand exceeds unity, a decrease in price increases the total expenditures of consumers and (what is the same thing) the total revenues of firms. Whenever this elasticity falls short of unity, a decrease

---

*For a calculus-based treatment of this material, see Section 3A of the Calculus Appendix at the back of this book.

TABLE 3.2

Effects of Price Changes on Total Revenue (TR)

Given Own-Price Elasticity of Demand (absolute values)	Price Increases	Price Decreases
Relatively elastic (>1)	*TR* falls	*TR* rises
Unit elastic (=1)	*TR* unchanged	*TR* unchanged
Relatively inelastic (<1)	*TR* rises	*TR* falls

The effect of a given price change on total revenue depends on elasticity of demand, which is why businesses and governments are interested in estimates of elasticity.

in price decreases the total expenditures of consumers and the total revenues of firms. An increase in price has the opposite effects in each case.

Consider Figure 3.17. Panels (a) and (b) feature the identical market-demand line. Panel (a) pictures the effect of a price cut in the region of relatively elastic demand. A 28-percent cut in price, from 0A to 0B, produces a 128-percent rise in quantity demanded, from 0C to 0D. As a result, the total expenditures of consumers (which equal price multiplied by quantity) rise from 0AEC to 0BFD. As firms see it, the revenue loss shown by the dotted rectangle is more than offset by the gain of the crosshatched region.

Panel (b), in contrast, pictures the effect of a price cut in the region of relatively inelastic demand. Even a 62-percent cut in price, from 0a to 0b, produces only a 35-percent rise in quantity demanded, from 0c to 0d. As a result, the total expenditures of consumers fall from 0aec to 0bfd. As firms see it, the revenue loss shown by the dotted rectangle is not made up by the gain of the crosshatched one. In each situation, obviously, a price rise would have the opposite effect. All this is summarized in Table 3.2.*

---

*For a calculus-based treatment of this material, see Section 3B of the Calculus Appendix at the back of this book.

EMPIRICAL MEASURES OF ELASTICITIES

Economics literature contains an abundance of empirical elasticity estimates. Tables 3.3 to 3.6 provide a small sample of elasticity estimates, mostly from the study of U.S. markets. As a look at the sources indicates, these studies were made at different times and places, and the estimates reflect, of course, the price-quantity relationships observed then and there. At other times or places, different results could well have been obtained. It is important, therefore, not to look upon these elasticity data as if they indicated some inherent and permanent characteristics of the goods involved.

Consider Table 3.3 on p. 82, which shows own-price elasticities. As is usual, one finds high elasticities for goods that have good substitutes, and low elasticities for those that do not. There are many substitutes for cottonseed oil; there are few for gasoline.

Two other matters should be noted. First, the narrowness with which a good is defined influences the number of substitutes it has and, therefore, the elasticity estimate. There may be few substitutes for gasoline in general, but there are many for Mobil gasoline and even more for Mobil gasoline sold at a particular station.

Second, the length of time under consideration also influences the number of substitutes available. A doubling of the price of gasoline this year may cut back gasoline consumption by only 14 percent, but over a period of 5, 10, or 50 years, the response would be much stronger. Given enough time, people can change their lifestyles and walk and bicycle more or take fewer and shorter trips. They can change the location of their residences and jobs. They can produce smaller and more efficient cars that use less gasoline per mile. They can discover new types of energy, and much more. Indeed, economists often make short-run and long-run estimates of elasticity, and these confirm that elasticity tends to be higher for longer periods, often dramatically so. Consider Table 3.4, which compares long-run and short-run elasticities.

Then turn to Table 3.5 on page 84, which shows estimates of income elasticities. It differentiates between inferior goods (with negative elasticities) and normal goods. Among normal goods, it differentiates between necessities (with positive elasticities below unity) and luxuries (with elasticities above unity).

Finally, Table 3.6 on p. 85 presents cross-price elasticities for a number of substitute and complementary goods. Note that similar estimates for independent goods would produce elasticities of zero.

THE MANIFOLD USES OF ELASTICITY ESTIMATES

The British economist Gregory King (1648–1712) noted that bumper crops always seem to spell bad times for farmers and that poor crops spelled good times. Anyone with a knowledge of the low own-price and income elasticities for farm products can easily solve the puzzle. Indeed, recognition of this fact led American farmers during this century, with the help of their

TABLE 3.3

Selected Estimates of Own-Price Elasticities of Demand in the United States (absolute values)

Good	|Elasticity|	Source*	Good	|Elasticity|	Source
Cottonseed oil	6.92	C	Air travel (foreign)	0.70	J
Tomatoes (fresh)	4.60	J	Shoes	0.70	J
Green peas (fresh)	2.80	J	Household appliances	0.67	J
Scrod	2.20	A	Legal services	0.61	J
Legal gambling	1.91	Q	Physicians' services	0.58	J
Lamb	1.90	G, O	Rail travel (commuter)	0.54	J
Restaurant meals	1.63	J	Jewelry, watches	0.54	J
Marijuana	1.51	M	Water	0.52	F
Peaches	1.50	G	Cigarettes	0.51	L
Butter	1.40	N	Stationery	0.47	J
Automobiles	1.35	S	Radio, TV repair	0.47	J
China, glassware	1.34	J	Sea scallops	0.46	A
Apples	1.30	G	Toilet articles	0.44	J
Giving to charity	1.29	E	Cabbage	0.40	J
Taxi service	1.24	J	Auto repair	0.36	J
Cable TV	1.20	B	Medical insurance	0.31	J
Chicken	1.20	G	Margarine	0.30	N
Radios, TV sets	1.19	J	Potatoes	0.30	D
Beer	1.13	I	Coffee	0.25	D
Furniture	1.01	J	Eggs	0.23	C
Housing	1.00	J	Spectator sports	0.21	J
Alcohol	0.92	J	Bus travel (intercity)	0.20	J
Beef	0.92	U	Theatre, opera	0.18	J
Telephone calls	0.89	B	Natural gas (residential)	0.15	J
Sports equipment, boats, etc.	0.88	J	Gasoline and oil	0.14	J
Movies	0.87	J	Milk	0.14	C
Flowers, seeds	0.82	J	Electricity (residential)	0.13	J
Citrus fruit	0.80	G	Newspapers, magazines	0.10	J
Bus travel (local)	0.77	J	Mail (letters)	0.05	B

*Sources follow Table 3.6.

government, to *restrict* output and *raise* their revenues. Take another look at panel (b) of Figure 3.17. Mentally reverse the arrows shown there, and interchange the ''gain'' and ''loss'' labels. When demand is own-price inelastic, a relatively small cut in quantity allows price to be raised so much that consumers spend, and producers receive, more money than before. In addition, the lower quantity lowers the producers' costs.

The Parker Pen Company followed this strategy in the 1950s when it realized the low own-price elasticity for its ink (called Quink). Various telephone companies in 1977 followed this strategy when they became aware of the low own-price elasticity for directory assistance calls and started charging for such calls. The owners of ball parks who are aware of the low own-price elasticity for spectator sports know what they are doing when they do *not* lower price to fill the empty seats [as from *Oc* to *Od* in panel (b) of Figure 3.17].

On the other hand, consider panel (a) of Figure 3.17. When demand is own-price elastic, a cut in price causes consumers to buy so much more that their expenditures, and the revenues of producers, rise. Henry Ford I followed this strategy

in the early decades of the auto company. So did the Columbia Record Company in the 1930s and AT&T's long-distance department in the 1960s.

Government officials find knowledge of elasticities to be just as crucial in their decision making. A nationwide tax hike that raises the price of a product with inelastic demand (such as alcohol, movies, cigarettes, water, coffee, or gasoline) will raise lots of extra revenue but may not cut quantity demanded very much. If a large cut in quantity is desired (to cure cancer from cigarettes or conserve water or gasoline) only a very large hike in the tax will do the trick. On the other hand, a tax hike that raises the price of a product with elastic demand (such as restaurant meals and legal gambling) will decrease government revenues and also cut quantity demanded very much, as people turn to substitutes (such as cooking at home and illegal gambling).

Business and government leaders who do not heed the crucial information embodied in elasticity estimates can make serious mistakes. When the railroads of the 1930s raised their fares (in the face of price-elastic demand), their revenues plummeted. When city government in the 1950s raised property tax rates (in the face of price-elastic demand), many businesses and house-

TABLE 3.4

Long-Run Versus Short-Run Elasticities[a]

Good	|Elasticity| Short-Run	|Elasticity| Long-Run	Good	|Elasticity| Short-Run	|Elasticity| Long-Run
China, glassware	1.34	8.80	Radio, TV repair	0.47	3.84
Alcohol	0.92	3.63	Toilet articles	0.44	2.42
Sports equipment, boats, etc.	0.88	2.39	Medical insurance	0.31	0.92
Movies	0.87	3.67	Bus travel (intercity)	0.20	2.17
Flowers, seeds	0.82	2.65	Theatre, opera	0.18	0.31
Bus travel (local)	0.77	3.54	Natural gas (residential)	0.15	10.74
Air travel (foreign)	0.70	4.00	Gasoline, oil	0.14	0.48
Shoes	0.70	1.20	Electricity (residential)	0.13	1.90
Rail travel (commuter)	0.54	1.70	Newspapers, magazines	0.10	0.52
Jewelry, watches	0.54	0.67			

[a]Own-price elasticities of demand, United States, absolute values; source for each item is the source for the same item in Table 3.3.

holds abandoned the cities, producing lowered city-property values and tax collections, as well as suburban sprawl, road congestion, and air pollution.

SUMMARY

1. A person's demand for a consumption good is a function of many variables, such as the good's own price, the prices of other goods, and the consumer's budget and tastes. With the help of indifference-curve analysis, one can, among other things, derive the demand for a good as a function of its own price alone. Normally, such demand curves follow the "law" of downward-sloping demand. A rare exception is Giffen's paradox.

2. Demand for a good can also be derived as a function of income alone. This demand is pictured by an Engel curve. Engel curves for normal goods are upward-sloping; those for inferior goods are downward-sloping.

3. Every price change—other prices, money income, and tastes being constant—can be considered to change quantity demanded for two different reasons: the substitution effect and the income effect. Given any initial level of real income, a utility-maximizing consumer facing a price change is bound to change the composition of the optimal bundle of consumption goods, substituting more of the now relatively cheaper good for less of other, now relatively more expensive goods. This is the substitution effect. Given money income, the price change, however, changes real income and thus changes the quantity demanded for that reason as well. This is the income effect. The substitution effect of lowered price, for example, always increases quantity demanded. The income effect of lowered price reinforces the substitution effect in the case of normal goods but works against it in the case of inferior goods. This may (but need not) produce Giffen's paradox. Depending on how real income is defined, the substitution and income effects can be measured in two different ways (the Hicksian way and Slutsky's way); accordingly, one can derive two different income-compensated demand curves (that only show the substitution effect of price changes).

TABLE 3.5

Selected Estimates of Income Elasticities of Demand in the United States

Good	Elasticity	Source	Good	Elasticity	Source
Automobiles	2.46	J	Giving to charity	0.70	E
Alcohol	1.54	J	Mail (letters)	0.65	B
Housing, owner-occupied	1.49	J	Tobacco	0.64	J
Furniture	1.48	J	Gasoline, oil	0.48	J
Books	1.44	J	Housing, rental	0.43	J
Dental services	1.42	J	Butter	0.42	T
Restaurant meals	1.40	J	Eggs	0.37	T
Shoes	1.10	J	Electricity, residential	0.20	R
Clothing	1.02	J	Coffee	0	K
Water	1.02	J	Margarine	−0.20	T
Medical insurance	0.92	J	Starchy roots	−0.20	K
Cable TV	0.83	B	Pig products	−0.20	K
Telephone calls	0.83	B	Flour	−0.36	T
Physicians' services	0.75	J	Whole milk	−0.50	K

TABLE 3.6

Selected Estimates of Cross-Price Elasticities of Demand in the United States and the United Kingdom

Good with Quantity Change	Good with Price Change	Elasticity	Source
Florida Interior oranges	Florida Indian River oranges	+1.56	H
Margarine	Butter	+0.81	T
Butter	Margarine	+0.67	T
Natural gas	Fuel oil	+0.44	R
Beef	Pork	+0.28	T
Electricity	Natural gas	+0.20	R
Pork	Beef	+0.14	T
California oranges	Florida Interior oranges	+0.14	H
Fruits	Sugar	−0.28	P
Cheese	Butter	−0.61	P

Sources to Tables 3.3 to 3.6:

A. Frederick W. Bell, "The Pope and the Price of Fish," *The American Economic Review,* December 1968.

B. Charles B. Blankart, "Towards an Economic Theory of Advice and Its Application to the Deregulation Issue," *Kyklos,* I, 1981, p. 101.

C. G. E. Brandow, "Interrelations among Demands for Farm Products and Implications for Control of Market Supply," *Bulletin* 680 (University Park: Pennsylvania State University Agricultural Experiment Station, 1961).

D. Rex F. Daly, "Coffee Consumption and Prices in the United States," *Agricultural Economic Research* (Washington, D.C.: U.S. Department of Agriculture, Economic Research Service, July 1958).

E. M. Feldstein and A. Taylor, "The Income Tax and Charitable Contributions," *Econometrica,* November 1976.

F. Henry S. Foster, Jr., and Bruce R. Beattie, "Urban Residential Demand for Water in the United States," *Land Economics,* February 1979.

G. Karl A. Fox, *The Analysis of Demand for Farm Products, Technical Bulletin 1081* (Washington, D.C.: U.S. Department of Agriculture, September 1953).

H. Marshall B. Godwin, W. Fred Chapman, Jr., and William T. Hanley, *Competition between Florida and California Valencia Oranges in the Fruit Market, Bulletin 704* (Washington, D.C.: U.S. Department of Agriculture, Economic Research Service, December 1965).

I. T. F. Hogarty and K. G. Elsinger, "The Demand for Beer," *The Review of Economics and Statistics,* May 1972.

J. H. S. Houthakker and Lester D. Taylor, *Consumer Demand in the United States: Analyses and Projections,* 2nd edition (Cambridge, Mass.: Harvard University Press, 1970).

K. Richard G. Lipsey and Peter O. Steiner, *Microeconomics,* 5th edition (New York: Harper and Row, 1979), p. 133.

L. Herbert L. Lyon and Julian L. Simon, "Price Elasticity of the Demand for Cigarettes in the United States," *American Journal of Agricultural Economics,* November 1968.

M. Charles T. Nisbet and Firouz Vakil, "Some Estimates of Price and Expenditure Elasticities of Demand for Marijuana among UCLA Students," *The Review of Economics and Statistics,* November 1972.

N. A. S. Rojko, *The Demand and Price Structure for Dairy Products, Technical Bulletin 1168* (Washington, D.C.: U.S. Department of Agriculture, 1957).

O. Henry Schultz, *The Theory and Measurement of Demand* (Chicago: Chicago University Press, 1938).

P. R. Stone, *The Measurement of Consumers' Expenditure and Behavior in the United Kingdom, 1920–1938,* vol. I (Cambridge, England: Cambridge University Press, 1954).

Q. Daniel B. Suits, "The Elasticity of Demand for Gambling," *The Quarterly Journal of Economics,* February 1979.

R. L. Taylor and R. Halvorsen, "Energy Substitution in U.S. Manufacturing," *The Review of Economics and Statistics,* November 1977.

S. U.S. Senate, Subcommittee on Antitrust and Monopoly, *Administered Prices: Automobiles* (Washington, D.C.: U.S. Government Printing Office, 1958).

T. H. Wold and L. Jureen, *Demand Analysis* (New York: Wiley, 1953).

U. Elmer Working, *The Demand for Meat* (Chicago: University of Chicago Press, 1951).

4. Indifference-curve analysis can also be used to derive the demand for a consumption good as a function of another good's price. This analysis will reveal whether any two goods are independents, complements, or substitutes.

5. The individual demands of all potential market participants can be added together to derive market demand. This procedure becomes complicated in the presence of bandwagon, snob, or Veblen effects. The Veblen effect is capable of producing an upward-sloping section in the market-demand line.

6. Empirical studies of market demand have used a number of approaches, including consumer interviews, consumer clinics, market experiments, time-series studies, and cross-section studies.

7. The study of market-demand relationships allows economists to answer a multitude of important questions posed by decision makers in business and government. Particularly important in answering such questions is the calculation of exact measures of the responsiveness of quantity demanded to other variables. Such measures include the own-price elasticity of demand, the cross-price elasticity of demand, and the income elasticity of demand.

8. Empirical measures of these elasticities have many uses in business and government.

KEY TERMS

arc elasticity
bandwagon effect
change in demand
change in quantity demanded
complementary goods
cross-price elasticity of demand
cross-section studies
demand
elasticities of demand
Engel curve
Engel's law
Giffen's paradox

Hicksian income-compensated demand curve
identification problem
income-consumption line
income effect
income elasticity of demand
independent goods
inferior goods
"law" of downward-sloping demand
luxuries
market demand
necessities
normal goods
ordinary demand curve
own-price elasticity of demand
point elasticity
price-consumption line
Slutsky's income-compensated demand curve
snob effect
substitute goods
substitution effect
time-series studies
Veblen effect

HANDS-ON PRACTICE

Exercise #1

State governments are forever looking for new revenue sources; one of them is provided by the fact that citizens demand personalized automobile license plates and states can produce them at a negligible cost. Given what you have learned in this chapter, what pricing strategy would you suggest to a state government seeking to gain revenue by selling these so-called "vanity plates"?

Solution:

The answer is evident from Figure 3.15 on page 78. Assuming a zero production cost, a state's profit would be maximized by maximizing sales revenue, which would occur at the point of unit elasticity. Any price above that would correspond to the region of relatively elastic demand (and revenue could be raised by lowering the price). Any price below the unit elasticity point would correspond to the region of inelastic demand (and revenue could be raised by raising the price).

Exercise #2

A recent study has, in fact, taken up the issue noted in Exercise 1. (See Neil O. Alper, Robert B. Archibald, and Eric Jensen, "At What Price Vanity? An Econometric Model of the Demand for Personalized License Plates," *National Tax Journal,* vol. XL, no. 1, 1987, pp. 103–109.) Among the data they collected were those of Table 3.7. Assuming, once again, negligible production costs, what advice would you give to the states involved?

TABLE 3.7

State	5-Year Fee for Vanity Plates	Own-Price Elasticity of Demand (absolute)
Ohio	$ 60.10	2.64
Mississippi	55.00	2.42
Alabama	50.00	2.20
Oregon	50.00	2.20
Tennessee	50.00	2.20
Indiana	40.00	1.76
Wyoming	30.00	1.32

Solution:

The solution is evident from panel (a) of Figure 3.17: Lower the price to below $30. As long as the elasticity is absolutely greater than 1, the marginal benefit of this action (revenue gain) will exceed the marginal cost (revenue loss).

Exercise #3

The same study noted in Exercise 2 also collected the data of Table 3.8. Still assuming negligible production costs for vanity plates, what advice would you give to those states?

TABLE 3.8

State	5-Year Fee for Vanity Plates	Own-Price Elasticity of Demand (absolute)
Georgia	$ 2.00	.09
Alaska	4.00	.17
Connecticut	7.60	.31
Kansas	8.00	.34
Montana	8.00	.34
Rhode Island	10.00	.42
Maine	15.00	.66

Solution:

The solution is evident from panel (b) of Figure 3.17: Raise the price above $15. As long as the elasticity is absolutely smaller than 1, the marginal benefit of this action (revenue gain from *raising* the price) will exceed the marginal cost (revenue loss from selling fewer plates).

Note: A $25 fee was associated with roughly unitary price elasticity in various states, ranging from Arkansas, Delaware, and Idaho to Maryland, New Hampshire, and West Virginia.

QUESTIONS AND PROBLEMS

✓ **1.** Consider Figure 3.1, panel (a), but imagine that the vertical axis measures *money* spent on all goods other than butter. In that case, a demand curve for butter must exhibit an own-price elasticity of greater than unity when the price-consumption line is sloping downward to the right and an own-price elasticity of less than unity when it is sloping upward to the right (elasticities measured in absolute values). Explain.

2. "The 'law' of downward-sloping demand is universally applicable and not just to things traded for money in the market: The longer the lines at the ski lift, the less often do people come back to ski; the more unpleasant are our neighbors, the less often do we visit them; the muddier the short cut across the lawn, the less often do we use it; the lower a professor's grades, the fewer the students who take the course; the higher are market wages, the less time do we give to friends, spouses, children, parents, and even to genuine reflection by ourselves; the more parking tickets are issued, the fewer the violations.'' Explain. Then make a list of your own examples of the ''law'' of downward-sloping demand outside the realm of money and markets. (*Hint:* Consider criminal activity, religious activity, extramarital affairs, having children. . . .)

3. Draw a budget line and an indifference curve to depict an initial consumer optimum. Let the price of one good rise.

a. Assuming the good is a normal good, graphically show the total effect on quantity demanded; then separate it into substitution and income effect using the Hicksian approach.

b. Using the graph derived in (a), determine the shape of the good's demand curve (i) while holding money income constant and (ii) while holding real income constant.

c. Show how your answer to (a) would differ when using the Slutsky approach.

d. Show how your answer to (a) would differ if the good were a Giffen good (but you used the Hicksian approach).

e. Using the graph derived in (d), determine the shape of the good's demand curve (i) while holding money income constant and (ii) while holding real income constant.

4. a. What do you think are the own-price and income elasticities of demand for the following: beer, Coca Cola, Diet Pepsi, gasoline, Levi jeans, required textbooks, safety pins, sports cars. Give reasons for your answers.

b. Which of the following are likely to have positive cross-price elasticities of demand: automobiles and oil, gin and tonic, a Harvard education and a Yale education, ham and cheese, men's shoes and women's shoes. Give reasons for your answers.

5. a. In the graph below, consider the two demand curves (D_1 and D_2) and the three Engel curves (E_1, E_2, and E_3). Determine the own-price elasticity of demand on D_1 at points a, c, g, and h, and on D_2 at points c and e. Then determine income elasticity at b, d, and f.

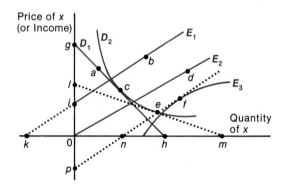

*b. Using calculus, prove that the income elasticity of demand on E_1 differs at every point. (You may assume that E_1 is described by the equation $Q_{D_x} = a + bY$.)

*c. Using calculus, prove that the own-price elasticity of demand on D_2 is the same at every point. (You may assume that D_2 is described by the equation $Q_{D_x} = aP_x^{-b}$.)

d. Using algebra, prove that the weighted average of the income elasticities of demand for all goods equals unity, provided the weights are the expenditure shares of the goods.

6. Assuming all other things are equal, calculate in each case below the magnitude of the own-price elasticity of demand:

a. In 1975, New York City's Taxi and Limousine Commission authorized a 17.5 percent increase in fares. Taxi company revenues went up by 10.5 percent.

b. In 1975, New York City's Metropolitan

Transportation Authority raised tolls for seven bridges and two tunnels with these results:

Facility	Toll Increase	Traffic Count*
Bronx Whitestone Bridge	50¢ to 75¢	1.791 to 1.765
Cross Bay Bridge	50¢ to 75¢	0.381 to 0.328
Henry Hudson Bridge	50¢ to 75¢	0.777 to 0.616
Marine Parkway Bridge	50¢ to 75¢	0.486 to 0.421
Throgs Neck Bridge	50¢ to 75¢	2.125 to 2.016
Triborough Bridge	50¢ to 75¢	3.400 to 3.000
Verrazano Narrows Bridge	75¢ to $1	2.390 to 2.328
Brooklyn Battery Tunnel	70¢ to 75¢	0.904 to 0.838
Queens Midtown Tunnel	50¢ to 75¢	1.360 to 1.240

*Million vehicles, Sept. 1–21, 1975, compared to same period in 1974.

Can you explain the differences in your results for the various facilities?

7. **a.** Consider the own-price elasticities of U.S. airline travel in the table below calculated separately for different lengths of trip.[3] Could the Civil Aeronautics Board have helped airlines by authorizing an "across-the-board" increase in fares? Explain.

Distances in Miles	Elasticity
28	0.76
400	1.02
650	1.07
1500	1.14
2500	1.17

b. In recent years, economists have calculated own-price elasticities of demand for gasoline to be much higher than in the 1960s (see the earlier and lower elasticities indicated in Table

3.4). These new estimates range in absolute values from .2 in the short run (1 year) to .4 for 5 years and .8 for 10 years.[4] On that basis, President Carter's advisors in late 1979 urged an increase in the federal gasoline tax from 4 cents to 50 cents per gallon. They argued that the new price of $1.50 per gallon would cut gasoline consumption by 7 million barrels per day within a year. (A barrel holds 42 gallons.) What must have been the daily consumption at the time of this advice? What gasoline savings could one expect in future years?

8. Determine whether each of the following statements is true or false:

a. In a world of two goods, both cannot be inferior; both cannot be luxury goods.

b. All inferior goods produce Giffen's paradox.

c. An indifference curve between perfect substitutes (of which one is as good as the other, as two nickels versus one dime) would be straight like a budget line.

d. An indifference curve between perfect complements (which must be consumed in fixed proportions to be any good at all, as right shoes and left shoes) would be right-angled like the two axes of a graph.

e. The snob effect makes the market-demand curve less (own-price) elastic at any given price.

f. The bandwagon effect makes the market-demand curve less (own-price) elastic at any given quantity.

g. Any demand curve that intersects both axes cannot have constant own-price elasticity throughout.

h. The demand curve for the output of a single firm in a perfectly competitive market

---

[3]Arthur de Vany, "The Revealed Value of Time in Air Travel," *The Review of Economics and Statistics,* February 1974, p. 80. Copyright 1974 by The President and Fellows of Harvard College. Reprinted by permission of North-Holland Publishing Company.

[4]*The New York Times,* November 25, 1979, pp. F1 and 18; Robert S. Pindyck, *The Structure of World Energy Demand* (Cambridge, Mass.: MIT Press, 1979).

must be horizontal (and exhibit an infinite own-price elasticity at every point).

i. On two parallel, downward-sloping demand curves, the own-price elasticity of demand is the same at any given price.

j. On two parallel, downward-sloping demand curves, the own-price elasticity of demand is the same at any given quantity.

k. Luxuries, unlike necessities, have an income elasticity of less than unity.

l. Positive cross-price elasticity denotes Giffen's paradox.

m. If your college has doubled its tuition in the last decade, but the number of student applications and enrollments remained the same, this indicates a zero own-price elasticity of demand.

*9. Consider the following demand function that relates the quantity of beef demanded, Q_{D_b}, to the price of beef, P_b, the price of lamb, P_l, and the price of pork, P_p:

$$Q_{D_b} = 52 - 1.8P_b + .2P_l + .9P_p$$

Using calculus (and your knowledge of relevant elasticity formulas), determine

a. the own-price elasticity of demand for beef

b. the cross-price elasticity of demand for beef with respect to the price of lamb

c. the cross-price elasticity of demand for beef with respect to the price of pork

d. the precise values of these three elasticities, given P_b = $10 per lb., P_l = $7 per lb., P_p = $5 per lb.

10. For many years, U.S. home owners have enjoyed federal tax benefits in the form of mortgage interest and property tax deductions on income tax returns. Assume these two items equal 75 percent of housing costs.

a. If you were a home owner so favored and you had a 25-percent marginal tax bracket, what percentage of your housing cost would be paid by Uncle Sam?

b. Assuming that the own-price elasticity of demand for housing equals −1.2 (as some studies have shown), and that your experience is typical of all home owners, by how much does the federal tax subsidy increase the quantity of housing demanded over what it would otherwise be (without the subsidy)?

11. The accompanying table contains data that describe a demand line. Using an appropriate formula, calculate the own-price elasticity of demand between each of the points given.

Point	P_x	Q_x
A	8	2
B	7	4
C	6	6
D	4	10
E	3.5	11
F	2.5	13
G	0	18

12. The accompanying table contains data that describe an Engel curve. Using an appropriate formula, calculate the income elasticity of demand between each of the points given. Is the good in question an inferior good, a necessity, a luxury? Explain your answer.

Point	Income	Quantity
A	4,000	200
B	6,000	400
C	8,000	600
D	10,000	700
E	12,000	760
F	14,000	780
G	16,000	700
H	18,000	500

13. Table 3.2 relates elasticity, price changes, and total revenue. Confirm the claims made by the table with the help of your answer to Question 11.

14. From the data in the accompanying table, calculate relevant elasticities by comparing A with B and C with D; then classify the goods as substitutes or complements. What might the goods be?

Good	Price	Quantity
A	.80	100
	1.20	60
B	.40	80
	.40	100
C	.20	40
	.40	30
D	.40	80
	.40	70

15. The accompanying Figure 3.18 shows the budget line of a worker who can work zero hours per week and earn nothing (point *B*) or (hypothetically) work continuously at $5 per hour all week long and earn $840 (point *A*). The worker in fact maximizes utility at point *C* (working $168 - 126 = 42$ hours and earning 42 ($5) = $210 per week. Let the government provide a *wage rate subsidy* of $2.50 per hour, swinging the budget line to *BD*. Let the worker, in response, move to *E* on higher indifference curve I_1 (working $168 - 110 = 58$ hours and earning 58 ($7.50) = $435 per week). Separate the observed total effect on leisure (a decline from 126 to 110 hours per week) into a Hicksian substitution and income effect.

16. The accompanying Figure 3.19 shows the budget line of a worker who can work zero hours per week and earn nothing (point *B*) or (hypothetically) work continuously at $5 per hour all week long and earn $840 (point *A*). The worker in fact maximizes utility at *C* (working $168 - 68 = 100$ hours and earning 100($5) = $500 per week. Let the government institute a *negative income tax* as follows: Everyone receives a basic $250 grant per week (*BD*), but the grant is reduced by 50¢ for every $1 earned from work. Thus, a person earning $500 pays back $250 and is not subsidized at all.

FIGURE 3.19

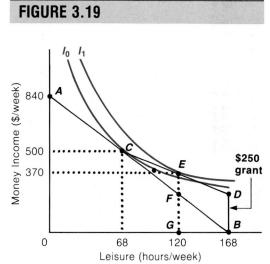

Hence the new budget line is *BDCA*. Let the worker, in response, move to *E* on higher indifference curve I_1 (working $168 - 120 = 48$ hours and earning 48($5) = $240 per week = *FG*, plus getting $250 - $120 = $130 from the government = *EF*). Separate the observed total effect on leisure (an increase from 68 to 120 hours per week) into a Hicksian substitution and income effect.

FIGURE 3.18

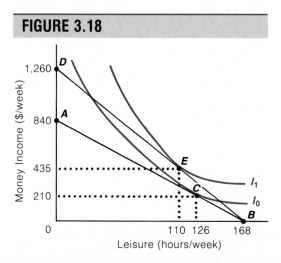

SELECTED READINGS

Allen, R. G. D. "The Work of Eugen Slutsky," *Econometrica,* July 1950, pp. 209–16.

Hicks, John R. *Value and Capital,* 2nd ed. London: Oxford University Press, 1946.

A classic work by the 1972 Nobel Prize winner in economics, on the materials discussed in Chapters 2 and 3 of this book.

Hicks, John R., and R. G. D. Allen. "A Reconsideration of the Theory of Value," *Economica,* February 1934, pp. 52–76 and May 1934, pp. 196–219.

A crucial article in value theory.

Houthakker, H. S., and Lester D. Taylor. *Consumer Demand in the United States: Analyses and Projections.* Cambridge, Mass.: Harvard University Press, 1970.

Estimation of demand equations for 82 expenditure categories, of Engel curves, price and income elasticities, etc.

Leibenstein, Harvey. *Beyond Economic Man: A New Foundation for Microeconomics.* Cambridge, Mass.: Harvard University Press, 1976, chap. 4.

A discussion of bandwagon, snob, and Veblen effects.

Samuelson, Paul A. "Complementarity—An Essay on the 40th Anniversary of the Hicks-Allen Revolution in Demand Theory," *Journal of Economic Literature,* December 1974, pp. 1255–89.

An important survey article on the concepts of substitutability and complementarity, written by the 1970 Nobel Prize winner in economics.

Seligman, Ben B. *The Reaffirmation of Tradition.* Main Currents in Modern Economics. vol. 2. Chicago: Quadrangle Books, 1971, pp. 403–21.

A critical discussion of the work of John R. Hicks.

Slutsky, Eugen. "On the Theory of the Budget of the Consumer," American Economic Association, *Readings in Price Theory.* Chicago: Irwin, 1952, pp. 27–56.

A translation of the famous 1915 article.

COMPUTER PROGRAMS

The KOHLER-3 personal-computer diskettes that accompany this book contain one program of particular interest to this chapter:

3. The Demand for Goods includes a 25-question multiple-choice test with immediate responses to incorrect answers as well as numerous exercises concerning the separation of income and substitution effects, the measurement of point elasticities, and more.

ANALYTICAL EXAMPLE 3.1

THE DEMAND ELASTICITY OF ANIMAL CONSUMERS

Biologists and psychologists have shown that the study of animal behavior can provide important insights for the study of human behavior. Economists are just beginning to realize that much can be learned from the similarities of the *economic* behavior of different species. The insights of the Slutsky-Hicks theory of (human) consumer choice, for example, have been duplicated by biologists while studying such diverse species as protozoa, bumblebees, sunfish, and deer mice. If one characterizes changes in the natural environment of such animals as changes in the relative prices of goods available to the animals, one can show that their changes in consumption patterns correspond precisely to the changes that economic theory would predict for human consumers under similar circumstances. Economists, therefore, should be able to study animals, as psychologists do, and derive conclusions about people.

The types of rat experiments described in Close-Up 3.1 have, for example, yielded estimates of demand elasticities that make a lot of sense for human consumers as well. Consider the accompanying table. Part (A) lists own-price elasticities and cross-price elasticities of demand by rats implied by so-called *income-compensated demand curves* (which only show the substitution effect of any price changes on the quantity demanded). Note that the own-price elasticity is lower for an essential good (food) than it is for a nonessential one (root beer), which is just what one would expect for people as well. Or consider the *cross-price* elasticities in part (B) in which all numbers are based on *ordinary* or *uncompensated* demand curves that show the substitution as well as income effect of any price changes on quantity demanded. The cross-price elasticities for essential goods (food and water) are negative, implying that these goods are complements. The cross-price elasticities of nonessential goods (root beer, collins mix, etc.), however, are positive or near zero, implying that these goods are substitutes or independents. Finally note that the *own-price* elasticities in part (B) are generally higher than in part (A), which is also as one would expect if the consumers were human and the goods involved were normal goods. The income effect, included in part (B) but not in (A), reinforces the substitution effect of any price change; hence the effect of any price change on quantity demanded (and measured own-price elasticity) is stronger.

(A) Based on Income-Compensated Demand (measures substitution effect of price changes only)

	Good	Own-Price Elasticity	Goods	Cross-Price Elasticity
Essential	Food	|.04| to |.18|	Water/food Saccharin solution/food	.03 to .13 .06 to .18
Nonessential	Root beer	|.31| to |2.22|	Collins mix/root beer Cherry cola/root beer	.76 to 4.12 .72

(B) Based on Ordinary Demand (measures substitution and income effect of price changes)

	Good	Own-Price Elasticity	Goods	Cross-Price Elasticity
Essential	Food Water	|.12| to |.20| |.90|	Water/food Food/water	−.13 to −.55 −.32
Nonessential	Root beer	|1.03| to |6.39|	Collins mix/root beer Cherry cola/root beer	.15 2.27
	Cherry cola	|1.05| to |3.98|	Root beer/cherry cola Saccharin solution/cherry cola	.83 .01
	Saccharin solution	|1.02|	Cherry cola/saccharin solution	−.01

Source: John H. Kagel, Raymond C. Battalio, Howard Rachlin, and Leonard Green, "Demand Curves for Animal Consumers," *The Quarterly Journal of Economics,* Vol. XCVI, No. 1, February 1981, pp. 1–15. Table (from pp. 6 and 12) © 1981 by the President and Fellows of Harvard College. Published by John Wiley & Sons, Inc.

ANALYTICAL EXAMPLE

ANALYTICAL EXAMPLE

ANALYTICAL EXAMPLE 3.2

THE DEMAND FOR SHAKESPEARE PERFORMANCES

One researcher recently estimated demand functions for performances by Britain's Royal Shakespeare Company during the 1965–1980 period and separately for the Aldwych Theater in London and the Shakespeare Memorial Theater in Stratford-on-Avon. The equations took the form

$$Q_{D_x} = a + bP_x + cP_y + dY$$

where Q_{D_x} was the quantity of cultural experiences demanded, P_x the real price per experience, P_y the real price of substitute experiences (such as movies), and Y real consumer income; the coefficients a through d being positive or negative constants. An own-price elasticity of demand of $-.657$ was calculated (implying that the Royal Shakespeare Company could have raised price *and revenue* thereby), while an income elasticity of 1.327 was calculated (implying that Shakespeare performances were a luxury item). The demand curves in P_x versus Q_{D_x} space, and the average price-quantity combination prevailing during the period, are shown in the accompanying graph.

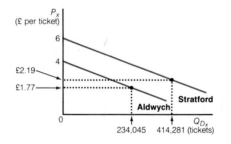

Source: James H. Gapinski, "The Economics of Performing Shakespeare," *The American Economic Review,* June 1984, pp. 458–66.

ANALYTICAL EXAMPLE 3.3

DESIGNING A NATIONAL DENTAL HEALTH INSURANCE

Designers of national health insurance proposals have been greatly concerned with a number of questions. What would happen to the quantity of various services demanded if prices to patients were cut to zero or were cut 75 percent? What would be the cost to government? Knowledge of elasticities is crucial to answering these questions. A 1970 national cross-sectional survey of the demand for dental care in

1970 revealed the ranges of elasticities (actual values) shown in the table below, which were calculated separately for (white) children, adult females, and adult males:

Service	Own-Price Elasticities	Income Elasticities
Examinations	-0.59 to -0.03	$+0.73$ to $+0.51$
Cleanings	-1.34 to -0.14	$+0.80$ to $+0.74$
Fillings	-0.95 to -0.58	$+0.88$ to $+0.28$
Crowns	-1.70 to $+0.89$	-0.08 to $+0.93$
Extractions	-1.51 to $+0.21$	-0.13 to $+0.47$
Dentures	-0.59 to $+2.20$	-0.08 to $+0.26$
Orthodontia	-0.08	$+1.24$

Extractions and dentures were found to be inferior goods for adults (poor person's dentistry); preventive care, fillings, and such exotic care as orthodontia being preferred at higher incomes. Most importantly, the researchers found that, due to relatively high price elasticities, visits to dentists would more than double for adults and more than triple for children if prices to patients were cut to zero. Quantity demanded would still increase considerably with patients paying 25 percent and the government paying 75 percent. It would be impossible to meet such demand with the current number of dentists in the population. To avoid long waiting periods before patients could see doctors, patients would have to pay rather high percentages of the payments until the supply of dental services was adjusted. Alternatively, because price elasticity was generally highest for children, the likely shortage could be alleviated if dental insurance was phased in slowly for children. (Such a strategy was followed in 1974 when Sweden inaugurated its national dental insurance plan.)

Source: Willard G. Manning, Jr. and Charles E. Phelps, "The Demand for Dental Care," *The Bell Journal of Economics,* Autumn 1979, pp. 503–25. Table (p. 512) copyright © 1979, American Telephone and Telegraph Company.

CLOSE-UP 3.1

SUBSTITUTION AND INCOME EFFECTS IN THE WORLD OF WHITE RATS

Sometimes even economists manage to devise controlled experiments. Consider the following one. Two white rats were placed in cages that contained levers to activate dipper cups. When its lever was depressed, one dipper cup provided a measured quantity of root beer; the other one provided collins mix. Each rat was given a fixed "income" of so many pushes on the levers per day, and experimenters set the "price" per unit of root beer and collins mix as the number of pushes the rats had to "spend" to get a unit.

Initially, the rats were given an income of 300 pushes per day; both liquids were priced at 20 pushes per unit. Rat 1 settled down to a pattern of drinking about 11 units of root beer per day and about 4 of collins mix. Rat 2 chose more than 14 units of root beer and less than 1 unit of collins mix per day.

CLOSE-UP

Experimenters then doubled the "price" of root beer to 40 pushes and halved the price of collins mix to 10. At the same time, Slutsky-like, they adjusted the income of each rat so it could afford to continue its old consumption pattern if it so chose. This eliminated any possible income effect of the price change. Would the pure substitution effect work as the theory of human consumer behavior predicts? Would the rats consume more of the cheaper collins mix and less of the dearer root beer, even though they could afford to drink as much of both goods as previously?

The answer was yes. Rat 1 changed its consumption to about 8 units of root beer and 17 of collins mix per day. Rat 2 ended up consuming about 9 units of root beer and 25 of collins mix per day. Even rats have downward-sloping demand curves.

Sources: John H. Kagel, Raymond C. Battalio, Howard Rachlin, Leonard Green, Robert L. Basemann, and W. R. Klemm, "Experimental Studies of Consumer Demand Behavior," *Economic Inquiry,* March 1975, pp. 22–38. *See also* Tom Alexander, "Economics According to the Rats," *Fortune,* December 1, 1980, pp. 127–32, for a discussion of other experiments.

CLOSE-UP 3.2

CROSS-PRICE ELASTICITY AND THE CELLOPHANE CASE

The U.S. Department of Justice brought suit against the du Pont Company (which sold 75 percent of the cellophane used in the United States) for having monopolized the sale of cellophane. In its defense, du Pont claimed that the relevant market was wider than that of cellophane and should include all flexible wrapping materials (of which du Pont sold less than 20 percent). To prove its point, du Pont produced cross-price elasticities between cellophane and close substitutes, such as aluminum foils, wax paper, and polyethylene. In a 1956 landmark decision, the U.S. Supreme Court agreed with du Pont.

Source: *U.S. Reports,* vol. 351 (Washington, D.C.: U.S. Government Printing Office, 1956), p. 400.

4

The Technology of the Firm

Chapters 2 and 3 explored the factors that determine the demand for goods by consumers, Chapters 4 and 5 now turn to those factors that determine the supply of such goods. The present chapter will focus on the *physical* aspects of the productive process by which firms make goods available to people when and where they are wanted; Chapter 5 will consider the *monetary* aspects as well.

The discussion of scarcity in Chapter 1 noted that in any given period a society's ability to produce goods is limited by the quantities of resources available and by the current state of its technology (the set of production methods known to people). Every single firm, we must now add, is similarly constrained by resources and technology—whether it is large or small, whether it produces airplane rides, apples, or medical care, whether it is run by a genius, a moron, or a group of either type. With the inevitably limited inputs chosen by it, the firm cannot produce a larger quantity of any given type of output than current technology allows. This physical constraint on the producer of every good can be summarized by a **production function.** The production function is the technical relationship, stated in physical and not in value terms, between all conceivable combinations of inputs used during a period and the associated *maximum* quan-

tities of some type of output, given the state of technology. This relationship can be expressed in the form of an equation, a table, or a graph.

If we denote, respectively, the quantities of human, capital, and natural resource services used in a given period by L, K, and T, the state of technology by t, and the maximum possible outputs obtainable from combinations of the above by Q, we can write a production function as

$$Q = f(L, K, T), \text{ given } t.$$

Naturally, any change in technology, t, will change the relationship between physical input combinations (L, K, and T) and the associated maximum output quantities, Q. That, however, is a matter to be discussed in Chapter 10. This chapter focuses on the production function under a *given* state of technology. Even with this restriction, the production function is a complicated relationship.

Consider the production of apples. Current technical knowledge allows firms to produce apples with a near-infinite variety of input combinations. Orchards can be located in many places—in Oregon or Michigan, in Maine or Virginia, at sea level or at high elevations. Accordingly, such natural resources as the inherent fertility of the soil, the amount of annual rainfall or sunshine, and the length of the growing season can be varied widely. A similar story can be told about capital resources. Orchards can be established on 1-acre lots or on 5,000-acre lots; they can be placed in the open (and usually are), but they can also be set up under glass. They can be planted with trees bred to resist disease or with ordinary ones that are sprayed with pesticides—by hand, by tank car, or even by plane. Orchards can be equipped with bee hives (to assist fertilization) or sprinkler systems (to prevent damage from frost), with irrigation equipment, rodent control, or cold-storage barns. The quantity of human resources used can, similarly, be adjusted almost without limit. People can be used to plant trees and fertilize them, to prune trees and harvest the crop, to store and market the crop, to run and repair equipment, to supervise operations, and much more.

Given enough time, a firm engaged in apple production can vary all of these inputs. Economists have a special name for this situation. A time period so long that a firm can vary the quantities of *all* of its inputs is called the **long run.** In contrast, a time period so short that the quantity of at least one of the firm's inputs cannot be varied is called the **short run.** Obviously, the length involved differs for firms in different industries. For example, an apple producer would require a minimum of five years to increase the number of fruit-bearing trees (they cannot be grown overnight); yet a street vendor selling apples might be able to increase all relevant inputs in a day. We will begin our study of the production function with a discussion of the short run. In the simplest possible case, a firm may be able to vary the quantity of only one of its inputs.

THE CASE OF A SINGLE VARIABLE INPUT

Imagine an apple producer who was limited, during a given period, not only by the current state of technology, but also by fixed quantities of capital and natural resources, $\overline{K}$ and $\overline{T}$. During a

given year, for instance, this producer may have available (and be unable to vary in quantity) 1,000 mature apple trees (on a 5-acre hilltop in Oregon), 3 tons of fertilizer, 2 orchard-spraying machines, and so on. The number of full-time laborers, L, may, however, be freely variable; by varying the number of workers, the firm may be able to vary its output. The production function of this firm can be written as

$$Q = f(L), \text{ given } \overline{K}, \overline{T}, t.$$

Alternatively, this relationship can be expressed by the type of data in columns (1) to (3) of Table 4.1. Rows (A) to (J) list 10 of many more conceivable combinations of fixed and variable inputs and the maximum total output associated with each. Consider row (A). The use for a year of 1,000 apple trees, 3 tons of fertilizer, etcetera is designated in column (1) as the use of 1 unit of fixed input. If no labor at all were performed, as shown by the 0 in column (2), the firm would end up producing no apples at all, as column (3) shows. An unholy alliance of winter storms, spring frost, summer drought, and various pests would ruin the unprotected trees. Even if apples grew on them, there would be no one to do the harvesting. Yet the firm has many alternatives. Some of them are shown in rows (B) through (J). If the firm used the work of even one person for a year—row (B)—the picture would be altered drastically. Sprinkling blossoms against frost and watering roots during the drought, perhaps, would reward the firm, eventually, with an apple harvest of 1,000 bushels.

There are other possibilities, of course. The use of two workers for a year would bring even better results. Two workers—row (C)—would be able to do what one alone could not accomplish: prune the tops of trees, fertilize their roots, and wrap their trunks to keep the rodents away. As a result, the trees would grow more and larger apples; total product would rise to 2,700 bushels a year. The hiring of three workers—row (D)— instead of two would yield even more spectacular success. There would now be time to fix and run the spraying machines, to harvest more of the

TABLE 4.1

A Simple Production Function

	Inputs per Year		Output per Year			
	Fixed (1,000 apple trees, 3 tons of fertilizer, etc.) (1)	Variable (workers) (2)	Maximum Total Product (bushels of apples) (3)	Marginal Product of Labor (bushels of apples per extra worker) (4) = Δ(3)/Δ(2)		Average Product of Labor (bushels of apples per worker) (5) = (3)/(2)
(A)	1	0	0			—
				1,000		
(B)	1	1	1,000		Increasing returns to labor	1,000
				1,700		
(C)	1	2	2,700			1,350
				2,300		
(D)	1	3	5,000			1,667
				2,000		
(E)	1	4	7,000			1,750
				1,300		
(F)	1	5	8,300		Decreasing returns to labor	1,660
				700		
(G)	1	6	9,000			1,500
				300		
(H)	1	7	9,300			1,329
				0		
(I)	1	8	9,300			1,163
				−300		
(J)	1	9	9,000			1,000

Each row of this table shows a conceivable combination of inputs used per year, columns (1) and (2), and the associated maximum total product, column (3), given the state of technology. Column (4) depicts the *law of eventually diminishing returns to a variable input:* Given technical knowledge and a fixed quantity of some input, such as the natural and capital resources listed in column (1), equal successive additions of another input, such as the labor listed in column (2), eventually yield declining additions to total output, such as the apple crop in column (3). As this example indicates, the law in question may operate only after a range of increasing returns has been passed. The returns involved refer to the variable input's *marginal product* and should not be confused with its *average product,* column (5). Note: As the pointers between columns (3) and (4) indicate, the marginal products shown refer to the intervals between rows.

apples, to take care of the cold-storage barn. Fewer apples would be eaten by worms, remain unharvested, or spoil before reaching the market. Total product would rise to 5,000 bushels a year.

And so it would go, but not forever. Proceeding on the path of hiring more labor, an orchardist would soon come face to face with a technological fact of life: Given fixed quantities of capital and natural resources, illustrated by the unchanging entries in column (1), equal successive additions of labor would be bound to yield, eventually, ever smaller additions to the crop, followed by zero additions or even negative ones, as shown by column (4). Sooner or later, there would be too many workers relative to the fixed number of trees and quantity of equipment. Once trees were saturated with fertilizer, water, and tender loving care, additional workers would have nothing to do except eat apples and get into each other's way! Inevitably, the principle of declining marginal benefit (first noted in Chapter 1) would come into play. When the benefit that is declining refers to physical product rather than utility, the principle is usually referred to as the **law of variable proportions** or the **law of diminishing returns.** Strictly speaking, it should be given the awkward name of *the law of eventually diminishing returns to a variable input.*

The Law of Diminishing Returns

The nature of the law of diminishing returns, which can be observed in all production functions, can be most clearly understood with the help of a new concept: **Marginal product** is the physical change in the total product attributable to a unit change in some input in the productive process, all else being equal. (In later chapters, when there is danger of confusing physical product with its market value, we will refer to this concept as **marginal physical product.** In this chapter, however, all units are measured in physical terms.)

The marginal product of labor in Table 4.1 can be calculated by noting the change in the total product evidenced by the difference between any two adjacent numbers in column (3), a difference that is always associated in our example with a unit change in labor input in column (2). The results are shown directly in column (4). As the brackets indicate, **diminishing returns to a variable input** always refer to declines in that input's *marginal* product as a larger quantity of the input is used. These declines should not be confused with possible declines of total product—column (3)— or of **average (physical) product**—column (5). Average product is the ratio of total product to the total quantity of an input used. The average product of the variable labor input is shown in column (5).

Table 4.1 also highlights the fact that the eventual inevitability of diminishing returns, as a variable input is added to a fixed input, does not preclude the existence of a limited range of **increasing returns to a variable input,** in which

use of a larger quantity of the input is associated with *increases* in its marginal product. Note how labor's marginal product in our orchard declines when three or more workers are employed but rises prior to this point. Similarly (though not shown in Table 4.1), there might exist a range of **constant returns to a variable input,** in which use of a larger quantity of the input is associated with constancy in its marginal product. This, too, would have to be a transitory stage, or it would be possible to add more and more workers to our 5-acre orchard (and receive ever constant amounts of extra output in return) until the entire world's apple crop was being produced there. The mental image of a thousand, a million, and, finally, a billion workers being crammed into our 5-acre piece of land should be enough to convince us that increasing and constant returns must *eventually* give way to diminishing returns. Because increasing or constant returns are a limited possibility, however, economists who do not wish to be misunderstood talk of the law of *eventually* diminishing returns.

Note: While the concepts of increasing, constant, or diminishing returns to a variable input refer to the behavior of the marginal product of a particular *type* of input (such as labor), it is not a good idea to link the marginal product of an input type to any particular *unit* of that input (such as a particular worker). In Table 4.1, each of the persons employed can be assumed to be an *equally good* worker. The sixth person hired should not be viewed as any weaker, lazier, or less intelligent than the first five, even though he or she would add so much less to the total crop. Nor need the ninth person be any different from the sixth. The different performances of workers would stem from the different *circumstances* existing when these workers arrived on the scene. If worker number nine were hired first, he or she, too, would produce a marginal product of +1,000 rather than −300 bushels. If worker number one were hired in eighth place, he or she, too, would produce a marginal product of zero rather than of 1,000 bushels. By the same token, if our orchardist were to fire any one of eight workers laboring in the orchard, no matter whether he or she was hired as the first, fourth, or eighth one, the total produced would not change at all, since the product associated with seven workers is the same as that for eight workers, as shown in column (3). This may seem surprising, but it is really little more than common sense. People by themselves produce nothing. How productive they are depends on the world into which they are placed. Their productivity depends on the quantity and quality of the natural, capital, and other human resources they find in this world. Ask yourself this: What would *your* marginal product be if you were to join the productive process—just as you are now—in Central Africa or in fourth-century Tibet rather than in the present-day United States? Thus a simple lesson emerges: To avoid confusion, one should never talk of, say, the marginal product of *the* sixth laborer, but rather of the marginal product of labor when six instead of five workers are employed.

A Graphical Exposition

Figure 4.1 is a graphical illustration of a simple production function. The heavy dots in panel (a) depict the data from columns (2) and (3) of Table 4.1; the heavy dots in panel (b) graph data from columns (2) and (4) and from columns (2) and (5). Note that the marginal products of labor have been plotted at the midpoints of the ranges to which they apply and that all the heavy dots have been connected by smooth curves. These curves give us additional information (about points between the heavy dots), which was not contained in Table 4.1; all of our subsequent discussions will be based on this more detailed information now available in the graph.

It is important to understand the nature of the relationships between (1) total product and marginal product, (2) total product and average product, (3) marginal product and average product, and, finally, (4) the average products of different inputs.

First, note that the *height* of labor's marginal-product curve measures nothing else but the *slope* of the total-product curve (because

that slope *is* the marginal product). As long as total product is rising with increased use of labor, all else being equal, the slope of the total-product curve is positive (as between 0 and *a*). Correspondingly, in panel (b), labor's marginal product is positive (as between 0 and *b*). You may wish to review Figure 1.4, ''Declining Marginal Benefit,'' which illustrates this relationship in a different way (see p. 11).

Observe how the total product is rising at an increasing rate between 0 and *c* (the point of inflection on the curve), but rising at a decreasing rate between *c* and *a*. Correspondingly, in panel (b), labor's marginal product is positive and rising up to point *d* (which is directly below *c*), but positive and falling between *d* and *b* (which is found directly below *a*). The input quantity corresponding to *d*, at which marginal product is maximized and beyond which it falls, is called the **point of diminishing returns.** Thus labor's marginal-product curve shows directly two ranges of labor inputs: the one producing increasing returns and the one producing diminishing but positive returns in terms of output. Finally, there exists, of course, a third range in which (excessive) labor inputs yield negative marginal products (to the right of *b*) and, therefore, cause total product to decline (to the right of *a*). These three *ranges* are indicated by the brackets underneath panel (b). They should not be confused with the three *stages* underneath panel (a), to be discussed below.

Second, consider the relationship between labor's total and average product. Because labor's average product always equals total product divided by corresponding labor input, its size can be gauged in panel (a) by the slope of a ray originating at 0 and going to any desired point on the total-product curve. Thus the average product of one worker (at point *e*) is 1,000 bushels (the height of *e*) divided by 1 worker, or 1,000 bushels. This average product of one worker is shown by point *h* in panel (b), but it can also be read as the slope of straight line 0*ef* in panel (a) or, mathematically, as tangent α. Because the ray through 0*e* also passes through *f*, the average product of nine workers must also be 1,000 bushels; indeed, 9,000 bushels (the height of f) divided by 9 workers does equal 1,000 bushels. The average product of 9 workers is shown by point i in panel (b) and, again, by tangent α in panel (a). Once this is understood, it is easy to imagine a series of rays emanating from point 0 in panel (a) and aiming, successively, at points farther and farther to the right along the total-product curve. These rays would cut the total-product curve at e, then c, then g, a, and f; the

ever changing angle α (formed by the rays and the abscissa of the graph) would trace out the size of labor's average product. Can you show how angle α (and labor's average product) would rise, with increasing use of labor, to a maximum for ray $0g$, but would decline once more than 4 workers were employed? Note how, in panel (b), labor's average product reflects this behavior of angle α. The average product rises to point k (directly below g) and then declines.

FIGURE 4.1

Total, Marginal, and Average Product

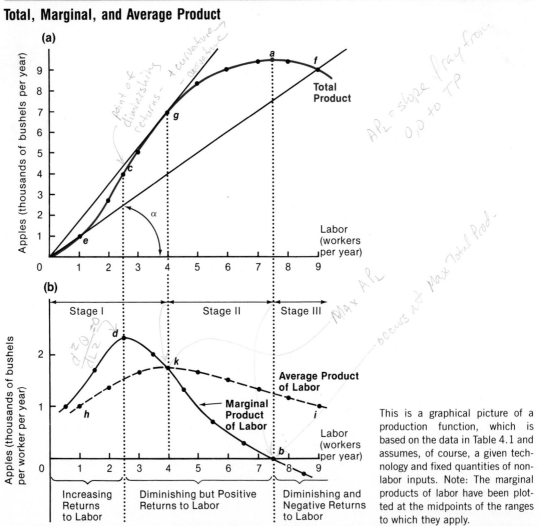

This is a graphical picture of a production function, which is based on the data in Table 4.1 and assumes, of course, a given technology and fixed quantities of non-labor inputs. Note: The marginal products of labor have been plotted at the midpoints of the ranges to which they apply.

Third, consider the relationship between labor's marginal and average products. As it turns out, the behavior of average "anything" (be it product or even a student's grades) is always related in the following way to the behavior of marginal "anything": When marginal is above average, it pulls up the average. When marginal is below average, it pulls down the average. As long as marginal is equal to average, average does not change.

You can verify this behavior by looking at Figure 4.1. Note that while marginal product exceeds average product, average product is rising (from *h* toward *k*). While marginal product falls short of average product, average product is falling (from *k* toward *i*). Average product reaches a maximum when it equals the marginal product (as it does at point *k*).

Students are apt to be quite familiar with this phenomenon without realizing it. Anyone receiving a new grade (which we might call a *marginal* grade) knows how it can pull one's grade *average* down or up. A marginal grade below average will pull down the average; one above average will pull up the average. This is true, furthermore, regardless of what the marginal grade itself is doing. Each new grade can be better than the last one (marginal grades are rising); yet if these new (and improving) grades are below the average, the average will still go down. Each new grade, on the other hand, can be worse than the last one (marginal grades are falling); yet if these new (and deteriorating) grades are above the average, the average will still go up. Observe this phenomenon in Figure 4.1: marginal product is falling between *d* and *k,* but because it is above average, it still pulls the average up.

Finally, the three stages of the production function, labeled I, II, and III, tell us something about the **productivity** of each type of input, which is the ratio of output produced to input quantity used, or the average product. Throughout stage I, while the use of labor is increased from 0 to 4 workers per year and the quantities of nonlabor inputs are held fixed, the productivities of both types of inputs increase. The increase in

labor's productivity is obvious from the stage I segment of the average-product curve in panel (b). The average product of labor rises up to maximum *k* at the dotted borderline between stages I and II. The increase in the average product of nonlabor inputs is not graphed directly, but it can be seen indirectly in panel (a). Because the quantity of nonlabor inputs is constant throughout, the increase in total product from 0 toward *g* must be associated with a corresponding increase in the ratio of total product to this constant amount of nonlabor inputs.

Now consider stage II, wherein the use of labor is increased further from 4 to between 7 and 8 units. The productivity of labor obviously declines to the right of *k* in panel (b). The productivity of nonlabor inputs, on the other hand, continues to rise to its maximum at the borderline between stages II and III. Again, this can be seen indirectly in panel (a). Because total product rises from *g* toward *a*, the ratio of total product to the constant amount of nonlabor inputs must also rise.

Note: Given the kind of production function introduced here, it is impossible to maximize simultaneously the productivity of *both* labor and nonlabor resources. (Whether anyone would ever *want* to do such a thing is another question, to which we will turn in the next chapter.)

Consider stage III. The productivities of both types of inputs decline. The average-product-of-labor curve in panel (b) tells us directly that labor productivity is declining. The declining total-product curve in panel (a) to the right of point *a* tells us indirectly that the productivity of nonlabor inputs is declining. Presumably, no firm will ever utilize input combinations such as those in stage III where greater use of variable inputs yields lower total product. Stage III is characterized by **technical inefficiency** because it is now possible, within a given firm, to produce a given output with less of one or more inputs without increasing the amount of other inputs. Economists usually assume (perhaps wrongly) that each firm by itself achieves **technical efficiency,** a situation in which it is impossible for a given firm to produce a given

TABLE 4.2

A Complex Production Function

Maximum Total Product
(bushels of wheat per year)

Capital (units per year)							
7	746 — 1055 — 1292 — 1492 — 1668 — 1828 — 1974
6	691 — 977 — 1196 — 1382 — 1545 — 1692 — 1828
5	631 — 892 — 1092 — 1261 — 1410 — 1545 — 1668
4	564 — 798 — 977 — 1128 — 1261 — 1382 — 1492
3	488 — 691 — 846 — 977 — 1092 — 1196 — 1292
2	399 — 564 — 691 — 798 — 892 — 977 — 1055
1	282 — 399 — 488 — 564 — 631 — 691 — 746
0	1 2 3 4 5 6 7 Labor (units per year)

Given technical knowledge and a fixed quantity of some input (such as natural resources not shown here), different combinations of two variable inputs (such as labor and capital) may yield the alternative total products shown in this grid. The production function shown here is subject throughout to diminishing returns to either labor (given capital) or capital (given labor). Its equation is $Q = 282 \sqrt{K \cdot L}$.

output with less of one or more inputs without increasing other inputs. Note: *Technical* efficiency should not be confused with *economic* efficiency (discussed in Chapter 14). Unlike technical efficiency, economic efficiency always involves the *comparison* of the circumstances of two or more firms or households.*

THE CASE OF TWO VARIABLE INPUTS

We are now ready to study a more complicated case in which two inputs vary. Consider a producer of wheat who is limited, during a given period, by the current state of technology, t, and

---

*For a calculus-based treatment of this material, see Section 4A of the Calculus Appendix at the back of this book.

by fixed natural resources, $\overline{T}$, but who can freely vary the quantities of both labor and capital, L and K. The firm's production function can be written as

$$Q = f(L, K), \text{ given } \overline{T} \text{ and } t.$$

This production function can be expressed by numerical data such as those in Table 4.2. The table can be read like a mileage chart. The use of 2 units of capital plus 5 units of labor, it tells us, would yield 892 bushels of wheat per year; 6 units of capital used with 3 units of labor would yield 1,196 bushels instead, and so on for all other combinations. Note: The production function shown here is subject to diminishing returns to either input. Holding capital constant at any level and increasing labor by equal units will raise output by ever decreasing amounts. (Mov-

[handwritten margin notes:] "class - used $Q = 100 \, L^{\frac{1}{2}} \, K^{\frac{1}{2}}$ (Cobb Douglass) $A = 100, \; a = b = \frac{1}{2}$)"

ing from left to right along any row, you might verify this fact by calculating the marginal products of labor.) Similarly, holding labor constant at any given level while capital is increased will also raise output by ever decreasing amounts. (Moving along any column from the bottom to the top, you may wish to calculate the marginal products of capital.)

A complex production function can be illustrated graphically in a number of ways. One way is to use a three-dimensional graph like the graph of the utility mountain in Figure 2.3 (see p. 34). Our firm could be viewed very much like the consumer in Chapter 2. Instead of consuming apples and butter to produce utility, it consumes the services of labor and capital to produce wheat. Table 4.2 could be treated like the firm's field of choice. A total-product mountain could be erected above this table in a third dimension, indicating by its height above each input combination the total quantity of wheat that this combination would yield. As the numbers in Table 4.2 indicate, this total-product mountain would start at a zero elevation in the lower left corner and rise to its highest point in the upper right one. Unlike in the case of total utility, furthermore, there would be no problem at all with *measuring* the total product involved because we do know how to measure such physical quantities as bushels, gallons, and tons of output. Thus each number in Table 4.2 can be considered a measurement of the height of the total-product mountain above that number.

Yet it is not necessary to construct such a mountain. Just as the utility mountain could be collapsed to a two-dimensional set of consumption-indifference curves, so the total-product mountain can be reduced to a set of **production-indifference curves.** Each of these curves shows all the alternative combinations of two inputs that yield the same maximum total product and among which a producer would be indifferent from a purely technical point of view. As we shall see later, this does not mean indifference from an economic, profit-maximizing point of

view. That is why it is probably wiser to call the production-indifference curve by one of its other names, such as **equal-product curve** or **isoquant.** The technical information highlighted in color in Table 4.2 has been transferred to Figure 4.2, which illustrates how a more complex production function can be presented graphically.

ISOQUANTS ANALYZED

To understand what isoquants reveal about the production function, it is important to understand a number of the characteristics of isoquants.

FIGURE 4.2

Isoquants

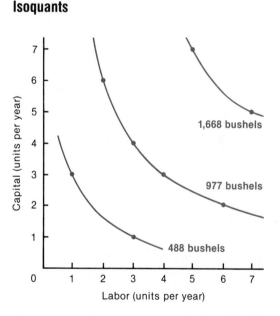

A set of isoquants is a graphic picture of a complex production function. Any given isoquant shows all the alternative combinations of two inputs (such as the services of labor and capital) that yield the same maximum total product (such as bushels of wheat). This set of isoquants assumes, of course, a given technology and fixed quantities of any other inputs.

Horizontal and Vertical Slopes Denote Zero Marginal Products

The right-angled isoquants pictured in panel (a) of Figure 4.3 are far from impossible, but consider what they tell us: A producer could produce at most 50 units of product with input combination A. If the same quantity of capital were used, but more labor (such as the amount corresponding to B), output would remain unchanged at 50 units. This unchanged output implies a zero marginal product of *labor* on the horizontal isoquant segment to the right of A. Similarly, if the same quantity of labor were used as in A, but more capital (such as the amount corresponding to C), output would still remain at 50 units. This unchanged output implies a zero marginal product of *capital* on the vertical isoquant segment above A. Surely, no producer would ever use additional labor or capital that added nothing to output. A producer would avoid the implied technical inefficiency (corresponding to the stage III borderline in Figure 4.1) and would produce 50 units of output *only* with input combination A. Correspondingly, 100, 150, or 200 units of output would be produced only with input combinations D, E, and F, respectively. All levels of output would be produced only with the technically efficient input combinations that lie on the dotted ray from 0 to F and beyond. That is, the product concerned would always be produced with the same capital-to-labor ratio (the one given by the slope of the dotted ray).

Positive Slope Denotes Negative Marginal Products

Consider the positively sloped isoquant segments found in the shaded area of panel (b) of Figure 4.3. If such isoquants existed, no producer would ever select an input combination in the shaded area for this reason: If a producer could produce 30 units of product with input combination a, the use of extra labor with capital unchanged (implied by a move from a to b) would *reduce* total output (b lies below the 30-unit isoquant). In

region ab, labor's marginal product is, therefore, negative. Output could be kept unchanged only if, along with the counterproductive extra labor, extra capital were added, too (by a move from b to c). But what producer, who could produce 30 units of some output with capital-labor combination a, would ever wish to produce the same output with combination c, which uses more of both inputs? All other input combinations below the dotted line from 0 to a and beyond, similarly, denote the presence of negative marginal products of labor.

An analogous story can be told for the area above the dotted line from 0 to d and beyond. In that region, capital, rather than labor, has negative marginal products: If a producer could produce 30 units of product with input combination d, the use of extra capital, with labor unchanged (as implied by a move from d to e) would *reduce* total output (e lies below the 30-unit isoquant). Output could be kept unchanged only if, along with the counterproductive capital, extra labor were added, too (by a move from e to f). At f, a producer would end up using more of *both* inputs than at d but would be getting the same output. All the technically efficient input combinations are, therefore, found in the unshaded lens-shaped area within which isoquants are negatively sloped.

Negative Slope Denotes Positive Marginal Products

We can assume that producers are interested in using inputs only as long as they yield positive marginal products. This implies that producers will focus on negatively sloped segments of isoquants when making input choices. Isoquant I_0 in panel (c) of Figure 4.3 illustrates one possibility.

Isoquant I_0 is analogous to the consumption-indifference curve analyzed in Chapter 2 (see pp. 36–38). This time, it is not apples and butter that are consumed to produce invisible utility; the services of capital and workers are consumed to produce a visible product, such as wheat. Con-

FIGURE 4.3

Isoquants Analyzed

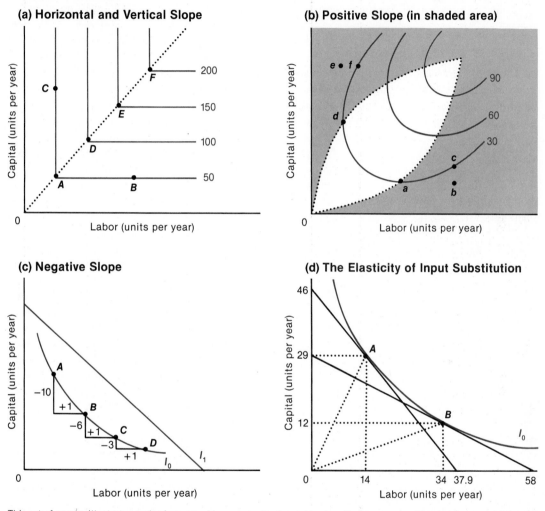

This set of graphs illustrates major features of isoquants: Horizontal and vertical segments of isoquants—panel (a)—and isoquant segments with positive slope—panel (b)—denote regions of technical inefficiency. Technically efficient segments of isoquants must be negatively sloped—panel (c). The ease or difficulty with which producers can switch among known techniques of production can be measured by the elasticity of input substitution—panel (d).

sider a producer who was producing the given output level represented by I_0 and was doing so with input combination A. If 10 units of capital were now removed from the process of production (and assuming capital's marginal product was positive), output would fall, but this fall might be compensated exactly by the addition of

1 unit of labor. That is why B is found on the same isoquant as A. The rate at which a producer is able to exchange, without affecting the quantity of output produced, a little bit of one input (say, capital) for a little bit of another input (say, labor) is called the **marginal rate of technical substitution (MRTS).** In our graph, the marginal

rate of technical substitution of labor for capital, $MRTS_{L/K}$, is pictured as the amount of capital the producer is able to sacrifice technically for an extra unit of labor, while keeping output unchanged. This ever changing $MRTS$ clearly equals the absolute value of the slope of the isoquant. In region AB, this comes to $\left|\frac{10}{1}\right|$, on the average.[1] It reflects, in turn, the ratio of the marginal products of the two inputs. Because the removal of 10 units of capital reduces output by some amount X, we can so denote the marginal product of 10 units of capital and say $MP_{10K} = X$. It follows that $MP_{1K} = .1X$. Because the addition of 1 unit of labor raises output by the same amount X, we can so denote the marginal product of 1 unit of labor and say $MP_{1L} = X$. Therefore, $MP_{1L}/MP_{1K} = X/.1X = 10/1.$*

$$|\textbf{Isoquant slope}| = MRTS_{L/K} = \frac{MP_L}{MP_K}$$

Note: Just as consumption-indifference curves in Chapter 2 were depicted as subject to a diminishing marginal rate of substitution, so isoquant I_0 in panel (c) depicts a frequently observed characteristic of production functions: a diminishing marginal rate of technical substitution. If our producer, having moved from A to B, wanted to substitute ever more labor for capital, output could be kept unchanged only if equal increases in labor went hand in hand with *ever*

smaller sacrifices of capital (or equal sacrifices of capital were compensated by *ever larger* increases of labor).

Consider, in contrast, the meaning of straight-line isoquant I_1. I_1 depicts a constant marginal rate of technical substitution, which implies that the two inputs are perfect substitutes for each other. In such a case, we might as well treat them as a single input.

Finally, note one other analogy to the theory of the consumer. Like consumption-indifference curves, the isoquants of a given producer cannot intersect. Any given input combination cannot, simultaneously, yield two different maximum output quantities.

The Elasticity of Input Substitution

Economists like to measure the ease or difficulty with which inputs can be substituted for each other and with which producers can switch, therefore, from one known technique of production to another. The **elasticity of input substitution,** usually denoted by σ, pronounced *sigma,* is a measure of this substitutability. It is the percentage change in the ratio of two inputs used in producing a given output quantity, divided by the associated percentage change in the marginal rate of technical substitution between these inputs.

Consider panel (d) of Figure 4.3. Let us calculate the elasticity between A and B on isoquant I_0. Because the inputs involved are labor, L, and capital, K, we can write the formula of Box 4.A.

---

[1]At any one point, P_0, on a convex isoquant, the slope is measured by a ratio such as a/b; between two points, P_1 and P_2, the (average) slope is measured by a ratio such as c/d.

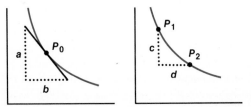

*For a calculus-based treatment of this material, see Section 4B of the Calculus Appendix at the back of this book.

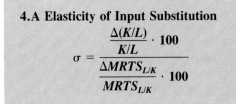

4.A Elasticity of Input Substitution

$$\sigma = \frac{\dfrac{\Delta(K/L)}{K/L} \cdot 100}{\dfrac{\Delta MRTS_{L/K}}{MRTS_{L/K}} \cdot 100}$$

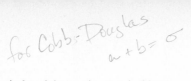
for Cobb-Douglas
$a + b = \sigma$

The capital-to-labor ratio at A is 29/14, or 2.07. It becomes 12/34 or .35 at B, making for a change of -1.72. For the same reasons noted in the Chapter 3 section on "Arc Elasticity Measures," it is customary to relate this absolute change to the *average* K/L ratio in the AB range, or to $(2.07 + .35)/2$, which equals 1.21 in our case. Thus the numerator in our example equals $(-1.72/1.21) \cdot 100 = -142$ percent. Turning to the denominator, we find that the $MRTS_{L/K}$ at A equals the slope of the isoquant at A and is given by the slope of the tangent at that point. Its absolute value is 46/37.9 or 1.21. The $MRTS_{L/K}$ becomes 29/58 or .5 at B, making for a change of $-.71$. Once again relating this absolute change to the *average* $MRTS_{L/K}$ in the AB range, or to $(1.21 + .5)/2$, which is .855, the denominator in our example equals $(-.71/.855) \cdot 100 = -83$ percent. Hence $\sigma = (-142/-83) = 1.71$. Because the input ratio and the marginal rate of technical substitution always move in the same direction, the elasticity of input substitution is always positive for isoquants that allow input substitution. The magnitude of σ is zero, for example, in the extreme case of right-angled isoquants, as in panel (a) of Figure 4.3, because, as we noted, input substitution is then ruled out. In that case, only one capital-to-labor ratio exists that is technically efficient (the one given by the slope of line $0F$), and the numerator in the above formula equals zero. In contrast, σ is infinite for straight-line isoquants, such as I_1 in panel (c), because the "two" inputs related in this way are perfect substitutes. In that case, only one $MRTS$ exists, and the denominator of the above formula equals zero.

The value of σ lies, therefore, between zero and infinity for normal convex isoquants, and it is larger the easier input substitution is. Hence σ roughly indicates which firms or industries, in the face of rising relative input prices, will be able to hold their costs down and which will incur increases in production costs that must ultimately increase output prices or reduce profits. A large σ indicates that the rising price of one input can be easily escaped by switching to a different technique of production that favors the use of another input that is relatively cheaper. In contrast, a low or even zero value of σ indicates that, for technological reasons, the producer is almost or completely unable to change the mix of inputs used.

THE CASE OF NOTHING BUT VARIABLE INPUTS

We now turn to the long run, in which all inputs can be varied at the same time. Economists have been particularly interested in the effects on output of variations in the *scale* of the productive process. Scale is said to vary when all inputs are not only changed at the same time, but in the same proportion as well. Three types of consequences occur when all inputs are changed simultaneously and in the same proportion: constant, increasing, or decreasing returns to scale.

Constant Returns to Scale

If a simultaneous and equal percentage change in the use of all physical inputs leads to an *identical* percentage change in physical output, a firm's production function is said to exhibit **constant returns to scale.** Under such circumstances, if $Q = f(L, K, T)$, given t, and c is some constant, it is also true that $cQ = f(cL, cK, cT)$, given t. Ordinarily, this is the kind of result one would expect. If a firm can combine, for example, 1,000 apple trees, 3 tons of fertilizer, 2 orchard-spraying machines, etcetera with 4 workers to produce 7,000 bushels of apples in a year, why shouldn't it be able to combine 2,000 apple trees, 6 tons of fertilizer, 4 orchard-spraying machines, and 2 etcetera with 8 workers to produce 14,000 bushels of apples in a year? Indeed, it might, as Table 4.3 illustrates. The data in columns (1) to (3) have been taken from Table 4.1. They might represent the original technical alternatives open to the firm, with the formerly fixed inputs in column (1) denoting 1,000 apple trees, 3 tons of fertilizer, and the like. The data in columns (4) to (6) then represent a different set of technical alternatives that would prevail if the firm doubled all inputs, including the previously fixed ones. Obviously, these data are only illustrative. Inputs can be changed by *any* percentage; there is nothing magic about *doubling* all inputs (an increase of 100 percent). For example, under constant returns to scale, a 5.2-percent increase (or decrease) in all inputs would increase (or decrease) output by 5.2 percent as well. Such constant returns to scale, however, do not always occur.

Increasing Returns to Scale

If a simultaneous and equal percentage change in the use of all physical inputs leads to a *larger* percentage change in physical output, a firm's production function is said to exhibit **increasing**

returns to scale. Under such circumstances, if $Q = f(L, K, T)$, given t, and c is some constant, we find that $cQ < f(cL, cK, cT)$, given t. Why should the average products of all inputs rise when scale is increased and, therefore, fall when scale is reduced? A number of possible reasons can be cited. Most important among these are the advantages inherent in a specialization of inputs and the operation of certain physical laws.

As the scale of production becomes larger, the process of production can be broken down into a multitude of ever narrower tasks, and more and more people and machines can specialize in performing these different tasks. As a result, people who have different inherent talents can concentrate on what they can do best. The person with a knack for mechanics can work full-time fixing orchard-spraying machines when there are 300 of them but could hardly make a full-time job out of fixing just 1. At the same time, other people can specialize in accounting, financing, marketing, apple picking, bee keeping, research, or perhaps even in worker dental care. Even

TABLE 4.3

Constant Returns to Scale Illustrated

	Scale 1			Scale 2		
	Inputs (respective units per year)		**Output** (bushels per year)	**Inputs** (respective units per year)		**Output** (bushels per year)
	Capital and Land (1)	Labor (2)	Apples (3)	Capital and Land (4)	Labor (5)	Apples (6)
(A)	1	0	0	2	0	0
(B)	1	1	1,000	2	2	2,000
(C)	1	2	2,700	2	4	5,400
(D)	1	3	5,000	2	6	10,000
(E)	1	4	7,000	2	8	14,000
(F)	1	5	8,300	2	10	16,600
(G)	1	6	9,000	2	12	18,000
(H)	1	7	9,300	2	14	18,600

If a simultaneous and equal percentage change in the use of all its physical inputs leads to an identical percentage change in its physical output, a firm's production function is said to exhibit *constant returns to scale.* Note how, in this example, the doubling of all inputs also doubles the return they bring; that is, total output. When columns (1) and (2) become columns (4) and (5), column (3) becomes column (6). The same process would, of course, work in reverse: If constant returns to scale existed, the halving of all inputs would halve the associated outputs.

when talents are not inherent, it is easier to create and then maintain skills in people when each person's work is reduced to a simple and repetitive operation: "Practice makes perfect." This advantage is lost to the Jack-of-all-trades who must pass from operation to operation, moving, possibly, among many different locations of work, using ever different sets of tools, and all the while losing valuable time in between tasks or while "warming up" for a new one.

The very simplicity and repetitiveness of narrowly specialized, large-scale operations encourage, in turn, the invention and use of machines. When only 900 bushels of apples are produced per year, who would think of installing an assembly line to sort and wash them? The introduction of all kinds of specialized capital equipment, from electric turbines and internal combustion engines to computers and servomechanisms, testifies to the endless possibilities of increasing productivity through the use of specialization.

The operation of certain physical laws is also responsible for increasing returns to scale. Consider a box that is 1 foot long, 1 foot wide, and 1 foot high. It has a surface area of 6 square feet and a volume of 1 cubic foot. If one quadruples the length, width, and height, the surface area becomes 96 square feet, and the volume grows to 64 cubic feet. A 16-fold increase in surface area produces a 64-fold increase in volume! Frequently, the input quantities needed to construct "containers," such as cargo ships, office buildings, or pipelines, depend on their surface area, but their output depends on their volume. Larger scale, therefore, yields more output per unit of input. Many similar examples can be cited: A 20-ton stamping machine can be more effective than 500 hammers made with the same inputs; high-temperature processes often work better on a larger scale; a 1,000-horsepower motor may take fewer inputs to build than two 500-horsepower motors do; firms may need fewer administrators or pieces of standby equipment per unit of output and fewer inventories per dollar of sales the larger are output and sales.

Decreasing Returns to Scale

If a simultaneous and equal percentage change in the use of all physical inputs leads to a *smaller* percentage change in physical output, a firm's production function is said to exhibit **decreasing returns to scale.** Under such circumstances, if $Q = f(L, K, T)$, given t, and c is some constant, we find that $cQ > f(cL, cK, cT)$, given t. Why should the average products of all inputs fall when scale is increased and, therefore, rise when scale is reduced? Specialization carries with it not only the benefit of greater productivity but also a cost: the need to devote some resources to the task of *coordinating* the specialized activities of different people. Within firms, this task is performed consciously by managers specifically appointed for the purpose, but such managerial coordination becomes ever more difficult the larger a firm is. And, thus, the most important reason for decreasing returns to scale is the increasing inability of management to make right things go right and keep wrong things from going wrong!

Consider this: How can each employee know at all times what he or she must do if the goal of the firm is to be achieved? Quite clearly, a multitude of knowledge fragments, dispersed in the minds of separate individuals and not available to a single mind in its totality, have to be used jointly. There are only two methods of doing this. First, one can convey to a single mind (or that of a very small group of persons) all the knowledge that should be used but is, in the first instance, given to others. That mind can then digest the knowledge, formulate a plan of action, and issue appropriate orders that tell everyone else what to do. Second, one can convey to each person whatever additional knowledge is needed to dovetail independent individual actions with those of all others.

While the market economy as a whole uses the second method to coordinate the actions of households and firms, each individual firm internally uses the first method instead. The employees of a firm do not make their own decisions on the basis of price signals. Rather, they are being paid for their willingness to obey the authority of central planners! A supervisor does not *induce* a worker to oil machine X in shop Y by offering to pay more for this task than for another one. Rather, he *orders* the oiling to be done and that's that! Thus a large firm may be viewed as countless people placed in an administrative hierarchy (reaching from the top echelon of executives down to the lowliest of night watchguards). They are all tied together by an elaborate system of communications channels through which information flows up and orders flow down.

This observation brings us to the main point: Since the decision-making power of top management would be paralyzed by any attempt to give it *all* the information that is contained in the minds of all employees and that is relevant to the joint productive enterprise, the function of the firm's hierarchy is to *prevent* information from reaching the upper ranks of management except in highly condensed and abstract form! Important as it is to know that machine X in shop Y needs oiling, top management must be spared the knowledge of this fact. The upward-bound information channels must operate like a stratified sieve. As information possessed by any employee travels up the hierarchy (such as worker A's knowledge about squeaky machine X in shop Y), it must be acted upon at the lowest available executive rank (as by a supervisor's order that the machine be oiled). Thus all information, wherever it originates, must be stopped at the next highest level and translated into instructions. But it must also be translated into more abstract and condensed form and passed on up the hierarchy. Our supervisor, for instance, must eventually order another 100 gallons of oil from the purchasing department. And the purchasing department must eventually report to the accounting department monthly costs of $10 million for all kinds of supplies, one of which was a 100-gallon drum of oil (which would be a detail of no interest to top management at all). But the accountants must eventually report figures on overall annual revenue and production cost to top management.

Thus the squeaky machine, in totally unrecognizable fashion, makes itself known at the top!

Communications flowing in the reverse direction must have a corresponding fate. General orders from the top (say, to cut costs) must eventually be translated into specific orders further down (such as to throw out that oil-guzzling machine X in shop Y and replace it with a brand-new machine Z).

Now imagine what happens when a firm grows and grows and grows. Some 76 employees turn into 760, and 760 turn into 7,600, and they, in turn, become 760,000. The channels of communication become longer and longer. And the chances that essential information will not get through become greater and greater! There are so many workers and supervisors and Vice-Presidents in Charge Of This-and-That! It becomes difficult to determine who is responsible for what. Some things are done 10 times; some not at all. Perhaps 50 different people waste a total of 10 valuable hours reporting and fixing that one squeaky machine. Perhaps no one at all bothers about the machine, since everyone expects someone else to be responsible. So a $50,000 machine turns into a $325 piece of scrap for lack of $7.16 worth of oil. Would you be surprised if that firm's average product went down?

Indeed, this incident may give rise to a new Office for Scientific Management. Reams of paper and hundreds of hours of labor may be devoted to producing exact job descriptions for every position in the firm that tell what each person must and must not do. Yet all this red tape may not help at all. Even though worker number 39,373 is supposed to oil machine X in shop Y (according to page 291 of *the* booklet), the next time machine X needs oil, worker number 39,373 may just happen to be ill, to be giving birth to a baby, or to be away on jury duty. The machine-destroying accident may happen all over again because it is impossible to lay down iron-clad rules for all conceivable contingencies. Would you be surprised if that firm's average product went down?

This new incident may cause a lot of bad blood. There may be charges and counter-charges. Who was responsible? Nobody, according to the rule book, of course, but this doesn't make sense to anybody. Before long, workers will feel caught up in and overwhelmed by a vast impersonal bureaucracy. Their morale will sag. Work will slow down. Absenteeism will rise. There will be careless work. Would you be surprised if that firm's average product went down?

There may also be trouble at the top. Information essential to the prosperity or even survival of the firm may be lost or garbled during its tortuous travels along ever longer communication routes. Or even this condensed information may become so voluminous as to be impossible to handle. As a result, top management may make wrong decisions: They may fail to be responsive to new opportunities or they may act at the wrong time—and mistakes at that level may cost billions of dollars! Indeed, at its worst, management may completely lose contact with reality. It may become the victim of a sort of organizational mental illness: Top people may come to be surrounded by aides eager to please their superiors, always ready to confirm their ideas. These aides may deliberately filter out information contradicting the top people's image of the world they guide. As a result, that image may become unshakable. Top management may become incapable of learning anything new. Thinking themselves to be looking out of a window, they may actually be looking at a mirror! Would you be surprised if that firm's average product went down?

Our earlier discussion of physical laws provides another way of thinking about decreasing returns to scale. It may in fact be impossible to make true scale changes in a firm. Recall the preceding discussion of the geometric properties of a box. When length, width, and height are scaled up from 1 to 4, surface area rises from 1 to 16, volume from 1 to 64. In what sense then is a larger box a scaled-up version of a smaller one? Something like scaling up a box may happen during the growth of a firm. When some of its dimensions (such as the numbers of workers and machines) are increased a thousandfold, other dimensions (such as the required length of communication channels and the required number of messages) may increase by a millionfold. If management increases a thousandfold, too, disaster may be close at hand. Perhaps the forgoing story about decreasing returns to scale simply reflects old-fashioned diminishing returns to variable inputs in the presence of the *relatively* fixed input of management.

Note: The forgoing speculation notwithstanding, one should not confuse constant, increasing, and decreasing returns *to scale* with constant, increasing, and decreasing returns *to a single variable input*. Returns to scale occur when all inputs change and do so in the same proportion. When all inputs are increased in this way, they yield, respectively, constant, increasing, or decreasing *average* products. Returns to a single variable input, on the other hand, occur while some other inputs are fixed. When this variable input is increased, it yields, respectively, constant, increasing, or decreasing *marginal* products.

Returns to Scale and Isoquants

Each of the three types of returns to scale produces a distinctive pattern on an isoquant map. Consider Figure 4.4. Panel (a) pictures a family of isoquants for a production function subject to *constant* returns to scale. Note how 50 units of output are produced by 3 units of capital and 1 unit of labor (point *A*). Double both inputs, and output doubles as well (point *B*). Triple them, and output triples (point *C*). When constant returns to scale prevail, distance $0A = AB = BC$ along any ray from the origin, indicating that any given percentage change in output requires an *identical* percentage change in all inputs.

Panel (b) pictures isoquants for a production function subject to *increasing* returns to scale. Note how 50 units of output are produced by 3 units of capital and 1 unit of labor (point *D*).

Double both inputs, and output quadruples (point *G*); triple them, and it rises 18-fold (point *H*). The isoquant (now dashed) for 100 units of output in panel (a) is labeled 200 units now; the one for 150 units in (a) carries a 900-unit label in (b). When increasing returns to scale prevail, successively numbered isoquants get ever closer along any ray from the origin. In our case, although the difference between the relevant isoquants remains at 50 units of output, distance $0D > DE > EF$, indicating that any given percentage change in output requires a *smaller* percentage change in all inputs.

Panel (c), finally, pictures isoquants for a production function subject to *decreasing* returns to scale. Note how 50 units of output are produced by 3 units of capital and 1 unit of labor (point *K*). Double both inputs, and output fails to double (point *L*); triple them, and it fails to triple (point *N*). The isoquant (now dashed) for 100 units of output in panel (a) is labeled 90 units now; the one for 150 units in (a) carries a 130-unit label in (c). When decreasing returns to scale prevail, successively numbered isoquants

lie farther and farther apart along any ray from the origin. In our case, although the difference between the relevant isoquants remains at 50 units of output, distance $0K < KM < MP$, indicating that any given percentage change in output requires a *larger* percentage change in all inputs.

Returns to Scale and the Distribution of Income

In the history of economic thought, the idea that most production functions are likely to exhibit constant returns to scale gave rise to the **marginal productivity theory of income distribution,** according to which the apportionment of total output among the suppliers of human, capital, and natural resource services that made the output can be explained by the quantities of these inputs that are employed, on the one hand, and their respective marginal products, on the other hand. Consider a so-called **homogeneous production function;** it has the property that multiplication of each of the variables in the function by a constant, *c*, multi-

FIGURE 4.4

The Spacing of Isoquants

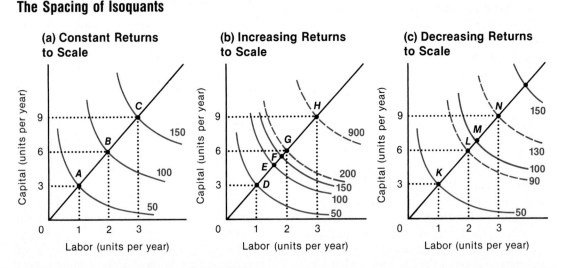

The presence of constant, increasing, or decreasing returns to scale, as in panels (a) to (c), respectively, can be recognized by looking at the spacing of isoquants.

plies the total function by some power, *n,* of that constant. For example, if $Q = f(L, K, T)$ is such a function, then $c^n Q = f(cL, cK, cT)$. When $n = 1$, this function displays constant returns to scale; when $n > 1$, it displays increasing returns to scale; and when $0 < n < 1$, it displays decreasing returns to scale. Only in the constant-returns-to-scale case do input quantities, multiplied by their respective marginal products, sum to the total product.*

EMPIRICAL STUDIES OF PRODUCTION FUNCTIONS

Economists derive their ideas about production functions in a variety of ways, including engineering estimates, market observations, time-series studies, and cross-section studies.

Engineering Estimates

Chapter 3 noted how consumer interviews and consumer clinics might be used to study demand. In an analogous approach, the economist turns to technical experts, such as engineers and agricultural scientists, to study production functions. Based on their day-to-day experience with the productive process or on the deliberate performance of controlled experiments, such experts may supply information about physical input-output relationships. For example, the German agricultural scientist Johann Heinrich von Thünen (1783–1850)—a Biography of whom appears in Chapter 4 of the *Student Workbook* that accompanies this text—was a pioneer in exploring the nature of production functions by careful experiment. He collected the kinds of data found in Table 4.1 by applying, in a given locale and year, different amounts of variable inputs to various plots of identical land. Each of the rows, labeled (A) through (J) in Table 4.1, might represent one of his experiments. In that fashion, Thünen in-

dependently discovered the law of first increasing, but eventually diminishing returns, which had been first stated (in 1767) by the French statesman, M. de Turgot (1727–1781).

Market Observations

A second approach to the study of production functions, somewhat analogous to the market experiments described in Chapter 3, is to observe the fate of firms in their respective markets. University of Chicago economist George Stigler has suggested the **survivor principle** as a method of making inferences about the production function in an industry.[2] The fundamental postulate of this principle is that competition among differently sized firms in an industry will, in the long run, allow only the technically most efficient firms to survive. Hence the characteristics of these survivors reveal those of the industry's production function.

If firms of many different sizes survive in an industry in the long run, Stigler argues, we can conclude that technical efficiency is not a function of the size of firms and that constant returns to scale exist. If, over time, firms of small size are supplanted by larger ones, we can suspect the presence of increasing returns to scale in small firms. On the other hand, if large firms eventually give way to smaller ones, the presence of decreasing returns to scale can be assumed.

Stigler studied firms in a number of industries, among them those making steel ingots by the open-hearth or Bessemer processes. He classified the firms involved by size, calculated the share of each class in industry output, and observed the historical trend of these shares. Table 4.4 is taken from his study. Stigler noted the persistent and rapid decline in the number of firms and their output shares in class (A), as well

---

*For a calculus-based treatment of this material, see Section 4C of the Calculus Appendix at the back of this book.

[2]George J. Stigler, ''The Economies of Scale,'' *The Journal of Law and Economics,* October 1958, pp. 54–71. For an appraisal, *see* William G. Shepherd, ''What Does the Survivor Technique Show about Economies of Scale?'' *The Southern Economic Journal,* July 1967, pp. 113–22.

as the less spectacular decline in classes (B), (C), and (G). Similarly, the growth in number and output shares of firms in classes (D) to (F) suggested to him constant returns to scale in this industry over a wide range of sizes of firms (from 2.5 to 25 percent of industry capacity).

Time-Series Studies

A third approach to the study of production functions is to gather statistical data for one firm or group of firms on inputs used and outputs produced in various past periods and assume that the different input-output relationships observed for these past periods can be considered alternatives available in the present. The major problem associated with this approach is *the identification problem,* the difficulty of identifying a large number of potential data from a few historical data each of which may belong to a different set of potential data. This problem has already been discussed in Chapter 3 in connection with demand functions. In the case of production-function measurement, additional problems arise. Apart from the possible unwillingness of firms to disclose the relevant data, economists

often find themselves unable to measure physical inputs and outputs. How does one measure and add together labor services when so many different types are being performed with varying degrees of skill? How is one to measure and add together capital services that come from a multitude of structures, machines, and the like, each unit of which, furthermore, is at a different stage in its life cycle? How is one to measure the output of a college, a hospital, a law firm, or a police department? How about that of the Equal Employment Opportunities Commission or the Department of Defense? Even the seemingly obvious output of an apple orchard might be difficult to measure, if not only apples, but also cider and jelly are produced, along with such by-products as hay and honey in the summer and sleigh rides in the winter. Economists, of course, do make such measurements, but these measurements are rarely immune to criticism.

Paul H. Douglas, an economist who later became a distinguished U.S. Senator, and Charles W. Cobb, a mathematician, were among the pioneers of the time-series approach to production-function measurement. Using U.S. 1899–1922 data on labor services, L, capital

TABLE 4.4

The Survivor Principle and the U.S. Steel Ingot Industry

Class	Each Firm in Class	Percentage of Industry Output Produced by: All Firms in Class			Number of Firms in Class		
		1930	1938	1951	1930	1938	1951
(A)	Under .5	7.16	6.11	4.65	39	29	22
(B)	.5 to 1	5.94	5.08	5.37	9	7	7
(C)	1 to 2.5	13.17	8.30	9.07	9	6	6
(D)	2.5 to 5	10.64	16.59	22.21	3	4	5
(E)	5 to 10	11.18	14.03	8.12	2	2	1
(F)	10 to 25	13.24	13.99	16.10	1	1	1
(G)	25 and over	38.67	35.91	34.50	1	1	1

Source: George J. Stigler, "The Economies of Scale," *The Journal of Law and Economics,* October 1958, pp. 54–71. Reprinted by permission of the University of Chicago Press. Copyright 1958 by the University of Chicago.

services, K, and aggregate real output, Q, they calculated an economywide production function for all firms in manufacturing. Their regression equation took the form $Q = AL^aK^b$, where A, a, and b were positive constants. This so-called **Cobb-Douglas production function** is a special type of constant-elasticity-of-substitution, or **CES production function.** Its elasticity of input substitution is always equal to unity. The sum of $a + b$, furthermore, is a returns-to-scale parameter. When there are constant returns to scale, the sum equals unity; $a + b$ exceeds unity for increasing returns to scale; $a + b$ falls short of unity in the presence of decreasing returns to scale.

The crucial parameters of the Cobb and Douglas study are given in row (A) of Table 4.5. The results of comparable studies by Douglas and other researchers are given in rows (B) through (E). Note that the size of a indicates the percentage increase in aggregate manufacturing output that could be expected from a 1-percent increase in labor services, all else being equal. The size of b indicates the increase in output expected from a 1-percent increase in capital services. Thus the Cobb and Douglas study, row (A), predicts a

.98-percent increase in manufacturing output from a 1-percent increase in both labor and capital inputs—almost constant returns to scale.

Cross-Section Studies

A fourth approach to the study of production functions is to gather statistical data for a given year on inputs used and outputs produced by different firms or groups of firms and assume that the different input-output relationships observed among these firms or groups can be considered present alternatives available to each of them. This approach has also been discussed in Chapter 3 in connection with the statistical measurement of demand. Table 4.6 brings together the results from a wide variety of cross-section studies.

Cross-section studies have also yielded important information about the elasticity of input substitution. While the mathematical property of the Cobb-Douglas function is such that the elasticity of substitution is always a constant equal to unity, some researchers have calculated CES production functions that allow the elasticity constant to be different from unity (or even **VES production functions** that allow for the possibil-

TABLE 4.5

Production Function Parameters: Time-Series Estimates

Country	Period	*a*	*b*	*a+b*
(A) United States	1899–1922	0.73	0.25	0.98
(B) Victoria	1907–29	0.84	0.23	1.07
(C) New South Wales	1901–27	0.78	0.20	0.98
(D) Norway	1900–55	0.76	0.20	0.96
(E) New Zealand	1915–35*	0.42	0.49	0.91

For aggregates of manufacturing firms, time-series regression studies (based on Cobb-Douglas functions of $Q = AL^aK^b$) consistently produce results close to constant returns to scale, shown by the fact that the sum of coefficients a and b approximates unity.

*Excluding 1917

Sources: Paul H. Douglas, "Are There Laws of Production?" *The American Economic Review,* March 1948, pp. 1–41; A. A. Walters, "Production and Cost Functions: An Econometric Survey," *Econometrica,* January–April 1963, pp. 1–66.

TABLE 4.6
Production Function Parameters: Cross-Section Estimates

Country	Year	Industry	*a*	*b*	*a + b*
(A) United States	1957	Furniture	0.90	0.20	1.10
		Chemicals	0.89	0.20	1.09
		Printing	0.62	0.46	1.08
		Food, beverages	0.51	0.56	1.07
	1909	Foods	0.72	0.35	1.07
	1957	Rubber, plastics	0.58	0.48	1.06
		Instruments	0.83	0.21	1.04
		Lumber	0.65	0.39	1.04
		Apparel	0.91	0.13	1.04
		Leather	0.96	0.08	1.04
		Stone, clay	0.40	0.63	1.03
		Fabricated metals	0.88	0.15	1.03
		Electrical machinery	0.66	0.38	1.03
		Nonelectrical machinery	0.62	0.40	1.02
		Transport equipment	0.79	0.23	1.02
	1919	Manufacturing	0.76	0.25	1.01
	1957	Textiles	0.88	0.12	1.00
		Paper, pulp	0.56	0.42	0.98
	1909	Metals, machinery	0.71	0.26	0.97
	1957	Primary metals	0.59	0.37	0.96
		Petroleum	0.64	0.31	0.95
(B) Canada	1952/67	Telephone	0.71	0.41	1.11
	1937	Manufacturing	0.43	0.58	1.01
(C) France	1945	Gas	0.80	0.14	0.94
(D) United Kingdom	1950	Coal	0.79	0.29	1.08
(E) South Africa	1937/38	Manufacturing	0.66	0.32	0.98
(F) India	1951	Basic chemicals	0.80	0.37	1.17
		Coal	0.71	0.44	1.15
		Paper	0.64	0.45	1.09
		Cotton	0.92	0.12	1.04
		Jute	0.84	0.14	0.98
		Sugar	0.59	0.33	0.92
		Electricity	0.20	0.67	0.87
(G) Australia	1912	Manufacturing	0.52	0.47	0.99

For firms in various industries and countries, cross-section regression studies (based on Cobb-Douglas functions of $Q = AL^a K^b$) consistently produce results suggesting the existence of close-to-constant returns to scale. This is shown by the fact that the sum of coefficients *a* and *b* approximates unity.

Sources: Same as Table 4.5; *also* A. Rodney Dobell et al., "Telephone Communications in Canada: Demand, Production, and Investment Decisions," *The Bell Journal of Economics and Management Science,* Spring 1972, pp. 175–219; John R. Moroney, "Cobb-Douglas Production Functions and Returns to Scale in U.S. Manufacturing Industry," *Western Economic Journal,* December 1967, pp. 39–51.

ity of a *variable elasticity of substitution*). Consider Table 4.7, which shows estimates of elasticities of capital-labor substitution. In general, the results indicate that capital-labor substitution is easier in primary production than in manufacturing.

SECOND THOUGHTS: THE MATTER OF X-INEFFICIENCY

In recent years, an admittedly controversial theory has become a subject of debate. If you take another look at the definition of the production function, you will notice that it is about the relationship of inputs to the *maximum* output obtainable from them. Statistical studies, however, look at *actual* output obtained. Unless we can assume that firms always get the maximum output from any given set of inputs they use, all statistical measurements of production functions are seriously flawed. In 1966, Harvey Leibenstein (1922–   )—a Biography of whom appears in Chapter 4 of the *Student Workbook* that accompanies this text—challenged economists to examine the possibility that firms do not always obtain the maximum possible output. For a century, he argued, economists have focused on the removal of *economic* inefficiency but have ignored another kind of inefficiency, which he called *X-inefficiency*. Although both of these concepts will be discussed later in more detail in Chapter 14, we can quickly establish what Leibenstein had in mind.

Economic inefficiency is a situation in which it is possible, through some reallocation of resources or goods among different firms or households, to make some or all people better off without making others worse off. Consider this example: Imagine two firms (Alpha and Beta) producing the same (or different) products with identical types of inputs (capital, K, and labor, L). If the marginal rate of technical substitution were $5K$ for $1L$ in Alpha but $1K$ for $1L$ in Beta, economic inefficiency would prevail. One could remove, for example, $5K$ from Alpha and give

TABLE 4.7

Selected Estimates of Elasticities of Capital-Labor Substitution

(A) Primary Production

Petroleum, natural gas	1.71
Metal mining	1.41
Agriculture	1.20
Nonmetallic minerals	1.18
Fishing	0.94
Coal mining	0.93

(B) Manufacturing

Coal	1.35
Publishing, printing	1.21
Paper	1.14
Nonferrous metals	1.10
Nonmetallic mineral production	1.08
Transport equipment	1.04
Petroleum products	1.04
Iron and steel	1.00
Rubber	0.98
Shipbuilding	0.97
Processed food	0.93
Machinery	0.93
Chemicals	0.90
Lumber and wood products	0.84
Grain milling production	0.81
Textiles	0.80
Leather products	0.72
Apparel	0.42

(C) Utilities and Services

Transport	1.74
Trade	1.12
Electric power	0.82

The elasticities shown above were estimated from CES-production functions calculated from U.S. and Japanese data.

Source: Adapted from K. J. Arrow, H. B. Chenery, B. S. Minhas, R. M. Solow, "Capital-Labor Substitution and Economic Efficiency," *The Review of Economics and Statistics,* August 1961, p. 240. Copyright 1961 by the President and Fellows of Harvard College.

$1K$ to Beta in return for $1L$ that would have to go to Alpha. This would leave Alpha's and Beta's outputs unchanged, while freeing $4K$. These additional units of capital, when used by Alpha, Beta, or any other firm, could then raise output somewhere in the economy. Because the removal of such economic inefficiency always involves a reallocation of resources or goods among different firms or households, this type of inefficiency is also called **allocative inefficiency.**

Leibenstein, in contrast, wanted economists to focus on a matter *internal* to a firm (and long studied in departments of business administration)—namely, the possibility that Alpha and Beta, regardless of the existence or absence of allocative inefficiency, and for reasons internal to each, might be getting less output from the resources at their disposal than was possible. Consider again our example. When Alpha's *MRTS* was 5*K* for 1*L,* its total output was, perhaps, 5,000 bushels of apples per year. Yet a better internal administration of given input quantities might have produced, let us suppose, 6,000 bushels per year. Similarly, when Beta's *MRTS* was 1*K* for 1*L,* its total output, perhaps, was 900 bushels of apples per year (or 500 bicycles per year). Yet the maximum output of Beta might have been 1,100 bushels (or 590 bicycles) instead. Naturally, this kind of situation might prevail even after the removal of allocative inefficiency, when, perhaps, Alpha's and Beta's marginal rates of technical substitution had been equalized at, say, 3*K* for 1*L*. Whenever the actual output a firm gets from given resources falls short of the maximum output it *could* get if it administered its resources better, **X-inefficiency** exists. It is measured by the gap between maximum and actual output and can be removed not by a reallocation of resources among different firms, but by a better administration of unchanged quantities of resources *within* each firm.

The Possible Cause of X-Inefficiency

Leibenstein suggested that the kind of slack or technical inefficiency just discussed was most likely to occur as firms grew beyond the stage at which a single owner could keep a watchful eye on everything. He focused on the distinction between *principals* (owners) and *agents* (people working for others). He argued that in multiperson firms exceeding, perhaps, 10 persons, agents are free to make many decisions. This is so because employment contracts clearly specify rates of pay in advance but cannot possibly specify every task workers must perform in return. These contracts are necessarily vague and incomplete on all matters relating to worker effort. As a result, workers have a lot of discretion as to the type of activities they perform, the pace of these activities, and their quality (Leibenstein called this area of worker discretion the *APQ bundle*—in reference to *activity type, pace,* and *quality*).

Consider a group of workers in any firm. Unless the group is small and the owner at all times works right along with the rest, the owner has limited control over what workers do. The larger the firm, the more owners there are likely to be, the farther removed from actual operations they must necessarily be, and the more vague must be their instructions. Consider what operating instructions can possibly be given by the owners of General Motors. Even in a much smaller firm, such as the orchard discussed early in the chapter, agents have a lot of discretion. A supervisor may send out workers to root-feed the trees, to prune, spray, or water them, to pick apples, to fix the truck, or to put a new roof on the storage barn. Or workers may be sent out to select their own activities. In either case, the activity types selected may not be the best ones for maximizing output; workers may do their work at a pace unreasonably slow; they may do a sloppy job. The effect on output can be disastrous. Trees improperly fertilized, pruned, sprayed, or watered may yield half their potential crop. Apples carelessly picked may rot in a week.

In most firms, the problem just discussed cannot possibly be removed by ensuring that a single boss knows all, sees all, controls all. The production process is too complex to eliminate all the discretion workers have over their effort. Yet,

Leibenstein contends, X-inefficiency can be reduced—for example, by motivating workers better. In contrast to his critics, furthermore, who tend to argue that it is hardly worthwhile to raise output from given resources if each $1 of extra output raises administrative cost by more than $1 (the typical case, critics contend), Leibenstein argues that X-inefficiency that can be *profitably* removed is widespread.

Evidence on X-Inefficiency

When a firm produces less output than is possible, using a given set of inputs, the firm's profit is lower than it could be. The profit is lower because inputs translate into costs, and output becomes revenue. If one could find two firms exactly alike, except for Leibenstein's X-factor (noted in Close-Up 4.2), the one with X-inefficiency should have a lower profit. Recently, an opportunity arose to test this X-inefficiency hypothesis under well-controlled conditions.[3] Investigators studied a string of restaurants operated by one company on a franchise basis. Because of the franchisor's desire to have a uniformly good reputation that would be associated with every eating place despite the fact that each was operated by a different owner, the parent company provided a great deal of direction. It prescribed the restaurant's architecture, each item on the menu, and all prices. Its head chef determined optimum recipes so that each franchisee would know exactly how many pounds of coffee to use in the coffee-making equipment, how many slices of bacon to use with an order of eggs, and how many ounces of meat to put in an entree. All ingredients, down to napkins and tableware, were supplied by the parent company, which also handled the accounting centrally. A service manual standardized service at each restaurant.

On 22 occasions, a franchisee quit, and the parent company assigned a company manager until a new franchisee could be found. These managers were invariably experienced, having worked with the parent company for many years. The investigators took such opportunities to compare the performance of identical restaurants when run by franchise-owners and when run by company managers. The results were clear-cut: Establishments run by owners made a profit of 9.5 percent on the average; those run by company managers made a profit of only 1.8 percent. Said a company executive: "When a restaurant is operated by a franchise-owner instead of a company manager . . . profits go up. This is because franchise-owners just watch the little things closer; they utilize the cooks and waitresses better; they reduce waste."

A note of caution: By itself, anecdotal evidence such as the above proves nothing about the overall importance of X-inefficiency. A more systematic evaluation will be undertaken in Chapter 14. In the meantime, however, we are warned of this important challenge to traditional production-function measurements.

SUMMARY

1. The technical relationship between inputs and output, which is called the *production function,* is a crucial factor in determining the supply of goods. The production function can be expressed in the form of an equation, a table, or a graph. It can refer to the short run or the long run. A simple, short-run production function, in which a single input only can vary, illustrates the *law of eventually diminishing returns* to increases in a variable input. Such diminishing returns might be preceded by a limited range of increasing or constant returns and always refer to the input's *marginal product.* A graphical exposition of the simple, short-run production function highlights a number of important relationships, including those between total product and mar-

---

[3]This example is based on John P. Shelton, "Allocative Efficiency vs. 'X-Efficiency': Comment," *The American Economic Review,* December 1967, pp. 1252–58.

ginal product, between total and average product, between marginal and average product, and between the average products of different inputs.

2. A more complex, short-run production function, in which two inputs can vary, shows diminishing returns to either input. It can be presented graphically by a set of isoquants.

3. An analysis of isoquants reveals *technical inefficiency* in segments with horizontal, vertical, or positive slope and *technical efficiency* in negatively sloped segments. Isoquants that are convex with respect to the origin are likely to be typical of real-world production functions. The slopes of isoquants equal the marginal rate of technical substitution of inputs and also the ratio of their marginal products. The ease or difficulty with which producers can switch among known techniques of production is measured by the *elasticity of input substitution*.

4. A long-run production function, in which all inputs are variable, can be subject to constant, increasing, or decreasing *returns to scale* (which must not be confused with constant, increasing, or decreasing *returns to a single variable input*). While the appearance of increasing returns to scale is usually associated with advantages from specialization and the operation of certain physical laws, decreasing returns to scale are generally attributed to the difficulties of managerial coordination. The presence of constant, increasing, or decreasing returns to scale is reflected in the spacing of isoquants.

5. Empirical investigations of production functions rely on engineering estimates, market observations (the survivor principle), time-series studies, and cross-section studies.

6. While the production function pertains to the relationship between input and the *maximum* output obtainable from them, statistical studies use data on actual output. Unless we can assume that firms always get the maximum output from any given set of inputs they use, all empirical measurements of production functions are seriously flawed. The theory of X-inefficiency addresses this issue.

KEY TERMS

allocative inefficiency

average (physical) product

CES production function

Cobb-Douglas production function

constant returns to a variable input

constant returns to scale

decreasing returns to scale

diminishing returns to a variable input

economic inefficiency

elasticity of input substitution

equal-product curve

homogeneous production function

increasing returns to a variable input

increasing returns to scale

isoquant

law of diminishing returns

law of variable proportions

long run

marginal (physical) product

marginal productivity theory of income distribution

marginal rate of technical substitution (*MRTS*)

point of diminishing returns

production function

production-indifference curve

productivity

short run

survivor principle

technical efficiency

technical inefficiency

VES production function

X-inefficiency

HANDS-ON PRACTICE

✓ Exercise #1

Consider the data of Table 4.8. Calculate the marginal and the average products of capital.

TABLE 4.8

Units of Capital Used (given constant labor and land)	Maximum Total Product
0	0
1	500
2	900
3	1200
4	1400
5	1500

Solution:

See Table 4.9.

TABLE 4.9

Units of Capital	Maximum Total Product	Marginal Product of Capital	Average Product of Capital
0	0		?
		500	
1	500		500
		400	
2	900		450
		300	
3	1200		400
		200	
4	1400		350
		100	
5	1500		300

Exercise #2

Consider Table 4.2, "A Complex Production Function." Calculate (a) a row for 8 units of capital, then (b) a column for 8 units of labor.

Finally, calculate (c) the marginal products of labor along the new capital row and then the marginal products of capital along the new labor column.

Solution:

a. Given the production function of $Q = 282 \sqrt{K \cdot L}$, the entries in the 8-units-of-capital row are $282\sqrt{8 \cdot 1} = 798$; $282\sqrt{8 \cdot 2} = 1128$; $282\sqrt{8 \cdot 3} = 1382$; $282\sqrt{8 \cdot 4} = 1595$; $282\sqrt{8 \cdot 5} = 1784$; $282\sqrt{8 \cdot 6} = 1954$; $282\sqrt{8 \cdot 7} = 2110$; and $282\sqrt{8 \cdot 8} = 2256$.

b. Similarly, the entries in the 8-units-of-labor column are $282 \sqrt{1 \cdot 8} = 798$; $282\sqrt{2 \cdot 8} = 1128$; $282 \sqrt{3 \cdot 8} = 1382$; $282 \sqrt{4 \cdot 8} = 1595$; $282 \sqrt{5 \cdot 8} = 1784$; $282 \sqrt{6 \cdot 8} = 1954$; $282 \sqrt{7 \cdot 8} = 2110$; and $282 \sqrt{8 \cdot 8} = 2256$.

c. Given the symmetry, the numbers, although measured in different units, are the same: 330, 254, 213, 189, 170, 156, 146. (Can you see why adding all these marginal products to the initial 798 yields the ultimate 2256?)

Exercise #3

The production function for picking wild raspberries is $Q = 100 \sqrt{L}$, where Q is the quantity picked and L represents units of labor input. Similar to text Figure 4.1, create a graph of total, average, and marginal product for 1 to 9 units of labor. (*Hint:* The marginal product equals $50/\sqrt{L}$.)

Solution:

One can calculate the necessary data as follows.

	Labor Units								
	1	2	3	4	5	6	7	8	9
Total Product, $Q = 100\sqrt{L}$	100	141.4	173.2	200	223.6	244.9	264.6	282.8	300
Average Product, Q/L	100	70.7	57.7	50	44.7	40.8	37.8	35.4	33.3
Marginal Product, $50/\sqrt{L}$	50	35.4	28.9	25	22.4	20.4	18.9	17.7	16.7

Figure 4.5 illustrates the relationships involved.

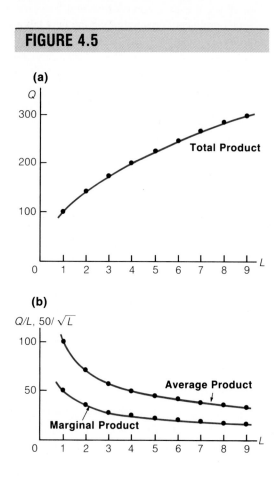

FIGURE 4.5

(a)

(b)

QUESTIONS AND PROBLEMS

1. Consider the data below. Assume other inputs and technology are fixed. Calculate the marginal and average products of labor.

Labor (hours per year)	Total Product (tons per year)
0	0
10	500
20	800
30	900

2. Take another look at Figure 4.1, ''Total, Marginal, and Average Product.''
  a. What do you think is the marginal product of *nonlabor* inputs in stages I, II, and III?
  b. How would the average-product and marginal-product lines in panel (b) look if the total-product line were straight, such as line 0*ef* in panel (a)?

3. Mr. A: If one increased the scale of a flea by a factor of 1,000, one would increase its strength by a million (strength of wings and muscles is proportional to their cross-section) but would increase its weight by a billion (weight is proportional to volume). Such a scaled-up flea, therefore, couldn't jump at all. There is a lesson in this for the large firm.

  Ms. B: Of course. And there is another lesson in the fate of the dinosaurs. They died out because their nervous systems and pea-sized brains couldn't keep up with their overgrown bodies.
Explain using the concepts of returns to scale.

4. John R. Moroney's cross-section study of U.S. manufacturing yielded the 1958 data given in the accompanying table.[4] Applying

Industry	Value Added (in thousands of dollars)	
	In Smallest Plant	In Largest Plant
Furniture	85.1	726.9
Chemicals	365.7	6,414.3
Printing	134.7	321.5
Food, beverages	191.5	774.6
Rubber, plastics	203.7	6,452.7
Instruments	148.0	1,528.5
Lumber	40.6	201.1
Apparel	88.6	1,013.9
Leather	202.0	1,475.9
Stone, clay	156.2	575.5
Fabricated metals	167.1	645.0
Transport equipment	194.0	5,196.4
Textiles	203.4	2,277.9
Paper, pulp	360.7	5,156.9
Primary metals	344.3	9,349.2
Petroleum	299.1	5,046.7

Stigler's survivor principle, the author concluded that the wide variation in plant sizes evidenced by these data provided independent confirmation of the existence in U.S. manufacturing of constant returns to scale (this story was also told by Table 4.1). Do you agree? Why or why not?

5. Consider Table 4.6, "Production Function Parameters: Cross-Section Estimates." What would happen to British coal output if labor and capital inputs each were increased by 1 percent? What if capital only was increased by 1 percent? What if capital was decreased by 1 percent?

6. To the extent that its existence can be traced to insufficient worker motivation, how, if at all, could one ever *eliminate* X-inefficiency? (*Hints:* Consider the possible role of external incentives, such as monetary rewards or public praise, or of internal incentives, such as feelings of joy or guilt. Consider the possible role of worker participation in management. If you know anything about them, draw on the Swedish, Soviet, or Yugoslav experiences.)

7. Are the following statements true or false?

a. In the presence of diminishing returns, a firm can do nothing to increase the marginal product of its variable input.

b. When marginal product rises, average product rises.

c. When marginal product falls, average product falls.

d. If the law of diminishing returns did not hold, one could grow the annual world crop of wheat in a single flower pot.

e. The elasticity of input substitution equals the slope of an isoquant.

8. Are the following statements true or false?

a. The existence of increasing returns to scale refutes the law of diminishing returns.

b. In the presence of decreasing returns to

scale, a firm can do nothing to increase the average product of its inputs.

c. If one constructed a total-product mountain, as suggested in the section on "The Case of Two Variable Inputs," the mountain would be very steep in the presence of increasing returns to scale and very flat in the presence of decreasing returns to scale.

d. In the presence of increasing returns to scale, a decrease in scale reduces the average products of all inputs.

e. In the presence of decreasing returns to scale, an increase in scale reduces the average products of all inputs.

f. X-inefficiency might be discovered by studying the operations of a single firm.

g. Allocative inefficiency can never be found by studying the operations of a single firm.

*9. Consider the following production functions; using calculus, calculate in each case the marginal products and the average products of all inputs.

a. $Q = f(L, K, T) = 100L^2KT$

b. $Q = f(L, K) = 10L + 5K - L^2 - 2K^2 + 3LK$

c. $Q = L^{.64}K^{.36}$ (a production function for Australia, 1934–35, estimated by Douglas and Gunn)

d. $Q = L^{.43}K^{.58}$ (a production function for Canada, 1937, estimated by Douglas and Daly)

e. $Q = L^aK^b$

In each case, what would your precise answers be if f. $L = 1.5$, $K = 2$, and (where applicable) $T = 8$, while $a = 2$ and $b = 3$?

10. Check each of the following for accuracy:

a. These production functions embody constant returns to scale:

i) $Q = 20L$

ii) the function given in Analytical Example 4.2

b. These production functions embody increasing returns to scale:

i) $Q = 3L^3 + 5LK^2 + K^3$

---

[4]John R. Moroney, "Cobb-Douglas Production Functions and Returns to Scale in U.S. Manufacturing Industry," *Western Economic Journal*, December 1967, p. 49. Copyright Western Economic Association, 1967 and 1968.

ii) $Q = 25K^6 - L^2K^4$

c. These production functions embody decreasing returns to scale:

i) $Q = \dfrac{14}{L} - \dfrac{20}{K}$

ii) $Q = \dfrac{3}{L^2} + \dfrac{25}{LK} + \dfrac{6}{K^2}$

11. Use the data of the accompanying table to compute the average (physical) product of labor as well as the marginal (physical) product of labor. (Assume other inputs are fixed.)

Point	Labor	Total Product
A	0	0
B	3	90
C	4.8	200
D	6	370
E	8.3	800
F	11.7	1130
G	13.6	1180 (maximum)
H	16.9	990

12. Graph the total, average, and marginal products from Problem 11 in a graph like Figure 4.1.

13. The accompanying table gives points on three different isoquants. Plot these points in a graph and connect them by smooth curves.

Isoquants					
I_0		I_1		I_2	
K	T	K	T	K	T
A: 12	1	F: 11.4	4.4	L: 13	7.7
B: 8	3	G: 8.2	7	M: 10.4	10
C: 3.3	8	H: 6	10	N: 8.4	13
D: 1.7	12	K: 4.8	13		
E: 1.1	15				

14. Between each of the adjacent points on isoquant I_0 compute the marginal rate of technical substitution of land, T, for capital, K. Then compute the elasticity of input substitution between H and K.

SELECTED READINGS

Alessi, Louis de. "Property Rights, Transaction Costs, and X-Efficiency: An Essay in Economic Theory," *The American Economic Review*, March 1983, pp. 64–81.

> A sharp critique of the X-efficiency concept. For a reply, *see* Harvey Leibenstein, "Property Rights and X-Efficiency: Comment," *The American Economic Review*, September 1983, pp. 831–42.

Cobb, Charles W., and Paul H. Douglas. "A Theory of Production," *The American Economic Review*, March 1928, pp. 139–65.

> The original article on what is now called the Cobb-Douglas production function.

Dempsey, Bernard W. *The Frontier Wage*. Chicago: Loyola University Press, 1960.

> A complete translation of volume 2, section 1 of Thünen's work on income distribution by marginal products, originally published in 1850.

Douglas, Paul H. *The Theory of Wages*. New York: Macmillan, 1934.

> A pathbreaking statistical study of U.S. production functions. *See also idem.* "Are There Laws of Production?" *The American Economic Review*, March 1948, pp. 1–41, the author's presidential address to the American Economic Association.

Leibenstein, Harvey. "Allocative Efficiency vs. 'X-Efficiency,' " *The American Economic Review*, June 1966, pp. 392–415.

> The original article on X-efficiency theory. It is reprinted in *idem.*, *Beyond Economic Man: A New Foundation for Microeconomics.* Cambridge, Mass.: Harvard University Press, 1976, chap. 3. For elaborations, see the Appendix to this book ("Toward a Mathematical Formalization of X-Efficiency Theory"), as well as *idem.* "Aspects of the X-Efficiency Theory of the Firm," *The Bell Journal of Economics and Management Science*, Autumn 1975, pp. 580–606; "On the Basic Proposition of X-Efficiency Theory," *The American Economic Review*, May 1978, p. 328–34; and "A Branch of Economics Is Missing: Micro-Micro Theory," *Journal of Economic Literature*, June 1979, pp. 477–502.

Lovell, C. A. Knox. "Estimation and Prediction with CES and VES Production Functions," *International Economic Review*, October 1973, pp. 676–92.

Moore, John H. "Agency Costs, Technological Change, and Soviet Central Planning," *The Journal of Law and Economics*, October 1981, pp. 189–214.

An interesting application of the X-efficiency concept to the Soviet economy—the largest hierarchical management system in the world. The attempt to run an entire economy like a single firm creates *agency costs* (less output and less technical innovation than possible) because agents (such as workers) who carry out activities on behalf of some principal (such as a boss or a central planing board), unless closely monitored, will maximize their own welfare and will behave nonoptimally from the principal's point of view.

Stigler, George J. "The Xistence of X-Efficiency," *The American Economic Review,* March 1976, pp. 213–16.

> The 1982 winner of the Nobel Prize in economics criticizes the Leibenstein theory. For a reply, *see* Harvey Leibenstein. "X-Inefficiency Xists—Reply to an Xorcist," *The American Economic Review,* March 1978, pp. 203–11; and "Microeconomics and X-Efficiency Theory: If There Is No Crisis, There Ought to Be," *The Public Interest, Special Issue 1980: The Crisis in Economic Theory,* pp. 97–110.

COMPUTER PROGRAMS

The KOHLER-3 personal-computer diskettes that accompany this book contain one program of particular interest to this chapter:

4. The Technology of the Firm includes a 25-question multiple-choice test with immediate responses to incorrect answers as well as numerous exercises concerning the production function.

ANALYTICAL EXAMPLE 4.1

MARGINAL PRODUCTS IN PROFESSIONAL BASKETBALL

Production functions can be estimated not only for orchards and steel plants but for more unusual types of producers, such as professional basketball teams. An unusual type of production function was calculated for the 1976–77 season of the National Basketball Association. Output was measured as the ratio of final scores of games; 10 types of inputs were entered in the production function, from the ratio of field-goal-shooting percentages to the ratio of turnovers, from play at home or in the opponent's court to the difference in the number of blocked shots. The accompanying table shows the estimated marginal products of all of these basketball inputs.

Inputs	League	Boston	Buffalo	N.Y. Knicks	N.Y. Nets
Field-goal–shooting percentage	.6245	.5445	.6637	.5262	.5858
Free-throw–shooting percentage	.1132	.0733	.1600	.0943	.1238
Offensive rebounds	.0737	.0636	.0792	.0565	.0734
Defensive rebounds	.0553	.0753	.0428	.1169	−.0036
Assists	.0121	.0326	−.0100	.0185	.0398
Personal fouls	−.1178	−.1590	−.1033	−.1182	−.1182
Steals	.0160	.0156	.0093	.0408	.0211
Turnovers	−.1094	−.0702	−.1129	−.1329	−.0739
Home court	.0135	.0147	.0071	.0298	−.0025
Blocked shots	.0008	.0022	−.0005	.0011	.0009

The first entry indicates, for the league as a whole, a .6245 increase in the ratio of final scores for a 1-unit increase in that of field-goal–shooting percentages. Note how personal fouls and turnovers had negative marginal products, while the advantage of the home court was much smaller than usually supposed.

Source: Thomas A. Zak, Cliff J. Huang, John J. Siegfried, "Production Efficiency: The Case of Professional Basketball," *Journal of Business,* July 1979, pp. 379–92. Table adapted by permission of the University of Chicago Press. Copyright 1979 by the University of Chicago.

ANALYTICAL EXAMPLE 4.2

THE PRODUCTION OF SHAKESPEARE PERFORMANCES

Analytical Example 3.2 discussed the estimation of a demand function for performances by Britain's Royal Shakespeare Company during the 1965–80 period. The same study estimated a production function as well. This function took the form

$$Q = e^{.39Z}L^{.62}K^{.33}$$

where Q was the quantity of cultural experiences produced (measured in paid attendance units), L was labor used (including the services of everyone involved, from designers, directors, and players to carpenters, program sellers, and secretaries), K was capital used (measured by depreciation, rental, utilities, and similar expenses), and Z was a shift variable ($=0$ for the Aldwych Theatre in London, $=1$ for the Memorial Theatre in Stratford-on-Avon). The production functions for the two theaters, and the average input-output combination prevailing during the period, are shown in the accompanying graph.

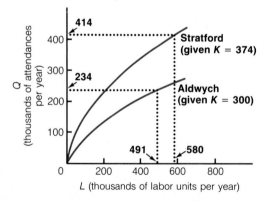

Source: James H. Gapinski, "The Economics of Performing Shakespeare," *The American Economic Review,* June 1984, pp. 458–66.

ANALYTICAL EXAMPLE 4.3

EMPIRICAL ESTIMATES OF ISOQUANTS

The accompanying graph shows empirical estimates of isoquants, based on U.S. and Japanese data.

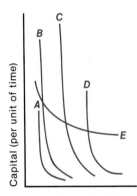

The isoquants can cross because five graphs have been superimposed on each other. Each isoquant refers to a different set of industries:

A = textiles, wood products, grain milling
B = agriculture, mining, paper, nonferrous metals
C = steel, rubber, transport equipment
D = apparel, personal services
E = electric power

Can you guess why isoquant E has such a different shape?

Source: K. J. Arrow, H. B. Chenery, B. S. Minhas, R. M. Solow, "Capital-Labor Substitution and Economic Efficiency," *The Review of Economics and Statistics,* August 1961, p. 240. Copyright 1961 by the President and Fellows of Harvard College. Reprinted by permission of North-Holland Publishing Company.

ANALYTICAL EXAMPLE 4.4

THE ENERGY CRISIS AND INPUT SUBSTITUTION IN U.S. AGRICULTURE

American agriculture during this century has experienced sizable increases in productivity, many of them related to increased use of energy. In 1979, U.S. farms were using more than 4 million tractors, 3 million trucks, and half a million combines. Some 35 million acres were irrigated; 20 million tons of fertilizer and almost half a million tons of pesticides were used. Because all these inputs require energy for their manufacture or operation, U.S. agriculture seems very susceptible to disruption in energy supplies. This seems all the more true because the biological nature of agriculture is such that serious output loss occurs unless operations are performed regularly or during critical periods. (Consider the importance of regularity in the environmental control of poultry housing or the importance of timing in the planting of corn and the harvesting of wheat.)

In order to gauge possibilities for input substitution that would make agriculture less dependent on regular and sufficient energy supplies, an agricultural production function was estimated. Agricultural output was taken to be a function of land, hired labor, mechanical energy (in the form of farm machinery and fuels), and chemical energy (fertilizers and pesticides). The accompanying table lists the elasticities of substitution derived from this function.

| Region | Elasticities of Substitution Between: | | | | |
	Land and Mechanical Energy (1)	Land and Chemical Energy (2)	Hired Labor and Mechanical Energy (3)	Hired Labor and Chemical Energy (4)	Mechanical Energy and Chemical Energy (5)
United States	1.36	0.78	1.91	0.27	1.19
Northeast	1.35	0.84	2.12	0.23	1.48
Appalachian	1.35	0.87	1.99	0.25	1.31
Southeast	1.33	0.92	1.97	0.26	1.38
Lake states	1.37	0.80	1.98	0.23	1.16
Corn belt	1.39	0.80	2.26	0.05	1.16
Delta states	1.35	0.85	2.00	0.25	1.33
Northern plains	1.37	0.72	2.05	0.60	0.96
Southern plains	1.35	0.76	1.79	0.31	1.06
Mountain	1.34	0.65	1.67	0.36	0.99
Pacific	1.35	0.72	1.98	0.18	1.42

As the frequency of rather high elasticity estimates indicates, there is a surprising degree of flexibility in the use of agricultural inputs. If energy supplies were seriously reduced, U.S. agricultural output could be maintained by substituting land or labor for mechanical energy, as in columns (1) and (3). It would be much harder to substitute them for chemical energy, as in columns (2) and (4). In the short run, it would, of course, be easiest to substitute one form of energy (say, tractor cultivation) for another (say, chemical weed control), as column (5) indicates.

Note the regional elasticity differences for any given policy. A policy maker would be well advised to take account of them. Consider the substitution of labor for machinery in column (3). This is considerably easier in the Corn Belt ($\sigma = 2.26$), where large-scale corn and soybean production takes place, than in the Mountain Region ($\sigma = 1.67$), where small-scale operations produce specialized crops on irrigated plots of land.

Source: Kerry Webb and Marvin Duncan, "Energy Alternatives in U.S. Crop Production," *Federal Reserve Bank of Kansas City Economic Review*, February 1979, pp. 14–23.

ANALYTICAL EXAMPLE

ANALYTICAL EXAMPLE 4.5

THE PRODUCTION OF CULTURE

One economist recently estimated production functions for five of the "fine arts": theater, opera, symphony, ballet, and modern dance. Using 1966–74 Ford Foundation data for 164 performing arts companies, James Gapinski measured output by the number of cultural experiences enjoyed by patrons and then related it to three types of inputs: labor services of artists, labor services of "adjuvants" (administrators, box office and maintenance help, parking lot attendants, promotional personnel, stage hands, ushers, and the like), and capital services (of structures, musical instruments, stage sets, costumes, scores, scripts, and the like).

The accompanying table shows excerpts from a multitude of fascinating implications of the estimated production functions.

Part A	Theater	Opera	Symphony	Ballet
Scale Coefficient				
$\lambda = 0.25$	0.2823	0.2802	0.3079	0.1315
$\lambda = 0.75$	0.7610	0.7640	0.7741	0.7309
$\lambda = 1.25$	1.2398	1.2359	1.2263	1.2036
$\lambda = 2.00$	1.9438	1.9517	1.9129	1.4531
$\lambda = 3.00$	2.7445	2.9391	2.8260	1.3347
$\lambda = 4.00$	3.2361	3.9701	3.6750	1.1139

Part B	Theater	Opera	Symphony	Ballet
Elasticity of Input Substitution				
1. Artists, capital	0.7533	0.7198	0.8510	0.7223
2. Adjuvants, capital	1.1225	1.3308	1.1189	1.7114
3. Artists, adjuvants	1.4134	3.6444	2.1612	1.5506

Part (A) shows what happened to output when all inputs were simultaneously multiplied by some coefficient, such as 0.25 or 4.00. Theater, opera, and symphony showed decreasing returns to scale for all scalar adjustments. (For example, the reduction of all theater inputs to 25 percent reduced theater output to only 28.23 percent; a 4-fold increase of all theater inputs raised theater output only 3.2361-fold.) Ballet, however, was a maverick, showing increasing returns to scale for input decreases and extreme decreasing returns to scale for input increases. (For example, a reduction of all ballet inputs to 25 percent reduced ballet output to 13.15 percent; a 4-fold increase of all ballet inputs raised ballet output only 1.1139-fold.)

Part (B) shows estimates of the elasticity of substitution for different input pairs. Note that this elasticity is uniformly low for artists and capital (1), indicating that they

ANALYTICAL EXAMPLE

cannot very easily be substituted for one another. Elasticity is not as low for adjuvants and capital (2). Finally, the elasticity is fairly high for artists and adjuvants (3): one type of labor can easily be substituted for another type.

Source: James H. Gapinski, "The Production of Culture," *The Review of Economics and Statistics,* November 1980, p. 584. Copyright © 1980 by the President and Fellows of Harvard College. Reprinted by permission of North-Holland Publishing Company.

ANALYTICAL EXAMPLE 4.6

CAPITAL-LABOR SUBSTITUTION IN SOVIET ECONOMIC GROWTH

In 1950, a 10-percent increase in capital by itself would have increased the output of Soviet industry (mining, manufacturing, power) by almost 9 percent; by 1969, the output response to a 10-percent increase in capital had dropped to only 4 percent. This phenomenon has been explained with the help of a CES-production function for Soviet industry for the 1950–69 period. The accompanying graph shows the estimated production isoquant between the services of capital, *K,* and labor, *L.* An elasticity of capital-labor substitution significantly less than unity was calculated. The low elasticity estimate ($\sigma = .403$) was interpreted as foreshadowing future difficulties with the traditional Soviet growth strategy of capital-labor substitution.

From 1950–69, Soviet capital inputs grew rapidly (at annual rates between 7.9 and 12.6 percent); labor inputs grew much more slowly, if at all (at annual rates from −1.3 to +5.8 percent). As one input rose relative to the other, the effect was the same as if it had risen while the other was constant: diminishing returns set in. Output increases based on further capital accumulation decreased.

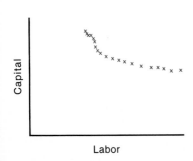

Source: Martin L. Weitzman, "Soviet Postwar Economic Growth and Capital-Labor Substitution," *American Economic Review,* September 1970, vol. LX, No. 4, pp. 676–92.

CLOSE-UP 4.1

THE OPTIMUM SIZE OF CARGO SHIPS

In recent years, the average size of cargo ships has been increasing rapidly, but a limit to this trend is in sight. The output of a ship can be viewed as the *quantity of cargo it hauls per mile.* Because the quantity of labor and materials required to build a container is a function of its surface area, while holding and hauling capacity is a function of the volume enclosed, the hauling operations of a ship tend to be subject to increasing returns to scale. The hauling cost per ton tends to *decrease* with larger ship size.

A ship in port, however, is a different matter from a ship at sea. The output of a ship in port is better viewed as the *quantity of cargo it loads or unloads per day.* The capacity to handle cargo in port tends to be a function of the length of the ship because length determines the number of possible hatches and cranes. Because length cannot grow in proportion to volume, the handling operations of a ship tend to be subject to decreasing returns to scale. The handling cost per ton tends to *increase* with larger ship size.

Economies of scale in *hauling* cargo must, therefore, be traded off against diseconomies in *handling* it. This yields an optimum ship size at which the marginal benefit of large size (lower hauling cost per ton) just equals the associated marginal cost (higher handling cost per ton).

In 1980, the Chevron Shipping Company subjected four of its supertankers to "downsizing," a process akin to removing the center leaf of a dining room table and shoving the table back together again. Four 200,000-ton ships were sliced apart, a 100-foot section was removed from the middle of each, and the remainder was re-welded together. The result was a set of four 150,000-ton tankers capable of operating in ports that were previously inaccessible.

Sources: Jan Owen Jansson and Dan Shneerson, "Economies of Scale of General Cargo Ships," *The Review of Economics and Statistics,* May 1978, pp. 287–93; "Shrinking the Oversized Supertanker," *The New York Times,* July 18, 1980, pp. D1 and 6.

CLOSE-UP 4.2

A TALE OF TWO FORD PLANTS: X-INEFFICIENCY

In the preface to his *Beyond Economic Man,* Leibenstein introduces his thoughts on X-efficiency with a quotation from Tolstoy's *War and Peace:*

> . . . military science assumes the strength of an army to be identical with its numbers. Military science says that the more troops the greater the strength. *Les gros battaillons ont toujours raison* (Large battalions are always victorious). . . .
>
> In military affairs the strength of an army is the product of its mass and some unknown X. . . .

> That unknown quantity is the spirit of the army, . . .
>
> The spirit of an army is the factor which multiplied by the mass gives the resulting force. To define and express the significance of this unknown factor—the spirit of an army—is a problem for science.
>
> This problem is only solvable if we cease arbitrarily to substitute for the unknown x itself the conditions under which that force becomes apparent—such as the commands of the general, the equipment employed, and so on—mistaking these for the real significance

of the factor, and if we recognize this unknown quantity in its entirety as being the greater or lesser desire to fight and to face danger.

Leibenstein expands:

Without straining his meaning too much, Tolstoy's argument is similar to one of the central theses of this volume, despite the fact that his concern is the art of war, and mine economics, one of the arts of peace. To shift to the common language of economics, what Tolstoy is saying is that merely knowing the observable *inputs* (the number of guns, men, the commands of the generals, and so on) does not tell you the outcome, contrary to the claims of the "military scientists." Something else is involved, an X-factor that Tolstoy equates with "spirit." Similarly, in . . . this volume I argue that knowing the allocation of inputs and the state of the arts of production is not enough, there is also something else involved—what I have called the X-efficiency element.

The recent experience of Ford Motor Company plants in Europe provides support for Leibenstein's contention. Two identical Ford plants were erected at Saarlouis, West Germany, and at Halewood, England. A casual visitor to the sleek gray buildings in either town finds them dominated by robot welders, vast automated presses, and shiny new cars rolling off the assembly line. Yet this is where the resemblance ends. Consider the accompanying data:

	Germany	Britain
Daily output		
anticipated	1,015 cars	1,015 cars
actual	1,200 cars	800 cars
Workers employed	7,762	10,040
Labor hours per identical car	21	40

Ford officials in Europe say that the difference between the two plants comes down to the *attitude of workers.* In England, strikes are frequent; in Germany, unknown. In England, workers are visible everywhere, often reading, eating, or even kicking soccer balls; in Germany, the plant appears almost depopulated and workers always seem hard at work. In England, workers get twice as many quality demerits as in their German sister plant. In England, featherbedding is rampant (a doctor certified that it takes two men to lift the hood onto the car body, but in fact one man does it, while the other one watches); in Germany, featherbedding is absent. In England, visitors are jeered (and worse); in Germany, they are treated with extreme courtesy. In England, despite many union-made safety rules, the injury rate is high; in Germany, it is the lowest in Ford's European operations. . . .

Sources: Steven Rattner, "A Tale of Two Ford Plants: German Unit Far Outpaces One in Britain," *The New York Times,* October 13, 1981, pp. D1 and D4; Harvey Leibenstein, *Beyond Economic Man: A New Foundation for Microeconomics* (Cambridge, Mass.: Harvard University Press, 1976).

CLOSE-UP 4.3

THE BATTLE FOR CORPORATE CONTROL

In the 1980s, corporate takeovers have been very big business. In the process, names of once obscure investors, such as Carl Icahn, David Murdock, and T. Boone Pickens, became household words. Some have praised the corporate raiders for identifying badly managed firms and cleaning house by firing bad managers and selling off unproductive assets. According to this view, takeovers and the threat of takeovers whips everybody into shape and eliminates technical inefficiency. Even though individual managers are displaced and may even lose their organization-specific human capital, society benefits. A contrary view claims that the modern financial buccaneers merely pirate their victims' assets, then depart leaving the companies in shambles.

Evidence suggests that the former view is more accurate. Successful takeovers, presumably by encouraging greater technical efficiency, have increased stockholder wealth by 20 to 35 percent, a total of $54 billion from 1981–86 alone. Corporate restructurings, prompted in large part by the *threat* of takeover, have had a similar effect. (The Phillips, Unocal, Arco restructuring alone created $6.6 billion in stockholder wealth.) On the contrary, stockholders of companies that prevented takeovers (and spent real resources for that purpose) have had losses.

What have been the weapons in the battles fought? Outsiders eager to gain control of corporate resources have used these:

a. mergers (the bidder negotiates a takeover agreement with the target company management; the stockholders then vote to accept or reject the terms)

b. tender offers (the bidder directly turns to the target company stockholders offering to buy some or all of their stock; the offer is termed "hostile" if opposed by target company management, "friendly" if approved by it)

c. proxy contests (a dissident stockholder group attempts to replace the corporate board of directors by persuading stockholders to vote accordingly)

d. leveraged buyouts (the shareholders' equity is bought with borrowed funds)

Managements opposing takeovers have, in turn, used weapons such as these:

a. litigation

b. the passing of state government antitakeover laws

c. the purchase at a premium of blocks of target company stock already held by hostile suitors (a practice called *greenmail*)

d. poison pills (shareholder rights amendments that make takeovers extremely costly)

Sources: Gregg A. Jarrell, James A. Brickley, and Jeffry M. Netter, "The Market for Corporate Control: The Empirical Evidence Since 1980," *Journal of Economic Perspectives,"* Winter 1988, pp. 49–68. For an earlier analysis, see Council of Economic Advisers to the President, "The Market for Corporate Control," *Economic Report of the President, 1985* (Washington, D.C.: U.S. Government Printing Office, 1985), pp. 187–216.

5

Costs and the Supply of Goods

The production function, discussed in the previous chapter, tells us what a firm *can* do, what kinds of input-to-output conversions lie in the realm of the possible. What a firm *will* do, however, is quite another matter. In order to predict which of many possible courses of action a firm will choose, we must also know what the firm seeks to accomplish.

THE MOTIVATION OF FIRMS

Throughout this book, we will assume that firms follow the optimization principle in order to *maximize the profit* they derive from their economic choices. We will assume, in short, that people setting up and running firms consider a high money income very important for achieving their particular goals in life. We will attribute to them the hope that the revenues they derive from the sale of goods will exceed, as much as possible, the costs they must incur during the production of these goods. In a world of uncertainty, running a firm clearly amounts to taking a chance: Hoped-for-profits may fail to materialize. Losses may take their place if lower-than-expected revenues or higher-than-expected costs

appear, at which point owners of firms may note belatedly that it would have been better not to have gone into business at all. It does not seem unreasonable, therefore, to assume that those people who nevertheless go into business—and by that very fact indicate a desire to increase their money incomes beyond what they would otherwise be—will conduct that business in such a fashion as to get the greatest possible profit. For this reason, we will assume that owners of firms or the managers they appoint keep a sharp eye on business affairs and are always ready to exploit whatever opportunity presents itself to increase profit to the maximum possible level.

However, as in the earlier discussion of utility maximization by consumers, a word of warning is in order. We are not assuming that all owners of firms must be selfish and exploitative, nor are we approving of such orientation. Nor are we assuming that those who make profits (rather than losses) will use their higher money incomes to promote selfish purposes. There is nothing to prevent the monetarily successful owners of a firm from using their profits to help the poor or to do any one of a million ''unselfish'' things. Nor is there anything, of course, to force profit makers into doing any of these ''socially responsible'' things. Just like wage income, profit can be large or small (and unlike wage income, it can even be negative); just like wage income, it represents power to pursue *whatever* goals the recipients wish to pursue.

It is easy to see how the profit-maximization goal can help us forge a link between the production function and the supply of goods in the market. Given the market prices of inputs, physical input quantities can be translated into costs of production. Given the market price of output, physical output quantities can be translated into revenues. As a result, the output quantity that maximizes the difference between total revenue and total cost can be identified, and, economists postulate, this is the output quantity a profit-maximizing firm will supply. (When the difference between total revenue and total cost is positive, such as $+100$ or $+21$, maximizing it ensures the highest of all possible profits. When the difference is negative, such as -15 or -60, maximizing it ensures the lowest of all possible losses.)

ACCOUNTING COST VERSUS OPPORTUNITY COST

Cost plays a very important role in the supply of goods, but cost means many things to many people. The proverbial person in the street, if asked to list costs of production, would most likely mention current expenditures, especially cash expenditures (like, perhaps, for wages or raw materials). Business accountants are more careful, recognizing as costs of production also items that may require neither current nor cash expenditures (such as periodic insurance premiums, property taxes, or depreciation allowances). Yet the accountant's concept remains far less sophisticated than the economist's notion of *opportunity cost,* which will be utilized here.

The accountant focuses on **explicit costs.** These are highly visible costs that the owners of firms incur when acquiring resource services from other households or when acquiring intermediate goods from other firms. These visible expenditures include wages and salaries paid for the use of other people's labor, rental payments for the use of other people's natural or capital resources, interest payments for the use of other people's money, payments for raw materials or services supplied by other firms, and payments of taxes. With the exception of depreciation allowances (which return to the owners of firms, over the lifetime of their plant and equipment, an amount of tax-free revenue equal to the historical cost of their assets), the accountant ignores a whole range of **implicit costs.** These are hidden costs that the owners of firms incur when using the services of their own resources in their own firms instead of hiring them out to collect the maximum income available elsewhere. When owners work in their firms or when they use their own land, equipment, and money in their firms, they forgo the wages, rent, and interest they might have earned in their best outside alternatives. The economist insists that such forgone incomes should be added to explicit costs whenever the costs of production are to be determined.

The economist, as we first learned in Chapter 1, always pictures costs in terms of forgone alternatives. When resources are used to produce one good, these resources cannot be used to make other goods; the lost opportunity of having these other goods represents *cost* in the economist's sense. Surely, economists argue, such opportunity cost is incurred regardless of whether the resources that make one good instead of another happen to be owned by outsiders or by the owners of the firm in which they are used and whether the right to their use is acquired for cash or cash plays no role at all. Indeed, picture the case of a Robinson Crusoe who produces goods by applying only his own labor to natural resources owned by no one. Accounting cost would be zero, but opportunity cost would be all too real. Economists, therefore, prefer measuring the cost of one good as the maximum value of other goods that could have been made instead. They estimate such cost always as the *sum* of explicit and implicit ones, or as the minimum payment necessary to keep all resources (regardless of ownership) in their present employment. This minimum payment equals, of course, the maximum payment these resources could get elsewhere. It measures, therefore, the value of output they could produce in their best alternative employment.

COSTS IN THE SHORT RUN

Let us return to the orchard discussed in the previous chapter. Table 4.1, "A Simple Production Function," depicted the orchard's operations in the short run when the firm was saddled with some productive inputs the quantities of which it could not vary (see p. 99). The number of trees, the quantity of fertilizer, the set of equipment, and the size of the management team, perhaps, were the fixed inputs; the number of hired workers was the only variable input. The potential levels of production associated with all the technically efficient input combinations, formerly listed in rows (A) to (H) of Table 4.1, have been reproduced as column (1) of Table 5.1. This table also shows the various types of cost associated with each of these potential crops.

TABLE 5.1

Short-Run Cost Alternatives

Total Product (bushels of apples per year)	Fixed Cost	Variable Cost	Total Cost	Average Fixed Cost	Average Variable Cost	Average Total Cost	Marginal Cost
	(dollars per year)			(dollars per bushel)			
(1)	(2)	(3)	(4) = (2) + (3)	$(5) = \frac{(2)}{(1)}$	$(6) = \frac{(3)}{(1)}$	$(7) = \frac{(4)}{(1)}$	$(8) = \frac{\Delta(4)}{\Delta(1)}$
(A) 0	25,000	0	25,000	?	?	?	
							10.00
(B) 1,000	25,000	10,000	35,000	25.00	10.00	35.00	
							5.88
(C) 2,700	25,000	20,000	45,000	9.26	7.41	16.67	
							4.35
(D) 5,000	25,000	30,000	55,000	5.00	6.00	11.00	
							5.00
(E) 7,000	25,000	40,000	65,000	3.57	5.71	9.29	
							7.69
(F) 8,300	25,000	50,000	75,000	3.01	6.02	9.04	
							14.29
(G) 9,000	25,000	60,000	85,000	2.78	6.67	9.44	
							33.33
(H) 9,300	25,000	70,000	95,000	2.69	7.53	10.22	

As long as a firm has at least one input it cannot vary (let us assume it operates an orchard with a given number of trees, quantity of fertilizer, set of equipment, and management team), that firm operates in the short run. In the short run, it is saddled with a fixed cost—column (2)—for these fixed inputs. Yet the firm might be able to vary other inputs (for example, hired labor). By varying such other inputs—and the associated costs represented by column (3)—the firm can vary its total cost (4), as well as the level of its production (1) and other types of cost dependent on the level of production (5–8). Note: As the pointers between columns (7) and (8) indicate, the marginal costs shown refer to the intervals between rows (A) through (H).

Fixed, Variable, and Total Costs

Columns (2) to (4) of Table 5.1 show the overall levels of three types of cost. **Fixed cost,** in column (2), does not vary with the level of production. It arises from the use of inputs the quantity of which is fixed during the period in question. In general, these costs are fixed because of long-term contractual agreements that cannot be cancelled without stiff penalties or because of the presence of resources so specialized that they are of no use anywhere else (such as buildings or machines made for a narrowly defined task). In the short run, a firm cannot escape its fixed cost, not even by shutting down and cutting production to zero. **Variable cost,** in column (3), in contrast, does vary with the level of production. It is associated with the use of inputs the quantity of which can be varied and the variation of which changes the level of production during a given period. **Total cost,** in column (4), is simply the sum of fixed and variable costs.

In principle, any particular type of cost can be fixed or variable. Consider labor cost. If the owner of a firm signed a 10-year employment contract with a worker, promising a $10,000 annual salary, the $10,000 would become a fixed cost *for those 10 years.* Regardless of whether the firm ended up producing 100 bushels of apples in a year, 100,000 bushels, or none at all, it would still have to pay out $10,000 a year. In the long run, of course, this cost could be escaped. After the contract period had elapsed, the salary contract would not have to be renewed. Thus the same labor cost, looked upon over a longer period, would be a variable cost.

Note: The economist's distinction between fixed and variable costs should not be confused with the accountant's distinction between indirect and direct costs. While the economist asks whether cost is variable with respect to the overall level of output in a given period, the accountant asks whether cost is attributable to the production of a particular unit of output. The use of labor, raw materials, and machine time is often attributable to the production of a specific unit of output, and the costs are then called **direct** or **prime costs.** Because administrative or heating expenses and the depreciation of buildings are usually not attributable to producing a specific unit of output, such costs are called **indirect** or **overhead costs.**

Table 5.2 explains how the fixed cost in column (2) of Table 5.1 could conceivably be

TABLE 5.2

Calculating Fixed Cost

	Dollars per Year
Explicit:	
Property taxes	$ 3,000
Implicit:	
Forgone potential income from selling the orchard and lending out the proceeds	4,000
Forgone potential salary as substitute teacher (spouse 1)	5,000
Forgone potential salary as newspaper reporter (spouse 2)	13,000
Total	**$25,000**

The opportunity cost of running a firm includes explicit costs as well as implicit ones, as shown here with reference to the fixed cost of an orchard. Taking account of implicit costs as well as explicit ones allows the owners of firms to make the best decisions on the long-run desirability of being in business.

calculated in the case of the orchard business. Our orchard might be owned and run by a married couple that is being billed each year for $3,000 of property taxes. Because these taxes have to be paid regardless of the level of production, they represent a fixed cost. They are an explicit cost, too, and every accountant would take note of them. Yet accountants would ignore the three implicit-cost entries in Table 5.2. They represent the maximum incomes our couple could receive if they quit the orchard business and turned to their best alternatives. They might be able to sell the orchard and all its equipment and lend out the proceeds to someone else for $4,000 a year. They might take up the best jobs they could get in a nearby town, one as a substitute teacher ($5,000 a year) and the other as a newspaper reporter ($13,000 a year). Thus the very fact of their being in business initially burdens our two owner-managers with $25,000 a year in disadvantages. If they didn't own and run the orchard, they would take in $22,000 per year in other income and spend $3,000 per year less because someone else would have to worry about the property taxes. Because every conceivable level of output is thus burdened with this $25,000 cost, the $25,000 entry is found in every row of column (2) of Table 5.1.

The story is different, of course, for column (3). Because hired workers, by assumption, are the only input our orchardists can vary, their variable cost depends entirely on the number of workers hired and the prevailing annual wage for this type of work. Assuming the annual wage to equal $10,000, and considering (from a glance at Table 4.1, ''A Simple Production Function'') how many workers are needed to produce any of the crops listed in column (1) of Table 5.1, we can calculate the variable cost associated with different potential crops (3). Thus a 1,000 bushel-per-year crop, requiring one worker for a year, would cost $10,000, and so on down the column. We can now calculate total cost in column (4) as the sum of the fixed and variable costs in columns (2) and (3). The relationships involved are summarized in Box 5.A.

5.A Fixed, Variable, and Total Costs

1. **Fixed Cost, $FC = c$,** where c is a constant equal to the sum of each fixed-input quantity times its price
2. **Variable Cost, $VC = f(Q)$,** where Q is quantity produced and varies with one or more inputs, while VC equals the sum of each variable-input quantity times its price
3. **Total Cost, $TC = FC + VC$**
$$= c + f(Q)$$

Thus, if a product were being produced with fixed capital and natural resources, $\overline{K}$ and $\overline{T}$, but variable labor, L, and if the respective resource prices were P_K, P_T, and P_L, the total cost of producing any given quantity, Q_1, would equal

$$TC = (P_K \cdot \overline{K} + P_T \cdot \overline{T}) + P_L \cdot L$$
$$= c + P_L \cdot L.$$

Average Fixed, Average Variable, Average Total, and Marginal Costs

From the information in columns (1) to (4) of Table 5.1 we can calculate four other types of cost. **Average fixed cost, AFC,** equals fixed cost divided by total product. Thus, in row (B), as long as our orchardists hire only one worker for a year and produce 1,000 bushels of apples, the average fixed cost comes to $25,000 per year divided by 1,000 bushels per year, or $25 per bushel (5). Similar calculations can be made for the other types of cost shown in the column (6) to (8) heads.

Average variable cost, AVC, equals variable cost divided by total product. Thus, in row (B), as long as our orchardists hire only one worker for a year and wages are the only variable cost, this comes to $10,000 per year divided by 1,000 bushels per year, or $10 per bushel (6). **Average total cost, ATC,** equals total cost divided by total product. Thus, in row (B), as long as our orchardists hire only one worker for a year, this comes to $35,000 per year divided by 1,000 bushels per year, or $35 per bushel (7). **Marginal cost, MC,** finally, is the *change* in total cost, as from $25,000 per year in row (A) to $35,000 per year in row (B) of column (4), divided by the corresponding *change* in total product, as from 0 to 1,000 bushels per year from rows (A) to (B) in column (1). In this case, it comes to $+$10,000 per year divided by $+$1,000 bushels per year, or $10 per bushel. This figure is an average for the range of output between 0 and 1,000 bushels a year; hence it appears between rows (A) and (B) in column (8).

Note: Marginal cost can also be calculated by dividing the change in *variable* cost by the corresponding change in total product. Because fixed cost does not change, the change in total cost always equals that in variable cost. These additional relationships are, in turn, summarized in Box 5.B.

FIGURE 5.1

Short-Run Cost Curves

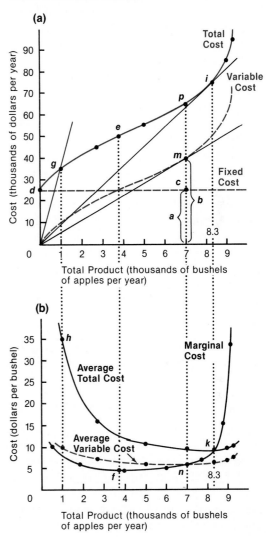

These graphs, based on Table 5.1, summarize the cost alternatives of a firm operating in the short run. Given technology and input prices, any firm can predict in this way the minimum levels of various types of cost associated with each potential level of production. Note: Marginal costs have been plotted at the midpoints of the ranges to which they apply, and all data plots have been connected by smooth curves. These curves give us additional information (about points between the heavy dots) that was not contained in Table 5.1. All subsequent discussions will be based on this more detailed information.

5.B Average Fixed, Average Variable, Average Total and Marginal Costs

1. $AFC = \dfrac{FC}{Q} = \dfrac{c}{Q}$

2. $AVC = \dfrac{VC}{Q} = \dfrac{f(Q)}{Q}$

3. $ATC = \dfrac{TC}{Q} = \dfrac{FC}{Q} + \dfrac{VC}{Q}$

   $= AFC + AVC$

4. $MC = \dfrac{\Delta TC}{\Delta Q} = \dfrac{\Delta VC}{\Delta Q}$

The Cost Curves

For purposes of analyzing the alternatives before our firm, it is useful to plot the data from Table 5.1 in a graph (see Figure 5.1). In panel (a), the fixed-cost and variable-cost data of columns (2) and (3) are plotted against total product from column (1). Note the horizontal (fixed cost) and upward-sloping (variable cost) dashed lines. The solid total-cost line is the vertical addition of the two dashed lines. Consider, for example, how a 7,000-bushel-a-year total product can be produced with $25,000 of fixed cost (distance *a*) plus $40,000 of variable cost (distance *b*). Distance *mp*, of course, equals distance *a*. Alternatively, distance *cp* equals distance *b*. These relationships are implied by equation (3) of Box 5.A.

In panel (b), the average-variable, average-total, and marginal-cost data are similarly plotted against total product. The heavy dots represent the data in columns (6) to (8) of Table 5.1.[1] The relationships between the total curves in panel (a) and the average or marginal curves in panel (b) are analogous to those noted when discussing total, marginal, and average product graphed in Figure 4.1 (see p. 102).[2]

---

[1]The column (5) data of average fixed cost have not been plotted in panel (b) because such a curve is of little interest in this particular chapter. But note equation (1) in Box 5.B, or look at the column (5) data in Table 5.1. These imply that *AFC* is forever declining as *Q* rises (the curve not shown is a rectangular hyperbola), and this fact is evidenced by the ever diminishing vertical distances, as *Q* rises, between *ATC* and *AVC* in panel (b). These distances, as equation (3), Box 5.B suggests, equal *AFC*.

[2]Indeed, under the perfectly competitive assumptions implicitly made so far, one can quickly derive the short-run total-cost curve of panel (a), Figure 5.1 by a series of manipulations of the underlying short-run production function of panel (a), Figure 4.1. By implication, the associated panel (b) curves are related as well. First, consider the production function of Figure 4.1:

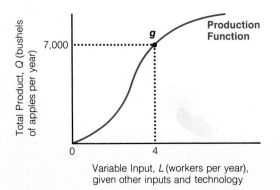

Second, reverse the axes and discover the identical relationship in a different way:

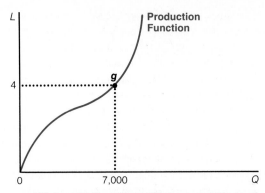

Third, multiply each variable-input quantity by the prevailing variable-input price. This changes the new vertical-axis entries from *L* (workers per year) to $L \cdot P_L$ (annual wage cost) or, in this example, into variable cost—without changing the color line of the graph. Physical information (*4 workers* produce 7,000 bushels, given other inputs and technology) is simply turned into monetary information (*$40,000 of wages* are associated with an output of 7,000 bushels, given other inputs and technology):

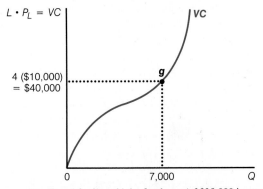

Fourth and finally, add the fixed cost (of $25,000 in our example) to the variable-cost function just derived. The resultant total-cost function in the last graph is the same one found in Figure 5.1:

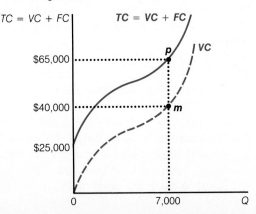

The slope of the total-cost curve equals marginal cost. Therefore, the *height* of the marginal-cost curve measures the *slope* of the total-cost curve. Because the slope of the total-cost curve is positive throughout, marginal cost is always positive as well. As long as increased production raises total cost at a decreasing rate (as between *d* and *e,* the point of inflection on the curve), marginal cost is falling to its minimum at *f* (point *f* is directly below *e*). On the other hand, once increased production raises total cost at an increasing rate (as it does to the right of *e*), marginal cost is rising (to the right of *f*). This increase of marginal cost reflects the appearance of diminishing returns to the variable input.

The relationship between total cost and average total cost can be gauged by the slope of a ray originating at 0 in panel (a) and going to any desired point on the total-cost curve. Thus the average total cost of 1,000 bushels is $35,000 per year divided by 1,000 bushels per year, or the slope of ray 0*g*. This $35-per-bushel value is shown by point *h* in panel (b). We can imagine a series of similar rays emanating from point 0 in panel (a) and aiming, successively, at points farther and farther to the right along the total-cost curve. The ever changing angle formed by this ray and the abscissa of the graph would trace out the behavior of average total cost. Can you show how this angle (and average total cost) would fall, with increasing production, to a minimum for ray 0*i* and would then rise? Note how, in panel (b), average total cost falls to point *k* (directly below *i*) and then rises.

We can also imagine a series of rays from 0 in panel (a) toward the dashed curve of variable cost; the ever changing slopes of these rays would trace out the size of average variable cost. Can you show how this slope (and average variable cost) would decline with increasing production, to a minimum for ray 0*m,* and would then rise? Note how in panel (b), average variable cost falls to point *n* (directly below *m*) and then rises.

Note how panel (b) also confirms our discussion, in the previous chapter, of the characteristic relationship between average and marginal. As long as marginal cost is below average variable cost (to the left of point *n*), it pulls down average variable cost (even when marginal cost itself is rising, as it does to the right of point *f*). As long as marginal cost is below average total cost (to the left of point *k*), it pulls down average total cost (even when marginal cost itself is rising). Similarly, marginal cost above either type of average cost (to the right of *n* or *k*, respectively) pulls up that average cost. Thus it is no accident that marginal cost equals the two types of average cost at their respective minima (points *n* and *k*). This is also visible in panel (a). Note how the slope of ray 0*i* (which measures minimum average total cost) equals the slope of the total-cost curve at *i* (and the slope of the total-cost curve, of course, always measures marginal cost). This is reflected by average total cost meeting marginal cost at *k* in panel (b). Similarly, note how the slope of ray 0*m* (which measures minimum average variable cost) equals the slope of the variable-cost curve at *m*. Because the total-cost curve and the variable-cost curve are vertical displacements of each other (the vertical difference between them being fixed cost), the slope at *m* equals that at *p* and thus, again, equals marginal cost. This is reflected by average variable cost meeting marginal cost at *n* in panel (b).*

THE PERFECTLY COMPETITIVE FIRM'S OPTIMUM IN THE SHORT RUN

It is easy to show how the graphical tools presented as Figure 5.1 can be used to determine a firm's optimum rate of production. If the firm operates in perfectly competitive markets (as we shall now assume), the only relevant information missing in our story is the market price of the firm's product. Because the perfectly competitive firm, acting alone, cannot influence that price, that market-determined price is not only the firm's **average revenue, AR** (or ratio of total

---

*For a calculus-based treatment of this material, see Section 5A of the Calculus Appendix at the back of this book.

revenue to total product), but it is also the firm's **marginal revenue, MR** (the ratio of any change in total revenue to the corresponding change in total product), as Box 5.C indicates.

5.C Total, Average, and Marginal Revenue Under Perfect Competition

$$TR = P*Q$$

$$AR = \frac{TR}{Q} = \frac{P*Q}{Q} = P*$$

$$MR = \frac{\Delta TR}{\Delta Q} = P*$$

where $P*$ is the market-determined price

The firm can maximize its **profit,** or the difference between its total revenue and the total (explicit and implicit) cost associated with producing that revenue, by following the optimization principle explained in Chapter 1:

> *The profit-maximizing firm must adjust its rate of production until the marginal benefit of production, which is the given price of its output, equals the rising marginal cost of production.*†

The orchard business can provide examples of a number of possible outcomes that will illustrate this profit-maximizing rule.

A Profitable Business

Figure 5.2 illustrates what would happen if our orchardists could sell apples at $12 per bushel. If the price were $12 per bushel, they could maximize their profit by choosing an 8,625-bushel-per-year production level.

Consider panel (a). If apples sold at $12 per bushel, 1,000 bushels would sell for $12,000 (point *a*), 3,000 bushels for $36,000 (point *b*), and so on along a straight line of total revenue. Because this line is not only straight, but also

---

†For a calculus-based treatment of this material, see Section 5B of the Calculus Appendix at the back of this book.

FIGURE 5.2

A Profitable Business

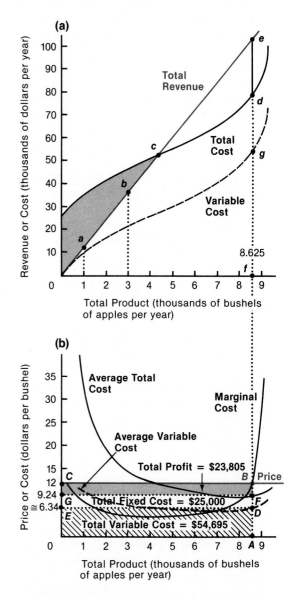

If product price were $12 per bushel, this firm would find its optimal rate of production at 8,625 bushels per year. Point *B,* therefore, is one point on its short-run supply curve.

goes through the origin of the graph, its slope simultaneously measures the ratio of total revenue to total product—that is, average revenue or product price—and the ratio of any change in total revenue to the corresponding change in total product—that is, marginal revenue. The graph shows that all potential output levels to the left of point *c* would yield a negative profit or **loss,** because total cost would exceed total revenue by various amounts. (Such losses can be measured, for any given output level, as the vertical difference between the total-cost and total-revenue lines in the shaded area.) As far as we can see in our graph, output levels to the right of point *c,* however, would yield profits because total revenue would exceed total cost. This difference would again vary, the maximum profit being associated with an output of 8,625 bushels of apples per year. At that output level, total revenue would equal $103,500 per year (distance *ef*), total cost $79,695 per year (distance *df*). Thus profit would equal $23,805 per year (distance *ed*). Distance *ed* represents the maximum possible profit because the total-revenue and total-cost lines diverge along *ce* and *cd,* respectively, but they converge to the right of points *e* and *d.* At these two points, their respective slopes are equal.

Because the slope of the total-revenue line equals marginal revenue as well as price and because the slope of the total-cost curve equals marginal cost, our orchardists could turn to panel (b) and search for an equality of price and marginal cost. Such equality can be found at point *B,* which indicates the same optimum output level of 8,625 bushels per year. Note how, in panel (b), rectangle 0*ABC* represents the total revenue associated with this optimum output: 8,625 bushels per year (distance 0*A*) times a price of $12 per bushel (distance *AB*), or $103,500 per year.

The graph in panel (b) provides a variety of other information. The orchard's variable cost, measured by distance *gf* in panel (a), equals the crosshatched rectangle 0*ADE,* or 8,625 bushels per year (distance 0*A*) times an average variable cost of slightly over $6.34 per bushel (distance

AD), or $54,695 per year. The orchard's total cost, measured by distance *df* in panel (a), can be seen to equal rectangle 0*AFG,* or 8,625 bushels per year (distance 0*A*) times an average total cost of $9.24 per bushel (distance *AF*), or $79,695 per year. Because total cost is the sum of fixed and variable costs, total fixed cost, measured by distance *dg* in panel (a), equals white rectangle *EDFG,* or 8,625 bushels per year (distance *ED*) times slightly under $2.90 per bushel (distance *DF*), or $25,000 per year. Distance *DF,* of course, equals average fixed cost (total fixed cost divided by total product) or, more simply, the difference between average total and average variable cost.

At a price of $12 per bushel (distance *AB*) but an average total cost of $9.24 per bushel (distance *AF*), **average profit**—that is, total profit divided by total product (or price minus average total cost)—equals $2.76 per bushel (distance *FB*). Hence total profit, measured by distance *ed* in panel (a), equals shaded rectangle *GFBC,* or 8,625 bushels per year (distance *GF*) times an average profit of $2.76 per bushel (distance *FB*), or $23,805 per year.

If our orchardists did face a price of $12 per bushel and, therefore, did produce 8,625 bushels per year, they would be doing well, indeed. They would take in revenue of $103,500 a year, while paying out $54,695 to hired workers and $3,000 in property taxes (as noted in Table 5.2). They would keep the remaining $45,805, and this amount, given our assumptions, would be the firm's taxable *accounting* profit. Only $23,805 of this amount, however, would represent *economic* profit, a gain over and above our orchardists' best alternative income of $22,000 (which is the sum of the implicit fixed-cost items in Table 5.2).

A Zero-Profit Business

Figure 5.3 depicts a zero-profit business. Our perfectly competitive orchardists (who would have no control over the market price of their product) might be less lucky than in Figure 5.2. Suppose the price of apples were only $9.04 per bushel, all else remaining equal. Under these circumstances, the total-revenue line has a lower slope than in Figure 5.2. In fact, it just touches the total-cost curve at a single point, *a*. Any output level other than 8,300 bushels per year would result in losses. As panel (a) indicates, this output level would yield total revenue of $75,032 per year (distance *ac*), and identical total cost, and zero profit. Note how the obvious equality of the slopes of the total-revenue and total-cost lines at point *a* once more confirms the optimization principle: The total net benefit of an activity (the profit from producing apples, in our case) is maximized when marginal benefit (the slope of our total-revenue line) just equals marginal cost (the slope of our total-cost curve).

Panel (b) tells the same story. Price equals marginal cost at point *I*, suggesting the same optimal output of 8,300 bushels per year. Rectangle 0*HIK* represents the associated total revenue of 8,300 bushels per year times a price of $9.04 per bushel (distance *HI*), or $75,032 per year. The orchard's variable cost, measured by distance *bc* in panel (a), equals crosshatched rectangle 0*HLM*, or 8,300 bushels per year times an average variable cost of slightly under $6.03 per bushel (distance *HL*), or $50,032 per year. The orchard's total cost, measured by distance *ac* in panel (a), can be seen to equal rectangle 0*HIK*, or 8,300 bushels per year times an average total cost of $9.04 per bushel (distance *HI*), or $75,032 per year. Thus total fixed cost, measured by distance *ab* in panel (a), equals the area of the white rectangle *MLIK*, or 8,300 bushels per year times an average fixed cost of slightly more than $3.01 per bushel (distance *LI*), or $25,000 per year.

At a price of $9.04 per bushel, the business would make no profit at all. Our orchardists could do no better than just break even. Indeed, an output level at which total revenue equals total cost (*a*) and at which price equals average total cost (*I*) is called a **break-even point.** When price also equals *minimum* average total cost (point *I*), a firm cannot escape choosing the break-even level of production. Under the circumstances, producing at zero profit, however, is preferable to

FIGURE 5.3

A Zero-Profit Business

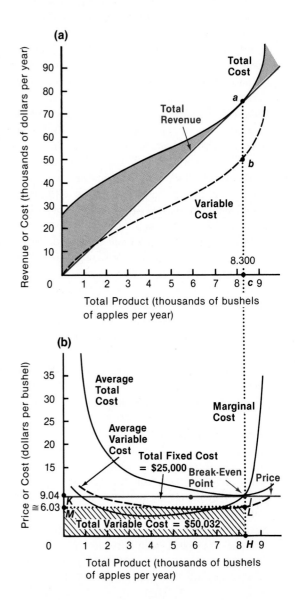

If product price were $9.04 per bushel, this firm would find its optimal rate of production at 8,300 bushels per year. Point *I*, therefore, is one point on its short-run supply curve.

closing down. If our friends closed down, they would lose all their revenue and would save their variable cost, but they would still be saddled with $25,000 per year of fixed cost, and hence a loss equal to this amount. Surely, it would be better to have a zero profit: If they produced 8,300 bushels per year, they would take in revenue of $75,032 per year, while paying out $50,032 to hired workers and $3,000 in property taxes. They would keep $22,000 and be just as well off as they could have been with their best alternative.

A Losing Business

In the short run, it could even be rational for the orchardists to stay in business while making a loss. Suppose the price of apples were $7.25 per bushel, all else remaining the same, as depicted in Figure 5.4. As the shaded gap between total cost and total revenue indicates in panel (a), the orchardists could then find no output level at all at which total revenue would be sufficient to cover total cost. Operating this business would mean operating it with a loss. But note: There exists a range of output levels (between point *a* and point *b*) that would yield total revenue more than sufficient to cover *variable* cost. Producing any one of these outputs would leave some revenue to cover a *portion* of fixed cost. As a result, the firm's loss (which would equal fixed cost, if it shut down at once) could be reduced to a figure below fixed cost. As long as fixed cost could not be escaped (the orchard could not be sold to escape property taxes, to cash in and lend out the owner's equity, and to free the owners for their alternative jobs), it would be wise to pursue a policy of loss minimization. Note how the shaded gap of loss could be narrowed the most (and the excess of total revenue over variable cost could be widened the most) by producing 7,680 bushels of apples per year. Our orchardists would gain total revenue of $55,680 per year (distance *cd*), incur a total cost of $70,000 per year (distance *ed*), and make a loss of $14,320 per year (distance *ec*). This loss would be preferable to that of $25,000 per year at the zero-production

FIGURE 5.4

A Losing Business

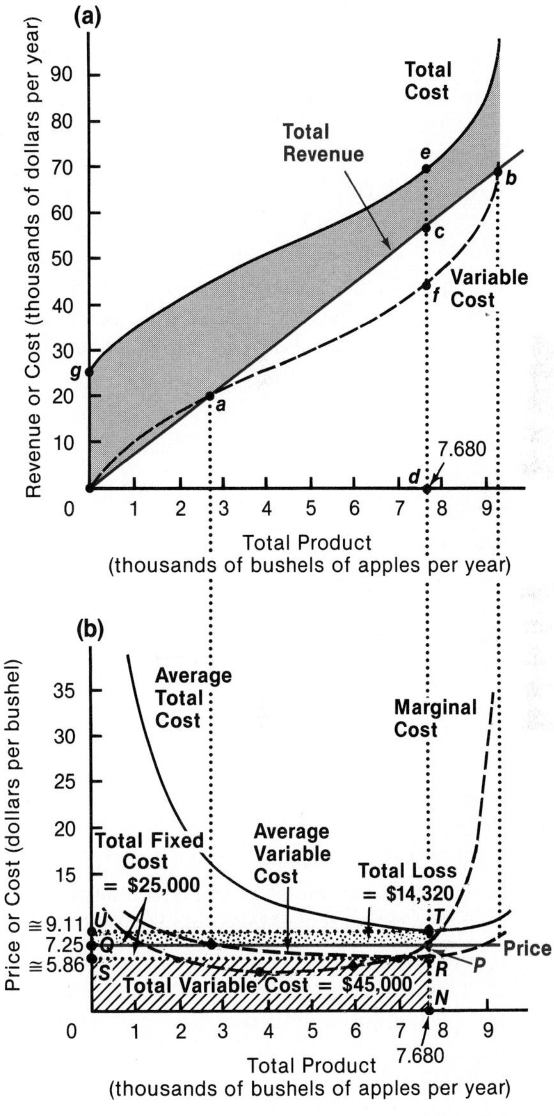

If product price were $7.25 per bushel, this firm would find its optimal rate of production at 7,680 bushels per year. Point *P*, therefore, is one point on its short-run supply curve.

level (distance 0g). This loss would be $10,680 per year lower than fixed cost ($ef = 0g$), and this improved performance equals the maximum possible excess of total revenue over variable cost (distance cf).

We can quickly check our results in panel (b). Price equals marginal cost at point P, confirming as optimal an output of 7,680 bushels per year. Rectangle 0NPQ shows the associated total revenue of 7,680 bushels per year times a price of $7.25 per bushel (distance NP), or $55,680 per year. The orchard's variable cost, measured by distance fd in panel (a), equals crosshatched rectangle 0NRS, or 7,680 bushels per year times an average variable cost of slightly under $5.86 per bushel (distance NR), or $45,000 per year. The orchard's total cost, measured by distance ed in panel (a), can be seen to equal rectangle 0NTU, or 7,680 bushels per year times an average total cost of slightly over $9.11 per bushel (distance NT), or $70,000 per year. Thus total fixed cost, measured by distance ef in panel (a), equals the combined area of the white and dotted rectangles, $SRTU$, or 7,680 bushels per year times an average fixed cost of slightly under $3.26 per bushel (distance RT), or $25,000 per year.

Because, at the optimal production level, price (distance NP) would fall short of average total cost (distance NT), a negative average profit, or **average loss** would be made, which would come to slightly more than $1.86 per bushel and yield a total loss of $14,320 per year, as shown by the dotted rectangle in panel (b) and by distance ec in panel (a). The white rectangle, of course, corresponds to distance cf in panel (a), the portion of fixed cost that is covered by revenue.

Note how our friends, if they produced 7,680 bushels per year, would take in $55,680 per year, while paying out $45,000 to hired workers and $3,000 in property taxes. They would keep $7,680, which is $14,320 less than alternatives available to them in the long run (as indicated by the calculated loss). For the time being, though, this would be better than nothing.

A Business on the Fence

The product price can be so low—slightly above $5.71 per bushel in our case—that whether to produce at a loss or to shut down operations at once would become a matter of indifference. The situation of a business on the fence is depicted in Figure 5.5. As the shaded gap between total cost and total revenue indicates in panel (a), our orchardists could find no output level at which total revenue would cover total cost. Indeed, as a comparison of the variable-cost and total-revenue lines indicates, with the single exception of the 7,000-bushels-a-year output level, total revenue would be insufficient even to cover variable cost. In the short run, producing 7,000 bushels a year would not be wrong, however. Our orchardists would receive total revenue of $40,000 per year (distance bc). They would incur variable costs of the same amount. Their total cost (distance ac) would equal $65,000 per year. They would make, therefore, a $25,000-per-year loss equal to fixed cost (distance ab). An immediate shutdown would produce an identical loss (distance 0d).

As always, panel (b) tells the same story as panel (a), but in a different way. Price equals marginal cost at point W. Rectangle 0VWX shows total revenue of 7,000 bushels per year times a price slightly above $5.71 per bushel (distance VW), or $40,000 per year. Variable cost, equal to distance bc in panel (a), equals crosshatched rectangle 0VWX, or 7,000 bushels per year times an average variable cost slightly over $5.71 per bushel (distance VW), or $40,000 per year. Total cost, measured by distance ac in panel (a), equals rectangle 0VYZ, or 7,000 bushels per year times an average total cost slightly under $9.29 per bushel (distance VY), or $65,000 per year. Total fixed cost, measured by distance ab in panel (a), therefore equals rectangle $XWYZ$, or 7,000 bushels per year times average fixed cost of slightly over $3.57 per bushel (distance WY), or $25,000 per year. This is also the total loss.

The owners of such a business would be "sitting on the fence." If they shut down, they would lose $25,000 compared to their best alter-

FIGURE 5.5

A Business on the Fence

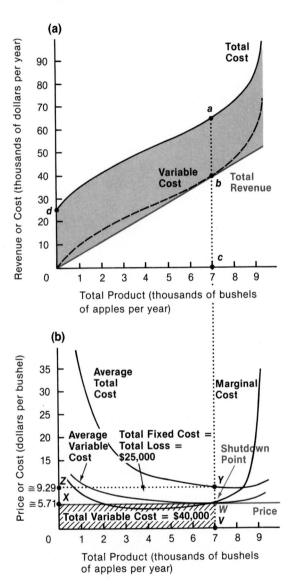

If product price were $5.71 per bushel, this firm would be indifferent about producing 7,000 bushels per year or shutting down at once. Point *W,* therefore, is the lowest point on its short-run supply curve.

native. If they operated, at the 7,000-bushel-a-year level, they would take in $40,000 of revenue, pay an equal amount to hired workers, and have nothing left to pay property taxes ($3,000) or to reimburse themselves for their forgone income alternatives. That is why our orchardists would be at the verge of shutting down at once. Indeed, an output level at which total revenue equals variable cost and at which price equals average variable cost (points *b* and *W,* respectively) is called a **shutdown point.** When price also equals *minimum* average variable cost (point *W*), a firm cannot escape choosing the shutdown level of production. Although whether to produce or shut down has become at this point a matter of indifference, even the slightest further deterioration of product price would cause the firm to cease operations immediately.

SUPPLY IN THE SHORT RUN

From the forgoing discussion, we can conclude that, in the short run, while firms are saddled with fixed cost that they cannot escape,

1. no firm will operate with a loss in excess of fixed cost, because there exists the alternative of closing down and making a loss equal to fixed cost;

2. a firm might operate with a loss equal to fixed cost, because the alternative of closing down would yield an identical loss (Figure 5.5);

3. a firm will operate with a loss falling short of fixed cost, because the alternative of closing down would yield a bigger loss equal to fixed cost (Figure 5.4);

4. a firm will operate with zero profit, because implicit costs (counted as part of fixed cost) are then fully covered by revenues; hence owners would earn from their resources in their own firm exactly what they could at best earn elsewhere, and shutting down would deprive them of these earnings (see Figure 5.3);

5. a firm will operate with a positive profit

because its presence indicates earnings in excess of the owners' best alternative (see Figure 5.2).

Indeed, we can be more precise. Notice in Figures 5.2 to 5.5 how the optimum level of production in each case corresponds exactly to the intersection (at points *B, I, P,* and *W,* respectively) of the price line with rising marginal cost. From this correspondence, we can conclude:

FIGURE 5.6

Short-Run Supply

Price or Cost
(dollars per bushel)

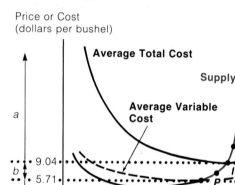

This graph, which is based on panel (b) of Figures 5.2 to 5.5, highlights an important fact: In the short run, the optimum levels of production corresponding to all conceivable product prices are always found on the rising arm, above minimum average variable cost, of the perfectly competitive firm's marginal-cost curve. This rising portion of the marginal-cost curve, which appears in color, is the firm's short-run supply. Note how the firm operates at an economic profit at any price above $9.04 per bushel (range *a*) because price then exceeds average total cost at the optimum (*P* = *MC*) position (such as *B*). In turn, the firm makes a loss but continues to operate, at any price between $5.71 and $9.04 per bushel (range *b*) because price then covers average variable cost but fails to cover average total cost at the optimum (*P* = *MC*) position (such as *P*). Finally, the firm shuts down at once at any price below $5.71 per bushel (range *c*) because the inevitable loss of fixed cost at zero output then falls short of the loss at all positive output levels.

In the short run and in a perfectly competitive market, the rising arm of a firm's marginal-cost curve, above the minimum level of average variable cost, shows how much the firm would produce and offer for sale at alternative product prices. This segment of the rising arm is the firm's short-run supply.

The concept of **supply,** like *demand,* thus refers to a set of many price-quantity combinations. *Supply* denotes the alternative amounts of an item that would be offered for sale during a given period at all conceivable prices of this item, all else (technology, fixed input quantities, and all input prices) being equal.

The colored line in Figure 5.6 depicts the **"law" of upward-sloping supply,** the tendency of sellers normally to offer for sale larger quantities of an item when its price is higher, all else being equal.

Note: Had we assumed, in our earlier discussions, a different technology, different amounts of fixed inputs, or different prices of fixed or variable inputs, we would have derived a different supply curve. That is why a change in technology, fixed inputs, and input prices *shifts* a good's short-run supply curve to the right or left and is referred to as a **change in supply.** In contrast, a change in the good's own price, while other factors remain unchanged (a situation we envisioned when moving from Figure 5.2 to Figure 5.5), causes a *movement along* a given supply curve (as from *B* to *W*) and is referred to as a **change in quantity supplied.**

COSTS AND SUPPLY IN THE LONG RUN

A firm operating in the short run, by definition, is operating with at least one input quantity that is fixed. As a result (even if it avoids X-inefficiency), it is not necessarily producing its output at as low a cost as could be achieved in the long run when all inputs are variable.

Let us illustrate the truth of this assertion by considering a firm that uses only two types of inputs, capital and labor, and that can produce any given quantity of its output with the help of many different combinations of these inputs. Some of this firm's production possibilities are illustrated, in panel (a) of Figure 5.7, by the three isoquants for output levels of 100, 150, and 200 bushels of product, respectively. As we noted in Chapter 3, the (absolute) value of the ever-changing isoquant slope equals the marginal rate of technical substitution of labor for capital, $MRTS_{L/K}$, or—what comes to the same thing—the ratio of the marginal product of labor to the marginal product of capital, MP_L/MP_K.

Let us imagine that this firm, being a perfect competitor in the resource markets, was faced with given input prices of $250 per year for a unit of capital service and of $125 per year for a unit of labor service. We can draw straight **isocost lines** (akin to the budget lines of Chapter 2), each of which shows all the alternative combinations of the two inputs that the firm is able to buy in a given period at current market prices, while incurring the same total cost. The panel (b) lines are labeled accordingly. Note, for example, how $500 could purchase 2 units of capital or 4 units of labor or any combination of them lying on the isocost line with the $500 label. The absolute value of the slope of every isocost line, therefore, reflects the ratio of the price of a unit of labor service, P_L, to that of a unit of capital service, P_K; in our case, $125/$250 or ½.

$$|\text{Isocost line slope}| = \frac{P_L}{P_K}$$

Note that every isocost line must satisfy the condition that $(P_L \cdot L) + (P_K \cdot K)$ equals a given level of total cost, TC_0, where P_L and P_K refer to the prices and L and K to the quantities of labor and capital services. Thus

$$(P_L \cdot L) + (P_K \cdot K) = TC_0.$$
$$P_K \cdot K = TC_0 - (P_L \cdot L)$$

This implies the Box 5.D formula.

FIGURE 5.7

Isoquants and Isocost Lines

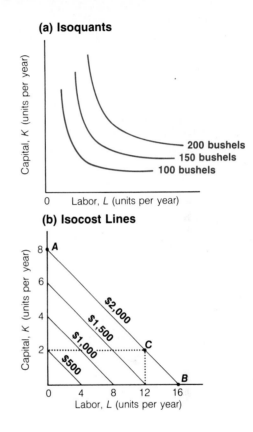

(a) Isoquants

Capital, K (units per year)

200 bushels
150 bushels
100 bushels

0   Labor, L (units per year)

(b) Isocost Lines

Capital, K (units per year)

8 A
6
4
2

$2,000
$1,500
$1,000
$500

C

B

0   4   8   12   16
Labor, L (units per year)

A firm that can vary all of its inputs (here capital and labor) can typically produce a multitude of output levels—each with a multitude of input combinations [panel (a)]. If it is a perfect competitor in the input markets, the firm faces given input prices (here $P_K = 250 and $P_L = 125) and can buy any of the input combinations lying on a straight isocost line for a given level of total cost, TC_0. Each isocost line can be described by the equation

$$K = \frac{TC_0}{P_K} - \left(\frac{P_L}{P_K} \cdot L\right)$$

where TC_0/P_K is the line's vertical intercept (such as point A), while $-P_L/P_K$ is the line's negative slope (of $-\frac{1}{2}$ in this example).

5.D The Isocost-Line Equation

$$K = \frac{TC_0}{P_K} - \left(\frac{P_L}{P_K} \cdot L\right)$$

This isocost-line equation tells us that the quantity of capital used always equals the difference between TC_0/P_K (which is the maximum possible quantity, such as that shown by point A on isocost line AB) and the isocost-line slope absolute value (P_L/P_K) times the quantity of labor used.

On line AB in panel (b), Figure 5.7, for example, if $L = 0$,

$$K = \frac{TC_0}{P_K} = \frac{\$2,000}{\$250} = 8 \text{ (point } A\text{)}.$$

On the other hand, if $K = 0$,

$$L = \frac{TC_0}{P_K}\left(\frac{P_K}{P_L}\right) = \frac{TC_0}{P_L} = \frac{\$2,000}{\$125}$$
$$= 16 \text{ (point } B\text{)}.$$

Similarly, if $L = 12$,

$$K = \frac{TC_0}{P_K} - \frac{P_L}{P_K} \cdot L = \frac{\$2,000}{\$250} - \frac{\$125}{\$250} \quad (12)$$
$$= 2 \text{ (point } C\text{)}.$$

Now consider that our firm wanted to produce the maximum possible output for a given level of cost (of, say, $1,500). Or imagine that it wanted to produce a given output (of, say, 100 bushels) at the lowest possible cost. In either case, the optimum solution can be found by superimposing isoquants and isocost lines, as in Figure 5.8.

In the first case, the firm's optimum is found at c, where the given $1,500 isocost line just touches the highest (150-bushel) isoquant it can reach. In the second case, the optimum is found at b, where the given 100-bushel isoquant just touches the lowest ($1,000) isocost line it can

FIGURE 5.8

The Firm's Optimum

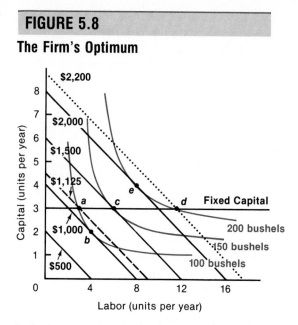

In the long run, when all inputs can be freely varied, a profit-maximizing firm would produce all levels of output at minimum possible cost, as by utilizing input combinations b, c, or e. These represent tangencies of isoquants and isocost lines and, therefore, positions in which the marginal product per dollar of one input equals that of any other input. In the short run, however, a firm may be forced by the fixity of one input (such as $K = 3$ shown by the black horizontal line) to produce many output levels at costs exceeding those achievable in the long run, as illustrated by points a and d.

reach. It is no accident that at these points of equal slopes the ratio of input prices equals the ratio of the inputs' marginal products, MP; and the result is analogous to the consumer's optimum discussed in Chapter 2, as a comparison of Box 2.C with 5.E can show.

5.E Condition for Firm's Optimum:

Slope of isocost line = slope of isoquant

$$\frac{P_L}{P_K} = \frac{MP_L}{MP_K}.$$

Therefore,

$$\frac{MP_L}{P_L} = \frac{MP_K}{P_K}$$

The last equation in Box 5.E is a condition for profit maximization, and it can be extended to any number of inputs:

$$\frac{MP_L}{P_L} = \frac{MP_K}{P_K} = \frac{MP_T}{P_T} = \ldots \ldots$$

Profit is maximized, this equation says, when the marginal product per dollar of input is the same regardless of the input type. Put differently, the marginal-benefit to marginal-cost ratio must be the same for all inputs (the marginal benefit being the extra physical output associated with a dollar's worth of an input, the marginal cost being the extra dollar spent on the input). A contrary example can illustrate the point: Let P_L = \$125 and P_K = \$250, while MP_L as well as MP_K equal 50 bushels. By substituting inputs, the firm could produce more output (hence more revenue and profit) from a given cost. Using 1 K less would release \$250 and lower output by 50 bushels, but spending \$250 more on labor would yield 2 L more, hence 2(50) = 100 extra bushels—a net gain of 50 bushels.*

Alternatively, given the same assumptions, the firm could lower cost (hence raise profit) from a given output (and revenue). Using 1 K less would release \$250 and lower output by 50 bushels, but spending \$125 more on labor would yield 1 L more, hence 50 extra bushels—a net reduction of \$125 in cost.†

Now consider this firm in the *short run* with, perhaps, a fixed quantity of 3 units of capital (in Figure 5.8, the firm cannot make choices above or below the black horizontal line). If it wanted to produce 100 bushels of product per year, it would have to use input combination *a,* and this would cost, as the dashed isocost line shows, \$1,125 per year. Average total cost would equal \$11.25 per bushel. Yet, as point *b* indicates, the same amount of output could be produced at a total cost of \$1,000 per year (and average total cost could be reduced to \$10 per bushel), if less

capital and more labor were utilized. A profit-maximizing firm, surely, would take advantage of this possibility in the *long run.*

What if our firm wanted to produce 150 bushels per year, given its 3-unit fixed capital? It could then optimize even in the short run because it would have to use (optimal) input combination *c* and would spend \$1,500 per year. Its average total cost would equal \$10 per bushel, and, by accident, this would be the lowest figure achievable with the firm's given **plant** or physical production facility, as defined by the set of fixed inputs available to the firm (K = 3). When a firm in this way produces the output level associated with the minimum average total cost achievable from a given plant, it is said to have an **optimal rate of plant operation** or to be producing its **capacity output.** Operation at break-even point *I* in the graph of a zero-profit business in Figure 5.3 also corresponds to this situation.

Yet a firm may have good reasons not to operate at capacity. Just as it may wish to operate below capacity at some product prices (note points *P* and *W* in Figures 5.4 and 5.5), so it may wish to operate above capacity at other product prices (note point *B* in Figure 5.2). Operation below capacity corresponds to point *a* in Figure 5.8. Operation above capacity corresponds to point *d.* The implications of operating at point *a* were noted above; operations at point *d* can be analyzed similarly. A firm with 3 units of fixed capital, that wanted to produce 200 bushels per year, would have to use input combination *d.* It would then spend \$2,200 per year. The average total cost would equal \$11 per bushel. In the long run, the use of less labor and more capital (at point *e*) could reduce average total cost to \$10.

Note: A special case of optimization, involving situations in which a firm's isoquants are not continuously curved, is discussed in Appendix 5.A, ''Linear Programming,'' which can be found in Chapter 5 of the *Student Workbook* that accompanies this text.

---

*For a calculus-based treatment of this material, see Section 5C of the Calculus Appendix at the back of this book.

†For a calculus-based treatment of this material, see Section 5D of the Calculus Appendix at the back of this book.

The Planning Curve under Constant Returns to Scale

Imagine the owners of a perfectly competitive firm still in its planning stage or, if you prefer, the owners of an existing firm who are contemplating major changes in the long run. They might imagine setting up plants of many different sizes, each one defined by a different-sized set of fixed inputs. Our orchardists, for example, might draw up one blueprint for a 5-acre lot with 1,000 apple trees (and the appropriate equipment to service them). They might draw up other blueprints for 50 acres and 10,000 trees, for 100 acres and

20,000 trees, and many more. And for each of these blueprints, they might produce a graph like Figure 5.1 to show short-run cost curves. The short-run average total cost and short-run marginal cost for blueprints 3, 10, and 21, for example, might appear as lines *SRATC* and *SRMC* in panel (a) of Figure 5.9. The subscripts refer to the numbers of the hypothetical blueprints; larger numbers refer to plants of larger sizes.

A picture like that in panel (a) would indicate the presence of constant returns to scale: The owners of our firm might determine that they could produce, at an average total cost of $10 per

---

FIGURE 5.9

Short-Run Versus Long-Run Costs and Long-Run Supply

(a) Constant Returns to Scale

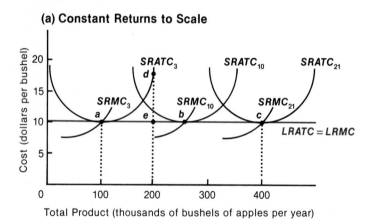

(b) Increasing and Decreasing Returns to Scale

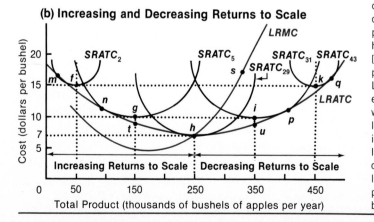

It is important to distinguish the minimum (short-run) average total cost achievable in a given plant (such as *g* for plant #5 or *i* for plant #31) from the minimum (long-run) average total cost achievable for a given rate of production (such as *t* for 150,000 and *u* for 350,000 bushels of apples per year). To achieve the latter and, thus, operate on the *LRATC* curve, may well require the underutilization or overutilization of some plant. Any given long-run average-total-cost curve implies, in turn, a long-run marginal-cost curve; and *LRMC*, at or above the level of *LRATC*, is the perfectly competitive firm's long-run supply. As long as economies or diseconomies of scale are the sole consequence, respectively, of increasing or decreasing returns to scale in the firm's production function, the following holds: Long-run supply is horizontal [and equal to *LRMC* in panel (a)] in the presence of constant returns to scale. Long-run supply is upward-sloping [and equal to *LRMC* above *h* in panel (b)] when increasing returns to scale at lower output levels give way to decreasing returns to scale at higher output levels. In the long run, no firm will continue to operate while making losses; nothing, therefore, is supplied at prices below average total cost, such as below point *h* in panel (b).

bushel, 100,000 bushels of apples per year, if they used 50 acres and 10,000 trees and operated this plant at capacity (point *a*). They might find that quadrupling all inputs would quadruple total cost but quadruple output as well, yielding the same minimum average total cost (point *c*). And they might discover that, given enough time to adjust all inputs appropriately, any other output level could be produced at an equivalent cost (point *b*).

Once fixed inputs corresponding to $SRATC_3$ were in place, the firm could, of course, produce an output of 200,000 bushels per year, but operating above capacity in this manner would drive short-run average total cost up from *a* to *d*. Given enough time for adjusting the number of trees and other inputs—perhaps by following a blueprint 6 (not shown)—these costs could be reduced to *e*. Under the circumstances, therefore, our firm's average total cost in the long run, *LRATC,* could always be reduced to $10 per bushel for any conceivable level of output. The long-run average-total-cost line is also called the **planning curve.** It helps owners of firms make long-range plans because it is tangent to all the curves of short-run average total cost and is, therefore, the *geometric locus* of the minimum achievable average total costs for all conceivable output levels. When the planning curve is horizontal, long-run marginal cost, *LRMC,* coincides with it. (Marginal above average would pull average up; marginal below average would pull average down.) While the upward-sloping lines of short-run marginal cost indicate our firm's short-run response to changes in product price (given alternative plant sizes), this horizontal *LRMC* is its long-run supply. Given enough time, this line tells us, our firm can supply *any* annual apple crop at $10 per bushel.

The Planning Curve under Increasing and Decreasing Returns to Scale

A perfectly competitive firm's long-run supply need not be a horizontal line, however. Consider panel (b) of Figure 5.9. The owners of our single-plant firm might determine that they could produce, at an average total cost of $15 per bushel, 50,000 bushels of apples per year, if they used 25 acres and 5,000 trees and operated this plant at capacity (point *f*). However, what they could do is not necessarily what they would do. They might find that doubling all inputs would double costs but triple output, yielding a lower minimum average total cost (point *g*). A further 17-percent increase in all inputs (and total cost) might raise output by 67 percent and also reveal the **optimum plant,** or that plant, among all conceivable ones, with the lowest possible minimum average total cost (point *h*). In our case, this figure would come to $7 per bushel. That, however, would be the end of increasing returns to scale.

Further proportionate increases in all inputs might bring about lesser increases in output. Starting from the optimum plant (29), operated at capacity (point *h*), a doubling of all inputs might raise output by only 40 percent, yielding a higher minimum average total cost of $10 per bushel (point *i*). A further 93-percent increase in all inputs might raise output by a mere 29 percent and raise minimum average total cost to $15 per bushel (point *k*). Decreasing returns to scale might thus follow on the heels of increasing returns to scale.

Once more, the owners of our firm could draw the planning curve. This time, however, this geometric locus of the minimum achievable average total costs for all conceivable output levels would not be a straight line. This line of long-run average total cost (*LRATC*), like the lines of short-run average total cost (*SRATC*), would be *U*-shaped, but the reason would differ: *short-run* average total cost curves are *U*-shaped because the fixity of some input gives rise, eventually, to diminishing returns to the variable input. The *long-run* average total cost curve may be *U*-shaped because, as was argued here, increasing returns to scale associated with a firm's growth are bound to give rise, eventually, to decreasing returns to scale. Because it envelops all the short-run curves, touching each only at a single point, the *U*-shaped *LRATC* curve is also called an **envelope curve.**

Two notes of caution must be sounded about this curve. First, in panel (b) of Figure 5.9, the downward-sloping part of the *LRATC* curve has been explained by increasing returns to scale and, thus, by such factors as the increased specialization of inputs (noted in Chapter 4) that a larger firm makes possible. This approach is likely to be sufficient for the perfectly competitive firm that is being discussed in this chapter. In principle, however, the downward slope (as between *m* and *h*) may also be explained by other factors, especially for imperfectly competitive firms. Consider the ability of such firms to depress input prices by means of volume discounts as they increase their plant sizes and input quantities purchased. Consider the ability of such firms to make economical use of by-products that a smaller firm would discard. [A small sawmill, for example, may well discard sawdust and wood scraps; a large one may turn these into artificial fireplace logs or kindling, respectively; the extra revenues would effectively reduce the cost of the main product, lumber. Large meat producers, similarly, market a host of by-products (fertilizer, glue, leather); so do large gasoline refiners (machine oil, lubricants, vaseline).]

Consider the ability of such firms to persuade local governments to build more or better support facilities, such as roads, which may decrease the firms' transportation costs. In all these cases, even constant returns to scale in the production function may go hand in hand with a *U*-shaped *LRATC* curve because larger plants mean lower and lower *SRATC* curves as the above-noted other factors come into play. Indeed, the great variety of factors that effectively reduce average total costs for the larger firm (whether increasing returns to scale in the production function, lower prices of materials or machines, the recovery of some costs through the sale of by-products, or the reduction in transport costs) are jointly referred to as **economies of scale** or **economies of mass production.** Similarly, all the factors (decreasing returns to scale and others) that cause the *LRATC* curve to slope upward are called **diseconomies of scale.** As long as we discuss the perfectly competitive firm, we will continue to ascribe a

U-shaped *LRATC* curve to increasing or decreasing returns to scale alone, however, as noted in Figure 5.9.

Second, unlike in the panel (a) case of constant returns to scale, the long-run average-total-cost curve in the presence of increasing or decreasing returns to scale (or, more generally, in the presence of economies of scale or diseconomies of scale) does not connect all the *minimum* points of short-run curves, such as *a*, *b*, or *c* in panel (a) or *f*, *g*, *h*, *i*, or *k* in panel (b). Except for point *h*, the long-run average-total-cost curve in panel (b) never coincides with the minima of short-run average-total-cost curves. Point *m* does not coincide with *f*, nor *n* with *g*, nor *p* with *i*, nor *q* with *k*.

A *U*-shaped curve of long-run average total cost implies the following:

1. When economies of scale exist (for example, as a result of increasing returns to scale in the production function), it is cheaper to produce a *given* output (such as that corresponding to point *m* or *n*) by running a larger plant *below* capacity (plant #2 at *m* instead of *f*, plant #5 at *n* instead of *g*) than by putting together an appropriately designed smaller plant (#1 or #3, not shown) that would produce this output when run at its capacity.

2. When diseconomies of scale exist (for example, as a result of decreasing returns to scale in the production function), it is similarly cheaper to produce a *given* output (such as that corresponding to point *p* or *q*) by running a smaller plant *above* capacity (plant #31 at *p* instead of *i*, plant #43 at *q* instead of *k*) than by putting together an appropriately designed larger plant (#39 or #47, not shown) that would produce this output when run at its capacity. Note: If you should find this material difficult to understand, be assured that it is. You may find comfort in reading the Biography of Jacob Viner (1892–1970), one of this century's great economists, which can be found in Chapter 5 of the *Student Workbook* that accompanies this text. As you will see, he, too, had difficulty!

3. A *U*-shaped curve of long-run average total cost implies a separate line of long-run

FIGURE 5.10

Isoquants and Long-Run Cost Curves

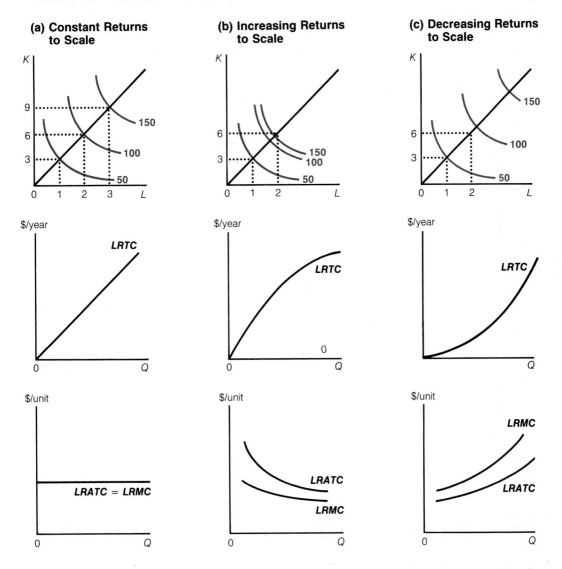

The nature of the perfectly competitive firm's long-run cost curves depends crucially on the nature of the firm's production function.

marginal cost, such as *LRMC* in panel (b). (Falling average implies marginal below it; rising average implies marginal above it.) Because firms will not stay in business in the long run when making losses, and because every product price below the lowest possible average total cost at *h* would create such losses, the firm's long-run supply curve equals the rising branch of its long-run marginal cost above long-run average total cost.

Isoquants and Long-Run Cost Curves

The nature of the perfectly competitive firm's long-run cost curves, as we have seen, depends crucially on the nature of the firm's production function. The relationship is summarized in Figure 5.10. The top row of graphs reproduces Figure 4.4 on the spacing of isoquants; in panel (a), a simultaneous doubling of all inputs doubles output precisely (constant returns to scale); in panel (b), a simultaneous doubling of all inputs clearly more than doubles output (increasing returns to scale); in panel (c), a simultaneous doubling of all inputs fails to double output (decreasing returns to scale). Underneath each of these graphs, the implications for cost curves are given. Under constant returns to scale, doubled output implies doubled total cost (input prices being given); the long-run total-cost curve is a straight line starting at origin 0 (there are no fixed costs!); the long-run average total cost, therefore, is depicted by a horizontal line (just as in panel *a* of Figure 5.9). Under increasing returns to scale, doubled output implies less-than-doubled total cost (given input prices); accordingly, *LRTC* rises at a decreasing rate as *Q* rises; both *LRATC* and *LRMC* (below it) are declining (just as in the left-hand side of panel *b* of Figure 5.9). Under decreasing returns to scale, finally, doubled output implies more-than-doubled total cost (given input prices); accordingly, *LRTC* rises at an increasing rate as *Q* rises; both *LRATC* and *LRMC* (*above*) are rising [just as in the right-hand side of panel (b) of Figure 5.9].

EMPIRICAL STUDIES OF COST AND SUPPLY

Empirical studies of costs and supply are plagued by the difficulties, discussed in Chapter 4, of estimating production functions. In addition, as noted earlier in this chapter, problems arise because the economist's notion of cost differs from that of the accountant. Economics researchers, who inevitably must use accounting data,

have to correct such data to bring them in line with the economist's idea of opportunity cost. This is a difficult task because accountants ignore most implicit costs and when they don't, as in the case of depreciation, they arrange the relevant numbers so as to reap tax advantages and not to reflect the economic life of the assets in question.

Table 5.3 reports on some of the major empirical studies of long-run cost conducted by economists. The table can be studied most profitably after glancing once more at panel (b) of

FIGURE 5.11

An Empirical Cost Function

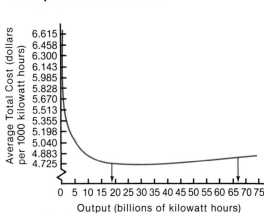

This L-shaped cost function for U.S. firms producing electric power was calculated from cross-section data for a 1970 sample of 114 firms. The bulk of electricity output was generated by firms operating in the essentially flat area of the average-total-cost curve. (The arrows indicate the boundaries of the region of no significant economies or diseconomies of scale.) The replacement of existing firms by a much smaller number of extremely large firms (operating at minimum average total cost) would have reduced total U.S. electricity generating costs by only 3 percent in 1970.

Source: From Laurits R. Christensen and William H. Greene, "Economies of Scale in U.S. Electric Power Generation," *Journal of Political Economy,* August 1976, p. 674. Reprinted by permission of The University of Chicago Press. © 1976 by The University of Chicago.

TABLE 5.3

Summary of Selected Long-Run Cost Studies

Country, Industry (1)		Long-Run Average Total Cost of Small Firms as a Percentage of Minimum Achieved by Large Firms (2)	Source (3)
United States	Hospitals (a)	130	C
	(b)	100	I
	Commercial banking		
	demand deposits	116	A
	installment loans	102	A
	Electric power	112	D
	Railroads (a) west	107 ⎫	
	south	100 ⎬	B
	east	83 ⎭	
	(b)	100	G
	Airlines (local service)	100	E
	Trucking	95	H
Canada	Life insurance	114	F
United Kingdom	Beer	155	J
	Dyes	144	
	Newspapers	140	
	Oil refineries	127	
	Bread	130	
	Bricks	130	
	Ethylene	130	
	Aircraft	125+	
	Polymer manufacture	123	
	Detergents	120	
	Electric motors	120	
	Sulfuric acid	119	
	Cement	117	
	Computers	113–116	
	Steel	112–117	
	Cars	110–113	
	Refrigerators, washers	112	
	Synthetic yarn extrusion	111	
	Iron foundry	110–115	
	Diesel engines	110+	
	Machine tools	110	
	Turbogenerators	110	
	Footwear	105	
	Bicycles ⎫		
	Book printing ⎪	$\approx$100	
	Cotton textiles ⎬		
	Plastics ⎭		

Sources:

A. F. W. Bell and N. B. Murphy, *Costs in Commercial Banking* (Boston: Federal Reserve Bank of Boston, Research Report No. 41, 1968).

B. George H. Borts, "The Estimation of Rail Cost Functions," *Econometrica,* January 1960, pp. 108–31.

C. Harold A. Cohen, "Hospital Cost Curves with Emphasis on Measuring Patient Care Output," in Herbert F. Klarman, ed., *Empirical Studies in Health Economics* (Baltimore, Md.: Johns Hopkins Press, 1970), pp. 279–93.

D. Laurits R. Christensen and William H. Greene, "Economies of Scale in U.S. Electric Power Generation," *Journal of Political Economy,* August 1976, pp. 655–76.

E. George Eads, Marc Nerlove, and William Raduchel, "A Long-Run Cost Function for the Local Service Airline Industry: An Experiment in Non-Linear Estimation," *The Review of Economics and Statistics,* August 1969, pp. 258–70.

F. Randall Geehan, "Returns to Scale in the Life Insurance Industry," *The Bell Journal of Economics,* Autumn 1977, pp. 497–514.

G. Zvi Griliches, "Cost Allocation in Railroad Regulation," *The Bell Journal of Economics and Management Science,* Spring 1972, pp. 26–41.

H. Roger Koenker, "Optimal Scale and the Size Distribution of American Trucking Firms," *Journal of Transport Economics and Policy,* January 1977, pp. 54–67.

I. Judith R. Lave and Lester B. Lave, "Hospital Cost Functions," *The American Economic Review,* June 1970, pp. 379–95.

J. Aubrey Silberston, "Economies of Scale in Theory and Practice," *The Economic Journal,* March 1972, pp. 369–91. (In this study, small firms are defined as those producing half the output volume at which minimum average total costs are reached.)

Figure 5.9. The long-run average total cost of a small or medium-sized firm in an industry may be that shown by points *m* or *n*, while larger firms enjoy costs as low as *h*. Column (2) of Table 5.3 shows this relative size for a number of industries studied. Evidence is overwhelming that long-run average-total-cost curves tend to be *L*-shaped, with the horizontal portion of the letter *L* covering a rather wide range of output. (This result, of course, reflects the widespread evidence on near constant returns to scale, which was reported in Chapter 4.)

Figure 5.11 is an example of a typical empirical cost function. There is little evidence of long-run average-total-cost curves turning up as in section *hpq* of Figure 5.9. This may be the consequence of the fact that many cost studies use input-output data supplied by *engineers*, and engineers may not be very good at picking up diseconomies of scale, which, as we argued, are likely to be caused by difficulties of *managerial* coordination. On the other hand, the absence of significant evidence on such diseconomies may instead reflect the fact that firms know when to stop their growth!

FROM INDIVIDUAL SUPPLY TO MARKET SUPPLY

As in the case of demand, economists focus attention not so much on the supply of an *individual* firm, but on **market supply,** the sum of the supplies of all market participants.

Short-Run Market Supply

As long as all firms supplying a given product face identical market prices for inputs as well as outputs (and this we assume in the perfectly competitive markets under study so far), individual supplies will differ due to differences in technology or fixed input quantities, but they can be added together at each product price. Table 5.4 demonstrates how the short-run market-supply schedule can be derived. Although we believe that thousands, perhaps millions, of sellers would appear in any perfectly competitive market, we need not concern ourselves with such large numbers. For the moment, and only to simplify the arithmetic, we can imagine only

FIGURE 5.12

Deriving Short-Run Market Supply

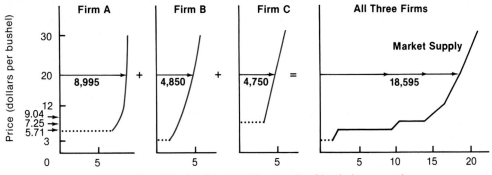

Quantity of Apples Supplied (thousands of bushels per year)

This graph, which is based on Table 5.4, shows how short-run market supply can be derived by adding horizontally, at each conceivable price, the quantities supplied by all market participants, all else being equal.

TABLE 5.4

Deriving the Short-Run Market Supply Schedule

Price (dollars per bushel) (1)	Quantity of Applies Supplied (bushels per year)			
	Firm A (2)	Firm B (3)	Firm C (4)	All Three Firms (5) = (2) + (3) + (4)
0	0	0	0	0
3.00	0	1,500	0	1,500
5.71	7,000	2,250	0	9,250
7.25	7,680	2,800	3,320	13,800
9.04	8,300 +	3,150 +	3,450 =	14,900
12.00	8,625	4,000	3,750	16,375
20.00	8,995	4,850	4,750	18,595
30.00	9,125	5,875	6,000	21,000

A short-run market supply schedule can be derived by adding, at each conceivable price, the quantities supplied by all potential market participants, all else being held equal. Note: Column (2) data refer to the firm depicted in Figure 5.6.

three sellers to exist in the market for apples. Their respective supply schedules might be those shown in columns (2) through (4) of Table 5.4. Their combined market-supply schedule is shown in column (5). Naturally, all this information can be graphed, as in Figure 5.12.

We have already noted a number of factors that will shift an individual firm's supply, such as changes in technology, the quantity of fixed inputs, and input prices. Because of the large number of sellers in a perfect market, such shifts in a single firm's supply will affect market supply only imperceptibly, but widespread changes in individual supplies will shift market supply noticeably. (Imagine what would happen to Figure 5.12 if a technical improvement in apple production became generally available, if the climate changed, or if the prices of inputs rose sharply.)

Long-Run Market Supply

While the simple horizontal addition of short-run supply curves of individual firms is a tolerably correct procedure for deriving *short-run* market supply, things are much more complicated in the case of *long-run* supply. In the long run, neither the number of firms nor the size of their plants is fixed. As a result, a possible problem emerges with the construction of a long-run market-supply curve. Given its production function, the prices of inputs, and the number and size of other firms, the long-run supply of each *individual firm* in an industry may be accurately depicted, as in Figure 5.9 by horizontal *LRMC* in panel (a) or by upward-sloping *LRMC* (above point *h*) in panel (b). Yet the *industry's* long-run supply curve need not necessarily look like either of these lines. If the production functions or input prices available to individual firms were affected by the number and size of other firms operating in the industry, the derivation of long-run market supply would involve the addition of individual market supplies that were changing in the very process of addition! The number and size of other firms can affect a firm's production function (*technological externalities*) or a firm's input prices (*pecuniary externalities*).

Technological Externalities. When the *production function* of one firm is affected, favorably or unfavorably, by the operation of other firms, a **technological externality** is said to exist. To illustrate the effect of a favorable externality, let us imagine our apple orchard being operated on swampy soil. Its production function may be that underlying panel (b) of Figure 5.9. Its long-run

supply curve may be *LRMC* above point *h* in that graph. Accordingly, an increase in the price of apples from $7 per bushel to $17 per bushel, would, in the long run, increase our firm's annual quantity supplied from 250,000 bushels (point *h*) to 330,000 bushels (point *s*). Yet the simultaneous appearance of many new or larger competitors might falsify this result.

Our orchardists might find that higher product prices were drawing in ever larger numbers of new competitors, who were all draining land to plant new orchards. Our orchardists' own land might be drained indirectly as well. As a consequence, any given set of inputs might yield more apples than before because apple trees flourish in drier soil. This would mean that any given cost yielded more apples than before; all cost curves would shift down as the industry grew in size. Our orchard's individual supply curve would end up below or to the right of its former position. The firm might supply 400,000 rather than 330,000 bushels per year at the $17 price.

The process involved will be discussed in detail in Chapter 6, but we can see now that *favorable* technological externalities make a long-run market-supply line much flatter than a simple horizontal addition of given upward-sloping *LRMC* curves would suggest. The market supply derived from such upward-sloping curves could even be horizontal or downward-sloping. Favorable technological externalities that caused horizontal individual supplies [corresponding to *LRMC* in panel (a) of Figure 5.9] to shift down during an industry's expansion would, similarly, produce a downward-sloping market-supply line.

Note: The presence of *unfavorable* technological externalities associated with industry growth would make the market-supply line *steeper* than otherwise. Consider an apple orchard in the desert, relying on irrigation from wells. The appearance, as a result of higher product price, of more or larger firms might drastically reduce the water available to the original firms, leading to less output from otherwise identical inputs. Less output for the same cost would cause individual supply lines to shift above previous ones in the very process of industry expansion. Similar examples of unfavorable technological externalities would be the increasing difficulty of catching fish the more boats are fishing, the increasing difficulty of oil producers to get oil out of the ground the more oil wells there are, and the increasing difficulty of power stations to find cool river water the more firms there are to use rivers for cooling purposes.

Pecuniary Externalities. When *input prices* paid by our firm are affected, favorably or unfavorably, by the operation of other firms, a **pecuniary externality** is said to exist. Our apple orchard can provide an example of the presence of an unfavorable externality. Imagine that any increase in product price caused additional firms to enter the apple industry or caused existing firms to expand. Their activities might raise the prices of inputs used in the industry: the wages of apple pickers, the rental rates of spraying machines, the prices of fertilizer and pesticides. As a consequence, any given set of inputs would yield the same quantity of apples as before but would cost more. Our orchard's cost curves would shift up as the industry grew in size; its supply curve would end up above or to the left of its former position. If, in panel (b) of Figure 5.9, the apple price rose from $7 per bushel to $17 per bushel, our firm's quantity supplied might rise from 250,000 bushels not to 330,000 bushels per year, but only to 260,000 bushels per year. The market-supply line would be steeper than otherwise.

Note: An analogous argument can be made with respect to *favorable* pecuniary externalities. Their presence would make the market-supply line flatter than otherwise, possibly even negatively sloped. Consider the possibility of *lowered* input prices as an industry expanded because, perhaps, the presence of a larger number of firms stimulated the development of more or better resources usable by the industry (see Chapter 6 for further discussion).

MARKET SUPPLY EXAMINED: ELASTICITY

As in the case of *quantity demanded,* economists are interested in measuring the responsiveness of a good's *quantity supplied* to the good's price. A good's **price elasticity of supply** is the percentage change in quantity supplied divided by the percentage change in the good's price, all else being equal. Denoting this elasticity by ϵ_S, quantity supplied by Q_S, price by P, and changes in these variables by Δ, the elasticity formula for any good, x, is analogous to the elasticity formula for demand, as a comparison of Box 5.F with 3.A can show.

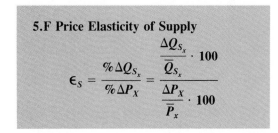

5.F Price Elasticity of Supply

$$\epsilon_S = \frac{\% \Delta Q_{S_x}}{\% \Delta P_X} = \frac{\dfrac{\Delta Q_{S_x}}{\overline{Q}_{S_x}} \cdot 100}{\dfrac{\Delta P_X}{\overline{P}_x} \cdot 100}$$

Indeed, the entire discussion of own-price elasticity in Chapter 3 (see pp. 74–76) is relevant here. As in the case of demand, *arc* elasticity is calculated by using the averages, $\overline{Q}_{S_x}$ and $\overline{P}_X$, respectively, of old and new quantities and prices in the denominators above. On the other hand, the *point* elasticity of supply can be read instantly at any point along a supply curve by applying the *PAPO* rule. (According to the *PAPO* rule, the elasticity at a given point equals the distance from the point to the abscissa, $P{\rightarrow}A$, divided by the distance from the point to the ordinate, $P{\rightarrow}O$, along a tangent to the curve at the point in question.) Consider Figure 5.13, which shows eight different supply lines, labeled S_1 through S_8. To measure the price elasticity of supply at point a on S_1, for example, we place a tangent on S_1 at a, which is conveniently provided by supply line S_2 and its dotted extension. The price elasticity of supply at a then equals distance ab (point to abscissa) divided by the distance ac (point to ordinate), or about $+2$. This means that a 1-percent change in price will elicit, in the immediate vicinity of a, a 2-percent change in quantity supplied in the same direction. By placing similar tangents at other points on S_1, similar calculations could be performed.

Now consider the straight supply line S_2. Obviously, at point a, the price elasticity of supply is also $+2$. To the left and below a, this elasticity is larger; to the right and above a, it is smaller, but it is always larger than unity. (Can you show why elasticity is always larger than unity along any straight supply line that intercepts the ordinate in quadrant I of our coordinates?)

In contrast, the price elasticity of supply at any point on lines S_3 and S_4 equals unity exactly.

FIGURE 5.13

Price Elasticity of Supply

Price
(dollars per bushel)

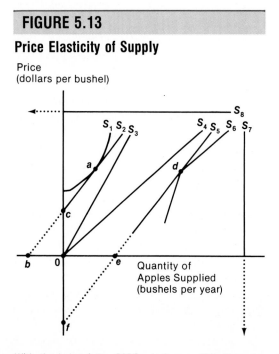

Quantity of
Apples Supplied
(bushels per year)

With the help of the *PAPO* rule (see p. 77), the price elasticity of supply can be determined instantly at any point on any supply curve.

Elasticity is unity for all points on any straight supply line going through the origin. The distance from any chosen point to the abscissa then always equals that from the point to the ordinate, because both axes are met at origin 0. Now consider the price elasticity of supply at d, on either line S_5 or S_6. It equals distance de (point to abscissa) divided by distance df (point to ordinate), or $+.56$. This means that a 1-percent change in price will elicit, in the immediate vicinity of d, only about a .5-percent change in quantity supplied in the same direction. Indeed, along any straight supply line that intercepts the abscissa in quadrant I of our coordinates, the price elasticity of supply, though changing, is less than unity because one quantity (such as de) is always divided by a larger one (such as df).

Finally, consider vertical supply line S_7 and horizontal line S_8. Price elasticity of supply equals zero at all points on the vertical line because point-to-abscissa distances of varying lengths are always divided by infinity (point to ordinate). Common sense tells us that a vertical supply line indicates that no change in price can elicit even the slightest change in quantity supplied. Such may be the situation in the very short run, as when fishing boats return from the sea (or berry pickers return from the forest) and offer a momentarily fixed quantity of perishable products for sale. Given more time, of course, boats can go to sea (or berry pickers to the forest) more or less frequently; hence the quantity they supply will become responsive to price. Not surprisingly, therefore, price elasticities of supply, like those of demand, tend to be larger in the long run than in the short run. The extreme case is illustrated by line S_8, which has an elasticity of infinity at all points. It corresponds to the constant-returns-to-scale long-run supply line of panel (a) in Figure 5.9.

Note: Supply elasticities can also be defined and calculated with respect to variables other than a good's own price. When goods are produced jointly (wool and mutton) or when goods are competitive in production (wheat and rye), economists calculate *cross-price elasticities* of

TABLE 5.5

Selected Estimates of Price Elasticities of Supply in the United States

Good	Elasticity		Good	Elasticity	
	Short Run	Long Run		Short Run	Long Run
Cantaloupes	0.02	0.04	Green snap beans	0.15	∞
Lettuce	0.03	0.16	Eggplant	0.16	0.34
Green peppers	0.07	0.26	Tomatoes	0.16	0.90
Green lima beans	0.10	1.70	Kale	0.20	0.23
Shallots	0.12	0.31	Spinach	0.20	4.70
Beets	0.13	1.00	Watermelons	0.23	0.48
Carrots	0.14	1.00	Green peas	0.31	4.40
Cauliflower	0.14	1.10	Onions	0.34	1.00
Celery	0.14	0.95	Cabbage	0.36	1.20

Source: Adapted from Marc Nerlove and William Addison, "Statistical Estimation of Long-Run Elasticities of Supply and Demand," *Journal of Farm Economics,* November 1958, Vol. XL, p. 872.

supply, which show the responsiveness of one good's quantity supplied to the price of another good. Similarly, various *income elasticities* of supply can be calculated—for example, the responsiveness of the supply of a good to incomes earned in the industry could be determined to see whether higher incomes reduce the quantity of inputs supplied to an industry and hence reduce the quantity supplied of the industry's product. In general, though, economists have been less inclined to calculate these other types of elasticities than in the case of demand because such estimates are less useful. Unlike demand elasticities, supply elasticities tell us nothing, for example, about the amount of money spent by buyers or taken in by sellers (see Chapter 3 for a discussion of the types of elasticity of demand).*

Table 5.5 brings together the results of supply studies for fresh vegetables during the 1919–55 period. The short-run elasticities were calculated for one growing period. Not surprisingly, long-run elasticities are larger, often considerably so. In the long run, each firm can change the quantities of formerly fixed inputs. In addition, the number of firms in the industry can change. More firms are likely to enter an industry as the price of the industry's product rises because that raises profit (all else being equal), and profit indicates the extra income owners of firms can earn in this industry as compared to other industries. Similarly, existing firms will leave an industry altogether if the price of the industry's product falls sufficiently to create losses. While firms may continue producing while making losses in the short run, they will never do so in the long run because losses (as economists define them) point to extra income the owners of firms could earn in other activities. Thus it is not surprising, as Table 5.5 tells us, that a 1-percent change in the price of spinach causes only a .2-percent change, in the same direction, in quantity supplied when a given growing season is considered. Yet, over a longer period, when the size and number of firms can change, the change in quantity supplied associated with a 1-percent price change rises to 4.7 percent.

SUMMARY

1. Economists postulate that the dominant goal of firms is the maximization of profits—of the difference, that is, between revenues and costs. Given the prices of output and inputs,

*For a calculus-based treatment of this material, see Section 5E of the Calculus Appendix at the back of this book.

production-function data can be translated into prospective revenues and costs. The relationship between revenue and cost, in turn, determines how much of a good a profit-maximizing firm will supply.

2. It is important to distinguish the accountant's concept of cost from that of the economist. With the exception of depreciation allowances, the accountant focuses on *explicit* costs. The economist, in order to derive a measure of opportunity cost, adds *implicit* costs to explicit costs.

The *total* cost incurred by a firm in the short run can be divided into *fixed* and *variable* costs (which should not be confused with *indirect* and *direct* costs). Economists use information about fixed, variable, and total cost to calculate *average fixed cost, average variable cost, average total cost,* and *marginal cost.*

3. Graphs of short-run cost curves can be used, along with revenue curves, to depict the optimum rate of production of a perfectly competitive firm in the short run. As long as product price equals or exceeds minimum average variable cost, the optimum output level is always found where product price and rising marginal cost are equal.

4. Analysis of short-run cost curves and product-price information leads to the identification of the rising arm of the marginal-cost curve (above minimum average variable cost) as the perfectly competitive firm's short-run supply curve.

5. A firm operating in the short run (even if it avoids X-inefficiency) is not necessarily producing its output at a cost as low as could be achieved in the long run when all conceivable input combinations can be realized. This difference between costs achievable in the short run and in the long run can be illustrated with the help of isoquants and isocost lines. A profit-maximizing firm's optimum input combination (which ensures minimum cost for any given output level) is always found where a relevant isoquant just touches an isocost line, and such optimum can usually be achieved only in the long run. The (horizontal or upward-sloping) long-run

marginal-cost curve of the perfectly competitive firm becomes its curve of long-run supply.

6. Evidence from a number of empirical studies of cost and supply indicates that curves of long-run average total cost tend to be L-shaped, with the horizontal portion of the letter L covering a rather wide range of output.

7. The supply curves of individual firms can be added together to yield market supply, although the presence of technological or pecuniary externalities may complicate the procedure.

8. The responsiveness of a good's quantity supplied to its price is measured by the price elasticity of supply. Empirical measures indicate higher elasticities for the long run than the short run.

KEY TERMS

average fixed cost (AFC)

average loss

average profit

average revenue (AR)

average total cost (ATC)

average variable cost (AVC)

break-even analysis

break-even point

capacity output

change in quantity supplied

change in supply

direct costs

diseconomies of scale

economies of mass production

economies of scale

envelope curve

explicit costs

fixed cost (FC)

implicit costs

incremental-profit analysis

indirect costs

isocost line

''law'' of upward-sloping supply

loss

marginal cost (*MC*)

marginal profit

marginal revenue (*MR*)

market supply

optimal rate of plant operation

optimum plant

overhead costs

pecuniary externality

planning curve

plant

price elasticity of supply

prime costs

profit

shutdown point

supply

technological externality

total cost (*TC*)

variable cost (*VC*)

HANDS-ON PRACTICE

Exercise #1

Consider Table 5.6. Given a fixed cost of $100 and a variable-input price of $50 per unit, compute variable cost and total cost for alternatives (A) through (H).

TABLE 5.6

	Units of Variable Input Used	Total Product (tons/year)
(A)	0	0
(B)	1	200
(C)	2	600
(D)	3	1200
(E)	4	1600
(F)	5	1900
(G)	6	2100
(H)	7	2200

Solution:

See Table 5.7.

TABLE 5.7

	Fixed Cost	Variable Cost	Total Cost
(A)	$100	$ 0	$100
(B)	100	50	150
(C)	100	100	200
(D)	100	150	250
(E)	100	200	300
(F)	100	250	350
(G)	100	300	400
(H)	100	350	450

Exercise #2

Still using the data from Exercise 1, calculate average fixed cost, average variable cost, average total cost, and marginal cost.

Solution:

See Table 5.8. All entries are rounded.

Exercise #3

If the data given in Exercises 1 and 2 referred to a perfectly competitive firm, what would be its short-run supply curve? Graph it.

Solution:

Supply in the short run would be marginal cost above minimum average variable cost. Figure 5.14 is a graph of the two relevant curves, based on the last column of Table 5.6 and the corresponding data in Table 5.8. Thus the supply curve is the marginal-cost curve between points *a* and *b*. (Marginal-cost data have been plotted over the midpoints of the output ranges to which they apply.)

TABLE 5.8

	Average Fixed Cost	Average Variable Cost	Average Total Cost	Marginal Cost
(A)	$ (100/0) = ?	$ (0/0) = ?	$ (100/0) = ?	
(B)	$ (100/200) = .500	$ (50/200) = .250	$ (150/200) = .750	A to B: $\frac{\$50}{200}$ = .250
(C)	$ (100/600) = .167	$ (100/600) = .167	$ (200/600) = .333	B to C: $\frac{\$50}{400}$ = .125
(D)	$(100/1200) = .083	$(150/1200) = .125	$(250/1200) = .208	C to D: $\frac{\$50}{600}$ = .083
(E)	$(100/1600) = .063	$(200/1600) = .125	$(300/1600) = .188	D to E: $\frac{\$50}{400}$ = .125
(F)	$(100/1900) = .053	$(250/1900) = .132	$(350/1900) = .184	E to F: $\frac{\$50}{300}$ = .167
(G)	$(100/2100) = .048	$(300/2100) = .143	$(400/2100) = .190	F to G: $\frac{\$50}{200}$ = .250
(H)	$(100/2200) = .045	$(350/2200) = .159	$(450/2200) = .205	G to H: $\frac{\$50}{100}$ = .500

FIGURE 5.14

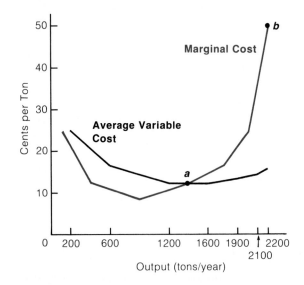

Output (tons/year)

QUESTIONS AND PROBLEMS

1. "Given the economist's definition of cost as *opportunity cost*, the average total costs of different firms in an industry cannot differ. If one firm, for example, had superior management or land, it would have lower average variable costs than its competitors, but its average fixed costs would be correspondingly higher." Discuss.

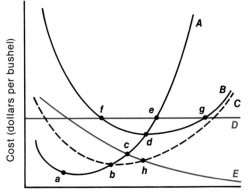

Total Product (bushels of apples per year)

2. Consider the graph above and identify:
a. the marginal-cost curve.
b. the average-total-cost curve.
c. the average-variable-cost curve.
d. the average-fixed-cost curve.
e. the short-run supply curve.
f. the marginal-revenue curve.
g. the average-revenue curve.
h. the capacity output level.
i. the break-even point on the short-run supply curve.

j. the shutdown point on the short-run supply curve.

3. Consider the profitable business in Figure 5.2.

a. What would happen to the firm's optimum, if government imposed a 50-percent tax on profit?

b. What if the government imposed a $20,000 license fee?

c. A $1 tax per bushel of output?

4. Suppose that each of the input combinations, A to D, in the table below could produce an output of 1,000 bushels of apples per year. Draw the 1,000-bushel isoquant in a graph. Assume that 1 pound of fertilizer sells for one-fifth as much as 1 hour of labor, and determine the minimum-cost combination of inputs for this level of output. What would the minimum-cost combination be if the price of labor halved?

	Fertilizer (pounds per year)	Labor (hours per year)
(A)	1,000	200
(B)	640	360
(C)	360	640
(D)	200	1,000

5. In Figures 5.1–5.5, *short-run* total-cost curves appear along with *short-run* average-total-cost and marginal-cost curves. Yet when *long-run* average total cost and marginal cost are depicted in Figure 5.9, no long-run total-cost curve is shown. How would you draw a long-run total-cost curve and why?

6. Review Analytical Example 5.1, "Break-Even Analysis."

a. Suppose the charter business were already a going concern, selling 700 hours a year (at an average total cost of $84.36). Would the ex-professor be wiser to accept or to reject someone's offer to pay $50 for an hour's ride? How about $20?

b. Produce a break-even analysis for the prospective publication of a college textbook.

7. In 1974, a quarter million baby turkeys were killed by turkey hatcheries in Georgia because the cost of raising turkeys (34 cents a pound) far outstripped what farmers could get for them (20 cents a pound). Analyze this event with the help of *incremental-profit analysis* (refer to Analytical Example 5.2).

8. Are each of the following true or false?

a. Direct costs equal prime costs.

b. Prime costs equal variable costs.

c. Indirect costs equal overhead costs.

d. Overhead costs equal fixed costs.

e. If marginal cost were to fall with higher output, average total cost would have to fall.

f. The total variable cost at any output level equals the sum of marginal costs up to that output level.

g. The most profitable level of production for any firm is the one at which average-total cost is minimized.

h. If the profitable apple orchard pictured in Figure 5.2 were run by a surgeon, its profit would instantly vanish.

i. The minimum point on a curve of short-run average total cost shows the lowest average total cost of production for a given fixed cost.

j. A rise in a good's price leads to an increase in its supply.

k. The long-run average-total-cost curve shows the lowest possible average cost for producing any given output when the firm has time to make all the adjustments in input combinations it wants to make.

l. The long-run supply curve of a firm is an envelope curve.

m. The lowest point on a firm's long-run supply curve can be found at the capacity output level of the optimum plant.

n. Technological externalities make the market-supply curve less price elastic at any given quantity.

o. Pecuniary externalities make the market-supply curve less price elastic at any given price.

p. All straight-line supply curves have the same price elasticity at every point on the curve.

q. The slope of a straight total-cost line equals marginal cost.

r. The slope of a straight total-cost line equals average variable cost.

s. The slope of a straight total-cost line equals average total cost.

t. The presence of X-inefficiency would push all cost curves vertically downward.

u. If one drew a curve of average fixed cost in a graph like Figure 5.1, it would decline and never rise, no matter how big production became.

*9. Use calculus as needed to answer the following questions:

a. For each of the following total-cost functions, determine the average-total-cost function and the marginal-cost function; then graph the total-cost function in one graph and the other two functions in another graph directly underneath. As in Figure 5.1, use the same scale horizontally.

1. $TC = a + bQ$
2. $TC = a + bQ + cQ^2$
3. $TC = 50 + 60Q - 5Q^2 + Q^3$

b. A perfectly competitive firm faces an output price of $30 per unit; its marginal-cost function is $10 + .5Q$.

1. Determine the profit-maximizing output, Q^*.

2. Graphically determine total variable cost, total revenue, and the difference between the two at Q^*. What does this difference represent?

c. For each of the following situations, calculate the profit-maximizing output level, Q^*, as well as the totals of revenue, fixed cost, variable cost, and profit at Q^*.

1. $TC - 2Q - Q^2 = 0$ and $TR = 3Q$
2. $TC = 200 + 5Q^2$ and $TR = 6Q$

*10. Use calculus as needed to solve the following optimization problems for a profit-maximizing firm:

a. The firm's production function is $Q = Q(K, L) = aK^bL^c = KL$; $P_K = 100$, $P_L = 300$; an output of $Q^* = 2400$ is to be produced at minimum cost. Determine L, K, and the minimum cost.

b. The firm's production function is $Q = 100K^2L^3$; $P_K = 100$, $P_L = 300$; output is to be maximized subject to a total-cost constraint of 90,000. Determine L, K, and the maximum output.

11. From the data in the accompanying table, determine average fixed cost, average variable cost, average total cost, and marginal cost.

Q	TFC	TVC
1	50	30
2	50	40
3	50	45
4	50	55
5	50	90

12. The accompanying table contains data for several short-run average-total-cost curves. Graph these curves; then draw in a long-run average-total-cost curve as well.

	Plant #1			Plant #2	
Point	Q	SRATC	Point	Q	SRATC
A	2	11.0	F	4.8	8.9
B	2.4	9.0	G	5.8	6.0
C	4.3	8.1	H	7.0	4.0
D	6.3	9.0	I	8.1	3.9
E	7.0	10.4	K	10.2	4.7
			L	12.0	6.8

	Plant #3			Plant #4	
Point	Q	SRATC	Point	Q	SRATC
M	9.2	6.1	T	15.9	8.9
K	10.2	4.7	U	17.1	7.0
N	11.7	3.2	S	20.4	5.8
P	14.1	2.1	V	23.2	6.2
Q	16.9	2.9	W	25.0	7.2
R	19.7	4.7	X	26.4	9.8
S	20.4	5.8			

13. A perfectly competitive firm faces a price and marginal revenue of $5 per unit. Its average total cost is given in the accompanying table. Graph these data; then figure out the profit-maximizing output. Show the firm's supply curve in the graph, if you can.

Q	ATC
100	5.10
200	3.00
300	2.10
400	2.00 (min.)
500	2.15
600	2.95
700	4.25
800	6.50

14. Once more consider your answer to Problem 12. Figure out the precise long-run marginal-cost data and also draw them in your graph.

SELECTED READINGS

Johnston, John. *Statistical Cost Analysis.* New York: McGraw-Hill, 1960.

An important work on cost functions and their empirical estimation.

Scherer, F. M., et al. *The Economics of Multi-Plant Operation.* Cambridge, Mass.: Harvard University Press, 1975.

While this chapter focuses on single-plant firms, Scherer's book discusses the determinants of multi-plant operation in the U.S. and six other countries.

Viner, Jacob. "Cost Curves and Supply Curves," American Economic Association. *Readings in Price Theory.* Chicago: Irwin, 1952, chap. 10.

A reprint of a famous article of 1931, with the addition of a supplementary note.

Walters, Alan A. "Production and Cost Functions: An Econometric Survey," *Econometrica,* January–April, 1963, pp. 1–66.

Tables VI–VIII summarize a large number of empirical cost studies. Includes an excellent bibliography.

COMPUTER PROGRAMS

The KOHLER-3 personal-computer diskettes that accompany this book contain two programs of particular interest to this chapter:

5. Costs and the Supply of Goods includes a 25-question multiple-choice test with immediate responses to incorrect answers as well as numerous exercises concerning various concepts of costs, isoquant analysis, and more.

Appendix A. Solving Simultaneous Equations can help with the exercises. Users of the *Student Workbook* may also wish to utilize *Appendix B. Linear Programming.*

ANALYTICAL EXAMPLE 5.1

BREAK-EVEN ANALYSIS: THE CASE OF THE FLYING PROFESSOR

The owners of existing or potential firms often use a simplified version of panel (a), Figures 5.2–5.5, to determine the minimum sales volume required to make a new type of business activity worthwhile. Consider the case of a professor who had saved $50,000 and was thinking of spending it on a small airplane. What were the prospects for entering the air charter business—the business of carrying freight or taking people to major air terminals, other small airports, or simply for scenic rides? The prospective 1985 finances of such a venture are shown in the accompanying table.

Fixed Cost (dollars per year)		Average Variable Cost (dollars per flight hour)		Average Revenue
Explicit				
Hangar rent	$ 1,000	Gasoline	$14.–	$75.–
Insurance	600	Aircraft repairs	5.–	
Telephone	150	Avionics repairs	3.–	
Taxes, licenses	100	Miscellaneous	3.–	
Aeronautical charts	100	(long-distance phone,		
Miscellaneous supplies	100	landing fees)		
Implicit		**Total**	**$25.–**	
Salary forgone	$30,000			
(college teaching)				
Interest forgone	5,000			
(on $50,000 investment)				
Depreciation (on	2,500			
$50,000 plane)				
Other income	2,000			
forgone (writing				
college texts)				
Total	**$41,550**			

Using the data in the table and assuming that hourly variable cost and revenue would be unaffected by the number of hours flown per year, the professor drew the accompanying graph.

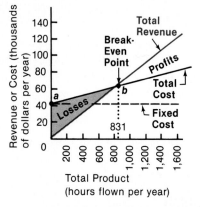

It became immediately obvious that the sale of fewer than 831 flight hours per year would yield losses (compared to the professor's alternatives). The sale of more than 831 flight hours would produce profits. At exactly 831 hours per year, the business would break even. Note how, at the break-even point (*b*), total revenue of 831 hours times $75 per hour, or $62,325, would be generated. Total cost would be the same: $41,550 (fixed) plus $20,775 (variable), the latter figure being equal to 831 times $25.

In this way, the expected-total-revenue and expected-total-cost lines for any prospective business can be juxtaposed in order to determine the minimum sales volume required to avoid losses. This procedure, called **break-even analysis,** is instantly adaptable to changes in the basic data. Note how any change in annual fixed cost changes the total-cost line's intercept at point *a*. A change in hourly variable cost

($25 per hour in our case) changes the slope of the total-cost line. A change in hourly revenue ($75 per hour in our case) changes the slope of the total-revenue line. In any of these cases, the new break-even output level can be determined at a glance by looking for the new break-even point. In many businesses, average variable cost and average revenue are in fact constant for wide ranges of output. For them, the kind of straight-line analysis used here can be an important decision-making tool.

Note: It does not follow, as the above graph seems to imply, that unlimited output yields infinite profit. Eventually, increases in output are bound to turn down the line of total revenue or turn up the line of total cost.

ANALYTICAL EXAMPLE 5.2

INCREMENTAL-PROFIT ANALYSIS: THE CASE OF CONTINENTAL AIR LINES

The owners of existing firms that are saddled with fixed costs often use a simplified version of panel (b), Figures 5.2–5.5, to determine whether they should take on a bit of extra business. Their approach is nothing else but an application of the optimization principle, usually known as **incremental-profit analysis.** Heeding the often cited advice of the British economist William S. Jevons with respect to fixed cost ("Bygones are bygones"), the analyst compares the expected *marginal revenue* with the expected *marginal cost* of a prospective action; the difference between the two is the extra, incremental, or **marginal profit** the action is likely to bring to the business.

Consider the case of Continental Air Lines, Inc. In 1962, it filled only half the available seats on its Boeing 707 jets, a number that was 15 percent worse than the national average. Yet running many half-empty flights *raised* the firm's profit. Here is why: The typical flight's total cost came to $4,500. Of this amount, $2,500 were the flight's share of fixed costs that would be incurred even if no flight were made; $2,000 were "out-of-pocket" costs. The typical flight's revenue came to $3,100. Thus each extra flight added to total revenue (produced a marginal revenue of) $3,100. Each flight added to total cost (produced a marginal cost of) $2,000. The difference between marginal revenue and marginal cost ($3,100 − $2,000) was the marginal or incremental profit ($1,100) from running an extra flight.

Source: "Airline Takes the Marginal Route," *Business Week,* April 20, 1963, pp. 111–14.

CLOSE-UP 5.1

THE PRICE OF SUGAR AND THE SUPPLY OF MOONSHINE

This chapter teaches that the supply of any product is affected by the prices of the inputs needed to make it. Consider the case of "moonshine"— illegal whiskey produced in regions of steep mountains and dense forests from Virginia to Georgia. For decades, agents of the Treasury Department's Bureau of Alcohol, Tobacco, and Firearms have been waging a seemingly hopeless battle against the elusive moonshiners. In recent times, the "revenuers" have been using airplane reconnaissance, infrared heat sensors, and dynamite to shut down the stills. The moonshiners, in turn, have abandoned wood and coke as fuel and have substituted propane gas because it produces no telltale smoke. Some of them have even camouflaged their operations against overflights with mock cemeteries, complete with fake tombstones and plastic flowers. In 1973, however, moonshiners were hit by a catastrophe that rivaled the appearance of federal agents: The price of sugar tripled, and it takes 10 pounds of sugar to make a gallon of illegal booze. Moonshine producers are always in a hurry to finish their batch and move on to another location. Unlike the producers of "government whiskey," they cannot rely on the slow process of drawing natural sugars from grain being distilled. Thus, in 1973, along with the price of sugar, the price of moonshine soared from $6 to $15 per gallon. At that level, its price was close to the price of legal whiskey, and the market for moonshine contracted severely.

Precisely the opposite happened in 1982. For one thing, as part of President Reagan's efforts to cut back government expenditures, the Bureau of Alcohol, Tobacco, and Firearms was scheduled to be disbanded and shifted its priorities away from moonshining toward firearms control. More importantly, new state and federal taxes on liquor raised the price of legal whiskey to $30 per gallon, raised the demand for the illegal "white lightning," and raised its street price to $20 per gallon—at the very time that the price of sugar was *declining*. All of these factors boosted the moonshining business. (In the course of a few months, agents of the Virginia Alcohol and Beverage Control Board discovered dozens of newly flourishing stills, one of them ready to ship 100,000 gallons of the drink.)

In the meantime, the same thing has been happening halfway around the globe. In pursuit of his temperance campaign, General Secretary Gorbachev sharply cut the production of liquor and raised prices. Before long, in such places as the hinterlands of *Soviet* Georgia, an estimated quarter million people were processing cheap Cuban sugar into a vodka-like home brew called *samogon,* which was stronger than but selling for much less than state-produced liquor. As a popular ditty put it, "Thank you, thank you, Cuba. All of Russia does proclaim, Ten ounces per kilo of sugar, And it burns with a bright blue flame."

Indeed, by 1988, the Soviet government was faced with enormous sugar shortages and introduced rationing of sugar.

Sources: *The Wall Street Journal,* July 30, 1975; *The New York Times,* January 23, 1980, p. A12; March 8, 1981, p. 11; December 27, 1981, p. 55; August 29, 1982, p. 37; November 16, 1987, p. A12; April 27, 1988, pp. A1 and 8.

CLOSE-UP 5.2

THE LONG-RUN PRICE ELASTICITY OF THE SUPPLY OF NEW HOUSING CONSTRUCTION

The purchase price of a new house is based essentially on two components: the price of the land and the price of the structure. Given that the price elasticity of the supply of land in urban areas is less than infinity, a rising demand for new homes inevitably drives up the price of land and consequently the price of housing. James R. Follain, Jr., wanted to know whether an increased demand for new homes would have a similar effect on the housing price by driving up the price of the structure component.

Using data for the 1947–75 period, he tested the hypothesis that the long-run supply of new residential construction had an elasticity of infinity. This would be true if the building industry, given enough time, could adjust its capabilities without limit at given minimum average total costs. Test results confirmed the hypothesis. The long-run supply curve for new construction was found to be horizontal. This suggested that the portion of recent increases in housing prices attributable to a lethargic response by builders would eventually dissipate. Note: This situation is depicted in panel (a) of Figure 5.9 by the rising short-run supply curves (*SRMC*) and by the horizontal long-run supply curve (*LRMC*).

Source: James R. Follain, Jr., "The Price Elasticity of the Long-Run Supply of New Housing Construction," *Land Economics,* May 1979, pp. 190–99.

PART

3

Markets for Goods

These chapters show how equilibrium prices and quantities are established when consumers who demand goods meet firms that supply them. The major types of market structures introduced here are distinguished from one another by the number of sellers, the homogeneity or differentiation of their products, the ease or difficulty of market entry, and more.

6

Perfect Competition

Utility-seeking households and profit-seeking firms are likely to meet one another in a multitude of markets. These markets, however, should not be envisioned as the open-air markets of old—with fish, flower, and vegetable stalls, under multicolored tents, located on the town square, and open only three days a week. As we will use the term, a **market** refers to an invisible framework within which people so inclined can make contact with one another for the purpose of trading something scarce and within which they jointly determine the price and quantity of what they are trading. Thus there are as many markets as there are scarce things—markets for apples, shoes, and airplane rides; markets for the use of workers, oil deposits, and turret lathes; markets for shares of stock and deeds to land. According to our definition, two shares of General Motors stock, traded in New York and Chicago, respectively, are being traded in the same market. But apples and shoes, traded in the same store, are being traded in two different markets.

For purposes of understanding the market economy, it is useful to classify markets into two broad classes: markets for goods (the economy's outputs) and markets for resources (the economy's inputs). While all the chapters of Part 3 focus on markets for goods, this chapter deals with a very special case, the **perfectly competitive market.**

DEFINING CHARACTERISTICS

To qualify as perfectly competitive, a market must possess the following four characteristics:

a. There is a large number of independent buyers and also of sellers.

b. All units of the traded item are viewed as identical.

c. All buyers and sellers possess full knowledge relevant to trading.

d. Nothing impedes entry into or exit from the market.

Let us consider each of these characteristics in turn.

There is a large number of independent buyers and also of sellers. Perfect competition requires that a large number of buyers and also of sellers can be found in a market and that each of these traders acts independently of all others.

This raises a difficult question about the meaning of largeness. Where do we draw the line? Is 1,000 a large number, while 999 is small? Fortunately, the issue is resolved quite easily: We can consider the number of buyers or sellers large if the ordinary transactions of any one buyer or seller do not appreciably affect the price at which transactions are made. This implies that even the largest buyer purchases only a trifling fraction of the total traded. Think of households buying oranges, for example. This also implies that even the largest seller sells only an insignificant percentage of the total traded. Consider farmers selling wheat, for example.

It is by no means difficult to find real-world markets in which the number of buyers is large in this sense and in which the number of sellers is large at the same time. Consider the organized stock or commodity exchanges or the foreign exchange markets. Any single buyer or seller of General Motors stock, of potatoes, or of German marks is in the very position with respect to price that has just been noted.

(Later chapters of this book, however, will demonstrate that there are other markets, not very well described by the examples found in this chapter, in which the number of buyers, or of sellers, or of both is small or in which large numbers of them act in collusion. The cigarette companies, meatpackers, or single employer in town are each an example of a small number of buyers; the auto companies, teamsters union, or OPEC cartel are examples of a small number of sellers.)

All units of the traded item are viewed as identical. Perfect competition also requires that, in the minds of buyers, all units of the item that are traded in any one market are identical. It is easy to find real-world markets that have this characteristic. Consider the market for beef or salt or Irish potatoes; for a given grade of coal, gasoline, or steel; of German marks or General Motors stock. So far as buyers are concerned, each unit is a perfect duplicate of any other unit. As a result, buyers never care from which par-

ticular seller they acquire the units they buy. They do not care whether they get farmer Brown's potatoes or farmer Green's, whether they buy the stock certificate of a given firm from a broker in Chicago or a lady next door.

Under such conditions, advertising by any one seller, aimed at taking customers away from other sellers in the same market, makes no sense. Imagine farmer Brown renting billboards, buying radio and television time, sending messages through the mail, taking out ads in magazines and newspapers, and employing an army of traveling sales representatives, telling us "Farmer Brown's Irish potatoes are the best," or (shading the truth somewhat) "Farmer Brown's Irish potatoes cure cancer," or even "Farmer Green's Irish potatoes cause cancer." With the possible exception of Green, people would just laugh at him, knowing full well that anybody's Irish potatoes were just as good as anybody else's. Brown would be pretty stupid wasting all that money.

(Once again, later chapters will show that other, *imperfectly* competitive markets exist as well—markets in which advertising is rampant and in which buyers care very much about the exact source of their supply. This is so when buyers see differences in different units of an item, regardless of whether this is objectively true. Think of aspirin brand A versus B; of autos, cigarettes, or soap; of toothpaste; and of labor. Think of products that buyers admit to be identical but that are linked to attributes that do matter: a store closer to home, free convenient parking, more and friendlier clerks, music while you shop, carpeted floors, more trading stamps, easier credit terms, prompter delivery, better warranties, faster repair and maintenance. . . .)

All buyers and sellers possess full knowledge relevant to trading. Perfect competition requires that all buyers and sellers are effectively linked with all potential trading partners and are fully aware of the characteristics of traded items and of prices offered and demanded. People are in close contact with each other, and their communication is continuous. The ticker tape of the Chicago

Board of Trade, showing—within seconds and all over the world—the current price of wheat and the quantities and qualities traded, is a good example of this situation.

(Once again, later chapters will consider other markets in which traders are very imperfectly informed about market conditions. Consider how traders in some markets can find each other only by incurring heavy costs for advertising or intermediary services. Consider how some market participants often know more about quality than their trading partners: Manufacturers may know that their appliances will break in four months, while purchasers do not; doctors may know of their limited experience or incompetence, while their patients do not; employers may know of risks attached to jobs, while employees do not; job applicants may know of their lack of talent or motivation, while their prospective employers do not. Such lack of knowledge about quality imposes costs on buyers in addition to those associated with simply finding out who the sellers are; thus, buyers who do not care to learn from bitter experience have to protect themselves against low quality by buying service contracts, warranties, or advice. Finally, consider how prices are often quoted deceptively and how they vary widely among sellers of identical items—a fact that buyers can discover only through an expensive search.)

Nothing impedes entry into and exit from the market. Perfect competition requires that anyone, at any time, is free to become a buyer or seller in a market, is free to enter the market on the same terms as existing traders. Similarly, it requires that there are no impediments that prevent anyone from ceasing to be a buyer or seller in a market and thus from leaving it.

There are many real-world markets in which this condition exists. If one possesses the requisite resources, one can become a buyer or seller of potatoes or piano lessons at any time, and the same holds for many other markets as well.

(Yet again, later chapters will look at exceptions that are just as frequent. Consider how technical conditions often dictate the existence of a single seller only, as in the case of electric power. Consider how sellers form cartels and then conspire to keep other sellers out of the market, as in the case of labor unions. Consider how governments grant exclusive franchises to limited numbers of sellers, as in the case of taxicabs, or how they place deliberate barriers in the way of some sellers, such as foreigners. Consider how government regulators sometimes force firms to continue serving certain markets even though the regulated firms would prefer otherwise.)

THE CONCEPT OF MARKET EQUILIBRIUM

Chapters 2 to 5 have shown why households and firms who face prices that they cannot affect by their individual actions will demand or supply, respectively, different quantities of goods at different potential prices. The current chapter, finally, brings together our previous analysis of market demand and that of market supply. We will now study the process by which, in a perfectly competitive market, only one of the many potential prices emerges as the actual market price at which people trade with one another. In this context, the concept of *equilibrium* becomes crucial. The British economist Alfred Marshall (1842–1924), whose Biography appears in Chapter 6 of the *Student Workbook* that accompanies this text, defined **market equilibrium** as a situation in which there is no innate tendency for price or quantity to change. In order to apply this definition, however, it is important to specify the time period. Marshall suggested a threefold classification of equilibrium: *momentary, short-run,* and *long-run* equilibrium.

Momentary equilibrium refers to market equilibrium in a period so short that the quantity supplied is absolutely fixed. **Short-run equilibrium** refers to a market equilibrium during a somewhat longer period in which a given number of firms can vary quantity supplied by changing the utilization rate of given plants.

Long-run equilibrium refers to market equilibrium in a period so long that new firms can enter the industry and old ones can leave it or change the size of their plants. The exact length of each period, of course, will vary with the industry in question.

MOMENTARY EQUILIBRIUM

To analyze momentary equilibrium, imagine a situation in which a given amount of a good already exists, in which the good in question cannot be stored, and in which time is too short to produce additional units. In such a situation, market supply is equal to a fixed quantity regardless of price. (The price elasticity of supply is zero.) This situation is illustrated by the vertical supply line in Figure 6.1. The supply shown there refers to 2,000 pounds of perishable fish that have just been landed by a number of fishing boats. Until their next trip out, the fishers cannot supply more. If the fish cannot be stored (and that we assume), the fishers might as well sell it for whatever it will bring. Given the market demand shown in the graph, point *e* denotes the equilibrium price and quantity. Only a price of $2.50 per pound can "clear" the market by balancing the quantities demanded and supplied.

If prices were higher, such as $3.50 per pound, the market would have a **surplus.** A surplus always denotes an amount by which the quantity demanded at a given price falls short of the quantity supplied. In this case, quantity demanded would equal 1,000 pounds per day (point *a*) and quantity supplied would be 2,000 pounds per day (point *b*). Trying to unload their wares, frustrated would-be sellers would underbid each other to attract customers. Price would fall, and quantity demanded would rise. (Note arrows *A* and *B*.)

If price were lower than $2.50 per pound, such as $1.50 per pound, the market would have a **shortage.** A shortage always denotes an amount by which the quantity demanded at a given price exceeds the quantity supplied. In this

FIGURE 6.1

Momentary Equilibrium

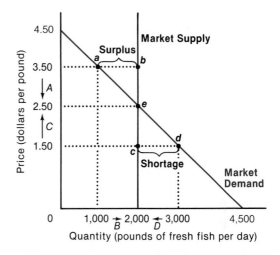

In a period so short that quantity supplied is absolutely fixed, momentary equilibrium is reached where vertical market supply intersects downward-sloping market demand (point *e*).

case, quantity demanded would equal 3,000 pounds per day (point *d*) and quantity supplied would be 2,000 pounds per day (point *c*). This time, frustrated would-be buyers would outbid each other, trying to buy what doesn't exist. Price would rise, and quantity demanded would fall (as indicated by arrows *C* and *D*).

All this can, of course, be shown algebraically as well. Our supply line can be represented by equation (1).

$$Q_S = 2,000 \qquad \textbf{(1)}$$

Our demand line can be represented by equation (2).

$$Q_D = 4,500 - \frac{4,500}{4.50} P \qquad \textbf{(2)}$$
$$= 4,500 - 1,000P$$

(Note how the values of the horizontal and vertical intercepts, such as 2,000, 4,500, and 4.50, appear in these equations.)

We can solve our equations with the help of the equilibrium condition that quantity supplied equal quantity demanded:

$$Q_S = Q_D \qquad (3)$$
$$2,000 = 4,500 - 1,000P$$
$$-2,500 = -1,000P$$
$$2.50 = P.$$

Substituting $P = 2.50$ in (2), we find $Q_D = Q_S = 2,000$.

Note: One must be careful not to apply the preceding analysis too freely. Many goods exist in absolutely fixed amounts, such as the paintings of old masters, back issues of *Time* magazine, or antique pieces of furniture. Yet the relevant market-supply curves can still be upward-sloping because these items (unlike fresh fish, fresh strawberries, or fresh mushrooms) can easily be stored. Thus owners are likely to vary the quantities put on the market with the prevailing price. (Fish, strawberries, or mushrooms can, of course, be preserved, but canned fish, frozen strawberries, and dried mushrooms are hardly the same products as their fresh counterparts.)

SHORT-RUN EQUILIBRIUM

The analysis of equilibrium is similar when we lengthen our time horizon to include the short run. In the short run, a given number of firms can respond to market prices by varying output within given plants. The market-supply line in Figure 6.2, therefore, is upward-sloping. In perfect analogy to our earlier discussion, point *e* alone depicts the equilibrium price and quantity. At the $6-per-bushel price, every buyer can find a seller, and every seller can find a buyer, for just the quantity each of them wishes to trade. Any higher price, such as $8 per bushel, would produce a surplus (and pressure for price to fall). Any lower price, such as $4 per bushel, would produce a shortage (and pressure for price to rise).

Because firms in the short run can adjust the utilization rate of their fixed plant, surpluses and

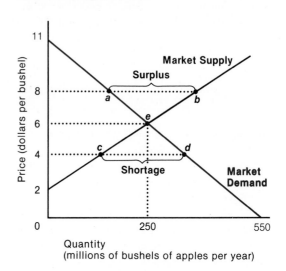

FIGURE 6.2

Short-Run Equilibrium

In a perfectly competitive market, short-run equilibrium is reached where upward-sloping market supply intersects downward-sloping market demand (point *e*). At any higher price, there would be surpluses, tending to depress price. At any lower price, there would be shortages, tending to raise price. Note: Figure 6.2 is a visual illustration of the story told in Chapter 1. Apples are *scarce* because, at a zero price, people's desire for this good (550 million bushels per year) exceeds the amount then available (zero). Yet, at a sufficiently high price, a scarce good can be in surplus, too.

shortages are eliminated not only by adjustments on the part of the buyers (as in the momentary run), but also by adjustments on the part of sellers. Thus a price fall from $8 per bushel to $6 per bushel would raise quantity demanded (from *a* to *e*), but it would also lower quantity supplied (from *b* to *e*). Similarly, a price rise from $4 per bushel to $6 per bushel would lower quantity demanded (from *d* to *e*), but it would also raise quantity supplied (from *c* to *e*). All of these adjustments, of course, would occur for the reasons already discussed in Chapters 3 and 5.

In a perfectly competitive market, furthermore, the equilibrium price and quantity are established by the collective action of all market participants despite the fact that no individual, acting alone, has the power to affect the equilibrium price.

Once equilibrium is reached, any one seller who simply announced a price above equilibrium would immediately lose all customers; they would know that they could find identical units being sold (at the equilibrium price) by thousands of other sellers. Once equilibrium is reached, any one buyer who simply announced a price below equilibrium would immediately drive away all sellers; they would know that they could find thousands of other buyers willing to pay the equilibrium price.

Nor can any one seller or buyer cause a shift of the equilibrium price by some positive *action,* like dropping out of the market entirely. Because the kind of market-demand line illustrated in Figure 6.2 would be the summation of thousands or millions of individual demand lines, the loss of any one of these components would shift the market-demand line to the left (and hence the intersection point down), but imperceptibly so. The boycotting of the market (in protest of too high a price) by any one of 70 million household-buyers of apples, for example, just would not make a big-enough dent. Perhaps this buyer could cause a surplus of 20 bushels a year at the $6-per-bushel price, but given the 250-million-bushel-per-year market volume, this might drop the equilibrium price only to $5.9999999 per bushel—that is, leave it unchanged! You are in this position yourself when it comes to buying apples. Do you think you could make the price of apples come down if you (alone) decided not to buy any?

Similarly, the market-supply line of Figure 6.2 is the summation of thousands upon thousands of individual supply lines. The loss of any one of these components would shift the market-supply line to the left (and hence the intersection point up), but imperceptibly so. If there were 60,000 competitors, the single orchardist who dropped out entirely (in protest of too low a price) might cause a shortage of 7,000 bushels

per year at the $6-per-bushel price, but given the 250-million-bushel-per-year market volume, this might raise the equilibrium price only to $6.0011 per bushel—that is, leave it unchanged as well. This is why economists talk of **atomistic competition** in perfectly competitive markets. The power of each market participant, like that of an atom in a vast ocean, is too insignificant to affect the equilibrium price.

Note once again that the story depicted by Figure 6.2 can be expressed mathematically as well. The supply line shown there can be expressed by equation (4)[1]

$$Q_S = -125 + 62.5P \qquad (4)$$

The demand line of Figure 6.2 can be expressed by equation (5).[2]

$$Q_D = 550 - 50P \qquad (5)$$

We can solve for the equilibrium values with the help of equation (6) as follows.

$$Q_S = Q_D \qquad (6)$$
$$-125 + 62.5P = 550 - 50P$$
$$112.5P = 675$$
$$P = 6$$

Substituting $P = 6$ in (5), we find $Q_D = Q_S = 250$.

---

[1]This equation can be derived from the graph by noting that the vertical intercept of market supply is 2, and its slope is 4/250. (A price rise of $4 from $2 to $6 is associated with a quantity rise of 250 million bushels per year.) Thus, an equation of the line can be written as $P = 2 + (4/250)Q_S$. Algebraic manipulation of this equation yields equation (4) above:

$$P - 2 = (4/250)Q_S, \text{ hence}$$
$$250P - 500 = 4Q_S, \text{ hence}$$
$$62.5P - 125 = Q_S.$$

[2]This equation can be derived from the graph by noting that the horizontal intercept of market demand is 550, while its slope is negative 6/300. (A price rise of $6 from 0 to $6 is associated with a quantity decline from 550 to 250, or of 300 million bushels per year.) Thus, an equation of the line can be written as $Q_D = 550 - (300/6)P$, which is the same as equation (5) above.

LONG-RUN EQUILIBRIUM

Once we extend our time horizon even further to include the long run, we may discover forces for inevitable change that are hidden in the short run. Given the conditions of a perfectly competitive market, which allows firms freely to enter or exit industries, the existence of *profits* in the short run would induce existing firms to expand their capacities, and induce new firms to enter the industry. Profit, after all, measures income to the owners of firms for the services of their own resources that exceeds the amount available from their best outside alternatives. Similarly, the existence of *losses* in the short run would induce existing firms to contract their capacities and even to leave their industry altogether. It would also discourage outsiders from establishing new firms in the industry. Losses, after all, measure the extent to which the owners of firms could get higher income for the services of their own resources in alternative pursuits. A perfectly competitive market will be in long-run equilibrium only when the producers in the industry make neither profits nor losses. In such a zero-profit situation, the owners of firms are, of course, earning from their own resources used in their own firms exactly as much income as they would earn in their best alternatives. They have, therefore, no reason to leave the industry for those alternatives. Nor have outsiders any reason to enter this industry and abandon those alternative pursuits.

A Profitable Industry Expands

Panels (a) and (b) of Figure 6.3 picture a short-run equilibrium that harbors within it the seeds for long-run change. Panel (a) shows market demand, *D*, market supply, *S*, and the equilibrium price and quantity corresponding to point *e*. Panel (b) illustrates the situation of a typical firm in this industry, very much like that in Figure 5.2, ''A Profitable Business'' (see p. 144). Faced with a market price of $8 per bushel, the firm produces

3,500 bushels of apples per year, a tiny fraction of the 170-million-bushel total supplied by all firms as a group. This particular level of the firm's output is, of course, selected because it equates (at point *a*) the marginal benefit of production (which is the apple price, *P*) with the marginal cost of production, *MC*. Note how point *a* is one point on the firm's supply curve, *s*, and how *s* is one of many components of market supply, *S*, and equals the rising branch of *MC* above the minimum point of average variable cost, *AVC*.

Note also: At the optimal output level, average total cost, *ATC*, equals $6.50 per bushel (point *b*). Hence an average profit of $8 − $6.50, or $1.50 per bushel is being made (distance *ab*); total profit equals $1.50 per bushel times 3,500 bushels per year, or $5,250 per year (the shaded area). It is not difficult to see why the owners of such a firm would be tempted to enlarge their productive capacity so as to reap even larger profits. Nor is it hard to see why all kinds of other people, not currently in the apple business at all, would also be planting new apple trees, building apple storage barns, and ordering orchard spraying machines. These others may be producers of bobby pins (making a loss on their investment) or enterprising taxi drivers (with houses on three-acre lots).

Over the years, as it enlarged its capacity, our firm's supply line, *s* (along with all the other cost lines) would, therefore, appear farther to the right (note the arrows). Market supply, *S*, would also shift right because there would be more firms and larger ones. As a result, given demand, intersection *e* would move, and the equilibrium price would fall. This process would continue until its ultimate cause (the existence of profits) was eliminated. Profits would be eliminated when the equilibrium price, then at intersection *e** (not shown) below and to the right of *e*, was just equal to the minimum average total cost of production (now at *c*).

Caution: During the process of industry expansion, the minimum level of *ATC* itself might change. This change in minimum *ATC*

FIGURE 6.3

A Profitable Industry Expands

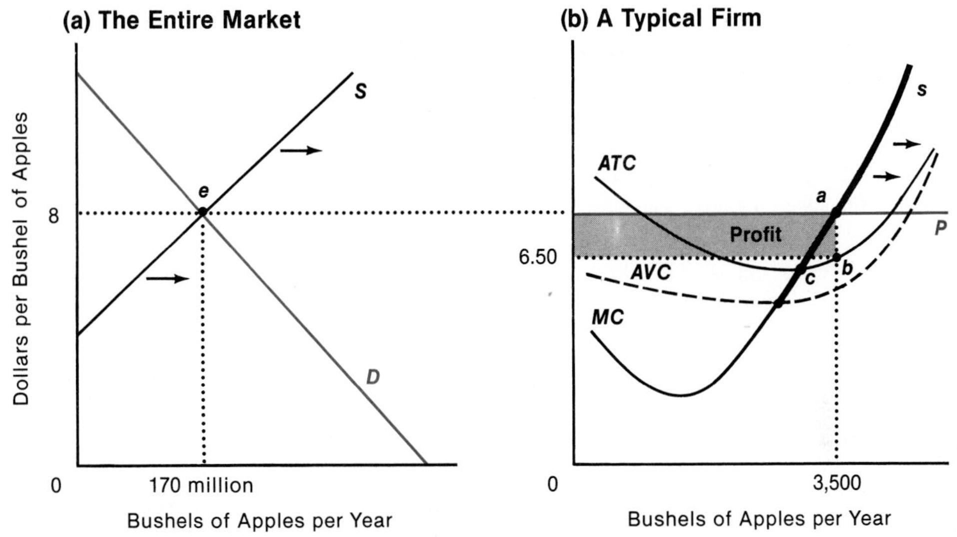

(a) The Entire Market

(b) A Typical Firm

When markets are perfectly competitive, a short-run equilibrium—panel (a)—in which the typical firm makes a profit—panel (b)—harbors within it the seeds for long-run change. The number and size of firms in the industry will grow, and this process will cease precisely when product price (now at *e*) has fallen to equal the minimum average total cost (*ATC*) of producing the product (now at *c*). *Caution:* The level of minimum *ATC* may change in the process of industry expansion.

---

might be due to **external economies**—that is, favorable technological or pecuniary externalities associated with industry growth—or it might be the result of **external diseconomies**—that is, unfavorable technological or pecuniary externalities associated with industry growth. These concepts must not be confused with **internal economies** (increasing returns to scale) or **internal diseconomies** (decreasing returns to scale), which determine the shape of the individual firm's long-run supply curves. (See Figure 5.9, "Short-Run Versus Long-Run Costs and Long-Run Supply," on p. 154.)

An Unprofitable Industry Contracts

Whether we have profits in the industry initially (as assumed in the preceding section) or whether we have losses in the industry (as about to be discussed), the end result is the same: zero profits. Panel (a) of Figure 6.4 shows market demand, *D*, market supply, *S*, and the equilibrium price and quantity, corresponding to point *e*. Panel (b) illustrates the unprofitable situation of a typical firm in this industry, very much like that in Figure 5.4. "A Losing Business" (see p. 147). Faced with a market price of $5 per bushel, the firm produces 2,700 bushels of apples per year, a tiny fraction of the 280-million-bushel total supplied by all firms as a group. This output level equates (at point *a*) product price, *P*, and marginal cost, *MC*.

At this optimal output level, average total cost, *ATC*, equals $6.10 per bushel (point *b*). Hence an average loss of $6.10 – $5, or $1.10 per bushel is being incurred (distance *ab*); total loss equals $1.10 per bushel times 2,700 bushels per year, or $2,970 per year (dotted area). Clearly, the owners of such a firm would wish to escape the loss by contracting their productive capacity and eventually leaving the industry altogether. And outsiders would have no desire to enter this field of activity.

After a number of years, the firm pictured in panel (b) may have disappeared—along, perhaps, with thousands of others—or its capacity may have been severely cut. In the latter case, its supply line, *s* (along with all the other cost lines), would appear farther to the left (note the arrows). Market supply, *S*, would also shift left because there would be fewer and smaller firms. As a result, intersection *e* would move, given demand, and the equilibrium price would rise. This process would continue until its ultimate cause (the existence of losses) was eliminated. Losses would be eliminated when the equilibrium price, then at intersection *e** (not shown) above and to the left of *e,* was just equal to minimum average total cost of production (now at *c*).

Note again that during the process of industry contraction the minimum level of *ATC* itself might change, depending on the existence or absence of external economies or diseconomies.

The Normal Price

As we have just seen, in an economy with perfectly competitive markets, profits or losses invite an expansion or contraction, respectively, of the affected industry. Because this process comes to a halt precisely when profits or losses have been eliminated, there exists the ever present tendency for equilibrium price to change until the volume of a good that is demanded is sold at a price equal to the lowest possible average total cost of producing it. This level of price is called the **normal price.** Once the normal price is reached, the owners of firms earn, from their own resources used in their own firms, neither more nor less than they could earn in their

FIGURE 6.4

An Unprofitable Industry Contracts

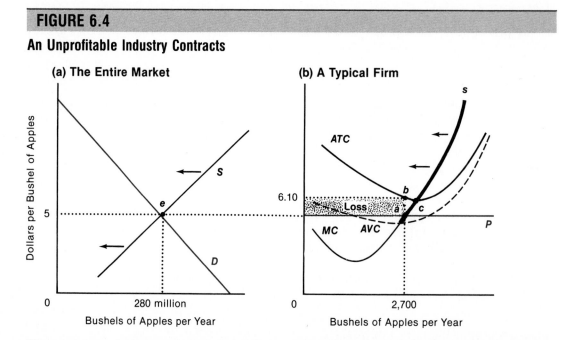

When markets are perfectly competitive, a short-run equilibrium—panel (a)—in which the typical firm makes a loss—panel (b)—harbors within it the seeds for long-run change. The number and size of firms in the industry will decline, and this process will cease when product price (now at *e*) has risen to equal the minimum average total cost (*ATC*) of producing the product (now at *c*). Note: The level of minimum *ATC* itself may change in the process of industry contraction.

best outside alternatives. As was shown in Figure 5.3, "A Zero-Profit Business" (p. 146), the revenue of firms then just covers their total cost, variable and fixed, including, of course, implicit cost. Figure 6.5 illustrates the nature of long-run equilibrium as well as a variety of ways in which it might be restored once it is upset.

A Constant-Cost Industry.   Consider panel (a) in Figure 6.5. Imagine market demand, D, and market supply, S, to prevail. According to intersection a, when apples sell at $6 per bushel and 250 million bushels are traded per year, we have a short-run equilibrium. We now assume that the typical firm's short-run and long-run cost curves look like those in panel (a) of Figure 5.9, "Short-Run Versus Long-Run Costs and Long-Run Supply." The typical firm, before industry growth, finds itself in long-run equilibrium as well: Faced with a $6-per-bushel price, such a firm equates price, P, with short-run and long-run marginal cost, $SRMC$ and $LRMC$, at b and produces 3,000 bushels per year. Because short-run and long-run average total cost ($SRATC$ and $LRATC$) equal P at b, the firm makes zero profit. There is no reason for new firms to enter the industry or for old ones to expand or contract. Because a and b are found at the same level, $6 is not only the short-run equilibrium price but also the long-run normal price.

Now imagine that demand rose to D^*. A new short-run equilibrium at c would be established, with price at $10 per bushel and quantity at 360 million bushels per year. The long-run equilibrium would be gone: The typical firm would now equate higher price, P^* (shown by the horizontal dashed line), with $SRMC$ at d, and produce 4,400 bushels per year. (The movement by the typical firm from b to d corresponds to the movement by all firms from a to c.) Yet short-run average total cost for the new optimal output volume would equal only $7 per bushel (point e). Thus the firm would make a profit of $3 per bushel (distance de) and a total profit of $13,200 per year (shaded). Indeed, the firm would notice that the long-run average total cost of producing the new output volume was only $6 per bushel (point f),

and the firm would wish to acquire a larger plant with minimum $SRATC$ at f. At the same time, new firms would be attracted into the industry by all the profit being made. The industry would begin to expand; supply curve, S, would shift to the right.

Panel (a) pictures the case of a **constant-cost industry,** so called because the normal price of its product is unchanged after the industry has ceased to expand or contract. This situation arises whenever technological or pecuniary externalities are absent. Under such circumstances, our expanding firm's cost curves simply shift to the right, as from $SRATC$ and $SRMC$ to $SRATC^*$ and $SRMC^*$. (Note that point g on the graph after industry growth corresponds to point f on that picturing the firm before industry growth.) The shift of $SRMC$ to $SRMC^*$ on the right-hand side of our graph is depicted, along with the entry of new firms, by the rightward shift of S to S^*. At the new equilibrium at h, product price has returned to $6 per bushel; larger and more numerous firms supply 525 million bushels per year. The typical firm, now larger, supplies 4,400 bushels per year, according to the new equality of P with $SRMC^* = LRMC$ (at $g = f$). Zero profit has returned; the equilibrium price equals the normal price.

Note how an increase in market demand from D to D^* has, in the long run, called forth such an increase in supply that market price remained unchanged. A constant-cost industry's long-run supply, therefore, is a horizontal line, such as the colored line through a and h.

An Increasing-Cost Industry.   Panel (b) of Figure 6.5 depicts the same initial situation as in panel (a), and the same intermediate position, caused by the increase in demand. Accordingly, identical curves and points have been given the same labels as in panel (a).

Panel (b), however, depicts the case of an **increasing-cost industry,** so called because the normal price of its product is higher after the industry has ceased to expand or is lower after it has ceased to contract. This situation arises whenever unfavorable technological or pecuniary externalities are associated with industry expansion. Under such circumstances, the cost curves of all firms shift up. Thus an expanding firm's cost curves are not only shifted right, but also up, as from short-run or long-run ATC and MC to ATC' and MC'. The shift of $SRMC$ to $SRMC'$, on the right-hand side of the graph, is again depicted, along with the entry of new firms, by the rightward shift of S, but this shift is weaker than in panel (a), halting at S' and equilibrium point k. This weaker shift of S to S' reflects the fact that the adjustment process is faster when profits are squeezed away not only by falling product price [as in panel (a)], but also by rising costs. In panel (b), therefore, the industry's expansion comes to a halt by the time product price has fallen to $9 per bushel and larger and more numerous firms supply 400 million bushels per year (point k). The typical firm, now larger, supplies 4,400 bushels per year, according to the equality of P' with $SRMC' = LRMC'$ (at i). Zero profit has returned; the equilibrium price equals the normal price.

This time, however, an increase in market demand from D to $D*$ has, in the long run, called forth an increase in supply so weak that market price rose. An increasing-cost industry's long-run supply, therefore, is an upward-sloping line, like the colored line through a and k.

A Decreasing-Cost Industry. Panel (c), finally, depicts the same initial situation as in panel (a), and the same intermediate position, caused by the increase in demand. Accordingly, identical curves and points have been given the same labels as in panel (a).

Panel (c) now depicts the case of a **decreasing-cost industry,** so called because the normal price of its product is lower after the industry has ceased to expand or is higher after it has ceased to contract. This situation arises whenever favorable technological or pecuniary externalities are associated with industry expansion. Under such circumstances, the cost curves of all firms shift down. Thus an expanding firm's cost curves are

not only shifted right, but also down, as from short-run or long-run ATC and MC to ATC'' and MC''. The shift of $SRMC$ to $SRMC''$ on the right-hand side of the graph is again depicted, along with the entry of new firms, by the rightward shift of S, but this shift is now stronger than in either panel (a) or (b), halting at S'' and equilibrium point n. This stronger shift from S to S'' reflects the fact that the adjustment process is slower when profits are squeezed away by falling product price but are enlarged by falling costs. In panel (c), therefore, the industry's expansion comes to a halt only by the time product price has fallen to $2 per bushel and larger and more numerous firms supply 660 million bushels per year (point n). The typical firm, now larger, supplies 4,400 bushels per year, according to the new equality of P'' with $SRMC'' = LRMC''$ (at m). Zero profit has returned; the equilibrium price equals the normal price.

This time, however, an increase in market demand from D to $D*$ has, in the long run, called forth an increase in supply so strong that market price fell. A decreasing-cost industry's long-run supply, therefore, is a downward-sloping line, such as the colored line through a and n.

TWO AGELESS DEBATES

When Alfred Marshall introduced the preceding analysis, he effectively put an end to a seemingly eternal debate about forces that determine the prices of goods in perfectly competitive markets.

Subjective-Utility Versus Objective-Cost Theories

For thousands of years, there have been those who argued that the price of a good is determined by *subjective factors;* that is, by the usefulness or utility the good has for people, which is reflected in demand. According to this argument, a pound of meat fetches a high price compared to a pound of mud because meat has greater usefulness. Unfortunately, this theory left too many ques-

FIGURE 6.5

Long-Run Industry Supply Curves

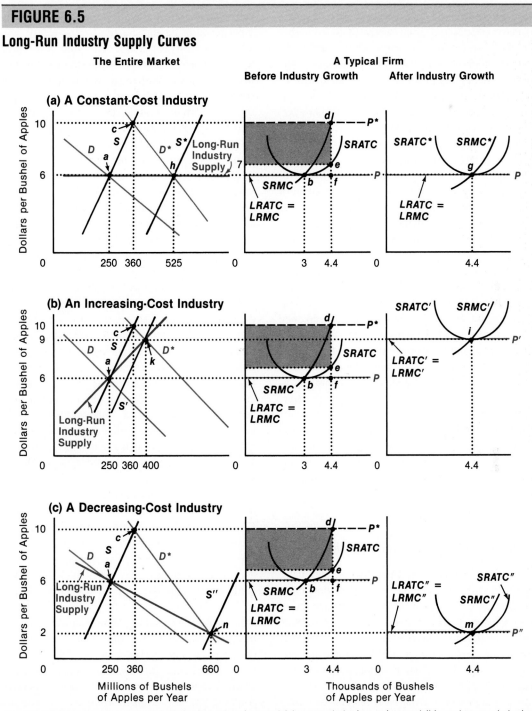

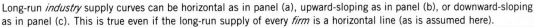

Long-run *industry* supply curves can be horizontal as in panel (a), upward-sloping as in panel (b), or downward-sloping as in panel (c). This is true even if the long-run supply of every *firm* is a horizontal line (as is assumed here).

tions unanswered: Don't people derive much greater satisfaction from water than from diamonds? Isn't life itself impossible without the former but quite tolerable without the latter? Why then does a pound of water fetch such a low price compared to a pound of diamonds?

Questions such as these gave rise to an alternative theory, according to which the price of a good is determined by *objective factors;* that is, by the cost of producing the good, which is reflected in supply. Because it costs so much more to produce a pound of meat than to produce a pound of mud, the argument went, meat has the higher price. Similarly, diamonds have a higher price than water because diamonds cost more to produce. Yet, again, there were counterexamples.

Alfred Marshall put an end to this fruitless debate by noting that demand and supply (subjective and objective factors) were *both* responsible for the level of a good's price. He likened the two forces to the blades on a pair of scissors. Just as it is pointless to say that a piece of paper is cut by the moving blade when the other is held stationary, Marshall argued, it is also pointless to claim that either demand or supply alone determines price.

Thus the principle of mutual determination of prices permanently superseded the idea of a single determinant. The Marshallian analysis did little, however, to end another debate about the morality of prices.

Just Price Versus Scarcity Price

For as long as there have been buyers, they have wished for lower prices. For as long as there have been sellers, they have wished for higher ones. Philosophers since Aristotle have argued about the "morally just" level of prices. Governments of all ages have attempted to define and impose such prices. The Roman emperor Diocletian prescribed "just prices" for all goods and executed sellers who overcharged buyers. A millenium later, St. Thomas Aquinas drew up rules of his own, and he assured violators of eternal damnation. Modern governments in all countries

continue to follow their lead, although punishment tends to be less drastic.

Economists, of course, are quite bewildered by this debate. They look upon the equilibrium prices discussed earlier in this chapter not as something to be moralized about, but as crucial bits of information about the degree of scarcity prevailing, information that allows vast numbers of people to work together in an orderly way. Consider the $6-per-bushel apple price depicted in Figure 6.2. It summarizes for all concerned a vast amount of dispersed knowledge. A household looking at this price is told, indirectly of course, that apples can be had for $6 a bushel because there happen to be another 90 million would-be apple buyers who value apples in millions of different ways, all of which is reflected in market demand which, for purposes of consistency, must equal market supply. In turn, the market supply reflects the different circumstances of some 60,000 orchardists who happen to be endowed with so many apple trees, who happen to possess certain kinds of technical knowledge, who happen to face certain weather conditions, who happen to be confronted with certain wage levels that must be paid to get people to pick apples rather than produce cars *. . . and much more!* Of course, no household really wants to be told all these things. That is why perfectly competitive markets eliminate the infinite detail and just provide, to each consumer, the most necessary information in capsule form: *"If you are willing to pay $6 per bushel, you can buy all the apples you like."*

This price implies, of course, that there are good reasons (not given to the household) why it could *not* have all the apples it wanted for $4 per bushel. The reason might be that many orchardists would then suffer losses and go out of business, and thus there would be fewer apples. Or perhaps other people would then want so many more apples (and would so quickly snap up available stores of them) that this household couldn't find any, even if orchardists did supply the same amount as before. A million and one reasons might be given. But our household would have neither the inclination nor the time to listen.

Thus the market economy saves the household the trouble of wasting its time hearing lengthy explanations. It just sends out its broadcast message!

The same message, of course, goes to all other households at the same time, and a similar message goes to each and every firm: *"If you are willing to accept $6 per bushel, you can sell all the apples you like."* This message, too, takes the place of lengthy detailed explanations. If a firm were unable to produce apples at anything less than $20 per bushel, it would quickly get the point: There are lots of other producers around who are smarter or more fortunate! They know more about putting together fertilizer, trees, and tender loving care, or they enjoy a better climate, or whatever. This price tells the firm: "The apple business is not for you!"

Naturally, any well-intentioned government that wanted to establish a "just price" of $8 (to help sellers) or of $4 (to help buyers) would upset the intricate mechanism that determines a proper indicator of scarcity in the $6-per-bushel equilibrium price. When establishing a "just price" other than the equilibrium price, such a government would inevitably create a surplus or a shortage and thus open a Pandora's box of problems. These problems would, ultimately, force the government to abandon its intervention or to replace the spontaneous market coordination of people's activities with a managerial coordination of its own. These are matters to which we will return in later chapters. The remainder of this chapter will describe a few of the manifold uses of the tools of analysis just discussed.

APPLICATIONS OF MARSHALLIAN ANALYSIS

Application 1: Abundance Versus Scarcity

Our simple discussion of momentary equilibrium (Figure 6.1) can be expanded to help us understand how abundance can turn into scarcity. Consider Figure 6.6. The vertical supply lines shown there are identical in the three panels; they represent the limited quantity of something that is available to people during the course of a year (and the availability of which, at least in the short run, is not influenced by price). All kinds of things might be measured along the horizontal axis: the number of college openings available for would-be freshmen; the number of apartments available in a city; the number of acres available on Manhattan Island; the number of satellites that can be placed in a given orbit without causing signal interference or collision hazards; the number of cars that can traverse a given stretch of highway safely (while driving at the speed limit); the number of whales that can be caught while keeping the whale population stationary; the number of human babies that can be born while keeping the human population stationary; or even the number of tons of sewage that can be dumped into a river without any adverse consequences on subsequent uses of the river.

The demand lines in our graphs are, however, downward-sloping; they depict the typical tendency of people to take all they want at zero price, but less and less at higher and higher *positive* prices.

Now focus on the succession of panels (a) through (c). Panel (a) pictures a world of abundance. Even at a zero price, people only want two units per year; yet four units are available. Everyone can take all he or she wants and then some! The right-hand circle in Figure 1.1 (on p. 5) exceeds the left-hand circle; there is no need to restrict the use of this good to anyone. There is no conflict, no need for government to clarify who may or may not enjoy the good. There is no need to economize the good, and no need for economists' telling people how to make careful choices. In such a situation, a zero price is a proper price because there is no scarcity. Does such a situation ever exist? Of course, it does. Consider Manhattan Island, or the entire North American continent for that matter, when the first European settlers arrived. There was more than enough land for everyone, at a zero price. Unlike today, there were no Registries of Deeds that could identify the owners of every single acre of land and, thus, guide a potential demander to a

FIGURE 6.6

When Abundance Turns into Scarcity

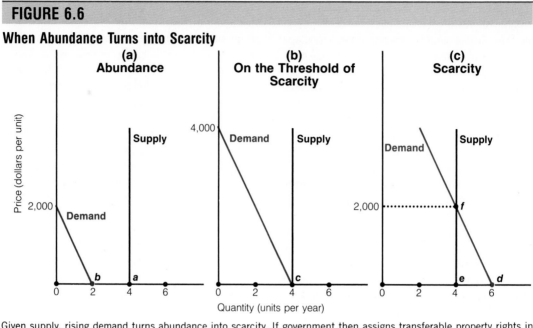

Given supply, rising demand turns abundance into scarcity. If government then assigns transferable property rights in things that are scarce, new markets emerge for the scarce things that were once free, and these things are traded at a positive price.

potential supplier of that land. Or consider almost any U.S. highway between midnight and 5 A.M. A stretch of that highway might accommodate 400 cars, properly spaced, going at the speed limit. Yet, even at a zero price, only 5 cars may be found on that road at any one time. Similar to the gap *ab* in panel (a) of Figure 6.6, supply exceeds demand at a zero price; the highway is a free good, not a scarce one. Or, consider, finally, the world in the past when, perhaps, 4,000 whales could be "harvested" per year while keeping their population unchanged (because natural births exceeded natural deaths to this extent), when, perhaps, 4 million human babies could be born each year while keeping human population growth small (because natural deaths equaled 3.9 million per year, let us say), or when, perhaps, a great river could easily absorb the annual dumping of 4,000 tons of raw sewage without any noticeable harm to anything and anyone (property, plants, animals, or people). What if, under these circumstances, people in fact were catching 2,000 whales per year, were

having 2 million babies per year, or were dumping 2,000 tons of sewage per year? Then, once again, the story of panel (a) would fully apply: There would have been no scarcity and certainly no need for any government to assign restrictive rights to the catching of whales, the having of babies, or the dumping of sewage.

Panel (b), in contrast, pictures a world on the threshold of scarcity. Supply (in this example) is unchanged, but demand has grown. (The entire demand line has shifted to the right; at any given price we care to consider, people now demand more of the good than before.) Still, everyone can get all he or she wants. (The right-hand circle in Figure 1.1 now equals the left-hand circle.)

Panel (c), finally, depicts the world in which we usually find ourselves, the world of scarcity. Note how demand has further shifted to the right. (The right-hand circle in Figure 1.1 now is smaller than the left-hand one, and conflict is bound to appear.) At a zero price, demand exceeds supply; point *d* lies to the right of *e* in panel (c). And now consider what happens if government does nothing at all: At a zero price, people now desire more places in college, more apartments, more acres of land, more satellite slots, more highway space, more whales, more babies, more sewage dumping grounds than are supplied (in the sense defined above). The law of the jungle takes hold. The strong or the cunning get into college, take over the apartments that are available, or the land that exists. Satellites, perhaps, are orbited without regard to the consequences, and signal interference and collisions become commonplace. Some 600 cars, perhaps, do crowd onto the highway designed to accommodate 400 cars, but driving at the speed limit and safely is a thing of the past. Some 6,000 whales are caught per year, but this exceeds the safe supply, and the whale population begins to decline. Some 6 million human babies, perhaps, are born, and the human population begins to rise rapidly. Some 6,000 tons of raw sewage, perhaps, are dumped, but the consequences cease to be nil. The fish die, as do birds that eat fish; there are ''no-swimming'' signs. Newspaper headlines talk of *crisis* everywhere: of violence in the cities and in the countryside (people are fighting over apartments and over land), of highway congestion and accidents, of whales' becoming extinct, of a human population explosion that promises standing-room-only in a hundred years, of dying rivers that stink.

But imagine instead that a government, at the very moment that the world crossed the threshold from abundance into scarcity, had clearly established property rights in the things newly scarce. (It might have issued 4,000 deeds to the available apartments, acres of land, or orbital slots, for instance; it might have issued limited numbers of 400 highway-user permits, 4,000 whaling permits, 4 million human-birth permits, and 4,000 one-ton sewage-dumping permits.) And suppose this government had stood ready to use its police power to enforce a new set of rules: Only the holders of property rights—be they original recipients or subsequent buyers thereof—could use the things now scarce. Under these circumstances, as panel (c) illustrates, the *shortage* of *ed* at a zero price would have driven

up the price to an equilibrium level of $2,000 per unit, cutting quantity demanded from the excessive amount at *d* to equal supply at *f*. As a result, anyone who wanted to go to college for a year could reserve an appropriate opening for a $2,000 fee; anyone who wanted an apartment for a year, an acre of land, an orbital slot, room on a highway, or the right to catch a whale, have a baby, or dump a ton of sewage could do so at the same $2,000 per unit price. As a result, the above-cited newspaper headlines would disappear; in each case, the positive price would cut back the quantity demanded at a zero price (would cut back the left-hand circle in Figure 1.1) to the available quantity supplied (to the smaller size of the right-hand circle). Thus the establishment of transferable property rights would eliminate the chaos that would otherwise ensue when scarcity prevails.

A final note: It is one thing to recognize that government must assign property rights in all scarce things and facilitate their voluntary exchange before a *market economy* can function well. It is also important to realize, however, that the task of assigning property rights is likely to be a painful one because it requires difficult choices. The task is also likely to surface anew in each generation as hitherto undreamed-of forms of scarcity develop. We are all used to the existence of property rights and markets with respect to apples, cars, college slots, houses, and land, for instance, but who has ever heard of property rights in orbital slots, in whale-hunting rights, baby-birth rights, or sewage-dumping rights? Such property rights could never be established and enforced, some people think, but one shouldn't be so sure. Seemingly preposterous things have happened before. (In 1912, when the United States had no federal income tax, critics of an income tax proposal argued that Americans would never pay it; yet soon Americans were obediently filling out income tax forms and sending billions of dollars to Uncle Sam every year.) As Chapter 15 will illustrate, new property rights are being born all the time. Nevertheless, it is true that governments often neglect the crucial tasks outlined in this section. When, as a consequence, markets fail to work, critics often talk of "market failure," but it may well be the failure of government to lay the proper foundations for markets, or it may be that the manifold governmental activities that hamper the free operation of markets are responsible for the alleged market failure.

Application 2: Cobweb Cycles

For centuries, interested observers have noted a curious phenomenon in many markets: In one period, quantity traded is small and price high. In the next period, quantity is high and price is low. Again and again this cycle repeats itself. This phenomenon applies to a wide variety of goods—from cattle, corn, and hogs to lumber, ships, and wine and even to new economics Ph.D.'s. All these goods have in common a considerable time lag between the decision to produce them and their final availability for sale in the market.

Marshall's analysis of market equilibrium provides a simple explanation—by pointing out that while movement to equilibrium is an ever present tendency, equilibrium is *not* a continuous state of affairs. More often than not, the world is not settled down nicely at an equilibrium, but *is in the process of moving toward one*. This movement can take many forms, including that of an *eternal cycle*, a *damped cycle*, or an *explosive cycle*, among others.

An Eternal Cycle. In panel (a) of Figure 6.7, the market demand for pork is represented by D; we assume the market supply to be fixed in an initial period at 2 million tons per year, represented by dashed line S_1. Point *a*, therefore, depicts a momentary equilibrium. Price equals $4,000 per ton. Compared with their past experience, hog producers may find this price very attractive. Accordingly, they may wish to increase quantity supplied, *but they cannot do it overnight*. In fact, there is a biologically determined lag of about one year between breeding and slaughter: Hogs have a gestation period of four months; it takes two months after birth

before they can be weaned, and another four to six months before they have reached marketable weight. Hog producers, therefore, inevitably make production decisions in the present that affect supply with a considerable lag. Once the future arrives, supply is again momentarily fixed. The decision in period 1 to supply not 2 million but 5 million tons of pork per year, for instance, yields market supply S_2 in period 2. If market demand has not changed (and that we assume), the increased supply cannot be sold at the $4,000 price (point *b*). A new momentary equilibrium is reached at *c*. Price plummets to $1,500 per ton. Almost certainly, hog producers will then contract their operations so as to supply, perhaps, only 2 million tons of pork per year. Period 3 supply, S_3, once more momentarily fixed, equals S_1, but it doesn't sell at $1,500 per ton (point *d*). Given demand, price soars to $4,000 per ton in period 3 (point *a*). From here, the cycle continues: from *a* not to *b* (as producers expect), but to *c;* from *c* not to *d*, but to *a*, and so on forever more—unless, of course, producers learn from their experience and change their ways of adjusting quantity supplied to price. Their present behavior is summarized by supply line S^*. Unlike the supply lines we have met before, this one indicates the quantity supplied in one period as a function of the price prevailing in an earlier period: Point *b* shows the quantity supplied in period 2 when price is $4,000 per ton in period 1; point *d* shows the quantity supplied in period 3 when price is $1,500 per ton in period 2. As long as producers continue to make decisions according to lagged supply line S^*, the potential equilibrium at *e* cannot be reached.

A Damped Cycle. In panel (b) of Figure 6.7, the cycle begins again at a momentary equilibrium with a price of $4,000 per ton and a quantity of 2 million tons, fixed for the year (point *f*). The producers' reaction to the high price, however, is not as strong as in panel (a): Distance *fg* is less than distance *ab;* the slope of S^{**} is larger than that of S^*. As a result, the price-quantity cycle *dampens* over time. Momentary equilibrium

FIGURE 6.7

Cobweb Cycles

(a) Eternal Cycle

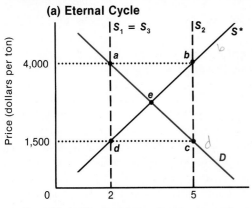

(b) Damped Cycle

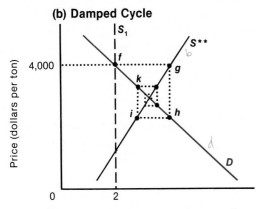

(c) Explosive Cycle

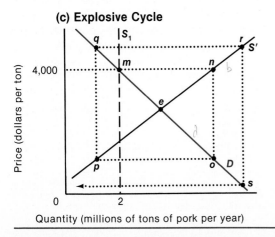

The tendency of the prices and quantities of some goods to rise above and then fall below some intermediate level in alternate periods produces patterns like cobwebs on demand and supply diagrams. Note: The slopes of the three demand lines are identical. In panel (a), the slope of supply line S^* equals the absolute value of the slope of D, providing the basis for an eternal cycle. In panel (b), the slope of S^{**} exceeds that of S^* (distance $fg < ab$), forming the basis for a damped cycle (all else being equal). In panel (c), the slope of S' is below that of S^* (distance $mn > ab$); this is the basis for an explosive cycle (all else being equal).

moves from *f* not to *g* (as producers expect), but to *h;* from *h* not to *i,* but to *k;* and from there along the dotted lines to an equilibrium at the intersection of *D* and *S*** in the center of the graph. We can see from the pattern in the graph why the tendency of the prices and quantities of some goods to rise above and then fall below some intermediate level in alternate periods is referred to as a **cobweb cycle.**

An Explosive Cycle. Finally, consider panel (c) of Figure 6.7. The cycle starts again at a momentary equilibrium with a price of $4,000 per ton and a quantity of 2 million tons, fixed for the year (point *m*). This time the producers' reaction to the high price is *stronger* than in panel (a): Distance *mn* exceeds distance *ab,* the slope of *S'* is smaller than that of *S*.* As a result, the price-quantity cycle *explodes* over time. Momentary equilibrium moves from *m* not to *n* (as producers expect), but to *o;* from *o* not to *p,* but to *q;* from *q* not to *r,* but to *s.* . . . Clearly, such a cycle cannot be maintained much longer than that! Its continued life would require negative prices and negative quantities; that is, economic nonsense. Sooner or later, therefore, an explosive cycle must cease, perhaps because the hog-raising industry disappears from the scene or because hog producers and consumers change the behavior depicted by *D* and *S'* in the graph.

Conclusion.   In all three cycles discussed, point *e* is a potential equilibrium. If the price-quantity combination at *e* ever prevailed, it could be maintained over time.[3]

------

[3]All of the preceding discussion of cobweb cycles can be presented mathematically as well. Similar to equation (4) given in the text, supply can be represented as

$$Q_{S_t} = -a + bP_{t-1} \qquad (7)$$

the only difference being that the quantity supplied at time *t* now is a function of price at time *t* − 1. Demand can be represented by a normal function like equation (5) in the text:

$$Q_{D_t} = c - dP_t \qquad (8)$$

The present period's equilibrium price is found from equation (9):

The real-world cattle cycles depicted in Figure 6.8 are a mixture of the three types of cycles just discussed; they are superimposed on an upward secular trend in the total number of cattle.

Application 3: Consumers' Surplus and Producers' Surplus

People often misunderstand the nature of the competitive process by which equilibrium is reached in perfectly competitive markets. From their own experience with competitive sports, they are apt to visualize competition as personal rivalry, as a situation of strife and conflict in which one party endeavors to gain what another endeavors to gain at the same time. Hence the

$$Q_{D_t} = Q_{S_t} \qquad (9)$$

Substituting (7) and (8) into (9), we get

$$c - dP_t = -a + bP_{t-1} \qquad (10)$$

Solving (10) for P_t produces

$$P_t = \left(-\frac{b}{d}\right)P_{t-1} + \frac{a+c}{d} \qquad (11)$$

It follows from equation (11) that prices in periods 1 and 2 are

$$P_1 = \left(-\frac{b}{d}\right)P_0 + \frac{a+c}{d} \qquad (12)$$

and

$$P_2 = \left(-\frac{b}{d}\right)P_1 + \frac{a+c}{d} \qquad (13)$$

Substituting (12) into (13), we get

$$P_2 = \left(-\frac{b}{d}\right)^2 P_0 + \left(-\frac{b}{d}\right)\frac{a+c}{d} + \frac{a+c}{d} \qquad (14)$$

Proceeding along this path, one can show the following by comparing the slope of the supply curve, *b*, with the absolute value of the slope of the demand curve $|d|$:

   a) When $b = |d|$, price will eternally oscillate from even to odd years,
   b) When $b < |d|$, price oscillates in a damped fashion,
   c) When $b > |d|$, price oscillates in an explosive fashion.

Caution: Unlike the caption to Figure 6.7, equations (7) and (8) express slope with respect to the independent variable, *P,* not relative to the dependent variable *Q.*

success of one party is believed to involve the failure of the other. Yet this view is quite inapplicable to the process of competition in perfectly competitive markets. This process is an *impersonal* one; it serves to ferret out possibilities that allow everyone to win at the same time.

Personal rivalry requires that rivals know each other and have the power to affect each other. But in perfectly competitive markets there are so many market participants that few of them know each other, and no one participant has the power to affect any other specific participant. Market participants are personally impotent (and know others to be equally impotent) concerning market prices because they are set by the collective actions of so many. Each buyer and seller rather looks upon other buyers and sellers the way you would look at other buyers when shopping, say, for apples. Would you know those millions of others who compete for apples with you? Even if you met one of your "competitors" in the store, would you view him or her as a personal enemy?

More important, the impersonal competition in perfectly competitive markets, far from creating a win-or-lose situation, allows large numbers of people to provide each other with mutual benefits. Obviously, in a world of scarcity, such provision with mutual benefits cannot possibly mean that everyone can have everything—as sellers could by charging infinite prices and buyers could by paying zero prices. Perfect competition helps people make deals—and only those deals from which one party benefits while simultaneously benefiting the other. The equilibrium price identifies these mutually beneficial possibilities. All who could gain from trading at this price are assured that they can so trade, that they are not reaching for the impossible, that their wishes are consistent with those of others who would also gain. The establishment of the equilibrium price, furthermore, also determines how the common gain is shared.

Figure 6.9, which illustrates the gains from trade, is based on Figure 6.2. Imagine all potentially traded bushels of apples as tokens in a game called *Exchange*. We line up, on the horizontal axis, each one of the bushels demanded according to the *maximum* price someone would be willing to pay for it (line *D*). A bushel for which someone most eager for apples would be willing to pay $11 is first in line, next to the vertical axis. A bushel for which someone else (or the same person) is only willing to pay $8 (or $2) is placed farther to the right (at *a* or *b*, respectively). Similarly, we line up horizontally bushels potentially supplied according to the *minimum* price someone would be willing to accept for them (line *S*). A bushel someone is willing to supply for the least amount, say $2, is first in line for

FIGURE 6.8

Cattle Cycles

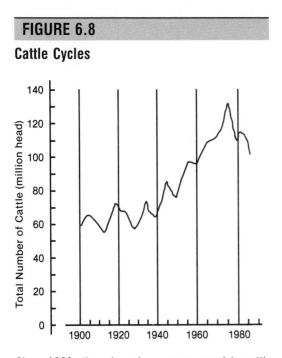

Since 1900, there have been seven complete cattle cycles in the United States. The typical cycle has lasted about 11 years, but no two cycles have been alike. **Source:** John Rosine, "Cattle Cycles—Past and Present," *Ninth District Quarterly* (Federal Reserve Bank of Minneapolis, November 1974), pp. 13–20; U.S. Bureau of the Census, *Statistical Abstract of the United States* 1988 (Washington, D.C.: U.S. Government Printing Office, 1987), p. 633.

trading (*c*). A bushel someone else (or the same firm) would be willing to supply for a higher price (say $7) appears farther to the right (at *d*) with less of a chance to be traded. The game is played by making all mutually beneficial trades and rejecting all trades that would cause one party to lose. Interestingly, a *vertical* line drawn through equilibrium point *e* discriminates between the trades that would be made and those that would be rejected. A *horizontal* line drawn through point *e* shows us how the traders split their joint gain (note the two dotted lines).

The Consumers' Surplus. Those bushels that would have been bought for the equilibrium price or more (such as *a*) are traded (at the equilibrium price). As Alfred Marshall saw it, however, to the extent that buyers are willing to pay more than they do pay, they each reap a little bit of a "consumer's surplus." Marshall measured the sum of these surpluses by the dotted triangle *fge*. He defined this **consumers' surplus** as the difference between the maximum sum of money consumers would pay for a given quantity (such as area 0*fei* for the 250-million-bushel equilibrium quantity in Figure 6.9) and the actual sum they do pay (such as area 0*gei* that represents the market value of that equilibrium quantity).*

The Producers' Surplus. Those bushels that would have been sold for the equilibrium price or less (such as *c*) are traded too (at the equilibrium price). To the extent that sellers are willing to accept less than they do receive, they each reap a little bit of a "producer's surplus." The sum of these surpluses is measured by the crosshatched triangle *ghe*. This **producers' surplus** is defined as the difference between the sum of money producers actually receive for a given quantity (such as area 0*gei* that represents the market value of the 250-million-bushel equilibrium quantity in Figure 6.9) and the minimum sum they would have accepted (such as area 0*hei* that represents the sum of marginal costs or the total

---

*For a calculus-based treatment of this material, see Section 6A of the Calculus Appendix at the back of this book.

FIGURE 6.9

The Gains from Trade

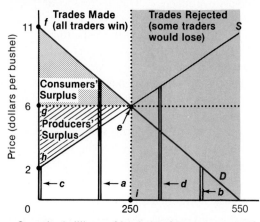

Quantity (millions of bushels of apples per year)

An age-old conflict between buyers and sellers must be resolved in any market. Buyers always want lower prices; sellers always want higher ones. Competition becomes the arbiter, setting price at the only level (here $6) that can be maintained. In the process, potential trades that involve a clear gain to both buyer and seller are, in fact, made (unshaded). Trades that would bring loss to either buyer or seller are rejected (shaded). Those who trade do so at a clear gain to themselves (note triangle *fhe*). The level of the equilibrium price determines how that gain is split among them (the dotted portion goes to buyers, and the crosshatched one goes to sellers).

---

variable cost of producing that equilibrium quantity).†

Conclusion. All bushels lined up in the unshaded area are traded at a clear gain to all buyers and sellers involved. The equilibrium price determines how buyers and sellers share the total gain from trade (triangle *fhe*).[4]

---

†For a calculus-based treatment of this material, see Section 6A of the Calculus Appendix at the back of this book.

[4]The demand and supply functions of Figure 6.9 can be represented by $P = 11 - .02Q_D$ and $P = 2 + .016Q_S$, respectively. (Compare footnotes 1 and 2.) Thus equilibrium price and quantity are found by equating Q_D and Q_S as $P^* = 6$ and $Q^* = 250$. For additional, calculus-based discussion, see Section 6A of the Calculus Appendix at the back of this book.

On the other hand, all potential bushels (such as *b*) that would have been bought only below the equilibrium price are not traded. The same holds for potential bushels (such as *d*) that would have been produced only if sale for more than the equilibrium price had been possible. All the bushels lined up in the shaded area are not traded at all, because such trade would require one of the trading parties to lose. In a world of scarcity, such discrimination concerning who can and cannot participate in an economic activity is inevitable. The higher-cost suppliers and less-eager demanders alike must be left out to avoid the chaos that would result if everyone tried to do what cannot possibly be done. Among the potential traders in the shaded area, there is not a single supplier who could cover marginal cost, even when being paid the highest price an excluded demander offered to pay. No *voluntary* exchange, therefore, can bring these people together.

Second Thoughts. The preceding analysis of consumers' and producers' surplus can be traced back to 1844, when a French engineer, Jules Dupuit, attempted to measure the social benefit of such public goods as roads, canals, and bridges. Alfred Marshall popularized these notions, and he entertained high hopes for their use as a tool for public policy. As will be shown in the next sections, one can analyze the effects of excise taxes or import quotas (and much more) by studying changes of the consumers' and producers' surpluses in the affected markets. Yet the concepts quickly became controversial and have remained so ever since. We can illustrate this controversy by focusing on the consumers' surplus.

Marshall himself had noted that the measurement of the consumers' surplus by a triangular area under demand curve, *D*, was correct only if certain assumptions held. One of these assumptions was the absence of an income effect for any change in the good's price. To the extent that a fall in price, for example, raised consumers' real income and, therefore (depending on whether the good was a normal or inferior one), added to or

subtracted from the substitution effect, the dotted triangle in Figure 6.9 would not provide a correct measure of consumers' surplus (but would overstate or understate its magnitude, respectively). Marshall defended himself against such possible error by confining his own discussions to changes of consumers' surplus resulting from small changes in prices and to such goods as matches, newspapers, postage stamps, salt, and tea (which are unimportant in the budgets of most consumers and might have zero income elasticities of demand). Yet such restrictions made a wide use of the concept impossible, and many economists have called it ''worse than useless'' (P. A. Samuelson) and ''no more than a theoretical toy'' (I. M. D. Little).

Yet the notion that the sum actually paid for a quantity of a good understates the satisfaction this quantity provides has proven too important to be abandoned because of measurement problems. John Hicks (a Biography of whom appears in Chapter 3 of the *Student Workbook* that accompanies this text) has tried to rescue the concept, at least at the level of the individual consumer.

The Hicksian Consumer Surpluses. John Hicks defined four possible measures of the consumer's surplus, each being a sum of money that, if taken from (or given to) a consumer, would offset the gain from a price fall (or substitute for the loss from a price rise). These four measures are illustrated, for the case of a price fall, in Figure 6.10. The horizontal axis measures the quantity of apples consumed by an individual; the vertical axis measures the consumer's income (or the quantities of ''all other goods'' consumed, at fixed prices). The consumer's income is assumed to equal $0A$. Given the initial price of apples, the budget line is AB. The consumer's initial optimum is at C, on indifference curve I_0. Then the price of apples falls, all else being equal. The budget line becomes AD, and the consumer's optimum shifts to E, on to higher indifference curve I_1.

The first of the Hicksian measures is the **price-compensating variation,** the *maximum* amount of income the consumer would *pay* for the privilege of buying (any desired quantity of) a good at a lower price. In our example, this measure equals *AF* because the consumer would, with only 0*F* of income left, reach income-apple combination *G* at the new price (dashed line *FH* parallels *AD*); *G* provides as much satisfaction as initial *C* (both are on indifference curve I_0).

An alternative measure is the **price-equivalent variation,** the *minimum* amount of income the consumer would *accept* for relinquishing the opportunity of buying (any desired quantity of) a good at a lower price. In our example, this measure equals *AK* because the

consumer could, with total income of 0*K,* reach income-apple combination *L* at the old price (dashed line *KJ* parallels *AB*); *L* provides as much satisfaction as *E* (both are on indifference curve I_1).

The third Hicksian measure is the **quantity-compensating variation,** the *maximum* amount of income the consumer would *pay* for the privilege of buying a good at a lower price, *while being constrained to buying the quantity (here* 0*Q) that the consumer would buy at the lower price in the absence of compensation.* In our example, this measure equals *EM,* because the consumer could, after paying this amount, reach income-apple combination *M*, which provides as much satisfaction as the initial position *C* (both are on indifference curve I_0).

Finally, there is the **quantity-equivalent variation,** the *minimum* amount of income the consumer would *accept* for relinquishing the opportunity of buying a good at a lower price, *while being constrained to buying the quantity (here* 0*P) that the consumer would buy at a higher price in the absence of compensation.* In our example, this measure equals *CN,* because the consumer could, after receiving this amount, reach income-apple combination *N,* which provides as much satisfaction as the new position *E* (both are on indifference curve I_1).

Hicks Versus Marshall. Hicksian indifference-curve analysis helps pinpoint a potential problem with measuring the consumers' surplus by the triangular area, dotted in Figure 6.9, under the Marshallian demand curve. Consider once again the derivation of a demand curve from indifference curves. (See the Chapter 3 section ''Substitution and Income Effects'' for detail.) Figure 6.11 involves the case of a good with zero income effect. In panel (a), we picture a consumer with income 0*A* facing a price of good *X* such that a maximum of 0*B* of *X* can be bought. Given indifference curves I_0 and I_1, the consumer optimizes at *A* on budget line *AB.* Assuming $P_x = 3$, the zero purchase of good *X* is pictured in panel (b) by point *M.* Let the price of good *X* fall to $P_x = 1$. The budget line swings to *AC;* the

FIGURE 6.10

Four Versions of the Consumer's Surplus

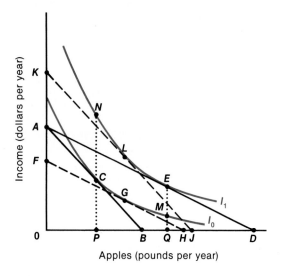

John Hicks expanded Alfred Marshall's notion of the consumer's surplus. Here a consumer moves from *C* to *E* in response to a decreased price of apples. The surplus might be measured by either a price-compensating or quantity-compensating variation (by *AF* or *EM*). Each leaves the consumer in the initial welfare position (*G* and *M* are found on indifference curve I_0, as is initial position *C*). This surplus might also be measured by either a price-equivalent or a quantity-equivalent variation (by *AK* or *CN*). Each of these leaves the consumer in the new welfare position (*L* and *N* are found on indifference curve I_1, as is new position *E*).

consumer's new optimum is H; a quantity $0L = 0R$ of good X is bought; point N is a second point on the consumer's ordinary demand curve (that holds money income constant). However, holding *real* income constant (in the Hicksian sense noted in Chapter 3), we find the consumer optimizing at point K where dashed budget line DE (parallel to AC) just touches the original indifference curve, I_0. Thus the substitution effect of the price fall is seen to equal the total effect. No part of the increased purchases of X (from zero to $0L = 0R$) is explained by any income effect. The indifference curves are vertically parallel; thus, the Hicksian income-compensated demand curve is identical with the ordinary demand curve.

In this rare case of identity, the dotted triangular area of consumer's surplus under the ordinary demand curve (panel b) is precisely equal to the Hicksian concept of price-compensating variation. In our example, the maximum amount of income the consumer would pay for the privilege of buying (any desired quantity of) good X at the lower \$1 price equals AD, because the consumer could, with only $0D$ of income left, reach income/good-X combination K at the new price, and K provides as much satisfaction as initial A (both are on indifference curve I_0). Can we find the panel (b) equivalent of this Hicksian surplus AD? Indeed, we can: Because combinations A and K provide the same total utility to the consumer, the utility gain from consuming $0L = 0R$ of good X is precisely equal to the utility loss of AG of income that the consumer is willing to sacrifice indifferently for $GK = 0L = 0R$. Thus AG is equivalent to area $0MNR$ in panel (b), because this area under the demand curve also measures the total utility derived from consuming $0R$. However, our consumer, in fact, gave up only AF of income to gain $FH = GK = 0L = 0R$ of good X. This amount actually given up equals the market value of $0R$ of good X, or the crosshatched area in panel (b). Our conclusion is close at hand. In panel (a), the difference between what the consumer was willing to give up (AG) and what the consumer did have to give up (AF) equals $FG = HK = AD$,

FIGURE 6.11

Hicksian and Marshallian Consumer Surplus: Zero Income Effect

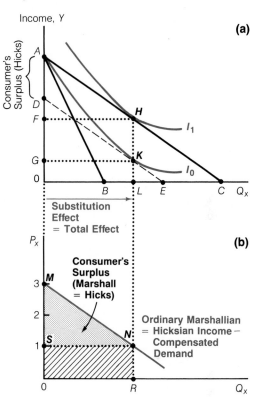

When the income effect of a price change is zero, the Hicksian concept of consumer's surplus [such as AD in panel (a)] is equal to a triangular area (here dotted) under the ordinary Marshallian demand curve that holds money income constant, but only because that demand curve is then equal to the Hicksian income-compensated demand that holds real income constant.

the previously identified Hicksian surplus. In panel (b), the corresponding magnitudes are areas $0MNR$ and $0SNR$, leaving dotted SMN as the consumer's surplus.

For goods with nonzero income effects, the conclusion stated in the caption of Figure 6.11 does not hold, however. Figure 6.12 illustrates the situation for a normal good for which the income effect reinforces the substitution effect. We picture a consumer at the identical initial positions A and M, respectively. As price falls, a new optimum is found at H, panel (a), making point S, panel (b), a second point on the ordinary demand curve. On that basis, one would identify the sum of the dotted and shaded areas, or triangle LMS, as the consumer's surplus. Yet given the positive income effect visible in panel (a), we find that the substitution effect alone moves the consumer from A to K, not to H; thus point N is a second point on the Hicksian income-compensated demand curve, which is, thus, seen to diverge from the ordinary one. As a result, the Hicksian measure of consumer's surplus now diverges from the previously identified triangle LMS. The Hicksian measure equals AD in panel

(a), as before. The equivalent in panel (b) is the dotted triangle alone (LMN), and here is why: To gain JK = 0R of good X, the consumer was willing to give up indifferently AJ of income; thus AJ equals 0MNR in panel (b). In fact, the consumer bought JK by sacrificing AF of income; thus AF equals crosshatched area 0LNR in panel (b). Therefore, the Hicksian consumer's surplus of AJ − AF = FJ = GK = AD in panel (a). The panel (b) equivalent must be the dotted triangle LMN.

Because income effects of price changes distort consumer's surplus estimates when ordinary demand curves are used for the purpose, economists are generally agreed that Hicksian

FIGURE 6.12

Hicksian and Marshallian Consumer Surplus: Positive Income Effect

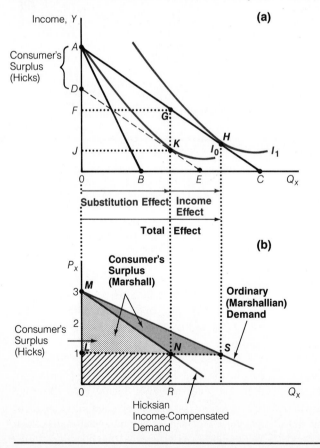

When the income effect of a price change is not zero, the Hicksian concept of consumer's surplus [such as AD in panel (a)] is equal to a triangular area (here dotted) under the Hicksian income-compensated demand curve, but differs from a corresponding measurement (here dotted plus shaded) that one would make with the help of an ordinary demand curve. In this example, the latter measurement exaggerates the consumer's surplus as defined by Hicks.

income-compensated demand curves should be used. Unfortunately, the Hicksian measurements of the consumer's surplus remain nonoperational. No one knows how to go about measuring the amounts involved for even a single consumer, let alone millions of them. Yet economists do make statistical measurements of market-demand curves. And many of them do continue to use the theoretically suspect Marshallian triangle in their policy evaluations, at least as a rough approximation of the theoretically purer Hicksian measures. Excise taxation, import quotas, and free trade are types of policies that are often evaluated using Marshallian rather than the Hicksian analysis, as the remaining applications show.

Application 4: Excise Taxation

The Marshallian analysis of demand and supply allows economists to predict the effects of government intervention in markets. Consider the imposition of an **excise tax,** a tax per unit of product equal to, say, $3 per bushel of apples sold.

Figure 6.13 is based on the diagram of short-run equilibrium in Figure 6.2. It shows an initial equilibrium at e, with price at $6 per

bushel and quantity at 250 million bushels of apples traded per year. What would happen if sellers were asked to deliver $3 to the government for every bushel of apples sold?

The Short Run. Given the short-run market demand and market supply pictured in Figure 6.13, price to buyers surely could not rise by $3 to $9 per bushel. If it did, quantity demanded would fall to 100 million bushels per year (point a), but sellers (who would collect $9 per bushel, pay $3 to the tax collector, and keep $6) would continue to supply 250 million bushels (point e). Thus a surplus of 250 − 100, or 150 million bushels per year, would develop (distance ab). Price to buyers would then fall below $9.

Nor could sellers bear the entire tax. If price to sellers fell by $3 to $3 per bushel, quantity supplied would fall to 62.5 million bushels per year (point c), but buyers (who would continue to be charged $6 per bushel, $3 of which would go to the tax collector) would continue to demand 250 million bushels per year (point e). Thus a shortage of 250 − 62.5, or 187.5 million bushels per year would develop (distance cd). Price to sellers would then rise above $3.

FIGURE 6.13

Imposing an Excise Tax

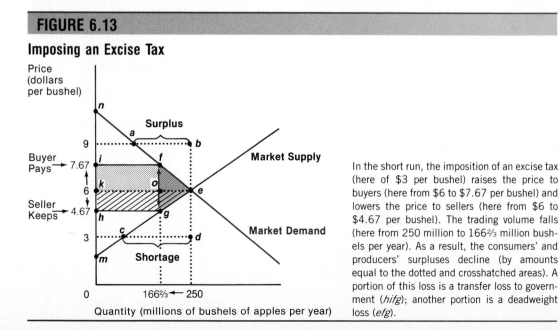

In the short run, the imposition of an excise tax (here of $3 per bushel) raises the price to buyers (here from $6 to $7.67 per bushel) and lowers the price to sellers (here from $6 to $4.67 per bushel). The trading volume falls (here from 250 million to 166⅔ million bushels per year). As a result, the consumers' and producers' surpluses decline (by amounts equal to the dotted and crosshatched areas). A portion of this loss is a transfer loss to government (hifg); another portion is a deadweight loss (efg).

We can find the solution by fitting a vertical wedge (*fg*) that is equal to the $3-per-bushel tax between the supply and demand curves to the left of equilibrium point *e*. The points where such a wedge meets the demand and supply curves indicate that the price to the buyer must rise from the original $6 to $7.67 per bushel, while the price kept by the seller (after paying the tax) must fall to $4.67. In our example, this is the only equilibrium possible, equating quantity demanded (point *f*) with quantity supplied (point *g*) at 166⅔ million bushels per year.

Government would collect a tax of 166⅔ million bushels per year times $3 per bushel, or $500 million per year (rectangle *fghi*). The consumers' surplus would decrease by dotted area *kefi* and the producers' surplus by crosshatched area *kegh*. The loss of consumers' and producers' surplus that results from the excise tax, furthermore, can be divided into two parts. A portion of this loss is offset by the government's gain (or that of the beneficiaries of governmental spending). This **transfer loss** equals the government's tax receipts and is shown by the unshaded rectangle *fghi*. Another portion of the loss, however, is *not offset by anybody else's gain*. It is called the **deadweight loss** and is shown by shaded triangle *feg*.

A final note: If demand had been perfectly inelastic with respect to price (a vertical line), the excise tax would have been shifted entirely onto buyers. Similarly, it would have been shifted entirely onto sellers if supply had been perfectly price-inelastic.[5]

The Long Run.   Our analysis has to be modified with respect to the long run. Imagine that the apple industry had been in long-run equilibrium prior to the imposition of the tax. Because the tax

lowers the net price to sellers, the typical firm would be making losses after the imposition of the tax. The industry's position would be precisely that of the unprofitable and therefore contracting industry pictured in Figure 6.4. This contraction would have to continue until the price to sellers was again equal to minimum average total cost (*ATC*). Another glance at Figure 6.5 shows three possible outcomes.

If the industry was one of constant cost, its contraction would not change the level of minimum *ATC*; hence price to sellers would ultimately return to $6 per bushel (given our example of Figure 6.13). In the long run, consumers would be paying $9 per bushel (and market supply would intersect line *ke* below *a*).

If the industry was one of increasing cost, its contraction would lower the level of minimum *ATC*; hence price to sellers would, ultimately, remain below $6 per bushel.

If the industry was one of decreasing cost, its contraction would raise the level of minimum *ATC*; hence price to sellers would, ultimately, have to *exceed* $6 per bushel. Because price to buyers would be even $3 higher than the sellers' above-$6 price, quantity demanded might then fall to zero. If it did, the entire industry would disappear. The power to tax is, indeed, the power to destroy!

Application 5: Import Quotas

The Marshallian tools also help economists predict the effects of *quantitative* market restrictions imposed by government. Consider the imposition of an **import quota,** a maximum physical limit on the amount of a good that may be imported.

The diagram of short-run equilibrium in Figure 6.14 shows an initial equilibrium at *e*,

---

[5]The results obtained from our graphical example can once again be found mathematically. Before the imposition of the tax, the price paid by the demander, P_D, equaled that received by the supplier, P_S. After the imposition of an excise tax of $t = \$3$ per bushel, however, $P_D - t = P_S$. Given the original demand and supply functions noted in footnote 4, the new equilibrium condition can be written as

$$P_D - t = 11 - .02Q_D - t = P_S = 2 + .016Q_S$$
$$11 - .02Q - 3 = 2 + .016Q$$
$$Q = 166\tfrac{2}{3}$$

By substitution, we find $P_D = 7.67$ and $P_S = 4.67$. Tax revenue, *T*, equals $t \cdot Q = 3 (166⅔) = 500$. For additional, calculus-based treatment of this material, see Section 6B of the Calculus Appendix at the back of this book.

with price at $200 per ton and quantity at 13 million tons of sugar traded per year. Of this amount, 5 million tons are supplied by domestic sources (distance *ab*) and another 8 million tons are imported (distance *be*). What would happen if the government imposed an import quota limiting sugar imports, regardless of price, to 4 million tons per year (distance *bd*)?

The Short Run. A shortage of *de* at the $200-per-ton price would drive the price up to $242 per ton (point *g*); quantity traded would fall to 10 million tons per year. (The straight line through points *d* and *g*, which parallels the U.S.-sources supply line by the amount of the quota *bd*, would be the new market supply.) Note how U.S.suppliers would increase quantity supplied by 1 million tons per year (from *b* to *h*). Together with quota imports of *hg* (equal to *bd*), quantity supplied at the new price would equal quantity demanded (point *g*).

There would, therefore, be a loss of consumers' surplus equal to area *igea*. U.S. producers would gain *ihba* of this amount in added producers' surplus (dotted). Foreign producers would gain crosshatched area *hgfc* because the identical 4 million tons (*hg* = *cf*) were imported before at the lower price of $200 per ton. That, however, would not be the whole story. Foreign producers also used to sell the 1 million tons now sold by U.S. producers (distance *bc*) and the 3 million tons now sold not at all (distance *fe*). On these accounts, foreigners would *lose* producers' surplus; and additional losses would occur if the quota was assigned not to those (low-marginal-cost) foreign producers who used to supply the 6 to 9 millionth tons, but to those others (with higher marginal costs) who supplied the 10 to 13 millionth tons.

So far as the United States is concerned, the effect is clear: Producers would gain; consumers would lose a much larger amount. The two shaded triangles, furthermore, would represent deadweight losses; area *bhc* being frittered away in higher-than-necessary production costs (because expensive domestic production would be

FIGURE 6.14

Imposing an Import Quota

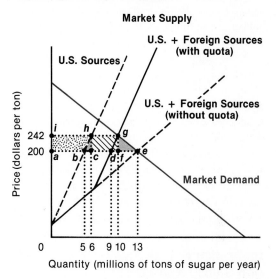

In the short run, the imposition of an import quota (here equal to *hg*) raises the market price (here from $200 to $242 per ton). The trading volume falls (here from 13 million to 10 million tons per year). As a result, the consumers' surplus declines (by area *igea*). A portion of this loss is transferred to domestic producers (dotted), another portion to foreign producers (crosshatched), and the rest is deadweight loss (shaded).

substituted for cheaper foreign production), area *fge* reflecting the surplus forgone as a result of the decline in the volume of trade.

The Long Run. The long-run effects would be analogous to those discussed in the section on excise taxation. This time, however, the effects would work in the opposite direction. If the domestic sugar industry was in long-run equilibrium prior to the quota imposition, the typical firm would find itself making profits after the quota had raised the price. The industry's position would be that of the profitable and therefore expanding industry pictured in Figure 6.3. This expansion would have to continue until the price was again equal to minimum average total cost. Figure 6.5 shows three possible outcomes.

In the case of a constant-cost industry, price would ultimately return to $200 per ton. Domestic supply plus the quota would intersect market demand at *e*. In the case of an increasing-cost industry, minimum *ATC* would rise with the industry's expansion, which would cease when domestic supply plus quota intersected market demand somewhere between *g* and *e*. In the case of a decreasing-cost industry, minimum *ATC* would fall with the industry's expansion, which would cease when domestic supply plus quota intersected market demand somewhere to the right and below *e*. Then consumers would be getting more sugar than before the quota, and at a lower price. (This possible outcome is often cited by those making the so-called "infant industry" argument in favor of quotas.)

Application 6: Free Trade: Who Gains, Who Loses?

Using the theory of comparative advantage, economists often argue that the opening up of free trade between two countries makes both countries better off and is, therefore, a good idea. Yet, in practice, despite the overall gain, *some* people in both countries are likely to be hurt, and this explains their opposition to such a free-trade policy. Once again, the concepts of *consumers' surplus* and *producers' surplus* are helpful for understanding the issue.

Consider two countries, the United States and China. Assume competitive markets for textiles and wheat, with price and marginal cost for both goods equal to $10 per unit in the United States prior to the opening of trade, but equal to 50 yen per unit of textiles and 100 yen per unit of wheat in China. Clearly, the United States has a comparative advantage in wheat, China in textiles. (If the United States produced 1 more unit of wheat, it would need $10 of extra resources and would have to produce 1 less unit of textiles. If China produced 1 less unit of wheat, it would release 100 yen of resources and, thus, be able to produce 2 more units of textiles. While having used the same resources, the world would be richer by 1 unit of textiles. Furthermore, if the United States then exported to China 1 unit of wheat for 1.5 units of textiles, *both* countries would have the same amount of wheat as before, but ½ unit of textiles more, providing the oft-cited *possibility* for making some people better off without making anyone worse off at all.)

If free trade is opened up and a free market in foreign exchange is allowed to flourish as well, a country with a *comparative* advantage in a given good will, at the equilibrium rate of exchange, also enjoy the *absolutely* lower price, and it will begin to export the good. (In our example, such an equilibrium exchange rate will lie between 5 yen per dollar and 10 yen per dollar and equal, say, 8 yen per dollar. Below 5 yen per dollar, everything will be cheaper in the United States, and there will be no supply of dollars to buy yen to buy Chinese goods, but plenty of demand for dollars with yen to buy American goods; the price of dollars will rise. Above 10 yen per dollar, everything will be cheaper in China, and there will be no demand for dollars with yen to buy American goods, but plenty of dollars to buy yen to buy Chinese goods; the price of dollars will fall.)

Figure 6.15 illustrates our example. Panels (a) to (c) are about textiles. Domestically, in the United States, supply and demand determine an equilibrium price of $10 per unit [panel (a)]; in China, the domestic price is 50 yen = $6.25 [panel (c)]. As trade opens up, American consumers are willing to buy textiles abroad below the domestic $10 price; their import demand is shown in panel (b). Follow the dashed line from point *f* to point *m* to find the starting point of import demand; then note that import demand at lower prices always equals the domestic shortage that would otherwise prevail. Thus *cd* = *ik*. Similarly, Chinese producers are willing to sell textiles abroad above the domestic $6.25 price; their export supply is also shown in panel (b).

Follow the dashed line from point *o* to point *h* to find the starting point of export supply; then note that export supply at higher prices always

FIGURE 6.15

Gains and Losses from Free Trade

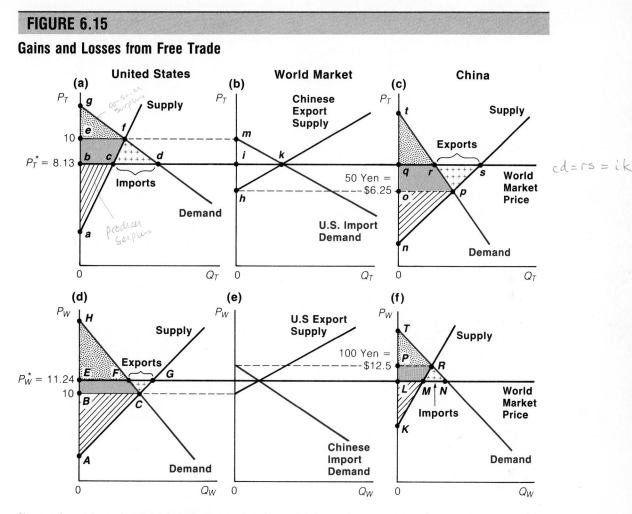

Changes in consumers' and producers' surpluses as free trade opens up can explain why consumers in exporting countries and producers in importing countries often oppose free trade, while consumers in importing countries and producers in exporting countries are in favor of free trade.

equals the domestic surplus that would otherwise prevail. Thus $rs = ik$. The intersection, in panel (b), of import demand and export supply at k points to the equilibrium world market price of $P_T^* = \$8.13$; its level is indicated by the horizontal line stretching across panels (a) to (c). We can summarize the consequences as follows.

Within the United States, the fall in price from \$10 to \$8.13 per unit of textiles raises quantity demanded from ef to bd. The consumers' surplus rises from egf (dotted) to bgd (dotted plus shaded plus crosses); American textile consumers will favor free trade. The same fall in price lowers the quantity supplied by *domestic* producers from ef to bc. The producers' surplus falls from aef (crosshatched plus shaded) to abc (crosshatched); American textile producers (broadly defined to include the owners of firms as well as workers and suppliers of raw materials) will oppose free trade. Yet the consumers' gain ($befd$) exceeds the producers' loss ($befc$) by cfd; it is possible to tax the gainers sufficiently to compensate the losers and leave nobody worse off in the end.

Within China, the rise in price from $6.25 to $8.13 per unit of textiles lowers quantity demanded from *op* to *qr*. The consumers' surplus falls from *otp* (dotted plus shaded) to *qtr* (dotted); Chinese textile consumers, unlike their American counterparts, will oppose free trade. The same rise in price raises the quantity supplied by producers from *op* to *qs*. The producers' surplus rises from *nop* (crosshatched) to *nqs* (crosshatched plus shaded plus crosses); Chinese textile producers (broadly defined), unlike their American counterparts, will favor free trade. Yet the producers' gain (*oqsp*) exceeds the consumers' loss (*oqrp*) by *rsp;* it is possible to tax the gainers sufficiently to compensate the losers and leave nobody worse off in the end.

Note that U.S. imports (*cd*) precisely equal Chinese exports (*rs*) and that the world's net gain from free trade is pictured by the sum of triangles *cfd* and *rsp* (the two areas filled with crosses). We can similarly analyze the effects of free trade on the wheat industry; consider panels (d) to (f). In the United States, free trade raises the domestic price of $10 per unit to $11.24. Quantity demanded falls; quantity supplied rises. The consumers' surplus falls from *BCH* (dotted plus shaded) to *EHF* (dotted); American wheat consumers oppose free trade. The producers' surplus, however, rises from *ABC* (crosshatched) to *AEG* (crosshatched plus shaded plus crosses); American wheat producers favor free trade. (This story reminds us precisely of what happened some years ago when the Russians bought up a large portion of the U.S. crop of wheat; U.S. farmers were overjoyed, U.S. consumers of bread and hamburger buns were not.) In China, free trade lowers the domestic price of $12.50 per unit to $11.24. Quantity demanded rises; the quantity supplied by domestic producers falls. The consumers' surplus rises from *PTR* (dotted) to *LTN* (dotted plus shaded plus crosses); Chinese wheat consumers favor free trade. The producers' surplus, however, falls from *KPR* (crosshatched plus shaded) to *KLM* (crosshatched); Chinese wheat producers oppose free trade.

SUMMARY

1. This chapter joins the analysis of market demand to that of market supply. It studies the nature of momentary, short-run, and long-run equilibrium in a perfectly competitive market. A *perfectly competitive market* is defined by the following four characteristics:

a. There is a large number of independent buyers and also of sellers.

b. All units of the traded item are viewed as identical.

c. All buyers and sellers possess full knowledge relevant to trading.

d. Nothing impedes entry into or exit from the market.

2. *Market equilibrium* is a situation in which there is no innate tendency for price or quantity traded to change.

3. *Momentary equilibrium* is the equilibrium reached in a period so short that the quantity supplied is absolutely fixed. Price is reduced by surpluses and raised by shortages, until quantity demanded equals that which is supplied.

4. *Short-run equilibrium* is the equilibrium reached in a period sufficiently long for a given number of firms to be able to vary quantity supplied by changing the utilization rate of given plants.

5. *Long-run equilibrium* is the equilibrium reached in a period so long that new firms can enter the industry and old ones can leave it or change the size of their plants. When markets are perfectly competitive, firms make zero economic profits in the long run because profitable industries expand, depressing product price, and unprofitable industries contract, raising product price, until product price equals *minimum average total cost;* that is, normal price. In the process of industry expansion or contraction, the normal price itself may change. Accordingly, the long-run industry supply curve can be horizontal, upward-sloping, or downward-sloping; the industry can be one of constant cost, increasing cost, or decreasing cost.

6. The Marshallian analysis of equilibrium-price determination put an effective end to the eternal conflict between the subjective-utility and objective-cost theories of price. It did not, however, hinder the ageless attempts by the powerful to replace the market equilibrium price, which properly reflects the degree of scarcity prevailing, with a "just" price, which is considered morally acceptable.

7. Applications of the Marshallian apparatus include explanations of abundance versus scarcity, cobweb cycles, the gains from exchange with the help of the consumers' and producers' surpluses, the effects of excise taxation, import quotas, and free trade.

KEY TERMS

atomistic competition
cobweb cycle
constant-cost industry
consumers' surplus
deadweight loss
decreasing-cost industry
excise tax
external diseconomies
external economies
import quota
increasing-cost industry
internal diseconomies
internal economies
long-run equilibrium
market
market equilibrium
momentary equilibrium
normal price
perfectly competitive market
price-compensating variation
price-equivalent variation
producers' surplus
quantity-compensating variation
quantity-equivalent variation
shortage

short-run equilibrium
surplus
transfer loss

HANDS-ON PRACTICE

Exercise #1

At New York's Kennedy Airport, the supply of landing slots on runway 31 Left is 60 per hour when the weather is clear. Assume that the slots are to be rationed by price. What is the proper landing fee between 5 P.M. and 6 P.M. on Fridays when the demand is $P = 600 - 5Q_D$? And Monday mornings between 10 A.M. and 11 A.M. when demand is $P = 100 - 2Q_D$?

Solution:

Between 5 P.M. and 6 P.M. on Fridays:

$$P = 600 - 5Q_D; \text{ hence}$$
$$Q_D = 120 - .2P$$
$$Q_S = 60$$

In equilibrium,

$$Q_D = Q_S$$
$$120 - .2P = 60$$
$$-.2P = -60$$
$$P = 300$$

Between 10 A.M. and 11 A.M. on Mondays:

$$P = 100 - 2Q_D; \text{ hence } Q_D = 50 - .5P$$

In equilibrium,

$$Q_D = Q_S$$
$$50 - .5P = 60$$
$$-.5P = 10$$
$$P = -20$$

In practice, this means that a *zero price* is proper. Then $Q_D = 50$, $Q_S = 60$, the runway is a free good.

Exercise #2

A bridge connecting New Jersey with New York City can accommodate 6,000 cars per hour if the cars move at the speed limit. The number of cars, N, wanting to use the bridge is related to the toll charged, T, as follows (weekdays, city-bound lanes): 7–9 A.M. $T = \$8 - \left(\frac{\$8}{11}\right)N$; 9–11 A.M. $T = \$9 - \$1.8N$, where N is measured in thousands of cars. If traffic congestion (more cars trying to use the bridge than it can accommodate at the speed limit) is to be avoided,
a. what is the proper toll for the 9–11 A.M. period?
b. what is the proper toll for the 7–9 A.M. period? In each case, show your answer graphically; then confirm it arithmetically.

Solution:

Arithmetical answer:
To equate supply ($N = 6$) with demand ($T = 9 - 1.8N$) at 9–11 A.M., $T = 9 - 1.8(6) = -1.8$. One would have to *pay* people \$1.80 per car to get 6,000 cars per hour to use the bridge! In practice, this means that a zero toll is indicated. Then only 5,000 cars will use the bridge (point a); it is a free good.

To equate supply ($N = 6$) with demand $\left(T = 8 - \left(\frac{\$8}{11}\right) N\right)$ at 7–9 A.M., $T = 8 - \left(\frac{\$8}{11}\right)6 = 3.64$. Only a toll of \$3.64 per car can eliminate traffic congestion. Can you see how there would be a shortage of bc at a zero toll? Eleven thousand cars would be trying to use a bridge designed for 6,000 cars; bumper-to-bumper, slow-moving traffic would exist at a zero toll.

Exercise #3

Reconsider Figure 6.13, "Imposing an Excise Tax," on p. 201. Calculate:
a. the consumers' surplus before and after the tax
b. the producers' surplus before and after the tax
c. the deadweight loss
d. the tax collected

Solution:

a. The consumers' surplus changes from *ken* to *ifn*; both are triangular areas that can be calculated by the familiar formula (base × height)/2. Distance ke = 250 million bushels/year; distance if, 166⅔ million bushels/year. The value of point n is missing, but can be deduced from the fact that the demand line (between e and f) rises by \$1.67/bushel when quantity falls by 250 – 166⅔ = 83⅓ million bushels. Thus, be-

Graphical answer

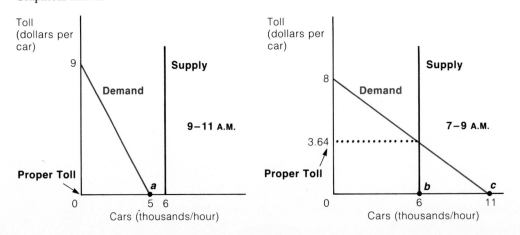

tween *f* and *n*, when quantity falls by 166⅔ million bushels, price must rise by 2($1.67) = $3.34 to a total of $11.01 at *n*. Hence distance *kn* = $5.01, and distance *in* = $3.34. Thus, *ken*, the consumers' surplus before the tax equals

$$\frac{(250 \text{ million bushels/year}) (\$5.01/\text{bushel})}{2}$$
$$= \$626.25 \text{ million/year.}$$

Similarly, *ifn*, the consumers' surplus after the tax equals

$$\frac{(166⅔ \text{ million bushels/year}) (\$3.34/\text{bushel})}{2}$$
$$= \$278.33 \text{ million/year.}$$

b. The producers' surplus changes from *mke* to *mhg;* both again triangular areas measurable by the formula noted in (a). While distances *ke* and *hg* are shown in the graph, the value of point *m* is missing, but can be deduced from the fact that the supply line (between *e* and *g*) falls by $1.33/bushel when quantity falls by 250 − 166⅔ = 83⅓ million bushels. Thus, between *g* and *m*, when quantity falls by 166⅔ million bushels, price must fall by 2($1.33) = $2.66 to a total of $2.01 at *m*. Hence distance *km* = $3.99, and distance *hm* = $2.66. Thus, *mke*, the producers' surplus before the tax equals

$$\frac{(250 \text{ million bushels/year}) (\$3.99/\text{bushel})}{2}$$
$$= \$498.75 \text{ million/year.}$$

Similarly, *mhg*, the producers' surplus after the tax equals

$$\frac{(166⅔ \text{ million bushels/year}) (\$2.66/\text{bushel})}{2}$$
$$= \$221.67 \text{ million/year.}$$

c. The deadweight loss equals triangles *efo* plus *ego*, or

$$\frac{(83⅓ \text{ million bushels/year}) (\$1.67/\text{bushel})}{2}$$
$$+ \frac{(83⅓ \text{ million bushels/year}) (\$1.33/\text{bushel})}{2}$$

This comes to

$69.58 million/year + $55.42 million/year
= $125 million/year.

d. The tax collected is area *ifgh*, or

(166⅔ million bushels/year) ($3/bushel)
= $500 million/year.

Note: It is no accident that the loss of consumers' surplus ($347.92 million/year) plus the loss of producers' surplus ($277.08 million/year) precisely add to $625 million per year, the combined deadweight loss plus tax revenue.

QUESTIONS AND PROBLEMS

1. In 1979, a 5-foot by 9-foot painting by Frederic Church, entitled *Icebergs*, was sold for $2.5 million at a New York auction. At the time, only two paintings had ever commanded more at auction: a Velazquez (*Portrait of Juan de Pareja*), which sold for $5.54 million in 1970 and a Titian (*Diana and Actaeon*), which sold for $4.0, million in 1971. Can you explain these prices with the help of the Marshallian tools of supply and demand?

2. All available tickets to athletic or artistic events are often sold out prior to the season. As the season progresses, these tickets are sometimes resold at higher-than-original prices (a phenomenon called "scalping") but at other times are sold at lower-than-original prices. Explain.

3. In mid-1972, the U.S. wheat price was $1.70 per bushel. Then the Russians entered the market, buying up 19 million metric tons of wheat (one-fourth of the U.S. crop). By the end of the summer, the price of wheat was $5 per bushel. Even the per-bushel price of rye (which the Russians did not buy) jumped from $1.01 to $3.86, that of oats from 80¢ to $2.06, and that of soybeans from $3.50 to $12. Can you explain these events?

4. When markets are pefectly competitive, what do you think would happen to an industry, given market demand for its product, if its inputs were gradually becoming exhausted? Explain.

5. Many observers have decried as immoral the existence of markets for babies, corneas, blood, or kidneys, in which the supply comes from paid donors and thus adds to the nonmarket supply from unpaid donors. What do you think about this "commercialism"? (*Hint:* Consider, for example, the effect of such a commercial delivery system on the price paid for blood and on the quantity available to those needing transfusions. What if you were told that the frequency of transfusion hepatitis among recipients of blood from paid donors was 10 times greater than among those receiving blood from unpaid donors?)

6. The equilibrium price depicted in Figure 6.2 is *stable;* that is, it would be reestablished through competition if, inadvertently, it ever rose above or fell below this level. What would competition do, however, if market demand had the peculiar position given in the accompanying graph and if the price moved away from its equilibrium at *e*?

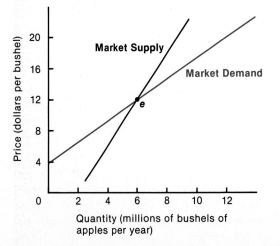

Quantity (millions of bushels of apples per year)

7. A society wishing to reduce the consumption of illegal drugs has two available strategies: (a) reducing demand by harassing buyers or (b) reducing supply by harassing sellers. Considering the fact that higher drug prices impose heavy costs on innocent bystanders (as addicts turn to robbery and murder to acquire additional funds), which is the better strategy? Explain.

8. Analyze the effect, in terms of consumers' and producers' surplus, of a governmentally imposed below-equilibrium limit on the quantity demanded.

9. Consider the following four sets of demand and supply functions:

(1)	(2)
$3Q_D + P - 10 = 0$ $P^2 - 10Q_S - 4 = 0$	$3Q_D + P - 100 = 0$ $Q_S - 2P + 40 = 0$

(3)	(4)
$Q_D = 50$ $P = 400$	$P = 20 - 4Q_D$ $P = 1.5Q_S + 1$

a.   Graph each set.
b.   For each set, determine the equilibrium price and quantity graphically. Check your results mathematically for sets (2) and (4).
c.   For each set, determine Q_D if $P = 5$; determine P if $Q_D = 5$.
d.   In each case, determine the price above which demand is zero, below which supply is zero.
e.   In each case, what is demanded at a zero price?
f.   For set (1), determine the effect of a price ceiling of $P_{max} = 3$.
g.   For set (2), determine the effect of a price floor of $P_{min} = 15$.
h.   For set (3), determine the price ceiling required in order to create a shortage of 2.
i.   For set (4), determine the effect of a

$1-per-unit tax. Who pays what percentage of the tax revenue?

j. For set (2), determine the effect of a $2-per-unit subsidy. Who receives what percentage of the total subsidy?

10. Consider these demand and supply functions:

$$Q_{D_t} = 200 - 30P_t$$
$$Q_{S_t} = 100 + 10P_{t-1}$$

a. Determine the long-run equilibrium price and quantity.

b. Given a price of $P_0 = 8$ at time 0, plot the cobweb diagram for times 0 through 4.

11. Consider panels (a) through (c) of Figure 6.6. Using simple arithmetic, express the demand and supply in each panel by an equation; then check the accuracy of your result by confirming the equilibrium positions.

12. "Economists are apt to praise markets as superb rationing devices for things that are scarce. They point to a graph, such as Figure 6.6, and note how one could organize markets not only for such commonplace things as apples and houses, but also for the apportionment of scarce broadcasting frequencies, landing slots at major airports, and space on bridges during the rush hour. Indeed, they argue that markets are good for preserving the purity of the air and continued existence of animal species, ranging from geese, sponges, and tuna to whales, zebras, and who knows what else. But I say this is nonsense. True enough, a state of anarchy is not a pretty thing to contemplate, but it is not inevitable. *People must be taught to be less selfish.* Then they would *voluntarily* restrict their desires for things that are scarce; one wouldn't have to price them out of the market with positive prices for things that ought to be free. All it takes is developing people's social consciousness, making them sensitive to the evil consequences of unrestrained behavior."

a. Explain how the types of markets discussed here could in fact be organized.

b. Evaluate the alternative approach to dealing with scarcity that is proposed here.

13. The Environmental Protection Agency has established that it is perfectly safe to dump 500 tons of arsenic into the air of a state, as long as it is done gradually during the course of a year. What fee should the agency charge would-be dumpers if the demand for dumping opportunities equals $P = 1,000 - 4Q_D$? What if the demand equals $P = 1,000 - Q_D$?

14. Recalculate your answers to Exercise 1 on p. 207 for foggy weather when only 30 planes per hour can land safely.

15. Figure 6.13 shows various effects of an excise tax from the standpoint of all market participants as a group. Among other things, consumers pay more per unit, get a lower quantity, and suffer a deadweight loss. Use indifference-curve analysis to assess the effect of an excise tax on an *individual* consumer.

16. Once again, consider the deadweight loss (area *efg*) in Figure 6.13. It clearly would be of different size if the slopes of market demand and market supply were different. Can you develop a formula that relates the deadweight loss to these slopes or even to the elasticities of demand and supply?

SELECTED READINGS

Baumol, William J., John C. Panzar, and Robert D. Willig. *Contestable Markets and the Theory of Industry Structure.* New York: Harcourt Brace Jovanovich, 1982.

> A generalization of the theory of perfect competition to multiproduct firms. For an important review, *see* Michael Spence, "Contestable Markets and the Theory of Industry Structure: A Review Article." *Journal of Economic Literature,* September 1983, pp. 981–90.

Dooley, Peter C. "Consumer's Surplus: Marshall and His Critics," *Canadian Journal of Economics,* February 1983, pp. 26–38.

Dupuit, Jules. "On the Measurement of the Utility of Public Works," in American Economic Association, *Readings in Welfare Economics.* Homewood, Ill.: Irwin, 1969, pp. 255–83.

> A translation of the famous article of 1844 on consumers' surplus.

Hicks, John R. "The Rehabilitation of Consumer's Surplus," *Review of Economic Studies,* February 1941, pp. 108–16; *idem.* "The Four Consumer's Surpluses," *Review of Economic Studies,* no. 1, 1943, pp. 31–41; *idem.* "The Generalized Theory of Consumer's Surplus," *Review of Economic Studies,* no. 2, 1946, pp. 68–74.

Marshall, Alfred. *Principles of Economics,* 9th ed., with annotations by C. W. Guillebaud, vols. I and II. London: Macmillan, 1961.

McKenzie, Richard B., and Gordon Tullock. *The New World of Economics.* Homewood, Ill.: Irwin, 1981.

> Filled with unusual applications of demand and supply analysis, involving sexual behavior, exploitation, marriage and divorce, child production, crime, and much more.

Mishan, E. J. *Welfare Economics: Five Introductory Essays.* New York: Random House, 1964, pp. 184–98.

> On realism and relevance in the theory of consumers' surplus.

Morey, Edward R. "Confuser Surplus," *The American Economic Review,* March 1984, pp. 163–73.

> A recent note on the consumers' surplus debate, with a good listing of the literature.

Smith, Vernon L. "An Experimental Study of Competitive Market Behavior," *The Journal of Political Economy,* April 1962, pp. 111–37.

> Reports on a six-year experiment designed to study the process by which a competitive equilibrium of demand and supply is attained. (For a more recent report on experiments of this type, see the article by Charles R. Plott cited at the end of Chapter 8.)

COMPUTER PROGRAMS

The KOHLER-3 personal-computer diskettes that accompany this book contain two programs of particular interest to this chapter:

6. Perfect Competition includes a 25-question multiple-choice test with immediate responses to incorrect answers as well as numerous exercises concerning supply and demand.

Appendix A. Solving Simultaneous Equations can be used for the exercises if a mathematical solution is desired.

ANALYTICAL EXAMPLE 6.1

THE POPE AND THE PRICE OF FISH

For more than 1000 years, the Catholic Church required its members to abstain from meat on Friday in the spirit of penance. In December of 1966, however, the American Catholic bishops, following prior authorization from Pope Paul VI, terminated obligatory meatless Fridays (except during Lent). One economist decided to test the impact of this decision on the fish market. Using data for New England, where a large quantity of fish is regularly landed and consumed and where 45 percent of the population is Catholic, Frederick W. Bell estimated two demand equations for a variety of fish: one for January 1957 to November 1966 (prior to the Church decree) and another one for December 1966 to August 1967. He isolated the effect on the price of each type of fish of such influences as the quantity landed, personal income, cold storage holdings, imports, meat and poultry prices, Lenten demand, other fish prices, and the Church decree. In accordance with theoretical expectations (that a fall in demand reduces price, all else being equal), he discovered a 12.5-percent average decline in fish prices *attributable to the decree.* The accompanying table shows some of his results.

ANALYTICAL EXAMPLE

Species	Percentage Change in Price Due to Church Decree
Sea scallops	− 17
Yellowtail flounder	− 14
Large haddock	− 21
Scrod	− 2
Cod	− 10
Ocean perch	− 10
Whiting	− 20

Source: Frederick W. Bell, "The Pope and the Price of Fish," *The American Economic Review,* December 1968, Vol. *LVIII,* No. 5, pp. 1346–50. Reprinted by permission.

ANALYTICAL EXAMPLE 6.2

THE POLITICAL ECONOMY OF MILK AND HOUSING

In many real-world markets, government intervention will not allow the equilibrium price to be established. In 1982, for example, the U.S. government had legislated an above-equilibrium minimum price for milk (and milk products) such as that shown in the accompanying graph. The predictable result was a surplus (such as *ab*) for butter, cheese, and milk; the government spent $2.4 billion to purchase it, and thereby spent more on otherwise unwanted dairy products than on numerous other programs deemed important by many. (The dairy subsidy was eight times larger than federal spending on the arts and humanities, three times larger than spending on the National Park Service, twice as large as spending on the National Science Foundation, and also twice as large as the Agency for International Development's spending on Third World development projects.) The program was rationalized as an aid to poor farmers, but, in fact, most of the money went to the biggest and richest farmers who had most of the milk to sell, while the higher price of dairy products hurt most the consumers with low incomes. Was there an explanation? Of course. The mere 500 dairy farmers per Congressional district were impressively organized and spent $1.8 million on 1982 federal election campaigns—given the $2.4 billion return, not a bad investment.

Or consider a typical government intervention at the local level. In many communities in the United States and abroad, rent controls have been imposed since World War II, such as the below-equilibrium maximum price for housing services in the accompanying graph. The predictable result is a shortage (such as *cd*). The result has been long waiting lists (in the late 1950s, it took an average of 40 months to get an apartment in Stockholm) and a deteriorating housing stock (in New York landlords spend half as much on repairs of rent-controlled apartments as on repairs of similar noncontrolled units). Typically, the rationale (landlords are rich, renters are poor) is not supported by the facts, but the policy is explained by the organized use of political power.

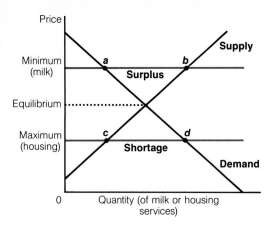

Sources: John D. Donahue, "The Political Economy of Milk," *The Atlantic Monthly,* October 1983, pp. 59–68; S. Rydenfelt, "Rent Control Thirty Years On," *Verdict on Rent Control* (London: Institute for Economic Affairs, 1972), p. 65; G. Sternlieb, *The Urban Housing Dilemma* (New York Housing and Development Administration, 1972), p. 202.

ANALYTICAL EXAMPLE 6.3

CONSUMERS' SURPLUS AND THE CONSTRUCTION OF AIR TRAFFIC CONTROL TOWERS

In 1985, there existed well over 13,000 airports in the United States, but many of them were privately owned and operated. Even among the airports owned by the federal government there were many that did not have airport control towers, yet the Federal Aviation Administration (FAA) was carrying out a program of building and staffing such towers. In deciding where to locate new towers, the FAA followed a simple rule: Build the next tower at the nontower airport with the highest traffic count (number of takeoffs and landings per year). This rule, the FAA reasoned, would maximize the benefit to the flying public from the scarce construction funds the agency had available. But quite possibly this reasoning was wrong!

Consider the accompanying graph. Given the typically zero price charged for using a federal facility with no control tower, the traffic count at one airport may be 0*F,* at another airport 0*B.* The FAA would build a tower at the former airport in preference over the latter. Yet the charging of positive prices might reveal the color demand curve for the former airport and the black demand curve for the latter. That is, users may have plenty of substitutes for the first airport and might cease using it altogether once the user fee reached 0*E.* On the other hand, users may have fewer alternatives for the second airport and would continue to use it until the user fee reached 0*A,* although in both cases quantity demanded decreases with higher price.

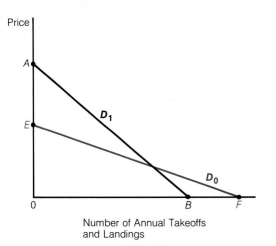

Number of Annual Takeoffs
and Landings

It is immediately clear that the total benefit and consumers' surplus from using the high-traffic-count airport at the zero price equals 0*EF,* while the corresponding measure for the low-traffic-count airport is 0*AB,* a *larger* amount. Building towers that maximize traffic count can clearly be wrong.

Note: Similar errors may well be made when TV programs with the highest ratings are kept going, while those with lower ratings are discarded, or when college departments with the largest student enrollment are given budgetary allocations in preference to others with fewer students. In each case, the consumers' surplus may be larger where the "traffic count" (TV viewers or enrolled students) is smaller.

ANALYTICAL EXAMPLE 6.4

THE WELFARE EFFECTS OF U.S. SUGAR QUOTAS

Ever since 1948, the U.S. government has imposed quotas on sugar imports. As a result, the U.S. price of sugar has exceeded the world market price, by 40 percent in 1970. One economist has calculated the effects of this policy, using 1970 data. The total loss of consumers' surplus (equivalent to area *igea* in Figure 6.14) equaled $585.96 million. Of this amount, domestic producers gained $228.73 million (the dotted area in Figure 6.14), foreign producers gained $267.28 (the crosshatched area). The deadweight loss due to lower trade volume (area *fge*) was $10.28 million; the deadweight loss due to increased production cost (area *bhc*) was $79.67 million.

Source: Ilse Mintz, *U.S. Import Quotas: Costs and Consequences* (Washington, D.C.: American Enterprise Institute for Public Policy Research, February 1973).

CLOSE-UP

CLOSE-UP 6.1

PROFIT AND INDUSTRY EXPANSION: DEPARTMENT STORE DENTISTRY

In 1979, 10 percent of the U.S. population had never seen a dentist; 50 percent hadn't seen one for more than a year; only 5 percent saw one regularly. Prices and profits in the industry were high. This situation induced a number of dental entrepreneurs to make sweeping changes, getting out of their low-volume, single-chair practices and setting up (with the increased use of technicians) high-volume, lower-priced operations in department stores.

Montgomery Ward first leased space in several West Coast stores to such dental centers. Sears, Roebuck and Co. soon did the same on the West Coast, while Korvettes and Times Square Stores Corporation opened similar centers in New York. Before long, the idea spread throughout the nation. Following store hours and relying on the huge potential market (some 100,000 people walk through a single department store in a month), the average department store dentist handled more than 750 patients a month (compared to 240 patients for the single-chair practitioner). Patients could usually see dentists at a moment's notice and at 20 to 40 percent lower fees. (Note: At some Montgomery Ward stores, lawyers have joined the move to department stores. Shoppers can go into the Law Store, pay $10, pick up a telephone in a private booth, and talk with a lawyer. Offering such services at a low price, which can be known in advance, has opened up a huge market of people who fear being hit by an unknown amount.)

Sources: Elizabeth Bailey, "The Department Store Dentist," *Forbes,* March 19, 1979, pp. 112 and 114; Anton Rupert, "Shopping-Center Shingles," *The Wall Street Journal,* October 16, 1979, p. 48; "Moving the Dentist's Chair to Retail Stores," *Business Week,* January 19, 1981, pp. 56 and 58.

CLOSE-UP 6.2

TICKET SCALPING AND OTHER CRIMES

The existence of consumers' surplus is evidenced by the frequent success of *ticket scalpers* who make a profit by buying tickets at the box office price and then reselling them at a much higher price. The phenomenon drew national attention in 1984 during an extended tour of singer Michael Jackson and his brothers. In New York, for example, some 167,000 tickets were sold out, at the official $28 price, within nine hours of going on sale. Eager fans found it easy, however, to buy tickets thereafter—anywhere from $100 to $700 apiece! New York and New Jersey authorities were kept busy prosecuting the "criminals" because their laws made such activity a misdemeanor punishable by heavy fines. Economists, on the other hand, tend to look at such reselling as evidence of mutually beneficial deals that occur because purchasers value the tickets much more highly, and sellers value them less highly, than the agreed-upon price.

Note: At about the same time, a similar phenomenon occurred in Boston where Glenn Heller, owner of a Beacon Hill Gulf station, started charging variable prices for his gasoline, $1.69 per gallon between 8 A.M. and 7 P.M., $2.59 between 7 P.M. and midnight, and $3.59—the highest price in the nation—between midnight and 8 A.M. While some people were outraged, customers kept coming.

Sources: Joseph Berger, "Variety of Scalpers Peddling Jackson Seats for up to $700," *The New York Times,* July 29, 1984; "His Gas Prices Still Highest in the Nation," *The Daily Hampshire Gazette,* May 18, 1981, p. 11.

CLOSE-UP 6.3

CONSUMERS' SURPLUS AND THE MARCH ON WASHINGTON

On November 15, 1969, the largest assembly of dissenters in U.S. history gathered in Washington, D.C., to urge an end to the Vietnam War. The intensity of their feeling was indicated by the fact that they came from every state, and they traveled long distances and spent much time and money in the process. A group of economists estimated a demand curve for this mass demonstration, plotting various prices of participation (calculated at $1 per hour of travel time plus 5.5¢ per person per mile) against the number of participants from different states. This enabled them to calculate the average price paid per marcher, as well as the total market value of the march ($7.1 million). From this information the researchers also calculated the consumers' surplus (from the area under the demand curve and above the price): $10.1 million.

Source: Charles J. Cicchetti, A. Myrick Freeman, III, Robert H. Haveman, and Jack Knetsch, "On the Economics of Mass Demonstrations: A Case Study of the November 1969 March on Washington," *The American Economic Review,* September 1971, pp. 719–24.

CLOSE-UP

7

Monopoly and Cartels

Barring gifts or loans from other societies, the people of any society (as a group) can increase the yearly flow of goods available to them in only one of three ways:

1. People can utilize the existing stocks of their resources at a higher rate. That is, they can opt for less leisure and less conservation of capital and natural resources.

2. People can increase the size of their resource stocks and then use them at the accustomed rate. For example, they can trade in lowered current consumption for greater investment in human and physical capital.

3. People can increase their productivity. Risk-bearing entrepreneurs, for example, can make innovative changes that coax a larger flow of goods from identical resource flows.

In an economy with perfectly competitive markets, what is true for people as a group is also true for every individual. Barring the receipt of gifts or loans from other people, every individual who wishes to have an increased command over goods must do one of the three things just mentioned. In an economy with perfectly competitive markets, every individual who wishes to have a larger piece of the pie and who cannot get it through gifts or loans must engage in an activity that enlarges the pie itself. In the absence of perfectly competitive markets, on the other hand, there is another way for individuals to increase their command over goods.

Regardless of the type of market prevailing, all individuals as a group can never get more goods unless the overall quantity of goods is larger. When markets are imperfectly competitive, however, a subset of all people can get more even from a constant or shrinking pie—*at the expense of other people*. In imperfectly competitive markets, some people can get more goods at others' expense through a cunning alteration of the prices at which exchanges take place. To the extent that individuals can raise the prices of things being sold or reduce the prices of things being bought purchasing power can be transferred to these manipulators of prices.

When all markets are perfectly competitive, no person, of course, has the power to manipulate prices in such a manner because trading partners have plenty of alternatives open to them. If any one seller, for example, tried to dictate a price above the competitive equilibrium level, all buyers would disappear. Buyers could find many other sellers able and willing to supply, at the competitive equilibrium price, as much as they wanted of any good. But now consider this: What if a seller were able to kill off competition in whatever was for sale (and in its close substitutes as well)? What if there were no other sellers or at least no other independently acting ones? In this situation, buyers would be trapped. Instead of finding innumerable sellers, buyers would find only a single seller (or a group of sellers acting as one). Buyers would be confronted by a **monopoly,** an industry that has only a single seller and the product of which has no close substitutes, or by a **cartel,** a group of conspiring sellers acting as one and making joint price-quantity decisions with a view toward earning a larger profit than competition would allow. This chapter will consider the effects of monopolies and cartels in the markets for goods; Chapter 11 will consider imperfectly competitive markets for resource services in turn.

THE SOURCES OF MONOPOLY POWER

Monopoly power is the ability of a seller to raise the price of something that is for sale above the perfectly competitive level. This power can originate from a number of technological and legal sources, including increasing returns to scale, exclusive ownership of key resources, patents and copyrights, and exclusive franchises.

Increasing Returns to Scale

Consider an industry subject to increasing returns to scale. As noted in Chapter 4, under such conditions, a simultaneous and equal percentage change in the use of all physical inputs leads to a larger percentage change in physical output. Chapter 5 showed how an increase in scale under such conditions of increasing returns shifts average-total (and marginal) cost curves not only to the right, but also down (see Figure 5.9 "Short-Run Versus Long-Run Costs and Long-Run Supply" on p. 154). This shift is now illustrated, with respect to a hypothetical producer of electric power, in Figure 7.1, which depicts a producer who is capable of setting up a multitude of different-sized power plants. Design number 41, for example, yields short-run

FIGURE 7.1

The Natural Monopoly

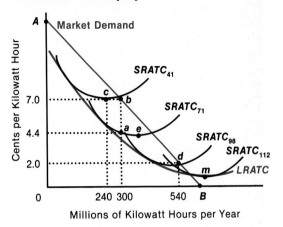

Whenever long-run average total cost is declining throughout the range of possible quantities demanded in the market, the first firm expanding its scale sufficiently to supply the entire market may secure for itself a natural monopoly.

average-total-cost curve $SRATC_{41}$, design number 71 yields curve $SRATC_{71}$, and so on, until design number 112 produces the optimum plant, the one that has taken advantage of all available economies of scale and yields the lowest possible minimum average total cost (at point m). The firm's long-run average-total-cost curve $LRATC$, therefore, is the color envelope curve labeled $LRATC$. Whenever long-run average total cost is in this way declining throughout the range of possible quantities demanded in the market (as shown here by market-demand line AB), the situation is one of **natural monopoly.**

The assumed technical facts—not uncommon for producers of electric power, gas, water, and telephone service—enable a single firm to produce more cheaply than two or more firms. The first firm to recognize and take advantage of such increasing returns to scale can profitably supply the entire market (instead of a negligible fraction thereof), while keeping additional firms out of the market by the certain prospect of losses. Consider how such a firm might design and construct plant number 71, produce 300 million kilowatt hours at 4.4 cents each (point *a*) and sell them at 7 cents each (point *b*). Any potential rival, in order to meet the 7-cents-per-kilowatt-hour price, would have to construct a plant of size number 41 at least and run it at its optimal rate (point *c*). All else being equal, such extra output of 240 million kilowatt hours would raise total quantity supplied to 540 million kilowatt hours, a quantity that could not be sold for more than 2 cents per kilowatt hour (point *d*). This price would inevitably engulf the new and the old firm in losses. (Both *c* and *e*, the minimum average total costs associated with plants 41 and 71, respectively, clearly exceed 2 cents.) These losses would be even larger should the potential newcomer build a plant as large as or larger than number 71, for the resultant market supply could not even be sold at the lowest of all possible average total costs, corresponding to point *m*. This sort of analysis would keep newcomers at bay, or this sort of scenario would, eventually, allow only one firm to survive. Monopoly need not, however, be the result of technical factors.

Exclusive Ownership of Key Resources

Sometimes firms become the only sellers in their industry because they have exclusive ownership of a key resource without which the industry's product cannot be produced. The Aluminum Company of America (Alcoa) once controlled most domestic bauxite deposits (from which aluminum is made), and it also controlled many strategic water power sites capable of generating the massive electric power needed for aluminum ingot production. American Metal Climax once controlled 90 percent of the world's molybdenum (all of it in one Colorado mountain); the International Nickel Company once owned a similar percentage of the world's nickel. And the de Beers Company of South Africa (see Close-Up 7.2) owns or leases most of the diamond mines in the world.

The exclusive ownership conducive to monopoly need not necessarily involve natural resources, however. Consider why New York's

Met long held a monopoly in American opera: All the experienced singers available were under long-run contracts to the Met. Professional baseball and football clubs, similarly, sign up all the talented players, making life rather impossible for potential competitors. The same kind of advantage would also accrue to any firm that could sign up all the possessors of some secret production recipe similar, perhaps, to that of making a genuine Stradivarius violin. On that account, however, government nowadays provides a helping hand.

Patents and Copyrights

Government frequently promotes the establishment of monopoly when it issues patents and copyrights. A **patent** is an exclusive right to the use of an invention. It is limited to a period of 17 years and permits the holder to prevent all others from producing a specified product or using a specified process. Patents are, of course, granted in order to encourage the production and disclosure of inventions and to stimulate innovation that is often risky and expensive to undertake but all too easy and cheap for others to copy. Many monopolies in the past have been based on patents, including patents for such products or processes as aluminum, cash registers, cellophane, instant photographic pictures, rayon, scotch tape, shoe machinery, and xerography. Monopolies can, similarly, be created with the help of a **copyright,** the exclusive right to the reproduction, publishing, or sale of a literary, musical, or artistic work. Although patents and copyrights are only granted for limited periods, the seller so favored often acquires an impregnable market position by the time this protection expires.

Exclusive Franchises

The most ancient source of monopoly, and one that often has the most enduring effect, is the **exclusive franchise,** a governmental grant to a single seller of the exclusive right to produce and sell a good. Kings throughout history have granted this privilege to their favored subjects, presumably because it provided a way to enrich them (by enabling them to charge their fellow citizens above-competitive prices) without any drain from the royal purse. For Americans, the monopoly of the British East India Company is, perhaps, of the greatest significance. That monopoly gave rise to the Boston Tea Party.

This type of contrived barrier to competition is common. Consider the exclusive franchises granted by the federal government to the U.S. Postal Service, by state governments to single restaurant chains operating along their turnpikes, and by city governments to cable television companies, garbage collectors, taxi companies, and various concessions (from airport car rentals to food service and parking at sports events).

THE PROFIT-MAXIMIZING MONOPOLY: THE SHORT RUN

Just as we analyzed in Chapter 5 the likely behavior of a profit-maximizing firm under perfect competition, we can predict the probable behavior of a profit-maximizing monopoly. Contrary to what many people think, no monopoly ever charges the highest possible price or "what the traffic will bear," which is easily seen by following the route of thought taken by A. A. Cournot (1801–77), who developed the theory of monopoly (and a Biography of whom can be found in Chapter 7 of the *Student Workbook* that accompanies this text).

The Demand Function and Total Revenue

A monopoly traps buyers in the sense that they cannot buy the given product from any other firm. Even a good substitute is unavailable. In another sense, however, buyers are free. They can always buy smaller quantities if prices are raised and even refuse to buy the product at all should the monopoly raise price by too much. A monopoly, therefore, has to reckon with the "law" of downward-sloping demand. Being the

only seller in its industry, it is confronted, furthermore, with the entire market demand, which might consist of the data in columns (1) and (2) of Table 7.1. Unlike the firm in perfect competition (which is a price taker), a monopoly can set price at whatever level it wishes. The monopoly is a price setter, but it must also live with the consequences: Given price, buyers decide what quantity they will take; this price-quantity combination determines the monopoly's total revenue and, by implication, its marginal revenue as well. Note: If our monopoly charged "the highest possible price" (an outrageous 50 cents per kilowatt hour, perhaps), it would sell nothing at all. Thus its total revenue would be zero, and it would soon go out of business!

The data of Table 7.1 can be plotted, as in Figure 7.2. In panel (b), for example, price-quantity combinations *A* to *F* have been plotted as the fat dots so labeled on the market-demand line. The demand line's midpoint, *M*, has also been indicated. The total-and marginal-revenue data of Table 7.1 have been similarly plotted. (Note the fat dots on the respective curves.)

As we learned from Figure 3.15, "How Elasticity Can Vary" (p. 78), the absolute value of the price elasticity of demand in segment *AM* exceeds unity; it equals unity at *M;* and it falls short of unity in segment *MF*. These elasticities imply that price reductions that start from the 50-cents-per-kilowatt-hour/no-sales combination at *A* and stop just shy of the 25-cents-per-kilowatt-hour/25-million-kilowatt-hours-per-day sales combination corresponding to point *M* will increase quantity demanded so much as to raise total revenue. Panel (a) shows that total revenue rises from 0 toward *m*. On the other hand, price reductions starting just below 25 cents per kilowatt hour do not lead to a proportionate increase in quantity demanded. Total revenue, therefore, falls, as from *m* toward *f* in panel (a). Maximum total revenue, found at point *m*, therefore, corresponds to the unitary price elasticity of demand that is found at midpoint *M* on our straight-line demand function. (Can you see why Cournot, who investigated the behavior of a profit-maximizing monopoly selling mineral water wanted for its healing power, argued that the monopoly would choose a price corresponding to midpoint *M* on its straight-line demand if any amount of water could be produced at zero cost from a natural spring?)

The Demand Function and Marginal Revenue

Note in Figure 7.2 that a monopoly's total-revenue line ceases to be a ray from the origin as is true for a firm under perfect competition (see Figure 5.2, "A Profitable Business" on p. 144). Correspondingly, a monopoly's marginal revenue ceases to be equal to the market price; marginal revenue for a monopoly cannot be depicted by a horizontal line. Our monopoly does not face, helplessly, a market-determined price. It sets its own price, but knows that quantity sold varies accordingly. If it charges 40 cents per kilowatt hour, for instance, it sells 10 million kilowatt hours per day (point *B* in our graph), and its total revenue is $4 million a day (point *b*). If it instead charges 30 cents per kilowatt hour, it sells 20

million kilowatt hours per day (point *C*), and its total revenue is $6 million a day (point *c*). Thus **marginal revenue,** or the change in total revenue divided by the associated change in total product, equals +$2 million per day divided by +10 million kilowatt hours per day, or 20 cents per kilowatt hour, as shown by "triangle" *abc* underneath the total-revenue curve in panel (a) of Figure 7.2 and by point *G* in panel (b). Marginal revenue is thus considerably smaller than either the old price of 40 cents or the new one of 30 cents per kilowatt hour. The relationships discussed so far are summarized in Box 7.A.

A comparison of Box 7.A with Box 5.C (on p. 144) immediately highlights the most significant difference between the monopoly and the perfectly competitive firm discussed so far: The former can choose its own price; the latter has to accept the equilibrium price established by competition among the many. As a result, the monopoly's marginal revenue, unlike the perfect competitor's, is always below price. The reason is simple and can be seen clearly by reviewing the Figure 7.2 example of lowering price from 40

TABLE 7.1

A Monopoly's Demand and Revenue

	Market Demand		Revenue	
	Price (cents per kilowatt hour) (1)	Quantity (million kilowatt hours per day) (2)	Total Revenue (million dollars per day) (3) = (1) × (2)	Marginal Revenue (cents per kilowatt hour) $(4) = \frac{\Delta 3}{\Delta 2}$
(A)	50	0	0	
				40
(B)	40	10	4	
				20
(C)	30	20	6	
				0
(D)	20	30	6	
				−20
(E)	10	40	4	
				−40
(F)	0	50	0	

A monopoly is confronted with the entire market demand, in columns (1) and (2). It can set price, in column (1), at whatever level it wishes but must then take the consequences, in columns (2)–(4).

cents to 30 cents (and thereby raising sales by 10 million kilowatt hours of electricity per day).

FIGURE 7.2

Monopoly: Total and Marginal Revenue

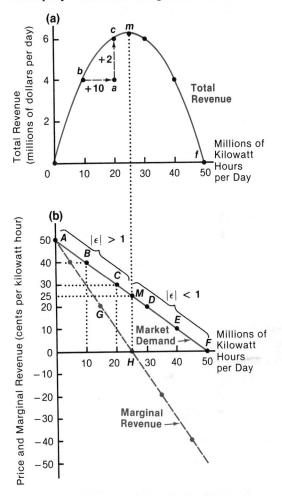

A monopoly is confronted with the entire market demand (line *AF*). It can set price at whatever level it wishes but must then live with the consequences: Quantity demanded varies with price; depending on the price elasticity of demand, any price reduction will raise, leave unchanged, or reduce total revenue and will thus be associated with positive, zero, or negative marginal revenue. This graph shows analogous implications for any price increase.

7.A Total, Average, and Marginal Revenue under Monopoly

$$TR = P \cdot Q$$

$$AR = \frac{TR}{Q} = \frac{P \cdot Q}{Q} = P$$

$$MR = \frac{\Delta TR}{\Delta Q} < P$$

where *P* is the market price that the monopoly is free to choose.

While the extra sales bring in extra revenue of $3 million per day (+10 million kilowatt hours per day at 30 cents each), these extra sales, we assumed, can be made only by lowering the price from 40 cents to 30 cents per kilowatt hour. Thus 10 cents are also lost for each of the 10 million kilowatt hours that would have been sold had the price remained at 40 cents per kilowatt hour. This loss from lower price comes to $1 million per day. When offset against the $3 million gain from larger sales, a net gain is made of only $2 million, or 20 cents per kilowatt hour, indicated, respectively, by distance *ac* in panel (a) and by point *G* in panel (b).

Indeed, when the price elasticity of demand has an absolute value of less than unity (as in section *MF* of our demand line), any revenue loss from lowered price exceeds any gain from larger sales. Then total revenue (to the right of *m*) declines; marginal revenue (to the right of *H*) is negative. (The reader may wish to review Figure 3.17, "Elasticity, Expenditure, and Revenue," on p. 80.)

Note: It is no accident that marginal revenue is zero (point *H*) exactly when the absolute value of the price elasticity of demand is unity (point *M*) and when total revenue is maximized (point *m*). The marginal revenue line associated with a *straight-line* demand function always connects the demand function's intercept on the vertical axis (point *A*) with a point such as *H*, midway between the origin 0 of the graph and the demand function's intercept on the horizontal axis (point

F). This is why Cournot's advice to the producer of costless mineral water could also be phrased as selecting a price that reduced marginal revenue to zero. Most monopolies, of course, do not have zero costs. Because profit maximization is then more complicated than maximizing total revenue or setting marginal revenue to zero, we must turn to costs.

Cost Curves

Our analysis in Chapter 5 of the perfectly competitive firm can now be extended: A monopoly, just like a perfectly competitive firm, faces a production function, must pay for its inputs, and can calculate the costs of producing various levels of output. These costs can be depicted by the types of curves shown in Figure 5.1, ''Short-Run Cost Curves'' (p. 141). The costs of producing any given quantity of any given product, however, will not necessarily be identical regardless of whether the producing firm is a perfect competitor or a monopoly. As we have seen, a monopoly's production costs may be lower due to economies of scale. On the other hand, these costs may also be higher due to a greater likelihood of X-inefficiency when the fear of competitors is absent (see Chapter 14 for further discussion). At the moment, we need accept only the fact that a monopoly's cost curves will have the same *general* shape as those of any other firm; thus the Box 5.A and 5.B summaries (pp. 140–141) fully apply.

Profit Maximization

Just like any other firm, a monopoly will maximize its profit by selecting an output volume that maximizes the difference, Π, between total revenue, *TR*, and total cost, *TC* (and, therefore, equates marginal revenue, *MR*, with marginal cost, *MC*, as the optimization principle suggests).* Figure 7.3 is a copy of Figure 7.2, but

---

*Section 7A of the Calculus Appendix at the back of this book provides an important qualification to the parenthetical statement for those who are concerned with mathematical precision.

with various cost curves superimposed upon it. Given the assumed conditions of revenue and cost, this monopoly would maximize profit by producing an output volume of 20 million kilowatt hours per day.

FIGURE 7.3

A Profit-Making Monopoly

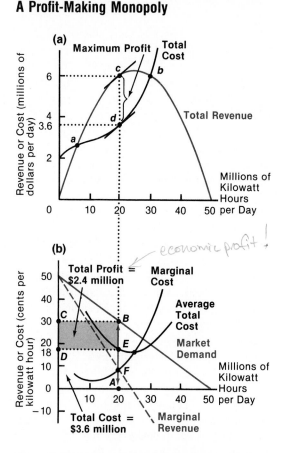

This profit-making monopoly finds its optimal rate of production where its rising marginal cost equals its falling marginal revenue. Given the short-run revenue and cost functions shown here, this equality occurs at points *c* and *d* in panel (a) and at *F* in panel (b). The corresponding optimal rate of production equals 20 million kilowatt hours per day; therefore, a price of 30¢ per kilowatt hour is set. In this example, total revenue exceeds total cost; thus a positive profit is made that is equal to $2.4 million per day (distance *cd* in the top panel; the shaded rectangle in the bottom panel).

Consider panel (a) of Figure 7.3. It is obvious that any output volume to the left of point *a* or to the right of point *b* would yield losses because total cost would exceed total revenue. All intermediate output levels would yield positive profits, but to varying degrees. The maximum possible profit would be $2.4 million per day (distance *cd*), corresponding to the 20-million-kilowatt-hour total noted above. It is no accident that the slope of the total-revenue curve at *c* exactly equals that of the total-cost curve at *d*. Between *a* on the one hand and *c* or *d* on the other, total revenue and total cost increasingly diverge from each other; so total profit grows. Between *c* or *d* on the one hand and *b* on the other, total revenue and total cost converge; so total profit declines.

Panel (b) of Figure 7.3 leads to the same conclusion, of course. The ever changing slope, at various potential output volumes, of the total-revenue curve is now reflected by the height of the marginal-revenue curve. The ever changing slope of the total-cost curve, similarly, shows up as the height of the marginal-cost curve. The equality of marginal cost and marginal revenue at *F* signifies maximum profit. Consider what would happen if the firm produced the associated 20 million kilowatt hours per day and set a 30-cents-per-kilowatt-hour price to make people demand just this (20-million-kilowatt-hour) quantity (point *B*). Total revenue would then equal rectangle 0*ABC*; that is, 20 million kilowatt hours times the 30-cents-per-kilowatt-hour price, or $6 million per day, also shown by point *c* in panel (a). Total cost would equal rectangle 0*AED*; that is, 20 million kilowatt hours times the 18-cents-per-kilowatt-hour average total cost, or $3.6 million per day, also shown by point *d* in panel (a). Total profit, therefore, would equal shaded rectangle *DEBC*; that is, 20 million kilowatt hours times the 12-cents-per-kilowatt hour average profit *BE*, or $2.4 million per day, also shown by distance *cd* in panel (a).

Note: The making of positive profit is not inevitable. Given identical demand but less favorable cost conditions, our monopoly could just as well be making zero profit, as illustrated

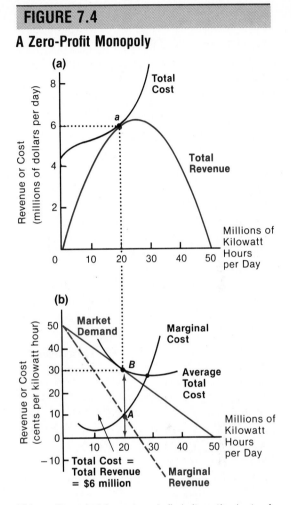

FIGURE 7.4

A Zero-Profit Monopoly

This profit-maximizing monopoly finds its optimal rate of production where its rising marginal cost equals its falling marginal revenue. Given the short-run revenue and cost functions shown here, this equality occurs at point *a* in panel (a) and at *A* in panel (b). The corresponding optimal rate of production equals 20 million kilowatt hours per day; therefore, a price of 30¢ per kilowatt hour is set, but zero profit is made: Total cost just equals total revenue (point *a*); average cost just equals average revenue or price (point *B*). Any other production volume would yield losses.

in Figure 7.4, or even a loss, as illustrated by Figure 7.5.*

---

*For a calculus-based treatment of this material, see Section 7A of the Calculus Appendix at the back of this book.

FIGURE 7.5

A Loss-Incurring Monopoly

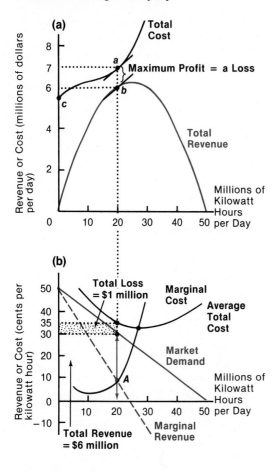

This profit-maximizing monopoly finds its optimal rate of production where its rising marginal cost equals its falling marginal revenue. Given the short-run revenue and cost functions shown here, this equality occurs at points *a* and *b* in panel (a) and at *A* in panel (b). The corresponding optimal rate of production equals 20 million kilowatt hours per day; therefore, a price of 30¢ per kilowatt hour is set, but a loss is incurred: Total cost exceeds total revenue by $1 million per day (distance *ab* in the top panel; the dotted rectangle in the lower panel). Any other production volume would yield larger losses. Note: This monopoly would cease to exist in the long run and would produce at the indicated output level in the short run only as long as its loss fell short of fixed cost, as is the case here. (Remember that fixed cost can be read off at the point where the total-cost curve intercepts the vertical axis, as at *c*.)

THE PROFIT-MAXIMIZING MONOPOLY: THE LONG RUN

A major difference between a perfectly competitive firm and a monopoly is evident in the long run. While both types of firms *will* go out of business rather than make losses in the long run, and while both *may* make zero profit permanently, the difference between the two concerns the possibility of making positive profit. As was illustrated in Figure 6.3, ''A Profitable Industry Expands'' (p. 183), competitive firms cannot expect to make positive profits in the long run. Quite the contrary is true for a monopoly. Its profit, if positive, may well be permanent because entry into the industry is blocked to other firms for one of the reasons already mentioned.

Figure 7.3, however, does not necessarily depict long-run equilibrium. (Figure 7.3 would represent long-run equilibrium only if all the curves shown there pertained to the long run.) Suppose, however, that the demand and marginal revenue in panel (b) were long-run curves, while the cost curves were short-run curves. The implications are analyzed in Figure 7.6, which is a copy of Figure 7.3, but the earlier curves of marginal and average total cost are now labeled $SRMC_1$ and $SRATC_1$. The short-run profit-maximizing output level (corresponding to point *F* and equal to 20 million kilowatt hours per day) is still shown, along with the associated profit of $2.4 million per day (rectangle *EBCD*).

We now postulate long-run curves of marginal and average total cost, such as color lines *LRMC* and *LRATC*. Under such conditions, our monopoly would wish to change its scale. (Note how the initial output volume could be produced, in a larger plant, at a lower average total cost shown by point *M*, which lies below *E*.) Given enough time, our monopoly would equate (at point *A*) long-run marginal cost with long-run marginal revenue. It would produce 24 million kilowatt hours per day, sell them at 26 cents each (point *H*), and take in total revenue of $6.24 million per day. All this output would be produced in the cheapest possible way, at an average total cost of 10 cents per kilowatt hour (point G), utilizing a larger plant with short-run curves of average and marginal cost, $SRATC_2$ and $SRMC_2$ (not shown). Thus a profit of 16 cents per kilowatt hour (distance GH) would yield total profit of $3.84 million per day (shaded rectangle $GHKL$). In the absence of changes in demand or costs, this profit would be permanent.

AN INDEX OF MONOPOLY POWER

Figure 6.5, "Long-Run Industry Supply Curves" (p. 187), demonstrated that the perfectly competitive firm in the long run will always produce an output volume at which economic profit is zero, at which price equals marginal cost, and at which price also equals minimum average total cost. Now consider a monopoly that faces the same type of downward-sloping market demand that perfectly competitive firms face as a group:

1. Such a monopoly, as we have just seen, may well earn positive profit in the long run.

The Monopoly in the Long Run

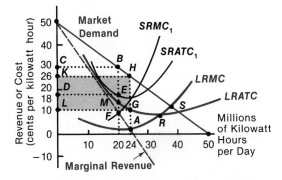

In the long run, a monopoly produces an output volume (here 24 million kilowatt hours per day) that equates long-run marginal cost with long-run marginal revenue (here at point A). Because entry into the industry is blocked to other firms, the resultant profit (shaded rectangle $GHKL$) is permanent.

2. In addition, because its marginal revenue always falls short of price and its profit is maximized when marginal revenue is equated with marginal cost, this monopoly will always choose to produce an output volume at which price exceeds marginal cost. (Note how H exceeds A in Figure 7.6 and how the firm would have to produce a quantity and charge a price corresponding to point S if it were to act like a perfect competitor, equating price with marginal cost.)

3. Finally, a monopoly may well not produce at minimum average total cost. (Note how, in Figure 7.6, G exceeds long-run minimum average total cost at R.)

Of these three characteristics of monopoly, the second one will always be present. For this reason, Abba P. Lerner, in 1934, suggested that the gap between price, P, and marginal cost, MC, could be used to measure *the degree of monopoly power exercised by a firm*. This **Lerner index** is usually calculated as the ratio of

$$\frac{P - MC}{P}.$$

Consider Figure 7.6. The final equilibrium price is 26 cents per kilowatt hour (point H). Long-run marginal cost at the chosen output volume equals 2.5 cents per kilowatt hour (point A). Thus the index comes to

$$\frac{26¢ - 2.5¢}{26¢} = .9$$

This contrasts with a maximum of 1 (for Cournot's zero-marginal-cost producer of mineral water) and a minimum of 0 (for the perfectly competitive firm that equates price and marginal cost).

Note: Because every profit-maximizing firm equates marginal cost, MC, and marginal revenue, MR, the Lerner index can be rewritten as

$$\frac{P - MR}{P}.$$

In addition, marginal revenue is always related to the (absolute value of the) price elasticity of demand, ϵ, such that

$$MR = P - \frac{P}{|\epsilon|}.$$

(The accuracy of this relationship can be gauged from the fact that the price elasticity of demand facing a *perfectly competitive* firm is infinite. In that case, P/ϵ becomes zero, and, as we know, $MR = P$ for such a firm.)* It follows that the Lerner index also equals

$$\frac{1}{|\epsilon|},$$

which makes intuitive sense. A firm facing an infinite price elasticity of demand (as perfect competitors do) would have zero power to raise price. A firm facing a very low elasticity would have a high degree of such power. (In Chapter 14, we will pursue further the significance of the gap between marginal cost and price.)

THE NATURE OF CARTELS

It is not difficult to see why firms in an otherwise competitive industry might be tempted to form a cartel. If such firms were lucky enough to imitate the behavior of a profit-making monopoly, their efforts would yield an important prize: permanent economic profit instead of the ever present tendency toward zero profit.

In principle, the formation of a cartel is easy. All it takes is an agreement among all the existing sellers to charge an identical and higher price and to restrict supply until it equals market demand at the cartel price. In practice, however, such would-be monopolists often run afoul of one or more of three obstacles: organizational difficulties, a high price elasticity of demand, or a high price elasticity of supply.

Organizational difficulties include the problem of getting all or most existing sellers to join

the cartel in the first place. When there are many sellers, this may be a hopeless task. Even when there are few, but they do not get along with each other (because of political differences, for example), the original formation of the cartel may not be possible. But organizational difficulties occur beyond this initial stage. Cartel members must frequently meet and agree on a common price to be charged; they must allocate among themselves the necessary reductions in quantity supplied; they must keep each other from cheating on the agreement. It takes a strong and lasting spirit of cooperation to achieve all this. Even when it is present, the cartel may fail.

No degree of organizational success can overcome a *high price elasticity of market demand.* Consider the extreme case of an infinite elasticity where buyers have plenty of good substitutes available for the cartel's product. Under such circumstances, any increase in price by the cartel leads to the total disappearance of quantity demanded. Selling nothing at a very high price will satisfy few sellers, indeed.

Finally, a cartel may be wrecked by a *high price elasticity of supply.* Even if cartel members are loyal and reduce quantity supplied in response to the higher price, newcomers who have no inclination to join the conspiracy may enter the industry, attracted, of course, by the very price rise engineered by the cartel. These new suppliers may offset or more than offset the supply reduction by the cartel. Then a glut will develop on the market, and buyers will find it easy to be supplied below the cartel price.

In spite of these likely difficulties, cartels have been formed throughout history through private efforts, with the help of government, and even as a result of international agreements. Not surprisingly, successful cartels have been rare.

Private Cartels

Consider the formation of a private price-fixing and output-restricting agreement among hundreds of thousands of wheat farmers. Their initial circumstances might be those depicted by point *e* in Figure 7.7. Some 2.5 billion bushels of wheat

---

*For a calculus-based treatment of this material, see Section 7B of the Calculus Appendix at the back of this book.

FIGURE 7.7

The Cartel

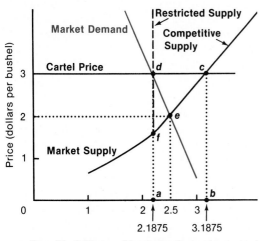

Competitive sellers of a good may improve their welfare at the expense of buyers by conspiring to raise price and by restricting the quantity supplied. If wheat farmers, for example, could agree to restrict supply so that the line going through *f, e,* and *c* was shifted to dashed line *fd,* they could escape the $2-per-bushel competitive equilibrium price (corresponding to *e*) and enjoy the $3-per-bushel cartel price (corresponding to *d*). In the process, they would replace, just as a monopoly does, a price equal to marginal cost (at *e*) with a price (at *d*) above marginal cost (at *f*).

might be traded in the year prior to the cartel's formation, and wheat might sell at a competitive equilibrium price of $2 per bushel. Yet, a bright organizer might note, a slight restriction of the yearly supply to 2.1875 billion bushels could raise price to $3 per bushel and benefit all the farmers. How could the organizer persuade all the wheat farmers in the nation to join and to agree on cutting next year's output by 12.5 percent below this year's crop so as to raise price from the old equilibrium level of $2 to an estimated new level of $3 per bushel? (In 1968, when the National Farmers' Organization tried to organize a cattle cartel, only 10 percent of the farmers joined.)

Even if the initial step could be taken, buyers could surely find farmers cheating on the agreement. Imagine yourself to be one of the farmers who has just voted on the above scheme. You used to produce, say, 5,000 bushels, getting $10,000 of gross revenue at the old $2-per-bushel price. Now you know that you will have to cut output by 12.5 percent (as everyone else has to). Then you will sell 4,375 bushels. If the price rises to $3, this will gross $13,125, a clear gain of $3,125. But you know something else. You know that you play an insignificant part in this whole scheme. Nobody would ever notice if you, just you, did not cut your output. Total supply would then be cut, you might figure, from 2.5 billion bushels to only 2.187500625 billion bushels (instead of the agreed-upon 2.1875 billion bushels). That would surely make no difference. As long as the others stuck to the agreement, price would still rise to $3, or almost that. And then your gross income would rise to almost $15,000, not just to $13,125. Even if you were caught (which would be unlikely), nobody could fine you or throw you in jail. Under the English common law (unwritten law), private conspiracies to fix output and market shares and prices cannot be enforced. It would pay you to cheat! (In 1968, some cattle farmers blew up cattle scales and sat on the roads obstructing cattle shipments by the "chiselers." But many more of them were marketing their cattle; some even used house trailers to conceal their shipments.)

As you might expect, there would be others who would have the same bright idea of cheating as you. There would even be some who were brighter than that. They would *raise* their output in the hope of making a killing when all others cut theirs and caused prices to go up. And even if the original conspirators were totally loyal to each other and honestly abided by the agreement, the scheme might fail: *New* sellers might appear on the scene, because of the new and higher price. Former potato farmers might grow wheat to get a piece of the loot. And foreign farmers might ship in huge quantities. Before long, a surplus of *dc* might appear in the market, putting strong pressure on price to fall. Thus a privately arranged price-fixing agreement has an excellent chance of breaking down.

Government-Sponsored National Cartels

It is not surprising that would-be cartel-makers turn to government for help against reluctant joiners, argumentative members, chiselers, and outsiders. More often than not, this government help is provided and takes the form of *legislating,* separately or in combination, the setting of a higher price, a cutback in supply, or even an increase in demand.

Legislatures that desire to fix prices above competitive equilibrium levels either enact special price laws or grant broad powers to specially designed departments of the executive to do such price fixing. Among such executive departments (past or present) are the multitude of federal "alphabet agencies"; the CAB, the FCC, the FMC, the FPC, the FTC, and the ICC, to name just a few! The Civil Aeronautics Board (CAB), now extinct, for many years was responsible for regulating interstate airline service. It set fares at notoriously high levels to accommodate even the higher-cost producers. On identical routes served by CAB-regulated interstate and by nonregulated *intrastate* airlines, the fares of the intrastate lines (such as California's *Pacific Southwest* and Texas's *Southwest*) were about 50 percent below the rates of CAB carriers. The Federal Communications Commission (FCC) has performed a similar role for telephone and telegraph companies and radio and television broadcasters. The Federal Maritime Commission (FMC) has done the same thing with respect to ocean shipping, and the Federal Power Commission (FPC) with respect to natural gas and electric power producers. The Federal Trade Commission (FTC) has long kept retail prices high enough to allow high-cost outlets to live side by side with lower-cost chain stores. The Interstate Commerce Commission (ICC) has promoted high prices for interstate barge and ship companies, buses, railroads, and (nonagricultural) truckers. (Chapter 15 will describe how some of these practices were being stopped in the early 1980s.)

The federal laws setting minimum prices of goods above competitive equilibrium levels have included, most notably, laws fixing prices for agricultural products. These products have ranged from almonds, barley, beans, butter, cheese, corn, cotton, dates, flax seed, honey, milk, lemons, mohair, raisins, sorghum, and oats to peanuts, potatoes, rice, rye, soybeans, sugar beets and cane, tung nuts, tobacco, walnuts, wheat, and wool. (See Analytical Example 6.2, "The Political Economy of Milk and Housing," for an earlier discussion of this practice.)

Many state and local governments, in addition, protect sellers beyond the reach of federal laws from the supposed ravages of competition. State liquor commissions set liquor prices; state public utility commissions set electric power and telephone rates. State insurance commissions set insurance rates; city transport commissions set rates on buses, subways, and taxis. For some 38 years prior to 1976 (when a federal law repealed them), states as well as cities promoted minimum retail prices for almost everything. Their so-called **fair-trade laws** allowed any manufacturer to fix a minimum price for a product and, if a single retailer agreed to it, to bind all retailers to it, even those who refused to sign an agreement with the manufacturer. Those selling for less could be enjoined, fined, and even jailed. As recently as 1974, 36 states, from California to New York, still had such laws.

Initial price-fixing moves have to be reinforced by further decrees or laws, as Figure 7.7 also illustrates. When price is raised above its equilibrium level (and kept there by law), a surplus develops because quantity demanded drops (along *ed* in the graph), while quantity supplied rises (along *ec*). To avoid the surplus, a government unwilling to let the price fall must either cut the supply or raise the demand; that is, it must bend the market-supply line left until it goes through point *d* or shift the market-demand line right until it goes through point *c*.

Supply has often been cut by denying or restricting market entry to new sellers and by forcing existing sellers to reduce their own supply. From its inception in 1938 until recently, for example, the CAB has not allowed the creation of a single new interstate airline, finding such a move "not required by the public interest, convenience, and necessity." The CAB also enforced market sharing or output restrictions among the existing 10 domestic airlines in order to give them "route security" and to avoid "excessive, destructive, and cut-throat competition." The other federal alphabet agencies, as well as their brethren at the lower levels of government, have performed identical supply-restricting functions.

Similarly, agricultural price legislation has been buttressed by restrictions on domestic output and on imports. Domestic farmers have been issued **acreage allotments** that restrict the total acreage that can be planted with particular crops to or below that achieved at a given date in the past. Farmers have also been given **marketing quotas** that set a maximum amount of a product that particular farmers can legally sell. (Marketing quotas were set when farmers with acreage allotments responded by, nevertheless, producing *more,* due to their flooding of the restricted acreage with fertilizer, pesticides, high-yield seeds, and tender, loving care.) In addition, under the old Soil Bank Program and more recent land-set-asides, farmers have been paid subsidies for taking land entirely out of production. This program has been reinforced by controls on agricultural imports that take the form of either high **tariffs** (import taxes) or low **import quotas** (maximum physical limits on the amounts of goods that may be imported).

The federal government has also helped non-agricultural sellers of goods by such "protective" foreign trade legislation. Even though, in many cases, minimum prices have not been legislated, such restrictions on the domestic market supply raise prices indirectly above the level that would otherwise pertain. Thus we have tariffs on cars, steel, and textiles; we have import quotas on baseball mitts, bicycles, and umbrellas; and we have persuaded foreign governments to impose, "voluntarily," export quotas on their firms (as in the case of Japanese steel and television sets). The list could easily be lengthened. Indeed, a whole range of other *nontariff* barriers (usually in the form of red tape that discourages foreign trade) serves to accomplish

the same goal of reducing alternative sources of supply to the domestic buyer and thus enabling favored domestic sellers to charge more.

State governments, similarly, have pushed up the prices of many goods by placing restrictions on the output produced or the number of producers. Under the Prorationing Program in Oklahoma and Texas, for instance, the number of days per month during which existing oil wells may pump is restricted by law (with the exception of offshore wells that are under federal jurisdiction). Every state in the union also requires the licensing of a multitude of "professions," broadly defined to include not just architects, doctors, dentists, lawyers, and psychologists, but also astrologers, barbers, bartenders, dancing instructors, egg graders, morticians, television aerial erectors, and yacht sellers!

In addition to reinforcing high prices with cuts in supply, governments can do something for sellers that even the most perfectly organized private cartel would find impossible to do: A government can actually force buyers to buy the same quantity (or even more) at the very time that price is raised. The most common approach is to tax people and then use the money to make purchases from or give outright gifts to the favored sellers. Under the agricultural programs in effect prior to 1974 and again since 1977, for instance, the federal government stands ready to purchase, at the prices officially legislated, butter, peanuts, sugar, wheat, and other products. In Figure 7.7, the government might set the price at $3 per bushel, while letting farmers produce what they like (point *c*) and letting them sell privately what they can (point *d*). The government might then buy the difference (*dc*), spending the taxpayers' money (equal to *abcd*). Taxes finance such purchases as well as the cost of their subsequent storage, destruction, or give-away (be it in the form of school lunches or aid to India). A host of other producers, such as airlines, bus companies, ocean shippers, railroads, and subways, are also subsidized by various levels of government. Thus taxpayers in all parts of the country who help finance subsidies to airlines or railroads or farmers are, in fact, being forced to "buy" airplane rides and railroad trips and butter without even realizing it. In this way, they are helping to maintain the government-sponsored high prices of air travel or railroad shipping or butter, which, of course, is the object of the monopoly game: for some people to gain at the expense of other people, without making an effort to reduce overall scarcity.

International Cartels

Often governments join with other governments to form cartels. The practice goes back to at least 1470 when the Vatican under Pope Paul II joined with King Ferdinand of Naples to form an *alum* cartel that lasted 30 years. (Alum is an astringent, crystalline double sulfate of aluminum and potassium that was used in medicine, leather tanning, cloth dyeing, and the arts. At the time, the Turks also supplied it, but the use of Turkish alum was declared un-Christian by the Pope.) In more recent times, OPEC (the Organization of Petroleum Exporting Countries) has, of course, provided a (temporary) example of spectacular success; it is discussed in detail in Analytical Example 7.3, "OPEC—the World's Most Successful Cartel?"

Similar success is not impossible, perhaps, for bauxite and uranium producers. Indeed, at the time of this writing, an International Bauxite Association (IBA) had succeeded in tripling the price of bauxite. The group was formed in 1974 by Australia, the Dominican Republic, Ghana, Guinea, Guyana, Haiti, Indonesia, Jamaica, Sierra Leone, Surinam, and Yugoslavia.

There has been much speculation about other international cartels, actual and potential, ranging from bananas (Central America, Ecuador), coffee (Brazil, Colombia), and grain (Australia, Canada, the United States) to natural rubber (Indonesia, Malaysia, Sri Lanka, Thailand), phosphate rock (Morocco, Tunisia), and tea (India, Sri Lanka). In general, though, the prospects for other international cartels are dim.

First, more often than not, some sellers in an industry do not wish to cooperate. (Consider the political differences between the Soviet Union and South Africa, both of which would have to join cartels for chromium, gold, or manganese. Consider how Iceland refused to join IATA, the International Air Transport Association, and how, as a consequence, until 1978 Icelandic Airlines provided the only low-priced scheduled service across the Atlantic but was also denied landing rights in Europe, except in Iceland and Luxembourg.)

Second, the price elasticity of demand is often high because substitutes are available. This availability has blocked the success of a copper cartel, the Conseil Intergouvernemental des Pays Exportateurs de Cuivre (CIPEC), formed by Chile, Peru, Zaire, and Zambia.

Finally, the price elasticity of supply is often high because the product can easily be produced in many places (consider grain). Therefore, it is not surprising that only about one-third of all the international cartels formed in the past have ever managed to raise price at all, and very few of these have managed to last more than five years.

A Final Note

Often governments aid the formation of cartels for reasons unrelated to the monopolistic consequences here discussed. Federal government programs relating to agriculture, for example, have been enacted for purposes of equity in order to maintain **parity,** defined as the 1910–14 relationship between the prices received by farmers for agricultural goods and the prices paid by them for nonagricultural goods. But regardless of the "good" intent, such policies have promoted monopoly, and that alone is our concern in this chapter. (The wisdom of the parity program can be questioned on other grounds. In 1910–14, the bushels-per-acre yields of U.S. farmers equaled, for example, 14.3 in wheat, 26 in corn, 200.3 in cotton. By 1972–76, these yields were 30.6, 86.7, and 477.2, respectively. Thus even substantial reductions in prices per bushel need not imply reduced farm income.)

State programs that have promoted monopoly, similarly, have often been enacted for other reasons. Consider the Texas restrictions on oil production. They emerged because oil is *fugacious;* it will migrate underground heedless of surface boundary lines. Prior to the state's prorationing law, landowners would produce as fast as possible, especially along the boundaries of their tracts, lest their neighbors drain away their oil. This runaway production dissipated underground pressure too rapidly; oil was bypassed by water and permanently lost. Thus the law was enacted to prevent this physical waste.

State and local licensing provisions, finally, have the admirable goal of certifying the competency of sellers to buyers. But they also restrict the number of practitioners unnecessarily. Examples abound, but here is just one: Of 2,149 aspiring general contractors who took the Florida construction industry licensing board exam in 1973, all failed. Another reason why licensing can be seen as a device to restrict trade rather than to protect the public from unscrupulous charlatans is that state licensing usually evaluates novices only at the start of their careers. Short of outright criminality, they are rarely unlicensed, even if they turn out to be undependable, incompetent, or senile! As the saying goes, the road to hell is paved with good intentions.

APPLICATIONS

Application 1:
The Author-Publisher Conflict

Authors, it is said, usually prefer a lower sales price for their books than do their publishers. If authors are paid a fixed and non-negotiable percentage of the list price, which is often the case, it is not difficult to see why. Consider Figure 7.8. Panel (b) shows a hypothetical market-demand function for a book (color line ab), along with the implied marginal-revenue line (ac). The solid color line in panel (a) shows the corresponding total-revenue function (before any royalty payments are made to the author). From the author's point of view, things are simple, indeed. Having written the book, the author's marginal cost of production is zero, as shown by line MC_A in panel (b) that coincides with the horizontal axis.

Being in the position of Cournot's owner of the costless mineral spring, the author, therefore, wants to equate zero marginal cost with zero marginal revenue, which can be done only at point c where the price elasticity of demand equals unity. Put differently, the author wants to maximize total revenue (before royalty payments) at point M because the author will receive a fixed percentage, say 20 percent, of this sum. In our example, by charging the author's preferred prices of $12.50 per copy, the firm will sell 25,000 copies and take in revenue of $312,500, thus assuring the author of the maximum possible royalty receipts of $62,500 (distance MN).

From the publisher's point of view things look different, however. Assume that the book is produced at a total fixed cost of $50,000 [point C in panel (a)], but at a constant marginal (and average-variable) cost of $8 per copy. The implied cost curves are as shown as the three black lines in the graphs. From the publisher's vantage point, furthermore, the assumed royalty payment of 20 percent of list price changes the effective average-revenue line from the market demand line, AR, to the dashed line, AR^*. (A price of $25 taken in from a buyer, for instance, after the royalty payment to the author of 20 percent, means only $20 to the publisher. Compare points a and d. Similarly, a price of $17.50 taken in means post-royalty receipts of only $14. Compare points h and g.) Accordingly, the publisher's total revenue line is the *dashed* color line in panel (a), and the publisher's effective marginal-revenue line is dashed line dc, not solid line ac in panel (b). Accordingly, the publisher will want to maximize profit by equating, at point e, the publisher's marginal cost, MC_p, with the publisher's marginal revenue, MR_p. This profit-maximizing decision calls for a price of $17.50 per copy and sales of 15,000 copies per year. Total revenue after royalty payments will then equal $210,000 (point B), total cost will equal $170,000 (point A), and profit will equal $40,000 (distance AB). The same profit can also be seen as the shaded rectangle in panel (b), because the sale of 15,000 copies brings an average post-royalty revenue of $14 (point g), while costing an average $11.33 (point *f*), making for an average profit of $2.67 (distance *fg*). Given the assumptions made, the publisher, presumably, will win, and the author will only receive 20 percent of the publisher's gross revenues (of $17.50 times 15,000, or $262,500), which equals $52,500 (rectangle *ghok*) and is clearly less than the potential maximum of $62,500 noted above.

But note: If the royalty contract is renegotia-

ble, author and publisher might agree on maximizing the joint sum of royalties and profit and could both become better off by selling a quantity and charging a price corresponding to point *n* in panel (b).*

---

*For a calculus-based treatment of this material, see Section 7C of the Calculus Appendix at the back of the book. For a detailed discussion of this issue and a listing of the

FIGURE 7.8

Author Versus Publisher

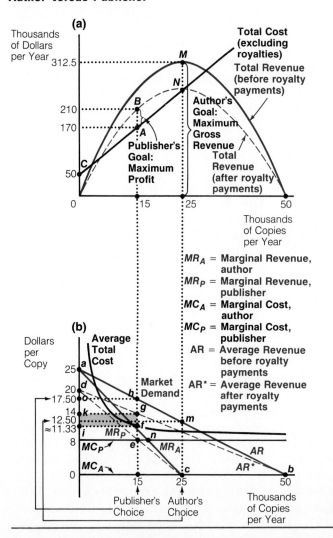

| MR$_A$ = Marginal Revenue, author |
| MR$_P$ = Marginal Revenue, publisher |
| MC$_A$ = Marginal Cost, author |
| MC$_P$ = Marginal Cost, publisher |
| AR = Average Revenue before royalty payments |
| AR* = Average Revenue after royalty payments |

Authors who receive royalties equal to a fixed percentage of the list price of their books—contrary to what one might guess—prefer a lower price than their publishers do.

Application 2: Price Discrimination

In the previous discussion of profit-max-imization, we implicitly assumed that monopolies, like perfect competitors, charge all customers identical prices, but often they do not. Whenever a seller charges a given buyer or different buyers different prices for different units of an identical good—even though such price differences cannot be justified by differences in the cost of serving these buyers—**price discrimination** is said to exist. Price discrimination can enhance a monopoly's possibilities for profit making.

Firms with the power to set prices (such firms need not necessarily be pure monopolies) can engage in price discrimination whenever they face customers with different price elasticities of demand and are able to segregate these customers accordingly. Obviously, sellers would not be successful in charging some people higher prices than other people, if those favored with the offer of low prices could resell their acquisitions to the less fortunate would-be buyers. The British economist A. C. Pigou (a Biography of whom appears in Chapter 16 of the *Student Workbook* that accompanies this text) first examined price discrimination in detail and identified three types of price discrimination: first-degree, second-degree, and third-degree.

First-Degree Price Discrimination. One refers to **first-degree price discrimination** or **perfect price discrimination** when a seller charges each buyer for each unit bought the maximum price the buyer is willing to pay for that unit. As a result, the seller can appropriate the entire consumer surplus and leave the buyer indifferent about buying or not buying. The

literature, *see* Stephen K. Layson, ''Is There a Conflict Between Authors and Publishers over Book Prices?'' *Southern Economic Journal*, April 1982, pp. 1057–60; and Michael A. Crew, ''Royalty Contracts: An Efficient Form of Contracting?'' *Southern Economic Journal*, January 1984, pp. 724–33.

FIGURE 7.9

First-Degree Price Discrimination

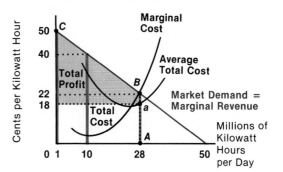

A seller practices *first-degree* or *perfect price discrimination* when each buyer is charged for each unit bought the maximum price the buyer is willing to pay for that unit. As a result, the seller appropriates the entire consumer surplus. The firm shown here, if it could practice such price discrimination, would produce 28 million kilowatt hours per day and reap a profit equal to the shaded area.

demand and cost conditions of the firm pictured in Figure 7.9 are identical to those given in panel (b) of Figure 7.3 for a profit-making monopoly. Yet we now assume that this firm is able to practice perfect price discrimination. It charges 50 cents for the first kilowatt hour sold (represented by the thin column next to the vertical axis). It charges the same customer or a different one slightly less than 50 cents for the second kilowatt hour, and so on along the downward slope of market demand until the 10 millionth kilowatt hour is sold for 40 cents and the 28 millionth one for 22 cents. As a result of this procedure, the divergence between price and marginal revenue disappears; the market-demand line becomes the marginal-revenue line as well.

As is true for all firms, our price-discriminating monopoly finds its profit-maximizing output volume by equating marginal cost and marginal revenue (point *B*). Thus it produces 28 million kilowatt hours per day, at an average total cost of 18 cents (point *a*). The graph clearly shows the division of our firm's total revenue (0*ABC*) between total cost (unshaded) and total profit (shaded). And there can be little doubt that the profit so achieved exceeds that of the identical firm in the absence of price discrimination, shown in panel (b) of Figure 7.3.

The achievement of such perfect price discrimination is, however, extremely difficult (and confined, perhaps, to the haggling that tourists experience in foreign bazaars), which is why would-be price discriminators usually turn to a cruder alternative.

Second-Degree Price Discrimination.   One refers to **second-degree price discrimination** when a seller partitions market demand into fairly large (but not necessarily equal-sized) blocks of product units and charges a given buyer or different buyers different prices for these blocks but uniform prices within the blocks. As a result, the firm captures only a portion of the consumer surplus (see Figure 7.10). Once more, the demand and cost conditions of the firm pictured in Figure 7.10 are identical to those in Figure 7.3. We now assume that this firm is able to practice second-degree price discrimination. Thus it announces a rate schedule according to which it charges 40 cents per kilowatt hour for the first 10 million kilowatt hours bought, 30 cents per kilowatt hour for the next 10 million, 22 cents per kilowatt hour for the next 8 million, and so on. As a result of this procedure, the firm's marginal-revenue line takes on a stair-step appearance.

Once more, the firm maximizes profit by choosing the output volume that equates marginal cost and marginal revenue (point *a*). Thus it produces 28 million kilowatt hours per day at an average total cost of 18 cents (point *b*). The graph again shows the division of the firm's total revenue (the *sum* of blocks *A*, *B*, and *C* up to the marginal-revenue line) between total cost (unshaded) and total profit (shaded). Clearly, the profit so achieved exceeds that of the identical firm in the absence of price discrimination, shown in panel (b) of Figure 7.3.

It is fairly easy to find examples of second-degree price discrimination. Consider how elec-

FIGURE 7.10

Second-Degree Price Discrimination

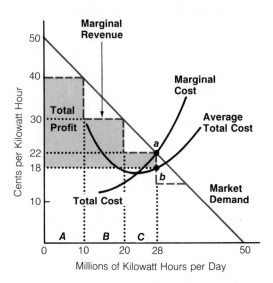

A seller practices *second-degree price discrimination* when market demand is partitioned into fairly large (but not necessarily equal-sized) blocks of product units and a given buyer or different buyers are charged different prices for these blocks but uniform prices within the blocks. As a result, the seller captures a portion of the consumer surplus. The firm shown here, if it could practice such price discrimination, would produce 28 million kilowatt hours per day and reap a profit equal to the shaded area, while selling block *A* at 40 cents per unit, block *B* at 30 cents a unit, and block *C* at 22 cents a unit.

tricity, natural gas, water, telephone, Xeroxing services, and even credit card loans are routinely sold in this way. People pay so much for the first 500 kilowatt hours, 1,000 cubic feet, three minutes of talking, 100 Xerox copies, or $500 of credit; they pay ever less for additional similar blocks. The same principle operates when drug stores sell vitamins at 100 for $1 and 200 for $1.01; when restaurants sell lunches at $1.25 per person and $2 per couple; when grocers sell cans of peas at 30¢ for one, 55¢ for two, and 75¢ for three, and when magazines offer subscriptions at

FIGURE 7.11

Third-Degree Price Discrimination

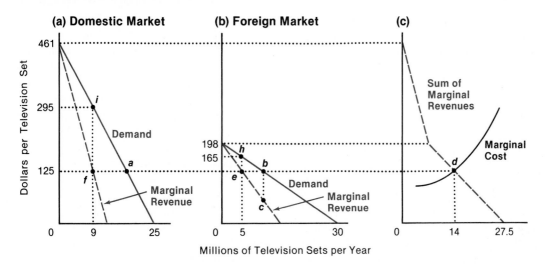

A seller practices *third-degree price discrimination* when market demand is partitioned into two or more groups of customers and different prices are charged for different groups, but uniform prices are charged within these groups. The firm shown here, if it could practice such price discrimination, would sell a total of 14 million television sets: 9 million for $295 each in the domestic market and 5 million for $165 each in the foreign market.

Caution: The horizontally combined marginal revenue only serves the purpose of helping the firm find the best output volume and hence the marginal cost (here $125) with which the price-discriminating firm then separately equates the marginal revenues of the two markets (at *f* and *e*). The kinked line of the combined marginal revenues should not be confused with the kinked demand curves (and their implied *discontinuous* marginal revenue curves) to be discussed in the next chapter. Those kinked demand curves refer to oligopolists who do *not* engage in price discrimination, but charge uniform prices.

$10 for a year, $18 for two years, and $24 for three years.

Note: Car dealers make no similar offers because it would be worthwhile for people to reject the offer of one car for $5,000 in favor of two cars for $8,000, only to resell the second car for less than $5,000 and thus to wreck the $5,000-car market entirely. In the case of canned peas, it isn't worth the trouble for the buyer to resell.

Third-Degree Price Discrimination. One refers to **third-degree price discrimination** when a seller partitions market demand into two or more groups of customers and charges different prices among, but uniform prices within, these groups. The firm pictured in Figure 7.11 is assumed to sell television sets at home and abroad but to face markets in which the price elasticity of demand differs at any given price. At a price of $125 per set, for example, the elasticity in the domestic market (at point *a*) equals |.38| and that in the foreign market (at point *b*) equals |1.79|. (The reader may wish to review in Chapter 3 the *PAPO* rule for calculating elasticity.)

If the firm charged an identical price in both markets, it would not be getting as much profit as it could get through price discrimination: uniform prices imply diverging marginal revenues when price elasticities differ. Note how, in panel (a) of Figure 7.11, the marginal revenue corresponding to a $125 price is negative (as measured by the intersection, not shown, of the dashed marginal-revenue line and a vertical line going through point *a*). In panel (b) of our graph, on the other hand, the marginal revenue corresponding to a $125 price is still positive (point *c*). Under such circumstances, the firm could increase profit by switching a unit from the market with the lower elasticity (and marginal revenue) to that with the higher elasticity (and marginal revenue). Profit maximization, therefore, requires identical marginal revenues in all markets served by a firm.

Profit maximization also requires, of course, an identity between marginal revenue and marginal cost, which is determined in panel (c) of our graph where the *horizontal sum* of marginal revenues is compared with marginal cost. The profit-maximizing output is thus found to be 14 million television sets per year. This output implies a marginal cost of $125 per set and, following the horizontal dotted line left from point *d*, sales of 5 and 9 million sets, respectively, in the foreign and domestic markets. As points *e* and *f* indicate, these sales volumes alone ensure for both markets identical marginal revenues, which, in turn, are identical with marginal cost.

The final solution is that 5 and 9 million sets per year can be sold in the two markets, respectively, at prices of $165 and $295 per set (points *h* and *i*). Thus a profit-maximizing price discriminator will charge a higher price in the market that has a lower price elasticity of demand at any given price. This strategy, of course, makes intuitive sense; examples abound.*

The very example just utilized is not far-fetched. In 1980, SONY of Japan was accused of making a profit by dumping television sets in the United States below cost. This was an unlikely story, for no one can ever make a profit by selling below (average total) cost. It was true, however, that SONY sold TVs at $180 in the United States and identical ones at $333 in Japan. Figure 7.11 can explain these facts. As we assumed in the

hypothetical graph, SONY faced much more competition abroad (and thus a higher price elasticity of demand) than at home.

The separation of markets on the basis of geography need not, however, involve international frontiers. Consider how state universities charge different fees to in-state and out-of-state students, how airport managers charge different gasoline prices to transient planes and those based on their field, how supermarket chains charge different prices in suburbs and central cities (and to a degree not justified by differences in cost). Nor is geography the only basis for price discrimination of the third degree.

Equally common is market separation on the basis of people's age, sex, and income. Think how children or the elderly are offered lower prices by airlines, banks, barbers, and cinemas. Consider ''ladies' day'' at the golf and tennis club, on the ski slopes; consider the lower prices some doctors and lawyers charge the poor and that journals and newspapers charge students or members of the armed forces.

Market separation on the basis of time is another favorite. New books and films are sold early to the most eager at high prices and much later to others at lower prices. Movie theaters have matinees, twilight hours, and regular showings; prices of electricity, telephone service, and vacation resorts vary by time of day or year. (Close-Up 6.2 on p. 216 contains another example.)

Indeed, every possible way in which people can be grouped by eagerness of demand might be used for price discrimination: Milk producers charge different prices to households and to butter or cheese manufacturers. Electric companies discriminate between residential and industrial customers; periodicals discriminate between new and old subscribers. Railroads transport goods with low *value density* (such as coal) for less than goods with high value per cubic foot; they charge more per mile on short hauls than on long hauls. The U.S. Postal Service charges more for first class mail than for equally heavy advertisements, books, or newspapers. Manufacturers sell branded gasoline and tires for more

---

*For a calculus-based treatment of this material, see Section 7D of the Calculus Appendix at the back of this book.

than physically identical unbranded ones. Airlines charge more for first-class seats on daytime trips than for night coach, group charters, or ''no frills'' flights (and the differences cannot be fully explained by differences in services rendered). At the stadium, box seats, grandstand seats, and bleachers do not cost the same.

Application 3: Markup Pricing

Firms frequently set their prices by simply adding a percentage markup to their average variable cost of production. Is this procedure inconsistent with Cournot's theory of monopoly, according to which firms maximize their profit only if they choose an output volume that equates marginal revenue with marginal cost? Not necessarily. As we noted in the section on ''An Index of Monopoly Power,''

$$MR = P - \frac{P}{|\epsilon|}.$$

Equating marginal revenue with marginal cost, therefore, implies that

$$MC = P - \frac{P}{|\epsilon|}.$$

This, in turn, can be written as

$$MC = P - \frac{P}{|\epsilon|} = P\left(1 - \frac{1}{|\epsilon|}\right).$$

Dividing by the parenthetical expression, we get

$$\frac{MC}{\left(1 - \frac{1}{|\epsilon|}\right)} = P;$$

hence

$$\frac{MC}{\frac{|\epsilon|}{|\epsilon|} - \frac{1}{|\epsilon|}} = P,$$

and

$$\frac{MC}{\frac{|\epsilon| - 1}{|\epsilon|}} = P.$$

Thus equating marginal revenue with marginal cost implies

$$P = MC \left(\frac{|\epsilon|}{|\epsilon| - 1}\right)$$

To the extent that a firm's marginal cost is constant over a wide range of output (as pictured, for example, in Figure 7.8), marginal cost equals average variable cost. Hence our equation comes to

$$P = AVC \left(\frac{|\epsilon|}{|\epsilon| - 1}\right),$$

which is precisely the formula for a percentage markup!

Let the price elasticity of demand equal $|4|$. Then

$$P = AVC \left(\frac{4}{4 - 1}\right) = AVC \left(\frac{4}{3}\right) = AVC\,(1.33).$$

If this firm sets price 33 percent above average variable cost, it, in effect, equates marginal revenue with marginal cost.

Note: As we have seen when discussing the author-publisher conflict, a firm with monopoly power and positive marginal cost will always choose an output volume at which price elasticity exceeds $|1|$. The optimal markup, from the point of view of a monopoly with positive and also constant marginal cost, is, therefore, the higher the less price-elastic demand is. Let $|\epsilon| = 1.1$ in the above formula. Then

$$P = AVC \left(\frac{1.1}{1.1 - 1}\right) = AVC \left(\frac{1.1}{0.1}\right)$$
$$= AVC\,(11),$$

calling for a markup of 1,000 percent.

Application 4: The "Captured" State

Some people argue that government officials are inevitably "captured" by would-be monopolists who want to be aided in securing monopoly power. We have seen plenty of examples above. Why does government help people acquire power over prices to gain income? Why doesn't it insist that people gain income only through productive contributions?

We all like to think of government as the impartial servant of the public good. We like to see government as the instrumentality by which the nation achieves *the national interest*—meaning, perhaps, an overall reduction in the realm of scarcity. But the nation does not talk to government officials; individuals do. Within the nation, there are many individuals whose interests conflict with those of other individuals. For each of these individuals, income can be gained more easily by taking it away from other people—given the overall degree of scarcity prevailing—than by making genuine contributions toward reducing the realm of scarcity by working harder, saving more, or making cost-reducing innovations. It is surprising that some of these individuals want the government to intercede for their *special interest* (which is to gain power to raise the prices of whatever they sell in order to raise their income in the easiest way)? To the extent that government responds to such requests, it does not govern in the national interest; it promotes a coalition of special interests. Sellers use many devices to get government to promote their special interest in above-equilibrium minimum prices, reduced supply, or increased demand for whatever they have to sell.

The "Capture" of Legislators. Sellers can induce legislators at all levels of government to rig markets directly—or to set up appropriate agencies to do the rigging—by channeling a number of rewards to them. Perhaps the most important reward is campaign contributions.

All legislators must be elected. Those with the "proper" attitude—toward minimum prices (for airplane trips, electricity, insurance, labor, liquor, milk, taxi rides, telephone service, or wheat), toward supply-restricting laws (ranging widely from those concerning cartels, copyrights, exclusive franchising, and immigration to others on import and marketing quotas, mergers, patents, professional licensing, tariffs, and union affairs), and toward demand-raising laws (awarding government contracts or subsidies for anything from peanuts to railroads to the unemployed)—can be rewarded by the beneficiaries of this "proper" attitude. Early rewards come in the form of votes and in the form of funds to finance expensive radio and TV campaigns designed to gather other people's votes. (A federal campaign cost a minimum of $100,000 in 1988). During the early 1970s, major corporations as well as other organizations —ranging from dairy farmers, dentists, and doctors to seafarers, teachers, and truckers—spent more than $100 million on federal election campaigns alone. Following rather aggressive solicitation of funds by top officials in the Nixon Administration, many corporations made illegal contributions. Among those who eventually admitted to such contributions publicly were American Airlines, Ashland Oil, Braniff Airlines, Goodyear Tire and Rubber, Gulf Oil, Minnesota Mining and Manufacturing (3M), and Phillips Petroleum.

Once elected, these officials are, of course, expected to show proper gratitude toward their beneficiaries. They are expected to vote in the "right" way and to lend a ready and sympathetic ear to professional lobbyists who will point out the "national interest" in all types of legislation under consideration, which is really the special interest of those who lobby and whose income position is being advanced by the legislation. Meanwhile, the voices of those whose income position is being eroded by the very same legislation go unheard. The interests of the organized special pleaders are visible and concentrated; their gain may be $100 million worth of extra revenues that would come to a single firm, or a small group of them, as a result of higher legal prices, a subsidy, or a government contract. On the contrary, the interest of their unorganized victims is invisible and diffuse; their loss may be 50 cents from each of 200 million consumers or taxpayers. The special-interest groups can afford to hire full-time professional lobbyists (together with large staffs of lawyers, public relations people, and so on). They can easily inundate the overworked staffs of every single legislator with good advice on the meaning of "sound public policy." They can orchestrate, if necessary, a letter campaign by thousands who have a lot to gain. The millions who lose are silent. Thus legislators get a nicely biased view of things. By following the "national interest" as represented by special-interest groups the compliant legislators can gather further rewards: more campaign funds in the future, more votes from those with new jobs in new plants built in their home districts by beneficiaries grateful for their help, job offers in case of a lost election, all-expenses-paid vacations, and, perhaps, even gifts of fur coats. Much of this, incidentally, is perfectly legal if financed from people's personal incomes (as in the case of a gift from a high-salaried corporate officer); it is quite illegal if it is financed by corporate funds.

The "Capture" of Regulators.   Now consider the regulatory bodies set up by the legislative branch of government (and discussed in more detail in Chapter 15). Their officials, too, are systematically influenced by those they are supposed to "regulate." They, too, receive rewards for being compliant when approached by the special interests.

Many regulators have strong bonds with the regulated. For example, it is not at all unusual to put doctors on a professional licensing board for practitioners of medicine, to put airline industry officials on the CAB, to place electric power company executives on the FPC. Even when such choices are not dictated by the need for expert knowledge, lobbyists will see to it that this is exactly what happens. (No wonder that regulators are frequently found to own securities and thus have a personal financial interest in compa-

nies they regulate. In 1974, for example, 19 officials of the FPC, which had raised natural gas prices, held natural gas company stock.)

Even when members of a regulated industry are not the regulators, chummy relations quickly develop. Regulators necessarily have frequent contact with the regulated at formal public hearings before the various commissions involved or at the more than 100,000 nonpublic meetings a year in which specific issues are "informally adjudicated."

The federal alphabet agencies, for instance, employ administrative law judges. They gather evidence, conduct hearings, and make decisions on the government-sponsored cartels about rates charged, the number of firms allowed, and so on. This procedure is typically lengthy and even then any decision can be appealed to the full regulatory commission or challenged in court or both. A recent railroad merger case took 3 years and 275 days of hearings to decide. It produced a veritable paper nightmare of 50,000 pages of transcripts and 100,000 pages of exhibits. There is plenty of occasion for regulators and the regulated to get to know each other not just during hearings, but also during informal contacts over lunch, at business conventions, and at social gatherings. Naturally, the CAB members (who awarded that new route bringing in $100 million in annual revenues) will be invited to the airline's inaugural flight. Naturally, the ICC members (who approved that railroad merger cutting costs by $100 million a year) will go on the inaugural ride, complete with fancy food, liquor, and entertainment. Before long, government officials and industry executives are personal friends. In 1974, the chairman of the CAB was taken on an all-expenses-paid golfing trip to Bermuda by Boeing and United Aircraft Company officials and journeyed through Europe with a TWA vice-president—all while issues vital to these firms were being decided by the CAB.

Sooner or later, it becomes obvious that friendly regulators (like friendly legislators whose reelection bids fail) can expect future jobs from those they now regulate. In 1971, for example, 12 of 24 former CAB members were employed by the firms they used to regulate. Could it be any clearer why government underwrites the monopoly game?

SUMMARY

1. If people as a group wish to increase their command over goods (barring the receipt of gifts or loans from other such groups), they must engage in some activity that enlarges the overall quantity of goods available. Any subset of all people can, however, always gain additional goods even if the total quantity thereof is unchanged. They can do so at the expense of other people, by forming *monopolies* or *cartels*. Monopolies and cartels have the ability to raise the price of something that is for sale above the perfectly competitive level. This *monopoly power* originates from technological or legal sources, including increasing returns to scale, exclusive ownership of key resources, patents and copyrights, and exclusive franchises.

2. Contrary to what many people think, a profit-maximizing monopoly does not charge the highest possible price, but one that corresponds to the quantity that equates (constant or rising) marginal cost with (falling) marginal revenue. Equating marginal cost and marginal revenue leads to maximum possible profit, but in the short run such profit can be positive, zero, or even negative.

3. A major difference between a perfectly competitive firm and a monopoly is that the monopoly may reap positive profit *even in the long run* when it equates long-run marginal cost and long-run marginal revenue.

4. There are other differences between a perfectly competitive firm and a monopoly: A monopoly will always choose an output volume at which price exceeds marginal cost; a monopoly is unlikely to produce at minimum average total cost. The gap between price and marginal cost (which is always present when firms are able to exercise monopoly power) provides the basis for constructing the Lerner index of monopoly power.

5. Firms also establish cartels in the hope of reaping permanent economic profit. The success of cartels, however, is often elusive because of organizational difficulties, a high price elasticity of demand, or a high price elasticity of supply. Yet firms try to overcome these obstacles—privately, with the help of various levels of government, and via international agreements.

6. Some applications of the theory of monopoly include the author-publisher conflict, price discrimination (of the first, second, and third degree), markup pricing, and the notion of the "captured" state.

KEY TERMS

acreage allotments

cartel

copyright

exclusive franchise

fair-trade laws

first-degree price discrimination

import quotas

Lerner index

marginal revenue (*MR*)

marketing quotas

monopoly

monopoly power

natural monopoly

parity

patent

perfect price discrimination

price discrimination

second-degree price discrimination

tariff

third-degree price discrimination

HANDS-ON PRACTICE

Exercise #1

Consider a monopoly facing the demand function given in Table 7.2. Assuming fixed costs of $100 and constant marginal costs of $20 regardless of output, what are the firm's profit-maximizing price and output quantity? How large is the profit?

TABLE 7.2

Price	Quantity Demanded
$100	0
75	5
50	10
25	15
0	20

Solution:

The demand function is graphed as Figure 7.12, which clearly implies the equation $P = 100 - \frac{100}{20} Q = 100 - 5Q$.

FIGURE 7.12

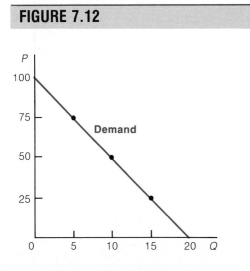

Because marginal revenue has twice the slope of demand, $MR = 100 - 10Q$, as shown in Figure 7.13.

FIGURE 7.13

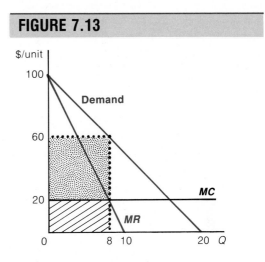

Profit is maximized when marginal revenue equals marginal cost, hence

$$MR = MC$$
$$100 - 10Q = 20$$
$$Q = 8$$

Substituting $Q = 8$ in the demand function yields

$$P = 100 - 5(8)$$
$$P = 60$$

This is shown in Figure 7.13 as well.

The constant marginal cost implies constant average variable cost equal to marginal cost; thus total variable cost at the profit-maximizing output level equals the crosshatched area, or $20(8) = 160$ per unit of time. Total revenue equals the crosshatched plus dotted areas, or $60(8) = 480$ per unit of time, implying a dotted area producer surplus of $40(8) = 320$ per unit of time. Given fixed costs of $100, the profit is $220 per unit of time.

Exercise #2

Still considering the data of Exercise 1, what would happen to the profit-maximizing price and quantity, as well as to fixed cost, variable cost, and profit, if the government imposed an excise tax of $15 per unit on the producer?

Solution:

Marginal cost, including tax, would equal $35; hence

$$MR = MC^*$$
$$100 - 10Q = 35$$
$$Q = 6.5$$

which implies

$$P = 100 - 5(6.5) = 67.5.$$

Thus total revenue would equal $TR = PQ = 67.5 (6.5) = \$438.75$. Of this amount, the government would collect $\$15 (6.5) = \$97.5$. Variable cost would equal $\$20(6.5) = \$130$, fixed cost $100, as before. Thus profit would equal the remaining $111.25.

QUESTIONS AND PROBLEMS

1. The text lists technological and legal sources of monopoly power. Can you think of illegal ones?

2. Consider the zero-profit monopoly in Figure 7.4. Could the firm pictured there make a positive profit with the help of first- or second-degree price discrimination? Explain.

3. Consider the profit-making monopoly depicted in Figure 7.3.
   a. At which point, to the left of E, must average total cost intersect market demand?
   b. To which point on the marginal-cost curve does the total-cost curve's point of inflection (between a and d) correspond?
Explain your answers.

4. Consider the following data for a monopoly and determine its profit-maximizing price.

Price	Quantity	Total Cost
8	5	30
7	6	32
6	7	34
5	8	36
4	9	38
3	10	48

5. The monopoly pictured in Figure 7.6 in the long run is not producing its output at the lowest of all possible average total costs (shown by point R). What would make a monopoly produce at a point such as R?

6. The section on third-degree price discrimination gives many examples. Examine them and try to determine in each case *why* such price discrimination is possible. (*Hint #1:* Children are more apt than adults to get homemade haircuts; thus their price elasticity of demand is relatively high and the price is lower than for adults. Barbers need not fear that children will resell their cheap haircuts to adults who are being charged more. *Hint #2:* Bulky books may not be mailed at all if the charge is high; thus the shipper's price elasticity of demand is high and the price is lower than for first-class mail. Those who mail books cannot resell these cheap postal services to others who are charged so much more per pound of first class mail. *Hint #3:* Executives traveling on expense accounts are unlikely to switch from first-class air transportation to third-rate buses; thus their price elasticity of demand is relatively low, and the price is higher—out of all proportion to any increased leg room and food consumption. Such executives, furthermore, cannot obtain this service more cheaply by buying a night coach passenger's ticket.)

7. Do you think price discrimination could ever be practiced by *buyers?* Explain.

8. Are each of the following true or false?

a. A monopoly that faces a price-inelastic demand at its chosen price cannot be maximizing profit.

b. The author of a book who received a fixed percentage of the publisher's profit would wish to price the book in such a way that price elasticity of demand was greater than $|1|$.

c. A monopoly that is suddenly taxed 20 percent of its profit will decrease quantity produced and raise its price.

*9. In each case below, calculate the profit-maximizing quantity and price and also the size of the maximum profit and do so in two ways, using the total-revenue and total-cost, but also the marginal-revenue and marginal-cost approach.

a. $P = 50 - 2Q - 4Q^2$ and $ATC = Q + 5$

b. $TR = 25Q - .8Q^2$ and $TC = 2 + 20Q + .1Q^2$

c. $P = 50 - 5Q$ and $TC = Q^2 + 4Q$

*10. Given the situation described by (9) above, assess the impact of taxation described below:

a. If a per-unit tax of $t = 2$ is imposed on (9a), what happens to the profit-maximizing quantity and price? What is the new profit? What is the size of the tax revenue, $T = tQ$?

b. If a 9.89-percent sales tax is imposed on (9b), what happens to the profit-maximizing quantity and price? What is the new profit? What is the size of the tax revenue, T? (*Hint:* The type of tax given here implies that for every $1 paid by the buyer the seller receives 91¢ because adding 9.89 percent to 91¢ yields $1.)

c. If a lump sum tax of $T = 3$ is imposed on (9c), what happens to the profit-maximizing quantity and price? What is the new profit?

11. A monopoly has collected the data in the accompanying table. Use them to determine the profit-maximizing levels of price and quantity (and do so graphically).

P	Q	SRMC	P	Q	SRMC
11	0	4.71	4.71	8	4.71
10.21	1	4.71	3.93	9	4.71
9.43	2	4.71	3.14	10	4.71
8.64	3	4.71	2.36	11	4.71
7.86	4	4.71	1.57	12	4.71
7.07	5	4.71	.79	13	4.71
6.29	6	4.71	0	14	4.71
5.50	7	4.71			

12. A monopoly has collected the data in the accompanying table. Use them to determine the maximum-profit quantity arithmetically.

Q	TR	TC	Q	TR	TC	Q	TR	TC
0	0	390	5	1,000	770	10	880	1,350
1	320	530	6	1,125	800	11	700	?
2	530	625	7	1,200	890	12	530	?
3	700	700	8	1,125	1,020	13	320	?
4	880	730	9	1,000	1,190	14	0	?

13. Consider again the data of Problem 11. What is the size of the maximum profit?

14. Consider again the data of Problem 12. Confirm your earlier answer graphically; then draw a profit-versus-quantity graph directly underneath the graph of total revenue and total cost, similar to the total-net-benefit graph in panel (c) of Figure 1.6, "Optimization," p. 13.

15. In 1988, the Japanese were accused of dumping trucks in the U.S. market; can you explain the facts cited?

Model	Factory Price Bound for	
	Japan	U.S.
Toyota, standard bed, 2 door pickup	$5,313	$3,988
Nissan, standard compact	5,194	4,009
Isuzu, 2-wheel drive pickup	5,488	3,888

Source: *New York Times,* March 31, 1988, p. D1.

SELECTED READINGS

Brennan, Geoffrey, James Buchanan, and Dwight Lee. "On Monopoly Price," *Kyklos,* 4, 1983, pp. 531–47.

Argues that the orthodox theory of monopoly price is incomplete and, in some respects at least, misleading (in that it fails to take account of the fact that buyer adjustment to price change takes time and that demand elasticity in the long run differs from the short run).

Brozen, Yale. "Is the Government the Source of Monopoly?" *Intercollegiate Review,* Winter 1968–69. Reprinted in Tibor R. Machan, ed. *The Libertarian Alternative: Essays in Social and Political Philosophy.* Chicago: Nelson-Hall, 1974, chap. 9.

Bulow, Jeremy I. "Durable-Goods Monopolists," *Journal of Political Economy,* April 1982, pp. 314–32.

Discusses the special problems faced by monopolists whose sale of durable goods creates a second-hand market that is not controlled by the monopolist.

Cournot, Antoine A. *Researches into the Mathematical Principles of the Theory of Wealth.* New York: Macmillan, 1897.

A translation of the 1838 classic that developed the theory of monopoly and much more.

Gemmell, Norman. "Is There a Conflict Between Authors and Publishers Over Royalty Terms?" *Economic Letters,* vol. 29, no. 1 (1989), pp. 7–11.

Discusses how the conflict noted in this chapter's Application 1 might be resolved.

Horvitz, Paul M. "The Pricing of Textbooks and the Remuneration of Authors," *The American Economic Review,* May 1966, pp. 812–20. Reprinted in Harry G. Johnson and Burton A. Weisbrod. *The Daily Economist.* Englewood Cliffs, N.J.: Prentice-Hall, 1973, pp. 22–29. *See also idem,* "A Note on Textbook Pricing," *The American Economic Review,* September 1965, pp. 844–48, which explores the possibilities of intertemporal price discrimination in the textbook market.

Kessel, Reuben A. "Price Discrimination in Medicine," *The Journal of Law and Economics,* October 1958, pp. 20–53.

A discussion of the cartel sponsored by the American Medical Association.

Lerner, Abba P. "The Concept of Monopoly and the Measurement of Monopoly Power," *Review of Economic Studies,* June 1934, pp. 157–75.

The original proposal of the Lerner index of monopoly power.

Pigou, A.C. *The Economics of Welfare,* 4th ed. London: Macmillan, 1950.

The first systematic discussion of the three degrees of price discrimination.

Silberman, Jonathan, and Gilbert Yochum. "The Market for Special Interest Campaign Funds: An Exploratory Approach," *Public Choice,* 1980, pp. 75–83.

Stocking, George W. *Cartels in Action: Case Studies of International Diplomacy.* New York: Twentieth Century Fund, 1946.

COMPUTER PROGRAMS

The KOHLER-3 personal-computer diskettes that accompany this book contain one program of particular interest to this chapter:

7. Monopoly and Cartels includes a 25-question multiple-choice test with immediate responses to incorrect answers as well as numerous exercises concerning the concept of marginal revenue, profit maximization under monopoly, and government intervention in otherwise competitive markets.

ANALYTICAL EXAMPLE 7.1

THE MARKET VALUE OF MONOPOLY POWER

As Chapter 6 has shown, economic profits in a perfectly competitive industry tend toward zero in the long run. Suppose, however, that the producers in an industry, say taxi drivers, perhaps with the help of government, restricted industry output below the perfectly competitive level and thereby gained the power to raise price above the competitive level. Such *monopoly power* might enable each member of the cartel to reap permanent economic profits of, say, $50,000 a year. If the current interest rate were 10 percent, this prospective profit stream is equivalent to that which one could derive from owning a $500,000 bank account (because, at the assumed 10-percent interest rate, the owner of the account could also earn $50,000 a year forever). The process of calculating the current dollar equivalent of a future income stream (of calculating the $500,000 figure in our example) is called *capitalization* and will be discussed in detail in the Chapter 12 section, "Fisher's Concept of Capital." We can, however, anticipate the following implication: Those who hold monopoly power effectively own a valuable asset (equal to the *present value,* such as our $500,000 above, of the extra future incomes derivable from that power), and, not surprisingly, this asset can be sold in the market. The table below indicates recent market prices people have paid in order to acquire monopoly power from its holders.

Sources of Monopoly Power	Market Price	Year
Boston taxicab licenses	$23,000	1967
Chicago taxicab licenses	$10,000–18,000	1968
New York taxicab licenses	$68,000	1980
American Baseball League franchises	$20–25.3 million	1981
National Baseball League franchises	$6–11 million	1971
National Basketball League franchises	$1–3 million	1971
Commodity Futures Exchange seats	$200,000–325,000	1980
New York Stock Exchange seats	$82,000–212,000	1979
Television station licenses	$2–50 million	1979
Tobacco growing rights (per acre)	$1,500–3,000	1960
Trucking operating rights (per route)	$5,000–2.5 million	1979

Note: If the government were to auction off monopoly rights at the time of their creation at the kind of prices indicated in the table, government would thereby recoup for its citizens as a group the present value of money to be taken from them in the future through the exercise of monopoly power. If government fails to do this initially (as is usually the case), it cannot easily do it later. Once the initial recipient of a monopoly right has sold it to someone else, the purchaser of this right will not make economic profits because cost will be so much higher. In New York City, for example, someone may pay $78,000 for a taxi, only $10,000 of which is for the physical car, the remainder going for the medallion needed to run it. If the present value of future monopoly profits equals the medallion's $68,000 market value, extra profit and extra cost just offset each other. Secondary owners of monopoly rights, therefore, would justifiably resent it if they suddenly had to pay the government for these rights.

The same facts make it difficult to deregulate an industry that was government-regulated in the past. Thus the impact of the Motor Carrier Act of 1980 on the balance sheets of trucking firms was swift and massive. The size of suddenly worthless monopoly-route privileges, carried as intangible "operating rights" assets on the books, ranged from a low of $3 million (Cooper-Jarrett) to a high of $34.9 million (Yellow Freight System).

Sources: Edmund W. Kitch et al., "The Regulation of Taxicabs in Chicago," *The Journal of Law and Economics,* October 1971, pp. 285–350; David A. Andelman, "New York's Taxi Industry Thriving on Some Controversial Economics," *The New York Times,* March 13, 1980, pp. A1 and

ANALYTICAL EXAMPLE

B8; R. G. Noll, ed., *Government and the Sports Business* (Washington, D.C.: Brookings, 1974); Laurel Sorenson, "Seats on Major Exchanges These Days Are Bringing Sellers Some Record Sums," *The Wall Street Journal,* September 3, 1980, p. 38; Karen W. Arenson, "New York Stock Exchange Faces Challenge," *The New York Times,* October 29, 1979, pp. A1 and D3; R. G. Noll et al., *Economic Aspects of Television Regulation* (Washington, D.C.: Brookings, 1973); Ronald Alsop, "Once-Shaky UHF Stations Lure Viewers, and Surging Profits Attract Eager Buyers," *The Wall Street Journal,* January 8, 1980, p. 46; F. H. Maier et al., "The Sale Value of Flue-Cured Tobacco Allotments," *Technical Bulletin* 148 (Agricultural Experiment Station, VPI, April 1960); M. Kafoglis, "A Paradox of Regulated Trucking," *Regulation,* September-October, 1977, pp. 27–32; Thomas Baker, "Reality Takes the Wheel," *Forbes,* October 27, 1980, pp. 133–34; *The New York Times,* June 17, 1981, p. 1.

ANALYTICAL EXAMPLE 7.2

DENTAL CARTELS

Dental practitioners in the United States must be licensed by state boards. Thirty-five states do not honor licenses granted in other jurisdictions. Consequently, dentists seeking to practice in those states must pass local examinations regardless of their previous experience. Large percentages of out-of-state applicants are typically denied licenses; most in-state graduates successfully complete dental board exams. This discriminating procedure has the effect of insulating practitioners from competition from nonresident dentists who might otherwise migrate. This competition-avoiding effect, however, is absent in the 15 states that have reciprocity agreements binding them to endorse each other's licenses. Do dentists in the "protected" states manage to charge higher prices? A study of 1970 prices based on a survey of 10,000 dental practitioners indicates that prices in protected states are higher.

Service	Average Price in Reciprocity States	Average Price in Nonreciprocity States	Percentage Difference
Periodic oral exam	$ 3.44	$ 3.75	+9.0
Complete series of X-rays	5.47	5.65	+3.3
Dental prophylaxis	7.61	8.26	+8.5
Simple tooth removal	6.32	7.45	+17.9
Root canal extirpation and filling	51.37	56.42	+9.8
Amalgam filling (1 surface)	6.33	6.52	+3.0
Amalgam filling (2 surfaces)	10.05	10.35	+3.0
Gold inlay (2 surfaces)	47.00	50.73	+7.9
Cast gold crown	70.38	74.72	+6.2
Bridge (2 units)	143.23	154.19	+7.7
Acrylic-base denture	147.50	150.33	+1.9
Denture repair	16.41	16.38	−0.2

Source: Lawrence Shepard, "Licensing Restrictions and the Cost of Dental Care," *The Journal of Law and Economics,* April 1978, pp. 187–201. Table reprinted by permission of the University of Chicago Press. Copyright 1973 by the University of Chicago Law School.

ANALYTICAL EXAMPLE 7.3

OPEC—THE WORLD'S MOST SUCCESSFUL CARTEL?

In 1960 at Baghdad, the governments of five major oil-exporting countries (Iran, Iraq, Kuwait, Saudi Arabia, and Venezuela) formed OPEC, the Organization of Petroleum Exporting Countries. By 1980, there were eight additional members: Algeria, Ecuador, Gabon, Indonesia, Libya, Nigeria, Qatar, and the United Arab Emirates. After having wielded little power for more than a decade, the organization demanded and received a higher price for oil and a greater share of profit from the oil companies in 1973. On January 1, 1973, the price of oil was $2.12 a barrel. By year's end (following an Arab-led embargo of oil exports to the United States that was seen to aid Israel in that year's Yom Kippur War), the price was $11.65 a barrel. By the end of 1980, it was $41 a barrel. An unprecedented transfer of income was occurring from oil-consuming to oil-producing nations. (By 1980, OPEC was producing 26.5 million barrels a day, at an average total cost of about 25 cents a barrel. OPEC's total revenue exceeded $300 billion a year, which would have been sufficient to buy up, in about three years, 100 percent of the shares of all companies listed on the New York Stock Exchange. The market value of these shares, on September 30, 1979, was $961.3 billion.) In the short run, without question, OPEC was a success.

In the long run, however, things were quite different. The power of OPEC was constrained by the responsiveness, to the higher price of oil, of the world's oil consumers as well as non-OPEC suppliers. The resultant downward pressure on price, in turn, destroyed the discipline of OPEC members. Consider the evidence so far: Consumers have conserved energy (for example, by turning to energy-efficient cars) and have switched to alternative fuels (for example, coal, gas, and nuclear power). Compare OPEC's 1975 demand forecast for 1985 (50 million barrels per day) with the 1985 reality (18 million barrels per day). On the other hand, vast new sources of supply have come onto the market, mainly from Alaska, the North Sea, and Mexico. By 1983, the world price of oil had declined to $29 a barrel. In response, and contrary to OPEC policy, Indonesia, Iran, Libya, Nigeria, and Venezuela *increased* production. It was unlikely that Saudi Arabia (owner of a third of OPEC's oil) would continue to cut its own output to compensate. Indeed, in 1985, the Saudis followed through on a long-standing threat to increase their own output as well unless others abided by the quota. By mid-1986, the price of oil hit a low of $10 per barrel.

While OPEC's power in the long run has been reduced substantially by forces such as these, economists have asked an interesting question: Are the consuming nations ever helpless in the face of an OPEC stranglehold? Their answer: Not really, although they have been acting as if they were. Consider a suggestion by M. A. Adelman.

His idea is illustrated by the graph in Figure A. Let world market demand for oil be represented by line *AB* and the associated marginal revenue by dashed line *AM.* Let the marginal cost of producing oil be zero (for it is almost that). Then the profit-maximizing position of the OPEC cartel is given by the marginal-cost and marginal-revenue intersection at *M*. Like Cournot's producer of mineral water, OPEC maximizes profit by maximizing revenue. Since average total cost of production is very low as well (*MF*), the maximum monopoly profit (shaded area *GFEK*) is just slightly lower than maximum revenue (*OMEK*).

In fact, however, OPEC never reached this position, having gradually moved from output-price combination *C* in 1970 to combination *D* in 1980. Output-price combination *E*, however, was OPEC's goal.

Now consider what would happen if consuming nations imposed a tax equal to a fixed percentage of market price. The market-demand line facing OPEC would swing left around point *B;* in the case of a 50-percent tax, it would swing from *BA* to *BK*. Whatever the price paid by consumers, such as *EM*, the consumers' government would collect half of it, such as *EH*. Accordingly, the marginal-revenue line facing OPEC would change from *AM* to *KM*, but the profit-maximizing output would remain at *M*!

Consumers would pay *EM* per barrel, the consumers' government would collect *EH* per barrel, and OPEC would earn *HM* per barrel. OPEC's profit would be cut from *GFEK* (shaded), to *GFHI*. Indeed, a steeper proportional tax, equal to the ratio *EF/EM*, or 91 percent in our example, would eliminate OPEC's profit entirely, and the transfer of income would be ended.

FIGURE A

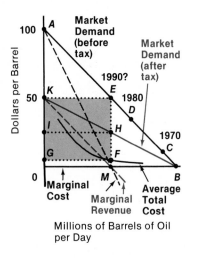

Millions of Barrels of Oil
per Day

Sources: Based on *The New York Times,* June 11, 1980, pp. 1 and D4; October 29, 1979, p. D3; October 28, 1984, pp. F1 and 26; M. A. Adelman, "Constraints on the World Oil Monopoly Price," *Resources and Energy* 1 (1978), pp. 3–19; Dermot Gately, "A Ten-Year Retrospective: OPEC and the World Oil Market," *Journal of Economic Literature,* September 1984, pp. 1100–1114.

CLOSE-UP 7.1

MONOPOLY IN "MONOPOLY"

Around 1900, Elizabeth Magee of Virginia devised "The Landlord's Game." Many versions of it were played for years. Eventually, Parker Brothers acquired the rights to the game, called it "Monopoly," and sold more than 80 million copies worldwide. In 1973, the monopoly in "Monopoly" was challenged. Ralph Anspach, professor of economics at San Francisco State, invented a new game, which he called "Anti-Monopoly". The object of the game was not the building but the breaking of monopolies. The game quickly sold more than 400,000 copies.

Parker Brothers filed suit, claiming infringement of its trademark. Anspach, Inc. filed a countersuit, claiming that the Parker Brothers trademark was invalid, that "Monopoly" had become part of the English language, and that the use of this word was free to all, like Kleenex or aspirin. A 10-year, see-saw battle took place in the courts. First, in 1977, a court ruled in favor of Parker Brothers. Under the gleeful eyes of its officials, all of the then remaining 7,000 "Anti-Monopoly" games were buried in a Minnesota landfill. In 1982, however, a California federal appeals court ruled otherwise. Like other words formerly protected as trademarks (cellophane, margarine, shredded wheat, or thermos), the court ruled, "Monopoly" was a generic name, without trademark status. In 1983, by refusing to review the case, the U.S. Supreme Court let the appeals court ruling stand. Parker Brothers paid damages to Anspach and consented to the sale of "Anti-Monopoly" anywhere.

Note: The case has created jitters among the holders of other trademarks, such as Coke, Formica, Teflon, and Xerox. (A Xerox Corporation ad admonishes users: "Don't 'Xerox' things, *copy* them.") Other former trademarks have already gone the way of "Monopoly": Eastern Airlines' "Air Shuttle" and Nestle's "Toll House cookies." And in 1988, the McDonald's Corporation sued Quality Inns International for naming a new chain of economy motels "McSleep Inns." The defendant denied trademark infringement and argued that "Mc" words had so saturated everyday language that the hamburger giant could no longer lay exclusive claim to the trademark. The lodging company provided the court with over 60 examples, ranging from McFashion and McPaper to McArt, McFuneral, and McTelevision—all denoting "basic, convenient, inexpensive, standardized" products.

Sources: *The New York Times,* June 12, 1976, p. 33; July 6, 1977, p. D9; June 20, 1982, p. F17; September 7, 1983, pp. D1 and D5; October 23, 1983, p. 45; July 22, 1988, p. A8; *Business Week,* March 7, 1983, p. 36.

CLOSE-UP 7.2

DE BEERS: DIAMONDS ARE FOREVER

De Beers Consolidated Mines, Ltd. of South Africa (founded in 1888 by Cecil Rhodes, who brought much of the African continent into the British empire) has run a worldwide diamond cartel for nearly a century. It now handles about 85 percent of the world's uncut diamonds, including even those produced by Communist countries, such as Angola and the Soviet Union. Frequently, de Beers earnings are impressive. In 1978, for example, de Beers netted $852 million, an impressive 44 percent on its stockholders' equity.

The company gets its diamonds for about $10 a carat; its selling price averages $80 a carat. (A *carat* equals 200 milligrams or 1/142 of an ounce.

It was named for a carob seed, noted for its consistency in weight.) Unlike OPEC's dealings, those of de Beers are secretive. The key to market control are the "sights," diamond sales to wholesalers and cutters that occur every five weeks in London, Kimberley, and Lucerne. Attendance is by invitation only, and invitations are issued to some 300 persons. They must follow de Beers policies on pricing and sales or they will be barred from the "sights"—and that means no access to diamonds anywhere. As a result,. no one speaks ill of the Central Selling Organization or the Syndicate. Nobody wants to offend the hand that feeds.

Over the years, de Beers has been successful when challenged. In 1982, for example, it became clear that the new Argyle mine in Northern Australia would be capable of raising world diamond output by 40 percent by the mid-1980s. Despite early objections by the Australian government, de Beers got the newcomer to sign up with the cartel. At the same time, Zaire pulled out of the cartel and began to sell its output independently. (Its output consists mostly of industrial-grade diamonds that are used for abrasive wheels, cutting tools, and phonograph needles and are referred to as *boart*.) Within no time at all, de Beers flooded the market with boart from its $1.7-billion inventory; the price dropped by two-thirds; and Zaire returned to the fold.

Sources: Paul Gibson, "De Beers: Can a Cartel Be Forever?" *Forbes,* May 28, 1979, pp. 45–56; "How de Beers Dominates the Diamonds," *The Economist,* February 23, 1980, pp. 101–2; *The Wall Street Journal,* February 22, 1982, p. 27 and July 7, 1983, pp. 1 and 16.

CLOSE-UP 7.3

ORANGE UPRISING

To Jacques Giddens, grower of navel oranges in Orange Cove, California, the federal marketing quotas were "crazy." Each year, he said, they forced him to throw away perfectly good food merely to hold up prices. In 1976, he rebelled.

After selling 3,441 cartons of oranges above his Department of Agriculture quota, Mr. Giddens was fined $12,620 by the government. He declined to pay, sued the government, and lost. He was broke but not broken. In fact, after his revolt, the rancher managed to exceed his marketing quota by leasing some of his trees directly to consumers at $16 apiece. He guaranteed each lessee 120 pounds of fruit. His ranch did the picking and packing; the lessee paid the shipping.

"This is exempt from the marketing order," Mr. Giddens explained, "because when you lease a tree from me, that's your tree, and all I do is ship you the fruit from it. I take care of it for you. It's not covered by the quota."

At the time, he said, he was the only orange grower in the country who leased trees. More recently, other farmers have joined the fight, using petitions and lawsuits to put an end to "1930s-bred socialism." As federal marketing orders prevented them from harvesting millions of oranges all across California's San Joaquin Valley, a farm spokesman said: "Even the Communists don't do what we're doing—destroying good food."

Source: Richard Haitch, "Orange Uprising," *The New York Times,* May 11, 1980, p. 37; Marj Charlier, "Fighting Quotas," *The Wall Street Journal,* June 17, 1987, pp. 1 and 13.

CLOSE-UP 7.4

SUPPORTING THE PRICE OF SUGAR

As the rain pelted the leaky old warehouse one summer day in 1978, a mysterious substance as viscous as lava and as dark as motor oil oozed under the doors and into the street of Riviera Beach, Florida, attracting swarms of flies and bees. The warehouse was filled with raw sugar acquired by the federal government under its new 1977 price support program; the scene of sugar spoiling in federal warehouses was repeated in many places all over the United States.

Under the new program, sugar growers could borrow money (at 14.73¢ a pound) from the government but had to turn over their crops as collateral. If later market prices were higher, they could reclaim the sugar; if they were not, they forfeited their crops; taxpayers, through the government, became the reluctant owners of the sugar. The stakes were large. At a time when the world price of sugar was less than 8¢ a pound, each penny increase in price added $224 million to the American sugar growers' revenue, but (as they said) this would "only" cost the average American one extra dollar per year.

Note: The world market price of sugar has fluctuated wildly, from 65¢ a pound in 1974 to 8¢ a pound in 1977 to 42¢ a pound in 1980 to 7¢ a pound in 1982. In the latter year, U.S. taxpayers were paying an average $215,000 in support money to U.S. sugar producers—far more than the analogous amount going to the average dairy farmer ($11,250) or the average wheat farmer ($475). See Analytical Example 6.2, "The Political Economy of Milk and Housing," for another discussion of this issue.

Sources: William Robbins, "Conflicting Interests Over Sugar Create Unwanted U.S. Surpluses," *The New York Times,* January 14, 1979, pp. 1 and 48; *idem,* "Lobbyists Worked Off Stage to Shape Sugar Laws," *The New York Times,* January 15, 1979, pp. A1 and D4; and *idem,* "Powerful Rivals Clash Over Sugar Price Supports," *The New York Times,* January 16, 1979, pp. A1 and D11; July 18, 1982.

8

Oligopoly and Monopolistic Competition

Chapter 7 explained why sellers of goods, seeking to gain economic profit on a permanent basis, may wish to eliminate all other sellers in their industry or at least to collude with them. We also noted the technological and legal foundations on which some firms manage to build successful monopolies or cartels. For many other firms, however, complete success remains elusive in this monopoly game, although they may succeed in part. As a result, most firms come to inhabit a "twilight zone," lying somewhere between monopoly or cartel on the one hand and perfect competition on the other. In all market economies, this middle ground, in which features of monopoly blend with those of competition, is of major importance. Although Cournot clearly pointed to it in 1838, it took another century before economists paid serious attention to it. In 1933, under the leadership of Edward H. Chamberlin (1899–1967) of Cambridge, Massachusetts and Joan V. Robinson (1903–83) of Cambridge, England (biographies of whom appear, respectively, in Chapters 8 and 11 of the *Student Workbook* that accompanies this text), a major revolution was launched in microeconomic theory, similar in importance to the macroeconomic one initiated by J. M. Keynes in 1936. Economists began to focus on **imperfect competition;** that is, market situations, other than pure monopoly and cartel, in which individual sellers nevertheless face downward-sloping demand curves and thus have some measure of control over price.

The Coca Cola Company, for example, because of its trademark, has a legal monopoly in this drink. No one else may produce it, and the firm can charge any price it likes for it. But when it does, it better be aware of its obvious rivals, from the makers of Pepsi Cola to those of orange juice. Because these rivals produce a whole range of fairly good substitutes, the Coca Cola Company does not enjoy a pure monopoly. The suburban corner drugstore, similarly, because of its location, has a local monopoly of sorts. It, too, can charge any price it wishes for its drugs. But it better be aware that if its prices get too much out of line, customers will trade in the advantage of short trips to the neighborhood store for lower prices at competing drugstores downtown. This chapter will discuss the types of situations illustrated by the Coca Cola Company and the corner drugstore.

We will first consider **oligopoly,** a market structure in which the entry of new firms is difficult and relatively few sellers compete with one another, offering either homogeneous products (cement, steel, rail transportation) or differentiated ones (cars, cigarettes, soap). Later in the chapter, we will turn to **monopolistic competition,** a market structure in which the entry of new firms is easy and large number of sellers compete with one another, offering differentiated products.

OLIGOPOLY AND STRATEGIC BEHAVIOR

In situations of oligopoly, one encounters **strategic behavior**—the type of behavior arising among a small number of actors who have conflicting interests and are mutually conscious of the interdependence of their decisions. There being so few sellers, each one of them has identifiable rivals, the actions of whom become known almost at once; every seller is intensely aware that the actions of any one significantly affect the fortunes of all others. Because collusion at the expense of buyers is either absent or so informal as to be imperfect, the decisions of any one seller on such matters as product quantity, price, quality, or advertising are bound to be viewed by the other sellers as attempts to gain at their expense. These decisions, therefore, are bound to call forth some sort of reaction, the type and extent of which is hard to predict. When any one move is likely to call forth a countermove, what will be the end result? Nobody knows! Economists have developed dozens of theories to capture this interdependence. As a group, these theories reflect the rich array of actual behavior patterns, but no single one is universally accepted as *the* theory of oligopoly. We will resist a Teutonic compulsion to list all the competing theories, but we will consider a few of the more important ones.

DECISION MAKING UNDER OLIGOPOLY: OUTPUT QUANTITY

Cournot himself considered the case of two competitors whose decision making focused on the *quantity* of output produced. Each of them was making output decisions on the assumption that its rival was supplying a fixed quantity that would not be adjusted in response to any output decision made by itself. Panel (a) of Figure 8.1 pictures a hypothetical market-demand line AB, which is based on the equation $Q = 100 - P$, where Q and P are quantity and price in the market as a whole. At a price of \$100, therefore, quantity demanded is zero (point A); at a zero price, quantity is 100 units per year (point B). Our graph also shows the implied marginal revenue as dashed line AC. Now let fixed cost as well as the marginal cost of production be zero (only to keep the graph uncluttered); marginal cost is shown by line $0B$. A pure monopolist would choose a quantity of 50 units per year (point C), charge a price of \$50 per unit (point D), and make a profit of \$2,500 per year (rectangle $0CDE$). Not so our two competitors.

Let Firm X believe that Firm Y is going to supply $q_Y = 60$. Then the demand facing X will be seen by X as market demand Q minus 60 or as $Q = 100 - P - 60 = 40 - P$. This demand line and its marginal-revenue line is shown in panel (b) as lines FG and FH, respectively. At zero marginal cost, Firm X would supply 20 units (point H), charge \$20 each (point I), and (still assuming zero fixed cost) make a profit of \$400 (rectangle $0HIK$). Note: At a price of \$20, market demand would equal 80, leaving exactly 60 units to be supplied by Firm Y, as we assumed.

In a similar fashion, one can calculate how much output X would supply for various other assumed quantities supplied by Y, and this output is shown by X's **reaction curve** in panel (c) of our graph, which shows the best quantity supplied from X's point of view for every possible quantity supplied by Y. The quantity combination calculated above (if $q_Y = 60$, then $q_X = 20$) is shown as point L.

When X supplies 20 units, firm Y, however, may not supply 60 units at all. Suppose, as Cournot assumed, that Y also believed that any quantity decision of its own would call forth no reaction from X. Noting X's decision to supply 20 units, Firm Y would then, by an analogous procedure, calculate its demand as $Q - 20 = 100 - P - 20 = 80 - P$ and would end up supplying 40 units instead; this output is shown by point M on Y's reaction curve. Analogously, Y would supply nothing if X supplied 100, 50 units if X supplied nothing, and so on. (The equations of the reaction curves are $q_X = 50 - .5q_Y$ and $q_Y = 50 - .5q_X$, respectively.)

As panel (c) of our graph shows, the only quantity combination that would not elicit further reactions from the two rivals is the **Cournot equilibrium,** which is found at the intersection of the two reaction curves. The Cournot equilibrium point reflects the decision, on the part of both firms, to supply 33⅓ units. Note: If a total of 66⅔ units were thus supplied, market price would equal $33.33, as seen clearly by point N in panel (a). Total revenue and (in this example) profit would come to $2,222.22, clearly less than the potential monopoly profit of $2,500 calculated above. Indeed, Cournot reckoned, a gradual increase in the number of competitors would in this way eventually reduce the price to marginal cost (to zero in our case). The case also shows, however, the "price" these firms are paying for not colluding with each other and the incentive that exists to form a cartel, cut production, and raise price.*

We should note in conclusion that it is fairly easy to find fault with almost all existing theories of oligopoly, including Cournot's. Consider what it takes for his equilibrium to be attained. No matter how stupidly wrong Firm X is (when counting on its rival to supply a fixed quantity $\bar{q}_Y$

---

*For a calculus-based treatment of this material, see Section 8A of the Calculus Appendix at the back of this book.

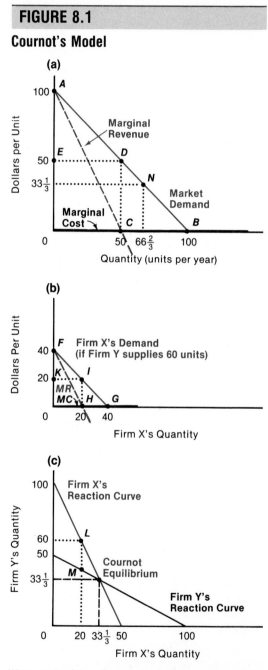

FIGURE 8.1

Cournot's Model

(a)

(b)

(c)

When each of two firms in an industry makes output decisions on the assumption that its rival is supplying a fixed quantity that will not be adjusted in response to any output decision made by itself, a Cournot equilibrium emerges.

but finding instead a quantity adjustment being made by Firm Y), it will continue to be steadily stupid to the end! The implied inability of each firm to learn from experience is not exactly credible. Next, we will turn to other models that focus attention not on adjustments in quantity, but on adjustments in price.

DECISION MAKING UNDER OLIGOPOLY: PRICE

In a situation of oligopoly, any seller's change in price in the downward direction can easily be interpreted by rivals as an attempt to eliminate them by luring away their customers. Rivals are unlikely to take this lying down. They will answer such "predatory price cutting" with price cuts of their own. This may give rise to a further price cut by the original firm, and so on in an endless chain. There are plenty of precedents for such a chain of price cuts. A **price war** in which rival firms successively cut their prices below those of competitors (and perhaps even below their own cost) occurred in the 1870s among railroads hauling freight between New York and Chicago. A price war raged among oil producers in the 1880s, among the makers of cigarettes in the 1930s, and among the makers of heavy electrical equipment in the 1950s. And in the 1970s, price wars have raged among New England banks (with respect to NOW accounts), transatlantic airlines and rent-a-car companies.

Sometimes the participants in such struggles end up pricing their product below cost and go bankrupt, leaving the field to their luckier competitors whose longer staying power may be the result of lower cost, greater financial reserves, or profitable lines of business in other industries. Like all wars, price wars are bitter experiences for the firms involved. They see their profits disappear and their very existence threatened, all the while knowing that monopoly profits could be ensured with the proper degree of cooperation.

On the other hand, any seller's change of price in the upward direction can be suicidal as

well. If the rivals simply sit back and do nothing, the seller who raises prices is likely to lose many customers to those rivals—and again there may be red ink as a result.

Some theorists, therefore, have argued that oligopolistic firms will have "sticky" prices, which they will be very reluctant to change.

The Kinked Demand Curve

Paul M. Sweezy, in 1939, developed the theory of the **kinked demand curve** to account for this expected price rigidity (see Figure 8.2). An oligopolistic firm is imagined to be selling 800 million packs of cigarettes per year at a price of $1 per pack (point *a*). It sees itself as facing two subjectively estimated demand lines. One of these, extending from *b* to *d* and beyond, indicates how much this firm expects to sell at various prices if its rivals exactly match any price change it cares to initiate. The other demand line, extending from *c* to *f* and beyond, indicates how much this firm expects to sell at various prices if its rivals do not react to any price change it cares to initiate. Note how a hypothetical price increase from $1 to $1.25 per pack would reduce quantity demanded from *a* to *d* if rivals raised their prices equally, while the same price hike would reduce quantity demanded from *a* to *c* if rivals held the line on their prices and thus lured customers away from our firm. Note how, similarly, a hypothetical price cut from $1 to 75 cents per pack would increase quantity demanded from *a* to *e* if rivals lowered their prices equally, while the same price cut would increase quantity demanded from *a* to *f* if rivals did not match the cut and thus allowed our firm to lure customers away from them.

As Sweezy saw it, any one firm is likely to reason as follows: If it raised its price, rivals could increase their market share by doing nothing, and that is exactly what the rivals would do. Thus the demand line relevant to our firm for any increase in price is color segment *ac* and not dashed segment *ad*. On the other hand, if the firm lowered its price, rivals would decrease their market share by doing nothing, and that is exactly what rivals would *not* do. Thus the demand line relevant to our firm for any decrease in price is color segment *ab* and not dashed segment *af*.

Our firm's entire demand line, therefore, is found when the irrelevant segments (dashed) are deleted. It is the kinked color line *cab,* with the kink occurring at the level of the present price (point *a*). Corresponding to this kinked line of demand, a strangely shaped marginal-revenue line, going from *c* to *g, h,* and *i,* can be derived.

As was shown with the help of Figure 7.2, "Monopoly: Total and Marginal Revenue" (p. 223), the marginal-revenue line corresponding to any straight demand line can always be found half-way between that demand line and the vertical axis. Thus the marginal revenue corresponding to demand segment *ca* equals *cg* (distance *kg,* for instance, being equal to *gf*). Because the pessimistic assumptions of our firm about the

behavior of its rivals make demand line *caf* inapplicable to the right of point *a,* its marginal-revenue line becomes similarly irrelevant to the right of point *g,* and this segment hasn't even been drawn. Analogously, the marginal revenue corresponding to demand segment *ab* goes from *h* to *i* and beyond (distance 0*i,* for instance, being equal to *ib,* distance *mh* equalling *hn,* and so on). Again, because demand line *bd* is inapplicable to the left of point *a,* its marginal-revenue line is irrelevant to the left of *h,* and this segment also has not been drawn.

We can now view our firm's profit picture by introducing cost curves. Because the firm has chosen to produce 800 million packs of cigarettes per year, marginal cost must equal marginal revenue at this quantity, and it does (point *o*). The average total cost corresponding to this output level (point *p*) is seen to equal 65 cents a pack. Thus a profit per pack of 35 cents is made

FIGURE 8.2

Sweezy's Model

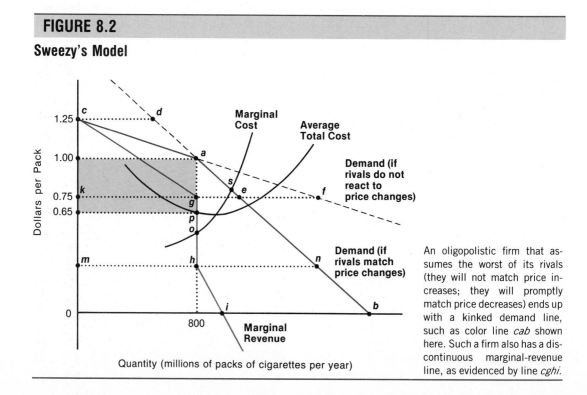

An oligopolistic firm that assumes the worst of its rivals (they will not match price increases; they will promptly match price decreases) ends up with a kinked demand line, such as color line *cab* shown here. Such a firm also has a discontinuous marginal-revenue line, as evidenced by line *cghi.*

(distance ap), and total profit equals $280 million per year (shaded rectangle).

Implications of the Kinked Demand Curve. The existence of a kinked demand curve implies, among other things, that oligopolistic firms, quite unlike perfect competitors or monopolists, may not change price even in the face of moderate changes in (a) marginal cost or (b) demand. These two implications are illustrated, respectively, in panels (a) and (b) of Figure 8.3. Panel (a) shows an original profit-maximizing equilibrium corresponding to the intersection, at point c, of marginal revenue, MR, and marginal cost, MC_0. The firm produces 800 million packs of cigarettes per year and sells each for $1. Let marginal cost rise as high as MC_1, or let it fall as low as MC_2. The MR-MC intersection changes (to b or d, respectively), but the profit-maximizing output and price remain the same.

Panel (b) pictures an identical initial equilibrium, corresponding to intersection e of original MC_0 and MR_0. Now let demand fall from D_0 to D_1, which changes marginal revenue from MR_0 to MR_1. A new equilibrium corresponds to the MC-MR intersection at f. Quantity produced is down to 525 million packs a year, but price (now corresponding to point h on D_1 rather than i on D_0) is the same.

Criticisms of the Sweezy Model.   As they did with Cournot's model, economists have found much in the Sweezy model with which to quarrel. Consider how the model does not explain how the initial price is derived in the first place. The model suggests that prices should be more rigid in oligopolistic industries than in those dominated by monopoly. Yet empirical studies by George J. Stigler, by Julian Simon, by Walter J. Primeaux, Jr., and Mark R. Bomball, and by

— a rationalization

FIGURE 8.3

Implications of Kinked Oligopoly Demand

(a) Change in Marginal Cost

(b) Change in Demand

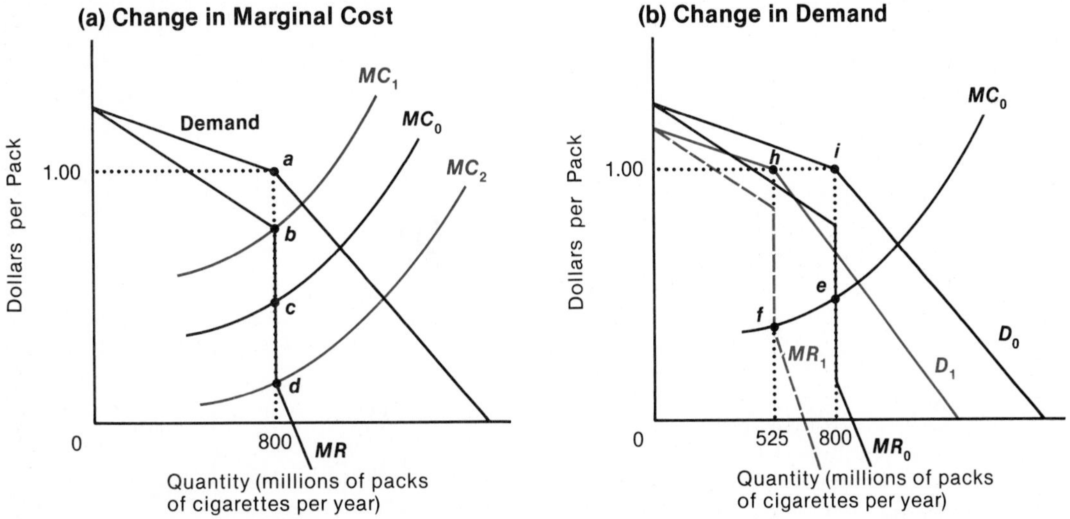

The existence of kinked oligopoly demand implies price rigidity even in the face of moderate changes in marginal cost [panel (a)] or demand [panel (b)].

others have shown exactly the opposite to be true.[1] No wonder that many economists prefer to explain oligopolistic pricing by means other than the Sweezy model.

Gentlemen's Agreements

Some economists argue that oligopolists who cannot manage to build a cartel, but recognize the inevitable interdependence of their actions, are most likely to construct some kind of communications network among themselves. (Consider the political analogies of NATO joining the Warsaw Pact versus détente and telephone hotlines.) As a result, oligopolists can, perhaps, make output and price decisions that are not instantly interpreted by their rivals as signs of aggression, but rather serve the purpose of mutual accommodation. Such communications may be overt, as in the case of **gentlemen's agreements** (ladies, presumably, can enter into them as well), informal oral understandings among oligopolists in the same industry that they will maintain a certain minimum price. These agreements are apt to be ratified by nothing more than a handshake over lunch, and they have in fact been made on many occasions. (When such overt communications are illegal, as is often the case, communications may be covert instead.)

In the 1880s, gentlemen's agreements involved the coal, cordage, rail transport, salt, and whiskey industries. Later, it was the cement and steel companies' turn. Between 1907 and 1911, for example, all the important steel industry executives regularly attended the celebrated din-

ners given by Judge Elbert J. Gary, then chairman of the board of directors of U.S. Steel. And for many years later, their **basing-point system,** called *Pittsburgh plus,* worked like a charm. Until 1948, all steel companies, regardless of their location, would quote prices equal to those charged by U.S. Steel at its Pittsburgh mills (the basing point) plus rail freight from the basing point to the buyer's location. No wonder that the U.S. Navy Department, when it opened 31 secret bids for a quantity of rolled steel on May 26, 1936, found 31 identical prices of $20,727.26 each. And in the same year, the U.S. Engineer's Office at Tucumcari, New Mexico, received 11 sealed bids for the delivery of 6,000 barrels of cement. Each one of them was identical, right up to the sixth decimal point: $3.286854 per barrel.[2] How often, do you think, is this going to happen by pure chance?

Today, Gary-style understandings are quite illegal in the United States, but this does not mean that they are uncommon. People of the same industry do meet at trade association conventions, and, as Adam Smith himself taught us long ago, ''people of the same trade seldom meet together, even for merriment and diversion, but the conversation ends in a conspiracy against the public, or in some contrivance to raise prices.'' In fact, the U.S. Department of Justice has estimated that a third of U.S. firms were involved in private, informal price-fixing activities in 1974. Food producers engaged in price fixing included the makers of beef, beer, bread and bakery products, eggs, milk and milk products, seafood, sugar, and soft drinks. Price fixing, however, was not confined to commodities. The professional societies of accountants, architects, doctors, engineers, lawyers, and real estate brokers routinely circulated schedules on minimum fees that no ''ethical'' member was supposed to violate. Yet oligopolistic price fixing can and does occur in even more subtle ways.

[1]George J. Stigler, ''The Kinky Oligopoly Demand Curve and Rigid Prices,'' *Journal of Political Economy,* October 1947, pp. 432–49; Julian L. Simon, ''A Further Test of the Kinky Oligopoly Demand Curve,'' *The American Economic Review,* December 1969, pp. 971–75; Walter J. Primeaux, Jr., and Mark R. Bomball, ''A Reexamination of the Kinky Oligopoly Demand Curve,'' *Journal of Political Economy,* July/August 1974, pp. 851–62; Walter J. Primeaux, Jr., and Mickey C. Smith, ''Pricing Patterns and the Kinky Demand Curve,'' *The Journal of Law and Economics,* April 1976, pp. 189–99.

[2]These charming examples are cited in Max E. Fletcher, *Economics and Social Problems* (Boston: Houghton Mifflin, 1979), pp. 172–73.

Price Leadership

According to a set of industry practices called **price leadership,** one firm, the price leader, announces and occasionally changes list prices, which the other firms immediately adopt as well. The whole process works tacitly, as if by telepathy. There is no written agreement, not even a handshake over lunch. Yet a clearly observable parallelism of action emerges. Examples of this practice abound. Industries (and their usual price leaders) involved have included banking (Chase Manhattan) and those making aluminum (Alcoa), automobiles (General Motors), cigarettes (Reynolds), ready-to-eat cereals (Kellogg), turbogenerators (General Electric), steel (U.S. Steel), and many more.

Note: As is true for all other theories of oligopoly pricing, those concerning gentlemen's agreements and their unspoken counterpart, price leadership, are far from complete. It is unclear, for example, how a price leader is selected (indeed, the position often changes hands, as it has among Kellogg, General Mills, and Post in the cereals industry). Nor is it clear how a particular price is determined. Is the monopoly price chosen? Is it a much lower **limit price** that prevents the entry into the industry of new rivals? Is it a matter of finding a **focal-point price,** one that has a compelling prominence for reasons of aesthetics, precedent, symmetry (round numbers, $199.95, splitting the difference)? On all these questions, the theory is silent.

Figures 8.4 to 8.6 present three alternative theories that have been advanced concerning the way in which the price leader sets the industry price. None of the theories is generally accepted, but each may well apply to particular situations.

FIGURE 8.4

Price Leadership: The Low-Cost-Firm Model

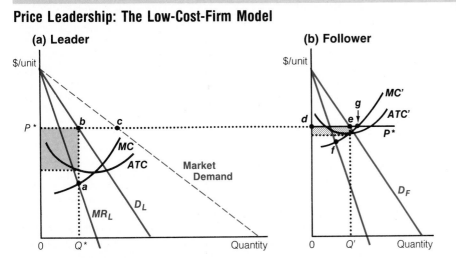

According to the low-cost-firm model, price leadership is exercised by the firm with the lowest cost curves, here *ATC* and *MC* in panel (a). The firm or firms with higher cost curves, here *ATC′* and *MC′* in panel (b), follow the leader. The leader, allegedly, decides on its own market share (here 50 percent, as evidenced by the position of D_L relative to market demand), and then maximizes profit by choosing the price/quantity combination (here P^*, Q^*) that corresponds to the *MC* and MR_L intersection (here at *a*). The follower, allegedly, accepts the leader's price, P^*, and supplies whatever part of market demand has been left unsatisfied by the leader (here $bc = de = Q'$). The follower, thus, acts neither like a monopolist (who would choose a price-quantity combination corresponding to *f*) nor like a perfect competitor (who would choose a combination corresponding to *g*). In our example, the leader's profit (shaded) greatly exceeds the follower's (dotted). It remains unclear why the leader behaves in this way. Why, for example, doesn't the leader charge a price below the follower's minimum *ATC′* and thus eliminate the follower from the scene? Is fear of antitrust action the answer?

According to the lowest-cost firm model, price leadership is exercised by the firm with the lowest cost curves. It chooses its own market share and, on that basis, maximizes profit by equating marginal revenue with marginal cost. As Figure 8.4 shows, the follower or followers accept the leader's price and then satisfy whatever market demand has been left unsatisfied by the leader.

According to the dominant-firm model, also named the **Stackelberg model** after the German economist Heinrich von Stackelberg who advanced it in 1934, a dominant firm, surrounded by a fringe of small firms, sets the price. It lets the other firms sell all they like at that price, but then supplies the rest of the market in a profit-maximizing fashion, as Figure 8.5 illustrates.

According to the entry-limit model, finally, colluding firms make a price/quantity decision that does *not* maximize short-run profit in order to keep potential entrants out of the market. The model is illustrated in Figure 8.6.

DECISION MAKING UNDER OLIGOPOLY: PRODUCT QUALITY

Some oligopolists (but not all) compete with each other on still another front. To the extent that this is possible, they go out of their way to differentiate their product from that of their competitors in the same industry. Such **product differentiation** can involve the physical aspects of goods (their color, durability, flavor, octane rating, size, style, and

---

FIGURE 8.5

Price Leadership: The Dominant-Firm Model (Stackelberg)

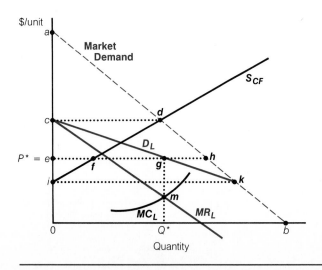

According to the Stackelberg model, a **dominant firm** that supplies at least half of the market and has no significant competitors, except for a fringe of numerous small firms, sets the industry price, but allows the other firms to sell all they like at that price. The dominant firm itself supplies the rest of the market in a profit-maximizing fashion. If market demand is *ab,* and if the horizontal summation of the competitive fringe firms' marginal costs (above their respective average variable costs) is S_{CF}, the fringe firms supply the entire market (*cd*) at a price of 0*c*. In that case, the demand remaining for the leader, D_L, is zero. The fringe firms, on the other hand, supply nothing at a price of 0*i* or below; the entire market demand then belongs to the leader. At intermediate prices between 0*c* and 0*i*, the market is shared between the leader and the competitive fringe. Thus the leader's demand, D_L, is kinked line *ckb*. The leader maximizes profit by equating (at *m*) marginal cost, MC_L, with marginal revenue, MR_L, thus setting a price of P^* and selling $Q^* = eg$. The competitive fringe, it is alleged, accepts the same price as a given and, like perfect competitors, supplies *ef = gh*. Puzzling questions remain: What determines who the leader is? What happens when a fringe firm challenges the leader for its position?

the like), the purely legal aspects (the introduction of a trademark), or the conditions of sale. These conditions of sale must be very broadly defined. Consider how firms seek to be pleasantly different (and thus gain a degree of monopoly power) by building a new store closer to your home, providing free convenient parking, more business hours per week, attractive reusable containers, more and friendlier clerks, music while you shop, carpeted floors, more trading stamps, easier credit terms, prompter delivery, better warranties, faster repair and maintenance—the list goes on. (See Analytical Example 8.1.)

Not all product differentiation involves genuine improvements in quality. New brand names, designs, or packaging may simply make people believe in differences that do not exist. Even when higher quality is fiction, when the belief in fiction is fact, sellers have a greater power over price. (See Close-Up 8.1.)

Product differentiation, whether fact or fic-tion, involves complex decisions that are even more difficult to analyze than decisions about output quantity and price. Quantity and price, after all, can only move in two directions—up or down—but, as the above list indicates, product quality can take on innumerable dimensions. It is not surprising, perhaps, that economic theorists have advanced little beyond Chamberlin, who pointed them to this important and hitherto neglected aspect of competition.

Indeed, one of the most interesting pieces of theoretical apparatus in this field precedes the publication of Chamberlin's book by four years and comes to us from Harold Hotelling.

The Hotelling Paradox

Panel (a) of Figure 8.7 represents a group of 19 buyers (but we can think of them as 19 million just as well). They are uniformly distributed along a straight line of geographic distance, from

FIGURE 8.6

Price Leadership: The Entry-Limit Model

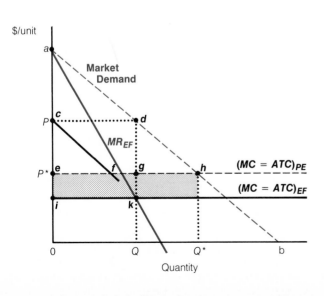

According to the entry-limit model, colluding existing firms, *EF*, set a price, *P**, and sell a quantity, *Q**, that does not maximize short-run profit. This is done deliberately to keep potential entrants, *PE*, out of the market. Accordingly, the price is set at or just below the level of minimum average total cost of the potential competitors. Given market demand, *ab*, and the existing firms' *MC = ATC* shown in the graph, the profit-maximizing choice (corresponding to the marginal-cost/marginal-revenue intersection *k*) is *P* and *Q*, with profit equal to *icdk*. Even if potential entrants had higher marginal and average total costs than the existing firms, as shown, they could make profits by entering the market, charging prices below *P*, and satisfying, at the very least, the additional quantity demanded (along *dh*, also shown by *cf*). The existing firms are said to choose a price such as *P** or below (that promises zero or negative economic profits to potential entrants). Charging *P** and selling *Q**, the existing firms' profit then equals only the dotted area, which is less than maximum short-run profit *icdk*.

west (W) to east (E). We can think of this line as Main Street or a transcontinental railroad or even a beach. Now let us imagine that only two sellers exist. They sell equally priced products, identical in the minds of all buyers except for the location of sale. No buyer, therefore, prefers one seller to the other except for one reason: to minimize the cost, in time or money, of transportation (and that cost is assumed uniform per unit of distance everywhere). We have thus reduced the enormously complex issue of product quality to one dimension only: product differentiation on the basis of seller location.

If one wanted to minimize the total cost, in time or money, of transportation, if all buyers wished to contact a seller once but could not pool their trips, Hotelling asked, where should the two sellers be located? The answer is shown in panel (a). Sellers should locate symmetrically at the quartile points of our line, seller A's position coinciding with the location of buyer #5 and seller B's with the location of buyer #15. Under these circumstances, buyers 1–9 would buy from

A, because it would be costlier for each one of them to go to B. Buyers 11–19 would buy from B, because it would be costlier for each one of these to go to A. Buyer #10, located on the line of indifference that would divide the market between the two sellers, would find it equally costly to go to A or B and would thus be indifferent between the two sources of supply. If one represented the transportation cost from one buyer's location to the next location by $1, the total cost of transportation for all buyers would equal $45. (Buyers 5 and 15 would spend nothing; buyers 4, 6, 14, and 16 would spend $1 each; buyers 3, 7, 13, and 17 $2 each, and so on.) The locational product differentiation given in panel (a) would thus be ideal for minimizing the total cost of all buyers, but the sellers would not choose these locations.

Imagine that seller A (a restaurant on Main Street, perhaps, or an ice cream vendor on a beach) first appeared and in fact located at location #5. Where would B locate? The answer is given in panel (b). Seller B would locate at

FIGURE 8.7

The Hotelling Paradox

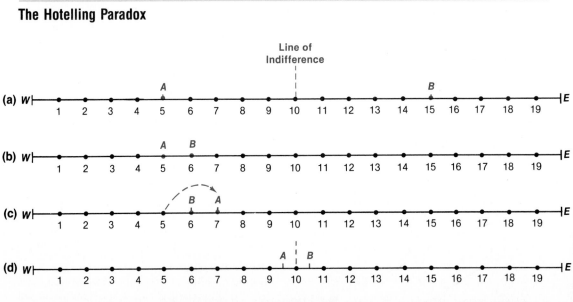

Under certain conditions, competition by means of product differentiation leads to products that are hardly differentiated at all. Similar "adjacencies" abound outside the area of economics proper.

location #6, between A and the mass of customers, as close to A as possible without erasing the (locational) difference between the two. As a result, only buyers 1–5 would buy from A, while buyers 6–19 would buy from B. Society's transportation cost would by far exceed the $45 minimum calculated above; it would equal $101 instead. (Can you show how this figure is derived?)

Yet this result would be unstable if relocation costs were zero (and this we will assume). As shown in panel (c), seller A could use the same strategy as B did. By now jumping over B and locating at #7, A could gain all the customers from 7–19, while B would be left with only 1–6. So far as total transportation costs are concerned, this would be an improvement (they would decline to $93), but the situation would still be unstable because B could, in turn, jump over A and locate at #8, thereby gaining a larger share of the market.

Where will it all end? Look at panel (d). Both sellers will end up in the geographic center of the market, near the line of indifference and only imperceptibly differentiated from each other. Total transportation cost will not be minimized (and will equal $81.50 in this example).

Hotelling's paradox is that competition by means of product differentiation may lead to products that are hardly differentiated at all. Hotelling was the first to realize that this theory had much wider applicability than has been indicated so far.

Wider Applications of Hotelling's Paradox

When one considers ''distance'' figuratively instead of literally, the above technique of analysis can be applied to competing sellers whose products are separated not geographically, but by any one of a host of other dimensions of quality. *W* in our graph, for example, might denote not the western edge of a market, but the extreme degree of blandness of a beer or sweetness of cider. *E*, correspondingly, might not denote the eastern edge of the market, but the extreme degree of

bitterness of a beer or sourness of cider. Consumers might then be viewed not as uniformly distributed along a *geographic* line, but as distributed along a line of ''characteristics space,'' differentiated from one another by tastes that indicate different degrees of preference for a characteristic such as bitterness, sourness, or the like. Thus buyer #1 might prefer the sweetest of all possible ciders (or the blandest of all possible beers) over all others, while buyer #19 would prefer the most sour cider (and the most bitter beer). Other buyers would have preferences between these two extremes. Again we could ask: Where would sellers ''locate''? Which one of 19 possible varieties of cider (or beer) would each of them produce and offer for sale? Again the answer would follow our earlier analysis.

Society's cost (now measured in terms of the dissatisfaction buyers feel when they cannot get exactly the quality of product that is most preferred) would be minimized if seller A produced the product quality most preferred by buyer #5 and if seller B produced the product quality that was first choice for buyer #15. As we learned from panel (a) before, dissatisfaction would then equal 45 units. No single buyer would have to buy a product quality more than 5 gradations away from the one that was most preferred; many buyers would get product qualities much closer to their first choice.

Yet the end result once more would not be the one pictured in panel (a). If seller A produced the product most liked by buyer #5, seller B would produce the product most liked by buyer #6, thereby getting buyers 7–19 to buy from B as well. Although none of them would rank B's product as their first choice, all of them would prefer B's to A's, for the latter would still be one notch farther away from their ideal. As panel (b) of our graph shows, #7 would almost get first choice when buying from B, while #19, extremely unhappy with B's product as well as A's, would still prefer B's. B's product characteristics would be a little bit closer to nonexistent product quality 19 than would be A's.

The end result, of course, would be the same old sameness depicted in panel (d). This undue tendency of competitors to imitate each other in product quality, Hotelling argued, explains a lot about the real world of economics and beyond. It explains why all shoes are so much alike but also why political parties and religions are so much alike. Anyone who takes a sharply contrasting position from a competitor (as when the Republicans or the Baptists locate at 5 in the belief that the Democrats or the Methodists will locate at 15) will find the competitor getting between this position and as many "customers" as possible (as when the Democrats or the Methodists locate at 6 instead). For an interesting case in point, see Close-Up 8.2.

DECISION MAKING UNDER OLIGOPOLY: ADVERTISING

Unlike individual firms under perfect competition, for whom it would make no sense to advertise, imperfect competitors do advertise, with a vengeance. In 1988, imperfect competitors spent several hundred dollars for every man, woman, and child in the United States on advertising. As used here, the term *advertising* includes not only newspaper and magazine ads, radio and television announcements, direct mail solicitations, roadside billboards, and Goodyear blimps, but also store window displays, the distribution of free samples and trading stamps, a variety of contests and games, the efforts of salespeople, and much more. All this activity, of course, is designed to increase the demand for a firm's product at the expense of that for the products of competitors or even entirely different products. Regardless of whether a firm's attempt to shift its demand curve to the right is successful or not, advertising raises that firm's costs. As Chamberlin envisioned it, **selling cost**—that is, cost designed to alter a firm's demand curve—can be added to the familiar curves of (average or marginal) production cost. Depending on the degree to which the demand curve is shifted at the same time, the firm's profit is or is not

increased as a result. Advertising, accordingly, will be continued or abandoned.

Advertising, it is often claimed, comes in two forms, but the two types are difficult to disentangle in practice. Some advertising is clearly **informative advertising,** which provides genuine information to buyers about the very existence of products or sellers, about price, and about quality. Because people are by nature less than omniscient, such advertising plays an important role in that it reduces people's ignorance and helps them make choices. As will be noted in detail in Chapter 9, information can be a very valuable commodity, indeed. Other types of advertising, however, are of more questionable value.

Persuasive advertising is designed to divert people's attention from facts to images and make them buy more as a result of imagined advantages. This persuasion occurs, perhaps, when products are associated with beautiful women, handsome men, gracious living, and the like and when people are gradually turned into Pavlovian dogs. In a thousand different ways, people are "brainwashed" into being loyal to a particular firm's particular product until they are ready to shout "We'd rather fight than switch." People get precious little information when they are told that "blondes have more fun," that a cigarette "has the honest taste," or that they can now "put a tiger in their tank." Yet even in advertisements like these, people do get some information; if nothing else, they learn about the existence of the product concerned. Those, therefore, who would ban persuasive advertising on the grounds that the resources devoted to it represent a social waste would have a hard time sorting out informative from persuasive statements.

This is not to say that there is no room for improvement. Along with government agencies, such as the Federal Trade Commission or the Food and Drug Administration, a business-sponsored National Advertising Review Board seeks to eliminate blatant deception from advertisements. In 1981, for example, one ad showed a picture of a slim actress and the words, "California Avocados. Only 17 calories a slice. Would this body lie to you?'' Apparently it would, because the ad also promised consumers specified quantities of vitamins plus potassium, but the size portion that would justify that claim would contain 132 calories. The ad was challenged and withdrawn. Yet subtle deception, half-truths, and ''little white lies'' persist. Thus we are told that ''Anacin contains 23 percent more pain reliever than other leading headache remedies,'' but we are not told that Anacin equals 400 mg. of plain aspirin (plus some caffeine) as compared with the 325 mg. content of the standard (and so much cheaper) aspirin tablet. Banks promise us ''the highest interest rate allowed by law'' but invariably fail to mention that almost all other banks offer identical rates. Even cleverly chosen brand names can deceive: ReaLemon sounds like the genuine article, yet all other brands of such (reconstituted) lemon juice are indistinguishable from it.

One issue has greatly interested economists in recent years: Does advertising *prevent* newcomers from entering an industry or does it *help* them to do so? Many cross-industry studies have shown a strong (positive) correlation between advertising intensity and (accounting) profit rates. This evidence has been interpreted by some to indicate that heavy advertising creates **brand loyalty** (the making of repeat purchases by consumers who have ceased sampling other brands) and thus discourages new firms from entering the market. To take customers away from the established firms, it is said, the newcomers would have to charge lower prices or make even heavier advertising expenditures; they cannot hope to make the kinds of profits existing firms are making; they do not enter the industry. Advertising, thus, is a barrier to entry.

The same evidence has been interpreted differently by others. They picture imperfectly informed customers sampling a few brands, then sticking with the best of the lot (exhibiting brand loyalty) not because they are psychologically attached to the chosen product or convinced that it is the best of all existing ones, but because they

consider further search too costly, given the probability of finding a better brand. Yet intense advertising under such circumstances that provides new information to consumers may well cause them to switch to a new brand and provide the advertising firm with extraordinary profits. Advertising, thus, is a means of overcoming brand loyalty rather than a means of creating it. Close-Up 8.3 and Analytical Examples 8.2 and 8.3 present recent evidence that advertising may lower prices and aid newcomers to gain a foothold in a market.

For a further discussion of advertising and other aspects of the theory of oligopoly, see Chapter 9.

MONOPOLISTIC COMPETITION

Much of what has been said so far about product differentiation and advertising applies to *monopolistic competitors* as well as oligopolists. Yet monopolistic competitors are distinguished from oligopolists by the absence of strategic behavior. Entry into a monopolistically competitive ''industry'' is easy; large numbers of firms compete in it; and no single firm need fear any noticeable impact of its actions on any one competitor (of whom there are so many). No single firm, therefore, need fear any reaction by these others. The retail trade and service sectors of the economy are prime examples of monopolistic competition.

Note: In the previous paragraph, the term *industry* appears in quotation marks and for a good reason. Traditionally, economists have considered an *industry* as composed of all firms producing an identical product. To the extent that the product of each firm is differentiated in a multitude of ways from that of every other firm, an obvious difficulty arises with this industry concept. Chamberlin attempted to overcome this problem by distinguishing **product groups**— groups of closely related but differentiated products that serve the same wants—and then treating all firms producing such products as if they belonged to an ''industry.'' Such product groups, he thought, are distinguishable from each other by obvious gaps in the endless chain of substitutes such that the similar products of any two firms within a Chamberlinian group are related by a high cross-price elasticity of demand, while the more dissimilar products of any two firms placed in different groups are related by a very low or zero cross-price elasticity.

Profit Maximization

The behavior of the monopolistically competitive firm can be analyzed very much like that of the pure monopoly, but there is a difference in the long run. Entry into the "industry" being easy, zero economic profit is the inevitable long-run result for a monopolistic competitor, as shown in Figure 8.8. Panel (a) depicts a barbershop's downward-sloping demand line. Unlike wheat

farmers, barbers do have their own identifiable products that cannot be duplicated perfectly. As a result, they have a group of more or less loyal patrons who prefer a particular firm's service, location, or whatever. Unlike wheat farmers, barbers, therefore, do have some measure of control over price. When they raise price, sales do not instantly fall to zero (as they would for the wheat farmer who insisted on getting more than the going price set at the Chicago Board of Trade). Yet our barber cannot raise price to infinity either. At $9.50 per haircut in our example, even the most loyal patrons will vanish for cheaper competitors. By the same token, monopolistically competitive barbers (unlike wheat farmers) will not gain all the world's customers by lowering price even a bit. Many people would continue to rely on their familiar (and now relatively more expensive) shops.

FIGURE 8.8

The Monopolistic Competitor

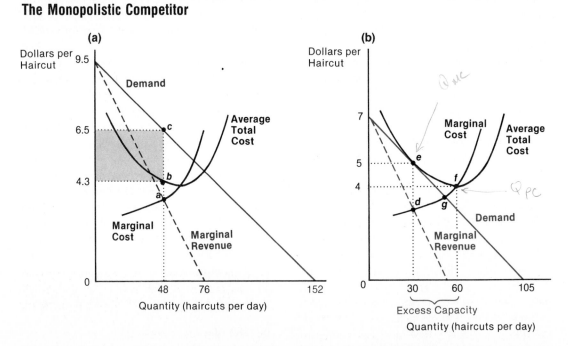

If monopolistically competitive firms make economic profit, as shown by the shaded rectangle in panel (a), entry of new firms into their "industry" will occur. This entry of new firms will reduce the demand for each firm and eliminate economic profit, as shown in panel (b). The inducement for entry being gone, entry into the "industry" will then cease.

Given our barber's demand, the implied marginal-revenue line (dashed), and the cost curves shown in panel (a) of Figure 8.8, profit is maximized (as it would be for a pure monopoly) according to intersection *a*. Every day, 48 haircuts are produced at an average cost of $4.30 (point *b*) and for a price of $6.50 (point *c*). Thus the barber makes a profit of $105.60 per day (shaded rectangle).

Yet this profit will not continue into the long run. When economic profit is being made and entry into the industry is easy, others enter the industry—in this case opening up other barbershops. These other barbers would also like to earn $105.60 a day over and above their next best alternative (which, be it remembered, is what economic profit indicates). Gradually, some of our barber's customers (who may discover these new stores and prefer their work or location) will drift away. Our friend's demand will shrink, as from the demand line in panel (a) to the lower one in panel (b). In the end, this barber will produce only 30 haircuts per day (point *d*), at a price and average total cost of $5 (point *e*). Economic profit will have disappeared, just as it would have in perfect competition. But monopolistic competition is distinguished from perfect competition by the occurrence of *excess capacity.*

Excess Capacity

As we saw in Chapter 6, in long-run equilibrium, perfectly competitive firms are producing at minimum average total cost. They operate their plants at the optimal rate; they produce capacity output. Not so for monopolistic competitors. Note how our firm in panel (b) produces 30 haircuts at an average total cost of $5 (point *e*), while its average total cost could be as low as $4 if it produced twice as much (point *f*). This difference between the monopolistically competitive firm's capacity output and its profit-maximizing lower actual output is called **excess capacity.**

This excess capacity can be seen in many places. Consider how hotels, movie houses, and restaurants are rarely filled, how gas station attendants and retail store clerks mostly have plenty of spare time left to serve other customers. But beware: The occurrence of excess capacity does not imply that the higher-than-minimum cost of production found in monopolistically competitive ''industries'' is a pure waste. What if, in our example, half the barbershops closed down? As panel (b) of Figure 8.8 shows, the other half could make up for this shutdown by producing twice as many haircuts each for $1 less on the average. But there would be a cost to buyers: Barbershops would be less conveniently located; customers would have to wait longer to be served; they would have a smaller selection of work quality to choose from. The opposite of this cost, of course, is the *benefit* buyers get when many firms operate permanently at a fraction of their capacity. Given people's genuine preference for diversity, this advantage may well make producing at higher-than-minimum average total cost worthwhile. Barbers, as you know, are not all alike. Would you rather have 10 barbers in your neighborhood, 2 of whom cut your hair just the way you like it and are always ready to serve you instantly because they are always underemployed; or would you prefer 5 who charge less, but none of whom ever manages to do the perfect job you crave and all of whom are always crowded? The answer, undoubtedly, will vary from product group to product group. This answer will depend on the extent to which an elimination of excess capacity can cut average total cost and prices (this will be the more likely, for example, the higher total fixed costs are); it will also depend on the degree to which products within their class can be substituted for one another (whether you think, for example, that all barbers are pretty much alike or that they differ as night does from day).

THE NEW THEORY OF CONTESTABLE MARKETS

In 1883, the French economist Joseph Bertrand severely criticized the Cournot model noted earlier in this chapter. Why, he argued, should we picture firms determining their output quantities—

given assumed quantities of their competitors—and then letting the market determine the equilibrium price? Isn't it just as possible that firms first determine their product price—given assumed *prices* of their competitors—and then let the market determine the quantity that can be sold and should, therefore, be produced? These questions gave rise to the **Bertrand model,** and it led to conclusions quite different from Cournot's. In fact, the Bertrand approach to modeling oligopoly behavior led to the conclusion that even oligopolists would charge prices equal to marginal cost!

Consider, argued Bertrand, two firms in an industry, both charging price above marginal cost initially. If the firms are selling a homogeneous product, Firm 1 can lower its price slightly below that of Firm 2 and will instantly gain the entire market. Firm 2 can then do the same, and the process will continue until both charge a price equal to marginal cost. Thus competition, even between two firms only, leads to the perfectly competitive end result.

Recently, the Bertrand model has been extended to include potential as opposed to actual competition. A number of economists have argued that the very threat of other firms entering a market will influence the behavior of existing firms in such a way as to bring about competitive results. And these economists have challenged the traditional classification of market types (ranging from the extremes of perfect competition and monopoly to the intermediate structures of oligopoly and monopolistic competition) and have suggested as more useful the study of **contestable markets.**[3] Entry into such a market is absolutely free and exit from it absolutely costless, just as in perfect competition, but the other aspects of perfect competition (the presence of large numbers of independent buyers and also of sellers, homogeneity of product, and perfect

knowledge relevant to trading) may well be absent. Contrary to what we have noted in the preceding sections of this chapter, if a market is thus contestable, even if it contains only a few firms (oligopoly) or many firms selling differentiated products (monopolistic competition), the long-run industry equilibrium cannot contain positive profit nor price above marginal cost.

This result becomes obvious, it is said, the moment one focuses not on the degree of competition among existing firms *in* the market, but on the possibility of competition among existing and potential firms *for* the market. Consider Figure 8.2 on p. 258. Under the assumptions of the oligopoly model (which include difficult entry), the profit shown there (shaded) could easily persist in the long run. If the market were contestable, however, outsiders could turn a quick profit by making hit-and-run attacks on the existing firms, charging some price below $1 for the current quantity (of 800 million packs of cigarettes), while selling additional units at prices along line *as* and producing them at marginal costs along *os*. Or consider panel (b) of Figure 8.8 on p. 268. According to the new theory, point *e* will not be the long-run equilibrium because new entrants can sell 30 haircuts below $5 each, while making up for the implied loss by selling additional units at prices (along *eg*) above marginal costs (along *dg*). We will not pursue the new theory here because its main usefulness seems to lie in analyses of multiproduct firms and returns to scale that go beyond the intended scope of this book.[4]

APPLICATIONS

Application 1: Mergers

An obvious way for oligopolistic firms to escape the uncertainty of rival reactions—if they cannot establish a formal cartel and if they do not wish to rely on such informal and inevitably imperfect

[3]William J. Baumol, "Contestable Markets: An Uprising in the Theory of Industry Structure," *The American Economic Review,* March 1982, pp. 1–15; and William J. Baumol, John C. Panzar, and Robert D. Willig, *Contestable Markets and the Theory of Industry Structure* (San Diego: Harcourt Brace Jovanovich, 1982).

[4]Michael Spence, "Contestable Markets and the Theory of Industry Structure: A Review Article," *Journal of Economic Literature,* September 1983, pp. 981–90.

means of collusion as price leadership—is to eliminate their rivals by merging with them. **Mergers** involve the direct purchase of the assets of one firm by another. Such mergers can be **horizontal mergers,** among firms that sell closely related products in the same geographic market—as when one of two electric power companies in a city merges with the other. Mergers can also be **vertical mergers,** in which the merging units are related as suppliers and users of each other's products—as when an electric power company merges, on the one hand, with the crude oil refiners and railroads that supply it with fuel oil and, on the other hand, with the aluminum producers that use electric power. Mergers can also be **conglomerate mergers** among firms that have neither competitive nor buyer-seller relations but operate in many industries and, perhaps, even countries. In the United States three distinct waves of merger activity can be identified.

The First Wave. A first wave of mergers, totaling 2,890, occurred during 1896–1903. These mergers were mostly horizontal ones. For example, the Standard Oil Company ended up with 90 percent of the U.S. petroleum refining capacity, U.S. Steel with 65 percent of U.S. steel-making capacity, the American Can Company with 90 percent of the tin can market, and American Tobacco with 90 percent of the tobacco products market. Similar successes were achieved by Allis-Chalmers, the Corn Products Refining Company (now CPC International), Du Pont, Eastman Kodak, International Harvester, International Paper, International Salt, National Lead (now NL Industries), Pittsburgh Plate Glass (now PPG Industries), Standard Sanitary (now American Standard), United Fruit (now United Brands), United Shoe Machinery, U.S. Gypsum, U.S. Rubber (now Uniroyal), and more.

The Second Wave. A second wave of 6,848 mergers occurred during 1923–33. These mergers were predominantly vertical ones and involved firms in such industries as automobiles, chemicals, food, metals, and petroleum.

The Third Wave. A third wave of mergers, totalling 17,307, occurred during 1950–69. Many of these mergers were conglomerate ones. Such mergers were not necessarily designed to gain monopoly, but served to reduce risk by diversifying operations. Sometimes, such diversification is achieved through **product-extension mergers,** as when the merging firms do not directly compete but use related production processes or marketing channels. (Consider how Procter and Gamble produced detergents and once tried to move into the liquid bleach market by merging with Clorox.) At other times, diversification is achieved through **market-extension mergers,** involving firms in the same line of business but in different geographic areas. (Consider how Kroger acquired more supermarkets in new geographic areas.) Other conglomerate mergers, however, cannot be classified as either of these two types. A classic example is the International Telephone and Telegraph Company (ITT). It started out as a communications company and still operates as such in 123 countries. As a natural move, it branched into the manufacture of telephone equipment. But before long it also rented cars (Avis); it built homes (Levitt and Sons); it baked bread (Continental); it operated hotels and motor inns (Sheraton); it made consumer loans; it produced glass and sand; it processed data; it sold insurance, ran secretarial schools, rented billboards, was active in publishing (Bobbs-Merrill, Putnam's), and much more! By 1980, ITT had sales of $18.5 billion and employed close to 350,000 workers, worldwide.

It is instructive to look at the annual listing in *Fortune* of the 500 largest industrial corporations. Ranked by sales in 1988, General Motors was first (with $121.1 billion in sales) and was followed (in this order) by Ford, Exxon, IBM, General Electric, Mobil, Chrysler, Texaco, du Pont, and Philip Morris (with $25.9 billion in sales). In many recent years, the sales of each of the 10 largest corporations have exceeded the revenues of each of the 50 states. And the top corporations have had sales exceeding the national income of most of the world's nations! In 1984, while corporations as a group made 91 percent of private business sales in the United States, the 100 largest industrial corporations alone accounted for almost 12 percent, and the 500 largest for more than 17 percent. Just 3,000 firms like them could have supplied *everything* all types of private firms were supplying.

Application 2: "False" Wants Versus "True" Needs

In recent years, some economists have moved the subject of advertising from the realm of *positive theory* (which, as we noted in Chapter 1, seeks to explain what *is*) into the realm of *normative statements* (which seek to teach us what *ought to be*). Harvard's John Kenneth Galbraith, groups of "radical" economists, and others have argued that advertising is bad for us. As they see it, advertising largely misinforms people; it manipulates them into wanting products they do not really need. Thus people buy white bread, we are told, and soft drinks and TV dinners, the nutritional values of which are pure fantasy. People waste money on deodorants, electric toothbrushes, liquor, and tobacco. And they suffocate themselves in machinery: airplanes, boats, cars, dishwashers, lawnmowers, snowmobiles, and vacuum cleaners. Such is the power of Madison Avenue! Indeed, without it, these critics assert, scarcity would be a thing of the past. (In terms of Figure 1.1, "The Scarcity Problem" on p. 5, without advertising the left-hand circle would presumably shrink to be equal to or smaller than the right-hand one.)

The Creation of "False" Wants.   Advertising critics admit that people do, of course, have certain legitimate material wants. They need enough food, clothing, shelter, and medical care to keep the body safe and sound. But, essentially, these "true" needs are simple and minimal. What then is the origin of "false" wants? That is a long story, according to these critics:

People are born with few innate desires, with wants that are *theirs* in the ultimate sense of being fixed in their genes. Beyond the liking of mother's milk and the disliking of loud noises

and such, it is inevitable that most preferences are learned from other people. Unfortunately, it is asserted, people are brought up to like and dislike the wrong things in our society. People are not being informed; they are being deformed. They are not taught what is good for them and then set free to be agents of their own will. Instead they are made into sheep that follow the interests of a host of hidden and not so hidden persuaders. Parents and playmates, neighbors and teachers, businesses and governments all join in a ceaseless effort to brainwash the young into "needing" a multitude of material things. Before they are grown up, such wants have become as natural as the very air they breathe. Yet most of these wants are false.

Consider, critics say, the sad example set by parents: They dare not reject the materialistic goals sought by their neighbors. The social isolation resulting from being "different" is considered worse than death itself. So they do what the majority does, wasting day after day, year after year, in the pursuit of gadgets to "keep up with the Joneses." Getting no support from their parents, children naturally cave in to a similar fear of ostracism. They keep up with their peers, accumulating lollipops and tricycles today, clothes and sports cars tomorrow. The drive to acquire things becomes an addiction before they even reach school. And teachers, it is said, lovingly nourish the poisonous seed that has been planted. They do not really care to take children on exciting adventures in human enlightenment or even to teach them cognitive abilities. Note, we are told, how often the natural curiosity of children is met with insincere answers, subtle condescension, and even open disrespect; note how original thinking is discouraged in favor of learning "the facts." Note how children in school are taught the very traits that will allow them to make money later in life to satisfy their "needs": They must be punctual and disciplined; they must patiently wait for rewards; above all, they must conform.

All this conditioning is further reinforced, we are told, by ceaseless advertising on the part of firms and by propaganda on the part of government. Business and government leaders join in exploiting for their own ends the materialist cravings instilled in people. Corporate executives or generals, seeking to build new empires for themselves, easily persuade people to spend their incomes on a new type of car today or to tax themselves for new types of weaponry tomorrow. And, crippled by their inability to think for themselves and to make decisions for their own good, people succumb to the deception of professional persuaders. Consumer sovereignty in the marketplace becomes a farce. Rather than calling the tune on what is produced, households dance to the siren song of Madison Avenue. Democracy becomes a mockery too. The whole process is *reversed:* At the ballot box, sovereign citizens do not instruct their government, but officials tell voters how to behave in a way the officials have already determined.

Thus, advertising critics conclude, people end up being automatons, helpless puppets moved by strings behind their backs. They veritably sleepwalk through life, dominated by false wants and falsely believing that their satisfaction will lead to happiness. How much better life would be, they say, if we would silence the intrusive, raucous, ugly voices of the advertisers!

Criticizing the Critics. Other observers of contemporary life, however, are disturbed by claims that advertisers create "false" wants. Sure enough, they say, firms and governments do advertise and propagandize, but they do not create "false" wants. They merely identify wants that already exist, and they try to persuade people to satisfy them in particular ways. For example, all people at all times and in all places want food. Although the "manipulators" have nothing to do with this fact, they might try to channel such a basic desire toward ice cream— and Baskin-Robbins ice cream at that. Similarly, all people want clothing, but they might be induced to satisfy this basic want with long skirts today, short ones tomorrow, and pants thereafter—Robert Hall pants at that. People

want beauty, cleanliness, excitement, mobility, shelter, and sex. The "manipulators" do not create these desires either, we are told, but they do their best to direct them: toward RCA Beethoven records, Sweet Life herbal essence shampoo, and scenic rides in Schweizer sailplanes; toward Ford Fiestas, American Barn homes, and *Playboy* magazines. Indeed, it is argued, the *limited* power of the alleged manipulators is evidenced by their preoccupation with market surveys, by their failure to launch 80 to 90 percent of all technically successful new products at all (because they do not survive market research) and by their withdrawal of a third to a half of those products that are launched (because they fail to sell sufficiently during the first year). At the same time, the *thoughtful* appraisal of their own choices by households is evidenced by their refusal to make repeat purchases where their basic desires have not been satisfied by a specific product, by their purchase of disinterested advice (an appraiser's, before buying a house and a mechanic's before buying a used car), and by their subscription to consumer magazines. The manipulation of votes is, similarly, highly exaggerated. Therefore, it is concluded, we better accept people's spending decisions and political votes as expressions of their "true" wants. Those who would deny the value of these decisions are simply would-be dictators who would love to impose their own tastes on others. These tastes are usually those of an arrogant culture élite that claims to *know* that Beaujolais is better than Budweiser, camping in the High Sierras is preferable to snowmobiling in Iowa, and a visit to the Louvre is more tasteful than one to Miami Beach.

There is simply no way, the critics' critics conclude, to separate "false" wants from "true" needs. Who among the billions of people on earth could possibly be trusted to do so? So we must, in the end, accept people's own words and consider every expression of material wants as an expression of true material need. There is simply no objective way of making moral judgments about the material wants people express, ranking material wants on a scale of better or worse, approving of some and disapproving of others. Certainly, their professional skills do not endow economists with any special ability to decide for others which goods are truly good for them and which are ''bads'' in disguise.

Application 3: Industrial Organization

Market structures that fall between the polar cases of perfect competition and pure monopoly are of obviously great importance. By pointing to this crucial middle area, Chamberlin revised microeconomic theory drastically and permanently. But he also set in motion a blending of abstract price theory with empirical research that gave rise to a new specialization within economic science: **industrial organization.** While microeconomic theorists thrive on simplicity and rigor and like best models focusing on the barest of essentials, the practitioners of industrial organization lean toward explanations of market structure, behavior, and performance that are rich in institutional and quantitative detail. Let us consider some of the institutional and quantitative detail that industrial organization economists would add to the theoretical apparatus discussed earlier in this chapter.

Indexes of Industrial Concentration. To study the exact extent to which particular markets are dominated by a few large firms, one can construct **concentration ratios,** each one of which equals the percentage of industry sales attributable to a given number of the largest firms, usually the 4, 8, 20, and 50 largest companies. Thus a 4-firm concentration ratio of 62 would indicate that the 4 largest firms in the industry accounted for 62 percent of industry sales in a given year.

A 1972 study of 450 U.S. industries revealed that this 4-firm concentration ratio was between 0 and 19 for 87 industries, between 20 and 39 for 168 of them, between 40 and 59 for another 118, and at 60 or above for the remaining 77 industries. Table 8.1 contains much richer detail.

To some extent, large concentration ratios, such as those of Table 8.1, may even *understate* the market power of firms, for the ratios refer to the nation as a whole. Many markets, however, are effectively limited to a much smaller area because of such factors as prohibitive transportation costs, perishable products, and so on. Suppose there were in a hypothetical industry 1,000 producers, all of equal size. Then the 4 ''largest'' companies would ship 4/1,000 of output, or .4 percent. If producers competed on a national scale, buyers everywhere would have 1,000 sellers to choose from, and the low concentration ratio might correctly indicate, at least so far as *numbers* are concerned, that perfect competition exists in the industry. Yet, if each firm was the sole supplier in a three-county area and transportation beyond that area was impossible or difficult, each firm would have something close to a monopoly. Yet, because the concentration ratio is calculated on a national basis, it would not reflect this monopoly situation.

However, a high concentration ratio does not necessarily denote imperfect competition. Imports from abroad (of great importance in the case of motor vehicles) may substantially alter the picture. Thus the 4 largest firms may account for 100 percent of domestic shipments, yet they may supply only 1 percent of the total sold, if imports are of overwhelming importance. Other perfect substitutes may also be available in large quantities domestically (such as recycled aluminum).

Finally, the meaning of the industry classification must be carefully assessed. ''Calculating/accounting machines'' (see Table 8.1), for instance, is a broad category. Although the 4 largest firms supply 73 percent of shipments, we might want to know what these shipments are. It may turn out that each of these firms supplies 100 percent of *particular* machines that have no good substitutes; then the ratio understates what it is supposed to test. Vice versa, ''cereal breakfast foods'' may be too narrow a category. There are undoubtedly excellent breakfast-food substitutes. Even though 4 companies make 90 percent of

TABLE 8.1

Concentration Ratios in the United States, 1972

Industry	4-Firm Ratio	8-Firm Ratio	Number of Firms
Electron receiving tubes	95	99	21
Motor vehicles, car bodies	93	99	165
Primary lead	93	99	12
Cereal breakfast foods	90	98	34
Electric lamps	90	94	103
Turbines and generators	90	96	59
Household refrigerators/freezers	85	98	30
Cigarettes	84	n.a.	13
Cathode-ray (TV) tubes	83	97	69
Household laundry equipment	83	98	20
Carbon/graphite products	80	91	58
Primary aluminum	79	92	12
Household vacuum cleaners	75	91	34
Chocolate, cocoa products	74	88	39
Calculating/accounting machines	73	89	74
Tires, inner tubes	73	90	136
Aircraft	66	86	141
Metal cans	66	79	134
Roasted coffee	65	79	162
Sanitary paper products	63	82	72
Soap and detergents	62	74	577
Storage batteries	57	85	138
Glass containers	55	76	27
Wine, brandy	53	68	183
Malt beverages	52	70	108
Pet food	51	71	147

In many U.S. industries, concentration ratios are high and the number of firms is small.

Source: U.S. Bureau of the Census, Census of Manufactures, 1972 *Special Report Series: Concentration Ratios in Manufacturing,* MC72(SR)-2 (Washington, D.C.: U.S. Government Printing Office, 1975).

shipments, their market power may be much less than the concentration ratio seems to indicate.

The Structure of the U.S. Economy. Industrial organization economists can also tell us much about the U.S. economy as a whole. Consider a recent study by William G. Shepherd that is summarized in Table 8.2. The first column of numbers in section (A) shows the amounts of 1978 national income that were attributable to the various sectors of the U.S. economy. The sectors are listed in the order in which they appear in government publications. (There are 89 standard-industrial-

classification or SIC categories; agriculture, forestry, and fisheries take categories 0–9; services take categories 70–89.) The numbers in the first column imply that agriculture, forestry, and fishing produced a mere 3.6 percent of national income; mining (including coal, crude oil, metal, natural gas, and nonmetallic minerals) produced another 1.6 percent. Some 5.8 percent of the national income came from construction, but a hefty 30.4 percent from manufacturing activity (involving everything from aircraft engines, breakfast foods, cars, and cement to gasoline, heavy machinery, steel, and soap). Transportation (by air, pipeline, rail, road, and water) and public utilities (electricity, gas, and sanitation services) accounted for 10.7 percent of the total; wholesale and retail trade for another 17.3 percent. Some 13.9 percent of national income, finally, originated in finance, insurance, and real estate, and the remaining 16.7 percent in the service sector (covering anything from auto repair, barbering, domestic service, and entertainment to hotels and restaurants, legal services, and medical care). Table 8.2 tells us more than that.

Competition in the U.S. Economy. Using detailed data, Shepherd was also able to classify various economic activities in accordance with the degree of competition prevailing in the relevant markets. He used four categories: An activity was classified as *pure monopoly* when the producer's market share was at or near 100 percent, entry into the market was effectively blocked, and control over price was exercised by the producer. An activity was classified as involving a *dominant firm* when one producer had a market share of between 50 and over 90 percent

TABLE 8.2

Trends of Competition in the U.S. Economy, 1939–80

A. Sectors of the Economy	National Income in Each Sector, 1978[a]	The Share of Each Sector That Was Effectively Competitive		
		1939	1958	1980[a]
	($ billion)	(%)	(%)	(%)
Agriculture, Forestry, and Fisheries	54.7	91.6	85.0	86.4
Mining	24.5	87.1	92.2	95.8
Construction	87.6	27.9	55.9	80.2
Manufacturing	459.5	51.5	55.9	69.0
Transportation and Public Utilities	162.3	8.7	26.1	39.1
Wholesale and Retail Trade	261.8	57.8	60.5	93.4
Finance, Insurance and Real Estate	210.7	61.5	63.8	94.1
Services	245.3	53.9	54.3	77.9
Totals	**1,512.4**	**52.4**	**56.4**	**76.7**

B. Competition Categories		The Share of Each Category in National Income		
		1939	1958	1980
	($ billion)	(%)	(%)	(%)
1. Pure Monopoly	38.2	6.2	3.1	2.5
2. Dominant Firm	42.2	5.0	5.0	2.8
3. Tight Oligopoly	272.1	36.4	35.6	18.0
4. Others: Effectively Competitive	1,157.9	52.4	56.3	76.7
Totals	**1,512.4**	**100.0**	**100.0**	**100.0**

[a]1980 figures reflect competitive conditions as of 1980. The industry weights are based on 1978 data for national income, the latest year available.

Source: William G. Shepherd, "Causes of Increased Competition in the U.S. Economy, 1939–1980," *The Review of Economics and Statistics,* November 1982, pp. 613–26.

and had control over price and high profits, and when entry barriers were high. An activity was characterized as *tight oligopoly* when the 4-firm concentration ratio exceeded 60 percent, there were medium to high entry barriers, and rigid (cooperatively set) prices existed. Government-regulated firms were included in this category as well, as were firms, such as milk producers, that were actively colluding with the help of government. The remaining economic activities (loosely oligopolistic, monopolistically competitive, and perfectly competitive) were classified as *effectively competitive*. All these had in common a 4-firm concentration ratio below 40 percent, low entry barriers and unstable market shares, little collusion, flexible prices, and low profits.

Having made this classification (for the years 1939, 1958, and 1980), Shepherd reached two major conclusions: Roughly three-quarters of the U.S. economy in 1980 was effectively competitive [see the last column of section (B)]. There has been a major advance in competitiveness since 1958 [see row 4, section (B)]. Shepherd attributed this development to vigorous antitrust action, increased import competition, and deregulation.

SUMMARY

1. This chapter focuses on *imperfect competition;* that is, market situations other than pure monopoly and cartel in which individual sellers, nevertheless, face downward-sloping demand curves and thus have some measure of control over price. Two market structures can be distinguished: (a) oligopoly, in which the entry of new firms is difficult and relatively few sellers compete with one another, offering either homogeneous or differentiated products, and (b) monopolistic competition, in which the entry of new firms is easy and large numbers of sellers compete with one another, offering differentiated products. In situations of oligopoly, strategic behavior takes on crucial importance. Because the number of actors is so small and because they have conflicting interests, they are mutually conscious of the interdependence of their decisions. Economists have developed dozens of theories to capture this interdependence.

2. In Cournot's model, decisions focus on output. Each oligopolistic firm assumes that its rivals supply a fixed quantity regardless of its own decisions. The Cournot equilibrium identifies a possible outcome in which the separate output decisions of firms are consistent with one another and with market demand.

3. In Sweezy's kinked-demand-curve model, decisions focus on price and on the avoidance of price wars. The Sweezy model has a number of implications, including the likelihood of rigid oligopoly prices, even in the face of moderate changes in marginal cost or demand. Because the Sweezy model does not stand up well to empirical verification, rival models of oligopolistic pricing abound. These rival models include those stressing the importance of gentlemen's agreements and of price leadership; these models, too, are far from perfect. Among those discussed here are the low-cost firm model, the dominant-firm (or Stackelberg) model, and the entry-limit model.

4. Some oligopolists compete with each other on still another front, that of product differentiation. This, too, gives them a degree of monopoly power—even when actual differences do not exist, but buyers only imagine them. Product differentiation is difficult to analyze because of its complexity; one theoretical attempt leads to the Hotelling paradox.

5. Oligopolists, finally, compete with each other by incurring selling costs, designed to alter the demand they face. Advertising can be informative as well as persuasive, but it is next to impossible to disentangle these two. Nor is it easy to determine whether advertising (by established firms) is a barrier to entry or whether advertising (by newcomers) is an effective means of entering a market. Some evidence (that advertising lowers prices) points to the latter interpretation.

6. *Monopolistic competitors* also compete on the basis of product differentiation and advertising; they are distinguished from oligopolists by the absence of strategic behavior. The behavior of the monopolistically competitive firm can be analyzed very much like that of the pure monopoly, but there is a difference in the long run: Zero long-run profit is inevitable for the monopolistic competitor. The long-run equilibrium of monopolistic competition is also different from that of perfect competition in that *excess capacity* occurs in monopolistic competition.

7. The new theory of contestable markets extends the Bertrand model of oligopolistic price competition from actual competition to the mere threat of it. The new theory blends some of the features of perfect competition (free entry and exit) with other features of imperfect competition and suggests that the long-run outcomes derived by traditional theories of oligopoly and monopolistic competition have to be modified when markets are contestable.

8. Some of the wider applications of the tools developed here include the story of business mergers, the debate on "false" wants versus "true" needs, and the birth and nature of a new field of specialization in economics: industrial organization. (Recent research by industrial-organization specialists suggests that the U.S. economy has become considerably more competitive since the late 1950s.)

KEY TERMS

basing-point system
Bertrand model
brand loyalty
concentration ratios
conglomerate mergers
contestable markets
Cournot equilibrium
dominant firm
excess capacity

focal-point price
gentlemen's agreements
horizontal mergers
Hotelling's paradox
imperfect competition
industrial organization
informative advertising
kinked demand curve
limit price
market-extension mergers
mergers
monopolistic competition
oligopoly
persuasive advertising
price leadership
price war
product differentiation
product-extension mergers
product groups
reaction curve
selling cost
Stackelberg model
strategic behavior
vertical mergers

HANDS-ON PRACTICE

Exercise #1

Consider the two reaction curves in Figure 8.9. Determine the Cournot equilibrium for the two-firm industry in question.

Solution:

The graph shows $Q_X = 60 - \dfrac{60}{80} Q_Y = 60 - .75 Q_Y$ for X's curve. It also shows $Q_Y = 30 - \dfrac{30}{100} Q_X = 30 - .30 Q_X$ for Y's curve. Substituting, we get

FIGURE 8.9

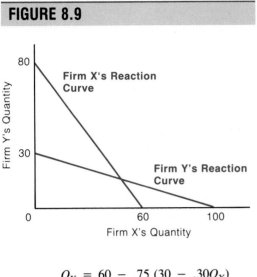

Firm X's Reaction Curve

Firm Y's Reaction Curve

Firm Y's Quantity

Firm X's Quantity

$$Q_X = 60 - .75 (30 - .30Q_X)$$
$$Q_X = 60 - 22.5 + .225Q_X$$
$$.775\,Q_X = 37.5$$
$$Q_X = 48.387$$

Hence $Q_Y = 30 - .30 (48.387) = 15.484$

Exercise #2

Consider the dominant-firm (or Stackelberg) model depicted in Figure 8.10. Graphically, determine the price set by the leader as well as the quantity sold by leader and competitive fringe.

FIGURE 8.10

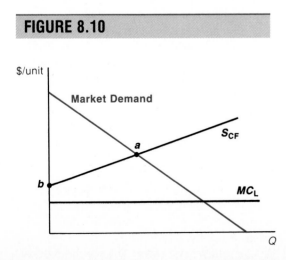

$/unit

Market Demand

S_{CF}

MC_L

Q

Solution:

See Figure 8.11. The leader's demand curve goes from c (left of intersection a) to d (right of intercept b) and on to e. This implies a relevant marginal revenue for the leader shown by MR_L. The leader maximizes profit by equating (at i) marginal revenue and marginal cost, producing quantity $Q_L = kn$ and charging price k (according to point n). At this price, the competitive fringe supplies $km = no = Q_{CF}$.

FIGURE 8.11

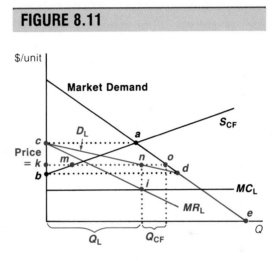

$/unit

Market Demand

D_L

S_{CF}

Price = k

MC_L

MR_L

Q_L Q_{CF}

Q

QUESTIONS AND PROBLEMS

1. In the section on Cournot's model, "Decision Making under Oligopoly: Output Quantity," it is claimed that the two firms discussed there have an incentive to form a cartel, cut production, and raise price. Write the perfect cartel agreement for this case: the quantity each firm must produce, the price it must charge, the increase in profit it can expect.

2. Figure 8.2, "Sweezy's Model," shows the conventional kinked demand curve for a timid, pessimistic oligopolist. Now draw a different kinked demand curve (and the associated curve of marginal revenue) for an aggressive, optimistic oligopolist.

3. Figure 8.3, "Implications of Kinked Oligopoly Demand," illustrates that price can be rigid even in the face of moderate changes in marginal cost or demand. Show the price and quantity effects for:

  a.   a profit-maximizing *oligopoly* of *major* changes in marginal cost and demand.

  b.   a profit-maximizing *monopoly* of *any* changes in marginal cost and demand.

  c.   a profit-maximizing *perfect competitor* of *any* changes in marginal cost and demand.

4. Consider Figure 8.7, "Hotelling's Paradox."

  a.   What would be the ideal and actual location of a third firm, C, that appeared on the scene?

  b.   How would you modify the entire analysis if the customers were not distributed uniformly over geographic space or along the continuum for any other characteristic?

  c.   Do you think there are "product-characteristics leaders" as there are price leaders?

5. Can you think of other examples besides the ones mentioned in the text where Hotelling's paradox is at work? (*Hints:* Look at a history book and study Goldwater's presidential campaign, then McGovern's. Consider the sameness of automobiles, economics texts, and television programs; consider why bars, barbershops, and gas stations locate right next to each other.)

6. **Mr. A:** Advertising, besides supporting product variety, provides another major benefit not mentioned in this chapter's text: It subsidizes the mass communications media. In recent years, it has provided 50 percent of periodical, 70 percent of newspaper, and almost 100 percent of (noneducational) radio and television station revenue.

Ms. B: You call that a benefit? Advertisers want to reach the largest possible audience; the media make sure to reach it by appealing to the lowest possible common denominator. So we get scandal sheets and television's wasteland.

What do you think?

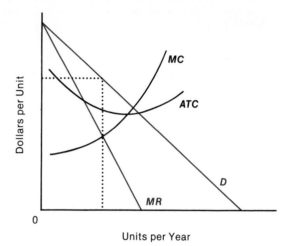

7. The accompanying graph shows a monopolistically competitive firm in short-run equilibrium.

  a.   Why is it in *short-run* equilibrium?

  b.   What will happen in the long run?

  c.   Given long-run equilibrium, how would advertising alter the picture? (Consider both successful and unsuccessful advertising.)

8. In 1972, the 4-firm concentration ratio in the ready-mixed concrete industry was 6, the 8-firm ratio was 10, and the number of firms was 3,978. The corresponding three numbers for bread and cake were 29, 39, 2,800; for fluid milk, 18, 26, and 2,024; for newspapers, 17, 28, and 7,461. Do you think these figures understate or overstate monopoly power? Why?

*9. In a market supplied by a dominant firm and a competitive fringe, market demand is $Q_M = 500,000 - 40P$. The supply by the fringe is $Q_F = 10P$. The dominant firm's total cost is $TC = 500,000 + 1,000Q_D + .004Q_D^2$, where Q_D is the demand as seen by the dominant firm.

  a.   Determine the market price that the profit-maximizing dominant firm will set.

  b.   What will be the dominant firm's market share?

  c.   What will be the size of its profit?

10. Table 8.3 below comes from the same source as Table 8.2. For each of the eight sectors of the economy, determine the 1939–1980 trend in competitiveness. (*Hint:* You will have to cal-

TABLE 8.3

The Trend of Competition by Sectors of the U.S. Economy, 1939–1980

SIC Category	Sector	Competition Category[a]	Amount of National Income in Each Category ($ million)		
			1939	1958	1980
0–9	Agriculture, Forestry, and Fisheries	1	0	0	0
		2	0	0	0
		3	507	2,681	7,462
		4	5,519	15,229	47,261
10–14	Mining	1	0	0	0
		2	0	0	0
		3	211	443	1,116
		4	1,422	5,254	25,354
15–17	Construction	1	0	0	0
		2	0	0	0
		3	1,688	8,367	17,346
		4	654	10,624	70,247
20–39	Manufacturing	1	135	372	0
		2	2,053	6,777	18,032
		3	6,588	40,358	124,428
		4	9,318	60,234	317,042
40–49	Transportation and Public Utilities	1	3,827	9,557	38,171
		2	120	7,974	24,133
		3	3,856	9,917	35,828
		4	743	9,683	64,186
50–59	Trade	1	0	0	0
		2	0	0	0
		3	5,313	23,019	17,238
		4	7,291	35,227	244,542
60–69	Finance, Insurance, and Real Estate	1	0	0	0
		2	880	203	0
		3	2,194	14,582	12,384
		4	4,917	26,090	198,351
70–89	Services	1	36	0	0
		2	213	1,185	0
		3	3,231	16,364	54,296
		4	4,074	20,831	190,950
Totals		1	3,998	9,929	38,171
		2	3,266	16,139	42,165
		3	23,588	115,731	272,098
		4	33,938	183,172	1,157,933
Percent of Total National Income		1	6.17	3.06	2.53
		2	5.04	4.97	2.79
		3	36.41	35.61	18.02
		4	52.38	56.37	76.66

[a] 1 is "pure monopoly," 2 is "dominant firm," 3 is "tight oligopoly," and 4 is "effectively competitive" (loose oligopoly, monopolistic competition, and pure competition).

culate percentage figures from the dollar figures similar to the analogous computation made in the color box at the bottom of the table for the economy as a whole.)

11. Depict your solutions to problem 9 graphically. Can you tell the fringe firms' *quasi-rent*, a term that refers to the excess of total revenue over variable costs?

SELECTED READINGS

Adams, Walter, ed. *The Structure of American Industry*, 5th edition. New York: Macmillan, 1977.

An example of industrial-organization economics at its best; contains studies of the structure, conduct, and performance of 13 industries.

Archibald, G. C. "Chamberlin vs. Chicago," *Review of Economic Studies*, October 1961, pp. 2–28.

Contrasts Chamberlin's views on imperfect competition with those of the Chicago school (*see* Stigler below).

Bain, J. S. *Barriers to New Competition*. Cambridge, Mass.: Harvard University Press, 1956.

An important work in industrial organization.

Baumol, William J., John C. Panzar, and Robert D. Willig, *Contestable Markets and the Theory of Industry Structure*. San Diego, Calif.: Harcourt Brace Jovanovich, 1982.

A major work on contestable markets. For a review, *see* Michael Spence, "Contestable Markets and the Theory of Industry Structure," *Journal of Economic Literature*, September 1983, pp. 981–90.

Chamberlin, Edward H. *The Theory of Monopolistic Competition: A Reorientation of the Theory of Value*, 8th edition. Cambridge, Mass.: Harvard University Press, 1965.

This edition of the work also contains a bibliography of some 1,500 articles about Chamberlin's work.

Comanor, William S., and Thomas Wilson. *Advertising and Market Power*. Cambridge, Mass.: Harvard University Press, 1975.

Dewey, Donald. *The Theory of Imperfect Competition: A Radical Reconstruction*. New York: Columbia University Press, 1969.

A critical review of the now widely accepted Chamberlin-Robinson achievement.

Galbraith, John Kenneth. *The Affluent Society*. Boston: Houghton Mifflin, 1958.

Contains the well-known attack on advertising as a violation of consumer sovereignty.

Hayek, Friedrich A. von. "The Non-Sequitur of the 'Dependence Effect,'" *Southern Economic Journal*, April 1961, pp. 346–48.

A critique of Galbraith's view on advertising and consumer sovereignty, written by the 1974 Nobel Prize winner in economics.

Kuenne, Robert E., ed. *Monopolistic Competition Theory: Studies in Impact*. New York: Wiley, 1967.

Contains 17 essays written by major scholars in honor of Chamberlin.

Lindbeck, Assar. *The Political Economy of the New Left*, 2nd edition. New York: Harper and Row, 1977.

Contains a superb discussion of the debate on "false" wants versus "true" needs.

Meade, James E. "The Optimal Balance Between Economies of Scale and Variety of Products: An Illustrative Model," *Economica*, August 1974, pp. 359–67.

The 1977 Nobel Prize winner in economics discusses the trade-off, in a monopolistically competitive industry, between excess capacity and product variety on the one hand and lower average cost but less variety on the other.

Nagle, Thomas T. "Do Advertising-Profitability Studies Really Show That Advertising Creates a Barrier to Entry?" *The Journal of Law and Economics*, October 1981, pp. 333–49.

Rejects the conclusions of cross-sectional empirical studies that depict advertising as a barrier to entry and presents limited evidence that advertising positively affects the competitiveness of an industry.

Nicholls, William. *Price Policies in the Cigarette Industry*. Nashville, Tenn.: Vanderbilt University Press, 1951.

One of many excellent case studies of price leadership.

Plott, Charles R. "Industrial Organization Theory and Experimental Economics," *Journal of Economic Literature*, December 1982, pp. 1485–1527.

A fascinating report on the insights gained from experimental studies that indicate how market institutions and practices influence market performance.

Robinson, Joan V. *The Economics of Imperfect Competition*. London: Macmillan, 1933.

Like Chamberlin's work noted above, a classic.

Schelling, Thomas C. *The Strategy of Conflict*. Cambridge, Mass.: Harvard University Press, 1960.

On the theory of focal points.

Stackelberg, Heinrich von. *The Theory of the Market Economy*. New York: Oxford University Press, 1952.

The Stackelberg model of oligopolistic behavior (pp. 195 ff.), first published in 1934.

Stigler, George J. "Monopolistic Competition in Retrospect." In *Five Lectures on Economic Problems.* New York: Macmillan, 1949.

> A severe criticism of the Chamberlinian revolution, written by the 1982 Nobel Prize winner in economics.

Stigler, George J. "The Literature of Economics: The Case of the Kinked Oligopoly Demand Curve," *Economic Inquiry,* April 1978, pp. 185–204.

> A superb summary with an excellent bibliography.

Stigler, George J., and Kenneth E. Boulding. *AEA Readings in Price Theory.* Chicago: Irwin, 1952.

> See especially Chap. 20 (Sweezy's model), Chap. 21 (Stigler's criticism of Sweezy), and Chap. 23 (Hotelling's paradox).

Stigler, George J., and James K. Kindahl. *The Behavior of Industrial Prices.* New York: National Bureau of Economic Research and Columbia University Press, 1970.

> Shows oligopolistic actual transactions prices are much more flexible than officially quoted prices.

Stiglitz, Joseph E., and G. Frank Mathewson. *New Developments in the Analysis of Market Structure.* Cambridge, Mass.: MIT Press, 1986.

COMPUTER PROGRAMS

The KOHLER-3 personal-computer diskettes that accompany this book contain two programs of particular interest to this chapter:

8. Oligopoly and Monopolistic Competition includes a 25-question multiple-choice test with immediate responses to incorrect answers as well as numerous exercises concerning the Cournot equilibrium and the dominant-firm model.

Appendix A. Solving Simultaneous Equations will be helpful in performing the exercises.

ANALYTICAL EXAMPLE 8.1

THE COST OF AUTOMOBILE MODEL CHANGES

The efforts by some firms to differentiate their product from those of competitors are very costly, indeed. Some people argue that this product differentiation represents a waste of resources that could better be used to produce other goods. Others maintain that the ability to choose among many versions of a basic product makes people better off. Three economists decided to investigate the factual side of the issue. They

Year (1)	Millions of Extra Dollars Compared to 1949 Model Cars				Extra Dollars per Car (6)
	Retooling Cost (2)	Producer's Direct Cost[a] (3)	Consumer's Gasoline Cost (4)	Total (5) = (2) + (3) + (4)	
1950	20	−27	13	6	1
1951	45	267	36	348	65
1952	82	460	102	644	148
1953	246	436	161	844	138
1954	264	1,072	240	1,576	362
1955	469	2,425	372	3,266	527
1956	336	3,040	590	3,966	630
1957	772	4,048	806	5,626	905
1958	626	2,354	949	3,924	922
1959	532	3,675	1,147	5,354	962
1960	537	3,456	1,346	5,339	888

[a]Extra factory and selling costs due to the production of larger and heavier cars with automatic transmissions, increased horsepower, power steering, power brakes.

estimated the annual cost of auto model changes from 1950–1960 compared to the 1949 model. As the table below shows, these extra costs reached a figure as high as $5.6 billion (in 1957). In many years, they amounted to almost a quarter of the total cost of a car.

Source: Franklin M. Fisher, Zvi Griliches, and Carl Kaysen, "The Cost of Automobile Model Changes Since 1949," *The Journal of Political Economy,* October 1962, pp. 433–51. Table adapted by permission of the University of Chicago Press. Copyright 1962 by the University of Chicago.

ANALYTICAL EXAMPLE 8.2

ADVERTISING AND THE PRICE OF EYEGLASSES

It is often claimed that advertising, by creating loyalty to brand names, supports the positions of would-be monopolists. Yet the fact that advertising can also be seen as an important weapon for those who want to challenge established firms by competing with them through lower prices was suggested recently by a study of the market for eyeglasses. The data of the accompanying table are based on a 1963 national sample of 634 individuals who obtained eyeglasses, had eye examinations, or both. The prices paid were compared for states in which professional societies of opticians and optometrists forbade their members to advertise (and in which this prohibition was even written into law) and for states that allowed such advertising—see rows (1)

Population Group	Average Prices in States with Complete Advertising Restrictions	Average Prices in States with No Advertising Restrictions	Difference
	Eyeglasses Alone		
(1) All individuals	$33.04	$26.34	$ 6.70
(2) Individuals in Texas, North Carolina, and the District of Columbia only	$37.48	$17.98	$19.50
	Eyeglasses and Eye Examinations Combined		
(3) All individuals	$40.96	$37.10	$ 3.86
(4) Individuals in Texas, North Carolina, and the District of Columbia only	$50.73	$29.97	$20.76

and (3). In every case, advertising went hand in hand with lower prices. This result showed even more strongly when comparing prices only in the most extreme cases—rows (2) and (4)— in which the ban on advertising was strictest (North Carolina) or the freedom to advertise was of longest standing (Texas, District of Columbia).

Postscript: In 1978, in the wake of a 1977 U.S. Supreme Court decision on advertising by lawyers (see Close-Up 8.3), the Federal Trade Commission ruled restrictions on eyeglass advertising illegal. The result was a widespread drop in eyeglass prices.

Source: Lee Benham, "The Effect of Advertising on the Price of Eyeglasses," *The Journal of Law and Economics,"* October 1972, pp. 337–52. Table adapted by permission of the University of Chicago Press. Copyright 1972 by the University of Chicago.

ANALYTICAL EXAMPLE 8.3

ADVERTISING AND THE PRICE AND QUALITY OF OPTOMETRIC SERVICES

Restrictions on advertising have been a long-standing feature of most markets for professional services, such as those supplied by physicians and optometrists. Professional associations have consistently argued that advertising should be forbidden because it would lead to an erosion of service quality: Price-cutting advertisers would attract more customers, hence spend less time with each and give less careful examinations; nonadvertisers would have to follow the same path lest they lose their clientele; and technically ignorant consumers would have no way of detecting the general quality deterioration and thus could not resist it.

Yet, in 1980, a federal appeals court opened the way for physicians and other professionals to advertise fees and services. One economist has tested the quality-erosion hypothesis by examining the first effects of the court's ruling on the market for optometric services. The crucial results are given in the accompanying table.

Optometrists Operating in Cities Where Advertising Is Allowed	Price Effect[a] (per exam)	Quality Effect[b] (per exam)
1. Not advertising (by choice)	$ −2.59	+11.71 min.
2. Advertising via storefront	−7.56	−.87 min.
3. Advertising via media (small firm)	−11.13	−3.14 min.
4. Advertising via media (national chain)	−12.35	−4.89 min.

[a]Compared to the $28.92 price in cities prohibiting advertising.
[b]Compared to the 41.23 minutes spent in cities prohibiting advertising.

Advertising caused a substantial decline in the average price per exam compared to cities where advertising was prohibited. This decline affected all optometrists, even those (row 1) that chose not to advertise and those (row 2) that only advertised via their storefronts. If quality is measured by the time spent per exam, the quality of work done by the advertisers (rows 2–4) did, indeed, decline, but—contrary to the above hypothesis—the quality of work done by nonadvertisers actually rose. In addition, nonadvertisers were so numerous that the *average* market quality in cities allowing advertising was greater, not smaller. Given the lower prices, this implies considerable social benefits from loosening restrictions on advertising.

Source: John E. Kwoka, Jr., "Advertising and the Price and Quality of Optometric Services," *The American Economic Review,* March 1984, pp. 211–16.

ANALYTICAL EXAMPLE 8.4

INDUSTRIAL CONCENTRATION BY PURE CHANCE

Among many other things, industrial-organization economists study the reasons for observed degrees of concentration. They find, of course, the expected reasons: economies of scale, legal barriers to entry. Yet one economist has pointed to an unusual possibility: the operation of sheer luck.

	4-Firm Concentration Ratio at Year:							
Simulation	1	20	40	60	80	100	120	140
Run 1	8.0	19.5	29.3	36.3	40.7	44.9	38.8	41.3
Run 2	8.0	20.3	21.4	28.1	37.5	41.6	50.8	55.6
Run 3	8.0	18.8	28.9	44.6	43.1	47.1	56.5	45.0
Run 4	8.0	20.9	26.7	31.8	41.9	41.0	64.5	59.8
Run 5	8.0	23.5	33.2	43.8	60.5	60.5	71.9	63.6
Run 6	8.0	21.3	26.6	29.7	35.8	51.2	59.1	72.9
Run 7	8.0	21.1	31.4	29.0	42.8	52.8	50.3	53.1
Run 8	8.0	21.6	23.5	42.2	47.3	64.4	73.1	76.6
Run 9	8.0	18.4	29.3	38.0	45.3	42.5	43.9	52.4
Run 10	8.0	20.0	29.7	43.7	40.1	43.1	42.9	42.9
Run 11	8.0	23.9	29.1	29.5	43.2	50.1	57.1	71.7
Run 12	8.0	15.7	23.3	24.1	34.5	41.1	42.9	53.1
Run 13	8.0	23.8	31.3	44.8	43.5	42.8	57.3	65.2
Run 14	8.0	17.8	23.3	29.3	54.2	51.4	56.0	64.7
Run 15	8.0	21.8	18.3	23.9	31.9	33.5	43.9	65.7
Run 16	8.0	17.5	27.1	28.3	30.7	39.9	37.7	35.3
Average	**8.0**	**20.4**	**27.0**	**33.8**	**42.1**	**46.7**	**52.9**	**57.4**

F. M. Scherer conducted a computer-simulation experiment for an imaginary industry containing 50 identical firms and having neither economies of scale nor legal entry barriers. Each firm initially held a market share of 2 percent. Scherer instructed his computer to let the industry grow at 6 percent per year but to give each individual firm a random probability of growing somewhat faster or slower than this average. (This average growth rate and the variability of individual firms' growth around the average were set equal to 1954–60 figures actually observed among *Fortune*'s list of 500 top industrial corporations.) The computer followed the fortunes of each firm through 140 years of simulated history; this experiment was repeated 16 times. The result, shown in the accompanying table, is truly amazing.

Within a few decades, the imaginary industry ended up with the very degree of concentration observed for real-world U.S. manufacturing industries—in spite of the assumed absence of the usual causes of concentration. After a simulated century had elapsed, it was not uncommon to find a single leading firm holding 25–35 percent of the market, while its former equals held .1 percent! How did Scherer explain it? By pure chance: Some firms got an early run of luck and grew faster than the average for several years in a row. Once they led the pack, it was harder for other firms to catch up because everybody had an equal chance to grow by a given percentage in every year.

Source: F. M. Scherer, *Industrial Market Structure and Economic Performance,* 2nd edition, p. 146. Copyright © 1980 Houghton Mifflin Company. Used by permission.

CLOSE-UP 8.1

BRAND LOYALTY: THE CASE OF TURKEY MEAT

In 1965, an experiment was conducted to test the reaction of consumers to brand names. In Part I of the experiment, subjects from Detroit were handed two plates, each with a slice of turkey meat. The slices were in fact from the same turkey, but they were labeled differently. One label was that of a heavily advertised brand well known in Detroit; the other one was given an unfamiliar name. The results: 10 percent thought the slices tasted alike; 34 percent preferred the unknown brand; 56 percent preferred the known brand. In Part II of the experiment, subjects were handed two plates with tender and tough turkey meat, respectively. There were no brand labels. The results: 13 percent thought the slices tasted alike; 7 percent preferred the tough meat; 80 percent preferred the tender meat. In Part III of the experiment, subjects were asked to guess which brand the Part II samples belonged to. Some 64 percent thought that the sample they had preferred must have been the familiar brand.

Many similar experiments have shown that people can perceive actual differences in product quality in the *absence* of brand names, but that they perceive identical goods as different in the *presence* of brand names—and then prefer the familiar brand.

Source: James C. Makens, "Effect of Brand Preference Upon Consumers' Perceived Taste of Turkey Meat," *Journal of Applied Psychology,* August 1965, pp. 261–63.

CLOSE-UP 8.2

THE CONVERGENCE OF PERSONAL COMPUTERS

Not so long ago, I.B.M. and Apple personal computers were as different as a utilitarian Volvo and a sporty Porsche. Not any more—they are becoming as alike as a Pontiac and a Chevy, just as predicted by Figure 8.7, "The Hotelling Paradox." Consider how Apple's Macintosh II has picked up many features previously confined to I.B.M.: The microprocessor has been made much more powerful, the internal memory has been raised to 8 megabytes, disk drives are faster, the machine is expandable (users can add on circuit boards); software once usable on I.B.M. only (such as Lotus 1–2–3) runs on the Macintosh, and the keyboard looks more professional and invites use by office workers. On the other hand, I.B.M. has picked up on Apple features in its new PS/2:

Former Apple software runs on it (such as the Microsoft Excel spreadsheet program or Aldus Corporation's Pagemaker program), the floppy disks are sturdier 3.5″ types, there is a high-resolution screen, there is a graphics-oriented operating system, complete with "windows" and "mouse" (a pointing device), and the user manual is both shorter and easier to learn (many instructions are right on the screen).

Source: David A. Sanger, "I.B.M. and Apple Converge," *The New York Times,* November 17, 1987, pp. D1 and 5. For a similar story involving Apple computers and Sun work stations see *The New York Times,* March 10, 1989, pp. D1 and 4.

CLOSE-UP 8.3

ADVERTISING AND THE PRICE OF LEGAL SERVICES

Advertising, it is often claimed, only raises costs and, therefore, prices, but this is decidedly too simplistic a view. Until recently, for example, there was no advertising in the market for legal services. Bar associations routinely threw out members who were so "unethical" as to compete with their colleagues by advertising their fees or the nature of their services. They argued that such ads encouraged "extravagant self-laudatory brashness" and "unscrupulous solicitation" that was not designed to uphold the dignity of the profession. The object of lawyers, it was argued, was to provide service, not to make profit (a fine distinction surely lost on consumers).

Along came John Bates and Van O'Steen, law partners in Phoenix, Arizona, who defied the advertising ban. They were promptly taken to court, but eventually, on June 27, 1977, the U.S. Su-

preme Court agreed with them, citing the First Amendment guarantee of free speech.

The results have been amazing. In Phoenix, the fee for an uncontested divorce has dropped from $350 to $150. Similar price reductions have resulted all over the country for the preparation of wills, title searches, and much more. And many innovative types of services are being offered as well, from do-it-yourself divorce kits at $16.95 (instructions and forms included) to telephone consultations at $9.95.

Sources: Warren Weaver, Jr., "Court Rules Lawyer May Advertise Fee for Routine Service," *The New York Times,* June 28, 1977, pp. 1 and 14; "Publicizing Fees," *ibid.,* July 1, 1977, p. 22; "Lawyers May Now Advertise," *ibid.,* July 3, 1977, p. E5; and Carol H. Falk, "Lawyers Are Facing Surge in Competition As Courts Drop Curbs," *The Wall Street Journal,* October 18, 1978, pp. 1 and 21.

PART

4

Special Topic: The Economics of Uncertainty

These chapters study situations of uncertainty, all too common in the real world, in which economic decision makers possess less-than-complete knowledge on matters relevant to their choices. Under such circumstances, special types of models help explain the behavior of people and, ultimately, the emergence of special types of markets for insurance, gambling, commodity futures, and more.

9

Decision Theory and Game Theory

Only rarely do the actions of economic decision makers lead to unique consequences that are known with certainty in advance. In countless situations, such decision makers face a serious problem: They are called upon to choose between two or more alternative courses of action at a time when the associated consequences cannot be foreseen with certainty because they depend on the nature of some future event over which the decision maker has no control. Under such circumstances of **uncertainty** it is difficult to make a rational decision.

In this chapter, we deal with **primary uncertainty,** or **event uncertainty,** which is said to exist when certain future events, which are bound to affect the outcome of present decisions, have not yet occurred and no one can possibly know what they will be like. Consider the farmer who must choose now among plantings of alternative crops but knows that some of these crops will flourish if the season turns out to be cool and dry, while others will do so only if it is hot and wet. Consider the manufacturer who must decide now whether to introduce a new production process or to continue using the old one but who also knows that the profit consequences of either decision will differ greatly, depending on whether future oil prices (or future wages) are

low or high. Consider the marketing manager whose advice about introducing a new product (or modifying the style, packaging, or labeling of an old product) is desired now but who knows the consequences of any of these actions to be dependent on as-yet-unknown levels of future demand (which, in turn, depend crucially on the behavior of competitors). Or think of the real-estate developer who must make a commitment now to a small- or medium-sized or large-scale project; the consulting firm that must decide now to install a small or a large computer; the oil company that must drill now or sell its rights; the record producer who must initiate a major sales campaign now or abort the production of a record altogether; the independent TV producer who can submit the pilot of a new program to a network now or sell the rights to someone else; the job applicant who must decide now to work for a fixed salary or on a commission basis. In all these cases and many more, the wisdom or foolishness of any present decision will ultimately be determined by (uncontrollable) future events: by the summer's weather, by the pricing or output decisions of rival producers, by whether the demand for housing (or consulting services) turns out to be high or low, by whether oil is found at the drilling site or the test hole is dry, by whether the new record (or TV show) becomes a hit or is a failure, by whether the new employee is successful at making sales or not.

In many situations such as these, decision makers inevitably face **risk,** an uncertainty-induced chance of variation in their welfare. But note: In the following sections we will *not* emphasize the distinction between uncertainty and risk that was introduced by Frank H. Knight (1885–1972), a Biography of whom appears in Chapter 9 of the *Student Workbook* that accompanies this text. This distinction, although once followed by many economists, has largely been abandoned. Knight reserved the term *risk* for situations in which people cannot foretell the specific outcome of an action because two or more outcomes are possible but in which people do know the types of outcomes and the associated objective probabilities of their occurrence. The **objective probability** of an event is the relative frequency with which it occurs in a series of trials repeated under identical conditions. Thus we do not know whether the toss of a single coin will produce heads or tails. But we do know that one and only one of these two events must occur (the events are collectively exhaustive and mutually exclusive) and that the probability of each equals one-half. (When tossed an infinite number of times, each of the two sides will show up half the time.) In the same way, we do not know whether the use of a particular house or car will be terminated by fire or accident this year, but we do know (from statistics on large numbers of similar cases) that, say, 1 out of 250 like objects will suffer this fate.

Knight suggested, on the other hand, that the term *uncertainty* be reserved for situations in which people cannot foretell the specific outcome of an action because two or more outcomes are possible and in which people neither know the types of outcomes nor the associated objective probability distribution. Research directed toward technical change provides a fitting example. Will such efforts lead to the discovery of a new source of abundant energy? Or to new strains of wheat? And if the former, will it lead to the availability of cheap solar cells, of fusion power,

or of as-yet-undreamed-of other energy sources? No one can know even the types of all outcomes, much less the objective probabilities of their occurrence. The uniqueness of the contemplated events makes the very concept of objective probability an inappropriate one. Under such circumstances, no two individuals may agree, but each person can still attach a **subjective probability** to every imaginable outcome—can attach, that is, to each outcome a measure of personal belief in the likelihood of its occurrence.

We will ignore Knight's distinction because it has proved sterile. All decision makers must somehow forecast the future, must assign probabilities to the possible outcomes of their actions. It matters little whether these probabilities are agreed upon by everyone and, therefore, *objective* (as in situations of **Knightian risk**) or whether they are controversial and *subjective* (as in situations of **Knightian uncertainty**).[1]

DECISION THEORY: BASIC CONCEPTS

A variety of methods, collectively referred to as **decision theory,** can be employed in the systematic analysis and solution of decision-making problems that arise because uncertainty exists about future events over which the decision maker has no control but which are bound to influence the ultimate outcome of a decision. In all of these methods, certain identical elements are present; it is helpful to focus on these elements systematically when searching for a solution to a decision-making problem.

Actions, Events, Payoffs

First, each decision maker has specific decision alternatives available. In the language of decision theory, the decision maker must make a choice among various mutually exclusive **actions,** a

---

[1]For a systematic discussion of probability concepts and probability distributions, *see* Heinz Kohler, *Statistics for Business and Economics,* 2nd ed. (Glenview, Ill.: Scott, Foresman and Co., 1988), chaps 5–7.

complete list of which is symbolized by A_1, A_2, ..., A_n. A business executive, for example, might be called upon to manufacture and market a new product by taking one of two actions: A_1 = constructing a small plant; A_2 = constructing a large plant.

Second, future occurrences, not under the control of the decision maker, will affect the outcome of any present action taken by the decision maker. These occurrences are commonly referred to as **states of nature** or, more simply, as **events;** a collectively exhaustive list of mutually exclusive events is symbolized by E_1, E_2, . . ., E_n. The production and marketing of a new product, for example, might be linked with one of two events: E_1 = an environment of weak demand; E_2 = an environment of strong demand. As we shall see, probability values about such events may or may not be employed by a decision maker at the time when a choice among actions is taken.

Third, positive or negative net benefits are associated with each possible action/event combination. These net benefits are the joint outcome of choice and chance and are commonly referred to as **payoffs.** Payoffs can be measured in any kind of unit appropriate to the problem at hand: in dollars, in time, or even in utility, as we shall see. The payoffs from constructing a small plant, for example, might be annual profits of $8 million if demand is weak or $5 million if demand is strong (the smaller payoff resulting from the need, perhaps, to then run the plant above its designed

capacity if demand is strong, which leads to extremely high unit costs of production). The corresponding payoffs from a large plant might be −$2 million or +$12 million instead (the smaller payoff again, perhaps, occurring because the running of a large plant *below* its capacity also involves unusually high unit costs of production).

The Payoff Table

A decision-making situation in the context of uncertainty can be summarized in a variety of ways; one popular summary is the **payoff table,** a tabular listing of the payoffs associated with all possible combinations of actions and events. Table 9.1 is such a tabular summary for our example. Each row corresponds to one of the two possible actions; each column corresponds to one of the two possible events. The four cells of the table show the associated annual profits (in millions of dollars).

Note: In this payoff table neither action is unambiguously superior to the other in the sense that it produces payoffs that are as good as or better than those of the alternative action no matter which event occurs. If such an unambiguously superior action exists, it is called a **dominant action,** and its existence turns the alternative into an **inadmissible action** that need not be considered further because of its obvious inferiority. In our example, A_1 would be dominant if, all else being equal, the A_1/E_2 cell contained an entry of

TABLE 9.1

A Payoff Table

Actions	Events	
	E_1 = weak demand for new product	E_2 = strong demand for new product
A_1 = constructing a small plant	8	5
A_2 = constructing a large plant	−2	12

This table shows the annual profits (in millions of dollars) associated with four possible action/event combinations.

12 instead of 5; if A_1 were dominant, A_2 would be inadmissible. Under those circumstances, the decision maker could choose A_1 without hesitation and would reap a profit of \$8 million if E_1 occurred or of \$12 million if E_2 occurred. The choice of A_2 would lead to worse or at best equally good results, as the A_2 row of Table 9.1 indicates.

The Decision Tree

Another popular summary of a decision-making situation is the **decision tree;** it illustrates a decision problem by showing, in chronological order from left to right, every potential action, event, and payoff. The decision-tree diagram is particularly useful when a decision problem involves a sequence of many decisions that extend over a long stretch of time.

It is customary in decision-tree diagrams to denote any point of *choice* (at which the decision maker is in control) by a square symbol from which branches representing the possible actions of the decision maker (and, therefore, called **action branches** or **decision branches**) emanate toward the right. Such an **action point** (also variously referred to as a **decision point, decision node,** or **decision fork**) is illustrated in panel (a) of Figure 9.1, along with the relevant branches. In contrast, any point of *chance* (at which the decision maker exercises no control, but "nature" is in charge) is denoted symbolically by a circle from which branches representing the possible events confronting the decision maker (and, therefore, called **event branches** or **state-of-nature branches**) emanate toward the right. Such an **event point** (also variously referred to as a **state-of-nature point, state-of-nature node,** or **state-of-nature fork**) is illustrated in panel (b) of Figure 9.1, again with the associated branches. Panel (c), finally, shows the entire decision tree that summarizes our example.

Summarizing a decision problem, either with the help of a payoff table or a decision tree, is helpful, but it is only the first step toward a solution. A best plan of action still remains to be chosen; the following sections consider some of the criteria that might be employed to find it.

DECISION MAKING WITHOUT PROBABILITIES

Consider a situation, such as that summarized by Table 9.1 or Figure 9.1, in which a decision must be made in the face of uncertainty, but nothing is known about the likelihood of occurrence of those alternative future events that are certain to affect the eventual outcome of the present decision. Imagine that the decision maker does not even care to guess what the event probabilities might be. In such a case, it is common practice to employ one of three decision criteria: *maximin (or minimax), maximax (or minimin),* or *minimax regret.*

Maximin (or Minimax)

The first of the nonprobabilistic criteria embodies a decidedly conservative approach to decision making. It guarantees that the decision maker does no worse than achieve the best among the poorest possible outcomes. This criterion takes one of two forms, depending on whether the decision maker aims to maximize benefit or minimize cost. If maximization of benefit is the objective (as in our example above), the criterion is called **maximin** because the decision maker is to find the lowest possible (or minimum) benefit associated with each possible action, identify the highest (or maximum) benefit among these minima, and then choose the action associated with this maximum of minima (which explains the name given to this criterion). Table 9.2 illustrates how the maximin criterion would be applied to our example.

If minimization of cost is the objective (as when a firm must choose, perhaps, between the installation of alternative antipollution devices), the analogous criterion is often referred to as **minimax** because the decision maker is to find the highest possible (or maximum) cost associated with each possible action, identify the lowest (or minimum) cost among these maxima, and then choose the action associated with this minimum of maxima (which explains the name given

FIGURE 9.1

A Decision Tree

(a) Action Point and Branches

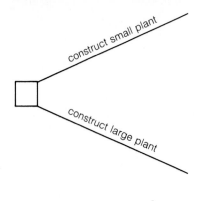

construct small plant

construct large plant

(b) Event Point and Branches

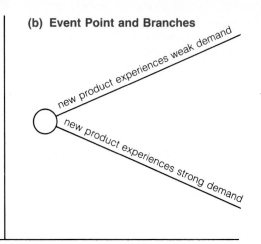

new product experiences weak demand

new product experiences strong demand

(c) Actions, Events, and Payoffs

Choice	+	Chance	=	Outcome
Action Point and Branches		**Event Points and Branches**		**Payoffs**

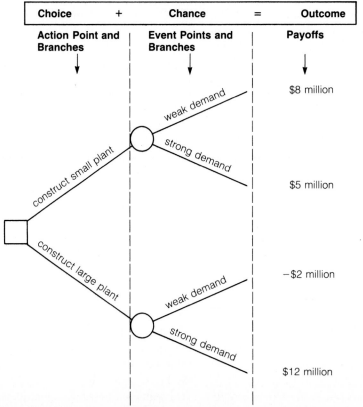

$8 million

$5 million

−$2 million

$12 million

weak demand

strong demand

construct small plant

construct large plant

weak demand

strong demand

As this illustration shows, the possible payoffs associated with a decision made under uncertainty result from a mixture of choice (square symbol) and chance (circular symbols). Note that the information contained in this diagram is precisely the same as that found in the payoff table (Table 9.1).

to the criterion in this instance). Table 9.3 illustrates how the minimax criterion would be applied.

Note that the maximin (or minimax) criterion is ideally suited to the born pessimist. If you always expect the worst, if you always suspect that "nature" or chance will work against you, then you cannot do better than employ this criterion. It will give you nothing worse than the best among all the worst things that can happen: the highest of the lowest possible profits in Table 9.2 and the lowest of the highest possible costs in Table 9.3.

Maximax (or Minimin)

The second among the nonprobabilistic criteria goes to the other extreme and seeks to achieve the best of the best possible outcomes. This criterion, too, comes in two forms. If maximization of benefit is the objective, the criterion is called **maximax** because the decision maker is to find the highest possible (or maximum) benefit associated with each possible action, identify the highest (or maximum) benefit among these maxima, and then choose the action associated with this maximum of maxima (as the name suggests).

TABLE 9.2

Maximizing Benefit: The Maximin Criterion

| Actions | Events | | Row Minimum |
	E_1 = weak demand for new product	E_2 = strong demand for new product	
A_1 = constructing a small plant	8	5	⑤ ←Maximin
A_2 = constructing a large plant	-2	12	-2

This table shows the annual profits (in millions of dollars) associated with four possible action/event combinations. The lowest of the possible profits associated with each action is shown in the last column; the maximin criterion suggests taking the best of these (encircled), or action A_1. Under the circumstances, the firm can do no worse than earn a profit of $5 million. It might even earn $8 million, if E_1 rather than E_2 occurs.

TABLE 9.3

Minimizing Cost: The Minimax Criterion

| Actions | Events | | Row Maximum |
	E_1 = low level of demand and production	E_2 = high level of demand and production	
A_1 = install small antipollution system	5	8	⑧ ←Minimax
A_2 = install large antipollution system	10	4	10

This table shows the annual costs (in millions of dollars) associated with four possible action/event combinations. The highest of the possible costs associated with each action is shown in the last column; the minimax criterion suggests taking the best of these (encircled), or action A_1. Under the circumstances, the firm can do no worse than incur a cost of $8 million. It might even pay as little as $5 million, if E_1 rather than E_2 occurs.

Table 9.4 illustrates how the maximax criterion would be applied to our first example.

If minimization of cost is the objective (as in our second example above), the analogous criterion is often referred to as **minimin** because the decision maker is to find the lowest possible (or minimum) cost associated with each possible action, identify the lowest (or minimum) cost among these minima, and then choose the action associated with this minimum of minima (as the name suggests). Table 9.5 illustrates how the minimin criterion would be applied to our second example.

Note that the maximax (or minimin) criterion is ideally suited to the born optimist. If you always expect the best, if you are always convinced that "nature" or chance will be on your side, then you might go after the best of the best in the fashion just shown: the highest of the highest possible profits in Table 9.4 and the lowest of the lowest possible costs in Table 9.5.

Minimax Regret

The third one among the nonprobabilistic criteria is just a bit more complicated. To understand it, we must first define the concept of **opportunity loss (OL)** or **regret.** When the decision maker aims to maximize benefit, the opportunity loss equals the difference between (a) the optimal payoff for a given event (the highest benefit in a given event column of our tables) and (b) the actual payoff achieved as a result of taking a specified action and the subsequent occurrence of that event. Consider, for example, the E_1 column of Table 9.4. If E_1 occurs, the optimal payoff is $8 million. If the decision maker has previously chosen A_1, the actual payoff will equal $8 million as well; hence, the opportunity loss will equal $8 million $-$ $8 million $= 0$. The decision maker has no reason to regret anything because given the occurrence of E_1, the best possible action had, in fact, been taken. If, on the other hand, the decision maker has previously chosen A_2, the actual payoff will equal $-$$2 million; hence, the opportunity loss will equal $8 million $-$ ($-$$2 million) $=$ $10 million. The decision maker has plenty of reason for regret because given the occurrence of E_1, if only A_1 had been chosen instead of A_2, the decision maker would be better off by $10 million (having a gain of $8 million instead of a loss of $2 million). Similar opportunity-loss values can be calculated for the E_2 column, of course, as is shown in Table 9.6 (which is also referred to as a **regret table**). The application of the criterion of **minimax regret** is also illustrated in that table. According to this criterion, the decision maker finds the highest possible (or maximum) regret value associated with each possible action, identifies the lowest (or minimum) value among these maxima, and

TABLE 9.4

Maximizing Benefit: The Maximax Criterion

| | Events | | **Row Maximum** |
Actions	E_1 = weak demand for new product	E_2 = strong demand for new product	
A_1 = constructing a small plant	8	5	8
A_2 = constructing a large plant	-2	12	⑫ ←Maximax

This table shows the annual profits (in millions of dollars) associated with four possible action/event combinations. The highest of the possible profits associated with each action is shown in the last column; the maximax criterion suggests taking the best of these (encircled), or action A_2. Under the circumstances, the firm might earn a profit of $12 million, but it might also have a loss of $2 million, if E_1 rather than E_2 occurs.

then chooses the action associated with this minimum of maximum-regret values. (Note the encircled figure in Table 9.6.)

The minimax-regret criterion is applied in the same way to cost-minimization problems, but the regret table itself is computed in a slightly different way. When the decision maker aims to minimize cost, the opportunity loss equals the difference between (a) the actual cost incurred as a result of taking a specified action and the sub-

sequent occurrence of an event and (b) the minimum cost achievable for that event (the lowest cost in a given event column of our tables). Table 9.7 gives the solution for our example.

Criticism

When we survey the above solutions to our decision-making problems, we discover that the results differ depending on the criterion that is

TABLE 9.5

Minimizing Cost: The Minimin Criterion

Actions	Events		Row Minimum
	E_1 = low level of demand and production	E_2 = high level of demand and production	
A_1 = install small antipollution system	5	8	5
A_2 = install large antipollution system	10	4	④←Minimin

This table shows the annual costs (in millions of dollars) associated with four possible action/event combinations. The lowest of the possible costs associated with each action is shown in the last column; the minimin criterion suggests taking the best of these (encircled), or action A_2. Under the circumstances, the firm might incur costs as low as \$4 million, but it might also have costs of \$10 million, if E_1 rather than E_2 occurs.

TABLE 9.6

Maximizing Benefit: The Minimax-Regret Criterion

Actions	Events		Row Maximum
	E_1 = weak demand for new product	E_2 = strong demand for new product	
A_1 = constructing a small plant	8 − 8 = 0	12 − 5 = 7	⑦←Minimax Regret
A_2 = constructing a large plant	8 − (−2) = 10	12 − 12 = 0	10

This table, based on Table 9.4, shows the opportunity loss or regret values (in millions of dollars) associated with four possible action/event combinations. The highest of the possible regret values associated with each action is shown in the last column; the minimax-regret criterion suggests taking the least painful of these (encircled), or action A_1. Under the circumstances, the decision maker might come to regret the lost opportunity of earning \$7 million in extra profit, but the regret might also be zero (if E_1 rather than E_2 occurs) and it could not be worse than \$7 million (as it would be if A_2 were chosen and E_1 were to occur).

applied. In our benefit-maximizing example, the maximin criterion suggests A_1 (the construction of a small plant), the maximax criterion suggests A_2 (the construction of a large plant), and the minimax-regret criterion suggests A_1 as well. Similarly, different results were obtained in the cost-minimizing case. Such differences, however, should not surprise us; they merely reflect the underlying differences in decision-making philosophies that stress, respectively, being careful, being daring, or minimizing future regret.

Nevertheless, all of the above criteria leave some critics unhappy. Consider how these criteria ignore all payoff values except certain extreme ones found in a given row. Take Table 9.2 and imagine, for example, that the 12 changed to 12,000. Despite the drastic change (and the sudden possibility of making a profit of $12 *billion* by constructing a large plant), the maximin criterion would continue to counsel that action A_1 be taken (that a small plant be built in order to avoid a possible $2 million loss).

In addition to placing undue reliance on extreme values, all of the above criteria ignore the probabilities of events, but, critics argue, even guesses could often be extremely helpful.

Such guesses about the likelihood of some events can be indicated by a subjective probability number between 0 and 1, which can be assigned to each possible event such that zero indicates belief in a zero chance of the event happening and unity indicates belief that the event is going to happen with certainty.

If, in the example just cited (Table 9.2 with the 12 changed to 12,000), E_1 had a low probability and E_2 had a high one, it would surely be foolish to apply the maximin criterion and forgo an almost certain $12 billion gain in order to avoid a highly unlikely $2 million loss. Indeed, many decision makers prefer the criteria discussed in the next sections because they do take probabilities into account.

DECISION MAKING WITH PROBABILITIES

Many times a decision maker can develop fairly good estimates for the probabilities of alternative future events. Decision criteria that make use of such estimates include the *maximum-likelihood criterion*, the *maximization* (or minimization) *of*

TABLE 9.7

Minimizing Cost: The Minimax-Regret Criterion

Actions	Events		Row Maximum
	E_1 = low level of demand and production	E_2 = high level of demand and production	
A_1 = install small antipollution system	5 − 5 = 0	8 − 4 = 4	④←Minimax Regret
A_2 = install large antipollution system	10 − 5 = 5	4 − 4 = 0	5

This table, based on Table 9.5, shows the opportunity-loss or regret values (in millions of dollars) associated with four possible action/event combinations. The highest of the possible regret values associated with each action is shown in the last column; the minimax-regret criterion suggests taking the least painful of these (encircled), or action A_1. Under the circumstances, the decision maker might come to regret the lost opportunity of reducing costs by $4 million more, but the regret might also be zero (if E_1 rather than E_2 occurs) and it could not be worse than $4 million (as it would be if A_2 were chosen and E_1 were to occur).

expected monetary value (depending on whether the objective is the maximization of some benefit or the minimization of some cost), the *minimization of expected opportunity loss* or regret value, and the *maximization of expected utility.*

Maximum Likelihood

A decision maker using the **maximum-likelihood criterion** simply ignores all the events that might occur except the most likely one and selects the action that produces the optimal result (maximum benefit or minimum cost) associated with this most likely event. Table 9.8, which is an adaptation of Table 9.1, illustrates the procedure.

Critics argue that the use of this criterion amounts to "playing ostrich" because so much that might happen is being ignored. In this example, the best of all possible outcomes (12) is never even considered; in other cases, the preoccupation with the event of the highest probability might lead the decision maker to focus on an event with a probability of .1, while ignoring other events with a combined probability of .9 (but individual probabilities of less than .1). This result is considered most unsatisfactory by critics of this criterion.

Proponents of this criterion, on the other hand, argue that people often do behave in precisely this fashion. They look at nothing but the most likely event, as evidenced, for example, in the famous *cobweb cycles* in agricultural and labor markets. Thus, according to *one* scenario (others are possible), farmers assume that the *most likely* future price of hogs is the one equal to the present price; hence, a low price in period 1 (because it is used as an indicator of a low price in period 2) discourages the raising of hogs in period 1 and leads to a shortage and an unexpectedly *high* price in period 2. This high price in period 2, in turn, encourages the raising of hogs in period 2 and leads to a surplus and an unexpectedly low price in period 3. And so it goes, low and high prices following one another eternally. (See the discussion of this phenomenon on pp. 192–195 and 371–373 of this text.)

Expected Monetary Value

A decision maker using the **expected-monetary-value criterion** determines an expected monetary value for each possible action and then selects the action with the optimal expected monetary value (the largest, if the objective is to maximize some benefit; the smallest, if the objective is to minimize some cost). The **expected monetary value (EMV)** of an action equals the sum of the weighted payoffs associated with that action, the weights being the probabilities of the alternative events that produce the various possible payoffs.

TABLE 9.8

Maximizing Benefit: The Maximum-Likelihood Criterion

	Events	
Actions	E_1 = weak demand for new product $p(E_1)$ = .7	E_2 = strong demand for new product $p(E_2)$ = .3
A_1 = constructing a small plant	⑧	5
A_2 = constructing a large plant	−2	12

This table shows the annual profits (in millions of dollars) associated with four possible action/event combinations. Given the assumed probabilities of the events [$p(E_1)$ = .7 and $p(E_2)$ = .3], the maximum-likelihood criterion leads a decision maker to focus entirely on the shaded E_1 column (because .7 is greater than .3) and to select the optimal result in that column (encircled). Thus A_1 is the action chosen by those who employ the maximum-likelihood criterion.

Tables 9.9 and 9.10, which are based on our earlier examples, illustrate the procedure.

Note how a decision maker who, when confronted with the type of situation given in Table 9.9, consistently chooses A_1 will, on average, gain $7.1 million per year because $8 million will be gained 70 percent of the time and $5 million 30 percent of the time. In contrast, a

consistent choice of nonoptimal A_2 would, in the long run, yield a gain of only $2.2 million per year because $2 million would be lost 70 percent of the time and $12 million would be gained 30 percent of the time in this type of situation. Similarly, a decision maker who, when confronted with the type of situation given in Table 9.10, consistently chooses A_1 will, on average,

TABLE 9.9

Maximizing Benefit: The Expected-Monetary-Value Criterion

Actions	Events		Expected Monetary Value, EMV
	E_1 = weak demand for new product $p(E_1) = .7$	E_2 = strong demand for new product $p(E_2) = .3$	
A_1 = constructing a small plant	8	5	$8(.7) + 5(.3) = $ (7.1) ←Optimum
A_2 = constructing a large plant	−2	12	$-2(.7) + 12(.3) = 2.2$

This table shows the annual profits (in millions of dollars) associated with four possible action/event combinations; it also shows the expected monetary value of each possible action, based on the assumed probabilities of the events [$p(E_1) = .7$ and $p(E_2) = .3$]. Because the objective is to maximize benefit, the *largest EMV* is optimal; thus A_1 is the action chosen by those who employ the expected-monetary-value criterion.

TABLE 9.10

Minimizing Cost: The Expected-Monetary-Value Criterion

Actions	Events		Expected Monetary Value, EMV
	E_1 = low level of demand and production $p(E_1) = .7$	E_2 = high level of demand and production $p(E_2) = .3$	
A_1 = install small antipollution system	5	8	$5(.7) + 8(.3) = $ (5.9) ←Optimum
A_2 = install large antipollution system	10	4	$10(.7) + 4(.3) = 8.2$

This table shows the annual costs (in millions of dollars) associated with four possible action/event combinations; it also shows the expected monetary value of each possible action, based on the assumed probabilities of the events [$p(E_1) = .7$ and $p(E_2) = .3$]. Because the objective is to minimize cost, the *smallest EMV* is optimal; thus A_1 is the action chosen by those who employ the *EMV* criterion.

incur costs of only $5.9 million per year, while the nonoptimal choice of A_2 would, in the long run, produce costs of $8.2 million.

Note also that the probabilities used in these examples are assumed to be the best guesses of the decision maker. It may well happen, however, that a decision maker has no idea about event probabilities whatsoever. In that case, many decision theorists recommend that equal probabilities be assigned to all events. Given a list of collectively exhaustive and mutually exclusive events, the probability assigned to each then equals 1 divided by the number of such events. This procedure is variously referred to as the **equal-likelihood criterion,** the **criterion of insufficient reason, Bayes's postulate,** or (because he popularized it, even though it was first suggested by Thomas Bayes) the **Laplace criterion.**

The use of the expected-monetary-value criterion can also be depicted graphically. Consider the decision tree of Figure 9.2. It is based on Figure 9.1 and, as the caption indicates, the decision-tree analysis leads to the same decision as Table 9.9. Because the graphical process of finding the optimal action involves starting at the terminal (ultimate-payoff) points of the tree

---

FIGURE 9.2

A Decision Tree and the Expected-Monetary-Value Criterion

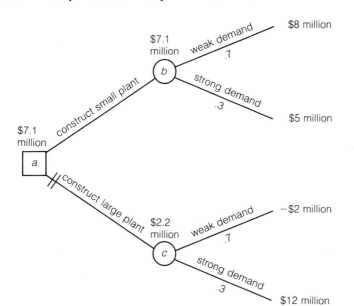

The application of the expected-monetary-value criterion is often depicted by means of a decision tree. Event probabilities are attached to each event branch and, by a process termed *backward induction,* the ultimate payoff values appearing at the tips of the branches are translated, using these probabilities, into expected monetary values at each fork of the tree (here, $7.1 million at event point *b,* $2.2 million at event point *c,* and, ultimately, $7.1 million at action point *a*). When maximizing benefit, a decision maker employing the *EMV* criterion will take the action leading to the highest *EMV* (in this case, the decision maker will follow the branch from action point *a* to event point *b*). By refusing to follow the alternative action branch (from *a* to *c*) that leads to the lower *EMV,* the benefit-maximizing decision maker is said to "cut off" or "prune" the nonoptimal path through the tree. (Note the colored line suggesting a cut by the pruning shears.) This pruning leaves intact only the optimal path from *a* to *b* and beyond and makes the expected monetary value of the decision maker's action equal to $7.1 million as well. *Caution:* Branch pruning can take place only at action points, never at event points, because only the former are controlled by the decision maker.

branches (at the "top" or right side of the tree) and then working backward along the branches to find expected monetary values for each fork, this type of graphical solution of a decision problem is called **backward induction.**

Expected Opportunity Loss

A decision maker using the **expected-opportunity-loss criterion** determines an expected opportunity loss (or expected regret value) for each possible action and then selects the action with the smallest of these values. This procedure *always* yields the same result as the expected-monetary-value criterion. The **expected opportunity loss (EOL),** or **expected regret value,** of an action equals the sum of the weighted opportunity-loss values associated with that action—the weights being the probabilities of the alternative events that produce the various possible opportunity losses. Tables 9.11 and 9.12, which are based on our familiar examples, illustrate the procedure.

Note how a decision maker who, when confronted with the type of situation given in Table 9.11, consistently chooses A_1 will, on average, incur an opportunity loss of $2.1 million per year because that loss will be zero 70 percent of the time and equal to $7 million 30 percent of the time. In contrast, a consistent choice of nonoptimal A_2 would, in the long run, produce an opportunity loss of $7 million per year because such a loss would equal $10 million 70 percent of the time and be zero 30 percent of the time. A similar analysis can be made with respect to Table 9.12.

Expected Utility

All of the decision-making criteria discussed so far have employed *monetary* outcome measures. Yet critics have argued that using money to measure outcomes is a mistake—that people will invariably take those actions that maximize their welfare or *utility,* and that actions that maximize monetary benefit or minimize monetary cost may well not coincide with those that maximize utility. The kind of situation depicted in Table 9.13 can be used to illustrate what these critics have in mind.

Would the typical decision maker really be indifferent between actions A_1 (investing $100 million in vineyards) and A_2 (investing $100 million in the auto industry) just because their expected monetary values are equal? Critics argue that the decision maker would not be indifferent because A_2, unlike A_1, involves *risk.* Choosing A_2 over A_1 is equivalent to taking a

TABLE 9.11

Maximizing Benefit: The Expected-Opportunity-Loss Criterion

	Events		Expected Opportunity Loss, EOL
Actions	E_1 = weak demand for new product $p(E_1) = .7$	E_2 = strong demand for new product $p(E_2) = .3$	
A_1 = constructing a small plant	$8 - 8 = 0$	$12 - 5 = 7$	$0(.7) + 7(.3) = 2.1$ ←Optimum
A_2 = constructing a large plant	$8 - (-2) = 10$	$12 - 12 = 0$	$10(.7) + 0(.3) = 7$

This table, based on Table 9.4, shows the opportunity-loss or regret values (in millions of dollars) associated with four possible action/event combinations; it also shows the expected opportunity loss for each possible action, based on the assumed probabilities of the events [$p(E_1) = .7$ and $p(E_2) = .3$]. The smallest *EOL* is optimal; thus A_1 is the action chosen by those who employ the expected-opportunity-loss criterion. It is no accident that this result is identical with that given by the expected-monetary-value criterion (Table 9.9).

gamble, to giving up a sure thing (a $15 million return from action A_1 regardless of which event occurs) for an uncertain thing (*either* a $25 million return if E_1 occurs *or* a $5 million return if E_2 occurs). Although such a gamble would be a **fair gamble** (in which the expected monetary value of what is given up—that is, the $15 million certain to be received from action A_1—is precisely equal to the expected monetary value of what is received—that is, the $15 million received, on the average, from action A_2), most people would not take the gamble. If critics are

---

TABLE 9.12

Minimizing Cost: The Expected-Opportunity-Loss Criterion

Actions	Events		Expected Opportunity Loss, *EOL*
	E_1 = low level of demand and production $p(E_1)$ = .7	E_2 = high level of demand and production $p(E_2)$ = .3	
A_1 = install small antipollution system	5 − 5 = 0	8 − 4 = 4	0(.7) + 4(.3) = (1.2)←Optimum
A_2 = install large antipollution system	10 − 5 = 5	4 − 4 = 0	5(.7) + 0(.3) = 3.5

This table, based on Table 9.5, shows the opportunity-loss or regret values (in millions of dollars) associated with four possible action/event combinations; it also shows the expected opportunity loss for each possible action, based on the assumed probabilities of the events [$p(E_1)$ = .7 and $p(E_2)$ = .3]. The smallest *EOL* is optimal; thus A_1 is the action chosen by those who employ the expected-opportunity-loss criterion. It is no accident that this result is identical with that given by the expected-monetary-value criterion (Table 9.10).

TABLE 9.13

Doubts about the Expected-Monetary-Value Criterion

Actions	Events		Expected Monetary Value, *EMV*
	E_1 = oil price rises moderately $p(E_1)$ = .5	E_2 = oil price rises sharply $p(E_2)$ = .5	
A_1 = investing $100 million in vineyards	15	15	15(.5) + 15(.5) = 15 ←Optimum?
A_2 = investing $100 million in the auto industry	25	5	25(.5) + 5(.5) = 15

This table shows the annual profits (in millions of dollars) associated with four possible action/event combinations; it also shows the expected monetary value of each possible action, based on the assumed probabilities of the events [$p(E_1)$ = $p(E_2)$ = .5]. According to the *EMV* criterion, a decision maker would be indifferent between the two actions, but critics argue that most people would decisively opt for A_1.

right, most people would be even less inclined to take an **unfair gamble** in which the expected monetary value of what is given up exceeds the expected monetary value of what is received. (By changing the two entries of 15 in Table 9.13 to 16, for example, action A_2 would be turned into an unfair gamble.) Indeed, many people, critics assert, would even reject a **more-than-fair gamble** in which the expected monetary value of what is given up is less than the expected monetary value of what is received. (By changing the two entries of 15 in Table 9.13 to 14, for example, action A_2 would be turned into a more-than-fair gamble.)

The St. Petersburg Paradox. The apparent paradox of people refusing to take fair gambles was first solved some 250 years ago. A Swiss mathematician, Daniel Bernoulli (1700–1782) studied gamblers at the casinos of St. Petersburg, and he considered the game described below between two persons, A and B:

> A fair coin is tossed until heads appears; if heads appears on the first toss, A pays B $1; if heads appears for the first time on the second toss, A pays B $2; if heads appears first on the third toss, A pays B $4; and so on, with A always paying 2^{n-1} at the nth toss if heads appears.

If playing this game is to be a fair gamble, what fee, Bernoulli asked, should B be willing to pay A for the privilege of playing this game? Because the player of a fair game is never asked to pay more than the expected monetary value of gain, this value can be calculated easily. Consider Table 9.14. Given a probability of .5 for heads to appear on the first toss, the expected monetary value of gain is $\$1(.5) = \$.50$ if the game ends after the first toss. Given a probability of $(.5)^2$ for heads to appear first on the second toss, the expected monetary value of gain is $\$2(.5)^2 = \$.50$ if the game ends after the second toss. And so it goes. Thus the expected monetary value of gain during the entire game is the sum of the expected monetary values of all possible outcomes, or the infinite series $\$.50 + \$.50 + \ldots = \infty$. Yet people are clearly not willing to pay such an infinite sum of money for the privilege of playing this game (even though such a payment would make the gamble precisely fair).

One probably could solve the paradox by postulating that gamblers cannot possibly be convinced to take this game seriously. How could they be so gullible as to believe that payoff would actually be made should they be lucky enough to win a large sum? (If heads did not appear until

TABLE 9.14

The St. Petersburg Game

Number of Toss (1)	Payoff if Heads First Appears at Given Toss (2)	Probability of Heads First Appearing at Given Toss (3)	Expected Monetary Value = Payoff × Probability (4) = (2) × (3)
1	$1	.5	$.50
2	2	$(.5)^2$	.50
3	4	$(.5)^3$	.50
4	8	$(.5)^4$	.50
5	16	$(.5)^5$	.50
.	.	.	.
.	.	.	.
.	.	.	.

The St. Petersburg game has an expected monetary value of gain of infinity (equal to the sum of the last column of this table).

the 42nd toss, for example, the required payoff would equal more than the entire U.S. gross national product!) Bernoulli, however, had a different idea. He argued that people making decisions under uncertainty were not attempting to maximize expected *monetary* values, but maximized expected *utilities* instead. He thought that the **total utility of money** (the overall welfare people derived from the possession of money) was rising the more money people had, while the **marginal utility of money** (the increase in total utility that was associated with a one-dollar increase in the quantity of money, for example) was declining the more money people had. Any person starting with $500, for example, would, therefore, place a smaller subjective value on gaining an extra sum than on losing an equal amount. Any game with an equal probability of gaining and losing a given amount was, therefore, fair in monetary terms, but unfair in utility terms. The game's expected utility was negative. No wonder people refused to play it!

Figure 9.3 contains a hypothetical person's **utility-of-money function**—the relationship, that is, between alternative amounts of money the person might possess and the different utility totals associated with these amounts. It is assumed, in accordance with Bernoulli's postulate, that the total utility of money rises with greater amounts of it, while its marginal utility (shown by the slope of the total utility curve) declines.

In Figure 9.3, the total utility of money, U, is related to the amount of money, $, by the equation $U = \sqrt{\$}$. Thus a person with $500 is assumed to receive $\sqrt{500}$, or 22.36 *utils* (units of utility) from it (point A). The same person would, however, receive only 5.92 extra utils from an added $300 (when moving from A to C) but would lose 8.22 utils by a loss of $300 (when moving from A to B). Given this type of utility function, the St. Petersburg paradox is easily solved. While the expected monetary value of the game equals infinity, its expected utility equals

FIGURE 9.3

The Utility of Money

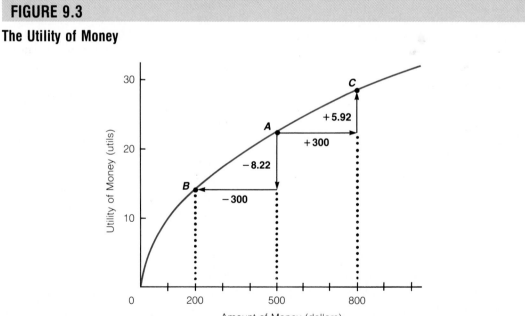

This graph illustrates a person's utility function that is characterized by declining marginal utility of money. The total utility of money, *U*, here is related to the amount of money, $, by the equation *U* = √$. Other relationships are, of course, also possible.

$$EU = \sqrt{1}(.5) + \sqrt{2}(.5)^2 + \sqrt{4}(.5)^3 +$$
$$\sqrt{8}(.5)^4 + \sqrt{16}(.5)^5 + \ldots$$
$$= 1(1/2) + \sqrt{2}(1/4) + 2(1/8) +$$
$$2\sqrt{2}(1/16) + 4(1/32) + \ldots$$
$$= 1/2 + \sqrt{2}(1/4) + 1/4 + \sqrt{2}(1/8) +$$
$$1/8 + \ldots$$
$$= 1 + \sqrt{2}(1/2) = 1.707 \text{ utils.}$$

By the above equation, $U = \sqrt{\$}$; hence $U^2 = \$$ and an expected utility of 1.707 translates into a dollar equivalent of $(1.707)^2 = \$2.91$. This $2.91, then, is the far-less-than-infinite amount that a person who maximized expected utility, and possessed the above utility function, would pay for the privilege of playing the St. Petersburg game.

Note: Someone else who also maximized expected utility, but who possessed a different utility function, would act quite differently. This difference brings us to an important conclusion: Even if people, as is likely, maximize the expected utility rather than the expected monetary value of an action when facing uncertainty, we cannot predict their behavior without a knowledge of their utility functions. Indeed, the shape of these functions reveals important information about people's attitudes concerning the spread of possible outcomes of their action around the action's expected value. The extent of such a spread (as from 15 down to 5 and up to 25 for action A_2 above) in fact measures the *risk* of an action, and people can view risk in one of three ways. They can be averse to it; they can be neutral toward it; they can seek it out.

Risk Aversion. Imagine for a moment that the investor whose choices were pictured in Table 9.13 possesses the type of utility function postulated by Bernoulli. This type of utility function is illustrated in panel (a) of Figure 9.4. Action A_2, as we noted earlier, would bring the investor a profit of $15,000 a year, regardless of what happens to the price of oil. This amount of money is associated, according to point B on the utility function, with a total utility of $0b$. Action A_1, on the other hand, would bring the investor, with equal probability, a profit of $5,000 a year *or* of $25,000 a year. As we can see from points A and C, respectively, the associated utilities equal $0a$ and $0c$. The *expected* utility from an equally weighted $5,000 or $25,000 a year, however, equals the sum of half of $0a$ plus half of $0c$, and this sum is shown in the graph by utility $0d$. It corresponds to point D, located on the dashed line connecting A and C and above the $15,000 expected monetary value of the $5,000 or $25,000 gamble. [Note: The expected utility of receiving $5,000 with a probability of .2 or $25,000 with a probability of .8 could similarly be read off of dashed line AC, but at a point above the $5,000(.2) + $25,000(.8) = $21,000 expected monetary value of this different gamble.]

Whenever a person in this way considers the utility (as at point B) of a certain prospect of money to be higher than the expected utility (as at point D) of an uncertain prospect of equal expected monetary value, the person is said to hold an attitude of **risk aversion.** This attitude is always present when a person's marginal utility of money (shown here by the slope of utility function $0ABC$) declines with larger amounts of money.

Risk aversion is, indeed, quite common. Consider how people do all kinds of things, small and large, to *escape* gambles: They place person-to-person calls instead of station-to-station calls; at airports, banks, and post offices, they prefer single lines feeding to many clerks to the chance of getting into a slow or fast line; they diversify their assets and do not "place all eggs in one basket"; they buy plenty of insurance; they reject fair gambles, as our risk-averse investor would by taking action A_1 (to gain utility $0b$) rather than action A_2 (that has an equal expected monetary value but a smaller expected utility $0d$).

Risk Neutrality. Let us imagine instead that our investor's utility function is illustrated by panel (b) of Figure 9.4. In this case, the utility of

FIGURE 9.4

Attitudes Toward Risk

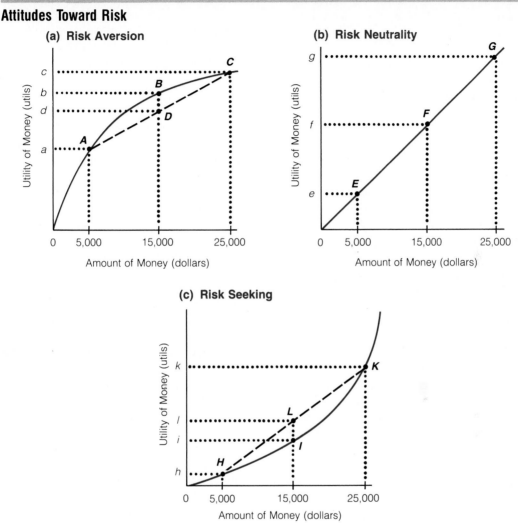

This set of graphs illustrates three basic attitudes toward risk: risk aversion in panel (a), risk neutrality in panel (b), and risk seeking in panel (c). These attitudes correspond, respectively, to declining, constant, and increasing marginal utilities of money.

action A_1, with its certain payoff of $15,000 a year, would equal 0*f*, corresponding to point *F*. Action A_2 would bring, according to points *E* and *G*, utility of 0*e* or 0*g*, and with equal probability. The expected utility of this gamble, however, would also equal 0*f*. (A straight line between *E* and *G* leads us to point *F* above the $15,000

expected monetary value of the $5,000 or $25,000 gamble.)

Whenever a person in this way considers the utility (as at point *F*) of a certain prospect of money to be equal to the expected utility (as at point *F*) of an uncertain prospect of equal expected monetary value, the person is said to hold an attitude of **risk neutrality.** This attitude is always present when a person's marginal utility of money (shown here by the slope of utility function 0EFG) remains constant with larger amounts of money.

Risk neutrality is not very common, but it is precisely the implicit assumption made by those who advocate the use of the expected-monetary-value criterion. If all people were risk neutral, our investor would be truly indifferent between actions A_1 and A_2 because, as we saw, their expected monetary values are equal. By the same token, a risk-neutral person would be willing to pay $100 for the privilege of taking each of the following fair gambles, for the expected monetary value of each of these is also $100:

a.   a 99-percent chance of getting $101.01 and a 1-percent chance of getting nothing;
b.   a 50-percent chance of getting $101 and a 50-percent chance of getting $99;
c.   a 1-percent chance of getting $10,000 and a 99-percent chance of getting nothing;
d.   a 1-percent chance of getting $1 million, a 1-percent chance of losing $990,000, and a 98-percent chance of getting nothing.

After thinking about it, you might pay the price for (a) and (b) or something close to it, but do you have the sweepstakes mentality to go after (c)? Are you ready for the Russian roulette of (d)?

Risk Seeking.   Now imagine that our investor's utility function is illustrated by panel (c) of Figure 9.4. In this case, the utility of action A_1, with its certain payoff of $15,000 a year, would equal 0i, corresponding to point I. Action A_2 would bring, according to points H and K, utility of 0h or 0k, and with equal probability. By the now familiar procedure, we can establish the expected utility of this gamble as 0l, corresponding to point L on dashed line HK.

Whenever a person in this way considers the utility (as at point I) of a certain prospect of money to be lower than the expected utility (as at point L) of an uncertain prospect of equal expected monetary value, the person is said to hold

an attitude of **risk seeking.** This attitude is always present when a person's marginal utility of money (shown here by the slope of utility function 0HIK) rises with larger amounts of money.

Risk seeking, like risk neutrality, is not very common. If all people were risk seekers, our investor would, of course, prefer action A_2 to A_1, and all of us would constantly seek out and accept huge riches-or-ruin gambles. In fact, of course, most of us have the opposite inclination and seek to buy insurance, a matter taken up in the next chapter.

Conclusion.   An evaluation of decision outcomes in terms of utility rather than money may well be a superior approach. If the investor depicted in Table 9.13, for example, were risk-averse and had Bernoulli's utility function, the decision problem could be laid out as in Table 9.15. This approach would explain why the investor would prefer A_1 to A_2, even though A_1 and A_2 have equal expected monetary values.

A decision maker using the **expected-utility criterion** thus determines the expected utility for each possible action and then selects the action that maximizes expected utility. The **expected utility** *(EU)* of an action equals the sum of the weighted utilities associated with that action—the weights being the probabilities of the alternative events that produce the various possible utility payoffs.

Note: Analytical Example 9.1 shows a real-world example of using the expected utility approach.

GAME THEORY

In the remainder of this chapter, we consider a special case of decision theory in which decision makers are pitted not against the anonymous "state of the world" but identifiable individuals instead.

More often than not, economic theorists describe the behavior of decision makers in terms

TABLE 9.15

Maximizing Expected Utility

Actions	Events		Expected Utility, *EU*
	E_1 = oil price rises moderately $p(E_1)$ = .5	E_2 = oil price rises sharply $p(E_2)$ = .5	
A_1 = investing \$100 million in vineyards	$\sqrt{15}$ = 3.87	$\sqrt{15}$ = 3.87	3.87(.5) + 3.87(.5) = ③.87 ←Optimum
A_2 = investing \$100 million in the auto industry	$\sqrt{25}$ = 5	$\sqrt{5}$ = 2.24	5(.5) + 2.24(.5) = 3.62

This table, based on Table 9.13, shows the utility associated with four possible action/event combinations for a risk-averse person with a utility function of $U = \sqrt{\$}$. The table also shows the expected utility of each possible action, based on the assumed probabilities of the events [$p(E_1) = p(E_2)$ = .5]. Because the objective is to maximize expected utility, the largest *EU* is optimal; thus A_1 is the action chosen by those who employ the expected-utility criterion.

of *maximization* (as of utility or profit) or *minimization* (as of disutility or cost). Yet, as the study of oligopoly has shown, this type of decision making gets to be very complex when the results achieved by one economic agent depend not only on this agent's own actions, but also on those of identifiable others who are conscious of this fact and may or may not be willing to cooperate. Thus one firm's desire to maximize profit may be opposed by other firms seeking to maximize their profits, and this *conscious conflict of wills* gives rise to a peculiar and disconcerting mixture of several interlocking maximization problems.

When people interact with specific other people and when these other people can actively seek to thwart the attainment of the first people's goals, all those involved must base their decisions on what they expect others to do and, therefore, on what they think others expect them to do, and perhaps even on what they think the others think they expect them to do. . . . Under such circumstances, when no actor is in complete control of the factors influencing the outcome, how can one even talk of an *individual's* rational behavior, much less predict its results?

No wonder that to this day there exists no satisfactory theory of oligopoly. There are bits and pieces, as Chapter 8 attests, but they do not make for a unified whole. There is, however, hope, based on a development that originated in 1944. In that year, two Princeton professors, a mathematician and an economist, joined forces to suggest a new approach to the problem of inter-locking decision making. One of them was John von Neumann (1903–1957), Hungarian-born mathematical genius and one of three coinventors of the U.S. hydrogen bomb. The other was Oskar Morgenstern (a Biography of whom appears in Chapter 9 of the *Student Workbook* that accompanies this text). They looked upon any decision-making situation in which the payoff to people's choices depends not only on them (and "nature") but also on other people's choices as a **game.** They developed a highly novel analytical apparatus, called **game theory,** which is a method for studying decision making in situations of conflict when the fates of those who seek different goals are interlocked. Game theory is a method with universal applicability—useful not only for analyzing the behavior of oligopolistic firms but also that of chess and poker players, cops and robbers, diplomats, military strategists, and politicians fighting for nomination. This section can do no more than provide a brief introduction to this fascinating subject.

The Two-Person Zero-Sum Game

The simplest of all possible games (and inevitably also the dullest) is one between two persons in which the winnings of one person are exactly matched by the losses of the other. Because the

sum of (positive) winnings and (negative) losses equals zero, this game is called a **zero-sum game.** Table 9.16 shows the major elements involved in every game: players, control variables, and payoffs. Consider part (I) first. The "players" are two firms that compete with each other by introducing newly differentiated products. Each firm has three "control variables." Each can introduce one of three products; Products A, B, or C in the case of Firm 1; Products D, E, or F in the case of Firm 2. The resultant "payoffs," in terms of market share gained or

TABLE 9.16

Zero-Sum Games

(I) Market-Share Game:		Matrix of Firm 1's Gain (+) or Loss (−) of Market Share (in percent)			
		Firm 2			Row Minimum
		Product D	Product E	Product F	
Firm 1	Product A	+3	0	+4	⓪ ← Maximin
	Product B	−4	−2	+8	−4
	Product C	+4	−1	−3	−3
Column Maximum		+4	⓪	+8	

Minimax

(II) Smuggling Game:		Matrix of Smugglers' Gain (+) or Loss (−) (in million dollars)			
		Border patrol			Row Minimum
		Guards freeway only	Guards mountain road only	Guards both lightly	
Smugglers	Take freeway	A −10	B +10	C −4	−10
	Take mountain road	D +4	E +2	F +2	(+2) ← Maximin
Column Maximum		+4	+10	(+2)	

Minimax

Both of the zero-sum games pictured here have a saddle point. Players, therefore, do best by pursuing a pure maximin or minimax strategy. These strategies lead to the results shown by the two shaded numbers.

lost by Firm 1, are shown in the body of the table. Because this is a zero-sum game, any gain to Firm 1 is a loss to Firm 2, and the opposite. Consider the first row. If Firm 1 introduced Product A and Firm 2 responded with Product D, it tells us, Firm 1 would gain (and Firm 2 lose) 3 percent of the market. On the other hand, if Firm 1 introduced Product A, while Firm 2 responded with Product E or F, Firm 1 would gain 0 or 4 percent of the market, respectively (and Firm 2 would lose identical shares). The entries in the next two rows of Table 9.16 are similarly interpreted.

How should a player act, given the likelihood of several different outcomes for any one action?

Pessimistic Assumptions. Von Neumann and Morgenstern suggested that each party would imagine itself in the place of its rival and ask: "What would I do in response to my own strategy if I was my own rival?" They also suggested this pessimistic answer: "If I was my rival, I would do what was best for this rival and worst for me; that is, I would choose the most damaging counterstrategy."

Thus if Firm 1 chose A, Firm 2 would choose E (giving Firm 1 a zero increase in market share). If Firm 1 chose B, Firm 2 would choose D (giving Firm 1 a 4-percent loss in market share and itself a 4-percent gain). And if Firm 1 chose C, Firm 2 would choose F (giving Firm 1 a 3-percent loss in market share and itself a 3-percent gain). All these terrible outcomes (terrible, that is, from the point of view of Firm 1) are shown in the last column of our table, labeled "Row Minimum."

We can, however, also look at all this from the point of view of Firm 2. Thus if Firm 2 chose to introduce Products D, E, or F, Firm 1 would choose Products C, A, or B, respectively, each time giving itself the best possible result and, by implication, handing the worst possible outcome to Firm 2. All these worst outcomes (worst from the point of view of Firm 2) are shown in the last row of our table, labeled "Column Maximum." Note: In this zero-sum game, these maxima for Firm 1 imply, of course, minima of −4, 0, and −8 for Firm 2.

Maximin and Minimax Strategies. Von Neumann and Morgenstern suggested that each firm (always expecting the worst) would now choose the strategy that made the worst possible outcome as good as possible. For Firm 1, as we have just seen, these worst possible outcomes are given in the last column. Thus Firm 1 would choose the encircled maximum of these minima (the *maximum minimorum*). According to this **maximin strategy,** it would introduce Product A. As you can see from Table 9.16, the worst that could then happen to Firm 1 would be a zero increase in market share.

In this zero-sum game, the worst possible outcomes for Firm 2 are, of course, the best possible ones for Firm 1. Firm 2, therefore, would choose the encircled minimum of the maxima (the *minimum maximorum*) shown in the last row. According to this **minimax strategy,** Firm 2 would introduce Product E. The worst that could then happen to Firm 2 would be a zero increase in Firm 1's market share and, therefore, a zero decrease in its own market share.

We can now easily see the result, which is shown by the shaded number in Table 9.16, part (I). Firm 1 would choose A and Firm 2 would choose E; neither firm would gain or lose any share of the market.

Review. We can quickly review what we have learned by now examining part (II) of Table 9.16. This time we imagine a group of smugglers who can brashly take their load by truck over the freeway or can sneakily take a smaller amount via a circuitous mountain road. The border patrol, on the other hand, can concentrate their forces on the freeway or on the mountain road or they can split them up between the two.

Here are the possible outcomes if the smugglers take the freeway: If they run into a heavy freeway guard (box A), they will be caught, lose their entire load, and be out $10 million. If the patrol only guards the mountain road, the smugglers will get through and gain $10 million (box B). If the smugglers find a light freeway guard, they will not be caught, but will not get through, and so they will be out $4 million in expenses (box C).

What if the smugglers take the mountain road? If the freeway is guarded heavily, the smugglers will get through, but their load will be smaller because of the terrain, so they gain only $4 million (box D). If the patrol guards the mountain road heavily or lightly the smugglers will get through, but they will also have to share their loot with the mountain people who help them (box E and F).

Let us assume that any gain (or loss) to the smugglers can be regarded as an equal loss (or gain) to the border patrol. Then our previous analysis applies fully. The smugglers will consider the worst that can happen to them (last column) and ''maximin'' by taking the mountain road. The border patrol will consider the best that can happen to the smugglers (last row) and ''minimax'' by guarding both roads lightly. The result: The smugglers will get through, but only with a small load and by paying heavy bribes. Their net gain will be $2 million (box F).

Saddle Point.   A game in which the maximin equals the minimax is said to have a **saddle point.** Note the zero in the last column of part (I) and the $+2$ in that column of part (II) versus the zero in the last row of part (I) and the $+2$ in that row of part (II). Such games end up being rather dull. Even if one player knows the other player's choice in advance (if Firm 1 knows that Firm 2 will introduce Product E or if Firm 2 knows that Firm 1 will introduce product A), the first player's own choice will not change. Neither can do better than making the saddle-point choice. Under such circumstances, neither has an incentive ever to change strategy. Each chooses the same strategy over and over again. Not all games, however, have a saddle point. Imagine inter-

changing the $+3$ and 0 in the first row of the market-share game. This change would not affect the maximin, which would still be zero, but it would affect the minimax, which would then be $+3$. Under such circumstances, Firm 1 would still introduce Product A; Firm 2 would still introduce Product E; but Firm 1 would gain (and Firm 2 lose) 3 percent of the market.

Note: Because there would be no saddle point in this example, one firm (namely, Firm 2) would then change its strategy if it knew the other's strategy in advance. If Firm 2 knew that Firm 1 will introduce Product A, Firm 2 could do better with Product D (which would then yield a zero market-share increase for Firm 1). But if Firm 1 knew that Firm 2 will introduce Product D, it would introduce Product C; and if Firm 2 knew *that* it would bring out F and that wouldn't be the end of the story yet!

When there is no saddle point, therefore, sticking to a given strategy does not work. Such rigidity in behavior would reveal precious information to the other player and upset the stability of the game. A no-saddle-point game, by introducing security aspects into the game, becomes much more interesting. As von Neumann and Morgenstern have shown (but which cannot be shown in this brief discussion), under such circumstances players can still employ an unbeatable **mixed strategy** that alternates at random between the available pure strategies and thereby avoids patterns of behavior that would reveal important information to the other players. (Why, do you think, do border patrols make their rounds at random instead of using a discernible pattern? Why do night watchguards and postal inspectors do the same? Why do professors pick quiz questions at random from a book?)

The Two-Person Nonzero-Sum Game

People can also play a **nonzero-sum game** in which the winnings and losses of all players add to a positive or negative number. The most famous game of this type is, perhaps, illustrated in Table 9.17. The game is called the **prisoners'**

TABLE 9.17

The Prisoners' Dilemma

Interrogation Game:		Matrix of Each Suspect's Loss of Free Time via Jail Sentence		
		Suspect 2		**Row Minimum** (for suspect 1)
		Confess	Keep quiet	
Suspect 1	Confess	A −8 years / −8 years	B −10 years / −1 year	−8 years (circled) / Maximin
	Keep quiet	C −1 year / −10 years	D −2 years / −2 years	−10 years
Column Minimum (for suspect 2)		−8 years (circled) / Maximin	−10 years	

The *prisoners' dilemma* illustrates game situations in which the best common choice of strategies (block D in this example) is unstable, offers great incentives to cheat, and leads to the worst choice possible (block A).

dilemma. The police, it is imagined, have arrested two men suspected of robbery. The District Attorney locks the men up in separate rooms, and then tells each man that the following deal is being offered to both of them:

If the man confesses, while his partner keeps quiet, the "cooperative" partner will be allowed to plead guilty to a lesser charge and get off with 1 year in jail, but the other partner will get 10 years (box B or C). They have one hour to decide.

The two men also know this: If they both confess, they will both get 10 years, but 2 years off for being so helpful. Thus they will both end up spending 8 years in jail (box A). If they both keep quiet, the D.A.'s evidence being less than perfect, they can only be nailed on the lesser charge (of possessing stolen goods), and both will get 2 years (box D).

What will they do? Consider the point of view of Suspect 1: If Suspect 2 kept quiet, then, by confessing, Suspect 1 could get 1 year (box B) instead of 2 years (box D). If Suspect 2 confessed, then, by confessing, Suspect 1 could get 8 years (box A) instead of 10 years (box C).

An analogous argument, of course, can be made for Suspect 2. Thus each will realize that he will be better off confessing no matter what his partner does. Both will "maximin"—that is, both will confess—and both will get 8 years!

From the prisoners' point of view, of course, box D would be a much better choice. Yet, while Suspect 1 tries for B, Suspect 2 tries for C; both get A. Thus are the wages of selfishness. Note: This type of game is being played every day, in a million different ways.

Consider Table 9.18. Part (I) pictures a situation common before the outbreak of a price war. Two competing firms are charging identical prices and would neither gain nor lose if they maintained the *status quo* (box D). Yet if Firm 1 maintained its price but Firm 2 cut its price by 10 percent, Firm 1 would lose $8 million, while Firm 2 would gain $6 million (box C). An analogous result would emerge, if Firm 2 maintained its price but Firm 1 made the price cut (box B). A simultaneous price cut, on the other hand, would bring equal $6 million losses to both firms (box A). Again, we have a prisoners' dilemma. Seeking to ensure the best of the worst that can happen (note the encircled number in the last column), Firm 1 will cut its price. Seeking to achieve the same goal (note the encircled number in the last row), Firm 2 will cut its price as well. They will end up in box A, while box D would have been so much better for them.

Part (II) pictures a similar story. Each of two competing firms is assumed to be spending $1

TABLE 9.18

Nonzero-Sum Games

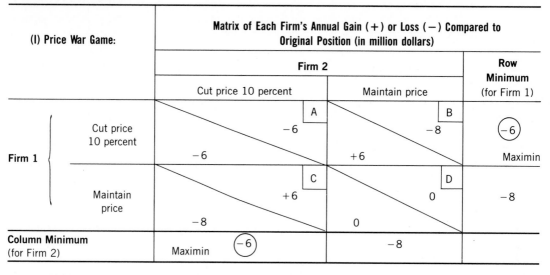

(I) Price War Game:		Matrix of Each Firm's Annual Gain (+) or Loss (−) Compared to Original Position (in million dollars)		Row Minimum (for Firm 1)
		Firm 2		
		Cut price 10 percent	Maintain price	
Firm 1	Cut price 10 percent	A −6 / −6	B −8 / +6	⊝−6 Maximin
	Maintain price	C +6 / −8	D 0 / 0	−8
Column Minimum (for Firm 2)		Maximin ⊝−6	−8	

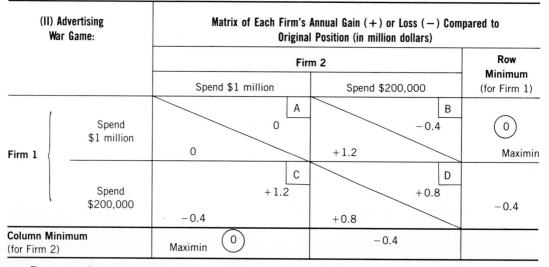

(II) Advertising War Game:		Matrix of Each Firm's Annual Gain (+) or Loss (−) Compared to Original Position (in million dollars)		Row Minimum (for Firm 1)
		Firm 2		
		Spend $1 million	Spend $200,000	
Firm 1	Spend $1 million	A 0 / 0	B −0.4 / +1.2	⊝0 Maximin
	Spend $200,000	C +1.2 / −0.4	D +0.8 / +0.8	−0.4
Column Minimum (for Firm 2)		Maximin ⊝0	−0.4	

The games pictured here also are prisoners' dilemma games. In part (I) as well as (II), the best common strategy is found in box D, but the worst one (box A) is chosen.

million per year on advertising. The extra revenue received by each as a result of advertising is $1 million, so the net effect is zero (box A). If Firm 2 now "disarmed" by spending only $200,000, while Firm 1 continued to spend $1 million, customers would abandon 2 for 1. Firm 1 would gain $1.2 million in sales; Firm 2 would lose $400,000, its $1.2 million loss in sales being partially offset by the $800,000 cut in advertising expenditures (box B). An analogous result would occur if only Firm 1 cut its advertising, while Firm 2 did not (box C). Yet if both firms "disarmed" at the same time and spent only $200,000 on advertising, neither would gain or lose customers and revenue, but both would have lowered costs and thus would gain $800,000 (box D).

With each firm going after the best of the worst, they end up in box A, spending $1 million each. Yet each could be so much better off by a simultaneous agreement to "disarm" and go after box D. (Can you see why U.S. tobacco companies were delighted, not grieved, when the government some years ago banned cigarette ads from television?)

Wide Applicability.   Games abound in which selfishness, uncooperativeness, hate, and suspicion put everyone in the worst possible spot (box A), while a dose of altruism, cooperation, love, and trust could make everyone better off (box D). Yet the great gains to be had from collusion (two years' jail instead of eight, zero loss instead of $6 million, an $800,000 gain instead of none) again and again remain unrealized because each player has an incentive to cheat and make an even greater gain (one year's jail instead of two years', $6 million gained instead of zero lost, $1.2 million gained instead of $800,000). Thus prisoners who could form an unspoken cartel and improve their common lot turn into stool pigeons, and firms that could form a cartel and raise profit by maintaining price (or by advertising less) end up with a price or advertising war instead (that is, with lowering prices and advertising as much as ever). People who could form a "cartel" and raise welfare by polluting less end up polluting more. And governments that could form a "cartel" and raise welfare by disarming end up in an arms race instead.

It is fairly easy to see what it would take to escape such prisoners' dilemma games.

Escaping the Dilemma.   There are at least three steps people could take to escape a prisoners' dilemma. One is to open up communications. If our prisoners could only have talked with one another! They could have reasoned together and ended up in situation D instead of A. The prisoners' dilemma feeds on uncertainty and distrust. Consider the international arms race. Early warning systems, telephone hot lines, and policies of détente, by opening up communications between the "prisoners" in separate rooms, have so far helped avoid nuclear holocaust. (See Close-Up 9.2 for a fascinating example.) On the other hand, nobody knows what goes on in foreign-weapons labs, and on that account suspicion thrives. We have not avoided the development of ever new weapons. Military leaders fear the worst. (Are "they" developing weapons to deliver poison gas? Deadly germs? The neutron bomb?) And thus is born the irresistible momentum to the arms race.

A second step toward escaping the dilemma is the institution of swift and certain punishment for those not choosing the best joint strategy. Betrayal and double cross must do more harm than good. Consider how "rat finks" are assassinated in the streets, how price cutters are threatened with even larger cuts, how the recipients of payola are fired on the spot, and how nuclear attackers are promised instant annihilation in turn. Consider, on the other hand, how those who know themselves to be immune from detection and punishment go ahead and do as they please. The secret developers of new weapons are a case in point. Once their weapons are revealed, they can count on years of undisturbed advantage. (Note: The certainty of swift punishment would worsen the entries in block A of the prisoners' dilemma tables, perhaps to -8 years plus death in Table 9.17 and to $-$9 million in both parts (I) and (II) of Table 9.18. The outcome would be a new game, called Chicken, and its solution would be quite a different one. Can you show why?)

A third step toward escape from the dilemma is to repeat the game. People can then *learn* to cooperate and to trust, which does not happen if the game is played only once. Consider how the same nuclear deterrence game is played anew on every single day, while the develop-a-new-weapon game is different every time.

Criticisms

Game theory has not brought permanent relief from the complexities of imperfect competition. Not everyone is happy with the kind of theory just introduced. Some would rather substitute less pessimistic assumptions about people's behavior. Do typical players of ''games,'' they ask, really choose the best of the worst for themselves or the worst of the best for their opponents? Do people fear the worst more than they hope for the best? Might they not fear regret more than disaster? Might the glittering prize of cooperative bliss not attract them more than the skeletons of earlier aspirants repel? If so, might one not do better by substituting still different strategies for those suggested by von Neumann and Morgenstern?

Of course one could. A wealth of alternative approaches exists. So far, no one of them has been universally accepted as the best theory for explaining the games people play.

SUMMARY

1. When people possess less than complete knowledge relevant to their decision making, they operate under uncertainty and, inevitably, face risk.

2. *Decision theory* consists of a variety of methods that can be employed in the systematic analysis and solution of decision-making problems that arise because uncertainty exists about future events over which the decision maker has no control, but which are bound to influence the ultimate outcome of a decision.

Certain identical elements are present in every decision problem involving uncertainty. They include the mutually exclusive decision alternatives, or *actions,* available to the decision maker, the mutually exclusive future occurrences, or *events,* that will affect the outcome of any present action taken but that are not under the control of a decision maker, and the positive or negative net benefits, or *payoffs,* that are associated with each possible action/event combination and that are thus the joint outcome of choice and chance.

A *payoff table* summarizes a decision-making situation in the context of uncertainty; it consists of a tabular listing of the payoffs associated with all possible combinations of actions and events. A *decision tree* provides an alternative summary; it shows graphically, and in chronological order from left to right, every potential action, event, and payoff. In such a tree diagram, any point of choice (at which the decision maker is in control) is denoted by a square symbol and is called an *action point* (from which *action branches* representing the possible actions emanate). In contrast, any point of chance (at which the decision maker exercises no control but at which ''nature'' is in charge) is denoted by a circle and is called an *event point* (from which *event branches* representing the possible events emanate).

3. When nothing is known about the likelihood of those alternative future events that are certain to affect the eventual outcome of a present decision, and if the decision maker does not even care to guess what the event probabilities might be, one of three decision criteria is commonly employed: maximin (or minimax), maximax (or minimin), or minimax regret.

a. According to the *maximin criterion,* a decision maker who seeks to maximize some benefit finds the minimum benefit associated with each possible action, identifies the maximum among these minima, and chooses the action associated with this maximum of minima. (The same criterion is called the *minimax criterion* when a decision maker seeks to minimize some cost; such a decision

Solution:

a. See Table 9.19. The minimax action is A_3.

b. See Table 9.19. The minimin action is A_1.

c. See Table 9.20. The minimax-regret action is A_3.

Exercise #2

Consider the price war game depicted in Table 9.21. If both firms follow the maximin strategy, what is the outcome?

Solution:

The row minima are -10, -5, -10 for Firm 1; it chooses A_5. The column minima are -10, -8, -13 for Firm 2; it chooses A_2. Thus both maintain their prices.

QUESTIONS AND PROBLEMS

1. The results obtained by the use of the nonprobabilistic decision criteria are easily affected by irrelevant factors. Consider Table 9.2 and imagine a government offering a fixed subsidy of $8 million, *regardless of the firm's action*, if demand should be weak. One would think that this incentive should not affect the firm's action, but under the maximin criterion it does. Explain.

2. Depending on whether future demand is low, moderate, or high, a real-estate developer foresees profits (in millions of dollars) of 4, 5, or 6 from a small project; of 1, 6, or 10 from a medium-sized project; and -5, 0, or 30 from a large project. Determine the best action under the criterion of

TABLE 9.19

Actions	Events			Row Maximum	Row Minimum
	E_1 = recession	E_2 = inflation	E_3 = stagflation		
A_1 = direct-mail campaign	75	20	40	75	20 (Minimin)
A_2 = newspaper campaign	50	60	30	60	30
A_3 = TV campaign	55	40	45	55 (Minimax)	40

TABLE 9.20

Actions	Events			Row Maximum
	E_1 = recession	E_2 = inflation	E_3 = stagflation	
A_1 = direct-mail campaign	75 − 50 = 25	20 − 20 = 0	40 − 30 = 10	25
A_2 = newspaper campaign	50 − 50 = 0	60 − 20 = 40	30 − 30 = 0	40
A_3 = TV campaign	55 − 50 = 5	40 − 20 = 20	45 − 30 = 15	20 (Minimax regret)

TABLE 9.21

Price War Game		Matrix of Each Firm's Annual Gain (+) or Loss (−) Compared to Original Position (in million dollars)		
		Firm 2		
		A_1 = cut price 20 percent	A_2 = maintain price	A_3 = raise price 20 percent
Firm 1	A_4 = cut price 20 percent	−10 / −10	+5 / −8	+10 / −13
	A_5 = maintain price	−5 / +4	0 / 0	+5 / −3
	A_6 = raise price 20 percent	−10 / +12	−5 / +3	+10 / +8

a. maximin.
b. maximax.

3. Depending on whether future demand is low, moderate, or high, a producer of aircraft emergency locator transmitters (ELTs) foresees profits (in thousands of dollars) of 15, 20, or 25 from a small production run; of 6, 20, or 35 from a medium-sized run; and of −10, 0, or 69 from a large run. Determine the best action under the criterion of

a. maximin.
b. maximax.

4. The Zoning Board of Appeals has granted permission to a builder to erect between 1 and 5 homes on a certain lot, but whatever the chosen number is, the homes must all be built now. The builder's cost is $100,000 per home; up to the number demanded, homes built can be sold at 25 percent above cost; any surplus homes can be sold to a real-estate firm at 60 percent of cost. How many homes should the profit-seeking builder erect, given that 1 home is the minimum and the criterion is

a. maximin.
b. maximax.

5. Rework Problem 4, but let the builder's cost be $60,000 per home, while regular sales are at 50 percent above cost and surplus sales at 80 percent of cost.

6. Rework Problem 4, but let the builder's cost be $120,000 per home, while regular sales are at 15 percent above cost and surplus sales at 50 percent of cost.

7. Reconsider Problem 3, but this time determine the best action under the criterion of minimax regret.

8. Reconsider Problem 3. Determine the best action under the expected-monetary-value criterion, assuming $p(E_1) = .1, p(E_2) = .7$, and $p(E_3) = .2$.

9. A business executive has determined that keeping the business in its present location is a disaster and that it must be moved to one of two new locations, east or west. Moving east will produce future net earnings with a present value of either $50 million or $10 million; moving the business west will produce future net earnings with a present value of either $100 million or zero—in each case, depending on whether the attempt to break into the new market will be a success or a failure.[1] Assuming that the chances for success or failure at the new locations are judged to be equal, determine the best action under the criterion of expected monetary value.

---

[1] In order to make comparable dollars of revenue and cost that pertain to different periods of time, it is customary to calculate payoffs in terms of "present value." For a detailed discussion of this concept, see Chapter 12 of this text.

10. Reconsider Problem 9. Determine the best action under the criterion of expected opportunity loss.

11. Reconsider Problem 9. Determine the best action under the criterion of expected utility, assuming the executive has a utility function of $U = \sqrt{\$}$.

12. Reconsider part II of Table 9.18. What would the outcome be if the entries in cell A were both equal to $+10$?

SELECTED READINGS

Bernoulli, Daniel. "Exposition of a New Theory on the Measurement of Risk," *Econometrica,* January 1954, pp. 23–36.

> A translation of Bernoulli's original solution (1738) of the St. Petersburg paradox.

Boulding, Kenneth E. *Conflict and Defense: A General Theory.* New York: Harper and Row, 1962.

Cross, John G. *The Economics of Bargaining.* New York: Basis Books, 1969.

Friedman, James W. *Oligopoly and the Theory of Games.* Amsterdam: North Holland, 1977.

Jacquemin, Alexis. *The New Industrial Organization: Market Forces and Strategic Behavior.* Cambridge, Mass.: MIT Press, 1987.

> Contrasts the classical approach to industrial organization (that studies market structure, behavior, and performance as emerging from a passive adaptation of industries to their environment) with a modern view (that sees complex games of power and economic domination manipulating the environment of industries).

Knight, Frank H. *Risk, Uncertainty and Profit.* Boston: Houghton Mifflin, 1921.

> A classic text.

Leibenstein, Harvey. *Beyond Economic Man: A New Foundation for Microeconomics.* Cambridge, Mass.: Harvard University Press, 1976, esp. chap. 9.

> Applies game theory to the analysis of X-inefficiency. *See also* his more recent article on the subject, "The Prisoner's Dilemma in the Invisible Hand: An Analysis of Intrafirm Productivity," *The American Economic Review,* May 1982, pp. 92–97.

Luce, R. Duncan, and Howard Raiffa. *Games and Decisions.* New York: Wiley, 1954.

McDonald, John. *Strategy in Poker, Business, and War.* New York: Norton, 1950.

Neumann, John von, and Oskar Morgenstern. *The Theory of Games and Economic Behavior,* rev. ed. Princeton, N.J.: Princeton University Press, 1953.

> The classic work on *game theory* that studies decision making under uncertainty that is complicated by a conscious conflict of wills so that the payoff to an action depends not only on the decision maker's choice and "nature," but also on the conscious choices made by other people.

Raiffa, Howard. *Decision Analysis: Introductory Lectures on Choices under Uncertainty.* Reading, Mass.: Addison-Wesley, 1968.

Rapoport, A. *Fights, Games, and Debates.* Ann Arbor, Mich.: University of Michigan Press, 1960.

Samuelson, Paul A. "St. Petersburg Paradoxes: Defanged, Dissected, and Historically Described," *Journal of Economic Literature,* March 1977, pp. 24–55.

> A superb discussion by the 1970 winner of the Nobel Prize in economics.

Schelling, T. C. *The Strategy of Conflict.* Cambridge, Mass.: Harvard University Press, 1960.

Schotter, Andrew, and Gerhard Schwödiauer. "Economics and the Theory of Games: A Survey." *Journal of Economic Literature,* June 1980, pp. 479–527.

Shackle, G. L. S. *Expectations in Economics.* Cambridge, England: Cambridge University Press, 1949.

> Postulates that decision makers in conflict situations compare two "focus outcomes" (hope for the best and fear of the worst) and make a choice between the two (instead of focusing on the latter alone).

Shubik, Martin. *Strategy and Market Structure.* New York: Wiley, 1959.

> The most ambitious application of game theory to the analysis of oligopoly.

Shubik, Martin. *Essays in Mathematical Economics: In Honor of Oskar Morgenstern.* Princeton, N.J.: Princeton University Press, 1967.

> Contains a 175-item bibliography of Morgenstern's work (through 1964) plus 27 essays on game theory, mathematical programming, decision theory, and more.

Shubik, Martin. *Game Theory in the Social Sciences: Concepts and Solutions.* Cambridge, Mass.: MIT Press, 1984.

Telser, Lester G. *Competition, Collusion, and Game Theory.* Chicago: Aldine-Atherton, 1972.

Tullock, Gordon. "Adam Smith and the Prisoners' Dilemma," *The Quarterly Journal of Economics,* Supplement 1985, pp. 1074–81.

Williams, J. D. *The Compleat Strategyst.* New York: McGraw-Hill, 1954.

COMPUTER PROGRAMS

The KOHLER-3 personal-computer diskettes that accompany this book contain one program of particular interest to this chapter:

9. *Decision Theory and Game Theory* in-

cludes a 25-question multiple-choice test with immediate responses to incorrect answers as well as numerous decision-making exercises. All of the exercises deal with uncertainty; some of them do and others do not assume a knowledge of event probabilities.

ANALYTICAL EXAMPLE 9.1

DECISION ANALYSIS COMES OF AGE

As recently as the early 1970s, decision analysis was still an experimental management technique. The idea that a choice facing a decision maker can be expressed as a mathematical function of probability and utility numbers (that measured, respectively, the decision maker's uncertainties and value judgments) and that the best action was the one with the highest expected utility had just begun to move out of business schools and into practical application in the business world. By the early 1980s, however, decision making with the help of quantitative models that incorporate personal judgment had gained acceptance in many large corporations and government departments.

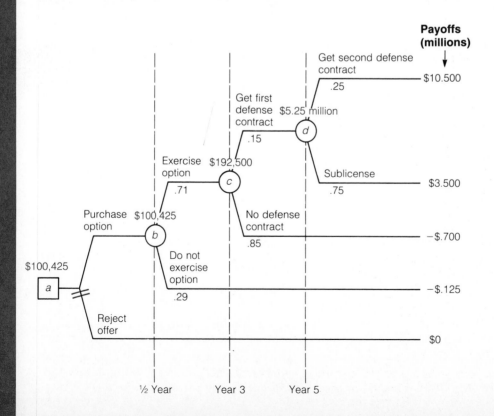

For example, in 1974, the AIL Division of Cutler-Hammer, Inc. was offered the opportunity to acquire the defense-market rights to a new flight-safety-system patent. The inventor claimed he had a strong patent position as well as technical superiority, but the market for the product depended on legislative action and was very uncertain. Management had to decide fast whether to purchase the rights to the new patent or to reject the offer; it used standard decision-tree techniques. Its initial analysis is illustrated in the accompanying diagram.

The immediate choice (at action point *a*) was the purchase of a six-month option on the patent rights or rejection of the offer. Six months hence, it was judged, there was (at event point *b*) a 71-percent chance of exercising the option and a 29-percent chance of not doing so. Three years down the road (at event point *c*), there was a 15-percent chance of getting, and an 85-percent chance of not getting, a first defense contract. Five years down the road (at event point *d*), finally, there was a 25-percent chance of getting a second defense contract and a 75-percent chance of being able to sublicense. Thus there were five possible outcomes. Using the technique of backward induction, the expected monetary values given in color were computed, and the tree was pruned as shown. Purchasing the option was shown to be worth $100,425; rejecting the offer was worth $0.

Upon further analysis, however, management discovered a third possible action at *a*—rejecting the offer and seeking a sublicense later on. That approach was shown to yield an expected value of $49,800, about half of the $100,425 expected monetary value of the option-purchase route. Nevertheless, being risk-averse, management chose the newly discovered third alternative: Its analysis showed the *EMV* of $49,800 to be composed of a 94-percent chance of zero gain or loss and a 6-percent chance of gaining $830,000. On the other hand, as we can figure from the diagram, the *EMV* of $100,425 is provided by a riskier route composed of a 29-percent chance of losing $125,000, a 60-percent chance of losing $700,000, and an 11-percent chance of a postive return with an expectation of $5.25 million. Thus management effectively maximized expected utility rather than monetary value.

Many other companies have also used the decision-tree technique. Ford has determined in this way whether to produce its own tires and whether to stop producing convertibles; Honeywell used it to decide whether to pursue certain new weapons programs; Pillsbury used the technique to determine whether to switch from a box to a bag for a certain grocery product (and whether it was worthwhile to make a market test of the issue); Southern Railway employed it to choose whether to electrify part of its system; Gulf Oil used it to decide whether to explore certain sites; ITT used decision trees in deciding whether to make certain capital investments.

Source: Jacob W. Ulvila and Rex V. Brown, "Decision Analysis Comes of Age," *Harvard Business Review,* September-October 1982, pp. 130–41.

CLOSE-UP 9.1

MARKETING AS WARFARE

In a world of oligopolies in which businesses look upon each other as rivals, executives are increasingly using the language of military science. They talk of price and advertising "wars," of "border clashes" and "market invasion," of an "escalating arms race" and "guerrilla warfare." Indeed, executives are studying the works of Clausewitz and Liddell Hart, military theorists who advocated, respectively, the enemy's total annihilation or merely subjugation. Having combed the military classics for ideas, marketing texts list offensive and defensive strategies such as these:

Offensive strategies:

1.   The *frontal attack* pits strength against strength and rarely succeeds. (Military strategists who have discovered only 6 successes in 280 campaigns of this sort since ancient times advise the would-be attacker to forget it, unless a 3:1 advantage in resources exists.) Firms that use this risky approach match the rival product by product, advertisement by advertisement, price cut by price cut. RCA, GE, and Xerox tried and lost against IBM; Helene Curtis's Suave Shampoo won against Procter and Gamble's Head and Shoulders.

2.   The *flanking attack* pits strength against weakness and attacks where the enemy least expects it. It can be *geographical* (as when IBM competitors focus on small and medium cities that are ill-served by IBM) or *segmental* (as when German and Japanese car makers entered the U.S. market for small cars when Detroit was focusing on large ones or when Miller introduced light beer neglected by Schlitz).

3.   The *encirclement attack* surrounds the enemy on all sides, diluting the enemy's strength. An attacking firm offers everything the rival has and more. Success came to Seiko when it saturated the world watch market with 2,300 models catering to every conceivable taste; success eluded Hunt's when it tried to outdo Heinz's ketchup line in a similar way.

4.   The *bypass attack* involves a decision not to fight. A firm diversifies toward unrelated products or new geographic regions. Thus Colgate, unable to outdo Procter and Gamble in soaps and detergents, did well in cosmetics, hospital products, sporting goods, and textiles.

5.   The *guerrilla attack* involves harrassing and demoralizing the enemy. A firm will cut prices selectively, hire away the executives of competitors, or engage in selective legal actions (even when lost, legal actions that delay the opponent's plans may destroy those plans).

Defensive strategies:

1.   A *position or static defense* is the riskiest of all; it is akin to the French Maginot Line, the German Siegfried Line, the Israeli Barlev Line, the forts of old. The belief in something being invincible is almost always proven wrong; Henry Ford's faith in his Model T is a case in point. The Coca Cola Company has recently taken this lesson to heart: Despite its selling of half the soft drinks in the world, it is countering attacks on its position by diversifying—into wines, fruit drinks, desalinization equipment, and plastics!

2.   A *mobile defense* is forever flexible. Similar to the Coca Cola case, a firm employing this defense broadens its market by focusing on an underlying generic need rather than a specific product. Thus a petroleum company will think of itself as an energy company and thus turn to coal or hydro power and more.

3.   A *flank-positioning defense* involves hedging one's bets. A supermarket, for instance, may preserve its appeal by merging with pharmacies or bookstores and selling their products along with regular groceries.

4.   A *counteroffensive* fights back with the same weapons that led the attack. Clearasil, for instance, successfully defended its market share when attacked by an advertising blitz of Oxy–5, another acne medication.

5.   The *hedgehog defense* employs strategic withdrawal. Firms under attack may prune their product lists, for example, and concentrate only on the best sellers. This approach was taken recently by Westinghouse (with respect to its refrigerator models) and by Campbell soups (with respect to its canned-product line).

Note: While some executives have been using strategies derived from Western military writers, others have turned to the East. They have been reading *A Book of Five Rings* by Miyamoto Musashi, a 16th-century Japanese samurai, in order to uncover the secrets of Japanese business prowess. (Musashi, a wandering swordsman who defeated more than 60 opponents in duels, emphasizes the importance of timing, keen observation of one's opponent, clear thinking, and dedication to mastering one's craft as the key ingredients to winning battles, military or commercial.)

Source: Philip Kotler and Ravi Singh, "Marketing Warfare," *The Journal of Business Strategy,* Winter 1981.

CLOSE-UP 9.2

THE MOSCOW–WASHINGTON HOTLINE

An excellent example of a prisoners' dilemma situation is provided by the Cuban missile crisis that brought the world to the brink of nuclear war. At the time, messages between President Kennedy and Premier Khrushchev took six hours to deliver. The crisis gave birth to the *hotline,* a 24-hour electronic link between Washington and Moscow through which leaders might defuse explosive situations.

Today the link consists of a teletype and facsimile system capable of transmitting messages, maps, charts, and photographs almost instantaneously between the Pentagon's National Military Command Center and the Communist Party Headquarters on Red Square. On this side of the line, messages are instantly translated and sent to the Situation Room of the White House; they can also be sent to the President wherever he goes, using special equipment that accompanies him at all times.

Ever since its inauguration in 1963, the system has been tested every hour of every day. According to one test message, "The quick brown fox jumped over the lazy dog's back 1234567890." Other messages have included Shakespeare, Mark Twain, and—on the Russian side—Chekhov and a poem about a Moscow sunset. Serious messages were exchanged during the 1967 Arab-Israeli Six-Day War, the 1971 Indo-Pakistani War, the 1974 Turkish invasion of Cyprus, the 1979 Soviet invasion of Afghanistan, and, more recently, the 1988 unrest in Poland. Thus, in 1967, Kosygin promised to keep the Soviets out of the war if the United States would do likewise. President Johnson readily agreed. Yet, a few days later, a U.S. ship was torpedoed off the Sinai peninsula. As a U.S. carrier task force moved in to pick up survivors, the Russians were reassured of U.S. neutrality. Again, when the Israelis seemed poised to take Damascus, the United States promised to attempt to keep the Israelis from continuing their drive. The Russians, in turn, pledged nonintervention on behalf of their Syrian ally.

As a defense program, the hotline has proved to be a real bargain; it cost a mere $1 million in 1988. No wonder that other countries have installed hotlines as well: France and the U.S.S.R., Great Britain and the U.S.S.R., Israel and Egypt, North and South Korea.

Source: Webster Stone, "Moscow's Still Holding: Twenty-Five Years on the Hot Line," *The New York Times Magazine,* September 18, 1988, pp. 58, 59, and 67.

10

Insurance and Gambling, Search and Futures Markets

In this chapter, we extend our earlier discussion of *primary* or *event uncertainty* and show how its existence gives rise to markets for insurance and gambling. Then we go a step further and note the existence of **secondary uncertainty** or **market uncertainty,** a situation in which certain facts about the present or future are known to some people but not to other people. Consider the consumer who wishes to buy a given type of car at the cheapest possible price but who does not know (as potential sellers do) at which places and prices it is presently available. Consider the manufacturer who plans to supply a commodity in the future but who does not know at which future price it can be sold. (If the present plans of all future buyers and suppliers could be revealed, the future equilibrium price could be known now.)

In the following sections, we will focus on four approaches people take toward the two types of uncertainty. We will note how people enter **contingent-claim markets** in which they trade rights to variable quantities of particular goods— the quantities being dependent on the occurrence of specified "states of the world." In such markets, people can *reduce* risk—the uncertainty-induced chance of variation in their welfare— through *insurance,* or they can *increase* risk through *gambling.* In addition to buying insur-

ance, people who dislike uncertainty can also mitigate it by *searching* for added information or entering **futures markets,** in which they commit themselves now to trade, at specified dates in the future, specified quantities and qualities of goods at specified prices. (These markets contrast with **spot markets,** in which people agree to trade specified quantities and qualities of goods at specified prices and do it now.)

FROM RISK AVERSION TO INSURANCE

As was noted in the previous chapter (pp. 306–308), people might hold any one of three attitudes toward risk. They might be averse to it; they might be neutral toward it; they might seek it out. The existence of risk aversion—by far the most common attitude—gives rise to a market for insurance.

The Demand Side

Consider Figure 10.1. The utility function shown there is that of the risk averter first pictured in panel (a) of Figure 9.4. Suppose that this person was assured of a $25,000 income but also saw a

FIGURE 10.1

Risk Aversion and Insurance

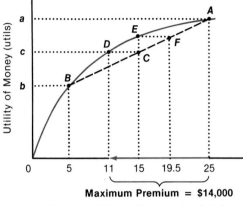

A risk-averse person can reduce risk (or the spread of possible outcomes around an expected value) by buying insurance. In this example, an equally probable $5,000 or $25,000 (with a $15,000 expected monetary value) could be escaped, without a change in welfare, by purchasing $20,000 of insurance for a premium of $14,000. (The resultant certain utility of $11,000, corresponding to point *D,* would then just equal the utility expected under uncertainty, corresponding to point *C.*) Any lower insurance premium would, of course, raise welfare in comparison with the situation of uncertainty.

50-50 chance of losing a $20,000 house through fire in a given year. (This rather unrealistic number has been chosen in order to produce an easily readable graph.) This person would, in fact, face a gamble between $25,000 (and its associated utility 0*a*) and $5,000 (and its lower utility 0*b*), both cases being considered of equal subjective probability. The expected monetary value of this gamble would equal $15,000 and, as point *C* tells us, provide an expected utility of 0*c*.

Note: The risk-averse person would derive equal expected utility from $11,000 to be received with certainty because point *D* on this person's utility function is found at the same level as *C*. Such a person, therefore, would be willing to pay up to $14,000 for a contingent claim according to which someone would contract to pay $20,000 if the house burned down.

The Supply Side

When risk averters, seeking to replace uncertainty with certainty, in this way offer to buy contingent claims, others may well supply them. An insurance company might notice that the objective probability of someone's house burning down in a given year is in fact not .5, but .004. In order to make good on claims, it would, therefore, have to collect $20,000 from every 250 home-owners like our risk-averse friend plus, let us say, an added 20 percent to cover operating costs. It could, therefore, offer to sell the contingent claim sought by our friend for as little as $24,000 per year divided by 250, or $96 per year—a far cry from the $14,000-a-year maximum premium our friend was willing to pay.

Indeed, even if the company's estimate of probability agreed with our home-owner's (and it would have to collect $20,000 plus expenses from every 2 persons), the premium could be as low as $12,000 per year. In either case, therefore, there would be room for a mutually profitable deal. Such a deal would leave our friend somewhere on the utility function to the right of *D* and to the left of *A*, and such a position would yield, with certainty, a utility greater than 0*c*, the utility expected in an uncertain world.

No wonder that insurance has been big business ever since ancient times. Even the Babylonians insured their caravans, the Greeks their sea trade. At the time of Queen Elizabeth I, the English followed suit. As an act of Parliament put it, "It cometh to passe that upon the losse or perishinge of any shippe, there followethe not the undoinge of any man, but the losse lighteth rather easilie upon many than heavilie upon few."[1] Before long, in 1688, Edward Lloyd opened a coffeehouse near the Thames River in the City of London, and merchants and shippers met there to negotiate marine insurance. From these humble beginnings, there developed Lloyd's of London,

---

[1]Timothy Green, "You Name It, Lloyd's of London Probably Insures It," *Best of Business,* Fall 1981, pp. 25–31, and Godfrey Hodgson, "Restoring the Lloyd's of London Mystique," *New York Times Magazine,* March 11, 1984, pp. 48ff.

now the world's largest insurance market. Housed in an imposing white stone building in the heart of London, Lloyd's in 1984 was not a company in the usual sense of the term, but an association of some 23,400 "names"—investors with a minimum wealth of £100,000 each who had formed several hundred "syndicates" to sell insurance policies and who were individually liable to the full extent of their assets. (The "names" included the Duke and Duchess of Marlborough, Arabian oil sheiks, Hong Kong shipowners, Nigerian tribal chiefs, tennis star Virginia Wade, and the Pink Floyd rock band!) The policies sold ranged from the expected to the highly unusual. Among the expected, one finds auto, aviation, burglary, fire, health, liability, and life insurance. But Lloyd's has also insured dancers, movie stars, and soccer players against damage to their legs; ball teams, ski resorts, and

vacationers against bad weather; international businesses against nationalization or contract cancellations after *coups d'état;* and even a Texan against death from the uncontrolled reentry of Skylab (that $1 million policy cost $250). In 1984, Lloyd's collected over $5 billion in premiums.

At the same time, plans were underway in many insurance companies to compete more effectively for Lloyd's business. In what was billed as "the most important change in the international insurance business in decades," a New York Insurance Exchange opened in 1980. Modeled after Lloyd's, it was scheduled to become primarily a marketplace for high-risk insurance, covering such things as offshore oil rigs and satellites. The exchange was designed to let insurance companies that had taken on such huge risks sell off smaller pieces of risk to many others and to attract to this type of reinsurance a multitude of individual investors.

Analytical Example 10.1 at the end of this chapter contains an interesting application.

FROM RISK SEEKING TO GAMBLING

Just as risk aversion gives rise to insurance, so risk seeking leads to a market for gambling.

The Demand Side

Consider Figure 10.2. The utility function shown there is that of the risk seeker first pictured in panel (c) of Figure 9.4.

Suppose that this person was assured of a $15,000 income but was also offered a bet to win or lose, with equal probability, $10,000 in a year. This person would compare utility 0a, associated with the $15,000 certain income, with higher utility 0b, associated with the $15,000 expected monetary value (or mathematical expectation) of the gamble. This person, therefore, would be willing to take the gamble. Indeed, the person would pay up to $3,500 for the privilege of taking the gamble.

If the person did pay the $3,500 fee, one of two things would happen (with equal probability,

FIGURE 10.2

Risk Seeking and Gambling

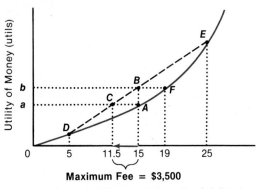

A risk-seeking person can increase risk (or the spread of possible outcomes around an expected value) by gambling. In this example, a certain prospect of $15,000 could be escaped, without a change in welfare, by paying a fee of $3,500 for the privilege of gambling for an equally probable loss or gain of $10,000. (The resultant expected utility of the gamble, corresponding to point *C,* would then just equal the utility received under certainty and corresponding to point *A.*) Any lower gambling fee would, of course, raise welfare in comparison with the situation of certainty.

we assumed): $10,000 would be lost (leaving the original $15,000 minus the $3,500 fee minus the $10,000 loss, or $1,500) or $10,000 would be won (leaving the original $15,000 minus the $3,500 fee plus the $10,000 gain, or $21,500). The expected monetary value of this gamble would equal $1,500 (.5) + $21,500 (.5) = $11,500, which (as point C indicates) has an expected utility of $0a$, just equal to the utility (at point A) of the $15,000 certain income.

Thus, such a person would be willing to pay up to $3,500 for the mere privilege of winning or losing $10,000 contingent upon an uncertain event, such as the performance of a race horse, roll of a die, or drawing of a lottery number.

The Supply Side

When risk seekers, seeking to replace certainty with uncertainty, in this way offer to buy contingent claims, others may well supply them. No wonder that all types of gambling have flourished for centuries and in many cultures. Like insurance, gambling is big business, too. Apart from betting on horse races and lotteries, which are legal in many states, Las Vegas long held a U.S. monopoly in casino gambling (1983 taxable casino revenue was $1.9 billion). Recently, Atlantic City established a number of casinos; by 1983, their taxable "take" almost matched Las Vegas with $1.8 billion. Indeed, as New Jersey was contemplating an extension of such gambling to the Meadowlands, a stone's throw from Manhattan, New York's Casino Gambling Study Panel in 1979 had recommended setting up some 40 casinos, from Niagara Falls and the Catskills to Manhattan and Coney Island. (The panel projected a taxable annual revenue of $3 billion.) Similar panels made similar suggestions from Pennsylvania to Massachusetts to Quebec. And, by 1988, some 29 states were actively marketing lottery tickets that brought in $15.6 billion in sales revenue. On the average, 37 percent of this revenue was profit and, thus, a painless alternative to higher taxes. Indeed, some state governments were even contemplating a multistate

lottery with jackpots in excess of $80 million! Close-Up 10.1 presents the big picture, but as Close-Up 10.2 shows, governments have a schizophrenic attitude toward gambling.

SIMULTANEOUS INSURING AND GAMBLING

It does not follow from the foregoing analysis that risk averters always buy insurance and never gamble. Nor does it follow that risk seekers always gamble and never buy insurance. What each group will do depends very much on whether the insurance or gambles they confront are more-than-fair, fair, or unfair.

Insurance and Gambles: From More-than-Fair to Unfair

We already noted that a gamble is called *fair* when its expected monetary value is zero, any expectation of gain being exactly offset by that of loss. The same definition applies to **fair insurance.** Accordingly, insurance contracts and gambles are called *more than fair* when their expected monetary value is positive, when the expectation of gain exceeds that of loss. Similarly, insurance contracts and gambles are *unfair* when their expected monetary value is negative and the expectation of gain falls short of that of loss. An analysis of our earlier examples can quickly establish how people with different attitudes toward risk will act when confronted with these three different types of insurance contracts or gambles.

The Risk Averter's Attitude Toward Insurance. Consider once more Figure 10.1, in which our house-owner was willing to replace the $5,000-versus-$25,000 gamble with a $25,000 certainty minus a premium of up to $14,000 a year. Because the $20,000 house was believed to have a 50-percent chance of burning down in a year, its owner had a mathematical expectation of gain from insurance of $10,000 a year (the owner could expect to collect from the insurance company $20,000 every second year). The insured owner's expectation of loss, on the other hand, was nothing else but the insurance premium.

If the premium were smaller than $10,000 a year (and the insurance, therefore, was more than fair), our owner would end up with a certain amount of money in excess of $15,000 and a utility corresponding to some point to the right of E. Surely, such would be better than the expected utility without insurance (corresponding to C). Risk averters, therefore, do buy insurance that is more than fair.

If the premium were exactly $10,000 a year (and the insurance, therefore, was fair), our owner would end up with exactly $15,000 and a utility corresponding to point E. This, too, would be better than the expected utility without insurance (corresponding to C). Risk averters, therefore, do buy insurance that is fair.

If the premium were larger than $10,000 a year (and the insurance, therefore, was unfair), premiums between $10,001 and $14,000 a year would leave the owner with $14,999 to $11,000 of money a year and a utility corresponding to some point between D and just to the left of E. Such would be as good as or better than the expected utility without insurance (corresponding to C). Risk averters, therefore, buy *some* insurance that is unfair. They won't buy it, however, if it is *too* unfair. Any premium above $14,000 a year would reduce the person's money to below $11,000 a year and reduce utility below 0c (below what it would be without insurance). Risk averters would not buy such insurance.

The Risk Seeker's Attitude Toward Insurance. Assume all circumstances to be the same as in the previous section, except that the home-owner is risk-seeking, and the utility function is depicted by Figure 10.2. Even the person depicted there would replace the $5,000-versus-$25,000 gamble with a $25,000 certain amount, minus insurance premium, as long as the premium was no more than $6,000 a year (such insurance would

be more than fair). The amount of money available with certainty would then lie between $19,000 and $25,000 a year, and the associated utility (corresponding to some point between F and E) would exceed the expected utility of the gamble (corresponding to B). Risk seekers, therefore, do buy *some* insurance that is more than fair.

By the same token, however, they reject other insurance contracts that are more than fair, and they reject all that are fair or less than fair. In our example, premiums between $6,001 and $9,999 (still leaving the insurance more than fair), of $10,000 (making the insurance fair), and in excess of $10,000 (making the insurance unfair) would all produce remaining money amounts below $19,000 a year. They would, therefore, produce utilities corresponding to points along the line from 0 to just left of F, always lower than the expected utility of the gamble (corresponding to B).

The Risk Averter's Attitude Toward Gambling. Just as risk seekers can be persuaded to buy insurance when it is considerably more than fair, so risk averters would take gambles if they were considerably more than fair. Consider, again, Figure 10.1. This time, a risk averter with a certain sum of $15,000 would reject the $5,000-versus-$25,000 equally probable and, therefore, fair gamble because E lies above C.

Since even this fair gamble would be rejected by the risk averter, obviously an unfair one, with an expected utility corresponding to some point between B and C, would be rejected all the more. These positions would also bring lower utility than E.

Indeed, *some* more-than-fair gambles, with expected utilities corresponding to points between C and F, would be rejected as well. Even these positions would bring lower utilities than E. Yet other more-than-fair gambles would be acceptable, even to the risk averter. In our example, these gambles are those with mathematical expectations between $19,500 and $25,000 a year, all of which produce expected utilities (on segment *FA*) as large as or larger than the utility of the $15,000-a-year certain sum assumed available initially.

The Risk Seeker's Attitude Toward Gambling.
Just as risk averters will reject insurance when it is extremely unfair, so risk seekers reject gambles that are considerably unfair, as implied in Figure 10.2. We already know why the person pictured there would reject the certainty of $15,000 in favor of a fair gamble—an equally probable $5,000 or $25,000: Point *B* lies above point *A*.

Since a fair gamble would be accepted, obviously a more-than-fair one, with an expected utility corresponding to some point between *B* and *E*, would be accepted all the more. These positions would also bring higher utility than *A*.

Indeed, as we have seen, *some* unfair gambles, with expected utilities corresponding to points between *B* and *C,* would be accepted as well. Even these positions would bring higher utilities than *A*. Yet other unfair gambles would not be acceptable, even to the risk seeker. In our example, these gambles are those with mathematical expectations between $5,000 and $11,499 a year, all of which produce expected utilities (on segment *DC*) smaller than the utility of the $15,000-a-year certain sum assumed available initially.

The attitudes of risk seekers and risk averters toward both gambling and insurance are summarized in Table 10.1, along with the attitudes of risk-neutral persons.

A Paradox

We now must face a paradox. Our analysis leads us to conclude that a risk averter will buy a fair insurance contract, and even a not-too-unfair one but will never take a fair or unfair gamble. Similarly, a risk seeker will never buy a fair or unfair insurance contract but will take a fair and not-too-unfair gamble. Yet real-world people do buy fair and unfair insurance and take fair and unfair gambles at the same time! How can they possibly be risk averters and risk seekers simultaneously?

A possible explanation for the paradox that most people are risk averters yet *do* take fair and not-too-unfair gambles, contrary to what Table 10.1 tells us, is that people gamble not only in order to change their wealth, but also for the very fun of it. The very activity of being at the races or visiting the casinos, perhaps, is recreational for them, like playing tennis or going to the beach. Thus there are consumption aspects to gambling that create additional utility not considered above. This explanation rings true when one considers the high frequency of repetitive small-

TABLE 10.1

Risk: Attitudes and Behavior

Person's Attitude Toward Risk	Person's View of					
	Insurance, if Contract Is			Gambling, if Contract Is		
	More than Fair	Fair	Unfair	More than Fair	Fair	Unfair
Risk aversion	Desirable	Desirable	Sometimes desirable	Sometimes desirable	Undesirable	Undesirable
Risk neutrality	Desirable	Indifferent	Undesirable	Desirable	Indifferent	Undesirable
Risk seeking	Sometimes desirable	Undesirable	Undesirable	Desirable	Desirable	Sometimes desirable

Regardless of their attitudes toward risk, people may find insurance or gambling desirable or undesirable depending on the type of contract offered them.

stakes gambling at casinos (which can hardly have significant impact on people's wealth). It doesn't ring true when one considers the purchase of state lottery tickets.

The most famous answer to this paradox, however, is provided by Milton Friedman and L. J. Savage. They suggest that people's utility functions may not look at all like those found in Figure 10.1, but may look like the one in Figure 10.3. The marginal utility of money declines, the hypothesis says, when the amount of money is below a certain level (such as A), rises between that level and a higher one (as between A and B), and falls again above that higher level.

Now consider a person with an amount of money equal to A. That person may face the possibility of a large loss of AC, as did our house-owner in Figure 10.1. For reasons indicated then, that person would buy insurance, trading in the gamble between C and A for the certainty of some intermediate amount, such as D. The utility of this certain amount, corresponding to point d, would exceed the utility expected from the gamble, corresponding to some point, such as b, on the dashed line between c and a. This is why the utility function from 0 to a is said to lie in the region of insurance.

The same person, on the other hand, may be attracted by a lottery, offering a large chance of losing a small sum (the ticket price AD) and a small chance of winning a large sum (a lottery price of AE). The expected monetary value of this gamble between D and E may equal the amount F. As can be seen in our graph, the expected utility derived from the gamble, corresponding to f, exceeds the utility at a of the certain amount of money held initially. The person will take the gamble; thus a given person may be found simultaneously in the first and last row of Table 10.1 (note the encircled portions).

MARKET UNCERTAINTY AND SEARCH

When people are confronted by uncertainty of the market, rather than uncertainty of events, they can try to overcome their ignorance of the facts by engaging in **search,** an activity designed to discover information already possessed by other people. Like all activities, the search for information absorbs resources and time, and there is therefore an optimum point beyond which a wise decision maker does not carry the effort. *Pigheadedness* (looking forever for that needle in the haystack) is sure to violate the optimization principle, but so is *faintheartedness* (not looking at all). Consider, for example, the search for the terms at which exchange can be carried out.

The Search for Price

George J. Stigler was among the first to emphasize how buyers and sellers alike must inevitably act before they have perfect knowledge of the best available price. Someone about to buy a new car, for example, can visit any number of dealers; each additional visit will bring with it not only an

FIGURE 10.3

The Friedman-Savage Hypothesis

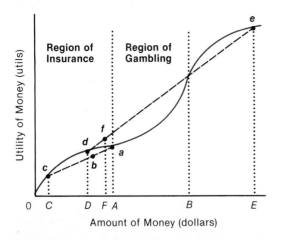

A person whose utility function looks like the one pictured here may buy fair and not-too-unfair insurance while simultaneously taking fair and not-too-unfair gambles.

ever increasing total cost of the search, but also an ever declining marginal benefit from extending the search. Consider Table 10.2. A buyer who had to spend an extra $150 to visit the fourth dealer, for example, would not find the added search worthwhile: The $150 marginal cost would exceed the $125 marginal benefit.

The phenomenon just described is, of course, widely applicable, and not only to buyers. Consider how people often engage in lengthy searches for the highest possible price when selling their homes or their labor. The fact that a wide dispersion of prices persists in such markets is an indicator of ignorance in these markets. This ignorance can be overcome in part by direct search of the type just described but also by the purchase of second-hand information (expert advice) and the monitoring of free information disseminated by others (which might be misinformation). Note: When markets are completely centralized, such as those for securities traded at major stock exchanges, everyone can know all the prices quoted by all traders at a given time. In that rare case, price dispersion disappears.

The Search for Quality

An even more interesting problem, highlighted by George A. Akerlof, is people's ignorance about the *quality* of things traded in markets. Consider the market for *used* cars. Why is it, Akerlof asked, that brand-new cars fetch such a low price when resold on the used-car market? The answer is fairly simple:

The buyer of a new car faces a (low) probability of *x* that the new car is a ''lemon.'' Once the car has been bought and used, the buyer knows the car's quality with certainty. Surely, buyers are more likely to resell their cars when they are lemons. Buyers of used cars, in turn, assume this to be so. They cannot differentiate good used cars (for which they would gladly pay a fairly high price) from bad used cars (for which they would pay almost nothing). As a result, they offer an average price that seems unreasonably low to the seller of a good used car and delightfully high to the seller of a bad used car. No wonder that good cars disappear from the used-car market, while lemons abound. The abundance of

TABLE 10.2

Searching for the Lowest Price

Number of Sellers Canvassed	Probability of Finding Minimum Price Equal to		Expected Minimum Price
	$4,000	$6,000	
1	.5	.5	$5,000
2	.75	.25	4,500
3	.875	.125	4,250
4	.9375	.0625	4,125
.	.	.	.
.	.	.	.
.	.	.	.
∞	1.0	0	$4,000

If sellers of a given type of car are equally divided between prices of $4,000 and $6,000, a buyer searching for the lowest possible price is ever more likely to find it the more sellers are canvassed.

Source: Based on George J. Stigler, ''The Economics of Information,'' *The Journal of Political Economy,* June 1961, p. 214. Reprinted by permission of the University of Chicago Press. © 1970 by the University of Chicago.

lemons, of course, only strengthens the determination of people to pay little for used cars. (For additional discussion, see Analytical Example 10.2 at the end of this chapter.)

Sellers who know the (high) quality of what they have to sell try to dispel the ignorance on the buyers' side by engaging in a variety of activities that would be irrational if the quality of their products was low. Such sellers engage in informational advertising (the citing of facts and the drawing of valid conclusions). They establish brand names whereby they make themselves vulnerable to loss of repeat sales if quality is low. They offer prepurchase inspection by experts of the buyers' choosing, money-back guarantees, or free service contracts. In the labor market, too, sellers engage in **signaling,** an activity designed to convince buyers of the high quality of what is being sold. Consider how workers advertise their high quality by acquiring educational credentials (which low-quality workers would find it difficult or impossible to get). Buyers, in turn, engage in **screening,** an activity designed to select high-quality sellers. Consider how employers select high-quality workers from an applicant pool with the help of educational credentials, even though the education itself may be totally unrelated to the immediate tasks to be performed. (Screening based on indices that cannot be altered at the discretion of individual workers, such as age, race, or sex, is typically illegal.)

MARKET UNCERTAINTY AND FUTURES MARKETS

When market uncertainty involves ignorance not about present facts, but about the future, people can sometimes dispel it with the help of futures markets. Note that unconditional rather than contingent claims are being traded in these markets. In futures markets, people commit themselves now to trade, at specified dates in the future, specified quantities and qualities of goods at specified prices; these agreements are not contingent on the occurrence of unforeseeable events,

such as a house burning down or lottery number 97,531 being drawn. Futures markets balance demand and supply *in advance;* on the basis of the combined information available to traders now, they produce the best possible estimates of future prices. Futures markets are windows on the future. They serve to redistribute uncertainty over the population, from hedgers who wish to minimize price risk to speculators who wish to assume it.

The Role of Hedging

Hedging is the taking of equal and opposite positions in the spot and futures markets, with the hope that this will prevent a loss due to price fluctuations. A hedger attempts to have neither a net asset or **long position** (in which more of something is owned than owed) nor a net liability or **short position** (in which more of something is owed than owned). A successful hedger's net worth is, therefore, unaffected by price changes.

The Selling Hedge or Short Hedge. Consider a farmer who wishes to fix the value, at the current spot price, of a 10,000-bushel wheat crop just before the harvest. This farmer is in a long position in the spot market, owning wheat and owing none at all. The farmer can protect the value of this existing inventory (at the spot price of, say, $2.77 per bushel) by selling in the futures market, thereby gaining a short position in it. The farmer's initial moves, we assume, are made on September 5, as indicated at the top of Table 10.3. Various consequences are possible, but we will consider only two:

Case I indicates what would happen if spot and futures prices both fell by equal amounts. While the farmer would lose 12¢ per bushel on the actual wheat (compared to the September 5 price), there would be a gain of 12¢ per bushel on the futures contracts. Thus the farmer in fact would receive $2.77 per bushel.

Case II is analogous to I. It indicates what would happen if spot and futures prices both rose by equal amounts. Once more, the farmer would

TABLE 10.3

The Selling Hedge

Spot Market	Futures Market
September 5 — Spot price is $2.77 per bushel; farmer owns 10,000 bushels of not-yet-harvested wheat	December futures price is $2.87 per bushel; farmer sells two contracts of December wheat futures (a single grain contract is 5,000 bushels)
Case I	
November 20 — Spot price is $2.65 per bushel; farmer sells 10,000 bushels of wheat	December futures price is $2.75 per bushel; farmer buys two contracts of December wheat
Loss: 12¢ per bushel	Gain: 12¢ per bushel
Net result: 0	
Case II	
November 20 — Spot price is $2.87 per bushel; farmer sells 10,000 bushels of wheat	December futures price is $2.97 per bushel; farmer buys two contracts of December wheat
Gain: 10¢ per bushel	Loss: 10¢ per bushel
Net result: 0	

The **selling hedge** or **short hedge** aims to provide price protection for producers, merchants, and warehousers while they hold inventories of commodities, as they inevitably must.

be successful in "locking in" the pre-harvest price.

Note: If the farmer hadn't hedged at all, the farmer would have lost $1,200 in Case I (compared to September 5) and would have gained $1,000 in Case II. A risk-averse individual may prefer the results of Table 10.3.

The Buying Hedge or Long Hedge. Just as sellers try to ensure their revenues, so buyers who need a continuing supply of raw materials can attempt through hedging to ensure their costs. Consider a builder who has just contracted to deliver a number of houses a year hence. The contract is based on the current spot prices of raw materials, including 10 carloads of plywood. The builder has, in effect, just sold plywood that isn't owned (and won't have to be bought until construction begins seven months hence). The builder is in a short position in the spot market. The builder could, of course, buy the plywood (and all other materials) right now. But buying

now would incur storage, insurance, and interest costs. The builder can instead "lock in" the current spot price by buying a futures contract and taking a long position in that market. Table 10.4 shows the initial moves and two possible consequences:

Case I indicates what would happen if spot and futures prices both rose by equal amounts. While the builder would lose $32 per thousand square feet (MSF) on the actual plywood (compared to the September 5 price), there would be a gain of $32 per MSF on the futures contracts. Thus the builder would, in fact, have "locked in" the plywood at $137 per MSF, the price on which the building contract was based.

Case II indicates what would happen if spot and futures prices both fell by equal amounts. Once again the builder's initial cost estimate would effectively be maintained.

If the builder hadn't hedged at all, the builder's housing construction cost would have been much higher and the profit margin much lower (compared to September 5) in Case I. The opposites would have been true in Case II. Presumably, a risk-averse builder does not desire to speculate in this way on plywood price fluctuations but only wants to protect the projected margin of profit from the building activity, which is what hedging allows.

The Role of Speculation

Speculating is the deliberate taking of long or short positions in spot or futures markets, with the hope that this will lead to profit from price fluctuations. Unlike hedgers, speculators do want price changes to affect their net worth.

Speculators, like hedgers, can work the short or the long side of the market. The speculator anticipating a decline in prices will sell futures at today's levels hoping to follow up this action with a later purchase of futures at a lower price, thus making a profit. The speculator anticipating a rise in prices will buy futures, aiming at a later

sale at a higher price and also making a profit. Consider these actual examples:

1. On January 7, 1974, a speculator sold one October, 1974, soybean meal futures contract (100 tons) at $180 per ton. The commodity exchange required a **margin deposit** (a good-faith payment to ensure performance on the contract) of 8.33 percent of the full value of the contract—$1,500. On June 14, 1974, the speculator bought an October, 1974, soybean meal futures contract at $101.50 per ton, realizing a gain of $78.50 per ton. The speculator made a profit, in just 5 months, of $7,850 on the invested $1,500.

2. On January 2, 1973, a speculator bought one December, 1973, soybean futures contract at $113.75 per ton. On August 13, 1973, the same contract could be sold at $284.20, at a gain of $170.45 per ton or $17,045 for the contract.

Note: First, gains such as these are far from automatic. Large losses are equally likely. Second, speculators, although often maligned as

TABLE 10.4

The Buying Hedge

	Spot Market	Futures Market
September 5	Spot price is $137 per MSF (1,000 square feet); builder in effect sells 10 carloads of plywood (when signing the building contract)	May futures price is $142 per MSF; builder buys 10 contracts of May plywood futures
Case I		
April 5	Spot price is $169 per MSF; builder buys 10 carloads of plywood (to carry out the construction contract)	May futures price is $174 per MSF; builder sells 10 contracts of May plywood futures
	Loss: $32 per MSF	Gain: $32 per MSF
	Net result: 0	
Case II		
April 5	Spot price is $117 per MSF; builder buys 10 carloads of plywood	May futures price is $122 per MSF; builder sells 10 contracts of May plywood futures
	Gain: $20 per MSF	Loss: $20 per MSF
	Net result: 0	

The **buying hedge** or **long hedge** aims to provide price protection for buyers who plan to buy materials in the future and have already contracted to make future delivery to others of these materials (or of goods made with them).

greedy gamblers, perform an extremely useful social function. Price fluctuations in a market economy are inevitable, and the associated risk must be borne by someone. Speculation permits these risks to be shifted from the producers and merchants of goods to others. Speculators are willing to assume the risk of price changes for the opportunity of making a profit. Their speculation in commodities is distinguishable from gambling because the risks assumed exist as an inevitable part of marketing commodities, whereas the risks in gambling are created for their own sake.

Besides taking risks off the shoulders of others, speculators normally help smooth out price fluctuations over time. When they buy in times of low prices, they tend to raise prices; when they sell in times of high prices, they tend to lower them—compared, in each case, to what prices would otherwise have been. Nevertheless, speculators are always denounced as ''scalpers'' who rip off people at times of intense scarcity by selling at high prices. Those critics do not realize that without speculators prices would be higher still. (On rare occasions, speculators do aggravate price fluctuations. The most famous recent example is discussed in Close-Up 10.3, ''The Great Silver Squeeze of 1980.'' An equally famous ancient example occurred in Holland in the 1630s when new tulip varieties were developed and tulip trading was introduced by the Amsterdam and Rotterdam stock exchanges. For a brief period, a rare type of bulb sold for $10,000 apiece, but the price fell precipitously thereafter.)

The Role of Organized Commodities Exchanges

To facilitate the trading of futures contracts by hedgers and speculators, organized commodities exchanges have been established. The first of these, the Chicago Board of Trade, came into existence in 1848. By now, there are many others, including the Chicago Mercantile Exchange, the Kansas City Board of Trade, the Minneapolis Grain Exchange, the Winnipeg

Commodity Exchange, and a number of others in New York: the Amex Commodities Exchange; the Comex or Commodity Exchange; the Coffee, Sugar, and Cocoa Exchange; the Cotton Exchange; the Mercantile Exchange; and, since 1980, the Futures Exchange.

On the floor of these exchanges, exchange members trade, in **open-outcry auctions** (using shouts and hand signals), more than 70 commodities, including: *primary commodities* (such as barley, cattle, cocoa, coffee, corn, cotton, crude oil, eggs, flax seed, hogs, lumber, oats, pepper, potatoes, rye, rubber, sorghum, soybeans, sugar, wheat, aluminum, copper, gold, lead, platinum, silver, tin, and zinc) and *processed commodities* (such as cottonseed and soybean oil, gasoline, heating oil, hides, iced broilers, lard, orange juice, plywood, pork bellies, and wool). Most recently, interest rate futures have been introduced with spectacular success, including U.S. Treasury bills, notes, and bonds; commercial paper; Ginnie Mae (Government National Mortgage Association) contracts; and Eurodollar CDs (certificates of deposit); equally popular have been the new stock index futures (contracts pegged to broad measures of stock market performance, such as the Value Line Stock Index, Standard and Poor's 500 Stock Index, and the New York Stock Exchange Composite Index).[2]

Each exchange standardizes the commodities (or financial instruments) in which it conducts futures trading with the help of detailed contract specifications. At the Chicago Board of Trade, for example, a plywood futures contract calls for a boxcar of 36 banded units of 66 pieces each (2,376 pieces), sized 48″ by 96″ (76,032 square feet total), four- or five-ply, half-inch thick, exterior glue 32/16, free on board, Portland, Oregon.

---

[2]The increasing popularity of *financial futures* (which involve trading in debt instruments, stocks, foreign currencies, and precious metals) is evidenced by the fact that they made up 32.4 percent of all futures contracts in 1980, but 60.1 percent in 1984. *See* James Sterngold, ''Hard Times for Commodities,'' *The New York Times,* October 21, 1984.

The volume of futures trading on all U.S. exchanges has increased rapidly in recent years, from 12 million contracts worth $145 billion in 1970 to 115 million contracts worth $6 trillion in 1984. The ever changing prices established through this trading reflect the ever changing knowledge, jointly possessed by all traders, about trends in demand and supply. Every bit of relevant news is immediately reflected in futures prices, whether it is news about a coming recession in U.S. home building, a Congressional defeat of sugar price supports, a drought in Thailand's sugar cane fields, the introduction of cotton planted in Alabama, the introduction of cocoa stockpiles on the Ivory Coast, labor troubles at El Salvador's coffee-drying plants, Mugabe's victory in platinum-rich Zimbabwe, a political shake-up and transportation breakdown in Uganda, Chinese cotton buying, the disappearance of anchovies from the coast of Peru, a planned orange-juice promotion campaign by a major producer, or Coca Cola's decision to replace sugar with corn sweeteners.

The resulting prices are continually reported in major newspapers around the world. Table 10.5 is an example of a typical futures market page; Close-Up 10.4 at the end of this chapter provides an interesting application.

APPLICATIONS

Application 1: Adverse Selection and Moral Hazard

We have seen how risk-averse individuals can improve their welfare with the help of insurance. What about insurance companies? Are they gambling? Not at all. The **law of large numbers** tells them that what is unpredictable and subject to chance for the individual is predictable and uniform in a mass of like individuals: Nobody knows whether John Doe's house will burn down this year. But if statistics tell us that only 1 of 250 like houses have burned down in the country in each of the past 50 years (and have done so for unrelated reasons), an insurance company that insures a sufficiently large random sample of the population can be virtually certain of the sample's behavior. All else being equal (no nuclear war, no invasion from outer space, no volcanic eruptions), the sample's behavior will be like that of the population at large. The company can, therefore, set premiums in such a way as to cover or more than cover benefits paid out.

Or can it? First, an insurance company must deal with two ageless problems: adverse selection and moral hazard.

Adverse Selection. An insurance company faces the problem of **adverse selection** when those who buy insurance make up a biased sample such that their probability of loss differs markedly and, from the point of view of the insurance company, adversely from the population at large. This problem can arise because of differential access to information similar to the used-car market discussed earlier. The would-be insured know their own riskiness: whether they are accident prone, subject to hereditary disease, thinking of suicide. The insurance company only knows what is true *on the average* for the population as a whole. If the company offers fair insurance, high-risk people will look upon the premiums as more than fair; low-risk people will see them as less than fair and *may* not buy insurance at all. As a result, it is quite possible for only "lemons" to seek out insurance!

Figure 10.4 graphically illustrates the insurance company's problem of adverse selection. Imagine that all people had the utility function shown in this graph and also owned an identical amount of $25,000 initially. All people also face the same potential loss of $20,000, but two equal-sized classes of people exist when it comes to probabilities. Class I people are low-risk; their probability of loss is only .2. Class II people are high-risk; their probability of loss is .8.

An uninsured class I person, therefore, faces a gamble between $5,000 (with a probability of .2) and $25,000 (with a probability of .8). The expected monetary value of the gamble equals $21,000. Such a person's expected utility corresponds to point C on dashed line AB. Such a person would be delighted to buy fair insurance;

TABLE 10.5

The Futures Market Page

GRAINS & OILS

WHEAT (CBT) 5,000 bu.; $ per bu.

Season High	Season Low		High	Low	Close	Chg.	Open Interest
4.96	3.84½	Jul	4.18	4.14½	4.16½	-.04	19716
5.06	3.98	Sep	4.31	4.27¾	4.29¼	-.03½	10340
5.23½	4.18½	Dec	4.50	4.46	4.47¾	-.04	7912
5.37½	4.33	Mar	4.64	4.62	4.62½	-.04	3254
4.96	4.40½	May	4.70½	4.68	4.68½	-.03½	378
4.75	4.62	Jul	4.63	4.62	4.63	-.05	9

Est. sales 12,112; sales Thur. 14,749.
Total open interest Thur. 41,658, off 285 from Wed.

SOYBEANS (CBT) 5,000 bu.; $ per bu.

Season High	Season Low		High	Low	Close	Chg.	Open Interest
8.57	5.95	Jul	6.33	6.26¾	6.32	+.01¾	37345
8.01½	6.06	Aug	6.39	6.34½	6.38¾	+.00¼	10297
7.95	6.15	Sep	6.47½	6.42¼	6.47	+.00½	4146
7.91	6.31	Nov	6.61	6.55¾	6.60½	-.00¼	22797
7.84½	6.49	Jan	6.74½	6.70½	6.74¼	-.01¾	12064
7.87	6.67½	Mar	6.89	6.85	6.88¾	-.01	8662
7.41½	6.81	May	6.99½	6.96	6.99½	-.01¼	4082
7.12	7.06	Jul	7.08	7.05	7.08	-.01½	154

Est. sales 18,358; sales Thur. 21,878.
Total open interest Thur. 99,584, up 83 from Wed.

SOYBEAN OIL (CBT) 60,000 lb.; ¢ per lb.

Season High	Season Low		High	Low	Close	Chg.	Open Interest
28.80	20.12	Jul	22.25	21.92	22.23	+ .06	25080
28.60	20.40	Aug	22.45	22.14	22.45	+ .08	8078
27.90	20.70	Sep	22.65	22.40	22.65	+ .08	5808
27.65	20.98	Oct	22.85	22.60	22.82	+ .07	5066
27.15	21.37	Dec	23.15	22.90	23.12	+ .05	7320
26.65	21.55	Jan	23.20	23.05	23.20	+ .07	4425
26.95	21.90	Mar	23.50	23.35	23.47	......	2287
27.00	22.35	May	23.65	23.60	23.65	- .10	1131
25.35	22.72	Jul	24.05	23.90	24.05	+ .12	524

Est. sales 8,015; sales Thur. 11,999.
Total open interest Thur. 59,778, up 201 from Wed.

LIVESTOCK

CATTLE, Feeder (CME)
42,000 lb.; ¢ per lb.

Season High	Season Low		High	Low	Close	Chg.	Open Interest
88.00	65.45	Aug	71.30	70.90	71.22	- .05	6689
87.25	65.17	Sep	71.25	70.80	71.25	+ .05	1548
86.80	64.55	Oct	71.10	70.75	70.97	- .08	2817
87.00	65.15	Nov	72.15	1.80	71.97	- .03	1026
75.00	69.10	Jan	.....	.....	73.25	......	43
75.00	72.00	Mar	73.75	73.75	73.75	......	22
75.25	70.00	Apr	.....	.....	74.55	+ .05	48

Est. sales 2,025; sales Fri. 3,687.
Total open interest Fri. 12,215, off 65 from Thur.

PORK BELLIES (CME)
38,000 lb; ¢ per lb.

Season High	Season Low		High	Low	Close	Chg.	Open Interest
58.85	30.90	Jul	32.75	32.00	32.25	- .35	12118
57.80	30.80	Aug	32.45	31.90	32.17	- .18	10662
57.15	45.80	Feb	47.25	46.55	46.85	+ .03	2033
57.50	38.75	Mar	47.00	46.65	46.90	+ .10	236
57.75	46.15	May	47.60	47.30	47.30	- .20	49
49.90	48.00	Jul	48.60	48.00	48.00	+ .05	13
48.90	47.30	Aug	47.85	47.45	47.45	......	19

Est. sales 4,836; sales Thur. 7,149.
Total open interest Thur. 25,245, up 961 from Wed.

ICED BROILERS (CME)
30,000 lb.; ¢ per lb.

Season High	Season Low		High	Low	Close	Chg.	Open Interest
48.00	40.65	Jun	43.10	43.00	43.10	- .25	268
47.50	41.65	Jul	44.60	44.35	44.40	......	246
46.60	41.70	Aug	43.90	43.75	43.90	+ .10	224
44.25	42.00	Oct	42.75	42.75	42.75	+ .20	175
43.95	42.87	Dec	42.90	42.90	42.90	- .10	82

Est. sales 36; sales Thur. 40.
Total open interest Thur. 1,000, off 14 from Wed.

FOODS

COFFEE (NYCSE) 37,500 lb. ¢ per lb.

Season High	Season Low		High	Low	Close	Chg.	Open Interest
215.65	149.25	Jul	203.00	200.0.	200.65	- 1.09	4943
214.78	168.50	Sep	210.40	207.25	208.07	- 1.35	6933
204.50	168.25	Dec	204.50	201.10	201.36	- 1.57	2049
199.00	165.50	Mar	196.95	194.00	194.37	- 1.13	1111
196.50	168.00	May	195.00	193.50	193.86	- 1.39	318
195.50	175.46	Jul	195.50	193.02	193.02	- 1.98	72
195.50	180.25	Sep	195.50	195.25	193.88	- 1.85	28

Est. sales 3,637; sales Thur. 3,190.
Total open interest Thur. 15,454 up 90 from Wed.
Spot 1.85.

EGGS, Shell (CME) 22,500 doz.; ¢ per doz.

Season High	Season Low		High	Low	Close	Chg.	Open Interest
53.95	41.25	Jun	.....	.....	45.00	......	6
51.00	48.00	Jul	.....	.....	48.00	......	1
60.90	54.50	Sep	58.50	58.00	58.50	+ .50	46
56.00	55.45	Oct	.....	.....	55.60	......	1
60.50	59.50	Dec	.....	.....	61.25	......	2
58.20	58.20	Jan	.....	.....	58.20	......	1

Est. sales 1; sales Thur. nil.
Total open interest Thur. 58, off 2 from Wed.

ORANGE JUICE (NYCTN, CA)
15,000 lb.; ¢ per lb.

Season High	Season Low		High	Low	Close	Chg.	Open Interest
113.75	83.70	May	94.55	94.55	94.60	+0.15	263
111.50	83.25	Jul	89.70	89.40	89.50	+0.25	2336
109.30	86.50	Sep	90.55	90.25	90.20	+0.05	1493
105.25	87.80	Nov	91.00	91.00	91.0+	......	618
107.75	87.30	Jan	92.80	92.65	92.80	+0.50	879
107.75	88.00	Mar	93.60	93.60	93.70	+0.20	572
107.90	89.25	May	.....	.....	95.50	+0 15	314
107.50	102.00	Jul	.....	.....	96.10	+0.15	5

Est. sales 120; sales Thur. 103.
Total open interest Thur. 6,480 up 3 from Wed.

SUGAR, World (NYCSE) 112,000 lb.; ¢ per lb.

Season High	Season Low		High	Low	Close	Chg.	Open Interest
36.65	7.60	Jul	36.65	35.60	36.58	+ 1.77	16078
35.65	7.85	Sep	34.99	34.99	34.99	+ 1.00	7553
35.79	10.03	Oct		35.62	35.62	+ 1.00	18720
6.45	17.05	Jan	36.45	36.45	36.45	+ 1.00	158
36.53	13.73	Mar	.....	.....	36.54	+ 1.00	17515
36.33	15.55	May	.....	.....	36.30	+ 1.00	6094
36.09	21.85	Jul	36.00	36.00	36.00	+ 1.00	2978
35.75	27.20	Sep	.....	.....	35.70	+ 1.00	426
35.45	28.75	Oct	.....	.....	35.48	+ 1.00	855

Est. sales 12,550; sales Thur. 14,452.
Total open interest Thur. 70,377 up 838 from Wed.
Sugar No. 11 spot 34.89.

WOOD

LUMBER (CME) 100,000 bd. ft.; $ per 1,000 bd. ft.

Season High	Season Low		High	Low	Close	Chg.	Open Interest
243.60	164.80	Jul	197.80	195.30	197.80	+5.00	3779
245.20	175.00	Sep	205.90	203.00	205.90	+5.00	2672
238.90	172.00	Nov	206.70	202.20	206.70	+5.00	1586
new contracts 130,00 bd. ft.							
226.50	156.50	Jan	198.40	195.00	198.40	+5.00	1867
228.10	160.00	Mar	211.40	207.50	211.30	+4.80	789
233.50	164.00	May	217.00	214.50	216.40	+4.10	397
225.00	169.00	Jul	221.00	219.50	220.50	+3.00	264
228.00	221.50	Sep	......	......	224.20	+2.70	5

PLYWOOD (CBT) 76,032 sq. ft.; $ per 1,000 sq. ft

Season High	Season Low		High	Low	Close	Chg.	Open Interest
209.00	160.20	Jul	193.50	190.20	191.40	+1.70	1771
211.20	164.70	Sep	197.00	194.50	195.00	g-1.70	1236
212.40	166.80	Nov	198.70	196.50	196.80	+1.80	575
214.00	170.50	Jan	203.00	201.50	201.50	+2.20	467
219.00	174.50	Mar	207.00	205.50	205.50	+2.50	584
223.00	178.50	May	211.00	208.50	210.50	+4.00	271
215.00	183.00	Jul	......	......	213.00	+3.50	99
211.00	189.00	Sep	......	......	212.00	+ .5	3

Est. sales 721; sales Thur. 1,022.
Total open interest Thur. 5,006, up 73 from Wed.

METALS

PLATINUM (NYM)
50 troy oz.; $ per troy oz.

Season High	Season Low		High	Low	Close	Chg.	Open Interest
763.5	501.00	May	551.50	551.50	543.80	- 0.50	9
1071.5	315.40	Jul	565.00	547.00	550.80	- 1.50	3224
1113.5	375.50	Oct	569.50	556.00	558.80	- 1.20	1526
1148.5	388.00	Jan	573.50	71.00	569.80	- 1.70	644
1189.5	579.00	Apr	......	......	581.00	.. 2.00	539
655.5	595.00	Jul	......	......	593.00	- 1.00	21

Est. sales 1,012; sales Thur. 865.
Total open interest Thur. 5,973 up 122 from Tues.

SILVER (NYCX) 5,000 troy oz.; ¢ per troy oz.

Season High	Season Low		High	Low	Close	Chg.	Open Interest
4100.00	610.50	May	1195.0	1125.0	1196.0	+036.0	395
1290.00	110.00	Jun	......	......	1198.0	+035.0	14
4240.00	642.40	Jul	1206.0	1135.0	1205.0	+038.0	6748
4280.00	666.00	Sep	1230.0	1170.0	1225.0	+037.0	4532
4437.00	796.00	Dec	1260.0	1200.0	1255.0	+036.0	3001
4183.00	843.50	Jan	1265.0	1250.0	1265.0	+035.0	1654
4493.50	924.00	Mar	1290.0	1265.0	1286.0	+035.0	3523
4530.50	1006.00	May	1306.0	1305.0	1306.0	+034.0	2154
4357.00	1229.00	Jul	1327.0	1273.0	1327.0	+034.0	1449
4200.00	1254.00	Sep	......	......	1348.0	+034.0	436
4140.00	1340.00	Dec	......	......	1379.0	+034.0	81
4164.00	4164.00	Jan	......	......	1390.0	+034.0	21
1468.00	1328.00	Mar	......	......	1411.0	+034.0	1

Est. sales 2,000; sales Thur. 2,754.
Total open interest Thur. 24,009 off 491 from Wed.

GOLD (IMM) 100 troy oz.; $ per troy oz.

Season High	Season Low		High	Low	Close	Chg.	Open Interest
914.50	226.00	Jun	515.30	509.00	510.30	- 3.90	5085
532.00	507.20	Jul	......	......	514.00	- 4.50	30
938.00	231.70	Sep	527.90	520.00	521.00	- 5.50	4622
550.00	528.00	Oct	......	......	525.00	- 5.50	10
957.50	262.50	Dec	541.00	534.50	535.30	- 3.70	3837
976.00	282.20	Mar	553.00	547.00	549.20	- 2.60	2664
578.00	551.00	Apr	555.80	553.20	553.20	- 2.60	12
993.90	351.70	Jun	566.50	560.00	563.20	- 1.20	3071
1011.20	455.90	Sep	580.00	573.00	577.20	- .20	1933
1031.90	559.10	Dec	592.00	589.00	591.20	+ .50	970
732.00	608.00	Mar	609.00	605.20	605. 0	+ .90	6

Est. sales 3,739; sales Thur. 6,015.
Total open interest Thur. 22,240, off 634 from Wed.

FIBERS

COTTON (NYCTN) 50,000 lb.; ¢ per lb.

Season High	Season Low		High	Low	Close	Chg.	Open Interest
90.67	64.00	Jul	78.45	77.40	77.59	-0.31	12214
90.50	64.25	Oct	76.30	75.30	75.55	-0.04	3753
90.75	66.00	Dec	74.15	73.15	73.46	+0.09	13323
91.00	70.00	Mar	75.25	74.30	74.75	+0.35	5149
92.10	74.80	May	.....	.....	75.55	+0.05	415
81.60	75.50	Jul	77.10	77.00	76.75	+0.55	125
79.95	76.50	Oct	78.00	77.00	77.50	......	4

st. sales 5,550; sales Thur. 10,098.
Total open interest Thur 34,983 off 711 from Wed.

FINANCIAL

LONG-TERM TREAS. BONDS (CBT)
8%-$100,000 prin.; pts. and 32d's of 100%

Season High	Season Low		High	Low	Close	Chg.	Open Interest
95-31	63-15	Jun	81-30	81-04	81-29	+63	9099
95-22	64-05	Sep	81-30	81-03	81-29	+63	16660
95-27	64-24	Dec	81-23	80-26	81-22	+62	11543
95-27	65-14	Mar	81-17	80-19	81-17	+64	8828
94-20	65-04	Jun	81-10	80-08	81-07	+61	7546
92-15	65-25	Sep	81-02	80-08	81-00	g-62	6670
91-18	65-19	Dec	80-28	80-04	80-28	+64	6248
91-15	65-23	Mar	80-23	79-25	80-23	+64	5562
88-08	65-23	Jun	80-19	80-05	80-19	+64	5525
83-09	65-24	Sep	80-16	80-02	80-16	+64	3354
82-16	69-25	Dec	80-13	79-31	80-13	+63	406

Est. sales 22,304; sales Thur. 19,117.
Total open interest Thur. 81,441, up 70 from Wed.

This table shows excerpts from newspaper reports on the May 23, 1980, trading in U.S. futures markets. Next to each commodity is a key to the exchange: CBT = Chicago Board of Trade, CME = Chicago Mercantile Exchange, NYCSE = New York Coffee and Sugar Exchange, NYCTN, CA = New York Cotton Exchange, Citrus Associates, NYM = New York Mercantile Exchange, NYCX = Comex or Commodity Exchange in New York, IMM = International Monetary Market of the CME. Then follows the contract size (5,000 bushels in the case of wheat) and the monetary units represented by the figures in the table (dollars per bushel in the case of wheat). Each row then gives, for the stated *future* month, the highest and lowest price contracted during the season and then the highest and lowest price contracted on the Friday of May 23, 1980, the closing price on that day, and the change from the previous trading day's closing price. **Open interest** is the number of contracts outstanding for the stated month and not yet liquidated by delivery of the commodity or by an offsetting contract. For most recent data, look at any issue of *The New York Times* or *The Wall Street Journal*.

that is, pay a premium of $4,000 and have a certain utility corresponding to point D (which exceeds C).

An uninsured class II person, on the other hand, faces a gamble between $5,000 (with a probability of .8) and $25,000 (with a probability of .2). The expected monetary value of this gamble equals $9,000. Such a person's expected utility corresponds to point E, and such a person would gladly pay a premium of $16,000 for fair insurance, thereby gaining certain utility corresponding to F.

The insurance company, unfortunately, may not be able to tell who is class I and who is class II. If it issued fair insurance, it would charge everyone the *average* premium of $10,000, thereby giving everyone an expected monetary value of $15,000. This would delight class II

people. They would be getting more-than-fair insurance. They would buy insurance, getting utility corresponding to G instead of F (and, as we saw, F already was preferred to uninsured utility at E). All this would, however, dismay class I people. They would be getting less-than-fair insurance. In *this* example, they would not buy it, for the utility corresponding to G is below H (which corresponds to that received without insurance at C).

As a result, the insurance company will get all the lemons (class II people), and it will make losses. It will raise premiums but thereby drive low-risk people away all the more!

One possible solution is this: Low-risk people might *signal* to the company that they are low-risk people by offering to accept high deductibles in their policies, a type of behavior irrational for high-risk people. (A **deductible** is a fixed dollar amount by which any insurance company benefit payment falls short of a loss suffered by an insured.) Or the low-risk people might offer to buy **coinsurance,** an arrangement whereby they commit themselves to shoulder a fixed percentage (rather than a fixed dollar amount) of any loss. In either case, the insurance company could *screen* applicants by their willingness to accept deductibles and coinsurance, and it could offer lower premiums to these people.

For an interesting application of the preceding material, see Close-Up 10.5 at the end of this chapter.

Moral Hazard.   An insurance company faces the problem of **moral hazard** when those who have bought insurance subsequently change their behavior in such a way as to increase the probability of the occurrence of any loss or of a larger loss. Once insured, people might relax protective measures and be less careful about their lives, health, and physical wealth. Insurance companies look upon this as something akin to fraud, but economists are more likely to view this "unwillingness to uphold moral values" as the simple result of the law of downward-sloping demand: Once having bought health insurance, for example, a person will view medical services

FIGURE 10.4

Adverse Selection

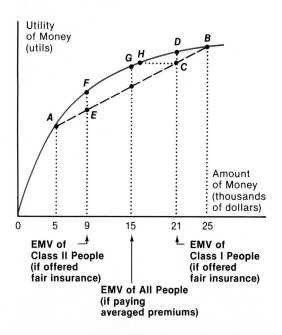

Under some conditions, it is quite possible for low-risk people *not* to insure and for only high-risk people to insure. Such an adversely selected population sample leads to insurance company losses.

TABLE 10.6

The Sources of U.S. Economic Growth

Factors Responsible for Observed Growth	Percentage of Growth Rate Explained by Given Factor	
	1909–1929	1929–1982
Increased labor hours	39	20
Increased human capital (education)	13	19
Increased physical capital	26	14
Technical advance	(12)	(31)
Others	10	16

As the encircled numbers indicate, technical advance during this century explains a significant (and increasing) proportion of the U.S. rate of economic growth.

Source: Derived from information in Edward F. Denison, *The Sources of Economic Growth in the United States and the Alternatives Before Us* (New York: Committee for Economic Development, 1962) and *idem, Trends in American Economic Growth, 1929–1982*. (Washington, D.C.: Brookings Institution, 1985).

as being offered at a low or zero price and will naturally demand a larger quantity.

Insurance companies attempt to counteract moral hazard by increasing people's incentive to avoid claims. They can do this, again, by using deductibles and coinsurance. They can include cancellation provisions, as when life insurance becomes invalid in the case of suicide or when fire insurance becomes invalid in the case of arson. They can reward people for loss-prevention behavior, as when premiums for burglary, flood, or life insurance are reduced when people, respectively, install alarm systems, build dikes, or refrain from smoking.

Application 2: Technical Advance and the Entrepreneur

As we noted in Chapter 9, Frank H. Knight stimulated many of the advances that led to our current understanding of behavior under uncertainty. His notion that profit was somehow a reward for the way a special type of person acts in the face of uncertainty is another case in point. Joseph A. Schumpeter (1883–1950), a Biography of whom appears in Chapter 10 of the *Student Workbook* that accompanies this text,

called such a person an *entrepreneur*, and he attributed the capitalist economy's remarkable rate of technical advance to this type of person.

Economic Growth and Technical Advance. Consider the fact that the U.S. real gross national product has grown more than 16-fold during this century. Measured at 1958 prices, the nation's output has grown from a mere $72 billion in 1900 to $1,187 billion in 1988. This comes to an average annual rate of growth of over 3.2 percent. Economists have studied the reasons for this performance. They have found that it cannot be explained merely by similar increases in inputs, such as labor hours, human capital, or physical capital. The *ratio* of total output to total inputs has risen over time. Economists have attributed the difference between the observed increase in total output and the smaller hypothetical increase that could have been expected as a result of observed increases in inputs to **technical advance,** an improvement in known methods of production. Table 10.6 summarizes the results of one major study of the sources of U.S. economic growth.

Technical Advance and the Production Function. Technical advance makes it possible to meet old wants in entirely new ways, either with the help of new products or by producing old products in new ways. The appearance of new products can be viewed as the birth of a new production function; producing an old product in a new way can be viewed as a fundamental change in a pre-existing production function. In Table 4.1, ''A Simple Production Function'' (p. 99), technical advance can be depicted as an event that left all data in columns (1) and (2) unchanged but raised those in column (3). This increase in column (3) data, of course, is equivalent to a decrease in column (1) and (2) data while column (3) data remain unchanged. Again, in Figure 4.2, ''Isoquants'' (p. 105), technical advance can be viewed as a relabeling, with larger output numbers, of all isoquants. The 488-bushel, 977-bushel, and 1,668-bushel figures might, for example, be replaced with 977-bushel, 1,954-bushel, and 3,337-bushel labels. Note: Such technical advance makes it possible to produce any given output at lower cost, all else being equal.

Invention Versus Innovation. The birth of new production functions or the change of old ones should not, however, be confused with **invention,** the intellectual act of generating a new idea. An act of invention may be the random result of hard work by gifted individuals who, driven by curiosity, work with little assistance and few resources. That's how the incandescent light bulb, the reaper, and the telegraph were invented. Yet invention today is less likely to emerge from the long, slow process of unsystematic trial and error engaged in by independent tinkerers. The first industrial research laboratory in the United States was established as late as 1876 by Thomas Edison. Nowadays, there are thousands of such laboratories, each one engaged in the *systematic* derivation of new knowledge. These laboratories carry on **basic research,** scientific inquiry not directed toward any specific ''useful'' discovery. Biologists may study why cells proliferate; physicists may study the laws of motion. Such laboratories also carry on **applied research,** the application to a particular problem of the knowledge gained in basic research. Biological principles may now be applied to the

creation of new varieties of plants or animals, physical principles to the design of new computers and communications via satellites.

Yet all this research has no effect on economic growth! Another step is needed: Someone must be the first to put new ideas to practical use; this person must move, so to speak, from the laboratory to the field or factory bench and translate inventions into new products, new qualities of old products, or new processes of production. Such an act of **innovation** is carried out by Schumpeter's **entrepreneur.** An entrepreneur is not like a manager-bureaucrat who keeps an established firm running in routine ways. Such a person, rather, employs imagination and daring, introduces commercially something that has never been tried before, and, in the process, deliberately accepts great risk.

The ''Gale of Creative Destruction.'' As Schumpeter saw it, risk-taking entrepreneurs, who introduce successful innovations, temporarily become single sellers, or monopolists. They introduce products that never existed before, or they produce old products at reduced cost, making it impossible for established firms to compete. Yet, over time, the monopoly is ended as a swarm of imitators also introduces the new product or process. Thus, in a ''gale of creative destruction,'' old products and processes disappear, and technical advance is diffused throughout the economy. And the innovating entrepreneurs, if their innovations prove a success, are rewarded for their risk bearing with economic profit, at least temporarily.

Thus Schumpeter viewed competition in the capitalist economy as the sequential creation and destruction of monopolies: the stagecoach being replaced by the railroad, the railroad by the automobile, the automobile by airplanes, and airplanes, perhaps, by rocketships.

Application 3: Marketing Weather Forecasts

As we noted earlier, people might deal with uncertainty by searching for information. Such search might involve the purchase of information

TABLE 10.7

A Payoff Matrix

	States of the World	
Individual Actions	S_1 = Much Rain	S_2 = Little Rain
A_1 = Fertilizing	25	5
A_2 = Not fertilizing	15	15
	Subjective probabilities	
	.5	.5

This payoff matrix shows a farm's net income (in thousands of dollars per year) dependent on the farmer's decision to fertilize or not to fertilize the land and on nature's provision of much or little rain during the growing season.

from others. Consider, for example, the case of a farmer depicted in Table 10.7. The farmer is faced with a choice between two actions (A_1 and A_2). Nature, in turn, is "choosing" between two possible "states of the world" (S_1 and S_2). Four possible consequences emerge in the body of the table and might represent the net income of the farm under the given combinations of actions and events.

The farmer's obvious dilemma could be resolved with a perfect weather forecast. If such a forecast could be produced and it predicted much rain, the farmer would take action A_1 (and collect $25,000). If the forecast predicted little rain, the farmer would take action A_2 (and collect $15,000). A private producer of such a forecast would, however, not divulge the content of the forecast without first being paid for it. How much would the farmer be willing to pay in advance of being told?

The Demand Side. The farmer would have to replace the subjective probabilities about the states of the world (given as .5 each in our table) with new probabilities relating to the likely content of the forecast. Suppose, however, that the farmer also judged the probability of a "heavy rain" forecast to be .5 and the probability of a "light rain" forecast to be .5. The expected monetary value of the farmer's actions would then be $20,000 or the sum of (.5)$25,000 (the

farmer's net income from action A_1, which would be taken after a "heavy rain" forecast) plus (.5)$15,000 (the farmer's net income from action A_2, which would be taken after a "light rain" forecast).

Presumably, the farmer would pay a maximum of $5,000 for a perfect forecast because $5,000 is the difference between the expected monetary values of the farmer's actions with a perfect forecast ($20,000) and without a perfect forecast ($15,000).

The Supply Side. Suppose someone could produce such a perfect forecast for $5,000 or less and offer it to our farmer: What if there were many farmers like our friend? Could a producer of weather information collect a maximum of $5,000 from each? This is unlikely. Because each farmer would know that he or she could get the information from any one of the others, no farmer would buy it; therefore it probably wouldn't be produced!

Why *probably?* A producer of forecasts who could not sell the information directly might still be able to appropriate the value of the forecast by suppressing the information and taking actions such as the following:

a. If the future weather (known as yet only to the forecaster) promised a large crop and very low future spot prices, the forecaster could become a speculator and sell futures contracts for this crop at their presently still-high prices and liquidate the contracts by later buying at the lower prices.

b.   If the future weather (known as yet only to the forecaster) promised a small crop and very high future spot prices, the forecaster could buy futures contracts at the presently still-low prices and liquidate the contracts by later selling at the higher prices.

Note: The very activity of selling futures short (or buying them long) would immediately tend to depress (or raise) the futures prices of this crop. In this way, the weather forecaster's private knowledge would be revealed to the world! Although they would not be given the reason, millions of others who were interested in this crop would be told to expect lower (or higher) prices in the future. Futures markets truly are windows on the future!

SUMMARY

1.   People can cope with uncertainty in numerous ways; these include entering contingent-claim markets, searching for information, or operating in futures markets.

2.   As was noted in the previous chapter, people have one of three attitudes toward risk: risk aversion, risk neutrality, or risk seeking. The existence of risk aversion gives rise to a demand for and supply of insurance.

3.   Conversely, the existence of risk seeking gives rise to a demand for and supply of gambling.

4.   Risk averters do not always buy insurance, while they avoid gambling. Risk seekers do not always gamble, while they avoid buying insurance. What either will do depends on whether the insurance or gambles they confront are more than fair, fair, or unfair. As the Friedman-Savage hypothesis indicates, some people may even buy insurance and gamble simultaneously.

5.   When people are confronted by uncertainty of the market rather than uncertainty of

events, they can try to overcome their ignorance of the facts by searching for information already possessed by other people. They may engage in the search for price, the search for quality, signaling, or screening.

When market uncertainty is caused by ignorance not about present facts, but about the future, people can sometimes dispel the uncertainty with the help of futures markets. These markets serve to redistribute uncertainty over the population, from hedgers who wish to minimize price risk to speculators who wish to assume it. Because price fluctuations in a market economy are inevitable, speculators perform extremely useful functions in shouldering price risks and (normally) smoothing out price fluctuations over time. Organized commodities exchanges facilitate the trading of futures contracts by hedgers and speculators.

6.   The analysis of uncertainty has a number of wider applications, including: the problems of adverse selection and moral hazard, the role of risk-taking entrepreneurs in economic growth, and the marketing of information.

KEY TERMS

adverse selection

applied research

basic research

buying hedge

coinsurance

contingent-claim markets

deductible

entrepreneur

fair insurance

futures markets

hedging

innovation

invention

law of large numbers

long hedge

long position

margin calls

margin deposit

market uncertainty

moral hazard

open interest

open-outcry auctions

screening

search

secondary uncertainty

selling hedge

short hedge

short position

signaling

speculating

spot markets

technical advance

HANDS-ON PRACTICE

Exercise #1

A risk averter faces the unpleasant prospect of a gamble between $50,000 (with a probability of .8) and $12,000 (with a probability of .2). What is the expected monetary value?

Solution:

It equals $50,000(.8) + $12,000(.2) = $42,400.

Exercise #2

Reconsider Table 10.7. Imagine the entries in the first column to be 33, 12, and .8, while those in the second column were 17, 29, and .2. Determine the maximum the farmer would pay for a perfect weather forecast.

Solution:

The farmer would pay a maximum of $2,400 and for this reason: *Without* a forecast, the expected monetary value of action A_1 is $33,000(.8)

+ $17,000(.2) = $29,800. Similarly, the *EMV* of A_2 is $12,000(.8) + $29,000(.2) = $15,400. If *EMV* is being maximized, action A_1 will be taken, yielding an *EMV* = $29,800. *With* a forecast, A_1 is taken with an S_1 forecast, but A_2 with an S_2 forecast. Thus the *EMV* is $33,000(.8) + $29,000(.2) = $32,200. The value of a perfect forecast is therefore $32,200 − $29,800 = $2,400.

QUESTIONS AND PROBLEMS

1. Calculate the expected monetary value for each of these games from your point of view:

a. We flip a coin; if heads appears, I get $1 from you; if tails appears, you get $1 from me.

b. We flip a coin; if heads appears, I get $1 from you; if tails appears, you get $10 from me.

How much would you pay me for the privilege of playing either game?

2. Psychiatrists distinguish calculated risk taking from neurotic risk taking. The former, they say, involves conscious deliberation, planning and training, the positive goal of personal achievement, and the taking of responsibility for the outcome (at least in part). The latter, they say, involves no deliberation, no planning and preparation, but the negative goal of escaping from something and letting pure chance determine the outcome. Which of these types of risk taking (if either) fits the astronaut, the cigarette smoker, the drug addict, the entrepreneur, the gambler, the hedger, the insurance company, the speculator?

3. Consider Figure 10.1.

a. Prove that the risk averter pictured in panel (a) would be even more averse to an equally probable $3,000 or $27,000 prospect than to the $5,000 or $25,000 one shown there.

b. How would this person value an equally probable $3,000 or $16,000 prospect? A prospect providing a probability of .2 for $3,000 and of .8 for $16,000?

c. Prove that the risk seeker pictured in Figure 10.2 would be even more thrilled about an equally probable $3,000 or $27,000 prospect than about the $5,000 or $25,000 one shown there.

4. Take another look at Figure 10.3, which involved an insurance purchase that replaced a gamble between *C* and *A* with the certainty of *D,* as well as a gamble that replaced the certainty of *A* with a gamble between *D* and *E.* Reread the discussion and determine whether

a. the insurance was fair or unfair.

b. the gamble was fair or unfair.

5. Consider Table 10.3. Work out the consequences for two other cases and prove that hedging need not be foolproof.

a. Imagine a Case III in which (on November 20) the spot price equals $2.82 and the December futures price equals $2.85 per bushel.

b. Imagine a Case IV in which (on November 20) the spot price equals $2.71 and the December futures price equals $2.94 per bushel.

6. Some economists have suggested that one might take notice of uncertain future *preferences* by creating markets for claims contingent on tastes. Suppose you were contemplating a trip at some time in your life to a scenic wonder similar to Yellowstone Park. If you were sure of going, you might wish to make sure that the scenic wonder was still there in the future (and wasn't going to be destroyed in the meantime by, say, uranium strip mining). Then you might be willing to pay, say, $100 for the option to purchase an entrance ticket in 20 years at a price specified now. Yet you might judge the probability of going to be .2 and that of not going to be .8. In the case of not going you wouldn't want to pay a cent for the option. Do you think one could set up a market here in which the owners of Scenic Wonder could sell contingency claims to potential future visitors now, thereby allowing the voice of future generations to speak and to provide enough money to resist would-be uranium miners? (*Hint:* think of moral hazard.)

7. In the 1860s, Gilbert, Henry, and Maxwell developed the theory of electromagnetism. In the 1880s, Hertz conducted laboratory demonstrations of the production and detection of wireless waves. In 1897, Marconi introduced the radio, based on the former work. Which one of these was an entrepreneur? Explain.

8. Consider a perfectly competitive industry in long-run equilibrium. With the help of graphs, similar to Figure 6.5, "Long-Run Industry Supply Curves" (p. 187), illustrate the "gale of creative destruction" that might be unleashed by a Schumpeterian entrepreneur.

9. Comment on the following exchange:

Mr. A: The author-publisher conflict (discussed in Application 1, Chapter 7) is blown all out of proportion. Whether we maximize sales (as authors allegedly desire) or maximize profit (the alleged publisher's goal), when marginal cost (a little bit of ink, paper, machine time, and binding) is tiny compared to price, while fixed cost (editing, composition, warehousing, selling) is huge, the result is practically the same.

Ms. B: Of course, and that's why it makes no difference to speak of whether the author gets 10 percent of sales or 10 percent of profit as a royalty. More importantly, however, you should consider that this royalty arrangement is a way for *risk sharing.* The author knows things the publisher doesn't know and can discover only at great cost (such as the author's true ability and the quality and sales prospects of the work); the publisher knows things the author doesn't know (such as production costs and the extent of planned promotional effort).

10. It has been argued that a correct measure of the social cost of monopoly power should include the size of monopoly profits because, in a rent-seeking environment, those who seek monopoly power will expend resources to get monopoly up to the expected monetary value of this profit. Thus monopoly profit is a good measure of the unobserved value of wasted resources. (*See* Close-Up 14.3 for a discussion.) Yet this calculation cannot be correct if those who seek monopoly power are risk averse (and, surely, risk is involved because not everyone's attempt to get such power is crowned with success). What do you think?

SELECTED READINGS

Akerlof, George A. "The Market for 'Lemons': Quality Uncertainty and the Market Mechanism," *The Quarterly Journal of Economics,* August 1970, pp. 488–500.

> A seminal article on which this chapter's discussion of quality uncertainty is based.

Arrow, Kenneth J. *Essays in the Theory of Risk-Bearing.* Chicago: Markham, 1971.

> Twelve essays by the 1972 winner of the Nobel Prize in economics, ranging from the intermediate to the advanced level. *See also* Arrow's presidential address to the American Economic Association: "Limited Knowledge and Economic Analysis," *The American Economic Review,* March 1974, pp. 1–10.

Fellner, William. *The Economics of Technical Advance.* New York: General Learning Press, 1971.

> A superb discussion of the meaning, measurement, and implications of technical progress.

Friedman, Milton, and L. J. Savage. "The Utility Analysis of Choices Involving Risk," *Journal of Politcal Economy,* August 1948, pp. 279–304. Reprinted in George J. Stigler and Kenneth E. Boulding, eds. *Readings in Price Theory.* Homewood, Ill.: Irwin, 1952, chap. 3.

> The source of this chapter's discussion of the Friedman-Savage hypothesis. (Friedman won the 1976 Nobel Prize in economics.)

Hirshleifer, Jack. "Speculation and Equilibrium: Information, Risk, and Markets," *The Quarterly Journal of Economics,* November 1975, pp. 519–42.

> Argues that the literature on uncertainty is preoccupied with price risks while ignoring quantity risks. *See also* the discussion of this article in the November 1976 issue of the same journal, pp. 667–96.

Hirshleifer, Jack, and John G. Riley. "The Analytics of Uncertainty and Information—An Expository Survey," *Journal of Economic Literature,* December 1979, pp. 1375–1421.

> An excellent summary of the literature.

Klein, Benjamin, and Keith B. Leffler. "The Role of Market Forces in Assuring Contractual Performance," *Journal of Political Economy,* August 1981, pp. 615–41.

> Discusses advertising as a way of signaling high quality.

Kohler, Heinz. *Statistics for Business and Economics,* 2nd edition. Glenview, Ill.: Scott, Foresman and Co., 1988.

> Chapter 17 contains a thorough treatment of modern decision theory (that develops criteria for dealing with uncertainty), including a section on the value of information.

Kolb, Robert W. *Understanding Futures Markets.* Glenview, Ill.: Scott, Foresman and Co., 1985.

> A superb text.

Leffler, Keith B. "Physician Licensure: Competition and Monopoly in American Medicine," *The Journal of Law and Economics,* April 1978, pp. 165–86.

> A further discussion, in light of Akerlof's "lemons" model, of Kessel's article, cited at the end of Chapter 7.

Maddison, Angus. "Growth and Slowdown in Advanced Capitalist Economies: Techniques of Quantitative Assessment," *Journal of Economic Literature,* June 1987, pp. 649–98.

> A thorough discussion of the kinds of issues raised in this chapter's Application 2.

Meade, James E. *The Theory of Indicative Planning.* Manchester, England: Manchester University Press, 1970; *idem. The Controlled Economy.* London: Allen and Unwin, 1971.

> Superb discussions of uncertainty and of reducing it via national economic planning, by the 1977 winner of the Nobel Prize in economics.

Schumpeter, Joseph A. *Capitalism, Socialism, and Democracy,* 3rd edition. New York: Harper, 1950. (Originally published in 1942.)

> A wide-ranging work that discusses, among other things, the key role played by risk-taking entrepreneurs.

Spence, Michael. "Job Market Signaling," *The Quarterly Journal of Economics,* August 1973, pp. 355–74.

> The first article on the subject.

Stigler, George. "The Economics of Information," *Journal of Political Economy,* June 1961, pp. 213–25; *idem.* "Information in the Labor Market," *Journal of Political Economy,* October 1962, pp. 94–105.

> The first articles on search, by the 1982 winner of the Nobel Prize in economics.

Williams, Jeffrey. "Futures Markets: A Consequence of Risk Aversion or Transactions Costs?" *Journal of Political Economy,* October 1987, pp. 1000–1023.

> Argues that risk aversion is not necessary to explain the salient features of commodity futures markets; transactions costs can explain their existence as well.

COMPUTER PROGRAMS

The KOHLER-3 personal-computer diskettes that accompany this book contain one program of particular interest to this chapter:

    10. *Insurance and Gambling, Search and*

Futures Markets includes a 25-question multiple-choice test with immediate responses to incorrect answers as well as numerous exercises concerning unfair, fair, and more-than-fair insurance contracts or gambles, the random walk of futures prices, and more.

ANALYTICAL EXAMPLE 10.1

SMOKE DETECTORS AS INSURANCE

People can and often do reduce the risk of death and injury by the voluntary purchase of safety devices. One economist recently studied people's behavior with respect to the purchase of smoke detectors. She estimated that in the United States in 1976 there would have been 6,492 deaths and 6,759 injuries from residential fires in the absence of smoke detectors. In fact, however, 13 percent of households voluntarily installed smoke detectors, 80 percent of which were operational and provided 45-percent protection against death and 30-percent protection against injury. (These surprisingly low numbers are explained by people's inability to escape in spite of being warned or by their failure to respond correctly to alarms.) As a result, actual fire deaths were reduced to 6,200 and injuries to 6,750 in 1976. (If all households had had detectors, the numbers of deaths and injuries would have been 4,155 and 5,089, respectively.)

It was also estimated how much people paid for this reduction in the fire hazard. The average purchase price of a smoke detector in 1976, for example, was $39.65, while the annual operating cost was $1.57 (for batteries). Present values for the stream of operating costs were determined for discount rates of 5 and 10 percent.

All these data were then used to estimate the implicit value the purchasers of smoke detectors had placed upon their lives. The results are shown (in part) in the

Weighting Scheme (importance attached to reducing death, *D*, versus injury, *I*)		Implicit Value of Life, Given a Discount Rate of	
D	*I*	5 Percent	10 Percent
1.0	0.5	$227,273	$271,562
1.0	0.1	287,611	343,658
1.0	0	308,544	368,671

Note: Readers may wish to compare these results with those noted in the section of Chapter 11 on "Wage Differentials and the Value of Life."

accompanying table for a variety of assumptions. These include the two discount rates noted above, as well as alternative weights people might attach to the relative importance of reducing the probability of death or injury.

Source: Rachel Dardis, "The Value of a Life: New Evidence from the Marketplace," *The American Economic Review,* December 1980, pp. 1077–82.

ANALYTICAL EXAMPLE 10.2

TESTING THE "LEMONS" MODEL: USED PICKUP TRUCKS

One economist recently tested the "lemons" model according to which bad products in a market drive out good ones when sellers know more about quality than buyers. (Given such asymmetric information, buyers don't know much about quality until after purchase; hence sellers have no incentive to provide good quality, it is argued.) The test focused on the market for used pickup trucks of the 1972–76 model years and utilized data from the 1977 Truck Inventory and Use Survey (which was part of the U.S. Census of Transportation). Controlling for characteristics that buyers could observe, such as the trucks' ages and mileages, the question was asked whether the proportion of trucks requiring maintenance was different between new trucks and used trucks. The accompanying table shows some of the results.

| | | | Proportion of Trucks Requiring Engine Maintenance | |
Year	Number in Sample	Proportion of Trucks Acquired Used	Bought New	Bought Used
1976	2,137	.11	.08	.05
1975	1,602	.27	.10	.11
1974	2,261	.37	.11	.13
1973	2,085	.48	.15	.15
1972	1,839	.53	.13	.15

It was concluded that pickup trucks that were purchased used required no more maintenance than trucks of similar age and lifetime mileage that had not been traded, and that, therefore, this market was *not* a market for "lemons." Note: It can be expected that the "lemons" result is avoided whenever institutions exist that counteract quality uncertainty, such as brand names, warranties, or search by buyers.

Sources: Eric W. Bond, "A Direct Test of the 'Lemons' Model: The Market for Used Pickup Trucks," *The American Economic Review,* September 1982, pp. 836–40. See *also* the ensuing controversy: Michael D. Pratt and George E. Hoffer, "Test of the 'Lemons' Model: Comment," and Eric W. Bond, "Test of the 'Lemons' Model: Reply," *The American Economic Review,* September 1984, pp. 798–804.

CLOSE-UP 10.1

THE GAMBLING BOOM

In 1985, as the accompanying table shows, Americans gambled an estimated $190.8 billion, over 83 percent of it quite legally.

1985 U.S. Gambling (in billions of dollars)

Legal		$159.2
casino table games	$99.5	
slot machines	26.2	
horse racing	12.2	
state lotteries	10.2	
other (bingo games, etc.)	11.1	
Illegal		31.6
bookies, numbers	31.6	
Total		$190.8

Some Americans did their best to improve their odds. Take Philip Anderson. In August of 1985, he was arrested by security guards at a Las Vegas casino for exhibiting "suspicious body movements." An investigation proved revealing: He was wearing "computer shoes," a tiny card-counting microcomputer strapped to his calf under his clothing and controlled by switches he manipulated with his feet. Tapping his toes, Mr. Anderson was able to tell the computer which cards from the blackjack deck had been played, The computer, calculating the cards remaining in the deck, sent back messages on how to play his hand. The electronic help came in an equally novel way: via a wire that delivered little electric shocks from the computer to the rear strap of his athletic supporter.

All this was ingenious, but also illegal. But Mr. Anderson went to court, arguing that current law violated both the First and Fourteenth Amendments by barring transmission of information between him and his computer and interfering with the practice of his profession.

Other forms of high-tech cheating abound as well. One gambler was recently seized with a tiny video camera, which, worn on a belt buckle, was often able to sneak a peek at a blackjack dealer's hole card as it was dealt face down off the deck. The image was relayed to an accomplice with a TV monitor in a van who, in turn, told the player via a tiny radio receiver in his ear. Yet another player was caught training lasers on the "big wheel," a spinning device in which payoffs are made on bets that the wheel will land on a certain number. The lasers were used to reveal whether the wheel had idiosyncrasies favoring particular numbers.

Sources: *The Daily Hampshire Gazette,* March 27, 1987, p. 6; *The Wall Street Journal,* January 13, 1988, pp. 1 and 12.

CLOSE-UP 10.2

CALIFORNIA PYRAMIDS AND THE FLORIDA POKER CASE

In 1980, "pyramid parties" became a fad that swept California with a revival-meeting intensity. Even 300 arrests and $250 fines for violating a state ban on "endless chain schemes" didn't cool the pyramid fever. The pyramid parties were an extension of the endless-chain-letter idea. A player paid $1,000 to enter the bottom of the pyramid. If two other players could be induced to do likewise, the initial outlay was recouped; if they, in turn, recruited enough others, the original player could rise to the top of a 64-person pyramid and collect $16,000. Party goers proselytized relatives, friends, neighbors, and anyone else interested in making a fast buck. And the Federal Reserve in Los Angeles noted double the normal demand for $50 and $100 denomination bills. Said the head of the fraud and forgery unit of the state's department of justice: "I've never seen anything like this, and nothing seems to end it. Arrests and publicity don't have the impact they normally would."

Note: Pyramid schemes were being investigated by New York police as well. In one Long Island raid, a former district attorney was discovered among the crowd. Upon his arrest, he promptly called the persecution of gamblers a misplaced priority of law enforcement agencies. "Everyone there fully realized the risk involved," he said. "They were there to socialize, have some fun, and hopefully win some money. There was no

fraud involved. The people there knew what they were doing." Meanwhile, in Florida, eight retired men, ranging in age from 63 to 70, were found guilty of violating Florida's gambling law by playing nickle-and-dime poker at their mobile home village; they were fined $75 each.

Sources: G. Christian Hill, "California Pyramids: Modern Wonders of Western World," *The Wall Street Journal,* May 29, 1980, pp. 1 and 29; Shawn G. Kennedy, "Pyramid Game on L.I. Raided," *The New York Times,* July 2, 1980, p. 81; "8 Convicted in 10¢ Poker Case," *The New York Times,* February 4, 1982, p. A16.

CLOSE-UP 10.3

THE GREAT SILVER SQUEEZE OF 1980

The most dramatic series of events ever to happen on the commodities exchanges reached a climax in 1980. Speculators bought large numbers of futures contracts for silver, gradually running up the futures price from $6 per ounce in the spring of 1979 to a peak of more than $50 per ounce in January, 1980. These speculators included the oil-rich Hunt brothers of Texas (Nelson Bunker, William Herbert, and Lamar), but they were not alone. Conticommodity Services (the brokerage arm of the Continental Grain Company), Kuwaiti "oil interests," and Hong Kong "elements" were playing the same game.

Normally, only a small percentage of futures trading leads to delivery of a commodity. Rather, the majority of contracts are matched up on the exchange floor before their expiration date: Speculators with long positions, for example, liquidate their rights to receive commodities by selling their contracts (at a higher price, it is hoped), while hedgers with short positions close out their positions by buying contracts, as illustrated in Table 10.3. In January, 1980, when open interest amounted to 105,187 contracts, or about 526 million ounces of silver, and when merchants had registered the availability of only 77 million ounces, however, speculators gave every impression of planning to take actual delivery of the

metal. They had *cornered* the market: Because the holders of short positions couldn't deliver what didn't exist, the speculators could insist on astronomical prices for giving up their contracts.

The directors of New York's Comex and Chicago's Board of Trade, where silver futures are traded, however, intervened. They limited each trader's allowable futures position to 600 contracts, restricted trading to the liquidation of contracts, raised margin deposits, and even suspended silver trading altogether. After its January peak, the price of silver futures plunged to about $10 per ounce in March. (Can you find evidence for this in Table 10.5?)

Brokers made **margin calls** requiring their speculating customers (the value of whose contract holdings was declining) to make additional good-faith cash deposits. This was bad for the Hunts, who at one point held more than $1 *billion* in silver contracts. By March, they couldn't meet a margin call, but by May 1980, they arranged a credit line of $1.1 billion with a group of 13 major U.S. banks to pay off their silver debts. In return for the favor, they had to sell 63 million ounces of silver and coal properties in North Dakota and Montana; they had to mortgage everything—from cotton plantations in Mississippi; parking lots in downtown Anchorage, Alaska; and the family

CLOSE-UP

jewel (the Placid Oil Company) to a bowling alley and shopping center in Dallas; interests in World Championship Tennis; 500 thoroughbred horses; and 75,000 head of cattle. Even personal items had to be put in hock, from the furniture in Bunker's Kentucky farm house to Herbert's Greek and Roman statues to Lamar's Rolex watch and Mercedes-Benz!

Note: The Hunts themselves vehemently denied that they had ever intended to corner the silver market. In 1988, the first of numerous lawsuits to decide the issue opened in New York. In the suit, Minpeco, a leading Peruvian mineral company, tried to regain a $150 million loss allegedly sustained because of the "greedy, power-

hungry, and unscrupulous" Hunts. Indeed, the jury found the Hunts guilty and they were ordered to pay $130 million in damages.

Sources: *The New York Times,* January 22, 1980, pp. D1 and 7; March 29, 1980, pp. 29 and 32; April 22, 1980, pp. D1 and 10; May 28, 1980, pp. D1 and 7; February 25, 1988, p. D2; August 21, 1988, pp. 1 and 34; *The Wall Street Journal,* May 27, 1980, pp. 1 and 35. For the Hunt's side of the story, *see* Roy Rowan, "A Talkfest with the Hunts," *Fortune,* August 11, 1980, pp. 163–68, and John A. Jenkins, "Battling a Billion-Dollar Debt," *The New York Times Magazine,* September 27, 1987, pp. 24ff.

CLOSE-UP 10.4

THE VALUE OF COMMON CENTS

In February 1980, the price of May 1980 copper futures at New York's Commodity Exchange reached an all-time high of $1.48 a pound. This worried one buyer of high-grade copper bars, the U.S. Mint. In 1979, the mint had produced 7 billion pennies, each bright new cent weighing 3.11 grams. There are 453.6 grams to the pound, which works out to 145.85 new (unworn) pennies to a pound, or 2.15 cents less than the futures price. When the intrinsic value of the common copper cent exceeds 1¢, people begin to melt down the coins. (Melting down pennies is relatively easy and doesn't require the high temperatures neces-

sary to reduce gold or silver.) While the U.S. Mint was contemplating a ban on unlicensed melting, the Canadian Mint quickly moved to make its 1¢ coins thinner instead. (Eventually, the United States turned to minting zinc pennies with copper plating.)

Sources: H. J. Maidenberg, "The Value of Common Cents," *The New York Times,* February 18, 1980, p. D4; Dylan Landis, "Currency: The Power of a Penny," *The New York Times,* October 11, 1981, p. F23.

CLOSE-UP 10.5

INSURANCE AND THE PRICE OF SEX

It is a fact of life that there *are* differences between men as a class and women as a class. For example, women at all ages have a higher life expectancy; they have fewer auto accidents; they have more frequent and more costly medical

problems; they are disabled more often and for longer periods. Insurance companies, as we have seen, work with the law of large numbers. They can't predict what will happen to an *individual* man or woman, but they can predict what will happen to the *average* man or woman. Accordingly, they *classify* people on the basis of the known characteristics of the group to which they belong and charge insurance premiums on that basis. Not surprisingly, women have long paid less for life insurance and auto insurance than men, but more for health insurance and disability benefits; and, for a given premium, have received lower monthly pension benefits than men (because women, on the average, collect these benefits for more months than do men who die earlier).

A number of women (among them Nathalie Norris in Arizona and Diana Spirt in New York) have filed suit, arguing that treating people as members of a class, rather than as individuals, constitutes precisely what the Civil Rights Act forbids: discrimination. They wanted the same monthly pension benefits as men were receiving. In 1983, the U.S. Supreme Court agreed with the Norris claim; in 1984, by refusing to review a lower court's ruling on the Spirt case, it effectively confirmed its earlier decision. All this opened up a Pandora's box because the basis of issuing insurance had always been the now suspect classification of people by group characteristics. Will it become illegal to classify people on the basis of anything, such as age? In the future, will the young have to pay the same life insurance premiums as the old? Will women get higher pension benefits than now and also have to pay higher premiums for auto insurance?

Sources: Daniel Seligman, "Insurance and the Price of Sex," *Fortune,* February 21, 1983, pp. 84–85; Stephen Wermiel, "Sex Discrimination Suit May Force Big Changes in Retirement Benefits," *The Wall Street Journal,* January 10, 1983, p. 21; *The Chronicle of Higher Education,* October 17, 1984, pp. 1 and 22.

5

Markets for Resources

These chapters show how equilibrium prices and quantities are established when households who supply resources meet firms that demand them. The focus is on labor and capital; both perfect competition and imperfect competition are considered.

11

Labor and Wages

In the previous chapters, we have discussed markets for *goods* and we have noted how their output and prices are established under a variety of conditions, ranging from the extremes of perfect competition and monopoly to such intermediate market forms as oligopoly and monopolistic competition. In this chapter and the next, we turn to markets in which the services of *resources* are traded. In such markets, firms rather than households appear as demanders; households rather than firms appear as suppliers.

The present chapter will concentrate on markets in which the services of human resources are traded. Much of what will be discussed here, however, could be applied, with minor changes, to other inputs as well, such as the services of natural resources, for example.

THE CASE OF PERFECT COMPETITION

In this section we will assume that the markets for labor, as well as those for the goods firms produce with labor's help, are perfectly competitive.

Demand: A Single Variable Input

The demand for resource services is invariably a **derived demand**—derived from the demand for goods. Unless there was a demand for apples, no firm would demand the services of human apple pickers or orchard-spraying machines, nor would it be interested in acquiring the right to use acres of land on which to plant apple trees. Indeed, firms can be expected to follow the optimization principle and always hire that quantity of any resource service that equates the marginal benefit of resource use with the associated marginal cost. As a result, the demand for the services of a resource, just like that for a consumer good, turns out to be not a single quantity, but a whole set of alternative price-quantity combinations. All this can be shown most easily in the case of a firm that can vary only a single input.

A Numerical Example. Consider a firm in the short run, subject to the production function given in Table 11.1. Given its technical know-how and fixed quantities of natural and capital resource services (1), the firm can vary labor services (2) and therefore its output (3). The

TABLE 11.1

The Input Decision

	Inputs per Year		Output per Year		Marginal Benefit and Marginal Cost of Input Use	
	Fixed (1,000 apple trees, 3 tons of fertilizer, etc.)	Variable (workers)	Maximum Total Product (bushels of apples)	Marginal Physical Product of Variable Input, MPP_i (bushels of apples per extra worker) $(4) = \frac{\Delta(3)}{\Delta(2)}$	Marginal Benefit = Marginal Value Product of Variable Input $MVP_i = MPP_i \cdot P_o$ (dollars per extra worker per year) $(5) = (4) \cdot \$12$	Marginal Cost = Price of Variable Input, P_i (6)
	(1)	(2)	(3)	(4)	(5)	(6)
(A)	1	0	0			
				1,000	$12,000	$10,000
(B)	1	1	1,000			
				1,700	20,400	10,000
(C)	1	2	2,700			
				2,300	27,600	10,000
(D)	1	3	5,000			
				2,000	24,000	10,000
(E)	1	4	7,000			
				1,300	15,600	10,000
(F)	1	5	8,300			
				700	8,400	10,000
(G)	1	6	9,000			
				300	3,600	10,000
(H)	1	7	9,300			
				0	0	10,000
(I)	1	8	9,300			

The data in columns (1) to (4), taken from Table 4.1, "A Simple Production Function," depict the technical possibilities open to a firm in the short run. Given the assumed price of output, P_o ($12 per bushel of apples), the firm can translate the variable input's marginal product from physical into value terms; column (4) becomes column (5). This marginal benefit of input use, MVP_i, can be compared with the associated marginal cost, which is the price of the input, P_i, in column (6). As long as MVP_i exceeds P_i, as in rows (A) to (F), the firm's profit can be increased by using more of the variable input. Once MVP_i falls short of P_i, as in rows (G) to (I), the firm's profit can be increased by using less of the variable input. The optimum variable-input quantity is found between rows (F) and (G), where MVP_i equals P_i and where both equal $10,000 (not shown). Note: As the pointers between columns (3) and (4) indicate, the entries in columns (4) to (6) refer to the intervals between rows (A) through (I).

marginal product of labor (4) is, in fact, the marginal benefit to the firm of using extra workers. When this benefit is measured in physical terms (as so many bushels of apples), it is called the marginal *physical* product of the variable input, MPP_i. The marginal benefit, however, can also be measured in dollars. Because the firm is assumed to operate in perfectly competitive markets, the volume of its activities will not affect the price of its output, P_o, of, say, $12 per bushel of apples. Thus each marginal physical product can be multiplied by the same product price of $12 to yield the *marginal value product* of the variable input, MVP_i (5). As long as it operates in perfectly competitive markets, the firm's volume of activities does not affect input prices either. Thus the price of the variable input, P_i, assumed at $10,000 per worker per year, is, in fact, the marginal cost (6) to the firm of using extra workers. The firm can always get another worker for a year for another $10,000.

Columns (5) and (6), clearly, contain all the information necessary for an optimal input decision. As long as the marginal value product of the variable input exceeds the input price, as in rows (A) to (F), the firm can raise its profit by hiring more units of the variable input. Thus the first worker hired raises the firm's revenue by $12,000 (because 1,000 bushels are added to output and sell for $12 each), but the firm's cost only rises by $10,000 (because that is the worker's wage). Thus the firm's profit rises (or its loss falls) by the $2,000 difference. Similarly, once the marginal value product falls short of the input price, the firm can raise its profit by hiring fewer units of the variable input, as in rows (G) to (I). Profit maximization calls for equating MVP_i with P_i: At some input combination between rows (F) and (G)—involving, perhaps, the hiring of five full-time workers and one part-time worker—both magnitudes will equal $10,000. The profit-maximizing firm must adjust its rate of resource use until the marginal benefit of resource use, which is the declining marginal value product of its variable input, equals the marginal cost of resource use, which is the given input price.*

A Graphical Exposition. Figure 11.1 is a graphical illustration of how to derive the demand curve for a single variable input. Panel (a) is a copy of panel (a), Figure 4.1 on p. 102, where a simple production function was depicted

---

*For a calculus-based treatment of this material, see Section 11A of the Calculus Appendix at the back of this book.

on the assumption that only labor could be varied and other inputs, such as capital and natural resources, were fixed. (The same production function is also shown in columns 1–3 of Table 11.1.) Panel (b) of Figure 11.1 is, in turn, a copy of panel (b), Figure 4.1, but, to avoid confusion with the value concepts to be discussed shortly, the two curves have now been labeled average and marginal *physical* product, respectively. Panel (c), finally, features the identical curves as panel (b), except that physical measures (bushels) have given way to values (dollars), each bushel-figure having been multiplied by the assumed product price of $12 per bushel. Thus average physical product times product price equals **average value product,** and marginal physical product times product price equals **marginal value product.** (The latter concept was already employed in the previous section, and the marginal-value-product-of-labor curve here can be viewed as a graphing of columns 2 and 5 of earlier Table 11.1.) Note that panel (c) contains a third line: the horizontal line at the $10,000 level of the assumed price of labor. (This line can be viewed as a graph of columns 2 and 6 of Table 11.1.) Clearly, our firm will find its optimal input quantity at point *e* where the declining marginal benefit of using labor (the marginal value product of labor) just equals the marginal cost of using labor (the $10,000 annual wage). Thus the firm will maximize profit by hiring 5.4 workers per year. And note: Given the same production function that is depicted in panels (a) and (b) of our graph, and given the same $12-per-bushel product price, and given, therefore, the marginal-value-product line of panel (c), our firm would hire different numbers of workers at different wages. If the price of labor were only $3,600 per year, the firm would optimize at point *f* and hire 6.5 workers. If the price of labor were $21,000 instead, the firm would hire 4 workers, in accordance with point *m*. (The firm would, however, incur losses in excess of fixed cost and therefore would *not* hire workers at wages above $21,000 per year in our example because the *average* value product of labor would then be smaller than the wage.) Thus

FIGURE 11.1

A Firm's Demand for Labor: The Simple Case

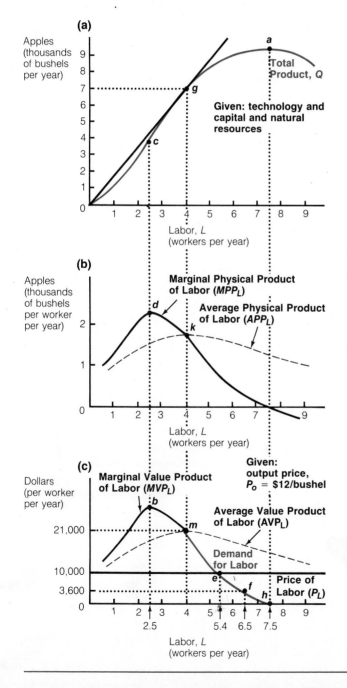

When a perfectly competitive firm uses a single variable input, a portion of the downward-sloping branch of the input's marginal-value-product curve is the demand curve for the input involved. The portion in question (below maximum average value product and above the horizontal axis) is highlighted in color in this graph [panel (c)]. Given technology, fixed quantities of other inputs, and output price, the firm pictured here demands the services of 5.4 workers per year when the price of labor is $10,000 per worker per year (point *e*). All else being equal, the firm would, however, demand the services of 4 or 6.5 or 7.5 workers per year, if the annual wage were $21,000 or $3,600 or zero, respectively (points *m*, *f*, and *h*). Why does the firm not demand any labor at wages above labor's maximum average value product at *m*? The answer is: For the same reason that the firm supplies nothing at output prices below minimum average variable cost—namely, that losses in excess of fixed cost would be made and the firm can then reduce losses to fixed cost by shutting down. Proof:

By definition, $\dfrac{Q}{L} = APP_L$ and

$$\frac{Q \cdot P_o}{L} = APP_L \cdot P_o = AVP_L,$$

where Q is total product, L is the quantity of labor used, and P_o is the price of output. For any price of labor, P_L, above point *m* it is true that $P_L > AVP_L$.

Hence $P_L > \dfrac{QP_o}{L}$ and

$$P_L L > QP_o.$$

When labor is the only variable input, this equals $VC > TR$

Hence $\dfrac{VC}{Q} > \dfrac{TR}{Q}$ and

$$AVC > P_o$$

the downward-sloping branch of labor's marginal-value-product curve, above the horizontal axis and at or below labor's average value product—noted in color in our graph—is the perfectly competitive firm's demand curve for labor when labor is the only variable input. Similar demand curves can be derived, in analogous fashion, for all other inputs. (See Analytical Example 11.1 at the end of this chapter for an interesting application.)

Before proceeding to the more complex case in which several inputs are variable, it is important to understand the relationship between change in quantity demanded and change in demand and the relationship between input decision and output decision.

Change in Quantity Demanded Versus Change in Demand. As we have just shown, the *quantity demanded* of any resource service varies with its price (and this is always illustrated by a *movement along* the demand curve, as from *m* to *e* to *f*). In addition, the *demand* for resource services changes (and the entire demand curve *shifts*) if there is a change in the underlying conditions determining the marginal value product of an input. Any change in technical knowledge, in the quantities of other inputs used, or in product price shifts the marginal-value-product curve of an input. This causes the firm to demand more or less of an input even at any given input price. Consider, for instance, a technical improvement that doubled all the entries in column (3) of Table 11.1, while leaving unaffected the inputs in columns (1) and (2). This doubling of maximum total product would double all the entries in column (4) and therefore all those in column (5) as well. Accordingly, a new marginal-value-product curve would appear in Figure 11.1 (along with new versions of all the other curves). The new demand curve for labor would lie above the one presently shown (except for point *h*). At the $10,000 price of labor, the profit-maximizing input quantity would change to more than 6 workers per year.

An increase in the quantity of nonlabor inputs in column (1) of Table 11.1 or a doubling of product price from $12 to $24 per bushel

would have identical results. The effect of doubling product price illustrates clearly how an increase in the demand for a good, by raising the good's price, translates itself into an increased demand for the inputs producing the good. Naturally, all of these effects can work in the direction of decreasing demand as well.

Input Decision Versus Output Decision. A firm's input decision is inextricably linked with its output decision. The profit-maximizing input decision depicted in Figure 11.1 corresponds exactly to the output decision depicted in Figure 5.2, "A Profitable Business" (p. 144), because both examples are based on identical assumptions concerning the production function and market prices (of $12 per bushel of apples and $10,000 per year per worker employed). The firm discussed in Figure 5.2 chose to produce 8,625 bushels of apples per year, and this output *implied* the use of about 5.4 workers per year. (Note the total variable cost of $54,695 given in Figure 5.2.) The firm discussed in Figure 11.1 chose to use about 5.4 workers per year, and this input *implied* the production of 8,625 bushels of apples per year.

Indeed, the profit-maximizing rule of the present chapter (under perfect competition, equate the declining marginal value product of an input, MVP_i, with input price, P_i) can be shown to be identical to the profit-maximizing rule of Chapter 5 (under perfect competition, equate the rising marginal cost of an output, MC_o, with output price, P_o).

The best input decision requires

$$MVP_i = P_i \qquad \textbf{(11.1)}$$

and this comes to $10,000 = $10,000 at *e* in panel (c) of Figure 11.1. Equation (11.1) can be rewritten as

$$MPP_i \cdot P_o = P_i \qquad \textbf{(11.2)}$$

or 833⅓ bushels · $12/bushel = $10,000, in our example. Rearranging terms, equation (11.2) becomes

$$P_o = \frac{P_i}{MPP_i} \qquad (11.3)$$

or $12/bushel = $10,000/833⅓ bushels.

Yet the price of an input, divided by the input's marginal physical product, is nothing else but the marginal cost of producing a unit of output with the help of this input. If labor is the only variable input, costs $10,000 a unit, and has a marginal product of 833⅓ bushels, the marginal cost of producing one bushel comes to $12. Hence it follows that

$$P_o = MC_o \qquad (11.4)$$

which, of course, is the best output decision of $12/bushel = $12/bushel at *B* in Figure 5.2. Thus the two profit-maximizing rules of equations (11.1) and (11.4) are one and the same.

Demand: Several Variable Inputs

If we assume the simultaneous variability of more than one input, a downward-sloping demand curve can still be derived for each input. The procedure, however, involves more than deriving individual curves for each input by the method discussed in the previous section. This added complexity results because few inputs are **independent inputs** such that a change in the quantity of one has no effect on the marginal physical products of other inputs. (Mass-production machines, on the one hand, and artisans who, on the other hand, work with their hands and simple tools may be an example of independent inputs.) Normally, inputs are **complementary inputs** such that a change in the quantity of one changes the marginal physical products of other inputs in the same direction. (Consider workers in an apple orchard. The more apple trees there are, the greater is the marginal productivity of any given number of workers likely to be; the more workers there are, the greater is the marginal productivity of any given number of trees likely to be.) Figure 11.2 depicts the demand for labor of a firm with two such complementary inputs, both of which

FIGURE 11.2

A Firm's Demand for Labor: A Complex Case

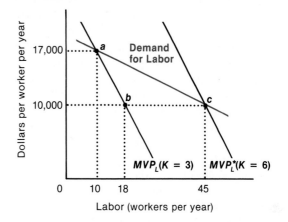

If a lower price of one input (here labor) causes a firm to hire additional amounts not only of this input but of complementary inputs as well (here capital services), the first input's marginal-value-product curve shifts up or to the right, as from MVP_L to $MVP_L{}^*$. The firm's demand curve for the input (here line *ac*) is, therefore, flatter than any given marginal-value-product (*MVP*) curve.

are variable. Let the firm use capital as well as labor services. As long as it uses 3 units of the former ($K = 3$), the marginal value product of labor, MVP_L, may vary with the quantity of labor employed in accordance with the line going through points *a* and *b*. At a price of $17,000 per worker per year, the firm would demand the services of 10 workers (point *a*). All else being equal, it would demand the services of 18 workers if labor's price dropped to $10,000 (point *b*). Yet line *ab* would not be the firm's demand curve for labor, if it always hired additional capital with additional labor. If the lower price of labor caused it to hire 6 units of capital services ($K = 6$) and labor's marginal value product of any given quantity of labor rose accordingly, the MVP_L line would shift up and right as indicated. The firm would demand 45 workers at the $10,000 price (point *c*). Thus its demand for labor would be the flatter line going through points *a* and *c*.

The demand for one input when several inputs are variable, can, however, also be derived more directly by a procedure akin to the derivation, in Figure 3.1 "The Price-Consumption Line" (p. 53), of a household's demand for a good.[1] Turn to panel (a) of Figure 3.1 and imagine that capital services are measured on the vertical axis, that labor services are measured on the horizontal one, and that lines I_0 to I_3 represent the capital-labor *isoquants* of a firm. An *isocost line* might swing around point A from AB to AC, to AD, and to AE, indicating successively lower prices of labor. A profit-maximizing firm would select the alternative optima shown by points a through d, and the implied demand curve for labor would appear exactly as in panel (b) of Figure 3.1. Indeed, this analogy to the theory of the household can be carried further.

Take another look at panel (a) of Figure 3.4 "Substitution and Income Effects" (p. 59). Once more imagine that capital services are on the vertical axis, that labor services are on the horizontal one, and that lines I_0 and I_1 are isoquants. With isocost line AB, a firm would choose an initial optimum at a but a new one at b once labor's price fell to produce isocost line AC. The increased quantity of labor demanded (the horizontal distance between a and b) could then be separated into two parts. As in the case of the household, the horizontal move from a to c is called the **substitution effect,** but the move from c to b is called the **scale effect** or the **output effect** (rather than the income effect).

The substitution effect makes a firm buy more of an output with a lowered price because the change in relative prices makes the firm substitute, in the optimal bundle of inputs used, more of the relatively cheaper input for less of the relatively more expensive one. Note how, in our imagined version of Figure 3.4, an unchanged output, represented by isoquant I_0, would be produced with input combination c rather than a, using less capital and more labor.

The scale or output effect, depicted by a move from c to b in Figure 3.4, on the other hand, makes the firm buy more of both inputs and produce a larger output after the price of one input has fallen. This increase in output occurs because the fall in the price of one input, here labor, effectively reduces the firm's marginal-cost curve. Given the price of output, this raises the profit-maximizing level of output. (As a glance at Figure 5.2, "A Profitable Business" on p. 144 can quickly confirm, a downward shift of the marginal-cost curve moves the profit-maximizing output level to the right of point B.)

Note: While the substitution effect always increases the quantity demanded of an input with lowered price, and while the output effect usually reinforces this result, the output effect could also operate in the *opposite* direction from the substitution effect. This counter movement would be analogous to the cases of inferior goods, illustrated in panels (b) and (c) of Figure 3.4. Those inputs for which the output effect works counter to the substitution effect are called **regressive inputs.**

For further discussion of substitution and scale effects, see Analytical Example 11.2 at the end of this chapter.

From Individual Demand to Market Demand

As was the case regarding the demand for consumer goods illustrated in Figure 3.7, "Deriving Market Demand" (p. 65), the demands of individual firms for inputs can be added together to derive market demand. The derivation of market demand for an input is slightly more complicated than for a consumer good, however. The input-demand curve of each firm is based on the assumption of a given product price (such as $12 per bushel in our example above). Given this product price, the firm pictured in Figure 11.1 [and now in panel (a) of Figure 11.3] would, indeed, increase quantity demanded from 4 to 6.5 workers per year if the annual price of labor fell from $21,000 to $3,600. Yet a simultaneous hiring of more labor by 100,000 other firms

---

[1]The following material makes use of the prior discussion of isoquants and isocost lines in the Chapter 5 section "Costs and Supply in the Long Run," on pp. 150–158.

FIGURE 11.3

Deriving the Market Demand for Labor

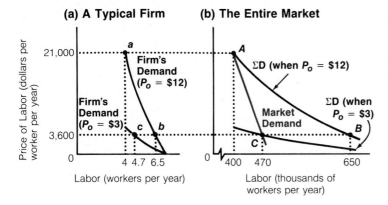

(a) A Typical Firm

(b) The Entire Market

Price of Labor (dollars per worker per year)

21,000

a

Firm's Demand $(P_o = \$12)$

Firm's Demand $(P_o = \$3)$

c   *b*

3,600

0   4 4.7 6.5

Labor (workers per year)

A

ΣD (when $P_o = \$12$)

ΣD (when $P_o = \$3$)

Market Demand

B

C

0   400   470   650

Labor (thousands of workers per year)

This graph illustrates how the market demand for labor (or any other input) can be derived from the individual demands of firms. Line *ab* in panel (a) represents a typical firm's demand for labor when the price of output equals $12 per bushel. The horizontal summation of this demand line for 100,000 similar firms is shown by line *AB* in panel (b). A similar individual demand line (and its summation for all firms) is shown for an output price of $3 per bushel. If labor's price is $21,000 a year initially, the typical firm demands 4 workers (point *a*); firms as a group demand 400,000 workers (point *A*). When labor's price falls to $3,600 a year, the individual firm would demand 6.5 workers, *all else being equal*. But if all firms hire more labor and raise output so much as to lower its price (to $3 per bushel as shown), the individual firm's demand line shifts. The firm then only demands 4.7 workers (point *c*), and firms as a group demand 470,000 of them (point *C*). Thus market demand is the steep line going through points *A* and *C*.

would raise industry output substantially and would almost certainly reduce product price from $12 to, say, $3 per bushel. This would shift our firm's marginal-value-product-of-labor curve down and to the left. The firm would hire, perhaps, only 4.7 workers at the $3,600 price. As a result, the *market* demand for labor is steeper than suggested by a horizontal summation of *given* marginal-value-product curves of individual firms [see Figure 11.3, panel (b)].

Individual Supply

What factors determine the supply of labor? Each individual, every day, has exactly 24 hours available, but obviously nobody can supply this much labor in a day on a regular basis. People have **reservation demands** for resources; that is, demands for purposes other than the sale of their services in the market. People certainly have reservation demands for their time. For want of a

better term, economists refer to such nonmarket uses of time as the consumption of **leisure**, but this term is used to describe more than sleeping, eating, going to the beach, and being with family and friends. It can also include study and hard work in the home. When analyzing a person's allocation of time between leisure so defined and work for pay, economists make use of the indifference-curve analysis introduced in Chapter 2. The individual is once more viewed as making a choice between two goods. This time, the choice is not between two specific consumer goods (such as apples and butter), but between income (or the set of *all* consumer goods that can be bought with that income) and leisure. Figure 11.4, which is analogous to Figure 2.6, "The Consumer's Optimum" (p. 39), shows that the individual is constrained by budget line *AB*. It divides the field of choice into attainable combinations (unshaded) of income and leisure and unattainable ones (shaded). The maximum amount of leisure available is obviously 24 hours per day (point *B*). The maximum income, however, depends on the prevailing wage. If it were $5 per hour (and that we assume), the individual could earn at most $120 per day, but that would require working 24 hours a day (point *A*). Note: The absolute value of the budget line's slope equals the prevailing wage; $120 per day divided by 24 hours per day comes to $5 per hour:

$$|\text{Budget line slope}| = \text{wage}$$

The *equation* of the budget line can be derived by noting that the line's vertical intercept equals the maximum possible income, $24w$, where w is the hourly price of labor or wage; while the horizontal intercept equals the maximum possible leisure time, 24 (hours per day). If we denote income by I and leisure hours by ℓ, the budget line is described by the intercepts as $I = 24w - \dfrac{24w}{24}\,\ell$, which simplifies to the expression given in Box 11.A.

11.A The Budget-Line Equation
$$I = 24w - w\ell$$

Consider how zero leisure, according to Box 11.A, implies an income of $I = 24w$ or $120 (point *A*) when $w = $5. Or note how 24 hours of leisure implies an income of $I = 24w - 24w = 0$ (point *B*). Any change in the wage would tilt the budget line around point *B* as an anchor point. A rise in the wage would tilt it upward (point *A* would move up along the vertical axis); any fall in the wage would tilt it downward (point *A* would move down toward 0). Correspondingly, the shaded world of the impossible would shrink or expand.

Figure 11.4 also includes a set of indifference curves, labeled I_0 to I_4. These curves display the characteristics discussed in Figure 2.5, "The Indifference Curve Analyzed" (p. 37). Each curve shows income-leisure combinations among which the individual is indifferent, but any combination on

FIGURE 11.4

An Individual's Income-Leisure Choice

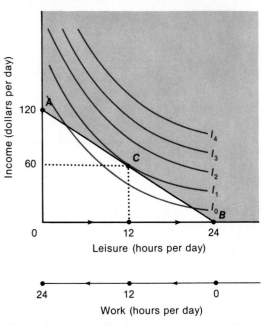

This graph brings together the elements involved when a utility-maximizing individual decides on the allocation of time between leisure and income-producing work. Budget line *AB* separates possible income-leisure choices (unshaded) from impossible ones (shaded). Indifference curves I_0 to I_4 depict the individual's preferences. Point *C* indicates the optimum income-leisure combination because, among all the possible combinations in triangle 0*AB*, it yields the highest total utility.

a higher-numbered curve is always preferred to one on a lower-numbered curve. The curvature of each indifference curve reflects the familiar diminishing marginal rate of substitution, now of leisure, ℓ, for income I. Thus the absolute value of an indifference curve's slope at any point also equals the ratio of marginal utilities of leisure to income.*

$$|\text{Indifference curve slope}|$$

$$= MRS_{\ell/I} = \frac{MU_\ell}{MU_I}$$

---

*For a calculus-based treatment of this material, see Section 11B of the Calculus Appendix at the back of this book.

Given the individual's opportunities and preferences (shown by the budget line and the indifference curves, respectively), the individual's optimum is found at point C. The consumption of 12 hours of leisure per day, which implies the supplying of 12 hours of labor per day and the receipt of $60 of income per day, maximizes the person's overall utility. At point C, the budget line is just tangent to the highest-numbered indifference curve that can be reached. Therefore, we have:

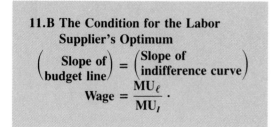

11.B The Condition for the Labor Supplier's Optimum

$$\left(\begin{matrix}\text{Slope of}\\\text{budget line}\end{matrix}\right) = \left(\begin{matrix}\text{Slope of}\\\text{indifference curve}\end{matrix}\right)$$

$$\text{Wage} = \frac{MU_\ell}{MU_I}.$$

At point C, our individual receives $5 per hour and is indifferent about exchanging, at the margin, 1 hour of leisure for $5 of income. Thus an hour of leisure is valued at the margin five times as highly as a dollar of income (or a dollar's worth of consumer goods).†

The preceding indifference-curve analysis can now be expanded to illustrate how the individual would vary the quantity of labor supplied with changes in a variety of factors—such as the wage rate or the amount of nonlabor income.

The Price-Consumption Line. Panel (a) of Figure 11.5 depicts a set of indifference curves identical to those in Figure 11.4, but Figure 11.5 illustrates the individual's behavior when confronted by different wage rates. If the hourly wage is $3, the lowest budget line is relevant and the maximum daily income is $72. The individual's optimum is then at point a where this

---

†For a calculus-based treatment of this material, see Section 11C of the Calculus Appendix at the back of this book.

FIGURE 11.5

The Price-Consumption Line

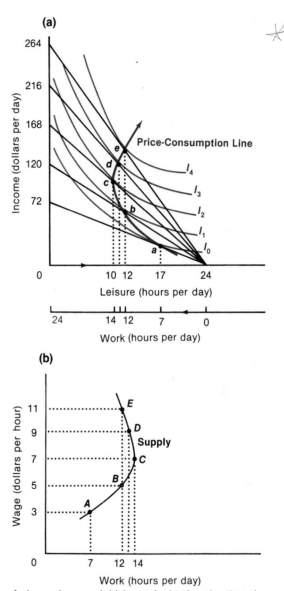

An increasing wage (which can also be viewed as the *price of leisure*) is pictured by a budget line swinging upward in panel (a). This wage increase gives rise at first to lower and later to higher quantities of leisure demanded, all else being equal. Note how the optima move from a to e along the price-consumption line. All this translates, in panel (b), to first higher and later lower quantities of labor supplied as labor's hourly wage rises from $3 to $11.

366 Chapter 11 Labor and Wages

budget line is tangent to the highest indifference curve (I_0) that can be reached with this budget. At point *a* the person chooses 17 hours of leisure and 7 hours of work per day; this labor quantity is indicated separately in panel (b) of our graph at point *A*.

If the hourly wage rises to $5, a new budget line that yields a maximum daily income of $120 becomes relevant. The individual's optimum moves to point *b* (which corresponds to point *C* in Figure 11.4). This choice is shown by point *B* in panel (b).

Successively higher wage rates of $7, $9, and $11 per hour keep moving the budget line up in panel (a) and yield new optima at *c*, *d*, and *e*. Once more, these choices are shown by points *C*, *D*, and *E* in panel (b).

In panel (a), the colored line that connects the various optima is the price-consumption line, already familiar to us from Chapter 3. The two consumption goods between which the individual chooses are in this case not apples and butter, but leisure on the one hand and all other consumption goods (represented by income) on the other hand. The price, of course, is the wage, which can also be viewed as the price of leisure: For every leisure hour that the individual chooses to consume, a price has to be paid equal to the wage that might have been earned instead.

Because the leisure-consumption choice implies a choice about hours worked, a labor-supply line can be derived as in panel (b). The particular supply curve is backward-bending, indicating that this individual would supply smaller quantities of labor at higher wages once the wage exceeded a certain level ($7 per hour). Such a phenomenon is frequently observed in labor markets, but it is not a logical necessity.

The Income-Consumption Line. We can, similarly, isolate the effect on the quantity of labor supplied of changes in other variables. Consider Figure 11.6. Indifference curves I_1 to I_4 in panel (a) depict once more a person's preferences concerning income and leisure. Point *C* represents an original optimum where nonlabor income is zero and the wage rate is $5 per hour.

FIGURE 11.6

The Income-Consumption Line

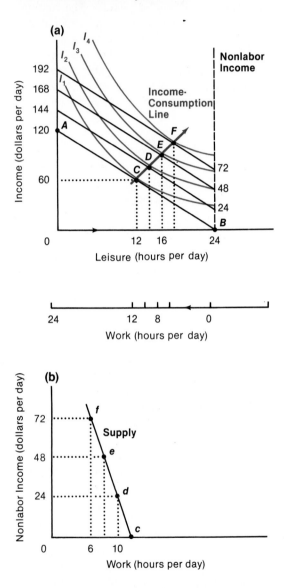

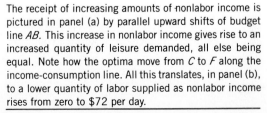

The receipt of increasing amounts of nonlabor income is pictured in panel (a) by parallel upward shifts of budget line *AB*. This increase in nonlabor income gives rise to an increased quantity of leisure demanded, all else being equal. Note how the optima move from *C* to *F* along the income-consumption line. All this translates, in panel (b), to a lower quantity of labor supplied as nonlabor income rises from zero to $72 per day.

Figure 11.6 shows the individual's behavior when confronted with different levels of nonlabor income, such as income from the sale of capital or natural resource services or a government grant.

When such income is zero, the individual works 12 hours a day—point C in panel (a), point c in panel (b). When nonlabor income equals $24 per day, budget line AB makes a parallel upward shift to this extent; the individual's new optimum is at D, implying more leisure and less work. This choice is shown at d in panel (b). Nonlabor incomes of $48 and $72 per day, similarly, shift the optimum to E and F in panel (a), and the quantity of labor supplied drops further to e and f in panel (b).

In panel (a), the colored line that connects the various optima is the income-consumption line, already familiar to us from Chapter 3. This line indicates increased consumption of leisure with rising income; leisure must then be a normal good for the individual concerned.

Close-Up 11.1 at the end of this chapter contains a further discussion of the types of labor supply curves found in Figures 11.5 and 11.6.

Substitution and Income Effects. We can separate the effect of a simple wage change on the consumption of leisure (and hence the supply of work) into a substitution effect and an income effect—just as we did in Chapter 3 for ordinary consumption goods that are bought in markets. Figure 11.7 illustrates the substitution and income effects of a wage increase. Consider panel (a). Given indifference curves I_0 and I_1 and an initial wage rate of $2 per hour, an individual's optimum is found at C on budget line AB. Sixteen hours of leisure are consumed; 8 hours of labor, therefore, are supplied. When the wage rate doubles, the budget line swings to BD; the new optimum is at E. Leisure falls to 12 hours a day and labor supplied rises to 12 hours also. This pattern of movement implies an upward-sloping supply curve of labor.

With the help of the dashed artificial budget line, the slope of which reflects the higher wage, the move from C to E can be analyzed.

The individual could have remained equally well off by moving from C to F, substituting more labor and income (and other consumption goods) for leisure to this extent. (Note how both C and F are found on indifference curve I_0.) This potential move represents the substitution effect, which always makes a person consume less of a good with higher price. In this case, the price of leisure has risen, and the individual is tempted to consume only 8 instead of 16 hours of it. Yet this is not the whole story. The wage hike has also given the individual a rise in real income, depicted by a parallel shift of the artificial dashed budget line to the actual one labeled BD. The income effect makes people buy more of normal goods if income rises. In this case, the individual buys extra leisure, moving from 8 to 12 hours per day. Thus the income effect partially offsets the substitution effect, and the final choice falls on E.

Indeed, it is possible for the income effect to overwhelm the substitution effect, as shown in panel (b). Given indifference curves I_0 and I_1, and an initial wage rate of $5 per hour, an individual's optimum is found at K on budget line GH. Sixteen hours of leisure are consumed, 8 hours of labor performed. Once more, the wage rate doubles, the budget line swings to HL; the new optimum is at M. Leisure rises to 20 hours a day, and labor supplied falls to 4 hours. This time, the supply of labor is backward-bending. Although the individual could have remained equally well off by moving from K to N (and would thus have supplied more labor), the income effect overwhelms the substitution effect.

Note: The income effect for ordinary consumption goods that are also normal goods *reinforces* the substitution effect (as noted in Chapter 3) because a higher price of those goods makes people poorer and thus makes them buy less on that account as well. The income effect for leisure always *works counter to* the substitution effect because a higher price of leisure (which is the wage) makes people richer, not poorer and thus makes them ''buy'' more leisure (assuming it is a normal good). The possibility of the income effect overpowering the substitution effect (which is rare for ordinary consumption goods because it requires the presence of Giffen's paradox) is fairly high in the case of leisure for the following reasons. Individuals are usually highly diversified when consuming ordinary goods. They consume small quantities of many goods. They consume small quantities of many

types of goods. Thus a change in the price of any one of them (be it butter, pigs' feet, or potatoes) affects the consumer's real income but usually to a minor degree. Individuals are, on the other hand, highly specialized when it comes to sup-

---

FIGURE 11.7

Substitution and Income Effects

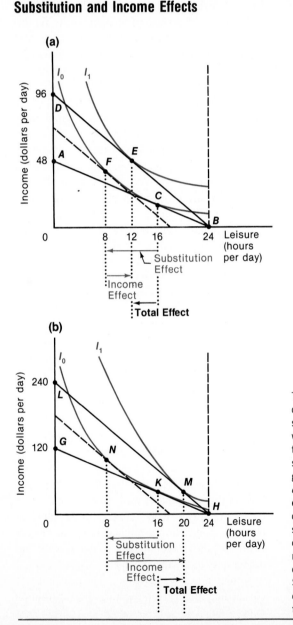

These two graphs illustrate the two effects on the quantity of leisure demanded (and therefore the quantity of labor supplied) of a higher price of leisure (that is, of a higher wage): The *substitution effect* of a higher wage decreases the quantity of leisure demanded and increases labor supplied. (Note the horizontal arrows so labeled in both graphs. They consistently point to the left.) The *income effect* of higher price works counter to the substitution effect and can offset it partially, as shown in panel (a), offset it exactly (not shown), or offset it more than fully, as shown in panel (b). Therefore, it is possible for a supply-of-labor curve (not shown) to have positively as well as negatively sloped segments. Note: Substitution and income effects are determined by the Hicksian rather than Slutsky's approach. (See Figure 3.5 on p. 61 for a discussion of these alternative approaches to splitting the total effect.)

plying resource services. Most of them supply relatively large quantities of services of a single resource only, usually labor. Thus a change in the price of labor is likely to have a substantial impact on the person's real income; hence a powerful income effect occurs. (See Close-Up 11.2 at the end of this chapter for further discussion.)

From Individual Supply to Market Supply

Individual labor supplies, like the one shown in panel (b) of Figure 11.5, can be added together horizontally to derive market supply. The market-supply line could have the same shape as the individual line shown in our graph; it could also be upward-sloping throughout. Indeed, market supply is likely to be upward-sloping because not all individuals have backward-bending supply curves, and, for those who do, the bend points will appear at different wage levels.

The Interaction of Demand and Supply

As in the market for goods, equilibrium is established in the markets for resource services through the interaction of the forces of demand and supply.

The Short Run.   Figure 11.8 illustrates how equilibrium is established in the labor market in the short run, in which the number of people is fixed.

Once again, if we wish, we can describe the equilibrium depicted in the graph mathematically instead. The supply line can be expressed as

$$Q_S = -90 + 45W \qquad (1)$$

where Q_S is the quantity of labor supplied and W is labor's price. The wage. The demand line can be written as

$$Q_D = 380 - 33\tfrac{1}{3}W \qquad (2)$$

where Q_D is the quantity of labor demanded and W, again, the wage. (The reader may wish to

FIGURE 11.8

The Market for Labor: The Short Run

In a perfectly competitive market for the services of a resource, equilibrium is reached where market supply intersects market demand (point *e*). At any higher price, there would be surpluses, tending to depress price. At any lower price, there would be shortages, bending to raise price. This is true not only for the services of this unspecified type of labor, but for the services of other resources as well.

consult footnotes 1 and 2 of Chapter 6 on p. 181 to see how these equations could be derived from our graph.) We can solve for the equilibrium values with the help of equation (3) as follows:

$$Q_S = Q_D \qquad (3)$$
$$-90 + 45W = 380 - 33\tfrac{1}{3}W$$
$$78\tfrac{1}{3}W = 470$$
$$W = 6$$

Substituting $W = 6$ in (2), we find $Q_D = Q_S = 180$.

The Long Run.   In the long run, the same principle of equating demand with supply applies, but demand and supply are likely to differ from their short-run counterparts. Until the markets for outputs are in long-run equilibrium (a matter discussed in Chapter 6), the demand for inputs, such as labor, will change. And the sellers of resource services have plenty of ways to change the supply of many inputs in the long run, too.

APPLICATIONS

Let us consider a number of applications of the perfectly competitive labor market model.

Application 1: Wage Differentials

When we look at the world around us, one thing is easily perceived: People earn vastly different wages in different occupations. Is this because real-world labor markets are far from perfectly competitive, or can such differentials exist even in perfectly competitive markets?

In the short run, certainly, such differentials can exist even under perfect competition. Market demand and market supply for janitors and truck drivers, for example, might just happen to intersect at different wage levels, as in panels (a) and (b) of Figure 11.9. Yet if people were alike and jobs were alike, the free mobility found in perfectly competitive markets would eliminate such differentials eventually. Janitors would leave their occupations; supply, S, in panel (a) of our graph would shift to the left. Given demand, D, janitorial wages would rise. As ex-janitors turned into truck drivers, supply, S^*, in panel (b) of our graph would shift to the right. Given demand, D^*, truck driver wages would fall. These changes would continue until the wage differential had disappeared.

Yet people are not alike; nor are jobs. That is why wage differentials could persist even in a world of perfectly competitive labor markets.

Differences in People.   There exist certain biological differences among people. People differ in physical strength, in size, and in intelligence. Some have a natural talent for athletics, music, or science; others are utterly inept in these fields. To the extent that these personal qualities cannot be acquired after birth, low-priced janitors cannot enter the occupations making use of these talents, and wage differentials can persist even in the long run.

FIGURE 11.9

Wage Differentials

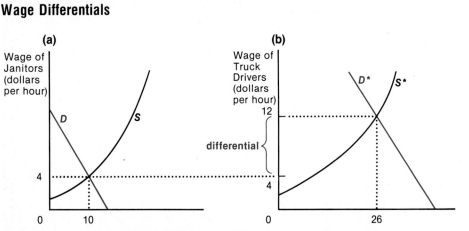

In perfectly competitive labor markets, the wage differential depicted here could not persist if all people and all jobs were alike. By the same token, biological differences in people and differences in the attractiveness of jobs can produce permanent wage differentials even when labor markets are perfectly competitive.

Differences in Jobs.   While people can sell the services of their natural and capital resources without being present when they are used, a seller of labor power must personally accompany what is being sold. For this reason, nonmonetary aspects of jobs become a crucial consideration. Jobs differ in a million ways: Some have to be performed in harsh northern climates; others in the humid South. Some must be done in urban areas; others in the countryside. Some can be carried out in small firms; others only in giant ones. Some jobs have regular hours; others require overtime, work on weekends and holidays or even at night. Some provide opportunities for advancement, responsibility, prestige, and power. Some are physically tiring, dirty, smelly, and noisy; others are boring, dull, and lonely. Some must be preceded by long periods of training and income forgone; others involve risks to health and life.

The list could be lengthened, but this much is clear: People have different preferences with respect to job characteristics. Some people like the northern climate; others hate it. Some love cities; others abhor them. Some seek out responsibility; others run from it. To the extent that monetary wage differentials only offset nonmonetary differences in the perceived attractiveness of jobs, the differentials can persist. Such wage differentials are then called **equalizing wage differentials** or **compensating wage differentials.** If all the janitors depicted in Figure 11.9 believed that they would rather lead a peaceful life than get paid $8 per hour more risking their lives on the highways, no shifts of supplies would occur in the two markets. Indeed, this sort of analysis has given rise to an interesting study about the value people place on human life.

Wage Differentials and the Value of Life. R. Thaler and S. Rosen examined 1967 U.S. wage differentials among a number of occupations, along with differentials in occupational death rates. Some of their results are shown in Table 11.2. The authors of this study concluded that workers were accepting, on the average, $176 in extra annual wages for the added risk that

1 out of 1,000 workers in their occupation would die at work during the year. This means that people put an implicit value of $176,000 on their own lives. This also means that a firm with 1,000 employees could, if these average data applied to it, save itself $176,000 in wage costs *per year* by eliminating the risk that killed 1 worker per year.[2]

Application 2: Cobweb Cycles for Labor

In Chapter 6, we noted the existence of cobweb cycles in the markets for certain commodities, such as cattle or corn (see pp. 192–195). A similar phenomenon exists in the markets for certain types of labor, and for the same reason, too. Whenever supply adjustments take a fairly long time (as they inevitably do in the case of highly skilled services, such as engineering or law, because of the long period of schooling required), cobweb cycles are likely to emerge.[3]

Consider Figure 11.10 that depicts the labor market for engineers. Let D represent the current demand and S_L the *long-run* supply. A current equilibrium exists at a; the wage is W_0 and the

---

[2]Although the risk premiums vary between $20 and $400 per year, a great number of studies have since confirmed the findings of Thaler and Rosen that wage differentials based on job hazards exist. *See,* for instance, W. Kip Viscusi, *Employment Hazards: An Investigation of Market Performance* (Cambridge, Mass.: Harvard University Press, 1979); Robert S. Smith, ''Compensating Wage Differentials and Public Policy: A Review,'' *Industrial and Labor Relations Review,* April 1979, pp. 339–52, which reviews eight studies; and Alan Marin and George Psacharopoulos, ''The Reward for Risk in the Labor Market: Evidence from the U.K. and a Reconciliation with Other Studies,'' *Journal of Political Economy,* August 1982, pp. 827–53. A study by John Garen, ''Compensating Wage Differentials and the Endogeneity of Job Riskiness,'' *The Review of Economics and Statistics,* February 1988, pp. 9–16, however, concludes that the types of differentials noted in Table 11.2 are downward-biased.

[3]The following discussion is based on Richard B. Freeman, ''A Cobweb Model of the Supply and Starting Salary of New Engineers,'' *Industrial and Labor Relations Review,* January 1976, pp. 236–46; and Robert J. Flanagan, Robert S. Smith, and Ronald Ehrenberg, *Labor Economics and Labor Relations* (Glenview, Ill.: Scott, Foresman and Co., 1984), pp. 212–15.

number of engineers employed is N_0. Let the demand for engineers rise to D'. The new long-run equilibrium, clearly, is at e, corresponding to W_1 and N_1, but in the short run the market moves to point b. This happens because the *short-run* supply of engineers is fixed at N_0 (and could be depicted by a vertical line going through a and b). The short-run wage thus moves to W_2, and this stimulates enrollments in engineering schools. A few years later, the quantity supplied corresponds to c, there being then N_2 engineers in the market. Given demand D', there exists a *surplus* of bc engineers at the wage of W_2; wages plummet to W_3 where the new short-run supply (line cd) meets the demand of D'. After a considerable lag of time and much soul-searching, some engineers will leave the field; the quantity supplied will become N_3 (not shown, but

corresponding to point f), and there will be a *shortage* of engineers equal to fd. This will drive the wage up to W_4 (not shown, but corresponding to point i). The market will thus follow the colored arrows and, perhaps, reach its final equilibrium (in this damped-cycle case) a few decades hence at point e.

Nor is this story pure fantasy. In the late 1950s, the U.S. market for engineers was said to be in surplus; by the end of the decade and into the early 1960s, there was an engineers' shortage, to be followed by a surplus in the late 1960s and a shortage in the 1970s. Wages (and enrollments in relevant educational institutions) fluctuated widely. To make matters worse, government agencies sometimes react to such events by *subsidizing* enrollments in fields of shortage labor. But consider what this implies: The shortage

TABLE 11.2

Differential Wages and Death Rates

Occupation	Occupational Annual Deaths per 100,000	Extra Annual Wage
Fishers	19	$ 33
Fire fighters	44	77
Police officers, detectives	78	137
Electricians	93	164
Teamsters	114	201
Sawyers	133	234
Crane or derrick operators	147	259
Sailors	163	287
Bartenders	176	310
Mine operatives	176	310
Taxicab drivers	182	320
Locomotive stokers	186	327
Structural ironworkers	204	359
Boilermakers	230	405
Lumberjacks	256	451
Guards, doorkeepers	267	470

Source: Adapted from Richard Thaler and Sherwin Rosen, *The Value of Saving a Life: Evidence from the Labor Market* (Rochester, N.Y.: University of Rochester, Department of Economics, December 1973). Reprinted in Nestor E. Terleckyj, ed., "Household Production and Consumption," *Studies in Income and Wealth,* vol. 40, p. 288. Copyright © 1976 National Bureau of Economic Research, Inc. Reprinted by permission.

(such as *fd* in Figure 11.10) already drives the wage up beyond its long-run equilibrium (such as to *i*, which lies above *e*). The government's policy only makes the excessive supply response worse.

Application 3: Using the Time-Allocation Model to Evaluate Government Programs

The time-allocation model introduced in Figure 11.4 can be used to evaluate a host of government programs that affect the labor market. Consider panel (a) of Figure 11.11. A worker's preferences are depicted by I_0 and I_1; the worker faces budget line *ac* and has chosen optimum *b*

FIGURE 11.10

Cobweb Cycle for Labor

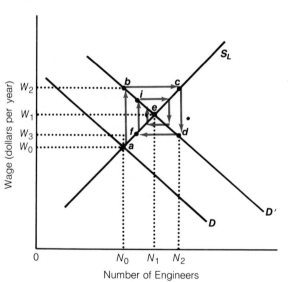

Cobweb cycles have been observed not only in the markets for commodities (see Figure 6.7 on p. 193), but in labor markets as well. *Caution:* Line S_L is *long-run* supply; short-run supply must be viewed as a vertical line (not shown) that shifts from a position above N_0 (and going through *ab*) to another above N_2 (and going through *dc*), then to a third (going through *fi*), and so on, always following the horizontal arrows.

FIGURE 11.11

Evaluating Income-Replacement Programs or Tax Programs

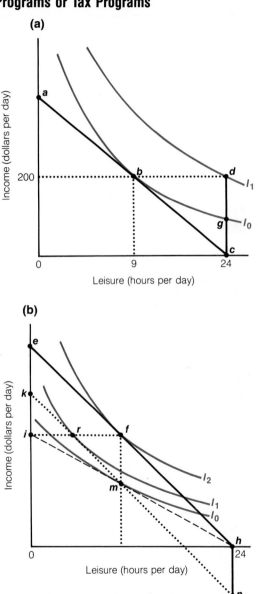

The time-allocation model can be used to show why it is *not* a good idea to replace 100 percent of the income lost by unemployed or injured workers [panel (a)] and why a lump-sum tax hurts workers less than a proportional income tax that collects the same revenue [panel (b)].

(working 15 hours and earning $200 per day). If the worker were laid off or were injured on the job so as to be unable to work, the worker would be positioned at *c*, with 24 hours of leisure and zero income, clearly worse off. Now let government introduce an *income-replacement program* that provides unemployment benefits or workers' compensation payments. Should 100 percent of the worker's lost earnings be replaced and a payment of *cd* be made to the worker, as many suggest? As the graph indicates, the worker would then be much better off, receiving, at point *d,* the original income along with 24 hours of leisure. Such a payment would clearly *overcompensate* the worker's utility loss; and this is likely to have a serious incentive effect. If unemployed, rather than take the first job offer that comes along, the worker may just take forever searching for a suitable job. If injured, but sufficiently healed to go back to work, the worker may elect to drag out the recovery time. Actual government programs of this type in the United States, therefore, pay only about one half of lost earnings (which might place the worker at a position such as *g*).

Now consider panel (b). A worker is at initial optimum *f*. The government introduces a *proportional income tax,* swinging original budget line *eh* around to *ih*. The worker moves to a new optimum at *m*; utility is down from the level of I_2 to the level of I_0. Could the government have done better? The answer is yes. It could have collected the same tax revenue of *fm* by imposing a *lump-sum tax* of *fm = hn = ek*. The after-tax budget line would have been dotted line *kn* instead of dashed line *ih*; the worker would have selected an optimum at *r* and would have been better off, enjoying the utility level implied by I_1 rather than I_0. The government's tax collection method was unnecessarily burdensome to the taxpayer. (Note that the income tax, by changing the slope of the budget line, distorted the worker's labor-supply decision toward more leisure at *m* than would be chosen with the lump-sum tax at *r*.) Note also the equally favorable conclusion

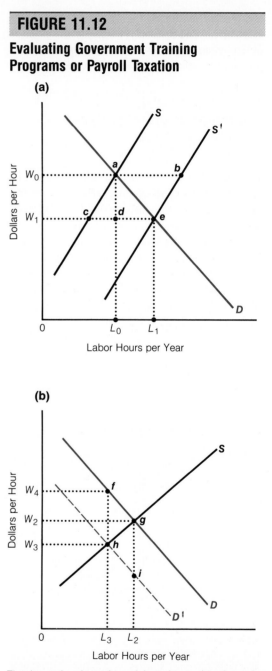

FIGURE 11.12

Evaluating Government Training Programs or Payroll Taxation

(a)

(b)

The demand-and-supply model can be used to show why a government training program will injure previously employed workers [panel (a)] and why a payroll tax levied on employers will hurt employees [panel (b)].

about the lump-sum tax that was reached in Chapter 2's section, "Application 1: Lump-Sum Versus Selective Sales Tax."

Application 4: Using the Demand-and-Supply Model to Evaluate Government Programs

The demand-and-supply model introduced in Figure 11.8 is equally useful for evaluating government programs affecting labor. Consider panel (a) of Figure 11.12. An original labor market equilibrium exists at a, with a wage of W_0 and labor employment of L_0, corresponding to demand, D, and supply, S. Let the government sponsor a *training program* for this type of labor, eventually releasing an additional $ab = ce$ units of such labor into the market. Even if all of the newly trained find employment (which we shall assume), not all is for the good. A new equilibrium emerges at e; it implies that some original workers who used to earn W_0 now earn only W_1 (along with the newly employed), while other original workers (cd) have left the market entirely. Only if the demand curve were extremely flat would this negative (and often overlooked) effect be negligible.

Now turn to panel (b). Consider an original equilibrium at g, with a wage of W_2 and labor employment of L_2. Let the government impose a *payroll tax* on the employers in order to finance (as our actual governments do) social security retirement, disability, and Medicare payments or unemployment benefits. Let the employer tax come to $gi = fh$ per hour. After paying the tax, the employer-demand curve for labor effectively equals dashed line D'. A new equilibrium is established at h, with a lower wage, W_3, received by workers and lower employment, L_3. Thus, contrary to intentions, the burden of the tax is partially shifted to workers. The employers are also worse off: They get less labor (L_3 rather than L_2), and they pay more per hour (W_4 rather than W_2). The government, of course, collects the difference, $W_4 - W_3$, between what employers

pay and what workers get. (Empirical studies show that somewhat less than half of employer payroll taxes are shifted to employees in the United States.) Note that the burden involved falls the more heavily on workers the more vertical the supply or the more horizontal the demand line is. Those who have few alternatives (workers with a near-vertical supply line who would supply roughly the same labor even with a huge cut in hourly pay), unlike those who have many (employers with a near-horizontal demand line who would demand next to no labor if its price went up even a little bit), are always the ones who end up paying a tax, regardless on whom it is officially levied. (The reader may wish to review a similar discussion in Chapter 6's Application 4, "Excise Taxation.")

THE CASE OF IMPERFECT COMPETITION

It is time to consider how the results obtained so far must be modified in the presence of imperfect competition. It would be possible to consider a great multitude of market imperfections; this section will focus on only four:

1. perfectly competitive sellers of labor confronting perfectly competitive buyers of labor, all of which buyers exert monopoly power in their respective product markets;

2. perfectly competitive sellers of labor confronting a single buyer only—a monopsony in the labor market—that is a perfectly competitive seller in the product market;

3. a single seller of labor—a monopoly in the labor market—confronting perfectly competitive buyers of labor; and

4. a single seller of labor confronting a monopsonistic buyer of labor.

(Monopoly power on the selling side of a labor market is usually exercised by workers who have formed a cartel for the joint sale of their labor; that is, a **labor union**.)

Competition in the Labor Market, Modified by Monopoly Power in the Product Market

Consider a firm with any degree of monopoly power. It may be an electric power company and a pure monopoly. It may be an oligopolistic automobile manufacturer or a monopolistically competitive restaurant. As we have learned in Chapters 7 and 8, one thing clearly differentiates such sellers from perfectly competitive ones: they face downward-sloping demand curves; and their marginal revenue, therefore, is lower than their product price.

When such firms enter the labor market, they often find themselves among innumerable buyers, however, and face just as many sellers.

Consider how the producers of many different goods frequently compete with each other for the same labor, whether unskilled or skilled, such as secretarial help. The monopoly power of such firms in their respective product markets has, however, a definite impact on their behavior in the labor market. The quantity of labor demanded by such firms will not be one that equates the given wage with labor's marginal value product, but a lower quantity that equates this wage with labor's **marginal revenue product (MRP)**, which is its marginal physical product multiplied by marginal revenue (rather than by product price), as will be shown with the help of Tables 11.3 and 11.4.

First, turn to Table 11.3; columns (1) and (2) illustrate a short-run production function for a

TABLE 11.3

The Labor Input Decision: Product Market Monopoly

Labor Quantity, L	Total Product, Q	Product Price, P	Total Revenue, $TR = Q \cdot P$	Marginal Benefit and Marginal Cost of Using Labor	
(number of workers per week)	(units per week)	(dollars per product unit)	(dollars per week)	Marginal Revenue Product of Labor[a] $MRP_L = \dfrac{\Delta TR}{\Delta L}$ (dollars per extra worker)	Labor's Wage W
(1)	(2)	(3)	(4) = (2) × (3)	(5) = Δ(4)/Δ(1)	(6)
0	0	1.20	0	—	112
1	500	1.00	500	500	112
2	950	.82	779	279	112
3	1,350	.66	891	112	112
4	1,700	.52	884	−7	112
5	2,000	.40	800	−84	112
6	2,250	.30	675	−125	112

[a]Strictly speaking, the entries in column (5) pertain to the *intervals* between the labor quantity of the given row and that of the preceding row.

A firm that possesses monopoly power in the product market will find that it can sell the extra output produced by extra labor only by lowering output price [columns (1)–(3)]. For such a firm total revenue [column (4)] will fail to rise in proportion to labor input not only because of the law of diminishing returns [evidenced in column (2)], but also because of the presence of monopoly power [evidenced by column (3)]. Given the conditions pictured here, the firm maximizes profit by hiring 3 workers and equating the marginal benefit of using labor (the declining MRP_L) with the associated marginal cost, here equal to the market wage (boxed numbers).

firm that can vary the quantity of labor used, but holds all other inputs constant. A comparison of columns (2) and (3) indicates the firm's monopoly power in the product market that we wish to assume. As the firm hires extra workers [column (1)] and therefore produces more output [column (2)], it finds itself able to sell the extra output only by lowering product price [column (3)]. The data of columns (2) and (3), in turn, allow us to compute the total revenue associated with different numbers of workers [column (4)]. The im-

plied *change* in total revenue, ΔTR, that is associated with a unit change in labor input, ΔL, is given in column (5); and this marginal revenue product clearly is the firm's marginal benefit of using labor.

Now assume that our firm faces a market wage of $112 per worker per week no matter how many workers it hires, as in column (6). This wage is our firm's constant marginal cost of acquiring labor. The profit-maximizing input decision is then indicated by the boxed numbers in

TABLE 11.4

The Relationship between Marginal Revenue Product, Marginal Physical Product, Marginal Revenue, and Marginal Value Product

Labor Quantity, L (number of workers per week)	Marginal Revenue Product of Labor, $MRP_L = \frac{\Delta TR}{\Delta L} = MPP_L \cdot MR$ (dollars per extra worker)	Marginal Physical Product of Labor, $MPP_L = \frac{\Delta Q}{\Delta L}$ (product per extra worker)	Marginal Revenue, $MR = \frac{\Delta TR}{\Delta Q} = (MRP_L)/(MPP_L)$ (dollars per extra product unit)	Marginal Value Product of Labor, $MVP_L = MPP_L \cdot P$ (dollars per extra worker)
(1)	$(2) = (3) \times (4) =$ Table 11.3, col. (5)	$(3) =$ Table 11.3, $\frac{\Delta(2)}{\Delta(1)}$	$(4) = \frac{(2)}{(3)} =$ Table 11.3, $\frac{\Delta(4)}{\Delta(2)}$	$(5) = (3) \times$ Table 11.3, col. (3)
1	500	500	1.00	500
2	279	450	.62	369
3	112	400	.28	264
4	−7	350	−.02	182
5	−84	300	−.28	120
6	−125	250	−.50	75

This table is based on the data of Table 11.3 and highlights the differences among a number of key concepts. Note, in particular, the differences between columns (2) and (5). When a firm possesses monopoly power in the product market, the marginal revenue product of labor declines much more rapidly than its marginal value product as more labor is used. This reflects the fact that a larger number of workers now brings not only a decline in marginal physical product, but also a decline in product price (without which the extra output could not be sold). Note that the marginal revenue product of labor can be determined in two ways: as $\Delta TR/\Delta L$ (as in Table 11.3), but also as follows: $MRP_L = \frac{\Delta TR}{\Delta L} =$

$\frac{\Delta TR}{\Delta Q} \cdot \frac{\Delta Q}{\Delta L} = MR \cdot MPP_L$. This implies, in turn, a second way of determining marginal revenue: $MR = \frac{MRP_L}{MPP_L}$.

our table. The firm does best for itself by hiring three workers. [A fourth worker would add 350 units to physical product [column (2)], but this extra output could be sold only be reducing the market price to 52 cents per unit [column (3)], which would actually lead to a *fall* in total revenue [column (4)]. No firm would want to pay $112 in extra cost in order to end up getting a marginal benefit of less than that amount, such as − $7 in our case.] Thus we conclude:

A firm that is a perfect competitor in the labor market but has monopoly power in the product market maximizes profit by hiring that quantity of labor which results in labor's marginal revenue product being equal to its wage.*

$$MRP_L = W$$

Second, turn to Table 11.4, which is based on the same data as Table 11.3. The table highlights the differences among a number of key concepts. Column (2) shows the *marginal revenue product of labor* that was just derived in column (5) of Table 11.3. It equals the change in total revenue that the firm can expect when it changes labor input by a unit. For example, when using 2 workers rather than than 1 worker, the firm's total revenue rises by $279 (and, clearly, this is the maximum amount the firm would pay to hire this second worker). Column (3) shows the *marginal physical product of labor* that is implied by the data in columns (1) and (2) of Table 11.3. For example, when using 2 workers rather than 1 worker, the firm can expect to get an extra 450 units of physical product. Column (4) shows the *marginal revenue,* a concept familiar to us from earlier chapters about the markets for goods and equal to the change in total revenue that the firm can expect when it changes output (rather than labor input) by a unit. For example, when the firm hires 2 workers rather than 1 worker, it gains, as we have just seen, $279 in

---

*For a calculus-based treatment of this material, see Section 11D of the Calculus Appendix at the back of this book.

extra revenue and 450 units of extra physical product; hence the extra revenue per extra unit of product is $279 divided by 450, or 62 cents. Column (5), finally, shows the *marginal value product of labor,* or the value of the marginal physical product at the current product price. For example, when 2 workers are hired rather than 1 worker, the marginal physical product is 450 units; the total product is 950 units and product price equals 82 cents (Table 11.3). Thus the market value of the marginal physical product is 82 cents per unit times 450 units, or $369, as shown in Table 11.4. (Because the firm can sell the extra 450 units only by cutting the price from $1 to 82 cents, it loses 18 cents on each of the original 500 units, and this $90 loss, together with the $369 gain, adds to the $279 marginal revenue product noted before.) Can you see why, under perfect competition, when extra output can be sold at an unchanged price (and marginal revenue *equals* price), the difference between marginal revenue product [column (2)] and marginal value product [column (5)] would disappear?

A Graphical Exposition. The profit-maximizing rule highlighted in color above can be demonstrated graphically as well. Figure 11.13 is a graph of Table 11.4, column (1) against columns (2) and (5); our assumed weekly wage of $112 per worker has been depicted too. The 3-worker profit-maximizing input quantity corresponds to intersection *b* of the two lines of labor's marginal revenue product and labor's wage. As a quick review of Figure 11.1, ''A Firm's Demand for Labor: The Simple Case'' (p. 359) can show, in the absence of product market monopoly power, the firm would demand the 5.3 workers corresponding to intersection *f.* The lower quantity demanded in the present case of a competitive buyer of labor whose labor market behavior is modified by its product market monopoly power should not surprise us.

Just as a firm with monopoly power restricts *output* below the level at which output price equals marginal cost (and thus raises output price above marginal cost), it also restricts *input* use below the level at which input price equals marginal value product (point f). Thus the gap between output price and marginal cost of production (which, we noted in Chapter 7, is the basis for Lerner's index of monopoly power) now reappears in the input market as a gap (bd in our graph) between input price and marginal value product. Economists have a special name for this gap.

Monopolistic Exploitation.   Many economists view the equality of an input's price with its marginal value product as the *absence* of exploitation. Correspondingly, such economists view a situation in which input price and marginal value product differ as one in which **exploitation** is present. When, as in our case, an input's marginal value product exceeds its price because the input's user possesses monopoly power in the product market (which makes the input's marginal revenue product fall short of its marginal value product), such economists talk of **monopolistic exploitation** of the input.

In the case of labor, we can write

Monopolistic exploitation of labor:

$$MVP > W \text{ because } MRP < MVP$$

and, for the perfect competitor in the labor market who has monopoly power in the product market, profit maximization dictates

$$MRP = W$$

The extent of labor's monopolistic exploitation is shown by the shaded area in Figure 11.13. Even though the weekly marginal product of 3 workers is worth $264 (point d), they each receive only $112. Thus they are said to be exploited by the $152 difference. Such a difference would not exist if our firm's product-market monopoly power did not exist and it hired the 5.3 workers corresponding to point f.

Note: Many economists are not very happy with this use of the emotionally laden term *exploitation*, popularized mainly by British economists like Joan Robinson (1903–83) and A. C. Pigou (1877–1959)—Biographies of whom ap-

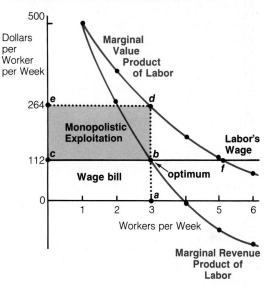

FIGURE 11.13

The Demand for Labor Reconsidered

This graph is a modification of panel (c), Figure 11.1, "A Firm's Demand for Labor: The Simple Case." It shows how a firm facing a market-determined wage in the labor market (here $112 per worker per week) but having monopoly power in its product market will demand labor according to its curve of labor's marginal *revenue* product, not marginal *value* product. Marginal revenue product, not marginal value product, measures such a firm's marginal benefit of using labor; the market-determined wage shows such a firm's marginal cost of acquiring labor. The optimum labor quantity hired by such a profit-maximizing firm, therefore, corresponds to intersection b (and equals 3 workers in this example). Note: When labor's marginal value product exceeds its wage because marginal revenue product falls short of marginal value product, labor is said to be subject to *monopolistic exploitation.*

pear, respectively, in Chapters 11 and 16 of the *Student Workbook* that accompanies this text. Indeed, as Figure 11.13 clearly shows (and as Table 11.4 attests as well), if our firm (positioned at optimum point b) were to fire any one of its 3 workers, it would lose revenue of $112, not of $264. Thus the firm is paying the marginal worker exactly what this worker is worth to the firm. So who is exploiting whom? Who is pocketing something that rightfully belongs to someone else? The consumers of our firm's product are really the ones to blame because they will take the extra output produced by a third worker only if product price is reduced from 82¢ per unit to 66¢ (note Table 11.3), which is why labor's marginal revenue product lies below its marginal value product. It would not be impossible for the consumers of the firm's product to be poorer than the workers who made it; in that case the poor would be exploiting the "rich." Clearly this situation is not what most people have in mind when hearing the word *exploitation*. Unfortunately, this use of the term is so entrenched in the literature of economics that it is impossible to change it now.

Monopsony in the Labor Market, but Competition in the Product Market

Consider a firm that sells its product in a competitive market but is the only buyer in a labor market in which a multitude of sellers compete with one another. Such a situation is far from unusual. A typical example given is the "company town," dominated by a single employer. Think of Seattle and the Boeing Company; Butte, Montana, and the Anaconda Copper Mining Company; Hershey, Pennsylvania, and the Hershey Chocolate Company; Barstow, California, and the Sante Fe Railway. Such dominant employers have "captured" work forces to the extent that such places are inhabited by workers who cannot or will not leave the area (being ignorant of alternatives, unable to find transportation, or reluctant to leave pretty scenery or good friends).

Just as *monopoly* means "single seller," so the buyer who is the only buyer in a market is referred to as **monopsony.** Monopsony need not necessarily be based on the geographic concentration of immobile resources, however. It can also arise out of an extreme degree of occupational immobility. Consider the options open to someone with specialized training, such as an astronaut, general, or designer of nuclear submarines. There is likely to be only a single employer

for such sellers of labor. Finally, monopsony in the labor market is often the result of employers who agree to act jointly in the hiring of labor and not to compete with each other for workers. Such **antipirating agreements** have been reached on a national basis by major league sports clubs and different departments of the federal government; on a regional basis by coal-mining firms and by those manufacturing furniture and garments; and on a local basis by colleges, construction firms, hospitals, hotels, newspapers, and restaurants.

As we noted in Chapter 7 when discussing the market for goods, one key difference between a perfect competitor and a monopoly derives from the fact that the latter faces a downward-sloping demand curve; as a consequence, the monopoly's marginal revenue lies below price as long as all customers are charged identical prices. Analogously, in the markets for inputs, such as labor, a similar difference between a perfect competitor and a monopsony exists. The monopsony does not face a market-determined wage (such as that represented by the horizontal black line in Figure 11.13), but faces instead the entire upward-sloping market-supply line. The monopsony can choose to pay any input price it wishes but must then take the consequences (must then be content with hiring whatever input quantity is being supplied at that price). If it wants to purchase a larger quantity, it must coax out a larger quantity supplied by offering a higher price. As long as all suppliers are paid the same, this fact has an important implication: The monopsonist's **marginal outlay,** or its change in total outlay divided by the corresponding change in the total input quantity purchased, will always *exceed* the input price it pays. It is easy to see why this is so by using a simple example. By setting a wage of $5 per hour, the monopsony may be able to attract 300 workers (hence its total wage bill is $1,500 per hour). In order to get 400 workers to work for it, the firm may have to raise its wage offer to $6 per hour. Assuming, as we do, that the firm cannot price-discriminate and pay $5 to some workers and $6 to other, equally skilled workers, the hiring of 400 workers im-

TABLE 11.5

The Labor Input Decision: Monopsony

Labor Quantity, L	Labor's Wage, W	Marginal Cost and Marginal Benefit of Using Labor	
		Marginal Outlay on Labor, MO_L	Marginal Value Product of Labor, MVP_L
(number of workers per week) (1)	(2)	(dollars per extra worker per week) (3)	(4)
100	50	100	700
200	100	200	600
300	150	300	500
400	200	400	400
500	250	500	300
600	300	600	200

For a firm with monopsony power in the labor market, labor's wage, in column (2), falls short of the marginal outlay on labor, in column (3). The latter is the marginal cost for such a firm of using labor. Such a firm hires extra workers as long as the marginal outlay on labor does not exceed the marginal benefit from using labor (which in this example equals labor's marginal value product). Given the conditions pictured here, a profit-maximizing firm hires 400 workers and thereby sets MO_L equal to MVP_L at $400 per worker per week (boxed numbers).

plies a total wage bill of $2,400 per hour. Thus the hiring of an extra 100 workers costs the firm an extra outlay of $2,400 minus $1,500, or $900 per hour, which comes to $9 per hour for each of the extra workers. This $9 figure is the marginal outlay, and it clearly exceeds the $6 wage that is being paid. How do we resolve the puzzle? We do so by noting that the extra 100 workers are receiving $6 per hour, making for a $600 total, but the 300 other workers receive a $1 *raise* per hour (price discrimination being ruled out), and this makes for another $300 expenditure. So far as the firm is concerned, the marginal cost of hiring the extra 100 workers is $9 per hour per worker (and it should not surprise us that the firm will not hire these workers unless they each add at least $9 to the firm's revenue).

Indeed, the presence of monopsony has a noticeable impact on the labor market, even when the firms involved have no monopoly power whatever in their product markets. The quantity of labor demanded by such firms will not

be one that equates any given wage with labor's marginal value product, but a lower quantity that equates the firm's marginal outlay on labor (implied by a wage the firm has set) with labor's marginal value product, as shown by Table 11.5. An assumed labor supply schedule is given in columns (1) and (2). Because our firm is the only buyer of labor in the market, it can set any wage it desires but must then take whatever number of workers present themselves. Because we assume that the firm can coax out a larger number of workers only by offering a higher wage to everyone, the firm's marginal outlay on labor, in column (3), exceeds the wage. (Example: If the firm set a wage of $50 per worker per week, it would get 100 workers and spend $5,000 per week. If the firm wanted 200 workers, it would have to offer $100 per week to all of them. Thus it would spend $20,000 instead. An extra outlay of $15,000 would bring forth 100 extra workers; thus a marginal outlay of $150 per worker per week would bring forth workers in the 100–200 worker range, and this number clearly exceeds the $100 wage paid to any one worker once 200 workers are employed.)[4]

Note: The marginal outlay on labor (which exceeds the wage) is clearly the marginal cost to such a firm of using labor. Unlike in earlier examples, this marginal cost is no longer a market-determined wage beyond the control of our firm.

If our firm, however, is a price taker in its product market, its marginal benefit of using labor is still labor's marginal value product, or labor's marginal physical product multiplied by a given market-determined product price. The

profit-maximizing input decision is again indicated by the boxed numbers in our table. The firm does best for itself by hiring 400 workers. (If it hired fewer of them, it would forgo profit unnecessarily because extra workers would then add less to the firm's total cost than to its total revenue. The reverse would be true if it hired more than the optimum number.)

A firm that is a perfect competitor in the product market but has monopsony power in the labor market maximizes profit by hiring the quantity of labor that results in labor's marginal value product being equal to the marginal outlay on labor.*

$$MVP_L = MO_L$$

---

[4]Column (3) of Table 11.5 gives the precise marginal outlay figures applicable to a small change in labor input when 100, 200, 300, etc. workers are employed. The $150 figure given in the text is the average marginal outlay incurred when successively hiring a 101st, 102nd, . . . and, finally, 200th worker.

---

*For a calculus-based treatment of this material, see Section 11E of the Calculus Appendix at the back of this book.

FIGURE 11.14

Monopsony in the Labor Market

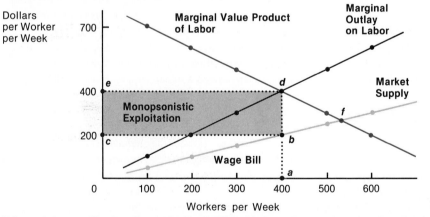

This graph is a modification of panel (c) Figure 11.1, "A Firm's Demand for Labor: The Simple Case." It shows how a firm facing a market-determined price in the product market but having monopsony power in the labor market will demand labor according to its curve of labor's marginal value product. The firm's marginal cost of acquiring labor, however, is not a horizontal line at a market-determined wage, but rather a rising line of marginal outlays that exceed the wages this firm can set. The optimum quantity hired by such a profit-maximizing firm, therefore, corresponds to intersection *d* (and equals 400 workers in this example who are paid $200 per week each). Note: When labor's marginal value product exceeds its wage because marginal outlay exceeds wage, labor is said to be subject to *monopsonistic exploitation*.

A Graphical Exposition. The above rule can be demonstrated graphically as well. Figure 11.14 is a graph of Table 11.5 column (1) against columns (2)–(4)—and all points between those in the table. The 400-worker profit-maximizing input quantity corresponds to intersection *d* of the two lines of marginal value product of labor and marginal outlay on labor. In the absence of monopsony power, the firm would, of course, demand the 533 workers corresponding to intersection *f* (and would do so at a market-determined wage of $267 per worker per week). As in the earlier example, we thus note a gap between labor's wage ($200 measured at *b*) and its marginal value product ($400 measured at *d*). This gap has a special name.

Monopsonistic Exploitation. Whenever an input's marginal value product exceeds its price because the input's user possesses monopsony power in the input market (which makes the marginal outlay on the input exceed its price), economists talk of **monopsonistic exploitation** of the input.

In the case of labor, we can write

Monopsonistic exploitation of labor:

$$MVP > W \text{ because } MO > W$$

and, for the monopsony in the labor market that is a perfect competitor in the product market, profit maximization dictates

$$MVP = MO$$

The extent of labor's monopsonistic exploitation is shown by the shaded area in Figure 11.14. Even though the weekly marginal value product of 400 workers equals $400 (point *d*), they each receive only $200. Once more, such a difference would not exist if our firm's labor market monopsony power did not exist and it hired the 533 workers corresponding to point *f*.

Note: In this instance, as in the previous one, the term ''exploitation'' can easily be misleading. The ''exploited'' workers need not be mi-grant farm workers or teenage waitresses; they may very well be star athletes or five-star generals, among the richest people in the country.

Labor Union Versus Competitive Buyers of Labor

How a union emerging in a previously competitive labor market will act depends, of course, on the goal the union wants to pursue. Labor unions pursue many goals, such as better working conditions, clear-cut grievance procedures, job security, and a host of fringe benefits, ranging from health and life insurance to paid vacations and pension plans. In the United States, however, their dominant goal has always been the achievement of higher money income for those employed.

One must not confuse labor's wage (a rate per unit of time) with labor's income (the wage multiplied by the number of time units worked). It is not at all obvious, therefore, how a union is to act when seeking to promote the best interests of workers. Can it hope to raise labor's income by increasing its wage and keeping employment unchanged? Must it accept a cut in employment when pushing wages up? If it must accept an employment cut, what is the ideal wage level from labor's point of view? To answer these questions we now turn to Figure 11.15. We assume that market demand and market supply equilibrate at a weekly wage of $250 per worker in the absence of a union (point *a*) and that 4,000 workers are then employed. Now let them form a union and threaten employers with a strike unless their wage is raised.

Pushing Up the Wage. As the market-demand line indicates, employers demand smaller quantities of labor as the wage rises above its competitive equilibrium level. At a weekly wage of $375 per worker, they demand only 3,000 workers (point *b*); at a weekly wage of $460, they demand 2,320 workers (point *c*), and so on. All else being equal, a union that pushes the wage up, therefore, is bound to lower the employment opportunities of workers. And the union has essentially three courses of action open to it: letting employers ration jobs, raising demand, and reducing supply.

Letting Employers Ration Jobs. First, the union can insist on a given above-equilibrium wage of, say, $460 per week and then let employers decide who is and who is not lucky enough to remain employed. In our example, employment would fall from 4,000 workers (point *a*) to 2,320 workers (point *c*). Those who would remain employed would clearly be better off; their unemployed fellow workers would be worse off. Indeed, unemployment would exceed the 1,680 workers thrown out of work (distance *cd*). As the upward-sloping market-supply curve

indicates, the higher wage would attract 4,410 additional workers into the market (distance *de*). Thus a labor surplus (or unemployment) of 1,680 + 4,410 = 6,090 workers would occur (distance *ce*).

Note: Unions have been instrumental in supporting either government programs of unemployment insurance and welfare assistance for the unemployed (represented by distance *ce* in our graph) or programs of public-service jobs. Such programs are equivalent, respectively, to subsidies paid farmers for *not* producing crops "supported" by governmentally set above-equilibrium prices or to government crop purchase plans. In either the labor or farmer case, taxpayers are made to protect members of cartels from undesirable consequences that follow upon their price-raising conspiracy.

FIGURE 11.15

Labor Union Versus Competitive Labor Market

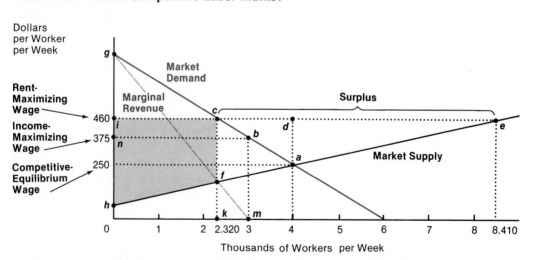

All else being equal, if a labor union is formed in a previously competitive market and pushes the wage above its equilibrium level ($250 per week in this example), the level of employment will fall. Beyond that, one can only speculate: The union might ignore the resultant labor surplus. It might also attempt to remove the labor surplus using policies designed to raise the demand for labor or reduce its supply. Nor can one predict which particular wage the union will set. The union may wish to maximize the total income of workers, given market demand (area 0*mbn*). It may wish instead to maximize the workers' economic rent (shaded); that is, seek the maximum possible excess of the workers' actual income (area 0*kci*) over their next best alternatives (area 0*kfh*). Or the union may pursue altogether different goals.

Raising Demand.   Our union's second option is to insist on a wage of, say, $460 per week but also to take measures to ensure that none of its present members lose their jobs. This happy result would occur if the union could manage to

1. bring about a rightward shift in the demand for labor until the demand line went through point *d* in our graph and
2. force employers never to use anyone but union members (while the union, of course, refused to admit to its rosters the 4,410 potential new workers represented by distance *de*).

Examples of policy 1 include: union support of government-mandated consumer purchases, regardless of whether consumers wish to buy the goods involved (automobile safety belts, aircraft emergency locator transmitters, household fire alarms); union-instigated governmental import restrictions, wage subsidies to employers, or tax cuts to consumers who buy the products of labor; and (as in the case of the International Ladies Garment Workers Union) cooperation with management to raise the productivity of labor or raise product price by advertising. (Remember that labor's marginal physical product and product price are the factors behind the market demand for labor.) Union attempts to shift the demand curve for labor to the right also include a whole range of practices that force employers to continue paying workers who are not really needed because their work is being done, or could be done, by fewer workers or by machines. Thus musicians have forced minimum orchestra sizes on film and opera producers regardless of the size actually needed and have forced broadcasters to employ ''standby orchestras'' while records were being played; stokers who used to feed steam boilers have forced railroads to keep them on, riding along on diesel locomotives that don't have steam boilers. Printers have insisted on setting ''dummy type'' for advertising copy, which newspapers never use when advertisers submit ready-to-print copy, and electricians have torn apart and rewired prewired equipment. Airline pilots have insisted on a third licensed pilot in the cockpit (where a flight engineer would do just fine), and bricklayers have restricted the number of bricks that can be laid in an hour. Textile workers have similarly limited the number of looms attended and painters the width of brushes. Such workers, who do not work or do unnecessary work, may as well take along a featherbed and sleep on the job, which is why this practice is called **featherbedding.**

Examples of policy 2 (forcing employers to use only union members) include the establishment of **closed shops** (in which only union members are hired) or of **union shops** (in which all employees, within 30 days after hiring, have to become union members or at least pay union dues as a condition of continued employment). Such policy is often reinforced by the restriction (common among construction and longshoring workers) of union membership to a few (4,000 in our case), by insisting on lengthy apprenticeships, charging high initiation fees, administering impossible entrance tests, or simply denying access to blacks, women, Jews, or any other easily identifiable group.

Reducing Supply.   The union's third option is to insist on a wage of, say, $460 per week, but also take measures to ensure that no more than the appropriate number of workers (2,320 of them in our example) apply for the job. This strategy would be equivalent to bending the market-supply curve at point *f* to coincide with line *fc*, which could be accomplished by restricting union membership even more severely by any of the aforementioned measures. Here, too, governmental support comes in handy. Consider how government (with the enthusiastic support of many unions) has restricted the supply of labor by setting maximum basic hours, prohibiting child labor, and severely limiting immigration.

Other laws have reduced the supply of labor in particular occupations: Until 1971, when the U.S. Supreme Court voided them, many so-called state protective laws barred designated persons from specified jobs. Women, for instance, were often barred from jobs requiring lifting of weights in excess of 25 pounds (but they were apparently free to lift heavier children at home) as well as from such "dangerous" occupations as bartending, bellhopping, coal mining, meter reading, pinsetting, shoe shining, and truck driving.

A Final Note. A union that pushes labor's wage above its competitive level will, of course, have to decide on the exact level it prefers, somewhere between points *a* and *g* in our graph. Many possibilities exist, but two of the more interesting ones have been indicated in Figure 11.15. A union may push the wage to $375 per week where the market demand for labor (point *b*) has a price elasticity of |1| and the marginal revenue to the union from selling labor is zero (point *m*). In this way, the union maximizes the total income of its members (area 0*mbn*). Given the assumed market demand, no other wage-employment combination can produce an income total as large as $1,125,000 per week (or $375 per week times 3,000 workers).

Or a union may push the wage to $460 per week (point *c*), where the union's marginal revenue of selling labor just equals the marginal cost of supplying it (point *f*). Note that the height of point *f* on the supply curve represents the lowest wage ($170) that worker #2,320 would accept for this type of work and thus, presumably, the highest wage that worker could get elsewhere. This worker's best alternative income is, therefore, the marginal cost of supplying his or her labor in this particular market. By implication, shaded area *cfhi* represents the maximum possible excess of workers' actual income over their next best alternatives (measured by the area under their supply curve, or 0*hfk* in this case). The shaded area is akin to the producers' surplus discussed in Chapter 6. It is also referred to as the workers' maximum possible **economic rent,** such rent being that portion of a payment to any resource that exceeds the minimum amount necessary to bring forth the quantity of services that is in fact supplied.

Labor Union Versus Labor Monopsony

What if a labor union emerges not in an otherwise competitive labor market, but in response to a labor monopsony? When a monopoly seller in this way meets a monopsony buyer, the situation is referred to as one of **bilateral monopoly,** although this is somewhat of a misnomer (since *monopoly* means "single seller," but a single buyer is involved here as well). Going beyond the semantics, we can say this: When a union has monopoly power over the supply of labor and a firm has monopsony power over the demand for it, no definite outcome can be predicted. What happens depends on the personalities involved and their bargaining skills. (Not surprisingly, game theory, discussed in Chapter 9, has been fruitfully applied in this area.) We can, however, imagine a number of possible outcomes, in response to a wage hike, including higher employment, unchanged employment, and lower employment.

Higher Employment. Panel (a) of Figure 11.16 is basically a copy of Figure 11.14. The upward-sloping line going through points *b* and *e* represents the competitive market supply faced by our monopsonist before the advent of the union. The upward-sloping line going through points *a* and *h*, accordingly, represents the monopsonist's marginal outlay on labor when there is no union. And the monopsonist's profit-maximizing position, before the union appears, corresponds to intersection *a*: At $400 per worker per week, the monopsonist equates the marginal value product of labor (marginal benefit) with the marginal outlay on labor (marginal cost), hires 400 workers, and pays each one $200 a week (point *b*). The resulting monopsonistic exploitation is the sum of the dotted and shaded rectangles (area *abcd*).

Now let a union appear and enforce a minimum wage of $300 per worker. The firm may pay more but never less, and, as the (old and new) supply line to the right of point *e* indicates, the

income (area 0*cde*); the remainder (shaded) is eliminated because the 301st to 400th workers are now unemployed.[5]

A Final Note. As the three graphs of Figure 11.16 show, a union that pushes labor's wage above the level a monopsony would voluntarily pay can eliminate monopsonistic exploitation. Yet, should it exist, monopolistic exploitation would continue. To see why, in your mind, relabel the three lines of labor's marginal value product in Figure 11.16 as "marginal revenue product of labor." The monopsony's optimum input choices would then be quite unaffected. The optimum input choices would correspond, as before, to points *i, a,* and *d,* respectively, in the three graphs. Yet as Figure 11.13 has shown,

there would then exist a marginal-value-product-of-labor curve *above* the ones presently shown. In each case, therefore, labor would receive a wage below its marginal value product. Monopolistic exploitation would persist because while the union can eliminate the divergence between wage and marginal outlay, it has no power to eliminate any divergence between product price and the marginal cost of production. The former divergence causes monopsonistic exploitation; the latter divergence, monopolistic exploitation. (For an interesting application, see Analytical Example 11.3 at the end of this chapter.)

APPLICATIONS

Let us, finally, consider two applications of the imperfectly competitive labor market model.

Application 5: The Baseball Players' Market

Baseball was the first sport to be organized professionally in the United States.[6] From the start, team owners recognized a common interest in preventing competition for players that would drive up salaries. Accordingly, the baseball players' market came to provide a perfect example of monopsony in action. Talented athletes who wanted to play professional baseball with a major league team found that the teams were not competing for the services of players. A player who wanted a first contract with a team had to sign a **reserve clause** handing over to the team's owners all rights to his future services. Thereafter, no other team would tamper with the player thusly "reserved" by the original team that signed him on. In future years, the owners of the original team could dispose of the player's services as they saw fit: They could keep the player

---

[5]The examples discussed so far show various possible outcomes of the bargaining process between monopoly and monopsony. Under certain assumptions, which may or may not hold in reality, one can, however, predict a *range* of wages and employment levels within which the final outcome will lie. The desires of the profit-maximizing firm dictate part of the answer: The firm in our example would like to equate the marginal value product of labor with the marginal outlay on labor at point *a* and thus pay a wage of $200, while hiring 400 workers. *If* the union wanted to maximize the workers' rent, its desire to do so would dictate the rest of the answer: In a fashion indicated in Figure 11.15, the union would then want to equate the marginal revenue from selling labor with the marginal cost of doing so. It would treat the monopsony's marginal-value-product-of-labor curve like a demand curve for labor, derive a corresponding marginal-revenue curve lying below it and find its intersection with labor's supply (and marginal-cost) curve. In our example, this intersection, similar to point *f* in Figure 11.15, would occur at $160 and an employment level of 320; the corresponding wage, similar to point *c* in Figure 11.15, would equal $480. Thus the bargaining would involve a wage level between $200 and $480 and an employment level between 320 and 400 workers. Those familiar with calculus can prove the union's rent-maximizing position as follows:

The union views the Figure 11.16 MVP_L curve as the demand for labor; its equation is $W = 800 - L$, where W is the wage and L is labor quantity. Total revenue from selling labor is $W \cdot L = 800L - L^2$ and marginal revenue is $MR = 800 - 2L$. Labor's market supply is its marginal-cost curve; its equation is $W = .5L$. Equating MR and MC, $800 - 2L = .5L$, and $L = 320$. Hence $W = 800 - 320 = 480$.

---

[6]This section is based in part on Simon Rottenberg, "The Baseball Players' Labor Market," *Journal of Political Economy,* June 1956, pp. 242–58; and Gerald W. Scully, "Pay and Performance in Major League Baseball," *The American Economic Review,* December 1974, pp. 915–30.

on (and either raise his salary, keep it unchanged, or cut it by a prearranged maximum percentage below that of the previous season); they could sell the contract to another team (and then the player had to report to the new owners within three days); they could terminate the contract (but even that was not certain to let the player off the hook because each team in the league, in inverse order of season standings, then had the opportunity to purchase the player's contract, and if any team did, the player was again bound to it). As long as a player was hooked (and that was the usual case), he could only play for the current owners of his contract and at whatever salary they offered him. His only alternative was not to play baseball at all. (Naturally, the contract owners' ability to depress player salaries was constrained by the need to maintain team morale.)

The Reserve Clause Challenged.   Not surprisingly, the reserve clause was challenged on several occasions. The Federal League before World War I tried to become a third major league but couldn't get players. Its challenge was defeated in court. In the 1940s, the Mexican League was dealt a similar blow. Curt Flood, star outfielder for the St. Louis Cardinals, didn't like being traded to Philadelphia. His court fight against the reserve clause was lost, too; he retired to Majorca. But in 1975, following a favorable arbitrator's ruling won by pitchers Andy Messersmith and Dave McNally, Jim "Catfish" Hunter, ace pitcher for the Oakland As, won a similar fight. The court invalidated his contract with the As; he became a free agent. Thus a new age dawned for professional athletes—the age of free agency.

Star Players' Salaries Explode.   Before long, more than 100 players had changed uniforms. Jim Hunter landed a 5-year $3.5 million contract with the New York Yankees. By 1978, Pete Rose left the Cincinnati Reds to get $800,000 a year from the Philadelphia Phillies. And by 1982, some 13 players were getting over $1 million a year each, Montreal's Gary Carter and the New York Mets' George Foster earning what was then the top ($2 million a year). The average player's

salary rose impressively, too, from $44,700 in 1975 to $146,500 in 1980.

It is easy to see why a single player may be worth that much to a team. If Pete Rose could draw even 10-percent more fans for home games alone (and he could), some 200,000 extra tickets per season would be sold for an average $4. In addition, the Phillies would get 40 percent of extra gate receipts from games on the road and extra broadcast fees as well.

Measuring Monopsonistic Exploitation.   Gerald W. Scully estimated the extent of monopsonistic exploitation of baseball players while the reserve clause was in effect. Some of his results are reproduced in Table 11.6. For players with different talents, in columns (1) and (2), Scully calculated first their contribution to the team's gross revenues [(3)], such as gate receipts, broadcast fees, and the like. He then figured the player's contribution to net revenue [(4)] by subtracting player training and development costs (which averaged $300,000 per player) as well as other costs, such as nonplayer salaries, transportation for away games, equipment and sales expenses, stadium rental, and imputed interest on the baseball franchise (worth $8.4 million for the average team).

As a comparison of columns (4) and (5) indicates, because average and star players received as salaries considerably less than their contribution to the team's net revenue, they were monopsonistically exploited. Mediocre players, however, exploited their teams instead!

For further discussions of free agency, see Analytical Example 11.4 at the end of this chapter.

Application 6: Teenage Unemployment and the Minimum Wage

As we have seen above, labor unions have acquired the power to push up money wages and have received much support from government. Government, however, can and does achieve wage increases even more directly by legislating above-equilibrium minimum wages. Thus a fed-

TABLE 11.6

The Monopsonistic Exploitation of Baseball Players, 1968–69

Type of Player (1)	Career Performance (2)	Marginal Revenue Product		Salary (5)
		Gross (3)	Net (4)	
	Lifetime Slugging Average			
Mediocre hitters	255	$121,200	$ – 39,100	$ 9,700
	283	135,000	– 25,300	20,000
Average hitters	338	256,600	128,300	29,100
	375	285,100	156,800	39,000
Star hitters	427	405,800	290,500	42,200
	525	499,000	383,700	68,000
	Lifetime Strikeout-to-Walk Ratio			
Mediocre pitchers	1.50	139,500	– 20,800	9,000
	1.66	154,300	– 6,000	18,100
Average pitchers	2.07	269,600	141,300	23,300
	2.46	316,000	187,700	43,700
Star pitchers	2.79	464,900	349,600	47,200
	3.54	595,000	479,700	86,300

When the reserve clause was in effect, all but mediocre U.S. baseball players were monopsonistically exploited. Note how, for average and star players, the data in column (5) fall short of those in column (4).

Source: Adapted from Gerald W. Scully, "Pay and Performance in Major League Baseball," *The American Economic Review,* December 1974, vol. 64, no. 6, pp. 915–30.

eral minimum wage was set at 25¢ per hour under the Fair Labor Standards Act of 1938; this minimum wage had risen to $3.35 per hour by 1984 (and was still there in early 1989). The original law did not by any means apply to all workers; employees of state and local government, farm workers, and household workers, for example, were excluded. Over the years, as Congress has raised the minimum with clocklike regularity, however, it has also extended the coverage of the law.

Economic theory predicts employment effects as a result of minimum-wage legislation precisely like those discussed above in connection with union-imposed wage hikes. If the labor markets affected by the imposition or increase of a minimum wage are competitive, the number of jobs declines (see Figure 11.15). If, on the other

hand, the affected labor markets are monopsonistic, the job effect is less certain. Employment may rise, remain unchanged, or fall (see Figure 11.16).

By now, U.S. economists have had plenty of experience with actual minimum-wage impositions or increases at both the federal and state levels. Subsequent to its enactment in 1938, the federal minimum wage, for example, has been increased 15 times between 1939 and 1984; it has been extended to new groups of workers 16 times. One economist, Yale Brozen, conducted a careful study of the actual employment effects of these minimum-wage changes.[7]

---

[7]Yale Brozen. "The Effect of Statutory Minimum Wage Increases on Teen-Age Employment," *The Journal of Law and Economics,* April 1969, pp. 109–22.

Brozen found that, because the overwhelming majority of workers have always enjoyed wages exceeding the legislated minimum, most people's wages and jobs have not been affected by changes in the statutory minima. The effects of minimum-wage laws have been primarily on the wages and employment of low-skilled workers. The largest single category of such workers are teenagers. Brozen noted that the monthly change in teenage unemployment, for some 20 years covered by his data, was down 123 times, up 111 times, zero 6 times. Yet, each time the minimum rose, teenage unemployment rose as well. Brozen was unable to attribute this relationship to coincidence.

In addition to these immediate increases in teenage unemployment, Brozen found a long-term upward trend in teenage unemployment relative to that of other people. This trend occurred despite a rising average level of education in this group and a declining rate of labor-force participation. For example, before the $1.15-per-hour minimum wage went into effect, unemployment among teenagers was 2.5 times the unemployment rate of the total labor force. In the year following the increase, it was 2.7 times as large. When the minimum wage rose further to $1.25 per hour, the teenage unemployment rate rose further to 3.1 times the general incidence of unemployment; by the time the minimum stood at $1.60 per hour, the multiple had risen to 3.6.

The minimum wage has affected employment opportunities more adversely even for nonwhite teenagers than for teenagers in general. For example, while the ratio of the incidence of general teenage unemployment to the unemployment of all workers rose by 64 percent from 1949–68, that for nonwhite teenage unemployment rose by 154 percent.

Brozen concluded that minimum-wage statutes, at the time of their imposition, have increased the incomes of some workers—namely, those who did not lose their jobs. These increases would, however, have come anyway within two to five years, as evidenced by studying the wage rates of noncovered workers, such as private household and agricultural workers. These rates have been rising 4 percent per year since 1949 despite the wage-depressing effects of additional workers looking for jobs in this sector after having been forced out of jobs covered by minimum wages. Apparently, successive amendments to the minimum-wage statute have raised wages particularly rapidly in the first year in the affected occupations, with very slow rises occurring thereafter. The total increase in the long run has differed little in covered and not-covered occupations. According to Brozen:

> If all that happened as a result of the minimum-wage statute was a change in the timing of wage rate increases, there would be little to concern us. However, in the interval between the time that the minimum wage is raised and the time that productivity and inflation catch up with the increase, thousands of people are jobless, many businesses fail which are never revived, people are forced to migrate who would prefer not to, cities find their slums deteriorating and becoming overpopulated, teenagers are barred from obtaining the opportunity to learn skills which would make them more productive, and permanent damage is done to their attitudes and their ambitions. This is a large price to pay for impatience.

Brozen's study does not stand alone. Numerous later ones have confirmed significant adverse effects of minimum wages on teenage employment.[8] Apparently, the attempt to help the working poor has proven to be the most effective way yet to keep teenagers idle. Because of their healthy propensity to test their abilities and op-

[8]As a partial listing only *see* Thomas G. Moore, ''The Effect of Minimum Wages on Teenage Unemployment Rates,'' *Journal of Political Economy,* July/August 1971, pp. 897–902; Douglas K. Adie, ''Teen-Age Unemployment and Real Federal Minimum Wages,'' *Journal of Political Economy,* March/April 1973, pp. 435–41; Finis Welch, ''Minimum Wage Legislation in the United States,'' *Economic Inquiry,* September 1974, pp. 285–318; Jacob Mincer, ''Unemployment Effects of Minimum Wages,'' *Journal of Political Economy,* August 1976, pp. S87–S104; James F. Ragan, ''Minimum Wages and the Youth Labor Market,'' *The Review of Economics and Statistics,* May 1977, pp. 129–36; Robert Swidinsky, ''Minimum Wages and Teenage Unem-

portunities, teenagers have always switched jobs more often than adults and therefore have always experienced higher rates of unemployment. Laws that have legislated teenage wages above teenagers' productivity, however, have given their jobs to more productive adults or to machines. Such laws have thus eliminated many traditional **entry-level jobs** that require little training or experience and allow untrained and inexperienced job seekers to find employment, gain experience, and depart these stepping-stones for better jobs.

What, finally, has the minimum wage done to relieve the incidence of poverty? Next to nothing, studies show. Here are some of the reasons: About half of all low-wage workers (especially teenagers) live in middle- and upper-income families; about one-third of the poor do not work because they are elderly or retired. The law fixes the *nominal* wage; even if it rises and a worker remains employed, employers can keep the real wage unchanged by reducing fringe benefits, such as low-cost meals, housing, or health insurance. The law is not strictly enforced and penalties for breaking it are small; apparently 30–50 percent of eligible workers work at illegally lower wages.[9]

SUMMARY

1. This chapter discusses labor markets. The demand for all inputs (derived as it is from the demand for output) is exercised by firms. Firms can be expected to hire that quantity of any

ployment,'' *Canadian Journal of Economics*, February 1980, pp. 158–71; and Robert H. Meyer and David A. Wise, "The Effects of the Minimum Wage on the Employment and Earnings of Youth," *Journal of Labor Economics*, no. 1, 1983, pp. 66–100. (According to the latter study, the 1973–78 employment of out-of-school men, aged 16–19, would have been 7 percent higher in the absence of the minimum wage.)

[9]Orley Ashenfelter and Robert S. Smith, "Compliance with the Minimum Wage Law," *Journal of Political Economy,* April 1979, pp. 335–50. *See also* Charles Brown, "Minimum Wage Laws: Are They Overrated?" *Journal of Economic Perspectives*, Summer 1988, pp. 133–45.

resource service that equates the marginal benefit of resource use with the associated marginal cost. In perfectly competitive markets, the marginal benefit is an input's *marginal value product;* the marginal cost is its price. The downward-sloping branch of an input's marginal-value-product curve (below average value product) becomes the perfectly competitive firm's demand for a single variable input.

2. When a firm can vary several inputs simultaneously, the derivation of the demand curve for any one input is only slightly more complex. The derivation involves the use of isoquants and isocost lines. The same graphical tools can be employed to show how the effect of a change in input price on quantity demanded can be divided into the *substitution effect* and *output effect.*

3. The demands of individual firms for any input can be added together to derive market demand. The procedure is slightly more complicated than the procedure for determining the market demand for consumer goods.

4. The individual's supply of labor can be derived from an analysis of the income-leisure choice (which leads a utility-maximizing person to equate the wage with the marginal rate of substitution of leisure for income). The supply can be derived with respect to the wage or any other variable, such as nonlabor income. The effect of any wage change can be separated into the familiar substitution and income effects. While the income effect for ordinary (and normal) consumption goods reinforces the substitution effect, the income effect works counter to the substitution effect in the case of leisure.

5. The supplies of services by individual resource owners can be added together to derive market supply.

6. Equilibrium is established for resource services through the interaction of demand and supply. The equilibrium in the short run can differ from that in the long run.

7. The theoretical tools noted so far can be applied widely. Examples are the analysis of wage differentials (and the implicit value people

place on their own lives when making occupational choices), of cobweb cycles in labor markets, and of all kinds of government programs,
ranging from income replacement and labor
training to various forms of taxation and more.

8.   Real-world labor markets contain numerous forms of market imperfections. In the
case of an otherwise competitive labor market in
which buyers appear who have monopoly power
in the product markets, the buyers determine the
best input quantity not by equating a given wage
with labor's marginal *value* product, but with
labor's marginal *revenue* product. As a result,
they employ less labor than otherwise, and labor
is *monopolistically exploited.*

9. . Another case of labor market imperfec-
tion arises when a perfectly competitive seller of
products is the only buyer of a given type of labor
but confronts a multitude of competitive sellers
of it. Such monopsony can arise as a result of
geographic isolation, extreme occupational specialization, or antipirating agreements among
employers. Such firms determine the best input
quantity not by equating a given wage with
labor's marginal value product, but by equating
marginal outlay on labor (implied by a wage the
firm itself has set) with labor's marginal value
product. As a result, these firms employ less
labor than otherwise, and labor is *monopsonistically exploited.*

10.   The sellers of labor, just as those of
products, can form cartels, which take the form
of labor unions. Labor unions pursue many
goals, chief among them being higher money
income for those employed. The effects of union-
imposed increases in wages differ with the type
of market. If the market is previously competitive, wage increases cause employment to fall;
unions can respond to the resulting unemployment by ignoring it or by various attempts to raise
the demand for or reduce the supply of labor.

11.   If a union imposes wage increases on a
monopsony, the effect on the level of employment cannot be predicted. Depending on the
extent of the wage hike, employment may rise,
remain unchanged, or fall.

12.   A number of wider applications of the

new theoretical tools include discussions of the
baseball players' market and of minimum-wage
effects on teenagers.

KEY TERMS

antipirating agreements
average value product (*AVP*)
bilateral monopoly
closed shops
compensating wage differentials
complementary inputs
derived demand
economic rent
entry-level jobs
equalizing wage differentials
exploitation
featherbedding
independent inputs
labor union
leisure
marginal outlay (*MO*)
marginal revenue product (*MRP*)
marginal value product (*MVP*)
monopolistic exploitation
monopsonistic exploitation
monopsony
output effect
regressive inputs
reservation demands
reserve clause
scale effect
substitution effect
union shops

HANDS-ON PRACTICE

Exercise #1

The manager of a department store was concerned about shoplifting and determined to do

something about it. The following experimental data were collected:[10]

TABLE 11.7

Number of Detectives on Duty during Store Hours	Total Value of Thefts Prevented per Day
0	$ 0
1	100
2	180
3	230
4	250
5	260

Derive the manager's demand curve for detectives, assuming the manager wants to follow the optimization principle.

Solution:

See Table 11.8. Note the marginal value products when detectives are added:

TABLE 11.8

Detectives	MVP
0 to 1	$100
1 to 2	80
2 to 3	50
3 to 4	20
4 to 5	10

The *MVP* column implies the demand curve: At a daily wage of $101 and above, it is not worthwhile to hire any detective (the marginal cost = wage then exceeds the marginal benefit = value of thefts prevented). At a daily wage of $100, it is just a matter of indifference to hire 1 detective; at a wage of $80, the manager will hire 2 detectives at most; at a wage of $10, as many as

[10]Adapted from Robert J. Flanagan, Robert S. Smith, and Ronald G. Ehrenberg, *Labor Economics and Labor Relations* (Glenview, Ill: Scott, Foresman and Co., 1984), pp. 56–58.

5 detectives could be hired. And note: All detectives can be assumed to be equally talented; the declining *MVP* simply reflects the fact that a first detective will spot all the easy cases; once these have been eliminated, it will become more and more difficult to counter the remaining, more sophisticated shoplifters. Thus any given wage helps define an *optimal amount* of shoplifting! At $50 per day per detective, for example, shoplifting that cannot be stopped by 3 detectives isn't worth worrying about. Hiring 5 detectives would then be just as wrong, from a profit-maximizing point of view, as hiring only 1 detective. In the former case, there would be too little shoplifting; in the latter case, too much. Paying out $50 to prevent $10 of shoplifting is just as foolish as *not* paying out $50 to prevent $80 of thefts.

Exercise #2

Consider columns (1) and (2) of Table 11.9. They show the total number of sandwiches that can be produced by a snack bar when employing different numbers of workers.

TABLE 11.9

(1) Number of Workers	(2) Number of Sandwiches per Day	(3) Wage per Worker per Day
1	80	$10
2	150	15
3	200	20
4	240	25
5	250	30
6	230	40

a. Assuming sandwiches brought in 50¢ each after ingredient costs are deducted, determine the schedule of labor's net marginal value product.

b. If workers were paid $20 per day, how many would be employed? How many at $35 per day?

c. What if sandwiches brought in 10¢ each and the daily wage were $10?

Solution:

a.   See Table 11.10.

TABLE 11.10

Number of Workers	Marginal Physical Product	Net Marginal Value Product
0–1	80	$40
1–2	70	35
2–3	50	25
3–4	40	20
4–5	10	5
5–6	−20	−10

b.   At $20 per day, 4 workers.
At $35 per day, 2 workers.
c.   The net marginal value product column would read: $8, 7, 5, 4, 1, and −2. At a wage of $10, nobody would be employed.

Exercise #3

Now consider also columns (1) and (3) of Table 11.9. They represent the labor supply.
a.   How many workers would be employed, and at what wage, if sandwiches brought in 50¢ each and the snack bar were a monopsony?
b.   What if a union were organized to fight the monopsony and it insisted on a wage of at least $30 per day?

Solution:

a.   Consider Table 11.11. Comparing marginal outlay with net marginal value product suggests profit-maximization by hiring 2 workers at $15 per day.
b.   The firm could then hire up to 5 workers at $30 per day. (The sixth worker insists on $40.) Up to 5 workers, the marginal outlay would be $30, and it would exceed the net marginal value product once there are 3 workers. Thus 2 workers per day would still be hired at $30 per day.

Exercise #4

Consider a negative-income tax scheme of the type discussed in Close-Up 11.2: Let the government provide a daily grant of $30 if a person earns nothing, but then take back 50¢ of the grant for every $1 earned. Illustrate graphically how an individual's welfare might be affected. Also show the effect on work effort and money income.

Solution:

Consider Figure 11.17. It provides one possible answer; others are conceivable. The individual depicted here faces a wage of $5 per hour and originally maximizes utility at point *a* on indifference curve I_0, sacrificing 12 hours of leisure and working 12 hours per day. Income is $60 per

TABLE 11.11

Number of Workers	Total Wage Bill	Marginal Outlay	Net Marginal Value Product
0	0		
		10	40
1	10		
		20	35
2	30		
		30	25
3	60		
		40	20
4	100		
		50	5
5	150		
		90	−10
6	240		

FIGURE 11.17

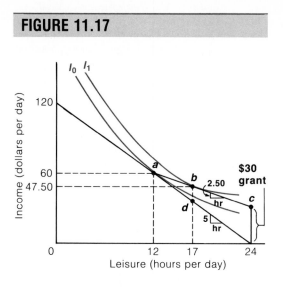

day. The negative-income tax scheme makes new opportunities available along line *ac*: At *c,* no work is done, but $30 per day are received. Every hour worked (for $5) only raises income by $2.50 because of the 50¢-per-dollar take back rule. Thus working 12 hours would bring only $30 on top of the $30 grant (point *a*). Our friend maximizes utility at *b* on indifference curve I_1. In sum, welfare is up (from I_0 to I_1), leisure is up (from 12 to 17 hours per day), work effort is down (from 12 to 7 hours per day), and income is down (from $60 to $47.50 per day).

Note that the individual gets a $30 grant, then earns 7 times $5 = $35, but pays half of that ($17.50) in additional taxes. The net effect is an income of $30 + $35 − $17.50 = $47.50 per day. The government's net payment is $30 − $17.50 = $12.50 (distance *bd*). This particular example illustrates an effect noted by some researchers: It is possible for the incidence of poverty to go *up* when a governmental welfare program is instituted.

QUESTIONS AND PROBLEMS

1. Figure 11.2 explains why the demand for an input would be flatter when two complementary inputs vary simultaneously than when a

single input alone varies. Show why the demand line would also be flatter (and not steeper) if inputs were *anti-complementary* such that the increased use of one decreased the marginal physical product of the other.

2. Figure 11.4 and many similar graphs found in this chapter contain indifference curves of people who give up leisure only for added income (and the prevalence of such people in the population is the reason why the old welfare programs that reduced recipients' welfare checks by a dollar whenever they earned a dollar on their own had such a problem with getting welfare recipients to go to work). Using the same graphical framework, draw an indifference-curve map for a *workaholic* who would give up income or accept zero pay for the privilege of working more; then show why the welfare-system incentive problem would disappear if all people were workaholics.

3. Figure 11.4 indicates the hours of work a person would choose if free to choose. How would one have to modify this analysis to account for such phenomena as moonlighting (holding two or more jobs) and overtime pay? (*Hints:* Imagine the workday in Figure 11.4 was inflexibly set at 8 hours. Then imagine that the workday was flexible, but the employer wanted the worker to work 16 hours.)

*4. A firm operates in perfectly competitive markets. Its output price is $40, its input price is $300, and it only uses one variable input, *K*. The firm's production function is $Q = 200K - K^2$. Using calculus as needed, determine the following profit-maximizing amounts:

 a. The amount of capital, *K*, employed.
 b. The total output produced.
 c. The total revenue, total cost, and total profit, given fixed cost of $300,000.

5. A firm has collected the accompanying data about an input's average value product (*AVP*) and marginal value product (*MVP*). Derive the firm's demand curve for this input graphically.

Input Quantity	AVP	MVP
1	3,900	7,500
3	5,900	8,990
4	—	9,200 (max.)
6	—	8,200
6.7	7,000	7,000
8	—	4,700
10	6,200	0
12	5,000	
14	3,300	

6. The following data pertain to three indifference curves that depict a person's tastes with respect to income and leisure. Plot the data in a graph, connecting the dots with smooth

	I_0	
Point	Income	Leisure
A	10,600	2
B	8,300	4
C	6,600	6
D	5,200	8
E	2,800	14
F	1,400	20
G	1,000	24

	I_1	
Point	Income	Leisure
H	12,000	5.6
I	10,000	7.6
K	7,000	12.8
L	5,000	19
M	4,000	24

	I_2	
Point	Income	Leisure
N	12,000	11.6
P	10,400	14
Q	8,600	18
R	7,400	22

curves. Determine the marginal rate of substitution of leisure for income in range DE.

7. Once again consider your answer to Problem 5. How many units of the input would the firm demand when faced with an input price of $4,700? What would the firm's profit then be?

8. Once again consider your answer to Problem 6. What would be the person's optimum leisure/income choice if the available wage were $271 per hour? What if the wage rose to $417 per hour?

9. Consider panels (a) through (c) of Figure 11.16, "Labor Union Versus Labor Monopsony." In each case, determine whether any involuntary unemployment would exist at the union-imposed wage. Explain.

10. **Mr. A:** The abolition of the reserve clause was a disaster. We will have baseball teams that are highly unbalanced as a result. All the rich teams will buy up all the star players; all the poor teams will end up with all the mediocre players.

Ms. B: That's absurd. Have you never heard of marginal revenue product?

With whom would you agree and why?

*11. Determine the following mathematically:

a. The three solutions represented by points a, b, and c in Figure 11.15, "Labor Union Versus Competitive Labor Market."

b. The competitive supply of labor to a firm is given by $L = 200W$, where L is labor quantity and W is labor's price or wage. The firm's marginal value product of labor or, when appropriate, demand for labor, is $L = 600 - 60W$.

1. If the firm is a monopsonist, what will be its profit-maximizing choice of L and W?

2. If a union now monopolizes the labor supply, what combination of L and W would maximize labor's income, $L \cdot W$?

3. What would be the union's choice if it cared to maximize labor's rent?

4. What would be the perfectly competitive outcome in this labor market?

5. What would be the outcome in a bilateral-monopoly case?

12. Let the demand for and supply of unskilled labor be

$$L = 500 - 25W \text{ and } L = -50 + 30W$$

a. Determine the equilibrium combination of L and W graphically.

b. Determine the amount of unemployment when a minimum wage is set at $4 per hour. At $14 per hour.

c. What happens to the total income of unskilled workers when a minimum wage of $14 per hour is imposed?

13. Graphically illustrate the equilibrium achieved by a perfectly competitive labor market, using your answer to Problem 11(b).

14. Graphically illustrate the equilibrium achieved when a rent-maximizing labor union monopoly faces perfectly competitive buyers of labor, using the answer to the relevant part of section (b), Problem 11, above.

15. Graphically illustrate the equilibrium achieved when a profit-maximizing monopsony faces perfectly competitive sellers of labor, using the answer to the relevant part of section (b), Problem 11, above.

16. Graphically illustrate the bilateral-monopoly case in the labor market, using the answer to the relevant part of section (b), Problem 11, above.

17. Babe Ruth is often called the greatest baseball player of all times. (He hit 714 home runs in his career, had a .342 lifetime batting average and an earned-run average of 2.28 as a pitcher.) He received a salary of $80,000 in 1930, equivalent at the consumer price index to $347,840 in 1979. Do you think he was exploited? Explain. (*Hint:* Pete Rose, not generally considered in the same category as Babe Ruth, earned $800,000 with the Phillies in 1979.)

SELECTED READINGS

Bailey, Martin J. *Reducing Risks to Life: Measurement of the Benefits.* Washington, D.C.: American Enterprise Institute, 1980.

A review of studies that estimate the value of human lives on the basis of people's willingness to accept riskier jobs at appropriately higher wages or to buy safety crash helmets, nonflammable pajamas, seat belts, smoke detectors, sprinkler systems, and the like. (*See also* Analytical Example 10.1, "Smoke Detectors as Insurance.")

Beeson, Patricia E., and Randall W. Eberts. "Identifying Amenity and Productivity Cities Using Wage and Rent Differentials," Federal Reserve Bank of Cleveland, *Economic Review,* 3, 1987, pp. 16–25.

A fascinating study of interregional wage differentials.

Brown, Charles, Curtis Gilroy, and Andrew Kohen. "The Effect of the Minimum Wage on Employment and Unemployment," *Journal of Economic Literature,* June 1982, pp. 487–528.

A superb summary of what economists know about the minimum wage.

Douglas, Paul H. *The Theory of Wages.* New York: Macmillan, 1934.

A pioneering study of econometric measurement concerning the demand for and supply of inputs.

Ferber, Robert, and Werner Z. Hirsch. "Social Experimentation and Economic Policy: A Survey," *Journal of Economic Literature,* December 1978, pp. 1379–1414.

A discussion of income-maintenance and other social experiments, such as Close-Up 11.2, "Negative Income Tax and Labor Supply."

Flanagan, Robert J., Robert S. Smith, and Ronald G. Ehrenberg. *Labor Economics and Labor Relations.* Glenview, Ill.: Scott, Foresman and Co., 1984.

An excellent text on all aspects of labor economics.

Freeman, Richard B. *The Market for College-Trained Manpower.* Cambridge, Mass.: Harvard University Press, 1971.

A study of career choice and cobweb adjustment patterns in markets for college-trained labor.

Linder, Staffan B. *The Harried Leisure Class.* New York: Columbia University Press, 1970.

An important and amusing discussion of the increasing scarcity of time. *See also* the symposium on this book in *Quarterly Journal of Economics,* November 1973, pp. 628–75.

Robinson, Joan V. *The Economics of Imperfect Competition.* London: Macmillan, 1933.

A classic; contains considerable discussion of the labor market and various types of exploitation.

Watts, Harold W., and Albert Rees. *The New Jersey Income-Maintenance Experiment, vol. 2: Labor-Supply Responses.* New York: Academic Press, 1977.

COMPUTER PROGRAMS

The KOHLER-3 personal-computer diskettes that accompany this book contain two programs of particular interest to this chapter:

11. Labor and Wages includes a 43-question multiple-choice test with immediate responses to incorrect answers as well as numerous exercises concerning optimum input quantities used by profit-maximizing firms under perfect competition as well as various forms of imperfect competition. *Appendix A. Solving Simultaneous Equations* will be helpful in performing the exercises.

ANALYTICAL EXAMPLE 11.1

INPUT DEMAND AND NONPROFIT FIRMS

Analytical Example 4.5, "The Production of Culture," reported on a recent estimate of production functions for various branches of the arts. The same study can be used to test whether performing arts companies use profit-maximizing input quantities as suggested by point *e* of Figure 11.1. If they did, we should expect the marginal value product of any input to equal its price (or the marginal physical product to equal the ratio of input to output price). Yet the accompanying table shows a consistent divergence between MPP_i and the ratio of P_i to P_o in the 164 companies studied.

	Theater	Opera	Symphony	Ballet
(A) Input: Artists				
Marginal physical product (MPP)	0.5943	0.2909	0.0870	0.5899
Ratio of input price to output price (P_i/P_o)	1.057	0.735	1.431	0.855
(B) Input: Capital				
Marginal physical product (MPP)	0.2051	0.0849	0.0347	0.1136
Ratio of input price to output price (P_i/P_o)	0.285	0.201	0.390	0.231

The marginal physical product was consistently below the relevant ratio of prices, implying marginal value product below input price. This implies an excessive use of these inputs from a profit-maximizing point of view, as would be the case if the firm depicted in Figure 11.1 used labor according to point *f* rather than *e*. Yet all this should not surprise us. Performing arts companies are frequently nonprofit organizations, heavily subsidized by private and public gifts, which augment revenues from ticket sales. If the price of labor depicted in Figure 11.1 were subsidized to the tune of $6,400 (the vertical difference between *e* and *f*), it would be perfectly rational to utilize a labor quantity corresponding to *f* (because the subsidy would effectively lower the price of labor to the $3,600 level shown there). The same, of course, holds true for capital as well.

Source: James H. Gapinski, "The Production of Culture," *The Review of Economics and Statistics,* November 1980, pp. 578–86. Reprinted by permission of North-Holland Publishing Company.

ANALYTICAL EXAMPLE 11.2

SUBSTITUTION AND SCALE EFFECTS IN THE BLACK LUNG PROGRAM

In 1969, the U.S. Congress passed the Coal Mine Health and Safety Act. A major purpose of the act was to address the issue of black lung disease that disabled and often killed coal miners whose lungs had become clogged with coal dust. The act made afflicted coal miners eligible for monthly benefits; they would be paid by the government until 1974, but thereafter employers were liable. A question arose concerning the employment effects of the increased labor costs that employers would soon face. The answer can be illustrated with the help of the accompanying graph.

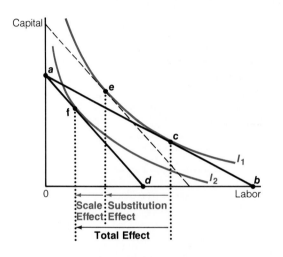

Coal mine operators might have faced an original isocost line *ab* and optimized on isoquant I_1 using the capital and labor amounts implied by point *c*. The higher labor cost (via insurance premiums or monthly benefits paid the disabled) would swing budget line *ab* to *ad*, given the price of capital services. A new optimum at *f* is chosen, implying a decrease in labor used by the horizontal difference between *c* and *f* (the total effect) and an increase in capital used (letting *machines* do the mining) equal to the *vertical* difference between *c* and *f*. The graph shows how the total effect on labor employment can be broken down into substitution effect and scale effect with the help of the hypothetical dashed isocost line. Investigators found that the substitution effect (that would make mine operators produce any given amount of coal with less labor and more capital because of the changed relative input prices) would reduce employment in underground mining by 4.5 percent. The scale effect (that would make people demand, and coal mine operators produce, less coal because of a higher price of coal) would reduce employment by another 6 percent. Including analogous changes in surface mining, the black lung program, it was found, would eliminate 11,700 coal-mining jobs.

Source: Ronald G. Ehrenberg and Robert S. Smith, *Modern Labor Economics: Theory and Public Policy* (Glenview, Ill.: Scott, Foresman and Co., 1982), pp. 94–96.

ANALYTICAL EXAMPLE 11.3

FIRE FIGHTERS FIGHT MONOPSONY

Using a large cross section of union and nonunion cities during 1960–66, Orley Ashenfelter followed the efforts of one of the largest unions in the public sector to counter the monopsony power of local governments. The accompanying table summarizes his observations about the International Association of Fire Fighters. Considering all cities studied, the author concluded that the 1966 average hourly wage of unionized firefighters had been raised from 6–16 percent above that of nonunion firefighters as a result of a 3–9 percent relative reduction of average annual duty hours of unionized firefighters and a 0–10 percent relative increase in their average annual salary.

	Percentage Difference between Union and Nonunion Cities, 1966	
	Small-Size Cities	Moderate-Size Cities
Average hourly wage	+16.0	+9.4
Average weekly duty hours	−5.8	−8.5
Average annual salary	+10.1	+1.0

Source: Orley Ashenfelter, "The Effect of Unionization on Wages in the Public Sector: The Case of Fire Fighters," *Industrial and Labor Relations Review*, January 1971, pp. 191–202.

ANALYTICAL EXAMPLE 11.4

BASEBALL PLAYERS' DEMAND FOR DISABILITY

As has been noted in Application 5: "The Baseball Players' Market," the advent of free agency has resulted in a remarkable redistribution of rents in the baseball players' market from club owners to players. Less observed has been a second effect, the reallocation of employment risk from players to owners. Prior to the days of free agency, virtually all of the 600 major league players had one-year contracts; the risk of not having it renewed if they were temporarily disabled was great; the *price* of being so disabled to baseball players was high. Now look at Table A and see what has happened since. Large numbers and percentages of players now have guaranteed multiyear contracts; the price of being disabled to baseball players has fallen. Have they "demanded" more disability as a result? This is the question one economist set out to answer.

TABLE A

Guaranteed Years on Contract, 1980	Number of Players	Percentage of Players
0	352	54
1	26	4
2	45	7
3	57	9
4	41	6
5	92	14
6	29	4
7	4	1
8	0	0
9	0	0
10	4	1

The answer was a definite yes, as Table B indicates:

TABLE B

Year	Total Number of Players Who Spent Time on Disabled List	Percentage of Players Who Spent Time on Disabled List	Total Number of Days Spent by All Players on Disabled List	Average Number of Days Spent by All Players on Disabled List
1974–76	267	14.8	14,087	7.826
1977–80	525	20.2	26,587	10.230

Several explanations for the players' increased disability rate have been offered by baseball executives, team physicians, sportswriters, and baseball fans:

1. *Artificial turf.* Allegedly, artificial turf results in more injuries.

2. *Advent of the "designated hitter" rule in the American League.* This rule apparently allows pitchers to pitch more innings per game than they would in the absence of the rule. It has been hypothesized that this places greater strain on pitchers' arms and thereby increases the likelihood of injuries among American League pitchers.

3. *Growing sophistication of sports medicine.* It has been hypothesized that injuries that previously went undetected are now diagnosed.

4. *The 1977 expansion of the American League.* This expansion supposedly has increased the proportion of younger players in the league. Proponents of this theory contend that young players, particularly young pitchers, are more susceptible to injuries than are older players.

Empirical evidence, however, does not support these explanations. (For example, the injury rate is *not* greater where there are more artificial turf fields.) An alternative explanation is this: The price of disability (being out of a job) having fallen, players

CLOSE-UP

"consume" more of it. How do they do it? For example, by working out less during the off-season, which increases their chances of pulling a muscle when they go back to play. The evidence on this hypothesis is amazing, as Table C indicates. At a given point in time, players with guaranteed long-term contracts are more likely to be disabled than players with short-term contracts. [See columns (1) and (2).] And players experience more disability after signing guaranteed long-term contracts than they do prior to signing such contracts. [See columns (3) and (4).]

TABLE C

Number of Guaranteed Years Remaining on Contract in 1980 (1)	Average Number of Days Players Spent on Disabled List in 1980 (2)	Average Number of Days Players Spent on Disabled List per Season prior to Contract (3)	Average Number of Days Players Spent on Disabled List per Season after Contract (4)
0–1	9.424	7.314	4.693
2	14.683	5.841	5.833
3	18.116	5.009	12.206
4	15.024	3.483	8.972
5+	21.189	5.019	13.849

There is even more to the story! Of the 155 players who signed contracts that were guaranteed for three or more years, 25 percent had contracts that specified bonuses related to the frequency of performance, the number of awards won, etcetera. For the players without incentive bonuses, the seasonal average number of days spent on the disabled list rose from 4.717 to 14.445 after signing the contract. For the players with the bonus incentive, the corresponding figures were 4.763 to 6.061 only.

Source: Kenneth Lehn, "Property Rights, Risk Sharing, and Player Disability in Major League Baseball," *Journal of Law and Economics,* October 1982, pp. 343–66.

CLOSE-UP 11.1

ECONOMICS ACCORDING TO THE RATS

The kinds of labor-supply curves found in panel (b) of Figure 11.5 and panel (b) of Figure 11.6 have been verified by experiments with rats and pigeons. Experimenters made these animals push levers (or peck at buttons) a certain number of times before they could obtain food. When the number of pushes or pecks was decreased for a given unit of food (that is, when the "wage" was increased per unit of effort), the hungry animals pushed and pecked faster and more diligently at first. The quantity of labor supplied rose, as from A to C in Figure 11.5. Further increases in the "wage," however, produced a slowing down of effort, a substitution of leisure for food income (as between C and E in Figure 11.5).

While holding the "wage" constant, the same animals were also supplied intermittently with various quantities of *free* food. As pictured in Figure 11.6, the rats and pigeons reduced their work output when they received free food while they worked. Interestingly, low-wage rats (who had to push a lot for a given amount of food) reduced

their work more than high-wage rats. Did high-wage rats love working for the sake of working?

Sources: These and other experiments are noted in Tom Alexander, "Economics According to the Rats," *Fortune,* December 1, 1980, pp. 127–32. *See also* Raymond C. Battalio, Leonard Green, and John H. Kagel, "Income-Leisure Tradeoffs of Animal Workers," *The American Economic Review,* September 1981, pp. 621–32, as well as Close-Up 3.1, "Substitution and Income Effects in the World of White Rats" (p. 95) and Analytical Example 3.1, "The Demand Elasticity of Animal Consumers" (p. 92).

CLOSE-UP 11.2

NEGATIVE INCOME TAX AND LABOR SUPPLY

In the late 1960s, the U.S. Congress debated the introduction of a negative-income-tax system designed to help the poor. Under such a program, families whose income falls below a given figure would receive cash grants from the government, and these grants would be reduced as the families' earned incomes rose. One thought has haunted the program's sponsors: Would the beneficiaries of such a program simply take the money and withdraw from the labor force? Would the rest of society then have to support these people permanently? Economists predicted two outcomes: (1) the receipt of nonlabor income in itself would tend to reduce work performed (consider Figure 11.6); (2) on the other hand, the reduction of the grant as *earned* income rose would in effect lower the recipients' wage rate. (If they took a job at $5 per hour, but then the original government grant was reduced by $3, the effective wage would fall to $2.) This lowered wage would produce both a substitution effect (less work) and an income effect (more work), a matter illustrated in Figure 11.7. What would be the *net* effect of all these forces? To answer these questions, the U.S. Congress funded a number of large-scale experiments—beginning in 1968—in New Jersey's six largest cities; in Gary, Indiana; in Seattle, Washington; in Denver, Colorado; and in rural Iowa and North Carolina.

The New Jersey results indicated that the labor-supply effects of such a program are small, involving a 5- to 10-percent reduction in the amount of work done by program participants. Even this reduction did not take the form of total withdrawal from work. Instead, recipients worked fewer hours, did less moonlighting, and took more time to search for jobs during periods of unemployment. Also, secondary workers in a family reduced their supply more than primary ones; English-speaking whites reduced their supply more than blacks or Spanish-speaking workers.

Sources: Joseph A. Pechman, Michael Timpane, eds., *Work Incentives and Income Guarantees: The New Jersey Negative Income Tax Experiment* (Washington, D.C.: Brookings Institution, 1975). *See also* Robert A. Moffitt, "The Labor Supply Response in the Gary Experiment," *The Journal of Human Resources,* Fall 1979, pp. 477–87. (In Gary, the work-reducing response of female household heads was found to be as high as 30 percent.) Reports on still other experiments can be found in "The Seattle and Denver Income Maintenance Experiments," *The Journal of Human Resources,* Fall 1980, entire issue. For a summary appraisal, *see* Philip K. Robins, "A Comparison of the Labor Supply Findings from the Four Negative Income Tax Experiments," *The Journal of Human Resources,* Fall 1985, pp. 567–82.

12

Capital and Interest

In Chapter 1, we noted that economists define *capital resources* as productive ingredients made by people, including structures, equipment, and inventories of raw materials. The creation of such capital goods invariably involves the processes of saving and investment and thus the passage of *time*. And that is why we must now turn to issues of greater complexity, to decisions that involve more than the comparison of *present* benefits with *present* costs. Consider households that exchange present consumption for future consumption by saving part of their income now and spending it in the future. Consider firms that similarly transform present consumption goods into future consumption goods by diverting resources now from the production of consumption goods to that of investment goods (which help produce future consumption goods, in turn). As a result of such intertemporal decision making, **capital markets** arise, sometimes also referred to as **asset markets.** In these markets, certificates of indebtedness are traded, along with ownership claims to the stocks of natural resources and of physical capital goods. (In a slave society, claims to people would be traded in such markets as well.) In the present chapter, we shall discuss these markets at length.

In order to focus on the essential features of intertemporal decision making, we shall assume that the markets about to be discussed are perfectly competitive. Thus we extend the condition of full knowledge on the part of traders to cover not only the present but also the future. We thereby assume away *uncertainty,* a complication that can be handled with the techniques noted in Part 4 of this book. In this chapter, however, we shall analyze how people would act in a world of certainty in which even the future outcomes of their decisions are known in advance. Just as people without parachutes know that they *will* be killed if they jump out of an airplane at 20,000 feet, so the households and firms in our world are imagined to anticipate the future perfectly.

HOUSEHOLDS AS SAVERS

Members of households typically save part of their incomes during their peak working years, as between the ages of 25 and 65. They often dissave during earlier years when they establish families or later when they have entered retirement. We shall focus on positive saving.

Households can save in a variety of ways; the simplest one is nothing else but the accumulation of coins, paper bills, and checking account balances that do not bear interest. Such money assets have **perfect liquidity,** an ability to be transformed without loss of value and at a moment's notice into any other asset. Yet households usually part with money savings and supply such funds to others. They can do so in the **loanable-funds market,** a market in which the money of some people is traded for **certificates of indebtedness** (or IOUs) issued by other people. These certificates are promises by the issuer to make future payments of money to the holder. Households act as suppliers in this market whenever they deposit money in savings accounts, buy corporate and government bonds, or acquire certificates of deposit, endowment life insurance, or pension claims. All of these actions amount to acquiring IOUs. Invariably, these IOUs are less liquid than money, but, unlike money, they provide an interest return so that more than one future dollar is received for every dollar given up now. However, households can and often do convert their money savings not into IOUs, but into **ownership claims.** These ownership claims are rights to the exclusive use of assets—assets that are often less liquid even than certificates of indebtedness. Such rights also yield streams of future income, in money or in kind. Consider corporate shares, deeds to natural resources and to physical capital goods, or even consumer durables and human capital (such as health, education, and training).

Regardless of whether households save in the form of money, IOUs, or ownership claims, the act of saving enables them to trade current consumption for future consumption: The money now not spent on restaurant meals, vacation trips, and apartment rentals (current consumption) can be set aside in a mattress and spent on these things later (future consumption). Or this money can be converted into such assets as bonds, skills, and furnished homes—assets that yield future interest, salaries, and income in kind (and thus future restaurant meals, vacation trips, and housing services). The household saving decision can be analyzed in a way analogous to Figure 2.6 "The Consumer's Optimum" (see p. 39). Instead of considering a choice, at a given time, between two different consumption goods (such

as apples and butter), we now consider a choice between identical sets of consumption goods at two different times. The time difference, however, makes these goods as different from each other as the apples and butter of our earlier example.

Market Opportunities

Figure 12.1 depicts a consumer's objective opportunities for exchanging current consumption, C_c, for future consumption, C_f. To facilitate the exposition, we shall let the present refer to this year and the future to next year, and, to eliminate any possible confusion because of changes in the general price level, we evaluate present and future sets of goods in *constant dollars*. The combinations of goods that are accessible to the consumer clearly depend on the consumer's initial endowment at E with current and future consumption goods and on the market rate of exchange between the two types of goods. That rate of exchange is determined by the effective annual real rate of interest; we assume it to equal 10 percent per year.

Note: It is crucial to distinguish between nominal, real, and effective rates of interest. The interest rate referred to in everyday usage is the **nominal rate of interest,** which indicates the percentage by which the dollar amount returned to a lender exceeds the dollar amount lent. Because of widespread inflation, an adjustment must be made to find the **real rate of interest,** which indicates the percentage by which the *purchasing power* (or actual quantity of consumption goods) returned to a lender exceeds the purchasing power lent. The real rate always equals the nominal rate minus the rate of inflation. Imagine, for example, that you lent $1,000 at a nominal rate of 20 percent per year. You would receive $1,200 worth of money a year hence. If the general price level was unchanged, you could actually buy 20 percent more goods; the real rate of interest would be 20 percent − 0 percent = 20 percent as well. If the general price level rose by 12 percent, 20 percent, or 30 percent, however, the real rate would equal, respectively, 8 percent, 0 percent, or −10 percent. In the case of a real rate of −10 percent, your purchasing power would actually have been reduced. *Throughout this chapter, we shall consider real rather than nominal rates of interest.* Surely, people who lend money and who operate under certainty, as we assume, cannot be expected to surrender current purchasing power for the promise of a positive nominal rate of interest alone; they must be assured of a positive real rate.

We further assume that people are not fooled by any particular way in which nominal interest contracts are expressed. We always refer to the **effective annual rate of interest,** which is the rate that is in effect paid *per year.* An interest contract, for example, may offer to pay "10 percent, compounded quarterly." This amounts to the payment of interest on the interest after the first quarter of the year and implies an effective *annual* rate of 10.19 percent. Similarly, nominal interest, which is paid less often than annually, implies lower-than-stated effective annual rates. Now picture our consumer at point E with $15,000 of current income (and potential current consumption) plus an ensured receipt of $5,500 of one-year-in-the-future income (and potential future consumption). This consumer *could* just consume $15,000 this year and $5,500 next year, but the consumer could also become a lender or borrower. At one extreme, the consumer could decide to consume nothing this year and lend the $15,000 saved (via the purchase of a risk-free bond, perhaps) at the assumed effective annual real rate of interest of 10 percent. This would yield a return of $15,000 (principal) plus $1,500 (interest) = $16,500 in a year and then enable the consumer to consume $5,500 + $16,500 = $22,000 of goods next year (and this maximum future consumption is shown by point A). At the other extreme, the consumer could decide to consume nothing *next* year and borrow $5,000 against the $5,500 claim on next year's income, thus in effect paying our assumed rate of 10

FIGURE 12.1

The Field of Intertemporal Choice

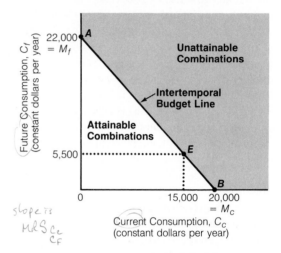

This graph shows all the alternative combinations of current and future consumption goods over which a consumer might conceivably exercise choice. Given an initial endowment (E) that consists of claims on $15,000 of consumption goods this year and $5,500 of consumption goods next year, and given an effective annual real interest rate of 10 percent, line AB becomes the intertemporal budget line that divides attainable combinations (unshaded) from unattainable ones (shaded). Note how this consumer could move from E to A by saving and lending $15,000 of current consumption goods for $16,500 of one-year-in-the-future consumption goods, thus choosing maximum future consumption of $M_f = $5,500 + $16,500 = $22,000. Or the consumer could move from E to B by dissaving and borrowing $5,000 of current consumption goods against the $5,500 one-year-in-the-future consumption goods, thus choosing maximum current consumption of $M_c = $15,000 + $5,000 = $20,000.

percent per year. This transaction would enable our consumer to consume $15,000 + $5,000 = $20,000 of goods this year (and this maximum current consumption is shown by point B). Clearly, our consumer could choose any other combination of current and future goods lying on or below line AB, which thereby is revealed as the intertemporal budget line or intertemporal consumption-possibilities frontier. As usual, combinations in the shaded area are unattainable, given initial endowment E and our interest rate of 10 percent per year. Changes in either one of these factors, however, can be expected to change the position of line AB.

Note that the absolute value of the slope of line AB (which is \$22,000/\$20,000, or 1.1) equals the value $1 + r$, where r is the effective annual real rate of interest. In our example, that rate is 10 percent, which literally means 10 per 100; and $1 + r$ thus equals $1 + (10/100) = 1.1$.

Intertemporal budget-line slope $= 1 + r$

The forgoing can be confirmed by considering the *equation* of our budget line. When inspecting Figure 12.1, we see that

$$C_f = M_f - \frac{M_f}{M_c} C_c$$

where C_f and C_c are the actual and M_f and M_c are the maximum possible levels of future and current consumption, respectively. This expression simplifies to that given in Box 12.A (because M_f/M_c is nothing else but $1 + r$).

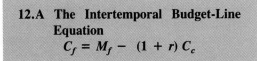

12.A The Intertemporal Budget-Line Equation
$$C_f = M_f - (1 + r) C_c$$

The budget-line equation tells us that the amount of future consumption always equals the maximum possible amount (M_f) minus the budget-line slope absolute value $(1 + r)$ times the amount of current consumption. In our Figure 12.1 example, if $C_c = 0$,

$$C_f = M_f = \$22,000 \text{ (point } A).$$

On the other hand, if $C_f = 0$,

$$0 = M_f - (1 + r) C_c \qquad \text{and}$$
$$C_c = \frac{M_f}{1 + r} = \frac{\$22,000}{1.1}$$
$$= \$20,000 \text{ (point } B).$$

Similarly, a $C_f = \$5,500$ implies

$$5,500 = M_f - (1 + r) C_c \qquad \text{and}$$
$$C_c = \frac{M_f - \$5,500}{1 + r} = \frac{\$16,500}{1.1}$$
$$= \$15,000 \text{ (point } E).$$

Time Preference

Figure 12.2 depicts three types of indifference curves between combinations of current consumption goods, C_c, and future consumption goods, C_f. Which one of the three curves, labeled I_0, I_1, and I_2, best describes a person's preferences between current and future consumption goods? When Eugen von Böhm-Bawerk (1851–1914), a Biography of whom appears in Chapter 12 of the *Student Workbook* that accompanies this text, first studied intertemporal decision making, he opted for the behavioral implications here described by I_0, and he rejected those implied by I_1 and I_2. Typical consumers, he argued, were *impatient* to consume now rather than later. They did not want to undertake the unpleasant task of abstinence and waiting. They subjectively valued present goods more highly than future goods of like kind and number. Böhm-Bawerk thought this was so for two reasons: (1) People often expected a more ample provision of goods in the future than in the present, and (2) people systematically underestimated their future wants (a matter Böhm-Bawerk attributed to "incomplete imagination" or a "defect of will," which gave imagined future wants not the same sharp reality as those presently felt). We can picture this by reviewing Figure 1.1, "The Scarcity Problem" on p. 5. As Böhm-Bawerk saw it, in people's imaginations future scarcity was usually less than present scarcity because the right-hand circle in our earlier graph was imagined as larger in the future and the left-hand one as smaller. Thus people's marginal utility of future income and consumption goods was lower than that of present ones, and, Böhm-Bawerk argued, they would indifferently trade a given set of present consumption goods only for a *larger* set of future ones.

This, of course, is exactly what is shown by indifference curve I_0, in contrast to I_1 and I_2. Consider, for instance, the slope of our three indifference curves along the 45° ray $0C$. At point A on curve I_0, a consumer is willing to trade, indifferently, 1 unit of current consumption goods for 1.5 units of future ones. (Note the dashed triangle constructed underneath point A.) Indifference curve I_0, which has an absolute slope of greater than one at all points, is said to depict a consumer who has a persistently **positive**

FIGURE 12.2

Time Preferences

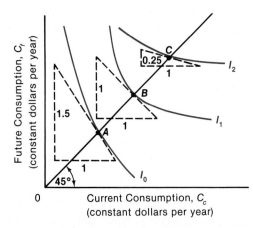

This graph depicts Böhm-Bawerk's distinction among intertemporal consumption-indifference curves that display (marginal) time preferences that are consistently positive (I_0), neutral (I_1), or consistently negative (I_2).

marginal time preference, a high preference for current over future consumption that leads lenders to exact more than 1 unit of future consumption for the sacrifice of 1 unit of present consumption. Note: Even this high price is increasing as more and more current consumption is sacrificed in return for more future consumption. Notice how the (absolute value of) the slope of indifference curve I_0 rises as one moves along it from right to left. The slope of an indifference curve relating current consumption to future consumption is the marginal rate of substitution between current and future consumption, also known as the **marginal time preference.**

If consumers were less impatient than Böhm-Bawerk saw them, they might, of course, have the kind of preferences depicted by line I_1 or I_2. Line I_2, which has an absolute slope of less than one at all points, depicts a consumer with **negative marginal time preference,** a high preference for future over current consumption that implies a lender's willingness to accept less than 1 unit of future consumption for the sacrifice of 1 unit of current consumption. (Note the dashed triangle underneath point C.) Such behavior is not impossible but is likely to be rare (especially under conditions of certainty about the future). Examples of persons with negative time preference might include extraordinarily miserly individuals or those whose present circumstances of abundance are believed to give way to future scarcity. (Consider a farmer's time preference for water if the farm land is flooded in the spring but subject to drought in the summer. Consider a consumer's time preference for bananas if a large quantity possessed now is certain to spoil fast.)

Finally, turn to line I_1, drawn symmetrically around the 45° line. It pictures a **neutral marginal time preference,** the lack of any intrinsic preference between current and future consumption. (Note the consumer's willingness, at point B, to trade indifferently 1 unit of current for 1 unit of future consumption, while positive time preference is found to the left of B and negative time preference to the right of it.)

In the next section, we shall employ the kind of indifference curves depicted by I_1 and we shall note how such a consumer will be induced by a positive rate of interest to choose an optimum position at which the marginal time preference is positive as well.

The Optimum

Figure 12.3, finally, brings opportunities and preferences together to depict the consumer's optimum. The consumer maximizes utility at C, where, as usual, budget line and indifference curve are tangent to each other. At that point, $1 + r$ equals the consumer's marginal rate of time preference and it is positive. (The consumer is indifferent about trading 1.1 units of future consumption for 1 unit of current consumption at point C.)

HOUSEHOLDS AS LENDERS

Changes in time preference and market opportunities will change a consumer's optimum. Consider, for instance, successive increases in the time premiums of real interest offered to the consumer, as depicted in Figure 12.4. Initially, given endowment E and a 10-percent rate of interest per year, the consumer can reach any point on line DF. For example, by giving up all claims on $15,000 of current consumption goods, the consumer could get 1.1 ($15,000) = $16,500 of next year's consumption goods *in addition to* the $5,500 of future goods corresponding to E. Thus the consumer could consume nothing now and $5,500 + $16,500 = $22,000 next year, thereby reaching point D. Alternatively, the consumer at E could trade in the entire claim on $5,500 of next year's consumption goods for an extra ($5,500/1.1) = $5,000 of current consumption goods. Thus the consumer could consume nothing in the future and $15,000 + $5,000 = $20,000 this year, thereby reaching point F. Given the indifference

FIGURE 12.3

The Consumer's Intertemporal Optimum

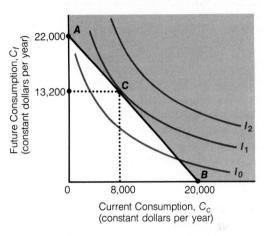

This graph summarizes the elements involved when a utility-maximizing consumer chooses between current and future consumption. Line AB (from Figure 12.1) depicts the consumer's intertemporal consumption-possibilities frontier. The colored intertemporal consumption-indifference curves (of type I_1 in Figure 12.2) depict the consumer's preferences. The optimum is found at point C that yields maximum total utility under the circumstances. This consumer will consume $8,000 of goods this year and $13,200 of goods next year. *Caution:* From this graph alone, we cannot tell whether the consumer is a lender or a borrower because that depends on the position of the initial endowment (is it between C and B or between C and A?). However, given endowment E from Figure 12.1, the consumer is saving and lending $15,000 − $8,000 = $7,000 this year in order to consume an extra $7,700 next year (on top of the initial future claim of $5,500 depicted in Figure 12.1).

curves shown, the consumer moves from E to neither extreme D nor F, but optimizes at A, consuming $8,000 in the current year and thus saving $7,000, just as noted earlier in Figure 12.3. The 10-percent interest and $7,000 saving (and lending) combination is depicted by point a in panel (b).

Let the interest rate rise first to 30 percent per year, and then to 50 percent, all else being equal. In panel (a), the budget line *pivots* at E, and new optima are found at B and then C. Correspondingly, the quantity of loanable funds supplied rises in panel (b) from a to b and then to c. By summing such supply curves for all individuals, a similar market-supply curve can be derived.

Note: An individual's supply of loanable funds could also be backward-sloping, similar to the supply of labor, depicted in panel (b) of Figure 11.5 "The Price-Consumption Line" (p. 365), because the income effect of higher real interest rates works counter to the substitution effect. Whenever the real interest rate goes up, more future consumption can be had for a given sacrifice of current consumption. This increased interest rate implies a fall in the price of a unit of

future consumption (measured in terms of the required sacrifice of current consumption). Thus the substitution effect makes the consumer "buy" more future consumption and less current consumption. Saving and lending rise. At the same time, however, the lowered price of future consumption makes the consumer richer. This income effect induces more future as well as more current consumption (hence less saving and lending). Unlike in Figure 12.4, the net effect might be a reduction in saving and lending. This would be the case, for example, if indifference curve I_3 were tangent to the dashed (50-percent interest) budget line not at C, but somewhere to the right and below B.

FIGURE 12.4

The Supply of Loanable Funds

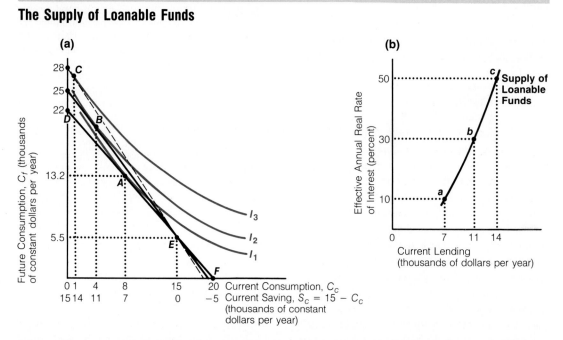

An increase in the effective annual real rate of interest from 10 percent to 30 percent to 50 percent is pictured in panel (a) by budget line *DF* pivoting around endowment position *E* to take on the steeper slope of *BE*, then *CE*. Given the consumer's preferences (depicted by I_1, I_2, and I_3), the consumer's optimum changes from *A* to *B* and to *C*. Correspondingly, current consumption drops from \$8,000 to \$4,000 and to \$1,000, while current saving rises from \$7,000 to \$11,000 and to \$14,000. When lent, these savings become the supply of loanable funds in panel (b). Note how points, *a*, *b*, and *c* reflect the interest rate/savings combinations implied by optima *A*, *B*, and *C*. respectively.

FIRMS AS INVESTORS

When Böhm-Bawerk wrote about interest, he gave a second reason for its existence besides the impatience of consumers who want to consume now rather than wait for future consumption. Present goods, he said, have a *technical superiority* over future goods. When current consumption goods are sacrificed to make current capital goods, future labor and natural resources, together with these capital goods, can produce a larger quantity of consumption goods, and can do so permanently.

Indirect, time-consuming, roundabout methods of production—methods that are capitalistic (in the literal sense of being capital-using)—Böhm-Bawerk argued, are superior to direct ones (that simply apply raw labor to natural resources). Consider Robinson Crusoe. Surrounded by nothing but natural resources, and using his bare hands only, he might catch 5 fishes a day. Over time, his daily food production would equal the series 5 . . . 5 . . . 5 . . . 5 . . . and so on, forever. Now suppose that Crusoe went hungry for a day and sacrificed the 5 fishes he might have caught. He might use his time to make a net and even build a canoe. Starting the next day, he might catch 10 fishes per day, and he might do so in half the time previously spent. He might spend the remainder of the time each day repairing net and canoe, thereby making his capital goods last as long as he lives. As a result, his daily food production would equal the series 0 . . . 10 . . . 10 . . . 10 and so on, forever. A 5-fish sacrifice on day 1 would thus yield a 5-fish increase in output on all future days—a real interest return of 100 percent per day! In this way, Böhm-Bawerk noted, the sacrifice of present consumption goods (like the 5 fishes sacrificed by Crusoe on day 1) can be productively transformed in every society through capital formation (like Crusoe's production and subsequent maintenance of net and canoe) into a *permanently* larger flow of future consumption goods. Present consumption goods thus have a **time productivity:** They have the ability, when sacrificed now for the sake of creating capital goods, to yield permanently more future consumption goods. This productivity, Böhm-Bawerk argued, is not only a physical productivity (as shown by the production of a permanently greater *quantity* of fish), but is also a value productivity. (Crusoe's investment would, in a market economy, yield a greater *value* of fish because his impatience to consume now rather than later would limit the sacrifice of current consumption. This would limit the production of current capital and future consumption goods long before the price of these future consumption goods had fallen sufficiently to turn the positive physical productivity of time into a negative value productivity.) Indeed, firms in our modern economy, similar to Robinson Crusoe and the planners of socialist economies, are continually engaged in the process of **capital budgeting:** identifying available investment opportunities, selecting investment projects to be carried out, and, finally, arranging for their financing.

Identifying Investment Opportunities

Robinson Crusoe's net-canoe investment project enabled him to get more fish (or "revenue") with a given effort (or "cost"). Put differently, it allowed him to get the same amount of fish with less effort. The managers of modern-day firms, similarly, can think of many investment projects that would raise revenue, given cost (or that would lower cost, given revenue). In either case, profit would be increased. Consider the case of a privately owned airport, the manager of which can think of five investment projects. We can describe each of these by a sequence of dated (positive or negative) cash flows. To keep things simple, we will make two assumptions. First, the projects are independent of each other in the sense that the outflows and inflows of cash associated with any one project are unaffected by the acceptance or rejection of the other projects.

Second, all cash flows occur on the last day of a given year.

The projects and their associated cash flows (excluding the cost of financing) are listed in rows (A) through (E) of Table 12.1.

Project (A) is the acquisition of three new airplanes at a cost of $300,000, their operation for five years in charter flights and teaching, and their subsequent sale. The positive numbers listed in the year 1 through 5 columns indicate revenues after annual costs of operation (fuel, maintenance, wages, taxes, and the like), and the last entry includes the salvage value. Project (B) is the construction of a new hangar at a cost of $100,000, the receipt of various annual net operating revenues in subsequent years (rental fees minus taxes, maintenance, and the like), and the sale of the hangar at the end of year 5. Project (C) is the purchase for $33,000 of a flight simulator and various audiovisual aids used in flight training. Net revenues are expected to rise as indicated from year 1 to year 4, to remain level at $10,000 through year 10, and then to cease.

Project (D) is the construction of a new runway at a total cost of $550,000. Net revenues (landing fees minus repair, snowplowing costs, taxes, and the like) of $50,000 a year are expected subsequently for 20 years. Project (E), finally, is the construction of a restaurant at a cost of $65,000. The restaurant is expected to yield net revenues of $20,000 for 4 years and to be sold for $50,000 at the end of year 5.

The listing of all possible investment projects is, however, only the first step in drawing up a capital budget. The next step is to select worthwhile projects from among possible ones.

Selecting Investment Projects to Be Carried Out

Our manager must now decide which of the possible investment projects are worth undertaking. If the firm's goal is to maximize profit (and this we still assume), each project's total revenue must somehow be compared with its total cost. This, however, can hardly be as simple as adding up all the numbers found in any one row and concluding, for instance, that project (A) is worthwhile because it produces an overall profit of $170,000. This figure would be correct only if the market rate of interest and, therefore, financing costs, were zero.

Financing costs are excluded from Table 12.1, but they are unlikely to be zero. Indeed, they equal forgone interest income if the firm finances its investment projects with its own funds (such as past depreciation allowances and retained profits), which could have been lent to others. And these costs equal the interest that must be paid to others if the firm borrows other

TABLE 12.1

A Firm's Investment Opportunities

Project	Net Cash Flows, Excluding Financing Cost (in thousands of dollars) at End of Year					
	0	1	2	3	4	5
(A) Airplanes	− 300	+ 50	+ 60	+ 70	+ 80	+ 210
(B) Hangar	− 100	+ 10	+ 12	+ 15	+ 20	+ 50
(C) Teaching aids	− 33	+ 2	+ 5	+ 8	+ 10	+ 10→through year 10
(D) Runway	− 550	+ 50	+ 50	+ 50	+ 50	+ 50→through year 20
(E) Restaurant	− 65	+ 20	+ 20	+ 20	+ 20	+ 50

A firm's investment opportunities can be described by sequences of dated cash flows.

people's funds. If the relevant interest rate were 10 percent per year, the $300,000 expenditure on project (A) would impose a $30,000 annual interest cost on the firm, regardless of whether it used its own funds or borrowed funds. Yet one should not now conclude that project (A) makes a profit of $20,000; that is, the $170,000 sum of all entries in row (A) minus the $150,000 interest cost over five years.

Dollars spent or received at different times are not of equal value in a world in which interest exists (for one or the other of Böhm-Bawerk's reasons). If the interest rate were 10 percent per year, a single dollar in year 0 could be lent and turned into $1.10 in year 1, into $1.21 in year 2, into $1.331 in year 3, into $1.4641 in year 4, and into $1.61051 in year 5. And the process can be reversed as well: Anyone expecting to receive with certainty $1.61051 in year 5 (and we assume certainty throughout this chapter) might just as well accept $1 now as an exact equivalent. (When lent at 10 percent per year, this present $1 would turn into $1.61051 five years hence). Similarly, of course, $1.4641, due to be received or spent in year 4, can be treated as $1 in year 0, as can $1.331 due in year 3, $1.21 due in year 2, and $1.10 due in year 1.

The process of making dollars of different dates comparable is called **compounding** when the interest rate is used to compute the *future value of present dollars*. The process of making dollars of different dates comparable is called **discounting** when the interest rate is used to compute the *present value of future dollars* (and the interest rate itself is then often referred to as the **discount rate**).

If the interest rate is r, the future value in year t (or FV_t) of any present value in year 0 (or PV_0) is thus given by the compound interest formula of Box 12.B.

12.B The Compound Interest Formula
$$FV_t = PV_0 \, (1 + r)^t$$

Note how $1 in year 0 was shown above to turn into $1.331 in year 3 at an interest rate of 10 percent per year. Our formula confirms this:

$$FV_3 = \$1\left(1 + \frac{10}{100}\right)^3 = \$1(1.1)^3 = \$1(1.331)$$
$$= \$1.331.$$

The above formula implies, of course, the discounting formula of Box 12.C.

12.C The Discounting Formula
$$PV_0 = \frac{FV_t}{(1 + r)^t}$$

Note how $1.61051 in year 5 was shown above to be the equivalent, at an interest rate of 10 percent per year, of $1 in year 0. The discounting formula confirms this result:

$$PV_0 = \frac{\$1.61051}{\left(1 + \dfrac{10}{100}\right)^5} = \frac{\$1.61051}{(1.1)^5}$$
$$= \frac{\$1.61051}{1.61051} = \$1$$

Table 12.2 shows the future equivalences of $1 for a variety of years and interest rates. By implication, it shows the discount factors by which future amounts must be divided to arrive at present-value equivalents. This table can be used to find the present value of each of the entries listed in Table 12.1.

Consider row (A) of Table 12.1 and apply to it, as the discounting formula demands, the discount factors of, say, the 10-percent column of Table 12.2. The −$300,000 in year 0 ("the present") must be divided by 1, which yields the present equivalent of −$300,000. The $50,000 of year 1, however, must be divided by 1.1, which yields a present equivalent of $45,454.55. (This sum, if available now and invested at 10 percent per year, would turn into $50,000 a year hence.) The $60,000 of year 2 must be divided by 1.21, and this yields $49,586.78. (This sum, if available now and invested at 10 percent per year, would turn into $60,000 two years hence.) The remaining entries in row (A), Table 12.1, are analogously divided by the remaining entries in the 10-percent column of Table 12.2, yielding present values, respectively, of $52,592.04, $54,641.08, and $130,394.28. These *comparable* dollars can, of course, be added together.

The addition of the present values of the negative and positive components of an investment project yields its **net present value.** The net present value for project (A) comes to − $300,000 + $332,668.73, which equals $32,668.73. This value implies that it is worthwhile to undertake project (A) at the assumed rate of interest of 10 percent per year. If the firm used its own funds to finance the project, it would earn, in terms of present dollars, $32,668.73 more than if it lent these funds to someone else. If it used borrowed funds, the firm would earn, in terms of present dollars, $32,668.73, even after paying others 10-percent per year on the borrowed funds.

The 10-percent column of Table 12.3 shows the net present values, similarly calculated, for all the projects of Table 12.1. The remaining columns of this table show what the net present values would be at alternative rates of interest.

Note how the profitability of each investment project varies with the prevailing rate of interest—the rate the firm could earn by lending its own funds to others or the rate it must pay to borrow other people's funds. If the market rate of interest were zero (the firm could neither earn a cent by lending its funds nor would have to pay a cent for borrowing all the funds it could use), all five investment projects would be worthwhile to undertake. They would then yield the profits indicated in the 0-percent column of Table 12.3. At the other extreme, a market rate of 25-percent per year would make all projects unprofitable. After counting in as costs the interest forgone on own funds or paid out on borrowed funds, the projects would yield the losses shown in the 25-percent column of Table 12.3. Other market rates imply other investment decisions that lie between these two extremes. At a market rate of 10 percent per year, projects (A), (C), and (E) would be worthwhile; projects (B) and (D) would be equivalent to losing, respectively, 25,000 and 124,000 presently available dollars.

TABLE 12.2

Compound Interest and Discount Factors

Year	Interest Rate per Year				
	5 Percent	10 Percent	15 Percent	20 Percent	25 Percent
0	1	1	1	1	1
1	1.0500	1.1000	1.1500	1.2000	1.2500
2	1.1025	1.2100	1.3225	1.4400	1.5625
3	1.1576	1.3310	1.5209	1.7280	1.9531
4	1.2155	1.4641	1.7490	2.0736	2.4414
5	1.2763	1.6105	2.0114	2.4883	3.0518

A single dollar will turn into various larger amounts when compounded at interest. (Note how $1 turns into $1.44 in 2 years at 20-percent interest per year.) Conversely, any given future amount can be discounted to find its earlier-period equivalent. (Note how, at 15-percent interest per year, $1.75 equals $1 four years earlier or $1.32 two years earlier.)

TABLE 12.3

Net Present Values of Investment Projects (in thousands of dollars)

Project	\ 0 Percent	\ 5 Percent	Rate of Interest per Year 10 Percent	\ 15 Percent	\ 20 Percent	\ 25 Percent
(A) Airplanes	170.0	92.9	32.7	−15.0	−53.2	−84.2
(B) Hangar	7.0	−11.0	−25.0	−36.1	−44.9	−52.1
(C) Teaching aids	52.0	30.3	15.5	5.1	−2.4	−7.9
(D) Runway	450.0	73.0	−124.0	−237.0	−307.0	−352.0
(E) Restaurant	65.0	45.1	29.4	17.0	6.9	−1.4

This table shows, for various rates of interest, the (year-0) net present values of the investment projects listed in Table 12.1. Note how, at an interest rate of 10 percent per year, the $32,668.73 net present value of project (A) (here rounded) would, together with the $300,000 initial cost of the project, produce exactly the stream of payments shown in row (A), Table 12.1: $332,668.73 invested at 10 percent per year, would turn into $365,935.60 in year 1. Taking out the $50,000 net revenue of year 1 (shown in Table 12.1) and investing the remainder would yield $347,529.16 in year 2. Taking out the $60,000 net revenue of year 2 and investing the remainder would yield $316,282.07 in year 3. Taking out the $70,000 net revenue of year 3 and investing the remainder would yield $270,910.27 in year 4. Taking out the $80,000 net revenue of year 4 and investing the remainder would yield $210,000 in year 5, the net revenue of that year. At a 10-percent-per-year rate of interest, therefore, project (A) is equivalent in year 0 to spending $300,000 and getting $332,668.73. Hence it is equivalent to a year-0 profit of $32,668.73, which is the net present value of project (A). Note: Close-Up 12.1, "Owning Versus Leasing Government Buildings," and Analytical Example 12.1, "Time Is Money," provide other examples of calculating net present value.

FIRMS AS BORROWERS

If our firm were interested in maximizing profit, it would include in its capital budget all investment projects with a positive net present value. It would be indifferent about undertaking those with a zero net present value. It would reject those with a negative net present value.

Under certain circumstances, one can also say that the firm would undertake all those projects that yielded an **internal rate of return** in excess of the current market rate of interest.[1] The internal rate of return is the interest rate that makes the net present value of an investment project just equal to zero. Hence it would be a matter of indifference to undertake or reject the project. Note in Table 12.3 that the internal rate of return for project (A) must lie somewhere between 10 percent and 15 percent, a range in which positive net present values give way to negative ones. In fact, the internal rate of return for project (A) equals 13.3 percent per year. The corresponding rates for projects (B) through (E) equal, respectively, 1.79 percent, 18.25 percent, 6.52 percent, and 24.09 percent per year.

Let us now assume, for the sake of illustration, that our firm uses borrowed funds exclusively. We can easily derive its demand for loanable funds from the forgoing data. At a zero rate of interest, Table 12.3 tells us, all projects are worthwhile; hence the firm borrows $1,048,000 (the sum of the year-0 data in Table 12.1) to carry out all the projects. This amount is shown by point *a* in Figure 12.5.

Once the market rate of interest exceeds 1.79 percent per year—the internal rate of return for project (B)—that project's net present value is negative. So the project is rejected and the quantity of funds demanded drops to $948,000 (point *b*). Again, once the market rate of interest

---

[1] A reservation to this statement will be noted in Application 1, "Conflicting Investment Criteria" (p. 423).

exceeds 6.52 percent per year—the internal rate of return for project (D)—the quantity of funds demanded drops to $398,000 (point *c*). When the market rate exceeds 13.3 percent per year, project (A) is eliminated; the quantity of funds demanded drops to $98,000 (point *d*). Similarly, market rates above 18.25 percent per year eliminate project (C) and reduce the quantity of funds demanded to $65,000 (point *e*). Finally, even project (E) cannot survive market rates above 24.09 percent per year, and the quantity of funds demanded by our firm vanishes altogether (point *f*). The firm's capital budget becomes zero.

A market-demand line can, of course, be derived in the usual fashion. More likely than not, if the demands of many individual firms were added horizontally at each rate of interest, the stairstep shape of the demand line shown here would give way to the usual smooth appearance.

THE PURE RATE OF INTEREST

The forgoing analysis of households as savers and lenders and firms as investors and borrowers can be used to explain the determination of the **pure rate of interest,** the interest rate that emerges in a perfectly competitive market for loanable funds when there is certainty (and, therefore, no risk).[2] Consider the market for loanable funds depicted in Figure 12.6. Imagine the market-supply line is derived from a multitude of individual ones, such as the one shown in panel (b) of Figure 12.4. Imagine, similarly, the market-demand line is derived from the summation, for many firms, of demand lines such as the one depicted by Figure 12.5. Because demand exceeds supply at a zero rate of interest, a positive rate emerges. This rate settles, in our example, at 10 percent per year because there are shortages at lower rates and surpluses at higher ones. Corresponding to equilibrium point *e*, $900 million worth of funds are traded per year.

[2]For a description of actual U.S. capital markets, see the Appendix to this chapter, "Markets for Bonds and Stocks," that appears in Chapter 12 of the *Student Workbook* that accompanies this text.

FIGURE 12.5

The Demand for Loanable Funds

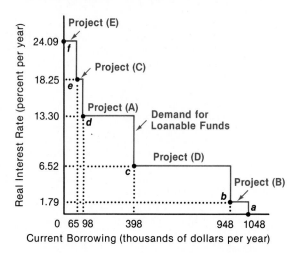

A firm's demand for loanable funds is downward-sloping. This shape reflects the increasing likelihood that the firm's investment projects are profitable (have positive net present values) as the market rate of interest declines.

At this equilibrium, all households with marginal rates of time preference of 10 percent per year or less (and, therefore, willing to lend at 10 percent) are able to lend their funds and to improve their lot. (Consider the lender of the dollar labeled *a* who would have been indifferent about lending it at 5 percent but who receives 10 percent.) All firms with marginal rates of time productivity of 10 percent per year or more (and therefore willing to borrow at 10 percent) are able to borrow all they wish and to profit as a result. (Consider the borrower of the dollar labeled *b* who would have been indifferent about borrowing it at 20 percent but who receives it at 10 percent.) Thus the marginal lender and borrower (of the 900 millionth dollar in our example) have, respectively, rates of time preference or time productivity just equal to the pure rate of interest. All those potential lenders (to the right and above *e*) who would sacrifice current consumption only at rates of interest above 10 percent per year are excluded from the market. So are all potential

FIGURE 12.6

The Market for Loanable Funds

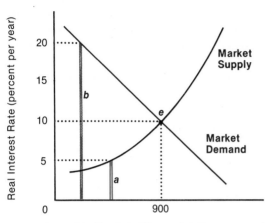

The pure rate of interest (here 10 percent per year) is determined by the interaction of supply and demand in a perfectly competitive market for loanable funds under conditions of certainty.

borrowers (to the right and below *e*) whose investment projects would yield returns of less than 10 percent per year. Thus the market brings together those who have funds (and thus control over resources) with those who have no funds (but are skilled in the use of resources), but only to the extent that the freeing of resources from current consumption and using them for investment (and the production of future consumption) is considered advantageous by all concerned. The establishment of the pure rate of interest can also be illustrated with the help of a famous diagram introduced by Irving Fisher (1867–1947), a Biography of whom also appears in Chapter 12 of the *Student Workbook* that accompanies this text.

Panel (a) of Figure 12.7 depicts a society's intertemporal production-possibilities frontier. Given their current resources and technology, the people in this society could produce only current consumption (point *A*). By sacrificing 1 unit of current consumption, people could carry out their

most productive investment projects and produce, eventually, 3.25 units of future consumption goods (point *B*). They could, similarly, move to points *C* or *D* by carrying out increasingly less productive investment projects. Note the absolute value of the slope of our intertemporal production-possibilities frontier. It declines from 3.25 in region *AB* (implying 3.25 future units − 1 current unit = 2.25 units return on the unit of consumption sacrificed) to 1 in region *BC* (implying a zero return) and to .5 in region *CD* (implying a negative return). This slope measures the **marginal time productivity** of present goods, or the additional future goods producers are able to create for a unit sacrifice of present ones. In our example, moving from *A* to *D*, this productivity declines progressively.

Yet long before profitable investment opportunities were exhausted in this way, Fisher argued, the impatience of consumers to consume now would put an end to sacrifices of current consumption goods. Panel (b) of Figure 12.7 depicts a communitywide intertemporal consumption-indifference curve. It illustrates, starting at *E* and moving toward *H*, how consumers as a group insist (in order to remain indifferent) on ever higher rewards of future consumption goods for successive equal sacrifices of current ones. The rise in their marginal time preference is shown by the changing slope of the indifference curve. Its absolute value rises from 1.05 in region *EF* to 1.1 in region *FG* to 2 in region *GH*.

Panel (c) shows Irving Fisher's way of illustrating Böhm-Bawerk's reasons for the emergence of interest. Superimposing panels (a) and (b), we find the community's optimum at point *I*, where the highest possible welfare is reached, given preferences and production possibilities. (Indifference curves below the one shown would imply lower welfare; curves above the one shown would be out of reach of the community's production possibilities.) At point *I*, the two curves are just touching each other, and their slopes equal that of the dashed line. This slope reflects a pure rate of interest of 10 percent per year, simultaneously equal to marginal time productivity and marginal time preference.

FISHER'S CONCEPT OF CAPITAL

Having focused on the essential nature of interest (as a phenomenon arising from time preference and time productivity), we now turn to the nature of capital. Irving Fisher generalized the concept to include more than physical capital goods, more than the structures, machines, and stocks of raw materials usually referred to as "capital resources." He viewed **capital** as the stock of all useful things or assets that yield streams of (net) income over time. And these assets can be *valued*, Fisher argued, with the help of the discounting process. **Capitalized value** can be derived by applying the pure rate of interest to the (net) income stream produced by each asset. Capitalized value is nothing else but *the present*

FIGURE 12.7

Fisher's Interest Diagram

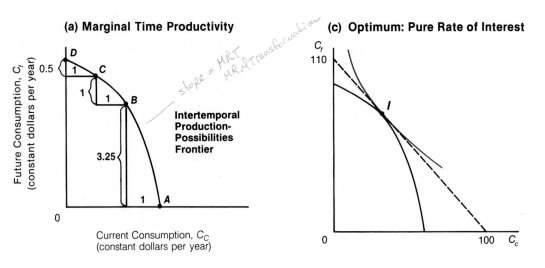

(a) Marginal Time Productivity

(c) Optimum: Pure Rate of Interest

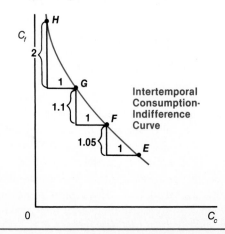

(b) Marginal Time Preference

This set of diagrams illustrates how the people of a community are able—panel (a)—and willing—panel (b)—to swap current consumption goods for future ones. At optimum point *I* in panel (c), marginal time preference is perfectly matched with marginal time productivity. The slope of the dashed line simultaneously equals the marginal time preference at *I* (measured by the slope of the intertemporal consumption-indifference curve) and the marginal time productivity at *I* (measured by the slope of the intertemporal production-possibilities frontier). The dashed line's slope (absolute value 1.1) implies a pure rate of interest of 10 percent per year.

value of the net income stream. Figure 12.8 provides a visual illustration of this process of **capitalization** (or deriving capitalized or present value).

Consider any income-producing asset (it is significant that it can be any asset at all): a bond, a share of common stock, an acre of land, a deposit of coal, a machine, a house, a car, even a skill embodied in a person. Let the asset produce, with certainty, a net income stream of

$100 at the end of each of 10 years (after which the asset disappears). If the pure rate of interest is 10 percent per year, and people can lend and borrow all the money they wish at this rate in a perfectly competitive market, the capitalized value of the asset at the end of year 0 is precisely $614.45. Figure 12.8 tells us why: The height of each column represents $100 received at the end of the stated year. But $100 at the end of year 1 is equivalent to only $90.91 now. (At 10-percent

FIGURE 12.8

How to Capitalize an Income Stream

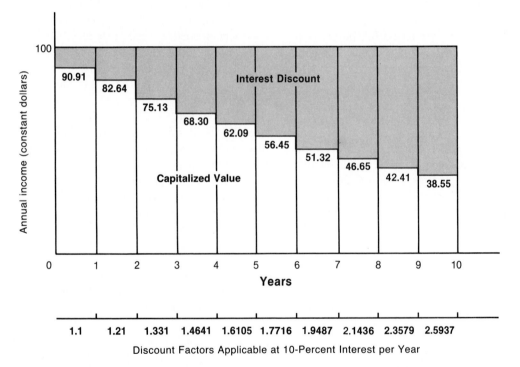

An income stream (represented here by 10 columns of $100) has a *present* or *capitalized value* that can be found by discounting separately each component part at the applicable rate of interest and then summing the results. In this example, the present value is given by the expression

$$PV_0 = \frac{FV_1}{(1 + r)} + \frac{FV_2}{(1 + r)^2} + \frac{FV_3}{(1 + r)^3} + \ldots + \frac{FV_{10}}{(1 + r)^{10}},$$

wherein each future value equals $100, $r = 10$ percent, and the 10 parts in the equation correspond to the white portions of the columns in the graph. Their sum is the capitalized value of $614.45 given by the lower white area. The upper shaded area of $385.55 has been discounted away. Note how later dollars shrink more than earlier ones as the time perspective of interest is applied (just as farther objects shrink more than nearer ones in spatial perspective).

interest per year, it will grow by a factor of 1.1 into $100 in a year.) Similarly, for all the other future receipts. Note how $100 to be received in 10 years is equivalent to only $38.55 now. (At 10-percent interest per year, it will grow by a factor of 2.5937 into $100 in 10 years.)

Figure 12.8 clearly shows why an increase in the interest rate instantly reduces the capitalized value of an income stream. It expands the shaded area of interest discount. A fall in the interest rate, for analogous reasons, raises capitalized value. The most dramatic example of how a change in the interest rate changes capitalized value is provided by the constant and perpetual income stream associated with government bonds (such as British ''consols'' and Canadian ''perps'') that are never repaid but pay a fixed sum of annual interest forever. The discount formula in this case simplifies to

$$PV = \frac{FV}{r}.$$

If interest of $100 per year is paid forever, the bond's capitalized value is $100/.10 at an interest rate of 10 percent per year, or $1,000. Raise this interest rate to 20 percent (or reduce it to 5 percent), and the bond's value instantly changes to $500 (or $2,000). Note: The values just computed, permanently invested at the respective interest rates, would yield the $100 annual stream forever.[3]

We are now ready to take Fisher's ideas a step further: In perfectly competitive markets and under conditions of certainty, the price of each asset will come to equal the asset's capitalized value and, in the case of reproducible assets in the long run, will come to equal the average cost of producing the asset as well.

Asset Prices in the Short Run

Asset prices will come to equal their capitalized values for a simple reason: Competition will bid asset prices up or down until they equal capitalized values. If the price of an asset exceeded its capitalized value, everyone would want to sell it, nobody would want to buy it, and its price would fall. Consider the asset depicted in Figure 12.8. If it were priced at $1,000, everyone holding this asset would want to sell it because $1,000, invested at the assumed going rate of interest of 10 percent per year, would yield a *permanent* (net) income stream of $100 a year, not just a limited stream of $100 a year for a decade. Nobody, however, would want to buy the asset because $1,000, invested to bring $100 for only 10 years would yield considerably less than the going rate of 10 percent per year.

Similarly, if the price of an asset fell short of its capitalized value (and equaled, perhaps, $500 in our example), everyone would want to buy it, nobody would want to sell it, and its price would rise. Note: When all asset prices equal the capitalized value of income streams derived from these assets, all assets yield the same annual percentage return. This return is the interest rate used to calculate the capitalized value.

---

[3]We can prove the accuracy of the simplified formula as follows, starting with the formula found in the Figure 12.8 caption:

$$PV_0 = \frac{FV_1}{(1 + r)} + \frac{FV_2}{(1 + r)^2} + \ldots + \frac{FV_n}{(1 + r)^n} \quad (1)$$

Multiplying both sides by $(1 + r)$ and recognizing that all future values are identical, we have

$$PV_0(1 + r) = FV + \frac{FV}{(1 + r)} + \ldots + \frac{FV}{(1 + r)^{n-1}} \quad (2)$$

Subtracting (1) from (2), we get

$$PV_0(1 + r) - PV_0 = FV - \frac{FV}{(1 + r)^n}$$

or

$$PV_0 \cdot r = FV\left[1 - \frac{1}{(1 + r)^n}\right] \quad (3)$$

When the financial instrument has no maturity date, n becomes infinity. Thus

$$\lim_{n \to \infty}\left[1 - \frac{1}{(1 + r)^n}\right] = 1 - 0 = 1$$

Thus equation (3) becomes

$$PV_0 \cdot r = FV \quad (4)$$

Dividing by r, we obtain the formula noted in the text.

Asset Prices in the Long Run

The prices of reproducible assets will come to equal their average costs of production in the long run because it will be profitable to change the rate of production whenever this equality does not hold. Consider again Figure 12.8. Imagine the asset was a machine priced (as expected) at $614.45. If someone could produce such machines for $500, more of them would be produced. This increase in production would eventually increase the supply of services of such machines and decrease the price of such services. Thus the annual net income derivable from the use of these machines would fall below the $100 shown in our graph. Accordingly, the capitalized value and, as we have argued, the price of the machine would fall. This price decline would continue until the price equaled production cost.

Similarly, if such machines could only be produced for $1,000, no one would produce them while their price was $614.45. This decline in production would eventually decrease the supply of services of such machines (as existing ones wore out) and would increase the price of such services. Thus the annual net income derivable from the use of these machines would rise above the $100 shown in the graph. Accordingly, the capitalized value and, therefore, the price of the machine would rise. This price increase would continue until the price equaled production cost.

APPLICATIONS

We now turn to a number of applications of the tools of interest and capital analysis developed so far.

Application 1: Conflicting Investment Criteria

Our earlier discussion yielded the "golden rule" of capital budgeting:

If you care to maximize the profit of your firm, carry out all investment projects that have a positive net present value at the current market rate of interest (*or that have an internal rate of return in excess of this market rate*).

Whenever a firm (1) is able to lend or borrow all the funds it wants at the current market rate of interest and (2) faces investment projects that are independent of each other and produce streams of returns that are first negative and then positive, a firm is well served by either of the criteria in the above rule. On occasions when these two conditions are not met, however, it is wise to ignore the parenthetical portion of the above rule because it conflicts with the positive-net-present-value criterion.

Net Present Value Versus Internal Rate of Return. The present-value criterion will appear to contradict the internal-rate-of-return criterion when a firm's investment funds are rationed by some device other than the equilibrium market rate of interest. Consider again Figure 12.5. Let the market rate of interest be 10 percent per year. The firm would then demand, as we noted earlier, $398,000 worth of funds in order to carry out projects (A), (C), and (E). (These projects alone would then have positive present values; these projects alone also have internal rates of return in excess of 10 percent per year.) Now let the firm's funds be restricted to $100,000. It would now be important to *rank* acceptable projects according to their profitability in order to pursue the most profitable ones first. Here a problem arises: A ranking by net present value changes with the market rate of interest; a ranking by internal rate of return is invariant with respect to that rate (see Table 12.4). According to the internal-rate-of-return criterion, the limited $100,000 are best spent on project (E), then (C), then (A). A consideration of project costs (shown in Table 12.1) effectively eliminates project (A). Yet the net-present-value criterion (at the 10-percent rate) counsels an ordering of projects (A), then (E), then (C).

Worse yet, in some instances, a meaningful internal rate of return cannot be calculated. The annual cash flow pattern of +$16,000,

− $20,000, and + $6,000, for example, has two negative internal rates of return of − 25 percent and − 50 percent per year, yet its net present value (at a market rate of 10 percent per year) equals *positive* $2,776.86.

It is also possible for an investment project to have *several* positive internal rates of return. The annual cash flow pattern of − $8,000, + $17,900, and − $10,000, for example, produces internal rates of return of 7.87 percent and 15.88 percent per year. At 10 percent, the net present value is $8.26.

As advanced treatises show, all these problems can be overcome by using only the net-present-value criterion. If unlimited funds are available at the current market rate of interest, all investment projects with positive net present values should be carried out. If funds are rationed (and because different projects involve different initial costs), profit is maximized by selecting that financially feasible subset of all profitable projects that maximizes net present value. In the example with the $100,000 spending limit, the projects that maximize net present value are project (E) that costs $65,000 and project (C) that costs $33,000, rather than *one-third* of project (A) that costs $300,000. At 10 percent per year, the net present value of one-third of project (A), according to Table 12.3, would be one-third of

$32,700, or $10,900, while the net present value of the combination of projects (E) and (C) would equal $46,900 (the sum of $29,400 plus $15,500 plus $2,000 of unspent funds).

Net Present Value Versus Payback Method. Many firms make investment decisions on the basis of the **payback method,** which rejects all investment projects the returns of which require more than a predetermined length of time to repay the initial investment outlay. Consider the projects in Table 12.1. If the payback period was set at 4 years, all projects but (E), which returns $80 on $65, would be rejected.

Note: This criterion is extremely crude. It completely ignores possible returns to the initial investment outlay in years after the payback period (such as in year 5 and later). The criterion also ignores the existence of interest. All payments and receipts within the payback period are treated as equivalent, regardless of their timing. Thus the method is almost certain to produce incorrect results for a profit-maximizing firm. As is evident from Figure 12.5, the choice of project (E) alone is correct only at market rates of interest in excess of 18.25 percent per year. At lower rates, other projects are worthwhile, too.

The only possible advantage of the payback method is that it might be used to select projects

TABLE 12.4

Alternative Rankings of Acceptable Investment Projects

Project	Internal Rate of Return (percent per year)	Ranking According to					
		Internal Rate of Return	Net Present Value, Given an Annual Market Rate of Interest of				
			0 Percent	5 Percent	10 Percent	15 Percent	20 Percent
(A) Airplanes	13.30	3	2	1	1	—	—
(B) Hangar	1.79	5	5	—	—	—	—
(C) Teaching aids	18.25	2	4	4	3	2	—
(D) Runway	6.52	4	1	2	—	—	—
(E) Restaurant	24.09	1	3	3	2	1	1

This table, which is based on Table 12.3, shows that rankings by internal rate of return do not vary with the market rate of interest but that rankings by net present value do vary with market interest.

yielding a quick return and from which a hasty exit can be made. Such a focus on a quick return may be desirable under conditions of uncertainty (assumed away in the present chapter) when late returns might be ignored because it is believed that they will be eroded by political upheaval, technological obsolescence, or competitive imitation. Otherwise the golden rule of capital budgeting remains most useful: Carry out all projects with positive net present value.

Note: Analytical Example 12.2 "Is There Interest Under Socialism?" discusses the use of the payback method in the context of the Soviet economy.

Application 2: The Separation Theorem

An isolated individual, such as Robinson Crusoe, inevitably must consume the identical combination of current and future consumption goods as

that which is being produced. If panel (c) of Figure 12.7 on p. 420 were to apply to such an individual, the choice of combination I on the intertemporal production-possibilities frontier (rather than any of the other points on that curve) would imply a welfare total corresponding to whatever indifference curve passes through point I as well. For an individual living in society, however, such need not be the case, and that individual's welfare can, therefore, be higher than it would otherwise be.

Consider Figure 12.9. An individual may be positioned at point E on the intertemporal production-possibilities frontier $CDEF$. If the individual were Robinson Crusoe, he would maximize utility by moving to some point between E and D on this frontier, the point where the highest reachable indifference curve (not shown) just touches the frontier. (Clearly, such a curve would lie somewhere between I_0 and I_1.) Being a member of society, however, the indi-

FIGURE 12.9

The Separation Theorem

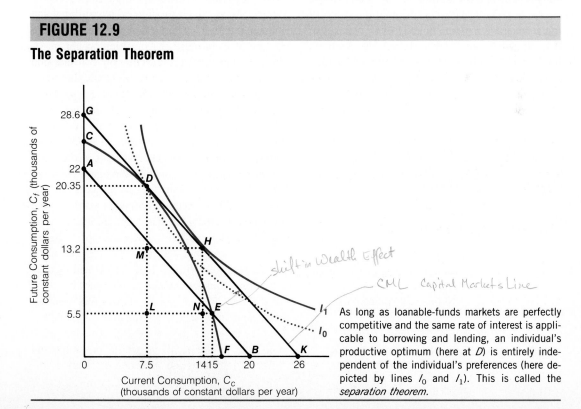

As long as loanable-funds markets are perfectly competitive and the same rate of interest is applicable to borrowing and lending, an individual's productive optimum (here at D) is entirely independent of the individual's preferences (here depicted by lines I_0 and I_1). This is called the *separation theorem.*

vidual has *both* intertemporal production opportunities (along line *CDEF*) and intertemporal market-exchange opportunities (along any line, such as *AB* or *GK*, with an absolute slope of $1 + r$, with r being the rate of interest at which borrowing and lending are possible—activities, it should be noted, that do require the existence of other people). By taking advantage of both opportunities, our individual could move to point *H* on indifference curve I_1 and be considerably better off than in isolation. Let us see how this result is possible.

First, our individual could optimize productive activities by moving from endowment position *E* to point *D*. This involves cutting back current consumption from $15,000 this year to $7,500 and (akin to Crusoe's not catching fish in order to build a canoe) to invest the savings instead to yield extra future consumption (like Crusoe's greater future catch of fish). Sacrificing $C_c = \$7,500$ (*EL*) later yields extra $C_f = \$14,850$ (*LD*). Why is point *D* the optimum? Because there alone exists an equality between the marginal rate of transformation in production ($1 of C_c for $1.1 of C_f), shown by the slope of the intertemporal production-possibilities frontier, and the market rate of exchange, as shown by the absolute slope of line *GK* ($1 + r = 1.1$). As a result of choosing *D*, our individual has maximized the present value of wealth. The present value of endowment *E* is:

$$PV_E = C_c + \frac{C_f}{(1 + r)} = 15 + \frac{5.5}{1.1}$$
$$= 15 + 5 = 20 \text{ (point } B).$$

The present value of combination *D* is

$$PV_D = C_c + \frac{C_f}{(1 + r)} = 7.5 + \frac{20.35}{1.1}$$
$$= 7.5 + 18.5 = 26 \text{ (point } K).$$

Second, our individual could optimize consumption activities by moving from production point *D* to point *H*. This involves trading in the market $7,150 of claims on future consumption, at the prevailing interest rate of 10 percent, for $6,500 of extra current consumption. Promising to repay $7,150 (*DM*), the individual gets $6,500 (*MH*) now, thereby reaching the highest indifference curve that can be reached under the circumstances (I_1). Naturally, point *H* is an optimum for the reasons indicated by Figure 12.3 on p. 411. Note that our individual has ultimately financed the $7,500 investment project (*EL*) by saving $1,000 (*EN*) and borrowing $6,500 (*NL* = *HM*). Thus, for an individual in society, unlike for an individual living alone, saving need not equal investment.

Now we are prepared to understand the **separation theorem** that notes that an individual's productive optimum position is entirely independent of the individual's preferences, as long as loanable-funds markets are perfectly competitive and borrowing and lending occur at a single rate of interest. In our example, no matter how much the individual's indifference curves shifted about, given production possibilities and market interest, the optimum production would remain at *D* because that position would maximize present value (at *K*). Only the consumption point (now *H*) would change, as would the extent of borrowing or lending. All this has, in turn, a crucial implication: Suppose that one individual (the "principal") delegates production decisions to another (the "agent"). Think of stockholders versus corporate managers. As long as the separation theorem is applicable, the agent need not know anything about the preferences of the principal. All the agent has to do is maximize the present value of what has been entrusted to the agent; this will suffice to make the principal as well off as possible. In terms of our graph, if the agent, endowed with *E*, moves to *D* and thereby maximizes present value at *K*, the agent has done all that can be done for the principal's welfare. (The same argument holds regardless of whether the agent works for a single principal or a multitude of them, all of whom possibly hold different intertemporal preferences. Thus a corporate manager who maximizes the wealth of the corporation, under the assumed conditions, maximizes the wealth increments that go to each one of the stockholders.)

Application 3: Investing in Human Capital

When studying economic growth, economists have become increasingly aware of an awkward "residual": The growth of real national output (in the United States, at an average rate of 3.12 percent per year from 1900–1960) could be explained only in part by the growth of inputs, as these were conventionally measured. (In the United States for the 1900–1960 period, labor hours accounted for 34.8 percent, the services of natural resources for 2.5 percent, and those of physical capital goods for 18.6 percent of the observed output growth.) What explained the remaining increase in output (or some 44.1 percent of the observed rate of growth)? Economists called it an "increase in productivity," but this only gave a name to their ignorance; it did not dispel it. Theodore W. Schultz (1902–), who won the 1979 Nobel Prize in economics and a Biography of whom appears in Chapter 12 of the *Student Workbook* that accompanies this text, took strong hints provided by Smith, von Thünen, and Fisher and argued that there was another, although invisible, input at work. This input, distinct from raw labor, was **human capital**—the health care, education, and training embodied in people. The very existence of this invisible capital could be deduced from the existence of an unexplained income stream, and the value of this human capital could be calculated with the help of Fisher's discounting technique. Schultz argued (and later studies by Edward F. Denison confirmed) that human capital had become an increasingly important input in the productive process. While owning little physical capital, most people owned a great deal of human capital and were thus capitalists. While it was customary to value physical capital and list it on balance sheets, Schultz noted, economists were hesitant to capitalize the income stream emanating from people and list it in a similar fashion. Capitalizing the income stream emanating from people smacked of valuing people like slaves and went counter to deep moral values. Yet Schultz urged his colleagues to overcome this reluctance and to study the investments *free people* were obviously making in themselves in order to enhance their welfare.

Physical Versus Human Capital. Indeed, there are many similarities between investing in physical goods and investing in people. Take another look at Table 12.1. Now imagine that the numbers referred to *household* investment projects instead. Such projects could include not airplanes, hangars, runways, and the like, but apprenticeship and on-the-job training, formal education (elementary school, high school, college), informal education (such as home-study courses), health maintenance or improvement, migration for better job opportunities. In each case, there would be a cost (such as the tuition, fees, and transportation expenses incurred and the labor income forgone while going to college). In each case, there would also be a later payoff (such as the higher lifetime income earned with a college degree, even after deducting health and education maintenance expenses). Thus human investments can be analyzed in precisely the same fashion as physical ones: Whenever the net present value of (negative and positive) cash flows is positive when the appropriate market rate of interest is applied, the investment is worth undertaking.

While the similarities are striking, it should be noted that human investments do differ from physical ones in a number of ways: A person's health, skills, and knowledge (unlike a machine) cannot easily be transferred to someone else.

Thus human capital cannot be confiscated or stolen, nor can it ordinarily be sold or bequeathed. (Even here there are exceptions: Consider how athletes sell the rights to their services to sports teams. Consider how parents with much human capital find it easier than parents without it to help their children acquire their own human capital.) Human capital is also portable and can usually be moved more easily than many types of physical capital. Human capital often provides a number of nonpecuniary benefits to its holder in addition to monetary ones. (Studies show, for example, that college graduates have happier marriages, less mental illness, and more enjoyable jobs than high-school graduates only. However, college graduates also work more hours and experience more pressure on the job.) Finally, human capital is subject to sudden and unexpected depreciation in the case of a person's death.

Returns on Human Capital. Statistical studies indicate that returns on investment in human capital are often substantial. Such studies begin with the type of data on schooling and lifetime income listed in Table 12.5. These studies must then tackle a number of statistical problems, such as the question of whether all educational expenditures are investments or some of them are consumption and whether all of the extra observed income can be attributed to extra schooling. (Perhaps those with more schooling are also more talented and more hardworking and would, therefore, have earned more income even without the extra schooling.) In addition, analysts must take into account, of course, the timing of extra income and of the investment expenditures made to achieve it. In the 1950s and 1960s, such studies calculated rates of return of 10–15 percent per year, showing investments in college education as very profitable indeed. In the 1970s and early 1980s, however (with college fees higher and many starting salaries relatively lower), net present values of college education projects plummeted, implying much lower rates of return of about 7.5 percent per year.

A final note: Even though the term itself may not be used, the concept of human capital is routinely employed the world over. Consider how juries determine damages in injury and death cases on the basis of the net present value of the victims' future income streams. Consider how New York's highest court recently ruled in a

TABLE 12.5

Schooling and Lifetime Incomes

Years of School Completed	Lifetime Income of Men from Age 18 to Death (1981 dollars)	Extra Lifetime Income over Previous Category
Fewer than 12 years	$ 601,000	—
High school, 4 years	861,000	$260,000
College, 1–3 years	957,000	96,000
College, 4 years	1,190,000	233,000
College, 5 years or more	1,301,000	111,000

Data such as these (referring to 1979) are only some of those needed to determine the worthwhileness of educational investments. Also needed are data on the cost of these investments, the exact timing of costs and receipts, and the appropriate interest rate for calculating net present value. Thus (ignoring nonmonetary benefits) a 1979 youngster may have been well advised *not* to finish high school if the discounted value of the $260,000 of extra income shown in the last column fell short of the cost of the last high-school year. Under such circumstances the cost in question, invested at interest, would generate more than $260,000 over the youngster's lifetime. Note: An amusing application of this material is found in Analytical Example 12.3, ''Are You Worth Your Weight in Gold?''

Source: U.S. Bureau of the Census, *Statistical Abstract of the United States: 1985* (Washington, D.C.: U.S. Government Printing Office, 1985), p. 453.

divorce case that the wife owned 40 percent of the net present value of the medical license of the husband whom she had supported during medical school.[4] Consider how governments of poor countries complain about the ''brain drain''; that is, the migration, by choice, of their healthier and more educated citizens to richer countries. These governments are aware of the fact that the emigrants take with them invisible capital and thus a stream of future output. Indeed, some governments argue that emigrants should *pay* for the invisible capital they take, especially if it was put in place by public expenditures. (Note how the Soviets demanded such payments from emigrating Jews; how the East Germans, from 1962–1984, sold 22,000 political prisoners to West Germany for $18,000 a head; and how the Cubans sold 1,113 men, prisoners from the Bay of Pigs invasion, to the United States for $55,950 each.) Consider how Mao Zedong's Red Guards, during the Great Proletarian Cultural Revolution in the late 1960s, attempted to create the classless society. All differences in income and status, they said, had to be eliminated: differences between males and females, old and young, leaders and followers, experts and lay persons, skilled and unskilled, mental and physical work, workers and managers, urban workers and peasants, the rich and the poor, teachers and students. As they moved through the countryside, the Red Guards turned student into teacher, teacher into worker, worker into manager, manager into peasant, and peasant into doctor. The common ownership of natural resources and physical capital was not enough to create socialism; they wanted to equalize the ownership of human capital as well.[5]

Application 4: The Exhaustion of Nonrenewable Natural Resources

In the 1970s, predictions of doomsday became popular. Because the world has finite stocks of nonrenewable natural resources (such as coal, metallic ores, natural gas, and oil) and because demand for them is positive and even growing, the argument went, one could confidently predict the complete exhaustion of these resources (and, it was implied, the collapse of modern civilization). The dates for this exhaustion and collapse were typically shown to be within the next 100 years.[6] Table 12.6 illustrates some of these doomsday predictions. The logic behind the table is impeccable: If the stocks of certain natural resources are finite (at whatever level), any positive rate of consumption (whether constant or growing) will exhaust the stocks. This conclusion follows from the assumption. Yet, with (almost) one voice, economists have characterized the doomsday models as utterly worthless because such models have one glaring defect: They completely ignore people's adaptive behavior in response to the workings of the price system.

The Role of the Price System.   In the absence of government intervention to prevent such an adjustment, economic analysis predicts, the gradual depletion of a nonrenewable natural resource will raise its price. This price increase will lead consumers to reduce the quantity demanded and will slow down the rate of depletion. The higher price will also encourage producers to initiate production from known stocks of resources that

[4]*The New York Times*, December, 27, 1985, p. 1.

[5]For a more thorough discussion, *see* Heinz Kohler, *Comparative Economic Systems* (Glenview, Ill.: Scott, Foresman and Co., 1989), chap. 10; and Steven N. S. Cheung, ''Irving Fisher and the Red Guards,'' *Journal of Political Economy*, May/June 1969, pp. 430–33.

[6]This line of argument can be found in Jay W. Forrester, *World Dynamics* (Cambridge, Mass.: Wright-Allen Press, 1971); Donella H. Meadows et al., *The Limits to Growth: A Report for the Club of Rome's Project on the Predicament of Mankind* (New York: Universe Books, 1972); and Mihajlo Mesarovic and Eduard Pestel, *Mankind at the Turning Point: The Second Report to the Club of Rome* (New York: New American Library, 1974).

have higher extraction costs, to step up exploration, and to develop substitutes.

Consider how, in recent years, sharply higher prices of crude oil have led consumers to substitute small cars for large ones, buses for private cars, insulation for heating or air conditioning, short trips for long trips. Consider how producers have found it profitable, because of higher prices, to find and extract natural resources that cost more to extract. (In the case of oil, producers have achieved ''enhanced recovery'' of oil from old reservoirs via the injection of water, steam, soap suds, and explosives or the replacement of rotary drills with jackhammers.

Oil producers are extracting ''synthetic'' oil from coal, shale rock, and tar sands. Producers are discovering and developing major new oil fields in faraway and forbidding places, such as Alaska's frigid North Slope, the Gulf of Mexico, and the stormy North Sea.)

The preceding examples show that the quantities of ''known global reserves,'' which are given in Table 12.6, are themselves a variable. Indeed, studies of *crustal abundance* of resources (their availability in the top 1 mile of the earth's crust) typically indicate quantities a million times the size of ''known global reserves.'' Raise the price (or improve technology) and previously

TABLE 12.6

Doomsday Predictions

Resource	Known Global Reserves	Number of Years Known Global Reserves Will Last:		
		At 1970 Global Consumption Rates	If Global Consumption Rates Grew as in the Past	If Global Consumption Rates Grew as in the Past and Reserves Were 5 Times Known Amounts
Coal	5×10^{12} tons	2,300	111	150
Aluminum	1.17×10^{9} tons	100	31	55
Chromium	7.75×10^{8} tons	420	95	154
Cobalt	4.8×10^{9} pounds	110	60	148
Copper	308×10^{6} tons	36	21	48
Gold	353×10^{6} troy ounces	11	9	29
Iron	1×10^{11} tons	240	93	173
Lead	91×10^{6} tons	26	21	64
Manganese	8×10^{8} tons	97	46	94
Mercury	3.34×10^{6} flasks	13	13	41
Molybdenum	10.8×10^{9} pounds	79	34	65
Nickel	147×10^{9} pounds	150	53	96
Platinum	429×10^{6} troy ounces	130	47	85
Silver	5.5×10^{9} troy ounces	16	13	42
Tin	4.3×10^{6} long tons	17	15	61
Tungsten	2.9×10^{9} pounds	40	28	72
Zinc	123×10^{6} tons	23	18	50
Natural gas	1.14×10^{15} cubic feet	38	22	49
Petroleum	455×10^{9} barrels	31	20	50

Doomsday modelers base their predictions on data such as those found in this table.

Source: Adapted from Donella H. Meadows et al., *The Limits to Growth: A Report for the Club of Rome's Project on the Predicament of Mankind.* A Potomac Associates book published by Universe Books, New York, 1972. Graphics by Potomac Associates.

known but "subeconomic" deposits become worthwhile candidates for extraction; previously unknown but "speculative" deposits are found. The appearance of these additional supplies explains that for many natural resources the ratio of known global reserves to consumption has remained constant over the decades, in spite of ever increasing rates of consumption. The reserve-consumption ratios in Table 12.7, which refers to non-Communist countries only, are typical.

Consider, finally, how the search for substitutes is accelerated by higher resource prices. Nothing can illustrate this accelerated search for substitutes more dramatically than the recent whirlwind of activity set off by higher crude oil prices, including: the construction of nuclear power plants (the fission of one gram of U^{235} produces energy equivalent to 14 barrels of oil); the production of biofuels (ethyl alcohol from cattails, corn, desert plants, seaweed, sugar beets, and wheat can be used to make gasohol); the burning of plant and animal wastes (from peanut shells and garbage to cow manure); the

harnessing of waterfalls, wind, and the sea (tides, waves, temperature gradients); research on solar cells, power stations in outer space, geothermal energy, and nuclear fusion.

Applying Our Tools.   We can utilize the tools discussed earlier in this chapter to illustrate why the prices of nonrenewable natural resources would, in fact, increase over time as depletion progressed, would thereby promote the adaptive behavior just discussed, and would prevent the type of sudden and unexpected resource exhaustion routinely pictured by the prophets of world cataclysm.

It is easiest to analyze the case of an identical annual demand for a resource, say copper ore, the stock of which is *not* increased as a result of higher output price and can be mined at a constant average total and marginal cost (see Figure 12.10). The average total and marginal cost of extracting a ton of copper ore, assumed constant at $0A$, is shown by the solid horizontal line in panel (a); the annual demand (assumed

TABLE 12.7

Reserve-Consumption Ratios

Resource	1950	1960	1969
Aluminum	—	252	279
Copper	63	49	59
Iron	527	686	>1,000
Lead	18	16	26
Nickel	140	195	135
Tin	25	25	25
Zinc	26	26	22
Petroleum	25	39	32

This table (applicable to non-Communist countries) shows that reserve-consumption ratios for natural resources are not declining over time. And note: If estimates of crustal abundance are substituted for *known* reserves, the years of potential consumption at current rates of consumption increase dramatically; in the early 1980s, to 68,066 for aluminum, 340 for copper, 2,657 for iron, 162 for lead, 618 for zinc.

Sources: Roy W. Wright, "Ferrous and Nonferrous Resources," *Centennial Volume, American Institute of Mining, Metallurgical and Petroleum Engineers* 1871–1970 (New York: American Institute of Mining, Metallurgical, and Petroleum Engineers, 1971), p. 18. Copyright © 1971 American Institute of Mining, Metallurgical, and Petroleum Engineers (Incorporated), reprinted by permission; Roy J. Ruffin and Paul R. Gregory, *Principles of Economics*, 3rd. ed. (Glenview, Ill.: Scott, Foresman and Co., 1988), p. 887.

equal every year) is shown in panel (b). Now consider the fact that the copper ore deposit is viewed by its owner as an asset (very much like a building, machine, or skill) that is capable of producing a stream of net benefits.

These net benefits are the difference (such as *AB* at time 0) between the price per ton of copper ore and the assumed average and marginal cost of extracting it. And these net benefits can be received, at the owner's discretion, at any point in time. That is, the owner can mine the entire deposit now, can mine part of it, or can leave it in the ground indefinitely (without incurring storage costs or having to worry about deterioration). Note: Every ton that is mined now yields the net price *AB*, which can be invested at the pure rate of interest (still assuming perfect capital markets

and certainty). If the net price per ton were $100 in year 0 (distance *AB*) and if funds could be lent at a pure rate of interest of 10 percent per year, any ton mined and sold now could in fact be turned into $110 in year 1, into $121 in year 2, and so on. To make the owner indifferent about mining this ton now or mining it later, *the net price must appreciate over time at a rate equal to the pure rate of interest.*

Given an interest rate of *r*, the schedule of net prices (*N*) from year 0 to year *n* (the year of resource exhaustion) must, therefore, be

$$N_0 \ldots N_0 (1 + r) \ldots N_0 (1 + r)^2 \ldots$$
$$N_0 (1 + r)^3 \ldots \text{ and, finally, } N_0 (1 + r)^n.$$

Such a schedule of rising net prices (shown in our graph by a rise of *AB* to *ED*) equalizes the present

FIGURE 12.10

The Exhaustion of a Nonrenewable Natural Resource

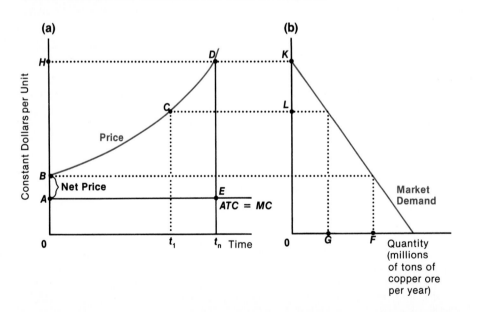

Under certain assumptions (such as perfectly competitive markets, certainty, constant average total and marginal costs of extraction, and constant market demand), the price of a nonrenewable resource rises over time at a rate equal to the pure rate of interest, as depicted by line *BD* in panel (a). Correspondingly, the annual quantity demanded (and mined) falls over time. Eventually, at time t_n, the last ton mined is also the last ton demanded. Resource exhaustion becomes a foreseen event, not an unexpected catastrophe.

values of all net prices. This schedule, therefore, equalizes the present value of all tons regardless of when they are mined; it maximizes the present value of the entire deposit.

Now consider this: Given market demand, a different gross price (measured by the height of line *BCD*) calls forth a different quantity demanded. If the price per ton of ore is *B*, quantity demanded is *F*. At higher price *C*, quantity demanded drops to *G*; at price *D*, nothing at all is demanded. Thus the rate of extraction can be expected to decline over time. Indeed, an owner will exhaust the deposit precisely at the moment at which price becomes so high (here *D*) as to eliminate demand.

The Timing of Exhaustion. How do we know that time t_n coincides with resource exhaustion? Suppose it didn't. If exhaustion had occurred earlier, as at time t_1, price thereafter (because of positive demand, zero supply) would have risen more rapidly than postulated by line segment *CD*. In our assumed world of certainty, owners would have foreseen this future rate of price rise exceeding the rate of interest. They would have reduced earlier supply—sacrificing, say $100 = N_0$ in year 0, or $133.10 = N_0 (1 + r)^3$ in year 3, in order to reap in year *n* a higher-valued net price in excess of $N_0 (1 + r)^n$. The earlier conservation would have ensured later availability and pushed the time of exhaustion from t_1 to t_n.

Correspondingly, if exhaustion had not yet occurred at time t_n, price thereafter (because of zero demand, positive supply) would have risen less rapidly than postulated by the line segment to the right of *D*. Owners would have foreseen this future rate of price rise falling short of the rate of interest. They would have reduced later supply—sacrificing in year *n* + 1, perhaps, an amount falling short of $N_0 (1 + r)^{n+1}$ in order to reap a higher-valued net price of $100 = N_0$ in year 0 or of $133.10 = N_0 (1 + r)^3$ in year 3. The later cut and earlier increase in supply would have pushed forward the time of exhaustion from t_{n+1} to t_n.

Extensions of the Analysis. The forgoing analysis can be extended in many ways. For example: What would be the effect of a higher rate of interest? Net price would have to rise at a faster rate, of course. With initial gross price *B*, the price line in panel (a) of Figure 12.10 would lie above line *BCD* to the right of *B*. Thus quantity demanded and mined would be lower in all but the initial period. Long before period t_n, the price line would cross dotted line *HK*, and demand would vanish. Yet some of the resource stock would then be unused! It would be in the interest of owners to charge an initial price lower than *B* (and sell more than *F* initially). This would make it impossible to sell as much later as in Figure 12.10. Later prices would have to be higher than in Figure 12.10. Indeed, as the smaller net price grew at the faster pace of the higher interest rate, the new price line in panel (a) would cross the old one and reach dotted line *HK* to the left of *D*. Once more, the last ton mined would become the last ton demanded, but the time of exhaustion would come earlier. (This makes intuitive sense: The higher pure rate of interest reflects greater impatience to consume now, which implies less conservation as well.)

What would be the effect of a constant extraction cost lower than *A*? An unchanged initial gross price of *B* would then produce a larger net price, and as it rose at the unchanged rate of interest, the price line would lie above *BD*. As above, this would lead to premature elimination of demand. Owners would charge an initial price lower than *B* (and sell more than *F* initially). Thus they would have to sell less later; once more, later prices would have to be above those in Figure 12.10. These higher later prices could occur only if the initial net price was larger than in Figure 12.10; that is, if not all of the decrease in cost was reflected in the lower gross price. The initially higher net price would then grow at the unchanged rate of interest, and the price line in panel (a) would start below *B*, cross line *BD*, and reach dotted line *HK* to the left of *D*. Once more, the time of exhaustion would come earlier.

In addition, one may, of course, wish to drop some of the assumptions made earlier and analyze situations in which demand and resource stock change. These changes might occur as higher output price stimulates the invention of substitutes or the discovery of new deposits.

SUMMARY

1. As a result of intertemporal decision making, capital markets arise in which certificates of indebtedness are traded, along with ownership claims to the stocks of natural resources and of physical capital goods. This chapter studies perfectly competitive capital markets under conditions of certainty. The household saving decision, a choice between present and future consumption goods, can be analyzed just like the choice between two present consumption goods by contrasting preferences with market opportunities. The preferences reflect impatience to consume now rather than later; the opportunities reflect the ability to earn interest by delaying consumption. The household's optimum combination of current and future consumption is found by equating the marginal rate of substitution of future for present goods with $1 + r$, where r is the effective annual real rate of interest.

2. The saving of households contributes to the supply of loanable funds. The quantity supplied changes with the interest rate, and the change can be separated into the substitution effect and the income effect.

3. While households have to balance their impatience to consume now with their ability to earn interest by consuming later, firms must balance their urge to take advantage of investment opportunities with their need to pay interest or forgo interest income. Their capital budgeting identifies available investment opportunities, selects investment projects to be carried out, and arranges for their financing. Given the prevailing interest rate (at which outside funds can be borrowed and the firm's own funds can be lent), a firm's investment projects can be evaluated on the basis of their *net present value*.

4. It is profitable for firms to undertake all investment projects with positive net present values. Because these values vary with the prevailing rate of interest, the quantity of loanable funds demanded by firms varies with the interest rate as well.

5. The interest rate that equates supply and demand in a perfectly competitive market for loanable funds under conditions of certainty is called the *pure rate of interest*. Its determination can also be depicted by Irving Fisher's famous diagram, contrasting a society's impatience to consume with its opportunities to invest.

6. While the essence of interest can be found by studying time preference and time productivity, the essence of capital can be found by studying income streams produced over time. With the help of the discounting process, such income streams can be used to establish the capitalized value of assets. In perfectly competitive markets and under conditions of certainty, the price of each asset will come to equal the asset's capitalized value. Each asset, therefore, will yield the same return as any other asset. In the case of reproducible assets, an asset's price will in the long run also come to equal the average total cost of producing the asset.

7. The tools discussed in this chapter can be applied to the analyses of different investment criteria (net present value versus internal rate of return, net present value versus payback method), of the separability of optimum intertemporal production and consumption decisions, of investments in human capital, and of doomsday models (predicting the sudden exhaustion of nonrenewable natural resources).

KEY TERMS

asset markets
capital
capital budgeting
capitalization
capitalized value

capital markets

certificates of indebtedness

coefficient of relative effectiveness

compounding

discounting

discount rate

effective annual rate of interest

human capital

internal rate of return

loanable-funds market

marginal time preference

marginal time productivity

negative marginal time preference

net present value

neutral marginal time preference

nominal rate of interest

norm of relative effectiveness

ownership claims

payback method

payback period

perfect liquidity

positive marginal time preference

pure rate of interest

real rate of interest

separation theorem

time productivity

HANDS-ON PRACTICE

Exercise #1

Review the section "Net Present Value Versus Internal Rate of Return." It claims that the annual cash flow pattern of +$16,000, −$20,000, and +$6,000 has two *negative* internal rates of return (−25 percent and −50 percent per year), yet has a net present value of *positive* $2,776.86 at 10-percent interest per year. Prove these claims, assuming the $16,000 is an initial receipt, followed by a $20,000 expenditure 1 year later and a $6,000 receipt 2 years later.

Solution:

a. −25-percent case: An initial balance of +$16,000 is followed 1 year later by a −25-percent return, or −$4,000, as well as a $20,000 expenditure. This produces a new balance of $16,000 − $4,000 − $20,000 = −$8,000. This is followed, in another year, by a −25-percent return (on −$8,000), or +$2,000, as well as a $6,000 receipt. This produces a new balance of −$8,000 + $2,000 + $6,000 = 0 at the end of the project.

b. −50-percent case: An initial balance of +$16,000 is followed 1 year later by a −50-percent return, or −$8,000, as well as a $20,000 expenditure. This produces a new balance of $16,000 − $8,000 − $20,000 = −$12,000. This is followed, in another year, by a −50-percent return (on −$12,000), or +$6,000, as well as a $6,000 receipt. This produces a new balance of −$12,000 + $6,000 + $6,000 = 0 at the end of the project.

c. $NPV = +\$16,000 - \dfrac{\$20,000}{1.1} + \dfrac{\$6,000}{1.21}$

$= \$16,000 - \$18,181.82 + \$4,958.68$

$= \$2,776.86.$

Exercise #2

The section noted in Exercise 1 also claims that the annual cash flow pattern of −$8,000, +$17,900, and −$10,000 has *two* positive internal rates of return (7.87 percent and 15.88 percent) and has a net present value of $8.26 at 10-percent interest per year. Prove these claims, assuming the $8,000 is an initial expenditure, followed 1 year later by the $17,900 receipt and, after another year, by the $10,000 expenditure.

Solution:

a. 7.87-percent case: An initial balance of −$8,000 is followed 1 year later by a 7.87-percent return, or −$629.60, as well as a $17,900 receipt. This produces a new balance of −$8,000 − $629.60 + $17,900

= + $9,270.40. This is followed, in another year, by a 7.87-percent return (on $9,270.40), or $729.58, as well as a $10,000 expenditure. This produces a new balance of $9,270.40 + $729.58 − $10,000 = 0 (rounded) at the end of the project.

b. 15.88-percent case: An initial balance of − $8,000 is followed 1 year later by a 15.88-percent return, or − $1,270.40, as well as a $17,900 receipt. This produces a new balance of − $8,000 − $1,270.40 + $17,900 = + $8,629.60. This is followed, in another year, by a 15.88-percent return (on $8,629.60), or $1,370.38, as well as a $10,000 expenditure. This produces a new balance of $8,629.60 + $1,370.38 − $10,000 = 0 (rounded) at the end of the project.

c. $NPV = -\$8,000 + \dfrac{\$17,900}{1.1} -$

$\dfrac{\$10,000}{1.21} = -\$8,000 + \$16,272.727 -$

$\$8,264.463 = \$8.26.$

Exercise #3

In 1623, Dutch settlers purchased Manhattan Island from American Indians for $24. If the Indians had invested these $24 at, say, 8 percent per year for the 366 years between 1623 and 1989, what would have been their principal in 1989?

Solution:

Applying the Box 12.B compound interest formula,

$$FV_{1989} = \$24\,(1.08)^{366}$$
$$= \$41,049,780,000,000.$$

More likely than not, this sum exceeds the value of Manhattan Island and all it contained in 1989.

(The Capital Budgeting computer program noted at the end of this chapter was used to generate the above answer.)

QUESTIONS AND PROBLEMS

1. Consider Figure 12.3. Let the consumer's initial position be at *A*. Where is the consumer's optimum? How can it be reached?

2. Consider this investment project: − 100, + 125 (where the expenditure occurs now and the receipt one year from now). What is the net present value at interest rates of 10 percent, 20 percent, and 30 percent? What is the highest interest rate at which it would be worth carrying out the project? Does your answer differ depending on whether you already have the funds or must borrow them?

3. Assuming a general level of interest of 5 percent per year, which is preferable:

a.   a $250 gift now or a $1,000 loan without interest for six years?

b.   a $1,000 gift now or a monthly salary increase of $50?

c.   a year's work in return for being paid $10,000 now or $1 million in 50 years?

d.   a lottery prize of $20,000 now or $1,000 per year for 30 years?

e.   buying a $5,000 car for cash now but at a discount of 5 percent or on credit with full payment required in 1 year?

4. "The pure rate of interest influences the length of time meat animals or trees are allowed to grow, the time wine or cheese is allowed to age, and the time durable goods are likely to last." Try to figure out why.

5. Compared to a decade earlier, the early 1980s brought a dramatic increase in the market price of medallions (government licenses) needed to run New York City taxicabs and in the market price of used-car rental firms (such as Rent-A-Wreck, Lease-A-Lemon, and Ugly-Duckling-Rent-A-Car). In Martin County, Kentucky, coal-mine operators became instant millionaires, and even the prices of car dealerships, mining supply stores, and houses soared. Simultaneously, hefty decreases occurred in the market price of seats on the New York Stock Exchange. Can you explain why? (*Hint:* Consider OPEC.)

6. The Passamaquoddy tidal power project has been viewed as a promising joint venture by the United States and Canada. Both parties agreed that the investment project would require heavy initial costs and would yield a flow of benefits stretching into the future. Using the same figures for costs and benefits, the Canadians calculated a negative present value for the project and rejected it, while the Americans calculated a positive present value and recommended carrying out the project. Can you explain the different results?

7. Do the following statements about *non-renewable* natural resources make sense?

a. ''Conservation means the greatest good of the greatest number, and that for the longest time'' (Gifford Pinchot, father of the American conservation movement).

b. ''Any divergence between the rate of increase over time of the net price and the rate of interest quickly leads to a retardation or speeding up of resource extraction (and an equalization of the two rates).''

8. Suppose that a campaign was mounted to recycle paper ''in order to save the trees.'' In the long run, would an increase in recycling save trees? (*Hint:* What would happen to the demand for and price of trees? To the value of tree lots?)

9. a. During a 1974 players' strike, the owners of National Football League teams rejected the charge of exploiting players and making excessive profits ($945,000 per team in 1973). Teams were then selling for $16 million, they said, which indicated a profit of only 5.9 percent per year. What do you think? (*Hints:* Remember what you have just learned about the capitalization of assets. Also consider the fact that a competing World Football League was being formed in 1973 and that many cities, including Seattle and Tampa, petitioned NFL owners for an expansion of franchises.)

b. Said the *Wall Street Journal* on March 17, 1982, p. 29: ''Proposition 13, passed in 1978, has eased the tax burden of California's property owners, but an unforseen side-effect of the tax-cutting initiative has been higher prices for new homes. . . . The median price of a new home in the state is $105,000 (half cost more, half less), compared with $69,000 for the nation as a whole.'' A statistical study confirmed that each $1 decrease in property taxes, all else being equal, had increased property values by about $7. Are you surprised? Explain.[7]

c. It has been suggested that urban renewal that takes the form of locating small public-housing projects in single-family residential areas will decrease property values near the project. Others have argued just the opposite, expecting an increase in property values. What do you think and why?

10. Draw a graph such as Figure 12.4, ''The Supply of Loanable Funds.'' Graphically, separate the income and substitution effects of a higher interest rate on saving. Is your answer unique, or might you have gotten a different one if you had drawn different indifference curves?

SELECTED READINGS

Bierman, Harold, Jr., and Seymour Smidt. *The Capital Budgeting Decision*, New York: Macmillan, 1984.

Bogachev, V., and L. Kantorovich. ''The Price of Time,'' *Problems of Economics,* February 1970, pp. 3–27.

> Translation of a 1969 article in *Kommunist,* indicating the Soviet discovery of interest.

Böhm-Bawerk, Eugen von. *The History and Critique of Interest Theories* (1884) and *The Positive Theory of Capital* (1889).

> These are volumes 1 and 2 of *Capital and Interest* (most recently published: South Holland, Ill.: Libertarian Press, 1959). The first volume provides a painstaking review of explanations for interest that have been proffered since ancient times; the second volume presents Böhm-Bawerk's own exposition.

[7]*See* Kenneth T. Rosen, ''The Impact of Proposition 13 on House Prices in Northern California: A Test of the Interjurisdictional Capitalization Hypothesis,'' *Journal of Political Economy,* February 1982, pp. 191–200.

Böhm-Bawerk, Eugen von. *Karl Marx and the Close of His System* (1896, published in English, New York: A. M. Kelley, 1949).

> A sharp attack on Marx. While Marx, the revolutionary, viewed interest as a form of exploitation that arose in the *process of production* (because a small number of capitalists exercised a monopoly in the ownership of physical capital goods badly needed by workers), Böhm-Bawerk, the theorist, views interest as arising in the *process of exchange* (as a phenomenon linked with barter across time of present for future goods), and he held that the concept would manifest itself in any economic system, regardless of time and place, even in socialism.

Denison, Edward F. *The Sources of Economic Growth in the United States and the Alternatives before Us.* New York: Committee for Economic Development, 1962; *idem. Why Growth Rates Differ: Postwar Experience in Nine Western Countries.* Washington, D.C.: Brookings Institution, 1967; and *idem. Accounting for United States Economic Growth, 1929–1969.* Washington, D.C.: Brookings Institution, 1974.

> Three of the original studies measuring the impact of human capital on growth. For a follow-up *see idem, Accounting for Slower Economic Growth: The United States in the 1970s.* Washington, D.C.: Brookings Institution, 1979; and *idem,* Trends in *American Economic Growth, 1929–1982.* Washington, D.C.: Brookings Institution, 1985.

Fisher, Irving. *The Theory of Interest.* New York: Macmillan, 1930.

> A revision of a 1907 book, dedicated "to the memory of John Rae and Eugen von Böhm-Bawerk who laid the foundations" and subtitled "As Determined by Impatience to Spend Income and Opportunity to Invest it."

Freeman, Richard B. *The Over-Educated American.* New York: Academic Press, 1976; *idem.* "The Decline in the Economic Rewards to College Education," *The Review of Economics and Statistics,* February 1977, pp. 18–29.

> A discussion of recent decreases in the returns to human investment; note the ensuing controversy in *The Journal of Human Resources,* Winter 1980.

Goeller, H. E., and Alvin M. Weinberg. "The Age of Substitutability," *The American Economic Review,* December 1978, pp. 1–11.

> A discussion of the principle of infinite substitutability, derived from a study of the crustal abundance of all elements, according to which humanity has almost inexhaustible natural resources for an infinite length of time.

Herfindahl, Orris C., and Allen V. Kneese. *Economic Theory of Natural Resources.* Columbus, Ohio: Merrill, 1974.

Hotelling, Harold. "The Economics of Exhaustible Resources," *The Journal of Political Economy,* April 1931, pp. 137–75.

Lecomber, Richard. *The Economics of Natural Resources.* New York: Wiley, 1979.

Nordhaus, William D. "World Dynamics: Measurement without Data," *Economic Journal,* December 1973, pp. 1156–83.

Schultz, Theodore W. "Investment in Human Capital," *The American Economic Review,* March 1961, pp. 1–17; *idem.* "Nobel Lecture: The Economics of Being Poor," *The Journal of Political Economy,* August 1980, pp. 639–51.

> The first of these is the presidential address to the American Economic Association.

Stigler, George J., and Gary S. Becker. "De Gustibus Non Est Disputandum," *The American Economic Review,* March 1977, pp. 76–90.

> An extension of the human capital concept to investments serving production in households rather than in firms. The capacity to appreciate music (or heroin) is shown to be increased (or decreased) by prior consumption thereof, which is seen to increase "music capital" (or decrease "euphoria capital"). Stigler won the 1982 Nobel Prize in economics.

Tietenberg, Tom. *Environmental and Natural Resource Economics.* Glenview, Ill.: Scott, Foresman and Co., 1984.

> A superb text that includes numerous chapters on depletable and renewable resources.

Tomes, Nigel. "Religion and the Rate of Return on Human Capital: The Evidence from Canada," *Canadian Journal of Economics,* February 1983, pp. 122–38.

> Analyzes 1971 census data and finds Jews with more average years of education (9.1) and a greater return on human capital (5.8 percent) than Protestants or Catholics.

Psacharopoulos, George. "Returns to Education: A Further International Update and Implications," *The Journal of Human Resources,* Fall 1985, pp. 583–604.

> Provides data for over 60 countries—for primary, secondary, and higher education.

COMPUTER PROGRAMS

The KOHLER-3 personal-computer diskettes that accompany this book contain two programs of particular interest to this chapter:

12. *Capital and Interest* includes a 28-question multiple-choice test with immediate responses to incorrect answers as well as numerous exercises concerning compounding, discounting, and capital budgeting.

Appendix C. Capital Budgeting is particularly helpful for exploring relationships among present value, future value, interest, and time.

Given any three of these values, and a compounding period of your choice, you can find the missing fourth value. The program can also be used to investigate the profitability of (negative and positive) cash flows that extend over time. It calculates an internal rate of return and also net present values at numerous discount rates of your choice.

ANALYTICAL EXAMPLE 12.1

TIME IS MONEY

In spite of the well-known saying, people often forget the time value of money. Such was the case in 1972 when *Consumer Reports* gave advice to home buyers. Builders of new homes, the magazine said, frequently offer to sell many appliances with the house: from clothes dryers, dishwashers, and garbage disposals to refrigerators, trash compactors, and washing machines. One such builder, said the magazine, offered appliances for $450, the cost of which could be added to a 27-year mortgage, increasing monthly payments by $3.32. Yet these appliances could be bought in the store for $675 and paid off in 2 years, by monthly payments of $32.71. Was the builder offering a good deal? No, said the magazine, one would be paying an extra $1,075.68 on one's mortgage (324 months × $3.32) if appliances were included on the mortgage but only $785.04 to the store (24 months × $32.71) if appliances were purchased separately.

The magazine's advice was surely wrong! Assume the homebuyer could easily have put money into a savings account at 5-percent interest per year. As Figure 12.8 so clearly shows, in the presence of interest, future dollars are less important than present ones, and this is more true the farther away the future is. When 5-percent annual interest is available, $1 payable in a year is equivalent to only $1/1.05 or about 95¢ now, $1 in 2 years to $1/1.05^2 or about 91¢ now, and $1 in 27 years to $1/1.05^{27} or about 27¢ now. If we calculate the present value of the above 2-year payment stream (assuming for convenience that one-half of $785.04 is paid at the end of each year), it comes to

$$\frac{\$392.52}{1.05} + \frac{\$392.52}{1.05^2} = \$373.83 + \$356.03 = \$729.86.$$

If we, similarly, calculate the present value of the 27-year payment stream (assuming for convenience that $\frac{1}{27}$ of $1,075.68 is paid at the end of each year), it comes to

$$\frac{\$39.84}{1.05} + \frac{\$39.84}{1.05^2} + \ldots + \frac{\$39.84}{1.05^{27}} = \$37.94 + \$36.14 +$$
$$\ldots + \$10.67 = \$583.38.$$

This means that someone could have put $583.38 at 5-percent interest per year into a savings account and taken out $39.84 at the end of each of 27 years and would have exactly exhausted the account. On the other hand, such a person would have had to place $729.86 into such an account in order to make the two near-term payments of $392.52. Thus the builder's deal was better after all. Note: Had we taken account of inflation, as we have not, our argument could have been strengthened.

Source: "Notes to Homebuyers on Financing Future Schlock," *Consumer Reports,* April 1972.

ANALYTICAL EXAMPLE 12.2

IS THERE INTEREST UNDER SOCIALISM?

Throughout history, there have been those who looked upon interest as something immoral. These include Moses and Aristotle, Mohammed and medieval scholastics, Karl Marx, and, more recently, the Ayatollah Khomeini. Marx taught socialists to associate interest with the idle rich; that is, with bloated bondholders, who were getting income for nothing. The Soviets, accordingly, claimed for decades that interest played no role in their system.

Yet, under socialism no less than under capitalism, there exist near-infinite opportunities to invest, and many of these must be forgone because people are impatient to consume now. Thus a pure rate of interest exists regardless of whether anyone is willing to admit it! As Soviet planners soon discovered, the basic truths depicted by Figure 12.7 are not confined to capitalism. Marxist ideology, however, prevented the Soviets from identifying, with the help of their economy's pure interest rate, the most productive investment projects. Planners, therefore, had no way to direct the limited resources released from present consumption to the most productive projects first. They added outlays to receipts without regard to their timing, and calculated, in effect, the net present values of investment projects at a zero-interest rate (akin to the zero-interest column of Table 12.3). As a result, planners found many more projects worthwhile than could possibly be carried out with the resources that could be spared from current consumption.

To choose among all these "worthwhile" investment projects, the planners calculated for each project a **payback period,** the number of years it takes for initial investment outlays to be paid back by (undiscounted) future receipts. (Thus a project with annual cash flows of $-100, +30, +30, +30, +30$ has a payback period of 3.33 years.) The planners then compared actual payback periods with an *arbitrary norm* (such as "4 years or sooner") and thereby reduced the potential number of projects to a feasible one.

As was noted in Application 1, "Conflicting Investment Criteria," the payback method involves, of course, the crude application of an interest rate without mentioning the term. (In medieval times, people similarly talked of making a "4-year purchase," instead of lending a sum at 25-percent interest per year, because four annual 25-unit payments of money returned an initial 100-unit sum.)

Indeed, Soviet planners have at times also calculated the *reciprocal* of the payback period (1/3.33 in our earlier example, or .30), and they have called this reciprocal the

coefficient of relative effectiveness. Planners compared it to an arbitrary **norm of relative effectiveness** (such as ".25 or more") to weed out investment projects. Note: These planners were, in effect, comparing something like an internal rate of return (of, say, 30 percent per year) with an interest rate (of, say, 25 percent per year).

Yet the Soviets utilized *different* norms of relative effectiveness for different industries. As a result, they rejected investment projects in some industries in favor of those in others, although the former could have contributed much more to net present value and hence economic growth. (Consider Table 12.3. Let the economy's pure rate of interest be 10 percent per year. Now imagine applying a "norm of relative effectiveness" of .05 to projects (A) and (B), of .15 to projects (C) and (D), and of .25 to project (E). If you recognize the given "norms" as code words for interest rates of 5 percent, 15 percent, and 25 percent per year, you see from Table 12.3 that projects (A) and (C) will be accepted but that projects (B), (D), and (E) will be rejected. Yet this is not the correct decision, as the 10-percent column reveals.) According to Soviet Nobel Prize winner L. V. Kantorovich (a Biography of whom appears in Chapter 5 of the *Student Workbook* that accompanies this text), the Soviet Union could have gotten, around 1960, from 30-percent to 50-percent more output from its existing resources. He attributed this fact in part to the planners' failure to make investment decisions with the help of an undisguised and uniform equilibrium interest rate. Perhaps his numbers were exaggerated to emphasize the importance of finally recognizing the crucial role of interest, even under socialism.[a]

[a]Judith Thornton, "Differential Capital Charges and Resource Allocation in Soviet Industry," *Journal of Political Economy,* May/June 1971, pp. 545–61. Her calculations were confined to Soviet industry for 1960–64. They suggested possible increases in value added of 3–4 percent if differential capital charges were eliminated. For further discussion of the issue, including the effects of recent economic reforms in the Soviet Union and China, *see* Heinz Kohler, *Comparative Economic Systems* (Glenview, Ill.: Scott, Foresman and Co., 1989).

ANALYTICAL EXAMPLE 12.3

ARE YOU WORTH YOUR WEIGHT IN GOLD?

Let us suppose you are 25 years old and have just graduated from college. Your lifetime income (in present dollars) may come to $800,000 (see Table 12.5). Yet this money will not be earned all at once. Suppose it comes to you in 40 annual installments of $20,000 each. If the pure rate of interest were 10 percent per year, you could calculate the present value of yourself as

$$\frac{\$20,000}{1.10} + \frac{\$20,000}{1.10^2} + \ldots + \frac{\$20,000}{1.10^{40}} = \$195,581.$$

Now suppose yours is one of the weights shown in column (1) below. Because 1 pound *avoirdupois* (in which humans are usually weighed) equals 14.58333 troy ounces (in which gold is weighed), your weight can be converted as shown in column (2). Let the present price of gold be $554 per troy ounce. Then column (3) indicates the gold value of your weight.

CLOSE-UP

Weight (pounds) (1)	Weight (troy ounces) (2)	Gold Value of Weight (3)
125	1822.92	$1,009,898
150	2187.50	1,211,875
175	2552.08	1,413,852
200	2916.67	1,615,835

A comparison of any number in column (3) with your present value calculated above indicates that you are *not* worth your weight in gold. But this can be remedied. If you went on a diet and brought your weight down to 353.03 troy ounces, or about 24 pounds, you would be worth your weight in gold!

Source: Adapted from Harry G. Johnson, "Are You Worth Your Weight in Gold?" in Harry G. Johnson and Burton A. Weisbrod, eds., *The Daily Economist* (Englewood Cliffs, N.J.: Prentice-Hall, 1973), pp. 30–33.

CLOSE-UP 12.1

OWNING VERSUS LEASING GOVERNMENT BUILDINGS

The calculation of present value can help government officials decide which is more advantageous: owning or leasing public buildings. Such a choice had to be made in the mid-1970s, when the federal government wanted to acquire a complex of buildings at the University of Virginia for use as the Civil Service Commission's Federal Executive Institute and Managerial Training Center. The General Services Administration (GSA), following guidelines issued by the Office of Management and Budget, used a 7-percent discount rate to calculate the net present value of construction and ownership costs at $27.2 million and then a 9-percent discount rate to calculate the net present value of lease payments at $17.2 million. The GSA recommended leasing the buildings. The General Accounting Office (GAO), however, argued that a single discount rate should be used—namely, one based on the Treasury's borrowing costs over a 30-year period. On that basis, the GAO calculated the net present value of ownership costs at $15.6 million and that of leasing at $16.0 million and recommended ownership of the buildings. (As the discussion of benefit-cost analysis in Chapter 16 will show, there exists much controversy on what constitutes the proper discount rate to evaluate public projects. Some argue that it should equal the rate of return that resources used in the public sector could earn in the private one instead. Others disagree. There is general agreement, however, that a *uniform* rate should be used for all government projects.)

Source: Charles J. Stokes, *Economics for Managers* (New York: McGraw-Hill, 1979), pp. 471–74. For additional discussion of this complex issue, see J. Callahan, "The Lease Versus Purchase Decision in the Public Sector," *National Tax Journal,* June 1981, pp. 235–39; and Mark A. Willis, "Leasing—A Financial Option for States and Localities?" Federal Reserve Bank of New York, *Quarterly Review,* Winter 1981–82, pp. 42–46.

12A

The Concept of Rent

Adam Smith and his immediate followers saw society as split into three distinct classes:

1. the *workers* (or proletariat), who supplied the services of human resources only (and received wages),

2. the *capitalists* (or bourgeoisie), who supplied the services of capital resources only (and received interest), and

3. the *landlords* (or aristocrats), who supplied the services of natural resources only (and received rents).

This scheme served the classical economists well. In their time, each of these classes of people performed a different function in society. These economists were interested, therefore, in the **functional distribution of income;** that is, the apportionment of national income among the owners of human resources, capital resources, and natural resources. Nowadays, however, it is not appropriate to equate this functional income distribution with a distribution among distinct social classes because any given individual can and often does own and supply the services of more than one type of resource. Thus any given individual is likely to be a member of more than one of the classical economists' classes of in-

come recipients. Modern economists, therefore, tend to pay more attention to the **personal distribution of income,** which is the apportionment of national income *among persons* (each of whom is likely to receive several types of income), as Chapter 14 will show.

Having discussed labor and wages in Chapter 11 and now capital and interest in Chapter 12, we shall *not* devote an entire chapter to natural resources and rents. There are at least two reasons. First, as was noted in Chapter 1, many resources considered natural resources by noneconomists are, in fact, considered capital resources by modern economists. Second, the term *rent* is used by hardly anyone nowadays in the strict original sense of a payment for the services of natural resources. In everyday usage, the term refers to payment for the use of apartments, cars, land, and similar items that are used by one person but owned by someone else. Economists use the term in a different sense still. They give the name **economic rent** to that *portion* of a payment for the services of any resource (human, capital, or natural) that exceeds the minimum amount necessary to bring forth the quantity that is in fact supplied. (Rent is thus analogous to *producer surplus* in the markets for goods.)

Consider Figure 12.11. Panels (a) through (c) picture three rather different market supplies of the services of three unspecified types of resources. Given demand, the price per hour of service turns out to be 0A in every case. The quantities actually supplied equal 0B, 0C, and 0D, respectively. Note: Given the vertical supply line in panel (a), which intersects the horizontal axis at B, the entire shaded area is economic rent as defined above because quantity 0B would be supplied even at a zero price. The situation is different in panel (b). The payment represented by the dotted rectangle is necessary to bring forth quantity 0C. The shaded area above it is economic rent. Finally, in panel (c), the necessary payments equal the dotted area: A first unit of resource service would be supplied for as little as 0E, a last unit for only DF. In fact, every unit is paid the price of 0A. The roughly triangular shaded area, therefore, measures the amount of economic rent. Economists are careful, however, to distinguish *pure rent* from *quasi rent*.

PURE RENT

The excess payment called economic rent is a **pure rent** when the quantity supplied *is totally unresponsive to its price in the long run* because the resource in question can neither be destroyed nor produced by people. The classical economists pointed to the "original and indestructible powers of the soil" as an example of such a resource. The British economist David Ricardo (1772–1823), in a famous debate about the high price of "corn" (a term then referring to grain), argued against those who blamed high corn prices on high rents charged tenant farmers by "greedy" landlords. Consider Figure 12.12. Because the Napoleonic Wars had interrupted foreign trade, argued Ricardo, England's supply of corn was unusually low, as at S. Given market demand, D, the price of corn was high (0a). Production was profitable on many farms. Farm A was producing quantity 0b, Farm B quantity 0c, and Farm C quantity 0d, and each equated

FIGURE 12.11

Economic Rents

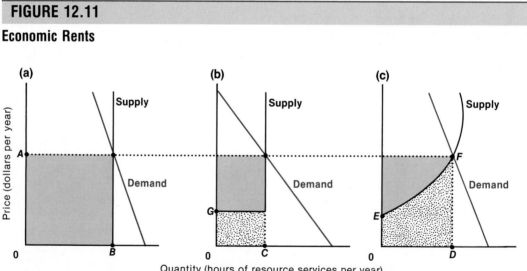

Economists give the name *economic rent* to that portion of a payment for the services of any resource (human, capital, or natural) that exceeds the minimum amount necessary to bring forth the quantity that is in fact supplied. Given the differently shaped supply and demand curves shown in the three markets pictured here, price (0A) is the same in all markets, but rents (shaded areas) and minimum necessary payments (dotted areas) differ in each market.

high market price with marginal cost. Now consider, Ricardo argued, each tenant farmer's position *prior* to the payment of rent to the owners of land. Because different plots of land have different fertility (an example of what Ricardo viewed as the "original and indestructible powers of the soil"), equal human effort applied to different plots of land is unequally rewarded: On Farm A, fertility is highest; output per unit of input is highest; the curve of average total cost (excluding rent) is lowest (ATC_x). On Farm C, fertility is lowest; output per unit of input is lowest; the curve of average total cost (excluding rent) is highest. Farm B's position is somewhere between the two. For Farm A, revenue minus cost (excluding rent), therefore, equals the shaded area; for Farm B, revenue minus cost (excluding rent) equals the crosshatched area; for Farm C, revenue minus cost (excluding rent) equals zero.

Who will collect the net revenue shown by the shaded and crosshatched areas? The landlords will collect this revenue in the form of rents, said Ricardo. Tenant farmer A will have no choice but to hand over the money represented by the shaded area, for the alternative is to farm inferior land, like C, which provides no net revenue. The tenant of Farm B will be in a similar position. Landlords therefore will pocket *differential* rent, reflecting precisely the different fertilities of their soil.

Would taxing the rents reduce the price of corn? Of course not, said Ricardo. Abolishing tariffs and allowing the free import of corn, however, *would* reduce the price. Supply would rise to S^*, and the price of corn would fall to $0e$. Domestic production would drop from $0g$ to $0f$, and imports would equal fh. Production on Farms B and C would cease, that on Farm A would contract to $0i$. Rents would be gone. Although the supply of the "powers of the soil" would be unchanged, like the vertical line in panel (a) of Figure 12.11, the decreased price of corn would so reduce the derived demand for corn-growing land that landlords would not be able to collect a penny of rent.

Modern economists are less likely to think of the fertility of the soil as conducive to payments of pure rent. They are too aware of humanity's

FIGURE 12.12

Ricardo's Differential Rents

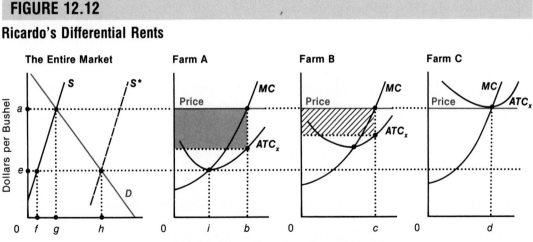

When the price of a product is high enough to generate strong demand for inputs in fixed supply (such as fertile plots of land), the owners of those inputs are able to collect rent. Plots of land with different fertility, argued Ricardo, will yield differential rent (equal to the shaded area for Farm A, the crosshatched area for Farm B, and zero for Farm C). These modern concepts and graphs illustrate Ricardo's verbal argument.

ability to destroy as well as produce this fertility. They point instead to such nonreproducible and unique aspects as the *location* of a plot of land or the special talents of famous athletes, models, movie actors, scientists, singers, or TV personalities. These special talents or unique features are best represented by the type of supply curve shown in panels (a) and (b) of Figure 12.11. Panel (a), for instance, might refer to the services provided by the parcel of land at the corner of New York City's 5th Avenue and 50th Street (site of Rockefeller Center and Saks Fifth Avenue). Or it might refer to an oil field or mineral deposit. Panel (b) might depict the supply of labor services by Muhammed Ali, Lauren Hutton, Marilyn Monroe, Albert Einstein, Joan Baez, or Dan Rather. As long as demand for such services is high enough—the quantity demanded exceeding $0B$ at a zero price in panel (a) and exceeding $0C$ at a price of $0G$ in panel (b)—their sellers receive pure rent. Pure rent serves the function, of course, of allocating the resource in question to the highest-valued use. Except by a fortuitous act of nature, even a huge pure rent will not call forth increased supply in the long run. On the other hand, even the complete elimination of pure rent will not reduce supply. The realization of this fact gave rise to the **single-tax movement** of Henry George.

THE SINGLE-TAXERS

Henry George (1837–1897) was an American seaman, journalist, and printer who argued for the finance of all governmental activities by a single tax on the ever rising incomes of the owners of land. He viewed these incomes as pure rents, land being absolutely fixed in supply, but subject to ever rising demand associated with population growth and its westward expansion. Landowners, he argued, contributed nothing to deserve such "windfall gains." George's ideas were popular among the poor, and his book, *Progress and Poverty,* became the all-time best-seller in economics. It sold millions of copies and brought him international fame. Indeed, as a

candidate of the Labor and Socialist parties, he was almost elected mayor of New York in 1886, outpolling another would-be politician, Theodore Roosevelt.

In the end, George's ideas proved unacceptable. For one thing, pure rents accrue to others besides the owners of land. Thus equity would call for taxing Muhammed Ali as much as the owner of a Wall Street parcel of land. Indeed, one might argue, the original owners of high-rent land are likely to have long sold it to others at a correspondingly high price, leaving current owners with nothing more than a normal interest return on their investment in the land. Real-world "rents," therefore, are a mixture of many types of payments, including implicit interest for the money owners have invested in land, buildings, and other improvements on this land, implicit wages for the work of landowners, reimbursement for air conditioning, heating, and general maintenance expenses, and, finally, pure rent. It is next to impossible to separate these elements. Furthermore, even the taxation of all pure rents would provide insufficient revenue to finance government.

Still, Henry George's ideas linger on. New York City's Henry George School of Social Science and a handful of George's supporters at the University of Missouri still promote these ideas. Some cities, such as Pittsburgh, place a higher tax on the assessed value of land than on the assessed value of buildings standing on it. And many cities, confusing real-world "rent" with pure rent, impose rent controls with disastrous results.[1] Similar disaster awaits those who confuse quasi rent with pure rent.

QUASI RENT

The excess payment defined by economists as economic rent is called a **quasi rent** when the quantity supplied *is responsive to its price in the*

---

[1]See Analytical Example 6.2, "The Political Economy of Milk and Housing," on p. 213.

long run because the resource in question can be destroyed and produced by people. For such resources, the elimination of rent does not change the quantity supplied in the short run but does change quantity supplied in the long run. All returns to human and real capital made by people are quasi rents as long as these resources are temporarily fixed in supply. While we cannot produce at will more parcels of land with the unique location of Wall Street, we can produce more apartment houses, oil tankers, and orchards planted with apple trees. While we cannot produce at will more people with the unique talents of Muhammed Ali or Albert Einstein, we can produce quite ordinary dentists and economics professors. Let panel (a) of Figure 12.11 represent the temporarily fixed supply, with no alternative uses, of the services of apartment houses, oil tankers, and apple orchards. Let panels (b) and (c) represent the supply of services, with some alternative uses, of dentists or economics professors. Imagine that a tax eliminated all of the rents. Surely, unlike in the pure rent case, supply would change in the long run. If the price for their services was cut to zero now, apartment houses, oil tankers, and apple orchards would eventually disappear because nobody would make the costly investment in their maintenance and replacement. Similarly, if the price for the services of dentists and professors was cut to eliminate rent and equal that of their best alternative employment, dentists and professors would eventually disappear because nobody would make the costly investment in the acquisition of the requisite type of human capital. By the same token, the payment of quasi rents so high that owners of apartment dwellings, oil tankers, or dental skills receive an unusually high return on their investment will eventually increase the stocks of these resources and the services supplied by them. The test of quasi rent versus pure rent is this: If the change in rent has no effect on long-run supply or has no predictable effect (because nature does the supplying), the rent is a pure rent. If the change in rent does affect long-run supply (because people do the supplying), the rent is a quasi rent.

KEY TERMS

economic rent
functional distribution of income
personal distribution of income
pure rent
quasi rent
single-tax movement

HANDS-ON PRACTICE

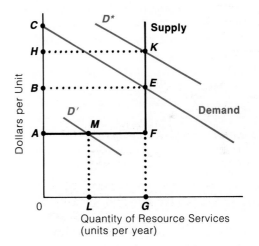

a. Given *demand* and *supply* intersecting at E, identify the income received by the resource in question. Is there any economic rent?

b. Would you change your answers if demand rose to D^*?

c. Would you change your answers if demand fell to D'?

d. What would you have to know in order to determine whether the economic rent in question was pure rent or quasi rent?

Solution:

a. Income: 0*BEG*. Yes, there is economic rent of *ABEF*.

b. Income would be larger: 0*HKG*. Rent would be larger: *AHKF*.

c. Income would be smaller: 0*AML*. There would be no economic rent at all.

d. One would have to know whether the supply of the resource in the long run could neither be reduced nor increased by people (rent would then be pure rent) or whether people could change the supply (making rent quasi rent).

Exercise #2

The graphs below pictures a perfectly competitive industry in long-run equilibrium.

a. Are the owners of these three cheese-producing firms (a sample of many more firms not shown) receiving economic rent? Explain.

b. How would you change your answer if demand rose to *D**?

c. If you have identified any economic rent, indicate whether it is pure rent or quasi rent.

Solution:

a. Yes, even though they are making zero economic profits. In the short run, any return above variable cost is economic rent. Even if

a firm could cover only part of its fixed cost, this would be preferable to shutting down at once and making a loss equal to fixed cost. The firms pictured here, of course, are covering all of this fixed cost precisely, and this return to fixed inputs is their economic rent. Note: The areas under the marginal-cost curves up to the chosen profit-maximizing (marginal-cost- and marginal-revenue- equating) quantities (0*A*, 0*B*, and 0*C*, respectively) measure the three firms' total variable costs (dotted). The roughly triangular shaded areas between the marginal-cost and marginal-revenue lines up to the chosen quantities measure these firms' fixed costs and, therefore, their rent. This must be so because total revenue (price 0*E* times chosen output levels) equals total cost in each case (price = average total cost at the chosen output levels).

b. If demand rose to *D**, each firm would have a higher price and marginal revenue (corresponding to the intersection of *D** with supply). Each firm would produce more (corresponding to the intersection of the higher marginal-revenue line with the given lines of marginal cost). Each firm would be making positive economic profit (because, in each case, at the newly chosen quantity, marginal revenue = price would exceed average total cost). Thus economic rent would

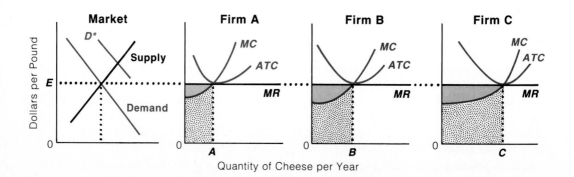

be higher (equal to fixed cost plus economic profit), and it would again be measured by the area between the lines of marginal cost and marginal revenue up to the chosen output quantity.

c. The rent is clearly quasi rent because people are quite capable, in the long run, of enlarging and multiplying cheese-producing enterprises or of reducing existing ones in size and numbers.

ANALYTICAL EXAMPLE 12A.1

THE COST OF THE DRAFT

In 1980, when Congress debated the renewal of the military draft, many argued that the draft would avoid the high budgetary cost of the volunteer army. Yet a draft army is also costly; the costs are simply borne by different people. Consider the 1965 cross-section study by Walter Oi, which is summarized (and simplified) in the accompanying graph. From geographic differences in enlistments, civilian incomes, and unemployment rates, Oi estimated the supply curve of military personnel shown here and juxtaposed it with demand. Under a volunteer army, the actual 1965 enlistments of 472,000 soldiers would have cost the taxpayers $5,900 per enlistee, or a total of $2.7848 billion (area 0abc). In fact, only $2,500 per enlistee was paid, or a total of $1.18 billion (area 0ade), an apparent saving of $1.6048 billion.

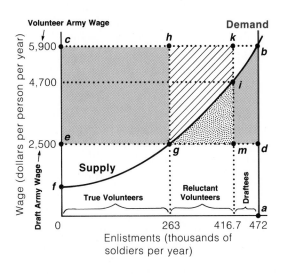

Yet an implicit tax on enlistees was being substituted for an explicit tax on all citizens: At the lower draft-army wage, only 263,000 of enlistees were true volunteers. Under the volunteer army, they would have received economic rent equal to area *fghc*; in the draft army they received only *fge* of economic rent, hence they lost *eghc* (shaded), or $894.2 million.

Another 153,700 enlistees were "reluctant volunteers," who enlisted only to avoid being drafted. They lost economic rent equal to *gikh* (crosshatched). They also lost an additional amount: One can always assume that the minimum price at which any unit of a resource is voluntarily supplied to a specific use—the height of the supply curve—equals that resource's next-best income opportunity, adjusted for compensating wage differentials. Thus the first enlistee in the graph is willing to enlist for as little as 0*f* and the last one only for *ab* because their alternative incomes or aversions to army life differ to this extent. It follows that reluctant volunteers also lost *gmi* (dotted), which represents pay these people require to volunteer for the army and be fully compensated for (1) the forgone alternative of the best civilian jobs they could get plus (2) any aversion they might have to army life. The total implicit tax on reluctant volunteers thus came to area *gmkh,* or $522.58 million.

There were, finally, 55,300 involuntary draftees. They lost economic rent of *ibk,* plus forgone civilian income or wage differentials of at least *mdbi* (shaded), or no less than $188.02 million. (Because the actual draftees probably were not the same people who would have volunteered at the $5,900 wage, but people on the supply curve to the right of point *b,* the implicit tax on them may have been much higher than *mdbi*).

Thus annual total losses to enlistees (area *edbc*) came to at least $1.6048 billion, easily matching the taxpayers' gain. Indeed, there were added losses, such as the costs to those taking less preferred, but draft-exempt jobs, to those staying in school to escape the draft, and to those engaging in illegal draft evasion, and to others.

Note again: The presentation here has been simplified in order to highlight the fact that the true cost of the draft is at least as high as the (seemingly higher) budgetary cost of the volunteer army. To the extent that reluctant volunteers as well as draftees occupy places under the supply curve far to the right of point *b,* and would truly volunteer only at a wage of, say, $50,000 per year, the true cost is even higher than shown above. (Can you see why the true cost of the draft would be reduced if randomly drafted individuals were allowed, as happened during the U.S. Civil War, to purchase substitutes? Then a draftee earning $50,000 in a civilian job, and facing $5,000 of military pay, could pay $20,000 to get someone earning $10,000 to volunteer in his place, and both individuals would be better off—barring the possibility that one of them is killed in action, of course!)

Note also: Those who have been fretting about the ever increasing (budgetary) cost of the U.S. volunteer army have pointed to the low cost of the Soviet army. Yet the seemingly low Soviet budgetary figures hide a much larger real cost: Ever since 1960, Soviet draftees have received monetary and in-kind income that equaled only one-half to one-third of their civilian income forgone.

Sources: Walter Y. Oi, "The Economic Cost of the Draft," *The American Economic Review,* May 1967, pp. 39–62; and Earl R. Brubaker, "The Opportunity Costs of Soviet Military Conscripts," in Joint Economic Committee, Congress of the United States, *Soviet Economic Prospects for the Seventies* (Washington, D.C.: U.S. Government Printing Office, 1973), pp. 163–74.

CLOSE-UP 12A.1

THE PRICE OF BEAUTY

"God makes models," it has been said, "and He doesn't make many of them." As a result, the market for models is depicted well by panel (b) of Figure 12.11. In 1980, four leading agencies—Ford Models, Inc., Wilhelmina Models, Inc., Elite Model Management, and Zoli—were battling each other for the limited supply of this gift of nature. Advertisers complained that the cost of buying status in the form of pretty faces had become outrageous. But the prices kept rising. New York's top three agencies each listed 15 to 20 models grossing over $100,000 a year. Most coveted were the exclusive contracts to represent cosmetic products. These contracts ranged from $50,000 to $300,000 annually and lasted up to 5 years, while requiring only 15 to 30 days of work a year. In 1979, Clotilde, a model representing Shiseido's flagship cosmetic line, was earning $190,000 a year. Lauren Hutton, representing Revlon's Ultima II cosmetics, was working under a $250,000 an-

nual contract. And Cheryl Tiegs was earning $300,000 a year, selling her lips, eyes, and face to Cover Girl makeup (Noxell Corporation). Even then, Noxell didn't get the rights to her hair or legs; they belonged to Bristol-Myers Clairesse hair coloring and, more recently, to Sears, Roebuck and Co., which paid a "seven figure" sum to get Ms. Tiegs to promote its "personality jeans." Unfortunately for the models, nature that giveth also taketh away. Beauty is perishable; a female model's career averages only 6 years. (Male models, such as William Loock, may work into their sixties but earn much less than women.)

Sources: Gwen Kinkead, "The Price of Beauty Is Getting Beyond Compare," *Fortune,* December 3, 1979, pp. 60–66; Dave Lindorff, "$125 an Hour: The Male Models," *The New York Times,* May 18, 1980, p. F3; "Cheryl Tiegs and Sears, Roebuck," *ibid.,* December 7, 1980, p. F19.

6

The Market
Economy as
a Whole

*These chapters show how all the different
markets found in the economy fit together in
an interdependent whole. In addition, the
overall performance of the market economy
is assessed by the two most popular criteria,
efficiency and equity.*

13

General Equilibrium

All modern economies are characterized by an incredible degree of interdependence because millions of households and firms participate in an intricate system of specialization and exchange. The activities of such multitudes of separate decision makers must be carefully coordinated; this coordination can be accomplished deliberately, with the help of central managers, or spontaneously, with the help of markets. In this book, we focus on the market economy entirely, but so far we have studied only pieces of it. One at a time, as if they existed in isolation from all the rest, we studied households in their dual roles as demanders of goods (Chapters 2 and 3) and suppliers of resource services (Chapters 11 and 12). We studied firms in their dual roles as suppliers of goods (Chapters 4 and 5) and demanders of resource services (Chapters 11 and 12). We also studied how equilibrium is established, both in the short run and in the long run, under a variety of conditions: perfect competition (Chapter 6) or imperfect competition (Chapters 7–9); certainty (Chapter 6) or uncertainty (Chapter 10).

Throughout these discussions, however, the basic approach was to focus on one decision maker or one market at a time and to ignore the many interrelationships among them.

Ceteris paribus, "all else being equal," became a key phrase as we studied, again and again, a **partial equilibrium,** a situation in one part of the economy that contained no innate tendency to change because, for example, an individual household had maximized utility, an individual firm maximized profit, or an individual market equated supply and demand—given, in each case, assumed data concerning the rest of the economy. Recall, for example, how the consumer's optimum was derived, *given* money income, the prices of goods, and preferences. Recall how the competitive producer's optimum was derived, *given* the price of output, the prices of inputs, and technology. Or recall how equilibrium in the market for a consumption good was derived, *given* market supply and demand and therefore the numbers of producers and consumers and all the factors that determine their individual supplies and demands.

For a wide range of problems, this partial equilibrium approach is, in fact, quite sufficient. Ignoring interrelationships often incurs only a small loss of predictive accuracy. The previous chapters have provided a multitude of examples. But the time has come to recognize that each partial equilibrium is part of a vast interdependent process. The economic problem of scarcity is not being tackled by a multitude of different processes occurring independently of each other, side by side, each one proceeding in its own track and being careful not to get in the way of the others. Nor are these processes occurring sequentially, with households deciding on the supply of resource services on Mondays, firms on their input demands on Tuesdays, market equilibrium established on Wednesdays, the incomes then earned giving rise to the demand for goods on Thursdays, which, perhaps, is satisfied by production and supply on Fridays. Instead, the price system is always busy fitting all these activities together, arranging a *simultaneous and mutual* determination of all prices and quantities. Economists wonder: Does the price system also produce a **general equilibrium,** a state of the economy in which billions of optimizing decisions by millions of decision makers are compatible with each other because all input and output markets are in equilibrium at the same time? Or does order in some markets, perhaps, *imply* disorder in others and utter chaos overall? Such is the subject of the present chapter. We begin by reviewing some of the basic features of economic systems just alluded to.

A UNIVERSAL FEATURE: LARGE-SCALE SPECIALIZATION

One thing that all modern economic systems have in common is that they are extremely complex because most people are participants in a vast scheme of specialization. Consider these facts about the United States in the 1980s: Its economy includes some 88 million households (mostly families, but also individuals living alone), some 20 million firms (single proprietorships, partnerships, and corporations), and over 80,000 separate governments (local, state, and federal). All

of these make economic choices about the production and apportionment of millions of goods and the utilization of as many resources. (Consider the many types and qualities of resources contained in each of the three broad classes of resources—human, natural, and capital—discussed in Chapter 1.)

Conceivably, of course, each and every good could be produced by the very same people who consume it. Each household, for instance, could be a totally self-sufficient unit of production and consumption, very much like Robinson Crusoe. It could use whatever resources it had, produce its own food, clothing, shelter, and so on, and be totally independent of the rest of humanity. In fact, however, this is the exception rather than the rule. In the United States, people consume little, if anything, of what they themselves produce. They are part of a grand division of labor. They exchange most or all of their own production with others who similarly specialize. These others, furthermore, are apt to be not a few identifiable persons, but literally hundreds of thousands of unknown people: farmers in Kansas, factory workers in Michigan, tin miners in Bolivia, sheep ranchers in Australia, oil workers in the North Sea, typists in California. All of these, in one way or another, help provide each of us with the goods we do consume.

Why this elaborate setup? Because we all get more goods when the process of production is organized on the basis of specialization and exchange rather than on the basis of self-sufficiency of every person or region. Imagine how few and primitive our goods would be if we insisted on making all of them ourselves or if, like Crusoe, we had to do so. A look at some of the small self-contained communities in this world, such as those of the African Bushmen, the Amazon Indians, or the Greenland Eskimos, illustrates this point.

Adam Smith (1723–90), a Biography of whom appears in Chapter 13 of the *Student Workbook* that accompanies this text, articulated the advantages of the division of labor 200 years

Smith — in Free Market, equilibrium established via price mechanism

ago when he pointed out that a pinmaker could not produce 20 pins in a day if he himself had to do everything that was required—drawing out the wire, straightening it, cutting it, pointing it, grinding it for receiving the head, making the head, and so on. Yet Smith observed that 10 people, only poorly equipped with machinery but with the proper division of labor among them, were able to make 48,000 pins in one day.

This particular example, of course, refers to specialization within a firm, but Smith was well aware of the benefits from specialization on a larger scale. He knew how the wealth of nations could be increased by the kind of regional cooperation involved in international trade among countries. Yet, as this very example serves to show, use of the division of labor is not a feature peculiar to the U.S. economy; it is a worldwide phenomenon. And the benefits, measured in greater production of goods, are enormous. Unfortunately, where there is a benefit, there is often a cost. And so it is here. Americans, Russians, and all other people who enjoy the obvious material benefits derived from a division of labor have to pay a price. They must divert valuable resources to deal with the complex problem of *coordination* to which the division of labor gives rise.

A UNIVERSAL PROBLEM: ENSURING COORDINATION

As people interact in their economic activities, not only within each firm and each nation, but even with people throughout the world, everything that one person does comes to intermingle with the actions of all others in an endless web. Any one action requires, directly and indirectly, appropriate complementary actions by thousands of other people. Think of a simple good—for example, a cake—and how it typically comes to you. Imagine the countless people and the countless types of natural and capital resources that are necessary to produce the ingredients of a cake. And trace in your mind the countless stages

through which each of these ingredients must travel before they turn into a cake. Consider how many more resources are involved in bringing it to you! Then think of the many other goods you consume, every day. How easy it would be for something to go wrong somewhere in the complicated sets of events that create these goods and transport them through space and time.

In 1845, Frédéric Bastiat, a famous French economist, was having just such thoughts.[1]

On coming to Paris for a visit, I said to myself: Here are a million human beings who would all die in a few days if supplies of all sorts did not flow into this great metropolis. It staggers the imagination to try to comprehend the vast multiplicity of objects that must pass through its gates tomorrow, if its inhabitants are to be preserved from the horrors of famine, insurrection, and pillage. And yet all are sleeping peacefully at this moment without being disturbed for a single instant by the idea of so frightful a prospect. . . .

How does each succeeding day manage to bring to this gigantic market just what is necessary—neither too much nor too little? What, then, is the resourceful and secret power that governs the amazing regularity of such complicated movements, a regularity in which everyone has such implicit faith, although his prosperity and his very life depend upon it?

One could write a similar story today. Think of New York. As in Bastiat's Paris, millions of people are living there. In a matter of days, they would all starve without a continual influx of goods. And what variety and quantity of goods these are! Thousands of tons of bread and fruit, trainloads of meat and coal, furniture and shirts, hairspray and bobby pins! These goods come not only from the surrounding countryside, but from the farthest corners of the globe. For days and months, by air, sea, and land, they are traveling, with New York as their destination. The same is

[1]Translated by the author from ''Il n'y a pas de principes absolus,'' in *Sophismes Économiques*, in *Oeuvres Complètes de Frédéric Bastiat*, vol. 4 (Paris: Guillaume, 1907), pp. 94–97. *See* Bastiat, *Economic Sophisms* (Princeton, N.J.: D. Van Nostrand Co., 1964) for an English edition.

true, on a smaller scale, for every city, town, and village in this country. But who is in charge of planning and guiding all this activity on which our existence depends? Who makes sure that the activities of every person mesh perfectly with those of all other persons?

For New York and the U.S. economy, the answer to these questions is ''nobody at all.'' For Moscow and the Soviet economy, the answer would be quite different. These two economic systems differ drastically in the way they try to achieve **economic order,** a state of affairs in which the specialized activities of all the people engaged in the division of labor are well coordinated.

Whenever people decide to engage in a division of labor, their separate activities can be coordinated in one of two ways: by **deliberate coordination** or by **spontaneous coordination.** The former approach is easier to understand; it tends to be the first solution that people consider when thinking about the coordination problem.

Characteristics of Deliberate Coordination

The separate economic activities of people engaged in a division of labor can be coordinated deliberately by a manager or a central planner. This deliberate coordination is also known as **managerial coordination** or the system of the **Visible Hand.** Under such circumstances, human reason is in charge (a matter most pleasing to human vanity). Ideally, the manager creates a social blueprint of everybody's activities to be performed during a future period. This blueprint is supposed to account for the concrete actions of all individuals at every moment and to ensure that the separate activities of all people mesh perfectly. If a manager decides to make locomotives, this manager would assign just the right number of other people, raw materials, and machines to produce just the right amounts of iron ore needed to make just the right amount of steel to make the locomotives. And, similarly, everything else that happens is to fit perfectly into the design: The

manager would order production of just the right amount of fuel to make just the right amount of electricity to run the machines that make the ball bearings for still other machines that make locomotive wheels. Once the plan is made, specific orders are issued to all individuals, and they are expected to do nothing but obey. The entire economy is thus run like one giant factory, by the Visible Hand of a manager.

Unfortunately, not everything that is logically conceivable is practically possible. The kind of task outlined above is an extremely difficult one. It can be carried out perfectly only by someone who is both omniscient and omnipotent, as a simple thought experiment can illustrate: Imagine that *you* were a country's economic dictator, and nothing could happen without your direction. Many millions of people were waiting for your commands. How would you decide what to produce and how and when and where and for whom? On what basis would you conclude that John Doe should mine iron ore to be made into steel to be made into locomotives? Why not use the steel to make orchard-spraying machines? Or plows to prepare a field for growing corn? Or should you grow red cabbages? If so, how many would you grow, where exactly should they go, and when? Your chance of making a complete mess of things would be excellent indeed. As would any central planner who is merely human, you would quickly run into the problem of being unable to gather, digest, and communicate all the knowledge that must be used to do a perfect job. Managerial coordination, therefore, has a number of inevitable costs. This is not the place to discuss them in detail, but they clearly include the need to establish an elaborate bureaucracy, staffed with tens of thousands of people and equipped with fancy communications and computing devices, and, thus, to divert resources from the production of other goods.[2]

---

[2]For a detailed discussion, see Heinz Kohler, *Comparitive Economic Systems* (Glenview, Ill.: Scott, Foresman and Co., 1989).

Characteristics of Spontaneous Coordination

Many economists, since the days of Adam Smith, have argued that the separate economic activities of people engaged in a division of labor can be coordinated spontaneously by price signals generated in markets. This is the system of **market coordination** or of the **Invisible Hand.** No central planner is put in charge of anything (a situation that dooms people, critics argue, to "irrationality" and "enslavement by blind forces"). In such a system, people do not cooperate with each other because someone issues commands reinforced, no doubt, by appropriate threats for noncompliance. Gone is the motto of the deliberate order: "You will do what I tell you, or I will do something bad to you." Instead, all individuals make their own plans on the basis of whatever limited knowledge they happen to possess. Then they meet in markets and make conditional offers to one another: "I will do something nice for you, if you do something nice for me."

Coordination of these independently decided but interdependent actions of different people is achieved and maintained by the **price system,** the set of interdependent prices in all the markets for goods and resources. These prices change as long as the independent actions of households and firms are not perfectly coordinated, making households and firms, in turn, change their behavior until coordination is achieved. Prices tell people indirectly what their inability to know everybody and everything intimately keeps them from knowing directly. Being keenly aware of how their welfare is affected by the prices they can get for what they sell and by the prices they must pay for what they want, all people are habitual price watchers. When people look for 16 million tons of apples, while only 8 million are being offered, anxious would-be buyers of apples will compete against each other and drive the price up. In response to these higher prices, two changes will occur: (1) some price-watching households will change their minds and decide to seek fewer apples at the higher price (using,

perhaps, oranges instead); (2) some price-watching owners of firms will change their minds, too, and decide to offer more apples at the higher price (producing more apples at the expense of something else, reducing apple inventories, increasing imports, and so on). Before you know it, a balance will be achieved between the production and consumption of apples. Similar adjustments will occur in all other realms of activity.

Adam Smith had this to say back in 1776:[3]

> It is not from the benevolence of the butcher, the brewer, or the baker that we expect our dinner, but from their regard of their own interest. We address ourselves not to their humanity, but to their self-love, and never talk to them of our own necessities but of their advantages. . . . Every individual is continually exerting himself to find out the most advantageous employment of whatever capital he can command. . . . he intends only his own gain, and he is in this . . . led by an invisible hand to promote an end which was no part of his intention. By pursuing his own interest, he frequently promotes that of the society more effectually than when he really intends to promote it.

And Bastiat answered his own question about the secret power that governs economic activity in the market economy:[4]

> That power . . . is the principle of free exchange. We put our faith in that inner light which Providence has placed in the hearts of all men, and to which has been entrusted the preservation and the unlimited improvement of our species, a light we term *self-interest,* which is so illuminating, so constant, and so penetrating, when it is left free of every hindrance. Where would you be, inhabitants of Paris, if some cabinet minister decided to substitute for that power contrivances of his own invention, however superior we might suppose them to be: if he proposed to subject this prodigious mechanism to his supreme direction, to take control of all of it into his own hands, to deter-

---

[3]Adam Smith, *An Inquiry into the Nature and Causes of the Wealth of Nations* (Homewood, Ill.: Irwin, 1963/1776), vol. 1, p. 12; vol. 2, pp. 21–23.

[4]Bastiat, *Sophismes Économiques.*

mine by whom, where, how, and under what conditions everything should be produced, transported, exchanged, and consumed? Although there may be much suffering within your walls, although misery, despair, and perhaps starvation, cause more tears to flow than your warmhearted charity can wipe away, it is probable, I dare say it is certain, that the arbitrary intervention of the government would infinitely multiply this suffering and spread among all of you the ills that now affect only a small number of your fellow citizens.

Thus it is in the United States. Basically, the economic choices made by a multitude of different households, firms, and governments are coordinated spontaneously, subconsciously, and without the intervention of any human commander-in-chief. Economic order is generated, as if by an Invisible Hand, because self-interested decision makers take their cues from the movement of market prices and adjust their activities as needed. However, spontaneous order, like the deliberate one, is not achieved without costs. Just as managerial coordination sacrifices output by tying up valuable resources in a bureaucracy to make possible the central planning and management of the economy, so market coordination sacrifices output by tying up valuable resources to make possible decentralized planning and management. Economists talk of **transactions costs,** or the **costs of exchange,** when output is sacrificed because resources are used to set up a system of voluntary exchanges and keep it functioning. As Chapter 15 will show, this involves governmental actions establishing property rights and facilitating widespread exchange.

MAPPING THE MARKET ECONOMY: THE BIG PICTURE

The market economy discussed in this book is assumed to operate under **capitalism,** an economic system in which most resources are privately owned. The major exchange relations that exist in such an economy can be depicted by the circular flows in Figure 13.1. Consider part (a). The left-hand box represents a likely multitude of households in whose adult members the property rights to most resources reside. (Even in capitalism, some resources must be owned by government so that it can perform whatever functions people assign to it.) The right-hand box in part (a) represents a large number of firms, which, under capitalism, any adventuresome individuals are free to form (and to liquidate).

Households and firms meet each other in two types of markets. Consider first the lower half of part (a). Its outer half-circle pictures households selling, and firms buying, services of the human, natural, and capital resource stocks that are owned by households. On a given day, perhaps, a particular household may sell 8 labor hours, 24 oil-deposit hours, and 24 turret-lathe hours—without, of course, giving up ownership of the person, oil deposit, or turret lathe as such. In return for the privilege of being allowed to use these resources temporarily, the firms involved pay out money in the form of wages and rental payments. This is a cost to them but income to the households involved. This income stream is augmented (or decreased) by positive (or negative) profits of the households that are also owners of firms. The shaded half-circle in the lower half represents this monetary counterflow to the flow of resource services.

Now consider the upper half of part (a). Its outer half-circle pictures firms selling, and households buying, consumption goods and human capital goods. As indicated, the consumption goods may be nondurable apples or airplane rides or durable cars; the human capital goods could be educational services. Once more, the shaded half-circle represents the monetary counterflow to this flow of goods.

Part (a) is fine as far as it goes; it tells the truth but not all of it. If we focused our attention more closely on the household box, we might discover the relationships pictured in part (b). In a capitalist market economy, frequent exchanges occur that involve only households. Households can sell outright the stocks of natural and capital resources they own (instead of just renting them

FIGURE 13.1

Circular Flows

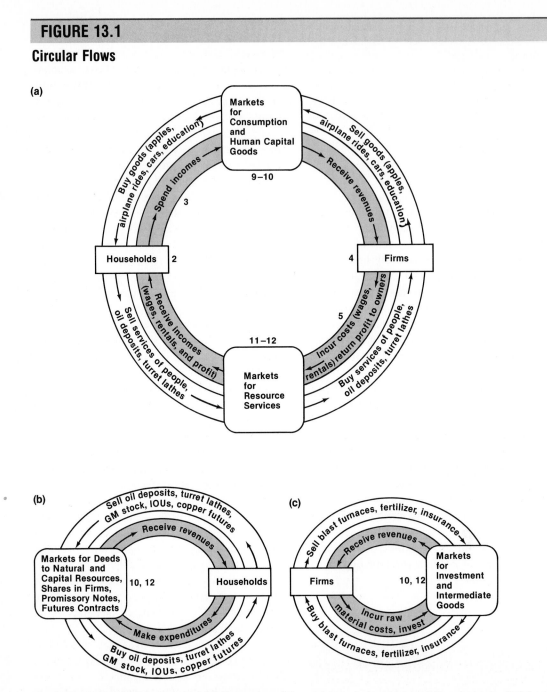

These circular-flow diagrams provide a bird's-eye view of the most important exchange relations in any capitalist market economy. They can be viewed as maps of this economy. (The numbers indicate the chapters that focus on the particular aspect of the economy shown. Additional chapters focus on other aspects, such as the interaction of many markets—Chapter 13—and the role of government—Chapters 15–16).

out to firms temporarily), but when they do, other households come to own them. Similarly, as part (b) illustrates, households often trade corporate stock among themselves; they lend to and borrow money from each other (which can be viewed as the buying and selling of promissory notes); and they even trade such strange things as copper futures (discussed in Chapter 10). Thus the circular flow in part (b) adds more detail to our bird's-eye view of the market economy.

Part (c) adds detail about the behavior of firms. Additional frequent exchanges occur that involve only firms. In particular, firms sell goods to other firms. Sometimes, these goods are used up right away by their recipients in the making of other goods (as perhaps the fertilizer or insurance service in our example). Such goods, which are produced by domestic producers during a period and then used up by the same or other domestic producers during the same period in the making of other goods, are called **intermediate goods.** Their purchase gives rise to raw material costs on the part of their buyers. At other times, firms sell **final goods,** goods produced by domestic producers during a period but *not* used up by the same or other domestic producers during the same period in the making of other goods. When final goods go to households, they are called *consumption* or *human capital goods,* as noted above, but when they go to firms, they are called *investment goods.* The blast furnaces in our example are a case in point. Their purchase gives rise to investment expenditures (financed, perhaps, with a portion of revenues corresponding to depreciation allowances or with the portion of profits not paid out to the owners of firms).

Having reviewed the big picture, we are now ready to meet general-equilibrium analysis.

A VERBAL-GRAPHICAL APPROACH

Nothing in economics is more difficult than the analysis of general equilibrium. This nonmathematical book cannot possibly do justice to this analysis, but two familiar tools—words and graphs—can help provide a basic understanding of what is involved.

Imagine a perfectly competitive economy that was, in fact, in a state of general equilibrium, as previously defined. When this state of affairs is upset, three types of effects can be observed: The **impact effect** is the effect of an initial change in supply or demand on the market concerned; the **spillout effect** is the effect of this change on other markets; and the **feedback effect** is the effect of these secondary changes in other markets on the market in which the initial change occurred. Consider these effects of a change in demand from beef to apples.

Impact Effects

A Lower Demand for Beef. Panels (a) to (c) of Figure 13.2 depict an original long-run equilibrium in the beef market. The sample household shown in panel (a) consumes 3 pounds of beef per week at the $2.50-per-pound price. That price, at which market demand D and market supply S are just equal in panel (b), is the equilibrium price. This equilibrium price equals the normal price, as shown in panel (c). Our sample firm, which, as always, produces where marginal cost of production equals marginal benefit (or product price), has a minimum average total cost just equal to price.

Note what would happen if this household's demand for beef fell, as suggested in panel (d), from the dashed to the solid line. As long as price remained unchanged (at $2.50), the household would cut purchases from the old quantity at point *a* to the new one at *b*, which illustrates its fall in demand. If, however, other households were cutting purchases too (and this we assume), market demand for beef would fall, as in panel (e), from D (now dashed) to D'. If the flow of beef from the market to households fell, while the flow of beef from producers to the market continued unabated, a *surplus* would develop at the old $2.50-per-pound price (shown by distance *de*). Storage facilities in the marketplace would fill up and overflow. Competition among sellers would reduce the price to $1.67 per pound (corresponding to intersection f). This lower price would be a signal to all involved to change their behavior.

Beef-eating households would, as households always do when the price of a good falls, increase their quantity demanded, as from b to c in panel (d). Beef-producing firms would, as firms always do when the price of a good falls, decrease their quantity supplied, as from g to h in panel (f). However, inherent in the situation would be a tendency for further change, because the new $1.67-per-pound equilibrium price

FIGURE 13.2

A Fall in the Demand for Beef

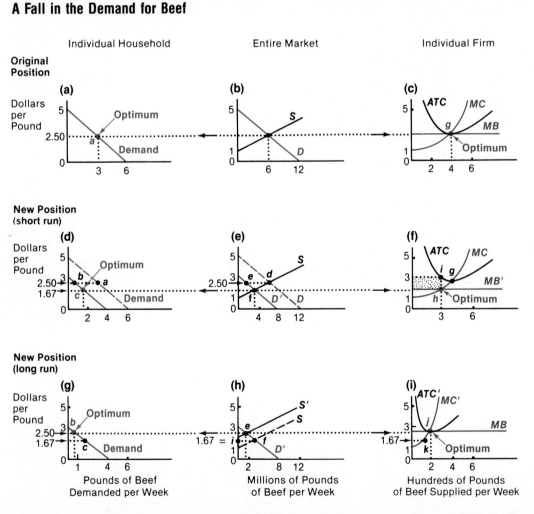

This set of graphs shows some of the adjustments, in a perfectly competitive market economy, to a fall in the demand for beef. If the industry involved is a constant-cost industry, as is assumed, the normal price of the product is unchanged after the industry has ceased to contract.

would no longer equal the $2.50-per-pound normal price. Consider how the typical firm would have turned from a zero-profit business into a losing business: Its price would have fallen (from point *g* to *h*), its average total cost would have risen (from point *g* to *i*), and it would then make losses, shown by the dotted rectangle in panel (f). The process described in Figure 6.4, "An Unprofitable Industry Contracts" (p. 184) would begin.

As soon as they could, firms would reduce their capacities or shut down completely. The particular firm illustrated here is assumed to reduce its capacity (a move akin to shifting from scale 2 to scale 1 in Table 4.3, "Constant Returns to Scale Illustrated" on p. 110), which is why panel (i) cost curves are to the *left* of their original position in panel (f). Compare *ATC′* and *MC′* with *ATC* and *MC*. Other firms, in ever increasing numbers, would also reduce capacity or even shut down entirely. As they did, market supply would fall as from *S* (now dashed) to *S′* in panel (h). But if the flow of beef from the producers to the market fell, while the flow of beef from the market to the households continued unchanged, a *shortage* would develop at the new $1.67-per-pound price (shown by distance *fi*). Storage facilities in the marketplace would empty out and, finally, be insufficient to meet demand. Competition among buyers would raise the price to $2.50 per pound (corresponding to intersection *e*). This higher price would be a new signal to all involved to change their behavior.

Beef-eating households would, as households always do when the price of a good rises, decrease their quantity demanded, as from *c* to *b* in panel (g). Beef-producing firms would, as firms always do when the price of a good rises, increase their quantity supplied, as from *k* to *j* in panel (i). Ignoring feedback effects, a final equilibrium would be reached when the firms remaining in the industry, as in panel (i), were again just covering cost with revenue. Their losses would have disappeared because the product price would be back at its old level, while average total cost (which had earlier risen to *i* above its

minimum) would in this constant-cost industry again have fallen to that minimum at *j*. In the end, beef producers would have done exactly what households had asked of them: produce less beef.

A Higher Demand for Apples.   Panels (a) to (c) of Figure 13.3 again picture an original long-run equilibrium. The household shown in panel (a) consumes 3 bushels of apples per year at the $12-per-bushel price. That price is the equilibrium price, in panel (b), and is also the normal price, in panel (c).

Note what would happen if this household's demand for apples rose, as suggested in panel (d), from the dashed to the solid line. As long as price remained unchanged (at $12), the household's higher demand would increase purchases from the old quantity at point *a* to the new one at *b*. If, however, other households were increasing purchases too (and this we assume), market demand for apples would rise, as in panel (e), from *D* (now dashed) to *D′*. And if the flow of apples from the market to households rose, while the flow of apples from producers to the market continued unchanged, a *shortage* would develop at the old $12-per-bushel price (shown by distance *de*). Apple storage facilities would empty out in no time, and demand would not be met. Competition among buyers would raise the price to $16 per bushel (corresponding to intersection *f*). This higher price would be a signal to all involved to change their behavior.

Apple-eating households would, as households always do when the price of a good rises, decrease their quantity demanded, as from *b* to *c* in panel (d). Apple-producing firms would, as firms always do when the price of a good rises, increase their quantity supplied, as from *g* to *h* in panel (f). However, inherent in the situation would be a tendency for further change, because the new $16-per-bushel price would no longer equal the $12-per-bushel normal price. Consider how the typical firm would have turned from a zero-profit business into a profitable business: Its price would have risen (from point g to h), its average total cost would have risen less (from point g to i), and it would now make a profit, shown by the shaded rectangle in panel (f). The process described in Figure 6.3 "A Profitable Industry Expands" (p. 183), would begin.

As soon as they could, existing firms would expand their capacities, and new firms would enter the industry. The particular firm shown here is assumed to expand its capacity (a move akin to going from scale 1 to scale 2 in Table 4.3, "Constant Returns to Scale Illustrated"), which

FIGURE 13.3

A Rise in the Demand for Apples

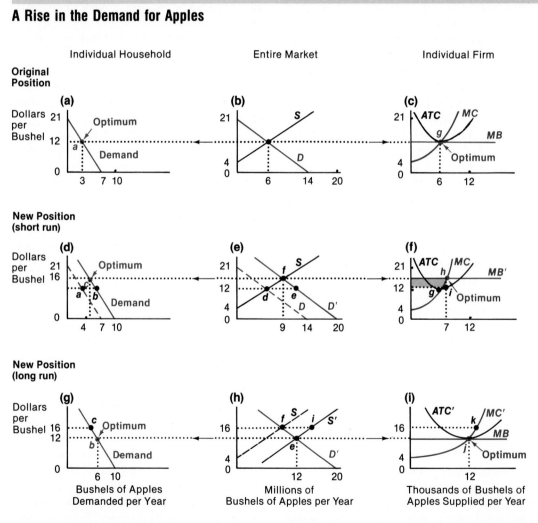

This set of graphs shows some of the adjustments, in a perfectly competitive market economy, to a rise in the demand for apples. If the industry involved is a constant-cost industry, as is assumed, the normal price of the product is unchanged after the industry has ceased to expand.

is why panel (i) cost curves are to the *right* of their original position in panel (f). Compare *ATC'* and *MC'* with *ATC* and *MC*. Other existing firms, in ever increasing numbers, would do the same, and new ones would enter the industry. As they did, market supply would rise as from *S* (now dashed) to *S'* in panel (h). But if the flow of apples from the producers to the market rose, while the flow of apples from the market to the households continued unchanged, a *surplus* would develop at the new $16-per-bushel price (shown by distance *fi*). Storage facilities would fill up and overflow. Competition among sellers would lower the price to $12 per bushel (corresponding to intersection *e*). This lower price would be a new signal to all involved to change their behavior.

Apple-eating households would, as households always do when the price of a good falls, increase their quantity demanded, as from *c* to *b* in panel (g). Apple-producing firms would, as firms always do when the price of a good falls, decrease their quantity supplied, as from *k* to *j* in panel (i). Ignoring feedback effects, a final equilibrium would be reached when the firms in the industry, as in panel (i), were again just covering cost with revenue. Their profits would have disappeared because the product price would be back at its old level, while average total cost (which had earlier risen to *i* above its minimum) would in this constant-cost industry again have fallen to that minimum at *j*. In the end, apple producers would have done exactly what households had asked of them: produce more apples.

Spillout Effects

Impact effects like those just described are only a tiny portion of the price system's work. The many firms that would reduce output or entirely leave the beef business, for instance, would, by their simultaneous actions, reduce the market demand for steers, butchers, ranch hands, veterinarians, pastures, feed lots, hay, corn, silos, harvesters, and much more. These reductions of

demand would, by themselves, tend to lower the prices of all these things and send out clear signals to all involved to change their behavior too in ways consistent with the households' desire to have less beef. Thus cattle breeders and owners of pastureland and makers of harvesters and all the rest would find their incomes falling, and they would have the incentive to put their resources into other, more remunerative fields. To be sure, each individual would be free to buck the trend. Individuals could do just the opposite of what price changes (and resultant income differentials) were asking of them. People could go *into* cattle breeding, pastureland, harvester production, and so on, just when the reverse was in the social interest; if they did, they should not be surprised if they were punished by exceptionally low incomes. Most people, therefore, could be expected to go in the direction pointed out by the Invisible Hand. Once enough inputs had thus been taken out of these declining fields, these input prices would, of course, go back up, and in the case of constant-cost industries, they would return to their original levels. Then the remaining (and fewer) cattle breeders, pasture owners, harvester producers, and so on, would again be receiving their old and higher incomes. The time of famine would be over.

In the same way, many old and new firms that would increase the output of the apple industry would, by their simultaneous actions, *increase* the demand for fertilizer, pesticides, baby apple trees, storage barns, apple pickers, spraying machines, rubber, steel, coal, iron ore, and much more. These increases in demand would, by themselves, tend to raise the prices of all these things and constitute clear signals to all involved to change their behavior too in ways consistent with the households' desire to have more apples. Thus producers of fertilizer, human apple pickers, makers of iron ore, and all the rest would find their incomes rising, and they would have the incentive to place more of their resources into such remunerative fields. To be sure, each individual would be free to go against the trend, but those who did go out of fertilizer manufacture, apple picking, iron ore mining, and so on, just when the reverse was in the social interest, would be punished by losing what, at least for a while, would be exceptionally high incomes. Most people, therefore, could be expected to go in the direction pointed out by the Invisible Hand. Once enough new inputs had thus been put into these expanding fields, these input prices would, of course, go back down, and, in the case of constant-cost industries, they would return to their original levels. Then the (greater number) of fertilizer producers, apple

pickers, and iron ore miners would again be receiving the lower incomes that once prevailed. The feast would have come to an end.

Finally, many seemingly unrelated effects would occur throughout the economy. Some households, such as the unlucky owners of pastureland, might react to their fall in income by demanding fewer yachts. The owners of profitable orchards might demand more furniture and airplane rides. The producers of cornflakes might supply more of them, because corn would be cheaper once there were fewer steers to be fed. Thus, in a billion unpredictable ways, the price

FIGURE 13.4

How Price Signals Would Spread

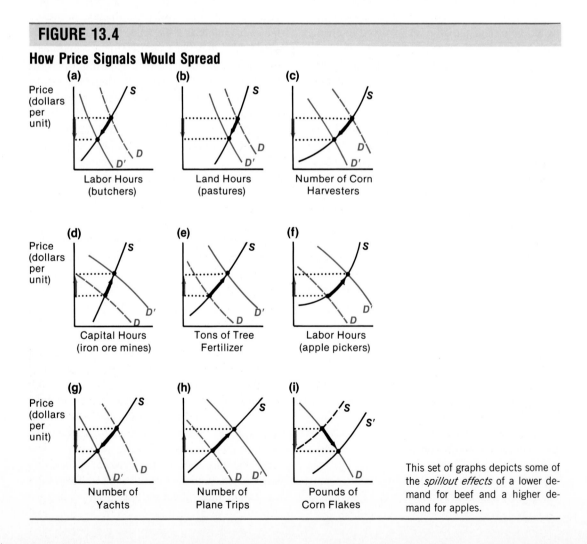

This set of graphs depicts some of the *spillout effects* of a lower demand for beef and a higher demand for apples.

system would tell just those from whom action was required what they should do. It would tell them in unmistakable ways (that appeal to their self-interests) to move in the direction of the ''carrot'' (higher income) and away from the ''stick'' (lower income). The price system would thus become the invisible *governor* of the competitive market economy, spreading its signals throughout.

The decreased demand for beef would reduce also the demand for things required, directly or indirectly, to make beef, as shown in panels (a) to (c) of Figure 13.4, by a shift of the dashed lines to the solid ones. In the same way, the increased demand for apples would increase also the demand for things required to make apples, as shown in panels (d) to (f). In addition, all kinds of seemingly unrelated effects would occur, as shown in panels (g) to (i). Thus the original change in household demand, akin to the ripple effect in a pond into which a stone has been thrown, would spread throughout the economy. The arrows in Figure 13.4 highlight the movements of the equilibrium points and the resultant price changes.

Feedback Effects

Figure 13.4 suggests why owners of iron ore mines, producers of tree fertilizer, human apple pickers, and people giving airplane rides would have higher incomes and would therefore (among many other things) demand more beef. This increase in the demand for beef forces us to reconsider the new long-run position shown in Figure 13.2 (which was based on the assumption of a *decreased* demand for beef by other people).

On the other hand, it is also possible that unlucky butchers, pastureland owners, and producers of corn harvesters or yachts or cornflakes would demand fewer apples. This decrease in demand forces us to reconsider Figure 13.3, which was based on the assumption of an initial *rise* in the demand for apples. All these new and offsetting changes in demand would, in turn, have spillout and feedback effects of their own!

Words and graphs can help illustrate the complexity of establishing a general equilibrium in the economy, but they cannot take us beyond this point. Because the full analysis of general equilibrium is an incredibly complex problem the solution of which is bound to escape the grasp of words and graphs, economists have turned to mathematics.

THE EQUATIONS OF WALRAS

In 1874, the French economist Léon Walras (the *s* is sounded) was the first to provide a precise formulation of the web of interconnections discussed and graphed in the preceding section. Walras (1834–1910), a Biography of whom appears in Chapter 13 of the *Student Workbook* that accompanies this text, viewed the economic system as a vast set of simultaneous equations. He described each household's demand for each good by a separate equation. He likewise described each household's supply of each resource service, each firm's supply of each good, and each firm's demand for each resource service using equations. He also formulated a market-clearing equation for the market of each good and of each resource service. Walras then showed, for a world of perfect competition, that it was theoretically possible to solve the resultant set of equations simultaneously for the prices and quantities of all inputs and outputs because *the number of independent equations equaled the number of the unknowns.*

The theoretical solution of Walras was, of course, nothing else but a general equilibrium of his hypothetical economy. When prices and quantities in all markets were thus in equilibrium simultaneously, short-run general equilibrium existed. When all firms in addition earned zero economic profit and no reproducible resources earned economic rent, long-run general equilibrium existed as well. Even though Walras's math was clumsy, he thus provided, as Joseph Schumpeter later put it, nothing less than ''the Magna Carta of exact economics.''

Walras was content with showing the theoretical possibility of a general equilibrium; he doubted the empirical usefulness of the analysis. Given the millions of equations involved, he saw no chance for filling them with numerical content. Yet his theory of *tâtonnement* or "groping" did provide a poetic vision of how an economy could solve the equations. He imagined price-taking buyers and sellers announcing the quantities they wanted to trade at prices *criés au hasard* (cried at random) by a price-making auctioneer. As long as the aggregate plans of buyers and sellers were in conflict, new prices would be "cried" and quantities would be adjusted. Only when an equilibrium set of prices was found would actual trading take place. Walras's theory, alas, hardly provided an accurate description of the real world. In addition, subsequent generations of economists were not satisfied with the Walrasian counting of equations and unknowns or, for that matter, with his assumption of universal perfect competition. Thus general-equilibrium analysis remained a difficult challenge.

WALRASIAN ECONOMICS SINCE WALRAS

Mathematical economists were not convinced by the Walrasian claim that a general equilibrium was possible because a solution "in principle" of his system of equations for a perfectly competitive economy was conceivable. Later economists argued that an equality of the numbers of independent equations and unknowns was neither a sufficient nor even a necessary condition for the existence of such a general equilibrium. To appreciate why an equal number of independent equations and unknowns may not be a *sufficient* condition for the existence of general equilibrium, consider the following two equations with two unknowns:

$$x^2 + y^2 = 0$$
$$x^2 - y^2 = 1$$

These equations have no solution in the realm of

real numbers, the only realm that has any economic meaning. The solution is $x = \sqrt{1/2}$ and $y = i\sqrt{1/2}$, where the imaginary number i satisfies $i^2 = -1$. How can we be sure, critics asked, that the Walrasian "solution in principle" wasn't a solution such as this one? Maybe his solution contained all sorts of imaginary or negative numbers that grossly violated economic reality. (In general, negative prices and quantities lack economic meaning.)

Now focus on the first of the two equations above. Even though we have one equation with *two* unknowns, it does have a solution in the realm of real numbers ($x = y = 0$); hence the Walrasian equation-and-unknown counting is not even a *necessary* condition for the existence of a general economic equilibrium.

In addition, economists wondered about the uniqueness or lack thereof of any general equilibrium. Might it not be possible, they asked, that many different sets of all prices and quantities equally satisfied the Walrasian equations? Thus economists set out to analyze the problem with rigor. Using topology and set theory, it was finally proved beyond doubt by Wald, von Neumann, Arrow, Debreu, and McKenzie that a general economic equilibrium can be achieved given a fairly wide set of assumptions (barring only a few conditions, such as increasing returns to scale, joint products, externalities, satiation of wants).[5]

Economists also investigated the stability of this general equilibrium: Would such an equilibrium, they asked, be reestablished once disturbed? This line of research originated in

---

[5]Abraham Wald, "On Some Systems of Equations of Mathematical Economics," *Econometrica*, October, 1951, pp. 368–403 (the translation of a 1936 paper); John von Neumann, "A Model of General Economic Equilibrium," *Review of Economic Studies* 1, 1945, 1–9 (translation of a 1937 article); Kenneth J. Arrow and Gerard Debreu, "Existence of an Equilibrium for a Competitive Economy," *Econometrica*, July 1954, pp. 265–90; Gerard Debreu, *Theory of Value: An Axiomatic Analysis of Economic Equilibrium* (New York: John Wiley & Sons, 1959); Lionel W. McKenzie, "On the Existence of General Equilibrium for a Competitive Market," *Econometrica*, January 1959, pp. 54–71.

Walras's theory of groping, was revived by Hicks, and was pursued by Samuelson, Arrow, Hurwicz, and others.[6]

More recently the theory of the whole economy has been developed on many fronts, incorporating the introduction of uncertainty,[7] a method for actually calculating general-equilibrium prices,[8] and consideration of imperfectly competitive markets.[9] (Given the nature of the mathematics involved, all these matters go beyond the level of this book.)

LEONTIEF'S INPUT-OUTPUT ANALYSIS

A major new departure in general-equilibrium analysis was made in 1941 by Wassily Leontief (1906–   ), who eventually won the 1973 Nobel Prize in economics for this work (and a Biography of whom can also be found in Chapter 13 of the *Student Workbook* that accompanies this

[6]John R. Hicks, *Value and Capital* (Oxford, England: Clarendon Press, 1939); Paul A. Samuelson, ''The Stability of Equilibrium: Comparative Statics and Dynamics,'' *Econometrica,* April 1941, pp. 97–120; *idem,* ''The Stability of Equilibrium: Linear and Nonlinear Systems,'' *Econometrica,* January 1942, pp. 1–25; and *idem,* ''The Relation Between Hicksian Stability and True Dynamic Stability,'' *Econometrica,* July–October 1944, pp. 256–57; Kenneth J. Arrow and Leo Hurwicz, ''On the Stability of the Competitive Equilibrium, Part I,'' *Econometrica,* October 1958, pp. 522–52; Kenneth J. Arrow, H. D. Block, and Leo Hurwicz, ''On the Stability of the Competitive Equilibrium, Part II,'' *Econometrica,* January 1959, pp. 82–109.

[7]Roy Radner, ''Competitive Equilibrium under Uncertainty,'' *Econometrica,* January 1968, pp. 31–58.

[8]Herbert Scarf, ''An Example of an Algorithm for Calculating General Equilibrium Prices,'' *The American Economic Review,* September 1969, pp. 669–77.

[9]Jean Jaskold-Gabszewicz and Jean-Philippe Vial, ''Oligopoly 'a la Cournot' in a General Equilibrium Analysis,'' *Journal of Economic Theory,* June 1972, pp. 381–400; Thomas Marschak and Reinhard Selten, *General Equilibrium with Price-Making Firms* (New York: Springer Verlag, 1974); Donald J. Roberts and Hugo Sonnenschein, ''On the Foundations of the Theory of Monopolistic Competition,'' *Econometrica,* January 1977, pp. 101–13; William Novshek and Hugo Sonnenschein, ''Cournot and Walras Equilibrium,'' *Journal of Economic Theory,* December 1978, pp. 223–66.

text). Leontief brought the Walrasian theory from the level of supreme abstraction down to a level that allowed the numerical specification of economic interdependencies in the U.S. economy. He invented the **input-output table,** which lists the flows of all newly produced goods and of resource services between all their suppliers and recipients, to illustrate the web of interrelationships in an economy.

The Input-Output Table

Leontief's new tool shows how the decisions of any one economic actor are intricately bound up with all other decisions. In general equilibrium, the decision to produce any one good, for instance, requires decisions to produce many other goods as well, because any one output, by requiring inputs, affects other outputs, and so on in an infinite chain. Table 13.1 represents a highly simplified version of such a table, depicting a hypothetical economy's interrelationships during a given past year. The table *columns* show *inputs* (that is, flows of newly produced goods and of resource services) received during the year by the parties listed on top from the parties listed on the left. The *rows* show *outputs;* each row shows how the total flow, in column (8), of any newly produced good or resource service (which came from the party listed on the left), was distributed during the year among the various recipients listed on top.

Obviously, any input-output table that is to be used for serious analysis or even centralized economic planning would have to contain millions of rows and columns. Besides the electric power, steel, and corn listed in rows (A) to (C) of our table, there would have to be separate rows for all other newly produced goods—from milk and shoes and electric motors to turret lathes and government office buildings and superhighways! Indeed, different types of any one product would have to be listed separately, too, right down to such detail as boys' tennis shoes size 10 and color blue. A complete table would similarly have to specify in detail the types of resource services required. The large categories listed in rows (D) to (F) would have to be broken down into all their different components. The quality of any worker, for instance, clearly varies with age, skill, and health; the quality of any piece of land varies with its location and the weather; and the quality of a machine varies with its wear and tear. All these factors would have to be accounted for.

Nevertheless, for purposes of illustration only, we shall assume that the oversimplified picture of Table 13.1 represents a complete picture of an economy in which only three goods were produced—rows (A) to (C)—and in which only three types of homogeneous resources were utilized—rows (D) to (F).

TABLE 13.1

The Input-Output Table

Recipients / Suppliers	Of Intermediate Goods and Primary Resources			Of Final Goods and Primary Resources				Total
	Electric power producers (1)	Steel producers (2)	Corn producers (3)	Domestic households (4)	Domestic producers (5)	Domestic government (6)	Foreigners (7)	(8)
(A) Electric power producers (millions of megawatt hours)	40	120	20	160		50	10	400
(B) Steel producers (millions of tons)	80	200	5	0	400	0	115	800
(C) Corn producers (millions of tons)	40	80	100	500	−120	200	−300	500
(D) Owners of human resources (millions of labor hours)	4	800	500	50		400	96	1,850
(E) Owners of natural resources (millions of acre hours)	4	200	2,500	200		600	0	3,504
(F) Owners of capital resources (millions of machine hours)	100	400	100	0		100	0	700

An input-output table is like a map of an economy. It gives an overview of the flows of commodities and services during a period between their suppliers (listed on the left) and their recipients (listed on top).

The Rows.   It is easy to interpret the meaning of each row of our table. Row (A), column (8), indicates that electric power producers were producing, during the year in question, some 400 million megawatt hours. Some 180 million of these megawatt hours were delivered to domestic producers, in columns (1) to (3), and *completely used up* in the making of other goods. This portion of electric power output, therefore, is placed in the category of *intermediate goods,* or goods produced by domestic producers during a period and then used up by the same or other domestic producers during the same period in the making of other goods. Another 220 million megawatt hours, however [listed in columns (4), (6), and (7)], were not used up domestically in the making of other goods. These hours are placed among *final goods,* or goods produced by domestic producers during a period but not used up by the same or other domestic producers during the same period in the making of other goods.

Note: Final goods may well have been used up (by households, government, or foreigners) or they may even have been sold to other producers in the country (and been added by them to their capital stock for *future* use). But goods can never be called final goods if they have been used up by *domestic producers* during the *same period* they were produced because that would make them intermediate goods.

Row (B), column (8) shows that 800 million tons of steel were produced this year. Of this total, some 285 million tons were completely used up by the makers of electric power (1), steel (2), and corn (3), leaving 515 million tons for final recipients. Of these 515 million tons, 400 million tons were received by domestic producers but not yet used up in the making of other goods (5), and 115 million tons were exported (7).

Row (C), column (8) shows that 500 million tons of corn were produced this year. However, another 300 million tons were imported from abroad—the negative entry in column (7)—while 120 million more tons were taken out of storage by domestic producers—the negative entry in column (5). Thus domestic supplies came to 500

+ 300 + 120 = 920 million tons. Of this total, 220 million tons were completely used up by the makers of electric power (1), steel (2), and corn (3), perhaps in the production of plastic parts used in electric generators and blast furnaces and, of course, as seed. The remaining 700 million tons were delivered to domestic households (4) and government agencies (6).

Row (D) shows that 1,850 million labor hours were performed during the year. Some 1,304 million of these were used in the making of electric power (1), steel (2), and corn (3). The remaining 546 million hours were directly used by domestic households (4), government agencies (6), and foreigners (7), perhaps in the form of services provided by barbers, typists, or technical advisers, respectively. Note: It is no accident that an X appears in row (D), column (5). Labor hours delivered to domestic producers must have been used up by them during the year in question in the making of goods; hence they appear in columns (1) to (3). Unlike steel or corn received (which might be used up or stored for future use), labor hours (just like acre hours, machine hours, and megawatt hours) cannot be stored for future use.

Rows (E) and (F), similarly, list the totals of acre hours and machine hours used during the year as well as the purposes to which they were put.

The Columns.   The columns of our table have, of course, been discussed by implication. Columns (1) to (3) show all the inputs used by our three types of producers while producing the output totals given in column (8) of rows (A) to (C). Electric power producers, for instance, produced this year 400 million megawatt hours—row (A), column (8)—by completely using up the newly produced goods and primary resource services listed in column (1): 40 million megawatt hours (electric power used to run electric generators), 80 million tons of steel (to build transmission towers), 40 million tons of corn (to make plastic parts used in generators), 4 million labor hours (which might have involved 1,515 workers working 8 hours a day for slightly over

11 months), 4 million acre hours (which might have involved using slightly under 457 acres year round as sites for electric power stations and transmission facilities); and 100 million machine hours (which might have involved using 11,416 machines year round to generate electricity). Columns (2) and (3) can be similarly interpreted.

Column (4) lists all the goods received for private consumption by households (electricity, corn, services of barbers and of private garden plots). Column (5) shows the change in the country's capital stock, or its annual investment (inventories of steel went up, inventories of corn went down). Column (6) lists goods received by government agencies and thus by people for collective consumption (electric light and heat for government offices, public schools, and hospitals; corn for the meals of soldiers; the services of clerks, doctors, and police officers; land used for parks and highways, and so on). Column (7), finally, lists the country's foreign trade (exports of electric power, steel, and labor services; imports of corn).

The input-output table can show us the effects of any disturbance of an initial equilibrium. Consider the effects of changes in the demands listed in columns (4) to (7).

Changes in Final Demands

Let households demand 80 million megawatt hours of electric power *less* next year, but let government agencies (in charge of street lighting and important research) demand some 120 million megawatt hours *more*. Let foreigners demand 55 million fewer tons of steel per year, while government agencies (in charge of a new space program) demand 95 million additional tons. Let domestic producers stop importing corn, while increasing corn inventories by 100 million tons per year (instead of drawing them down at a rate of 120 million tons). And let government demand 400 million fewer acre hours of natural resources, while private households (eager to set up garden plots) demand 400 million acre hours more.

All these changes to Table 13.1 are incorporated in columns (4) to (7) of Table 13.2. To understand how Leontief would figure the effects of our contemplated changes in demand, the reader should now imagine this table to be completely blank—except, of course, for the new compositions of final demand that we have just assumed in columns (4) to (7). The assumed changes in demand (compared to Table 13.1) have been highlighted by the encircled numbers in Table 13.2. Obviously each of these changes requires other changes in the original data of Table 13.1.

The increase by 40 million megawatt hours a year of the row (A) entries in columns (4) to (7) from 220 to 260, for instance, requires at the very least a corresponding increase from 400 to 440 in the total output of electric power in column (8) of row (A). That increase in total electric power output, in turn, requires increases in all the inputs used by electric power producers in column (1), which raises all the totals in column (8) and, in due course, all the other entries! This chain reaction illustrates why Leontief would quickly examine the technical facts of life.

Technical Coefficients

Leontief would use the type of information found in columns (1) to (3) of Table 13.1 to calculate **technical coefficients** for all goods. Technical coefficients are numbers showing the quantities of inputs producers in an industry require on the average per unit of output. The technical coefficients in Table 13.3 have been derived from Table 13.1. Every entry in column (1) of Table 13.1, for instance, has been divided by the 400-million-megawatt-hour total of electric power output shown in row (A), column (8). This division yielded column (1) of the new table: Because it took 40 million megawatt hours to produce 400 million megawatt hours, it took on the average .10 megawatt hour to produce 1 megawatt hour. Because it took 80 million tons of steel to produce 400 million megawatt hours, it took on the average .20 ton to produce 1 mega-

TABLE 13.2

A New Input-Output Table

Suppliers \ Recipients	Of Intermediate Goods and Primary Resources			Of Final Goods and Primary Resources				Total
	Electric power producers (1)	Steel producers (2)	Corn producers (3)	Domestic house-holds (4)	Domestic producers (5)	Domestic govern-ment (6)	Foreigners (7)	(8)
(A) Electric power producers (millions of megawatt hours)	48.862	132.889	46.873	(80)	✕	(170)	10	304.685 134.638 49.301 488.624
(B) Steel producers (millions of tons)	97.725	221.481	11.718	0	400	(95)	(60)	81.894 777.423 26.607 885.924
(C) Corn producers (millions of tons)	48.862	88.592	234.364	500	(100)	200	(0)	48.322 114.008 1,009.488 1,171.818
(D) Owners of human resources (millions of labor hours)	4.886	885.924	1,171.818	50	✕	400	96	2,608.628
(E) Owners of natural resources (millions of acre hours)	4.886	221.481	5,859.09	(600)	✕	(200)	0	6,885.457
(F) Owners of capital resources (millions of machine hours)	122.156	442.962	234.364	0	✕	100	0	899.482

This new input-output table shows the effects, throughout our hypothetical economy, of the changes in final demand highlighted by the encircled numbers. As a comparison with Table 13.1 indicates, the *impact, spillout,* and *feedback effects* leave no part of the economy untouched.

watt hour. And so on. Columns (2) and (3) of Table 13.3 have been similarly derived.

Armed with technical coefficients, Leontief would figure, to begin with, that increasing annual electric power output by 40 million mega-watt hours to accommodate the changes contemplated in row (A), columns (4) to (7) requires extra inputs equal to 40 million times all the entries in column (1) of Table 13.3. But increasing inputs in this way would only be a first approximation of the truth. As one can see in the very first entry in column (1) of Table 13.3, in this economy electric power requires electric power for its production! Thus any 40-million megawatt-hour increase in electric power output requires *another* 40 million times .10, or another 4-million-megawatt-hour increase in electric power production; this, in turn, requires another 4 million times .10, or a .4-million-megawatt-hour increase; and so on in an ever dwindling chain. Even *further* electric power is needed to help produce the additional steel and corn!

It is easy to see how this sort of computation would quickly get out of hand if it were to be pursued by mentally following chains of reasoning such as the one above. Fortunately, however, the mathematical technique of *matrix inversion* is a tool that enables analysts to calculate speedily all the effects, direct and indirect, of the types of changes envisioned in the example above. Matrix inversion produces, from the technical coeffi-

cients for intermediate goods (the top half of our Table 13.3), the so-called **Leontief inverse matrix,** a table showing, for those goods of which a portion of output is used up in the process of production itself (electric power, steel, and corn in our example), the total outputs ultimately required if one unit of such a good is to be delivered to final users. For serious analysis of general equilibrium, the Leontief inverse matrix is an indispensable tool. (The derivation of the Leontief inverse matrix is discussed in an Appendix to this chapter in the *Student Workbook* that accompanies this text.)

Interpreting the Leontief Inverse Matrix

Column (1) of Table 13.4 indicates that the recipients of final goods in our hypothetical economy could get 1 megawatt hour of electric power provided total electric power output equaled 1.1718673 megawatt hours, total steel

TABLE 13.3

Technical Coefficients

	Inputs Required on the Average to Make		
	1 Megawatt Hour of Electric Power (1)	**1 Ton of Steel** (2)	**1 Ton of Corn** (3)
(A) **Electric power** (megawatt hours)	$\frac{40}{400} = 0.10$	$\frac{120}{800} = 0.15$	$\frac{20}{500} = 0.04$
(B) **Steel** (tons)	$\frac{80}{400} = 0.20$	$\frac{200}{800} = 0.25$	$\frac{5}{500} = 0.01$
(C) **Corn** (tons)	$\frac{40}{400} = 0.10$	$\frac{80}{800} = 0.10$	$\frac{100}{500} = 0.20$
(D) **Human resources** (labor hours)	$\frac{4}{400} = 0.01$	$\frac{800}{800} = 1.00$	$\frac{500}{500} = 1.00$
(E) **Natural resources** (acre hours)	$\frac{4}{400} = 0.01$	$\frac{200}{800} = 0.25$	$\frac{2500}{500} = 5.00$
(F) **Capital resources** (machine hours)	$\frac{100}{400} = 0.25$	$\frac{400}{800} = 0.50$	$\frac{100}{500} = 0.20$

Technical coefficients can be calculated from an input-output table. The figures shown here are based on Table 13.1, columns (1)—(3) and (8). No attempt has been made to depict realistic production functions.

output equaled .314976 ton, and total corn output equaled .1858554 ton. These production levels would ensure sufficient raw materials throughout the economy to accommodate the ultimate delivery of 1 megawatt hour to a final user. In addition, of course, the services of human, natural, and capital resources would be needed.

Note how easily an analyst or central planner, looking only at the technical coefficients table, could have come to incorrect conclusions. Providing some final user with 1 extra megawatt hour of power, such a planner might have figured, would *directly* require the production of 1 extra megawatt hour (a matter of common sense), and would *indirectly* require the raw material production of another .10 megawatt hour of power, .20 ton of steel, and .10 ton of corn, as the entries in column (1) of Table 13.3 seem to indicate. Yet this conclusion would be wrong! As column (1) of the Leontief inverse tells us, providing a final user with 1 extra megawatt hour of power requires extra total output of not 1.1 but 1.1718673 megawatt hours of power; of not .20 but .314976 ton of steel; and of not .10 but .1858554 ton of corn! The inverse makes us aware not only of the direct extra output requirements (which common sense indicates) and not only of the most obvious

indirect ones (which the technical coefficients point out), but also of those that are far from obvious (and which are too complex to be grasped by any human mind).

Completing the New Input-Output Table

Total Output Requirements.   Armed with the Leontief inverse, it is easy to work out the total output requirements implied by our hypothetical new set of final demands. Imagine in Table 13.2 that columns (1) to (3) plus (8) were still empty. Using the Leontief inverse, we can now fill in the top three cells in column (8) as follows.

Noting in columns (4) to (7) of row (A) how final users now demand $80 + 170 + 10 = 260$ million megawatt hours, multiplying each of the column (1) entries in Table 13.4 by 260 million yields the total production levels of electric power, steel, and corn that accommodate this goal. The resultant figures, rounded to three decimals, are shown in column (8) of Table 13.2: 304.68549 million megawatt hours of power, 81.89376 million tons of steel, and 48.322404 million tons of corn.

Final demanders also seek to obtain $400 + 95 + 60 = 555$ million tons of steel. Multiply-

TABLE 13.4

The Leontief Inverse Matrix

	Total Output Required if Delivery to Final Users Is to Equal		
	1 Megawatt Hour of Electric Power (1)	1 Ton of Steel (2)	1 Ton of Corn (3)
(A) **Electric power** (megawatt hours)	1.1718673	0.2425902	0.0616257
(B) **Steel** (tons)	0.314976	1.4007629	0.0332583
(C) **Corn** (tons)	0.1858554	0.2054191	1.2618605

The Leontief inverse can be calculated from a table of technical coefficients with the help of matrix algebra. This table is based on Table 13.3 and, ultimately, on Table 13.1. All figures are rounded.

ing each of the column (2) entries in Table 13.4 by 555 million yields, the *additional* total output of electric power, steel, and corn required to accommodate this additional goal. The resultant figures—134.63756 million megawatt hours of power, 777.4234 million tons of steel, and 114.0076 million tons of corn—are also shown in Table 13.2.

Finally, final demanders also seek to acquire $500 + 100 + 200 = 800$ million tons of corn. Multiplying each of the column (3) entries in Table 13.4 by 800 million reveals further total output requirements for the three goods put out by this economy. The results—49.30056 million megawatt hours of power, 26.60664 million tons of steel, and 1,009.4884 million tons of corn—are shown in column (8) of Table 13.2, along with the totals of the entries we have just imagined making in the top three rows.

Input Requirements of Intermediate Goods.

At this point, we must imagine that columns (1) to (3) of Table 13.2, as well as the lower half of column (8), are still blank. Knowing the total output requirements of all goods produced by the economy from rows (A) to (C) of column (8), we can simply use the technical coefficients in Table 13.3 to calculate all the inputs required by each type of producer—assuming, of course, that the technical relationships between inputs and outputs that were observed in the past also hold in the future (even if the volume of production, and thus perhaps even the number of producers, should be different). Leontief's method does, in fact, assume such constant returns to scale.

Multiplying the 488.624-million-megawatt-hour total output of electric power by all the entries in column (1) of Table 13.3 yields the entries in column (1) of Table 13.2. Similar multiplications—of the 885.924-million-ton total output of steel by the column (2) entries in Table 13.3 and of the 1,171.818-million-ton total output of corn by the column (3) entries in Table 13.3—yields all the data for columns (2) and (3) of Table 13.2.

At this point, a quick accuracy check can be made. Do the column (8) totals of rows (A) to (C), which were independently derived with the help of the Leontief inverse, equal the sum of all the entries in their respective rows? They do.

Input Requirements of Primary Resource Services. At this point, only three cells in our table remain blank: the column (8) totals of rows (D) to (F) can be calculated by simple addition of all the entries in these three rows, yielding the three boxed numbers in column (8). If the economy can come up with the flows of resource services represented by these boxes, Table 13.2 can provide a feasible as well as a well-coordinated outline of economic activities that must be performed to accommodate the imagined set of new demands.

Wider Applications

The above example provides only the barest outline of Leontief's innovation, but it is sufficient to suggest why economists the world over have embraced the new technique with considerable success. Economic analysts in advanced economies have used input-output tables to estimate the consequences for different economic sectors of disarmament agreements or price hikes by the OPEC cartel. They have made such estimates by working through, as we have, the implications of changes in final demands likely to be brought about by these events. Economists in poor countries have used the technique to plan strategies of economic development; those in centrally planned economies have used the technique to formulate coordinated sets of commands likely to guide households and firms toward producing politically determined sets of final goods. (Consider Analytical Examples 13.1, "The Economic Effects of Disarmament," and 13.2, "The Structure of Development.") Thus economic science, in the past few decades, has made giant steps beyond earlier approaches to general economic equilibrium. These earlier approaches included the famous

[margin notes, handwritten:]

A = matrix of tech coeff.
(see table 13.3)
d = changes in demand

$Ax = d$

$x = A^{-1}d$

next (i) x

Tableau Économique of François Quesnay (1694–1774), which mapped the flows of goods and money among economic sectors (and was inspired by physician Quesnay's study of the circulation of blood in the human body), the reproduction schema of Karl Marx (1818–83), and the equations of Walras (1834–1910). Yet none of these theoretical tools enabled analysts to handle the empirical content of general equilibrium as Leontief's technique does.

SUMMARY

1. Modern economies are characterized by an incredible degree of interdependence because millions of households and firms participate in an intricate system of specialization and exchange. This interdependence is easily forgotten in the study of partial equilibrium situations that involve only one part of the economy. This chapter focuses on the attainment of *general equilibrium*, a state of the economy in which billions of optimizing decisions by millions of decision makers are compatible with each other because all input and output markets are in equilibrium at the same time.

2. The large-scale division of labor that is characteristic of modern economic systems brings the benefit of greater production along with a cost: the problem of having to coordinate the specialized activities of people, of having to ensure economic order.

3. The separate activities of people engaged in a division of labor can be coordinated deliberately by a human manager. *Managerial coordination*, while making possible increased output through a division of labor, inevitably sacrifices output by tying up resources in a planning bureaucracy.

The separate activities of people engaged in a division of labor can also be coordinated spontaneously by price signals generated in markets. *Market coordination*, while making possible increased output through a division of labor, inevitably sacrifices output by tying up resources

to set up a system of voluntary exchanges and keep it functioning.

4. The major exchange relations that exist in any capitalist market economy can be mapped in circular-flow diagrams. These diagrams picture households exchanging the services of resources and, ultimately, the products of resources with firms; they also picture exchanges among households or among firms.

5. The nature of general-equilibrium analysis is first explored by following, verbally and graphically, the *impact, spillout,* and *feedback effects* of a change in the composition of demand. This exploration illustrates that the "Invisible Hand" notion of Adam Smith was in fact a poetic expression of general-equilibrium analysis.

6. Because words and graphs ultimately cannot express the complex interrelationships in an economy, economists turn to mathematics. Léon Walras was a brilliant pioneer in developing a mathematical theory of general-economic equilibrium.

7. By now, mathematical economists have carried general-equilibrium analysis far beyond Walras. They have investigated various properties of the general equilibrium, ranging from its existence and economic meaningfulness to its uniqueness and stability. Mathematical economists have also extended the analysis to encompass uncertainty and imperfectly competitive markets.

8. Wassily Leontief's input-output analysis is a major new departure in general-equilibrium theory. Unlike the Walrasian equations, input-output analysis allows the numerical specification of an economy's interdependencies.

KEY TERMS

capitalism
costs of exchange
deliberate coordination

economic order

feedback effect

final goods

general equilibrium

impact effect

input-output table

intermediate goods

Invisible Hand

Leontief inverse matrix

managerial coordination

market coordination

partial equilibrium

price system

spillout effect

spontaneous coordination

technical coefficients

transactions costs

Visible Hand

HANDS-ON PRACTICE

Exercise #1

Consider the economy depicted in this chapter's Tables 13.1 to 13.4. How much would the output of this economy's three goods have to be increased if one wanted to export an additional 1,000 tons of corn?

Solution:

The answer can be found by multiplying all the entries in column (3) of Table 13.4 by 1,000: 61.6257 megawatt hours of electricity plus 33.2583 tons of steel plus 1,261.8605 tons of corn.

Exercise #2

Still pursuing the question raised in Exercise 1, by how much would the quantities of primary resources have to be increased?

Solution:

The answer can be found by multiplying the row (D) to (F) information of Table 13.3 by the respective output increases just calculated in Exercise 1:

One would need 61.6257 (.01) labor hours to make the extra electricity plus 33.2583 (1) labor hours to make the extra steel plus 1,261.8605 (1) labor hours to make the extra corn, or a total of 1,295.735 extra labor hours.

One would also need 61.6257 (.01) acre hours to make the extra electricity plus 33.2583 (.25) acre hours to make the extra steel plus 1,261.8605 (5) acre hours to make the extra corn, or a total of 6,318.2333 extra acre hours.

Finally, one would need 61.6257 (.25) machine hours to make the extra electricity plus 33.2583 (.5) machine hours to make the extra steel plus 1,261.8605 (.2) machine hours to make the extra corn, or a total of 284.40767 extra machine hours.

Exercise #3

Still pursuing the question raised in Exercise 1, where would all that newly produced corn go?

Solution:

The electric power industry would use .1 (61.6257) tons, the steel industry .1 (33.2583) tons, and the corn industry .2 (1,261.8605) tons as intermediate inputs. These uses add to 261.8605 tons; the remainder (1,000 tons) is exported. Note: These results are obtained by multiplying row (C) of Table 13.3 by the respective output increases found in Exercise 1.

QUESTIONS AND PROBLEMS

1. "Everything in a market economy depends on everything else! One can't even stir a flower without troubling a star. That's why a change in the demand for fish might well affect the wages of carpenters, and a change in the supply of crude oil might well affect the price of cereal.'' Explain.

2.   Mr. A: The price system is like a vast computer. It continually selects those sets of prices that are closer to general equilibrium while rejecting others further away.

Ms. B: It is impossible to prove this beyond a doubt.

What do you think?

3.   Consider an input-output table (refer to Tables 13.1 or 13.2).

a.   Could a column (4) entry be negative? What would a negative entry there mean?

b.   If all entries were in monetary terms, what would be the meaning of the sums of the various rows and columns?

4.   ''General equilibrium economics is undoubtedly a splendid intellectual achievement. But it is not by any means on the level of Newtonian mechanics. In a world with large complicated corporations, selling thousands of goods and services . . . the way we stick to our simple models (which at best cover one simple limiting case) is ludicrous. I am reminded of . . . the drunk who had lost his keys at night and spent his time searching for them under a streetlamp fifty yards from where he had lost them because that was the only place where he could see anything.''[10] Do you agree or disagree with this observer? Why?

5.   Respond to the following question posed by a central planner: ''What is wrong with taking account only of *direct* input requirements when planning an output target? After all, if each car requires five tires (including one spare) and if I want one more car, I need only plan for five more tires. If I produced six or seven more tires, I would have a surplus.''

---

[10]Martin Shubik, ''A Curmudgeon's Guide to Microeconomics,'' *Journal of Economic Literature*, June 1970, p. 415.

6.   ''I am confused. The caption to Table 13.3 says that the figures are based on Table 13.1, columns (1) to (3) and (8). Yet when I calculate technical coefficients from Table 13.2, I get the same answer.'' Explain why.

7.   Explain what would happen with input-output analysis if constant returns to scale did *not* prevail.

8.   Explain the meaning of column (3), Table 13.4.

9.   Consider panel (a) of Figure 13.1, ''Circular Flows,'' on p. 460. Suppose there were *H* households who were demanding *G* types of goods and supplying *R* types of resources in markets all of which were perfectly competitive. If you wanted to describe this economy by Walrasian equations, what kinds of equations would you write down? (*Hint:* Walras used three types of equations to set up his general-equilibrium model. A first set represented the demand by consumers for goods. A second set ensured that the total amount of each resource used by firms was equal to the total amount supplied by households. A third set described the conditions of long-run perfectly competitive equilibrium.) Give it a try; then you can look at a possible answer at the back of the book.

10.   Given your answer to Problem 9, determine whether your number of equations equals the number of unknowns to be determined.

11.   Mr. A: Now I have heard everything: People in the market economy are not supposed to coordinate their activities in a rational way, but they should simply submit to the blind forces of the market and all would work out for the good! That's just like announcing, as the fundamental principle of the whole system, that, *''in order to make a perfect and beautiful machine, it is not requisite to know how to make it.''* This proposition will be found, on careful examination, to summarize the essential idea of the Invisible Hand. In short, Absolute Ignorance is fully qualified to take the place of Absolute Wisdom.

Ms. B: Poor A, as usual, you don't see what it's all about. Why *not* submit to something that works well, even if you don't understand it rationally? As A. N. Whitehead used to say, "Civilization advances by extending the number of important operations we can perform *without* thinking about them." Knowing full well the limitations of human reason, I vote for the Invisible Hand.

Evaluate these two opposing positions.

SELECTED READINGS

Arrow, Kenneth J., and F. H. Hahn. *General Competitive Analysis.* San Francisco: Holden-Day, 1972.

> A comprehensive theoretical treatment that includes historical notes. (Arrow won the 1972 Nobel Prize in economics.)

Jaffé, William. "Walras's Economics as Others See It," *Journal of Economic Literature,* June 1980, pp. 528–49.

> In this article, the translator of Walras opposes the common view that Walras constructed a model by the use of which we can examine how the capitalist system works. Instead, he claims, Walras's *Eléments* were intended to be a *realistic utopia,* a delineation of a state of affairs nowhere to be found in the actual world, independent of time and place, ideally perfect in certain respects and yet composed of realistic psychological and material ingredients.

Kohler, Heinz. *Comparative Economic Systems.* Glenview, Ill.: Scott, Foresman and Co., 1989, chap. 6.

> An application of input-output techniques to Soviet central economic planning.

Kuenne, Robert E. *Microeconomic Theory of the Market Mechanism: A General Equilibrium Approach.* New York: Macmillan, 1968.

> A study, from the point of view of general-equilibrium analysis, of the theory of the consumer, of the firm (under perfect and imperfect competition), and of the complete market mechanism.

Kuenne, Robert E. *The Theory of General Equilibrium.* Princeton, N.J.: Princeton University Press, 1963.

> A thorough discussion of the neoclassical construction of the theory, as well as recent extensions into static linear systems, spatial models, and dynamic ones.

Leontief, Wassily W. *The Structure of [the] American Economy, 1919–1939: An Empirical Application of Equilibrium Analysis,* 2nd edition. New York: Oxford University Press, 1951.

> The first major work on input-output analysis by the 1973 winner of the Nobel Prize in economics.

Leontief, Wassily W. *Essays in Economics, vol. 1: Theories and Theorizing.* New York: Oxford University Press, 1966; *vol. 2: Theories, Facts, and Policies.* New York: Sharpe, 1977.

> Essays on a variety of subjects from history to mathematical economics; from the economics of Marx to that of Keynes; from international trade, economic development, and growth to Soviet economic science; from dynamic input-output analysis to national economic planning.

Leontief, Wassily W., et al. *Studies in the Structure of the American Economy: Theoretical and Empirical Explorations in Input-Output Analysis,* 2nd edition, New York: Oxford University Press, 1977.

> Essays by Leontief and others.

Miller, Ronald E., and Peter D. Blair. *Input-Output Analysis: Foundations and Extensions.* Englewood Cliffs, N.J.: Prentice-Hall, 1985.

> A comprehensive text, including applications and the U.S. input-output tables for 1947–77.

Morishima, Michio. *Walras' Economics: A Pure Theory of Capital and Money.* Cambridge, Mass.: Cambridge University Press, 1977.

> The author of *Marx's Economics* argues that Marx should be ranked as high as Walras in the history of mathematical economics and that Walrasian economists have misunderstood Walras just as Marxists often misunderstood Marx.

Morishima, Michio. "W. Jaffé on Léon Walras: A Comment," *Journal of Economic Literature,* June 1980, pp. 550–58.

> A strong critique of Jaffé's interpretation of Walras's work.

The Public Interest, Special Issue 1980. Articles by Kirzner, Hahn, and Arrow on "General Equilibrium and Beyond."

U.S. Bureau of the Census. "The Input-Output Structure of the U.S. Economy: 1967," *Survey of Current Business,* February 1974, pp. 24–56.

> An actual input-output table, complete with technical coefficients and inverse.

Walras, Léon. *Elements of Pure Economics.* Translated by William Jaffé. Homewood, Ill.: Irwin, 1954.

Weintraub, E. Roy. "On the Existence of a Competitive Equilibrium: 1930–1954," *Journal of Economic Literature,* March 1983, pp. 1–39.

> A fascinating survey of the existence-of-equilibrium literature that culminated in the work of Arrow-Debreu and McKenzie, with a link to the creation of game theory, fixed point theory, and linear programming.

COMPUTER PROGRAMS

The KOHLER-3 personal-computer diskettes that accompany this book contain three programs of particular interest to this chapter:

13. General Equilibrium includes a 31-question multiple-choice test with immediate re-

sponses to incorrect answers as well as numerous exercises concerning the concept of economic interdependence.

Appendix A. Solving Simultaneous Equations and *Appendix D. Matrix Operations* will be helpful in performing input-output analysis.

ANALYTICAL EXAMPLE 13.1

THE ECONOMIC EFFECTS OF DISARMAMENT

Input-output analysis has been used to predict the major economic effects certain to follow an international agreement to disarm. The accompanying table, based on 1958 U.S. data, shows some of the predicted results. For example, the 1958 military expenditures on food and kindred products in fact equaled $536 million (at 1947

Industry (1)	Military Demand (millions of 1947 dollars)	
	Direct (2)	Direct and Indirect (3)
Food and kindred products	536	1,513
Apparel and textile-mill products	143	575
Leather products	24	116
Paper and allied products	—	788
Chemicals and allied products	85	877
Fuel and power	991	2,633
Rubber and rubber products	6	244
Lumber and wood products	19	451
Nonmetallic minerals and products	—	337
Primary metals	—	3,384
Fabricated metal products	106	1,281
Machinery (except electrical)	166	823
Electrical machinery	915	3,110
Transportation equipment and ordnance	9,478	10,609
Instruments and allied products	22	370
Miscellaneous manufacturing industries	—	119
Transportation	730	1,486
Trade	78	735
Service and finance	705	1,886
Construction	967	967
Unallocated and waste products	742	2,144

prices). Yet a complete cessation of military spending would have reduced demand in that industry by $1,513 million because other industries, depending on military demand, would also reduce their demands for food and kindred products. All other entries can be similarly interpreted.

Clearly, disarmament by itself would produce massive but differential cuts in industry sales, as indicated in column (3), and thus cuts in output and employment. Yet the same analysis can be used to indicate the opposite effects of any increase in nonmilitary demands and can help guide policy makers toward actions that minimize adjustment effects.

Source: Wassily W. Leontief and Marvin Hoffenberg, "The Economic Effects of Disarmament," *Scientific American,* April 1961, pp. 47–55. Copyright © 1961 by Scientific American, Inc. All rights reserved. Reprinted by permission. Regional aspects of the same issue are explored by Walter Isard and Eugene W. Schooler in "An Economic Analysis of Local and Regional Impacts of Reduction of Military Expenditures," *Peace Research Society Papers,* 1, 1964, pp. 15–45. International impacts are investigated in Emile Benoit, ed., *Disarmament and World Economic Interdependence* (New York: Columbia University Press, 1967).

ANALYTICAL EXAMPLE 13.2

THE STRUCTURE OF DEVELOPMENT

Input-output analysis, by facilitating comparisons of the internal structures of developed and undeveloped economies, can help map out paths to economic development. The accompanying input-output tables (Figure A) indicate internal structures of model economies symbolically. Each number (at the head of a column or row) represents a different economic sector, O stands for "output," I for "input," D for "final demand," T for "total output," and H for "household-supplied resource services." The color squares represent numerical entries in the various cells of the table.

Panel (a) of Figure A shows a completely interdependent economy. Each sector supplies outputs to all others and draws inputs from all others. Panel (b), on the other hand, shows a random pattern of interindustry transactions. Some boxes are empty because no transactions occur between the affected sectors. In panel (c), panel (b) reappears with sectors rearranged (note the sequence of sector "call numbers"). This rearrangement, called "triangulation," reveals a hierarchical pattern of interindustry transactions. Note how sector 9 delivers its entire output to itself or to final demands but absorbs inputs from all sectors. Sector 8, on the other hand, delivers output to everyone but uses as inputs only its own output and household-supplied resource services. Thus the sectors above a given row in panel (c) are that row's customers; the sectors below a given row are suppliers. Thus any increase in final demand for a sector generates indirect demands that cascade down the diagonal slope of the matrix and leave the sectors above unaffected.

Panel (d), finally, shows a "block triangular" economy with interdependence of industries within blocks and hierarchical relationships among them. The analysis of

FIGURE A

Internal Structures of Model Economies

(a) Interdependent Pattern

(b) Random Pattern

(c) Hierarchical Pattern

(d) Block Triangular Pattern

such tables shows development planners in economically less developed countries which "working parts" typically found in developed economies are lacking in their country and also the sequence in which sectors must be developed.

Source: Wassily W. Leontief, "The Structure of Development," *Scientific American,* September 1963, pp. 148–66. Copyright © 1963 by Scientific American, Inc. All rights reserved. Recently, Leontief has developed the first input-output model of the world economy. Interested readers may wish to study his associated discussion of the economic prospects of the less developed nations. See "The World Economy of the Year 2000," *Scientific American,* September 1980, pp. 207–31.

14

Efficiency and Equity

Scarcity, as noted in Chapter 1, affects all present-day societies. Everywhere, resources and technical knowledge are insufficient to produce all of the goods people want. Under such circumstances, some desires for goods must remain unsatisfied even if no resources or goods are ever wasted by anyone.

This chapter will focus on an important implication of that early lesson: People who dislike scarcity should use their resources and goods as carefully as possible; they should *economize* them. Yet people are quite capable of making foolish choices with the resources and goods at their disposal. When they do, scarcity is more intense than necessary. Economists, therefore, have long been interested in developing criteria capable of judging the performance of economies and of highlighting the existence of *avoidable* scarcity. Numerous criteria have been proposed and are being applied; they include a full utilization of available resources, an efficient employment of resources, a rapid growth of output over time, an equitable apportionment of output among people, and others still. In this chapter, we shall concentrate on two of these criteria, economic efficiency and economic equity, which have been traditionally of greatest interest to microeconomists.

EFFICIENCY

In one way or another, the concept of efficiency is always concerned with the possibility of getting more output from given inputs. When the criterion of efficiency is applied, for instance, to the operations of a single firm, economists compare physical output with physical inputs. This we did in Chapter 4 when discussing **technical efficiency** or **X-efficiency,** a situation in which a single firm finds it impossible to produce a given output with less of at least one input without increasing the amount of other inputs. Put differently, such efficiency exists in a firm when it is impossible, with given technical knowledge, to produce a larger output from a given set of inputs.

When the yardstick of efficiency, however, is applied to an entire economy, economists compare the *total economic welfare* of all people (which is the ultimate output of the economy) with the *total of resource services utilized* (or the economy's inputs). In perfect analogy to the concept of technical efficiency, economists say that economy-wide or **economic efficiency** exists when it is impossible, with given technology, to produce a larger welfare total from given stocks of resources.

And note: The concept of economic efficiency is also referred to as **allocative efficiency** (because it is about the best allocation of given resources and the goods made with their help) and as **static efficiency** (because it is applied to a short time period (called "the present") in which the economy's stocks of resources and technical knowledge are fixed).

While it is easy enough to define economic efficiency as we just have, it is much more difficult to apply the concept to the world around us. The reason will become clear presently.

The Slippery Concept of a Change in Total Economic Welfare

If total economic welfare is defined as the sum of the welfares of all individuals, a reallocation of resources or goods that affects more than one person may well affect total economic welfare in an ambiguous fashion. Some potential changes, to be sure, would raise total economic welfare with certainty because they would bring to *each* person affected a marginal benefit that, in the judgment of that person, exceeded the associated marginal cost. Other potential changes, however, would affect total economic welfare in an ambiguous way, since they would bring a marginal benefit in excess of marginal cost to only some persons, while imposing a marginal cost in excess of the marginal benefit on other persons.

In the case where changes brought to *each* person a marginal benefit in excess of marginal cost, harmony would reign supreme. Each of the affected persons would agree to the potential change. If a vote were taken, it would be unanimous, because every single person affected by the change would expect to gain from it. Thus total economic welfare would rise with certainty.

In the case where some of the people affected by the change expected to experience a net gain and others a net loss, a unanimous vote would be inconceivable. Conflict rather than harmony would reign. Those people who would get a marginal benefit in excess of marginal cost would vote for the change. Others who would get a marginal cost exceeding the marginal benefit would vote against it. The effect of the change on total economic welfare would be ambiguous. Would the gainers gain more than the losers would lose, or the opposite? Would gains just balance losses in welfare? Unless we found a way of measuring each person's welfare and of then comparing it with that of other people (and, contrary to Bentham's hope, no one has found one yet), we could not tell what happened to the magnitude of total economic welfare.

Escaping the Ambiguity

The sort of situation in which the effect of a reallocation of resources or goods on total economic welfare was *ambiguous* would cause confrontation and struggle and, ultimately, victory for some and defeat for others. Economists have little to say about such ambiguous situations. Indeed, economists have decided to focus attention on those contrasting situations in which appropriate changes would raise total economic welfare *with certainty.* In such situations, people's energies could be channeled away from conflicts (from which some people would be certain to lose) and toward agreeable changes (from which no one would lose and some or all would gain).

At the turn of the century, the Italian economist Vilfredo Pareto (1848–1923), a Biography of whom appears in Chapter 14 of the *Student Workbook* that accompanies this text, suggested that economists define **economic inefficiency** as those situations in which it is possible, through some reallocation of resources or goods, to make some or all people better off (in their own judgment) *without making others worse off* (in *their* own judgment).

And note: By rewriting Pareto's definition of economic inefficiency, we can also develop an operational definition of economic efficiency that does not require us to make precise measurements and comparisons of the utilities of different people. Thus we can define **economic efficiency** as a situation in which it is *impossible,* through some reallocation of resources or goods, to make some people better off (in their own judgment) without making others worse off (in *their* own judgment).

Indeed, Pareto spelled out a number of so-called **marginal conditions** that must be met if economic inefficiency is to be avoided and if economic efficiency is to be achieved. By testing the degree to which any society fulfills these marginal conditions, economists can determine whether that society has managed to exhaust all *unambiguous* possibilities for increasing the total economic welfare of its people.

PARETO'S MARGINAL CONDITIONS OF ECONOMIC EFFICIENCY

Pareto's marginal conditions can be stated with the help of two key concepts. The first of these is the **marginal rate of transformation *(MRT)*,** the rate at which a producer is technically able to exchange, in the process of production, a little bit of one variable (say, labor or butter) for a little bit of another variable (say, apples produced with the help of that labor or produced in place of that butter). The second crucial concept is the **marginal rate of**

substitution *(MRS)*, the rate at which a consumer is willing to exchange, as a matter of indifference, a little bit of one variable (say, the consumption of leisure or butter) for a little bit of another variable (say, the consumption of apples received for the sacrifice of leisure or butter). Let us consider how Pareto used these concepts to talk about economic efficiency.

Condition 1: The Optimum Allocation of a Resource among Producers of the Same Good

One marginal condition of economic efficiency deals with the optimum allocation of a resource among producers of the same good:

> *1. Economic efficiency requires that the marginal rate of transformation* (MRT) *between any resource* x *and any good* a *be the same for any two producers,* α *and* β, *producing this good with that resource.*

$$MRT^{\alpha}_{x,a} = MRT^{\beta}_{x,a}$$

This condition is illustrated with the help of two production functions in Figure 14.1. Two

FIGURE 14.1

Pareto's First Condition

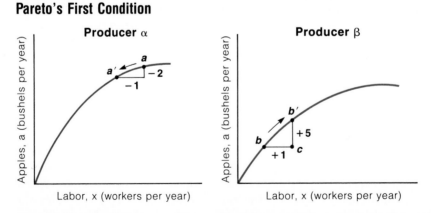

This set of graphs illustrates the violation of Pareto's first marginal condition of economic efficiency. Let producer α operate at point *a* initially, while producer β operates at *b*. Note that α's *MRT* equals 1*x* for 2*a*, while β's *MRT* equals 1*x* for 5*a*. Thus it is possible for α to release 1*x* in favor of β; this reduces α's output by 2*a*, while raising β's output by 5*a*. The economy as a whole has extra output of 3*a*. The possibility exists to make someone better off (by 3*a*) without making anyone else worse off.

producers, α and β, are initially operating at *technically* efficient points *a* and *b*, respectively. (Operating at a point such as *c* would be technically inefficient because it would be possible to raise output by 5*a* from the given amount of labor employed—a move from *c* to *b'*—or to lower input by 1*x*, while keeping output unchanged—a move from *c* to *b*.) Yet while each producer, in isolation, is doing as well as is possible, *economic* inefficiency exists. The caption tells us why.

Wide Applicability.   Although this example involved labor and apples, the first marginal condition is applicable to literally billions of situations. Resource *x* can be labor, but it can also be fertilizer or steel or turret lathes. Good *a* can be apples, but it can also be airplanes, haircuts, or residential houses. Even the term "producer" can refer to more than the ordinary business firm; it might refer to a region or even a country! Suppose α meant "Oregon" (or even "China"), while β stood for "Vermont" (or the "United States"). It is easy to imagine circumstances under which the shift of at least some units of labor (or any resource) from Oregon to Vermont

(or from China to the United States) would increase the world's output of goods. Artificial political boundaries that prevent such shifts make scarcity more severe than it has to be. The abolition of such boundaries (as within the United States or within a Common Market) helps raise the material welfare of people.

Condition 2: The Optimum Specialization of Production among Producers of the Same Goods

A second marginal condition of economic efficiency concerns the optimum specialization of production among producers of the same goods:

> *2. Economic efficiency requires that the marginal rate of transformation* (**MRT**) *between any two goods* **a** *and* **b**, *be the same for any two producers,* α *and* β, *producing both goods.*

$$MRT_{a,b}^{\alpha} = MRT_{a,b}^{\beta}$$

This condition is illustrated with the help of two production possibilities curves in Figure 14.2. Two producers, α and β, are initially

FIGURE 14.2

Pareto's Second Condition

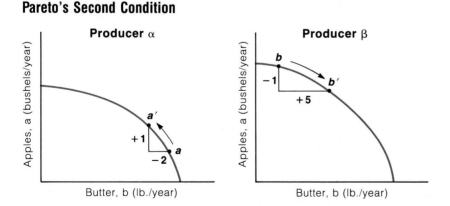

This set of graphs illustrates the violation of Pareto's second marginal condition of economic efficiency. Let producer α operate at point *a* initially, while producer β operates at *b*. Note that α's *MRT* equals 1*a* for 2*b*, while β's *MRT* equals 1*a* for 5*b*. Thus it is possible for α to produce an extra 1*a*, while sacrificing 2*b*. At the same time, β could produce an extra 5*b*, while sacrificing 1*a*. The economy as a whole would have extra output of 3*b* from identical resources, differently allocated. The possibility exists to make someone better off (by 3*b*) without making anyone else worse off.

operating at full-employment and technically efficient points *a* and *b*, respectively. Yet while each producer, in isolation, is doing as well as possible, *economic* inefficiency exists. The caption tells us why.

Wide Applicability. As was true for the first marginal condition, so this second one is applicable to billions of situations. Not only can goods *a* and *b* represent any two goods, but α and β can again refer to any two "producers," including regions or countries. Consider how international trading in goods might substitute for the international movement of resources should the latter prove impossible. If, in Figure 14.2, α stood for China and β for the United States, an *internal* shift of resources from the initial situations to the final ones could be followed by trade: The Chinese could export 1*a* to the United States in return for 3.5*b*, for example. This would leave both countries better off at the same time. (Can you show that both countries would end up with the same amount of apples as initially, but with an extra 1.5 units of butter each?)

Close-Up 14.1, "Stalin and Comecon," provides another illustration of the potential gains from international trade.

Condition 3: The Optimum Composition of Production and Consumption

Other Pareto conditions of economic efficiency are more subtle than the two just discussed. Economic welfare can possibly be increased, not because a greater quantity of goods could be made available, but because a different and preferred set of goods could be produced:

> *3. Economic efficiency requires that the marginal rate of transformation (MRT) between any two goods, **a** and **b**, produced by any producer, α, be equal to the marginal rate of substitution (MRS) between these two goods for any consumer, X, who consumes both.*

$$MRT^{\alpha}_{a,b} = MRS^{X}_{a,b}$$

FIGURE 14.3

Pareto's Third Condition

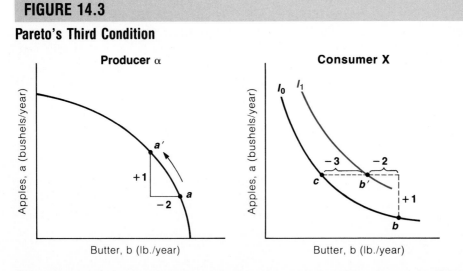

This set of graphs illustrates the violation of Pareto's third marginal condition of economic efficiency. Let producer α operate at point *a* initially, while consumer X operates at *b*. Note that α's *MRT* equals 1*a* for 2*b*, while X's *MRS* equals 1*a* for 5*b* (both points *b* and *c* lie on indifference curve I_0). Thus it is possible for α to produce an extra 1*a*, while sacrificing 2*b*. This would require that some consumer, such as X, consume 2*b* less while receiving 1*a* more. Yet this would make X better off (point *b'* lies on a higher indifference curve) without making anyone else worse off.

FIGURE 14.4

Pareto's Fourth Condition

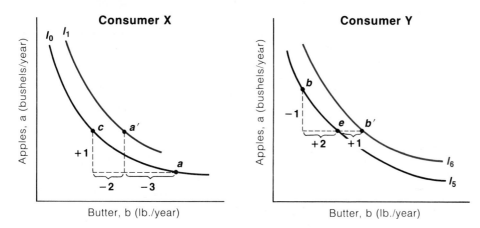

This set of graphs illustrates the violation of Pareto's fourth marginal condition of economic efficiency. Let consumers X and Y operate at points *a* and *b* initially. Note that X's *MRS* equals 1*a* for 5*b* (both points *a* and *c* lie on indifference curve I_0), while Y's *MRS* equals 1*a* for 2*b* (both points *b* and *e* lie on indifference curve I_5). It is possible to arrange an exchange of, say, 1*a* for 3*b*: If X moved from *a* to *a'* (giving up 3*b* and getting 1*a*), while Y moved from *b* to *b'* (giving up 1*a* and getting 3*b*), both consumers would be better off at the same time, reaching higher indifference curves I_1 and I_6, respectively. No one would be worse off as a result of the exchange.

This condition is illustrated with the help of a production-possibilities curve and two indifference curves in Figure 14.3. A producer α and a consumer X are initially operating at points *a* and *b*, respectively. Yet while each, in isolation, is doing as well as possible, *economic* inefficiency exists. The caption tells us why.

Condition 4: The Optimum Allocation of Goods among Consumers of the Same Goods

Given the overall quantity of production and even each person's share in this total, another important requirement of economic efficiency is that each person has the best combination of specific goods. According to Pareto:

> *4. Economic efficiency requires that the marginal rate of substitution* **(MRS)** *between any two goods,* **a** *and* **b,** *be the same for any two consumers,* **X** *and* **Y,** *consuming both goods.*

$$MRS^X_{a,b} = MRS^Y_{a,b}$$

This condition is illustrated with the help of two sets of indifference curves in Figure 14.4. Two consumers, X and Y, are initially operating at points *a* and *b*, respectively. Yet while each, in isolation, is doing as well as possible, *economic* inefficiency exists. The caption tells us why.* Close-Up 14.2, "The POW Camp," provides a real-world illustration.

THE PARETO OPTIMUM: SUMMARY AND CRITICISMS

When all the marginal conditions of economic efficiency are fulfilled simultaneously, a society is said to have reached its **Pareto optimum.** One

---

*For a mathematical treatment of the fourth Pareto condition, see Section 14A of the Calculus Appendix at the back of this book.

can, however, find efficiency conditions other than the four described above; as Pareto noted, a near-infinite number exists. All such efficiency conditions, however, can be summarized by the following two propositions:

1. All equivalent marginal rates of technical transformation or of indifferent substitution must be equal. That is, any *MRT* must equal anybody else's corresponding *MRT;* any *MRS* must equal anybody else's corresponding *MRS.*

2. Whenever one can technically transform a little bit of one variable into a little bit of another, the marginal rate of technical transformation (the amount of one variable one can obtain objectively by sacrificing a unit of the other) must equal the marginal rate of indifferent substitution (the amount of one variable a person could substitute for a unit of the other without a feeling of gain or loss). That is, any *MRT* must equal any corresponding *MRS.*

Note how the first, second, and fourth conditions are perfectly described by proposition 1, while the third Pareto condition is covered by proposition 2. As long as these two propositions are not fulfilled and marginal inequalities persist, Pareto tells us, a reallocation of resources or goods is possible that raises total economic welfare with certainty. Although most present-day economists would agree, Pareto is not without his critics.

The Pareto definition of economic efficiency is based on a number of value judgments. Some economists do not share these values. They do not consider economic efficiency, as defined by Pareto, to be a worthy goal to pursue.

First, Pareto defines total economic welfare in terms of the welfare of all the individuals that make up society. Total economic welfare is somehow the sum of individual welfares; it is not a separate concept independent of these individual building blocks. Pareto's critics often look upon society as an entity independent of the individuals constituting it, and they talk of ''the social good'' as separate from the sum of individual welfares.

Second, Pareto assumes that adult individuals (with the rarest of exceptions) are the best judges of their own welfares. An increase or decrease in the welfare of an individual is counted as such only when the affected individual so testifies. Pareto's critics often believe that the preferences of some people are superior to those of others and that everybody's welfare should be judged on the basis of these superior tastes.

Third, Pareto assumes, contrary to Bentham (see Chapter 2), that the welfare of one individual cannot be compared with that of another. As a result, Pareto is willing to make pronouncements about changes in total economic welfare only when the welfares of all individuals (in their own judgments) have remained unchanged or moved in the same direction. Pareto remains silent on all other comparisons. Even if a million people said they were better off as a result of a reallocation of resources or goods, a single statement to the contrary would lead Pareto to claim ignorance about the effect on *total* economic welfare.

As a consequence, the Pareto optimum, unlike Bentham's welfare maximum, is not a unique situation. Many possible situations would be considered optimal by the Pareto criterion. For example, the final situation depicted by points *a'* and *b'* in Figure 14.4 would be considered *efficient* by Pareto as long as the indifference-curve *slopes* at these points were equal. (As we learned in Chapter 2, these slopes measure the respective *MRS*s.) According to Pareto, given an equality of *MRS*s, no further changes could be recommended by economists because such changes would not increase total economic welfare *with certainty.* But now consider a situation in which the two individuals consumed completely different shares of the *total* quantities of the goods available. Suppose X at *a'* consumed 50*a* and 30*b*, while Y at *b'* consumed 500*a* and 300*b*. If the marginal rates of substitution were still equal, the Pareto criterion would not endorse any change because such change would not raise total economic welfare *unambiguously.* Yet helping poor X at the expense of rich Y would almost surely change a Benthamite measure of welfare (which measured and added together each person's welfare with the help of a cardinal number). Quite possibly, Pareto's critics assert, making poor X richer at the expense of rich Y would raise the total of economic welfare by giving, say, 300 units of extra satisfaction to poor X, while taking 20 units from rich Y. Yet Pareto, crippled by his own assumptions, would support the status quo and refuse to endorse any change in the (legitimate) fear that poor X might gain 300 and rich Y lose 800 units of satisfaction in the process. Since we cannot measure these changes in satisfaction but can only speculate about them, Pareto refuses to make a judgment. Any distribution of goods among consumers that is associated with equal marginal rates of substitution is, therefore, considered equally acceptable by his efficiency criterion, which exasperates Pareto's critics.

Later in this chapter, we shall discuss various criteria of *equity* that can be used to make the kinds of moral judgments Pareto's critics demand and to distinguish among the many situations that cannot be ranked on a scale of better or worse by the Pareto criterion.

THE ECONOMIC EFFICIENCY OF PERFECTLY COMPETITIVE MARKETS

We now turn to a crucial question: How can one ensure that a real-world economy achieves economic efficiency? One certainly cannot do it by having government bureaucrats identify all conceivable violations of Pareto's conditions (such as those illustrated in Figures 14.1 to 14.4) and then order appropriate reallocations of resources or goods. Friedrich A. von Hayek (1899–   ), who won the 1974 Nobel Prize in economics (and whose Biography appears in Chapter 14 of the *Student Workbook* that accompanies this text), has been particularly eloquent in pointing out the reason for this impossibility. Would-be central planners would be paralyzed by the **knowledge problem,** the difficulty of making use jointly of all the knowledge relevant to achieving economic efficiency because such knowledge is not available to a single mind in its totality but is found, in billions of dispersed fragments, in the minds of

countless separate individuals. The knowledge about which Hayek is concerned is, of course, those *MRT*s and *MRS*s we have just met; it is what he calls the vast reservoir of *unorganized* knowledge of particular applicability, the fleeting knowledge of the particular circumstances of place and time. Consider knowledge of *production possibilities* and *preferences* that refers only to particular places and people and moments. Each individual inevitably possesses unique bits of such information. And there are billions of *MRT*s and billions of *MRS*s, ever changing.

No central planner (or group of planners) can ever possess this unorganized type of knowledge. It must always remain dispersed. The central planner (or group of planners) will always be ignorant of most of what is known to all others taken together.

Yet Hayek notes a close link between perfectly competitive markets and the achievement of economic efficiency. Indeed, every conceivable Pareto condition of economic efficiency would tend to be fulfilled if profit-maximizing firms and utility-maximizing households were to determine the optimum quantities they wished to trade with the help of equilibrium prices established in such markets. A consideration of two of the marginal conditions discussed above will illustrate why the behavior of firms and households in perfectly competitive markets is linked to economic efficiency.

The First Pareto Condition

Consider Figure 14.5. Panel (a) depicts a competitive labor market that has established a wage of $3.10 per unit of labor. This wage would become the marginal cost of acquiring labor that would be a given to all firms, including α and β, depicted in panels (b) and (c). According to the input rule first illustrated in Figure 11.1, "A Firm's Demand for Labor: The Simple Case" (p. 359), each firm would maximize profit by buying that input quantity at which the input's declining marginal value product, MVP_i, just equaled the input's price, P_i. Thus firm α would choose to employ 9 units of labor (in accordance with intersection a); firm β would choose 21 units of labor (intersection b). As a result, the marginal value product of labor in one firm (distance A) would exactly equal that in the other firm (distance B).

$$MVP^\alpha_i = \$3.10 = MVP^\beta_i$$

Because an input's marginal value product equals its marginal physical product, MPP_i, multiplied by output price, P_o, the above equality implies that

$$MPP^\alpha_i \cdot P_o = \$3.10 = MPP^\beta_i \cdot P_o.$$

Because, furthermore, the output price is the same for all perfectly competitive firms (and assumed here to equal $1 per unit of apples), it also follows that labor's marginal physical product would be the same in the two firms.

$$MPP^\alpha_i = 3.1 \text{ units of apples} = MPP^\beta_i$$

Yet the marginal physical product of an input is nothing else but Pareto's marginal rate of transformation between this input and the output it makes. Thus

$$MRT^\alpha_{x,a} = 3.1 \text{ units of apples} = MRT^\beta_{x,a}.$$

Profit maximization under perfect competition, therefore, would keep α and β away from the kind of choices that spell economic inefficiency for the economy, which are depicted in Figure 14.1 and by points c and d in Figure 14.5.

The Second Pareto Condition

Consider Figure 14.6. Panels (a) and (d), respectively, depict competitive markets for apples and butter in which prices of $1 per unit of apples and 27.8¢ per unit of butter have been established. These prices would become the marginal benefit of selling these products for all firms, including α

FIGURE 14.5

Perfect Competition and Pareto's First Condition

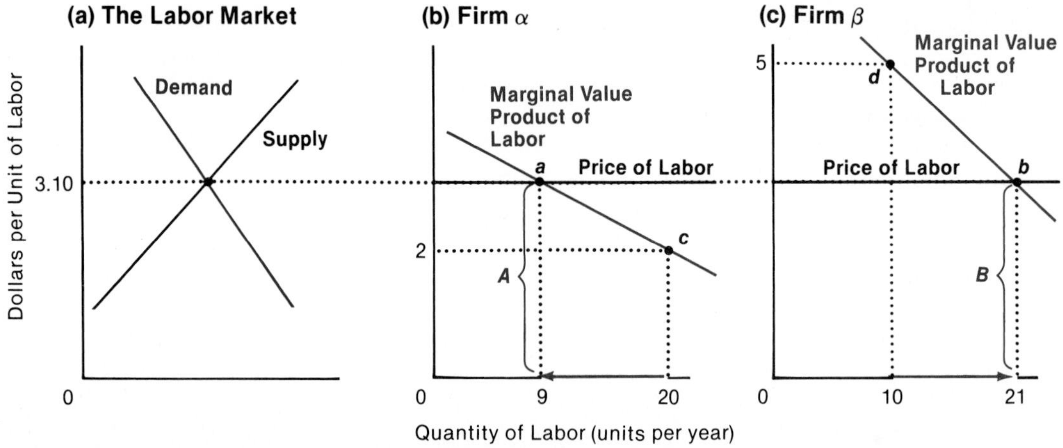

Perfectly competitive firms maximize profit by buying input quantities at which an input's declining marginal value product, MVP_i, just equals the input's price, P_i (points a and b). Because all firms face the identical input price, any input's marginal value product comes to be the same in all firms ($A = B$). Because an input's marginal value product, in turn, equals its marginal physical product, MPP_i, multiplied by output price, P_o, and because output price is the same for all firms, any input's marginal physical product comes to be the same in all firms as well. This equality fulfills Pareto's first condition because the marginal physical product of an input is the marginal rate of transformation of the input into output. > MRT and β, depicted in panels (b) and (e) or (c) and (f), respectively. According to the output rule first illustrated in Figure 5.2, ''A Profitable Business,'' (p. 144), each firm would maximize profit by producing and selling that output quantity at which the output's rising marginal cost, MC, just equaled its price, P. Thus firm α would choose to produce 27 units of apples (intersection a) and 11 units of butter (intersection b). Firm β would choose to produce 43 units of apples (intersection

FIGURE 14.6

Perfect Competition and Pareto's Second Condition

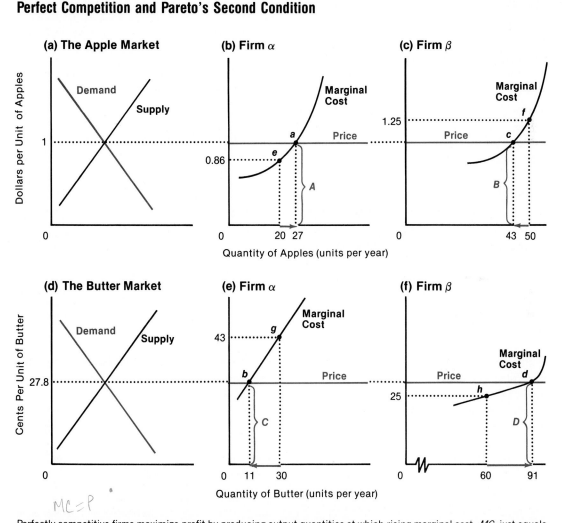

Perfectly competitive firms maximize profit by producing output quantities at which rising marginal cost, MC, just equals output price, P (points a through d). Because they face the identical output prices in any given market, all firms in effect equate each other's marginal costs of producing any good ($A = B$ and $C = D$). As a result, firms equate the marginal cost ratio of any two goods: $\dfrac{A}{C} = \dfrac{B}{D}$. This equality fulfills Pareto's second condition because each marginal cost ratio is a marginal rate of transformation of one good into another.

c) and 91 units of butter (intersection *d*). As a result, the marginal cost of producing apples in one firm (distance *A*) would exactly equal that in the other firm (distance *B*).

$$MC_a^\alpha = \$1 = MC_a^\beta$$

The same would be true with respect to the marginal cost of butter (distance $C = D$).

$$MC_b^\alpha = 27.8¢ = MC_b^\beta$$

By implication, one firm's marginal cost ratio (*A/C*) would also equal that of the other (*B/D*), each being equated with the identical ratio of market prices.

$$\left(\frac{MC_a}{MC_b}\right)^\alpha = \frac{\$1}{27.8¢} = \frac{3.6}{1} = \left(\frac{MC_a}{MC_b}\right)^\beta$$

Yet the reciprocal of the marginal cost ratio of two goods is nothing else but Pareto's marginal rate of transformation between them. If, at the margin, it costs 3.6 times as much to produce a unit of apples as to produce a unit of butter, one can transform 1 unit of apples into 3.6 units of butter. Thus the above implies

$$MRT_{a,b}^\alpha = 1a \text{ for } 3.6 \, b = MRT_{a,b}^\beta.$$

Profit maximization under perfect competition, therefore, would keep α and β away from the kind of choices that spell economic inefficiency for the economy, which are depicted in Figure 14.2 and by points *e* through *h* in Figure 14.6.

All Other Pareto Conditions

It can be shown that all other Pareto conditions would similarly be fulfilled in a world in which all decision makers faced identical equilibrium prices of resources and goods and were given the freedom to pursue their self-interest. Thus Pareto's third condition would be fulfilled for two reasons: (1) As we have just seen, profit-maximizing firms would equate marginal costs of

production with product prices and therefore would equate marginal cost ratios (or marginal rates of transformation between any two goods) with the price ratios of these goods. (2) As we learned in Chapter 2, utility-maximizing households would equate marginal rates of substitution between any two goods with their price ratios as well and with the very ratios of prices faced by firms. Thus any firm's *MRT* between goods would equal any household's *MRS:*

producer
$$MRT_{a,b}^\alpha = MRS_{a,b}^X \quad \text{consumer}$$

because each would be equated with the identical ratio of $\frac{P_a}{P_b}$.

Pareto's fourth condition would also be fulfilled in perfectly competitive markets because all households would face identical prices for any given good. Thus any households that maximized utility by equating the marginal rate of substitution between goods with their price ratio would by that very fact equate its marginal rate of substitution with that of any other household that would act in the same way:

$$MRS_{a,b}^X = MRS_{a,b}^Y$$

because each would be equated with the identical ratio of $\frac{P_a}{P_b}$.

All other Pareto conditions would be fulfilled in a similar fashion. Not surprisingly, this way of achieving economic efficiency is seen as an enormous advantage of an economic system with perfectly competitive markets. Such a system would not require saints to run it; ordinary mortals would do quite well! As Adam Smith described such a system,

> Every individual . . . endeavours . . . to employ his [resources] . . . that [their] produce may be of the greatest value. . . . He generally . . . neither intends to promote the public interest, nor knows how much he is promoting it. . . . He intends only his own security, . . . only his own gain. And he is in this . . . led by an Invisible Hand to promote an end which was not part of his inten-

FIGURE 14.7

Imperfect Competition and Pareto's First Condition

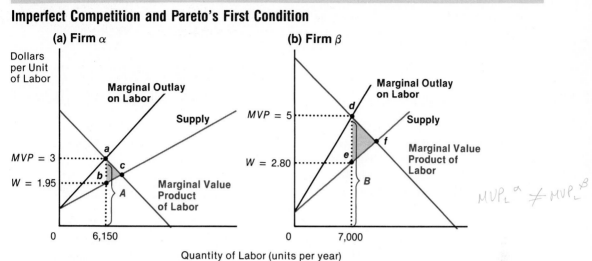

Input buyers that have monopsony power but act as perfect competitors in the output market maximize profit by buying input quantities at which an input's declining marginal value product just equals the marginal outlay on the input (points *a* and *d*). Under such circumstances, firms are unlikely to equate the input's marginal value products. Note how, in this example, $A \neq B$. Because an input's marginal value product, in turn, equals its marginal physical product multiplied by output price (and because output price is the same for all) the input's marginal physical products also differ between the firms. This inequality of the marginal physical products violates Pareto's first condition.

tion. . . . By pursuing his own interest he frequently promotes that of the society more effectually than when he really intends to promote it.[1]

THE ECONOMIC INEFFICIENCY OF IMPERFECTLY COMPETITIVE MARKETS

In the presence of monopoly, cartels, oligopoly, and all other forms of imperfect competition, economic efficiency would *not* emerge automatically as the happy by-product of self-interested behavior. Economic efficiency would occur only by sheer accident, if at all. Consider the Pareto conditions just discussed.

The First Pareto Condition

Figure 14.7 pictures the profit-maximizing behavior of two firms that are perfect competitors in the product market but have monopsony power in

the labor market. For reasons discussed in Chapter 11, each would equate its marginal outlay on labor with labor's marginal value product. Firm α would do so at intersection *a*; firm β at intersection *d*. Accordingly, α would hire 6,150 units of labor (at a wage of $1.95); β would hire 7,000 units (at a wage of $2.80).

Note: Unlike in Figure 14.5, which depicts the fulfillment of the first condition in the case of perfect competition, labor's marginal value product would now diverge between the two firms $A \neq B$). At α, the marginal unit of labor would add $3 to revenue and—with a competitive product price of $1 per unit—3 units to output. At β, the marginal unit of labor would add $5 to revenue and—given the same product price—5 units to output. Call labor *x* and product *a*, and a clear violation of Pareto's first condition emerges:

[1] Adam Smith, *An Inquiry into the Nature and Causes of the Wealth of Nations*, vol. 2 (Homewood, Ill.: Richard D. Irwin, 1963), pp. 22–23.

$$MRT_{x,a}^{\alpha}(=1x \text{ for } 3a) \neq MRT_{x,a}^{\beta}(=1x \text{ for } 5a).$$

Despite the inefficiency, neither firm would have any incentive to change its behavior because each would be maximizing profit. Thus economic inefficiency would persist.

The Second Pareto Condition

Figure 14.8 represents the profit-maximizing behavior of two firms that are imperfect competitors in the markets for two goods. For reasons discussed in Chapters 7 and 8, such firms would equate their marginal costs of production with marginal revenue. Firm α would do so at intersections a and g; firm β at intersections d and k. Accordingly, α would produce 10,000 refrigerators and 16,000 washers per year, while β would produce 18,000 and 26,000 units, respectively.

Note: Unlike in Figure 14.6, which illustrates the fulfillment of the second condition in the case of perfect competition, the two firms' marginal costs, as well as their ratios, would now diverge ($A \neq B$, $C \neq D$, and $A/C \neq B/D$). Realizing that these ratios are closely linked to the marginal rates of transformation between the two goods (and denoting refrigerators by r and washers by w), a clear violation of Pareto's second condition can be observed:

$$\left(\frac{MC_r}{MC_w}\right)^{\alpha} = \frac{\$150}{\$150}, \text{ hence } MRT_{r,w}^{\alpha} \text{ is } 1r \text{ for } 1w.$$

$$\left(\frac{MC_r}{MC_w}\right)^{\beta} = \frac{\$50}{\$100}, \text{ hence } MRT_{r,w}^{\beta} \text{ is } 1r \text{ for } .5w.$$

Therefore $MRT_{r,w}^{\alpha} \neq MRT_{r,w}^{\beta}$. In spite of this violation, neither firm would have any incentive to change its behavior because each would be maximizing profit. Thus economic inefficiency would persist.

Analogous problems can arise with all other Pareto conditions as well. Given the prevalence of imperfect competition [see section (B) of Table 8.2, "Trends of Competition in the U.S. Economy, 1939–80," on p. 276], such theoretical conclusions are, of course, disturbing. Not surprisingly, therefore, economists have attempted to measure in our economy the extent of unnecessary scarcity that economic inefficiency implies.

MEASURING THE WELFARE LOSS FROM ECONOMIC INEFFICIENCY

Arnold Harberger, about 35 years ago, made the first attempt to measure the welfare loss implied by economic inefficiency.[2]

Harberger's Measure

Harberger focused on the fact, visible in Figure 14.8, that firms with monopoly power in the goods market usually choose output levels at which price exceeds marginal cost. (A price-discriminating firm might be an exception.) As a result, units of output that potential consumers would value more highly than other goods are not produced, and potential welfare is unnecessarily forgone. Note in Figure 14.8 how firm α could push the production of refrigerators and washers beyond the chosen quantities to higher levels corresponding to points b and h, respectively. Each one of these extra units would be valued (along demand-line segments cb or ih) more highly than the resources needed to make them (as measured along marginal-cost line segments ab or gh). The height of marginal cost reflects, in turn, the most highly valued alternative goods that could be produced with the resources involved. The shaded "triangles" thus measure the loss of potential consumer welfare. They are a measure of the inefficiency caused by monopoly power. (For firm β, of course, "triangles" def and kmn can be similarly interpreted.)

When Harberger set out to measure the extent of inefficiency, however, he made a num-

[2]Arnold C. Harberger, "Monopoly and Resource Allocation," *The American Economic Review*, May 1954, pp. 77–87. *Note also* the discussion on pp. 88–92.

FIGURE 14.8

Imperfect Competition and Pareto's Second Condition

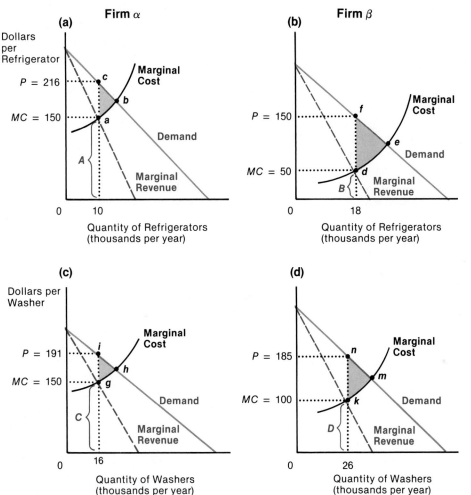

Sellers that have monopoly power maximize profit on the goods they sell by producing output quantities at which rising marginal cost just equals falling marginal revenue (points *a, d, g, k*). Under such circumstances, firms are unlikely to equate their marginal costs. Note how, in this example, $A \neq B$ and $C \neq D$. Because the marginal rate of transformation between any two goods is, in turn, closely linked to the ratio of marginal production costs, the *MRT*s are also unlikely to be the same for any two firms producing the same goods. This inequality of the *MRT*s violates Pareto's second condition.

ber of special assumptions, which are illustrated in Figure 14.9. Harberger assumed that demand was unit-elastic, that producers did not engage in price discrimination, and that long-run average total cost was constant (and therefore equal to long-run marginal cost) for both firms and indus-

tries. (The reader may wish to review the discussion of such a case in Figure 5.9, "Short-Run Versus Long-Run Costs and Long-Run Supply," on p. 154.)

Using data for 1924–28, Harberger calculated the deadweight welfare loss imposed by

Constant return to scale

monopoly power (and shown by the shaded "triangle" in Figure 14.9) for each of 73 U.S. manufacturing industries. He summed the results to $26.5 million. Expanding his sample result to all of manufacturing, he reached an estimate of $59 million, equal to about .1 percent of the gross national product (GNP).

An equivalent loss in 1988 would have come to $4.9 billion; that is, to $19.77 for every person in the United States or just about enough to take everyone to a restaurant once a year. If the size of this loss does not seem very impressive, be assured that the initial impact of Harberger's research was similar: The results of his research seemed to suggest that economists who concerned themselves with economic inefficiency were wasting their time with trivia.

Harberger Confirmed

A number of scholars followed in Harberger's footsteps and subsequently derived similarly trivial estimates of the extent of economic inefficiency. Some of them focused on goods markets as Harberger had done.[3] Others approached the matter by studying input markets[4] and the effects of trade barriers.[5] They, too, calculated minute welfare losses, usually below 1 percent of GNP.

Figure 14.7 can be used to illustrate the input-market approach to estimating economic

---

[3]*See,* for instance, David Schwartzman, "The Burden of Monopoly," *Journal of Political Economy,* December 1960, pp. 627–30; *idem,* "The Effect of Monopoly: A Correction," *Journal of Political Economy,* October 1961, p. 494; Dean A. Worcester, Jr., "New Estimates of the Welfare Loss to Monopoly, United States, 1956–1969," *Southern Economic Journal,* October 1973, pp. 234–45; John J. Siegfried and Thomas K. Tiemann, "The Welfare Cost of Monopoly: An Inter-Industry Analysis," *Economic Inquiry,* June 1974, pp. 190–202.

[4]*See,* for instance, Albert Rees, "The Effects of Unions on Resource Allocation," *The Journal of Law and Economics,* October 1963, pp. 69–78.

[5]A summary of such studies can be found in Charles P. Kindleberger and Peter H. Lindert, *International Economics,* 6th edition. (Homewood, Ill.: Irwin, 1978), p. 120. For a graphic illustration of the loss involved *see* "Application 5: Import Quotas" in Chapter 6 and Analytical Example 6.4, "The Welfare Effects of U.S. Sugar Quotas."

---

inefficiency. Note how firms with monopsony power in the input market always choose input-levels at which an input's marginal value product exceeds the wage paid to the input ($a > b$ and $d > e$). As a result, units of input that could produce output valued more highly than alternatives (such as leisure or other goods) are not used, and potential welfare is unnecessarily forgone. Note how firm α could push the use of labor beyond the chosen quantity to the higher level corresponding to point c. Each of these extra units would produce output valued more highly (along line segment ac) than alternatives (measured along line segment $bc,$ which indicates the minimum wages people are willing to accept in this market and thus the best alternatives they must have available elsewhere). The shaded triangle abc thus measures the welfare loss. (A similar interpretation can be made of firm β's triangle $def.$)

Harberger Criticized

While some researchers confirmed Harberger's estimate, other scholars seriously disagreed.[6] Three of the many criticisms of Harberger's estimate were: (1) Harberger understated the monopoly price distortion ΔP; (2) his assumption of unitary elasticity was too low and brought down the calculated quantity distortion, ΔQ; (3) manufacturing accounts for only a quarter of the GNP, and monopoly power is exercised in other sectors as well.

First, critics argued that Harberger had understated the monopoly price distortion, ΔP, for two reasons: He had used the average rate of return on invested capital in manufacturing as a

---

[6]*See,* for instance, George J. Stigler, "The Statistics of Monopoly and Merger," *Journal of Political Economy,* February 1956, pp. 33–40; Charles K. Rowley, *Antitrust and Economic Efficiency* (London: Macmillan, 1973); Abram Bergson, "On Monopoly Welfare Losses," *The American Economic Review,* December 1973, pp. 853–70 (but note the subsequent discussion in the December 1975 issue, pp. 1008–31); Richard Hartman, "On Monopoly Welfare Losses, Once Again," *Economic Inquiry,* April 1978, pp. 293–301.

FIGURE 14.9

Harberger's Measure of Welfare Loss

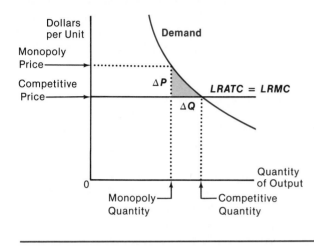

Because the area of a triangle equals its base times its height, divided by 2, the welfare loss of the roughly triangular shaded area in this graph can be approximated by $L = \dfrac{\Delta P \cdot \Delta Q}{2}$. Harberger assumed that firms that received his sample's average rate of return on invested capital were receiving zero *economic* profits and were charging a competitive price equal to long-run average total cost. He assumed that firms with greater returns were charging a monopoly price that exceeded the competitive price by ΔP. Assuming a price elasticity of demand equal to 1, Harberger used the elasticity formula $\left(\epsilon = \dfrac{\Delta Q}{Q} : \dfrac{\Delta P}{P} \right)$, along with his estimate of ΔP and industry data on P and Q, to calculate the monopoly output restriction ΔQ, and thus L.

proxy for the normal interest return on invested capital that competitive conditions would produce. Quite possibly the typically lower average rate of return on invested capital in such sectors as agriculture and services should have been used to approximate implicit interest costs. Harberger had also insufficiently accounted for the fact that monopoly power is a valuable asset (recall Analytical Example 7.1, ''The Market Value of Monopoly Power''). More often than not, this asset is not acquired for nothing, and it has to be continually defended against would-be competitors. Thus firms spend money on campaign contributions, legislative lobbying, even outright bribes (recall ''Application 4: The 'Captured' State'' in Chapter 7 or note Close-Up 14.3, ''The Economics of Rent Seeking''). Firms also spend large sums on persuasive advertising, antitrust and patent lawyers, and government licenses. Firms invest in deliberate excess capacity to deter new entrants into the industry or to secure higher cartel quotas (a practice once common among U.S. cement and oil producers). In addition, critics said, firms engage in a great deal of useless product differentiation. Note: It does not matter whether such expenditures are successful

in attaining or defending monopoly power. What matters is the fact that such costs would not exist under perfect competition and should be deducted from observed accounting costs before competitive costs are estimated. Barring such adjustments, the costs of an imperfectly competitive firm may appear so high as to make its profit look merely like a competitive return on invested capital.

For example, consider a person buying a New York taxi for $10,000. Such a person would also have to buy the $68,000 medallion (license) to run it. Let annual revenues equal $50,000 and explicit costs (wages, fuel, repairs, insurance, and the like) $42,200. The $7,800 difference between annual revenues and explicit costs will then appear as a mere 10-percent return on the $78,000 capital investment—just equal, perhaps, to the implicit return on capital a competitive market might require in the long run. Yet, instead of adding $7,800 of implicit cost to $42,200 of explicit costs (and thus deriving a $50,000 estimate of long-run cost), one may wish to treat only $1,000 as legitimate implicit interest on the $10,000 taxi. Adding this $1,000 to the explicit costs of $42,200 would yield a long-run cost estimate of $43,200 and reveal not a competitive firm's zero economic profit (and a zero price distortion ΔP), but a monopolistic profit of $6,800 (and a significant ΔP).

Second, Harberger's critics argued that his assumption of unitary elasticity was too low and thus biased downward the calculated quantity distortion, ΔQ. This criticism can be appreciated by picturing imperfectly competitive firms that face downward-sloping demand curves as well as downward-sloping marginal-revenue curves. As long as the price elasticity of demand exceeds $|\ 1\ |$, marginal revenue (although declining with higher output) is positive; marginal revenue reaches zero precisely at an output volume that corresponds to unitary price elasticity. Such a firm, if short-run profit-maximizing, will, however, choose an output volume that equates marginal cost (which will, surely, be positive) with marginal revenue (which will, therefore, be positive as well). As a result, such a profit-maximizing firm will choose an output volume at which not only is marginal revenue positive, but price elasticity of demand is also greater than $|\ 1\ |$. By estimating this elasticity as equal to $|\ 1\ |$, Harberger implicitly assumed zero marginal revenue—a situation such profit-maximizing firms would choose only in the unusual case of their having zero marginal costs. (*Caution:* The preceding argument is that of Harberger's critics, but one can think of various possible flaws in it; two examples will suffice. (1) A downward-sloping demand curve that is a rectangular hyperbola—and looks like that in Figure 14.9—does *not* imply a downward-sloping marginal-revenue curve because every possible price/quantity combination then yields the same total revenue, hence marginal revenue is always zero and elasticity always $|\ 1\ |$. (2) Some firms may *not* be maximizing short-run profit but long-run profit and may therefore choose a price/quantity combination with elasticity less than $|\ 1\ |$, as illustrated by Figure 8.6, "Price Leadership: The Entry-Limit Model," on p. 263).

Third, Harberger's critics maintained that manufacturing accounts for only 30 percent of national income and that monopoly power is surely exercised in other sectors as well. (A look at Table 8.2, "Trends of Competition in the U.S. Economy, 1939–80" on p. 276 and at Table 8.3 accompanying problem 10, Chapter 8, on p. 281 will confirm both of these assertions.) Because Harberger focused on manufacturing in calculating his estimate, his calculation of the welfare loss was considered to be too low.

Harberger Corrected

Not surprisingly, some of Harberger's critics have calculated welfare losses as high as 4–8 percent of the GNP. Their calculations, however, have also remained controversial.[7] Figure 14.10 summarizes the arguments just reviewed. Harberger estimated the competitive price at the level of *LRATC* by using accounting data of cost and adding a competitive return on capital equal to the average return earned by his sample. Using a lower estimate of the proper rate of return based on other sectors in the economy, might yield *LRATC'* instead. Applying this lower rate of

[7]*See*, for instance, David R. Kamerschen, "An Estimation of the 'Welfare Losses' from Monopoly in the American Economy," *Western Economic Journal*, Summer 1966, pp. 221–36 (with critical comments by Dean A. Worcester, Jr., "Innovations in the Calculation of Welfare Loss to Monopoly," *Western Economic Journal*, September 1969, pp. 234–43, and Victor P. Goldberg, "Welfare Loss and Monopoly: The Unmaking of an Estimate," *Economic Inquiry*, April 1978, pp. 310–12); Gordon Tullock, "The Welfare Costs of Tariffs, Monopolies, and Theft," *Western Economic Journal*, June 1967, pp. 224–32 (with comments by E. J. Mishan, "A Note on the Costs of Tariffs, Monopolies, and Thefts" in the September 1969 issue, pp. 230–33); David R. Kamerschen and Richard L. Wallace, "The Costs of Monopoly," *Antitrust Bulletin*, Summer 1972, pp. 485–96; Anne O. Krueger, "The Political Economy of the Rent-Seeking Society," *The American Economic Review*, June 1974, pp. 291–303; Richard A. Posner, "The Social Costs of Monopoly and Regulation," *Journal of Political Economy*, August 1975, pp. 807–27; Keith Cowling and Dennis C. Mueller, "The Social Costs of Monopoly Power," *The Economic Journal*, December 1978, pp. 727–48, and September 1981, pp. 721–25; Robert T. Masson and Joseph Shaanan, "Social Costs of Oligopoly and the Value of Competition," *The Economic Journal*, September 1984, pp. 520–35.

FIGURE 14.10

Correcting Harberger's Estimate

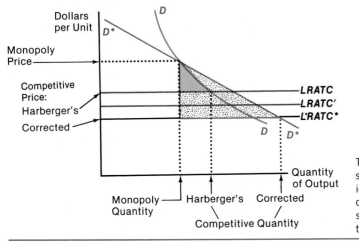

This graph is a copy of Figure 14.9, with some of the corrections suggested by critics indicated as well. The result of these corrections is a larger loss estimate, consisting not only of the shaded area, but the dotted one as well.

return to a lower total of invested capital (that excluded the capitalized value of monopoly power itself) might yield *LRATC** as the likeliest level of long-run average total cost and price under perfect competition. Finally, replacing demand line *DD* by *D*D** (which is more elastic in the relevant range) raises the loss triangle from the shaded area to the shaded-plus-dotted one.

X-EFFICIENCY VERSUS ECONOMIC EFFICIENCY

The preceding section described controversial estimates of economic welfare unnecessarily lost because of economic inefficiency. Equally controversial are estimates of welfare losses due to technical inefficiency within the boundaries of individual firms. As a result of the work of Harvey Leibenstein and his imitators, many economists have come to view X-inefficiency as all-pervasive and as much more significant in scope than economic inefficiency, but others disagree.[8]

Firms with monopoly power, it is believed, not only incur considerable expenses to obtain, strengthen, and defend that power (as discussed in the previous section), but they are generally lax on cost control because they do not face intense competitive pressure. Before long, such extravagances as lavish offices, high entertainment budgets, and long coffee breaks push costs to unnecessary levels.

The kinds of examples of X-inefficiency given in Chapter 4 have been confirmed by a number of investigations. One recent study investigated electric power producers.[9] In 49 U.S. cities that had two or more competing companies, average total cost was 11 percent lower, all else being equal, than in cities without such competition. Another study focused on banks.[10] In 34 U.S. metropolitan areas, banks with little competition had larger staffs and higher labor

---

[8]Note the discussion of X-Inefficiency in "Second Thoughts: The Matter of X-Inefficiency" in Chapter 4 as well as the writings by Leibenstein and Stigler cited at the end of Chapter 4.

[9]Walter J. Primeaux, "An Assessment of X-Efficiency Gained Through Competition," *Review of Economics and Statistics,* February 1977, pp. 105–08.

[10]Franklin R. Edwards, "Managerial Objectives in Regulated Industries: Expense-Preference Behavior in Banking," *Journal of Political Economy,* February 1977, pp. 147–62.

costs, all else being equal, than banks located in places with competition. Indeed, business news papers, magazines, and trade journals—from the *Wall Street Journal, Barron's, Business Week, Forbes,* and *Fortune* to *Computerworld* and *Iron Age*—fill their pages with sad stories of sleeping giants, stuck in old modes of operation, lacking new ideas, lethargic, and inbred. Yet it is difficult to interpret such anecdotal evidence.

Note: The waste of resources due to X-inefficiency may be much more significant than that from economic inefficiency. Comanor and Leibenstein believe that if half of national production were produced by firms with some degree of monopoly power (a conservative estimate), if their long-run average total and marginal cost were on the average 6 percent below price, and if the price elasticity of demand were | 2 |, a Harberger-type estimate of welfare loss would equal .18 percent of national product.[11] If the actual costs of these firms, however, were inflated by X-inefficiency so that true costs were 18 percent below price, a corrected Harberger-type loss estimate would equal 3 percent of national product. At the same time, the pure waste of resources from X-inefficiency would come to another 9 percent of national product. The overall waste of 12 percent of national product would have come, in 1988, to a quite respectable $2,373 for every person in the United States (see Figure 14.11).

EQUITY

Once economic efficiency has been achieved, total economic welfare cannot be raised further by increasing the welfare of some people *without* decreasing that of others. Some claim, however, that total economic welfare can often be raised even in such circumstances, namely by increasing the welfare of some people *at the expense of* that of others. Inevitably, such an increase in the

welfare of some at the expense of others requires moral judgments about the very situations among which Pareto would not choose. Because Pareto wanted to be an objective scientist, he would not rank, on a scale of better or worse, alternative allocations of resources or goods if such ranking required comparison of the welfare gains of some people with the welfare losses of others. Prophets and poets, philosophers and politicians, on the other hand, rarely exercise Pareto's restraint. They urge us to pursue **economic equity** or **economic justice,** a situation in which the apportionment of resources or goods among people is considered *fair*.

THE EFFICIENCY-EQUITY DISTINCTION

The mapping of preferences with the help of indifference curves (see Chapter 2) allows us to highlight the crucial distinction between economic efficiency and economic equity. Panel (a) of Figure 14.12 depicts the circumstances of Mr. Jones, who is consuming 6 pounds of apples and 45 pounds of butter per year (point A). The single indifference curve going through A shows the marginal rate of substitution to be .5/1 in the vicinity of A. Panel (b) presents similar information for Ms. Smith. She consumes 44 pounds of apples and 35 pounds of butter per year (point B), but her *MRS* equals 3/1. The inequality of the two *MRS*s spells inefficiency (see "Condition 4: The Optimum Allocation of Goods among Consumers of the Same Goods" on p. 489).

The diagram in panel (c), the **Edgeworth box,** depicts the same situation in a novel way. Jones's situation in panel (a) has been reproduced in the lower left-hand corner of the box, the origin of which is labeled 0_J. The position of Jones is again shown at point A, but a whole family of Jones's indifference curves has been added to the curve going through point A (see the solid lines convex with respect to 0_J).

Smith's situation in panel (b) has also been reproduced in panel (c), but panel (b) has been rotated 180 degrees, and point B of that graph has

[11]William S. Comanor and Harvey Leibenstein, "Allocative Efficiency, X-Efficiency, and the Measurement of Welfare Losses," *Economica,* August 1969, pp. 304–09.

FIGURE 14.11

X-Inefficiency and Economic Inefficiency

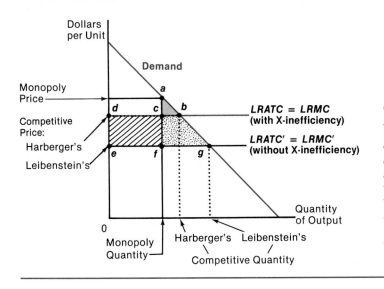

Given demand and observed costs *LRATC*, Harberger's procedure would identify shaded rectangle *abc* as the welfare loss due to economic inefficiency. Acceptance of Leibenstein's argument that monopoly power allows firms not only to raise price, but also to raise cost (as from *LRATC'* to *LRATC*) raises the estimate of economic inefficiency to include dotted area *bcfg*; an added welfare loss of pure X-inefficiency appears (cross-hatched area *cdef*).

been positioned to coincide with point *A*. As a result, the origin of panel (b) now appears at the upper right-hand corner of the box, labeled 0_S. The position of Smith is now also seen at *A*, but with respect to origin 0_S; a whole family of Smith's indifference curves has been added to the one going through point *A* (see the dashed lines convex with respect to 0_S).

The dimensions of the box, it should be noted, correspond exactly to the total annual quantities consumed by the two people. The vertical distance measures 50 pounds of apples per year. As the brackets indicate, Jones consumes 6 of these (measured up from 0_J), and Smith consumes 44 (measured down from 0_S). The horizontal distance measures 80 pounds of butter per year. Jones consumes 45 of these (measured right from 0_J); Smith consumes 35 (measured left from 0_S).

The inefficiency of the situation is immediately evidenced by the obviously different slopes, at point *A*, of the two people's indifference curves. (Recall that the slope of an indifference curve equals the *MRS*.) Now notice the manifold possibilities for improvement: If Smith gave up,

in favor of Jones, an amount of apples equal to *AF* and received an amount of butter equal to *FC* in return, both people would end up at point *C*. Smith would be equally well off (as evidenced by the fact that *C* is found on the same dashed indifference curve as *A*), but Jones would be better off. (With respect to 0_J, the solid indifference curve going through *C* is higher than the one going through *A*.) At point *C*, the slopes of the two people's indifference curves are equal; therefore their *MRS*s would be equal and efficiency would prevail.

Another alternative to *A* is found at point *D*: If Jones gave up, in favor of Smith, an amount of butter equal to *AG* and received an amount of apples equal to *GD* in return, both people would end up at point *D*. Jones would be equally well off (as evidenced by the fact that *D* is found on the same solid indifference curve as *A*), but Smith would be better off. (With respect to 0_S, the dashed indifference curve going through *D* is higher than the one going through *A*.) At point *D*, the slopes of the two people's indifference curves are equal; therefore, their *MRS*s would again be equal and efficiency would prevail.

FIGURE 14.12

The Edgeworth Box

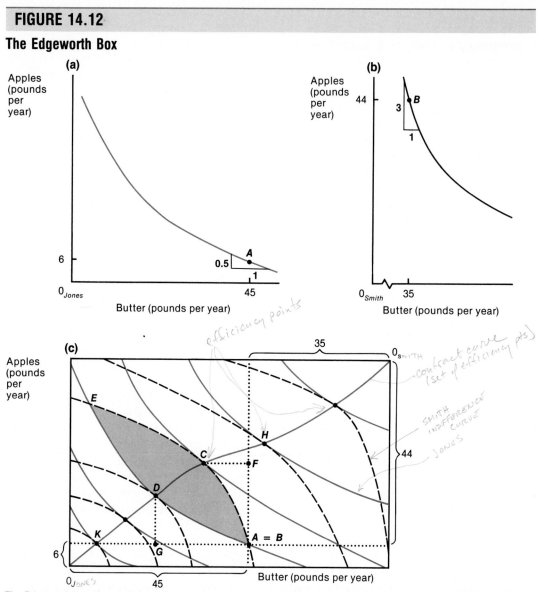

The Edgeworth box diagram[a] highlights the crucial distinctions between economic efficiency and economic inefficiency, and between economic efficiency and economic equity. Situations of inefficiency, evident by comparing panels (a) and (b), can be depicted as lying off a contract curve, as at point *A* (which equals *B*) in panel (c). Such situations of inefficiency can be removed through peaceful trading that can make everyone better off at one of the many efficient positions on the contract curve. Moves *along* this curve, however, affect the equity of the situation and inevitably cause conflict.

[a]Although it is named for him, this box diagram does not appear in any of Edgeworth's writings; it was first used by Pareto in 1893. *See* Vincent J. Tarascio, "A Correction: On the Genealogy of the So-Called Edgeworth-Bowley Diagram," *Western Economic Journal,* June 1972, pp. 193–97; and William Jaffé, "Edgeworth's Contract Curve," Parts I and II, *History of Political Economy,* Fall and Winter 1974, pp. 343–59 and 381–404.

As a matter of fact, if Jones and Smith traded with each other in such a way as to arrive at any point within the lens-shaped shaded area *ADEC*, both would reach a higher indifference curve at the same time! As Pareto taught us, however, economic efficiency requires *equality* of the *MRS*s of different people. In the Edgeworth box, the two *MRS*s are equal wherever the two persons' indifference curves have the same slope. All such efficient points (including *K*, *D*, *C*, or *H*) have been linked by a color line, which economists call the **contract curve.*** They use this term because people who find themselves in inefficient positions not on the curve (as at point *A*) can *contract* to trade with each other so that one or both can become better off at a position on the contract curve (as between *C* and *D* in our example). All positions that are not on the contract curve are inefficient; they make it possible for people to play a **positive-sum game,** in which no one wins utility at someone else's expense and the sum of (positive) winnings and (nonexisting negative) losses is positive.

The Edgeworth box diagram in panel (c) illustrates an important matter: Efficiency does not depict a single position, but a whole range of them. Any position on the contract curve is equally efficient. Once the *MRS*s are equalized, possibilities for simultaneous mutual gain are exhausted, regardless of the *total* quantities of goods consumed by the two individuals. Point *K* is efficient, as are *D*, *C*, and *H*.

Note: Once efficiency has been achieved by moving from positions off the contract curve to positions on it, any one person can become better off *only at the expense of another.* Quite possibly, people can then play only a **zero-sum game,** in which the winnings of utility of some are exactly matched by the losses of others and the sum of (positive) winnings and (negative) losses is zero. As long as we cannot measure and compare utilities, we can never be sure if winnings balance losses, but we can be sure of conflict all

along the contract curve. The contract curve, therefore, can also be called a **conflict curve.** People who find themselves in positions on the curve (as at point *C*) find themselves *fighting* with one another about moving (as from *C* to *H* or *C* to *K*) because in such a case one person becomes better off only at the expense of the other. Note how at *H*, Jones's indifference curve is so much higher than at *C*, but that of Smith is so much lower. The opposite is the case at *K*. A move along the conflict curve raises the issue of *equity.*

The importance of the efficiency-equity distinction, which is brought out so clearly in the box diagram, cannot be overemphasized. In many potential conflict situations, which might give rise to divorces or strikes or even wars, there exist in fact possibilities for peaceful accommodation, for mutually beneficial trade, akin to a move from point *A* not on the contract curve to a point between *C* and *D* lying on it. Awareness of such possibilities can avoid many an unnecessary conflict because conflict is inevitable only if one is already on the contract curve and determined to move.

Note: The advocates of equity do not agree among themselves on the meaning of their goal. Two major arguments dominate their debate about the proper slice of the ''pie'' that should go to any one person. One group seeks to promote *distributive* economic justice; another group pursues *commutative* economic justice.

NOTIONS OF DISTRIBUTIVE JUSTICE

The advocates of **distributive justice** argue that goods should be apportioned among people by some authority seeking to act justly. Such an authority is said to be acting justly whenever the percentage of all goods going to any one person is determined by this authority with reference to some personal characteristic that establishes the recipient as meritorious.

There is little agreement, however, as to who that authority should be or what characteristic it

---

*For the mathematics of the contract curve, see Section 14A of the Calculus Appendix at the back of this book.

should consult. There are some who argue that each person should receive a share of society's total output corresponding to the number of hours that person worked. This policy requires that someone keeps track of hours of labor performed. If a janitor, a farmer, and a surgeon each worked 40 hours a week, it would only be fair according to this view to give the same income to each. Someone who worked 20 hours should then get half the amount given to the former three.

Others disagree and hold that equity is served best when all people receive goods in accordance with their needs. No one, probably, has popularized this idea more than Karl Marx (1818–83), a Biography of whom appears in Chapter 14 of the *Student Workbook* that accompanies this text. Marx thought that goods would be apportioned according to need after the establishment of communism, an event he predicted to occur at the end of a long period of historical development and after the demise of both capitalism and socialism.

Still others define equity as equality; they would give all people, as a basic human right, an exactly equal share of the total set of goods produced in any one year. When the argument is presented as a matter of moral judgment, little can be said about it. However, two of the more complex arguments for the equal apportionment of goods were presented by an economist, Abba P. Lerner, and by a philosopher, John Rawls.

Abba Lerner

In order to illustrate Lerner's argument, let us suppose that a society's annual output of a multitude of goods were to be apportioned among 200 million persons. If the goods involved had freely flexible prices, one could distribute them most easily by apportioning among people an amount of, say, 2 trillion *dollars* and letting each person buy whatever quantities of whatever goods he or she could afford at whatever equilibrium prices emerged. Clearly, this method of distributing the available goods would work regardless of how much money income was given to any one person.

However, argues Lerner, it would surely be desirable to apportion the dollars (and hence the goods they can buy) in such a way as to maximize the total satisfaction people *as a group* derived from the goods available. For the sake of this desirable goal, says Lerner, one would have to give every person an exactly equal dollar amount (of $2 trillion divided by 200 million people, or of $10,000 per person in our example). This conclusion is based on Lerner's use of the principle of diminishing marginal utility, first discussed in the section on "The Concept of Utility: A Historic Note" in Chapter 2. Consider the effect of giving money income to any one person: Presumably, the first dollar received would be spent to satisfy that person's most urgent material desire (as defined by that person), the second dollar would be spent on the next urgent desire, and so on. Each additional dollar of income would thus raise the person's overall satisfaction (or utility) but by less and less. In other words, while the person's *total* utility derived from income would rise with higher income, the person's *marginal* utility of income would fall with higher income. For any one person, A, the declining marginal utility of income is illustrated by line MU_A in Figure 14.13.

The first dollar received by person A would bring utility represented by the thin column *la*. Additional dollars would bring smaller *extra* or marginal utility, even though total utility would rise. Thus the 8,000th dollar received in a year would bring marginal utility of *mb* (which is smaller than *la*), but it would bring the total utility of all 8,000 dollars received up to area *lmba*, the *sum* of all those thin columns of marginal utility associated with the 1st, 2nd, 3rd, and, eventually, the 8,000th dollar received. Similarly, if person A were to receive 20,000 dollars per year, the 20,000th dollar would bring still lower marginal utility of *qf*, which would be but the last addition to a utility total then equaling *lqfa*.

According to Lerner, a similar story could be told about any other person, B. The first dollar given to B would bring utility represented by thin column *qg*. If B received a 5,000th dollar (mea-

FIGURE 14.13

The Equal Income Argument

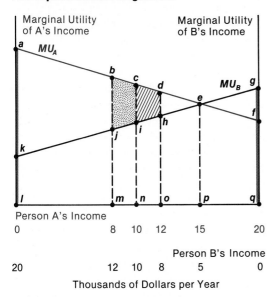

All agree that one could hypothetically maximize the total welfare derived from a society's annual production of goods by apportioning the money income that can buy those goods in such a way (point p) as to equalize the marginal utility of money income among all persons (point e). Since one cannot in fact measure and compare people's marginal utility of income, however, it is argued by some that an absolutely equal income distribution (point n) is preferable to unequal distributions: In the face of uncertainty about the location of point e, it is said, equal dollar deviations from equality raise total welfare as often as they lower it, but each time total welfare is raised, it is raised by less (crosshatched area) than it is reduced (dotted area) when the total is lowered. This entire argument rests on the operation of the principle of diminishing marginal utility.

sured from right to left in the graph), B's marginal utility of income would be only pe, but B's total utility would then equal $qgep$. And if B received 20,000 dollars, marginal utility would be only lk, but total utility $qgkl$.

How then, asks Lerner, can one possibly conclude that A and B and all others in this 200-million-person population should get an exactly equal $10,000 annual share of the 2 trillion dollars available (and of the goods they represent)? Surely, to squeeze the greatest possible

amount of human welfare from the available goods would require, *in principle,* giving more income to those who could enjoy it more than to others who would enjoy it less. In our example, this principle seems to lead to a clear-cut conclusion: Because B's enjoyment at any given income level is always below A's, the total utility of $20,000 of income would be maximized if A (a more efficient pleasure machine) received $15,000 of income and B received only $5,000. (Note: If A and B received these amounts, their marginal utilities would be *pe* and equal to each other. Thus no reallocation of income could raise total utility.)

In real-life situations, however, we do not know people's marginal-utility-of-income lines, continues the argument. There exists no way to measure the satisfaction a person receives from the goods acquired by means of the spending of money income. One can measure a person's weight (as so many pounds), a person's height (as so many inches), and a person's temperature (as so many degrees), but one cannot measure a person's satisfaction (as so many ''utils''?). Hence a graph such as Figure 14.13 must forever remain hypothetical. One can only *imagine* measuring A's marginal utilities for a 1st, 8,000th, and 20,000th dollar, plotting them as distances *la, mb,* and *qf,* and comparing them with similar data for B (such as *qg, oh,* and *lk*). Hence one cannot know whether B's marginal utility line intersects A's marginal utility line at *e,* as in our example, or at some other point. One cannot know the true social-utility-maximizing apportionment of income.

If, however, each person received an identical income (of $10,000 in our example) corresponding to midpoint *n,* there would be a 50–50 chance that the distribution of income that would maximize utility in society (because A's and B's marginal utilities were equal to each other) was in fact to the right or to the left of our chosen point *n.* Every time the actual distribution of income deviated from the equal income distribution point *n* in the direction of the true (but unknown) point of equality of marginal utilities, total utility in society would go up. Thus moving income distribution from *n* to *o* (closer to ideal point *p*) would give A $2000 of additional income at the expense of B. As a result, A's total utility would rise by *ncdo,* but B's total utility would fall by *niho,* resulting in a social net gain in utility equal to crosshatched area *icdh.*

On the other hand, every time the actual distribution of income deviated from the equal income distribution point *n* in a direction away from the true but unknown point of equality of marginal utilities, total utility in society would go down. Thus, moving income distribution from *n* to *m* (farther from ideal point *p*) would give B $2000 of additional income at the expense of A. As a result, B's total utility would rise by *mjin,* but A's total utility would fall by more, namely *mbcn,* resulting in a social net loss in utility equal to dotted area *jbci.*

The argument concludes by noting that the *size* of the loss associated with an incorrect deviation from equality (the dotted area) would exceed the size of the gain associated with an equal correct deviation from equality (the crosshatched area). Since, in a large population, frequent deviations from equality can be expected to result in the same frequency of losses as of gains, such deviations would create a decline in social welfare *with certainty:* 100 million crosshatched-area gains would be overpowered by 100 million dotted-area losses. Thus, in the face of our inability to measure people's ability to enjoy income, a policy of absolute income equality is preferable to a policy of inequality.

Note: The validity of the Lerner argument is by no means universally accepted. To name just one criticism, many economists have been troubled by the thought that different people's marginal-utility-of-income schedules may be interdependent and that the lines drawn in Figure 14.13 may shift during the very process of income redistribution.

John Rawls

Rawls asks us to imagine people ''in a state of nature'' in which they all rely, individually, on their own efforts. Because these people realize that social cooperation could give everyone a better life, they decide to form a society. They meet in an assembly for the purpose of drawing up a ''social contract'' that is to govern their relations with one another, including the way the benefits of their cooperation are to be apportioned among them. What rule of division will they agree upon?

People in this ''original position,'' Rawls argues, cannot know what kind of personal position they will have in the new society about to be formed. They cannot know whether they will end up as butchers, coal miners, deep sea divers, cleaners of sewers, judges, tax assessors, captains of industry, inventors of life-saving drugs, or pilots of jets. Therefore they will consider the matter impartially, and they will reject income inequality. Each person will fear ending up with the lowest-paying job and will want to press for a ''maximin'' rule that makes as large as possible the lowest income any person can get.

Rawls concludes that impartial people who do not have an ax to grind (because they do not know what their position in society will be) would come to agree unanimously on income equality. According to Rawls, income equality would therefore be the proper rule for our society in which such a unanimous agreement cannot be reached because real people do know their actual positions in society. Those with above-average incomes will defend inequality because it is in their interest to do so. (Rawls recognizes, however, that everyone might agree on inequality of income, if, in comparison to an egalitarian division, it made possible an improvement of everyone's position at the same time, as will be illustrated in Figure 14.15).

THE NOTION OF COMMUTATIVE JUSTICE

All the advocates of distributive justice focus on some *human authority acting justly* to establish a tight link between the output shares the authority allots to people and some personal characteristic of these people—their industry, their needs, their humanity. The advocates of **commutative justice** instead focus on the *just nature of an impersonal process* that generates any given apportionment of output. To them, the output shares ultimately received by people would be fair (even if they should be highly unequal) as long as these shares had been determined by the free choices of all people, all of whom enjoyed *equal opportunities* to influence the process of allocating resources to the production of goods.

For example, the advocates of commutative justice would be happy with a world in which all persons were given the chance, as far as possible, to own equal quantities of all resources and were given an equal freedom to use these resources to produce goods and to trade resources and goods with others. However, the advocates of commutative justice hasten to add, people so privileged should also be held responsible for the consequences of their choices.

In short, the advocates of commutative justice conceive of economic activity as something like a card game, and they intend to make it fair. As long as one distributes cards at the beginning of the game fairly (equal quantities of resources to all) and as long as one follows rules equally applicable to all (equal freedom to use resources, to trade resources and goods), the end result is seen as just. But in a fair card game, some win and others lose! Similarly, in a society aspiring to commutative justice, the incomes of people (and thus their share of output) can be expected to differ in the end.

THE PERSONAL DISTRIBUTION OF INCOME IN THE UNITED STATES

People who have embraced one or another of the notions of economic equity discussed above usually cite statistics to prove how badly the world falls short of their standards of equity. Table 14.1 contains typical data on the personal distribution of income. The table shows a highly unequal distribution of income. Note how the poorest 20 percent of all families (with 1987 incomes under $14,450) received only 4.6 percent of that year's

TABLE 14.1

The Distribution of Money Income Before Taxes among U.S. Families in 1987

Income Class (1)	Percent of Families in Class (2)	Percent of Total Income Received by Families in Class (3)	Percent of Families in Class or Lower Ones (4)	Percent of Total Income Received by Families in Class or Lower Ones (5)
Under $14,450	20	4.6	20	4.6
$14,450–$25,100	20	10.8	40	15.4
$25,101–$36,600	20	16.9	60	32.3
$36,601–$52,910	20	24.1	80	56.4
$52,911–$86,299	15	26.7	95	83.1
$86,300 and over	5	16.9	100	100.0

[handwritten annotation: does not include non-families (ie, individuals)]

In 1987, some $2,382 billion of aggregate family income was distributed in the highly uneven fashion shown here among 65 million U.S. families. (An additional $554 billion of income went to some 33 million individuals not living in families.)

Source: U.S. Bureau of the Census, *Current Population Reports,* Series P-60, No. 162, "Money Income of Households, Families, and Persons in the United States: 1987" (Washington, D.C.: U.S. Government Printing Office, 1989), pp. 42 and 43.

aggregate family income, while the richest 5 percent of families (with incomes above $86,300) received 16.9 percent of the total.

The Lorenz Curve

The **Lorenz curve** is a graphical device that shows the way in which income (in this case) or wealth (in other cases) is apportioned among the members of any group and highlights the extent of equality or inequality among them. Figure 14.14 shows how to graph the data in Table 14.1 by drawing a square measuring percentage of total money income received on the vertical axis and the percentage of families on the horizontal axis. Families are arranged from left to right from the one with the lowest to the one with the highest income.

The straight line that has been drawn from the bottom left corner at 0 to the top right corner at *e* is the **line of perfect equality** because it represents the hypothetical position of the Lorenz

FIGURE 14.14

The Lorenz Curve

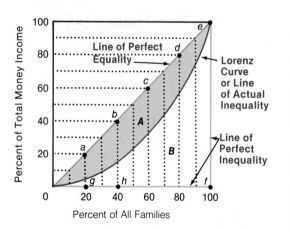

This Lorenz curve is a representation of the way in which money income was apportioned among U.S. families in 1987. The ratio of area *A* to *A* + *B* is the *Gini coefficient.* (The data used to plot this graph were taken from the fourth and fifth columns of Table 14.1.)

curve if the same amount of money income went to each family. If all families in the country shared total income equally, 20 percent of the families would share 20 percent of total income (at *a*), 40 percent of all families would share 40 percent of total income (at *b*), and so on, until 100 percent of all families shared 100 percent of total income (at *e*).

Note: This line of perfect equality should not be called one of perfect *equity,* or *justice,* for there is no objective way of defining what apportionment of income is perfectly just. One can, however, determine objectively whether income is apportioned perfectly equally, be that considered just or not.

At the other extreme, if one family received all the money income while all the others received none of it, what would the Lorenz curve look like? If we arranged the families on the horizontal axis as before on the basis of income, we would find that the poorest 20 percent of all families received 0 percent of total income (at *g* rather than at *a*), that the poorest 40 percent of all families similarly shared 0 percent of total income (at *h* rather than *b*), and so on. Even 99 percent of all families would still share 0 percent of total income (just a little bit to the left of *f* rather than to the left and below *e*). Yet when we considered all families, including the one having all the income, we would find that 100 percent of families had 100 percent of income (at *e*). Thus we could call the line 0*fe* a **line of perfect inequality,** because it represents the hypothetical position of the Lorenz curve if all the income went to one family and none of it to all the others.

In reality, 1987 money income in the United States was distributed neither perfectly equally (as would be shown by the line of perfect equality) nor perfectly unequally (as shown by the line of perfect inequality). Plotting the data of columns (4) and (5) of Table 14.1 reveals the actual Lorenz curve or the **line of actual inequality.** Like a loose string fastened to points 0 and *e*, this line hanging below the line of perfect equality (0*e*), and above that of perfect inequality (0*fe*), provides a visual representation of actual income inequality in the

United States. Any increase in equality would shift it toward 0e, any decrease toward 0fe. In fact, the extent of income inequality has been unchanged for many decades, if one looks at the data at given points in time, but consider Analytical Example 14.1, ''Income Dynamics,'' for another perspective.

The Gini Coefficient

Economists often summarize the extent of personal income inequality with the help of the **Gini coefficient,** the ratio of shaded area A (between the lines of perfect equality and actual inequality) to areas A + B (between the lines of perfect equality and perfect inequality). Thus the Gini coefficient can hypothetically range from 0 (perfect equality) to 1 (perfect inequality), but in the United States it typically lies in the .35 to .45 range. Whether one considers such a distribution fair or not depends entirely on which criterion of equity one wishes to embrace.

CREATING ECONOMIC JUSTICE

It is hardly surprising that proposals abound for turning perceived economic injustice into economic justice. Nor is it surprising that two basic approaches are recommended: promoting both commutative justice and distributive justice.

Promoting Commutative Justice

Some people argue for government intervention to promote equal opportunity. To enhance a more equal distribution of resource stocks, they support measures such as public education, job training, and health care. They also support any and all measures to eliminate monopolistic practices (by private individuals and groups as well as by government) that differentially restrict people's opportunities to utilize their resources.

Promoting Distributive Justice

Other people argue for government intervention to promote not equal *opportunity,* but equal or less unequal *end results.* They usually support some kind of ''Robin Hood scheme,'' taxing the rich and subsidizing the poor. They are not willing to rely on private charity to redress the inequality they observe. Rejecting private handouts to beggars as well as soup kitchens, church missions, and even the extended family, they opt for governmental aid in kind (commodity distributions, medical clinics, public housing) or in cash (agricultural subsidies, negative income taxes, rent supplements, welfare payments, and the like). Schemes of this sort, if pushed vigorously enough, can, however, pose a problem.

A significant amount of governmental redistribution can destroy the important incentives the price system creates, as we already noted in Chapter 10 when discussing Close-Up 11.1, ''Economics According to the Rats,'' and Close-Up 11.2, ''Negative Income Tax and Labor Supply.'' Consider, for example, the effects in our market economy of a change in demand from beef to apples that would ordinarily lower prices and incomes in the beef industry and raise them in the apple industry. These changes would provide the incentives to switch resources from one industry to the other. What if government intervened for reasons of equity? If it taxed suddenly rich apple pickers and orchardland owners and subsidized suddenly poor butchers and pastureland owners, why should butchers still move to become apple pickers? Why should pastureland owners bother about planting apple trees? The attempt to be ''fair'' would take the heart out of the price system's message. Instead of telling people that they could recapture their once-higher incomes only by doing what sovereign dollar-voting consumers had decreed (taking resources out of the beef industry and putting them into the apple industry instead), people would be getting quite a different message: ''*No matter whether you produce apples or beef, your income will be, more or less, the same.*'' Of course, people would then have little reason to change their behavior; resources would *not* be used efficiently for the purposes most wanted by households.

In short, as long as the payment of income is tied to contributions made to society's output, *differential* payments are necessary based not on effort put in, but on the objective result achieved; that is, based on whether the right kind of output is produced. Without differential payments, there couldn't be rewards and penalties to entice required changes in behavior.

The incentive problem is even greater if the tie between income received and contribution is broken entirely. Suppose all persons were guaranteed, through an appropriate program of government taxation and subsidies, an exactly identical income, independent of their contribution to production. Such a policy would effectively countermand *all* the orders of the price system with this single message: "*No matter what you do, your income will, ultimately, be the same!*" Under such circumstances, people may wonder about working only three hours a day, if at all. The nation's production-possibilities frontier would suddenly collapse on itself. Everyone would be contributing fewer resources for use in the process of production. Society's output and therefore society's total money income would fall. Like children fighting over a pie and spilling half of it on the floor, our egalitarian crusaders would have destroyed the very thing they wanted to distribute. The latest message to all, printed above in italics, would turn out to have been a classic Delphic oracle indeed. Everyone's income would ultimately be *the same* all right, but the same *as everyone else's* (and close to zero), not the same *as before!*

Many thoughtful economists, therefore, are hesitant to recommend creating perfect income equality and breaking the link between income and productive contribution. They recognize that people generally must be given rewards in order to contribute to the process of production at all. Without such rewards, the world's work simply would not get done. They also recognize that

people must be given differential rewards if the right things are to be done. Most economists do not rule out, of course, a *limited* redistribution to offset income differences arising from factors beyond people's control, such as inheritance or monopolistic practices.

Figure 14.15 illustrates the fairness-incentive problem graphically. Consider the case of two persons (or groups of persons), P and R. Let P be poor and have no earning capacity at all (or a low one). Let R earn $20 per hour and be rich. In

FIGURE 14.15

The Limits to Redistribution

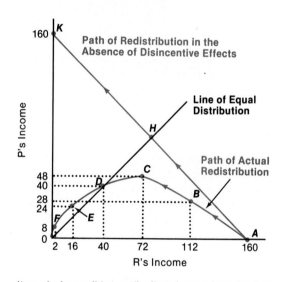

It may be impossible to redistribute income from rich R to poor P along line *AHK* (which implies an unchanged income total). It may only be possible to redistribute along line *ACF* (because the very act of redistribution has disincentive effects that reduce the income total). Under the circumstances, any attempt to redistribute a *given* income from a position of extreme inequality (*A*) to absolute equality (*H*) is bound to fail; an equal distribution of a *lower* income is possible (*D*), but this makes all people worse off than would be possible while maintaining some degree of inequality (*C*). The difference between *C* and *D* illustrates the exception to the Rawlsian absolute-equality rule.

accordance with our analysis in Figure 11.4 "An Individual's Income-Leisure Choice" (p. 364), we would not be surprised if R, when taxed to support P (and when thus receiving an effectively lower wage), were (1) to reduce hours worked and (2) to reduce hours worked all the more the higher was the tax. Some of the possibilities are shown in Table 14.2. In this example, society's income is maximized (at $160) if R is not taxed at all and P receives nothing, as in row (A). In row (D), society's income is cut in half (to $80) if a tax rate of 50 percent is introduced and P and R are given identical incomes (of $40 each). Yet in row (C), a less strict goal that maintains some income inequality enables P as well as R to be better off (with $48 and $72, respectively). Note that Figure 14.15 is based on columns (4) and (5) of Table 14.2.

SUMMARY

1. Scarcity may be unavoidable, but people who make foolish choices with the resources and goods at their disposal can make scarcity more intense than necessary. Economists measure the existence of avoidable scarcity with the help of various performance criteria, including efficiency and equity.

2. *Economic efficiency* is a situation in which it is impossible, through some reallocation of resources or goods, to make some people better off (in their own judgment) without making others worse off (in *their* own judgment).

3. Economic inefficiency can be eliminated, and economic efficiency be attained, by fulfilling certain marginal conditions first stated by Pareto, including those concerning:

a. the optimum allocation of a resource among producers of the same good;

b. the optimum specialization of production among producers of the same good;

c. the optimum composition of production and consumption;

d. the optimum allocation of goods among consumers of the same goods.

4. A general requirement for the achievement of the Pareto optimum is: Whenever one can technically transform a little bit of one variable into a little bit of another, the marginal rate of technical transformation must equal the marginal rate of indifferent substitution. All equivalent marginal rates of technical transformation or of indifferent substitution must be

TABLE 14.2

Hypothetical Income Redistribution

	Tax Rate on R (1)	Hours Worked by R (2)	Pre-Tax Income of R (3) = (2) × $20	Tax Revenue and Transfer to P (4) = (1) × (3)	After-Tax Income of R (5) = (3) − (4)
(A)	0%	8	$160	$ 0	$160
(B)	20%	7	140	28	112
(C)	40%	6	120	48	72
(D)	50%	4	80	40	40
(E)	60%	2	40	24	16
(F)	80%	0.5	10	8	2
(G)	100%	0	0	0	0

Redistributive taxation that changes extreme income inequality, in row (A), to absolute equality, in row (D), may well produce disincentive effects so strong that all people are worse off than would be possible under some degree of inequality, as in row (C).

equal. Pareto's efficiency criterion for judging the desirability of any given allocation of resources or goods enjoys wide assent among economists, but there are critics who do not accept the value judgments from which Pareto's criterion is derived.

5. A close relationship exists between market structure and the extent of economic efficiency achieved. When profit-maximizing firms and utility-maximizing households, *with the help of equilibrium prices established in perfectly competitive markets,* determine the optimum quantities they wish to trade, all conceivable Pareto conditions of economic efficiency come to be fulfilled.

6. *In imperfectly competitive markets,* the pursuit by firms and households of identical goals has no such beneficial effect. Indeed, economic efficiency then occurs only by accident, if at all.

7. Starting more than three decades ago, economists made their first attempts to measure the welfare loss implied by the prevalence of imperfectly competitive markets in the economy. An early measurement by Harberger put the loss at .1 percent of GNP, but a number of critics disagreed with this trivial estimate and supplied larger ones.

8. While exact measurements of economic inefficiency remain controversial, Leibenstein's claim that X-inefficiency is all-pervasive and much more significant in scope than economic inefficiency is equally controversial.

9. The advocates of economic *efficiency* aim to raise total economic welfare by reallocating resources or goods whenever this results in some people feeling better off while nobody feels worse off. The advocates of economic *equity* (who do not accept the taboo against interpersonal comparisons of welfare) aim to raise total economic welfare by reallocating resources or goods whenever this results in some people feeling better off, while others are judged to feel worse off *to a lesser degree.* The crucial distinction between economic efficiency and economic equity can most clearly be seen with the help of the Edgeworth box diagram.

Movements to its *contract curve,* illustrate moves toward economic efficiency from which all can gain at the same time. Movements along its *conflict curve* illustrate alleged moves toward economic equity from which some people gain, while others lose.

10. The advocates of equity do not agree among themselves. Some urge the creation of *distributive justice,* a situation in which goods are apportioned among people by some authority seeking to act justly, preferably by consulting some personal characteristic that measures the recipient's merit. This personal characteristic could be the number of hours a person works, a person's ''needs,'' or even a person's ''basic human right to an equal output share.''

11. The advocates of *commutative justice* aim to create a situation in which goods are apportioned among people as a result of free choices by all people, all of whom enjoy as nearly equal opportunities as possible in the process of resource allocation. They view equity as *fairness of the process* that produces and distributes goods rather than as *fairness of the end result* of that process.

12. The actual distribution of money income among households in the United States at any one point in time is highly unequal. This inequality can be illustrated in tabular form and also with the help of the *Lorenz curve* or the *Gini coefficient.*

13. It is hardly surprising that proposals abound for turning perceived economic injustice into economic justice. The proponents of commutative justice seek to achieve equal opportunity; those of distributive justice seek equal or less unequal end results. The latter approach, if pursued vigorously enough with the help of government, however, runs into the fairness-incentive dilemma.

KEY TERMS

allocative efficiency
commutative justice

conflict curve

contract curve

distributive justice

economic efficiency

economic equity

economic inefficiency

economic justice

Edgeworth box

Gini coefficient

knowledge problem

line of actual inequality

line of perfect equality

line of perfect inequality

Lorenz curve

marginal conditions

marginal rate of substitution *(MRS)*

marginal rate of transformation *(MRT)*

Pareto optimum

positive-sum game

rent seeking

static efficiency

technical efficiency

X-efficiency

zero-sum game

HANDS-ON PRACTICE

Exercise #1

The text claims that the economic inefficiency depicted at *a* and *b* in Figure 14.1 corresponds to firms operating at *c* and *d* in Figure 14.5. Explain.

Solution:

If α operates at *c*, Figure 14.5, labor's marginal value product is $2 and, at the assumed product price of $1 per bushel, the marginal physical product is 2 bushels, just as the left-hand graph of Figure 14.1 indicates.

If β operates at *d*, Figure 14.5, $MVP_L = \$5$; hence $MPP_L = 5$ bushels, just as shown by the right-hand graph of Figure 14.1.

Exercise #2

The text claims that the economic inefficiency depicted at *a* and *b* in Figure 14.2 corresponds to firms operating at *e*, *g*, *f*, and *h* in figure 14.6. Explain.

Solution:

If α operates at *e* and *g* in Figure 14.6, the apple-butter marginal-cost ratio is 86¢/43¢; this implies the *MRT* of 1*a* for 2*b* shown in Figure 14.2. Likewise, if β operates at *f* and *h* in Figure 14.6, the apple-butter marginal-cost ratio is 125¢/25¢; this implies the *MRT* of 1*a* for 5*b* shown in Figure 14.2.

Exercise #3

A *production-possibilities frontier,* we noted in Chapter 1, depicts all the alternative combinations of two groups of goods that people in a society are capable of producing in a given period by using a given flow of resources fully and in the best possible way, given their present state of technology. The phrase "in the best possible way" was not defined with precision in Chapter 1, but we can now do so by noting that it refers to nothing else but "an economically efficient way."

Try to adapt the Edgeworth box diagram of Figure 14.12 so that a production-possibilities frontier can be derived from it.

Solution:

Admittedly, this is a difficult exercise and requires much imagination. Here is one possible answer:

Consider panel (a) of the accompanying graph. Its dimensions might represent a society's given flow of resources during a period, such as

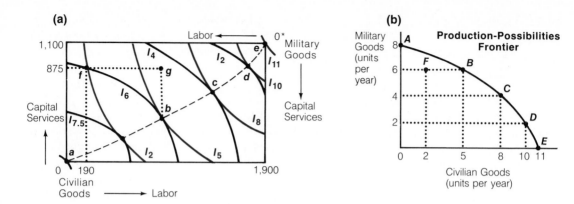

1,900 units of labor and 1,100 units of capital services. The society is producing two types of goods, civilian and military, and the quantities of resource services expended in the production of one or the other of the two types of goods are measured from origin 0 and 0*, respectively, as the arrows indicate. Any point inside the box represents full employment of resources: point f, for example, denotes that 190 units of labor and 875 units of capital services are used in the making of civilian goods; by implication, the remaining $1,900 - 190 = 1,710$ units of labor and $1,100 - 875 = 225$ units of capital services are used in the making of military goods. Not every point in the box, however, is economically efficient. Let us see why.

The society's technical knowledge is depicted by two sets of isoquants; the color isoquants, drawn with respect to the origin, 0, for civilian goods, show input combinations that can produce 2, 5, 8, etcetera units of civilian goods. The black isoquants, drawn with respect to origin, 0*, for military goods, show input combinations that can produce 2, 4, 6, etcetera units of military goods. Now picture the economy at f: 2 units of civilian goods would be produced, along with 6 units of military goods, as the relevant isoquant labels indicate. This output combination is shown in panel (b) by point F, but it does not represent an economically efficient use of the society's resources. Note how one could move from point f to point b in panel (a), sliding down along military-goods isoquant I_6, and end up

producing, at b, the same 6 units of military goods, but 5 rather than 2 units of civilian goods. This could be accomplished simply by reallocating given resources; specifically, by switching fg units of labor from military to civilian uses, while also switching gb units of capital services from civilian to military uses. Clearly, society's welfare would be up; there would be more civilian goods and no fewer military goods; society would have moved from F to B in our panel (b) graph.

At point b in panel (a), furthermore, the allocation of resources would be economically efficient and the kind of output-raising change that was just illustrated by the move from f to b would not be possible. What is different between f and b? At f, the slopes of the two isoquants differ; at b, they are identical; and identical slopes denote an identity of the marginal rates of technical substitution between labor and capital services in both industries (which is yet another Pareto condition of economic efficiency). As a result, point B in panel (b) [which depicts the 5-units-civilian-goods/6-units-military-goods combination of point b in panel (a)] lies *on* the production-possibilities frontier. Similar points of tangency in panel (a), such as a, c, d, and e, all of which are lying on the dashed black line, similarly translate into points A, C, D, and E in panel (b). Thus efficient resource allocations yield points on the production-possibilities frontier; inefficient ones yield points inside it, such as F.

QUESTIONS AND PROBLEMS

1.   Ms. A: When Pareto advocates a move towards economic efficiency, he is urging us to get a marginal benefit at a zero marginal cost.

Mr. B: Right. And he wants us to forgo any change in which a marginal benefit comes at a positive marginal cost because we can't measure the size of the marginal cost.

Evaluate these statements.

2. Invent a marginal rate of transformation between fishing vessels and sewing machines for the Soviet Union and another such *MRT* for Bulgaria so that it would pay the Soviet Union to specialize in producing fishing vessels, while Bulgaria specialized in sewing machines. Using your numbers, prove that specialization and trade could make everyone better off at the same time. Review Close-Up 14.1 and ask yourself what kind of data economic planners in Comecon would need to determine marginal rates of transformation.

3. Suppose a gasoline shortage developed this winter and the U.S. government (''in the interest of fairness'') were to allocate equal quantities of gasoline to each driver. Would this allocation be economically efficient? What difference would it make whether the government allowed or forbade people to trade its rations?

4. ''If one family consumed, each month, 10 times as much of each and every good as another family, the situation would be very unjust, even though it would be economically efficient.'' Comment on the validity of this statement.

5. The following is another marginal condition of economic efficiency: *Economic efficiency requires that the marginal rate of transformation between any two resources, x and y, be the same for any two producers, α and β, using both resources (to produce identical or different goods).*

a.   Explain this condition. (*Hints:* The *MRT* in this case refers to the rate at which a little bit of, say, labor can be exchanged for a little bit of, say, machine time in the process of production while output remains unaffected. This *MRT* is equivalent to the marginal rate of technical substitution discussed in Chapter 4.)

b.   Show why this condition would be fulfilled under perfect competition but probably not under imperfect competition.

6.   Ms. A: All that glitters is not gold. I can see a real problem with *implementing* moves away from economic inefficiency: Even if two parties wanted to get together and make themselves better off, third parties (who would become no worse off by objective standards) would interfere because these third parties would *feel* worse off. After all, most people look at their own welfare *relative to* that of others. They rejoice when others get worse off, and they resent it when others get better off. Hence they will do their best to obstruct any changes that improve the lot of others.

Mr. B: You are much too cynical. People aren't as malevolent as you depict them. Most people rejoice when others rejoice.

What do you think? Does the existence of malevolence or benevolence destroy the applicability of the Pareto criterion?

7.   Ms. A: There is nothing impossible about interpersonal comparisons of utility. When there is one orange left at the end of a long hike, I know exactly which family member needs it the most. When some people have mink coats and others starve, I know exactly who should be helped at the expense of whom. It just takes a little bit of imaginative empathy, of which Pareto seems to have none.

Discuss. (*Hint:* Consider the difference between making scientific statements and moral judgments.)

8.   Mr. A: Interpersonal comparisons of utility are impossible. No one can say with confidence: ''Your headache is worse than mine,'' or ''I enjoy apple pie more than you.'' Therefore no one can ever tell which apportionment of goods among people is fair.

Ms. B: I can. When some people can afford private planes and yachts, while others lack insulin or milk, economic injustice prevails. Evaluate these two positions.

9. Consider panel (c) of Figure 14.12, "The Edgeworth Box."

a. Indicate the positions to which Jones and Smith might move, without either of them becoming worse off, if their initial position was at E. What if their initial position was at F or G?

b. Imagine that one could measure total utility in the third dimension above the diagram. What would the utility mountain look like above the contract curve?

c. Imagine that Jones and Smith had identical tastes and therefore identical sets of indifference curves. Would mutually beneficial trade between them still be possible? Explain.

d. Change "Jones" to "labor union" and "Smith" to "employer." Change "apples" to "wages" and "butter" to "vacations." Re-interpret the diagram as a model of collective bargaining. What would happen if union and employer *started out* at a position on the contract curve?

e. Some diplomats like to "trade" with their counterparts; others call this "appeasement" and cry: "Millions for defense, not a penny for tribute!" Illustrate these attitudes with the help of the Edgeworth box.

f. Draw a new Edgeworth box to depict the following: "Jack Sprat can eat no fat, his wife can eat no lean."

10.   Mr. A: Lerner's income-equality argument is a farce. He argues for equality allegedly because we can't measure people's capacity to enjoy income, hence cannot justify departures from equality. Do you seriously think he would argue against equality, if we could make such measurement? Suppose we could prove some day that one person was an extremely efficient pleasure machine (was so much better than all other people at deriving utility from the consumption of goods). Suppose social welfare would be maximized if this person received 99 percent of output. Would Lerner agree with such inequality?

Ms. B: There are other problems with his argument, too: Why can't the marginal utility of income (unlike that of apples) *rise* with higher income? Why must the utility each person derives from income be dependent only on that person's income, and not on other people's? Evaluate these two criticisms.

11.   Mr. A: Rawls is wrong. What makes him think people are unwilling to gamble? Instead of being fearful lest they end up with the smallest income (which makes them favor equality), most people I know are attracted by the chance of getting a higher income than anyone else (which makes them favor inequality).

Ms. B: So true; all those income-equality arguments are nothing but rationalizations for envy. Note how the advocates of equality usually offer their advice to "society" in the sense of the United States. Why not to the world at large? Because that would give everyone (in 1988 purchasing power) a mere $2,750 a year share of world output.

Evaluate these two criticisms.

12. Consider Analytical Example 14.1, "Income Dynamics," and interpret each of the following: Row (1) of Table B, column (1) of Table C.

13. Figure 14.13, "The Equal Income Argument," presents Lerner's argument on the assumption of an initial deviation of actual income from equality of $no = nm$. Would the entire argument be affected in any way if the assumed initial deviation were different; for example, substantially larger? Explain.

SELECTED READINGS

Boulding, Kenneth E. "The Grants Economy." In *Collected Papers*, vol. 2. Boulder, Colo.: Colorado Associated University Press, 1971, pp. 477–85.

Urges economists to study not only two-way exchanges, but also the ever increasing importance of one-way transfers (coerced and voluntary) of exchangeables. *See also* his *The Economy of Love and Fear: A Preface to Grants Economics.* Belmont, Calif.: Wadsworth, 1973.

Boulding, Kenneth E., and Pfaff, Martin. *Redistribution to the Rich and the Poor: The Grants Economics of Income Distribution.* Belmont, Calif.: Wadsworth, 1972.

>A fascinating discussion of explicit and implicit grants that sometimes increase and at other times decrease income equality.

Buchanan, James M., et al., eds. *Toward a Theory of the Rent-Seeking Society.* College Station, Tex.: Texas A & M University Press, 1981.

>A collection of 18 essays on the resource-wasting activities by which people seek transfers of wealth through the aegis of the state.

Colander, David C. "Some Simple Geometry of the Welfare Loss from Competitive Monopolies," *Public Choice,* 45, 1985, pp. 199–206.

>An interesting contribution to the study of rent-seeking behavior.

Frey, Bruno S. "Economists Favour the Price System—Who Else Does?" *Kyklos,* 4, 1986, pp. 537–63.

>Most people, except professional economists who favor Pareto optimality, reject the use of the price system. The article asks why.

Harberger, Arnold C. "Three Basic Postulates for Applied Welfare Economics: An Interpretive Essay," *Journal of Economic Literature,* September 1971, pp. 785–97.

>A vigorous defense of the much criticized consumer surplus approach to measuring welfare effects.

Hayek, Friedrich von. *The Constitution of Liberty.* Chicago: University of Chicago Press, 1960; *Studies in Philosophy, Politics, and Economics.* Chicago: University of Chicago Press, 1967; and *Law, Legislation, and Liberty, vol. 2: The Mirage of Social Justice.* Chicago: University of Chicago Press, 1976.

>The 1974 winner of the Nobel Prize in economics discusses many concepts of economic justice and argues in favor of commutative justice.

Kohler, Heinz. *Comparative Economic Systems.* Glenview, Ill.: Scott, Foresman and Co., 1989.

>Discusses the concepts of efficiency and equity at length.

Lerner, Abba P. *The Economics of Control: Principles of Welfare Economics.* New York: Macmillan, 1944, chap. 3.

>Presents the argument noted in the text. For a particularly interesting criticism, *see* John Bennett, "The Probable Gain from Egalitarian Redistribution," *Oxford Economic Papers,* March 1981, pp. 165–69.

Marx, Karl, and Friedrich Engels. *Manifesto of the Communist Party,* in Robert C. Tucker, ed., *The Marx-Engels Reader,* 2nd edition. New York: Norton, 1978.

>Marx argues that, under capitalism, the *bourgeoisie* exploits the *proletariat;* and that this exploitation does not arise from individual circumstances, occasionally and accidentally, but from the logic of the capitalist system—unavoidably and independently of individual intention; socialism and communism is the cure.

Mishan, E. J. *Welfare Economics: Five Introductory Essays.* New York: Random House, 1964.

>A more advanced treatment of Pareto's ideas.

Pareto, Vilfredo. *Manual of Political Economy.* New York: Augustus M. Kelley, 1971.

>This is the only one of Pareto's works available in English. *Note* William Jaffé, "Pareto Translated: A Review Article," *Journal of Economic Literature,* December 1972, as well as the controversy elicited by this review (same journal, March 1974).

Rawls, John. *A Theory of Justice.* Cambridge, Mass.: Harvard University Press, 1971.

>Presents the argument described in the text. *See also* Norman Daniels, ed., *Reading Rawls: Critical Studies on Rawls' "A Theory of Justice."* New York: Basic Books, 1975.

COMPUTER PROGRAMS

The KOHLER-3 personal-computer diskettes that accompany this book contain one program of particular interest to this chapter:

14. Efficiency and Equity includes a 32-question multiple-choice test with immediate responses to incorrect answers as well as numerous exercises concerning Pareto's efficiency conditions and the issue of income redistribution versus disincentive effects.

ANALYTICAL EXAMPLE 14.1

INCOME DYNAMICS

Data on the personal distribution of income, such as those embodied in Table 14.1 or Figure 14.14, can easily be misleading and not only for the obvious reason that money-income measures neglect income in kind. More importantly, such data are likely to be misleading because most individuals go through a *cycle* of earning low incomes during their youth, growing incomes thereafter (with a peak just before retirement) and lower incomes late in life. Thus it is *possible* for every individual to have the same lifetime income, while income-distribution statistics look precisely as in Table 14.1, year after year. The apparent income inequality then reflects nothing more than the age distribution of the population! Each year, x percent of the population seems to live in poverty, and y percent seems to enjoy great riches, *but the people who are poor or rich at one time are frequently not the same people who are poor or rich at another time.* Surely, we would want to know whether this hypothetical scenario is applicable to the United States.

Fortunately, a group of researchers at the University of Michigan's Survey Research Center has been working diligently since the late 1960s on the first truly adequate study of income dynamics in the United States. Under the direction of James N. Morgan and Greg J. Duncan, researchers associated with the Panel Study on Income Dynamics (PSID) have conducted lengthy yearly interviews with the heads of 5,000 American families—the *same* families—in order to track the changes of their economic fortunes. (The original sample was indistinguishable from the American population as a whole and has been studied ever since 1968, including families that split off, such as children living alone or starting their own families, widows and widowers, separated and divorced partners, and so on. By 1983, the panel included 6,500 families and 16,000 people.) The results up to date are remarkable. They show that the "freeze-frame" character of yearly income-distribution data (such as Table 14.1) makes for a real distortion and causes us to miss the importance of mobility in the U.S. economy and thus muddles our thinking about poverty, equality, and economic justice.

Dynamic Poverty. Surely, if a significant proportion of the people poor in, say, 1985 were neither poor in 1984 nor destined to be poor in 1986, then the character of American poverty is radically different from what it would be if there were no

TABLE A

Percent of Individuals in Families with Incomes below Official Poverty Level, 1969–78

Poor in 1978	6.8%
Poor 1 or more years	24.4%
Poor 5 or more years	5.4%
"Persistently poor" (8 or more years)	2.6%
Poor all 10 years	0.7%

turnover in the poverty population. The PSID study made it possible for the first time to distinguish among families poor for a single year, a multi-year spell, or persistently. As Table A indicates, while nearly a quarter of the families were poor at least during one year of the 1969–78 period, only 5 percent were poor for five or more years, and fewer than 1 percent were poor during the entire decade. The most surprising result is that such a large proportion of American families (a proportion demographically indistinguishable from the population as a whole) falls below the poverty level at *some* time. This is caused not by some long-term problem, such as lack of education, but by short-term occurrences, such as divorce, death, layoffs, or returning to school. A second result of significance is the small percentage of the persistently poor. Clearly, all this has important implications for public policy.

Dynamic Equality. The PSID study also shows an astonishing degree of movement within the American income distribution. Consider the stunning changes indicated in Table B. The table shows the percentage of people in family income quintiles that remained in the same (1971) quintile and the percentage that rose or fell to another. Thus, of those who were either at the top or the bottom levels in 1971, only about half remained in those relative positions by 1978. Change in the middle income groups was even more dramatic: Only about a third remained in the same place; the rest rose or fell. (If there were no mobility in the American economy, the encircled numbers in Table B would be 100 percent; as can be seen, none is higher than 56 percent.) Given these persistent changes, the "half-life" of the American income distribution (as measured in quintiles) is at most seven years!

TABLE B

Changes in Family Income, 1971–78

Family Income Quintile, 1971	Family Income Quintile, 1978					
	Highest	Second	Third	Fourth	Lowest	Total
Highest	48.5	29.5	14.0	4.5	3.5	100%
Second	22.0	31.5	25.5	15.0	6.0	100%
Third	14.0	18.5	30.5	23.5	13.5	100%
Fourth	9.0	13.5	21.5	34.5	21.5	100%
Lowest	6.0	7.0	9.5	22.0	55.5	100%

Dynamic Justice. The PSID study also makes it possible to compare the economic status of a large group of people with that of its parents. Consider Table C, which makes this comparison for those who formed new households by 1981. As one can see, only just over a third of young adults with parents in the highest income group ended up in the same group, while fewer than half of those with parents in the lowest group remained there. (Again, if there were no mobility in the American economy, the encircled numbers in Table C would be 100 percent.) It may well be that the strong intergenerational mobility indicated here (which, no doubt, has something to do with the greater degree to which *equal opportunity* is realized in the United States compared to other countries) leads to long-term equality of *results*.

TABLE C

Intergenerational Economic Mobility, 1969–81

Parents' Average Family Income Quintile	Young Adult's Average Family Income Quintile					
	Highest	Second	Third	Fourth	Lowest	Total
Highest	(36)	23	19	13	9	100%
Second	25	(26)	22	17	10	100%
Third	17	26	(23)	23	11	100%
Fourth	15	19	19	(24)	23	100%
Lowest	2	9	18	27	(44)	100%

Economists can learn a great deal from this study, not least of all that the "movie" of an open economy is not simply the sum of the "still shots" they are used to studying.

Source: Mark Lilla, "Why the 'Income Distribution' Is So Misleading," *The Public Interest,* Fall 1984, pp. 62–76. For a first report on the study itself, *see* Greg J. Duncan et al., *Years of Poverty, Years of Plenty: The Changing Fortunes of American Workers and Families* (Ann Arbor, Mich.: University of Michigan Institute for Social Research, 1984). For a recent study of the representativeness of the current panel, see Sean Becketti et al., "The Panel Study of Income Dynamics after Fourteen Years: An Evaluation," *Journal of Labor Economics,* October 1988, pp. 472–92. (The study concludes that the distribution of demographic characteristics within the panel compares well with that derived from the official Current Population Survey.)

CLOSE-UP 14.1

STALIN AND COMECON

Stalin's changing attitudes toward foreign trade provide an illustration of the second Pareto condition discussed in Figure 14.2. Until the end of World War II, Stalin viewed foreign trade with suspicion. He looked upon it as a "safety valve" that would ensure the fulfillment of the national economic plan. Foreign trade allowed the import of essential items that could not be produced at home; exports were a necessary evil to pay for these imports. Ideally, though, a zero volume of foreign trade would ensure total independence from a hostile world surrounding the Soviet Union, while Stalin built "socialism in one country."

After 1945, other socialist countries emerged: Poland, Rumania, Bulgaria, Albania, Yugoslavia, Hungary, Czechoslovakia, East Germany—and in Asia others still. There is nothing wrong, argued Stalin's economists, with being dependent on friends. These economists urged abandonment of the old policy of minimizing foreign trade in favor of a grand international division of labor in "the socialist camp." Starting in 1949, the above-named countries joined the Soviet Union in a Council for Mutual Economic Aid (frequently abbreviated as Comecon or CMEA). They attempted to specialize in production in accordance with differences in their technical circumstances. The *MRT* data in Figure 14.2 are an indication of such differences. For example, Albania would specialize in early potatoes, Bulgaria in industrial sewing machines, Czechoslovakia in sugar-beet combines, East Germany in plastics, Hungary in aluminum products, Poland in horticultural tractors, Rumania in reed cellulose, and the Soviet Union in fishing vessels. In this way, given resources would yield higher output than a policy of national self-sufficiency would provide.[a]

[a]For a detailed listing of specialization decisions, *see* Heinz Kohler, *Economic Integration in the Soviet Bloc* (New York: Praeger, 1965), pp. 127–40.

CLOSE-UP 14.2

THE POW CAMP

Word War II prisoner-of-war camps provide an illustration of the fourth Pareto condition of economic efficiency—the optimum allocation of goods among consumers of the same goods—discussed in Figure 14.4. In these POW camps, almost no production occurred. Yet prisoners received many products, ranging from canned milk, beef, biscuits, butter, and jam to cigarettes, chocolate, sugar, clothing, razor blades, and writing paper. Like manna from heaven, these products came in the form of rations handed out by the detaining power, through Red Cross packages and private parcels. More often than not, everyone received almost identical quantities of all items. Yet within seconds

of receipt, widespread and spontaneous exchange of products occurred. People placed different personal evaluations on the items in their possession. The *MRS* data in Figure 14.4 are an indication of such differences. Through exchange, the prisoners reallocated a given quantity of goods in such a way that the comfort of everyone was increased at the same time.

Source: R. A. Radford, "The Economic Organization of a POW Camp," *Economica,* November 1945, pp. 189–201.

CLOSE-UP 14.3

THE ECONOMICS OF RENT SEEKING

As was noted in Chapters 11 and 12A, resource services that manage to receive a payment in excess of their best alternative are said to be receiving an *economic rent* equal to the difference between the actual payment and the best opportunity forgone. Such rents arise naturally in any price system as the result of the particular configurations of supply and demand; a given supply that meets a relatively strong demand, for example, might generate a large rent, and that rent may be permanent (be a *pure rent*) or temporary (be a *quasi rent*), depending on whether supply in the long run is or is not responsive to price. What

would be a temporary quasi rent in a free market could, however, be made permanent through the deliberate and artificial restriction of supply. Such restriction is often accomplished with the help of government, and people who expend scarce resources in order to create a situation in which they can increase their own income at the expense of other people's income are said to engage in **rent seeking.**

From the individual point of view, it is perfectly rational to expend resources for the purpose of gaining an asset that produces economic rent. Monopoly power created by government (in the form of a limited number of import licenses, off-shore oil-drilling rights, taxi medallions, and the like) is an example of such an asset; this power enables its holder to gain higher income than otherwise. From the point of view of society, resources expended on rent seeking (such as the lobbying efforts of would-be monopolists) are wasted. Such resources do not contribute to an increase in social welfare; they merely help transfer welfare from some people to other people. In his *Cours d'Économie Politique,* Pareto says:

> Let us suppose that in a country of thirty million inhabitants it is proposed, under some pretext or other, to get each citizen to pay out one franc a year, and to distribute the total amount amongst thirty persons. Every one of the donors will give up one franc a year; every one of the beneficiaries will receive one million francs a year. The two groups will differ very greatly in their response to this situation. Those who hope to gain a million a year . . . will win newspapers over to their interest by financial inducements and drum up support from all quarters. A discreet hand will warm the palms of needy legislators, even of ministers. . . . Those who hope to gain a million apiece have agents everywhere, who descend in swarms on the electorate, urging the voters that sound and enlightened patriotism calls for the success of their modest proposal. . . . In contrast, the individual who is threatened with losing one franc a year—even if he is fully aware of what is afoot—will not for so small a thing forgo a picnic in the country, or fall out with useful or congenial friends. . . . In these circumstances the outcome is not in doubt: the spoliators will win hands down.

More recently, Jeffrey Brennen, an economist at the Virginia Polytechnic Institute, devised a classroom game to demonstrate the social waste created by rent seeking.[a] In the game the instructor offers a prize of, say, $2 for which students in the class can bid. The students are told to write the amount of money they are willing to pay on a signed piece of paper and hand it in. They are also told that the highest bidder will take the prize, that they must pay the instructor the amount of their bid regardless of whether they are the highest bidder, and that they are free not to participate at all. The prize can, of course, be viewed as the classroom equivalent of the net present value of a stream of monopoly profits offered by government and sought by rent seekers. The bids students make can be viewed as the value of resources expended in efforts to acquire monopoly power.

The results of the game say much about the real world: The total of bids submitted tends to rise with the size of the class (the number of competitors seeking to gain monopoly). In classes of more than 40 students, the high bid tends to be close to $2, and the sum of bids is often several times the value of the prize. In one instance, this sum came to $24.37.

Interestingly, the first (and admittedly crude) estimate of the value of resources wasted in the U.S. economy on unproductive rent seeking is also very high: It came to 22 percent of the 1985 GNP.[b]

---

[a]As reported in Richard B. McKenzie, *Economic Issues in Public Policies* (New York: McGraw-Hill, 1980), pp. 70–71.

[b]David N. Laband and John P. Sophocleus, "The Social Cost of Rent-seeking: First Estimates," *Public Choice,* September 1988, pp. 269–75.

7

The Economic Role of Government

These chapters show how government must play a crucial role if the market economy is to work well. Government must assign and enforce property rights in all scarce things; it must promote competition; it must deal with externalities and provide public goods.

15

Property Rights, Antitrust, and Regulation

It is a mistake to think that a market economy can prosper in the complete absence of government. In fact, a market economy cannot function well unless there is a government successfully performing two crucial tasks, the establishment of transferable property rights in all things that are scarce and the promotion of a competitive environment that facilitates unrestricted voluntary exchanges among people. This chapter will explore these important economic roles of government.

ESTABLISHING PROPERTY RIGHTS

It is easy to see why market exchanges cannot flourish unless government assigns **property rights**; that is, rights to the exclusive, but perhaps socially circumscribed, use of scarce things: Scarcity creates a basic conflict situation. During any given period, once resources and technical knowledge have been applied in the best possible way and a set of goods has been produced,

people as a group cannot get additional goods. But any one person can always hope to get more goods at the expense of other persons. In the absence of government, there would surely emerge a wild scramble to appropriate those scarce, goods-yielding resources (or the good made with their help). Undoubtedly, the strong and the cunning would then end up with most resources and goods at the expense of the weak and not-so-clever. Life for many would be "nasty, brutish, and short." To avoid this situation, government is needed to bully the bullies, to banish the law of the jungle.

By assigning property rights, government establishes a boundary line for the social behavior of every person and makes clear who has disposition over any particular resource or good at any one moment. In fact, by establishing property rights, government distributes **economic power,** the capacity to make and enforce decisions on the allocation of resources and the apportioning of goods.

If you were given the exclusive right to yourself (no slavery was allowed) and also to 10 acres of land, a truck, and a house, these things would delineate your area of responsibility. These would be the things with which you could make choices, the things you could use to pursue your own welfare as you cared to define it. All other scarce things would be none of your business. They would be assigned to others and would establish *their* economic power.

It is also obvious why property rights have to be *transferable* from one person to another. If that were not so, nobody could ever succeed in selling or buying anything.

Anyone who has grown up in a market economy is, of course, familiar with the widespread existence of property rights that have been created in some distant past, but, as Close-Ups 15.1 to 15.4 indicate, new property rights are being born even in our time, and the process is never an easy one.

PROMOTING COMPETITION

Having defined property rights in all scarce things (and, presumably, having established a system of law, police, and courts to enforce them), there is another thing the government can do to make the market economy flourish: It can restrain monopoly and foster competition, thereby ensuring that the exchange of scarce things, at terms freely agreed upon by the parties involved, is equally open to all. If exchange at freely agreed-upon terms is not open to all, some people, unlike others, are coerced into uses of property rights they do not consider optimal or are prevented from uses that they do prefer.

As the remaining sections of this chapter will show, antitrust policy, the regulation of natural monopolies, even the regulation of certain competitive industries (to prevent the deterioration of "excessive" competition into no competition, or to promote full knowledge on the part of market participants)—all these governmental actions can be viewed as part of a grand design to ensure a competitive environment. As we shall also see, however, government is quite capable of playing an altogether different role. Recall the Chapter 7 discussion of the "captured" state (on pp. 240–42). Government regulation can also serve the purpose—promoted by special interests—of *destroying* competition. Recognition of this fact has given rise, in recent years, to a movement favoring deregulation.

ANTITRUST POLICY

In the past 100 years, the U.S. Congress has enacted a series of **antitrust laws** designed to restrain monopoly and foster competition and thereby to increase the likelihood that product prices will reflect marginal costs (economic efficiency), will equal lowest possible average total costs (technical efficiency), and will leave no room for long-run economic profits (economic equity). Consider how it all started.

THE IMPETUS TO ANTITRUST LEGISLATION

Late in the last century, private firms in the United States used a number of innovative devices in attempts to replace competition with monopoly. One of these was the horizontal merger, already discussed in Chapter 8, "Application 1: Mergers." A second method of eliminating competition was the formation of a **holding company,** a corporation established for the sole purpose of acquiring a controlling stock interest in two or more competing corporations in an industry and then jointly running their affairs. Holding companies were made possible by an 1888 New Jersey law permitting one corporation to buy stock in another, which was supplemented by a later law permitting a New Jersey corporation to do business anywhere. As a result of this legislation, a New Jersey corporation could be formed for the sole purpose of buying a controlling share of stock in a variety of other corporations. The holding company did not have to own any productive assets directly, but with a minimum of financial investment and some luck its owners could control a vast industrial empire.

Consider the example of an oil company with real estate and equipment of $1 billion. Assume the company has acquired its assets with the cash received from selling $500 million worth of bonds and $500 million worth of stock certificates. Suppose further that half the stock is nonvoting preferred stock. (The holders of a corporation's preferred stock, compared to the holders of common stock, receive preferential treatment—as to the payment of dividends, for example—but in return may give up their right to vote on corporate affairs. Further detail may be found in the *Student Workbook* accompanying this text, in Appendix 12A, "Markets for Bonds and Stocks.") Someone can control the corporation with certainty by owning just a little bit more than half of the *common* stock that alone carries the right to vote. That is, that person can control all of the $1 billion worth of assets by owning just a little more than $125 million worth of common stock. Because in fact most stockholders do not bother to vote, especially if the common stock ownership is widely dispersed, someone can probably control the company by owning a much smaller block of common stock. Suppose instead of owning a fraction above 50 percent, a person can get away with owning as little as 10 percent and still control the firm. That person can control the $1 billion worth of assets with only $25 million worth of common stock and, similarly, can control 10 companies that have $10 billion worth of assets with only $250 million worth of common stock.

Next, let a holding company A own those $250 million worth of common stock. A person who is smart and lucky can endow company A with the 250 million *dollars* needed to buy that much common stock of the 10 operating companies by again selling bonds (worth, say, $125 million), nonvoting preferred stock (worth, say, $62.5 million), and voting common stock (worth, say, the remaining $62.5 million). Making the same assumptions as above, such a person can control company A (and indirectly all 10 oil companies) with as little as 10 percent of its common stock, or $6.25 million.

One can, in fact, go further and pyramid holding company upon holding company. For example, let holding company B hold those $6.25 million worth of common stock. By the same procedure used above, a person can control company B (and hence A and hence all 10 oil producers) with as little as $156,250. Or the person can let holding company C own those $156,250 worth of common stock of B, and then control C, *and ultimately $10 billion worth of oil companies,* with no more than $3,906.25.

Fantastic as it may seem, many actual holding companies (including American Can, American Tobacco, U.S. Rubber, and U.S. Steel) vastly exceeded the above example in complexity. The $1 billion Associated Gas and Electric Company was controlled by a man holding $100,000 worth of voting stock.

A third device employed in the late 1800s to escape competition was the **trust,** a combination of several corporations under the trusteeship of a single board of directors that manages their affairs jointly. Stockholders of competing companies would surrender their stock certificates (and the right to run enterprise affairs) to a group of "trustees" in return for **trust certificates,** or nonvoting ownership shares in the trust. The trustees would then run all the companies as if they were a single enterprise. Holders of trust certificates would, as before, be entitled to all the profits made. Because most stockholders were more interested in earning something on their financial investment than in running a business, and because the elimination of competition through the device of the trust was expected to raise profits, the number of trusts grew rapidly. Most famous was the oil trust under John D.

Rockefeller. Other large ones existed in whiskey, cordage, lead, and sugar. The first laws designed to save competition got their name—*antitrust laws*—from the trust, but these laws were designed to counter forms of anticompetitive behavior other than trusts as well.

ANTITRUST LAWS AND THEIR APPLICATIONS

The first antitrust law, passed in 1890, is probably one of the shortest laws on record.

The Sherman Act

Section 1. Every contract, combination in the form of trust or otherwise, or conspiracy, in restraint of trade or commerce among the several States, or with foreign nations, is hereby declared to be illegal. Every person who shall make any such contract or engage in any such combination or conspiracy, shall be deemed guilty of a misdemeanor, and, on conviction thereof, shall be punished by fine not exceeding five thousand dollars, or by imprisonment not exceeding one year, or by both said punishments, in the discretion of the court.

Section 2. Every person who shall monopolize, or attempt to monopolize, or combine or conspire with any other person or persons, to monopolize any part of the trade or commerce among the several States, or with foreign nations, shall be deemed guilty of a misdemeanor, and, on conviction thereof, shall be punished by fine not exceeding five thousand dollars, or by imprisonment not exceeding one year, or by both said punishments, in the discretion of the court.

Without defining its terms, the Sherman Act thus forbade individual or joint efforts to restrain trade and to "monopolize." The act did not make clear, however, whether it outlawed already *existing* monopolies (that is, certain *market structures*) or only the attempt or only the *successful* attempt to establish monopoly (that is, certain types of business *conduct*). This uncertainty about the law's intent has haunted antitrust policy ever since. Certainly, the act's vague language gave wide latitude of interpretation to the courts.

The Rule of Reason

Not until 1911 did the U.S. Supreme Court enunciate its famous **rule of reason,** according to which only deliberate and unreasonable restraint of trade was illegal under the Sherman Act, not *bigness* per se. To be guilty of monopolization, the court said, a firm must have the *intent* to exercise monopoly power and on that basis engage in actions that restrain trade *unreasonably.* Both the Rockefeller family's Standard Oil Company (then owning 91 percent of refining industry capacity) and the Duke family's American Tobacco Company (supplying 90 percent of the market for most tobacco products) were found guilty under this rule (and were dissolved into several independent firms). These companies were guilty by virtue of the vicious tactics used to dispose of smaller competitors. This interpretation by the court narrowed the scope of the Sherman Act considerably. Subsequently, International Harvester, United Shoe Machinery Corporation, Eastman Kodak, and U.S. Steel were found *not* guilty, precisely because they held near-monopolies that had been "thrust upon them"; that is, without their having made predatory attacks on competitors. Mere size or the existence of unexerted power, the court held in 1920, was no offense.

Market Dominance Illegal Per Se

In 1945, in a case involving Alcoa (then supplying 90 percent of new aluminum production), the court reversed tradition. Alcoa was found guilty because of bigness alone, even though its conduct had not been offensive. Under this new interpretation, du Pont was found innocent in 1956, but the United Shoe Machinery Corporation was forced, in 1969, to set up two rival companies.

With court decisions aimed at shaping *market structure* (that is, the number and size of competing firms in the market), certain difficult problems have inevitably emerged. One of these problems has been the definition of the relevant market in which the accused firm is supposedly exercising monopoly power. For example, Alcoa believed it had a 33-percent share of the aluminum ingot market because it considered the market to include production for sale from new ore and from scrap plus imports, but the government calculated that Alcoa had a 90-percent market share because it considered the market to include only production from new ore, regardless of whether it was for sale or for Alcoa's internal use. Similarly, du Pont was accused of having a monopoly in cellophane (which, given its patent, was strictly speaking true), but the company argued successfully that the relevant market included other flexible wrapping materials as well and that its share of this larger market was less than 20 percent (see Close-Up 3.2, "Cross-Price Elasticity and the Cellophane Case"). Such problems have come up again and again. Was the 1963 market relevant to the Philadelphia National Bank national banking (4 percent share) or Philadelphia banking (36 percent)? Was the 1975 market relevant to Xerox that for all copying equipment (65 percent share) or that for plain-paper copiers (90 percent)?

Explicit Collusion Illegal Per Se

The courts have been less uncertain about the Sherman Act's intent on matters of collusion. They have consistently held explicit collusive agreements on prices, output, or market shares to be illegal *per se*; that is, they have been considered illegal regardless of motives or consequences. Such have been the rulings by the U.S. Supreme Court on price fixing in the Trans-Missouri Freight Association case of 1897, the Addyston Pipe and Steel Co. case of 1899, the Trenton Potteries case of 1927, the Socony-

Vacuum Oil Co. case of 1940, and many more. (The Court has been less consistent on pricing behavior that is consciously parallel but involves no direct communication. The accused were found guilty in the Interstate Circuit case of 1939, the American Tobacco case of 1946, the Cement Institute case of 1948, the General Electric-Westinghouse case of 1976, but most cases of tacit collusion since the 1950s have been viewed as exempt.) The courts, finally, have ruled illegal any joint venture by competitors (in the Penn-Olin Chemical Co. case of 1964) and any territorial allocations among them (in the Topco Associates case of 1972).

The Clayton Act

In the years following the enactment of the Sherman Act, powerful new business combinations came into being in many industries (steel, farm machinery, tin cans, etcetera). Again and again, practices used to achieve these combinations were held not to violate the act. So Congress enacted another law that focused on conduct rather than market structure and spelled out certain illegal acts. The Clayton Act of 1914 forbade sellers "to discriminate in price between different purchasers of commodities" but permitted such discrimination if differential prices were due to "differences in the grade, quality, or quantity of the commodity sold," if lower prices made "only due allowance for differences in the cost of selling or transportation," or if lower prices were offered "in good faith to meet competition" (see Chapter 7, "Application 2: Price Discrimination"). This prohibition was designed to protect small firms from larger rivals who frequently slashed prices on particular goods in particular markets only for the purpose of eliminating small competitors.

The Clayton Act also outlawed **exclusive contracts** by which sellers agree to "lease or make a sale or contract for sale of . . . commodities . . . on the condition that the lessee or purchaser thereof shall not use or deal in the . . .

commodity . . . of a competitor.'' Such contracts were common, for instance, in automobile retailing and soft-drink bottling. The Clayton Act similarly outlawed **requirements contracts,** according to which buyers agreed to purchase all of their requirements of a commodity from a given seller only. Gas stations often had to sign such a contract with suppliers of gasoline, batteries, tires; electric utilities had to sign such contracts with suppliers of coal or oil. Also outlawed were **tying contracts,** according to which buyers of one good agreed to purchase another good from the same seller as well. Under such contracts, for example, buyers of IBM card-sorting machines might be made to purchase IBM tabulating cards; buyers of tin-can closing machines to buy tin cans; buyers of TV antennas to buy antenna servicing; buyers of electrostatic copying machines to buy specially coated paper; buyers of a popular movie, *Gone with the Wind,* also to buy a terrible one, *Getting Gertie's Garter*; buyers of land to buy the services of a railroad to ship all products produced on the land.

The Clayton Act also forbade any corporation engaged in commerce to acquire the shares of a competing corporation or to purchase the stocks of two or more corporations that were competitors. The act enjoined large, directly competing firms from having **interlocking directorates,** an arrangement under which two or more competing corporations have in common some of the members of their boards of directors.

None of these specific prohibitions, however, was absolute. They applied where the stated conduct would ''substantially lessen competition or tend to create a monopoly.''

The Federal Trade Commission Act

Also in 1914, the Federal Trade Commission Act was passed, forbidding all ''unfair methods of competition.'' The commission newly created was empowered to issue ''cease and desist'' orders against violators. (The Wheeler-Lea Act of 1938, in addition to ''unfair methods of competition,'' also outlawed ''unfair or deceptive acts or practices'' in and of themselves, even if they did not hurt competitors. This later act enabled the Federal Trade Commission to control deceptive advertising practices.)

Close-Ups 15.5, ''The United States Versus IBM,'' and 15.6, ''The Breakup of Ma Bell,'' provide case studies of how the laws discussed so far have been applied.

The Robinson-Patman Act

As an amendment to the Clayton Act, the Robinson-Patman Act of 1936 was to protect small independent wholesalers and retailers from mass distributors (such as chain stores or mail-order houses). The bargaining strength of mass distributors (argued the smaller independent distributors) enabled them to pay ''unjustified'' lower prices for their purchases and then to undercut competitors. (In fact, as subsequent developments showed, much of their superior competitive strength came from streamlining internal operations.) The Robinson-Patman Act forbade differential quantity discounts among buyers buying the same quantity. It forbade *any* quantity discounts and the charging in one locality of lower prices than elsewhere if they helped to create monopoly.

Not surprisingly, this law created great uncertainty for firms ready to engage in vigorous price competition. Court decisions have since determined that price discrimination is illegal when practiced by dominant firms (United Shoe Machinery case of 1953), but it is allowed when practiced sporadically by smaller firms.

The Celler-Kefauver Act

The Celler-Kefauver Act of 1950, designed to discourage mergers, returned to the control of market structure rather than business conduct. It closed a loophole in the Clayton Act, forbidding not only the acquisition, for purposes of monopolization, of competitors' shares of stock, but also the use of such stock by proxy and the direct acquisition of the assets of a competitive firm. The Celler-Kefauver Act has been used to challenge all types of mergers, ranging from horizontal ones (Bethlehem-Youngstown Steel case of 1956) to vertical ones (Brown and Kinney Shoe case of 1962) to conglomerate ones (Procter and Gamble/Clorox case of 1967).

ANTITRUST POLICY ASSESSED

Have antitrust laws effectively promoted competition and restrained the growth of monopoly power? Many critics doubt it.

The Government's Critics

First, these critics argue that the Antitrust Division of the U.S. Department of Justice has been traditionally starved of funds. Until the 1930s, funds were sufficient to go after only a dozen cases per year. Since then, fewer than 50 cases per year have undergone intensive investigation and litigation—still an insignificant number. Why should most firms worry about being indicted?

Furthermore, many of the big cases against monopoly take an incredibly long time (5.5 years on the average) and create an impossible volume of evidence (hundreds of thousands of pages). Conviction, therefore, follows indictment only after a considerable lag and is far from certain. (After 5 years, the jury in the Memorex versus IBM case couldn't reach a verdict. Given the complexities, said the judge, no jury could have made a rational decision.)

Even when cases are carried through the courts to their ultimate conclusion, penalties imposed upon conviction have traditionally been negligible and have rarely taken the form of imprisonment. (In a 1961 electrical equipment industry case, executives were sentenced to 30 days in jail, but 9 of those days were remitted for good behavior. The defendants were viewed as martyrs by their peers!) Most penalties have taken the form of fines, but they have been incredibly insignificant. A 1950 *Study of Monopoly Power* by the House Committee on the Judiciary, for instance, revealed the following facts about a group of 25 major companies: During the preceding 12 years, they had been given fines on 77 occasions for violating the antitrust laws. The total of fines paid by a single firm ranged from $3,500 (Socony-Vacuum Oil Company) to $75,000 (A & P). Relating the total of fines paid over 12 years to the firms' assets as of 1948, the percentages ranged from .0002 percent (Socony-Vacuum Oil Company) to .05 percent (Bausch and Lomb Optical Company). Relating the total of fines paid over 12 years to the firms' *net* profits of a *single* year (1948), the percentages ranged from .002 percent (General Motors) to 2.402 percent (Bausch and Lomb Optical Company).

Since that time, these critics argue, things have not changed. From 1955 to 1965, the average fine handed corporations was $12,778; the average fine for individuals was $3,226. True enough, this does not tell the whole story. Convicted firms incur other costs, which are much more substantial. These other costs range from lawyers' fees, treble damage action by injured parties, and consumer brand switching (due to injury to the firm's "image") to refusal of the government to do business with such firms and sanctions by administrative agencies (such as refusal to renew licenses for broadcasting). Yet such costs are often avoided because not all cases are disposed of by the courts. Frequently, the government prosecutor and the accused reach a **consent agreement,** according to which the suit is dropped in exchange for voluntary ameliorative action by the accused party, such as spinning off a subdivision or withdrawing a deceptive advertisement. This kind of agreement short-circuits a long court proceeding and spares the accused open court embarrassment and the other consequences should conviction occur. Needless to say, the possibility of reaching consent agreements also opens up vast possibilities for corruption. The accused parties, who have potentially hundreds of millions of dollars to lose, might engineer a favorable outcome outside of court for a much smaller sum of campaign contributions or other favors. Three government suits against ITT, including one seeking the divestiture of the Hartford Fire Insurance Company, for instance, were dropped in 1971 on President Nixon's orders after ITT had promised, in repeated secret meetings with top administration officials, to underwrite a planned Republican national convention to the tune of $400,000, as well as to rid itself of Avis, the Canteen Corporation, Levitt and Sons, the fire protection division of the Grinnell Corporation, and two smaller insurance companies. Before this agreement was finalized, ITT and the White House tried to prevent a Securities and Exchange Commission subpoena of ITT memos and letters on the above deal; when their attempts failed, the commission joined ITT and the White House in foiling the investigations of the House Commerce Committee and the Senate Judiciary Committee. In the end, top ITT and Administration officials committed perjury before the Senate committee. (Close-Up 15.7, ''A Phone Call about Prices,'' provides another interesting example of what is probably commonplace illegal activity.)

Last but not least, critics say, the stress on controlling *conduct* rather than *market structure* is unfortunate. Aspiring monopolists who have the slightest amount of imagination can always discover new ways of accomplishing their purposes without violating the law. The only effective policy is one that enforces a competitive market structure by ensuring free entry into and exit from every market. Such a market structure has not been achieved since the enactment of the Sherman Act. Indeed, critics conclude, present policy can only be described as an utter perversion of the act's intent. Despite the fact that the intent of the Sherman Act was to restrain the output-restricting and price-raising actions of would-be monopolists, firms that *expand* trade by producing more output, by producing new types of output, or by selling it at lower prices (and which gain larger market shares as a result) find themselves indicted for *restraint* of trade. Surely, Alcoa expanded trade in 1945 when it built ingot production capacity ahead of anticipated increases in demand. Surely, du Pont expanded trade in 1978 when it developed a low-cost method for producing titanium dioxide pigments, built a new plant, *lowered* price, and gained 40 percent of the market. Surely, Kellogg, General Foods, and General Mills expanded trade when they gained 75 percent of the market for ready-to-eat cereals by introducing new varieties, such as bran, high-protein, vitamin-enriched, and presweetened cereals. Yet all of these firms were indicted for restraint of trade. American firms, critics say, are understandably confused. Are they supposed to reduce capacity, cut back production, raise price, reduce product variety?

The Government's Position

Government officials respond to critics by pointing to recent improvements. For example, the 1974 Antitrust Procedures and Penalties Act changed antitrust violations from misdemeanors to felonies and raised the maximum fines to $1 million for corporations and $100,000 and three years in jail for individuals. Also, in order to stem possible government-business collusion, new procedures were established for reaching consent agreements: The accused firm must file with the judge involved in a case a list of all contacts with government officials; the government prosecutor must give the judge (and publish in major newspapers) a 60-day advance notice of any proposed out-of-court settlement, spelling out how the settlement will cure the problems giving rise to the suit in the first place; the judge can accept or reject the settlement proposal after noting public response.

Furthermore, argue government defenders, the ghost of Senator Sherman is an *ex officio* member of every board of directors, which is supposed to mean that business executives think twice before any action on pricing, expansion, and the like in order not to come in conflict with the law. According to this view, the law has primarily preventive effects. Yet there is overwhelming evidence that the laws are continually violated on a large scale. It may well be, how-ever, that they would be violated even more without the threat of jail or fines, without the frequent use of court injunctions halting "unde-sirable" behavior, and without the fear of the other indirect effects of indictment or conviction.

THE REGULATION OF NATURAL MONOPOLY

In some situations, like those first depicted in Figure 7.1, "The Natural Monopoly" (p. 219), the long-run average total cost of producing a good is declining throughout the range of quan-tities that might be demanded in the market. In situations of such persistent economies of scale, the breakup of monopoly and the promotion of competition is undesirable because the lowest possible production cost can only be achieved by a monopoly. Government often protects such firms from competition, but it also attempts to regulate their behavior in order to achieve eco-nomic efficiency and equity.

The Theory

The graph in Figure 15.1 refers to an electric power company but could just as well be applied to gas distribution, telephone service, pipeline transport, or certain railroads for which the optimum plant equals or exceeds the size of the market. In the absence of government regulation, such a firm would, of course, maximize profit by equating marginal revenue, *MR*, with long-run marginal cost, *LRMC*, as at point *a*. This firm would produce 375 million kilowatt hours per year and sell them at 10 cents each (point *b*). Given long-run average total cost, *LRATC*, this price-output combination would produce an eco-nomic profit of 2.5 cents per kilowatt hour (distance *bf*), or a total of $9.375 million per year (crosshatched area). This combination would also imply a deadweight efficiency loss of the roughly triangular area *abe* (shaded).

If government regulators wanted to eliminate this deadweight loss by setting a competitive

FIGURE 15.1

Regulating the Natural Monopoly

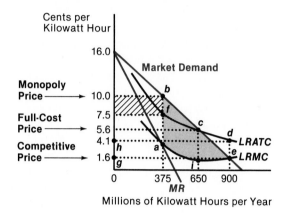

In the absence of government regulation, the natural monopoly pictured here maximizes profit by equating at point *a* the marginal benefit of production (or marginal revenue, *MR*) with its marginal cost (*LRMC*). It selects a price of 10 cents and produces an output of 375 million kilowatt hours per year, creating monopoly profit (cross-hatched) as well as a deadweight efficiency loss (shaded). If government regulators were to set a 1.6-cent competi-tive price equal to marginal cost, they would drive the firm into bankruptcy because average total cost (point *d*) would then exceed price (point *e*). Regulators can, how-ever, select a compromise, such as the full-cost price of 5.6 cents. This price produces neither profit nor loss but eliminates only a portion of the deadweight loss (area *abci*).

price equal to marginal cost, they would have to set the price at 1.6 cents per kilowatt hour (point *e*). This price would expand quantity demanded to 900 million kilowatt hours per year; the larger output would reduce long-run average total cost from *f* to *d*. Note: Under conditions of increasing returns to scale, long-run marginal cost lies below long-run average total cost; hence a price set equal to marginal cost produces a loss (here equal to *de*) on every unit of output sold. Thus government regulators could eliminate the shaded efficiency loss (and also the crosshatched monopoly profit) in the fashion just indicated, but if they did, they would drive our firm into bankruptcy. The firm would lose $22.5 million per year (area *degh*).

FIGURE 15.2

A Price-Discriminating Natural Monopoly

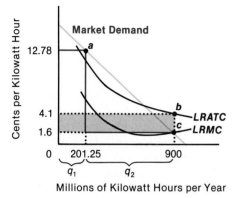

Marginal-cost pricing (point *c*) inevitably saddles a natural monopoly with a loss (shaded). The loss can be avoided by increasing revenue through price discrimination. In this example, quantity q_1 sold at 12.78 cents per kilowatt hour plus quantity q_2 sold at 1.6 cents per kilowatt hour yields total revenue just equal to total cost (of $36.9 million per year).

For this reason, government regulators attempt instead to set a full-cost price that just covers average total cost (point *c*). In our example, this price would be 5.6 cents per kilowatt hour and would lead to the production of 650 million kilowatt hours per year. At this price, total revenue would just equal total cost; monopoly profit would be gone. A portion of economic inefficiency would remain (portion *cei* of the shaded area).

One possibility for removing even the last remnants of economic inefficiency here would be for regulators to permit price discrimination. The demand and cost curves in Figure 15.2 are identical with those of Figure 15.1, but in Figure 15.2 we assume that regulators would institute a two-tier price structure. They would let the electric company charge 12.78 cents per kilowatt hour for what the market would take, and this quantity (q_1) would equal 201.25 million kilowatt hours per year (point *a*). In addition, however, a quantity (q_2) of 698.75 million kilowatt hours would be sold at 1.6 cents per kilowatt

hour, bringing the total to 900 million kilowatt hours per year. Thus marginal buyers would pay a price equal to marginal cost (point *c*). Average total cost would equal 4.1 cents (point *b*), and total cost would come to $36.9 million per year. Yet total revenue would add to the same sum: Total revenue would equal q_1 times 12.78 cents (or $25.72 million per year) plus q_2 times 1.6 cents (or $11.18 million per year). The practice of price discrimination would avoid the loss (shaded) that marginal-cost pricing would otherwise produce.

Unfortunately, government regulators are not omniscient. They do not possess the complete information about demand and cost conditions given to us in Figures 15.1 and 15.2.

Practical Problems

Government regulators who do not have access to all the information implied by the ready-made graphs of the textbook typically seek to set the price charged by a public utility in a way that produces zero economic profit. They attempt to select a price that generates just the revenue needed to attract and keep the resources used by the monopoly firm. This revenue must be sufficient to cover normal operating costs (such as wages, fuel, and depreciation) as well as a ''fair'' return on the investment made by the firm's owners. Such a policy, of course, makes a lot of sense. An inability to cover the costs mentioned would put an end to the firm. It would be unable to attract workers, buy raw materials, replace its equipment, and keep or expand its capital. Yet the determination of the ''fair'' return has produced no end of problems.

Regulators must, of course, first determine the desirable *rate* of return, which is not too difficult. If investors can find comparable investments elsewhere in the economy that return 10 percent per year, a similar percentage might be selected. If the return was less than 10 percent, present investors would want to withdraw their investment from the firm; the firm would find it impossible to attract additional funds should it ever wish to expand. Much more difficult to determine is the **rate base,** or the value of the investment on which the owners of the regulated firm are to receive a "fair" return and to which the selected rate of return is to be applied. What is the value of the owners' investment? Should it be, regulators have asked, the dollars ever received by the firm through the sale of common stock? Should it be the original cost of the firm's assets, minus depreciation thereon? Should it be the current replacement cost of these assets, given their present conditions? Each of these approaches is likely to yield a different figure; in times of inflation, current replacement cost is higher, for example, than original cost.

Nor is the determination of the "fair" return the only problem regulators face. Having once settled on a "fair" rate of return of, say, 10 percent per year and on an original cost of, say, $100 million, the regulators might announce their intention to select a price that generates revenues equal to operating costs plus $10 million a year (the "fair" return). Such a cost-plus procedure does little for managerial incentives. Indeed, it is likely to foster both X-inefficiency and technical stagnation. Why should any manager keep tight control over costs, or even reduce them, when regulators, in the end, are bound to change price so as to keep the owners' returns at exactly $10 million a year? Thus managers may grant large wage increases to unions whenever so asked and ensure themselves a quiet life. They may give jobs to incompetent relatives and live lavishly on the company expense account. Any gains in economic efficiency through regulation may thus quickly be eaten up by cost curves that shift up (X-inefficiency) or fail to shift down (lack of dynamic efficiency).

All this inefficiency is conceivably mitigated in the short run by **regulatory lag,** the length of time, sometimes years, that it takes government regulators to review a firm's performance and possibly change its price. The existence of this lag may attenuate the inefficiency effects just noted. If the lag is long, the owners of well-managed regulated firms that reduce costs can earn more than "fair" returns—that is, they will make economic profits—at least until the regula-

tors catch up and lower prices. (Note: Such profits are the very thing many regulators wish to eliminate; hence the restoration of incentives through regulatory lag also implies regulatory failure.) On the other hand, owners of well-managed regulated firms the costs of which are rising (because of inflation, perhaps) will earn less than "fair" returns—that is, they will incur economic losses. Such firms will be unable to attract new funds for expansion, and they are likely to cut costs by reducing the *quality* of the goods they supply.

Regulation is likely to have another undesirable consequence: the **Averch-Johnson effect.** If the return guaranteed by the regulators exceeds the cost of capital, the owners of a natural monopoly will substitute capital for other inputs and will not produce a given output at minimum cost.[1] They will undertake new investment in the firm regardless of whether it increases output. Consider the earlier example of regulators having selected a target rate of return of 10 percent a year. If the cost of capital is only 7 percent, any $1 million addition to the monopoly's capital yields a pure gain of $30,000 a year to investors. (These investors will get $100,000 from the monopoly; they would earn only $70,000 elsewhere.) Indeed, there are other distortions as well. In order to increase the value of the base on which regulators calculate allowable profit, natural monopolies have understated depreciation charges and allowed their suppliers to overcharge them on equipment purchases.

Note: All these problems are compounded when regulators attempt the much more complex task of setting not just one price, but a structure of prices, as a competitive market would in response to fluctuating demand. Consider how the demand for electricity, telephone service, or

---

[1]Harvey Averch and Leland L. Johnson, "Behavior of the Firm under Regulatory Constraint," *The American Economic Review,* December 1962, pp. 1052–69. *Note also* Robert M. Spann, "Rate of Return Regulation and Efficiency in Production: An Empirical Test of the Averch-Johnson Thesis," *The Bell Journal of Economics and Management Science,* Spring 1974, pp. 38–52.

rail transportation is bound to vary with the time of day, the day of the week, or the season of the year. Proper regulation requires, therefore, appropriately fluctuating prices.

THE REGULATION OF COMPETITION

Ever since 1887, when the Interstate Commerce Commission was set up to regulate the railroads, the number of regulatory bodies at all levels of government and their responsibilities have grown. Consider this partial listing of federal regulatory agencies:

1. The Civil Aeronautics Board (CAB) was set up to regulate airlines;

2. the Federal Communications Commission (FCC) was established to oversee telephone and telegraph companies, radio and television broadcasters, and then cable TV, CB radios, and ham operators;

3. the Federal Maritime Commission (FMC) was formed to regulate ocean shipping;

4. the Federal Power Commission (FPC) was set up to regulate natural gas and electric power producers;

5. the Nuclear Regulatory Commission (NRC) functions to regulate the nuclear industry;

6. the Interstate Commerce Commission (ICC) was formed to regulate railroads, inland water and coastal shipping, intercity buses, nonagricultural truckers, and pipelines.

By no stretch of the imagination can all of the above industries be described as natural monopolies. Why then were they subjected to regulation by government? Two competing theories—the public-interest theory and the special-interest theory—attempt to explain the regulation of competitive industries.

The Public-Interest Theory

Some observers believe that government regulates (perfectly or imperfectly) competitive industries "in the public interest." The phrase *the public interest* usually remains undefined, but

advocates of this theory often suggest that for reasons of economic equity, government regulators set out to "correct" the distribution of income in favor of buyers by commanding lower than market-clearing prices for goods considered "vital necessities" and "too important" to be priced by the market. Consider the recent federal price ceilings on natural gas and oil or the long-standing state and local controls over interest rates charged by lenders or rents charged by landlords. Often regulators also promote price discrimination to subsidize "the worthy," as when railroads are made to carry bulky raw materials at lower rates than finished products or when airlines are made to charge less per passenger mile for short flights or flights to small cities than for longer hauls and flights to large cities.

Not surprisingly, this type of "public interest" regulation causes no end of problems. The below-equilibrium price encourages consumption while discouraging production. As a result, shortages of natural gas and oil occur, students (or veterans) cannot find banks willing to make tuition (or mortgage) loans, and renters cannot find apartments. Shippers of bulky products face a boxcar shortage; short flights to small cities are crammed while long flights are plagued with empty seats. Before long, regulators can find plenty of reasons to expand their bureaucracy: they must now deal with "unexpected" shortages, with "price gouging" and black markets, with sudden deterioration in the quality of products (which is, of course, one way by which regulated firms can raise prices surreptitiously). Why does rent-controlled housing always deteriorate? Why have many operators of price-controlled gas stations ceased to check under the hood, wash windows, offer convenient hours, or accept all credit cards?

The Special Interest Theory

Economist George J. Stigler, who won the 1982 Nobel Prize (and a Biography of whom appears in Chapter 15 of the *Student Workbook* that accompanies this text), proposes another explanation for government regulation of competition.[2] Stigler argues that most of the time, regulation in competitive industries is not thrust upon firms, but procured by them. Firms seek to escape the rigors of competition (see the discussion of government-sponsored cartels and the ''captured'' state in Chapter 7). Firms want entry restrictions and cartel prices. They want subsidies. (Airlines, for example, have procured air mail subsidies even when they didn't carry mail.) They want to suppress substitutes. (Commercial TV stations, for example, want to keep out pay-TV provided by cable companies.) They want to promote complements. (Airlines, for example, want more and bigger airports; truckers want better highways.) From such desires arises the *demand* for regulation.

Firms are also willing to pay a price in campaign contributions, job offers, and votes. In response to this price arises the *supply* of regulation by politicians and bureaucrats. Even when regulation is initiated for other reasons (such as the avoidance of radio-spectrum interference), it soon comes to serve the special interests of the regulated themselves. As long as these special interests are being served, regulation persists, even when officially announced goals are not achieved and a multitude of perverse effects appear.

A Graphical Summary

Panel (a) of Figure 15.3 depicts a hypothetical competitive market for natural gas, housing space, and the like with a competitive price of $0A$ and quantity $0D$. Let regulators set a below-equilibrium *price ceiling* of $0B$ ''in the public interest,'' and quantity supplied falls to $0C$, while quantity demanded rises to $0E$. Thus a shortage of CE occurs. The shaded triangle represents potential welfare unnecessarily forgone.

---

[2]George J. Stigler, ''The Theory of Economic Regulation,'' *The Bell Journal of Economics and Management Science,* Spring 1971, pp. 3–21. *See also* Richard A. Posner, ''Theories of Economic Regulation,'' *The Bell Journal,* Autumn 1974, pp. 335–58; and Sam Peltzman, ''Toward a More General Theory of Regulation,'' *The Journal of Law and Economics,* August 1976, pp. 211–40.

Panel (b) depicts a hypothetical competitive market for air or truck transport services with a competitive price of $0F$ and quantity $0I$. This time regulators set an above-equilibrium *price floor* of $0G$ in the special interest of producers. Regulators also command a restricted quantity supplied equal to $0H$. The efficiency loss is shown by the shaded area, and the monopoly quasi rent is shown by area $GKLM$. Note: The owners of the regulated firms may have to share some of this rent with others, such as the politicians and regulators who make this gain possible and, perhaps, even with unionized workers, such as airline pilots or teamsters who insist on a piece of the cake. In the presence of such X-inefficiency, line KL (representing, say, long-run marginal and average total costs) will shift up, perhaps to dashed line PQ. Then a smaller output ($0H$ instead of $0I$) is produced at a higher-than-necessary cost ($0P$ instead of $0K$) and sold at a higher-than-competitive price ($0G$ instead of $0F$).

THE REGULATION OF HEALTH AND SAFETY

A new type of governmental regulation has mushroomed recently that is not tied to specific industries. The regulation of health and safety is concerned not with the control of prices or market entry, but rather with the control of the types of goods produced and the ways in which they are produced. While concern with health and safety is not new (the Food and Drug Administration was formed in 1906), a large number of new agencies have sprung up since 1970. A partial listing includes the Consumer Products Safety Commission (CPSC), the Environmental Protection Agency (EPA), the National Highway and Traffic Safety Administration (NHTSA), and the Occupational Safety and Health Administration (OSHA).

Much of the work of these agencies, some critics suggest, is based on the following normative judgments made by self-proclaimed representatives of ''the public interest'':

FIGURE 15.3

Regulating Competition

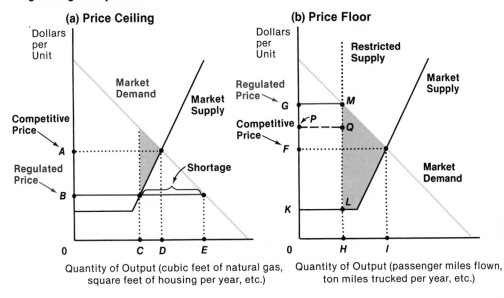

When government regulates competitive markets, it may favor buyers and set a below-equilibrium *price ceiling,* as in panel (a); it may instead favor sellers and set an above-equilibrium *price floor,* as in panel (b). In either case, there are other consequences: In the first case, not all buyers can buy what they wish; in the second case, not all suppliers can be allowed to supply what they wish. In both cases, potential welfare is unnecessarily forgone (shaded areas). Note that government outlaws prices *above* the ceiling [panel (a)] or *below* the floor [panel (b)].

1. It is never morally defensible to trade off human health and safety for material goods.

2. Because few private individuals possess the necessary information, governmental experts should determine which trade-offs of this type must be avoided.

The advocates of the above agencies, in contrast, reject this type of criticism as much too harsh. These agencies, they say, serve the important function of disseminating information to market participants and thus help make competition more perfect. They do for us collectively what we could do individually only by engaging in lengthy and costly *search*: assure us of the quality of products, the safety of working conditions, the effectiveness of drugs, and the like. (Close-Up 15.8 "Can Education Replace Regulation of Health and Safety?" has more to say on the matter.)

REGULATION ASSESSED

In recent years, economists have seriously questioned the worth of many types of regulation. Again and again, they have found the benefits to be low or nonexistent and the costs to be high or unnecessary.

Low Benefits of Regulating Natural Monopolies

George Stigler and Claire Friedland[3] have shown, for instance, that regulators of electric utilities have neither succeeded in changing price

[3]George J. Stigler and Claire Friedland, "What Can Regulators Regulate? The Case of Electricity," *The Journal of Law and Economics,* October 1962, pp. 1–16; reprinted in George J. Stigler, *The Citizen and the State: Essays on Regulation* (Chicago: The University of Chicago Press, 1975), pp. 61–77.

(as they might hope with a view toward achieving economic efficiency) nor profitability (as they might hope with a view toward achieving equity). Comparing data from states in which electric utilities were regulated with data from states in which electric utilities were unregulated, they found no significant differences in utility rates or stockholder experience. In spite of a professed desire to make a difference, the authors concluded, regulators were in fact regulating nothing.

The Theory of the Second Best

Other economists have had second thoughts on theoretical grounds about the desirability of regulating natural monopolies (or pursuing a vigorous antitrust policy). In a celebrated article,[4] Richard G. Lipsey and Kelvin Lancaster showed that if one or more Pareto conditions cannot be satisfied, it is in general not true that the cause of economic efficiency is served by satisfying as many of the other conditions as possible. This **theory of the second best** deals a fatal blow to any policy that attempts to approach the best-of-all-possible worlds by bringing price in line with marginal cost for as many goods as possible and doing so in a piecemeal fashion.

Abram Bergson[5] worked out the implications of the theory for an economy with competitive labor markets in which at least one industry (A) always charges a price above marginal cost, but in which government can affect the relation between price and marginal cost in other industries (B). The implications are complex; they will

only be summarized briefly here. To achieve economic efficiency, government must set the price of B-goods, P_B, to equal marginal cost, MC_B, if goods A and B are independent goods. If A and B goods are substitutes (or complements), however, P_B must exceed (or fall short of) MC_B. If different industries produce a mixture of independent, substitute, and complementary goods, the proper policy depends on the magnitudes of cross-price elasticities of demand, of the output in industry A, and the excess of P_A over MC_A. Therefore, a first-best policy (which simultaneously equates all prices with marginal costs) being out of reach, the equating of price and marginal cost in only some industries is almost surely not the second-best approach. What is second best, however, requires more information than any government is ever likely to possess.

The Theory of the Third Best

To escape the confusion and uncertainty imparted by the theory of the second best, some economists have retreated to a new position.[6] They suggest a **theory of the third best,** according to which policy makers are well advised to eschew *specific* policies (such as bringing prices in line with marginal costs) in favor of *general* policies (such as promoting free-market entry and exit) that on average are likely to have desired effects. Because there is no reason to believe that monopoly promotes efficiency or equity, they say, policies such as those that promote free entry into or exit from markets should be encouraged. This theory does not imply that every existing monopoly must be broken up or regulated.

This new approach is reminiscent not only of recent writings about *contestable markets* (see p. 269), but also of the much earlier suggestion

[4]Richard G. Lipsey and Kelvin Lancaster, "The General Theory of the Second Best," *The Review of Economic Studies*, vol. 1, 1956, pp. 11–32. For an elegant statement *see also* Edward Foster and Hugo Sonnenschein, "Price Distortion and Economic Welfare," *Econometrica*, March 1970, pp. 281–97; and Kunio Kawamata, "Price Distortion and Potential Welfare," *Econometrica*, May 1974, pp. 435–60.

[5]Abram Bergson, "Optimal Pricing for Public Enterprise," *Quarterly Journal of Economics*, November 1972, pp. 519–44.

[6]F. M. Scherer, *Industrial Market Structure and Economic Performance*, 2nd edition (Chicago: Rand McNally, 1980), p. 28; L. Athanasiou, "Some Notes on the Theory of Second Best," *Oxford Economic Papers*, March 1966, pp. 83–87; and Yew-Kwang Ng, "Towards a Theory of Third Best," *Public Finance*, vol. 1, 1977, pp. 1–15.

that policy makers be content with promoting **workable competition,** any market structure in which, taking into account structural characteristics and the dynamic factors that shaped them, no clearly indicated change can be effected through public policy that would result in greater social gains than losses.[7]

Because this advice relies so heavily on subjective judgments by policy makers, it is far from universally accepted by economists. George Stigler says with characteristic cynicism:[8]

> To determine whether any industry is workably competitive, therefore, simply have a good graduate student write his dissertation on the industry and render a verdict. It is crucial to this test, of course, that no second graduate student be allowed to study the industry.

Questionable Benefits of Other Types of Regulation

The benefits from regulating competition or health and safety have also been questioned. The regulation of competition redistributes income, the desirability of which depends on one's concept of equity. But one thing is objectively clear: Regulation (rather than the tax system) is a poor method of income redistribution. Regulation usually takes several dollars from some people in order to give one dollar to favored recipients. A study of trucking regulation, for example, showed that it had raised freight rates from 10–20 percent above the competitive level and

cost shippers an extra \$4 billion a year.[9] Yet of this amount truck operators gained only \$1.4 billion per year, or \$1 for each \$2.86 of increased cost to shippers. The remainder went to members of the teamsters' union (\$1.2 billion) or was dissipated in pure waste (\$1.4 billion), which resulted from driving the circuitous routes, from making the empty return trips, and from obeying the other regulations prescribed by the regulators.

The benefits of many health and safety regulations have similarly been questioned. Why shouldn't people be free, some critics have argued, to trade in health and safety for other things? People do it every day. Consider how people travel in private cars even though buses are safer. Consider how they eat cheap food at the Greasy Spoon even though food poisoning is less likely at the Fancy Restaurant. Consider how they take high-paying jobs in smoggy cities, even though lower-paying ones are available in country towns with cleaner air. (See Table 11.3, "Differential Wages and Death Rates" on p. 376 or Analytical Example 10.1, "Smoke Detectors as Insurance" on p. 348.) Why, critics ask, should *government* decide on the trade-offs made? Why not warn people of any and all hazards and let them decide whether they wish to avoid them? Must individual ignorance be used as an excuse for paternalism? Indeed, might individuals not possess *more* information than government bureaucrats whose inevitable ignorance of detailed circumstances is bound to make them treat all people alike even if it makes no sense? (For example, why should a person without children be forced to pay for safety caps on aspirin bottles designed to protect children? Why should a public library be forced to spend twice its annual budget on making itself accessible to the handicapped if there aren't any handicapped persons in town? Why should city subway systems provide elevators to make stations accessible to wheelchairs when it would be vastly cheaper to offer such people free taxi service?)

[7]John M. Clark, "Toward a Concept of Workable Competition," *The American Economic Review,* June 1940, pp. 241–56; Jesse W. Markham, "An Alternative Approach to the Concept of Workable Competition," *The American Economic Review,* June 1950, pp. 349–61; Stephen H. Sosnick, "A Critique of Concepts of Workable Competition," *Quarterly Journal of Economics,* August 1958, pp. 380–423; and Stephen H. Sosnick, "Toward a Concrete Concept of Effective Competition," *American Journal of Agricultural Economics,* November 1968, pp. 827–53.

[8]George J. Stigler, "Report on Antitrust Policy: Discussion," *The American Economic Review,* May 1956, p. 505.

[9]Thomas Gale Moore, "The Beneficiaries of Trucking Regulation," *The Journal of Law and Economics,* October 1978, pp. 327–44.

The High Costs of Regulation

The doubtful benefits of many regulations go hand in hand with very high costs. These costs can be grouped into three categories: (1) the direct costs of administering the regulatory agencies, (2) the direct costs of compliance by the affected parties, and (3) indirect costs. The first two are easiest to quantify.[10] In fiscal 1979, the budgets of the 55 federal regulatory agencies (the 80,000 employees of which managed to fill an equal number of pages of the *Federal Register* with new regulations) came to $4.8 billion. The private sector compliance costs came to a whopping $97.9 billion. This total of compliance costs included 7 cents for every pound of hamburger, $22 for the average hospital bill, $666 for every new car, and $2,000 for every new home. This compliance cost also included the cost to firms—at least $25 billion—of filling out more than 4,400 federal forms. The total of direct costs, almost $103 billion, thus came to about $500 for every person in the country. (Analytical Example 15.1, ''Regulation and the Price of Cars,'' provides more detail on the $666 figure just noted.)

The indirect costs of regulation may be more important still. It is impossible to list them all, and they are impossible to quantify. Indirect costs include the increased likelihood of X-inefficiency from the regulation of natural monopoly; the economic inefficiency created by regulating competition; and a slowdown in technical advance because an ever larger share of research and development expenditures is devoted to dealing with the governmental approval process. (Particularly affected are the drug and chemical industries. One drug company's application for approval of a muscle relaxant came to 456 volumes, weighed more than a ton, and stood taller than 8 stories. This is not an unusual case.) The indirect costs also include a slowdown in the growth of productivity caused by the rising claim government regulations make on resources available for investments in plant and equipment. Investment is also discouraged by heightened uncertainty regarding future regulations of new processes and products. A study by Edward Denision shows that pollution and job safety standards alone cut the annual rise in productivity by almost a quarter in the mid-1970s.[11] No wonder that many economists view government regulation with skepticism.

TIME FOR DEREGULATION

The 1980s may well be remembered as roundup time for runaway regulators—but only for some of them. The number of regulatory agencies, programs, and authorizing statutes, and the size of regulatory budgets, continue on their upward trajectory. Nevertheless, Congress has taken a number of steps—not, generally, to end regulation of natural monopoly or health and safety, but to end regulation of competition.

The Natural Gas Policy Act of 1978, while extending regulation to intrastate gas temporarily, provided for the deregulation of all gas by 1985. (Crude oil prices were deregulated by 1981). The Airline Deregulation Act of 1978 provided for the gradual removal of all government controls on market entry or exit, routing, fares, and the like; it even mandated the abolition of the CAB by 1985. A 1980 trucking deregulation law, along with a 1982 intercity bus deregulation law, severely clipped the powers of the ICC. The law on trucking provided for an end to the antitrust exemption of the industry's rate-setting bureaus. It promoted free market entry and exit, and it

---

[10]Murray L. Weidenbaum, ''The Costs of Government Regulation of Business,'' in *The Cost of Government Regulation*, Hearings before the Subcommittee on Economic Growth and Stabilization of the Joint Economic Committee, Congress of the United States (Washington, D.C.: U.S. Government Printing Office, 1978), pp. 31–59.

[11]Edward F. Denison, ''Effects of Selected Changes in the Institutional and Human Environment upon Output per Unit of Input,'' *Survey of Current Business*, January 1978, pp. 21–44.

returned to truckers the right to set prices, determine routes, and choose the type of cargo they carry. A railroad deregulation law was enacted as well; and the FCC has similarly moved to end most regulation of radio and television broadcasters, of cable TV companies, and of telecommunications.[12]

Close-Up 15.9, "Airline Deregulation: The Experience So Far," provides an interesting case study.

SUMMARY

1. To make a market economy function well, government must perform two crucial tasks. It must assign and protect property rights in all scarce things, and it must promote a competitive environment in which voluntary exchanges can flourish.

2. Late in the last century, private firms in the United States used a number of innovative devices in an attempt to replace competition with monopoly. These devices included horizontal mergers, holding companies, and trusts. In response to these devices, antitrust laws were designed to restrain monopoly and foster competition.

3. The Sherman Act of 1890 was the first antitrust law. Its vague language gave the courts wide latitude of interpretation. The courts first established, and later reversed, the "rule of reason," according to which not bigness *per se,* but only deliberate and unreasonable restraint of trade was illegal. The courts, however, have always held explicit collusion to be illegal *per se.* The Clayton Act of 1914 used conduct, rather than market structure, as a criterion and explicitly banned specified acts if they fostered monopoly, including price discrimination; exclusive, requirements, and tying contracts; intercorporate stockholdings; and interlocking

directorates. Other antitrust laws (Federal Trade Commission, Wheeler-Lea, Robinson-Patman, Celler-Kefauver) mainly deal with advertising, price discrimination, and mergers.

4. Critics doubt that antitrust laws have effectively promoted competition. They point to the relatively few indictments, the lengthy trials, the few convictions, and the low penalties. They view consent agreements as a cheap escape route for violators of the laws. They believe the government perverts the laws' intent when firms that *expand* trade by producing more, introducing new types of output, or selling for less are nevertheless indicted for *restraint* of trade. Defenders of antitrust policy point to recent increases in penalties and a tightening of procedures for consent agreements. They argue that antitrust laws have, in any case, mainly preventive effects.

5. In situations of natural monopoly, the promotion of competition is undesirable for technical reasons. Government usually seeks to regulate the behavior of such firms. According to economic theory, unless price discrimination is practiced, marginal-cost pricing (for purposes of achieving economic efficiency) produces losses. Full-cost pricing is a likely compromise. Regulation of natural monopoly, however, encounters a number of practical problems: the determination of a "fair" return, the unwitting encouragement of X-inefficiency and dynamic inefficiency (possibly attenuated by regulatory lag), and the Averch-Johnson effect.

6. Government regulation reaches beyond the natural monopolies into the realm of competition. At times, regulation of competitive industries can be explained by the *public interest theory* according to which regulation is thrust upon unwilling firms. According to this view, government intervenes for reasons of economic equity and commands lower-than-equilibrium prices in order to help buyers. (As critics note, such a policy causes no end of problems.) More often, the regulation of competition can be explained by the *special interest theory,* according

---

[12]"Has the FCC Gone Too Far?" *Business Week,* August 5, 1985, pp. 48–54; "Is Deregulation Working?" *Business Week,* December 22, 1986, pp. 50–55.

to which regulation is deliberately procured by firms that want to escape competition.

7. A new kind of regulation—the regulation of health and safety—is often supported by those who argue that trading off health and safety for other things is unjustified no matter what the cost.

8. In recent years, economists have seriously questioned the worth of many types of regulation. Empirical study has failed to show benefits from natural monopoly regulation. Theoretical advance has brought into question the desirability of piecemeal policies designed to strengthen competition (the theory of the second best); some economists, therefore, favor less specific general policies (the theory of the third best), which is reminiscent of an older and controversial suggestion to promote "workable competition." The benefits of regulating competition or health and safety are also far from certain. The doubtful benefits of many regulations go hand in hand with very high costs, including the costs of administering regulatory agencies, private sector compliance costs, and such indirect costs as heightened X-inefficiency, economic inefficiency, and dynamic inefficiency.

9. Since the late 1970s, the U.S. government has embarked upon a limited program of deregulation.

KEY TERMS

antitrust laws
Averch-Johnson effect
consent agreement
economic power
exclusive contracts
holding company
interlocking directorates
property rights
rate base
regulatory lag
requirements contracts
rule of reason
theory of the second best
theory of the third best
trust
trust certificates
tying contracts
workable competition

HANDS-ON PRACTICE

Exercise #1

Consider Figure 15.1, "Regulating the Natural Monopoly."

a. How big would be the firm's profit in the absence of regulation?

b. What would profit be if regulators set price equal to long-run marginal cost?

Solution:

a. The profit is given by the crosshatched area, or 2.5¢ (375 million) = $9.375 million per year.

b. There would be a *loss* equal to area *edhg*, or 2.5¢ (900 million) = $22.5 million per year.

Exercise #2

Consider Figure 15.3, "Regulating Competition." What would be the quantity traded in case (a)? In case (b)?

Solution:

a. Given price *OB*, quantity traded would be *OC*. (Even though people would *like* to buy *OE*, quantity *CE* is not being supplied.)

b. Given price O*G*, quantity traded would be O*H* = *GM*. (Even though people would ordinarily like to supply a larger quantity at that price, it wouldn't be demanded.)

QUESTIONS AND PROBLEMS

1. "The Clayton Act provisions against exclusive, requirements, and tying contracts are undesirable. Exclusive contracts make it easier for retailers to provide factory-authorized parts and service because they can establish a good working relationship with a single manufacturer. Requirements contracts reduce uncertainty; they enable buyers to count on the receipt of specified quantities at agreed-upon prices. Tying contracts help sellers make sure that their products' reputation is not sullied by breakdowns caused by the use of incompatible raw materials supplied by other firms." Evaluate this position.

2. "I have a better way for establishing a natural monopoly's rate base: Regulators should simply look at such a firm's actual profit and capitalize it according to Fisher's formula at the chosen fair rate of return. Then they don't have to debate endlessly on whether they should use the original or the reproduction cost of the firm's assets." Evaluate this position.

3. "If government can regulate a natural monopoly (in order to eliminate economic profit and economic inefficiency), it surely can equally regulate a monopoly that has increasing marginal and average total costs, such as the one depicted in panel (b) of Figure 7.3, 'A Profit-Making Monopoly' (p. 224)."

With the help of Figure 7.3(b), consider the effects on economic profit and on economic efficiency of each of the following types of regulation:

a. Setting a market-clearing price equal to marginal cost.

b. Setting a price equal to minimum average total cost.

c. Providing a per-unit subsidy that encourages an expansion of output equal to (a) above.

d. Setting a lump-sum tax, in conjunction with (c) above, that reduces economic profit to zero.

4. "The theory of natural-monopoly regulation has a fatal flaw: Even though increasing returns to scale imply that the industry's output can be produced most cheaply by a single firm, it does not follow that such a firm will inevitably charge a monopoly price unless it is regulated. Government can auction off the right to be this single producer to the firm that agrees to sell the good in question at the lowest price. As long as the inputs required for production are available to many potential firms and firms do not collude, there can be vigorous competition among many firms at the bidding stage. More likely than not, such franchising will produce the competitive price, and subsequently no regulation is needed."[13]

Evaluate this position. How would this procedure affect the likelihood of X-efficiency and dynamic efficiency?

5. "The government should adopt *sunset laws* that terminate the life of regulatory agencies after a specified number of years, unless the agency can justify its continued existence by proving that it has in the past produced benefits in excess of costs. Sunset laws would quickly put an end to nit-picking regulations that impose huge costs for tiny benefits."

Evaluate this position for each of the three forms of regulation discussed in this chapter.

6. Certain groups of individuals, by custom or law, are exempted from the antitrust laws. These exempt groups include agricultural cooperatives, defense suppliers, educational institutions, export associations, health-care suppliers,

[13]Based on Harold Demsetz, "Why Regulate Utilities?" *The Journal of Law and Economics,* April 1968, pp. 55–65.

intrastate commerce, labor unions, professional sports, regulated industries. Do you think exemptions are ever justified?

7. "Ralph Nader and all the governmental regulators of health and safety whom he has spawned are best described as fanatics. Fanatics always know what is good for us better than we do, and they always know their duty: make us do what is good for us (with our money of course)." Evaluate this position.

8. "The deregulation of competition hurts many innocent people because the elimination of monopoly power destroys valuable assets. The people who are hurt naturally oppose deregulation. They ought to be compensated."

Evaluate this position. (*Suggestion:* Review Analytical Example 7.1, "The Market Value of Monopoly Power" on p. 246. Then ask yourself: Should the owners of such power be compensated (a) if they received it as a gift originally, and (b) if they paid for it by purchasing it from the original recipients? Should others who shared the benefits of this power be compensated? Consider airline pilots, teamsters, electricians working for once regulated firms. Consider owners of restaurants at air and truck terminals positioned on once mandated and now abandoned routes. Consider owners of houses with once limited natural-gas hookups.)

9. Courts used to define "predatory pricing" as the charging of a price below average total cost in order to damage or destroy a competitor. In a number of cases, the courts have changed this position. A federal court in Denver in a 1977 case against Kerr-McGee, a federal court in San Francisco in a 1979 case against IBM, and a federal court in New York in a 1981 case against AT&T, used the Areeda-Turner test (named after two Harvard professors) and looked at average *variable* costs only. Would you agree?

10. It has been suggested that contestability theory (noted in Chapter 8) might be used to select industries for deregulation or continued regulation. When markets could easily be contested because capital comes in small units (airplanes, trucks, microwave transmission sets) and is mobile, deregulation is called for; otherwise it is not. What do you think?

11. "It is one thing for government, in order to certify competence, to require the licensing of people in certain occupations (doctors, lawyers, barbers, and taxi drivers). It is quite another to restrict, at the same time, the number of persons who are allowed to engage in these occupations. The former promotes perfectly competitive markets; the latter destroys them." Evaluate this position.

12. Mr. A: There are instances in which the assignment of property rights is clearly impossible. Consider the case of anadromous species of fish (fish that swim upstream to mate, like salmon), much debated during the Law of the Sea conference. Such fish spawn in the freshwater streams of "countries of origin," then migrate beyond the 200-mile economic zone to the high seas where everyone might catch them. How could one possibly protect such property?

Mr. B: You are so right; here is another case in point: the wife who invested heavily when she helped her husband get his Ph.D. This is a valuable asset that produces income for years to come; yet when her husband divorces her, she is out in the cold. She is allowed to share the family debts all right, but she has no property right in the asset she helped create.
Evaluate.

SELECTED READINGS

Bailey, Elizabeth, and William Baumol. "Deregulation and the Theory of Contestable Markets," *Yale Journal of Regulation*, 1984, pp. 111–37.

Bork, Robert H. *The Antitrust Paradox: A Policy at War with Itself.* New York: Basic Books, 1978.

A criticism of antitrust policy by the former Solicitor General of the United States.

Fisher, Franklin M., John J. McGowan, and Joen E. Greenwood. *Folded, Spindled, and Mutilated: Economic Analysis and U.S. v. IBM*. Cambridge, Mass.: MIT Press, 1983.

The primary economic witness (Fisher) for IBM presents the case against an IBM breakup.

Israilevich, Philip, and K. J. Kowalewski. "The Effect of Regulation on Ohio Electric Utilities," Federal Reserve Bank of Cleveland, *Economic Review,* 1, 1987, pp. 10–19.

An empirical test of the Averch-Johnson effect and more.

Joskow, Paul L., and Roger G. Noll. "Regulation in Theory and Practice: An Overview," *The Economics of Regulation*. New York: National Bureau of Economic Research, 1980.

A survey of the latest developments in regulation.

Journal of Law and Economics, December 1981.

Entire issue devoted to consumer protection regulation.

Kahn, Alfred E. *The Economics of Regulation*, 2 vols. New York: Wiley, 1971.

The definitive treatise at the time, written by the later chairman of the CAB and the President's Council on Wage and Price Stability.

Kaysen, Carl, and Donald F. Turner. *Antitrust Policy*. Cambridge, Mass.: Harvard University Press, 1959.

A superb text.

Kohler, Heinz. *Comparative Economic Systems,* Glenview, Ill.: Scott, Foresman and Co., 1989, cha. 8.

A study of the ultimate form of regulation: Oskar Lange's socialist market economy.

Kwoka, John E., and Lawrence J. White, eds. *The Antitrust Revolution*. Glenview, Ill.: Scott, Foresman and Co., 1989.

A set of 13 case studies. Economists involved in major recent antitrust proceedings set out the economic analyses employed by both sides.

Manne, Henry G. *The Economics of Legal Relationships: Readings in the Theory of Property Rights*. St. Paul, Minn.: West Publishing Co., 1975.

An excellent set of 37 readings on property rights.

Miller, James C. III, and Bruce Yandle, *Benefit-Cost Analysis of Social Regulation*. Washington, D.C.: American Enterprise Institute, 1979.

A selection of case studies on health and safety regulation.

Nozick, Robert. *Anarchy, State, and Utopia*. New York: Basic Books, 1974.

A discussion of the role of government in the economy.

Owen, Bruce M., and Ronald Braeutigam. *The Regulation Game: Strategic Use of the Administrative Process*. Cambridge, Mass.: Ballinger, 1978.

Presents the provocative hypothesis that regulation, at the cost of some efficiency, provides substantial benefits by protecting individuals from the risk they would otherwise face from the operation of the efficient but ruthless free market.

Peltzman, Sam. "The Growth of Government," *Journal of Law and Economics,* October 1980, pp. 204–89.

Argues that government regulation is a rich source of income to special interests whose rent-seeking is gradually replacing profit-seeking.

Petersen, H. Craig. *Business and Government.* New York: Harper & Row, 1981.

A good text focusing an antitrust and regulation.

Shepherd, William G., and Clair Wilcox. *Public Policies Toward Business,* 6th edition, Homewood, Ill.: Richard D. Irwin, 1979.

A classic text.

Stelzer, Irwin M. *Selected Antitrust Cases,* 5th edition. Homewood, Ill.: Richard D. Irwin, 1976.

Stigler, George J. *The Citizen and the State: Essays on Regulation*. Chicago: University of Chicago Press, 1975.

Thought-provoking essays by the 1982 winner of the Nobel Prize in economics.

Weiss, Leonard W., and Michael W. Klass. *Case Studies in Regulation: Revolution and Reform*. Boston: Little, Brown, 1981.

Nine case studies by experts in their respective fields.

COMPUTER PROGRAMS

The KOHLER-3 personal-computer diskettes that accompany this book contain one program of particular interest to this chapter:

15. Property Rights, Antitrust and Regulation includes a 25-question multiple-choice test with immediate responses to incorrect answers as well as numerous exercises concerning natural monopolies and government regulation.

ANALYTICAL EXAMPLE

ANALYTICAL EXAMPLE 15.1

REGULATION AND THE PRICE OF CARS

Government regulations raise the prices of many products. One study shows the cumulative effect of a decade of federal safety regulations on the price of an American-made car. As the table below indicates, these regulations raised the price by $666, when measured in 1977 dollars.

Year of Regulation	Government-Mandated Equipment	Estimated Increase in Retail Price (in 1977 dollars)
1968	Seat and shoulder belts, standards for exhaust emissions	$ 47.84
1968–69	Windshield defrosting systems, door latches, lamps, etc.	14.53
1969	Head restraints	27.48
1970	Reflective devices and further emission standards	14.77
1968–70	Ignition locking and buzzing systems, interior impact protection	12.75
1971	Fuel evaporative systems	28.33
1972	Improved exhaust emissions and warranty changes; seat-belt warning system	42.37
1972–73	Exterior protection	95.29
1973	Reduced flammability materials, etc.	8.72
1969–73	Improved side-door strength	20.85
1974	Interlock system and improved exhaust emissions	133.50
1975	Additional safety features and catalytic converter	146.66
1976	Hydraulic brakes, improved bumpers, removal of interlock system, etc.	41.54
1977	Leak-resistant fuel system, etc.	21.25
1978	Redesign of emissions controls	9.99
	Total	$665.87

Source: Murray L. Weidenbaum, "The Costs of Government Regulation of Business," in *The Cost of Government Regulation,* Hearings before the Subcommittee on Economic Growth and Stabilization of the Joint Economic Committee, Congress of the United States (Washington, D.C.: U.S. Government Printing Office, 1978), p. 44. Note: Weidenbaum's estimates have been called "inflated" by William K. Tabb, "Government Regulations: Two Sides to the Story," *Challenge,* November–December 1980, pp. 40–48. More recent estimates, including the above data plus substantially tightened 1980/81 emission standards, put the extra cost of a new car that is attributable to health and safety regulations at $2,000 in the early 1980s (current dollars). Additional and equally substantial price increases were caused by an entirely different type of regulation: import quotas. On both of these estimates, *see* Robert W. Crandall, "What Have Auto-Import Quotas Wrought?" *Challenge,* January–February 1985, pp. 40–47.

CLOSE-UP

CLOSE-UP 15.1

THE PAINFUL BIRTH OF PROPERTY RIGHTS: THE ELECTROMAGNETIC SPECTRUM

Like the air, the world's radio spectrum used to be taken for granted. But it is a very scarce resource now. If everyone who wished to broadcast just did so freely, there would be serious overcrowding and bad reception around the globe. As a result, property rights in radio frequencies (for voice communication, navigation, and data transmission) are sought by the military, by space agencies, by multinational manufacturing corporations and international banks, by airlines and ocean shippers, by radio and television broadcasters, by amateurs, and by many others.

In 1979, a 140-nation General World Administrative Radio Conference convened in Geneva to assign property rights in radio frequencies for the remainder of this century. A conflict emerged because nations wanted more frequencies than

are available but also because nations had ideological differences. While Western, developed nations favored the free global flow of information, the poor and Soviet-bloc nations favored a "new world information order" that would enable them to control strictly all information flows within their borders. They linked agreement on the allocation of scarce frequencies to agreements restricting the flow of information. They argued that the beaming of radio and television broadcasts by one country to another should occur only with the latter's consent and that the transmission of news via satellite should occur only with the consent of the country in which the news originates.

Source: *The New York Times,* September 23, 1979, p. E8; September 25, 1979, p. A1.

CLOSE-UP 15.2

THE PAINFUL BIRTH OF PROPERTY RIGHTS: THE LAW OF THE SEA

In the absence of a government that assigns property rights, the law of the jungle is likely to prevail; that is, the strong are likely to appropriate scarce resources. The world's oceans, which cover 70 percent of the earth's surface, are a case in point.

Because there has never been a world government, property rights in the ocean have been virtually nonexistent. Coastal nations used to claim sovereignty over a zone that extended 3 miles from the coast (the distance that a 17th century land-based cannon could shoot) and later claimed sovereignty over a 12-mile zone. Beyond that, "freedom of the sea" was the rule. Anyone was free to use the oceans as cheap routes of transport or for fishing, whaling, and the like.

During the 20th century, however, significant improvements in maritime technology have produced long-range fishing fleets that can even pinpoint schools of fish electronically. It did not take long for conflicts of interest to arise among the developed nations (the fishing fleets of which meet each other on the richest fishing grounds around the world) and between the developed nations and the poor nations (many of which are finding that the fish near their coasts are approaching extinction).

This conflict has been exacerbated by the discovery of oil and gas on the continental shelves and in the deep sea, and by the discovery of consolidated minerals, available in potato-sized nodules that lie scattered on the Pacific Ocean floor but at depths of 12,000 to 20,000 feet. Nodules of phosphate, ferro-manganese, and manganese (with cobalt, copper, and nickel) have attracted particular interest. Additional conflicts have arisen about the uses of oceans as dumping sites, about the accidental pollution of coastal zones as a consequence of oil drilling, and about the uses of over 100 merchant and naval straits for transit.

Given the military and economic strength of the developed nations, some of these conflicts could easily be resolved in favor of the strong. For example, because certain developed nations (notably the United States, West Germany, and Japan) alone have the capability of mining deep-sea nodules, these nations possess *de facto* property rights. The poor countries, hoping for a share in the ocean's Eldoradolike riches, have, however, pressed for an international agreement on property rights in the sea. In 1970, a United Nations resolution declared that the resources of the deep sea are "the common heritage of mankind," not just happy hunting grounds for the developed nations. This resolution was interpreted to signify not that every nation had an equal right to stake a claim to a mineral site on the ocean floor, but that every nation had an equal right of ownership in the sea bed and, therefore, an equal claim on the financial proceeds from a mineral site regardless

of who did the mining. Not surprisingly, a 158-nation U.N. conference on the Law of the Sea remained deadlocked for over a decade. In 1982, over U.S. opposition, a treaty was voted in, but many industrialized nations refused to sign it. (The treaty handed the sea bed, and thus more than two-thirds of the earth's surface, over to an International Sea Bed Authority that could restrict access to would-be miners and also require them to share their technology and revenues with poor countries.)

In the meantime, coastal nations, in a sudden rush of unilateral declarations, have claimed exclusive rights to economic zones extending 200 nautical miles outward from their coasts. After initial challenges, this new limit of sovereignty has become the norm, at least for fishing and oil-drilling operations. However, even in these zones, conflicts persist on such matters as shipping lanes, overflights, and marine scientific research.

Sources: Walter Berns, "Mining the Sea for a Brave New World," and Northcutt Ely, "One OPEC Is Enough," *Regulation,* November/December 1981, pp. 15–24; Stephen Chapman, "Underwater Plunder," *The Best of Business,* Fall 1982, pp. 105–08; Bernard H. Oxman, David D. Caron, and Charles L. O. Buderi, eds. *Law of the Sea: U.S. Policy Dilemma* (San Francisco: ICS Press, 1983).

CLOSE-UP 15.3

THE PAINFUL BIRTH OF PROPERTY RIGHTS: THE GEOSTATIONARY ARC

A precise orbit in space, positioned about 22,300 miles from earth and going around the equator, has been likened to a "mouth-watering delicacy" for the telecommunications industry. It is easy to see why. When a satellite occupies this orbit, its velocity not only perfectly offsets the earth's gravitational pull but also exactly matches the 24-hour rotation of the earth. As viewed from earth, the satellite appears to be stationary and can be seen from half the globe. Earth stations, therefore, need aim their antennae only once to be able to provide long-distance communications via satellite much more cheaply than by any other alternative. (The

alternative to satellite telephone service, for instance, is a complex system of terrestrial microwave facilities that includes large numbers of transmitters, amplifiers, and relay stations.) Not surprisingly, telephone companies, television and radio broadcasters, weather forecasters, newspaper publishers, and many others want to own a piece of this galactic real estate.

Unfortunately, the arc can accommodate only a finite number of satellites. Given the worldwide desire to use the arc, scarcity has appeared. To deal with this scarcity, the United Nations International Telecommunications Union has divvied up the worldwide arc. The U.S. share of the arc has been further divided between governmental and private uses by the Commerce Department's National Telecommunications and Information Administration. The Federal Communications Commission, in turn, has allocated orbital slots among the many private would-be users. The latter division has been controversial, indeed. First, the FCC must decide on the number of slots it distributes, which involves the issue of the allowable spacing of satellites within the U.S. portion of the arc so as to avoid collisions and signal interference. Second, the FCC must decide on the method of distributing the slots. Should they be handed out as free gifts to a few lucky users (on a first-come, first-served basis, perhaps)? Should they be auctioned off to the highest bidder? At the time of this writing, the matter remained unresolved; a 1982 auction of seven satellite channels by one earlier recipient, RCA, was later invalidated by the FCC. (That auction had brought in $90.1 million.)

Sources: Molly K. Macauley and Paul R.Portney, "Property Rights in Orbit," *Regulation,* July/August 1984, pp. 14–18 and 51–52; *The New York Times,* December 1, 1981, p. D2; January 28, 1982, p. D4; January 29, 1982, p. 12.

CLOSE-UP 15.4

THE PAINFUL BIRTH OF PROPERTY RIGHTS: THE MOON'S RICHES

In 1979, after seven years' labor, an international treaty on the exploitation of the moon's resources was approved by the 47-member United Nations Committee on Outer Space. The agreement seeks to ensure that smaller powers lacking the ability to explore space will have a stake in the mineral wealth of the moon and other celestial bodies by proclaiming these resources to be the "common heritage of mankind." Any commercial exploitation, however, is considered to be decades away.

Agreement on the new treaty was stalled for years because the Soviet Union was unwilling to accept the concept that the moon's resources should be a common heritage. The third world countries pressed for a commitment from the space powers similar to the one they sought on the mining of seabed minerals.

The controversial article designating the moon and its resources as "a common heritage" stipulates that neither the surface nor subsurface shall become the property of any country, although countries retain the right to conduct lunar explorations. Once commercial exploitation "is about to become feasible," the treaty commits countries to establishing an international regime to see that the benefits of lunar exploitation are shared equitably.

Source: *The New York Times,* July 4, 1979.

CLOSE-UP 15.5

THE UNITED STATES VERSUS IBM

In 1969, the U.S. government initiated an antitrust suit against the giant International Business Machines Corporation. At the time, IBM's stock had the highest aggregate value of any company's in the world, equal to that of all the companies traded on the American Stock Exchange. This fact, however, did not exhaust the superlatives connected with the case, for it promised to be the most complex and lengthy suit of its kind.

Even before the trial began in 1975, the government had collected more than 50 million documents for it. The government spent three years presenting its side, which filled 72,000 pages of trial transcript. It took another three years to present IBM's defense.

The government's argument raised the issue of market structure. In 1972, the government charged, IBM unduly dominated the market for "general-purpose electronic digital computer systems" by holding a 72-percent share. IBM, in turn, calculated a 32-percent market share by also including in the relevant market military computers, programmable hand-held calculators, computer leasing and servicing, and more.

The government also took up matters of business conduct. IBM, it charged, went out of its way to erect obstacles to the entry and growth of rivals: It "bundled" computer hardware with programming and maintenance, selling this combination at a single price and thereby keeping out independent programming and servicing firms. It stressed leasing rather than sale of machines, thereby imposing heavier capital requirements on potential imitators. When rival leasing companies bought up IBM computers and leased them for less than IBM rentals, IBM introduced "fighting machines," a new family of System 370 computers, which outdated the leasing companies' System 360s overnight. When makers of accessory equipment, such as California Computer Products and Telex, took away 10 percent of IBM's accessories market, IBM changed the design of its computers so that related equipment provided by other firms wouldn't work with IBM hardware. It also introduced new accessories of its own that were cheaper and more difficult to imitate. IBM reinforced its "fighting machine" strategy with price discrimination. It accepted slimmer profit margins and even losses on computers facing effective competition—for example, on the 360/90 super-power machine (in competition with Control Data Corporation) and the 360/67 time-sharing machine (with General Electric as the competitor). IBM sharply reduced prices on peripheral equipment (in competition with Telex and Memorex) if customers accepted two-year instead of one-month leases on mainframe computers. When rivals, such as Amdahl Corporation and Itel Corporation, introduced imitation IBM computers, IBM cut its prices substantially and instantly. Before long, IBM introduced new and better-working computers and sold them for less than the imitation machines. Overall, IBM left a trail of badly hurt, complaining rivals.

Not so, said IBM. IBM claimed its foremost position in the market was the result of good performance; of skill, industry, and foresight; of producing excellent and ever better products, with reliable service, at ever lower prices. A calculation costing $1.50 in the 1950s now costs a fraction of a penny. So far as the allegedly predatory practices go, said IBM, customers want them. Customers want "bundling" because the closest possible working relationship with IBM is valuable to them. Customers want leasing because they are risk-averse and unwilling to own machines when rapid technological advance in the industry is common.

When the two sides rested their arguments in mid-1981, no one expected a judgment soon; appeals, it was believed, would carry the case into the next century. Then, suddenly, the case began to unravel. The very court that would have to hear any appeal upheld as legal many practices (by AT&T and Eastman Kodak) disputed in the IBM trial. The costs of litigation were tremendous (the government had already spent $10 million and IBM $100 million), but the benefits were now being questioned. The Sherman Act, some argued, declares *restraint* of trade and *monopolizing* to be illegal, yet unlike monopolies that restrict output and raise price, IBM's output had grown by leaps and bounds; its prices had steadily fallen (two facts that even the government did not contest). No wonder one law professor (Robert H. Bork) dubbed the case "the antitrust division's Vietnam." In 1982, the government dropped the case, declaring the evidence "flimsy" and the suit "without merit."

Postscript: Since then, IBM has taken on the Japanese leviathans like Fujitsu, Hitachi, and NEC by pouring an unprecedented flood of new products onto the computer market, making frequent deep price cuts, and using "muscular marketing ploys" (disparaging rival products, chilling rival sales by announcing new IBM products way in advance, attempting to break rival sales contracts after the fact). By 1984, the major domestic rivals (Burroughs, Univac, NCR, Control Data, and Honeywell—collectively known by their initials as the "Bunch") were discussing an antitrust suit; a Congressional hearing on the matter was deemed inevitable.

Sources: *The New York Times,* numerous issues; Bro Uttal, "Is IBM Playing Too Tough?" *Fortune,* December 10, 1984, pp. 34–37.

CLOSE-UP 15.6

THE BREAKUP OF MA BELL

In 1974, the U.S. Department of Justice filed suit against American Telephone and Telegraph (AT&T), commonly known as the Bell System or Ma Bell. The company was charged with illegally attempting to monopolize the telephone business. Unlike the suit against IBM (see Close-Up 15.5), this one succeeded. On January 1, 1984, some $153.5 *billion* of assets were dismantled, one-third going to a new AT&T, two-thirds to seven regional holding companies (U.S. West, Pacific Telephone, Southwestern Bell, Bell South, Bell Atlantic, Nynex, and Ameritech). The remaining AT&T even had to give up the name Bell that it had carried ever since Alexander Graham Bell invented the telephone in 1876. (The bell in the circle has been replaced by a new corporate logo: a blue globe crossed by wavy white lines; the old symbol is being used by local companies.)

What have been the consequences so far? First, there has been a noticeable increase in competition on all fronts. Companies such as MCI and GTE-Sprint have entered the long-distance market, even though AT&T ("the right choice") maintained a market share of over 80 percent. Nevertheless, the 1980s brought sharp declines in long-distance rates, and this trend is likely to continue and even accelerate in the next few years with the advent of *equal access* (the ability of phone customers to dial any long-distance carrier without extra digits). Competition has also appeared in the area of private telephone systems, given the arrival of such new companies as Northern Telecom and Rolm. In addition, local Bell companies have found that they can buy equipment for much less from new U.S. and foreign vendors than it used to cost when Western Electric, now AT&T Technologies, had a monopoly. The new AT&T, in the meantime, is aggressively moving to tie office computers into a worldwide telecommunications system.

Second, local phone rates and fees for equipment installation and service have been rising sharply. This is not surprising because Ma Bell used to price long-distance service way above and local service way below marginal cost. (In 1981, this cross-subsidy came to over $10 billion.) Given the fact that there exists no further legal tie between the local companies and the providers of long-distance service, the subsidy is being phased out (as part of the AT&T divestiture); the increase in local rates is certain to continue. Some customers, such as the Boeing Company, have reacted by building their own local networks to bypass the local Bell companies. And the American public, as a 1984 Business Week/Harris poll showed, argued 64 percent against 25 percent (with 11 percent abstaining) that the Bell system breakup had been a ghastly mistake!

Sources: Andrew Pollack, "AT&T, U.S. Agree on Final Aspects of Bell Breakup," *The New York Times,* August 4, 1983, pp. 1 and D4; *idem,* "Jostling in the Overcrowded Phone Market," *The New York Times,* October 21, 1984, pp. F1 and 8; Alfred E. Kahn, "The Road to More Intelligent Telephone Pricing," *Yale Journal on Regulation,* 2, 1984, pp. 139–57; "Did It Make Sense to Break Up AT&T?" *Business Week,* December 3, 1984, pp. 86–124.

CLOSE-UP 15.7

A PHONE CALL ABOUT PRICES

In 1982, the U.S. government charged American Airlines with trying to enlist Braniff Airways in a scheme of "collusive monopolization." At the time, Robert L. Crandall was American Airlines president; Howard D. Putnam was Braniff's chairman. The government held a transcript of the following phone conversation:

Mr. Crandall: I think it's dumb as hell for Christ's sake, all right, to sit here and pound the [expletive] out of each other and neither one of us making a [expletive] dime.

Mr. Putnam: Well . . .

Mr. Crandall: I mean, you know, goddamn, what the [expletive] is the point of it?

Mr. Putnam: Nobody asked American to serve Harlingen, nobody asked American to serve Kansas City, and there were low fares in there, you know, before. So . . .

Mr. Crandall: You better believe it, Howard. But, you . . . you . . . you know, the complex is here—ain't gonna change a goddamn thing, all right. We can . . . we can both live here and there ain't no room for Delta. But there's, ah, no reason that I can see, all right, to put both companies out of business.

Mr. Putnam: But if you're going to overlay every route of American's on top of, over, on top of every route that Braniff has—I can't just sit here and allow you to bury us without giving our best effort.

Mr. Crandall: Oh sure, but Eastern and Delta do the same thing in Atlanta and have for years.

Mr. Putnam: Do you have a suggestion for me?

Mr. Crandall: Yes, I have a suggestion for you. Raise your goddamn fares 20 percent. I'll raise mine the next morning.

Mr. Putnam: Robert, we . . .

Mr. Crandall: You'll make more money and I will, too.

Mr. Putnam: We can't talk about pricing.

Mr. Crandall: Oh [expletive], Howard. We can talk about any goddamn thing we want to talk about.

Source: Robert D. Hershey, Jr., "American Airlines Accused in Pricing," *The New York Times*, February 24, 1983, pp. 1 and D4.

CLOSE-UP 15.8

CAN EDUCATION REPLACE REGULATION OF HEALTH AND SAFETY?

It is sometimes argued that government regulation in the realm of health and safety is not needed, that government should simply *educate* the public about risks and let them choose. Critics of this suggestion counter that even state-of-the-art persuasion techniques (such as a TV campaign) will not promote health and safety as well as regulation, if at all. This is so, these critics say, because there exists a fundamental difference between commercial-product advertising and promoting health and safety. A few million dollars spent on persuading consumers to switch from *Camels* to *Kool* will meet with a fair degree of success because the benefits are tangible and the message goes to people (smokers) who are already favorably inclined toward it. The same amount of money spent on a similar message to get consumers to give up smoking is an entirely different matter. The benefit (such as a longer life) is intangible; the recipient of the message is basically hostile toward it. Unless a one-time consumer action is required (such as installing smoke detectors or safety latches on medicine cabinets), these critics say, education about health and safety is unlikely to be as effective as regulation.

This hypothesis was tested (and affirmed) in three careful studies conducted recently. The first study was conducted by the National Highway Traffic Safety Administration (NHTSA). It involved a 1981–84 seatbelt education campaign. (The importance of the issue is obvious once one considers the annual toll of over 34,000 dead and over 500,000 badly injured.) Only 11 percent of automobile occupants wear seat belts, the campaign stressed, yet death and injury rates would be cut by 50 to 65 percent if everyone wore belts. Still, after carefully pretesting the program messages to ensure their effective transmission and after three years of effort, the percentage of car occupants using seat belts rose to only 13.9.

A second campaign was conducted by the Consumer Products Safety Commission (CPSC).

Its 1974–78 effort was designed to reduce the U.S. fire death rate, the highest in the world. (Each year, there are 5,000 deaths and 21,000 injuries from residential fires.) When carefully evaluated, the campaign was seen to have achieved no measurable decrease in the frequency and severity of the problem.

A third campaign, the Stanford Three Community Study, tried to attack heart disease, the leading cause of nonaccidental death in the United States. The campaign saturated two California towns with information and advice on smoking, cholesterol, hypertension, and the like; the third town served as a control. Involved were all the media as well as face-to-face counseling. After five years, some success was noted, as measured by changes in people's lifestyles, but it was minor.

Source: Robert S. Adler and R. David Pittle, "Cajolery or Command: Are Education Campaigns an Adequate Substitute for Regulation?" *Yale Journal on Regulation,* 2, 1984, pp. 159–93.

CLOSE-UP 15.9

AIRLINE DEREGULATION: THE EXPERIENCE SO FAR

Although the process of airline deregulation was begun in 1978, it was not completed until the end of 1984, when the Civil Aeronautics Board (CAB) ceased to exist. Deregulation had been supported by three Presidents (Ford, Carter, and Reagan), by the CAB itself (under economist Alfred E. Kahn), by influential members of Congress (such as Senator Edward Kennedy), and by most economists. They all predicted decreased costs and fares, higher traffic volume, and reasonable industry profits.

Deregulation was opposed (at least initially) by the major airlines and organized labor. (Review this chapter's section on the special interest theory of regulation for a possible explanation.) The opponents predicted higher fares, less traffic, plummeting profitability, loss of service to small communities, unemployment of airline labor, and

greater industry concentration. Consider what actually happened.

As expected, dozens of new airlines entered the industry. They viewed the established firms as cumbersome dinosaurs, unable to respond to the unaccustomed competition; and they challenged them on all fronts.

Costs. Despite such hard-to-control elements as debt service, soaring fuel prices, and landing fees, the new entrants achieved substantially lower average costs per seat mile. By late 1984, this cost was 5.3¢ for People's Express and 6¢ for Continental, but 8¢ for the major carriers. The upstarts gained this advantage in part because they were not burdened by high-wage union contracts and because of their "no frills" service to customers, but also because of innovative management. People's Express, for example, had no labor union, but a generous employee stock ownership plan; it made passengers pay $3 for each bag they checked and 50¢ for a cup of coffee; it cross-utilized labor (while not flying, pilots might do accounting and flight attendants might take care of the ticket counter), and it arranged for aircraft maintenance and baggage handling on the basis of the lowest bids received from outside contractors. (The airline boasted of not having a single secretary.) This competition had its effect on the major carriers. American and United, jointly accounting for a third of domestic air travel in 1984, negotiated new contracts with their unions that allowed lower pay for newly hired employees and more flexible work rules; Eastern and TWA announced that they could not survive without similar concessions.

Fares. The lower costs of many new entrants translated into lower fares. On the San Francisco-Los Angeles route, for instance, PSA had long charged $69, but lowered the ticket price to $44 when upstart Pacific Express charged $49. In response to similar competition, the major carriers slashed prices on the most heavily traveled routes throughout the United States. Thus Pan Am offered a $99 ticket to anywhere within the domestic system in 1982/83; by 1984, one could fly New York–Chicago for $59 and coast-to-coast for $119. (The fusillade of ad campaigns promoting these new bargain fares rarely noted, however, associated advance-purchase and length-of-stay restrictions, the availability of such tickets for off-peak hours only, and higher fares on routes lacking competition.) By 1986, over 90 percent of all passengers were taking advantage of discount fares. As a recent study noted, in the first decade of deregulation, consumers gained $100 billion via lower prices.

Traffic Volume. Increased traffic volume went hand-in-hand with lower fares. On its New York–Boston route, for example, People's Express carried 2.2 million passengers in 1981, but 4.3 million by 1984. Overall, there were 291 million passengers and 14.7 million flights in 1982; by 1986, there were 395 million passengers and 19.2 million flights. (Not surprisingly, the increased traffic volume overtaxed many airport facilities, leading to delays in bad weather. In 1986, for example, there were 62 *scheduled* departures at Newark between 8 and 9 A.M.)

Profits. As one would expect, recession, soaring fuel prices, and the rapid entry of new firms into the previously regulated market produced a mixed profit picture. For example, in 1983, the industry as a whole sustained losses of $1 billion; in 1984, there were profits. Some major carriers (United, American, Delta) did well; others (Eastern, Pan Am, TWA) were ailing. There has been a rash of bankruptcies (Braniff, Continental, Pacific Express, Air 1), but some of these firms re-emerged later (as did Continental) *without* a union contract. Many airlines improved their profit picture by merging with others. Thus, by 1988, American had swallowed Air Cal, Delta took in Western, TWA acquired Ozark, Northwestern bought Republic, and United took over Pan Am's Pacific routes. Texas Air bought Eastern as well as Continental, then merged the latter with Frontier, People's Express, and New York Air! Overall, the first decade produced industry net profits of less than 1 percent. (The swarm of new entrants forced the established airlines to cut fares which, in turn, brought about the explosion in volume noted previously.)

Service to Small Communities. Service to small towns (measured in available seat-miles) has, in fact, risen, but there are more commuter airlines and fewer majors at these places. All this is part of a major route realignment that has seen airlines enter and leave hundreds of routes. The favorite structure now is the *hub-and-spokes* system. Numerous flights (the spokes) feed passengers from all directions into a large central airport (the hub) where they change to other flights (on the same airline it is hoped). Thus even losses made on short flights *to* the hub can be made up by high *load factors* (high percentages of filled seats) on flights *from* the hub. Consider how American has created a hub at Dallas/Fort Worth, Continental at Houston, Delta at Atlanta, Eastern at Miami, Northwest at Memphis, People's Express at Newark, TWA at St. Louis, United at Chicago and Denver, USAir at Pittsburgh. Also consider that airlines that failed to follow this strategy did not do well. Thus, in 1978, airline representatives lined up on a Washington street outside the CAB building to bid for routes; United was first in line and asked for 1; Braniff was seventh and asked for 626; the costs involved killed it.

Unemployment.   Employment at new airlines has increased more than employment at old airlines has declined.

Industry Concentration.   In the early 1980s, it looked as if a three-tiered industry would be emerging: There would be major airlines, such as American and United; their market share had dropped from 90 percent in 1970 to 79 percent in 1982. There would be older regional airlines, such as Alaska, Piedmont, PSA, and USAir. There would be newcomers, such as People's Express, New York Air, and Midway. The market share of the latter two groups had been increasing. They had filled niches in the market not served by the majors (serving small cities, such as Atlantic City and its casinos; providing no frills or the opposite—plenty of seating room and gourmet snacks). But the industry shakeout (who will survive, who will disappear) surely had not been completed. By the late 1980s, industry analysts foresaw a different future, a future of a tight oligopoly in which six carriers (American, Delta, Northwest, Texas Air, TWA, and United) would have a combined market share in excess of 90 percent. (Indeed, the government has not challenged the 1985–87 merger of 20 airlines which has created near-monopolies at some hubs. For example, after the acquisition of Ozark gave TWA 75 percent of St. Louis airport gates, it raised fares 18 percent.)

Sources: *The New York Times* and *The Wall Street Journal,* numerous issues; Kenneth Labich, "Fare Wars: Have the Big Airlines Learned to Win?" *Fortune,* October 29, 1984, pp. 24–28, *Business Week,* January 9, 1989, p. 88, and *The Economist,* February 4, 1989, pp. 68 and 71. *See also* Alfred E. Kahn, "Applications of Economics to an Imperfect World," *The American Economic Review,* May 1979, pp. 1–13.

16

Externalities and Public Goods

When discussing the supply curve of a perfectly competitive industry in Chapter 5, we met situations of pecuniary (or technological) externalities in which the input prices paid by (or the production functions available to) some firms were affected, favorably or unfavorably, by the operation of other firms. This chapter returns to the issue of externalities, but its concern is at once broader and narrower than in Chapter 5. It is broader because we concentrate on interactions involving not only firms, but also households and government, and we consider the provision, in response to certain externalities, of public goods by government. This chapter's concern is narrower because we do not deal with pecuniary externalities that occur when the behavior of some households or firms affects the *market prices* faced by other households or firms; instead we focus on real or **nonpecuniary externalities,** which include, but are not confined to, the technological ones discussed in Chapter 5.

EXTERNALITIES

The **real externalities** discussed in this chapter are direct effects, independent of any price changes, that the actions of some households or firms have on the utility of other households or on the output of other firms, none of whom have invited these effects. Because real externalities occur when the independent actions of some people quite unintentionally spill over onto the lives of their neighbors, economists also call them **spillovers** or **neighborhood effects.** These effects, furthermore, can be of two kinds. They can be detrimental, unfavorable or **negative externalities** that impose costs in the form of decreased utility or output on bystanders who are not being compensated for this injury, to their dismay. Real externalities, however, can also be beneficial, favorable or **positive externalities** that provide benefits in the form of increased utility or output for bystanders who are not being charged for this favor, to their delight. Examples of both negative and positive externalities abound.

Negative Externalities

Examples of negative externalities include the decrease in utility imposed on some people as a result of economic development, such as the incessant growth of cities, highways, and parking lots—of oil derricks, strip mines, and transmission lines. As the natural beauty, purity, and serenity of mountain valleys, lakes, and woods give way to endless expanses of look-alike tract houses on treeless lots or to the ugly noisy world of blast furnaces, railroad yards, and glass and steel office towers or to commercial strips with garish signs, flapping pennants, and circus colors, some people, at least, will feel worse off. Another example is the widespread pollution of air, water, and land with thousands of wastes, ranging from hydrocarbons, fly ash, and sulfur dioxide to nitrates, pesticides, and sewage. Finally, consider how people reduce each other's welfare by crowding on beaches, freeways, and ski slopes, while firms reduce each other's *output* by crowding onto grazing lands, oil-bearing lands, and ocean fisheries.

Positive Externalities

Luckily, a similar story can be told about positive externalities. Consider how people provide free benefits to other people by planting beautiful flowers and trees, installing telephones, getting vaccinated, and becoming educated. Lumber companies that plant trees provide recreational benefits and possibly modify the weather favorably for nearby farms; firms that drain mines may also raise the productivity of neighboring ones; beekeepers raise the output of nearby orchards; firms that bury high-tension wires to reduce maintenance costs also remove eyesores to passersby and increase the safety of aircraft operations at nearby airports.

THE ANALYSIS OF PIGOU

In 1912, British economist A. C. Pigou (1877–1959), a Biography of whom appears in Chapter 16 of the *Student Workbook* that accompanies this text, became the first to deal with externalities in a systematic way. In the presence of externalities, Pigou argued, perfect competition would not produce a Pareto-type welfare maximum.

Consider, for example, the third Pareto condition discussed in Chapter 14. According to this condition, it is impossible to make someone better off without making someone else worse off, once the marginal rate of transformation between any two goods, $MRT_{a,b}$, equals the corresponding marginal rate of substitution, $MRS_{a,b}$. According to Pareto, such equality would be brought about under perfect competition because all producers and consumers of a and b would face identical market prices of these two goods, P_a and P_b.

Every profit-maximizing firm would adjust output until marginal cost, MC, equaled that given price. In equilibrium, therefore, MC_a would equal P_a and MC_b would equal P_b. If P_a equaled \$10, so would MC_a; if P_b equaled \$5, so would MC_b; therefore, within a firm producing both goods, $1a$ would be technically exchangeable for $2b$ (because both quantities would be taking \$10 of resources). Thus each firm's MRT would equal $1a$ for $2b$ when profit was maximized.

Similarly, every utility-maximizing household facing the prices just noted would adjust purchases until $1a$ and $2b$ were considered to provide the same utility at the margin (both quantities costing \$10 in the market). Thus each household's MRS would equal $1a$ for $2b$ when utility was maximized. When externalities are present, however, this grand conclusion about the automatic achievement of Pareto efficiency through perfect competition is upset.

Marginal Private Cost Versus Marginal Social Cost

Each one of the above marginal costs, Pigou noted, was a **marginal private cost** or **marginal internal cost,** which is the marginal cost borne by the firm (or household) actually producing (or consuming) a good. But now suppose that the production of good a involved a negative externality: The production of another unit of a required not only \$10 of additional resources within the firm that produced a (the marginal private cost), but it also forced another firm to spend an additional \$5 to defend itself against a reduction in its output as a result of the first firm's activity. Pigou called such change in the total cost of some firms (or households) that was associated with a unit change in the output (or consumption) of others the **marginal external cost.** And he called the sum of the marginal private cost, MPC, and marginal external cost, MEC, the **marginal social cost, MSC.** The MSC is, in fact, the marginal cost of an activity as seen from the viewpoint of society.

$$MPC + MEC = MSC$$

$$MPB + MEB = MSB$$

In our example, MSC_a would thus equal $15, which indicates that it would take $15 of extra resources to produce an extra $1a$ in society—$10 of these resources in the firm producing a and $5 elsewhere. As long as externalities were not involved in the production of good b, this MSC_a implies, of course, that the true marginal rate of transformation would equal not $1a$ for $2b$, but $1a$ for $3b$ (both quantities taking $15 of resources). Because consumers would value $1a$ indifferently with $2b$ (in accordance with the postulated market prices), society's welfare would not be maximized: If $1a$ less were produced, $15 of resources would be released ($10 at the producing firm, $5 elsewhere), and these resources could produce an additional $3b$. Any consumer indifferent about $1a$ and $2b$ could be made better off.

The same argument, Pigou noted, could be made (in analogous fashion) about positive externalities among producers and about (positive or negative) externalities in the realm of consumption.

Marginal Private Benefit Versus Marginal Social Benefit

In the case of externalities in the realm of consumption, a wedge would appear between **marginal private benefit** or **marginal internal benefit** (the marginal benefit enjoyed by a household actually consuming a good) and **marginal social benefit** (the marginal benefit of this activ-

ity as seen from the viewpoint of society). This difference would, of course, be the **marginal external benefit,** the change in the total benefit of some households that was associated with a unit change in the consumption of others.

The marginal external benefit, in turn, could be negative, as when neighbors are harmed by noisy snowmobiles, or it could be positive, as when neighbors benefit from the beautiful flower gardens of others.

The Golden Rule

Having made these observations, Pigou added this golden rule to Pareto's conditions:

> *In order to maximize total economic welfare, all divergences between any activity's marginal social benefit and marginal social cost must be eliminated.*

Pigou thought that government should design appropriate taxes and subsidies to close this gap.

$$MSC = MSB$$

The Role of Taxes on Producers

Panel (a) of Figure 16.1 depicts the market for paper, which, we now assume, involves a negative externality among producers: The producers of paper pollute a river and reduce the output of fishers, who must incur heavy additional costs if they wish to produce as much as before. The competitive paper industry's supply is shown by line S; it represents, of course, the sum (above minimum average variable costs) of the paper companies' marginal private costs, ΣMPC. If we add the fishers' marginal external costs (which vary with the amount of paper produced), we discover the higher marginal social cost of paper production, MSC. Line D represents, in turn, market demand, the sum of marginal private benefits and (we assume) marginal social benefits, $\Sigma MPB = MSB$.

A competitive market would clearly induce production of quantity q_1 at price p_1, corresponding to intersection a. Note: Marginal social cost would exceed marginal social benefit for all units produced beyond q_2, as is indicated by line segments bc and ba. Thus a competitive market would induce production too large for a welfare maximum. The last unit produced, q_1, would, for instance, yield a benefit to a paper consumer of p_1; this last unit would cost an equal amount in the paper factory but would cost an additional amount of ac elsewhere, resulting in a net social loss of ac on that unit. Similar and smaller losses would be made on all units between q_2 and q_1. Neglect of marginal external costs would produce a social net benefit from paper production that fell short of its possible maximum (the *MSB—MSC* difference up to q_2) by shaded area *abc*.

Government, Pigou would argue, could remove the gap ac between marginal private and marginal social cost by imposing upon paper producers a *per-unit tax* equal to bd, or the *MPC—MSC* gap at the optimal output volume q_2. This tax would raise the marginal-private-cost curve to the dashed line, making it the paper producers' new market supply, S'. Paper producers would then produce lower quantity q_2 (note the arrow) and sell it at higher price p_2. Because of the higher price (point b), paper consumers would consume less. Because of the lower net price (point d), paper producers would produce less. Both would have been made aware of the negative aspects of their behavior on other people in society. Marginal social benefit would equal marginal social cost (point b).

The Role of Taxes on Consumers

Panel (b) of Figure 16.1 depicts the market for snowmobiling, which, we assume, involves a negative externality among consumers: The users of snowmobiles create noise and reduce the welfare of many households affected by it. The snowmobilers' demand is shown by D; it represents the sum of the snowmobilers' marginal private benefits, ΣMPB. If we consider their neighbors' negative marginal external benefits (which vary with the amount of snowmobiling), we discover the lower marginal social benefit of snowmobiling, *MSB*. Line S represents, in turn,

market supply, the sum of marginal private costs and (we assume) marginal social costs, $\Sigma MPC = MSC$.

A competitive market would clearly induce production of quantity q_3 at price p_3, corresponding to intersection e. Note: Marginal social cost would exceed marginal social benefit for all units produced beyond q_4, as is indicated by line segments fe and fg. Thus a competitive market would induce consumption too large for a welfare maximum. The last unit consumed, q_3, would, for instance, yield a benefit to a snowmobiler of p_3; this last unit would cost an equal amount to produce, but it would also impose a negative benefit of eg on someone else, resulting in a net social loss of eg on that unit. Similar and smaller losses would be made on all units between q_3 and q_4. Neglect of (negative) marginal external benefits would thus produce a social net benefit from snowmobiling that fell short of its possible maximum (the *MSB—MSC* difference up to q_4) by shaded area *efg*.

Government, Pigou would argue, could remove the gap eg between marginal private and marginal social benefit by imposing upon snowmobilers a *per-unit tax* equal to fh, or the *MPB—MSB* gap at the optimal output volume q_4. This tax would lower the marginal private benefit curve to the dashed line, making it the snowmobilers' new market demand, D'. Snowmobile producers would then produce lower quantity q_4 (note the arrow) and sell it at lower price p_4. Snowmobilers, however, would pay more than before, p_4 plus the tax. Marginal social benefit would equal marginal social cost (point f).

The Role of Subsidies for Producers

Panel (c) of Figure 16.1 depicts the market for honey, which, we assume, involves a positive externality among producers: The presence of many bees raises the output of orchardists who can reduce their costs if they wish to produce as much as before. Thus the situation in panel (c) is analogous to that in panel (a), except that marginal social cost now lies *below* marginal private

FIGURE 16.1

Pigou's Golden Rule

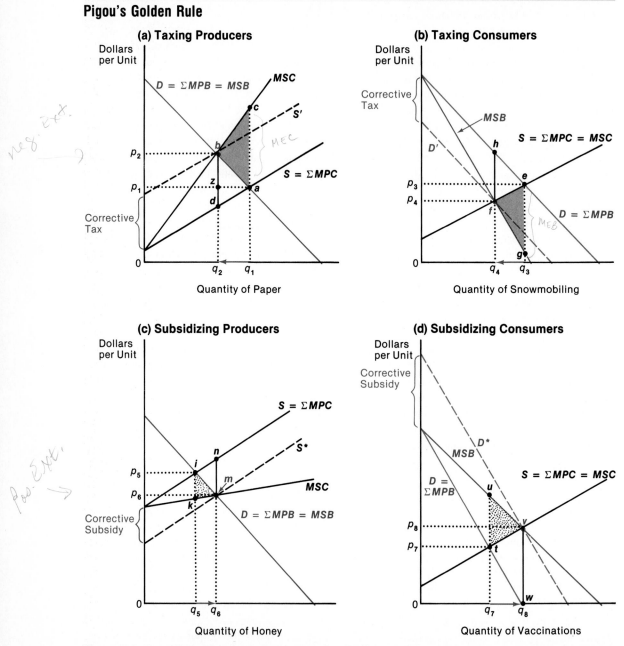

(a) Taxing Producers

Dollars per Unit

$D = \Sigma MPB = MSB$

MSC

S'

MEC

p_2

b

S = ΣMPC

p_1

z

c

a

d

Corrective Tax

0   q_2 q_1

Quantity of Paper

neg. Ext.

(b) Taxing Consumers

Dollars per Unit

Corrective Tax

MSB

S = $\Sigma MPC = MSC$

D'

h

p_3

e

p_4

i

MEB

D = ΣMPB

g

0   q_4 q_3

Quantity of Snowmobiling

(c) Subsidizing Producers

Dollars per Unit

S = ΣMPC

S*

n

p_5 i

m

p_6

MSC

k

D = $\Sigma MPB = MSB$

Corrective Subsidy

0   q_5 q_6

Quantity of Honey

Pos. Ext.

(d) Subsidizing Consumers

Dollars per Unit

Corrective Subsidy

D*

MSB

S = $\Sigma MPC = MSC$

D = ΣMPB

u

p_8

v

p_7

t

w

0   q_7 q_8

Quantity of Vaccinations

Pigou noted that self-interest easily eliminates divergences between marginal private benefits and costs in competitive markets but fails to eliminate divergences between marginal social benefits and costs. As a result, self-interest fails to maximize total economic welfare in the presence of externalities: When producers or consumers impose uncompensated cost. A competitive market would induce production q_5 at p_5, corresponding to intersection i. Marginal social cost would fall short of marginal social benefit not only for all units up to q_5, but also for all units between q_5 and q_6, as is indicated by line segments km and im. Thus a competitive market would induce production too small for a welfare maximum. The last unit produced, q_5, would, for instance, yield a benefit to a honey consumer of p_5; this last unit would cost an equal amount in the *apiary* (where bee hives are kept) but would *reduce* costs by ik in the orchards, resulting in a net social gain of ik on that unit. Similar and smaller gains would be forgone for all units between q_5 and q_6. Neglect of (negative) marginal external costs would thus produce a social net benefit from honey that fell short of its possible maximum (the *MSB—MSC* difference up to q_6) by dotted area ikm.

Government, Pigou would argue, could remove the gap ik between marginal private and marginal social cost by offering to honey producers a *per-unit subsidy* equal to mn, or the *MPC—MSC* gap at the optimal output volume q_6. This subsidy would lower the marginal private cost curve to the dashed line, making it the honey producers' new market supply, S^*. Honey producers would thus produce larger quantity q_6 (note the arrow) and sell it at lower price p_6. Honey producers, however, would receive more than before, p_6 plus the subsidy. Marginal social benefit would equal marginal social cost (m).

The Role of Subsidies for Consumers

Panel (d) of Figure 16.1 depicts the market for vaccinations, which, we assume, involves a positive externality among consumers: Those who get vaccinated are less likely to get sick, and therefore they raise the welfare of other households who are less likely to catch disease. The situation in panel (d) is analogous to that in panel (b), except that marginal social benefit now lies *above* marginal private benefit. A competitive market would induce production q_7 at p_7, corresponding to intersection t. Marginal social cost would fall short of marginal social benefit not only for all units up to q_7, but also for all units between q_7 and q_8, as is indicated by line segments tv and uv. Thus a competitive market would induce production too small for a welfare maximum. The last unit produced, q_7, would, for instance, yield a benefit to a vaccinated person of p_7; this last unit would cost an equal amount to produce but would yield an additional benefit of tu to other people. There would be a net social gain of tu on that unit. Similar and smaller gains would be forgone for all units between q_7 and q_8. Neglect of marginal external benefits would thus produce a social net benefit from vaccinations that fell short of its possible maximum (the *MSB—MSC* difference up to q_8) by dotted area tuv.

Government, Pigou would argue, could remove the gap tu between marginal private and

costs on others, competitive markets allow production and consumption to exceed the amount at which marginal social cost just equals marginal social benefit (points b and f). On the other hand, when producers or consumers provide free benefits to others, competitive markets allow production and consumption to fall short of the amount at which marginal social cost just equals marginal social benefit (points m and v). The implied economic inefficiencies (shaded and dotted areas), argued Pigou, can be eliminated through taxation whenever production and consumption are excessive, as in panels (a) and (b), and through subsidies whenever production and consumption are insufficient, as in panels (c) and (d).

Note: In these examples, the divergence between marginal private cost and marginal social cost, in panels (a) and (c), or between marginal private benefit and marginal social benefit, in panels (b) and (d), is itself increasing with the level of activity in question. This particular condition, however, is not the only one possible. Pigou's argument would be just as valid if the divergence in question were the same at all activity levels. Nor does the corrective tax or subsidy have to be a constant per unit, as shown here. Properly designed per-unit taxes or subsidies that vary with the activity level could accomplish the desired correction as well.

marginal social benefit by offering to consumers of vaccinations a *per-unit subsidy* equal to *vw*, or the *MPB—MSB* gap at the optimal output volume q_8. This subsidy would raise the marginal-private-benefit curve to the dashed line, making it the vaccination consumers' new market demand, D^*. The producers of vaccinations would then increase quantity to q_8 (note the arrow) and charge price p_8. The consumers involved, however, would pay less than before, p_8 minus the subsidy (or nothing at all in this case). Marginal social benefit would equal marginal social cost (point *v*).

THE CHALLENGE OF COASE

For nearly half a century, Pigou's analysis went unchallenged. Then Ronald Coase (1910–   ), a Biography of whom also appears in Chapter 16 of the *Student Workbook* accompanying this text, in a celebrated 1960 article, pointed out what is quite obvious in retrospect: Pigou's argument about the government's ability to raise social welfare implicitly assumes that the proposed tax-subsidy scheme is costless—which it is unlikely to be. The very costs of administrating the scheme might well exceed the gains to be had from eliminating economic inefficiency (which gains are shown by the shaded and dotted triangles in Figure 16.1).

In addition, Coase pointed out, if government simply assigned unambiguous and transferable property rights, competitive markets might well overcome the externalities problem and achieve economic efficiency without any further government intervention. When formulating his recommendations for government intervention, Pigou had implicitly assumed that the parties affected by externalities could not privately negotiate with one another. In fact, they have plenty of reasons to do just that. Whenever total economic welfare can be raised by reducing the output and consumption of goods with negative externalities, as in panels (a) and (b) of Figure

16.1, and whenever total economic welfare can be raised by increasing the output and consumption of goods with positive externalities, as in panels (c) and (d), the affected parties can negotiate for a change in the allocation of resources that makes everyone better off at the same time.

The Possibility of Private Deals

The vertical differences between *MSC* and *MPC* in panel (a) represent the value of extra outputs lost by fishers for various additions to paper production. Thus the production of paper unit q_2 raises the injury to fishers by *db*; the production of paper unit q_1 raises the injury by another *ac*, and increasing paper output all the way from q_2 to q_1 reduces fish output by *bdac*—which is also the value of output fishers would *gain* if paper production was cut from q_1 to q_2. If paper production was so cut, producers of paper would then lose producer surplus of only *adz* (market price being p_1), and consumers of paper would lose consumer surplus of *abz*. Surely the fisher's potential gain of *bdac* would be more than enough to compensate or overcompensate the losers in a way that made everyone as well off as or better off than before. Unless the transactions cost of finding each other, carrying out the negotiations, signing the contract, and enforcing it were larger than the potential net gain (area *abc*), such a private deal would be made and the welfare-maximizing output mix would be achieved—quite without governmental taxing or subsidizing. (Analytical Example 16.1, "The Economics of Bees," provides a real-world illustration.)

The Coase Theorem

As Coase pointed out, it would make no difference to the allocation of resources how government assigned property rights in a contested resource, such as the river in our example.

Let the government state that fishers had the right not to have fish harmed, that they owned the right to unhindered use of the river. If the river was also wanted by paper companies for purposes of waste dumping, the paper companies would have to pay compensation to fishers for any output losses brought about by paper-company pollution. The production of paper unit number q_2, for example, would cause a fishing loss valued at db; the production of paper unit number q_1 would cause a fishing loss valued at ac; and so on. Each time, paper producers would have to make a corresponding payment to fishers. The paper producers, therefore, would have to reckon these damage payments as an explicit cost of doing business. Their marginal private costs would come to equal MSC. They would "internalize" the externality; the divergence of private and social cost would disappear. Paper companies would choose to produce the Pareto-optimal quantity q_2 because the production of even one additional unit would bring a price (just below b on the demand curve) insufficient to cover the extra production cost, now including damage payments (just *above* b on the MSC line).

Amazingly, this resource allocation would not be changed at all if government were to assign property rights in the river to the paper companies and thus gave them the *right* to dump wastes into it and generate harmful externalities affecting fishers. Fishers would then have to *bribe* the paper companies into not exercising their rights. Because the production of paper unit number q_2 would cause a fishing loss valued at db (and that of paper unit number q_1 one of ac), fishers could make themselves better off by offering bribes up to this magnitude to prevent the production of these units of paper. Paper companies, however, would now have to consider forgone potential bribes as *implicit* costs of doing business. Thus the production of paper unit q_2 would cost them not only an added amount (shown by point d) of wages, materials, and the like, but also the loss of db that might have been received from fishers had unit q_2 not been produced. Once more, profit-maximizing paper companies would view MSC as the relevant indicator of their marginal private cost. Once

more they would choose to produce no more than q_2 units. The next unit produced would cost them more (including bribes forgone) than consumers of paper would be willing to pay. Thus paper production would be expanded (and the production of fish restricted) exactly up to the point at which the marginal unit of paper produced just equaled in value the marginal unit of fish sacrificed for its sake. In this way the total value of output would be maximized.

The **Coase theorem** on the allocative neutrality of property rights can be summarized as follows:

Under perfect competition, and in the absence of income effects and transactions costs, voluntary negotiated agreements among private parties generating or being affected by externalities will lead to the same resource allocation (and output mix) regardless of how property rights are assigned among these parties.

Limitations of the Coase Theorem

Coase recognized that his neutrality theorem might be falsified in the presence of income effects. It would surely make a difference to the distribution of income and wealth whether fishers or paper companies had property rights in our river. The assignment of these rights would determine whether fishers had to be paid damages *by* paper companies or had to pay bribes *to* them. If the income elasticity of demand differed for fishers and paper-company owners, the pattern of demand, and hence of equilibrium prices *and of outputs*, would differ under the two possible assignments of property rights.

Coase also recognized that the presence of high **transactions costs** (costs of setting up a system of voluntary exchanges and keeping it functioning) might preclude the reaching of voluntary agreements to internalize externalities, especially if the number of parties generating or being affected by externalities was large.

THE LARGE-NUMBERS PROBLEM: THE CASE OF POLLUTION

Consider the case of river pollution that involves not a small number of fishers and paper companies who know each other, but literally tens of thousands of people who cannot possibly know each other. Such large numbers of people, all of whom generate wastes or are adversely affected by them, will find voluntary agreements simply too costly to reach. Even identifying all the parties will be prohibitively difficult, as will be the measurement of externalities, the negotiations, and the subsequent policing of agreements. The production of the welfare-maximizing outputs mix, therefore, is not ensured. High transactions costs become the root of all evil; they explain why externalities persist. The recognition of high transactions costs leads directly to the modern post-Pigouvian theory of government intervention, which can be illustrated by considering possible policies for reducing the pollution of a large river.

The Optimum Level of Pollution

It is usually suggested that government should first identify the optimum level of pollution. Although in practice identifying optimum pollution is a costly procedure, the theoretical argument is clear enough (see Figure 16.2). The line labeled *MSB* represents the declining marginal social benefit of waste dumping. Thus the first unit dumped in a year saves society $50 of other goods that would have to be forgone if resources were diverted to treating or recycling that unit of waste (point *a*). By the same token, dumping the 48-millionth, 72-millionth, or 96-millionth unit saves society, respectively, $30, $20, or $10 of other goods (points *b*, *c*, and *d*). The decline in the dollar figures just cited reflects the fact that it is often very easy to reduce waste emissions by a unit when there is a lot of waste, while it is often very difficult to reduce waste emissions by a unit when there is little waste left. Thus cutting 1 unit

FIGURE 16.2

Optimum Pollution

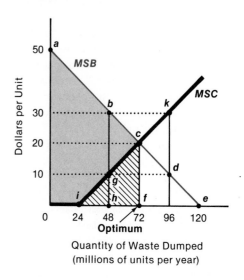

Quantity of Waste Dumped
(millions of units per year)

The optimum level of pollution is one at which the declining marginal social benefit from waste dumping just equals its rising marginal social cost (point *c*). This level maximizes society's net gain from dumping wastes (shaded area). Those who insist on zero pollution are asking society to sacrifice this net gain: They are asking to save goods destroyed by pollution and worth *cfi* (crosshatched) by sacrificing goods that could be produced if resources were not diverted to pollution abatement and that are worth 0*acf* (shaded plus crosshatched).

of waste out of 96 million units may cost a mere $10; for this reason the 96-millionth unit, *when dumped*, benefits society to the extent of $10 of other goods (point *d*). Yet cutting out the first unit (which is the last remaining unit of waste) may cost $50; for this reason the first unit, when dumped, benefits society to the extent of $50 of other goods (point *a*). Note: The area under the *MSB* line up to any chosen quantity equals the sum of marginal benefits; thus it shows the total benefit (in terms of other goods *not* sacrificed) of dumping the given quantity. Dumping 72-million units of waste per year saves society 0*acf* of other goods; dumping 120-million units saves society 0*ae* of goods.

The line labeled *MSC* represents the rising marginal social cost of waste dumping. Thus the first 24-million units dumped in a year have no harmful effect on anything; the natural environment absorbs these wastes easily (and line *MSC* coincides with the horizontal axis). Further dumping begins to cause damages—first to riverfront property perhaps, then to boats and fish, and, finally, to human health. Thus the 48-millionth unit dumped adds $10 to the damage already sustained and brings the total to *ghi*. The 72-millionth unit, in turn, adds $20 to damages and raises the total to *cfi*. The 96-millionth unit adds $30 (point *k*) to the damage total.

The optimum level of pollution equals the dumping of 72-million units of waste per year for the following reason: Up to this quantity, every unit dumped saves society goods valued more highly than those destroyed by pollution damage. Points on line *ac* lie above those on line *0ic*; the optimum amount of dumping brings society a net gain shown by shaded area *0aci*. Dumping *more* than 72-million units a year, however, reduces society's net gain because after that point each additional unit dumped destroys goods valued more highly (along line *ck*) than those saved by dumping rather than abating wastes (and valued along line *ce*). Without government intervention, however, the actual level of pollution will not equal the optimum.

The Actual Level of Pollution

Figure 16.3 is a copy of Figure 16.2, but the line showing the marginal social benefit of dumping is now viewed as the *demand for pollution opportunities*. The change of view is legitimate because the value of other goods that waste dumpers can save by dumping ($50 for the first unit dumped, $20 for the 72-millionth unit, and so on) is also the maximum amount they would pay for the right simply to dump the unit.

Now assume that property rights in our river are ill-defined. Anyone who wants to use the river can do so for any purpose whatever. In that case, potential waste dumpers face a *supply of*

FIGURE 16.3

Actual Pollution

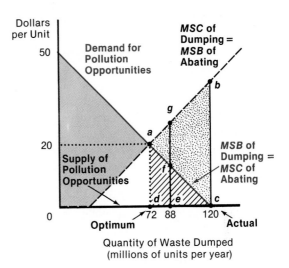

When property rights are ill-defined, actual pollution may well exceed optimum pollution. Beyond the optimum, society is then losing to pollution goods (dotted plus cross-hatched areas *abcd*) that exceed in value the goods that would have to be sacrificed in order to carry out pollution abatement (crosshatched area *acd*). The dotted area shows the net loss from excessive pollution (and the net gain from its potential abatement to the optimum level). This net loss offsets in whole or in part the maximum potential net benefit of waste dumping (shaded).

pollution opportunities that coincides with the horizontal axis: They may do all the dumping they like and at a zero price.

Because demand and supply meet at point *c*, 120-million units will in fact be dumped per year. Each one of these dumped units saves dumpers some resources that would otherwise have had to be spent on treating or recycling wastes and that could not have been spent on producing other goods.

Figure 16.3 also demonstrates that actual pollution in excess of optimal pollution is just as foolish as actual pollution falling short of the optimum. Imagine moving left from point *c* toward *d* by instituting a program of pollution abatement. The line of marginal social *benefit* of waste *dumping* (declining as one moves to the right from the level of zero waste dumping at origin 0) can then be viewed as a line of marginal social *cost* of waste *abating* (rising as one moves to the left from the level of actual waste dumping at point *c*). The line of marginal social cost of waste dumping (rising as one moves to the right from origin 0) can similarly be viewed as a line of marginal social benefit of waste abating (falling as one moves left from point *b*). Abatement of the 120-millionth unit of waste thus would bring a benefit of *bc* (pollution damage avoided), and it would cost nothing (point *c*)—it would be worthwhile. Abating the 88-millionth unit would bring a smaller benefit *(eg)* of pollution damage avoided; it would result in a positive but lower cost *(ef)* of other goods now sacrificed, so it would still be worthwhile (the marginal net gain being *fg*). By reducing actual pollution from the actual to the optimal level, society would save goods worth *abcd* (because they would not be destroyed by pollution). Society would sacrifice goods worth *acd* (because resources to make them would be diverted to pollution abatement). At the optimum level, there would be a net gain of *abc* (the dotted area). Without government action, however, society is likely to forgo this net gain.

POLLUTION-ABATEMENT POLICIES

It is one thing to discuss the optimal level of pollution as if all the relevant information were available. It is quite another matter in the real world. Government frequently has access to only fragmentary data. Many of the data are subjective. (How, for instance, is one to evaluate the effects of waste dumping that offend our aesthetic sensibilities: rivers covered with green, blue, and red iridescent splotches or topped with floating debris, ranging from trash and steel drums to tires and old rubber boots?) In addition, government is more likely to get data on totals

and averages than on the marginal quantities our theory demands. Nevertheless, let us consider some of the policy options open to a government that wishes to reduce waste dumping from an excessive level to an optimal one.

Moral Suasion

Government can try voluntarism by appealing to people's consciences and exhort them not to litter or incinerate trash or wear the furs of endangered species. It can urge people to treat their sewage; make less noise; conserve fuel, paper, or water; use unleaded gas and phosphate-free detergents; recycle bottles; and prevent forest fires. Unfortunately, altruism is a notoriously weak force for social change.

The Outright Ban

Much more reliable than moral suasion is an outright ban on polluting activities, supported by penalties for noncompliance, such as fines and prison terms. It would, of course, be impractical to ban all polluting activities at once. Consider the extreme chaos that would result if Congress were to outlaw all polluting internal combustion engines (as one of its members once seriously proposed). But limited bans are possible.

Setting Standards

The most popular approach of governments in the U.S. to pollution abatement has been the setting of standards. At the federal level, this started when Congress passed the National Environmental Policy Act, which declared that it is the policy of the U.S. government ''to create and maintain conditions under which man and nature can exist in productive harmony.'' The act created, in the office of the President, a permanent three-member Council of Environmental Quality to recommend environmental policies to the President. The act also gave birth, in 1970, to the Environmental Protection Agency (EPA). The EPA has set a variety of standards concerning many types of pollutants. **Input standards** specify the types of input polluters may use (for example, fuel with specified sulfur content). **Emission standards** specify maximum quantities of pollutants that may be released by any one polluter, and **ambient standards** specify the quantity the environment may contain.

Taxing the Dumping of Waste

Government can also use financial incentives, as Pigou taught us, to curb pollution. Figure 16.4 is based on Figure 16.3. As before, optimum pollution equals 72-million units per year, corresponding to the equality at point *a* of the marginal social benefit and cost of dumping. As before, actual dumping prior to government intervention equals 120-million units per year (point *b*). We now suppose that government imposes a tax of $20 for each unit dumped, equal to the marginal social cost of dumping *(ac)* for the optimal amount of dumping *(0c)*. This action effectively raises the supply of pollution opportunities from the horizontal axis (where it was in Figure 16.3) to the parallel line going through point *a*.

The message to polluters is clear. Instead of being given the right to dump all they want at a zero price, they can dump all they want at $20 per unit of wastes. Government has implicitly bestowed a property right in the environment on the public at large, but it stands ready, as the public's agent, to sell this right to individual would-be users.

Polluters, as a result, will reduce dumping to the optimal amount: Units dumped beyond the optimum save resources *from* abatement uses and *for* the production of other goods, which are valued along line *ab*. The values of these other goods are lower than the tax, which is measured along line *ad*. Polluters would rather lose goods worth *abc* (by diverting the resources that could have made these goods to a reduction in waste dumping from *b* to *c*) than face a tax of *acbd* (for dumping quantity *cb*). On the other hand, polluters would rather pay a tax of *0eac* for dumping *0c* than lose goods worth *0fac* (which the resources capable of abating *0c* can produce).

FIGURE 16.4

Pollution Abatement Through Taxation

The imposition of a tax per unit of waste dumped (here of $20) might reduce excessive pollution (point *b*) to the optimal level (point *c*).

Subsidizing Waste Abatement

Pigou's second approach has not escaped notice either. Figure 16.5 is again based on Figure 16.3. Optimum pollution equals 72-million units per year, corresponding to point *a;* actual pollution, prior to government intervention, equals 120-million units (point *b*). We will now suppose that government grants a subsidy of $20 for each unit of abated waste, equal to the marginal social benefit of abating *(ac)* for the optimal amount of abatement *(bc)*. This action effectively lowers the demand for pollution opportunities from where it was (dashed line *db*) to the parallel line going through point *c*.

The message to pollution abaters is clear. As before, they can dump all they want at a zero price (the supply of pollution opportunities again lies on the horizontal axis). But instead of having to bear the marginal social costs of abatement shown on line *bd,* abaters only need bear this cost minus $20 for each unit of abated waste. Government has implicitly bestowed a property right in the environment on the polluters, but it stands ready, as the public's agent, to buy back this right.

Polluters, as a result, will increase abatement from zero (point *b*) to the optimal amount *(bc):* Abatement from *b* to *c* will bring a subsidy equal to *abec* but will require resources capable of producing goods worth *abc.* Abatement is preferable, but abatement of the remaining waste *c0,* on the other hand, is not worthwhile. This further abatement would bring a subsidy equal to *dacf* but require resources capable of producing higher valued goods worth 0*dac.*

Marketing Pollution Rights

Yet another possibility for achieving optimum pollution is illustrated in Figure 16.6. A government that had determined as optimal the dumping of 72-million units of wastes per year could simply outlaw all dumping except by holders of **pollution licenses** or **pollution rights.** The government could then auction off 72 million of these rights, each one a transferable certificate allowing the holder to dump one unit of specified wastes into a specified environment. As Figure 16.6 shows, the strictly limited supply of rights would ensure a reduction of dumping to the optimal level. The demand for pollution opportunities would drive the price per right to $20 (point *a*), and (like a per-unit dumping tax) this

---

FIGURE 16.5

Pollution Abatement Through Subsidies

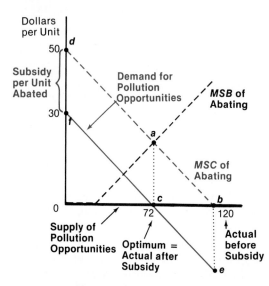

The granting of a subsidy (here, of $20) per unit of waste abated might reduce excessive pollution (point *b*) to the optimal level (point *c*).

FIGURE 16.6

A Market for Pollution Rights

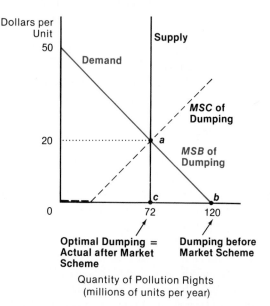

The introduction of a market for pollution rights might reduce excessive pollution (point *b*) to the optimal level (point *c*).

price would discourage all dumping beyond the optimum.

Note: Under this scheme, *any* party that wanted rights to nature's capacity to receive wastes and wanted them badly enough to pay the equilibrium price could acquire them. In most cases, these buyers of pollution rights would be polluters. But the purchasers could also be special-interest groups such as conservationists, who—disagreeing with the government's decision to allow *some* pollution—could buy up pollution rights for the purpose of *not* using them, of keeping them out of the hands of potential users.

PUBLIC GOODS

As the previous sections have demonstrated, when private firms or households produce or consume goods, they may well impose unwanted costs on outside parties—or they may enable them to snatch free benefits. Many a good, therefore, is not a **pure private good** in the sense that its producer or consumer alone bears all of the cost and enjoys all of the benefit associated with it. In the presence of externalities, goods have a certain element of "publicness" about them. The remainder of this chapter deals with certain extreme cases of goods that have *positive* externalities that affect not only a few people, but literally all members of society. The benefits of such goods lie in the public domain almost entirely.

In a number of papers written in the 1950s, Paul Samuelson (1915–   ), who won the 1970 Nobel Prize in economics and a Biography of whom also appears in Chapter 16 of the *Student Workbook* that accompanies this text, formalized the concept of a **pure public good.**[1] He defined it as a good that provides nonexcludable and nonrival benefits to all people in a given society, be it a locality, state, or nation. **Nonexcludability** is the property of a pure public good that makes it technically impossible or extremely costly to exclude any individual from the enjoyment of the good. Once a given amount of the good is available for anyone, it is available to everyone—simultaneously, automatically, and regardless of whether any payment is made for the privilege by any individual consumer. Should a larger amount of the good be produced, this larger amount is available to everyone as well. The good's benefit always and indivisibly embraces all (which is why economists say that public goods are characterized by **indivisibilities**).

Nonrivalness is the property of a pure public good that prevents rivalry among its consumers because the enjoyment of the good by any one person does not deplete its availability to others. Given the overall quantity of the good, the appearance of new consumers does not lead to a correspondingly diminished consumption by others, as is the case with pure private goods, such as chocolate bars or hamburgers. Given any overall quantity of such private goods, the increased consumption by one person does reduce that of others. A pure public good, in contrast, is nondepletable. One can add extra users, yet previous users will not have less on that account. A public good is like the legendary widow's cruse that remains full no matter how many people use its contents. Do such goods really exist?

Examples of such goods on the national level are: an automated air-traffic-control system, a clean natural environment, economic justice (as produced by domestic welfare or foreign aid programs), certain types of knowledge (as of mathematical theorems or weather forecasts), law and order, military security, prestige (as produced

---

[1]Paul A. Samuelson, "The Pure Theory of Public Expenditure," *Review of Economics and Statistics,* November 1954, pp 387–89; "Diagrammatic Exposition of a Theory of Public Expenditure," *Review of Economics and Statistics,* November 1955, pp. 350–56; and "Aspects of Public Expenditure Theories," *Review of Economics and Statistics,* November 1958, pp. 332–38.

by great architecture, national parks, or space exploration), radio and television signals (in the absence of electronic scramblers or cable transmission), and, finally, sound money. Locally, public goods are: flood control, fire and police protection, firework displays, open air concerts, snow removal on public streets, the town hall clock, townwide mosquito spraying, and traffic control (ranging from buoys on the river to lighthouses on the shore to traffic lights at road intersections). All these goods have in common the features of nonexcludability and nonrivalness. Once produced, it is next to impossible to exclude any particular citizen from the benefits: Your clean air is my clean air, your weather forecast is mine, your snow-free street is mine as well. Nor does the appearance of additional consumers detract from the consumption of others: When additional citizens make use of a mathematical theorem, others are not prevented from its continued use; when they derive pride from our explorer on the moon, others need not be less proud; when they tune in TV signals or glance at the town's clock, others can do so at the same time.

PURE PUBLIC GOODS AND MARKET FAILURE

Earlier sections showed why goods with positive externalities tend to be produced in quantities insufficient to yield the maximum possible economic welfare. Pigou therefore recommended governmental subsidies to stimulate the private provision of such goods (see Figure 16.1, "Pigou's Golden Rule" on p. 562). In the case of pure public goods, which involve positive externalities to an extreme degree, the Pigouvian problem returns with a vengeance: Unless government intervenes, private firms do not only produce such goods in amounts insufficient to secure maximum economic welfare; they do not produce them at all! The private market fails altogether.

The Free-Rider Problem

Consider a case in which everyone agrees that the collective benefit from a pure public good exceeds its cost. Who is going to produce such a good? A pure private good can be parceled out to individual buyers and withheld from them unless payment is made, but the very act of producing a pure public good makes it instantly and equally available to all. How then is a private producer going to collect a positive price from all the benefited parties? These beneficiaries can say, "We won't pay, and if you don't like it, withhold the benefit from us." The benefit-producing party must either share the benefit with everyone and bear the cost alone (because this party cannot withhold the good) or must stop producing the good (if this party does not want to give free benefits to others or cannot bear the cost alone).

This unwillingness of individuals voluntarily to help cover the cost of a pure public good, and their eagerness to let others produce the good so they can enjoy its benefits at a zero cost, is called the **free-rider problem.** The name has its origin in the Old West, in the days of cattle rustling. The ranchers of Dodge City banded together to form a vigilante group to catch (and hang) cattle thieves. Everyone contributed to the cost of the security force on horseback—that is, until rustling had been sufficiently discouraged by the existence of this group. Then individual ranchers began to withdraw, realizing that they could benefit just as much if they didn't pay. They became "free-riders" instead. Before long, the security force collapsed, and cattle rustling resumed. The rational behavior of each rancher thus led to the irrational behavior of the entire group, which is where government might have helped.

A Role for Government

Victims of the free-rider problem can agree mutually to coerce themselves: They can instruct their government to use its coercive powers for the purpose of securing the public good's net benefit, which the private market fails to deliver. If cattle rustling cost a group of 100 ranchers $5,000 a month, and if the maintenance of a security force that would prevent this loss cost $1,000 a month, the course of action would be clear: Every rancher could be taxed $10 a month, the security force could be hired with the proceeds, and each rancher would receive a benefit five times the cost.

In the same way, modern-day governments engage in the **public finance** of pure public goods, or the governmental collection of taxes from all those believed to benefit from the provision of pure public goods and the subsequent channeling of these funds toward the production of such goods, either by government agencies or private firms.

Note: Actual governments often arrange for the tax-financed production of many goods that are hardly pure public ones. These goods, financed by government and supplied free of charge on the grounds that all citizens merit a share of them, are called **merit goods.** Examples are public education, health care, housing, and social security. In addition, government agencies often produce goods that are sold in markets in competition with private firms, such as electric power, liquor, and sanitation services.

THE OPTIMUM QUANTITY OF A PUBLIC GOOD

Imagine a government determined to step in where the private market fails and eager to arrange for the production of a pure public good. What kind of information would such a government have to have to identify the welfare-maximizing quantity to be produced? In principle, Samuelson tells us, the answer is simple enough: The optimum quantity is the one at which the rising marginal social cost of producing the public good, *MSC,* just equals the good's falling marginal social benefit, *MSB.* The marginal social cost, as always, reflects the opportunity cost of producing the good; that is,

the maximum value of other goods that must be forgone to produce it. This marginal social cost is found in the same way for a pure public good as for a pure private one. Nothing new here.

The marginal social benefit of a pure public good, however, is a different sort of thing from that of a pure private good. A given unit of a pure private good (which has no externalities) can only be consumed by one individual; the marginal social benefit of a unit of a pure private good, therefore, equals the marginal private benefit received by a single person only. In contrast, a given unit of a pure public good can be consumed simultaneously by everyone; the marginal social benefit of a unit of a pure public good, therefore, equals the *sum* of the marginal private benefits received by all of its consumers.

The Marginal Social Benefit

Consider Figure 16.7. Panels (a)–(c) refer to a pure private good. Panel (a) depicts the situation for Consumer 1, whose increased consumption is associated with the declining marginal private benefits represented by blocks *a* through *e.* The color line along the top of the blocks thus indicates the maximum prices this consumer would pay in the market for various units of the good and is this consumer's demand curve for the private good. Panel (b) is similarly constructed but for Consumer 2. Given only two consumers (to keep things manageable), the market-demand curve is derived in panel (c) in the usual manner: by the *horizontal* summation of the individual demand curves at each price. This procedure was first illustrated in Figure 3.7 ''Deriving Market Demand'' (p. 65), and it is now highlighted by the labeling and shading of each individual block of marginal private benefit. The color line in panel (c), therefore, shows the marginal social benefits associated with various quantities of the pure private good.

Panels (d)–(f) refer to a pure public good. Panel (d) shows the situation for Consumer 1; blocks *i* through *m* represent the declining marginal private benefits of various quantities of the

FIGURE 16.7

Marginal Social Benefit: Pure Private Versus Pure Public Good

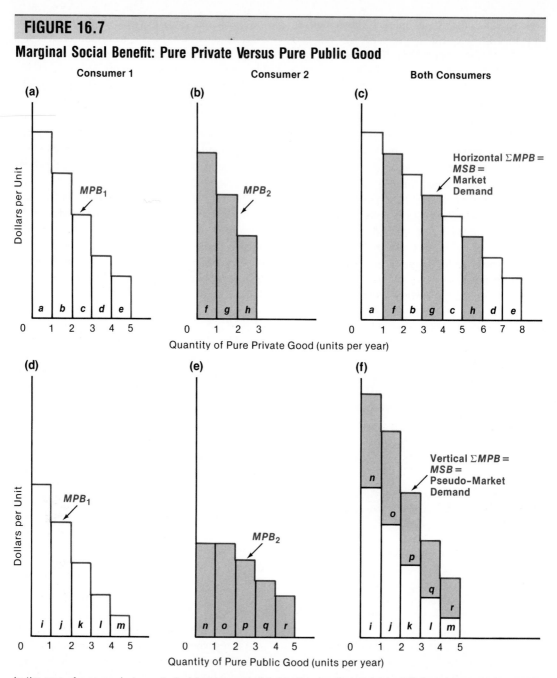

In the case of a pure private good, depicted in panels (a)–(c), the marginal social benefit is derived by the horizontal summation of all consumers' marginal private benefits.

In the case of a pure public good, depicted in panels (d)–(f), a vertical summation of marginal private benefits is in order. Each of the 8 units depicted in panels (a) and (b) is indeed a different unit, consumed privately. In contrast, what appear to be 10 different units in panels (d) and (e) are really 5 units only, each being consumed by both consumers at the same time. Therefore the total quantity shown in panel (c) is 8, while the total quantity in panel (f) is 5 and not 10.

public good. The color line along the top of the blocks again indicates the maximum prices this consumer would pay in a market for various units of the good, but it is a *pseudo*-demand curve only because the good is in fact not offered in the market. The color line in panel (e) must be similarly interpreted, with respect to Consumer 2. Panel (f) once more combines the two consumers' pseudo-demands into a pseudo–market demand that shows the marginal social benefits associated with various quantities of the pure public good. As the labeling and shading of the individual blocks indicates, the summing of marginal private benefits must now be *vertical* rather than horizontal because the first unit of the public good (10 minutes of a fireworks display, perhaps) is consumed *simultaneously* by Consumer 1 and Consumer 2. Thus it yields a marginal social benefit of *i* plus *n*. The second unit consumed by Consumer 1 is, similarly, identical to the second unit consumed by Consumer 2; hence its marginal social benefit equals *j* plus *o*. And so it goes for all other units as well. The calculation of the marginal social benefit of a pure public good thus contrasts sharply with that of a pure private good. The first unit (perhaps a chocolate bar) consumed by Consumer 1 in panel (a), for example, is a *different* unit from the first unit consumed by Consumer 2 in panel (b).

Identifying the Optimum

Panel (a) of Figure 16.8 contains a streamlined version of panel (f) of Figure 16.7, with the stairstep lines replaced by smooth ones. We now engage in a thought experiment. Let us imagine a fully informed government: This government knows the marginal social cost of producing the public good, line *MSC*. In addition, our consumers have truthfully revealed to government the maximum contributions they would make for added units of the good, reflected in lines *AB* and *CD*. Line *AB* shows the marginal private benefits Consumer 1 derives from various quantities of the public good, and this line corresponds to panel (d) in Figure 16.7. Line *CD* shows the marginal private benefits Consumer 2 derives

from the public good, and this line corresponds to panel (e) in the earlier graph. By the vertical addition of these private marginal benefits, our omniscient government can derive line *EFD*, which indicates, of course, the position of marginal social benefit, *MSB*.

Note: It is no accident that Consumer 2's marginal private benefit coincides with the marginal social benefit in range *FD* for public good quantities larger than *0B*. In that range, Consumer 1's marginal private benefit, we assume, is zero. If it were negative, but added quantities of the public good could be disposed of at no cost (as, perhaps, by the turning off of a TV set), the same result would pertain. If it were negative and disposal costs were prohibitive (as, perhaps, for added units of national defense received by a "dove"), Consumer 1's marginal private benefits would have to be subtracted from those of Consumer 2 to find marginal social benefits.

Possessing the knowledge embodied in panel (a) of our graph, our government can, of course, identify quantity *0G* as the optimum amount of the public good. That quantity corresponds to the intersection of *MSC* and *MSB* at point *H*.

The Fruits of Omniscience

A government that was benevolent as well as omniscient would arrange for the production of the optimum quantity. In our example, this optimum quantity would yield total social benefits of *0EHG* at a total social cost of *0IHG*. There would be a net benefit of *EHI* (shaded). Because private markets produce zero amounts of pure public goods, this net benefit depicts the potential gain in total economic welfare from the intervention by an omniscient and benevolent government.

A Comparison

This result can be contrasted with that of a perfectly competitive market providing a pure private good. Panel (b) of Figure 16.8 contains a streamlined version of panel (c) of Figure 16.7. Lines *MN* and *PQ* represent, respectively, the marginal-private-benefit and demand curves of

Consumers 1 and 2, which correspond to panels (a) and (b) of Figure 16.7. The *horizontal* addition of these lines yields line *PRS*, the marginal social benefit as well as the market demand.

Given competitive market supply, an equilibrium price of 0*T* and an equilibrium quantity of

0*U* would emerge. The latter corresponds to the optimum point at which marginal social benefit just equals marginal social cost. Thus the competitive market would yield a total social benefit of 0*PRVU* at a total social cost of 0*WVU*, and there would be a net benefit of *WPRV* (shaded).

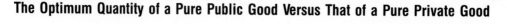

FIGURE 16.8

The Optimum Quantity of a Pure Public Good Versus That of a Pure Private Good

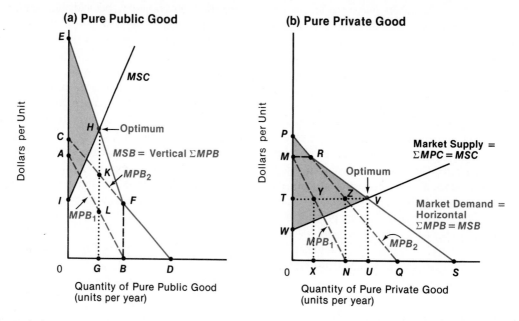

An omniscient government can quickly identify as optimal that amount of a pure public good, 0*G* in panel (a), at which its rising marginal social cost just equals its falling marginal social benefit (point *H*). Thus the optimum requires that marginal social cost equals the *vertical* sum of marginal private benefits:

$$MSC = MPB_1 + MPB_2. \text{ (Note how } GH = GL + GK.)$$

In contrast, a competitive market for a pure private good produces an optimum at which marginal social cost separately equals each consumer's marginal private benefit (and thus equals the *horizontal* sum of marginal private benefits):

$$MSC = MPB_1 = MPB_2. \text{ (Note how } UV = XY = NZ.)$$

Warning: Look closely at the notation in color. In one case, marginal benefits are related by summation; in the other they are related by equality. This difference summarizes the lesson of the previous graph (Figure 16.7) and highlights the distinction between pure public goods, which are consumed jointly by all, and pure private goods, which are consumed separately by each.

This net benefit would be achieved without any government action (beyond the initial assignment of transferable property rights and the facilitation of unrestricted exchange).

THE PROBLEM OF IGNORANCE

In the real world, governments, no matter how benevolent they are, are far from omniscient. How then are they going to discover people's preferences and identify the marginal social benefit associated with various possible quantities of a public good?

The very necessity to arrange for the provision of public goods by collecting taxes will, in fact, hamper the government's attempt to overcome its ignorance. Consider a government that wanted to imitate the pricing rule of the competitive market. Note how, in panel (b) of Figure 16.8, the competitive market establishes a uniform price of $0T$. While consumers face the same price, different consumers buy different amounts of private goods: Consumer 1 purchases $0X$; Consumer 2 buys $0N$; together, they purchase $0U$. Suppose government wanted to act accordingly and charge each consumer for all units of the public good a uniform tax-price, equal to the marginal private benefit derived by this consumer. Such an attempt would quickly spell trouble because consumers of a pure public good cannot possibly buy different amounts at a given tax-price. By definition, a pure public good is consumed in the same amount by all. Hence, as a result of the above pricing rule, consumers (who by necessity would receive the *identical quantity* of the public good) would enjoy *different marginal private benefits*. (Consider how "hawks" and "doves" are likely to evaluate any given quantity of national defense.) Thus the desire to tax in accordance with marginal private benefit would make it necessary to impose different taxes on different consumers.

Under this scheme, as we can see in panel (a) of Figure 16.8, Consumer 1 would have to be charged GL per unit for quantity $0G$, while Consumer 2 would have to be charged GK per unit for the same amount. (The two charges would add up to the marginal social benefit, GH.) Yet such differential taxation, equitable as it may seem, would lead to a serious problem. Consumers who expected to be taxed in accordance with their marginal private benefit (GL in the case of Consumer 1, GK in the case of Consumer 2) would not reveal the true intensity of their preference to the government. They would understate it, hoping to receive a lower tax bill and be a free-rider, at least in part. Hence a government following such a "pricing" rule could not identify the true marginal social benefit, nor the optimum amount of the public good to be provided.

Nor could this problem be solved by pretending, as government officials often do, that public goods are free. If people were convinced that they could get public goods for nothing, they would be apt to *overstate* their true preferences, which is why opinion polls that ask people about new (and allegedly free) government programs never fail to elicit huge majorities in favor of such programs.

How *do* real-world governments, which are not omniscient, in fact find out about people's preferences concerning public goods so that the optimum amounts can be identified?

THE PROCESS OF PUBLIC CHOICE AND GOVERNMENT FAILURE

In the past three decades, economists have become increasingly interested in the process of *public choice*, by which large groups of people decide on the overall quantity of public goods to be provided, on the particular types of such goods, and on the sharing of the associated tax burdens. The choice of a collective decision-making procedure is in itself an economic choice because every possible procedure has its own advantages and disadvantages, its own benefits and costs.

Decisions about public goods, for example, can be made on the basis of custom, by a dictator, or through democratic voting. If individual preferences are to be channeled into social decisions by voting, people must still choose from among a multitude of possible arrangements. They may favor *direct democracy,* in which all affected citizens vote on every possible governmental action. Or people may prefer a *representative democracy,* in which only a group of representatives, who are elected by all citizens, vote on governmental actions. Indeed, these representatives may turn over many decisions to a permanent group of civil servants, a *bureaucracy.* Real-world governments, of course, use a combination of these arrangements.

What then is the likelihood that people's true preferences for pure public goods will be identified and that optimum amounts will be produced?

Many economists now believe that the likelihood is low. They grant readily that an omniscient government could identify the optimum amounts of pure public goods (as we have done above). They grant also that such a government could then take the necessary actions to raise total economic welfare. But they hesitate to recommend that real-world, less-than-omniscient governments be entrusted with such a task. Such governments, they fear, may lower economic welfare instead. Under such circumstances, it would be preferable to have government do nothing and allow people to live with the bad effects of market failure than to have people suffer the worse effects of *government* failure.

It is not possible to do justice to the vast and fascinating literature on public choice in the context of this chapter, but we can give one example of possible government failure.

The Problem of Bureaucracy

One reason why the process of public choice may fail to identify and deliver the optimum quantity of pure public goods is that elected officials, wisely or foolishly, allocate dollar amounts to the provision of public goods, but *someone else* implements their decisions. The entire institutional structure through which political decisions are implemented is known as the **bureaucracy;** all the people working for these government agencies (or bureaus) are known as **bureaucrats.** Many economists argue that bureaucrats, too, are best viewed as engaged in the rational pursuit of self-interest. Just like consumers, the owners of firms, voters, and elected officials, bureaucrats are best seen as seeking to use existing institutions to their own advantage. Economists such as James Buchanan (1919–   ), a Biography of whom is also featured in Chapter 16 of the *Student Workbook* accompanying this text, have found that this view of bureaucrats is vastly more productive of explaining their behavior than an alternative view that regards their actions as "impartial service for the common good."

Bureaucrats Maximize Utility. Above all, Buchanan argues, bureaucrats seek to maximize their own utility by preserving and advancing their own careers, which means seeking higher salaries through promotion and seeking lower work loads for a given amount of pay. In hierarchical organizations, both goals can be achieved by multiplying the numbers of subordinates (and titles). Bureaucrats also seek job tenure, prestige, and various fringe benefits (ranging from insurance and pension plans to long coffee breaks, luxurious offices, and trips to important conferences in Rome). The achievement of these and similar goals, invariably, is a function of the agency's budget. As a result, utility maximization translates into budget maximization: "More is always better."

The Iron Triangle. Before long, a bargaining situation develops between bureaucrats on the one hand and legislators on the other. Because few bureaus receive revenue from sales, bureaucrats need legislators to make periodic grants of money. In the background are the "clients" served by the bureaucrats, the special interests for whom the bureaucrats soon become effective in-house lobbyists. Thus the Department of Defense begins to serve defense contractors; the Department of Agriculture serves farmers; the

Department of Education serves schools and colleges. Legislators with strong special-interest constituencies (and large numbers of apathetic voters) have, in turn, a powerful incentive to sit on committees that deal with the special-interest groups. These legislators will logroll until they find themselves appointed. Over time, legislative committees will be dominated by legislators who favor the special interests. Thus an "iron triangle" is formed: special interests, bureaucrats, and legislators, each seeking their own interests, will jointly promote overgenerous budgets for pure public goods. The consequences of the pursuit by government officials of their internal, private goals instead of publicly announced, official goals have been termed **internalities.** Internalities are associated with government failure, just as externalities are associated with market failure.

A Graphical Exposition. Panel (a) of Figure 16.9 depicts the ideal situation that government officials would bring about if they were omniscient, benevolent, and endowed with the strictest sense of public duty. They would identify the optimum quantity of the public good as $0D$ by comparing falling marginal social benefit, *MSB*, with rising marginal social cost, *MSC*. Because the private market would fail to produce any amount of the public good, government officials would impose upon people a total cost of $0ACD$ to procure a total benefit of $0BCD$. The shaded triangle *ABC* depicts the net benefit.

Panel (b) pictures an added element: the provision of an excess amount of the public good because public officials pursue private goals, as noted above. In this case, the total amount provided is not $0E,$ the optimum, but $0I$. The difference between $0E$ and $0I$ indicates that people are getting an *added* benefit of *EFHI*, but at an *added* cost of *EFGI*. Thus they are receiving, on the excess quantity, a net loss of crosshatched triangle *FGH*. Overall, people are getting a net benefit of the shaded minus the crosshatched area. They are still better off than without government intervention, but government has now failed to maximize the potential net

benefit from the provision of the pure public good.

Panel (c) depicts a situation in which the government's failure to optimize is so extreme that living with market failure and forgoing the shaded net benefit pictured in panel (a) would be preferable. In this case, government officials present people with a net social loss: As in panel (b), bureaucrats again provide for an above-optimal amount, $0P$. But this time, they also produce it at an excessive cost, pictured by *MSC**. This cost reflects the bureaucrats' tolerance of X-inefficiency: excess staffing, luxury offices, unnecessary trips to Rome. As a result, the public receives total benefits of $0LNP$ at a total cost of $0KMP$. The net result is a net loss equal to the shaded minus the crosshatched area. People are worse off than they would be if government had done nothing at all. Are there remedies? Perhaps, as the next sections show.

SHAKING UP THE BUREAUCRATS

It is difficult to judge the performance of government bureaus. They do not have annual statements of profit and loss. They do not issue stock certificates, the prices of which can be monitored. They do not go bankrupt when competitors do better. Yet there is an obvious need for monitoring performance and improving it where indicated. In recent years, a number of approaches have been much discussed, including (1) benefit-cost analysis, (2) competition among government bureaus, (3) replacing government production with government provision, and (4) introducing direct competition between bureaus and private firms.

Benefit-Cost Analysis

According to an old saying, the attitude of bureaucrats is: "If we have the money, let's do it." The optimization principle, introduced in the very first chapter of this book, requires otherwise. Even when a government project produces

FIGURE 16.9

Internalities

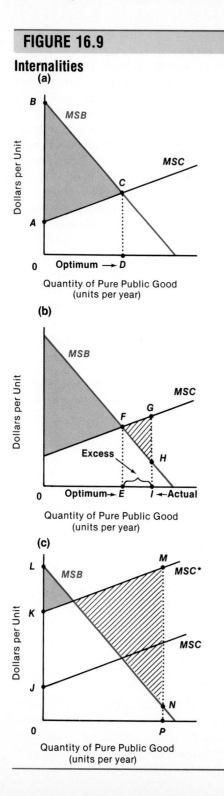

(a)

(vertical axis) Dollars per Unit

B
MSB
MSC
C
A
0   Optimum → D
Quantity of Pure Public Good
(units per year)

(b)

(vertical axis) Dollars per Unit

MSB
MSC
F   G
Excess
H
0   Optimum → E   I ← Actual
Quantity of Pure Public Good
(units per year)

(c)

(vertical axis) Dollars per Unit

M
L
MSB   MSC*
K
MSC
J
N
0   P
Quantity of Pure Public Good
(units per year)

Government officials may well fail to provide the optimum quantity of a pure public good because they are ill-informed about marginal social benefits and costs. But even if they were omniscient, they might fail to do so as a result of their pursuit of internal, private goals. They might then provide for an excessive amount of such a good, perhaps even at an excessive cost. As a result, the net benefit available to society under ideal conditions, or the shaded area in panel (a), might be offset partially by the crosshatched area in panel (b) or might give way to a net overall loss, represented by the shaded minus the crosshatched area in panel (c).

obvious benefits, they may not be worth the cost; the forgone alternative benefits may be larger. In an attempt to force bureaucrats to examine benefits in relation to costs, the U.S. federal government began introducing Planning-Programming-Budgeting Systems (PPBS) in its agencies in 1965; these systems have now spread to state and local governments as well. These systems require bureaucrats to engage in **benefit-cost analysis,** also referred to as **cost-effectiveness studies,** which is the quantification of the benefits and costs of all contemplated government projects, the rejection of those with benefit-cost ratios below unity, and the apportionment of the budget among those remaining projects that have the highest benefit-cost ratios.

For reasons noted in Chapter 12, benefits and costs that are spread out over time must, of course, be discounted to the present. So it is the *present* values of streams of benefits and costs that are compared. Projects with negative net present values are rejected (their benefit-cost ratio is below unity); projects with the highest positive net present values are carried out.

In this way, bureaucrats are forced to focus on the three major ingredients of intertemporal choice: benefits, costs, and the discount rate. Unfortunately, this procedure conveys an aura of precision that may not be justified. A benefit-cost ratio of 1.792 looks very precise and seems to suggest that the public project provides public benefits that exceed the forgone private ones by 79.2 percent. Yet this is true only if the benefits and costs have been estimated correctly and the proper discount rate has been applied. Often the analyst has much discretion in the estimation of benefits, costs, and discount rates and therefore can influence the outcome as well.

Consider estimating the benefits of a flood-control program. Some of the benefits are tangible and not too difficult to calculate: increased farm output, increased generation of electric power, decreased damages to residences and roads. Other benefits, however, are intangible and hard to estimate in dollars and cents: improved recreational opportunities or enhanced scenic beauty.

Similarly, many costs can be difficult to estimate. Estimating the cost of concrete or labor going into a dam is one thing; estimating long-run ecological damage is quite another. Even the market prices of concrete and labor may not be the proper ingredients for finding the opportunity cost of providing flood control: What if the price of concrete exceeds the marginal private cost of producing it? What if the marginal social cost of producing concrete falls short of or exceeds the marginal private cost? What if there is massive unemployment of labor, and the use of labor in the flood-control project in no way reduces output anywhere else?

Selecting the proper rate for discounting future benefits and costs is the most difficult task of all. Theoretical considerations, noted in Chapter 12, suggest the *pure rate of interest* is the proper rate for discounting. The pure rate of interest is the rate one would find in perfectly competitive capital markets. This rate would reflect the private sector's marginal time preference and marginal time productivity and would indicate the rate of return that resources used in the public sector could earn in the private one instead. But the real world provides the analyst with a bewildering complexity of rates of return, reflecting differences in risk, in maturity, in market imperfections, and in taxation. Thus one can find rates from 0–8 percent a year on short-term liquid assets and from 30–40 percent, perhaps, on investments in the most profitable industries. Which of these is the proper rate of discount therefore depends on the part of the private sector from which the resources to be used on the public project are to be withdrawn. Predicting the sectors from which resources will be withdrawn is next to impossible. A flood-control program may be carried out with resources withdrawn from private consumption, from private investment in low-risk sector A, or from private investment in high-risk sector B. . . . As a result, analysts typically prepare benefit-cost analyses with a range of "plausible" discount rates. And some analysts even argue that government should ignore rates of return in the private sector entirely. They think these rates are "artificial" (influenced by "arbitrary" monetary policy) or "unacceptable" (reflective of people's indifference to the fate of future generations). These analysts favor a conscious value judgment that establishes a "social" rate of discount through which government arbitrates the conflicting claims of present and future generations.

Enough has been said to indicate that benefit-cost analysis, even though seemingly precise, still does not hinder much of the subjective decision making by bureaucrats. The framework of PPBS in no way prevents bureaucrats, who are eager to justify their projects, from exaggerating benefits and understating costs. (For a real-world example, see Analytical Example 16.2, "Flooding Hell's Canyon, Draining Hetch Hetchy.")

Competition Among Government Bureaus

Competition among government bureaus has been suggested as a means of discouraging an unnecessary inflation of cost and of providing legislators with a yardstick by which to judge performance. Thus it has been argued that the competition among Air Force, Army, and Navy (all of which once procured their own planes) produced better-quality products at lower cost.

Government Provision, not Production

While it is true that pure public goods would not be provided by the private market and must be *provided* by government, it does not follow that they must be *produced* by government. Government provision simply requires the collection of taxes and the exercise of demand (because people as individuals would fail to spend money on pure public goods). Yet the *producers* of public goods could well be private firms.

To some extent, government has always been contracting out the production of pure public goods to the private sector. The most notable example is defense—military equipment is pro-

duced and research is even conducted by private firms. In the days of the Old West, government contracted out law enforcement in the same way. It collected taxes and then paid bounties to private hunters of criminals. In recent years, many American towns have begun to contract out many of their traditional activities, ranging from fire protection, highway construction, and janitorial services for public buildings to the operation of parking lots, prisons, and sanitation services. The private production of fire protection has been accomplished at half the original cost and the private production of garbage collection at two-thirds the cost.[2]

Competition Between Bureaus and Private Firms

Finally, placing existing government bureaus in direct competition with private firms is another possible approach to reducing government failure. Two possible candidates for this approach are the U.S. Postal Service and the local public schools.

The operations of the U.S. Postal Service have been described as unbelievably inefficient. Critics believe that private competition could improve matters drastically. United Parcel Service (a private firm) already handles more parcels than the U.S. Postal Service. The Federal Express (another private firm) is handling the high-speed delivery of an ever increasing number of

---

[2]Roger Ahlbrandt, *Municipal Fire Protection Services: Comparison of Alternative Organizational Forms* (Beverly Hills, Calif.: Sage, 1973); and E. S. Savas, *The Organization and Efficiency of Solid Waste Collection* (Lexington, Mass.: D. C. Heath, 1977). The latter study, covering 260 cities, noted that private contractors used smaller crews and more productive vehicles than municipal agencies. The former also had fewer absences and used incentive systems to serve more households per hour. Citing such "incentives for efficiency," the nation's governors in 1985 cautiously endorsed the private operation of prisons. (*The New York Times*, March 3, 1985, p. 26.) A private firm, Corrections Corporation of America, offered to run the entire Tennessee prison system for 99 years. (*The Wall Street Journal*, September 13, 1985, p. 45.)

small packages, as are the Airborne Express, Purolator Courier, and Emery. *Better Homes and Gardens, Business Week, Time,* and *The Wall Street Journal* have switched to private delivery of their publications (at an average 10 cents a copy compared to the Postal Service's 16.5 cents). Advertisers have abandoned the mails for the telephone. Many firms are eager to take on the letter business as well, but the Postal Service enjoys a legal monopoly. (No matter who delivers a first-class letter, it must carry U.S. postage.) Some suggest that this monopoly be lifted by Congress. Others believe that technological change will do the trick. The Postal Service, they argue, is employing antediluvian methods to carry the mails. Internal combustion engines and human backs lug around an essentially weightless commodity: information. This information could be transported much better via wire, radio, and satellite. Already an IBM-Comsat-Aetna consortium has proposed a Satellite Business System to replace interoffice mail communications by electronic means. In 1979, the Postal Service accordingly moved to protect its monopoly by requesting that the definition of "letters" be extended to "orientations of magnetic particles in a manner having a predetermined significance." The request was denied, but the Postal Service did initiate its own electronic mail service in 1982.

Many people are also unhappy with the local public schools. Milton Friedman (1912–   ), who won the 1976 Nobel Prize in economics and a Biography of whom appears in Chapter 1 of the *Student Workbook* that accompanies this text, has suggested a simple solution: that the funds currently collected in taxes be withheld from public school administrators and handed to parents of school children in the form of **education vouchers.**[3] These vouchers would be divisible certificates earmarked for the purchase of educational services only and might be "spent" by

their recipients in one or several accredited private or public schools (which could cash them in at the public treasury). As a result of such a voucher system, it is imagined, many different types of schools would emerge: large schools and small ones, schools stressing the arts and schools stressing science, schools stressing general education and others vocational training, morning schools and afternoon schools, segregated schools and integrated ones. Instead of taking whatever a public school board decreed, parents could tailor their children's curriculum to their own tastes! They could spend a part of their certificates on a Monday-morning all-boy art school, another part on a Tuesday-to-Thursday-afternoon coeducational science school, and another part on a Friday all-black vocational school. Parents could buy whatever services they deemed best for their children.

There would be room, too, it is argued, for teachers and administrators to experiment and make greater progress in their fields. Those who had a brand-new idea could open a school and test it out. They would not have to launch a full-scale political campaign to persuade the school board, other civil servants, or legislators of the soundness of their ideas. If successful, they would be swamped with applicants, have big revenues, and expand. Other less successful schools would find their pupils and revenues evaporating and would have to conform to the consumers' choice or go out of business! This important feature of competition is entirely lacking in *public* schools. Because they operate on tax revenue, they can provide bad services and still survive.

Such a voucher system might be used for all goods with positive externalities, resulting in a combination of the best of the public and private sectors. Such goods might be publicly financed (to ensure the provision of an optimum quantity), privately demanded with public money (to ensure that consumers keep as much freedom of choice as possible), and then produced by competing private and public firms (to ensure that production occurs in the cheapest way).

[3]Milton Friedman, *Capitalism and Freedom* (Chicago: University of Chicago Press, 1962), ch. 6; and *Free to Choose* (New York: Harcourt Brace Jovanovich, 1980), ch. 6.

SUMMARY

1. Nonpecuniary or real externalities are direct effects, independent of any price changes, of the actions of some households or firms on the utility of other households or on the output of other firms, none of whom have invited these effects. Such externalities are said to be negative when costs are imposed in the form of decreased utility or output on bystanders who are not being compensated for this injury. These externalities are said to be positive when benefits are provided in the form of increased utility or output for bystanders who are not being charged for this favor.

2. The British economist A. C. Pigou was the first to deal with externalities in a systematic way. In the presence of externalities, he argued perfect competition would not produce a Pareto-type welfare maximum. Marginal private cost would diverge from marginal social cost, and marginal private benefit would diverge from marginal social benefit. Pigou argued that government could close the gaps between marginal private and social costs or benefits (and restore the Pareto welfare maximum) by taxing producers and consumers who generated negative externalities and by subsidizing those who generated positive externalities.

3. For nearly half a century, Pigou's analysis went unchallenged. Then Ronald Coase noted two flaws: (a) the administration of the tax-subsidy scheme might be too costly to make it worthwhile; (b) if government assigned unambiguous and transferable property rights, and as long as transactions costs were low enough, private parties could negotiate among themselves about eliminating externalities—without any further intervention of government. Coase established the theorem that under perfect competition and in the absence of income effects and transactions costs, voluntary negotiated agreements among private parties generating or being affected by externalities will lead to the same resource allocation (and output mix) regardless of how property rights are assigned among these parties.

4. Pollution by and affecting large numbers exemplifies a case in which high transactions costs prevent a negotiated internalization of externalities. In this case, post-Pigouvian theorists also recommend government intervention. The government is urged, first, to determine the optimum level of pollution—which is likely to be smaller than the actual level.

5. Governmental policies to induce pollution abatement to the optimum level include moral suasion, outright prohibition, setting standards, taxing waste dumping, subsidizing waste treatment, and marketing pollution rights.

6. There exist certain goods with positive externalities that affect not only a few people, but literally all members of society. Such *pure public goods* provide *nonexcludable* and *nonrival* benefits to all people in a given society.

7. Pigou has shown us that goods with positive externalities tend to be produced in amounts insufficient to secure maximum economic welfare. In the case of pure public goods, which involve positive externalities to an extreme degree, the Pigouvian problem returns with a vengeance: Left to themselves, private firms do not produce such goods at all because of *the free-rider problem;* in principle, this problem can be overcome by government intervention.

8. In principle, it is simple enough to determine the quantity of a pure public good that maximizes social welfare. At this optimum quantity the rising marginal social cost of producing the public good just equals the good's falling marginal social benefit, which, in turn, equals the sum of the marginal private benefits received by all of its consumers.

9. In practice, it is next to impossible to get people to reveal their true preferences for pure public goods: If they are taxed according to expected benefits, people will understate their expected benefits. If people are taxed less, they will overstate them.

10. In recent decades, economists have become interested in the process of public choice by which large groups of people decide on the overall quantity of public goods to be provided, on the particular types of such goods, and on the sharing of the associated tax burdens. The study of this process has led economists to conclude that real-world government may well fail to provide optimal amounts of pure public goods.

11. One reason among many for government failure is the fact that political decisions are implemented by a bureaucracy; bureaucrats, like all people, are engaged in the rational pursuit of self-interest. An iron triangle develops, consisting of bureaucrats, legislators, and special interests, each of whom seek to promote their own interests. Jointly, they are likely to promote overgenerous budgets for pure public goods. Bureaucrats are likely to produce this excess quantity of public goods at an excess cost as well.

12. Possibilities for improving the performance of government bureaucracy include benefit-cost analysis; competition among government bureaus; government provision, but not production of public goods; and competition between bureaus and private firms.

KEY TERMS

ambient standards
benefit-cost analysis
bureaucracy
bureaucrats
Coase theorem
cost-effectiveness studies
education vouchers
emission standards
free-rider problem
indivisibilities
input standards
internalities
marginal external benefit (*MEB*)
marginal external cost (*MEC*)
marginal internal benefit
marginal internal cost
marginal private benefit (*MPB*)
marginal private cost (*MPC*)
marginal social benefit (*MSB*)

marginal social cost (*MSC*)
merit goods
negative externalities
neighborhood effects
nonexcludability
nonpecuniary externalities
nonrivalness
pollution licenses
pollution rights
positive externalities
public finance
pure private good
pure public good
real externalities
spillovers

HANDS-ON PRACTICE

Exercise #1

Consider Figure 16.1, "Pigou's Golden Rule," on p. 562. Identify the size of the tax the government would collect in cases (a) and (b) and the size of the subsidy it would disperse in cases (c) and (d).

Solution:

a. The tax would be *bd* times q_2.
b. The tax would be *hf* times q_4.
c. The subsidy would be *mn* times q_6.
d. The subsidy would be *vw* times q_8.

Exercise #2

Suppose a government project involves the following costs and benefits. At a discount rate of 10 percent per year, what is the current ratio of total benefit to total cost?

	Now	1 Year from Now	2 Years from Now	5 Years from Now
Costs	$200	$200	$200	$ 10
Benefits	—	—	$500	$500

Solution:

The present value of costs equals

$$PV_C = \$200 + \frac{\$200}{(1.1)^1} + \frac{\$200}{(1.1)^2} + \frac{\$10}{(1.1)^5}$$

$$= \$200 + \frac{\$200}{1.1} + \frac{\$200}{1.21} + \frac{\$10}{1.61}$$

$$= \$200 + \$181.82 + \$165.29 + \$6.21$$

$$= \$553.32$$

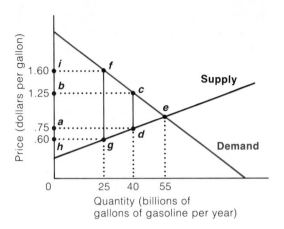

The present value of benefits equals

$$PV_B = \frac{\$500}{(1.1)^2} + \frac{\$500}{(1.1)^5} = \frac{\$500}{1.21} + \frac{\$500}{1.61} =$$

$$\$413.22 + \$310.56 = \$723.78$$

The ratio is $\dfrac{PV_B}{PV_C} = \dfrac{\$723.78}{\$553.32} = 1.31.$

Exercise #3

"A proper calculation of the marginal social cost of government projects should include not only the obvious tax expenditure (on, say, the labor and materials needed to construct another mile of interstate highway); it should also include the less obvious (such as the additional deadweight loss created by extra tax collection)." Evaluate the argument.

Solution:

The argument makes sense—provided the added taxes do create such deadweight loss. Consider an excise tax, similar to that discussed in Chapter 6, Application 4, on pp. 201–202. Consider the accompanying graph.

Originally, an excise tax of 50¢ per gallon of gasoline *(cd)* may have reduced purchases from pre-tax 55 billion to 40 billion gallons per year. Buyers face a $1.25-per-gallon price; sellers get 75¢ per gallon. Tax collections *(abcd)* equal $.50(40) = $20 billion per year; the deadweight loss *(cde)* equals $.50(15) divided by 2, or $3.75 billion per year. Thus each dollar collected cre-

ates 18.75¢ of deadweight loss on the average (divide 3.75 by 20).

Now let government double the excise tax to finance additional highways. The new tax is *fg* per unit. Total tax collections change to *hifg* = $1(25) = $25 billion a year; but the deadweight loss changes to *efg* = $1(30) divided by 2, or $15 billion per year. The doubling of the tax rate quadruples the deadweight loss! Now each dollar collected creates 60¢ of deadweight loss on the average (divide 15 by 25). At the margin, an added deadweight loss *(cdgf)* of $15 − 3.75 = $11.25 billion has been associated with an added $25 − 20 = $5 billion in tax collections. Thus the marginal deadweight-loss cost has been $11.25 billion divided by $5 billion, or $2.25 per extra tax dollar collected—hardly an insignificant amount.

QUESTIONS AND PROBLEMS

1. "In the presence of a negative externality, perfect competition cannot be relied upon automatically to produce a Pareto-type welfare maximum." This statement was illustrated numerically in the section on "The Analysis of Pigou." Invent an analogous example for the case of a positive externality.

2. Panel (a) of Figure 16.1 shows how the imposition of a per-unit tax on the output of perfectly competitive producers who create negative externalities leads to an increase in total economic welfare (equal to shaded triangle *abc*). Could the same argument be made if the output in question was produced by a monopoly? Explain.

3. "Pigou assumed away a common human trait: altruism. To the extent that people love their neighbors as themselves, they mentally add marginal external costs to marginal private costs and determine the extent of their activities on that basis. In the case of such altruism, any governmental tax on people supposedly creating negative externalities destroys rather than ensures a Pareto welfare maximum."

Evaluate this view.

4. Coase imagined the following situation: A rancher and wheat farmer operate side by side on unfenced land. Depending on how one looks at it, each is imposing negative externalities on the other. When the farmer grows more wheat, more cultivated fields stand in the way of the cattle, and the production of meat must be restricted. When the rancher increases the size of the herd, more cattle stray onto wheat fields and trample them; thus more meat implies less wheat. The facts, let us suppose, are as follows:

Size of Herd (number of steers)	Crop Loss (tons per year)
1	1
2	3
3	6
4	10

Assume that each steer brings a profit of $30, that each ton of wheat brings a profit of $10, and that transactions costs are zero. Then show that

a. the externalities will be internalized once property rights are clearly assigned either to the farmer (who now has a right not to have the wheat harmed) or to the rancher (who now has a right to let the cattle roam);
b. the Coase theorem applies to this case.

5. "When the reserve clause was in effect in organized baseball, people argued that it was needed to prevent wealthy baseball clubs from acquiring too large a share of the good players. This assertion can be refuted with the help of the Coase theorem."

Explain. (*Hint:* You may wish to review Chapter 11, "Application 5: The Baseball Players' Market." Then address the question of whether the team for which a player plays would differ with the identity of the owner of his services.)

6. "Coase is wrong. The mere possibility of mutual advantage does not ensure its achievement, even in the small-numbers (low-transaction-cost) case. Negotiations will break down because of strategic behavior: Waste-dumping paper companies will threaten to produce more paper (even if they have no such plans), merely in order to extort more bribe money from fishing companies. Or fishing companies will make untrue claims about fish killed in order to extort more damage payments from paper companies."

Evaluate this position.

7. "Although practical within limits, outright prohibitions are unlikely to achieve optimum pollution."

Comment.

8. In 1980, governments were worrying about a traffic jam in outer space because 80 satellites were all in the choicest orbit (a narrow region 22,300 miles above the equator where satellites make one revolution every 24 hours and thus remain stationary above the same spot, while being in optical range of nearly half the earth's surface). In order for ground stations to be able to discriminate among signals, these satellites had to be separated by 200–270 miles, and the demand for orbital slots was rising fast. As an economist, can you think of ways to deal with orbital crowding?

9. In a graph, draw a downward-sloping marginal social benefit line for the dumping of wastes by a chemicals plant, measuring wastes dumped on the horizontal axis. Also draw an upward-sloping marginal social cost line that depicts the damages done to a nearby computer firm that requires exceptionally clean air for its manufacturing process but finds the air continually polluted by the chemicals plant. Use your graph to illustrate the Coase theorem, assuming that transactions costs are negligible.

10. **Mr. A:** As the answer to Question 9 has shown, the Coase theorem will ensure optimal pollution levels in the short run, provided certain conditions are met, but pollution will not be optimal in the long run regardless of which party is endowed with property rights.

Ms. B: You are so right. Take the above case. In the long run, if the right to dump wastes is given to the chemicals plant, optimal pollution will occur, but if that right is given to the computer firm, the chemicals plant will go out of business and waste dumping will fall to a nonoptimal level of zero.

What do you think? Does Coasian bargaining break down in the long run when firms can enter and leave an industry (and *will* leave when losses are the alternative)?

11. "The free-rider problem discussed in this chapter throws new light on the right-to-work versus union-security debate (according to which unions want to restrict job openings to union members). The reason that unions insist on union shops or closed shops is that they are producing a public good that affects all employees equally whether they pay union dues or not."

Do you agree or disagree with this position? (*Hint:* Consider how unions "produce" working conditions, including rules about safety, lighting, heating, layoffs, promotions, discharge, and pace of work.)

12. "The distinction between pure public goods and merit goods is not a happy one. Quite obviously, the purchase by government of such merit goods as social security or public education, health care, and housing serves the purpose of producing the pure public good of *economic justice*. Thus merit goods are seen to be *ingredients* in the production of pure public goods in the same way that courthouses, jails, police cruisers, and polaris submarines are ingredients used in the production of internal or external security."

Evaluate this position.

13. "In 1976, the city government of New York chose to permit 1,622 murders, 3,400 rapes, 27,456 assaults, 77,940 robberies, and 195,243 burglaries. Today's figures are not any better. These crime rates are outrageous. When there are such obvious added benefits to be derived from additional crime prevention activities, the city ought to produce more of this public good."

What do you think? [*Hint:* Frame your answer with the help of panel (a) in Figure 16.8.]

14. "The educational voucher plan would be a disaster: most parents wouldn't know how to pick the best schooling for their children; the rich and the poor wouldn't get the same education; education is too important to trust to profit-seeking business; church schools and racially segregated schools might spring up as a result." What do you think?

15. **Mr. A:** Although city buses are not a pure public good, the consumption of bus trips by some people provides benefits not only to the bus riders in question but also to other people who do not ride buses. Consider the decrease in road congestion, accidents, and pollution. Therefore the public at large should properly pay for at least a part of bus transportation.

Ms. B: Of course. Furthermore, a properly designed subsidy of this sort will induce the production of an optimal level of bus transportation.

Illustrate this argument graphically. [Panel (a) of Figure 16.8 might prove helpful.]

16. In 1983, the Environmental Protection Agency asked the citizens of Tacoma, Washington, to take part in a difficult decision: Should it order the local Asarco copper smelter to reduce arsenic emissions into the air from 282 million grams per year to 172 million grams per year (thereby reducing arsenic-related lung cancer deaths from 4 to 1 per year), or should it order the plant shut down and thus save even that one last life per year? What do you think and why?

17. In 1969, different agencies of the federal government used different discount rates in their respective benefit-cost analyses. Thus the Office of Economic Opportunity used a 3- to

5-percent rate in evaluating its jobs corps, "upward bound," and family planning programs; the Department of Agriculture used a 4.875-percent rate for rural conservation and electrification programs. The Department of Defense used a 10-percent rate for air-station and shipyard projects; and the Department of Health, Education, and Welfare used rates between 0 and 10 percent in evaluating programs concerning tuberculosis, cancer, syphilis, arthritis, and motor vehicle injury. Evaluate this use of different discount rates.

SELECTED READINGS

Borcherding, Thomas E., ed. *Budgets and Bureaucrats: The Sources of Government Growth.* Durham, N.C.: Duke University Press, 1977.

Browning, Edgar K., and Jacquelene M. Browning. *Public Finance and the Price System,* 3rd edition. New York: Macmillan, 1987.

> An excellent text.

Buchanan, James M. *Economics: Between Predictive Science and Moral Philosophy.* College Station, Tex.: Texas A & M University Press, 1988.

> Some 26 papers by the 1986 Nobel Prize winner in economics.

Buchanan, James M. "An Economic Theory of Clubs," *Economica,* February 1965, pp. 1–14.

> A discussion of goods that are neither pure private nor pure public ones because they are excludable but also nonrival. *See also* comments by Y.-K Ng, *Economica,* August 1973 and August 1974.

Buchanan, James M., and Gordon Tullock. *The Calculus of Consent: Logical Foundations of Constitutional Democracy.* Ann Arbor, Mich.: University of Michigan Press, 1962.

> An analysis of political behavior under different decision rules.

Coase, Ronald H. "The Lighthouse in Economics," *The Journal of Law and Economics,* October 1974, pp. 357–76.

> A fascinating discussion of economists' favorite example of a public good—and why their usual conclusion (the need for government intervention) may well be wrong.

Coase, Ronald H. "The Problem of Social Cost," *The Journal of Law and Economics,* October 1960, pp. 1–44.

> The seminal article on the Coase theorem. *See also the* "Coase Theory Symposium," in the *Natural Resources Journal,* October 1973 and January 1974.

Council on Environmental Quality. *Environmental Quality — The Tenth Annual Report.* Washington, D.C.: U.S. Government Printing Office, 1979.

> A detailed review of 10 years of environmental policy. *See also* the subsequent reports.

Downs, Anthony. *An Economic Theory of Democracy.* New York: Harper and Row, 1957.

> Argues that people in the public sector, too, will engage in the rational pursuit of self-interest.

Fisher, Anthony C., and Frederick M. Peterson. "The Environment in Economics: A Survey," *Journal of Economic Literature,* March 1976, pp. 1–33.

Furubotn, Eirik, and Svetozar Pejovich. "Property Rights and Economic Theory: A Survey of Recent Literature," *Journal of Economic Literature,* December 1972, pp. 1137–62.

Galbraith, John Kenneth. *The Affluent Society.* Boston: Houghton Mifflin, 1958.

> Argues that public "needs" are underfinanced, while private "wants" are overindulged.

Leontief, Wassily. "Environmental Repercussions and the Economic Structure: An Input-Output Approach," *Review of Economics and Statistics,* August 1970, pp. 262–71.

> The 1973 winner of the Nobel Prize in economics extends input-output analysis (discussed in Chapter 13) to take into account the flow of materials between the economy and the environment.

Manne, Henry G. *The Economics of Legal Relationships: Readings in the Theory of Property Rights.* St. Paul, Minn.: West, 1975.

> A superb set of 37 articles.

Meyer, Richard, and Bruce Yandle. "The Political Economy of Acid Rain," *Cato Journal,* Fall 1987, pp. 527–45.

> A fascinating analysis of Congressional behavior.

Mishan, Ezra J. "The Postwar Literature on Externalities: An Interpretative Essay," *Journal of Economic Literature,* March 1971, pp. 1–28.

> *See also* the controversy about this article in the same publication, March 1972, pp. 57–62.

Musgrave, Richard A. "Public Goods," in E. Cary Brown and Robert M. Solow, *Paul Samuelson and*

ANALYTICAL EXAMPLE

Modern Economic Theory. New York: McGraw-Hill, 1983, pp. 141–56.

> A review and praise of Samuelson's contribution to public goods theory.

Niskanen, William A. *Bureaucracy and Representative Government.* Chicago: Aldine-Atherton, 1971.

> Argues that social gains from government intervention are apt to be consumed by an expansion of the bureaucracy itself.

Pigou, Arthur C. *The Economics of Welfare,* 4th edition. London: Macmillan, 1946.

> A classic text.

Proxmire, William. *The Fleecing of America.* Boston: Houghton Mifflin, 1980.

> The influential U.S. senator tells the story of his Golden Fleece Awards (which highlight absurd government projects).

Sandler, Todd, and John T. Tschirhart. "The Economic Theory of Clubs: An Evaluative Survey," *Journal of Economic Literature,* December 1980, pp. 1481–1521.

> A superb discussion of voluntary groups the members of which derive mutual benefit from sharing impure public goods (goods that are characterized by partial rivalry or some excludability of benefits).

Staaf, Robert J., and Francis X. Tannian. *Externalities: Theoretical Dimensions of Political Economy.* New York: Dunellen, 1974.

> A collection of 27 major articles on externalities.

Tietenberg, Tom. *Environmental and Natural Resource Economics.* Glenview, Ill.: Scott, Foresman and Co., 1984.

> A superb text that includes numerous chapters on externalities.

U.S. Congress, Joint Economic Committee. *The Analysis and Evaluation of Public Expenditures: The PPB System,* vols. 1–3. Washington, D.C.: U.S. Government Printing Office, 1969.

> An important collection of papers on all aspects of PPBS.

U.S. Congress, Joint Economic Committee. *Innovations in Planning, Programming, and Budgeting in State and Local Governments.* Washington, D.C.: U.S. Government Printing Office, 1969.

> A discussion of the use of PPBS by states, counties, and cities.

Wolf, Charles, Jr. "A Theory of Nonmarket Failure: Framework for Implementation Analysis," *The Journal of Law and Economics,* April 1979, pp. 107–39.

> An important discussion of government failure.

COMPUTER PROGRAMS

The KOHLER-3 personal-computer diskettes that accompany this book contain two programs of particular interest to this chapter:

16. Externalities and Public Goods includes a 31-question multiple-choice test with immediate responses to incorrect answers as well as numerous exercises concerning externalities associated with production or consumption, remedies suggested by Pigou or Coase, and cost-benefit analysis.

Appendix C. Capital Budgeting can be used to carry out benefit-cost analysis.

ANALYTICAL EXAMPLE 16.1

THE ECONOMICS OF BEES

The Coasean prediction that externalities are likely to be removed through private bargaining unless transactions costs are prohibitive has recently been confirmed by a study of bees. Beekeepers receive advantages from farmers who grow plants the nectar of which is likely to increase the production of honey. Accordingly, beekeepers pay "apiary rent" for the right to place their hives on the growers' land. But farmers also receive advantages from bees that aid pollination and thereby help increase certain crops, and these farmers pay "pollination fees" for the privilege of having bees on their land.

In the United States, contractual arrangements between the two parties are routine. Sometimes payments are made in one direction, as in the case of mint that helps yield honey but does not require pollination services. At other times payments are made in the other direction, as in the case of apples that require pollination services but do not improve honey output. Sometimes payments go both ways, as in the case of alfalfa and red clover.

The accompanying table shows some of the data collected during 1970–71 in this study of Coasean contracts in the state of Washington.

Seasons	Plants	Pollination Fees	Approximate Apiary Rent per Hive
Early Spring	Almond (California)	$5–$8	0
	Cherry	$6–$8	0
Late spring (major pollination season)	Apple and soft fruits	$9–$10	0
	Blueberry (with maple)	$5	0
	Cabbage	$8	0
	Cherry	$9–$10	0
	Cranberry	$9	0
Summer and early fall (major honey season)	Alfalfa	0	13¢–60¢
	Alfalfa (with pollination)	$3–$5	0
	Fireweed	0	25¢–63¢
	Mint	0	15¢–65¢
	Pasture	0	15¢– 65¢
	Red clover	0	65¢
	Red clover (with pollination)	$3–$6	0
	Sweet clover	0	20¢–25¢

Source: Steven N. S. Cheung, "The Fable of the Bees: An Economic Investigation," *The Journal of Law and Economics,* April 1973, pp. 11–33. Table adapted by permission of the University of Chicago Press. Copyright 1973 by the University of Chicago.

ANALYTICAL EXAMPLE 16.2

FLOODING HELL'S CANYON, DRAINING HETCH HETCHY

The Snake River between Idaho and Oregon passes through 200 miles of a geological formation known as Hell's Canyon—the deepest canyon in North America, including the Grand Canyon. From the canyon to the towering Seven Devils Peaks of Idaho and the beautiful Wallowa Mountains of Oregon, the area provides some of the most spectacular scenery in the country. The canyon is also the habitat of large numbers of elk, deer, and bighorn sheep, of huge flocks of redleg partridges, and, in the river itself, of salmon, steelhead, and sturgeon.

Hell's Canyon is also the best remaining site for developing hydroelectric power. Not surprisingly, plans were made in the 1960s to construct either two low dams (at the Mountain Sheep and Pleasant Valley sites) or one high dam (at Mountain Sheep). Conventional benefit-cost analysis, which *ignored* environmental costs, showed the high dam project to be worthwhile. The accompanying table weighs power and flood-control benefits against generating and transmission costs. The Federal Power Commission licensed the construction of the high dam, but the Secretary of the Interior appealed. The U.S. Supreme Court eventually ordered a reconsideration of the entire project that would assess the benefits of *not* developing the canyon.

The initial year's benefits from preserving the canyon for fishing, hunting, and the like were subsequently estimated at $.895 million. No reliable estimates could be made for the considerable value of the site for scientific research materials and opportunities. (Owing to the great vertical distance between the canyon floor and tops of adjacent rim crags, for example, virtually all of North America's ecological life zones can be found within only half a mile.) Nor was it possible to quantify the value people place on retaining the option (for themselves or future generations) of being able to visit such a remarkable site and not having it irrevocably destroyed. Nor was it possible to evaluate the destruction of the wildlife habitat (for migratory fish, waterfowl, and mammals). It seemed certain, however, that the present value of all environmental costs would exceed the present value of the high dam, shown in the table. Eventually, Congress passed a law prohibiting construction of the dam.

	Hell's Canyon Projects (in thousands of dollars per year, rounded)	
	Low Mountain Sheep–Pleasant Valley Complex	High Mountain Sheep Project
1976–80		
Benefits	38,985	40,901
Costs	44,513	39,597
Net benefits	− 5,441	1,304
1981–90		
Benefits	46,133	41,244
Costs	51,074	39,597
Net benefits	− 4,941	1,647
1991–2025		
Benefits	57,758	40,241
Costs	62,335	39,597
Net benefits	− 4,577	644
1976 present value for 1976–2025 period (discounted at 9 percent per year)	− 55,042	+ 13,809

Note: In 1987, a battle to save the spectacular Hetch Hetchy Valley of Yosemite National Park, fought and lost 74 years earlier, was reopened. Interior Secretary Hodel suggested that the reservoir that flooded the valley in the early 1900s to provide water for San Francisco be drained and the Hetch Hetchy restored as closely as possible to its original condition, including removal of the dam. Said Mayor Feinstein of San Francisco: "I think this is the worst idea I have heard since the sale of weapons to Iran."

Sources: Based on John V. Krutilla and Anthony C. Fisher, *The Economics of Natural Environments: Studies in the Valuation of Commodity and Amenity Resources* (Baltimore, Md.: The Johns Hopkins University Press, 1975), pp. 101–103. Copyright © 1975 by Resources for the Future, Inc. Published by The Johns Hopkins University Press. Adapted by permission. For recent developments, see *The New York Times,* August 6, 1987, p. 16.

Calculus Appendix

The material found in this appendix is provided for those who desire a calculus-based treatment of appropriate text sections.

SECTION 1A, p. 13. The *optimization principle* can be illustrated with calculus as follows: A total benefit curve, as in panel (a) of Figure 1.6, might be described by

$$TB = 10Q - .4Q^2$$

and total cost might be represented by an equation such as

$$TC = 5Q + .6Q^2$$

where Q represents the quantity of the activity in question. Then marginal benefit is

$$MB = \frac{dTB}{dQ} = 10 - .8Q$$

a line with negative slope as in panel (b), Figure 1.6. Then marginal cost is

$$MC = \frac{dTC}{dQ} = 5 + 1.2Q$$

a line with positive slope as in panel (b). The optimum comes at $MB = MC$, or when

$$10 - .8Q = 5 + 1.2Q$$
$$10 - 5 = 1.2Q + .8Q$$
$$5 = 2Q$$
$$Q = 2.5$$

The optimum Q can also be found by focusing on the net benefit, shown in panel (c), Figure 1.6. Given the above equations,

$$NB = TB - TC$$
$$= 10Q - .4Q^2 - (5Q + .6Q^2)$$
$$= 5Q - 1Q^2$$

For a maximum, the first derivative is set equal to zero; the second derivative is negative. Thus

$$\frac{dNB}{dQ} = 5 - 2Q = 0$$
$$5 = 2Q$$
$$Q = 2.5$$

as noted above. Furthermore,

$$\frac{d^2NB}{dQ^2} = -2$$

which confirms a maximum.

SECTION 2A, p. 38. When a choice between two consumption goods is involved, the meaning of the *indifference-curve slope* can be established with calculus as follows: Along any one indifference curve, total utility is a constant, $\overline{U}$. It is also a function of the quantities of good a and good b consumed, $U = U(Q_a, Q_b)$. The total differential of this function is

$$dU = \frac{\delta U}{\delta Q_a} dQ_a + \frac{\delta U}{\delta Q_b} dQ_b$$

and, because total utility is constant, $dU = 0$. Thus

$$-\frac{\delta U}{\delta Q_a} \cdot dQ_a = \frac{\delta U}{\delta Q_b} dQ_b \text{ and}$$

$$-\frac{dQ_a}{dQ_b} = \frac{\delta U/\delta Q_b}{\delta U/\delta Q_a} = \frac{MU_b}{MU_a}$$

This means that the (negative) indifference-curve slope (or $-dQ_a/dQ_b$), which is the marginal rate of substitution of b for a, equals the marginal-utility-b-to-a ratio.

SECTION 2B, p. 40. The *consumer's optimum* (Box 2.C) can be confirmed with calculus as follows: The utility function is $U = U(Q_a, Q_b)$; it is to be maximized subject to the budget constraint of $B = P_a Q_a + P_b Q_b$, while budget, B, and prices, P_a and P_b, are constants. The budget constraint can also be written as $B - P_a Q_a - P_b Q_b = 0$ and appears as such in the Lagrangian expression

$$\mathscr{L} = U(Q_a, Q_b) + \lambda(B - P_a Q_a - P_b Q_b) \quad (1)$$

This expression is to be maximized; the first-order conditions involve finding the partial derivatives with respect to the three unknowns (Q_a, Q_b, and the Lagrangian multiplier, λ) and setting them equal to zero:

$$\frac{\delta \mathscr{L}}{\delta Q_a} = \frac{\delta U}{\delta Q_a} - \lambda P_a = 0 \quad (2)$$

$$\frac{\delta \mathscr{L}}{\delta Q_b} = \frac{\delta U}{\delta Q_b} - \lambda P_b = 0 \quad (3)$$

$$\frac{\delta \mathscr{L}}{\delta \lambda} = B - P_a Q_a - P_b Q_b = 0 \quad (4)$$

Dividing (3) by (2),

$$\frac{P_b}{P_a} = \frac{\delta U/\delta Q_b}{\delta U/\delta Q_a} \quad (5)$$

Budget-line slope must equal indifference-curve slope for maximum utility.

SECTION 3A, p. 80. Given the equation of any demand function, *point elasticity* can be determined with calculus as follows: The kind of demand line featured in panel (a) of Figure 3.16, for example, might be represented by the equation $Q_{D_x} = a - bP_x$, where a is the horizontal intercept of the demand line and $-b$ is the reciprocal of the slope. Thus

$$\frac{dQ_{D_x}}{dP_x} = -b. \quad (1)$$

Yet it follows from our earlier formula that the own-price elasticity of demand *at a point* equals

$$\epsilon_D^{o-p} = \frac{dQ_{D_x}/Q_{D_x}}{dP_x/P_x} = \frac{dQ_{D_x}}{dP_x} \cdot \frac{P_x}{Q_{D_x}}. \quad (2)$$

Substituting (1) into (2), we get

$$\epsilon_D^{o-p} = \frac{-bP_x}{Q_{D_x}}. \quad (3)$$

This result confirms the lesson of Figure 3.15. Given a constant slope, $-b$ is a constant, but P_x and Q_{D_x} differ from one point on the demand line to the next; hence elasticity differs accordingly. As Q_{D_x} approaches zero, equation (3) tells us, elasticity approaches infinity; we move from point B toward A in Figure 3.15. Conversely, as

P_x approaches zero, equation (3) tells us, elasticity approaches zero as well; we move from point A toward B in Figure 3.15.

Now apply calculus to a linear demand function that relates the quantity demanded to the prices of two goods: $Q_{D_x} = a + bP_x + cP_y$. Then

$$\frac{\delta Q_{D_x}}{\delta P_y} = c, \qquad (4)$$

all else being equal. It follows from our earlier formula that the cross-price elasticity of demand *at a point* equals

$$\epsilon_D^{c-p} = \frac{dQ_{D_x}/Q_{D_x}}{dP_y/P_y} = \frac{dQ_{D_x}}{dP_y} \cdot \frac{P_y}{Q_{D_x}}. \qquad (5)$$

Substituting (4) into (5), we get

$$\epsilon_D^{c-p} = \frac{cP_y}{Q_{D_x}}. \qquad (6)$$

Depending on whether c is zero, less than zero, or greater than zero, goods x and y are independent, complements, or substitutes.

Consider, finally, a nonlinear Engel curve with the equation $Q_{D_x} = aY^c$. Then

$$\frac{dQ_{D_x}}{dY} = acY^{c-1}. \qquad (7)$$

It follows from our earlier formula that the income elasticity of demand *at a point* equals

$$\epsilon_D^Y = \frac{dQ_{D_x}/Q_{D_x}}{dY/Y} = \frac{dQ_{D_x}}{dY} \cdot \frac{Y}{Q_{D_x}}. \qquad (8)$$

Substituting (7) into (8), and noting that $aY^c = Q_{D_x}$, we get

$$\epsilon_D^Y = acY^{c-1}\left(\frac{Y}{Q_{D_x}}\right) = \frac{acY^c}{Q_{D_x}} = c. \qquad (9)$$

Similar determinations can be made for any other demand function.

SECTION 3B, p. 81. The relationship between *elasticity of demand and total revenue* can be confirmed with calculus thusly: Total revenue, $TR = P \cdot Q$. Therefore

$$\frac{dTR}{dQ} = P + Q\frac{dP}{dQ} = P + P\left(\frac{Q}{P} \cdot \frac{dP}{dQ}\right) \qquad (1)$$

$$= P + \frac{P}{\dfrac{P}{Q} \cdot \dfrac{dQ}{dP}}.$$

Given that elasticity of demand equals

$$\epsilon_D^{o-p} = \frac{dQ/Q}{dP/P} = \frac{P}{Q} \cdot \frac{dQ}{dP} \qquad (2)$$

we can substitute (2) into (1) to get

$$\frac{dTR}{dQ} = P + \frac{P}{\epsilon} = P - \frac{P}{|\epsilon|}. \qquad (3)$$

Thus, when

$$|\epsilon| > 1, \frac{dTR}{dQ} > 0.$$

TR moves in the same direction as Q (and, for a normal demand line, in the opposite direction from P).
When

$$|\epsilon| = 1, \frac{dTR}{dQ} = 0.$$

TR does not change as Q changes.
When

$$|\epsilon| < 1, \frac{dTR}{dQ} < 0.$$

TR moves in the opposite direction from Q (and, for a normal demand line, in the same direction as P).

SECTION 4A, p. 104. Consider how the text propositions about the production function can be verified with calculus: A *simple production* *function* of the type depicted in Figure 4.1 might be written as $Q = f(L)$, given $\overline{K}$, $\overline{T}$, and t, which means that maximum possible output, Q, is a function of (or depends on) the quantity of labor input, L, given fixed quantities of capital, K, and natural resources, T, along with a specified state of technology, t. Specifically, a function that exhibits first increasing and then diminishing returns to labor might take the form $Q = 100L^2 - 20L^3$. The corresponding *marginal product of labor* is the first derivative of this total-product function,

$$MPL = \frac{dQ}{dL} = 200L - 60L^2,$$

while the *average product of labor* is

$$APL = \frac{Q}{L} = 100L - 20L^2.$$

Sometimes these expressions are written as

$$MPL = \frac{dQ}{dL}\bigg|_{\overline{K},\overline{T},t} \text{ and } APL = \frac{Q}{L}\bigg|_{\overline{K},\overline{T},t,}$$

re-spectively, in order to remind the reader of the assumed constancy of other (nonlabor) inputs and technology. Note how easily one can determine the *maximum total product* (corresponding to a point such as *a* in Figure 4.1); namely, by setting the first derivative of the total-product function (or the marginal-product function) equal to zero (point *b*); while ensuring that the second derivative is negative. In the example, maximum Q comes at $MPL = 200L - 60L^2 = 0$, or when $L = 3.33$ and $Q = 370.37$. Furthermore, $\frac{d^2Q}{dL^2} = 200 - 120L$, which is negative at $L = 3.33$.

One can similarly determine the *maximum marginal product* (corresponding to a point such as *d* in Figure 4.1); namely, by setting the first derivative of the marginal-product function equal to zero; while ensuring that its second derivative is negative. In the example, maximum MPL comes at $\frac{dMPL}{dL} = \frac{d(dQ/dL)}{dL} = 200 - 120L =$

0, or when $L = 1.67$ and $Q = 185.74$. Note that $\frac{d^2MPL}{dL^2} = -120$.

Or consider the *maximum average product* (corresponding to a point such as *k* in Figure 4.1). All we need do is set the first derivative of the average-product function equal to zero, while ensuring that its second derivative is negative. In the example, maximum APL comes at $\frac{dAPL}{dL} = \frac{d(Q/L)}{dL} = 100 - 40L = 0$, or when $L = 2.5$ and $Q = 312.5$. Note that $\frac{d^2APL}{dL^2} = -40$. Note that the *slope of the average-product-of-labor curve* can also be described as

$$\frac{dAPL}{dL} = \frac{d(Q/L)}{dL} = \frac{L\left(\frac{dQ}{dL}\right) - Q\left(\frac{dL}{dL}\right)}{L^2}$$
$$= \frac{\frac{dQ}{dL} - \frac{Q}{L}}{L} = \frac{MPL - APL}{L}.$$

This implies that APL rises as L rises (and that $dAPL/dL$ is positive) as long as $MPL > APL$ (to the left of *k* in Figure 4.1). Similarly, APL falls as L rises (and $dAPL/dL$ is negative) as long as $MPL < APL$ (to the right of *k*). Finally, APL is at a maximum (and $dAPL/dL$ is zero) when $MPL = APL$ (at point *k* precisely). Indeed, in our current example, as noted above, maximum APL comes at $L = 2.5$ and equals $(312.5/2.5) = 125$. Yet at $L = 2.5$, MPL equals $200L - 60L^2 = 125$ as well. This is not surprising because, at the APL maximum, $\frac{dAPL}{dL} = 0$; hence $\frac{MPL - APL}{L} = 0$ and $MPL - APL = 0$ and $MPL = APL$.

SECTION 4B, p. 108. Note how calculus can help us interpret the meaning of the *isoquant slope:* Along any one isoquant, total output is a constant, $\overline{Q}$. It is also a function of the quantities of, say, capital and labor used, $Q = Q(K, L)$ The total differential of this function is

$$dQ = \frac{\delta Q}{\delta K}dK + \frac{\delta Q}{\delta L} \cdot dL$$

and, because total output is constant, $dQ = 0$. Thus

$$-\frac{\delta Q}{\delta K} \cdot dK = \frac{\delta Q}{\delta L} \cdot dL \text{ and}$$

$$-\frac{dK}{dL} = \frac{\delta Q/\delta L}{\delta Q/\delta K} = \frac{MPL}{MPK}$$

This means that the (negative) isoquant slope (or $-dK/dL$), which is the marginal rate of technical substitution of L for K, equals the marginal-product-of-labor-to-capital ratio.

SECTION 4C, pp. 114–15. The *product exhaustion theorem* can be proven quickly with the help of calculus: Given constant returns to scale,

$$\frac{dQ}{Q} = \frac{dL}{L} = \frac{dK}{K} = \frac{dT}{T} = c.$$

By the theorem of ratios, whenever

$$\frac{A}{B} = \frac{C}{D} = \frac{E}{F} = c,$$

then

$$\frac{xA + yC + zE}{xB + yD + zF} = c$$

as well. Therefore

$$\frac{dQ}{Q} = \frac{\frac{\delta Q}{\delta L} \cdot dL + \frac{\delta Q}{\delta K} \cdot dK + \frac{\delta Q}{\delta T} \cdot dT}{\frac{\delta Q}{\delta L} \cdot L + \frac{\delta Q}{\delta K} \cdot K + \frac{\delta Q}{\delta T} \cdot T} = c.$$

This implies, in turn, that

$$(MPL \cdot L) + (MPK \cdot K) + (MPT \cdot T) = Q$$

because the numerator of the last ratio is identical to the total differential, dQ. One can, similarly, show that rewarding inputs by their respective marginal products fails to exhaust the total product in the presence of increasing returns to scale, but more than exhausts it in the case of decreasing returns to scale.

SECTION 5A, p. 143. The *relationship between average and marginal* that is illustrated in panel (b), Figure 5.1 can be confirmed quickly with the help of calculus: Consider average total cost, $ATC = (TC/Q)$. When ATC is declining (as between h and k),

$$\frac{d\left(\frac{TC}{Q}\right)}{dQ} = \frac{\frac{dTC}{dQ} \cdot Q - \frac{dQ}{dQ} \cdot TC}{Q^2} < 0.$$

This means

$$\frac{dTC}{dQ} \cdot Q - TC < 0$$

and

$$\frac{dTC}{dQ} - \frac{TC}{Q} < 0.$$

Thus

$$MC - ATC < 0$$

and

$$MC < ATC.$$

When ATC is constant (at k),

$$\frac{d\left(\frac{TC}{Q}\right)}{dQ} = \frac{\frac{dTC}{dQ} \cdot Q - \frac{dQ}{dQ} \cdot TC}{Q^2} = 0.$$

This means

$$\frac{dTC}{dQ} \cdot Q - TC = 0$$

and

$$\frac{dTC}{dQ} - \frac{TC}{Q} = 0$$

Thus

$$MC - ATC = 0$$

and

$$\boldsymbol{MC = ATC.}$$

When ATC is rising (as to the right of k),

$$\frac{d\left(\dfrac{TC}{Q}\right)}{dQ} = \frac{\dfrac{dTC}{dQ} \cdot Q - \dfrac{dQ}{dQ} \cdot TC}{Q^2} > 0.$$

This means

$$\frac{dTC}{dQ} \cdot Q - TC > 0$$

and

$$\frac{dTC}{dQ} - \frac{TC}{Q} > 0.$$

Thus

$$MC - ATC > 0$$

and

$$\boldsymbol{MC > ATC.}$$

SECTION 5B, p. 144. A firm's *profit-maximizing rule* can be verified thusly with the help of calculus: The total net benefit from production is profit, Π, or the difference between total revenue, TR, and total cost, TC. To maximize Π, the first derivative of the profit function, $\Pi = TR - TC = f(Q) - g(Q)$ must be set equal to zero; the second derivative must be negative. [Note that total revenue is one function of

quantity produced, $TR = f(Q)$, while total cost is a different function of quantity, $TC = g(Q)$.] Thus $\dfrac{d\Pi}{dQ} = f'(Q) - g'(Q) = \dfrac{dTR}{dQ} - \dfrac{dTC}{dQ}$ $= MR - MC = 0$. Hence profit maximization requires $MR = MC$ or, in this case, $P = MC$. This corresponds to rule (c), Box 1.A. In addition, a maximum requires that

$$\frac{d^2\Pi}{dQ^2} = \frac{d^2TR}{dQ^2} - \frac{d^2TC}{dQ^2} < 0$$

or that

$$\frac{d^2TR}{dQ^2} < \frac{d^2TC}{dQ^2}.$$

This means that, at the profit-maximizing quantity, the rate of change of MR must be less than the rate of change of MC. Put differently, the marginal-cost curve must cut the marginal-revenue curve from below or when price is a given and thus has a zero rate of change; marginal cost must be rising as quantity produced is increased.

SECTION 5C, p. 153. A *firm's optimum* (Box 5.E) can be confirmed with the help of calculus: The production function is $Q = Q(L, K)$; it is to be maximized subject to the cost constraint of $TC_0 = P_L L + P_K K$, while total cost, TC_0, and input prices, P_L and P_K, are constants. The cost constraint can also be written as $TC_0 - P_L L - P_K K = 0$ and appears as such in the Lagrangian expression

$$\mathscr{L} = Q(L, K) + \lambda(TC_0 - P_L L - P_K K) \qquad \textbf{(1)}$$

This expression is to be maximized; the first-order conditions involve finding the partial derivatives with respect to the three unknowns (L, K, and the Lagrangian multiplier, λ) and setting them equal to zero:

$$\frac{\delta\mathscr{L}}{\delta L} = \frac{\delta Q}{\delta L} - \lambda P_L = 0 \qquad \textbf{(2)}$$

$$\frac{\delta \mathcal{L}}{\delta K} = \frac{\delta Q}{\delta K} - \lambda P_K = 0 \qquad (3)$$

$$\frac{\delta \mathcal{L}}{\delta \lambda} = TC_0 - P_L L - P_K K = 0 \qquad (4)$$

Dividing (2) by (3),

$$\frac{P_L}{P_K} = \frac{\delta Q/\delta L}{\delta Q/\delta K} = \frac{MP_L}{MP_K} = MRTS_{L/K} \qquad (5)$$

Isocost-line slope must equal isoquant slope for maximum output quantity, given a cost constraint. And note: Because $\dfrac{\delta \mathcal{L}}{\delta TC_0} = \lambda$, the value of λ indicates the extra output possible by relaxing the cost constraint by \$1 (that is, the *marginal product* associated with a \$1 change in inputs).

SECTION 5D, p. 153. When the optimization problem is not the maximization of output, given cost, but the minimization of cost, given output, a mathematical procedure similar to that used in Section 5C can be employed: The cost function is $TC = P_L L + P_K K$; it is to be minimized subject to the output constraint of $Q_0 = Q(L, K)$, while the input prices, P_L and P_K, and the output level, Q_0, are constants. The output constraint can also be written as $Q_0 - Q(L, K) = 0$ and appears as such in the Lagrangian expression

$$\mathcal{L} = P_L L + P_K K + \lambda[Q_0 - Q(L, K)] \qquad (1)$$

This expression is to be minimized; the first-order conditions involve finding the partial derivatives with respect to the three unknowns (L, K, and the Lagrangian multiplier, λ) and setting them equal to zero:

$$\frac{\delta \mathcal{L}}{\delta L} = P_L - \lambda \frac{\delta Q}{\delta L} = 0 \qquad (2)$$

$$\frac{\delta \mathcal{L}}{\delta K} = P_K - \lambda \frac{\delta Q}{\delta K} = 0 \qquad (3)$$

$$\frac{\delta \mathcal{L}}{\delta \lambda} = Q_0 - Q(L, K) = 0 \qquad (4)$$

Dividing (2) by (3),

$$\frac{P_L}{P_K} = \frac{\delta Q/\delta L}{\delta Q/\delta K} = \frac{MP_L}{MP_K} = MRTS_{L/K} \qquad (5)$$

Isocost-line slope must equal isoquant slope for minimum total cost, given an output constraint. And note: Because $\dfrac{\delta \mathcal{L}}{\delta Q_0} = \lambda$, the value of λ indicates the extra cost needed when relaxing the output constraint by 1 unit (that is, the *marginal cost* associated with a 1-unit change in output).

SECTION 5E, p. 165. Given the equation of any supply function, *point elasticity* can be determined with the help of calculus: Consider a linear supply function that is represented by the equation $Q_{S_x} = a + bP_x$, where a is the horizontal intercept of the supply line and b is the reciprocal of the slope. Thus

$$\frac{dQ_{S_x}}{dP_x} = b. \qquad (1)$$

Yet it follows from the Box 5.F formula that the price elasticity of supply *at a point* equals

$$\epsilon_S = \frac{dQ_{S_x}/Q_{S_x}}{dP_x/P_x} = \frac{dQ_{S_x}}{dP_x} \cdot \frac{P_x}{Q_{S_x}}. \qquad (2)$$

Substituting (1) into (2), we get

$$\epsilon_S = b \cdot \frac{P_x}{Q_{S_x}}. \qquad (3)$$

Since $Q_{S_x} = a + bP_x$, it follows that

$$\epsilon_S = \frac{bP_x}{a + bP_x}. \qquad (4)$$

Thus if a (the horizontal intercept) $= 0$, $\epsilon_S = 1$, regardless of slope and price (see

S_3 or S_4 in Figure 5.13). If $a > 0$, $\epsilon_S < 1$ at all points, but varies with price (see S_5 in Figure 5.13). If $a < 0$, $\epsilon_S > 1$ at all points, but again varies with price (see S_2 in Figure 5.13).

SECTION 6A, p. 196. Integral calculus can help us determine *consumers' and producers' surplus.* In Figure 6.8, if we denote the demand function by $P = f(Q)$ and equilibrium price and quantity by P^* and Q^*, respectively, the dotted triangle of consumers' surplus is

consumers' surplus

$$= \int_0^{Q^*} f(Q)dQ - P^*Q^*$$

If we denote the supply function by $P = g(Q)$ and equilibrium price and quantity by P^* and Q^*, respectively, the crosshatched triangle of producers' surplus is

producers' surplus

$$\mathscr{L} = P^*Q^* - \int_0^{Q^*} g(Q)dQ$$

Furthermore, given the precise demand and supply functions noted in Chapter 6, footnote 4,

consumers' surplus

$$= \int_0^{250}(11 - .02Q)dQ - 6(250)$$

$$= \left(11Q - \frac{.02Q^2}{2}\right)\Big]_0^{250} - 1500$$

$$= (2750 - 625) - 1500 = 625$$

producers' surplus

$$= 6(250) - \int_0^{250}(2 + .016Q)\, dQ$$

$$= 1500 - \left(2Q + \frac{.016Q^2}{2}\right)\Big]_0^{250}$$

$$= 1500 - (500 + 500) = 500$$

Both of these results can easily be checked geometrically in Figure 6.9 (by multiplying the respective triangles' base by height and dividing by 2).

SECTION 6B, p. 202. Figure 6.13 can also be analyzed with calculus. For example, we can determine (a) the excise tax that *maximizes* tax revenue and (b) what this maximum is. Given that

$$t = P_D - P_S$$
$$= 11 - .02Q_D - (2 + .016Q_S)$$
$$= 9 - .036Q$$

we know that $T = tQ = 9Q - .036Q^2$. To maximize T, the first derivative is set equal to zero; the second derivative must be negative:

$$\frac{dT}{dQ} = 9 - .072Q = 0$$

$$Q = 125$$

$$\frac{d^2T}{dQ^2} = -.072$$

Given $t = 9 - .036Q$, and a tax-revenue maximizing $Q = 125$, the ideal t, from the government's point of view, is $t = 4.5$. Thus maximum $T = 4.5(125) = 562.5$. (In that case, $P_D = 11 - .02(125) = 8.5$ and $P_S = 2 + .016(125) = 4$.)

SECTION 7A, p. 224–25. The *monopoly's profit-maximization rule* can be expressed succinctly with the help of calculus. Total revenue is a function of quantity produced, $TR = f(Q)$; total cost is a different function of quantity, $TC = g(Q)$; thus total profit is $\Pi = TR - TC = f(Q) - g(Q)$. Maximum profit occurs when the first derivative of the profit function equals zero, while the second derivative is negative. Thus $\dfrac{d\Pi}{dQ} =$

$$f'(Q) - g'(Q) = \frac{dTR}{dQ} - \frac{dTC}{dQ} = MR -$$

$MC = 0$. Hence profit maximization requires $MR = MC$. In addition, a maximum requires that

$$\frac{d^2\Pi}{dQ^2} = \frac{d^2TR}{dQ^2} - \frac{d^2TC}{dQ^2} < 0$$

or that

$$\frac{d^2TR}{dQ^2} < \frac{d^2TC}{dQ^2} .$$

This means that, at the profit-maximizing quantity, the rate of change of *MR* (the slope of the marginal-revenue line) must be less than the rate of change of *MC* (the slope of the marginal-cost line). Put differently, *MC* must cut *MR* from below, which is obviously the case in Figures 7.3 to 7.5 where, at the intersection points, the *MR* slope is negative, but the *MC* slope is positive. Consider, however, the accompanying graphs. Intersections *a* and *c* do, intersection *b* does not, denote profit maximization.

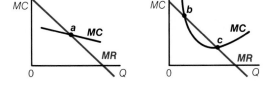

SECTION 7B, p. 228. For a calculus-based derivation of the *Lerner index of monopoly power* consider the following: A firm's total revenue is

$$TR = P \cdot Q. \qquad (1)$$

Marginal revenue, therefore, is

$$\frac{dTR}{dQ} = \frac{dP}{dQ} \cdot Q + \frac{dQ}{dQ} \cdot P \qquad (2)$$

$$MR = \frac{dP}{dQ} \cdot Q + P \qquad (3)$$

[For the perfect competitor, $(dP/dQ) = 0$, hence $MR = P$. For the monopoly, $(dP/dQ) \neq 0$, hence $MR \neq P$.] Recall from sections 4A and 4B that the (own-price) price elasticity of demand is

$$\epsilon = \frac{dQ}{dP} \cdot \frac{P}{Q} \qquad (4)$$

It follows that

$$\frac{dQ}{dP} = \epsilon\frac{Q}{P} \qquad (5)$$

and that

$$\frac{dP}{dQ} = \frac{1}{\epsilon} \cdot \frac{P}{Q} \qquad (6)$$

Combining (3) and (6), we get

$$MR = P + Q\left(\frac{1}{\epsilon} \cdot \frac{P}{Q}\right) = P + \frac{P}{\epsilon} \qquad (7)$$

Given that ϵ is typically negative, this implies

$$MR = P - \frac{P}{|\epsilon|} \qquad (8)$$

which is the expression given in the text.

SECTION 7C, p. 234. The text's *author versus publisher controversy* can also be analyzed with the help of calculus: The Figure 7.8 market demand line is $P = 25 - .5Q$; hence total revenue before royalty payments is $TR_b = PQ = 25Q - .5Q^2$. Accordingly, the author's marginal revenue is $MR_A = \frac{dTR_b}{dQ} = 25 - Q$. Given the author's marginal cost of $MC_A = 0$, the author's optimal position is confirmed as

$$MR_A = MC_A$$
$$25 - Q = 0$$
$$Q = 25, \text{ which implies}$$
$$P = 25 - .5(25) = 12.5.$$

If the author receives a fixed royalty payment of 20 percent of gross revenues, we can call the royalty rate $r = .2$ and confirm the maximum possible royalties as $R = rPQ = .2(12.5)\ 25 = 62.5$.

We can, similarly, confirm the text assertions concerning the publisher. Profit, Π, equals total revenue after royalty payments minus total cost. $TR_a = TR_b - R = TR_b - rTR_b = (1 - r)\ TR_b = .8(25Q - .5Q^2) = 20Q - .4Q^2 \cdot TC = 50 + 8Q$. Accordingly, $MR_p = 20 - .8Q$ and $MC_P = 8$. The publisher's optimal position is confirmed as

$$MR_P = MC_P$$
$$20 - .8Q = 8$$
$$12 = .8Q$$
$$Q = 15, \text{ which implies}$$
$$P = 25 - .5(15) = 17.5.$$

The publisher's profit equals

$$\Pi = TR_a - TC$$
$$= 20Q - .4Q^2 - (50 + 8Q)$$
$$= 12Q - .4Q^2 - 50$$
$$= 40.$$

Now imagine maximizing the *sum* of $\Pi + R$. We note that $\Pi + R = TR_a - TC + R$, but $TR_b = TR_a + R$, hence $\Pi + R = TR_b - TC$. To maximize $\Pi + R$, we differentiate with respect to Q and set equal to zero:

$$\frac{d(\Pi + R)}{dQ} = \frac{dTR_b}{dQ} - \frac{dTC}{dQ}$$
$$= MR_A - MC_P$$
$$= 0.$$

Thus maximum $\Pi + R$ requires $MR_A = MC_P$ (a quantity corresponding to n in Fig. 7.8). We can figure the results for our example:

$$MR_A = 25 - Q = MC_P = 8$$
$$Q = 17, \text{ which implies}$$
$$P = 25 - .5(17)$$
$$= 16.5$$

The implied total revenue, $TR_b = 16.5(17) = 280.5$; the implied total cost, $TC = 50 + 8(17) = 186$; hence maximum $\Pi + R = 94.5$. This exceeds the $\Pi + R$ found in the text when the publisher's choice prevails ($\Pi + R = 40 + 52.5 = 92.5$). Thus a mutually beneficial deal is conceivable.

SECTION 7D, p. 238. A mathematical exposition of *third-degree price discrimination* is not difficult: A firm operating in two markets, A and B, such that the absolute values of own-price elasticities are $|\epsilon_A| > |\epsilon_B|$, will have total-revenue, total-cost, and total-profit functions of

$$TR_A = f(Q_A) \tag{1}$$
$$TR_B = f(Q_B) \tag{2}$$
$$TC = f(Q_A + Q_B) \tag{3}$$
$$\Pi = TR_A + TR_B - TC \tag{4}$$
$$= f(Q_A) + f(Q_B) - f(Q_A + Q_B)$$

To maximize profit, we find, and set equal to zero, the partial derivatives with respect to Q_A and Q_B, respectively. Thus

$$\frac{\delta\Pi}{\delta Q_A} = \frac{\delta TR_A}{\delta Q_A} - \frac{\delta TC}{\delta Q_A} = 0 \tag{5}$$

$$\frac{\delta\Pi}{\delta Q_B} = \frac{\delta TR_B}{\delta Q_B} - \frac{\delta TC}{\delta Q_B} = 0 \tag{6}$$

According to (5), maximum profit requires $MR_A = MC$; according to (6), it requires $MR_B = MC$; hence it requires

$$MR_A = MR_B = MC \qquad (7)$$

as noted in the text. Now recall equation (8) of Section 7B: $MR = P - \dfrac{P}{|\epsilon|}$. This can be written as

$$MR = P\left(1 - \frac{1}{|\epsilon|}\right) \qquad (8)$$

Combining (7) and (8), we get this profit-maximizing condition:

$$P_A\left(1 - \frac{1}{|\epsilon_A|}\right) = P_B\left(1 - \frac{1}{|\epsilon_B|}\right) \qquad (9)$$

which means that

$$\frac{P_A}{P_B} = \frac{1 - \dfrac{1}{|\epsilon_B|}}{1 - \dfrac{1}{|\epsilon_A|}} \qquad (10)$$

This implies that $|\epsilon_A| > |\epsilon_B|$ goes with $P_A < P_B$ if profit is to be maximized. Just as noted in the text, higher price elasticity of demand calls for a lower price, lower price elasticity for a higher price.

SECTION 8A, p. 256. The text discussion of the *Cournot equilibrium* can be stated with the help of calculus: Cournot, who considered the sale of costless mineral water flowing from one or more privately owned springs, assumed $ATC = MC = 0$. Let the demand function be $P = 100 - Q$, as in Figure 8.1. Then total revenue *as well as total profit* equals $TR = \Pi = P \cdot Q = 100Q - Q^2$. If there is a single seller (monopoly), the first-order condition for profit maximization calls for

$$\frac{d\Pi}{dQ} = 100 - 2Q = 0;$$ hence $Q = 50$, hence $P = 50$, hence $\Pi = P \cdot Q = 2{,}500$ (as noted in the text). If there are two sellers (duopoly), $Q = q_1 + q_2$; and there are two profit functions:

$$\begin{aligned}\Pi_1 &= Pq_1 = (100 - Q)q_1 \\ &= (100 - q_1 - q_2)q_1 \\ &= 100q_1 - q_1^2 - q_1q_2\end{aligned}$$

$$\begin{aligned}\Pi_2 &= Pq_2 = (100 - Q)q_2 \\ &= (100 - q_1 - q_2)q_2 \\ &= 100q_2 - q_1q_2 - q_2^2\end{aligned}$$

Given the assumption about the behavior of sellers that $(\delta q_1/\delta q_2) = (\delta q_2/\delta q_1) = 0$, the corresponding first-order conditions for profit maximization are:

$$\frac{\delta\Pi_1}{\delta q_1} = 100 - 2q_1 - q_2 = 0$$

and

$$\frac{\delta\Pi_2}{\delta q_2} = 100 - q_1 - 2q_2 = 0.$$

This implies $q_1 = q_2 = 33\frac{1}{3}$, $Q = 66\frac{2}{3}$, $P = 33\frac{1}{3}$, and $\Pi = \Pi_1 + \Pi_2 = 1{,}111.11 + 1{,}111.11 = 2{,}222.22$ (as noted in the text).

Cournot showed that the equilibrium market quantity always equaled $Q = \dfrac{n}{n+1}Q^*$, where n is the number of sellers and Q^* is demand when price equals marginal cost (the perfectly competitive case). In our example, $Q^* = 100$ because $MC = 0$ and the horizontal market-demand-curve intercept at $P = 0$ is 100 (Figure 8.1, panel a). Thus,

when $n = 1$, $Q = \frac{1}{2}Q^* = 50$

when $n = 2$, $Q = \frac{2}{3}Q^* = 66\frac{2}{3}$

when $n = 3$, $Q = \frac{3}{4}Q^* = 75$

and, in the limit,

when $n \to \infty$, $Q = 1Q^* = 100$.

SECTION 11A, p. 358. Consider how calculus can verify the text discussion of selecting an *optimum input quantity:* The total net benefit from resource use is profit, Π, or the difference between total revenue, TR, and total cost, TC. To maximize profit, the first derivative of the profit function, $\Pi = TR - TC = f(L) - g(L)$ must be set equal to zero; the second derivative must be negative. [Note that total revenue, TR (which equals output quantity, Q, times output price, P_0), is one function of labor input, L, because $Q = f(L)$, given technology and other inputs, while total cost, TC (which equals variable cost, VC, plus fixed cost, FC), is another function of L, because $VC = h(L) = L \cdot P_L$, where L is the quantity and P_L is the price of labor.] Thus $\Pi = TR - TC = f(L) - g(L) = QP_0 - LP_L - FC$. Hence for maximum profit $\dfrac{d\Pi}{dL} = \left(\dfrac{dQ}{dL} \cdot P_0\right) - P_L = 0$ and $(MPP_L \cdot P_0) - P_L = 0$ and $MVP_L = P_L$. In addition, a maximum requires that $\dfrac{d^2\Pi}{dL^2} = \dfrac{d^2Q}{dL^2} < 0$. Marginal physical (and, therefore, marginal value) product must be falling.

SECTION 11B, p. 364. When a choice between income and leisure is involved, the meaning of the *indifference-curve slope* can be established with calculus as follows: Along any one indifference curve, total utility is constant, $\overline{U}$. It is also a function of income, I (or the implied quantities of consumer goods that can be consumed), and of leisure time, ℓ. Thus $U = U(I, \ell)$. The total differential of this function is

$$dU = \frac{\delta U}{\delta I}dI + \frac{\delta U}{\delta \ell}d\ell$$

and, because total utility is constant, $dU = 0$. Thus

$$-\frac{\delta U}{\delta I} \cdot dI = \frac{\delta U}{\delta \ell}d\ell \text{ and}$$

$$-\frac{dI}{d\ell} = \frac{\delta U/\delta \ell}{\delta U/\delta I} = \frac{MU_\ell}{MU_I}.$$

This means that the (negative) indifference-curve slope (or $-dI/d\ell$), which is the marginal rate of

substitution of ℓ for I, equals the marginal-utility-of-I-to-ℓ ratio.

SECTION 11C, p. 365. The *labor supplier's optimum* (Box 11.B) can be confirmed with calculus: The utility function is $U = U(I, \ )$; it is to be maximized subject to the budget constraint of $I = 24w - w\ell$, which can be written as $I - 24w + w\ell = 0$, and appears as such in the Lagrangian expression

$$\mathscr{L} = U(I, \ell) + \lambda(I - 24w + w\ell) \quad (1)$$

This expression is to be maximized; the first-order conditions involve finding the partial derivatives with respect to the three unknowns (I, ℓ, and the Lagrangian multiplier, λ) and setting them equal to zero:

$$\frac{\delta \mathscr{L}}{\delta I} = \frac{\delta U}{\delta I} + \lambda = 0 \quad (2)$$

$$\frac{\delta \mathscr{L}}{\delta \ell} = \frac{\delta U}{\delta \ell} + \lambda w = 0 \quad (3)$$

$$\frac{\delta \mathscr{L}}{\delta \lambda} = I - 24w + w\ell = 0 \quad (4)$$

Dividing (3) by (2),

$$w = \frac{\delta U/\delta \ell}{\delta U/\delta I} \quad (5)$$

Budget-line slope (the wage) must equal indifference-curve slope for maximum utility.

SECTION 11D, p. 378. The *profit-maximization rule* for a perfect competitor in the labor market who has monopoly power in the goods market ($MRP_L = W$) can be derived with calculus: A firm's profit, Π, equals total revenue, TR, minus total cost, TC. The latter, in our example, equals the sum of (variable) labor cost, $L \cdot W$, plus fixed cost, FC. Total revenue equals output, Q, times product price, P, the latter being itself a decreasing function of Q, hence of L. Thus the firm wants to maximize $\Pi = QP - LW - FC$, where W and FC are constants. The first derivative with respect to the variable labor input is

$$\frac{d\Pi}{dL} = \left(\frac{dQ}{dL} \cdot P\right) + \left(\frac{dP}{dQ} \cdot \frac{dQ}{dL} \cdot Q\right) - W.$$

Setting it equal to zero, we get

$$\underbrace{\frac{dQ}{dL}}_{MPP_L} \underbrace{\left(P + \frac{dP}{dQ} \cdot Q\right)}_{MR} = W$$

$$\underbrace{MPP_L \quad \cdot \quad MR}_{MRP_L} \qquad = W$$

$$MRP_L \qquad\qquad = W$$

And note: If, as happens under perfect competition, $(dP/dQ) = 0$, the above expression simplifies to

$$\frac{dQ}{dL}(P) = W \text{ and}$$

$$MPP_L \cdot P = W \text{ and}$$

$$MVP_L = W$$

which is the profit-maximizing condition noted in Chapter 11.

SECTION 11E, p. 382. The *profit-maximization rule* for a perfect competitor in the product market who has monopsony power in the labor market $(MVP_L = MO_L)$ can be derived with calculus, using the same notation as in Section 11D: $\Pi = TR - TC = QP - LW - FC$, as before, but this time P and FC are constants, while W is a function of labor quantity, L. Thus

$$\frac{d\Pi}{dL} = \frac{dQ}{dL} \cdot P - \left(W + L\frac{dW}{dL}\right).$$

Setting this first derivative equal to zero, we get

$$\underbrace{\frac{dQ}{dL} \cdot P}_{MVP_L} = \underbrace{W + L\frac{dW}{dL}}_{MO_L}$$

And note: If, as happens under perfect competition, $(dW/dL) = 0$, the above expression simplifies to

$$\frac{dQ}{dL} \cdot P = W \text{ or } MVP_L = W$$

which is the profit-maximizing condition noted in Chapter 11.

SECTION 14A, pp. 489 and 505. *Pareto's efficiency condition 4* can be derived as follows with the help of calculus: Because economic inefficiency exists as long as it is possible to increase the welfare of consumer X without decreasing that of consumer Y, let us maximize $U_X = f_X(a_X, b_X)$ or the utility of X that is a function of the quantities of good a and good b consumed by X, subject to the constraints that the utility of Y is constant and the total amounts of a and b available are fixed. These constraints can be written as

$$\overline{U}_Y = f_Y(a_Y, b_Y)$$

$$\overline{A} = a_X + a_Y$$

$$\overline{B} = b_X + b_Y.$$

To find the maximum, we create the Lagrangian expression

$$\begin{aligned}\mathcal{L} = &f_X(a_X, b_X) + \lambda_1[f_Y(a_Y, b_Y) - \overline{U}_Y]\\ &+ \lambda_2(a_X + a_Y - \overline{A})\\ &+ \lambda_3(b_X + b_Y - \overline{B}),\end{aligned}$$

differentiate partially with respect to $a_X,\ b_X,\ a_Y,$ and $b_Y,$ and set the respective results equal to zero. The results are

$$\frac{\delta\mathcal{L}}{\delta a_X} = \frac{\delta f_X}{\delta a_X} + \lambda_2 = 0$$

$$\frac{\delta\mathcal{L}}{\delta b_X} = \frac{\delta f_X}{\delta b_X} + \lambda_3 = 0$$

$$\frac{\delta\mathcal{L}}{\delta a_Y} = \lambda_1\frac{\delta f_Y}{\delta a_Y} + \lambda_2 = 0$$

$$\frac{\delta\mathcal{L}}{\delta b_Y} = \lambda_1\frac{\delta f_Y}{\delta b_Y} + \lambda_3 = 0$$

These last four expressions are equivalent to

$$MU_a^X = -\lambda_2$$

$$MU_b^X = -\lambda_3$$

$$MU_a^Y = -\frac{\lambda_2}{\lambda_1}$$

$$MU_b^Y = -\frac{\lambda_3}{\lambda_1}$$

where MU_a^X is the marginal utility of a consumed by X, etcetera. By division, we get

$$\frac{MU_a^X}{MU_b^X} = \frac{\lambda_2}{\lambda_3}$$

and also

$$\frac{MU_a^Y}{MU_b^Y} = \frac{\lambda_2}{\lambda_3}$$

Hence economic efficiency requires

$$\frac{MU_a^X}{MU_b^X} = \frac{MU_a^Y}{MU_b^Y}$$

which equals the condition given in the text

$$MRS_{a,b}^X = MRS_{a,b}^Y.$$

All other Pareto conditions of economic efficiency can be derived in an analogous fashion. In every case, the procedure is the same. And whenever we want to maximize the sum of two items, such as U_X and U_Y that cannot be measured cardinally and added together, we simply maximize one of them, such as U_X, while keeping the other constant (such as $\overline{U}_Y$ in our case).

Glossary*

acreage allotments government restrictions of the acreage that farmers may plant with a particular crop (7)

action branches branches emanating from an action point in a decision-tree diagram and representing the possible actions of the decision maker (9)

action point in a decision-tree diagram, a point of choice (at which the decision maker is in control), symbolized by a square (9)

actions in decision theory, the mutually exclusive decision alternatives open to a decision maker (9)

adverse selection a problem faced by insurance companies when those who buy insurance make up a biased sample such that their probability of loss differs markedly and, from the point of view of the company, adversely from the population at large (10)

allocative efficiency *see* **economic efficiency** (14)

allocative inefficiency *see* **economic inefficiency** (4)

ambient standards government rules specifying maximum quantities of pollutants a unit of the environment may contain (16)

antipirating agreements agreements among employers to act jointly in the hiring of labor and not to compete with each other for workers (11)

antitrust laws a series of laws, beginning with the Sherman Act of 1890, designed to restrain monopoly and foster competition (15)

applied research the application to a particular problem of the knowledge gained in basic research (10)

arc elasticity an (average) elasticity measure that refers to a section of a demand (or supply) line rather than a single point (3)

asset markets *see* **capital markets** (12)

atomistic competition the type of competition among buyers or among sellers in perfectly competitive markets in which each individual is too insignificant (like an atom in a large universe) to affect the equilibrium price (6)

average fixed cost (*AFC*) total fixed cost divided by total product, or the difference between average total and average variable costs (5)

average loss negative average profit (5)

average (physical) product (*APP*) the ratio of total product to the total quantity of an input used to produce the product (4)

---

*Chapter numbers appear in parentheses

average profit   total profit divided by total product, or price minus average total cost   (5)

average revenue (*AR*)   total revenue divided by total product; equals product price   (5)

average total cost (*ATC*)   total cost divided by total product   (5)

average value product (*AVP*)   the average physical product (*APP*) multiplied by product price   (11)

average variable cost (*AVC*)   total variable cost divided by total product   (5)

Averch-Johnson effect   production of a given output at higher-than-minimum cost by a regulated firm as a result of wasteful investment whenever the guaranteed return on investment exceeds the cost of capital   (15)

backward induction   a process by which a decision problem is solved with the help of a decision-tree diagram and that involves the computation, with the help of ultimate payoff values and event-branch probability values, of expected payoff values at each fork of the tree   (9)

bandwagon effect   a situation in which the demand for a good by each individual varies directly with the quantity others are seen to demand   (3)

basic research   scientific inquiry not directed toward any ''useful'' discovery   (10)

basing-point system   a system according to which oligopolists, regardless of their location, quote prices equal to those charged by one firm at a given place (the basing point) plus freight from the basing point to the buyer's location   (8)

Bayes's postulate   *see* **equal-likelihood criterion**   (9)

benefit   the advantage derived from an act of choice; an opportunity realized   (1)

benefit-cost analysis   the quantification of the benefits and costs of all contemplated government projects, the rejection of those with benefit-cost ratios below unity, and the apportionment of the budget among those remaining projects that have the highest benefit-cost ratios   (16)

Bertrand model   a model of oligopolistic behavior that focuses on price rather than quantity adjustments   (8)

bilateral monopoly   a situation in which a market contains not only a single seller (monopoly), but in which this seller also faces a single buyer (monopsony)   (11)

brand loyalty   the making of repeat purchases of a given brand by consumers who have ceased to sample other brands   (8)

break-even analysis   the graphical juxtaposition of expected-total-revenue and expected-total-cost lines for a prospective business, in order to determine the minimum sales volume required to avoid losses   (5)

break-even point   a level of output at which total revenue equals total cost and at which price equals average total cost   (5)

budget line   a graph of all the alternative combinations of two goods that a consumer is able to buy in a given period at current market prices by fully using a given budget   (2)

bureaucracy   the entire institutional structure through which political decisions are implemented   (16)

bureaucrats   people who work for government agencies   (16)

buying hedge   hedging a short position in the spot market by buying futures contracts now and selling them later   (10)

capacity output   the output level associated with the minimum average total cost achievable from a given plant   (5)

capital   the stock of all useful things or assets that yield streams of income over time   (12); *see also* **capital resources, financial capital,** and **human capital**

capital budgeting   the process of identifying available investment opportunities, selecting investment projects to be carried out, and arranging for their financing   (12)

capitalism   an economic system in which most resources are privately owned   (13)

capitalization   the process of calculating capitalized value   (12)

capitalized value   the present value of an income stream produced by an asset   (12)

capital markets   markets in which certificates of indebtedness are traded, along with ownership claims to the stocks of natural resources and of physical capital goods   (12)

capital resources   productive ingredients made by people, including structures, equipment, inventories   (1)

cartel   a group of conspiring sellers acting as one and making joint price-quantity decisions with a view toward earning a larger profit than competition would allow   (7)

certificate of indebtedness   an IOU or promise by the issuer to make future payments of money to the holder   (12)

CES production function   a production function with a constant elasticity of input substitution   (4)

change in demand   a shift in a demand line indicating a change in the amount of something people wish to buy in a period—in spite of unchanged price and because of other factors, such as a change in the number of buyers or in their unique circumstances   (3)

change in quantity demanded   a movement, in response to a change in an item's own price, along a given demand line (that relates the quantity demanded of an item to its own price, all else being equal)   (3)

change in quantity supplied   a movement, in response to a change in an item's own price, along a given supply line (that relates the quantity supplied of an item to its own price, all else being equal)   (5)

change in supply   a shift in a supply line that indicates a change in the amount of something people wish to sell in a period—in spite of unchanged price and because of other factors, such as a change in the number of sellers or a change in their unique circumstances   (5)

closed shops   firms operating under a collective bargaining agreement that forbids the hiring of nonunion workers   (11)

Coase theorem   ''under perfect competition and in the absence of income effects and transactions costs, voluntary negotiated agreements among private parties generating or being affected by externalities will lead to the same resource allocation (and output mix) regardless of how property rights are assigned among these parties''   (16)

Cobb-Douglas production function   a production function relating output, Q, to labor and capital inputs, L and K, in the form of $Q = AL^a K^b$, which has a constant elasticity of input substitution equal to unity and in which the sum of parameters $a + b$, if equal to, greater than, or smaller than unity, indicates the presence of constant, increasing, or decreasing returns to scale, respectively   (4)

cobweb cycle   the tendency of the prices and quantities of some goods to rise above and then fall below some intermediate level in alternate periods   (6)

coefficient of relative effectiveness   the reciprocal of the **payback period**   (12)

coinsurance   an arrangement whereby the insured commit themselves to shoulder a fixed percentage of any loss   (10)

commutative justice   a situation in which goods are apportioned among people as a result of free choices by people all of whom enjoy as nearly equal opportunities as possible in the process of resource allocation   (14)

compensating wage differentials   wage differences that offset nonmonetary differences in the perceived attractiveness of jobs   (11)

complementary goods   two goods such that the quantity demanded of one varies inversely with the price of the other, all else being equal; goods with a negative cross-price elasticity   (3)

complementary inputs   inputs with the characteristic that a change in the quantity of one changes the marginal physical products of other inputs in the same direction   (11)

compounding   the process of computing, with

the help of the interest rate, the future value of present dollars   (12)

concentration ratio   the percentage of industry sales attributable to a given number of largest firms, usually the 4, 8, 20, and 50 largest companies   (8)

conflict curve   another name for the **contract curve** in the Edgeworth box diagram, so called because people in efficient positions on the curve can make utility gains only at the expense of other people   (14)

conglomerate mergers   mergers of firms that have neither competitive nor buyer-seller relations   (8)

consent agreement   an agreement between a prosecutor and an accused party according to which a suit is dropped in exchange for voluntary ameliorative action by the accused   (15)

constant-cost industry   an industry in which the product's normal price is unchanged after the industry has ceased to expand or contract   (6)

constant returns to a variable input   constancy in an input's marginal (physical) product as a larger quantity of the input is used, all else being equal   (4)

constant returns to scale   a characteristic of the production function such that a simultaneous and equal percentage change in the use of all physical inputs leads to an identical percentage change in physical output   (4)

consumers' surplus   the difference between the maximum sum of money consumers would pay for a given quantity and the actual sum they do pay   (6)

consumption-indifference curve   a graph of all the alternative combinations of two consumption goods that yield the same total of utility and among which a utility-maximizing consumer would be indifferent   (2)

consumption-possibilities frontier   *see* **budget line**   (2)

contestable markets   markets into which entry is free and from which exit is costless   (8)

contingent-claim markets   markets in which people trade rights to variable quantities of

particular goods—the quantities being dependent on the occurrence of specified "states of the world"   (10)

contract curve   the locus of all the efficient points in the Edgeworth box diagram, so called because people in inefficient positions not on the curve can make mutually beneficial contracts to achieve efficiency on the curve   (14)

copyright   the exclusive right to the production, publishing, or sale of a literary, musical, or artistic work   (7)

cost   the disadvantage associated with an act of choice; the most highly valued alternative benefit forgone; an opportunity lost   (1)

costs of exchange   *see* **transactions costs**   (13)

cost-effectiveness studies   *see* **benefit-cost analysis**   (16)

Cournot equilibrium   that output combination between two oligopolists that does not elicit further reactions from either one of them   (8)

criterion of insufficient reason   *see* **equal-likelihood criterion**   (9)

cross-price elasticity of demand   the percentage change in quantity demanded of one good divided by the percentage change in the price of another good, all else being equal   (3)

cross-section studies   studies comparing economic data pertaining to different populations during the same past period of time   (3)

deadweight loss   a loss of consumers' or producers' surplus that is not offset by anyone else's gain   (6)

decision branches   *see* **action branches**   (9)

decision fork   *see* **action point**   (9)

decision node   *see* **action point**   (9)

decision point   *see* **action point**   (9)

decision theory   a variety of methods that can be employed in the systematic analysis and solution of decision-making problems that arise because uncertainty exists about future events over which the decision maker has no control, but which are bound to influence the ultimate outcome of a decision   (9)

decision tree a summary of a decision-making situation in the context of uncertainty, showing graphically and in chronological order from left to right every potential action, event, and payoff (9)

decreasing-cost industry an industry in which the product's normal price is lower after the industry has ceased to expand or is higher after it has ceased to contract (6)

decreasing returns to scale a characteristic of the production function such that a simultaneous and equal percentage change in the use of all physical inputs leads to a smaller percentage change in physical output (4)

deductible a fixed dollar amount by which any insurance company benefit payment falls short of a loss suffered by an insured (10)

deliberate coordination *see* **managerial coordination** (13)

demand a set of price-quantity combinations that represents the alternative amounts of an item that would be bought during a given period at all conceivable prices of this item, all else being equal (3)

derived demand a demand (such as the demand for resource services) that is derived from the demand in other markets (such as the demand for goods) (11)

desire for goods the quantities of goods people would take if all goods were available at zero prices (1)

diminishing returns to a variable input declines in an input's marginal (physical) product as a larger quantity of the input is used, all else being equal (4)

direct costs costs that can be attributed to the production of a particular unit of output (5)

discounting the process of computing, with the help of the interest rate, the present value of future dollars (12)

discount rate the interest rate used in discounting (12)

discrimination the making of irrelevant distinctions, as on the basis of race or sex, as a result of malevolent tastes (11)

diseconomies of scale factors, such as decreasing returns to scale and others, that cause the long-run average-total-cost curve to slope upward as output is increased (5)

distributive justice a situation in which goods are apportioned by an authority seeking to act justly, usually by consulting a personal characteristic (such as hours worked) that measures the recipient's merit (14)

dominant action in decision theory, an action that is unambiguously superior to an alternative action because it produces payoffs that are as good as or better than those of the alternative action no matter which event occurs (9)

dominant firm a firm that supplies at least half of the market and has no significant competitors, except for a fringe of numerous small firms that sell all they like at the dominant firm's price (8)

economic efficiency a situation within an economy in which it is impossible, with given technology, to produce a larger welfare total from given stocks of resources, and, therefore, in which it is impossible, through some reallocation of resources or goods among different households or firms, to make some or all people better off (in their own judgment) without making others worse off (in *their* own judgment) (14)

economic equity a situation in which the apportionment of resources or goods among people is considered fair (14)

economic inefficiency a situation within an economy in which it is possible, with given technology, to produce a larger welfare total from given stocks of resources and, therefore, in which it is possible, through some reallocation of resources or goods among diffferent households or firms, to make some or all people better off (in their own judgment) without making others worse off (in *their* own judgment) (4, 14)

economic justice *see* **commutative justice** and **distributive justice,** or **economic equity** (14)

economic order state in which the specialized activities of all the people engaged in the division of labor are well coordinated (13)

economic power   the capacity to make and enforce decisions on the allocation of resources and the apportioning of goods   (15)

economic rent   that portion of a payment for the services of any resource (human, natural, or capital) that exceeds the minimum amount necessary to bring forth the quantity that is in fact supplied; *see also* **pure rent** and **quasi rent**   (11, 12A)

economics   the study of how people allocate scarce resources (that usually have many alternative uses) to produce goods and of how they apportion these scarce goods among themselves   (1)

economies of mass production   *see* **economies of scale**   (5)

economies of scale   factors, such as increasing returns to scale and others, that cause the long-run average-total-cost curve to slope downward as output is increased (5)

Edgeworth box   a diagram that highlights the crucial distinctions between economic efficiency and inefficiency and between economic efficiency and economic equity   (14)

education vouchers   divisible certificates earmarked for the purchase of educational services   (16)

effective annual rate of interest   the interest rate that is in effect paid *per year*   (12)

elasticities of demand   exact measures of the responsiveness of quantity demanded to other variables; *see* **own-price elasticity of demand, income elasticity of demand,** and **cross-price elasticity of demand**   (3)

elasticity of input substitution   the percentage change in the ratio of two inputs used in producing a given output quantity, divided by the associated percentage change in the marginal rate of technical substitution between these inputs   (4)

emission standards   government rules specifying maximum quantities of pollutants that may be released by any one polluter   (16)

Engel curve   a graph of the alternative amounts of an item a person (or group of persons) would buy during a given period at all conceivable incomes, all else being equal   (3)

Engel's law   the observation that food expenditures take a smaller percentage of income the larger income is   (3)

entrepreneur   a special type of person acting in the face of uncertainty; an innovator who first puts new ideas to practical use, translating inventions into new products, new qualities of old products, and new processes of production   (10)

entry-level jobs   jobs that require little training or experience and allow untrained and inexperienced job seekers to find employment, gain experience, and depart these stepping-stones for better jobs   (11)

envelope curve   a curve to which other curves are invariantly tangent, such as the **planning curve,** which is tangent to all the curves of short-run average total cost   (5)

equal-likelihood criterion   in decision theory, the assignment of equal prior probabilities to all possible events when absolutely nothing is known about the likelihood of occurrence of these events   (9)

equal-product curve   *see* **isoquant**   (4)

equalizing wage differentials   *see* **compensating wage differentials**   (11)

event branches   branches emanating from an event point in a decision-tree diagram and representing the possible events confronting the decision maker   (9)

event point   in a decision-tree diagram, a point of chance (at which the decision maker exercises no control but at which ''nature'' is in charge), symbolized by a circle   (9)

events   in decision theory, the mutually exclusive future occurrences that will affect the outcome of any present action taken but that are not under the control of a decision maker   (9)

event uncertainty   uncertainty that exists when future events, which affect the outcome of present decisions, have not yet occurred and no one knows what they will be like   (9)

excess burden   a decrease in utility that is unnecessary in order to collect a given tax revenue and that could be avoided by the use of a different type of tax   (2)

excess capacity   the difference between a monopolistically competitive firm's capacity output and its profit-maximizing lower actual output   (8)

excise tax   a tax per unit of product   (6)

exclusive contracts   contracts by which sellers agree to lease or sell a commodity on the condition that the lessees or purchasers thereof shall not use or deal in the commodity of competitors   (15)

exclusive franchise   a governmental grant to a single seller of the exclusive right to produce and sell a good (7)

expected monetary value (*EMV*)   the sum of the weighted payoffs associated with an action, the weights being the probabilities of the alternative events that produce the various possible payoffs   (9)

expected-monetary-value criterion   one of several probabilistic criteria for making decisions under uncertainty according to which a decision maker determines an expected monetary value for each possible action and selects the action with the optimal expected monetary value (the largest *EMV* is optimal if the objective is to maximize some benefit; the smallest *EMV* is optimal if the objective is to minimize some cost)   (9)

expected opportunity loss (*EOL*)   the sum of the weighted opportunity-loss values associated with an action, the weights being the probabilities of the alternative events that produce the various possible opportunity losses   (9)

expected-opportunity-loss criterion   one of several probabilistic criteria for making decisions under uncertainty according to which a decision maker determines an expected opportunity loss for each possible action and selects the action with the smallest of these values   (9)

expected regret value   *see* **expected opportunity loss**   (9)

expected utility (*EU*)   the sum of the weighted utilities associated with an action, the weights being the probabilities of the alternative events that produce the various possible utility payoffs   (9)

expected-utility criterion   one of several probabilistic criteria for making decisions under uncertainty according to which a decision maker determines the expected utility for each possible action and selects the action that maximizes it   (9)

explicit costs   costs that the owners of firms incur when acquiring resource services from other households or when acquiring intermediate goods from other firms   (5)

exploitation   according to J. B. Clark, a situation in which the price for a unit of resource service falls short of the unit's marginal value product; according to Karl Marx, a situation in which workers as a group do not receive the entire national product   (11)

external diseconomies   unfavorable technological or pecuniary externalities   (6)

external economies   favorable technological or pecuniary externalities   (6)

fair gamble   a gamble with an expected monetary value of zero, any expectation of gain being exactly offset by an expectation of loss   (9)

fair insurance   an insurance with an expected monetary value of zero, any expectation of gain being exactly offset by an expectation of loss   (10)

fair-trade laws   laws allowing manufacturers to fix minimum prices for their products and, if a single retailer agrees to it, to bind all retailers to it   (7)

featherbedding   labor-union practices that force employers to continue paying workers who are not really needed because their work is being done, or could be done, by fewer workers or by machines   (11)

feedback effect   the effect of secondary changes in other markets on the market in which an initial change in supply or demand occurred   (13)

field of choice   the set of all alternative combinations of two goods over which a consumer might conceivably exercise choice   (2)

final goods   goods produced by domestic producers during a period and not used up by the same or other domestic producers during the same period in the making of other goods (13)

financial capital claims (such as money, stocks, deeds, or bonds) against real resources (1)

first-degree price discrimination a situation in which a seller charges each buyer for each unit bought the maximum price the buyer is willing to pay for that unit (7)

fixed cost (*FC*) cost that does not vary with the level of production during a given period and that is attributable to the use of fixed inputs (5)

focal-point price a price that has a compelling prominence for reasons of aesthetics, precedent, or symmetry (8)

free-rider problem the unwillingness of individuals voluntarily to help cover the cost of a pure public good and their eagerness to let others produce the good so they can enjoy its benefits at a zero cost (16)

functional distribution of income the apportionment of national income among the owners of human, natural, and capital resources (12A)

futures markets markets in which people commit themselves now to trade, at specified dates in the future, specified quantities and qualities of goods at specified prices (10)

game any decision-making situation in which the payoff to people's choices depends not only on them (and nature), but also on other people's choices (9)

game theory a method of studying decision making in situations of conflict when the fates of those who seek different goals are interlocked (9)

general equilibrium a state of the economy in which billions of optimizing decisions by millions of decision makers are compatible with each other because all input and output markets are in equilibrium at the same time (13)

gentlemen's agreements informal oral understandings among oligopolists in the same industry that they will maintain a certain minimum price (8)

Giffen's paradox a situation in which consumers buy less of an item when its price is lower and more when it is higher, all else being equal (3)

Gini coefficient the ratio of two areas in the Lorenz curve graph that summarizes the extent of income or wealth inequality; the ratio of the area between the line of perfect equality and actual inequality to the area between the line of perfect equality and the line of perfect inequality (14)

goods the means by which people satisfy their material wants, including tangible commodities as well as intangible services (1)

hedging the taking of equal and opposite positions in the spot and futures markets, with the hope that this will prevent a loss due to price fluctuations (10)

Hicksian income-compensated demand curve a demand curve relating price and quantity, while holding *real* income constant because the utility-increasing consequence of any price cut is immediately compensated (and precisely offset) by a cut in money income that leaves overall utility unchanged; the utility-decreasing consequence of a price increase is similarly compensated by an increase in money income (3)

holding company a corporation established for the sole purpose of acquiring a controlling stock interest in two or more competing corporations in an industry and then jointly running their affairs (15)

homogeneous production function a production function such that multiplication of each of the variables in the function by a constant, c, multiplies the total function by some power, n, of that constant; for example, given $Q = f(L,K,T)$, $c^nQ = f(cL, cK, cT)$ (4)

horizontal mergers mergers of firms selling closely related products in the same geographic market (8)

Hotelling's paradox the fact that, under certain conditions, competition by means of product differentiation leads to products that are hardly differentiated at all (8)

human capital the health care, education, and training embodied in people (1, 12)

human resources people able and willing to participate in the process of production (1)

identification problem the difficulty, encountered in time-series and cross-section studies, of identifying a large number of potential data (such as those on a market-demand line) from a few historical data, each of which may belong to a different set of potential data (3)

impact effect the effect of an initial change in supply or demand on the market concerned (13)

imperfect competition a market situation, other than pure monopoly or cartel, in which individual sellers, nevertheless, face downward-sloping demand curves and thus have some measure of control over price (8)

implicit costs hidden costs that the owners of firms incur when using the services of their own resources in their own firm instead of hiring them out to collect the maximum income available elsewhere (5)

import quota a maximum physical limit on the amount of a good that may be imported (6, 7)

inadmissible action in decision theory, an action that is unambiguously inferior to an alternative action because it produces payoffs that are at best as good as and often worse than those of the alternative action no matter which event occurs (9)

income-consumption line a line indicating how the optimum quantities of two consumption goods change in response to a change in income, all else being equal (3)

income effect one of two effects resulting from a price change: given money income, the income effect causes a consumer, for example, to buy more of a normal and less of an inferior good when a price falls (which implies an increase in real income) and the opposites (3)

income elasticity of demand the percentage change in quantity demanded of a good divided by the percentage change in the income of consumers, all else being equal (3)

increasing-cost industry an industry in which the product's normal price is higher after the industry has ceased to expand or is lower after it has ceased to contract (6)

increasing returns to a variable input increases in an input's marginal (physical) product as a larger quantity of the input is used, all else being equal (4)

increasing returns to scale a characteristic of the production function such that a simultaneous and equal percentage change in the use of all physical inputs leads to a larger percentage change in physical output (4)

incremental-profit analysis the comparison of the expected marginal revenue with the expected marginal cost of a prospective action in order to determine the difference between the two (which is the extra, incremental, or marginal profit the action is likely to bring to the business) (5)

independent goods two goods such that the quantity demanded of one does not respond to a changed price of the other, all else being equal; goods with zero cross-price elasticity (3)

independent inputs inputs with the characteristic that a change in the quantity of one has no effect on the marginal physical products of other inputs (11)

indifference curve *see* **consumption-indifference curve** (2)

indirect costs costs that cannot be attributed to the production of a particular unit of output (5)

indivisibilities the characteristic of pure public goods that makes their benefits indivisibly available to all people in society (16)

industrial organization a specialized field of economic study that blends abstract price theory with empirical research (8)

inferior goods goods of which smaller physical quantities are consumed at higher than at lower incomes, all else being equal; goods with a negative income elasticity (3)

informative advertising advertising that provides genuine information to buyers about the very existence of products or sellers, about price, and about quality (8)

innovation the activity of an entrepreneur who first puts a new idea to practical use (10)

input-output table a table that lists the flows of all newly produced goods and of resource services between all their suppliers and recipients and thereby illustrates the web of interrelationships in an economy (13)

input standards government rules specifying the types of inputs polluters may use (16)

interlocking directorates an arrangement under which two or more competing corporations have in common some of the members of their boards of directors (15)

intermediate goods goods produced by domestic producers during a period and then used up by the same or other domestic producers during the same period in the making of other goods (13)

internal diseconomies *see* **decreasing returns to scale** (6)

internal economies *see* **increasing returns to scale** (6)

internalities the consequences of the pursuit by government officials of their internal, private goals instead of publicly announced, official ones (16)

internal rate of return the interest rate that makes the net present value of an investment project just equal to zero (12)

invention the intellectual act of generating a new idea (10)

Invisible Hand *see* **market coordination** (13)

isocost line a graph of all the alternative combinations of two inputs that a firm can buy in a given period at current market prices, while incurring the same total cost (5)

isoquant a graph of all the alternative combinations of two inputs that yield the same maximum total product and among which a producer would be indifferent from a purely technical point of view (4)

kinked demand curve the demand curve faced by an oligopolist who believes that rivals will not match increases of the present price but will promptly match price decreases (8)

Knightian risk a situation in which people cannot foretell the specific outcome of an action because two or more outcomes are possible but in which people do know the types of outcomes and the associated objective probability distribution (9)

Knightian uncertainty a situation in which people cannot foretell the specific outcome of an action because two or more outcomes are possible and in which people neither know the types of outcomes nor the associated probability distribution (9)

knowledge problem the difficulty of making use jointly of all the knowledge relevant to achieving economic efficiency because such knowledge is not available to a single mind in its totality but is found, in billions of dispersed fragments, in the minds of countless separate individuals (14)

labor union a cartel among workers for the joint sale of their labor (11)

Laplace criterion *see* **equal-likelihood criterion** (9)

law of diminishing returns ''given technical knowledge and a fixed quantity of some input, equal successive additions of another input to the process of production eventually yield diminishing additions to total output'' (4)

''law'' of downward-sloping demand the tendency of buyers normally to buy larger quantities of something when its price is lower, all else being equal (3)

law of large numbers the observation that what is unpredictable and subject to chance for the individual is predictable and uniform in a mass of like individuals (10)

''law'' of upward-sloping supply the tendency of sellers normally to offer for sale larger quantities of an item when its price is higher, all else being equal (5)

law of variable proportions *see* **law of diminishing returns** (4)

leisure all nonmarket uses of time (11)

Leontief inverse matrix a table showing, for those goods of which a portion of output is used up in the process of production itself, the total outputs ultimately required if one unit of such a good is to be delivered to final users (13)

Lerner index a measure of the degree of monopoly power exercised by a firm, equal to $\dfrac{P - MC}{P}$ or $\dfrac{1}{|\epsilon|}$, where P is price, MC is marginal cost, and $|\epsilon|$ is the absolute value of the price elasticity of demand (7)

limit price a price that prevents the entry of new rivals into an oligopolistic industry (8)

line of actual inequality *see* **Lorenz curve** (14)

line of perfect equality the hypothetical position of the Lorenz curve if the same amount of income (or wealth) went to each member of the group in question (14)

line of perfect inequality the hypothetical position of the Lorenz curve if all of income (or wealth) went to one member of a group and none of it to other members (14)

loanable-funds market a market in which the money of some people is traded for certificates of indebtedness (or IOUs) issued by other people (12)

long hedge *see* **buying hedge** (10)

long position a net asset position in which more of something is owned than owed (10)

long run a time period so long that a firm can vary the quantities of all its inputs (4)

long-run equilibrium market equilibrium in a period so long that new firms can enter the industry and old ones can leave it or change the size of their plants (6)

Lorenz curve a graphical device that shows the way in which income (or wealth) is apportioned among the members of any group and highlights the extent of equality or inequality among them (14)

loss negative profit (5)

lump-sum tax a fixed dollar levy imposed on people regardless of what they do (2)

luxuries normal goods the consumption of which rises more rapidly than income; goods with a positive income elasticity above unity (3)

macroeconomics the study of the aggregate flows of resources and goods and of the overall level of prices (1)

managerial coordination the deliberate coordination by a manager or central planner of the separate economic activities of people engaged in a division of labor; also called the system of the **Visible Hand** (13)

marginal benefit (*MB*) the increase (or decrease) in an activity's overall benefit that is attributable to a unit increase (or decrease) in the level of that activity, all else being equal (1)

marginal conditions conditions that must be fulfilled to achieve economic efficiency (14)

marginal cost (*MC*) an increase (or decrease) in an activity's overall cost that is attributable to a unit increase (or decrease) in the level of that activity, all else being equal (1, 5)

marginal external benefit (*MEB*) the change in the total benefit of some households (or firms) that is associated with a unit change in the consumption (or output) of others (16)

marginal external costs (*MEC*) the change in the total cost of some firms (or households) that is associated with a unit change in the output (or consumption) of others (16)

marginal internal benefit *see* **marginal private benefit** (16)

marginal internal cost *see* **marginal private cost** (16)

marginalist thinking thinking about the objective possibility and subjective welfare implication of small changes in variables (1)

marginal outlay (*MO*) the change in a buyer's total outlay divided by the corresponding change in the total quantity purchased (11)

marginal (physical) product (*MPP*)   the physical change in the total product attributable to a unit change in some input in the productive process, all else being equal   (4)

marginal private benefit (*MPB*)   the marginal benefit enjoyed by the household (or firm) actually consuming (or producing) a good   (16)

marginal private cost (*MPC*)   the marginal cost borne by the firm (or household) actually producing (or consuming) a good   (16)

marginal productivity theory of income distribution   a theory according to which the apportionment of total output among the suppliers of human, capital, and natural resource services that made the output can be explained by the quantities of these inputs that are employed, on the one hand, and their respective marginal products, on the other hand   (4)

marginal profit   the difference between marginal revenue and marginal cost   (5)

marginal rate of substitution (*MRS*)   the rate at which a consumer is willing to exchange, as a matter of indifference, a little bit of one variable (say, the consumption of leisure or butter) for a little bit of another variable (say, the consumption of apples received for the sacrifice of leisure or butter)   (14)

marginal rate of technical substitution (*MRTS*)   the rate at which a producer is able to exchange, without affecting the quantity of output produced, a little bit of one input (say, labor) for a little bit of another input (say, capital)   (4)

marginal rate of transformation (*MRT*)   the rate at which a producer is technically able to exchange, in the process of production, a little bit of one variable (say, labor or butter) for a little bit of another variable (say, apples produced with the help of that labor or produced in place of that butter)   (14)

marginal revenue (*MR*)   any change in total revenue divided by the corresponding change in total product (in perfectly competitive markets, equal to product price; in imperfectly competitive markets, less than product price)   (5, 7)

marginal revenue product (*MRP*)   marginal physical product multiplied by marginal revenue   (11)

marginal social benefit (*MSB*)   the marginal benefit of an activity as seen from the viewpoint of society; the sum of marginal private benefit and marginal external benefit   (16)

marginal social cost (*MSC*)   the marginal cost of an activity as seen from the viewpoint of society; the sum of marginal private cost and marginal external cost   (16)

marginal time preference   the slope of an indifference curve relating current consumption to future consumption; the marginal rate of substitution between current and future consumption, or the additional future goods consumers are willing to accept, as a matter of indifference, for a unit sacrifice of present ones   (12)

marginal time productivity   the slope of a production-possibilities frontier relating current consumption to future consumption; the marginal rate of transformation between current and future consumption or the additional future goods producers are able to create for a unit sacrifice of present ones   (12)

marginal utility (*MU*)   the increase (or decrease) in an activity's overall utility that is attributable to a unit increase (or decrease) in the level of that activity, all else being equal   (2)

marginal utility of money   the change in the total utility of money that is associated with a unit change in the quantity of money   (9)

marginal value product (*MVP*)   marginal physical product multiplied by product price   (11)

margin calls   requests by commodity futures brokers for additional customer margin deposits   (10)

margin deposit   a good-faith payment to ensure performance on a futures contract   (10)

market   an invisible framework within which owners of property rights can make contact with one another for the purpose of trading something scarce and within which they jointly determine the price of what they are trading   (6)

market coordination   the spontaneous coordination, by price signals generated in markets, of the separate economic activities of people engaged in a division of labor; also called the system of the **Invisible Hand**   (13)

market demand   the sum of the demands of all potential market participants   (3)

market equilibrium   a situation in which there is no innate tendency for price or quantity to change   (6)

market-extension merger   a type of conglomerate merger involving firms in the same line of business but in different geographic areas   (8)

marketing quotas   maximum amounts of a product that farmers can legally sell   (7)

market supply   the sum of the supplies of all potential market participants   (5)

market uncertainty   uncertainty that exists when certain facts about the present or future are known to some people but not to other people   (10)

mathematical expectation   *see* **expected monetary value**   (16)

maximax (strategy)   one of several nonprobabilistic criteria for decision making under uncertainty according to which a decision maker who seeks to maximize some benefit finds the maximum benefit associated with each possible action, identifies the maximum among these maxima, and chooses the action associated with this maximum of maxima   (9)

maximin (strategy)   one of several nonprobabilistic criteria for decision making under uncertainty according to which a decision maker who seeks to maximize some benefit finds the minimum benefit associated with each possible action, identifies the maximum among these minima, and chooses the action associated with this maximum of minima   (9)

maximum-likelihood criterion   one of several probabilistic criteria for making decisions under uncertainty according to which a decision maker simply ignores all the events that might occur except the most likely one and selects the action that produces the optimal result (maximum benefit or minimum cost) associated with this most likely event   (9)

merger   the direct purchase of the assets of one firm by another   (8)

merit goods   goods the production of which is financed by government and that are supplied free of charge on the grounds that all citizens merit a share of them   (16)

microeconomics   the study of the behavior of decision makers in households, firms, and governments who, individually or in groups, make the kinds of choices that determine not only the detailed composition of the aggregate flows of resources and goods, but also the relative prices among individual resources and goods   (1)

minimax (strategy)   one of several nonprobabilistic criteria for making decisions under uncertainty according to which a decision maker who seeks to minimize some cost finds the maximum cost associated with each possible action, identifies the minimum among these maxima, and chooses the action associated with this minimum of maxima   (9)

minimax regret (strategy)   one of several nonprobabilistic criteria for making decisions under uncertainty according to which a decision maker finds the maximum regret value associated with each possible action, identifies the minimum among these maxima, and chooses the action associated with this minimum of maximum regret values   (9)

minimin (strategy)   one of several nonprobabilistic criteria for making decisions under uncertainty according to which a decision maker who seeks to minimize some cost finds the minimum cost associated with each possible action, identifies the minimum among these minima, and chooses the action associated with this minimum of minima   (9)

mixed strategy   a strategy, recommended for games without saddle points, that shifts at random among the available pure strategies   (9)

momentary equilibrium   market equilibrium in a period so short that the quantity supplied is absolutely fixed   (6)

monopolistic competition   a market structure in which the entry of new firms is easy; large numbers of sellers compete with one another, offering differentiated products   (8)

monopolistic exploitation   a situation in which an input's marginal value product exceeds its price because the input's user possesses monopoly power in the product market (which makes the input's marginal revenue product fall short of its marginal value product)   (11)

monopoly   an industry that has only a single seller the product of which has no close substitutes   (7)

monopoly power   the ability of a seller to raise the price of something that is for sale above the perfectly competitive level   (7)

monopsonistic exploitation   a situation in which an input's marginal value product exceeds its price because the input's user possesses monopsony power in the input market (which makes the marginal outlay on the input exceed its price)   (11)

monopsony   a buyer who is the only buyer in a market   (11)

moral hazard   a problem faced by insurance companies when those who have bought insurance subsequently change their behavior so as to increase the probability of the occurrence of any loss or of a larger loss   (10)

more-than-fair gamble   a gamble in which the expected monetary value of what is given up is less than the expected monetary value of what is received   (9)

natural monopoly   a situation in which long-run average total cost is declining with higher output throughout the range of possible quantities demanded in the market   (7)

natural resources   productive ingredients not made by people and untouched by them; gifts of nature in their natural state   (1)

necessities   normal goods the consumption of which rises less rapidly than income; goods with a positive income elasticity below unity   (3)

negative externalities   real externalities that impose costs in the form of decreased utility or output on bystanders who are not being compensated for this injury   (16)

negative marginal time preference   a high preference for future over current consumption that implies a lender's willingness to accept less than one unit of future consumption for the sacrifice of one unit of current consumption   (12)

neighborhood effects   *see* **real externalities**   (16)

net benefit   the difference between the total benefit and total cost of an activity   (1)

net present value   the sum of the present values of the negative and positive components of an investment project   (12)

neutral marginal time preference   the lack of any intrinsic preference between current and future consumption   (12)

nominal rate of interest   the percentage by which the dollar amount returned to a lender exceeds the dollar amount lent   (12)

nonexcludability   the property of a pure public good that makes it technically impossible or extremely costly to exclude any individual from the enjoyment of the good   (16)

nonpecuniary externalities   *see* **real externalities**   (16)

nonrivalness   the property of pure public goods that prevents rivalry among its consumers because the enjoyment of the good by any one person does not deplete its availability to others   (16)

nonzero-sum game   a game in which the winnings and losses of all players add to a positive or negative number   (9)

normal goods   goods of which larger physical quantities are consumed at higher than at lower incomes, all else being equal; goods with a positive income elasticity   (3)

normal price   a good's price that is equal to the lowest possible average total cost of production   (6)

normative statements   prescriptive statements akin to preaching; value judgments that tell us what ought to be, what is good and what is bad   (1)

norm of relative effectiveness   an arbitrarily selected coefficient of relative effectiveness   (12)

objective probability   a numerical measure of chance that estimates the likelihood of a specific occurrence (event A) in a repeatable random experiment; according to the classical approach, it is equal to the number of equally likely basic outcomes favorable to the occurrence of event A divided by the number of equally likely basic outcomes possible; according to the empirical approach, it is equal to the number of times event A did occur in the past during a large number of experiments divided by the maximum number of times event A could have occurred during these experiments   (9)

oligopoly   a market structure in which the entry of new firms is difficult and relatively few sellers compete with one another, offering either homogeneous or differentiated products   (8)

open interest   the number of outstanding futures contracts not yet liquidated by delivery of the commodity or by an offsetting contract   (10)

open-outcry auctions   auctions held on the floors of securities and commodities exchanges using shouts and hand signals   (10)

opportunity cost   the disadvantage associated with an act of choice, an opportunity lost; for example, the forgone quantity of one thing that might have been made possible with the resources that were, in fact, used to do another thing   (1)

opportunity loss (*OL*)   when a decision maker maximizes benefit, the difference between (a) the optimal payoff for a given event and (b) the actual payoff achieved as a result of taking a specified action and the subsequent occurrence of that event; when a decision maker minimizes cost, the difference between (a) the actual cost incurred as a result of taking a specified action and the subsequent occurrence of an event and (b) the minimum cost achievable for that event   (9)

optimal rate of plant operation   *see* **capacity output**   (5)

optimization principle   "people desiring to maximize the welfare they obtain from scarce resources must change the level of any activity as long as they do not value equally its marginal benefit, *MB,* and its marginal cost, *MC.* Whenever they value the marginal benefit more than the marginal cost, an expansion of the activity will raise their total welfare. Whenever they value the marginal benefit less than the marginal cost, a contraction of the activity will raise their total welfare. Whenever they consider the marginal benefit and marginal cost of equal value, the best possible (or optimum) level of the activity has been reached"   (1)

optimum plant   that plant, among all conceivable ones, with the lowest possible minimum average total cost   (5)

ordinary demand curve   a demand curve relating price and quantity, while holding money (rather than real) income constant   (3)

output effect   one of two effects resulting from an input price change, all else being equal; the output effect causes a firm to buy more of a normal and less of a regressive input as a result of a fall in its price (because of the implied decrease in marginal cost that raises the profit-maximizing output level)   (11)

overhead costs *see* **indirect costs** (5)

ownership claims rights to the exclusive use of assets (12)

own-price elasticity of demand the percentage change in quantity demanded of an item divided by the percentage change in its price, all else being equal (3)

Pareto optimum a situation in which all marginal conditions of economic efficiency are fulfilled simultaneously (14)

parity the 1910–14 relationship between the prices received by U.S. farmers for agricultural goods and the prices paid by them for nonagricultural goods (7)

partial equilibrium a situation in one part of the economy that contains no innate tendency to change because, for example, an individual household has maximized utility, an individual firm maximized profit, or an individual market equated supply and demand—given, in each case, assumed data concerning the rest of the economy (13)

patent an exclusive right to the use of an invention (7)

payback method a criterion for selecting investment projects that rejects all projects the returns of which require more than a predetermined length of time to repay the initial investment outlay (12)

payback period the number of years it takes for initial investment outlays to be paid back by (undiscounted) future receipts (12)

payoffs in decision theory, the positive or negative net benefits that are associated with each possible action/event combination and that are thus the joint outcome of choice and chance (9)

payoff table a summary of a decision-making situation in the context of uncertainty, consisting of a tabular listing of the payoffs associated with all possible combinations of actions and events (9)

pecuniary externality a situation in which the input prices paid by one firm are affected, favorably or unfavorably, by the operation of other firms (5)

perfect liquidity the ability of an asset to be transformed without loss of value and at a moment's notice into any other asset (12)

perfectly competitive market a market in which there is a large number of independent buyers and also of sellers, all units of the traded item are viewed as identical, all buyers and sellers possess full knowledge relevant to trading, and nothing impedes entry into and exit from the market (6)

perfect price discrimination *see* **first-degree price discrimination** (7)

personal distribution of income the apportionment of national income among persons, each of whom is likely to receive several types of income (12A)

persuasive advertising advertising that is designed to divert people's attention from facts to images and make them buy more as a result of imagined advantages (8)

planning curve the curve of long-run average total cost, which is tangent to all the curves of short-run average total cost and which is the geometric locus of the minimum achievable average total costs for all conceivable output levels a firm might produce (5)

plant a physical production facility, as defined by a set of fixed inputs, available to a firm (5)

point elasticity an elasticity measure that refers to a point (rather than arc) on a demand or supply curve (3)

point of diminishing returns the input quantity at which marginal product is maximized and beyond which it falls (4)

pollution licenses *see* **pollution rights** (16)

pollution rights transferable certificates each of which allows the holder to dump one unit of specified wastes into a specified environment (16)

positive externalities real externalities that provide benefits in the form of increased utility or output for bystanders who are not charged for this favor, to their delight (16)

positive-sum game a game in which no one wins at someone else's expense and the sum of (positive) winnings and (nonexisting negative) losses is positive   (14)

positive theory   a theory that makes purely descriptive statements and predictions; it explains what is and what causes what   (1)

positive marginal time preference   a high preference for current over future consumption that leads lenders to exact more than one unit of future consumption for the sacrifice of one unit of present consumption   (12)

prejudice   preconceived irrational opinion that leads to unfair partiality toward some people and bias against others or, for some, an attitude that facilitates rational behavior in the face of imperfect and costly information   (11)

price-compensating variation   one of four Hicksian measures of the consumer's surplus, equal to the maximum amount of income the consumer would pay for the privilege of buying any desired quantity of a good at a lower price   (6)

price-consumption line   a line indicating how the optimum quantities of two consumption goods change in response to a change in the price of one of these goods, all else being equal   (3)

price discrimination   a situation in which a seller charges a given buyer or different buyers different prices for different units of an identical good—even though such price differences cannot be justified by differences in the cost of serving these buyers   (7)

price elasticity of demand   *see* **own-price elasticity of demand** and **cross-price elasticity of demand**   (4)

price elasticity of supply   the percentage change in quantity supplied of an item divided by the percentage change in its price, all else being equal   (5)

price-equivalent variation   one of four Hicksian measures of the consumer's surplus, equal to the minimum amount of income the consumer would accept for relinquishing the opportunity of buying any desired quantity of a good at a lower price   (6)

price leadership   a set of oligopolistic industry practices according to which one firm, the price leader, announces and occasionally changes list prices that the other firms immediately adopt as well   (8)

price system   the set of interdependent prices in all the markets for goods and resources, which changes as long as the independent actions of households and firms are not perfectly coordinated, making households and firms, in turn, change their behavior until coordination is achieved   (13)

price war   a situation in which rival oligopolists successfully cut their prices below those of competitors (and perhaps even below their own cost)   (8)

primary uncertainty   *see* **event uncertainty**   (9)

prime costs   *see* **direct costs**   (5)

principle of declining marginal benefit   ''all other relevant factors being equal, the greater the overall level of any activity during a given period, the smaller will its marginal benefit usually be''   (1)

principle of diminishing marginal utility   ''given the quantities of all other goods being consumed, and given a person's tastes, successive additions of equal units of a good to the process of consumption eventually yield ever smaller additions to total utility''   (2)

prisoners' dilemma   a game situation in which the best common choice of strategies is unstable, offers great incentives to cheat, and leads to the worst choice possible   (9)

process of production   the set of activities deliberately designed to make goods available to people where and when they are wanted   (1)

producers' surplus   the difference between the sum of money producers actually receive for a given quantity and the minimum sum they would have accepted   (6)

product differentiation   the differentiation of products, on the basis of physical aspects, legal matters, or conditions of sale, among all the sellers in an industry   (8)

product-extension mergers a type of conglomerate merger in which the merging firms do not directly compete but use related production processes or marketing channels (8)

product groups groups of closely related but differentiated products that serve the same wants (8)

production function a technical relationship, stated in physical terms, between all conceivable combinations of inputs used during a period and the associated maximum quantities of some type of output, given the state of technology (4)

production-indifference curve *see* **isoquant** (4)

production-possibilities frontier all the alternative combinations of two goods or groups of goods that the people in a society are capable of producing in a given period by using their flow of resources fully and in the best possible way, given their present state of technology (1)

productivity *see* **average physical product** (4)

profit the difference between a firm's total revenue and the total (explicit and implicit) cost associated with producing that revenue (5)

property rights rights to the exclusive, but perhaps socially circumscribed, use of scarce things (15)

public finance the governmental collection of taxes from all those believed to benefit from the provision of pure public goods and the subsequent channeling of these funds toward the production of these goods, either by government agencies or private firms (16)

pure private good a good that generates no externalities and the producer or consumer of which alone bears all of the cost and enjoys all of the benefit associated with it (16)

pure public good a good that provides nonexcludable and nonrival benefits to all people in a given society (16)

pure rate of interest the interest rate that emerges in a perfectly competitive market for loanable funds when there is certainty (and, therefore, no risk) (12)

pure rent the rent received for the use of a resource the supply of which is totally unresponsive to resource price in the long run because the resource in question can neither be destroyed nor produced by people (12A)

quantity-compensating variation one of four Hicksian measures of the consumer's surplus, equal to the maximum amount of income the consumer would pay for the privilege of buying any desired good at a lower price, while constrained to buying the quantity the consumer would buy at the lower price in the absence of compensation (6)

quantity-equivalent variation one of four Hicksian measures of the consumer's surplus, equal to the minimum amount of income the consumer would accept for relinquishing the opportunity of buying any desired good at a lower price, while being constrained to buying the quantity that the consumer would buy at a higher price in the absence of compensation (6)

quasi rent the rent received for the use of a resource the supply of which is responsive to resource price in the long run because the resource in question can be destroyed and produced by people (12A)

rate base the value of the investment on which the owners of a regulated firm are to receive a "fair" return (15)

reaction curve a curve showing how much output one oligopolist will supply, given all possible outputs supplied by another (8)

real externalities direct effects, independent of any price changes, that the actions of some households or firms have on the utility of other households or on the output of other firms, none of whom have invited these effects (16)

real rate of interest the percentage by which the purchasing power (or actual quantity of consumption goods) returned to a lender exceeds the purchasing power lent (12)

regressive inputs inputs for which the output effect counteracts the substitution effect (11)

regret *see* **opportunity loss** (9)

regret table in decision theory, a table showing the opportunity-loss values associated with each possible action/event combination (9)

regulatory lag the length of time, sometimes years, that it takes government regulators to review a firm's performance and possibly change the price of the firm's product (15)

rent that portion of a payment for the services of any resource (human, natural, or capital) that exceeds the minimum amount necessary to bring forth the quantity that is in fact supplied (11)

rent seeking the expenditure of scarce resources for the purpose of gaining an asset (e.g., an exclusive franchise) that produces economic rent (14)

requirements contracts contracts according to which buyers agree to purchase all of their requirements of a commodity from given sellers only (15)

reservation demands demands for resources for purposes other than the sale of their services in the market (11)

reserve clause a clause in a labor contract that gives all rights to the future services of a worker to the worker's original employer (11)

resources ingredients used in the process of production; resources can be human, natural, or capital (1)

revealed-preference approach a method of deriving indifference curves by observing the actual market behavior of people (2)

right-to-work laws state laws outlawing the union shop (11)

risk an uncertainty-induced chance of variation in people's welfare; the extent of the spread of possible outcomes of an action around the action's expected value (9)

risk aversion an attitude according to which a person considers the utility of a certain prospect of money to be *higher than* the expected utility of an uncertain prospect of equal expected monetary value (9)

risk neutrality an attitude according to which a person considers the utility of a certain prospect of money to be *equal* to the expected utility of an uncertain prospect of equal expected monetary value (9)

risk seeking an attitude according to which a person considers the utility of a certain prospect of money to be *lower than* the expected utility of an uncertain prospect of equal expected monetary value (9)

Rule of Reason a 1911 U.S. Supreme Court interpretation of the Sherman Act, according to which only deliberate and unreasonable restraint of trade was considered illegal (15)

saddle point the combination of strategies that equates maximin and minimax (in a game) (9)

satiation that level of any activity at which its marginal benefit equals zero and at which its total benefit is maximized (1)

scale effect *see* **output effect** (11)

scarcity the economic problem arising from the fact that in all nations on earth today the limited set of goods that can be produced in a period is insufficient to satisfy, simultaneously, the desire for goods by all the people (1)

screening an activity by buyers designed to select high-quality sellers (10)

search an activity designed to discover information already possessed by other people (10)

secondary uncertainty *see* **market uncertainty** (10)

second-degree price discrimination a situation in which a seller partitions market demand into fairly large (but not necessarily equal-sized) blocks of product units and charges a given buyer or different buyers different prices for these blocks but uniform prices within the blocks (7)

selective sales tax a tax levied on the purchase of a particular good only (2)

selling cost cost designed to alter a firm's demand curve (8)

selling hedge hedging a long position in the

spot market by selling futures contracts now and buying them later   (10)

separation theorem   "as long as loanable funds markets are perfectly competitive, and the same rate of interest is applicable to borrowing and lending, an individual's productive optimum is entirely independent of the individual's preferences''   (12)

shortage   the amount by which the quantity demanded at a given price exceeds the quantity supplied   (6)

short hedge   *see* **selling hedge**   (10)

short position   a net liability position in which more of something is owed than owned   (10)

short run   a time period so short that the quantity of at least one of a firm's inputs cannot be varied   (4)

short-run equilibrium   market equilibrium in a period too short to vary the number or size of firms but sufficiently long for a given number of firms to be able to vary quantity supplied by changing the utilization rate of given plants   (6)

shutdown point   an output level at which total revenue equals variable cost and at which price equals average variable cost   (5)

signaling   an activity by sellers designed to convince buyers of the high quality of what is being sold   (10)

single-tax movement   a political movement led by Henry George, favoring the finance of all governmental activities by a single tax on land   (12A)

Slutsky's income-compensated demand curve   a demand curve relating price and quantity, while holding *real* income constant in the sense that any price changes are always compensated by money income changes in such a way that the consumer can, if desired, buy precisely the quantities that were bought prior to the price changes   (3)

snob effect   a situation in which the demand for a good by each individual varies inversely with the quantity others are seen to demand   (3)

speculating   the deliberate taking of long or short positions in spot or futures markets, with the hope that this will lead to profit from price fluctuations   (10)

spillout effect   the effect of a change in supply or demand on markets other than the one in which it occurs   (13)

spillovers   *see* **real externalities**   (16)

spontaneous coordination   *see* **market coordination**   (13)

spot markets   markets in which people agree to trade specified quantities and qualities of goods at specified prices and do it now   (10)

Stackelberg model   the dominant-firm model of oligopolistic behavior   (8)

state-of-nature branches   *see* **event branches**   (9)

state-of-nature fork   *see* **event point**   (9)

state-of-nature node   *see* **event point**   (9)

state-of-nature point   *see* **event point**   (9)

states of nature   *see* **events**   (9)

static efficiency   *see* **economic efficiency**   (14)

strategic behavior   behavior arising among a small number of actors who have conflicting interests and are mutually conscious of the interdependence of their decisions   (8)

subjective probability   a numerical measure of chance that expresses a purely personal degree of belief in the likelihood of a specific occurrence in a unique random experiment   (9)

substitute goods   two goods such that the quantity demanded of one varies in the same direction as the price of the other, all else being equal; goods with a positive cross-price elasticity   (3)

substitution effect   one of two effects resulting from a price change: the substitution effect causes a consumer (or a firm) to buy more of a good (or an input) with a relatively lower price and less of other goods (or inputs), given any initial level of real income (or output)   (3, 11)

supply   a set of price-quantity combinations that represents the alternative amounts of an item that would be offered for sale during a given period at all conceivable prices of this item, all else being equal   (5)

surplus   the amount by which the quantity demanded at a given price falls short of the quantity supplied   (6)

survivor principle   a method of making inferences about the production function in an industry that postulates that the technically most efficient production method is revealed by the characteristics of firms surviving competition in that industry in the long run   (4)

tariff   a tax on imports   (7)

technical advance   an improvement in known methods of production   (10)

technical coefficients   numbers showing the quantity of inputs producers in an industry require on the average per unit of output   (13)

technical efficiency   a situation in which it is impossible for a given firm, with given technical knowledge, to produce a larger output from a given set of inputs (or in which it is impossible to produce a given output with less of one or more inputs without increasing the amount of other inputs)   (4, 14)

technical inefficiency   a situation within a firm in which it is possible, with given technical knowledge, to produce a larger output from a given set of inputs (or to produce a given output with less of one or more inputs without increasing the amount of other inputs)   (4)

technological externality   a situation in which the production function of one firm is affected, favorably or unfavorably, by the operation of other firms   (5)

technology   the set of known methods of production   (1)

theory   a set of propositions intended to serve as an explanation of observed phenomena; a simplified representation of reality   (1)

theory of the second best   if one or more Pareto conditions cannot be satisfied, it is in general not true that the cause of economic efficiency is served by satisfying as many of the other conditions as possible   (15)

theory of the third best   policy makers are well advised to eschew specific policies (such as bringing prices in line with marginal costs) in favor of general policies (such as promoting free market entry and exit) that on average are likely to have desired effects   (15)

third-degree price discrimination   a situation in which a seller partitions market demand into two or more groups of customers and charges different prices among, but uniform prices within, these groups   (7)

time productivity   the ability of present consumption goods, when sacrificed now for the sake of creating capital goods, to yield permanently more future consumption goods   (12)

time-series studies   investigations of economic data pertaining to a given population during different past periods of time   (3)

total cost (*TC*)   the sum of fixed and variable cost   (5)

total utility of money   the overall welfare a person derives from the possession of a given quantity of money   (9)

transactions costs   output sacrificed because resources are used to set up a system of voluntary exchanges and keep it functioning   (13)

transfer loss   a loss of consumers' or producers' surplus that is offset by somebody else's gain   (6)

transitivity   a characteristic of choice denoting consistency or absence of contradiction   (2)

trust   a combination of several corporations under the trusteeship of a single board of directors that manages their affairs jointly   (15)

trust certificates   nonvoting ownership shares in a trust   (15)

tying contracts   contracts according to which buyers of one good agree to purchase another good from the same sellers as well   (15)

uncertainty   a situation in which people possess less-than-complete knowledge relevant to their decision making   (9)

unfair gamble   a gamble in which the expected monetary value of what is given up exceeds the expected monetary value of what is received   (9)

union shops   firms in which all employees, within 30 days after hiring, must become union members or at least pay union dues as a condition of continued employment   (11)

utility   the satisfaction a person derives from an activity   (2)

utility contour   *see* **consumption-indifference curve**   (2)

utility-of-money function   the relationship between alternative amounts of money a person might possess and the different utility totals associated with these amounts   (9)

variable cost (*VC*)   cost that varies with the level of production during a given period, attributable to the use of variable inputs   (5)

Veblen effect   a situation in which the demand for a good by each individual varies directly with the prevailing market price   (3)

vertical mergers   mergers of firms that are related as suppliers and users of each other's products   (8)

VES production function   a production function with a variable elasticity of input substitution   (4)

Visible Hand   *see* **managerial coordination**   (13)

workable competition   any market structure in which, taking into account structural characteristics and the dynamic factors that shaped them, no clearly indicated change can be effected through public policy that would result in greater social gains than losses   (15)

X-efficiency   *see* **technical efficiency**   (14)

X-inefficiency   a situation in which the actual output a firm gets from given resources falls short of the maximum output it could get, if it administered its resources better   (4)

zero-sum game   a game in which the winnings of some are exactly matched by the losses of others and the sum of (positive) winnings and (negative) losses is zero   (9, 14)

Answers and Comments
Odd-Numbered Questions

CHAPTER 1

1. **a.** *Always:* sand at a beach not yet discovered by people, sunshine, a school of tuna in the ocean. (See the text and glossary definition of natural resources.) *Never:* a highway, a college building, a can of peas. (The first two are capital resources; the can of peas is a capital resource as long as it is part of a firm's inventory and not yet in the possession of a household. Once in the possession of a household, the can of peas is a consumption good.) *Maybe:* 100 cubic feet of coal, if unmined; a cow, if wild; an acre of land, if virgin. (Coal in the factory yard, a domesticated cow, and cultivated land would be capital resources.)

   b. *Always:* an automobile-assembly plant, unsold refrigerators held by an appliance dealer, an inventory of groceries held by a food store. (See the text and glossary definition of capital resources.) *Never:* Ford Motor Company stock, a natural waterfall, a truck driver (the first of these may be called *financial* capital, while the last one can be said to embody *human* capital). *Maybe:* a toy truck or a wristwatch, if part of a store's inventory rather than held by a household; a horse, if domesticated rather than wild.

3. **a.** When $M = 0$, the largest amount of C is possible; then $5C^2 = 80$ and $C^2 = 16$; hence maximum $C = 4$. When $C = 0$, the largest amount of M is possible; then $2M^2 = 80$ and $M^2 = 40$, which implies $M = \pm \sqrt{40} = \pm 6.32$. Negative production making no economic sense, the maximum M sought is $M = 6.32$.

   b. Substituting $C = 4M$ in $5C^2 + 2M^2 = 80$, we find

$$5(4M)^2 + 2M^2 = 80$$
$$80M^2 + 2M^2 = 80$$
$$82M^2 = 80$$
$$M^2 = (80/82) = .9756$$
$$M = \pm .9877$$

Given the economically meaningful $M = .9877$, $C = 3.9508$. These values satisfy the equation given in the question.

   c. If $C = 2$, then

$$5(2)^2 + 2M^2 = 80$$
$$20 + 2M^2 = 80$$
$$2M^2 = 60$$
$$M^2 = 30$$
$$M = \pm 5.4772$$

If $C = 3$, then

$$5(3)^2 + 2M^2 = 80$$
$$45 + 2M^2 = 80$$
$$2M^2 = 35$$
$$M^2 = 17.5$$
$$M = \pm 4.1833$$

Using the economically meaningful values of M, the opportunity cost of producing 3C rather than 2C is 5.4772 − 4.1833 = 1.2939M.

5. **a.** The most highly valued alternative, *b* or *c*.

b. Once more, the most highly valued alternative would be the opportunity cost. It could literally be anything: in the case of foreign aid, perhaps, less aid to the domestic poor, less defense spending, fewer highways (if the foreign aid must be financed from a given government-budget) or less housing, less medical care, less investment in new factories (if the aid must be financed by higher taxes on the private sector).

c. If people cared to, they could spend every waking minute working for pay. To the extent that they devote their time to other things, they give up potential money income.

7.   I would vote for Mr. A, with sympathy for Ms. B. All the items mentioned have benefits and costs, probably falling marginal benefits and rising marginal costs, just as shown in Figure 1.6. I doubt that either maximization (of total benefit) or minimization (of total cost) produces optimization in any of these instances—a point that was also made more abstractly in Question 6. Consider some of the examples given:

a. *The size of people's wealth.* Few people are extremely wealthy. So most people think "the more wealth the better." Would more wealth be better if they were already very rich?

b. *The size of business organizations.* Owners of small firms often wish them to be larger. But when firms grow really large, people complain about the impersonality of human relationships within them. This is no accident. Due to the complexity of relationships among large numbers of people, these relations must be stripped down to the barest essentials lest the large organization die of communications failure. It cannot survive and also ensure the blossoming of full personal relations among all. (This matter is further discussed in the Chapter 4 section on decreasing returns to scale.)

c. *Pollution.* The notion of optimum pollution is discussed in detail in Chapter 16.

d. *The length of people's lives.* So far in history, people have lived rather short lives. Thus we naturally consider longer lives better. Would this be so if we lived to be 200? or 500? (Note Boulding's article on The Menace of Methuselah, referred to in the "Selected Readings" of Chapter 1).

Note: James G. March, in "Bounded Rationality, Ambiguity, and the Engineering of Choice," *The Bell Journal of Economics,* Autumn 1978, pp. 587–608, discusses many other types of choice, including such notions as optimal ambition, optimal clarity, optimal sin, and optimal rationality.

9.   There is no single correct answer.

CHAPTER 2

1.   The original budget line is solid line *AB*.
   a. The budget line changes to dashed line *AC*.

b. Yes, for all nonzero quantities of good *a*. The new budget line would then be dotted line *DB*.

FIGURE A-1

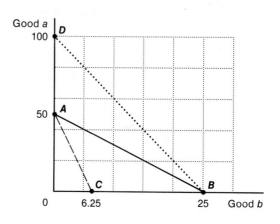

c. The consumer's choices would be legally limited to combinations within the dashed or dotted boxes, respectively. Combinations to the right of line *AB* would, of course, remain financially unattainable.

FIGURE A-2

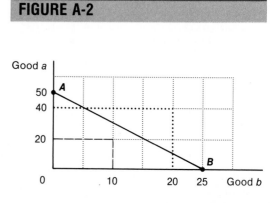

d. The consumer would be restrained, simultaneously, by dollar budget line *AB* and dashed coupon budget line *CD*. Thus only combinations in shaded area 0*AED* would be attainable.

FIGURE A-3

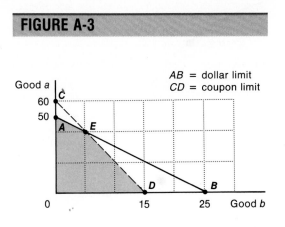

AB = dollar limit
CD = coupon limit

Good a

Units Consumed, cont.	Utils per Dollar, cont.	
(pounds)	Good *a*	Good *b*
25	4.0	1.5
30	3.5	1.25
35	3.0	1.0
40	(2.5)	0.75

Thus it is preferable to buy as many as 40 units of good *a* before the first 5 units of good *b* are bought. Indeed, the answer is: 40*a* (costing $400) plus 5*b* (costing $100) exhaust the budget and also equate marginal utilities per dollar (at 2.5 utils).

e. The consumer would be restrained, simultaneously, by solid dollar budget line *AB* and dashed time budget line *CD* and beyond. Thus only combinations in shaded area 0*CDB* would be attainable.

5. **a.** $150
   b. $7.50
   c. 1*a* for 2*b* or .5*a* for 1*b*
   d. The budget is spent, but utility is less than it could be (corresponding to I_0 rather than I_1). Point *B*, although preferable to optimum *C*, is not attainable.
   e. If the price of *a* were $7.50 and that of *b* were $15, their *MRS* would be 1*a* for .5*b* or 2*a* for 1*b* (because *at the optimum* the *MRS* corresponds to the price ratio).
7. Figure A-5 illustrates the possibility with a different set of indifference curves. The original budget line is *ab*, the original optimum *h*. Free food stamps for $75 of food produce new budget line *cdb* and new optimum *d*. Yet, in this case, a cash subsidy of $37.50 yields new budget line *ef* and produces at *i* utility equivalent to *d*.

FIGURE A-4

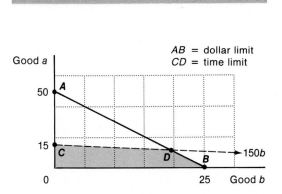

AB = dollar limit
CD = time limit

Good a

3. In the case of good *a*, the utils per pound convert into utils per $10; in the case of good *b*, they convert into utils per $20. Thus utils per $1 (which Jevons would have us equate) can be calculated as follows:

FIGURE A-5

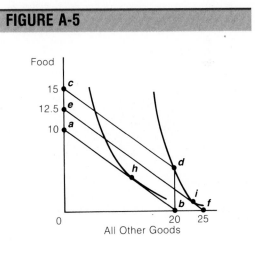

Units Consumed	Utils per Dollar	
(pounds)	Good *a*	Good *b*
5	6.0	(2.5)
10	5.5	2.25
15	5.0	2.0
20	4.5	1.75

b. The previous graph can be used to make the point. Just relabel the vertical axis "dental care." An original employee position at *h* on budget line *ab* might give way to a new optimum at *d* after an employer provided free dental care equal to *ac* = *bd*. Yet half as much added cash would give employees a new budget line *ef* and an optimum at *i* equivalent to *d*. Yet fringe benefits might be preferred if cash is taxable, while fringe benefits are not. Then the after-tax cash budget line might lie below *ef*.

9. The procedure noted in Section 2B of the Calculus Appendix can be applied.

a. The budget constraint is $100 - 10Q_a - 5Q_b = 0$. The Lagrangian is

$$\mathcal{L} = 4Q_a + 15Q_b - Q_a{}^2 - Q_aQ_b$$
$$- 3Q_b{}^2 + \lambda(100 - 10Q_a - 5Q_b).$$

Therefore,

$$\frac{\delta\mathcal{L}}{\delta Q_a} = 4 - 2Q_a - Q_b - 10\lambda = 0 \qquad (1)$$

$$\frac{\delta\mathcal{L}}{\delta Q_b} = 15 - Q_a - 6Q_b - 5\lambda = 0 \qquad (2)$$

$$\frac{\delta\mathcal{L}}{\delta\lambda} = 100 - 10Q_a - 5Q_b = 0 \qquad (3)$$

From the above, one can compute:

$$4 - 2Q_a - Q_b - 10\lambda = 30 - 2Q_a - 12Q_b - 10\lambda$$
$$11Q_b = 26$$
$$Q_b = 2.36$$
$$100 - 10Q_a - 5(2.36) = 0$$
$$-10Q_a = -88.2$$
$$Q_a = 8.82$$

b. The Lagrangian expression can also be written as

$$\mathcal{L} = U(Q_a \cdot Q_b) + \lambda(B - P_aQ_a - P_bQ_b).$$

Therefore equation (1) is

$$\frac{\delta\mathcal{L}}{\delta Q_a} = \frac{\delta U}{\delta Q_a} - \lambda P_a = 0.$$

Similarly, equation (2) is

$$\frac{\delta\mathcal{L}}{\delta Q_b} = \frac{\delta U}{\delta Q_b} - \lambda P_b = 0$$

It follows that

$$\frac{\delta U}{\delta Q_a} = \lambda P_a \text{ and } \frac{\delta U/\delta Q_a}{P_a} = \lambda$$

Also,

$$\frac{\delta U}{\delta Q_b} = \lambda P_b \text{ and } \frac{\delta U/\delta Q_b}{P_b} = \lambda$$

Thus λ is the marginal utility of any good per $1 of that good; it is the marginal utility of money.

11. *Panel (a):* Line *AB* is $Q_a = 120 - 4Q_b$;
line *AC* is $Q_a = 120 - 2Q_b$.

Panel (b): Line *AB* is $Q_a = 120 - 4Q_b$;
line *DB* is $Q_a = 60 - 2Q_b$.

Panel (c): Line *AB* is $Q_a = 120 - 4Q_b$;
line *EF* is $Q_a = 240 - 4Q_b$.

13. The $MRS_{b/a}$ is $\Delta Q_b / \Delta Q_a$. Thus the MRSs on the three indifference curves are:

I_0		I_1		I_2	
$\frac{+.9}{-2}$	$= -.45$	$\frac{+2}{-3.1}$	$= -.65$	$\frac{+3}{-3}$	$= -1.00$
$\frac{+1}{-2}$	$= -.50$	$\frac{+2}{-2.3}$	$= -.87$	$\frac{+2}{-1.2}$	$= -1.67$
$\frac{+1.2}{-2}$	$= -.60$	$\frac{+2}{-1.3}$	$= -1.54$	$\frac{+4}{-1.8}$	$= -2.22$
$\frac{+1.9}{-2}$	$= -.95$	$\frac{+2}{-1}$	$= -2.00$	$\frac{+2}{-.8}$	$= -2.50$
$\frac{+3.3}{-2}$	$= -1.65$	$\frac{+2}{-.8}$	$= -2.50$		
$\frac{+3.8}{-1}$	$= -3.80$	$\frac{+2}{-.6}$	$= -3.33$		
$\frac{+3}{-.1}$	$= -30.00$	$\frac{+2}{-.4}$	$= -5.00$		

CHAPTER 3

1. When the price-consumption line is sloping downward to the right, less money would be spent on all goods other than butter. Hence more money would be spent on butter from the given budget. Given the simultaneous fall in the price of butter, an own-price elasticity of greater than unity is implied.

Similarly, when the price-consumption line is sloping upward to the right, more money would be spent on all goods other than butter. Hence less money would be spent on butter from the given budget. Given the simultaneous fall in the price of butter, an own-price elasticity of less than unity is implied.

3. **a.** See Figure A-6. Initial budget line *AB*, initial indifference curve I_0, optimum at *C*. Price rise of good *b* changes budget line to *AD*, optimum to *F* on I_1. The three effects are shown in the graph.

b. Assume, for example, an initial budget of $150; given maximum $Q_b = 15$ at *B*, the initial $P_b = 10$, the initial $Q_b = 8$ at optimum *C*. This combination is shown by point *G*. Given the same money income and budget, and maximum $Q_b = 7$ at *D* after the price rise, the new price must be $P_b = (150/7) = 21.43$. The new $Q_b = 3.2$ at new optimum *F*. This combination is shown by point *H*. Line *HG* is the demand, given constant money income. However, holding real income constant (in the Hicksian utility sense), we move from *C* to *E* as a result

FIGURE A-6

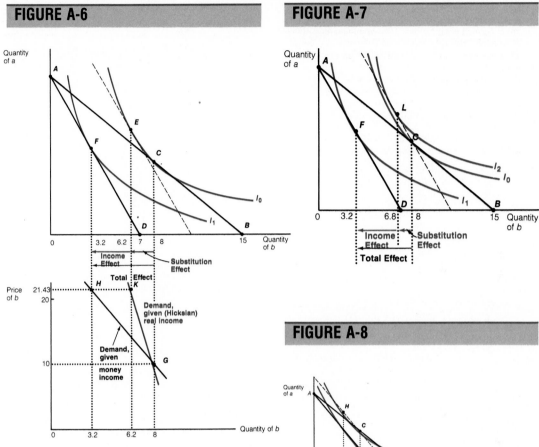

FIGURE A-7

FIGURE A-8

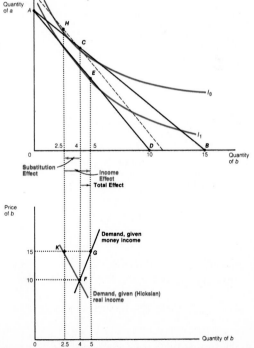

of this price rise; quantity falls to Q_b = 6.2 at E. This combination is shown by K. Line KG is the demand, given constant (Hicksian) real income (along indifference curve I_0)

c. See Figure A-7. Initial budget line is again AB; initial optimum is again at C on indifference curve I_0. Price rise of good b changes budget line to AD, optimum to F on I_1. Thus the *total effect* is the same (the horizontal difference between C and F). Slutsky defines unchanged real income not as unchanged utility level (as does Hicks), but as ability to buy initial combination (point C) at new prices. Given such ability (shown by dashed budget line), the optimum is L, not C; their horizontal difference is the Slutsky *substitution effect*, leaving the horizontal difference between L and F as the Slutsky *income effect*.

d. See Figure A-8. The initial budget line is AB; the initial optimum is at C on I_0. The price rise of good b changes the budget line to AD; the new optimum is at E on I_1. The three effects are shown in the graph. Note how the income effect works counter to and overwhelms the substitution effect (Giffen good).

e. Assume, for example, an initial budget of $150; given maximum $Q_b = 15$ at B, the initial $P_b = 10$; the initial $Q_b = 4$ at optimum C. This combination is shown by point F. Given the same money income and budget, and maximum $Q_b = 10$ at D after the price rise, the new price must be $P_b = (150/10) = 15$. The new $Q_b = 5$ at optimum E. This combination is shown by point G. Line FG is the demand, given constant money income. However, holding real income constant (in the Hicksian utility sense), we move from C to H as a result of this price rise; quantity falls to $Q_b = 2.5$ at H: This combination is shown by K. Line KF is the demand, given constant (Hicksian) real income (along indifference curve I_0).

5. a.   On line D_1 at a: $\dfrac{ah}{ag} > |\,1\,|$

On line D_1 at c: $\dfrac{ch}{cg} = |\,1\,|$

On line D_1 at g: $\dfrac{gh}{0} = |\,\infty\,|$

On line D_1 at h: $\dfrac{0}{hg} = 0$

On line D_2 at c: $\dfrac{ch}{cg} = |\,1\,|$

On line D_2 at e: $\dfrac{em}{el} < |\,1\,|$

On line E_1 at b: $\dfrac{bk}{bi} > 1$

On line E_2 at d: $\dfrac{d0}{d0} = 1$

On line E_3 at f: $\dfrac{fn}{fp} < 1$

b.   Income elasticity is defined as

$$\epsilon_D^Y = \frac{\dfrac{dQ_{D_x}}{Q_{D_x}}}{\dfrac{dY}{Y}} = \frac{dQ_{D_x}}{Q_{D_x}} \cdot \frac{Y}{dY}$$

$$= \frac{dQ_{D_x}}{dY} \cdot \frac{Y}{Q_{D_x}}.$$

Given $Q_{D_x} = a + bY$, it follows that $\dfrac{dQ_{D_x}}{dY} = b$. Hence the elasticity equals

$$\epsilon_D^Y = b\,\frac{Y}{Q_{D_x}}.$$

Since b is a constant and Y and Q_{D_x} differ at every point on the Engel curve, elasticity itself differs at every point.

c.   The own-price elasticity is defined as

$$\epsilon_D^{O\text{-}P} = \frac{\dfrac{dQ_{D_x}}{Q_{D_x}}}{\dfrac{dP_x}{P_x}} = \frac{dQ_{D_x}}{dP_x} \cdot \frac{P_x}{Q_{D_x}}$$

$$= \frac{dQ_{D_x}}{dP_x} \cdot \frac{P_x}{Q_{D_x}}.$$

Given $Q_{D_x} = aP_x^{-b}$, it follows that $\dfrac{dQ_{D_x}}{dP_x} = -abP_x^{-b-1}$. Hence the elasticity equals

$$\epsilon_D^{O\text{-}P} = -abP_x^{-b-1}\left(\frac{P_x}{Q_{D_x}}\right)$$

$$= \frac{-abP_x^{-b}}{Q_{D_x}} = \frac{-abP_x^{-b}}{aP_x^{-b}} = -b.$$

Thus elasticity equals the negative constant b. Note: If demand curve D_2 were a rectangular hyperbola, b would equal 1. Then the following would hold:

$$Q_{D_x} = aP_x^{-1} = \frac{a}{P_x}.$$

Therefore $P_x \cdot Q_{D_x} = a$. Price times quantity would be a constant.

d.   Take two goods, a and b. Given money income, Y, their expenditure shares are $\dfrac{P_a \cdot Q_{D_a}}{Y}$ and $\dfrac{P_b \cdot Q_{D_b}}{Y}$. We are to prove that

$$\frac{P_a \cdot Q_{D_a}}{Y}(\epsilon_{D_a}^Y) + \frac{P_b \cdot Q_{D_b}}{Y}(\epsilon_{D_b}^Y) = 1.$$

Applying the elasticity formula, the foregoing also equals

$$\frac{P_a \cdot Q_{D_a}}{Y}\left(\frac{\Delta Q_{D_a}}{Q_{D_a}} \middle/ \frac{\Delta Y}{Y}\right) + \frac{P_b \cdot Q_{D_b}}{Y}\left(\frac{\Delta Q_{D_b}}{Q_{D_b}} \middle/ \frac{\Delta Y}{Y}\right) = 1$$

and

$$\frac{P_a \cdot Q_{D_a}}{Y} \cdot \frac{\Delta Q_{D_a}}{Q_{D_a}} \cdot \frac{Y}{\Delta Y} + \frac{P_b \cdot Q_{D_b}}{Y} \cdot \frac{\Delta Q_{D_b}}{Q_{D_b}} \cdot \frac{Y}{\Delta Y} = 1$$

and

$$\frac{P_a \cdot \Delta Q_{D_a}}{\Delta Y} + \frac{P_b \cdot \Delta Q_{D_b}}{\Delta Y} = 1$$

$$\frac{P_a \cdot \Delta Q_{D_a} + P_b \cdot \Delta Q_{D_b}}{\Delta Y} = 1$$

If income can only be spent on a or b (as we assumed), any increase in income, ΔY, can only be spent on increased purchases of a or b (on ΔQ_{D_a} or ΔQ_{D_b}); hence the last equation's numerator equals the denominator:

$P_a \cdot \Delta Q_{D_a} + P_b \cdot \Delta Q_{D_b} = \Delta Y$, which completes the proof. This proof can, of course, be extended to any number of goods.

7. **a.** No. Given these elasticity estimates, such an increase would raise revenues only for very short trips and would actually lower them in all other cases.

b. Given the elasticity formula of $\epsilon_D^{O-P} = \dfrac{\Delta Q_D}{\overline{Q}_D} : \dfrac{\Delta P}{\overline{P}}$,

we can calculate $\overline{Q}_D = (\Delta Q_D \cdot \overline{P})/(\epsilon \cdot \Delta P)$. We are told that $\epsilon = -.2$ in the 1-year case and that $\Delta Q_D = -7$ million barrels per day. The information also implies an old price of $1.04 per gallon, a price hike of $\Delta P = 46¢$ per gallon, hence an average price of $\overline{P} = 1.27$ per gallon. Hence $\overline{Q}_D = (-7 \times 1.27)/(-.2 \times .46) = 96.63$ million barrels per day. Since $\overline{Q}_D = \dfrac{Q_0 + Q_1}{2}$, it follows that $Q_0 + Q_1 = 2(96.63) = 193.26$. Since also $Q_0 - 7 = Q_1$, it follows that

$$Q_0 + (Q_0 - 7) = 193.26$$
$$2Q_0 = 200.26$$

Daily consumption at time of advice:

$Q_0 = 100.13$ million barrels
per day.

$$\left[\text{Check: } \epsilon_D^{O-P} = \frac{\Delta Q_D}{\overline{Q}_D} : \frac{\Delta P}{\overline{P}} = \frac{-7}{96.63} : \frac{.46}{1.27} = -.2 \right]$$

The 5-year gasoline savings can be computed by noting that $\dfrac{\Delta Q_D}{\overline{Q}_D} = \dfrac{\epsilon \cdot \Delta P}{\overline{P}} = \dfrac{-.4(.46)}{1.27}$ in that case and that $\overline{Q}_D = \dfrac{Q_0 + Q_5}{2}$, where $Q_0 + \Delta Q_D = Q_5$. Hence

$$\overline{Q}_D = \frac{Q_0 + (Q_0 + \Delta Q_D)}{2} = \frac{2Q_0 + \Delta Q_D}{2}$$
$$= \frac{200.26 + \Delta Q_D}{2}.$$

Thus $\dfrac{2\Delta Q_D}{200.26 + \Delta Q_D} = \dfrac{-.4(.46)}{1.27}$, which implies $\Delta Q_D = -13.53$. Five-year savings are 13.53 million barrels per day.

$$\left[\text{Check: } \epsilon_D^{O-P} = \frac{\Delta Q_D}{\overline{Q}_D} : \frac{\Delta P}{\overline{P}} = \frac{-13.53}{93.365} : \frac{.46}{1.27} = -.4 \right]$$

The 10-year gasoline savings can be computed similarly: $\dfrac{2\Delta Q_D}{200.26 + \Delta Q_D} = \dfrac{\approx .8(.46)}{1.27}$, which implies $\Delta Q_D = -25.34$. Ten-year savings are 25.34 million barrels per day.

$$\left[\text{Check: } \epsilon_D^{O-P} = \frac{\Delta Q_D}{\overline{Q}_D} : \frac{\Delta P}{\overline{P}} = \frac{-25.34}{87.46} : \frac{.46}{1.27} = -.8 \right]$$

9. **a.** $\epsilon_{Db}^{O-P} = \dfrac{\delta Q_{Db}}{Q_{Db}} : \dfrac{\delta P_b}{P_b} = \dfrac{\delta Q_{Db}}{\delta P_b} \cdot \dfrac{P_b}{Q_{Db}}$

$= \dfrac{-1.8P_b}{52 - 1.8P_b + .2P_\ell + .9P_P}$

b. $\epsilon_{Db}^{C-P} = \dfrac{\delta Q_{Db}}{Q_{Db}} : \dfrac{\delta P_\ell}{P_\ell} = \dfrac{\delta Q_{Db}}{\delta P_\ell} \cdot \dfrac{P_\ell}{Q_{Db}}$

$= \dfrac{.2P_\ell}{52 - 1.8P_b + .2P_\ell + .9P_P}$

c. $\epsilon_{Db}^{C-P} = \dfrac{\delta Q_{Db}}{Q_{Db}} : \dfrac{\delta P_P}{P_P} = \dfrac{\delta Q_{Db}}{\delta P_P} \cdot \dfrac{P_P}{Q_{Db}}$

$= \dfrac{.9P_P}{52 - 1.8P_b + .2P_\ell + .9P_P}$

d. For (a): $\dfrac{-1.8(10)}{52 - 1.8(10) + .2(7) + .9(5)} = \dfrac{-18}{39.9}$

$= -.451$

For (b): $\dfrac{.2(7)}{39.9} = .035$

For (c): $\dfrac{.9(5)}{39.9} = .113$

11. The arc elasticity formula (Box 3.A or 3.B) applies.

Arc	Elasticity (via Box 3.B)
AB	$\left(\dfrac{2}{6}\right) : \left(\dfrac{-1}{15}\right) = -5.00$
BC	$\left(\dfrac{2}{10}\right) : \left(\dfrac{-1}{13}\right) = -2.60$
CD	$\left(\dfrac{4}{16}\right) : \left(\dfrac{-2}{10}\right) = -1.25$
DE	$\left(\dfrac{1}{21}\right) : \left(\dfrac{-.5}{7.5}\right) = -.71$
EF	$\left(\dfrac{2}{24}\right) : \left(\dfrac{-1}{6}\right) = -.50$
FG	$\left(\dfrac{5}{31}\right) : \left(\dfrac{-2.5}{2.5}\right) = -.16$

13.

Elasticity	Change in Total Revenue from Price Fall
Relatively elastic	
AB	from 16 to 28 = +12
BC	from 28 to 36 = +8
CD	from 36 to 40 = +4
Relatively inelastic	
DE	from 40 to 38.5 = −1.5
EF	from 38.5 to 32.5 = −6
FG	from 32.5 to 0 = −32.5

15. The substitution effect is the horizontal distance between *C* and *F*. (The higher wage rate induces $126 - 84 = 42$ extra hours of work.) The income effect is the horizontal distance between *F* and *E*. (The higher real income induces increased consumption of leisure or $110 - 84 = 26$ fewer hours of work.) The net effect: 16 more work hours, as noted in Figure 3.18.

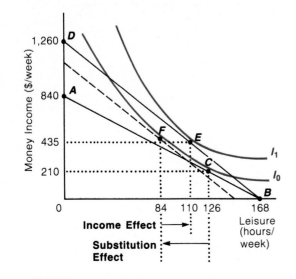

Income Effect ⟶
Substitution Effect ⟵

CHAPTER 4

1. Marginal products of labor (averages for given ranges): 50, 30, 10. Average products of labor: ?, 50, 40, 30.

3. The lesson is, of course, that it may not be possible to make genuine scale changes. The required communication channels in a growing firm may have to grow more than proportionally to the number of cooperating persons lest the kind of diseconomies discussed in the text set in.

5. If each were increased by 1 percent, coal output would increase by 1.08 percent. If capital only were increased by 1 percent, coal output would increase by .29 percent. If capital were decreased by 1 percent, coal output would decrease by .29 percent.

7. **a.** F **d.** T
   b. F **e.** F
   c. F

9. **a.** $\dfrac{\delta Q}{\delta L} = 200LKT$ $\dfrac{Q}{L} = 100LKT$

   $\dfrac{\delta Q}{\delta K} = 100L^2T$ $\dfrac{Q}{K} = 100L^2T$

   $\dfrac{\delta Q}{\delta T} = 100L^2K$ $\dfrac{Q}{T} = 100L^2K$

   b. $\dfrac{\delta Q}{\delta L} = 10 - 2L + 3K$

   $\dfrac{Q}{L} = 10 + \dfrac{5K}{L} - L - \dfrac{2K^2}{L} + 3K$

$\dfrac{\delta Q}{\delta K} = 5 - 4K + 3L$

$\dfrac{Q}{K} = \dfrac{10L}{K} + 5 - \dfrac{L^2}{K} - 2K + 3L$

c. $\dfrac{\delta Q}{\delta L} = .64L^{-.36}K^{.36}$

$\dfrac{Q}{L} = \dfrac{L^{.64}K^{.36}}{L} = L^{-.36} \cdot K^{.36}$

$\dfrac{\delta Q}{\delta K} = .36K^{-.64}L^{.64}$

$\dfrac{Q}{K} = \dfrac{L^{.64}K^{.36}}{K} = L^{.64} \cdot K^{-.64}$

d. $\dfrac{\delta Q}{\delta L} = .43L^{-.57}K^{.58}$ $\dfrac{Q}{L} = \dfrac{L^{.43}K^{.58}}{L} = L^{-.57}K^{.58}$

$\dfrac{\delta Q}{\delta K} = .58K^{-.42}L^{.43}$ $\dfrac{Q}{K} = \dfrac{L^{.43}K^{.58}}{K} = L^{.43}K^{-.42}$

e. $\dfrac{\delta Q}{\delta L} = aL^{a-1}K^b$ $\dfrac{Q}{L} = \dfrac{L^aK^b}{L} = L^{a-1}K^b$

$\dfrac{\delta Q}{\delta K} = bK^{b-1}L^a$ $\dfrac{Q}{K} = \dfrac{L^aK^b}{K} = L^aK^{b-1}$

f. *Case (a):*

MPL = 4,800	APL = 2,400
MPK = 1,800	APK = 1,800
MPT = 450	APT = 450

Case (b):

MPL = 13	APL = 15.833
MPK = 1.5	APK = 11.875

Case (c):

log MPL = log .64 $-$ .36 log 1.5 + .36 log 2
      = .08062 $-$ .36(.1761) + .36(.301)
log MPL = .1256
   MPL = 1.338

log APL = $-$.36 log 1.5 + .36 log 2
      = $-$.36(.1761) + .36(.301) = .0450
   APL = 1.109

log MPK = log .36 $-$ .64 log 2 + .64 log 1.5
      = .05563 $-$ .64(.301) + .64(.1761)
log MPK = $-$.0243
   MPK = $-$1.058

log APK =   .64 log 1.5 $-$ .64 log 2
      = .64(.1761) $-$ .64(.301) = $-$.0799
   APK = $-$1.202

Case (d):

$$\log MPL = \log .43 - .57 \log 1.5 + .58 \log 2$$
$$= .06335 - .57(.1761) + .58(.301)$$
$$\log MPL = .1376$$
$$MPL = 1.373$$

$$\log APL = -.57 \log 1.5 + .58 \log 2$$
$$= -.57(.1761) + .58(.301) = .0742$$
$$APL = 1.186$$

$$\log MPK = \log .58 - .42 \log 2 + .43 \log 1.5$$
$$= .07634 - .42(.301) + .43(.1761)$$
$$\log MPK = .0256$$
$$MPK = 1.061$$

$$\log APK = .43 \log 1.5 - .42 \log 2$$
$$= .43(.1761) - .42(.301) = -.0507$$
$$APK = -1.124$$

Case (e):

$$MPL = 2(1.5)(2)^3 = 24 \qquad APL = 1.5(2)^3 = 12$$
$$MPK = 3(2)^2(1.5)^2 = 27 \qquad APK = (1.5)^2(2)^2 = 9$$

11.

Point	APP_L	MPP_L
A	$\left(\dfrac{0}{0}\right) = ?$	
		$\dfrac{90}{3} = 30$
B	$\left(\dfrac{90}{3}\right) = 30$	
		$\dfrac{110}{1.8} = 61.1$
C	$\left(\dfrac{200}{4.8}\right) = 41.7$	
		$\dfrac{170}{1.2} = 141.7$
D	$\left(\dfrac{370}{6}\right) = 61.7$	
		$\dfrac{430}{2.3} = 187.0$
E	$\left(\dfrac{800}{8.3}\right) = 96.4$	
		$\dfrac{330}{3.4} = 97.1$
F	$\left(\dfrac{1130}{11.7}\right) = 96.6$	
		$\dfrac{50}{1.9} = 26.3$
G	$\left(\dfrac{1180}{13.6}\right) = 86.8$	
		$\dfrac{-190}{3.3} = -57.6$
H	$\left(\dfrac{990}{16.9}\right) = 58.6$	

13.

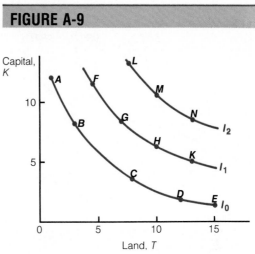

CHAPTER 5

1. True, in equilibrium. Review Table 5.1, "Short-Run Cost Alternatives," and Table 5.2, "Calculating Fixed Cost." Suppose a superior manager could reduce the variable inputs for any chosen level of total product so that variable cost was halved. Other firms would bid for this rare talent until our owner-manager's forgone potential salary (included, in this example, as implicit fixed cost) had risen precisely to offset the previously noted cost advantage.

3. Effect on optimum output quantity:

 a. In the case of a 50-percent profit tax, none. No effect on marginal cost and price.

 b. In the case of a $20,000 license fee, none. A $20,000 increase in fixed cost and an upward parallel shift of the total-cost curve would reduce profit *ed* by this amount in panel (a). A rise in average total cost would move *F* toward *B* and reduce the total-profit rectangle by $20,000 in panel (b).

 c. In the case of a $1 tax per bushel of output, the optimum output level would fall. The variable and total cost curves in panel (a) would shift up, but not in a parallel fashion. All the cost curves in panel (b) would shift up as well; *MC* itself would shift up by $1.

5. The curve of long-run total cost would go through the origin because of the absence of fixed cost in the long run. It would envelop short-run total cost curves based on varying levels of fixed cost as shown in Figure A-10. It would show the lowest total cost of producing any given quantity.

7. The marginal revenue from killing a baby turkey was 34 cents per pound (a reduction in feed cost). The marginal cost was 20 cents per pound (a reduction in sales revenue). Thus a marginal profit of 14 cents per pound was made.

FIGURE A-10

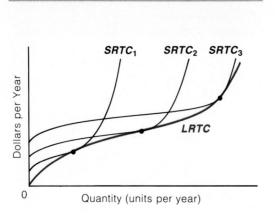

9. **a.** The average-total-cost functions and marginal-cost functions are:

1. $ATC = \dfrac{TC}{Q} = \dfrac{a}{Q} + b$

   $MC = \dfrac{dTC}{dQ} = b$

2. $ATC = \dfrac{TC}{Q} = \dfrac{a}{Q} + b + cQ$

   $MC = \dfrac{dTC}{dQ} = b + 2cQ$

3. $ATC = \dfrac{TC}{Q} = \dfrac{50}{Q} + 60 - 5Q + Q^2$

   $MC = \dfrac{dTC}{dQ} = 60 - 10Q + 3Q^2$

These are graphed in Figure A-11.

FIGURE A-11

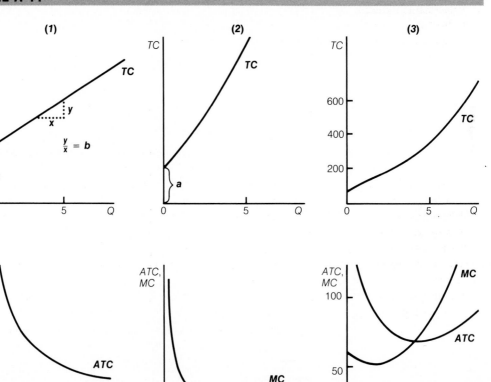

b. *1.* For profit maximization, $P = MC$

$$30 = 10 + .5Q$$
$$Q^* = 40$$

2. See Figure A-12.

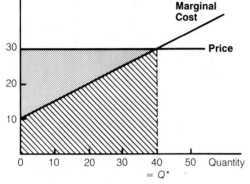

Total variable cost: the crosshatched area.
Total revenue: the crosshatched plus dotted areas.
The difference (dotted) must equal fixed cost plus profit because

$$TR - TC = \Pi$$
$$TR - FC - VC = \Pi$$
$$TR - VC = FC + \Pi$$

(If fixed cost, FC, exceeds the dotted area, the profit, Π, is negative, and the firm shuts down in the long run.)

c. In each case, profit, Π, equals $TR - TC$. Thus

1. $\Pi = 3Q - (2Q + Q^2)$
$\quad = Q - Q^2$

For maximum profit, $\dfrac{d\Pi}{dQ} = 1 - 2Q = 0$

$$Q^* = .5$$

The maximum is confirmed by $\dfrac{d^2\Pi}{dQ^2} = -2$.

At Q^*, $TR = 3(.5) = 1.5$; $FC = 0$, $VC = 2Q + Q^2 = 1.25$; $\Pi = .25$.

2. $\Pi = 6Q - (200 + 5Q^2)$
$\quad = 6Q - 200 - 5Q^2$

For maximum profit, $\dfrac{d\Pi}{dQ} = 6 - 10Q = 0$

$$Q^* = .6$$

The maximum is confirmed by $\dfrac{d^2\Pi}{dQ^2} = -10$.

At Q^*, $TR = 3.6$; $FC = 200$, $VC = 5Q^2 = 1.8$; $\Pi = -198.2$.

11.

Q	AFC = TFC/Q	AVC = TVC/Q	ATC = TC/Q	MC = ΔTC/ΔQ
1	50	30	80	
				10
2	25	20	45	
				5
3	16.7	15	31.7	
				10
4	12.5	13.8	26.3	
				35
5	10	18	28	

13.

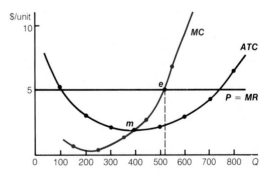

The data are graphed in Figure A-13 as the *ATC* and $P = MR$ lines. The tabular data allow the calculation of total cost, hence marginal cost, as follows:

Q	ATC	TC = Q × ATC	MC = $\dfrac{\Delta TC}{\Delta Q}$
100	5.10	510	
			.90
200	3.00	600	
			.30
300	2.10	630	
			1.70
400	2.00	800	
			2.75
500	2.15	1,075	
			6.95
600	2.95	1,770	
			12.05
700	4.25	2,975	
			22.25
800	6.50	5,200	

The graph suggests, once *MC* data are plotted, a profit-maximizing quantity of about 520. The firm's supply curve equals *MC* above minimum average variable cost (not known). Certainly, all of *MC* above *m* is part of the supply curve.

CHAPTER 6

1. Yes, text Figure 6.1, "Momentary Equilibrium," could be used for the explanation, although the supply line would undoubtedly not go down all the way to the horizontal axis in this case. Owners of paintings undoubtedly have a minimum supply price below which they will not sell.

3. Yes, text Figure 6.2, "Short-Run Equilibrium" could be used for the explanation. An increase in Russian demand for wheat raised the wheat price directly. The higher price induced other purchasers to decrease quantity demanded and possibly increase their demand for substitutes, causing the higher prices for rye, oats, and soybeans.

5. On a typical demand-supply diagram, if one graphs the quantity demanded at a zero price as a dot on the horizontal axis and if one graphs the quantity supplied by unpaid donors to the left of that demanded, a shortage is seen to exist. Some form of nonprice rationing must be employed. Many will go without babies, corneas, etcetera.

Now imagine the introduction of a market. Even if the quantity demanded were unchanged at all conceivable positive prices (an unlikely story often imagined by people), higher prices are bound to coax out larger quantities supplied. Equilibrium will be established where positively-sloped supply intersects vertical demand. The price will be positive, but *all* who previously wanted the goods in question (and many of whom did not get them) will not get what they want.

The fear of hepatitis might shift the demand to the left, leading to lower price and quantity.

7. The reduction of demand is the better strategy. All else being equal, this strategy reduces price along with quantity. The reduction in supply raises price, while reducing quantity.

9. **a.** See Figure A-14.

b. In each case, we equate demand and supply, $Q_D = Q_S$, at point *e*. Case *(1)* $P_e = 4.66$, $Q_e = 1.78$; Case *(2)* $P_e = 31.43$, $Q_e = 22.86$; Case *(3)* $P_e = 400$, $Q_e = 50$; Case *(4)* $P_e = 6.18$, $Q_e = 3.45$ (all numbers rounded). Mathematical determination:

Case (2) $100 - 3Q = 20 + .5Q$, given that (at *e*) $Q_D = Q_S$. Hence

$$80 = 3.5Q$$
$$Q_e = 22.857$$

Therefore $P = 100 - 3(22.857) = 31.429$.

Case (4) $20 - 4Q = 1 + 1.5Q$, given that (at *e*) $Q_D = Q_S$. Hence

$$19 = 5.5Q$$
$$Q_e = 3.454$$

Therefore $P = 20 - 4(3.454) = 6.184$.

c. Q_D at $P = 5$: For *(1)*, $5 = 10 - 3Q_D$; hence $Q_D = 1.67$. For *(2)*, $5 = 100 - 3Q_D$; hence $Q_D = 31.67$. For *(3)*, $Q_D = 50$ regardless of price. For *(4)*, $5 = 20 - 4Q_D$; hence $Q_D = 3.75$.

P at $Q_D = 5$: For *(1)*, $P = 10 - 3(5) = -5$ (which indicates that one would have to *pay* people to take more than what they want at zero price; namely, 3.33 units). For *(2)*, $P = 100 - 3(5) = 85$. For *(3)*, $P = 400$ regardless of quantity demanded. For *(4)*, $P = 20 - 4(5) = 0$ (as the horizontal intercept at the demand line confirms).

d. *Price above which demand is zero* equals the demand lines' vertical intercepts: 10, 100, ∞, and 20, respectively, for cases *(1)-(4)*. The answer to *(3)*, although mathematically correct, is, however, an unlikely story; the "law" of downward-sloping demand will undoubtedly assert itself eventually at higher prices. *Price below which supply is zero* equals the supply lines' vertical intercepts: 2, 20, 400, and 1 respectively, for cases *(1)-(4)*.

e. The demand lines' *horizontal* intercepts give the answers: 3.33, 33.33, 50, and 5 for cases *(1)-(4)*, respectively.

f. At $P = 3$, the quantity demanded can be calculated from $3 = 10 - 3Q_D$; hence $Q_D = 2.33$. The quantity supplied can be calculated from $3 = \sqrt{4 + 10Q_S}$, hence $Q_S = .5$. The effect would be a shortage of $2.33 - .50 = 1.83$.

g. There would be no effect because the equilibrium price is above the floor.

h. This cannot be done; any price below equilibrium instantly creates a shortage of 50 because supply disappears, while demand is unchanged.

i. We can rewrite the supply equation as $P = 2 + 1.5Q_S$ and solve: $20 - 4Q = 2 + 1.5Q$ at equilibrium. Hence

$$18 = 5.5Q$$
$$Q_e = 3.27$$

FIGURE A-14

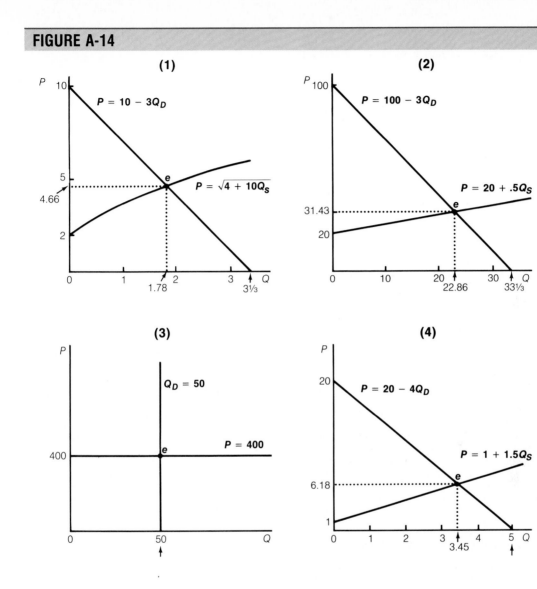

(1)

$P = 10 - 3Q_D$

$P = \sqrt{4 + 10Q_S}$

(2)

$P = 100 - 3Q_D$

$P = 20 + .5Q_S$

(3)

$Q_D = 50$

$P = 400$

(4)

$P = 20 - 4Q_D$

$P = 1 + 1.5Q_S$

Therefore, $P_e = 20 - 4Q_D = 6.92$ for buyers, but $P_e = 1 + 1.5Q_S = 5.92$ for sellers; the government taking the difference, or a total of $1(3.27) = \$3.27$. Compared to the old equilibrium price, the buyers pay $6.92 - \$6.18 = 74¢$ per unit more, while the after-tax receipts of sellers are $6.18 - \$5.92 = 26¢$ per unit less. Thus buyers bear 74 percent, and sellers 26 percent, of the tax burden, even though sellers may send the checks to the government.

j. We can rewrite the supply equation as $P = 18 + .5Q_S$ and solve: $100 - 3Q = 18 + .5Q$ at equilibrium. Hence

$$82 = 3.5Q$$
$$Q_e = 23.43$$

Therefore, $P_e = 100 - 3Q_D = 29.71$ for buyers, but $P_e = 20 + .5Q_S = 31.71$ for sellers, the government paying the difference, or a total of $2(23.43) = \$46.86$. Compared to the old equilibrium price, the buyers pay $31.43 - \$29.71 = \$1.72$ less per unit, while the post-subsidy receipts of sellers are $31.71 - \$31.43 = 28¢$ per unit more. Thus buyers enjoy 86 percent, and sellers 14 percent of the subsidy, even though sellers receive the entire government check.

Note: The answers given in (i) and (j) would have been the same if the tax had been imposed on buyers officially (and we would have shifted the demand line down rather than the supply line) or if the subsidy had been paid to buyers (and we would have shifted the demand line up rather than the supply line). Watch the wording here: What looks like an *upward* shift in supply (because the line shifts vertically up) is called a *decrease* in supply (because Q is less at each price). What looks like a *downward* shift in supply (because the line shifts vertically down) is called an *increase* in supply (because Q is higher at each price).

11.   *Panel (a):* Demand is $P = 2000 - \dfrac{2000}{2} Q_D$

$$P = 2000 - 1000 Q_D$$

Supply is $Q_S = 4$
At equilibrium, $Q_D = Q_S$. Thus $P = 2000 - 1000(4)$ $= -2,000$, but a negative equilibrium price denotes the absence of scarcity. A zero price can be charged and there will be more than enough for all.

Panel (b): Demand is $P = 4000 - \dfrac{4000}{4} Q_D$

$$P = 4000 - 1000 Q_D$$

Supply is $Q_S = 4$
At equilibrium, $Q_D = Q_S$. Thus $P = 4000 - 1000(4)$ $= 0$ (point c).

Panel (c): Demand is $P = 6000 - \dfrac{6000}{6} Q_D$

$$P = 6000 - 1000 Q_D$$

Supply is $Q_S = 4$
At equilibrium, $Q_D = Q_S$. Thus $P = 6000 - 1000(4)$ $= +2000$ (point f).

13.   Supply is $Q_S = 500$. At equilibrium, $Q_S = Q_D$. If $P = 1000 - 4Q_D$, $P = 1000 - 4(500) = -1000$. (There is no scarcity; a zero price can be charged; people can dump all they want.) If $P = 1000 - Q_D$, $P = 1000 - 500 = 500$. The agency must now charge a dumping fee of $500 per ton. Then people will want to dump only 500 tons per year.

15.   The accompanying Figure A-15 makes the analysis. Given a $10,000 annual budget, this consumer could buy $10,000 of other goods and no tires (point A) or no other goods and 200 tires (point B). Thus budget line AB implies a tire price of $50. The consumer's optimum is at C on indifference curve I_2. Let the government impose an excise tax of $50 per tire. The budget line swings to AD; the consumer's new optimum moves to E, which implies higher price and lower quantity (and lower utility on I_0). The government's tax collection is the value of EF, or EG dollars. Yet the government could have imposed a lump-sum tax of EG that was independent of the consumer's behavior. Then the budget line would have been dashed line HEK and the consumer would have found an optimum at L, being better off on I_1. The unnecessary utility loss (I_0 utility instead of I_1 utility) is the excise tax deadweight welfare loss.

CHAPTER 7

1.   Physical force (the murder of key personnel of competitors, the sabotage of their operations) or various forms of collusion (price fixing, tying contracts, et cetera) are illegal

FIGURE A-15

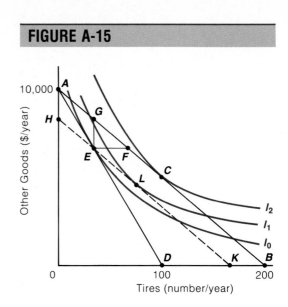

sources of monopoly power. The student may wish to look ahead to Chapter 15, which discusses various illegal activities designed to gain monopoly power.

3.   **a.**   *ATC* must intersect demand at a point vertically below a in panel (a) because total cost = total revenue implies average total cost = average revenue (or price).
   b.   The total-cost curve's point of inflection corresponds to minimum marginal cost, because declining *MC* implies total cost rising at a decreasing rate, while rising *MC* implies total cost rising at an increasing rate.

5.   If long-run marginal revenue intersected R, the firm would produce there.

7.   Of course. Consider a *monopsony* (which is an only buyer) paying, for each unit bought, the lowest possible price at which someone might supply that unit (as along some supplier's curve of marginal cost). Note how employers often keep the salary paid to any one employee secret from all other employees or how they pay overtime for extra units of labor. This issue is discussed in more detail in Chapter 11.

9.   **a.**   *Total appproach:*
$$TR = P{\cdot}Q = 50Q - 2Q^2 - 4Q^3$$
$$TC = ATC{\cdot}Q = Q^2 + 5Q$$
$$\Pi = TR - TC = 45Q - 3Q^2 - 4Q^3$$

For maximum, $\dfrac{d\Pi}{dQ} = 45 - 6Q - 12Q^2 = 0$

and $\dfrac{d^2\Pi}{dQ^2} = -6 - 24Q < 0$

By implication, $Q^* = 1.7026$ and $P^* = 35$ and $\Pi^* = 48.18$.
Marginal approach:

$$MR = \dfrac{dTR}{dQ} = 50 - 4Q - 12Q^2$$

$$MC = \dfrac{dTC}{dQ} = 2Q + 5$$

For maximum, $MR = MC$

$$\text{and} \frac{d^2TR}{dQ^2} < \frac{d^2TC}{dQ^2}$$

$$-4 - 24Q < 2$$

Given $50 - 4Q - 12Q^2 = 2Q + 5$, we have $45 - 6Q - 12Q^2 = 0$, as above.

b. *Total approach:*
$$TR = 25Q - .8Q^2$$
$$TC = 2 + 20Q + .1Q^2$$
$$\Pi = TR - TC = -2 + 5Q - .9Q^2$$

For maximum, $\dfrac{d\Pi}{dQ} = 5 - 1.8Q = 0$

$$\text{and} \frac{d^2\Pi}{dQ^2} = -1.8 < 0$$

By implication, $Q^* = 2.7777$ and $P^* = 22.78$ and $\Pi^* = 4.94$.

Marginal approach:

$$MR = \frac{dTR}{dQ} = 25 - 1.6Q$$

$$MC = \frac{dTC}{dQ} = 20 + .2Q$$

For maximum, $MR = MC$

$$\text{and} \frac{d^2TR}{dQ^2} < \frac{d^2TC}{dQ^2}$$

$$-1.6 < .2$$

Given $25 - 1.6Q = 20 + .2Q$, we have $5 - 1.8Q = 0$, as above.

c. *Total approach:*
$$TR = P \cdot Q = 50Q - 5Q^2$$
$$TC = Q^2 + 4Q$$
$$\Pi = TR - TC = 46Q - 6Q^2$$

FIGURE A-16

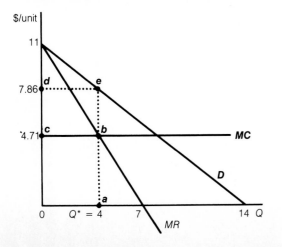

For maximum, $\dfrac{d\Pi}{dQ} = 46 - 12Q = 0$

$$\text{and} \frac{d^2\Pi}{dQ^2} = -12 < 0$$

By implication, $Q^* = 3.8333$ and $P^* = 30.83$ and $\Pi^* = 88.17$.

Marginal approach:

$$MR = \frac{dTR}{dQ} = 50 - 10Q$$

$$MC = \frac{dTC}{dQ} = 2Q + 4$$

For maximum, $MR = MC$

$$\text{and} \frac{d^2TR}{dQ^2} < \frac{d^2TC}{dQ^2}$$

$$-10 < 2$$

Given $50 - 10Q = 2Q + 4$, we have $46 - 12Q = 0$, as above.

11. See Figure A-16. The data allow us to plot demand and marginal cost; this implies the marginal revenue shown and the profit-maximizing combination of $Q^* = 4$, $P^* = 7.86$.

13. We cannot tell the size of the maximum profit, but we know this (from Figure A-16): Total revenue is $0aed = \$31.44$. Total variable cost is the sum of marginal costs up to the chosen level of $Q^* = 4$, equal to $0abc = \$18.84$. Thus area *bcde* represents the excess of total revenue over total variable cost. This excess of \$12.60 is available to cover fixed cost and profit. If fixed cost were \$10, for example, profit would be \$2.60. If fixed cost were \$20, profit would be $-\$7.40$.

15. See the text discussion of SONY television sets on page 238. It applies here. But also note that the factory price, bound for the United States, excludes advertising, freight, tariffs, and dealer incentives.

CHAPTER 8

1. "Agreed: Each of us will produce 25 units per year and charge a price of \$50 per unit." Given zero costs, each firm could expect a profit of \$1,250 per year, which would be \$138.89 per year better than the \$1,111.11 gained under the Cournot equilibrium.

3. a. Major changes in marginal cost and demand might shift the *MC-MR* intersection to a new quantity and, therefore, a new price. Presumably, the kink is supposed to reestablish itself at the new price-quantity combination.

   b. For a monopoly, any increase in marginal cost lowers quantity and raises price, *ceteris paribus*. The opposites occur for a decrease in marginal cost. Any increase in demand increases quantity and price; any decrease has opposite effects.

   c. For a perfect competitor, any increase (or decrease) in marginal cost lowers (or increases) quantity only, price being market-determined. Any increase (or decrease) in demand (presumably meaning market price and horizontal marginal revenue) raises (or lowers) quantity.

5.   The hints lead the way. (Goldwater's and McGovern's campaigns, of course, both of which resulted in landslide victories for their opponents, illustrate the dangers of locating at an extreme "right" or "left" position on Hotelling's characteristics space. Taking an extreme position allows an opponent to locate in a position that will attract the vast majority of "customers.")

7. **a.** Because the firm is making economic profit.

b. New firms will enter the "industry" (or Chamberlinian product group). This firm's demand will fall until economic profit is eliminated. See panel (b) of text Figure 8.8, "The Monopolistic Competitor," as an example of the end result.

c. Advertising would raise costs. If successful, it would raise demand sufficiently to recreate economic profit. If unsuccessful, it would fail to raise demand sufficiently and would bring losses.

9. **a.** In this model, the demand for the dominant firm's output, Q_D, is viewed as market demand minus fringe supply:

$$Q_D = Q_M - Q_F = 500,000 - 40P - 10P$$
$$= 500,000 - 50P$$

This is the same as $P = 10,000 - .02Q_D$; hence the dominant firm's marginal revenue is $MR_D = 10,000 - .04Q_D$. From the dominant firm's total-cost function we can determine $MC_D = 1,000 + .008Q_D$. To maximize profit, the dominant firm will equate

$$MR_D = MC_D$$
$$10,000 - .04Q_D = 1,000 + .008Q_D. \text{ Thus}$$
$$Q_D = 187,500$$
$$P = 6,250$$

b. At the industry price set by the dominant firm, total quantity demanded is $Q_M = 500,000 - 40P = 250,000$. The fringe firms supply $Q_F = 10P = 62,500$, leaving $Q_D = 500,000 - 50P = 187,500$ to the dominant firm—a market share of 75 percent.

c. The dominant firm's total revenue is $TR = P \cdot Q_D = 1,171,875,000$. Its total cost is $TC = 500,000 + 1000Q_D + .004Q_D^2 = 328,625,000$. Thus its profit is 843,250,000.

11.   See Figure A-17. All lines have been drawn on the basis of equations supplied in Problem 9. The dominant firm equates marginal revenue with marginal cost at a, then chooses the price/quantity combination at b. The dominant firm sells db units at chosen P^*; the fringe firms sell an additional $bc = de$. The dominant firm's total revenue is $0hbd$; its total cost is crosshatched area $0hik$ (because the above total-cost and quantity data imply an average total cost of about 1,753 per unit). By implication, the dotted area $ikdb$ is profit. The fringe firms' excess of total revenue over variable cost is area $hbcn$ (total revenue) minus area hcn (total variable cost), or area hbc (total fixed cost plus profit). Can you see that the unlabeled dashed line through hc is the fringe firms' supply curve with new origin h (that is, it is a horizontal displacement of line $0e$)? The area under this line, in the range of quantities supplied by the fringe (hn), is the sum of the fringe firms' marginal costs; that is, their total variable cost (hcn).

FIGURE A-17

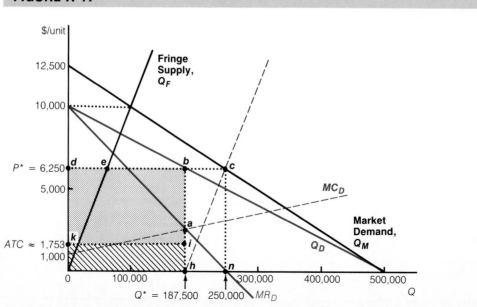

CHAPTER 9

1.   The E_1 column entries change from 8 and -2 to 16 and 6, the row minima change from 5 and -2 to 5 and 6, and the maximin action changes from A_1 to A_2.

Consider the same subsidy in the context of Table 9.3. The E_1 column entries (being costs) change from 5 and 10 to -3 and 2, the row maxima change from 8 and 10 to 8 and 4, and the minimax action changes from A_1 to A_2.

Although a fixed subsidy would not change the minimax-regret action, some other irrelevant factor easily might. Imagine that Table 9.2 contained a third possible action, $A_3 = $ buying an established plant, with payoffs (in millions of dollars) of -5 and $+20$, respectively, for E_1 and E_2. The existence of this third alternative would change the Table 9.6

entries in the E_1 column from 0 and 10 to 0, 10, and 13, and it would change the E_2 column from 7 and 0 to 15, 8, and 0. Hence the row maxima would become 15, 10, and 13, and the minimax-regret action would change from A_1 to A_2. But why should the mere existence of another (and rejected) alternative change the choice between the remaining alternatives?

3.   As Table 9.A shows, the maximin action is A_1; the maximax action is A_3.

5.   See Table 9.B. (The cell entries show revenue minus cost equaling profit, in thousands of dollars.) The maximin action is A_1; the maximax action is A_5.

7.   See Table 9.C. The minimax-regret action is A_3.

9.   See Table 9.D. The expected-monetary-value action is A_2.

11.   See Table 9.E. The expected-utility action is A_1.

TABLE 9.A

Actions	Events			Row Min.	Row Max.
	E_1 = low demand	E_2 = moderate demand	E_3 = high demand		
A_1 = small run	15	20	25	⑮	25
A_2 = medium run	6	20	35	6	35
A_3 = large run	-10	0	69	-10	㊿69

TABLE 9.B

Actions	Events					
	E_0 Demand = 0	E_1 Demand = 1	E_2 Demand = 2	E_3 Demand = 3	E_4 Demand = 4	E_5 Demand = 5
A_1 = build 1	48 − 60 = −12	90 − 60 = 30	90 − 60 = 30	90 − 60 = 30	90 − 60 = 30	90 − 60 = 30
A_2 = build 2	96 − 120 = −24	138 − 120 = 18	180 − 120 = 60	180 − 120 = 60	180 − 120 = 60	180 − 120 = 60
A_3 = build 3	144 − 180 = −36	186 − 180 = 6	228 − 180 = 48	270 − 180 = 90	270 − 180 = 90	270 − 180 = 90
A_4 = build 4	192 − 240 = −48	234 − 240 = −6	276 − 240 = 36	318 − 240 = 78	360 − 240 = 120	360 − 240 = 120
A_5 = build 5	240 − 300 = −60	282 − 300 = −18	324 − 300 = 24	366 − 300 = 66	408 − 300 = 108	450 − 300 = 150

TABLE 9.C

	Events			
Actions	E_1 = low demand	E_2 = moderate demand	E_3 = high demand	Row Maximum
A_1 = small run	15 − 15 = 0	20 − 20 = 0	69 − 25 = 44	44
A_2 = medium run	15 − 6 = 9	20 − 20 = 0	69 − 35 = 34	34
A_3 = large run	15 − (−10) = 25	20 − 0 = 20	69 − 69 = 0	(25)

TABLE 9.D

	Events		
Actions	E_1 = Success at New Location; $p(E_1)$ = .5	E_2 = Failure at New Location; $p(E_2)$ = .5	EMV
A_1 = move East	50	10	30
A_2 = move West	100	0	(50) Optimum

TABLE 9.E

	Events		
Actions	E_1 = Success at New Location; $p(E_1)$ = .5	E_2 = Failure at New Location; $p(E_2)$ = .5	EU
A_1 = move East	$\sqrt{50}$ = 7.07	$\sqrt{10}$ = 3.16	(5.12) Optimum
A_2 = move West	$\sqrt{100}$ = 10.00	$\sqrt{0}$ = 0	5.00

CHAPTER 10

1. **a.**   You have a 50-50 chance of losing or gaining $1. The expected monetary value is −$1(.5) + $1(.5) = 0.
b.   You have a 50-50 chance of losing $1 or gaining $10. The expected monetary value is −$1(.5) + $10(.5) = 4.50. How much you would pay me would depend on whether you were risk-averse, risk-neutral, or risk-seeking. If you were risk-averse, you would pay less than the expected monetary value; for example, −$1 for game (a) and $2 for game (b). If you were risk-neutral, you would pay at most the expected monetary value. If you were risk-seeking, you would pay more than the expected monetary value (up to a limit).

3. **a.**   See Figure A-18. The expected monetary value would be $3,000(.5) + $27,000(.5) = $15,000, but the associated expected utility would be less than D (on straight line FG at E).
b.   The expected monetary value of an equally probable $3,000 or $16,000 would equal $9,500. Its expected utility can be found at K on line FH in Figure A-18. The expected monetary value of $3,000 (p = .2) and $16,000 (p = .8) would equal $3,000(.2) + $16,000(.8) = $13,400. Its expected utility can be found at L on line FH.
c.   See Figure A-19. As in (a) above, the expected monetary value would be $15,000, but the associated expected utility would be more than L (on straight line MN at P).

FIGURE A-18

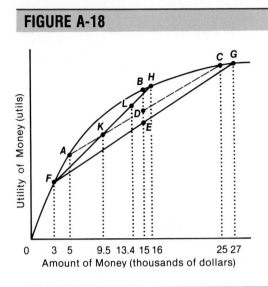

FIGURE A-19

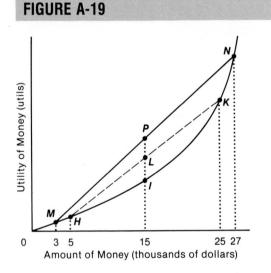

5. Text Table 10.3 modified:

Case III	
Nov. 20 Spot price is $2.82 per bushel; farmer sells 10,000 bushels of wheat.	December futures price is $2.85 per bushel; farmer buys two contracts of December wheat.
Gain: 5¢ per bushel	Gain: 2¢ per bushel
Net result: 7¢ per bushel gain	

Case IV	
Nov. 20 Spot price is $2.71 per bushel; farmer sells 10,000 bushels of wheat.	December futures price is $2.94 per bushel; farmer buys two contracts of December wheat.
Loss: 6¢ per bushel	Loss: 7¢ per bushel
Net result: 13¢ per bushel loss	

7. Marconi, because he put the new ideas into practical use, translating the earlier discoveries into a new product and acting in the face of uncertainty.

9. Both A and B have a point. As to Mr. A, consider Figure A-20. Let the demand for a book be $P = 40 - .02Q$; then marginal revenue is $MR = 40 - .04Q$, as shown. Let fixed cost be $10,000, but marginal cost a constant and tiny $1. Then *sales maximization* (the author's alleged preference) calls for zero marginal revenue:

$$MR = 40 - .04Q = 0$$
$$Q = 1000$$

The implied price (point *b*) is $P = 40 - .02(1000) = 20$. Total revenue is $TR = P \cdot Q = 20(1000) = 20,000$, and the author who receives 10 percent of sales gets $2,000. On the other hand, *profit maximization* (the publisher's alleged preference) calls for marginal revenue equal to marginal cost:

$$MR = 40 - .04Q = MC = 1$$
$$Q = 975$$

The implied price (point *a*) is $P = 40 - .02(975) = 20.50$. Total revenue is $TR = P \cdot Q = 20.50(975) = 19,987.50$, and

FIGURE A-20

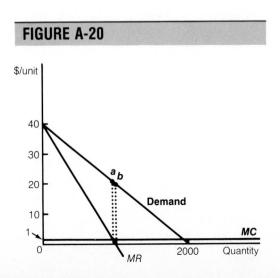

the author who receives 10 percent of sales gets $1,998.75. To the author, surely, the difference is negligible.

Ms. B is *wrong* about the author's indifference between 10 percent of sales or 10 percent of profit. Under sales maximization, profit is

$$
\begin{aligned}
TR &= 20,000 \\
- FC &= 10,000 \\
- VC &= 1,000 \ (1,000 \text{ copies} \times \$1) \\
\hline
\Pi &= 9,000; \text{ the author would get} \\
& \qquad \$900, \text{ not } \$2,000
\end{aligned}
$$

Under profit maximization, profit is

$$
\begin{aligned}
TR &= 19,987.50 \\
- FC &= 10,000.— \\
- VC &= 975.— (975 \text{ copies} \times \$1) \\
\hline
\Pi &= 9,012.50
\end{aligned}
$$

The author would get $901.25, not $1,998.75. Thus the author is indifferent between sales maximization and profit maximization, but not between getting 10 percent of sales and getting 10 percent of profit.

Ms. B may well be *right* on the issue of risk sharing. A royalty contract provides an incentive for both parties to promote sales (for example, by producing a high-quality book or engaging in heavy advertising, respectively). For more on this issue, see Michael A. Crew, ''Royalty Contracts: An Efficient Form of Contracting?'' *Southern Economic Journal*, January 1984, pp. 724–33, from which this example is taken.

CHAPTER 11

1. Take the case of two types of labor, *a* and *b*, which interfere with each other. Let the marginal-physical-product-to-input-price ratio be equalized initially: $MPP_a/P_a = MPP_b/P_b$. Now let the price of *a* fall. All else being equal, the profit-maximizing user will want to use more *a*. But this lowers the marginal-physical-(and value-) product *curve* of *b* (by assumption of anti-complementarity). Given the price of *b*, this leads to the use of less *b*. This, in turn, raises the marginal-physical-(and value-) product curve of *a*. The result is similar to text Figure 11.2. The lower price of one input (here labor type *a*) sets in motion forces that also shift the demand curve to the right (in this case not because more of another input is being used, but because less of it is being used).

3. **a.** If the work day were inflexibly set at 8 hours (= leisure of 16 hours), our friend would receive less total utility (at some point to the right of C on the budget line AB) than at optimum C. At such a position, an indifference curve, lying between I_1 and I_0, would *cross* the budget line. The marginal rate of indifferent substitution might then equal $2.50 per leisure hour; certainly any second job offering more than $2.50 per hour net (after extra transportation costs, et cetera) would be taken up, moving the worker in the direction of optimum C. If the

secondary job offered a wage between $5 per hour (implied by budget line slope AB) and $2.50 per hour, the total hours worked would be less than optimum C. If the secondary job offered a wage in excess of $5 per hour, the total hours worked would exceed optimum C. In that case, barring time limits on the secondary job, the secondary one would be substituted for the primary one (note how people often turn their avocation into their vocation). Often, of course, secondary jobs do have time limitations (for example, seasonal work, after-hour tutoring that complements the primary job).

b. If our friend worked 16 hours (= leisure of 8 hours), less total utility would be received also (at some point to the *left* of C on budget line AB). At such a position, an indifference curve, lying between I_1 and I_0, would again cross the budget line. The marginal rate of indifferent substitution might then equal $7.50 per leisure hour. Only steep overtime pay, tilting the budget line upward to the left of C until it was tangent, say, to I_2, would bring forth additional voluntary work.

5. See Figure A-21. The demand curve is section *eg*.

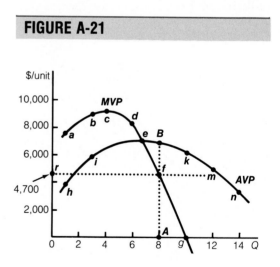

7. A horizontal wage line at $4,700 goes through *f*. Accordingly, 8 units would be demanded. We cannot tell what profit would be, but we know this: Total variable input costs would be $37,600 (area 0*Afr*). Total revenue would be 8 times *AB*, slightly under $56,000. The remaining amount (equal to 8 times *fB* and equal to slightly under $18,400) would equal fixed cost plus profit.

9. *Panel (a):* Unemployment of *ie* would exist. *Panel (b):* Unemployment would exist equal to the distance, along horizontal line *da*, from *a* to the line's intersection with market supply. *Panel (c):* Unemployment would exist equal to the distance, along horizontal line *ed*, from *d* to the line's intersection with market supply.

11.**a.**   *Point a:* The demand curve can be described by $W = 750 - .125\ Q_D$; the supply curve by $W = 59.52 + .04762\ Q_S$. At equilibrium a, $Q_D = Q_S$, hence

$$750 - .125\ Q = 59.52 + .04762\ Q$$
$$690.48 = .17262\ Q$$
$$Q = 4,000$$

Inserting this value in either demand or supply yields $W = 250$.

Point b: Given the above demand, the total revenue is

$$TR = W \cdot Q = 750\ Q_D - .125\ Q_D{}^2.$$

Thus marginal revenue is

$$MR = \frac{dTR}{dQ} = 750 - .25Q_D.$$

To maximize labor's total revenue,

$$MR = 750 - .25\ Q_D = 0$$
$$Q_D = 3,000$$

This implies a wage of $W = 750 - .125Q_D = 375$.

Point c: To maximize rent, we treat the supply curve as labor's marginal cost and equate it with marginal revenue:

$$MC = MR$$
$$59.52 + .04762\ Q = 750 - .25\ Q$$
$$.29762\ Q = 690.48$$
$$Q = 2,320$$

This implies a wage of $W = 750 - .125Q_D = 460$.

b.   *Case 1.:* The firm's MVP_L can be written as $W = 10 - .01666L$. The supply of labor to the firm can also be written as $W = .005L$, making total outlay, $TO = W \cdot L = .005L^2$ and marginal outlay equal to

$$MO = \frac{dTO}{dL} = .01L.$$

Equating this MO with MVP,

$$.01L = 10 - .01666L$$
$$L = 375$$

The required wage is $W = .005L = 1.875$

Case 2.: Given demand of $W = 10 - .01666L$, labor's total revenue is $TR = WL = 10L - .01666L^2$ and marginal revenue is

$$MR = \frac{dTR}{dL} = 10 - .03333L.$$

To maximize TR, MR must equal zero:

$$10 - .03333L = 0$$
$$L = 300$$

The implied wage is $W = 10 - .01666L = 5$.

Case 3.: The union would equate labor's marginal cost (supply) with the above marginal revenue; thus

$$.005L = 10 - .03333L$$
$$L = 260.89$$

The implied wage is $W = 10 - .01666\ L = 5.65$.

Case 4.: We equate demand and supply and find

$$10 - .01666L = .005L$$
$$L = 461.68$$

The implied wage is

$$W = 10 - .01666L = 2.31\ or\ is$$
$$W = .005L = 2.31$$

Case 5.: There is no clear-cut outcome because this is a combination of cases *1.* and *3.* The wage will lie between 1.875 and 5.65; the labor quantity between 260.89 and 375.

13.   See Figure A-22. It corresponds to case *4.*

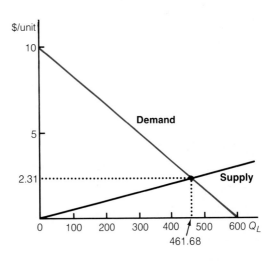

FIGURE A-22

15.   See Figure A-23. It corresponds to case *1.*
17.   yes. He was monopsonistically exploited, as it is explained in the text section, "Application 5: The Baseball Players' Market."

FIGURE A-23

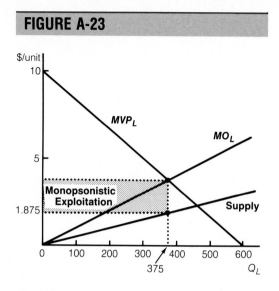

$/unit

MVP$_L$

MO$_L$

Monopsonistic Exploitation

Supply

1.875

0   100   200   300   375   400   500   600 Q_L

CHAPTER 12

1. The consumer's optimum is still at *C*. The consumer (who has no current income and lots of claims on future goods) can borrow *DC*, promising to pay back larger amount *DA* in the future.

3. **a.** A $1,000 loan without interest for six years is preferable. It is equivalent to a $50 income stream for 6 years. The present value of the stream equals

$$\frac{50}{1.05} + \frac{50}{1.05^2} + \ldots \frac{50}{1.05^6}$$
$$= \$47.62 + \$45.35 + \$43.19 + \$41.14$$
$$+ \ \$39.18 + \$37.31$$
$$= \$253.79$$

b. It depends on the length of time the person can expect to keep the job. If this length is 1 year only, an extra $600 will be earned, hardly as good as $1,000 now. On the other hand, an extra $600 for even 2 years (given the 5-percent interest rate) has a present value of $1,115.65.
c. The $1 million in 50 years is preferable. Its present value equals $1 million/$1.05^{50}$ = $87,203.79.
d. $20,000 now is preferable. The present value of the $1,000 income stream equals

$$\frac{1,000}{1.05} + \frac{1,000}{1.05^2} + \ldots \frac{1,000}{1.05^{30}} = \$15,372.49$$

e. Buying for cash is preferable. The choice is between $4,750 now or (presumably) $5,250 in a year (which, of course, has a present value of $5,000). Even if no interest were charged on the full price, cash buying would be preferable because the present value of $5,000 in a year would be $4,761.90.

5. OPEC had a major impact on the pattern of demand. Thus increased (or decreased) demands for the services of various assets affected not only the prices of these services, but also those of the assets in question. Note the text discussion surrounding Figure 12.8, ''How to Capitalize an Income Stream.''
7. **a.** A meaningless statement.
  b. True. Consider a copper ore mine. If the net price of, say, $100 per ton rose at 20 percent per year, while the rate of interest was 10 percent per year, an owner would rather hold a ton in the ground now and mine it in a year. At present, $100 would be forgone, but $120 would be gained through sale in a year. This would be better than selling for net $100 now and earning $10 of interest during the year. Yet such action would decrease the supply of copper ore now and, given demand, raise the current price. And it would increase the supply next year, and, given demand, lower next year's price. As a result, the rate of increase in the net price would decline. This postponement of mining now in favor of mining later would continue until the net price, too, was growing at 10 percent per year. Analogously, a net price increase at 5 percent per year, all else being the same, would speed up extraction.
9. **a.** The hint says it: The market value of a team adjusts to reflect the expected stream of future income and the rate that can be earned on any other asset of comparable riskiness. The attempted entry of new firms is a strong indication of economic profits in the industry.
  b. You shouldn't be surprised. Anyone who expects an eternal annual return of $1 (for example, as a result of a $1 property-tax reduction) will find that a one-time receipt of $7 (for example, when the affected house is sold) is precisely equivalent to this future flow of returns, provided the applicable interest rate is (1/7) 100, or 14.29 percent. (In fact, rates were 12–15 percent at the time.) This is so because $7, when invested at this rate, will generate a $1 return annually, forever.
  c. Property values will decrease if the demand for nearby real estate falls, for example, because of increased area noise, congestion, and the like, or because the influx of lower-income people or minorities causes the exodus of previous residents (''white flight''). Property values will increase if the demand for nearby real estate rises, for example, because more children make a nearby school possible, more people in general make nearby shops viable, more parks and public transport make the area attractive. For an actual study, see William A. Rabiega, Ta-Win Lin, and Linda M. Robinson, ''The Property Value Impacts of Public Housing Projects in Low and Moderate Density Residential Neighborhoods,'' *Land Economics*, May 1984, pp. 174–79.

CHAPTER 13

1. The statement may be overly poetic for some readers, but it does convey the basic truth of economic interdependence. Students should be able to construct any reasonable scenario that shows the statement to be correct.

3. **a.** It rarely would be negative, but it is not impossible, at least for rows (A)–(C). Commodities, for example, could be taken away from households, as has happened in this author's youth in Nazi Germany. (Private cars, cameras, radios, clothing, and stocks of food were confiscated for the war effort.)

b. The sums of rows would designate total sales revenue (from selling, say, electric power, labor, or machine hours). The sums of rows (D) to (F) would measure the gross national income. The sums of columns would designate total expenditures (on, say, raw materials and primary resources by electric power producers or on consumption goods by households). The sums of columns (4)–(7) would measure the gross national expenditure, as the familiar $C + I + G + (X - M)$.

5. The statement is incorrect. The production of one more car, for instance, requires extra tires in many places throughout the economy; for instance, on cars to transport extra workers to coal mines to mine extra coal needed for extra steel production to make the extra car. . . . Review the section on ''Interpreting the Leontief Inverse Matrix.''

7. It would be much more complicated, because the technical coefficients would vary with the volume of production.

9. Let d_{GC} represent the demand for the Gth good by the Cth consumer-household. This will depend on the prices of all goods and the tastes of the Cth consumer. It will also depend on the prices of all resource services because they determine, along with the amounts supplied by the consumer, the consumer's income. Hence there are $G \times C$ equations like

$$d_{GC} = f(P_1, P_2 \ldots P_G; p_1, p_2 \ldots p_R), \quad \text{(1)}$$

where $P_1, P_2 \ldots P_G$ are the prices of G goods and $p_1, p_2 \ldots p_R$ are the prices of R types of resource services, and where the consumer's tastes and input quantities determine the specific form of the equation.

The total quantity of the Gth good demanded by all consumers, then, is

$$D_G = d_{G1} + d_{G2} + \ldots d_{GC} \quad \text{(2)}$$

It follows from (1) and (2) that the total quantity demanded of each good depends on all goods and resource prices, but the specific relationship differs from one good to the next:

$$D_G = g(P_1, P_2 \ldots P_G; p_1, p_2 \ldots p_R) \quad \text{(3)}$$

Another set of equations must ensure that the total amount of each resource service supplied by consumer-households equals the total used by firms. Thus the quantity of the Rth input supplied, I_R, must equal the amount needed per unit of good 1 times the amount of good 1 produced plus the amount needed per unit of good 2 times the amount of good 2 produced, and so on for G goods:

$$I_R = u_{1R} \cdot D_1 + u_{2R} \cdot D_2 + \ldots + u_{GR} \cdot D_G \quad \text{(4)}$$

Finally, the long-run conditions of perfect competition are met if profit is zero because price equals average total cost for each good. The average total cost of producing the Gth good is

$$ATC_G = u_{G1} \cdot p_1 + u_{G2} \cdot p_2 + \ldots u_{GR} \cdot p_R \quad \text{(5)}$$

where the p's are the prices of the R resource types and u_{G1}, $u_{G2} \ldots u_{GR}$ represent the amounts of inputs 1, 2 . . . R needed per unit of good G. This average total cost must equal the good's price:

$$P_G = ATC_G \quad \text{(6)}$$

11. I vote with Ms. B. Mr. A's statement, incidentally, paraphrases an early book review, in the *Athenaeum*, of Charles Darwin's *On the Origin of Species*. The reviewer could not accept the notion of evolution, which to him meant accepting a universe under the rule of Absolute Ignorance. He preferred belief in a Master Artificer, endowed with Absolute Wisdom, who created and maintained the universe by reason.

CHAPTER 14

1. Both are correct. A move to a Pareto-superior position involves making one or more people better off in their own estimation (a marginal benefit) without making anyone worse off (a zero marginal cost). Pareto could not support as clearly desirable a positive marginal benefit (making someone better off) at a positive marginal cost (making someone else worse off) because we have no way of measuring either this benefit or that cost and of then comparing them.

3. This allocation almost certainly would *not* be economically efficient because different people's marginal rates of substitution between gasoline and other goods would diverge. Hence the kind of inefficiency depicted in Figure 14.4, ''Pareto's Fourth Condition,'' points *a* and *b*, would exist. Outlawing the trading of rations would perpetuate the inefficiency; allowing it would enable people to overcome inefficiency through exchange, as shown in Figure 14.4 as well.

5. **a.** One can adapt Figure 14.4 for an answer imagining producers to ''eat up'' labor and machine time to produce visible products, just as consumers eat apples and butter to produce invisible satisfaction. Just change consumers X and Y to producers α and β, change apples and butter to labor and machine time. Then the curves drawn in the graphs represent isoquants of the type first found in Figure 5.7(a) on page 151. Firm α might initially produce 100 bicycles per day at point *a*, while β produces 300 bicycles (or, significantly, 300 lawnmowers) at *b*. By trading 1 unit of labor for 3 units of machine time, the two firms could move to *a'* and *b'*, respectively, both producing a higher output.

b. *Under perfect competition,* both firms would face identical prices for labor and capital services. To maximize profit, both would use labor and capital services in such amounts as to equate their inputs' marginal value products (MVP_x and MVP_y) with their prices (P_x and P_y). Hence for Firm α:

$$P_x = MVP_x \text{ and } P_y = MVP_y.$$

Therefore

$$\frac{P_x}{P_y} = \frac{MVP_x}{MVP_y} = \frac{MPP_x \cdot P_0}{MPP_y \cdot P_0} = \frac{MPP_x}{MPP_y}$$

where P_0 is the price of output and MPP the marginal physical product. The same would hold for Firm β. Therefore the ratio of marginal physical products of the two inputs would be the same for both firms (each being equated with the identical input price ratio). This implies equal marginal rates of technical substitution as well. *Under imperfect competition,* the automatic (and unintended) achievement of economic efficiency would not be ensured. Both firms might maximize profit by using input quantities such that the marginal outlay on any input equaled its marginal revenue product. Hence for Firm α

$$P_x < MRP_x = MO_x < MVP_x$$

and

$$P_y < MRP_y = MO_y < MVP_y$$

Therefore it would be *possible* that

$$\frac{P_x}{P_y} \neq \frac{MRP_x}{MRP_y} = \frac{MO_x}{MO_y} \neq \frac{MVP_x}{MVP_y} = \frac{MPP_x}{MPP_y}$$

The same would hold for Firm β. Even if both firms paid the same input prices (not a necessity), the ratio of their inputs' marginal physical products and therefore their inputs' marginal rates of technical substitution might diverge at the point of profit maximization, eliminating any incentive for change.

7. Pareto wanted to make scientific statements; the speaker here is making moral judgments.

9. **a.** From *E,* Jones and Smith could move to any point within shaded, lens-shaped area *EDAC,* including points on the indifference curves enclosing this area. From *F* or *G,* they could move to any point within a similar lens-shaped area formed by the two persons' indifference curves (not shown) going through *F* or *G.*

b. A cross-cut of the utility mountain above the contract curve is shown by the top line in the Figure A-24 graph, wherein the horizontal axis represents the straightened-out contract curve. Note how various points on the contract curve along the path from 0_J to 0_S (such as *K, D, C,* and *H*) appear in this graph as well. Obviously, Jones's total utility rises along the path from 0_J toward 0_S, while that of Smith rises from 0_S toward 0_J as ever higher indifference curves are reached. If utility were not only measurable, but also interpersonally comparable, one could construct the top line of social utility, $U_J + U_S$. *Caution:* Students should not confuse this graph with text Figure 14.13, "The Equal Income Argument," which measures *marginal* utility (of income).

c. Yes, as long as the two consumers' marginal rates of substitution diverged (and they were thus positioned off the contract curve).

FIGURE A-24

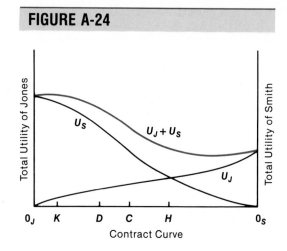

d. If they started out on the contract curve, but were determined to move, conflict would be inevitable. Quite possibly, during a long strike or lockout, everyone's tastes would change; that is, two new sets of indifference curves (and thus a newly positioned contract curve) would emerge. As a result, the original position *on* the original contract curve might become a position *off* the new contract curve. Then mutually beneficial trading would again be possible.

e. The two attitudes might be characterized as positions off or on the contract curve, respectively.

f. If this were literally true (and Jack Sprat received infinite disutility from eating fat, while his wife received infinite disutility from eating lean meat), Jack's indifference curves would shrink to the successive dots on the horizontal axis. Those of his wife would shrink to the successive dots on the right-hand vertical axis. Their ideal position would be at *E* (which would represent a shrunk contract curve): Jack would get all of the "lean," his wife all of the fat (see the Figure A-25 graph).

FIGURE A-25

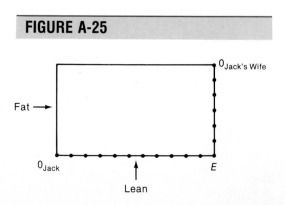

11.   A variety of arguments can be made to support either position. Note: The $1,250-a-year share of world output equals the per capita world GNP (a $5 trillion GNP divided by 4 billion people); it does not refer to private consumption goods only. If we excluded investment and government goods from the above figure (to approximate per capita private consumption goods available in a regime of world-wide equality), the per capita figure would be much lower. It would be lower still if we considered the disincentive effects of such a drastic redistribution.

13.   Yes. See Figure A-26. Picture a very large initial deviation from equality at *D* or *F*, respectively. Moving from *D* to *E*, person A gains utility of *a* + *b*; person B loses *b*, making for a net *gain* of *a* (dotted). Moving from equally likely *F* to *E*, person B gains utility of *f* + *g* + *d*; person A loses *g* + *d* + *c*, making again for a net *gain of* (*f* − *c*). In this example, there is *certainty* of gain from a move to equality. For further discussion, see John Bennett, "The Probable Gain from Egalitarian Redistribution." *Oxford Economic Papers*, March 1981, pp. 165–69.

FIGURE A-27

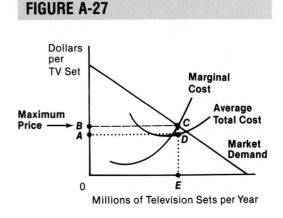

FIGURE A-26

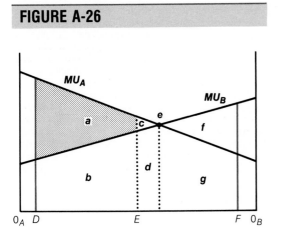

CHAPTER 15

1.   These are, indeed, important counter arguments to the Clayton Act provisions.

3.   **a.**   Consider Figure A-27, which is a modification of text Figure 7.3(b). By setting a maximum price of $0B$, the regulators would make inaccessible the market-demand line to the left of *C* and make *BC* into a new marginal revenue and demand line. The firm would produce quantity $0E$, corresponding to point *C*. The deadweight welfare loss would be gone; there would still be economic profit equal to *ABCD*.

b.   Consider Figure A-28, which again is a modification of text Figure 7.3(b). By setting a maximum price of $0F$, the regulators would annihilate the market-demand curve to the left of *K* and make *FK* into a new marginal revenue and demand line. The firm would produce quantity $0I$,

FIGURE A-28

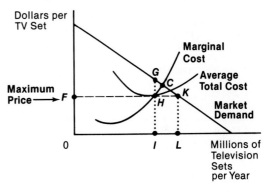

corresponding to point *H*. The deadweight welfare loss would then equal *GHC;* economic profit would be zero. There would also be a shortage of *HK* = *IL*.

c.   Consider Figure A-29, once more a modification of text Figure 7.3(b). By providing a per-unit subsidy equal to *CM* (the difference between original marginal cost MC_0 and marginal revenue at the output level that eliminates the deadweight welfare loss), a regulator could get the firm to produce output $0E$, and charge price $0B$. However, this would be equivalent to a parallel downward shift of MC_0 and ATC_0 to MC_1 and ATC_1; hence the firm would make an economic profit of *BCNP*.

d.   A lump-sum tax of *BCNP* would eliminate the economic profit, while not affecting marginal revenue and marginal cost and the firm's output/price decision. Such a tax would shift ATC_1 up in a nonparallel fashion, making it go through point *C* and making it intersect MC_1 at the new *ATC* minimum (not shown).

5.   Sunset laws would probably be a good idea for all three types of regulation discussed in the text.

FIGURE A-29

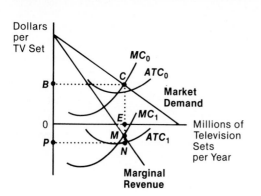

7. A variety of arguments can be made to support or oppose this position (which paraphrases the position of Milton Friedman—see Biography 1.1 in the *Student Workbook* that accompanies this text).

9. As was noted in text Chapter 5, a competitive firm's supply curve begins at minimum average variable cost in the short run (and equals the marginal-cost curve above this point). A case can be made for ignoring fixed costs in the short run (they would be there no matter what the firm was doing) and for designating any price that covered average variable costs as nonpredatory.

11. True. Licensing for competence promotes—while licensing for restricting numbers hinders—unrestricted voluntary exchanges. The former sets standards and norms; the latter restricts market entry.

CHAPTER 16

1. We can use the same example, slightly modified: Goal: $MRT_{a,b} = MRS_{a,b}$. In the absence of externalities, let $P_a = MPC_a = \$10$, and let $P_b = MPC_b = \$5$. Thus $MRT_{a,b} = 1a$ for $2b$ follows from profit maximization; $MRS_{a,b} = 1a$ for $2b$ follows from utility maximization. Now let the production of a involve a positive externality, such that $MPC_a = \$10$, but $MSC_a = \$5$. Hence true $MRT_{a,b} = 1a$ for $1b$. All else being the same, this implies economic inefficiency. By producing $2b$ less, one could in fact produce $2a$ more, making any consumer better off (because consumers still value $2b$ as much as $1a$ at the margin).

3. It is unlikely that people would be that altruistic. Even if they were, they would not have the knowledge necessary to make the adjustment properly. (This does not mean, of course, that government officials have that knowledge either.)

5. The hint leads the way. The team for which the player would play would be the same regardless of who owned his services. Suppose the reserve clause were not in effect. A player might be playing for Club A for a salary of $50,000 a year. If Club B offered $80,000, the player might move to Club B—provided he wasn't worth more than that to Club A, which would make a counter offer. The player would end up playing for the club that most highly valued his services. With the reserve clause, the same would be true. If the above player were worth $60,000 to Club A, which owned his contract, but $100,000 to Club B, Club B could offer $10,000 a year to Club A for the contract and would get it. (Club A would be no worse off than before, gaining *net* revenue of $10,000 a year in either case.) Club B could then pay the player's $50,000 annual salary, and the club would be better off, gaining $100,000 and paying $10,000 (to Club A) + $50,000 (to the player) = $60,000 a year. Once more, the player would be playing for the club that most highly valued his services. (For further reading on this issue, see Harold Demsetz, "When Does the Rule of Liability Matter?" *Journal of Legal Studies* 1 (1972): 13ff.)

7. True—unless, of course, the optimum is at the zero dumping point. Pollution that imposes extreme hazards might have such a zero dumping optimum point. (In that case, the MSC line in Figure 16.2 would start above point a on the vertical axis.) In general, though, risk-averse governments have chosen the ban when the cost of discovering the optimum level was itself prohibitive and they had to choose an arbitrary level between zero and unchecked pollution.

9. See Figure A-30. As long as pollution rights are marketable, the optimum dumping will occur. If the polluting plant gets the legal right to pollute, it could dump $0M$ legally. Yet the benefit C that it gets from dumping the above-optimal amount EM falls short of the extra damage to the computer firm $(C + D)$. The computer firm will pay some amount greater than C and smaller than $C + D$ to buy up the EM pollution rights (and *not* use them). Dumping will be reduced to the optimum; both parties will be better off at E than at M.

FIGURE A-30

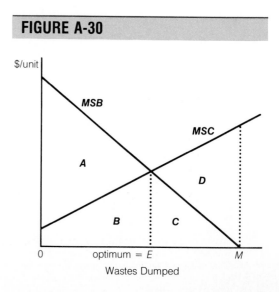

Wastes Dumped

If the computer firm gets the legal right to pollute, the chemicals plant will buy 0E rights because it can pay as much as A + B, while imposing damages of only B. Again, both parties will be better off at E than at 0.

11. There is a lot of truth to this. Public goods can be defined with respect to any society at all, be it all people on earth, all Americans, all residents of Michigan or of Boston, or all the workers in a given firm. Hence a *local* public good is not a self-contradictory term, as students sometimes think. All that matters is that such goods provide nonexcludable and nonrival benefits to all members of the society in question, however defined.

13. Although we do not know it, the city may well have produced the optimal quantity of this public good, such as 0G in text Figure 16.8. Although additional benefits might have been procured (totaling GHFD in Figure 16.8), the additional costs might have been larger, as is clearly the case in Figure 16.8 (the area under MSC between G and D exceeds GHFD). To prevent the 1,622 murders, for instance, the city might have had to spend $x billion, which were in fact spent, perhaps, on cardiac arrest units that saved 3,900 lives. (Note: students may wish to review the general discussion of the optimization principle in Chapter 1.)

15. See Figure A-31. Let the marginal private benefit (to bus riders) be MPB. Given marginal cost, MC, 0A bus trips will be made at a fare of Aa. If outsiders have an external benefit of MEB, the marginal social benefit, MSB, is the vertical sum of MPB + MEB; the social optimum is 0B bus trips. They will be produced only if nonriders subsidize the

FIGURE A-31

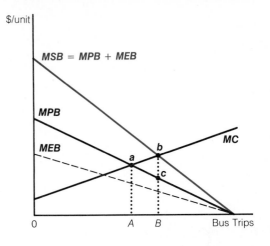

necessary fare, Bb, by bc (which equals the height of the dashed MEB line at B).

17. Almost certainly, this practice was nonsensical. (See the text discussion of benefit-cost analysis.)

Credits

p. 71   Reprinted with permission of Macmillan Publishing Company from *The Structure of American Industry* by Walter Adams, ed. Copyright © 1986 by Walter Adams.

p. 116   Table from George J. Stigler, "The Economies of Scale," *The Journal of Law and Economics,* October 1958, pp. 54–71. Copyright © 1958 by The University of Chicago Press.

p. 130   Table from Kerry Webb and Marvin Duncan, "Energy Alternatives in U.S. Crop Production," Federal Reserve Bank of Kansas City Economic Review, February 1979. Reprinted by permission of the Federal Reserve Bank of Kansas City.

p. 158   Figure from Laurits Christensen and William Greene, "Economies of Scale in U.S. Electric Power Generation," *Journal of Political Economy,* August 1976, p. 674. Reprinted by permission of The University of Chicago Press. Copyright © 1976 by the University of Chicago.

p. 165   Table adapted from Marc Nerlove and William Addison, "Statistical Estimation of Long-Run Elasticities of Supply and Demand," *Journal of Farm Economics,* November 1958, p. 872. Reprinted by permission of the American Economic Association.

p. 248   Table from Lawrence Shepard, "Licensing Restrictions and the Cost of Dental Care," *The Journal of Law and Economics,* April 1978, pp. 187–201. Reprinted by permission of The University of Chicago Press. Copyright © 1973 by the University of Chicago Law School.

p. 283   Table from Franklin Fisher, Griliches, and Kaysen, "The Cost of Automobile Model Changes Since 1949," *The Journal of Political Economy,* October 1962, pp. 433–51. Adapted by permission of The University of Chicago Press. Copyright © 1962 by the University of Chicago.

p. 284   Table from Lee Benham, "The Effect of Advertising on the Price of Eyeglasses," *The Journal of Law and Economics,* October 1972. Adapted by permission of The University of Chicago Press. Copyright © 1972 by the University of Chicago.

p. 285   Table from John E. Kwoka, Jr., "Advertising and the Price and Quality of Optometric Services," *The American Economic Review,* March 1984, pp. 211–16. Reprinted by permission of the American Economic Association.

p. 333   Table from George Stigler, "The Economics of Information," *The Journal of Political Economy,* June 1961, p. 214. Reprinted by permission of The University of Chicago Press. Copyright © 1970 by the University of Chicago.

p. 430   *The Limits to Growth: A Report for The Club of Rome's Project on the Predicament of Mankind,* by Donella H. Meadows, Dennis L. Meadows, Jorgen Randers, William W. Behrens, III. A Potomac Associates book published by Universe Books, N.Y., 1972. Graphics by Potomac Associates.

p. 479   Quotation from Martin Shubik, "A Curmudgeon's Guide to Microeconomics," *Journal of Economic Literature,* June 1970, p. 415. Reprinted by permission of the American Economic Association.

p. 481   From "The Economic Effects of Disarmament," by Wassily Leontief and Marvin Hoffenberg. Copyright © 1961 by *Scientific American, Inc.* All rights reserved.

p. 483   From "The Structure of Development," by Wassily W. Leontief. Copyright © 1963 by *Scientific American, Inc.* All rights reserved.

Subject Index

Name Index